The Book of
WINNERS

The Book of
WINNERS

By Claire Walter

Indexed by Felice D. Levy and Cynthia Crippen

A HARVEST/HBJ BOOK
HARCOURT BRACE JOVANOVICH
NEW YORK AND LONDON

© Facts on File, Inc., 1978

All rights reserved. No part of this publication may be
reproduced or transmitted in any form or by any means,
electronic or mechanical, including photocopy, recording,
or any information storage and retrieval system, without
permission in writing from Facts On File, Inc.,
119 West 57th Street, New York, NY 10019.

Published by arrangement with Facts On File, Inc.

Printed in the United States of America

LIBRARY OF CONGRESS CATALOGING IN PUBLICATION DATA
Walter, Claire.
The book of winners.
(A Harvest/HBJ book)
First published (c1978) under title: Winners, the
blue ribbon encyclopedia of awards.
Includes index.
1. Rewards (Prizes, etc.)—Directories. I. Title.
AS8.W34   1979   001.4′4   79-14237
ISBN 0-15-697208-5

First Harvest/HBJ edition 1979
A B C D E F G H I J

Contents

Preface

When a book such as THE BOOK OF WINNERS is issued, some words of explanation are required on how the volume was compiled, what has been included and what—perhaps—has been left out.

Every topical reference book must have a cutoff date, even though the story may be incomplete. For almost all of the awards and prizes included in this volume, the last word can never be written: there are, of course, new winners year after year. Facts On File's intention is to issue an up-to-date revised edition of THE BOOK OF WINNERS every two years. Subsequent editions will include new winners for the awards already in our data bank, new awards and prizes that have not yet been instituted as well as any significant awards or prizes that might have been overlooked in the preparation of this first edition. We welcome suggestions for additions, supplementary information, corrections and the names of subsequent award winners. Such information should be sent to: Awards Editor, Facts On File Publications, 119 W. 57th St., New York, N.Y. 10019.

THE BOOK OF WINNERS fills a gap in reference material by compiling and indexing available information about awards, the organizations that give them and the people or institutions that have received them. Obviously, it has been impossible to include all the world's awards and prizes. We have concentrated on major American honors in various fields of endeavor, as well as important awards given abroad, particularly those of international scope. Humorous as well as serious honors are included.

THE BOOK OF WINNERS comprises awards given on the basis of judgment rather than for measurable or objectively defined achievements. Therefore, we have included books which have won literary prizes but not those that topped the best seller list, the baseball star voted the Most Valuable Player in the league rather than the athlete with the highest batting average, movies and people in the film industry honored with an Oscar or at Cannes but not a list of the highest grossing pictures at the box office and people cited for public service achievements rather than those who won elections. Most, but not all, halls of fame have been excluded. This decision was based in part on necessity: there are literally thousands of halls of fame covering every field of endeavor imaginable. (In fact, R.R. Bowker has recently published the multi-volume *The Big Book of Halls of Fame in the United States and Canada* by Paul Soderberg and Helen Washington, which thoroughly covers this area.) Another factor in this decision was that the process of selection by ballot or election differs markedly from that used to determine the winners of most awards. We have, however, included a few halls of fame where in our judgment the selection process or the nature of the honor is more similar to those of awards than to those commonly associated with halls of fame. This was particularly true where the sponsoring organization itself describes or treats such an honor as comparable to its other awards. Significance also affected our decision on whether or not a hall of fame should be included.

We contacted by mail, phone or both thousands of award-giving organizations, asking them to describe the selection process for their major awards, what the individual honored receives (plaque, trophy, statuette, amount of money, etc.), a complete chronological list of all winners from the inception of the award through 1977 and, if possible, in each case the achievement for which the honor was granted. Every effort was made to track down information on awards whose sponsors chose not to reply to our series of questionnaires as well as to answer questions raised by discrepancies in the material we had received.

The vast majority of the material included in THE BOOK OF WINNERS has as its original source the organizations that gave the award. We have taken their word on spellings of names of individuals they have honored, except when the recipients were public figures whose names could be cross-checked in other reference sources. In most cases the year listed is the year in which the award was won. In the case of a few honors, an award for a particular year is issued at a later date. In all cases, we have followed the practice of the sponsors of the awards in our listings.

For the sake of consistency, given the scores of languages involved, we have eliminated all accent marks in foreign names and words rather than mislead readers by including some and omitting others. Except for awards of valor, where the recipient's death was one reason for the honor, we have deleted all references as to whether the award was made posthumously or whether the recipient is alive at this writing. Again for reasons of consistency, we have eliminated the titles "Dr." and "Professor." Where available, we have kept military rank, titles of nobility, clerical designations and, frequently, indications of elective office—all at the time of presentation of the award. When an honor included an expense-paid trip to an organization's meeting to accept the honor, or to present an address, we have not included this information in the descriptions of what the winner received except when these facts were especially significant.

We have organized the awards in what we believe are logical categories. In many cases, an individual award could have been placed logically in any one of several chapters. For example, an award to an author of a work of history might be included either in the "Books & Literature" chapter or in the chapter encompassing "Humanities & the Social Sciences." In such cases, we have asked ourselves and at times the sponsor whether the award is made *primarily* on the basis of literary merit, historical significance, the quality of scholarship or all three. On this basis, the National Book Award and the Pulitzer Prize for history were placed in the chapter on "Books & Literature," while those awards made by the American Historical Association to the authors of various historical works were placed in the chapter on the "Humanities & the Social Sciences." Inevitably, the final placement of some borderline cases reflects subjective judgments by the author and editor. We have attempted to compensate for this by cross-referencing and inclusion of an extensive index.

Within the chapters established, we have tried to group awards into logical packages, not alphabetically or by the name of the granting organization or of the award. For instance, sports awards are grouped first for general athletic achievement ("Athlete of the Year"-type honors) and then by sport. Within these categories and sub-categories, which are spelled out at the opening of each section, we attempted to alphabetize by the key word. Therefore, the order will sometimes be by the award's official name, sometimes by a well-known nickname and occasionally by the organization that grants it. Discrepancies between our judgment and that of the reader on what constitutes the key word will be reconciled by the index. We opted for ease of use rather than for a rigidly disciplined organizational approach.

In addition to the assistance granted us by hundreds of people who took the time to answer our queries, we would like to acknowledge several publications we found useful in doublechecking information about award-giving organizations and the people they honored: *Awards, Honors and Prizes* by Paul Wasserman and Krystyna Wasserman published by Gale Research Company, *Literary and Library Prizes* published by R.R. Bowker Company and Sandra Lee Stuart's *Who Won What* published by Lyle Stuart.

For aid in preparation of this complicated and lengthy manuscript, I feel deepest appreciation for the editorial guidance and judgments of Ed Knappman, the organization and patience of Nancy Fishelberg and the sharp eye and retentive memory of my husband, Burns E. Cameron, who was conscripted for proofreading assistance.

Claire Walter
Hoboken, New Jersey
August 1978

The Book of

WINNERS

General

Achievement

Contents

Related Awards

Boy of the Year

BOYS' CLUBS OF AMERICA
771 First Ave., New York, N.Y. 10017 (212/557-8593)

The "Boy of the Year" is an honor for demonstrated leadership and service to "home, church, community, school and Boys' Club" by a youngster between the ages of 13 and 18. Supported by the Reader's Digest Foundation and carrying a $5,000 scholarship award, the Boy-of-the-Year presentation is traditionally made by the President of the United States. A system of regional and national nomination and judging is used to select the winner.

1963	Ignacio Chavez
1964	Michael Rapinchuck
1965	Edwin Bassemier
1966	Peter Arroyo
1967	Gerald Simila
1968	William Beigl
1969	Perry Ludy
1970	James Heath
1971	Pelton Stewart
1972	Rodrigo Guerra, Jr.
1973	Gilbert Baez
1974	George Clark
1975	Kenneth Ivory
1976	Robert Fisher
1977	Gregory Baron

Cosmos Club Award

COSMOS CLUB
212 Massachusetts Ave. NW, Washington, D.C. 20008
(202/DU 7-7783)

The Cosmos Club Award is given annually to further the Club's cultural objectives and honors significant contributions in science, literature, the learned professions or public service. The award consists of $1,000 and a citation. The winner is selected by the Board of Management from nominations by the Awards Committee.

1964	Elvin C. Stakman,	Biologist
1965	Henry Allen Moe,	Humanitarian
1966	Merle Antony Tuve,	Geophysicist
1967	McGeorge Bundy,	Foundation Executive
1968	Samuel Eliot Morison,	Historian
1969	Robert D. Calkins,	Economist
1970	Edwin Herbert Land,	Scientist
1971	Kenneth Mackenzie Clark,	Art Historian
1972	Howard A. Rusk,	Physician
1973	Louis B. Wright,	Historian
1974	Horace M. Albright,	Conservationist
1975	Helen Hayes,	Performing Arts
1976	Roger Tory Peterson,	Ornithologist-Artist
1977	Archibald MacLeish,	Poet

Award of Merit

DECALOGUE SOCIETY OF LAWYERS
180 W. Washington St., Chicago, Ill. 60602 (312/263-6493)

The Award of Merit, which consists of a scroll, annually honors contributions to the Jewish community, the nation and the world through achievements in the arts, science, culture, public service or leadership.

1941	Barnet Hodes
1942	Marshall Field
1943	Col. Frank Knox
1944	Wendell L. Willkie
1945	Leo Lerner
1946	Bartley C. Crum
1947	Bishop Bernard J. Sheil
1948	Rabbi Stephen S. Wise
1949	Col. Jacob M. Arvey
1950	Percy L. Julian
1951	Judge Harry M. Fisher
1952	Gov. Adlai E. Stevenson
1953	Albert Einstein
1954	Hon. Harry S. Truman
1955	Sen. Herbert Lehman
1956	Edward J. Sparling
1957	Eleanor Roosevelt
1958	Judge Simon E. Sobeloff
1959	Philip M. Klutznick
1960	Judge Julius H. Miner
1961	Hon. Arthur J. Goldberg
1962	Sen. Jacob K. Javits
1963	Hon. Michael A. Musmanno
1964	Rabbi Mordecai M. Kaplan
1965	Albert B. Sabin
1966	Hon. Paul H. Douglas
1967	Hon. Abraham L. Marovitz
1968	Sen. Charles H. Percy
1969	Rene Cassin
1970	Ramsey Clark
1971	Sir Georg Solti
1972	Hon. Sidney R. Yates
1973	Justice William O. Douglas
1974	No award
1975	Saul Bellow
1976	Hon. Samuel B. Epstein
1977	Simon Wiesenthal

Antonio Felterinelli Prizes: Italian Citizens Award International Prize Gold Medal

ACCADEMIA NAZIONALE DEI LINCEI
Via Della Lungara 10, 00165-Rome, Italy

The Academy annually gives Antonio Felterinelli prizes in rotation for accomplishments in moral and historical sciences; physical, natural and mathematical sciences; letters; the arts; medicine; and, as merited, for exceptional humanitarian or moral achievement. Substantial cash honoraria are made, the amount varying according to the year's income from the Antonio Felterinelli Fund, which supports the awards. Members of the National Academy, presidents of other Italian academies and, in the case of the international awards, presidents of foreign academies may make nominations for consideration by a five-member committee convened to vote on the recipient.

ITALIAN CITIZENS AWARD

1950 Paola Zancani Montuoro and Umberto Zanotti Bianco, Archeology
1951 Gleb Wataghin, Mathematics, astronomy and physics
     Vincenzo Diamare, Biology

1952 Marino Moretti, Narrative prose
Emilio Cecchi, Letters
Ferdinando Neri, Criticism and history
1953 Filippo de Pisis, Painting
Giacomo Manzu, Sculpture
Mario Ridolfi, Architecture
Lorenzo Perosi, Music
Fausto Torrefranca, Art criticism
1954 Alberto Ascoli, Medicine
Luigi Califano, Medicine
Vittorio Erspamer, Medicine
Massimiliano Aloisi, Medicine
1955 Gianfranco Contini, Philology and history
Francesco Gabrieli, Philology and history
Federico Chabod, History
Nicola Turchi, History
Tullio Ascarelli, Jurisprudence
Salvatore Pugliatti, Jurisprudence
Augusta Guzzo, Philosophy
Bruno Nardi, Philosophy
Gaetano Pieraccini, Economics and social science
Livio Livi, Economics and social science
1956 Beppo Levi, Mathematics
Bruno Finzi, Mechanical science
Livio Gratton, Astronomy
Antonio Rostagni, Physics
Pietro Caloi, Geodesics and geophysics
Gino Bozza, Chemistry
Giovanni Merla, Geology and paleontology
Paolo Gallitelli, Minerology
Francesco D'Amato, Botany
Giuseppe Moruzzi, Physiology
1957 Antonio Baldini, Letters
Virgilio Giotti, Letters
Vasco Pratolini, Letters
1958 Mirko Basaldella, Sculpture
Giovanni Michelucci, Architecture
1959 Angelo Bairati, Medicine
Giovanni di Guglielmo, Medicine
Alessandro Rossi-Fanelli, Medicine
1960 Mario Praz, Philology, history and literary criticism
Arnaldo Momigliano, Historical science
Guido Calogero, Philosophical science
1961 Francesco G. Tricomi, Mathematics and mechanics
Giampietro Puppi, Astronomy, geology and geophysics
Livio Trevisan, Geology, paleontology and minerology
1962 Bruno Cicognani, Letters
Giuseppe de Robertis, Letters
Carlo Emilio Gadda, Letters
Camillo Sbarbaro, Letters
1963 Mino Maccari, Painting
Giorgio Federico Ghedini, Music
Luchino Visconti, Cinematography
1964 Antonio Ascenzi, Morphology
Luigi Musajo, Physiology and biochemistry
Enrico Ciaranfi, Pathology
1965 Giuseppe Billanovich, Philology
1966 Guido Stampacchia, Mathematics, mechanics and their application
Luigi Radicati di Brozolo, Physics, chemistry and their application
Vittorio Capraro, Biological science and its application
1967 Carlo Betocchi, Poetry
Giacomo Debenedetti, Essay
Quintino Cataudella and Ezio Raimondi, Criticism and history
1968 Pericle Fazzini, Sculpture

Luigi Moretti, Architecture
Francesco Arcangeli, Art criticism
Gian Francesco Malipiero, Music
1969 Giovanni Moruzzi, Medicine
Giacomo Mottura, Medicine
Oreste Pinotti, Medicine
Giulio Raffaele, Medicine
1970 Giorgio Petrocchi, Linguistics and philology
Eugenio Garin, Philosophical science
Giuseppe de Meo, Social and political science
1971 Aldo Andreotti, Mathematics, mechanics and their application
Giuseppe Colombo, Astronomy, geology, geophysics and their application
Adriano Gozzini, Geology, paleontology, minerology and their application
Pasquale Pasquini, Biological science and its application
1972 Italo Calvino, Fiction
Italo Siciliano, History and literary criticism
Gianfranco Folena, Theory and history of linguistics
Vittorio Sereni, Poetry
1973 Alberto Burri, Graphics
Pier Luigi Cervellati, City planning
Luigi Dallapiccola, Music
Umberto Mastroianni, Sculpture
1974 Emilio Agostoni, Medicine
Eraldo Antonini, Medicine
Luigi Donato, Medicine
Ottavio Pompeiano, Medicine
Gaetano Salvatore, Medicine
1975 Dinu Adamestreanu, Archeology
Fabrizio Sergio Donadoni, Archeology
Rolando Quadri, Jurisprudence
Giulio Capodaglio, Social and political science
Giuseppi di Nardi, Social and political science
Maria Floriani Squarciapino, Archeology (unpublished work)
1976 Enrico Bombieri, Mathematics, mechanics and their application
Gaetano Fichera, Mathematics, mechanics and their application
Michele Caputo, Astronomy, geology, geophysics and their application
Ferdinando Amman, Physics, chemistry and their application
Massimilla Baldo Ceolin, Physics, chemistry and their application
Raffaello Fusco, Physics, chemistry and their application
Ezio Tongiorgi, Geology, paleontology and their application
Giorgio Forti, Biological science and its application
Emanuele Padoa, Biological science and its application
Leo Pardi, Biological science and its application
1977 Diego Fabbri, Theater
Giovanni Macchia, Literary history

INTERNATIONAL PRIZE

1951 Jacques Hadamard, Mathematics and astronomy
1952 Thomas Mann, Letters
Ramon Menedez Pidal, History and criticism
1953 Ludwig Mies van der Rohe, Architecture
Igor Stravinsky, Music
1954 Alfred Blalock and Helen Taussig, Medicine
H.R. Griffith and A.R. MacIntyre, Medicine
1955 Leo Spitzer, Philology and literary history
Gaetano Salvemini, History
Ernst Rabel, Jurisprudence

Werner Jaeger, Philosophy
A.C. Pigou, Economics and social science
1956 Solomon Lefschetz, Mathematics, mechanics and their application
Sydney Chapman, Astronomy, geology, geophysics and their application
Giuseppe P.S. Occhialini, Physics, chemistry and their application
Bruno Sander, Geology, paleontology, minerology and their application
Ross Granville Henderson, Biological science and its application
1957 Wystan Hugh Auden, Letters
Aldo Palazzeschi, Letters
1958 Georges Braque, Painting
Ildebrando Pizzetti, Music
1959 Gaston Ramon, Medicine
1960 Hans Kelsen, Jurisprudence
1961 Pierre Auger, Physics and chemistry
John Burdon Sanderson Haldane, Biological science
1962 Eugenio Montale, Letters
1963 Henry Moore, Sculpture
1964 Wallace O. Fenn, Experimental medicine
Albert Bruce Sabin, Medical science and surgical application
1965 John Davidson Beazley, Archeology
1966 Harry Hammond Hess, Geology
1967 John Dos Passos, Fiction
1968 Pier Luigi Nervi, Architecture
1969 Rita Levi Montalcini, Medicine
1970 Claudio Sanchez Albornoz, History, historical geography and anthropology
1971 Jean Leray, Mathematics and its application
Bruno Rossi, Physics and astrophysics
1972 Eduardo de Filippo, Theater
1973 Richard Krautheimer, Criticism and art history
1974 Hugh Esmore Huxley, Medicine
1975 Alfred Verdross, Jurisprudence
1976 Edgar Bright Wilson, Jr., Chemistry
1977 Jorge Guillen, Poetry

PRIZE FOR OUTSTANDING HIGH MORAL OR HUMANITARIAN DEEDS

1954 Assn. Nazionale per gli Interessi del Mezzogiorno d'Italia (Assn. for the Interests of the Mezzogiorno of Italy)
1959 Unione Nazionale per la Lotta Contro l'Analfabetismo (National Union for the Fight Against Illiteracy)
1969 Coretta Scott King
1975 Piccola Casa della Divina Providenza "Il Cottolengo" (Il Cottolengo, Little House of the Divine Providence)

GOLD MEDAL

1969 Comitato Internazionale Croce Rossa (International Committee of the Red Cross)
Rubrica "Specchio dei Tempi" ("Mirror of Time" Directory)
Danilo Dolci

Hall of Fame Induction

HALL OF FAME FOR GREAT AMERICANS
Mailing Address: c/o New York University Public Affairs Dept., 21 Washington Place, New York, N.Y. 10013
(212/598-7733 or 212/367-7300)

The Hall of Fame Colonnade is a museum, open to the public, on the campus of the Bronx Community College, that commemorates achievements of American citizens of historical significance in the arts, sciences, humanities, government, business or labor. The public is invited to propose names for nomination and selection by the Electors of the Hall of Fame, which is now done every three years. To be nominated, a candidate must be dead at least 25 years. The dates to the left below indicate the years of selection.

1900 John Adams (1735-1826), Second President of the U.S.
John James Audubon (1785?-1851), Ornithologist and artist
Henry Ward Beecher (1813-87), Theologian
William Ellery Channing (1780-1842), Theologian
Henry Clay (1777-1852), Statesman
Peter Cooper (1791-1883), Philanthropist
Jonathan Edwards (1703-58), Theologian
Ralph Waldo Emerson (1803-82), Poet and essayist
David Glasgow Farragut (1801-70), Naval commander
Benjamin Franklin (1706-90), Statesman and inventor
Robert Fulton (1765-1815), Inventor
Ulysses S. Grant (1822-85), Union general and 18th President of the U.S.
Asa Gray (1810-88), Botanist
Nathaniel Hawthorne (1804-64), Author
Washington Irving (1783-1859), Author and diplomat
Thomas Jefferson (1743-1826), Third President of the U.S.
James Kent (1763-1847), Jurist
Robert E. Lee (1807-70), Confederate general
Abraham Lincoln (1809-65), Sixteenth President of the U.S.
Henry Wadsworth Longfellow (1807-82), Poet
Horace Mann (1796-1859), Educator
John Marshall (1755-1835), Chief Justice, U.S. Supreme Court
Samuel F.B. Morse (1791-1872), Inventor
George Peabody (1795-1869), Financier and philanthropist
Joseph Story (1779-1845), Jurist and Associate Justice, U.S. Supreme Court
Gilbert Stuart (1755-1845), Painter
George Washington (1732-99), Revolutionary War general and first President of the U.S.
Daniel Webster (1782-1852), Statesman
Eli Whitney (1765-1825), Inventor
1905 John Quincy Adams (1767-1848), Sixth President of the U.S.
James Russell Lowell (1819-91), Poet, critic and editor
Mary Lyon (1797-1849), Educator
James Madison (1751-1836), Fourth President of the U.S.
Maria Mitchell (1818-89), Astronomer
John Greenleaf Whittier (1807-92), Poet
William Tecumseh Sherman (1820-91), Union general
Emma Willard (1787-1870), Educator
1910 George Bancroft (1800-91), Historian and diplomat
Phillips Brooks (1835-93), Theologian
William Cullen Bryant (1794-1878), Poet and editor
James Fenimore Cooper (1789-1842), Novelist

Oliver Wendell Holmes (1809-94), Essayist and poet
Andrew Jackson (1767-1845), Statesman and seventh President of the U.S.
John Lothrop Motley (1814-77), Historian
Edgar Allen Poe (1809-49), Poet, writer and critic
Harriet Beecher Stowe (1811-96), Author and humanitarian
Frances Elizabeth Willard (1839-98), Social reformer
1915 Louis Agassiz (1807-73), Naturalist
Daniel Boone (1734-1820), Frontiersman
Rufus Choate (1799-1859), Lawyer and legislator
Charlotte Cushman (1816-75), Actress
Alexander Hamilton (1755?-1804), Statesman
Joseph Henry (1797-1878), Physicist
Mark Hopkins (1802-87), Educator
Elias Howe (1819-67), Inventor
Francis Parkman (1823-93), Historian
1920 Samuel Langhorne Clemens (Mark Twain, 1835-1910), Novelist
James Eads (1820-87), Engineer
Patrick Henry (1736-99), Statesman
William Morton (1819-68), Dentist
Alice Palmer (1855-1902), Educator
Augustus Saint-Gaudens (1848-1907), Sculptor
Roger Williams (1603?-83), Colonial leader and theologian
1925 Edwin Booth (1833-93), Actor
John Paul Jones (1747-92), Naval commander
1930 Matthew Fontaine Maury (1806-73), Naval officer and oceanographer
James Monroe (1758-1831), Fifth President of the U.S.
James A. McNeill Whistler (1834-1903), Painter
Walt Whitman (1819-92), Poet
1935 Grover Cleveland (1837-1908), Twenty-second and 24th President of the U.S.
Simon Newcomb (1835-1909), Astronomer
William Penn (1644-1718), Colonial leader and statesman
1940 Stephen Foster (1826-64), Composer
1945 Sidney Lanier (1842-81), Poet and musician
Thomas Paine (1737-1809), Political writer and pamphleteer
Walter Reed (1851-1902), Physician
Booker T. Washington (1856-1915), Educator
1950 Susan B. Anthony (1820-1906), Social reformer
Alexander Graham Bell (1848-1922), Inventor and scientist
Josiah Gibbs (1839-1903), Physicist
William Crawford Gorgas (1854-1920), Physician and scientist
Theodore Roosevelt (1858-1919), Twenty-sixth President of the U.S.
Woodrow Wilson (1856-1924), Twenty-eighth President of the U.S.
1955 Thomas J. (Stonewall) Jackson (1824-63), Confederate general
George Westinghouse (1846-1914), Inventor
Wilbur Wright (1867-1912), Inventor
1960 Thomas Alva Edison (1847-1931), Inventor
Edward Alexander McDowell (1861-1908), Composer
Henry David Thoreau (1817-62), Poet and essayist
1965 Jane Addams (1860-1935), Social reformer
Oliver Wendell Holmes, Jr. (1841-1935), Associate Justice, U.S. Supreme Court
Sylvanus Thayer (1785-1872), Soldier
Orville Wright (1871-1948), Inventor
1970 Albert Michelson (1852-1931), Physicist

Lillian Wald (1867-1940), Social worker
1973 Louis D. Brandeis (1856-1941), Jurist
George Washington Carver (1859?-1943), Agricultural chemist
Franklin Delano Roosevelt (1882-1945), Thirty-second President of the U.S.
John Philip Sousa (1854-1932), Composer
1976 Clara Barton (1821-1912), Founder of the American Red Cross
Luther Burbank (1849-1926), Horticulturalist
Andrew Carnegie (1835-1919), Steel-maker and philanthropist

Alexander Hamilton Medal

COLUMBIA COLLEGE ALUMNI ASSOCIATION
Hamilton Hall, Columbia University, New York, N.Y. 10027
(212/280-1754)

The Alexander Hamilton Medal, which is of bronze, is awarded annually to a distinguished alumnus or past or present faculty member for service and accomplishment in any field of endeavor. (Class year in parentheses.)

1947 Nicholas Murray Butler ('82)
1948 Frank Diehl Fackenthal ('06)
1949 Vi Kyuin Wellington Koo ('09)
1950 William Joseph Donovan ('05)
1951 Harry James Carman
1952 Carlton Joseph Huntley Hayes ('04)
1953 Arthur Hays Sulzberger ('13)
1954 Frank Smithwick Hogan ('24)
1955 Frederick Coykendall ('95)
Marcellus Hartley Dodge ('03)
1956 Richard Rodgers ('23)
Oscar Hammerstein 2nd ('16)
1957 Grayson Kirk
1958 Edmund Astley Prentis ('06)
1959 Mark Van Doren
1960 Ward Melville ('09)
1961 Columbia College's Nobel Prize-winning Faculty Members and Alumni:
Edward Charles Kendall ('08)
Polykarp Kush
Willis Eugene Lamb, Jr.
Joshua Lederberg ('44)
Hermann Joseph Muller ('10)
John Howard Northrop ('12)
Isidor Isaac Rabi
Harold Clayton Urey
1962 John Allen Krout
1963 Dwight David Eisenhower
1964 William Towson Taylor ('21)
1965 Peter Grimm ('11)
1966 Alfred A. Knopf ('12)
1967 Benjamin J. Buttenwieser ('19)
1968 Allan Nevins
1969 Arthur F. Burns ('25)
Joseph Wood Krutch
1970 Andrew W. Cordier
1971 Lionel Trilling ('25)
1972 No award
1973 Emanuel Celler ('10)
1974 Nicholas McD. McKnight ('21)
1975 Meyer Schapiro ('24)
1976 Arthur B. Krim ('30)
1977 George E. Jonas ('19)

Harvey Prize
TECHNION—ISRAEL INSTITUTE OF
TECHNOLOGY
Technion City, Haifa, Israel (Tel: 227 111)

The $35,000 Harvey Prize is awarded annually for excellence in science, technology or human health, for advancement of peace in the Middle East or for a literary work with profound insight into the life and mores of the Middle Eastern peoples. Two awards are made annually, based on a selection by the Harvey Prize Council, the Technion Senate and the American Technion Society.

1972 Willem J. Kolff, U.S.A., Invention of artificial kidney
Claude E. Shannon, U.S.A., Mathematical theory of communication known as Information Theory
1973 No award
1974 Alan Howard Cotrell, Great Britain, Comprehensive theories concerning the medical properties of materials
Gershom Scholem, Israel, Illuminating studies of Jewish mysticism
1975 George Klein, Sweden, Discoveries in cancer immunology
Edward Teller, U.S.A., Discoveries in atomic, nuclear and solid state physics and their practical application for the production of energy
1976 Saul Lieberman, U.S.A., Investigations into the civilizations of the peoples of the Middle East in the Hellenistic and Roman periods, and commentaries on the sources of Talmudic literature
Herman F. Mark, U.S.A., Research in polymers and plastics
1977 Seymour Benzer, U.S.A., Discoveries in molecular genetics and behavior
Freeman John Dyson, U.S.A., Studies in quantum electrodynamics, ferromagnetism, field theory, statistical mechanics and stability of matter

Lessing Prize
CITY OF HAMBURG
Rathaus, D-2000 Hamburg-1, Federal Republic of Germany

The Lessing Prize of the Free Hanseatic City of Hamburg is awarded every two years for meritorious achievement. The amount of the honorarium is currently 20,000 German marks.

1971 Werner Haftmann, Achievements as museum director and art historian
1973 Hannah Arendt, Work in political thought and philosophy
1975 Gustave Heinemann, Political writings
1977 Jean Amery, Author

Mademoiselle Awards
MADEMOISELLE MAGAZINE
350 Madison Ave., New York, N.Y. 10017 (212/692-5500)

The editors of *Mademoiselle* magazine annually select up to 14 women to receive Mademoiselle Awards honoring outstanding career achievement. Winners are recognized editorially in the magazine and receive a trophy.

1943 Agnes de Mille
Lena Horne
1944 Lauren Bacall
1945 Barbara Bel Geddes
Blanche Thebom
1946 Judy Holliday
Ceil Chapman
1947 Santha Rama Rau
Carson McCullers
1948 No award
1949 Margot Fonteyn
Julie Harris
1950 Marguerite Higgins
Florence Chadwick
Anne Fogarty
1951 Maria Tallchief
Shelley Winters
Maureen Stapleton
1952 Geraldine Page
Melissa Hayden
1953 Audrey Hepburn
Maria Callas
1954 Eva Marie Saint
Anne Klein
1955 Kim Stanley
Leontyne Price
Francoise Sagan
1956 Julie Andrews
Doris Day
1957 Althea Gibson
Carol Lawrence
1958 Anne Bancroft
1959 Ingrid Thulin
Gael Greene
1960 Elaine May
Wilma Rudolph
1961 Monica Vitti
Joan Baez
1962 Barbara Harris
Edna O'Brian
Margaret Court Smith
1963 Deanna Littell
Susan Sontag
Barbra Streisand
1964 Shirley Knight
Renata Adler
Emmanuelle Khanh
Patricia McBride
1965 Suzanne Farrell
Lesley Ann Warren
1966 Betsey Johnson
Jane Marsh
1967 Cecelia Holland
Bobbie Gentry
Faye Dunaway
Frances FitzGerald
1968 Jacqueline du Pre
Sondra Locke
Laura Nyro
Joyce Carol Oates
Wyomia Tyus
1969 Bernadette Devlin
Ali MacGraw
Kay Mazzo
Stephanie Mills
Blythe Danner
Liza Minnelli
Joan Murray
Bernadette Peters
Gloria Rojas
The Urban Corps
1970 Marion Edey

Peggy Cooper
Alice Tepper
Bonnie Sherk
Florette Angel
Eva Jefferson
Mary Breasted
1971 Alicia Bay Laurel
Nikki Giovanni
Marjorie Crow
Sherri Winter Kaplan
Glenda Copes
Susan Davis
Pamela Gentry
1972 Cynthia Buchanan
Suzy Chaffee
Judy Chicago
Micki Grant
Barbara Haskell
Elizabeth Holtzman
Brenda Itta
Bobbie Greene Kilberg
Lesley Oelsner
Amalie R. Rothschild
Actresses of the National Theatre of the Deaf
1973 Kathryn Burkhart
Lisa Connolly
Karol Hope
Sharon Curtin
Mary Emmons
Mary Beth Sheak
Anne Grant
Bette Midler
Carol Ruckdeschel
Claudia Weill
Laura X
Boston Women's Health Book Collective
1974 Rachel Scott
Leslie Crocker Snyder
Thea Lammers
Francine Prose
Sylvia Law
Karen Petersen
J. J. Wilson
Jill Godmilow
Judy Collins
Donna Karan
Colleen Myers
Carol Vittert
1975 Ruth Welting
Twyla Tharp
Louise McAllister Merritt
Susan Brownmiller
Diana Nyad
Gayl Jones
Pamela Zekman
Women Who Formed the First Women's Bank
1976 Lynn Sherr
Martha Coolidge
Ntozake Shange
Trazana Beverley
Lynn B. Jordan
Kristina Nordstrom
Lea Laiman
Eve Sonneman
Clamma Dale
Barbara Kopple
Meryl Streep
Kristina Mailliard
1977 Maxine Hung Kingston

France Moore Lappe
Karen Sauvigne
Susan Meyer
Anne Sutherland Harris
Linda Nochlin
Carol Bellamy
Elizabeth Swados
Marcia Tucker
Lynn Meadow
Linda Weir-Enegren
Carole Brill
Gilda Radner

Man of the Year

TIME MAGAZINE
Time-Life Bldg., 1271 Ave. of the Americas, New York, N.Y. 10019 (212/586-1212)

The editors of *Time* annually select the individual who has had the greatest influence on the course of the previous year as its Man of the Year. A portrait of this person appears on the magazine's year-end cover. The concept of great influence does not always imply praise. Occasionally, groups have also been selected for year-end review.

1927 Charles A. Lindbergh
1928 Walter P. Chrysler
1929 Owen D. Young
1930 Mohandas K. Gandhi
1931 Pierre Laval
1932 Franklin D. Roosevelt
1933 Hugh S. Johnson
1934 Franklin D. Roosevelt
1935 Haile Selassie
1936 Wallis Warfield Simpson
1937 General and Mme. Chiang Kai-Shek
1938 Adolf Hitler
1939 Joseph Stalin
1940 Winston Churchill
1941 Franklin D. Roosevelt
1942 Joseph Stalin
1943 George C. Marshall
1944 Dwight D. Eisenhower
1945 Harry S. Truman
1946 James F. Byrnes
1947 George C. Marshall
1948 Harry S. Truman
1949 Winston Churchill
1950 G.I. Joe
1951 Mohammed Mossadegh
1952 Queen Elizabeth II
1953 Konrad Adenauer
1954 John Foster Dulles
1955 Harlow Curtice
1956 Hungarian Freedom Fighter
1957 Nikita Khrushchev
1958 Charles de Gaulle
1959 Dwight D. Eisenhower
1960 15 Top U.S. Scientists
1961 John F. Kennedy
1962 Pope John XXIII
1963 Martin Luther King
1964 Lyndon B. Johnson
1965 Gen. William Westmoreland
1966 Youth, 25 years and under
1967 Lyndon B. Johnson
1968 Astronauts Anders, Borman and Lovell

1969 Middle Americans
1970 Willy Brandt
1971 Richard Nixon
1972 Richard Nixon and Henry Kissinger
1973 Judge John Sirica
1974 King Faisal
1975 Women of the Year (12)
1976 Jimmy Carter
1977 Anwar Sadat

Molson Prizes
CANADA COUNCIL
151 Sparks St., Box 1047, Ottawa, Ont. K1P 5V8, Canada
(613/237-3400)

The Molson Prizes now each carry a $20,000 honorarium from the Molson Foundation and annually recognize cultural achievement and contributions to the arts, social sciences, the humanities and national unity in Canada.

1963 Donald Creighton
      Alain Grandbois
1964 No award
1965 Jean Gascon
      Frank Scott
1966 Rev. Georges-Henri Levesque
      Hugh McLennan
1967 Arthur Erickson
      Anne Hebert
      Marshall McLuhan
1968 Glenn Gould
      Jean Le Moyne
1970 Jean-Paul Audet
      Morley Callaghan
      Arnold Spohr
1971 Maureen Forrester
      Rina Lasnier
      Norman McLaren
1972 John James Deutsch
      Alfred Pellan
      George Woodcock
1973 Celia Franca
      W. A. C. H. Dobson
      Jean-Paul Lemieux
1974 Alex Colville
      Pierre Dansereau
      Margaret Laurence
1975 Denise Pelletier
      Oxford String Quartet (Andrew Dawes, Terrence Helmer, Kenneth Perkins and Marcel St.-Cyr)
      Jon Vickers
1976 John Hirsch
      Bill Reid
      Jean-Louis Roux
1977 Jack Shadbolt
      George Story
      Gabrielle Roy

Omega Achievers Award
SAMSONITE CORPORATION
Attn: Peter van Der Noot, 1120 E. 45th Ave., Denver, Colo. 80239 (303/344-6262)

As a Bicentennial gesture, 10,000 editors, Congressmen and educators were polled to choose American nominees in 16 categories for the Omega Achievers Award. The award consisted of a sculpture and a commemorative attache case. The awards were made in 1977 "as America enters its third century."

Frank Borman, Aerospace
Norman Borlaug, Agriculture
R. Buckminster Fuller, Architecture
Henry Ford, Sr., Business and Industry
Margaret Mead, Education
Levi Strauss, Fashion
Earl Warren, Law
Alex Haley, Literature
Beverly Sills, Performing Arts
Robert Woodward and Carl Bernstein, The Press
Harry Truman, Public Service
Martin Luther King, Religion
James Cash Penney, Retailing
Jonas Salk, Science and Medicine
General David Sarnoff, Television/Radio
Lowell Thomas, Travel

Orden pour le Merite
MINISTRY OF THE INTERIOR
Rheindorferstrasse 198, D-5300 Bonn, Federal Republic of Germany

The insignia of the Orden pour le Merite is given each year to several individuals for outstanding achievement in art or science.

1974 W. Gentner, Physics
      T.G. Georgiades, Music history
      Fritz Lippmann, Biochemistry
      Sir Ronald Syme, History
1975 Pierre Boulez, Composition and conducting
      Richard Ettinghausen, Art history
      Gyoorg Ligeti, Composition
      Kenzo Tange, Architecture
1976 Not Available
1977 Not Available

Presidential Medal of Freedom
UNITED STATES EXECUTIVE OFFICE OF THE PRESIDENT
The White House, Washington, D.C. 20015 (202/456-1414)

The Presidential Medal of Freedom, which is of gold, is the highest civilian honor given in the United States and recognizes contributions to the national interest or security of the United States, the advancement of world peace or endeavors in the field of culture or other public or private endeavors beneficial to the nation. The Medal is presented in White House ceremonies. The award was established in 1963, replacing the Medal of Freedom. The first group of candidates was selected by the administration of John F. Kennedy but received their awards after his death from President Lyndon B. Johnson, who added posthumous honors both for his predecessor and for Pope John XXIII.

AWARDS BY PRESIDENT KENNEDY
1963 Marian Anderson, singer
      Ralph J. Bunche, United Nations undersecretary
      Ellsworth Bunker, diplomat
      Pablo Casals, cellist
      Genevieve Caulfield, educator
      James B. Conant, educator

John F. Enders, bacteriologist
Felix Frankfurter, jurist
Karl Holton, youth authority
Pope John XXIII
John F. Kennedy, President of U.S.
Robert J. Kiphuth, athletic director
Edwin H. Land, inventor
Herbert H. Lehman, statesman
Robert A. Lovett, statesman
J. Clifford MacDonald, educator
John J. McCloy, banker and statesman
George Meany, labor leader
Alexander Meiklejohn, philosopher
Ludwig Mies van der Rohe, architect
Jean Monnet, European statesman
Luis Muñoz-Marin, Governor, Puerto Rico
Clarence B. Randall, industrialist
Rudolf Serkin, pianist
Edward Steichen, photographer
George W. Taylor, educator
Alan T. Waterman, scientist
Mark S. Watson, journalist
Annie D. Wauneka, public health worker
E. B. White, author
Thornton Wilder, author
Edmund Wilson, author and critic
Andrew N. Wyeth, artist

AWARDS BY PRESIDENT JOHNSON

1964 Dean Acheson, statesman
Detlev W. Bronk, neurophysiologist
Aaron Copland, composer
Willem de Kooning, painter
Walt Disney, animated cartoonist and film producer
J. Frank Dobie, author
Lena F. Edwards, physician and humanitarian
Thomas Stearns Eliot, poet
Lynn Fontanne, actress
John W. Gardner, educator
Rev. Theodore M. Hesburgh, educator
Clarence L. Johnson, aircraft engineer
Frederick R. Kappel, telephone executive
Helen A. Keller, educator and author
John L. Lewis, labor leader
Walter Lippmann, journalist
Alfred Lunt, actor
Ralph Emerson McGill, journalist
Samuel Eliot Morison, historian
Lewis Mumford, urban planner and critic
Edward R. Murrow, radio-TV commentator
Reinhold Niebuhr, theologian
Leontyne Price, soprano
A. Philip Randolph, labor leader
Carl Sandburg, poet and biographer
John Steinbeck, author
Helen B. Taussig, pediatrician
Carl Vinson, legislator
Thomas J. Watson, Jr., industrialist
Paul Dudley White, physician

AWARDS BY PRESIDENT JOHNSON

1967 Ellsworth Bunker, diplomat
Eugene M. Locke, diplomat
Robert W. Komer, government official

AWARDS BY PRESIDENT JOHNSON

1968 Robert S. McNamara, government official
James Webb, NASA administrator

AWARDS BY PRESIDENT JOHNSON

1969 Eugene R. Black, banker
McGeorge Bundy, government official
Clark M. Clifford, statesman
Michael E. DeBakey, surgeon
David Dubinsky, labor leader
Henry Ford II, industrialist
Ralph Ellison, author
W. Averell Harriman, statesman
Bob Hope, comedian
Edgar Kaiser, industrialist
Mary Lasker, philanthropist
John W. Macy, Jr., government official
Gregory Peck, actor
Laurance S. Rockefeller, conservationist
Walt W. Rostow, government official
Dean Rusk, statesman
Merriman Smith, journalist
Cyrus R. Vance, government official
William S. White, journalist
Roy Wilkins, social welfare executive
Whitney M. Young, social welfare executive

AWARDS BY PRESIDENT NIXON

1969 Col. Edwin E. Aldrin, Jr., astronaut
Neil A. Armstrong, astronaut
Lt. Col. Michael Collins, astronaut
Duke Ellington, musician

AWARDS BY PRESIDENT NIXON

1970 Apollo 13 Mission Operations Team
Earl Charles Behrens, journalist
Edward T. Folliard, journalist
Fred Wallace Haise, Jr., astronaut
William M. Henry, journalist
Arthur Krock, journalist
David Lawrence, journalist
George Gould Lincoln, journalist
James A. Lovell, Jr., astronaut
Raymond Moley, journalist
Eugene Ormandy, conductor
Adela Rogers St. Johns, journalist
John Leonard Swigert, Jr., astronaut

AWARDS BY PRESIDENT NIXON

1971 Samuel Goldwyn, film producer
Manlio Brosio, NATO Secretary General
William J. Hopkins, White House executive clerk

AWARDS BY PRESIDENT NIXON

1972 Lila and DeWitt Wallace, founders of *Reader's Digest*
John Paul Vann, adviser in Vietnam war

AWARDS BY PRESIDENT NIXON

1973 John Ford, film director
William P. Rogers, diplomat

AWARDS BY PRESIDENT NIXON

1974 Melvin R. Laird, government official
Charles L. Lowman, orthopedist
Paul G. Hoffman, statesman
1975 No award

AWARDS BY PRESIDENT FORD

1976 David K.E. Bruce, diplomat
Martha Graham, dancer and choreographer
Jesse Owens, track and field champion
Arthur Rubinstein, pianist

AWARDS BY PRESIDENT FORD

1977 I. W. Abel, labor leader
John Bardeen, physicist
Irving Berlin, composer
Norman Borlaug, agricultural scientist
Omar N. Bradley, national security
Arleigh Burke, national security
Alexander Calder, sculptor
Bruce Catton, historian
Joseph P. DiMaggio, baseball star
Ariel Durant, author
Will Durant, author
Arthur Fiedler, conductor
Henry J. Friendly, jurist
Claudia "Lady Bird" Johnson, service to U.S. scenic beauty
Henry A. Kissinger, statesman
Archibald MacLeish, poet
James A. Michener, author
Georgia O'Keeffe, artist
Nelson A. Rockefeller, for government service
Norman Rockwell, illustrator
Donald H. Rumsfeld, for government service
Katherine Filene Shouse, for service to the performing arts
Lowell Thomas, radio-TV commentator and author
James D. Watson, biochemist

AWARDS BY PRESIDENT CARTER

1977 Rev. Martin Luther King, Jr., civil rights leader
Jonas Salk, medical researcher

Smithson Medal

SMITHSONIAN INSTITUTION
1000 Jefferson Dr. SW, Washington, D.C. 20560
(202/628-4422)

The Smithson Medal is the Smithsonian's highest honor and recognizes outstanding contributions to art, science, history, education or technology. The golden medal, which is awarded as merited, carries an honorarium "when appropriate."

1965 Royal Society of London, For outstanding contributions "to the increase and diffusion of knowledge among men"
1968 Edgar P. Richardson, Former director of the Detroit Institute of Arts and Henry Francis duPont Winterthur Museum and chairman of the Smithsonian Art Commission, "for helping to shape the course of art scholarship in this country, interweaving the two streams of history and men into effective unity"
1975 Nancy Hanks, Chairman of the National Endowment for the Arts and the National Council on the Arts, "for her effective leadership . . . in increasing the interest and support of both the Congress and the public in cultural programs for all Americans"
1976 Ralph E. Becker, Washington attorney, in recognition of his donation to the Smithsonian of his valuable collection of political campaign materials, as well as other services to the Institution

Spingarn Medal

NATIONAL ASSOCIATION FOR THE
ADVANCEMENT OF COLORED PEOPLE
1790 Broadway, New York, N.Y. 10019 (212/245-2100)

The Spingarn Medal is awarded annually for the "highest or noblest achievement by an American Negro" for the preceeding year or years. A Committee of Award selects the winner in a scientific, spiritual, commercial, educational, artistic or other field of endeavor. The medal is presented at the NAACP annual convention by a distiguished citizen.

1915 Ernest D. Just, Head of Department of Physiology, Howard University, for research in biology
1916 Maj. Charles Young, U.S. Army, for services organizing the Liberian constabulary and developing roads in the Republic of Liberia
1917 Harry T. Burleigh, Composer, pianist and singer, for excellence in creative music
1918 William Stanley Braithwaite, Poet, literary critic and editor, for distinguished achievement in literature
1919 Archibald H. Grimke, Former U.S. Consul to Santo Domingo, for distinguished service to his race and country
1920 W. E. B. DuBois, Author, editor, for the founding and calling of the Pan-African Congress
1921 Charles S. Gilpin, Actor, for his performance in the title role of The Emperor Jones by Eugene O'Neill
1922 Mary B. Talbert, Former president of the National Assn. of Colored Women, for service to the women of her race and for restoration of the Frederick Douglass Home
1923 George Washington Carver, Head, Department of Research, Tuskegee Institute, for distinguished research in agricultural chemistry
1924 Roland Hayes, Singer, for his interpretations of Negro folk music and work as a soloist with the Boston Symphony Orchestra
1925 James Weldon Johnson, Former U.S. Consul in Venezuela and Nicaragua, former editor and secretary of the NAACP, for distinguished achievements
1926 Carter G. Woodson, Historian, founder of the Assn. for the Study of Negro Life and editor, for 10 years' service in collecting and publishing records of the Negro in America
1927 Anthony Overton, Businessman, president of Victory Life Insurance Co., for his successful business career
1928 Charles W. Chesnutt, Author, for his pioneer work depicting the life and struggle of the American Negro
1929 Mordecai Wyatt Johnson, President, Howard University, for his successful administration as the first Negro president of the University and for his success in securing federal appropriations for the University
1930 Henry A. Hunt, Principal, Fort Valley High School, for devotion in the education of Negroes in rural Georgia
1931 Richard Berry Harrison, Actor, for his "fine and reverent characterization of the Lord" in The Green Pastures and for his long achievement interpreting English drama "for the mass of colored people"
1932 Robert Russa Moton, Principal, Tuskegee Institute, for his leadership at home, his stand on education in Haiti, his support of equal opportunity for the Negro in the American public school system and his expression of the best ideals of the Negro in his book, What the Negro Thinks
1933 Max Yergan, Missionary, for his 10 years as American YMCA secretary among the native students of South Africa and his efforts toward interracial understanding
1934 William Taylor Burwell Williams, Dean, Tuskegee Institute, for his long service in Negro education

1935 **Mary McLeod Bethune,** Founder and president of Bethune-Cookman College, for surmounting difficulties in creating an educational institution in Daytona Beach, Fla.

1936 **Howard Hope,** President, Atlanta University, for his leadership and distinguished role in education

1937 **Walter White,** Executive secretary of the NAACP, for his personal investigation of 41 lynchings and eight race riots and for lobbying for a federal anti-lynching bill

1938 **No award**

1939 **Marian Anderson,** Singer, for her special achievement in music and for "her magnificent dignity as a human being"

1940 **Louis T. Wright,** Surgeon, for his contributions and high standards as a medical man

1941 **Richard Wright,** Author, for his depiction of the effects of proscription, segregation and denial of opportunities of the American Negro in his books, *Uncle Tom's Children* and *Native Son*

1942 **A. Philip Randolph,** Labor leader and international president of the Brotherhood of Sleeping Car Porters

1943 **Wiliam H. Hastie,** Jurist and educator, for being an uncompromising champion of equal justice

1944 **Charles R. Drew,** Scientist, for his outstanding work with blood plasma

1945 **Paul Robeson,** Singer and actor, for his achievement in theater and on the concert stage

1946 **Thurgood Marshall,** Special counsel of the NAACP, for his service as a lawyer before many courts, especially in the Texas Primary Case, which influenced the end of disenfranchisement because of race

1947 **Percy L. Julian,** Research chemist, for his technical skill and for his discoveries to benefit mankind

1948 **Channing H. Tobias,** "For his consistent role as a defender of fundamental civil liberties" and his contributions to the President's Council on Civil Liberties

1949 **Ralph J. Bunche,** International civil servant, for his service as U.N. mediator in Palestine, his distinguished scholarship, his contributions in fashioning sections of the U.N. Charter and his efforts as director of the Trusteeship Council

1950 **Charles Hamilton Houston,** Chairman, NAACP Legal Committee, for his championship of equal rights

1951 **Mabel Keaton Staupers,** Leader National Assn. of Colored Graduate Nurses, for spearheading the integration of Negro nurses into American life

1952 **Henry T. Moore,** NAACP leader in Florida; "a martyr in the crusade for freedom"; assassinated by a bomb in his home, Christmas Eve 1951

1953 **Paul R. Williams,** Architect

1954 **Theodore K. Lawless,** Physician, educator and philanthropist

1955 **Carl Murphy,** Editor, publisher and civic leader

1956 **Jackie Robinson,** Athlete

1957 **Martin Luther King, Jr.,** "Dedicated and selfless clergyman," for creative contributions and outstanding leadership in the Montgomery bus boycott

1958 **Daisy Bates and the Little Rock Nine,** For "their pioneer role in upholding the basic ideals of American democracy in the face of continuing harassment"

1959 **Edward Kennedy (Duke) Ellington,** Composer and orchestra leader

1960 **Langston Hughes,** Poet, author and playwright

1961 **Kenneth B. Clark,** Professor of Psychology at the College of the City of New York; founder and director of the Northside Center for Child Development

1962 **Robert C. Weaver,** Administrator, Housing and Home Finance Agency

1963 **Medgar Wiley Evers,** NAACP Field Secretary for Mississippi; World War II veteran; "hero and martyr felled by an assassin's bullet" on June 12, 1963

1964 **Roy Wilkins,** Executive Director of the NAACP, "for the militancy of his leadership, the integrity of his performance, his determined and persistent pursuit of clearly perceived goals, his dedication and intelligence"

1965 **Leontyne Price,** Metropolitan Opera star

1966 **John H. Johnson,** Founder and president of the Johnson Publishing Co.

1967 **Edward W. Brooke III,** "First Negro to win popular election to the United States Senate"

1968 **Sammy Davis, Jr.,** Broadway and Hollywood star, civil rights activist

1969 **Clarence M. Mitchell, Jr.,** Director, NAACP Washington Bureau; lobbyist; specifically for role in passage of the Civil Rights Act of 1968 with its fair housing provisions

1970 **Jacob Lawrence,** Artist, teacher and humanitarian

1971 **Leon Howard Sullivan,** Clergyman, activist and prophet

1972 **Gordon Alexander Buchanan Parks,** "Twentieth Century Renaissance Man"

1973 **Wilson C. Riles,** Educator

1974 **Damon J. Keith,** Jurist

1975 **No award**

1976 **Hank Aaron,** Athlete

1977 **Alvin Ailey,** Dancer, choreographer and artistic director

UCLA Alumnus of the Year Award
Professional Achievement Award
UCLA ALUMNI ASSOCIATION
405 Hilgard Dr., Los Angeles, Calif. 90024 (213/825-3901)

The Alumnus of the Year Award honors a graduate who has "rendered a special and outstanding service to UCLA, or who, by personal achievement, has brought honor and distinction to the University." The Alumni Awards Selection Committee picks the winner from nominations of alumni and friends. (Class year in parentheses.)

1946 **M. Philip Davis** ('28)
1947 **William C. Ackerman** ('24)
1948 **Frederick F. Houser** ('26)
1949 **Ralph Bunche** ('27)
1950 **Victor Hansen** ('26)
1951 **Bruce Russell** ('26)
1952 **Glenn T. Seaborg** ('34)
1953 **Agnes DeMille** ('26)
1954 **Edward W. Carter** ('32)
1955 **Wilbur C. Johns** ('25)
1956 **John E. Canaday** ('27)
1957 **Cyril C. Nigg** ('27)
1958 **Saul Winstein** ('34)
1959 **Warren H. Crowell** ('27)
1960 **Charles I. Schottland** ('27)
1961 **Thomas J. Cunningham** ('28)
1962 **Jack R. Robinson** ('42)
1963 **Waldo E. Lyon** ('36)
1964 **Arjay R. Miller** ('37)
1965 **Jerome Hines** ('43)
1966 **Louis Banks** ('37)
1967 **William E. Forbes** ('28)
1968 **Carol Burnett** ('54)
1969 **W. Thomas Davis** ('31)

1970 H.R. Haldeman ('48)
1971 John V. Vaughn ('32)
1972 M.J. Frankovich ('34)
1973 John R. Wooden (Honorary Alumnus)
1974 Thomas Bradley ('41)
1975 Francis Ford Coppola MFA ('67)
1976 Fred L. Whipple ('27)
1977 E. Cardon Walker ('38)

Professional Achievement Awards honor the distinguished career achievement of a UCLA alumnus. Selection is made by a subcommittee of the Alumni Awards Selection Committee from nominations, and awards are given in more than a dozen fields, although not all fields are represented in any given year. (Class year in parentheses.)

1962 Dudley E. Browne ('34) Business
      Dean E. McHenry ('32) Education
      Ernest H. Martin ('42) Entertainment
      Frank S. Balthis ('26) Judiciary
1963 William P. Gray ('34) Law
      Louise Seyler Geyer ('27), MA ('38), Ph.D. ('45)
      Education
1964 Glenn M. Anderson ('36) Government
      Thomas P. Phelan ('29) Business
      Hale Sparks ('30) Education
1965 Scribner Birlenbach ('28) Business
      Jules Gregory Charney ('38), MS ('40), Ph. D.
      ('46) Science
      John D. French, MD ('33) Medicine
      Augustus F. Hawkins ('31) Government
      Lt. Gen. William R. Peers ('37) Military
      Charles E. Rickershauser, Jr. ('49), LLB ('57)
      Public Service
      Robert Waterfield ('45) Athletics
      Charles Wellman ('37) Finance
1966 Walter Dunbar ('38) Public Service
      Kenneth Kroehler ('39) Business
      Maj. Gen. Edward G. Lansdale ('30) Military
      J.D. Morgan ('41) Athletics
      Bertram L. Perkins ('47) Business
      Maxwell L. Rafferty ('38) Education
      Judge David W. Williams ('34) Jurisprudence
      Elliot McKay See, Jr. ('62) Special Professional
      Achievement Award, Astronaut
1967 Maj. Gen. Norman J. Anderson ('34) Military
      M.J. Frankovich ('34) Business and Entertainment
      Chancellor Glenn S. Dumke ('42) Education
      John D. Roberts ('41), MD ('44) Science
1968 Vincent M. Barnett, Jr. ('35) Education
      Congressman James S. Corman ('42) Government
      Maurice J. Dahlem ('34) Business
1969 Walter Cunningham MA ('61) Astronaut
      Maj. Gen. Salve H. Matheson ('42) Military
      Dorothy Wright Nelson ('50), LLB ('53) Law
      and Education
1970 Joseph Blatchford ('56) Government
      Madeline C. Hunter ('36), M.Ed. ('51), Ed.D.
      ('66) Education
      Donn D. Moomaw Ministry
1971 Frank T. Cary ('43) Business
      Lawrence E. Irell ('32) Law
      Joseph Jerome Kaufman ('42) Medicine
      Chauncey J. Medberry III ('38) Finance
      Maj. Gen. John Kirk Singlaub ('58) Military
      Sen. Ted Stevens ('47) Government

1972 Jeanne Quint Benoliel, D.N.S., M.S. ('55) Nursing
      Thomas Bradley ('41) Government
      Rita Milaw Lawrence ('40) Business
      E. Cardon Walker ('38) Entertainment
      Harold M. Williams ('46) Business and Education
1973 Gladys Ancrum, M.P.H. ('65), Dr. P.H. ('68)
      Nursing
      Josephine Miles ('32) Education
      Paul Ichira Terasaki ('50), MA ('52), Ph. D. ('56)
      Medicine
1974 Arthur Ashe, Jr. ('66) Athletics
      Yvonne Braithwaite Burke ('53) Government
      R. Bruce Merrifield ('43), Ph.D. ('49) Science
      Robert W. Rand ('45), Ph.D., M.D. Medicine
      Donald M. Small M.D. ('60) Medicine
1975 Ralph E. Crump ('50) Science
      Lamont Johnson (1942-43) Entertainment
      Judge Joan Dempsey Klein, LL.B ('55) Law
1976 Ross M. Blakely ('40) Finance
      William Frederickson, Jr. ('31) Recreation
      Bernard S. Jefferson ('31) Judiciary
      Elias George Theros ('47), MD ('57) Medicine
1977 Howard L. Berman ('62), LLB ('65)
      Roy Huggins ('39)
      William B. Keene ('49), LLB ('52)
      Walter H. Munk Ph. D. ('47)
      Page Ackerman ('29-31)
      Louise M. Darling ('33)

International Prize

JENNY AND ANTTI WIHURI FOUNDATION
Arkadiankatu 21 B 25, 00100-Helsinki 10, Finland (Tel: 444 145)

The Foundation awards prizes as merited for contributions to art, culture, science and economics, as determined by the organization and its Research Institute in consultation with experts from the field where appropriate.

1958 Rolf Nevanlinna
1961 Pentti Halonen
      Vaino Hovi
      Joonas Kokkonen
1968 J. McMichael
      Lars Ahlfors
1971 P. B. Hirsh
1976 Georg Henrik von Wright
      Jaakko Hintikka

Woman of Conscience Award

NATIONAL COUNCIL OF WOMEN OF THE U.S.
345 E. 46th St., New York, N.Y. 10017 (212/697-1278)

The $1,500 Woman of Conscience Award, which is funded by Clairol and administered by the National Council of Women, honors achievements in which women responded to a compelling community problem, demonstrated courage or made an unusual contribution. The winner is selected by a committee consisting of some members of the Council's Executive Committee and additional judges.

1963 Rachel Carson, Author

1964 **Hazel Brannon Smith,** Mississippi newspaper editor
1965 **Virginia Sanders,** Minnesota Plan author and advocate of education for women
1966 **Judge Florence M. Kelley,** New York City Family Court
1967 **Ellen Jackson,** Creative community program leadership
1968 **Dorothy Ainsworth**
     Mrs. Andrew Brown
     Mary S. Calderone
     Mrs. Edward Carter
     Mme. Marcel De Gallaix
     Mrs. D. Joe Hendrickson
     Florence Smith Jacobsen
     May Hall James
     Mrs. Martin Luther King, Jr.
     Dorothy M. Lewis
     Margaret Moore
     Jan Papenek
     Mamie B. Reese
     Mrs. Harold E. Rodden
     Mrs. Dean Rusk
     Dorothea W. Sitley
     Hilda Torrop
     Mrs. Raphael Tuorover
     Helen F. Winfield
     Mrs. William Volker
     Lt. Violet Hill Whyte
1969 **Annie May Bankhead,** Black leader
1970 **Ellen Sulzberger Straus,** Creator of *Call for Action,* New York radio program
1971 **No award**
1972 **Sister Ruth Dowd,** Educator of teenagers in Harlem
1973 **Patricia Smith,** Hospital and medical work in Vietnam
1974 **Frances F. Pauley,** Civil Rights worker
1975 **Margaret Mead,** Anthropologist
1976 **Barbara Jordan,** Congresswoman
1977 **Nancy Hanks,** Chairman, National Endowment for the Arts

Woman of the Year
LADIES' HOME JOURNAL
641 Lexington Ave., New York, N.Y. 10022 (212/935-6160)

Selection as a Ladies' Home Journal Woman of the Year gives recognition to women in various fields who are United States citizens for involved and accomplished leadership that provides an inspiring example to other women. The readers of *Ladies' Home Journal* return a ballot to the magazine for selections reviewed by a jury panel. Women selected receive a gold pin studded with a diamond "W."

1973 **Helen Hayes,** Arts and Humanities
     Shirley Chisholm, Public Affairs
     Katharine Graham, Economy and Business
     Nikki Giovanni, Youth Leadership
     Ellen Sulzberger Straus, Voluntary Action
     LaDonna Harris, Human Rights
     Mary Lasker, Quality of Life
     Virginia Apgar, Science and Research
1974 **Martha W. Griffiths,** Public Affairs
     Patricia Roberts Harris, Business and Professions
     Dorothy Height, Human Rights
     Katharine Hepburn, Creative Arts
     Billie Jean King, Sports
     Barbara McDonald, Community Service
     Dixy Lee Ray, Science and Research
     Barbara Walters, Communications
1975 **Maj. Gen. Jeanne M. Holm,** Government and Diplomacy
     Barbara Jordan, Political Life
     Sylvia Porter, Business and Economics
     Joan Ganz Cooney, Education
     Helen Thomas, Communications
     Lillian Hellman, Creative Arts
     Lady Bird Johnson, Quality of Life
     LaRue Diaforli, Humanitarian and Community Service
1976 **Betty Furness,** Business and Economics
     Margaret Mead, Science and Research
     Beverly Sills, Performing Arts
     Capt. Micki King, Sports
     Shirley Hufstedler, Government and Diplomacy
     Gov. Ella Grasso, Political Life
     Maya Angelou, Communications
     Annie Dodge Wauneka, Educational Leadership
     Betty Ford, Humanitarian and Community Service
1977 **Ruth C. Clusen,** Political Life
     Elisabeth Kubler-Ross, Science and Research
     Gloria Scott, Humanitarian and Community Service
     Liz Carpenter, Government and Public Affairs
     Elizabeth Drew, Communications
     Margaret McNamara, Education
     Addie Wyatt, Business and Economy
     Marian Anderson, Creative Arts
     Sheila Young Ochowicz, Sports

Contents

Books & Literature

Related Awards

Grand Prix du Roman

ACADEMIE FRANCAISE
INSTITUTE DE FRANCE
23 Quai de Conti, 75006-Paris, France (Tel: 326-02-92)

Of the dozens of literary prizes awarded by the Academy, the 10,000-franc Grand Prix du Roman is one of the most important. It annually honors an author or poet for a body of work displaying notable style and significant thought. A committee chooses the winner.

1915 Paul Acker, Collected works
1916 Avesnes, L'ile hereuse
1917 Charles Geniaux, Collected works
1918 Camille Mayran, Gotton
1919 Pierre Benoit, L'Atlantide
1920 Andre Corthis, Pour moi seul
1921 Pierre Villetard, Monsieur Bille dans la tourmente
1922 Francis Carco, L'homme traque
1923 Alphonse de Chateaubriant, La Briere
1924 Emile Henriot, Aricie Brun ou les Vertus
1925 Francois Dourourcau, L'Enfant de la Victoire
1926 Francois Mauriac, Le Desert de l'amour
1927 Joseph Kessel, Les Captifs
1928 Jean Balde, Reine d'Arbieu
1929 Andre Demaison, Le Livre des betes qu'on appelle sauvages
1930 Jacques de Lacretelle, Amour nuptial
1931 Henri Pourrat, Gaspard des montagnes
1932 Jacques Chardonne, Claire
1933 Roger Chacvire, Mademoiselle de Bois-Dauphin
1934 Paul Regnier, L'Abbaye d'Evolayne
1935 Albert Touchard, La Guepe
1936 Georges Bernanos, Journal d'un cure de campagne
1937 Guy de Poutales, La Peche miraculeuse
1938 Jean de la Varende, Le Centaure de Dieu
1939 Antoine de Saint-Exupery, Terre des hommes
1940 Edouard Peisson, Le Voyage d'Edgar
1941 Robert Bourget-Pailleron, La Folie d'Hubert
1942 Jean Blanzat, L'Orage du matin
1943 J.H. Louwyck, Danse pour ton ombre
1944 Pierre de Lagarde, Valmaurie
1945 Marc Blancpain, Le Solitaire
1946 Jean Orieux, Fontagre
1947 Philippe Heriat, La Famille Bousardel
1948 Yves Gandon, Ginevre
1949 Yvonne Pagniez, Evasion
1950 Joseph Jolinon, Les Provinciaux
1951 Bernard Barbey, Chevaux abandonnes sur le champ de bataille
1952 Henri Castillou, Le Feu de l'Eina
1953 Jean Hougron, Mort en fraude
1954 Pierre Moinot, La Chasse royale
1955 Michel de Saint-Pierre, Les Aristocrates
1956 Paul Guth, Le Naif localaire
1957 Jacques de Bourbon-Busset, Le Silence et la Joie
1958 Henri Queffelec, Un royaume sous la mer
1959 Gabriel d'Aubarede, La Foi de notre enfance
1960 Christian Marciaux, Notre Dame de Desempaies
1961 Pham Van Ky, Perdre la demeure
1962 Michel Mohrt, La prison maritime
1963 Robert Margerit, La Revolution
1964 Michel Droit, Le Retour
1965 Jean Husson, Le Cheval d'Herbeleau
1966 Francois Nourissier, Une histoire
1967 Michel Tourier, Vendredi ou les Limbes du Pacifique
1968 Albert Cohen, Belle du Seigneur
1969 Pierre Moustiers, La Parole
1970 Bertrand Poirot-Delpech, La Folle de Lituanie

1971 Jean d'Ormesson, La Gloire de l'Empire
1972 Patrick Modiano, Les Boulevards de ceinture
1973 Michel Deon, Un taxi mauve
1974 Kleber Headens, Adios
1975 No award
1976 Pierre Schoendoerffer, Le crabe-tambour
1977 Camille Bourniquel, Tempo

Jane Addams Children's Book Award

JANE ADDAMS PEACE ASSOCIATION
345 E. 46th St., New York, N.Y. 10017 (212/MU 2-8830)

The Jane Addams Children's Book Award is given annually by the Jane Addams Peace Association and the Women's International League for Peace and Freedom to honor the book that most effectively promotes peace, social justice and world community in the eyes of a committee of judges drawn from individuals concerned with children's books. A scroll is awarded to the recipient. Books may be submitted for consideration.

1953 Eva Knox, People Are Important
1954 Jean Ketchum, Stick-In-The-Mud
1955 Elizabeth Yates, Rainbow Around The World
1956 Arna Bontemps, Story Of The Negro
1957 Margot Benary-Isbert, Blue Mystery
1958 William O. Steele, The Perilous Road
1959 No award
1960 Edith Patterson Meyer, Champions Of Peace
1961 Shirley L. Arora, What Then, Raman?
1962 Aimee Sommerfelt, The Road To Agra
1963 Ryerson Johnson, Monkey And The Wild, Wild Wind
1964 John F. Kennedy, Profiles In Courage
1965 Duane Bradley, Meeting With A Stranger
1966 Emily Cheney Neville, Berries Goodman
1967 Robert Burch, Queenie Peavy
1968 Erik Christian Haugaard, The Little Fishes
1969 Esther Hautzig, The Endless Steppe
1970 No award
1971 Cornelia Meigs, Jane Addams: Pioneer Of Social Justice
1972 Betty Underwood, The Tamarack Tree
1973 S. Carl Hirsch, The Riddle Of Racism
1974 Nicholasa Mohr, Nilda
1975 Charlotte Pomerantz, The Princess And The Admiral
1976 Eloise Greenfield, Paul Robeson
1977 Milton Meltzer, Never To Forget: The Jews Of The Holocaust

Arts and Letters Awards

AMERICAN ACADEMY AND INSTITUTE OF
ARTS AND LETTERS
633 W. 155th St., New York, N.Y. 10032 (212/286-1480)

To encourage qualified writers and help them continue their creative work, the Institute annually gives $3,000 in awards to non-members. These Arts and Letters Awards may not be applied for. Similar awards are given in art and music.

The National Institute of Arts and Letters administered the National Book Awards in 1975 and 1976. These are now administered by the Association of American Publishers and are found on pp. 39-41.

In addition to these specific literature awards, the American Academy and Institute of Arts and Letters gives several awards for achievements in various arts and belles lettres, which will be found on pp. 30, 36, 53 and 57.

1941
Mary M. Colum — Jesse Stuart

1942
Hermann Broch — Norman Corwin
Edgar Lee Masters — Muriel Rukeyser

1943
Virgil Geddes — Carson McCullers
Jose Garcia Villa — Joseph Wittlin

1944
Hugo Ignotus — Jeremy Ingalls
Thomas Sancton — Karl Shapiro
Eudora Welty — Tennessee Williams

1945
Kenneth Fearing — Feike Feikema
Alexander Greendale — Norman Rosten
Jean Stafford — Marguerite Young

1946
Gwendolyn Brooks — Kenneth Burke
Malcolm Cowley — Peter DeVries
Langston Hughes — Arthur Laurents
Marianne Craig Moore — Arthur Schlesinger, Jr.
Irwin Shaw

1947
Nelson Algren — Eleanor Clark
Lloyd Frankenberg — Robert Lowell
Elizabeth Parsons — James Still

1948
Bertolt Brecht — Dudley Fitts
Harry Levin — James F. Powers
Genevieve Taggard — Allen Tate

1949
Leonie Adams — James Agee
Joseph Campbell — Alfred Kazin
Vincent McHugh — James Stern

1950
John Berryman — Paul Bowles
Maxwell David Geismar — Caroline Gordon
Shirley Graham — Hyam Plutzik

1951
Newton Arvin — Elizabeth Bishop
Louise Bogan — Brendan Gill
Randall Jarrell — Vladimir Nabokov

1952
Saul Bellow — Alfred Hayes
Theodore Roethke — Elizabeth Spencer
Peter Taylor — Yvor Winters

1953
Eric Bentley — Isabel Bolton
Richard Chase — Francis Fergusson

Paul Goodman — Delmore Schwartz

1954
Hannah Arendt — Ray Bradbury
Richmond Lattimore — David Riesman
Ruthven Todd — C. Vann Woodward

1955
Richard Eberhart — Robert Horan
Chester Kallman — William Krasner
Milton Lott — Morton D. Zabel

1956
James Baldwin — John Cheever
Henry Russell Hitchcock — Joseph Kerman
Josephine Miles — Priscilla Robertson
Frank Rooney

1957
Leslie Fiedler — Robert Fitzgerald
Mary McCarthy — W.S. Merwin
Flannery O'Connor — Robert Pack

1958
Joseph Frank — Herbert Gold
R.W.B. Lewis — William Maxwell
William Meredith — James Purdy
Francis Steegmuller

1959
Truman Capote — Leon Edel
Charles Jackson — Stanley J. Kunitz
Conrad Richter — Isaac Bashevis Singer
James Wright

1960
Irving Howe — Norman Mailer
Wright Morris — Adrienne Rich
Philip Roth — W.D. Snodgrass
May Swenson

1961
Edward Dahlberg — Jean Garrigue
Mark Harris — David McCord
Warren Miller — Brian Moore
Howard Nemerov

1962
Daniel Fuchs — John Hawkes
Galway Kinnell — Edwin O'Connor
Frank O'Connor — Joan Williams
John A. Williams

1963
Richard Bankowsky — William Gaddis
Joseph Heller — John Hollander
William Humphrey — Peter Matthiessen
Richard Yates

1964
Lionel Abel — Dorothy Baker
Norman Fruchter — Thom Gunn
Eric Hoffer — David Ignatow
Kenneth Rexroth

1965
Ben Belitt — Robert Bly

J. V. Cunningham
Joseph Mitchell
Henry Roth

Denise Levertov
P. M. Pasinetti
Harvey Swados

1966
William Alfred
James Dickey
Josephine Herbst
Gary Snyder

John Barth
Shirley Hazzard
Edwin Honig
M. B. Tolson

1967
Philip Booth
Daniel Hoffman
Stanley Edgar Hyman
David Wagoner

Hortense Calisher
Bernard Knox
Walker Percy

1968
John Malcolm Brinnin
Reuel Denny
John Frederick Nims
Richard G. Stern

Fred Chappell
Howard Moss
Julia Randall
Eleanor Ross Taylor

1969
John Ashbery
Allen Ginsberg
L. E. Sissman

George P. Elliott
Hugh Kenner

1970
Brewster Ghiselin
Richard Howard
Jerzy Kosinski
N. Scott Momaday
F. D. Reeve

Gordon S. Haight
Pauline Kael
James A. McPherson
Grace Paley
Kurt Vonnegut, Jr.

1971
Wendell Berry
Martin Duberman
Charles Gordone
Arthur Kopit
Leonard Nathan
Wilfrid Sheed

Stanley Burnshaw
Ronald Fair
Barbara Howes
Leonard Michaels
Reynolds Price

1972
Harry Crews
Paula Fox
Pauline Hanson
Israel Horovitz
Gilbert Rogin

Peter Davison
Penelope Gilliatt
Michael S. Harper
Walter Kerr
Ann Stanford

1973
Marius Bewley
Irving Feldman
Dorothy Hughes
Daniel P. Mannix
Jonathan Schell

Maeve Brennan
Frances FitzGerald
Philip Levine
Cynthia Ozick
Austin Warren

1974
Ann Cornelisen
Elizabeth Hardwick
Donald Justice
Charles Rosen
James Tate
Lanford Wilson

Stanley Elkin
Josephine Johnson
David Rabe
Sam Shepard
Henry Van Dyke

1975
William S. Burroughs
John Gardner
Terrence McNally

J. P. Donleavy
William H. Gass
Tillie Olsen

John Peck
Colin M. Turnbull

Mark Strand
Helen Hennessy Vendler

1976
Robert Coover
E. L. Doctorow
Kenneth Koch
John Simon
Susan Sontag

Robert Craft
Eugene D. Genovese
Charles Simic
Louis Simpson
Louis Zukofsky

1977
A. R. Ammons
Cynthia Macdonald
John McPhee
Paul Theroux
Robert Watson

Walter J. Bate
Joseph McElroy
James Schuyler
Anne Tyler
Charles Wright

Hans Christian Andersen International Medal

INTERNATIONAL BOARD ON BOOKS FOR
YOUNG PEOPLE
Leonhardsgraben 38A, CH-4051 Basel, Switzerland

The Hans Christian Andersen International Medal is
given every two years to a living author and a living
artist for an outstanding body of work that has made
an important contribution to children's literature. An
international jury appointed by the board's executive
committee makes the selection.

1956 Eleanor Farjeon, (United Kingdom)
1958 Astrid Lindgren, (Sweden)
1960 Erich Kastner, (Germany)
1962 Meindert DeJong, (U.S.A.)
1964 Rene Guillot, (France)
1966 Alois Carigiet, (author) (Switzerland)
     Tove Jansson, (illustrator) (Finland)
1968 James Kriiss, (author) (Germany)
     Jose Maria Sanchez Silva, (author) (Spain)
     Jiri Trnka, (illustrator) (Czechoslovakia)
1970 Gianni Rodari, (author) (Italy)
     Maurice Sendak, (illustrator) (U.S.A.)
1972 Scott O'Dell, (author) (U.S.A.)
     Ib Spang Olsen, (illustrator) (Denmark)
1974 Maria Gripe, (author) (Sweden)
     Farshid Misghali, (illustrator) (Iran)
1976 Cecil Bodker, (author) (Denmark)
     Tatjana Mawrina, (illustrator) (USSR)

Anisfield-Wolf Awards

CLEVELAND FOUNDATION
National City Bank Bldg., Cleveland, Ohio 44114
(216/861-3810)

The Anisfield-Wolf Awards, with cash prizes of $1,500,
are given annually for books published during the
previous year that lead to improved intergroup relations in the judgment of an awards committee. Awards
are given for scholarly books and for fiction, drama,
poetry, biography, autobiography or any other form of
creative writing. The award initially was sponsored by
The Saturday Review.

1935 Harold Gosnell, *Negro Politicians: The Rise of Negro
     Politics in Chicago*

1936 Julian Huxley and A. C. Haddon, *We Europeans: A Survey of "Racial" Problems*
1937 No award
1938 No award
1939 E. Franklin Frazier, *The Negro Family in the United States*
1940 No award
1941 Leopold Infeld, *Quest*
James G. Leyburn, *The Haitian People*
1942 Zora Neale Hurston, *Dust Tracks on a Road*
Donald Pierson, *Negroes in Brazil*
1943 Maurice Samuel, *The World of Sholom Aleichem*
Roi Ottley, *New World A-Coming*
1944 Gwethalyn Graham, *Earth and High Heaven*
Gunnar Myrdal, *An American Dilemma*
1945 Wallace Stegner and the editors of *Look*, *One Nation*
St. Clair Drake and Horace Cayton, *Black Metropolis*
1946 Sholem Asch, *East River*
Pauline R. Kibbe, *Latin Americans in Texas*
1947 Worth Tuttle Hedden, *The Other Room*
John Collier, *The Indians of the Americas*
1948 Alan Paton, *Cry the Beloved Country*
J. C. Furnas, *Anatomy of Paradise*
1949 S. Andhil Fineberg, *Punishment Without Crime*
Shirley Graham, *Your Most Humble Servant*
1950 John Hersey, *The Wall*
Henry Gibbs, *Twilight in South Africa*
1951 Laurens van der Post, *Venture to the Interior*
Brewton Berry, *Race Relations*
1952 Han Suyin, *A Many-Splendored Thing*
Farley Mowat, *People of the Deer*
1953 Vernon Bartlett, *Struggle for Africa*
Langston Hughes, *Simple Takes a Wife*
1954 Oden Meeker, *Report on Africa*
Lyle Saunders, *Cultural Difference and Medical Care*
1955 John P. Dean and Alex Rosen, *A Manual of Intergroup Relations*
George W. Shepherd, Jr., *They Wait in Darkness*
1956 Father Trevor Huddleston, *Naught for Your Comfort*
Gilberto Freyre, *The Masters and the Slaves: A Study in the Development of Brazilian Civilization*
1957 Jessie B. Sams, *White Mother*
South African Institute of Race Relations, *Handbook on Race Relations*
1958 Martin Luther King, Jr., *Stride Toward Freedom*
George Eaton Simpson and J. Milton Yinger, *Racial and Cultural Minorities*
1959 John Haynes Holmes, *I Speak for Myself*
Basil Davidson, *The Lost Cities of Africa*
1960 E. R. Braithwaite, *To Sir, With Love*
Louis E. Lomax, *The Reluctant African*
1961 Dwight L. Dumond, *Antislavery*
John Howard Griffin, *Black Like Me*
Gina Allen, *The Forbidden Man*
1962 Theodosius Dobzhansky, *Mankind Evolving*
1963 Bernhard E. Olson, *Faith and Prejudice*
Harold R. Isaacs, *The New World of Negro Americans*
Nathan Glazer and Daniel P. Moynihan, *Beyond the Melting Pot*
1964 James W. Silver, *Mississippi: The Closed Society*
Milton M. Gordon, *Assimilation in American Life*
James M. McPherson, *The Struggle for Equality: Abolitionists and the Negro in the Civil War and Reconstruction*
Abram L. Sachar, *A History of the Jews*
1965 Amram Scheinfeld, *Your Heredity and Environment*
Claude Brown, *Manchild in the Promised Land*

Malcolm X and Alex Haley, *Autobiography of Malcolm X*
H. C. Baldry, *Unity of Mankind in Greek Thought*
1966 Oscar Lewis, *La Vida*
David Brion Davis, *The Problem of Slavery in Western Culture*
1967 Raul Hilberg, *The Destruction of European Jews*
Norman Cohn, *Warrant for Genocide: The Myth of the Jewish World Conspiracy and The Protocols of the Elders of Zion*
Robert Coles, *Children of Crisis: A Study of Courage and Fear*
1968 Gwendolyn Brooks, *In the Mecca*
E. Earl Baughman and W. Grant Dahlstrom, *Negro and White Children*
Stuart Levine and Nancy O. Lurie, *The American Indian Today*
Leonard Dinnerstein, *The Leo Frank Case*
1969 Florestan Fernandes, *The Negro in Brazilian Society*
Vine Deloria, Jr., *Custer Died for Your Sins*
Dan T. Carter, *Scottsboro*
Audrie Girdner and Anne Loftis, *The Great Betrayal*
1972 Lee Rainwater, *Behind Ghetto Walls*
Betty Fladeland, *Men and Brothers*
Pat Conroy, *The Water is Wide*
1973 Naboth Mokgatle, *The Biography of an Unknown South American*
Michel Fabre, *The Unfinished Quest of Richard Wright*
Louis L. Snyder, *The Dreyfus Case*
Charles Duguid, *Doctor and the Aborigines*
Albie Sachs, *Justice in South Africa*
1974 Leon Poliakov, *The Aryan Myth*
Eugene D. Genovese, *Roll, Jordan, Roll*
1975 Lucy S. Dawidowicz, *The War Against the Jews, 1933-1945*
Raphael Patai and Jennifer P. Wing, *The Myth of the Jewish Race*
Thomas Kiernan, *The Arabs: Their History, Aims and Challenge to the Industrialized World*
1976 Richard Kluger, *Simple Justice*
Michi Weglyn, *Years of Infamy*
1977 Maxine Hong Kingston, *The Woman Warrior*
Allan Chase, *The Legacy of Malthus: The Social Costs of the New Scientific Racism*

Art Publishing Award

ART LIBRARIES SOCIETY OF NORTH AMERICA
Box 3692, Glendale, Calif. 91201

The Art Publishing Award is given annually for the trade book(s) on art that display the best design, workmanship, illustrations and scholarly quality (indexes, bibliographies, etc.). The book, which must have been published in North America, is honored with a certificate.

1973 Jonathon Green, *Camera Work: A Critical Anthology* (Aperture)
Coy Ludwig, *Maxfield Parrish* (Watson-Guptill)
1974 Lincoln Kirstein, *Elle Nadelman* (Eakins Foundation Press)
Pierpont Morgan Library, *Major Acquisitions of the Pierpont Morgan Library, 1927-1974*
1975 Dan Burne Jones, *The Prints of Rockwell Kent* (University of Chicago Press)

1976   Robert A Sobieszek and Odette M. Appel, *The Spirit of Fact: Daquerrotypes of Southworth & Hawes, 1843-1862* (David R. Godine)
1977   Detroit Institute of Arts and St. Louis Art Museum, *Henri Matisse: Paper Cut-Outs*

Athenaeum Literary Award
Fellow of the Athenaeum Honor
THE ATHENAEUM OF PHILADELPHIA
219 S. Sixth St., Philadelphia, Pa. 19106 (215/WA 5-2688)

The Athenaeum Literary Award medal is presented annually to authors residing within 30 miles of the Philadelphia City Hall at the time of writing an outstanding work of fiction or non-fiction and published during the previous year. A committee selects the winner of the bronze medal.

1949   John L. LaMonte, *The World of the Middle Ages*
1950   Henry N. Paul, *The Royal Play of MacBeth*
1951   Arthur Hobson Quinn, *The Literature of the American People*
1952   Nicholas B. Wainwright, *A Philadelphia Story*
1953   Lawrence Henry Gipson, *The British Empire Before the American Revolution*, Volume VIII
1954   Davis Grubb, *The Night of the Hunter*
1955   Conyers Read, *Mr. Secretary Cecil and Queen Elizabeth*
1956   Samuel N. Kramer, *From The Tablets of Sumer*
        Livingston Biddle, Jr., *The Village Beyond*
1957   Catherine D. Bowen, *The Lion and the Throne*
        Bettina Linn, *A Letter to Elizabeth*
1958   Loren Eiseley, *Darwin's Century*
        L. Sprague DeCamp, *An Elephant for Aristotle*
1959   John Canaday, *Mainstreams of Modern Art*
1960   Edwin Wolf II, *Rosenbach: A Biography*
        David Taylor, *Storm the Last Rampart*
1961   Lauren R. Stevens, *The Double Axe*
        Roy F. Nichols, *The Stakes of Power*
1962   Curtis Bok, *Maria*
        Carleton S. Coon, *The Origins of Races*
        Richard S. Dunn, *Puritans and Yankees*
1963   Samuel N. Kramer, *The Sumerians*
        Daniel Hoffman, *The City of Satisfaction*
1964   Dorothy S. White, *Seeds of Discord*
        Kristin Hunter, *God Bless the Child*
        Elizabeth G. Vining, *Take Heed of Loving Me*
1965   Laurence Lafore, *The Long Fuse*
1966   Edward S. Gifford, *Father Against the Devil*
1967   Edmund N. Bacon, *Design of Cities*
        Daniel P. Mannix, *The Fox and the Hound*
1968   Robert C. Smith, *Art of Portugal*
        E. Earnest, *Expatriates and Patriots*
1969   C. Henry Pitz, *Brandywine Tradition*
        Chaim Potok, *The Promise*
1970   No award
1971   Loren Eiseley, *The Night Country*
1972   Jerre Mangione, *The Dream and The Deal*
1973   John Maass, *The Glorious Enterprise*
1974   John R. Coleman, *Blue-Collar Journal*
1975   Martin P. Snyder, *City of Independence*
1976   No award

The Fellow of the Athenaeum Honor is bestowed annually for outstanding contribution to 19th-century studies. It consists of a scroll and lifetime membership in the Athenaeum.

1977   Henry Russell Hitchcock, Author, historian
        Nathaniel Burt, Author

Atlantic "First" Award
THE ATLANTIC MONTHLY
8 Arlington St., Boston, Mass. 02116 (617/536-9500)

The Atlantic "First" Award is given every one, two or three years as official recognition of the author of the most distinguished short story by a previously unpublished author to appear in *The Atlantic Monthly*. The editors decide who will receive the awards, which consist of a $750 and a $250 honorarium each year that the award is made. Winners of the $750 award are listed here.

1972   Wallace Knight, *The Way We Went*
        David Black, *Laud*
1973   James Polk, *The Phrenology of Love*
        Tracy Kidder, *The Death of Major Great*
1974   No award
1975   No award
1976   L. M. Rosenberg, *Memory*
1977   No award

Bancroft Prize
COLUMBIA UNIVERSITY
202 Low Library, New York, N.Y. 10027 (212/280-1754)

The Bancroft Prize, which now carries a $4,000 honorarium, is awarded annually for one or more works on American history (including biography) and for one work on diplomacy published during the previous year. While the books may deal with North, Central or South America, they must be written in English. Books may be submitted for consideration by the Bancroft Prize jury.

1948   Allan Nevins, *Ordeal of the Union*
        Bernard DeVoto, *Across the Wide Missouri*
1949   Robert E. Sherwood, *Roosevelt and Hopkins*
        Samuel Eliot Morison, *The Rising Sun in the Pacific*
1950   Lawrence H. Gipson, *The Great War For the Empire*, Vol. III: *The Victorious Years, 1758-1760*
        Herbert E. Bolton, *Coronado*
1951   Arthur N. Holcombe, *Our More Perfect Union*
        Henry N. Smith, *Virgin Land*
1952   Merlo J. Pusey, *Charles Evans Hughes*
        C. Vann Woodward, *Origins of the New South*
1953   George Dangerfield, *The Era of Good Feelings*
        Eric F. Goldman, *Rendezvous With Destiny*
1954   Clinton Rossiter, *Seedtime of the Republic*
        William L. Langer and S. Everett Gleason, *The Undeclared War*
1955   Paul Horgan, *Great River, The Rio Grande*
        Leonard D. White, *The Jacksonians*
1956   Elizabeth Stevenson, *Henry Adams*
        J.G. Randall and Richard N. Current, *Last Full Measure: Lincoln the President*
1957   George F. Kennan, *Russia Leaves the War*
        Arthur S. Link, *The New Freedom*
1958   Arthur M. Schlesinger, Jr., *The Crisis of the Old Order*
        Frank Luther Mott, *A History of American Magazines*, Vol. IV
1959   Ernest Samuels, *Henry Adams, the Middle Years*
        Daniel J. Boorstin, *The Americans, The Colonial Experience*

1960 R.R. Palmer, *The Age of the Democratic Revolution, A Political History of Europe and America, 1760-1800*
Margaret Leech, *In the Days of McKinley*
1961 Merrill D. Peterson, *The Jefferson Image in the American Mind*
Arthur S. Link, *The Struggle for Neutrality, 1914-1915*
1962 Lawrence A. Cremin, *The Transformation of the School*
Felix Gilbert, *To the Farewell Address: Ideas of Early American Foreign Policy*
Martin B. Duberman, *Charles Francis Adams, 1807-1866*
1963 Page Smith, *John Adams*
Roberta Wohlstetter, *Pearl Harbor: Warning and Decision*
John G. Stoessinger, *The Might of Nations: World Politics in Our Time*
1964 William E. Leuchtenberg, *Franklin D. Roosevelt and the New Deal, 1932-1940*
John L. Thomas, *The Liberator: William Lloyd Garrison*
Paul Seabury, *The Foreign Policy of the United States of America*
1965 Bradford Perkins, *Castlereagh and Adams: England and the United States, 1812-1823*
William B. Willcox, *Portrait of a General: Sir Henry Clinton in the War of Independence*
Dorothy Borg, *The United States and the Far Eastern Crisis of 1933-1938*
1966 Richard B. Morris, *The Peacemakers: The Great Powers and American Independence*
Theodore W. Friend III, *Between Two Empires: The Ordeal of the Philippines*
1967 William W. Freehling, *Prelude to Civil War: The Nullification Controversy in South Carolina, 1816-1836*
Charles Sellers, *James K. Polk, Continentalist, 1843-1846*, Vol. II
James Sterling Young, *The Washington Community, 1800-1828*
1968 Henry Allan Bullock, *The History of Negro Education in the South from 1619 to the Present*
Richard L. Bushman, *From Puritan to Yankee: Character and Social Order in Connecticut, 1690-1765*
Bernard Bailyn, *The Ideological Origins of the American Revolution*
1969 Winthrop D. Jordon, *White Over Black: American Attitudes Toward the Negro, 1550-1812*
N. Gordon Levin, Jr., *Woodrow Wilson and World Politics: America's Response to War and Revolution*
Rexford Guy Tugwell, *The Brain Trust*
1970 Charles Coleman Sellers, *Charles Willson Peale*
Gordon S. Wood, *The Creation of the American Republic, 1776-1787*
Dan T. Carter, *Scottsboro: A Tragedy of the American South*
1971 Erik Barnouw, *The Image Empire: A History of Broadcasting in the United States*, Vol. III
David M. Kennedy, *Birth Control in America: The Career of Margaret Sanger*
Joseph Frazier Wall, *Andrew Carnegie*
1972 Carl N. Degler, *Neither Black Nor White*
Robert Middlekauff, *The Mathers: Three Generations of Puritan Intellectuals, 1696-1728*
Samuel Eliot Morison, *The European Discovery of America: The Northern Voyages*
1973 Frances FitzGerald, *Fire in the Lake: The Vietnamese and the Americans in Vietnam*
John Lewis Gaddis, *The United States and the Origins of the Cold War*

Louis R. Harlan, *Booker T. Washington*
1974 Ray Allen Billington, *Frederick Jackson Turner: Historian, Scholar, Teacher*
Townsend Hoopes, *The Devil and John Foster Dulles*
Stephen Thernstrom, *The Other Bostonians: Poverty and Progress in the American Metropolis, 1880-1970*
1975 Robert William Fogel and Stanley L. Engerman, *Time on the Cross: The Economics of American Negro Slavery* and *Time on the Cross: Evidence and Methods —A Supplement*
Alexander L. George and Richard Smoke, *Deterrence in American Foreign Policy: Theory and Practice*
Eugene Genovese, *Roll, Jordan, Roll*
1976 David Brion Davis, *The Problem of Slavery in the Age of Revolution, 1770-1823*
R.W.B. Lewis, *Edith Wharton*
1977 Alan Dawley, *Class and Community: The Industrial Revolution*
Robert A. Gross, *The Minutemen and Their World*
Barry W. Higman, *Slave Population and the Economy in Jamaica, 1807-1834*

Mildred L. Batchelder Award

AMERICAN LIBRARY ASSOCIATION
CHILDREN'S SERVICES DIVISION
50 E. Huron St., Chicago, Ill. 60611 (312/944-6780)

The Mildred L. Batchelder Award is given annually to the publisher of the children's book considered to be the most outstanding of those originally issued in a foreign language and subsequently published in the U.S. within the previous two years. A committee of the Division's members makes nominations and the membership of the Children's Services Division votes on the winner, who receives an engraved citation.

1968 Alfred A. Knopf, *The Little Man* by Erich Kastner
1969 Scribner's, *Don't Take Teddy* by Babbis-Friis Baastad
1970 Holt, Rinehart & Winston, *Wildcat Under Glass* by Eliki Zei
1971 Pantheon, *In the Land of Ur* by Hans Baumann
1972 Holt, Rinehart & Winston, *Friedrich* by Hans P. Richter
1973 William Morrow, *Pulga* by S.R. Van Herson
1974 E.P. Dutton, *Petros' War* by Eliki Zei
1975 Crown Publishers, *An Old Tale Carved Out of Stone* by A. Linevski
1976 Henry Z. Walck, *The Cat and the Mouse Who Lived in a House* by Ruth Hurlimann
1977 Atheneum, *The Leopard* by Cecil Bodker

Curtis G. Benjamin Award for Creative Publishing

ASSOCIATION OF AMERICAN PUBLISHERS
One Park Ave., New York, N.Y. 10016 (212/689-8920)

The Curtis G. Benjamin Award for Creative Publishing is given annually for creative service to the industry from any area of publishing — editorial, marketing or general management. A nine-member committee and an AAP representative select the winner.

1976 Charles Scribner
1977 William Kaufmann

Bennett Award

HUDSON REVIEW
65 E. 55th St., New York, N.Y. 10022 (212/755-9040)

The Bennett Award honors a writer of any nationality who is at a critical stage at which a substantial cash grant might be useful and who has not received full recognition for past work. The first award totaled $12,500. It is anticipated that the prizes will be given every two years.

1976   Jorge Gullen, Spain

Benson Medal

ROYAL SOCIETY OF LITERATURE
1 Hyde Park Gardens, London W2, United Kingdom (Tel: 01-723-5104)

The Benson Medal, which is of silver, is presented at the discretion of the Society's council for distinguished work in belles lettres, biography, fiction, history or poetry.

1917	Gabrielle d'Annunzio
	Benito Perez Galdos
	Maurice Parres
1923	Lytton Strachey
1926	Percy Lubbock
	Robert Lynd
	Harold Nicolson
1928	Gordon Bottomley
	George Santayana
1929	F. A. Simpson
	Helen Waddell
1932	Stella Benson
1934	Dame Edith Sitwell
1938	E. M. Forster
	G. M. Young
1939	F. L. Lucas
	Andrew Young
1940	John Galsworthy
	Christopher Hassall
1941	Christopher La Farge
1952	Frederick S. Boas
1966	J. R. R. Tolkien
	Dame Rebecca West
1968	E. V. Rieu
1969	C. Woodham-Smith
1975	Philip Larkin

James Tait Black Memorial Prizes

UNIVERSITY OF EDINBURGH
Old College, Edinburgh, Scotland, United Kingdom

The James Tait Black Memorial Prizes, which are among the largest in the United Kingdom, go to the authors of the best novel and best biography published in Britain during the previous year. A professor of English at the University of Glasgow or a regis professor of English literature at the University of Edinburgh selects the winners, who receive income from the award endowment.

FICTION

1920   Hugh Walpole, *The Secret City*
1921   D. H. Lawrence, *The Lost Girl*
1922   Walter de la Mare, *Memoirs of a Midget*
1923   David Garnett, *Lady into Fox*
1924   Arnold Bennett, *Riceyman Steps*
1925   E. M. Forster, *A Passage to India*
1926   Liam O'Flaherty, *The Informer*
1927   Radclyffe Hall, *Adam's Breed*
1928   Francis Brett Young, *Love Is Enough* (British Title: *Portrait of Clare*)
1929   Siegfried Sassoon, *Memoirs of a Fox-Hunting Man*
1930   J. B. Priestley, *The Good Companions*
1931   E. H. Young, *Miss Mole*
1932   Kate O'Brien, *Without My Cloak*
1933   Helen Simpson, *Boomerang*
1934   A. G. Macdonell, *England, Their England*
1935   Robert Graves, *I, Claudius* and *Claudius the God*
1936   L. H. Myers, *The Root and the Flower*
1937   Winifred Holtby, *South Riding*
1938   Neil M. Gunn, *Highland River*
1939   C. S. Forester, *A Ship of the Line* and *Flying Colours*
1940   Aldous Huxley, *After Many a Summer Dies the Swan*
1941   Charles Morgan, *The Voyage*
1942   Joyce Cary, *A House of Children*
1943   Arthur Waley, trans., *Monkey* by Wu Ch'eng-en
1944   Mary Lavin, *Tales from Bective Bridge*
1945   Forrest Reid, *Young Tom*
1946   L. A. G. Strong, *Travellers*
1947   Oliver Onions, *Poor Man's Tapestry*
1948   L. P. Hartley, *Eustace and Hilda*
1949   Graham Greene, *The Heart of the Matter*
1950   Emma Smith, *The Far Cry*
1951   Robert Henriques, *Too Little Love* (British title: *Through the Valley*)
1952   W. C. Chapman-Mortimer, *Father Goose*
1953   Evelyn Waugh, *Men at Arms*
1954   Margaret Kennedy, *Troy Chimneys*
1955   C. P. Snow, *The New Men* and *The Masters*
1956   Ivy Compton-Burnett, *Mother and Son*
1957   Rose Macaulay, *The Towers of Trebizond*
1958   Anthony Powell, *At Lady Molly's*
1959   Angus Wilson, *The Middle Age of Mrs. Eliot*
1960   Morris West, *The Devil's Advocate*
1961   Rex Warner, *Imperial Caesar*
1962   Jennifer Dawson, *The Ha-Ha*
1963   Ronald Hardy, *Act of Destruction*
1964   Gerda Charles, *A Slanting Light*
1965   Frank Tuohy, *The Ice Saints*
1966   Muriel Spark, *The Mandelbaum Gate*
1967   Christine Brooke-Rose, *Such*
          Aidan Higgins, *Langrishe, Go Down*
1968   Margaret Drabble, *Jerusalem the Golden*
1969   Maggie Ross, *The Gasteropod*
1970   Elizabeth Bowen, *Eva Trout*
1971   Lily Powell, *The Bird of Paradise*
1972   Nadine Gordimer, *A Guest of Honour*
1973   John Berger, *G*
1974   Iris Murdoch, *The Black Prince*
1975   Lawrence Durrell, *Monsieur, or The Prince of Darkness*
1976   Brian Moore, *The Great Victorian Collection*
1977   John Le Carre, *The Honourable Schoolboy*

BIOGRAPHY

1920   H. Festing Jones, *Samuel Butler*
1921   G. M. Trevelyan, *Lord Grey of the Reform Bill*
1922   Lytton Strachey, *Queen Victoria*
1923   Percy Lubbock, *Earlham*
1924   Ronald Ross, *Memoirs*
1925   William Wilson, *The House of Airlis*
1926   Geoffrey Scott, *The Portrait of Zelide*
1927   H. B. Workman, *John Wyclif*

1928 H. A. L. Fisher, *James Bryce*
1929 John Buchan, *Montrose*
1930 Lord David Cecil, *The Stricken Deer: or The Life of Cowper*
1931 Francis Yeats-Brown, *Lives of a Bengal Lancer*
1932 J. Y. T. Greig, *David Hume*
1933 Stephen Gwynn, *The Life of Mary Kingsley*
1934 Violet Clifton, *The Book of Talbot*
1935 J. A. Neale, *Queen Elizabeth*
1936 R. W. Chambers, *Thomas More*
1937 E. Sackville-West, *A Flame in Sunlight: The Life and Work of Thomas de Quincey*
1938 Lord Eustace Percy, *John Knox*
1939 Sir Edmund Chambers, *Samuel Taylor Coleridge*
1940 David C. Douglas, *English Scholars*
1941 Hilda F. M. Prescott, *Spanish Tudor*
1942 John Gore, *King George V*
1943 Lord Ponsonby of Shulbrede, *Henry Ponsonby: Queen Victoria's Private Secretary*
1944 G. G. Coulton, *Fourscore Years*
1945 C. V. Wedgwood, *William the Silent*
1946 D. S. McColl, *Philip Wilson Steer*
1947 Richard Aldington, *The Duke* (British title: *Wellington*)
1948 Canon C. E. Raven, *English Naturalists*
1949 Percy A. Scholes, *The Great Dr. Burney*
1950 John Connell, *W. E. Henley*
1951 Mrs. Cecil Woodham-Smith, *Florence Nightingale*
1952 Noel G. Annan, *Leslie Stephen*
1953 G. M. Young, *Stanley Baldwin*
1954 Carola Oman, *Sir John Moore*
1955 Keith Feiling, *Warren Hastings*
1956 R. W. Ketton-Cremer, *Thomas Gray*
1957 St. John Ervine, *George Bernard Shaw*
1958 Maurice Cranston, *John Locke*
1959 Joyce Hemlow, *History of Fanny Burney*
1960 Christopher Hassall, *Edward Marsh*
1961 Canon Adam Fox, *Dean Inge* (British title: *Life of Dean Inge)*
1962 M. K. Ashby, *Joseph Ashby of Tysoe*
1963 Meriol Trevor, *Newman, The Pillar and the Cloud, Vol. 1; Light in Winter, Vol. 2*
1964 Georgina Battiscombe, *John Keble: A Study in Limitations*
1965 Elizabeth Longford, *Queen Victoria*
1966 Mary Moorman, *William Wordsworth: The Later Years 1803-1850*
1967 Geoffrey Keynes, *The Life of William Harvey*
1968 Winifred Gerin, *Charlotte Bronte*
1969 Gordon S. Haight, *George Eliot*
1970 Lady Antonia Fraser, *Mary Queen of Scots*
1971 Jasper Ridley, *Lord Palmerston*
1972 Lady Julia Namier, *Lewis Namier*
1973 Quentin Bell, *Virginia Woolf*
1974 Robin Lane Fox, *Alexander the Great*
1975 John Wain, *Samuel Johnson*
1976 Karl Miller, *Cockburn's Millennium*
1977 John Branville, *Doctor Copernicus*

Critici in Erba Prize
Graphic Prize Fiera de Bologna

FIERA DEL LIBRO PER RAGAZZI
Ente Autonomo per le Fiere de Bologna (Bologna Trade Fair Association), Piazza Constituzione 6, 40128 Bologna, Italy (Tel: 50-30-50)

The Critici in Erba Prize, which consists of a gold plate, is given annually for the best illustrated book pre-sented at the International Bologna Children's Book Fair. A committee of nine children between six and nine years of age from the schools of Bologna selects the winner.

1966 Xavier Saint-Justh, *L'album de Bambi*
1967 Franco Barberis, *Ich schenk Dir einen Papagei*
1968 Folco Quilici, *Alla scoperta dell'Africa*
1969 Jan Wahl, *Pocahontas in London*
1970 N.A. *La Storia di Francesco e Chiara raccontata dai bimbi di Groce*
1971 N.A. *Alle meine blatter . . .*
1972 N.A. *Waltzing Matilda*
1973 N.A. *Snow White and the Seven Dwarfs*
1974 N.A. *A Year in the Woods*
1975 N.A. *Il Principe Felice*
1976 Grere Janus Hertz, *Das Gelbe Haus*
1977 Jean de Brunhoff, *Die Geschichte von Babar*

The Graphic Prize Fiera de Bologna for Children and the Graphic Prize Fiera de Bologna for Youth, each of which is a gold plate, are given for works with outstanding graphic value based on graphic, artistic and technical criteria as judged by a committee of experts from the G.B. Bodoni Study Center in Parma. In the list below, "I" signifies works for young children while "Y" is for older children.

1966 Emilio Radius, *I/Y-Gesu oggi*
1967 Hilde Heyduck, *I-Drei Vogel*
       Hilde Heyduck, *Y-Die Alte Linde Gondula*
1968 Karin Brandt, *I-Die Wichtelmanner*
       Karin Brandt, *Y-Pribehy*
1969 Samad Bahrang, *I-The Little Black Fish*
       Michel Ragon *Y-La cite de l'an 2000*
1970 Eric Carle, *I-1,2,3, Ein Zug Zum Zoo*
       N.A. *Y-Vertel het uw kinderen*
1971 Remy Charlip, *I-Arm in Arm*
       N.A. *Y-Tutto su Gerusalemme biblica*
1972 Ruth Hurlimann, *I-Stadtmaus und Landmaus*
       N.A. *Y-Slavische Marchen*
1973 N.A. *I-Kopfblumen*
       N.A. *Y-Hodina Nachove Ruze*
1974 N.A. *I-Rotkappchen*
       N.A. *Y-The Last of the Mohicans*
1975 N.A. *I-Trois petit flocons*
       N.A. *Y-Das Spraehbastelbuch*
1976 Tsuguo Okuda, *I-Magic for Sale*
       Pushkin, *Y-Il cavallo di bronzo*
1977 N.A. *I-Schorschi Schrumpft*
       N.A. *Y-Takeru*

Booker Prize for Fiction

NATIONAL BOOK LEAGUE
7 Albemarle St., London W1X 4BB, United Kingdom (Tel: 01 493 9001)

The Booker Prize for Fiction is given annually for the best English language novel published before November 23/24 of the year of presentation and written by a citizen of the Commonwealth, Eire, Pakistan or South Africa. A five-judge panel selects the winner of the £ 5,000 award.

1969 P.H. Newby, *Something To Answer For*
1970 Bernice Rubens, *The Elected Member*
1971 V.S. Naipaul, *In A Free State*
1972 John Berger, *G*
1973 J.G. Farrell, *The Siege Of Krishnapur*

1974   Nadine Gordimer, *The Conservationist*
       Stanley Middleton, *Holiday*
1975   Ruth Prawer Jhabvala, *Heat And Dust*
1976   David Storey, *Saville*
1977   Paul Scott, *Staying On*

Boston Globe/Horn Book Awards

BOSTON GLOBE/HORN BOOK, INC.
Boston Globe, 135 Morrissey Blvd., Boston, Mass. 02107
(617/288-8000); Horn Book, Inc., 31 St. James Ave., Boston,
Mass. 02116 (617/482-5198)

The Boston Globe/Horn Book Awards, which carry
$200 honoraria, go to the authors of non-fiction and
fiction books and illustrators of books for children. Publishers may submit entries for consideration. A three-
person committee selects the winners.

AUTHOR (fiction)

1967   Erik Christian Haugaard, *The Little Fishes*
1968   John Lawson, *The Spring Rider*
1969   Ursula K. LeGuin, *The Wizard of Earthsea*
1970   John Rowe Townsend, *The Intruder*
1971   Eleanor Cameron, *A Room Made of Windows*
1972   Rosemary Sutcliff, *Tristan and Iseult*
1973   Susan Cooper, *The Dark is Rising*
1974   Virginia Hamilton, *M.C. Higgins, the Great*
1975   T. Degens, *Transport 7-41-R*
1976   Jill Paton Walsh, *Unleaving*
1977   Laurence Yep, *Child of the Owl*

ILLUSTRATOR

1967   Peter Spier, *London Bridge is Falling Down*
1968   Blair Lent, *Tikki Tikki Tembo*
1969   John S. Goodall, *The Adventures of Paddy Pork*
1970   Ezra Jack Keats, *Hi, Cat!*
1971   John Burningham, *Mr. Grumpy's Outing*
1972   Karue Mizumura, *If I Built A Village*
1973   Howard Pyle, *King Stork*
1974   Muriel Feelings, *Jambo Means Hello: Swahili Alpha-
       bet Book*
1975   Mitsuma Anno, *Anno's Alphabet*
1976   Remy Charlip and Jerry Joyner, *Thirteen*
1977   Wallace Tripp, *Grandfa' Grig Had a Pig, and Other
       Rhymes Without Reason from Mother Goose*

AUTHOR (non-fiction)

1976   Alfred Tamarin and Shirley Glubok, *Voyaging to
       Cathay: Americans in the China Trade*
1977   Peter Dickinson, *Chance, Luck and Destiny*

Georg-Buchner Prize

DEUTSCHE AKADEMIE FUR SPRACHE UND
DICHTUNG
Alexanderweg 23, D-6100 Darmstadt, Federal Republic of
Germany

The German Academy of Speech and Poetry's Georg-
Buchner Prize, which carries an honorarium of 10,000
German marks, is given annually for outstanding con-
tributions to German literature, either prose or poetry.

1971   Uwe Johnson
1972   Elias Canetti
1973   Peter Handke
1974   Hermann Kestes

1975   Manes Sperber
1976   Heinz Piontek
1977   Reiner Kunze

Caldecott Medal

AMERICAN LIBRARY ASSOCIATION
CHILDREN'S SERVICES DIVISION
50 E. Huron St., Chicago, Ill. 60611 (312/944-6780)

The Caldecott Medal is given to the artist or illustrator
of the most distinguished American picture book for
children published in the preceding year. The artist
must be a citizen or resident of the United States.
While the text need not be the work of the artist, it
must be worthy of the book. The Medal is a reproduction of the work of the 19th-century British illustrator,
Randolph Caldecott.

1938   Dorothy Lathrop, *Animals of the Bible.*
1939   Thomas Handforth, *Mei Li*
1940   Ingri and Edgar d'Aulaire, *Abraham Lincoln*
1941   Robert Lawson, *They Were Strong and Good*
1942   Robert McCloskey *Make Way for Ducklings*
1943   Virginia Lee Burton, *The Little House*
1944   Louis Slobodkin, *Many Moons*, by James Thurber
1945   Elizabeth Orton Jones *Prayer for a Child*, by Rachel
       Field
1946   Maud and Miska Petersham, *The Rooster Crows*
1947   Leonard Weisgard, *The Little Island*, by Golden
       MacDonald
1948   Roger Duvoisin, *White Snow, Bright Snow*, by Alvin
       Tresselt
1949   Berta and Elmer Hader, *The Big Snow*
1950   Leo Politi, *Song of the Swallows*
1951   Katherine Milhous, *The Egg Tree*
1952   Nicolas Mordvinoff, *Finders Keepers*, by Will Lip-
       kind and Nicolas Mordvinoff
1953   Lynd Ward, *The Biggest Bear*
1954   Ludwig Bemelmans, *Madeline's Rescue*
1955   Marcia Brown, *Cinderella*
1956   Feodor Rojankovsky, *Frog Went A-Courtin*, by John
       Langstaff
1957   Marc Simont, *A Tree Is Nice*, by Janice May Udry
1958   Robert McCloskey, *Time of Wonder*
1959   Barbara Cooney, *Chanticleer and the Fox*
1960   Marie Hall Ets, *Nine Days to Christmas*
1961   Nicolas Sidjakov, *Baboushka and the Three Kings*
1962   Marcia Brown, *Once a Mouse*
1963   Ezra Jack Keats, *The Snowy Day*
1964   Maurice Sendak, *Where the Wild Things Are*
1965   Beni Montresor, *May I Bring a Friend?*, by Beatrice
       S. de Regniers
1966   Nonny Hogrogian, *Always Room for One More*
1967   Evaline Ness, *Sam, Bangs & Moonshine*
1968   Ed Emberley, *Drummer Hoff*
1969   Uri Shulevitz, *The Fool of the World and the Flying
       Ship*, by Arthur Ransome
1970   William Steig, *Sylvester and the Magic Pebble*
1971   Gail E. Haley, *A Story-A Story*
1972   Nonny Hogrogian, *One Fine Day*
1973   Blair Lent, *The Funny Little Woman*, retold by Ar-
       lene Mosel
1974   Margot Zemach, *Duffy and the Devil*, retold by Har-
       vey Zemach
1975   Gerald McDermott, *Arrow to the Sun: A Pueblo In-
       dian Tale*
1976   Leo Dillon and Diane Dillon, *Why Mosquitoes Buzz
       in People's Ears*, retold by Verna Aardema

1977 Leo and Diane Dillon, *Ashanti to Zulu: African Traditions*, retold by Margaret Musgrove

Campion Award
CATHOLIC BOOK CLUB
106 W. 56th St., New York, N.Y. 10019 (212/581-4640)

The Campion Award, which consists of a medallion, is awarded annually for long and distinguished service to Catholic letters. The club's editorial board selects the winner.

1955	Jacques Maritain
1956	Helen C. White
1957	Paul Horgan
1958	James Brodrick, S.J.
1959	Sister Mary Madeleva
1960	Frank J. Sheed
	Maisie Ward
1961	John La Farge, S.J.
1962	Harold C. Gardiner, S.J.
1963	T.S. Eliot
1964	Barbara Ward
1965	Msgr. John T. Ellis
1966	John Courtney Murray, S.J.
1967	Phyllis McGinley
1968	George N. Shuster
1969	No award
1970	G.B. Harrison
1971	Walter and Jean Kerr
1972	No award
1973	No award
1974	Karl Rahner, S.J.
1975	No award
1976	John Delaney
1977	No award

Canada-Belgium Literary Prize
Governor General's Literary Awards
Children's Literature Prizes
Translation Prize
Canada-Australia Literary Prize
CANADA COUNCIL
151 Sparks St., Box 1647, Ottawa, Ont. K1P 5V8, Canada (613/237-3400)

The Canada-Belgium Literary Prize, which carries a $2,000 honorarium, is given alternately to a Canadian and a Belgian writing in the French language. The governments of the two countries administer the award, which is given for an author's complete works.

1971	Geo Norge, Belgian poet
1972	Gaston Miron, Canadian poet
1973	Suzanne Lilar, Belgian author
1974	Rejean Ducharme, Canadian novelist
1975	Pierre Mertens, Belgian writer
1976	Marie-Claire Blais, Canadian writer
1977	Not available at press time

The Governor General's Literary Awards are $5,000 cash prizes now given annually to a maximum of six authors, three each for meritorious books in English and in French. An 18-member selection committee

chooses a fiction, a non-fiction and a poetry/drama volume in each language.

1937 Bertram Brooker, *Think of the Earth*
T.B. Roberton, *T.B.R.—Newspaper Pieces*
1938 Laura G. Salverson, *The Dark Weaver*
E. J. Pratt, *The Fable of the Goats*
Stephen Leacock, *My Discovery of the West*
1939 Gwethalyn Graham, *Swiss Sonata*
Kenneth Leslie, *By Stubborn Stars*
John Murray Gibbon, *Canadian Mosaic*
1940 Franklin D. McDowell, *The Champlain Road*
Arthur S. Bourinot, *Under the Sun*
Laura G. Salverson, *Confessions of an Immigrant's Daughter*
1941 Ringuet (pseudonym), *Thirty Acres*
E. J. Pratt, *Brebeuf and His Brethren*
J. F. C. Wright, *Slava Bohu*
1942 Alan Sullivan, *Three Came to Ville Marie*
Anne Marriott, *Calling Adventurers*
Emily Carr, *Klee Wyck*
1943 G. Herbert Sallans, *Little Man*
Earle Birney, *David and Other Poems*
Bruce Hutchison, *The Unknown Country*
Edgar McInnis, *The Unguarded Frontier*
1944 Thomas H. Raddall, *The Pied Piper of Dipper Creek*
A. J. M. Smith, *News of the Phoenix*
John D. Robins, *The Incomplete Anglers*
E. K. Brown, *On Canadian Poetry*
1945 Gwethalyn Graham, *Earth and High Heaven*
Dorothy Livesay, *Day and Night*
Dorothy Duncan, *Partner in Three Worlds*
Edgar McInnis, *The War: Fourth Year*
1946 Hugh MacLennan, *Two Solitudes*
Earle Birney, *Now is Time*
Evelyn M. Richardson, *We Keep a Light*
Ross Munro, *Gauntlet to Overlord*
1947 Winifred Bambrick, *Continental Revue*
Robert Finch, *Poems*
Frederick Philip Grove, *In Search of Myself*
A. R. M. Lower, *Colony to Nation*
1948 Gabrielle Roy, *The Tin Flute*
Dorothy Livesay, *Poems for People*
William Sclater, *Haida*
R. MacGregor Dawson, *The Government of Canada*
1949 Hugh MacLennan, *The Precipice*
A. M. Klein, *The Rocking Chair and Other Poems*
Thomas H. Raddall, *Halifax, Warden of the North*
C. P. Stacey, *The Canadian Army, 1939-1945*
1950 Philip Child, *Mr. Ames Against Time*
James Reaney, *The Red Heart*
Hugh MacLennan, *Cross-country*
R. MacGregor Dawson, *Democratic Government in Canada*
R. S. Lambert, *Franklin of the Arctic*
1951 Germaine Guevremont, *The Outlander*
James Wreford Watson, *Of Time and the Lover*
Marjorie Wilkins Campbell, *The Saskatchewan*
W. L. Morton, *The Progressive Party in Canada*
Donalda Dickie, *The Great Adventure*
1952 Morley Callaghan, *The Loved and the Lost*
Charles Bruce, *The Mulgrave Road*
Josephine Phelan, *The Ardent Exile*
Frank MacKinnon, *The Government of Prince Edward Island*
John F. Hayes, *A Land Divided*
1953 David Walker, *The Pillar*
E. J. Pratt, *Towards the Last Spike*
Bruce Hutchison, *The Incredible Canadian*

Donald G. Creighton, *John A. Macdonald, The Young Politician*
Marie McPhedran, *Cargoes on the Great Lakes*
1954 David Walker, *Digby*
Douglas Le Pan, *The Net and the Sword*
N. J. Berrill, *Sex and the Nature of Things*
J. M. S. Careless, *Canada, A Story of Challenge*
John F. Hayes, *Rebels Ride at Night*
1955 Igor Gouzenko, *The Fall of a Titan*
P. K. Page, *The Metal and the Flower*
Hugh MacLennan, *Thirty and Three*
A. R. M. Lower, *The Most Famous Stream*
Marjorie Wilkins Campbell, *The Nor'westers*
1956 Lionel Shapiro, *The Sixth of June*
Wilfred Watson, *Friday's Child*
N. J. Berrill, *Man's Emerging Mind*
Donald G. Creighton, *John A. Macdonald, The Old Chieftain*
Kerry Wood, *The Map-Maker*
1957 Adele Wiseman, *The Sacrifice*
Robert A. D. Ford, *A Window on the North*
Pierre Berton, *The Mysterious North*
Joseph Lister Rutledge, *Century of Conflict*
Farley Mowat, *Lost in the Barrens*
1958 Gabrielle Roy, *Street of Riches*
Jay Macpherson, *The Boatman*
Bruce Hutchison, *Canada: Tomorrow's Giant*
Thomas H. Raddall, *The Path of Destiny*
Kerry Wood, *The Great Chief*
1959 Colin McDougall, *Execution*
James Reaney, *A Suit of Nettles*
Pierre Berton, *Klondike*
Joyce Hemlow, *The History of Fanny Burney*
Edith Lambert Sharp, *Nkwala*
1960 Hugh MacLennan, *The Watch That Ends the Night*
Irving Layton, *Red Carpet for the Sun*
Andre Giroux, *Malgre tout, la joie*
Felix Antoine Savard, *Le barachois*
1961 Brian Moore, *The Luck of Ginger Coffey*
Frank Underhill, *In Search of Canadian Liberalism*
Margaret Avison, *Winter Sun*
Paul Toupin, *Souvenirs pour demain*
Anne Hebert, *Poemes*
1962 Malcolm Lowry, *Hear Us O Lord from Heaven Thy Dwelling Place*
T. A. Goudge, *The Ascent of Life*
Robert Finch, *Acis in Oxford*
Yves Theriault, *Ashini*
Jean Le Moyne, *Convergences*
1963 Kildare Dobbs, *Running to Paradise*
Marshall McLuhan, *The Gutenberg Galaxy*
James Reaney, *Twelve Letters to a Small Town* and *The Killdeer and Other Plays*
Jacques Ferron, *Contes du pays incertain*
Gilles Marcotte, *Une litterature qui se fait*
Jacques Languirand, *Les insolites et les violons de l'automne*
1964 Hugh Garner, *Hugh Garner's Best Stories*
J. M. S. Careless, *Brown of the Globe*
Gatien Lapointe, *Ode au Saint-Laurent*
Gustave Lanctot, *Histoire du Canada*
1965 Douglas Le Pan, *The Deserter*
Phyllis Grosskurth, *John Addington Symonds*
Raymond Souster, *The Colour of the Times*
Jean-Paul Pinsonneault, *Les terres seches*
Rejean Robidoux, *Roger Martin du Gard et la religion*
Pierre Perrault, *Au coeur de la rose*
1966 Alfred Purdy, *The Cariboo Horses*
James Eayrs, *In Defence of Canada*

Gilles Vigneault, *Quand les bateaux s'en vont*
Gerard Bessette, *L'incubation*
Andre S. Vachon, *Le Temps et l'espace dans l'oeuvre de Paul Claudel*
1967 Margaret Atwood, *The Circle Game*
Rejean Ducharme, *L'avalee des avales*
Margaret Laurence, *A Jest of God*
Claire Martin, *La joue droite*
Marcel Trudel, *Le Comptoir, 1604-1627* (Vol. II of *Histoire de la Nouvelle France)*
George Woodcock, *The Crystal Spirit: A Study of George Orwell*
1968 Jacques Godbout, *Salut Galarneau*
Francoise Loranger, *Encore cinq minutes*
Eli Mandel, *An Idiot Joy*
Alden Nowlan, *Bread, Wine and Salt*
Robert-Lionel Seguin, *La Civilisation traditionnelle de l'"Habitant" aux XVIIe et XVIIIe siecles*
Norah Story, *The Oxford Companion to Canadian History and Literature*
1969 Marie-Claire Blais, *Manuscrits de Pauline Archange*
Fernand Dumont, *Le lieu de l'homme*
Alice Munro, *Dance of the Happy Shades*
Mordecai Richler, *Cocksure and Hunting Tigers Under Glass*
1970 George Bowering, *Rocky Mountain Foot* and *The Gangs of Kosmos*
Michel Brunet, *Les Canadiens apres la conquete*
Robert Kroetsch, *The Studhorse Man*
Gwendolyn MacEwen, *The Shadow-Maker*
Louise Maheux-Forcier, *Une foret pour Zoe*
Jean-Guy Pilon, *Comme eau retenue*
1971 Monique Bosco, *La femme de Loth*
Jacques Brault, *Quand nous serons heureux*
Dave Godfrey, *The New Ancestors*
B. P. Nichol, *Still Water, The True Eventual Story of Billy the Kid, Beach Head* and *The Cosmic Chef: An Evening of Concrete*
Michael Ondaatje, *The Collected Works of Billy the Kid*
1972 Pierre Berton, *The Last Spike*
Gerard Bessette, *Le cycle*
Gerald Fortin, *La fin d'un regne*
John Glassco, *Selected Poems*
Paul-Marie Lapointe, *Le reel absolu*
Mordecai Richler, *St. Urbain's Horseman*
1973 Robertson Davies, *The Manticore*
Dennis Lee, *Civil Elegies and Other Poems*
John Newlove, *Lies*
Jean Hamelin and Yves Roby, *Histoire economique du Quebec 1851-1896*
Gilles Henault, *Signaux pour les voyants*
Antoinine Maillet, *Don l'Orignal*
1974 Ralph Gustafson, *Fire on Stone*
Margaret Laurence, *The Diviners*
Charles Ritchie, *The Siren Years*
Victor-Levy Beaulieu, *Don Quichotte de la demanche*
Nicole Brossard, *Mecanique jongleuse suivi de Masculin grammaticale*
Louise Dechene, *Habitants et marchands de Montreal au XVIIe siecle*
1975 Milton Acorn, *The Island Means Minago*
Marion MacRae and Anthony Adamson, *Hallowed Walls*
Brian Moore, *The Great Victorian Collection*
Louis-Edmond Hamelin, *Nordicite canadienne*
Anne Hebert, *Les enfants du sabbat*
Pierre Perrault, *Chouennes*
1976 Carl Berger, *The Writing of Canadian History*
Marian Engel, *Bear*

Joe Rosenblatt, *Top Soil*
Andre Major, *Les rescapes*
Fernand Ouelett, *Les Bas Canada 1791-1840*
Alphonse Piche, *Poemes 1946-1968*
1977 Timothy Findley, *The Wars*
Gabrielle Roy, *Ces Enfants de Ma Vie*
Frank Scott, *Essays on the Constitution*
Denis Moniere, *Le Development des Ideologies au Quebec des Origines a Nos Jours*
O. G. Jones, *Under the Thunder, The Flowers Light Up the Earth*
Michel Garneau, *Les Celebrations (Adidou Adidouce)*

The $5,000 Children's Literature Prizes are given annually to two Canadian writers, one who writes in English and one in French, for books for young people, whether or not these works were published in Canada.

1975 Bill Freeman, *Shantyman of Cache Lake*
Louise Aylwin, *Raminagradu*
1976 Myra Paperny, *The Wooden People*
Bernadette Renaud, *Emilie, la baignoire a pattes*
1977 Jean Little, *Listen for the Singing*
Denise Houle, *Lune de neige*
Claude La Fortune, *L'evangile en papier*

The Translation Prize, which carries a $5,000 honorarium, is awarded annually for the best translation of a Canadian book. Now, one prize is given a year, alternately for an English-to-French and a French-to-English translation. Initially, two $2,500 prizes were given each year, one in each translation category. Textbooks and manuals are not considered for this award.

1974 Sheila Fischman, English translation of *Le deux-millieme etage* by Roch Carrier and *Le Loup* by Marie-Claire Blais under the titles *They Won't Demolish Me* and *The Wolf*
Michelle Tisseyre, French translation of *Such is My Beloved* and *Winter* by Morley Callaghan and *Seasons of the Eskimo* by Fred Bremmer under the titles *Telle est ma belle-aimee, L'hiver* and *L'Eskimo*
1975 John Glassco, English translation of the collected works of Saint-Denys Garneau under the title *Complete Poems of Saint-Denys Garneau*
Jean Simard, French translation of *Son of a Smaller Hero* by Mordecai Richler under the title *Mon pere, ce heros*
1976 Joyce Marshall, English translation of *Cet ete qui chantait* by Gabrielle Roy under the title *Enchanted Summer*
1977 Frank Scott, English translation of *Poems of French Canada* by Jean Pare, French translation of *L'homme de weekend (The Weekend Man)*

The annual $2,500 Canada-Australia Literary Prize alternately honors a Canadian and an Australian author writing in the English language. Each year an author from one country is chosen by a panel of judges from the other country on the basis of the writer's complete works.

1976 John Romeril, Australian playwright
1977 Not available at press time

Carey-Thomas Awards

PUBLISHERS' WEEKLY
1180 Ave. of the Americas, New York, N.Y. 10019
(212/764-5154)

The Carey-Thomas Awards honor creative book publishing in its various aspects—editorial judgment, initiative, imagination, manufacture, promotion and marketing. The magazine's review staff makes nominations for selection by a three- to five-member jury of authors, critics, librarians and booksellers. The winner, a publishing company, receives a certificate.

1942 Farrar & Rinehart, *Rivers of America* series
1943 University of Chicago Press, *A Dictionary of American English on Historical Principles*
1944 E. P. Dutton & Co., Inc., *The World of Washington Irving,* by Van Wyck Brooks
1945 Alfred A. Knopf, Inc. *The American Language,* by H. L. Mencken
1946 Duell, Sloan & Pearce, Inc., *The New World,* by Stefan Lorant
1947 Oxford University Press, *A Study of History,* by Arnold Toynbee
1948 William Sloane Associates, American Men of Letters series
1949 Rand McNally & Co., *Cosmopolitan World Atlas*
1950 Princeton University Press, *The Papers of Thomas Jefferson,* edited by J. P. Boyd and others
1951 Houghton Mifflin Co., *Life in America,* by Marshall B. Davidson
1952 The Macmillan Co., *The Diary of George Templeton Strong, 1835-1875,* edited by Allan Nevins and Milton H. Thomas
1953 Houghton Mifflin Co., *The Second World War,* by Sir Winston Churchill
1954 Doubleday & Co., Anchor Books series
1955 Belknap Press of Harvard University Press, *The Poems of Emily Dickinson,* edited by T. H. Johnson
1956 Doubleday & Co., Mainstream of America series
1957 Frederick A. Praeger, Inc., *The New Class,* by Milovan Djilas
1958 New York Graphic Society, *Complete Letters,* by Vincent Van Gogh
1959 Oxford University Press, *James Joyce,* by Richard Ellmann
1960 Simon & Schuster, *The Rise and Fall of the Third Reich,* by William L. Shirer
1961 Belknap Press of Harvard University Press, *The Adams Papers: Diary and Autobiography of John Adams*
1962 Shorewood Publishers, *Great Drawings of All Time*
1963 Wesleyan University Press, *New York Landmarks,* edited by Alan Burnham
1964 Sierra Club, Sierra Club Exhibit Format series, edited by David Brower
1965 Doubleday & Co., Anchor Bibles, edited by William Foxwell Albright and David Noel Freedman
1966 George Braziller, Inc., *The Hours of Catherine of Cleves,* introduction by John Plummer
1967 Holt, Rinehart & Winston, *Wilderness Kingdom: The Journals and Paintings of Father Nicolas Point,* translated by Joseph P. Donnelly, S.J.
1968 W. W. Norton & Co., *The Norton Facsimile: The First Folio of Shakespeare,* prepared by Charlton Hinman
1969 Alfred A. Knopf, Inc., *Huey Long,* by T. Harry Williams
1970 Random House with Maecenas Press and Chanticleer Press, *Picasso 347*
1971 Oxford University Press, *The Compact Edition of the Oxford English Dictionary: Complete Text Micrographically Reproduced*
1972 Yale University Press, *The Children of Pride: A True Story of Georgia and the Civil War*
1973 Princeton University Press, The Bollingen Series

1974 McGraw-Hill Book Company, *Madrid Codices of Leonardo da Vinci* and *The Unknown Leonardo,* edited by Ladislao Reti
1975 Pierpont Morgan Library of New York in association with David R. Godine, *Early Children's Books and Their Illustration*
1976 Basic Books, *Berggasse 19,* by Edmund Engelman
1977 Horizon Press, *An Autobiography,* by Frank Lloyd Wright

Carr P. Collins Award

TEXAS INSTITUTE OF LETTERS
Box 7219, Austin, Tex. 78712 (512/471-1833)

The Carr P. Collins Award, which carries a $1,000 honorarium, is given to honor a non-fiction book by a Texas author or on a Texas subject that, in the judges' opinion, is the most outstanding of the previous year.

1946 Green Peyton, *San Antonio in the Sun*
1947 John A. Lomax, *Adventures of a Ballad Hunter*
1948 Herbert Gambrell, *Anson Jones: The Last President of Texas*
1949 Tom Lea, *The Brave Bulls*
1950 Roy Bedichek, *Karankaway Country*
1951 Joe B. Frantz, *Gail Borden, Dairyman to a Nation*
1952 J. Frank Dobie, *The Mustangs*
1953 Walter Prescott Webb, *The Great Frontier*
1954 Paul Horgan, *Great River: The Rio Grande in American History*
1955 John S. Spratt, *The Road to Spindletop*
1956 Roy Bedichek, *Educational Competition: The Story of the University Interscholastic League*
1957 Frank Vandiver, *Mighty Stonewall*
1958 Lon Tinkle, *Thirteen Days to Glory*
1959 Lewis Hanke, *Aristotle and the American Indian*
1960 John Graves, *Goodbye to a River*
1961 Frances S. Mossiker, *The Queen's Necklace*
1962 Rebecca Smith Lee, *Mary Austin Holley*
1963 Ellen Maury Slayden, *Washington Wife*
1964 Frances S. Mossiker, *Napoleon and Josephine*
1965 Henry D. and Frances T. McCallum, *The Wire that Fenced the West*
1966 William A. Owens, *This Stubborn Soil*
1967 Willie Morris, *North Toward Home*
1968 Tom Lea, *A Picture Gallery*
1969 The Reverend C. C. White and Ada Morehead Holland, *No Quittin' Sense*
1970 Gene Schulze, *The Third Face of War*
1971 Charles W. Ferguson, *Organizing to Beat the Devil: Methodists and the Making of America*
1972 Joseph C. Goulden, *The Superlawyers*
1973 Lewis L. Gould, *Progressives and Prohibitionists, Texas Democrats in the Wilson Era*
1974 John Graves, *Hard Scrabble*
1975 Paul Horgan, *Lamy of Santa Fe*
1976 Thomas Thompson, *Blood and Money*
1977 William Humphrey, *Farther off from Heaven*

Companion of Literature

ROYAL SOCIETY OF LITERATURE
1 Hyde Park Gardens, London W2, United Kingdom (Tel. 01-723-5104)

The highest honor of the Royal Society of Literature is an invitation to become a Companion of Literature. This honor, which was initiated in 1961, is limited to 10 individuals at a time. The first seven names listed here were members in 1977, while the last three were invited to accept this honor in 1977.

Sir John Betjeman
Dame Rebecca West
Lord David Cecil
Angus Wilson
Lord Kenneth Clark
Arthur Koestler
Ruth Pittner
Philip Larkin
Stephen Spender
David Garnett

CIBC Award for Unpublished Writers

COUNCIL ON INTERRACIAL BOOKS FOR CHILDREN
1841 Broadway, New York, N.Y. 10023 (212/757-5339)

The Annual CIBC Award for Unpublished Writers is given to a U.S. writer from a racial minority whose manuscript best challenges stereotypes, supplies role models and/or portrays some distinctive aspect of their culture, as well as displays literary merit. Prize-winners in each of five ethnic categories receive $500 each. Judges who are members of the author's ethnic group evaluate manuscripts submitted to the Council and select the winners. Most of the winning manuscripts have ultimately been published. (* In the first years of the award, the only ethnic category was black, but winners were selected for books for different age groups.)

BLACK

1969 Walter D. Myers, *Where Does the Day Go*
      Kristin Hunter, *Soul Brothers and Sister Lou*
1970 Virginia Cox, *ABC: Story of the Alphabet*
      Sharon Bell Mathis, *Sidewalk Story*
      Margot S. Webb, *Letters from Uncle David: Underground Hero*
1971 Ray Anthony Shepard, *Sneakers*
1972 Florenz Webb Marshall, *The Rock Cried Out*
1973 Mildred D. Taylor, *Song of the Trees*
1974 Aishah Abdullah, *Midnight Simba Mweusi*
1975 Emily R. Moore, *Letters to a Friend on a Brown Paper Bag*
1976 No award
1977 Not available at press time

NATIVE AMERICAN

1971 Virginia Driving and Hawk Sneve, *Jimmy Yellowhawk*
1972 No award
1973 Nanabah Chee Dodge, *Morning Arrow*
      Michele P. Robinson, *Grandfather's Bridge*
1974 No award
1975 No award
1976 No award
1977 Not available at press time

CHICANO

1971 Juan Valenzuela, *I Am Magic*
1972 No award
1973 No award
1974 Abelardo Delgado, *My Father Hijacked a Plane*
1975 No award
1976 No award

1977 Not available at press time

ASIAN-AMERICAN

1972 Minfong Ho, *Sing to the Dawn*
1973 Dorothy Tomiye Okamoto, *Eyak*
1974 No award
1975 No award
1976 No award
1977 Not available at press time

PUERTO RICAN

1972 Theodor Languer-Franceschi, *The Unusual Puerto Rican*
      Cruz Martel, *Yagua Days* (Special Award)
1973 Jack Agueros, *El Pito de Plata de Pito*
1974 Antonia Hernandez, *Yari*
1975 No award
1976 Lydia Milagros Gonzalez, *El Mundo Maravilloso de Macu*
1977 Not available at press time

Decennial Prize

BROSS FOUNDATION
Lake Forest College, North Hall, Lake Forest, Ill. 60045
(312/234-3100)

The Foundation's $7,500 Decennial Prize is now given every 10 years for a published book or a manuscript on a subject in the humanities, social sciences or any other branch of study as it relates to Christianity as interpreted by the Presbyterian Church or other American evangelical church. A committee of judges selected by the college chooses the winner.

1880 Mark Hopkins, *The Evidence of Christianity*
1903 Marcus Dodds, *The Bible, Its Origins and Nature*
1906 Rev. James Orr, *The Problem of the Old Testament*
1907 J. Arthur Thomson, *The Bible of Nature*
1908 Frederick Bliss, *Religions of Modern Syria and Palestine*
1911 Josiah Royce, *The Sources of Religious Insight*
1915 Rev. Thomas J. Thoburn, *The Mystical Interpretation of the Gospel*
      Rev. John Neville Figgis, *The Will to Freedom*
1916 Henry Wilkes Wright, *Faith Justified by Progress*
1920 (Several authors; names unknown), *Christianity and Problems of Today*
1921 Rev. John P. Peters, *Bible and Spade*
1940 Harris Franklin Rall, *Christianity: An Inquiry Into Its Nature*
1950 Amos Wilder, *Modern Poetry and the Christian Traditions*
1960 John A. Hutchinson, *Language and Faith: An Essay in Sign, Symbol and Meaning*
1970 Claude Welch, *Protestant Thought in the Nineteenth Century, Vol. I*

Emerson-Thoreau Medal

AMERICAN ACADEMY OF ARTS AND SCIENCES
165 Allendale St., Jamaica Plain, Mass. 02130
(617/522-2400)

The Emerson-Thoreau Medal, which carries a $1,000 honorarium, is given annually to recognize distinguished achievement in literature and honors the over-

all body of an author's or poet's work. An academy committee selects the winner.

1959 Robert Frost
1960 T. S. Eliot
1961 Henry Beston
1962 Samuel Eliot Morison
1963 Katherine Anne Porter
1964 Mark Van Doren
1965 Lewis Mumford
1966 Edmund Wilson
1967 Joseph Wood Krutch
1968 John Crowe Ransom
1969 Hannah Arendt
1970 Ivor Armstrong Richards
1971 No award
1972 No award
1973 No award
1974 No award
1975 Robert Penn Warren
1976 No award
1977 Saul Bellow

Book Award

ENGLISH-SPEAKING UNION
16 E. 69th St., New York, N.Y. 10021 (212/879-6800)

The English-Speaking Union Book Award, administered in conjuction with *Books Abroad,* is given annually to the author of a book published in English although his or her native language is not English. The award carries a $2,000 honorarium.

1973 Kamala Markandaya, *Two Virgins*
1974 R.K. Narayan, *My Days*
1975 No award
1976 No award
1977 T. Obinkram Echewa, *The Land's Lord*

Esso Prize

LE CERCLE DU LIVRE DE FRANCE
8955 Blvd. Saint-Laurent, Montreal 435, Quebec, Canada
(514/384-4131)

The Esso Prize is a $5,000 award given annually for an outstanding French-Canadian novel. Through 1975, the award was known as the Prix du Cercle du Livre de France (French Book Guild Prize) and carried a $1,000 honorarium. A jury of critics and authors from France and Canada selects the winner.

1949 Francoise Loranger, *Mathieu*
1950 Bertrand Vac, *Louise Genest*
1951 Andre Langevin, *Evade de la Nuit*
1952 Bertrand Vac, *Deux Portes, Une Adresse*
1953 Andre Langevin, *Poussiere sur la Ville (Dust over the City)*
1954 Jean Vaillancourt, *Les Canadiens Errants*
1955 Jean Filiatrault, *Chaines*
1956 Eugene Cloutier, *Les Inutiles*
      Jean Simard, *Mon Fils Poutant Heureux*
      Maurice Gagnon, *L'Echeance*
1957 J. Marie Poirier, *Le Prix du Souvenir*
1958 Claire Martin, *Avec ou sans Amour*
1959 Pierre Gelinas, *Les Vivants, les Morts et les Autres*
1960 Claude Jasmin, *La Corde au Cou*
1961 Diane Giguere, *Le Temps des Jeux*
1962 No award

1963 Louise Maheux-Forcier, *Amadou*
1964 Georges Cartier, *Le Poisson Peche*
1965 Bertrand Vac, *Histoires Galantes*
1966 Andre Berthiaume, *La Fugue*
1967 Anne Bernard, *Cancer*
1968 Yvette Naubert, *L'Ete de la Cigale*
1969 Jovette Bernier, *Non Monsieur*
1970 No award
1971 Lise Parent, *Les Iles Flottantes*
1972 No award
1973 Huguette Legare, *La Conversation entre Hommes*
1974 Jean-Pierre Guay, *Mise en Liberte*
1975 Pierre Stewart, *L'Amour d'Une Autre*
1976 No award
1977 Simone Piuze, *Les Cercles Concentriques*

Geoffrey Faber Memorial Prize

FABER AND FABER LTD.
3 Queen Sq., London WCl N-3AU, United Kingdom (Tel: 01-278-6881)

The £250 Geoffrey Faber Memorial Prize is given yearly, alternately for fiction and poetry, to an author 40 years of age or under who is a citizen of the United Kingdom, any Commonwealth country, a British colony, Eire or the Republic of South Africa. Editors of publications which regularly run literary reviews select a three-judge panel, which chooses the winner.

1964 Christopher Middleton, *Torse Three*
     George Macbeth, *The Broken Places*
1965 Frank Tuohy, *The Ice Saints*
1966 Jon Silkin, *Nature with Man*
1967 William McIlvanney, *Remedy is None*
     John Noone, *The Man with the Chocolate Egg*
1968 Seamus Heaney, *Death of a Naturalist*
1969 Piers Paul Read, *The Junkers*
1970 Geoffrey Hill, *King Log*
1971 J. G. Farrell, *Troubles*
1972 Tony Harrison, *The Loiners*
1973 David Storey, *Pasmore*
1974 John Fuller, *Cannibals and Missionaries: Epistles to Several Persons*
1975 Richard Wright, *The Middle of a Life*
1976 Douglas Dunn, *Love or Nothing*
1977 Carolyn Slaughter, *The Story of the Weasel*

E. M. Forster Award

AMERICAN ACADEMY AND INSTITUTE OF ARTS AND LETTERS
633 W. 155th St. New York, N.Y. 10032 (212/286-1480)

The E.M. Forster Award, based on a bequest of the American rights and royalties of the author's posthumous novel *Maurice,* is given as merited to a young English writer for a stay in the United States.

1972 Frank Tuohy
1973 Margaret Drabble
1974 Paul Bailey
1975 Seamus Heaney
1976 Jon Stallworthy
1977 David Cook

International Publishers' Prize

FRANKFURT BOOK FAIR
Frankfurt, Federal Republic of Germany

The International Publishers' Prize, which carries an honorarium of about $5,000, is awarded annually for serious modern literature, often of a controversial political nature. The honor was instituted by a group of publishers from seven countries whose lists reflect interests in that type of literature. All members of this publishers' group plan publication of the winning author's work.

1977 Erich Fried, German poet

A second award is also made, resulting in planned publication of the author's work by the seven publishers in the group.

1977 Breyten Breytenbach, South African poet

Friends of American Writers Award Honorarium

FRIENDS OF AMERICAN WRITERS
c/o Mrs. William D. Wiener, 2650 Lakeview Ave., Chicago, Ill. 60614 (312/871-5143)

The Friends of American Writers Award was established to encourage authors in the north-central and south-central states, either natives or current residents, or those who have written about the Midwestern region. A $1,000 cash prize is given to the winner. In addition to the first-place award, a $300 runner-up prize is given. A 17-member committee evaluates books considered for the award and chooses the winner.

1938 William Maxwell, *They Came Like Swallows*
1939 Herbert Krause, *Wind without Rain*
1940 Elgin Groseclose, *Ararat*
1941 Marcus Goodrich, *Delilah*
1942 Paul Engle, *West of Midnight*
1943 Kenneth S. Davis, *In the Forests of the Night*
1944 Paul Hughes, *Retreat from Rostov*
1945 Warren Beck, *Final Score*
1946 Dorothy Langley, *Dark Medallion*
1947 Walter Havighurst, *Land of Promise*
1948 A. B. Guthrie, Jr., *The Big Sky*
1949 Michael De Capite, *The Bennett Place*
1950 Edward Nicholas, *The Hours and the Ages*
1951 Leon Statham, *Welcome Darkness*
1952 Vern Sneider, *The Teahouse of the August Moon*
1953 Leonard Dubkin, *The White Lady*
1954 Alma Routsong, *A Gradual Joy*
1955 Harriette Arnow, *The Dollmaker*
1956 Carol Brink, *The Headland*
1957 Thomas and Marva Belden, *So Fell the Angels*
1958 William F. Steuber, Jr., *The Landlooker*
1959 Paul Darcy Boles, *Parton's Island*
1960 Otis Carney, *Yesterday's Hero*
1961 James McCague, *Fiddle Hill*
1962 A. E. Johnson (Annabel and Edgar Johnson), *The Secret Gift*
1963 Lois Phillips Hudson, *The Bones of Plenty*
1964 Harry Mark Petrakis, *The Odyssey of Kostas Volakis*
1965 William H. A. Carr, *The Duponts of Delaware*
1966 Jamie Lee Cooper, *Shadow of a Star*
1967 Frederick J. Lipp, *Rulers of Darkness*

1968 Allan W. Eckert, *Wild Season* and *The Frontiersman*
1969 Ellis K. Meacham, *The East Indiaman*
1970 Richard Marius, *The Coming of Rain*
1971 Edward Robb Ellis, *A Nation in Torment*
1972 Keyes Beech, *Not Without the Americans*
1973 Thomas Rogers, *The Confession of a Child of the Century* by Samuel Heather
1974 Robert Boston, *A Thorn for the Flesh*
1975 Wendell Berry, *A Memory of Old Jack*
1976 Margot Peters, *Unquiet Soul*
1977 Jon Hassler, *Staggerford*

A $100 honorarium is given to the author of a meritorious children's book based on the same criteria.

1960 Clifford B. Hicks, *First Boy on the Moon*
1961 Dorothea J. Snow, *Sequoyah, Young Cherokee Guide*
1962 Mary Evans Andrews, *Hostage to Alexander*
1963 Nora Tully MacAlvay, *Cathie and the Paddy Boy*
1964 Ruth Painter Randall, *I Jessie*
1965 Rebecca Caudill, *The Far-Off Land*
1966 No award
1967 No award
1968 No award
1969 Charles Raymond, *Jud*
1970 Jean Maddern Pitrone, *Trailblazer*
1971 Anne E. Neimark, *A Touch of Light*
1972 Zibby Oneal, *War Work*
1973 Howard Knotts, *The Winter Cat*
       Peter Z. Cohen, *Foal Creek*
1974 Betty Biesterveld, *Six Days from Sunday*
1975 Eric A. Kimmel, *The Tartar's Sword*
1976 Anne Snyder, *First Step*
1977 Audree Distal, *The Dream Runner*

Gavel Awards

AMERICAN BAR ASSOCIATION
1155 E. 60th St., Chicago, Ill. 60637 (312/974-4000)

The Gavel Awards are given annually to honor films, the media and books for their depiction of or reportage on the law and the legal profession. The Bar Association recognizes achievements which foster greater public understanding of the American legal and judicial system, disclose areas in need of improvement or correction and encourage efforts of all levels of government to update laws. Engraved gavels are given to the winners, and Certificates of Merit go to authors.

1964 American Heritage Publishing Co., Series analyzing historic decisions of U.S. Supreme Court which helped shape American democracy
       J.B. Lippincott Co., *The Man Who Rode the Tiger*, biography of Samuel Seabury, recounting his dedication and influence as a lawyer, judge and exposer of municipal corruption, by Herber Mitgang
1965 McGraw-Hill Co., *Justice on Trial*, history of the U.S. Senate fight in 1916 leading to the confirmation of Supreme Court Justice Louis D. Brandeis, by A.L. Todd
1966 No award
1967 No award
1968 No award
1969 No award
1970 No award
1971 Macmillan Co., *The Self-Inflicted Wound*, which examines the due process and human rights revolution of the previous decade as a result of the Supreme Court's landmark cases

1972 University of Michigan Press, *The Assault on Privacy: Computers, Data Banks and Dossiers*
1973 No award
1974 David McKay Co., *In His Own Image: The Supreme Court in Richard Nixon's America*, tracing the Court's philosophical transition under Chief Justice Warren Burger, by James F. Simon
1975 Charles Scribner's Sons, *The Appearance of Justice* on past judicial ethics, by John P. MacKenzie
1976 Yale University Press, *The Morality of Consent* outlining how democracy can survive, by Alexander M. Bickel
1977 Oxford University Press, *The Role of the Supreme Court in American Government*, by Archibald Cox

Prix Goncourt

ACADEMIE GONCOURT
2 rue Mabillon, Paris 6, France

The Goncourt Prize is awarded annually, generally to a younger writer, for a novel or other work of prose published during the previous year. It is given to encourage upcoming French writers. Although the 50-franc honorarium is not a significant sum, the prize is prestigious in France. A seven-member committee of literary experts selects the winner.

1903 John-Antoine Nau, *Force Ennemie*
1904 Leon Frapie, *La Maternelle*
1905 Claude Farrere, *Les Civilises*
1906 Jerome and Jean Tharaud, *Dingley, l'illustre ecrivain*
1907 Emilie Moselly, *Terres lorraines*
1908 Francois de Miomandre, *Ecrit sur de l'eau*
1909 Martius and Ary Leblond, *En France*
1910 Louis Pergaud, *De Goupil a Margot*
1911 Alphonse de Chateaubriant, *Monsieur de Lourines*
1912 Andre Savignon, *Filles de la pluie*
1913 Marc Elder, *Le Peuple de la mer*
1914 Henri Barbusse, *Le Feu*
1915 Rene Benjamin, *Gaspard*
1916 Adrien Bertrand, *L'Appel du sol*
1917 Henri Malherbe, *La Flamme au poing*
1918 George Duhamel, *Civilisation*
1919 Marcel Proust, *L'ombre des jeunes filles en fleur*
1920 Ernest Perochon, *Nene*
1921 Rene Maran, *Batouala*
1922 Henri Beraud, *La Marigre de l'obese*
1923 Lucien Fabre, *Rabevel*
1924 Thierry Sandre, *Le Chevrefeuilles*
1925 Maurice Genevoix, *Raboliot*
1926 Henri Deberly, *Le Supplice de Phedre*
1927 Maurice Bedel, *Jerome 60° latitude Nord*
1928 Maurice Constantin-Weyer, *Un homme se penche sur son passe*
1929 Marcel Arland, *L'Ordre*
1930 Henri Fauconnier, *Nalaisie*
1931 Jean Fayard, *Mai d'amour*
1932 Guy Mazeline, *Les Loups*
1933 Andre Malraux, *La Condition*
1934 Roger Vercel, *Capitaine Conan*
1935 Joseph Peyre, *Sang et Lumieres*
1936 Maxence van der Meersch, *L'Empreinte du Dieu*
1937 Charles Plisnier, *Faux Passeports*
1938 Henri Troyat, *L'Araigne*
1939 Philippe Heriat, *Les Enfants gates*
1940 Francis Ambriere, *Les Grandes Vacances*
1941 Henri Pourrat, *Vent de mars*

1942 Marc Bernard, *Pareils a des enfants*
1943 Marius Grout, *Passage de l'homme*
1944 Elsa Triolet, *Le Premier Accrucoute*
1945 Jean-Louis Bory, *Mon village a l'heure*
1946 Jean-Jacques Gautier, *Histoire d'un fait divers*
1947 Jean-Louis Curtis, *Les forets de la nuit*
1948 Maurice Druon, *Les Grands Familles*
1949 Robert Merle, *Week-end a Zuydcoote*
1950 Paul Colin, *Les Jeux sauvages*
1951 Julien Gracq, *Le Rivage des Syrtes* (prize declined)
1952 Beatrix Beck, *Leon Morin pretre*
1953 Pierre Gascar, *Le Temps des morts*
1954 Simone de Beauvoir, *Les Mandarins*
1955 Roger Ikor, *Les eaux melees*
1956 Romain Gary, *Les racines du ciel*
1957 Roger Vailland, *La Loi*
1958 Francis Walder, *St.-Germain ou la Negociation*
1959 Andre Schwartz-Bart, *Le Dernier des justes*
1960 Vintila Horia, *Dieu est ne en exil*
1961 Jean Cau, *La Pitie de Dieu*
1962 Ann Langfus, *Les Bagages de sable*
1963 Armand Lanoux, *Quand la mer se retire*
1964 Georges Conchon, *L'Etat sauvage*
1965 Jacques Borel, *L'Adoration*
1966 Edmonde Charles-Roux, *Oublier Palerme*
1967 Andre Pieyre de Mandiargues, *La Marge*
1968 Bernard Clavel, *Les fruits de l'hiver*
1969 Felicien Marceau, *Creezy*
1970 Michel Tourier, *Le Roi des auines*
1971 Jacques Laurent, *Les Betises*
1972 Jean Carriere, *L'Epervier de Maheux*
1973 Jacques Chessex, *L'Ogre*
1974 Pascal Laine, *La Dentelliere*
1975 Emilie Ajar, *La Vie devant soi*
1976 Patrick Grainville, *Les Flamboyants*
1977 Didier Decoin, *John l'Enfer*

New Writers Award

GREAT LAKES COLLEGES ASSOCIATION
220 Collingwood, Ste. 240, Ann Arbor, Mich. 48103
(313/761-4833)

A panel of literature and writing professors from the Association's 12 member colleges annually selects a work of fiction and a work of poetry from books solicited from publishers of each writer's first work in any one particular field. The winners receive and are committed to accept an expense-paid speaking tour of member campuses, for which they receive $100 from each college. The award was first given in 1969 in three categories (novel, short story and poetry), but winners of early years are not available.

1973 Daniel Halpern, *Traveling on Credit* (poetry)
Inge Trachtenberg, *So Slow the Dawning* (novel)
1974 Margaret Craven, *I Heard an Owl Call My Name* (novel)
Alice Munro, *Dance of the Happy Shades* (short story)
1975 Elisauitta Ritchie, *Tightening the Circle Over Eel Country* (poetry)
Hilma Wolitzer, *Ending* (novel)
1976 Betty Adcock, *Walking Out* (poetry)
Rosellen Brown, *The Autobiography of My Mother* (novel)
1977 David St. John *Hush* (poetry)
Richard Ford, *A Piece of My Heart* (novel)

Sarah Josepha Hale Award

RICHARDS FREE LIBRARY
Newport, N.H. 03773 (603/863-3430)

The recipient of the Sarah Josepha Hale Award receives a medal in recognition of distinguished work in arts and letters reflecting New England atmosphere or influence. A committee of men and women in the book world selects the winner.

1956 Robert Frost
1957 John P. Marquand
1958 Archibald MacLeish
Dorothy Canfield Fisher
1959 Mary Ellen Chase
1960 Mark Van Doren
1961 Catherine Drinker Bowen
1962 David McCord
1963 John Hersey
1964 Ogden Nash
1965 Louis Untermeyer
Raymond Holden (Special Award)
1966 Robert Lowell
1967 John Kenneth Galbraith
1968 Richard Wilbur
1969 Lawrance Thompson
1970 Elizabeth Yates
1971 Norman Cousins
1972 May Sarton
1973 Henry Steele Commager
1974 Nancy Hale
1975 Edwin Way Teale
1976 John Ciardi
1977 Roger Tory Peterson

Faculty Prize
Robert Troup Paine Prize

HARVARD UNIVERSITY PRESS
79 Garden St., Cambridge, Mass. 02138 (617/495-2600)

The $2,000 Faculty Prize is awarded annually to a member of the Harvard University teaching or research staff for a book-length manuscript in a scholarly field. A committee at the University Press selects the recipient. The award has been suspended.

1956 Harry A. Wolfson, *Faith, Trinity, Incarnation, The Philosophy of the Church Fathers*, Vol. 1
1957 Mark DeWolfe Howe *Justice Holmes: The Shaping Years, 1841-1870*
1958 Franklin L. Ford, *Strasbourg in Transition, 1648-1789*
1959 Merle Fainsod, *Smolensk Under Soviet Rule*
1960 Renato Poggioli, *The Poets of Russia, 1890-1930*
1961 Sydney J. Freedberg, *Painting of the High Renaissance in Rome and Florence, 1475-1521*
1962 Herschel Baker, *William Hazlitt*
1963 Walter Kaiser, *Praisers of Folly*
Barry Dean Karl, *Executive Reorganization and Reform*
1964 Walter Jackson Bate, *John Keats*
1965 Bernard Bailyn, *Pamphlets of the American Revolution*, Vol. 1
1966 Don K. Price, *The Scientific Estate*
1967 Alfred B. Harbage, *Conceptions of Shakespeare*
1968 Giles Constable, *The Letters of Peter the Venerable*
1969 No award
1970 W. K. Jordan, *Edward VI*

Simon Kuznets, *Economic Growth of Nations*
1971 I. Bernard Cohen, *Introduction to Newton's Principia*
John Rawls, *A Theory of Justice*
1972 No award
1973 George M. A. Hanfmann, *Letters from Sardis*
1974 Stephan Thernstrom, *The Other Bostonians: Poverty and Progress in the American Metropolis, 1880-1970*
1975 Paul C. Mangelsdorf, *Corn: Its Origin, Evolution and Improvement*

The Robert Troup Paine Prize is given every four years for an outstanding unpublished work on a subject specified by the Harvard University Press during the previous four years. The award consist of $3,000 over and above the royalties derived from publication by the Press.

1962 Heiko A. Oberman, *The Harvest of Medieval Theology*
1966 Raymond A. M. DeRoover, *The Rise and Decline of the Medici Bank, 1397-1494*
Alasdair I. MacBean, *Export Instability and Economic Development*
1970 Ralph C. Croizier, *Traditional Medicine in Modern China*
1974 John Rawls, *A Theory of Justice*

Heinemann Awards
ROYAL SOCIETY OF LITERATURE
1 Hyde Park Gardens, London W2 2LT, United Kingdom (Tel:01-723-5104)

The Heinemann Awards, which each carry £ 200 cash prizes, are presented annually to individuals whose literary achievements have been in the less renumerative areas, such as poetry, biography and history. A committee selects the recipients on the basis of a work they have read.

1945 Norman Nicholson, *Five Rivers*
1946 D. Colston-Baynes, *In Search of Two Characters*
Andrew Young, *Prospect of Flowers*
1947 Bertrand Russell, *History of Western Philosophy*
V. Sackville-West, *The Garden*
1948 J. Stuart Collis, *Down to Earth*
Martyn Skinner, *Letters to Malaya*
1949 John Betjeman, *Selected Poems*
Frances Cornford, *Travelling Home*
1950 John Guest, *Broken Images*
Peter Quennell, *John Ruskin*
1951 Patrick Leigh-Fermor, *Travellers Tree*
Mervyn Peake, *Glassblowers and Gormanghast*
1952 Nicholas Monsarrat, *The Cruel Sea*
G. Winthrop Young, *Mountains with a Difference*
1953 Edwin Muir, *Collected Poems*
Reginald Pound, *Arnold Bennett*
1954 Ruth Pitter, *The Ermine*
L. P. Hartley, *The Go-Between*
1955 Robert Gittings, *John Keats: The Living Years*
R. S. Thomas, *Song at the Years Turning*
1956 Vincent Cronin, *Wise Man from the West*
R. W. Ketton-Cremer, *Thomas Gray*
1957 Harold Acton, *The Bourbons of Naples*
James Lees-Milne, *Roman Mornings*
1958 Peter Green, *Sword of Pleasure*
Gavin Maxwell, *A Reed Shaken by the Wind*
1959 Hester Chapman, *The Last Tudor King*
John Press, *The Chequer'd Shade*
1960 C. A. Trypanis, *The Cocks of Hades*

Morris West, *The Devil's Advocate*
1961 James Morris, *World of Venice* (English title: *Venice*)
Vernon Scannel, *The Masks of Love*
1962 Christopher Fry, *Curtmantle*
Christopher Hibbert, *The Destruction of Lord Raglan*
1963 Alethea Hayter, *Mrs. Browning*
1964 Robert Rhodes James, *Rosebery*
Alan Moorehead, *Cooper's Creek*
1965 Harold Owen, *Journey from Obscurity, II, Youth*
Wilfred Thesiger, *The Marsh Arabs*
1966 Nigel Dennis, *Jonathan Swift*
Derek Walcott, *The Castaway*
1967 Jean Rhys, *Wide Sargasso Sea*
Norman MacCaig, *Surroundings*
John Bayley, *Tolstoy and the Novel*
1968 W. Gerin, *Charlotte Bronte*
Michael Ayrton, *The Maze Maker*
1969 Gordon S. Haight, *George Eliot*
Jasmine Rose Innes, *Writing in the Dust*
V. S. Pritchett, *A Cab at the Door*
1970 Ronald Blythe, *Akenfield: Portrait of an English Village*
Brian Fothergill, *Sir William Hamilton*
Nicolas Wollaston, *Pharaoh's Chicken*
1971 Corelli Barnett, *Britain and Her Army*
R. W. Southern, *Medieval Humanism*
1972 Dorothy Carrington, *Granite Islands: Portrait of Corsica*
Geoffrey Hill, *Mercian Hymns*
Thomas Kilroy, *The Big Chapel*
1973 William St. Clair, *That Greece Might Still Be Free*
Thomas Keneally, *The Chant of Jimmy Blacksmith*
1974 Robin Lane Fox, *Alexander the Great*
Alistair MacLean, *From the Wilderness*
Barry Unsworth, *Mooncranker's Gift*
1975 John Wain, *Samuel Johnson*
Robin Furneaux, *William Wilberforce*
1976 Malcolm Bradbury, *The History Man*
William Trevor, *Angels at the Ritz*
1977 Philip Ziegler, *Melbourne*
Edward Crankshaw, *The Shadow of the Winter Palace*

Ernest Hemingway Foundation Award
P.E.N. AMERICAN CENTER
156 Fifth Ave., New York, N.Y. 10010 (212/255-1977)

The $6,000 Ernest Hemingway Foundation Award is given to the best first novel or collection of short stories in the English language by an American author. Mysteries and Westerns are ineligible unless their genre is secondary to their overall literary merit; children's books are not considered.

1975 Loyd Little, *Parthian Shot*
1976 Renata Adler, *Speedboat*
1977 Darcy O'Brien, *A Way of Life, Like Any Other*

David Higham Prize for Fiction
NATIONAL BOOK LEAGUE
7 Albemarle St., London W1X 4BB, United Kingdom (Tel: 01 493 9001)

The David Higham Prize for Fiction is given annually to a resident of Great Britain, the Commonwealth or Eire for a first novel or first book of short stories published in the year of presentation. A three-judge panel selects the recipient of the £500 award.

1975 Jane Gardam, *Black Faces, White Faces*
  Matthew Vaughan, *Chalky*
1976 Caroline Blackwood, *The Stepdaughter*
1977 Not available at press time

Winifred Holtby Medal

ROYAL SOCIETY OF LITERATURE
1 Hyde Park Gardens, London W22LT, United Kingdom (Tel: 01-723-5104)

The Winifred Holtby Medal, which carries a £100 honorarium, is given annually for the best regional novel of the year.

1967 David Bean, *The Big Meeting*
1968 Catherine Cookson, *The Round Tower*
1969 Ian MacDonald, *The Humming Bird Tree*
1970 Shiva Naipaul, *Fireflies*
1971 John Stewart, *Last Cove Days*
1972 No award
1973 No award
1974 Ronald Harwood, *Articles of Faith*
  Peter Tinniswood, *I Didn't Know You Cared*
1975 Graham King, *The Pandora Valley*
1976 Eugene McCabe, *Victims*
1977 Not available at press time

Howells Medal

AMERICAN ACADEMY AND INSTITUTE OF ARTS AND LETTERS
633 W. 155th St., New York, N.Y. 10032 (212/286-1480)

The Howells Medal of the Academy is given every five years for the most distinguished American fiction of the period.

1925 Mary E. Wilkins Freeman
1930 Willa Cather
1935 Pearl S. Buck
1940 Ellen Glasgow
1945 Booth Tarkington
1950 William Faulkner
1955 Eudora Welty
1960 James Gould Cozzens
1965 John Cheever
1970 William Styron
1975 Thomas Pynchon

Hugo Awards

WORLD SCIENCE FICTION SOCIETY
c/o Howard DeVore, 4705 Weddel St., Dearborn Heights, Mich. 48125 (313/565-4157)

Hugo Awards are given annually for the best science fiction works of various lengths and to individuals for contributions to science fiction writing, art and publishing. The winners are determined by a vote of the people who attend the Science Fiction Convention. The award, informally named after Hugo Gernsback, an early science fiction publisher, is a rocket ship-shaped tro-phy, whose official name is the Science Fiction Achievement Award.

NOVEL

1953 Alfred Bester, *The Demolished Man*
1954 No award
1955 Mark Clifton and Frank Riley, *They'd Rather Be Right*
1956 Robert A. Heinlein, *Double Star*
1957 No award
1958 Fritz Leiber, *The Big Time*
1959 James Blish, *A Case of Conscience*
1960 Robert A. Heinlein, *Starship Troopers*
1961 Walter M. Miller, Jr., *A Canticle for Leibowitz*
1962 Robert A. Heinlein, *Stranger in a Strange Land*
1963 Phillip K. Dick, *The Man in the High Castle*
1964 Clifford Simak, *Way Station*
1965 Fritz Leiber, *The Wanderer*
1966 Roger Zelazny, *This Immortal*
  Frank Herbert, *Dune*
1967 Robert A. Heinlein, *The Moon is a Harsh Mistress*
1968 Roger Zelazny, *Lord of Light*
1969 John Brunner, *Stand on Zanzibar*
1970 Ursula K. LeGuin, *The Left Hand of Darkness*
1971 Larry Niven, *Ringworld*
1972 Philip Jose Farmer, *To Your Scattered Bodies Go*
1973 Isaac Asimov, *The Gods Themselves*
1974 Arthur C. Clarke, *Rendezvous with Rama*
1975 Ursula K. LeGuin, *The Dispossessed*
1976 Joe Haldeman, *The Forever War*
1977 Kate Wilhelm, *Where Late the Sweet Birds Sang*

NOVELLA

1968 Philip Jose Farmer, *Riders of the Purple Wage*
  Anne McCaffrey, *Weyr Search*
1969 Robert Silverberg, *Nightwings*
1970 Fritz Leiber, *Ship of Shadows*
1971 Fritz Leiber, *Ill Met in Lankhmar*
1972 Poul Anderson, *The Queen of Air and Darkness*
1973 Ursula K. LeGuin, *The Word for World is Forest*
1974 James Tiptree, Jr., *The Girl Who Was Plugged In*
1975 George R.R. Martin, *A Song for Lya*
1976 Roger Zelazny, *Home Is the Hangman*
1977 James Tiptree, Jr., *Houston, Houston, Do You Read?*
  Spider Robinson, *By Any Other Name*

BEST NOVELETTE/SHORT FICTION/SHORT STORY
(Sometimes one award; sometimes separate)

1955 Walter M. Miller, Jr., "The Darfsteller"*
  Eric Frank Russell, "Allamagoosa"**
1956 Murray Leinster, "Exploration Team"*
  Arthur C. Clarke, "The Star"**
1957 No award
1958 Avram Davidson, "Or All the Seas With Oysters"**
1959 Clifford D. Simak, "The Big Front Yard"*
  Robert Block, "That Hell-Bound Train"**
1960 Daniel Keyes, "Flowers for Algernon"
1961 Poul Anderson, "The Longest Voyage"
1962 Brian W. Aldiss, "The Hothouse" (series)
1963 Jack Vance, "The Dragon Masters"
1964 Poul Anderson, "No Truce With Kings"
1965 Gordon R. Dickson, "Soldier, Ask Not"
1966 Harlan Ellison, " 'Repent Harlequin!' Said the Tick-tockman"
1967 Jack Vance, "The Last Castle"*
  Larry Niven, "Neutron Star"**
1968 Fritz Leiber, "Gonna Roll Them Bones"*
  Harlan Ellison, "I Have No Mouth, and I Must Scream"**

1969 **Poul Anderson,** "The Sharing of Flesh"*
Harlan Ellison, "The Beast That Shouted Love at the Heart of the World"**
1970 **Samuel R. Delany,** "Time Considered as a Helix of Semi-Precious Stones"***
1971 **Theodore Sturgeon,** "Slow Sculpture"*
1972 **Larry Niven,** "Inconstant Moon"***
1973 **Poul Anderson,** "Goat Song"*
R.A. Lafferty, "Eurema's Dam"**
Frederik Pohl and Cyril M. Kornbluth, "The Meeting"**
1974 **Harlan Ellison,** "The Deathbird"*
Ursula K. LeGuin, "The Ones Who Walk Away From Omelas"**
1975 **Harlan Ellison,** "Adrift Just Off the Islets of Langerhans, Latitude 38°54'N, 77°00'13" W"
Larry Niven, "The Hole Man"***
1976 **Larry Niven,** "The Borderland of Sol"*
Fritz Leiber, "Catch That Zeppelin"***
1977 **Isaac Asimov,** "The Bicentennial Man"*
Joe Haldeman, "Tricentennial"**

*Novelette **Short Story All others: Short Fiction

BEST PROFESSIONAL MAGAZINE

1953 *Astounding*
Galaxy
1954 *No award*
1955 *Astounding*
1956 *Astounding*
1957 *Astounding*
New Worlds (British)
1958 *Fantasy and Science Fiction*
1959 *Fantasy and Science Fiction*
1960 *Fantasy and Science Fiction*
1961 *Astounding/Analog**
1962 *Analog*
1963 *Fantasy and Science Fiction*
1964 *Analog*
1965 *Fantasy and Science Fiction*
1966 *If*
1967 *If*
1968 *If*
1969 *Fantasy and Science Fiction*
1970 *Fantasy and Science Fiction*
1971 *Fantasy and Science Fiction*
1972 *Fantasy and Science Fiction*

*Name changed in mid-year

BEST PROFESSIONAL EDITOR

1973 **Ben Bova**
1974 **Ben Bova**
1975 **Ben Bova**
1976 **Ben Bova**
1977 **Ben Bova**

BEST PROFESSIONAL ARTIST

1953 **Virgil Finlay**
Ed Emshwiller*
Hannes Bok*
1954 **No award**
1955 **Frank Kelly Freas**
1956 **Frank Kelly Freas**
1957 **No award**
1958 **Frank Kelly Freas**
1959 **Frank Kelly Freas**
1960 **Ed Emshwiller**
1961 **Ed Emshwiller**
1962 **Ed Emshwiller**

1963 **Roy Krenkel**
1964 **Ed Emshwiller**
1965 **John Schoenherr**
1966 **Frank Fazetta**
1967 **Jack Gaughan**
1968 **Jack Gaughan**
1969 **Jack Gaughan**
1970 **Frank Kelly Freas**
1971 **Leo and Diane Dillon**
1972 **Frank Kelly Freas**
1973 **Frank Kelly Freas**
1974 **Frank Kelly Freas**
1975 **Frank Kelly Freas**
1976 **Frank Kelly Freas**
1977 **Rick Sternbach**

*Best Cover Artists

BEST FANZINE, FAN MAGAZINE OR AMATEUR MAGAZINE (Titles and Editors)

1955 *Fantasy-Times,* James V. Taurasi Sr., and Ray Van Houten
1956 *Inside & Science Fiction Advertiser,* Ron Smith
1957 *Science-Fiction Times,* Taurasi, Van Houten and Prieto
1958 **No award**
1959 *Fanac,* Terry Carr and Ron Ellik
1960 *Cry of the Nameless,* F.M. and E. Busby, Toskey & Weber
1961 *Who Killed Science Fiction?,* Earl Kemp
1962 *Warhoon,* Richard Bergeron
1963 *Xero,* Pat and Dick Lupoff
1964 *Amra,* George Scithers
1965 *Yandro,* Robert and Juanita Coulson
1966 *ERB-dom,* Camille Cazedessus, Jr.
1967 *Niekas,* Edmund R. Meskys and Felice Rolfe
1968 *Amra,* George Scithers
1969 *Science Fiction Review,* Richard E. Geis
1970 *Science Fiction Review,* Richard E. Geis
1971 *Locus,* Charles and Dena Brown
1972 *Locus,* Charles and Dena Brown
1973 *Energumen,* Michael and Susan Glicksohn
1974 *Algol,* Andy Porter
The Alien Critic, Richard E. Geis
1975 *The Alien Critic,* Richard E. Geis
1976 *Locus,* Charles and Dena Brown
1977 *Science Fiction Review,* Richard E. Geis

BEST FAN ARTIST

1967 **Jack Gaughan**
1968 **George Barr**
1969 **Vaughn Bode**
1970 **Tim Kirk**
1971 **Alicia Austin**
1972 **Tim Kirk**
1973 **Tim Kirk**
1974 **Tim Kirk**
1975 **Bill Rotsler**
1976 **Tim Kirk**
1977 **No award**

BEST FAN WRITER

1967 **Alexei Panshin**
1968 **Ted White**
1969 **Harry Warner, Jr.**
1970 **Bob Tucker**
1971 **Richard E. Geis**
1972 **Harry Warner, Jr.**
1973 **Terry Carr**
1974 **Susan Wood**

1975   Richard E. Geis
1976   Richard E. Geis
1977   Richard E. Geis

MISCELLANEOUS AWARDS (Recipient and Achievement)

1953   Willy Ley, Factual Articles
       Philip Jose Farmer, Best New Science Fiction Author or Artist
       Forrest J. Ackermann, Number 1 Fan Personality
1954   No award
1955   No award
1956   Willy Ley, Best Feature Writer
       Damon Knight, Best Book Reviewer
       Robert Silverberg, Most Promising New Author
1957   No award
1958   Walter A. Willis, Outstanding Actifan
1959   No award
1960   No award
1961   No award
1962   No award
1963   No award
1964   Ace, Best Science Fiction Book Publisher
1965   Ballantine, Best Publisher
1966   "Foundation" series by Isaac Asimov, Best All-time Series

JOHN CAMPBELL AWARD FOR BEST NEW WRITER

1973   Jerry Pournelle
1974   Spider Robinson
       Lisa Tuttle
1975   P.J. Plauger
1976   Tom Reamy
1977   C.J. Cherryl

GANDALF AWARD FOR GRAND MASTER OF FANTASY

1974   J.R.R. Tolkien
1975   Fritz Leiber
1976   L. Sprague de Camp
1977   Andre Norton

SPECIAL HUGOS AND OTHER SPECIAL AWARDS

1955   Sam Moskowitz
1960   Hugo Gernsback
1962   Cele Goldsmith
       Donald H. Tuck
1963   P. Schuyler Miller
       Isaac Asimov
1967   CBS Television for *21st Century*
1968   Harlan Ellison
       Gene Roddenberry
1969   Neil Armstrong, Michael Collins and Edwin "Buzz"Aldrin
1973   Pierre Versins
1974   Chesley Bonestell
1975   Donald A. Wollheim
       Walt Lee
1976   James Gunn
1977   George Lucas

Children's Book Award

INTERNATIONAL READING ASSOCIATION
800 Barksdale Rd., Newark, Del. 19711 (206/543-6636)

The Children's Book Award, which carries a $1,000 honorarium, is given annually for the first or second book of fiction or non-fiction by an author who shows unusual promise in the children's book field. A selection committee chooses the winners from entries submitted to the Association.

1975   T. Degens, *Transport T-41-R*
1976   Laurence Yep, *Dragonwings*
1977   Nancy Bond, *A String on the Harp*

Award for Short Fiction

IOWA SCHOOL OF LETTERS
Dept. of English, University of Iowa, Iowa City, Iowa 52242

The $1,000 Award for Short Fiction is given annually to a writer who has not previously published a volume of prose fiction. Writers may submit new or revised manuscripts for preliminary screening by the Writers Workshop and final selection by a prominent writer or critic. In addition to the cash award, the winning manuscript is published by the University of Iowa Press.

1970   Cyrus Colter, *The Beach Umbrella*
1971   Philip F. O'Connor, *Old Morals, Small Continents*
1972   Jack Cady, *The Burning & Other Stories*
1973   H.E. Francis, *The Itinerary of Beggars*
1974   Natalie L.M. Petesch, *After the First Death, There is No Other*
1975   Barry Targan, *Harry Belten and the Mendelssohn Violin Concerto*
1976   C.E. Poverman, *The Black Velvet Girl*
1977   Pat M. Carr, Untitled

Jewish Heritage Award

B'NAI B'RITH
1640 Rhode Island Ave. NW, Washington, D.C. 20036
(202/857-6600)

The $1,000 Jewish Heritage Award is given annually for a body of literary work on Jewish life or Jewish thought. An awards committee selects the winner, who may be of any nationality and write originally in any language.

1966   Elie Wiesel
1967   Maurice Samuel
1968   Saul Bellow
1969   Salo W. Baron
1970   Isaac Babel
1971   Abraham J. Heschel
1972   Jacob Glatstein
1973   Nahum N. Glatzer
1974   Gershom Scholem
1975   Eliezer Greenberg
       Irving Howe
1976   Chaim Grade
1977   Bernard Malamud

Coretta Scott King Award

CORETTA SCOTT KING AWARD COMMITTEE
1236 Oakcrest Dr. SW, Atlanta, Ga. 30311 (404/344-7265)

This award is given annually for an inspirational and educational work that promotes better understanding and appreciation of the culture and contribution of all peoples to the realization of the American dream, as symbolized by the life, works and dreams of the late Dr. Martin Luther King, Jr. The award consists of a $250 honorarium, a plaque and a set of the *Encyclopaedia Britannica.*

1970 Lille Patterson, *Dr. Martin Luther King, Jr.: Man of Peace*
1971 Charlemae Rollins, *Black Treasure: Langston Hughes*
1972 Elton C. Fax, *17 Black Artists*
1973 Al Duckett, *I Never Had It Made: The Autobiography of Jackie Robinson*
1974 Sharon Bell Mathis, *Ray Charles*
1975 Dorothy Robinson, *The Legend of Africania*
1976 Pearl Bailey, *Duey's Tale*
1977 James Haskins, *The Story of Stevie Wonder*

James Russell Lowell Prize
MODERN LANGUAGE ASSOCIATION
62 Fifth Ave., New York, N.Y. 10011 (212/741-7854)

The $1,000 James Russell Lowell Prize is given annually to an MLA member for an outstanding linguistic or literary study, a critical edition or a critical biography. The five-member James Russell Lowell Prize Selection Committee gives the award to a person nominated by an individual or a publisher.

1969 Helen Vendler, *On Extended Wings*
1970 Bruce A. Rosenberg, *The Art of the American Folk Preacher*
1971 Meyer H. Abrams, *Natural Supernaturalism*
1972 Theodore J. Ziolkowski, *Fictional Transfigurations of Jesus*
1973 Leslie A. Marchand, *Byron's Letters and Journals*
1974 Josephine Miles, *Poetry and Change*
1975 Jonathan Culler, *Structuralist Poetics: Structuralism, Linguistics, and the Study of Literature*
1976 Joseph Frank, *Dostoevsky: The Seeds of Revolt, 1821-1849*
1977 Not available at press time

Howard R. Marraro Prize
MODERN LANGUAGE ASSOCIATION
62 Fifth Ave., New York, N.Y. 10011 (212/741-7854)

The $750 Howard R. Marraro Prize has been given annually for outstanding achievement in Italian studies to an MLA member for scholarly study in Italian literature or comparative literature involving Italian. In the future, it will be a biennial honor. Members submit nominations which are voted on by the Howard R. Marraro Prize Selection Committee.

1973 Bernard Weinberg, *Trattati di poetica e retorica del Cinquecento*
1974 Thomas G. Bergin, Lifetime achievement
1975 Beatrice Corrigan, Lifetime achievement
1976 Joseph G. Fucilla, Lifetime achievement

Medicis Prizes
c/o Francine Mallet, 25 Rue Dombasle, Paris 15, France
(Tel: 828-76-90)

The Medicis Prize, which is accompanied by a cash honorarium, is awarded annually for avant-garde prose, which may be a novel or a collection of shorter works. It is given to a relatively unknown but talented French author. In 1970, a second award was added for a notable non-French author.

FRENCH AUTHOR
1958 Claude Ollier, *La mise en scene*
1959 Claude Mauriac, *Le Diner en ville*
1960 Henri Thomas, *John Perkins*
1961 Philippe Sollers, *Le Parc*
1962 Colette Audry, *Derriere la baignoir*
1963 Gerard Jarlot, *Un chat qui aboie*
1964 Monique Wittig, *L'Opoponax*
1965 Rene-Victor Pilnes, *La Rhubarbe*
1966 Marie-Claire Blais, *Une saison dans la vie d'Emmanuel*
1967 Claude Simon, *Histoire*
1968 Elie Wiesel, *Le Mendiant de Jerusalem*
1969 Helene Gixous, *Dedans*
1970 Camille Bourniquel, *Seinonte ou la Chambre imperiale*
1971 Pascal Laine, *L'irrevolution*
1972 Maurice Clavel, *Le Tiers des etoiles*
1973 Tony Duvert, *Paysage de fantasie*
1974 Dominique Fernandez, *Porporino ou les Mysteres de Naples*
1975 Jacques Almira, *La voyage a Naucratis*
1976 Marc Cholodenko, *Les Etats du desert*
1977 Michel Butel, *L'Autre Amour*

FOREIGN AUTHOR
1970 Luigi Malerba, *Saut de la Mort*
1971 James Dickey, *Deliverance*
1972 Severo Sarduy, *Cobra*
1973 Milan Kundera, *La vie est ailleurs*
1974 Julio Cortazar, *Livre de Manuel*
1975 Steven Millhauser, *La Vie trop breve d'Edwin Mulhouse*
1976 Doris Lessing, *The Golden Notebook*
1977 Hector Bianciotti, *Le traite des saisons*

Samuel Eliot Morison Award
AMERICAN HERITAGE PUBLISHING CO.
10 Rockefeller Plaza, New York, N.Y. 10020 (212/399-8990)

The $5,000 Samuel Eliot Morison Award is given annually for the best book on American history by an American author that sustains the tradition of history as literature as well as scholarship. A panel of judges selects the winner.

1977 Joseph Lash, *Roosevelt and Churchill; 1939-1941: The Partnership That Saved the West*

National Book Awards
ASSOCIATION OF AMERICAN PUBLISHERS
One Park Ave., New York, N.Y. 10016 (212/689-8920)

The $1,000 National Book Awards are given annually for books by U.S. citizens "that have contributed most significantly to human awareness, to the vitality of our national culture and to the spirit of excellence." Panels of three judges select the winners from works that were published during the previous calendar year. Until 1975, the National Book Committee administered the award. For the next two years, until the Association took it over, it was handled by the American Academy and Institute of Arts and Letters. The categories have changed over the years. Poetry awards will be found on p. 59.

FICTION

1950 Nelson Algren, *The Man with the Golden Arm*
1951 William Faulkner, *The Collected Stories of William Faulkner*
        Brendan Gill, *The Trouble of One House*
1952 James Jones, *From Here to Eternity*
1953 Ralph Ellison, *Invisible Man*
1954 Saul Bellow, *The Adventures of Augie March*
1955 William Faulkner, *A Fable*
1956 John O'Hara, *Ten North Frederick*
1957 Wright Morris, *The Field of Vision*
1958 John Cheever, *The Wapshot Chronicle*
1959 Bernard Malamud, *The Magic Barrel*
1960 Philip Roth, *Goodbye, Columbus*
1961 Conrad Richter, *The Waters of Kronos*
1962 Walker Percy, *The Moviegoer*
1963 J. F. Powers, *Morte D'Urban*
1964 John Updike, *The Centaur*
1965 Saul Bellow, *Herzog*
1966 Katherine Anne Porter, *The Collected Stories of Katherine Anne Porter*
1967 Bernard Malamud, *The Fixer*
1968 Thornton Wilder, *The Eighth Day*
1969 Jerzy Kosinski, *Steps*
1970 Joyce Carol Oates, *Them*
1971 Saul Bellow, *Mr. Sammler's Planet*
1972 Flannery O'Connor, *Flannery O'Connor: The Complete Stories*
1973 John Barth, *Chimera*
        John Williams, *Augustus*
1974 Isaac Bashevis Singer, *A Crown of Feathers and Other Stories*
        Thomas Pynchon, *Gravity's Rainbow*
1975 Robert Stone, *Dog Soldiers*
        Thomas Williams, *The Hair of Harold Roux*
1976 William Gaddis, *JR*
1977 Wallace Stegner, *The Spectator Bird*

NON-FICTION

1950 Ralph L. Rusk, *Ralph Waldo Emerson*
1951 Newton Arvin, *Herman Melville*
1952 Rachel L. Carson, *The Sea Around Us*
1953 Bernard De Voto, *The Course of Empire*
1954 Bruce Catton, *A Stillness at Appomattox*
1955 Joseph Wood Krutch, *The Measure of Man*
1956 Herbert Kubly, *American in Italy*
1957 George F. Kennan, *Russia Leaves the War*
1958 Catherine Drinker Bowen, *The Lion and the Throne*
1959 J. Christopher Herold, *Mistress to an Age: A Life of Madame de Stael*
1960 Richard Ellmann, *James Joyce*
1961 William L. Shirer, *The Rise and Fall of the Third Reich*
1962 Lewis Mumford, *The City in History*
1963 Leon Edel, *Henry James: The Conquest of London* and *Henry James: The Middle Years*

ARTS AND LETTERS

1964 Aileen Ward, *John Keats: The Making of a Poet*
1965 Eleanor Clark, *The Oysters of Locmariaquer*
1966 Janet Flanner (Genet), *Paris Journal (1944-1965)*
1967 Justin Kaplan, *Mr. Clemens and Mark Twain*
1968 William Troy, *Selected Essays*

1969 Norman Mailer, *The Armies of the Night*
1970 Lillian Hellman, *An Unfinished Woman*
1971 Francis Steegmuller, *Cocteau*
1972 Charles Rosen, *The Classical Style: Haydn, Mozart, Beethoven*
1973 Arthur M. Wilson, *Diderot*
1974 Pauline Kael, *Deeper into the Movies*
1975 Roger Shattuck, *Marcel Proust*
        Lewis Thomas, *The Lives of a Cell: Notes of a Biology Watcher*
1976 Paul Fussell, *The Great War and Modern Memory*

HISTORY AND BIOGRAPHY

1964 William H. McNeill, *The Rise of the West*
1965 Louis Fischer, *The Life of Lenin*
1966 Arthur M. Schlesinger, Jr., *A Thousand Days*
1967 Peter Gay, *The Enlightenment*
1968 George F. Kennan, *Memoirs: 1925-1950*
1969 Winthrop D. Jordan, *White Over Black: American Attitudes Toward the Negro, 1550-1812*
1970 T. Harry Williams, *Huey Long*
1971 James MacGregor Burns, *Roosevelt: The Soldier of Freedom*

BIOGRAPHY

1972 Joseph P. Lash, *Eleanor and Franklin: The Story of Their Relationship Based on Eleanor Roosevelt's Private Papers*
1973 James Thomas Flexner, *George Washington: Anguish and Farewell (1793-1799)*
1974 Douglas Day, *Malcolm Lowry*
1975 Richard Sewall, *The Life of Emily Dickinson*

BIOGRAPHY AND AUTOBIOGRAPHY

1977 W.A. Swanberg, *Norman Thomas: The Last Idealist*

HISTORY

1972 Allan Nevins, Ordeal of the Union series—Vol. 7, *The War for the Union: The Organized War, 1863-64*; Vol. 8, *The War for the Union: The Organized War to Victory, 1864-65*
1973 Robert Manson Myers, *The Children of Pride*
        Isaiah Trunk, *Judenrat*
1974 John Clive, *Macauley: The Shaping of the Historian*
1975 Bernard Bailyn, *The Ordeal of Thomas Hutchinson*
1976 David B. Davis, *The Problem of Slavery in an Age of Revolution: 1770-1823*
1977 Irving Howe, *World of Our Fathers*

SCIENCE, PHILOSOPHY AND RELIGION

1964 Christopher Tunnard and Boris Pushkarev, *Man-Made America: Chaos or Control?*
1965 Norbert Wiener, *God and Golem, Inc.*
1966 No award
1967 Oscar Lewis, *La Vida*
1968 Jonathan Kozol, *Death at an Early Age*
1969 R. J. Lifton, *Death in Life: Survivors of Hiroshima*
1970 Erik H. Erikson, *Gandhi's Truth: On the Origins of Militant Nonviolence*

THE SCIENCES

1971 Raymond Phineas Stearns, *Science in the British Colonies of America*
1972 George L. Small, *The Blue Whale*
1973 George B. Schaller, *The Serengeti Lion: A Study of Predator-Prey Relations*
1974 S. E. Luria, *Life: The Unfinished Experiment*
1975 Silvano Arieti, *Interpretation of Schizophrenia*

PHILOSOPHY AND RELIGION

1972 Martin E. Marty, *Righteous Empire: The Protestant Experience in America*
1973 Sydney E. Ahlstrom, *A Religious History of the American People*
1974 Maurice Natanson, *Edmund Husserl: Philosopher of Infinite Tasks*
1975 Robert Nozick, *Anarchy, State and Utopia*

CONTEMPORARY AFFAIRS

1972 Stewart Brand, *The Last Whole Earth Catalog: Access to Tools*
1973 Frances FitzGerald, *Fire in the Lake: The Vietnamese and the Americans in Vietnam*
1974 Murray Kempton, *The Briar Patch: The People of the State of New York vs. Lumumba Shakur et al*
1975 Theodore Rosengarten, *All God's Dangers: The Life of Nate Shaw*
1976 Michael J. Arlen, *Passage to Ararat*

CONTEMPORARY THOUGHT

1977 Bruno Bettelheim, *The Uses of Enchantment: The Meaning and Importance of Fairy Tales*

CHILDREN'S LITERATURE

1969 Meindert DeJong, *Journey from Peppermint Street*
1970 Isaac Bashevis Singer, *A Day of Pleasure: Stories of a Boy Growing Up in Warsaw*
1971 Lloyd Alexander, *The Marvelous Misadventures of Sebastian*
1972 Donald Barthelme, *The Slightly Irregular Fire Engine or the Hithering Thithering Djinn*
1973 Ursula K. LeGuin, *The Farthest Shore*
1974 Eleanor Cameron, *The Court of the Stone Children*
1975 Virginia Hamilton, *M. C. Higgins the Great*
1976 Walter D. Edmonds, *Bert Breen's Barn*
1977 Katherine Patterson, *The Master Puppeteer*

TRANSLATION

1967 Willard Trask, *History of My Life* by Casanova
      Gregory Rabassa, *Hopscotch* by Julio Cortazar
1968 Howard and Edna Hong, *Soren Kierkegaard's Journals and Papers*, Vol. 1
1969 William Weaver, *Cosmicomics* by Italo Calvino
1970 Ralph Manheim, *Castle to Castle* by Louis-Ferdinand Celine
1971 Frank Jones, *Saint Joan of the Stockyards* by Bertolt Brecht
      Edward G. Seidensticker, *The Sound of the Mountain* by Yasunari Kawabata
1972 Austryn Wainhouse, *Chance and Necessity: An Essay on the Natural Philosophy of Modern Biology* by Jacques Monad
1973 Allen Mandelbaum, *The Aeneid of Virgil*
1974 Karen Brazell, *The Confessions of Lady Nijo*
      Helen Lane, *Alternating Currents* by Octavio Paz
      Jackson Mathews, *Monsieur Teste* by Paul Valery
1975 Anthony Kerrigan, *The Agony of Christianity and Essays on Faith* by Miguel de Unamuno
1976 No award
1977 Li-li Ch'en, *Master Tung's Western Chamber Romance: A Chinese Chantefable*

SPECIAL MERIT

1977 Alex Haley, *Roots*.

Frank and Ethel S. Cohen Award
William and Janet Epstein Fiction Award
Rabbi Jacob Freedman Award
Leon Jolson Award
Morris J. Kaplun Memorial Award
Bernard H. Marks Award
Charles and Bertie G. Schwartz Award

NATIONAL JEWISH WELFARE BOARD
15 E. 26th St., New York, N.Y. 10010 (212/532-4949)

The $500 Frank and Ethel S. Cohen Award is given annually for the best work on Jewish thought written in English by an American or Canadian resident as determined by a committee of judges appointed by the board's Jewish Book Council.

1963 Moses Ricshin, *The Promised City*
1964 Ben Zion Bokser, *Judaism: Profile of a Faith*
1965 Israel Efros, *Ancient Jewish Philosophy*
1966 David Polish, *The Higher Freedom, A New Turning Point in Jewish History*
1967 Nahum M. Sarna, *Understanding Genesis: The Heritage of Biblical Israel*
1968 Michael A. Mayer, *Origins of the Modern Jew*
1969 Emil L. Fackenheim, *Quest for Past and Future: Essays in Jewish Theology*
1970 Abraham Joshua Heschel, *Israel: An Echo of Eternity*
1971 Mordecai M. Kaplan, *The Religion of Ethical Nationhood: Judaism's Contribution to World Peace*
1972 Abraham E. Millgram, *Jewish Worship*
1973 Elie Wiesel, *Souls on Fire*
      Samuel Sandmel, *Two Living Traditions: Essays on Religion and the Bible*
1974 Eugene B. Borowitz, *The Mask Jews Wear, The Self-Deceptions of American Jewry*
1975 Eliezer Berkovits, *Major Themes in Modern Philosophies of Judaism*
1976 Solomon B. Frehoff, *Contemporary Reform Response*
1977 David Hartman, *Maimonodes: Torah and Philosophic Quest*

The $500 Bernard H. Marks Award annually honors a work which deals with some aspect of Jewish history written by a resident or citizen of the United States or Canada in English, Hebrew or Yiddish. Books on Israel or the Holocaust are not considered by the panel of judges appointed by the Jewish Book Council.

1973 Arthur J. Zuckerman, *A Jewish Princedom in Feudal France*
1974 Bernard D. Weinryb, *The Jews of Poland: A Social and Economic History of the Jewish Community in Poland from 1100 to 1800*
1975 Solomon Seitlin, Cumulative contribution to Jewish history
1976 Rafael Patai and Jennifer Patai Wing, *The Myth of the Jewish Race*
1977 Irving Howe, *World of Our Fathers*

The $500 Morris J. Kaplun Memorial Award recognizes the most outstanding book on Israel published during the previous year in English, Hebrew or Yiddish by a resident of the United States or Canada. A panel of judges selects the winner.

1974 Isaiah Friedman, *The Question of Palestine, 1914-1918: British-Jewish-Arab Relations*
1975 Arnold Kammer, *The Forgotten Friendship: Israel and the Soviet Bloc, 1947-1953*
1976 Melvin I. Urofsky, *American Zionism from Herzl to the Holocaust*
1977 Howard M. Sachar, *A History of Israel: Israel from the Rise of Zionism to Our Time*

The $500 Leon Jolson Award for a book on the Nazi Holocaust honors the best non-fiction book about this period published during the three previous years, rotating annually for a book published in English, in Hebrew and in Yiddish. Works translated into either of these languages are eligible. The author must be a resident of the United States or Canada. A panel of judges selects the winner.

1966 Zosa Szajkowski, *Analytical Franco-Jewish Gazetteer, 1939-45*
1967 Abraham Kin, Mordecai Kosover, and Isaiah Trunk, eds., *Algemeyne Entisklopedye: Yidn VII*
1968 Jacob Robinson, *And the Crooked Shall Be Made Straight*
1969 Judah Pilch, *The Jewish Catastrophe in Europe*
     Nora Levin, *The Holocaust: The Destruction of European Jewry*
1970 Zalman Zylbercweig, *Lexicon of the Yiddish Theater: Martyrs Volume*
1971 Rabbi Ephraim Oshry, *Sheelot u-Teshuvot: Mi-Maamakim*
1972 Henry L. Feingold, *The Politics of Rescue: The Roosevelt Administration and the Holocaust, 1938-1945*
1973 Aaron Zeitlin, *Vaiterdike Lider fun Hurban un Lider fun Gloiben in Yanish Korshaks Letze Gang*
1974 No award
1975 Isaiah Trunk, *Judenrat: The Jewish Councils in Eastern Europe under Nazi Occupation*
1976 Leyzer Ran, *Yerushalayim de Lite: Jerusalem of Lithuania*
1977 Rabbi Ephraim Oshry, *Sefer Sheelot U'Teshuvot Mi-Maamakim, Part IV*

The $500 William and Janet Epstein Fiction Award annually honors the previous year's best new fiction book by an American or Canadian citizen or resident on a Jewish theme and is sometimes given for an author's cumulative body of work, as determined by a committee of judges appointed by the board's Jewish Book Council. Until 1972, this award was called the Harry and Ethel Daroff Memorial Fiction Award.

1949 Howard Fast, *My Glorious Brothers*
1950 John Hersey, *The Wall*
1951 Soma Morgenstern, *The Testament of the Lost Son*
1952 Zelda Popkin, *Quiet Street*
1953 Michael Blankfort, *The Juggler*
1954 Charles Angoff, *In the Morning Light*
1955 Louis Zara, *Blessed Is the Land*
1956 Jo Sinclair, *The Changelings*
1957 Lion Feuchtwanger, *Raquel: The Jewess of Toledo*
1958 Bernard Malamud, *The Assistant*
1959 Leon Uris, *Exodus*
1960 Philip Roth, *Goodbye, Columbus*
1961 Edward L. Wallant, *The Human Season*
1962 Samuel Yellen, *The Wedding Band*

1963 Isaac Bashevis Singer, *The Slave*
1964 Joanne Greenberg, *The King's Persons*
1965 Elie Wiesel, *The Town Beyond the Wall*
1966 Meyer Levin, *The Stronghold*
1967 No award
1968 Chaim Grade, *The Well*
1969 Charles Angoff, *Memory of Autumn*
1970 Leo Litwak, *Waiting for the News*
1971 No award
1972 Cynthia Ozick, *The Pagan Rabbi and Other Stories*
1973 Robert Kotlowitz, *Somewhere Else*
1974 Francine Prose, *Judah the Pious*
1975 Jean Karsavina, *White Eagle, Dark Skies*
1976 Johanna Kaplan, *Other People's Lives*
1977 Cynthia Ozick, *Bloodshed and Three Novellas*

The $500 Rabbi Jacob Freedman Award is given annually to the translator of a book that is considered a Jewish classic for an English translation of literary merit. The book must have been translated into English during the previous two years by a citizen or resident of the United States or Canada from a work written before 1920 in any language. A panel of judges selects the winner.

1976 Jewish Publication Society Committee of Translators of the Prophets (Max Arzt, Bernard J. Bamberger, Harry Freedman, H.L. Ginsberg, Solomon Grayzel and Harry Orlinsky), *The Book of Isaiah*
1977 Zvi L. Lampel, *Maimonides' Introduction to the Talmud*

The $500 Charles and Bertie G. Schwartz Award honors a juvenile book on a Jewish theme that combines literary merit with an affirmative expression of Jewish thought. The book must be written by a United States or Canadian citizen or resident and have been published during the previous year. A panel of judges selects the winner. (The award has undergone several name changes.)

1952 Sydney Taylor, *All-of-a-Kind Family*
1953 Lillian S. Freehof, *Stories of King David; Star Light Stories*
1954 Deborah Pessin, *The Jewish People: Book Three*
1955 Nora Benjamin Kubie, *King Solomon's Navy*
1956 Sadie Rose Weilerstein, Cumulative contributions to Jewish juvenile literature
1957 Elma Ehrlich Levinger, Cumulative contributions to Jewish juvenile literature
1958 Naomi Ben-Asher and Hayim Leaf, *Junior Jewish Encyclopedia*
1959 Lloyd Alexander, *Border Hawk: August Bondi*
1960 Sylvia Rothchild, *Keys to a Magic Door: Isaac Leib Peretz*
1961 Regina Tor, *Discovering Israel*
1962 Sadie Rose Weilerstein, *Ten and a Kid*
1963 Josephine Kamm, *Return to Freedom*
1964 Sulamith Ish-Kishor, *A Boy of Old Prague*
1965 Azriel Eisenberg and Dov Peretz Elkins, *Worlds Lost and Found*
1966 Betty Schechter, *The Dreyfus Affair*
1967 Meyer Levin, *The Story of Israel*
1968 No award
1969 No award
1970 Gerald Gottlieb, *The Story of Masada by Yigael Yadin: Retold for Young Readers*
     Charlie May Simon, *Martin Buber: Wisdom in Our Time*

1971 Sonia Levitin, *Journey to America*
1972 Sulamith Ish-Kishor, *The Master of Miracle: A New Novel of the Golem*
1973 Johanna Reiss, *The Upstairs Room*
1974 Yuri Suhl, *Uncle Misha's Partisans*
1975 Bea Stadtler, *The Holocaust: A History of Courage and Resistance*
1976 Shirley Milgrim, *Haym Salomon: Liberty's Son*
1977 Chaya Burstein, *Rifka Grows Up*

Nebula Awards

SCIENCE FICTION WRITERS OF AMERICA
68 Countryside Apts., Hackettstown, N.J. 07840
(201/852-8531)

The Nebula Awards, which consist of Lucite trophies designed by artist Judy Blish, are given annually for outstanding science fiction writing of various lengths. The membership nominates and votes on the winners, who themselves need not be members of the organization.

GRAND MASTER AWARD (Given as merited for lifetime achievement)

1974 Robert A. Heinlein
1975 Jack Williamson
1976 Clifford D. Simak

NOVEL (40,000 words or more)

1965 Frank Herbert, *Dune*
1966 Samuel R. Delany, *Babel 17*
     Daniel Keyes, *Flowers for Algernon*
1967 Samuel R. Delany, *The Einstein Intersection*
1968 Alexei Panshin, *Rite of Passage*
1969 Ursula K. LeGuin, *The Left Hand of Darkness*
1970 Larry Niven, *Ringworld*
1971 Robert Silverberg, *A Time of Changes*
1972 Isaac Asimov, *The Gods Themselves*
1973 Arthur C. Clarke, *Rendezvous with Rama*
1974 Ursula K. LeGuin, *The Dispossessed*
1975 Joe Haldeman, *The Forever War*
1976 Frederik Pohl, *Man Plus*
1977 Frederik Pohl, *Gateway*

NOVELLA (17,550-40,000 words)

1965 Brian Aldiss, "The Saliva Tree"
     Roger Zelazny, "He Who Shapes"
1966 Jack Vance, "The Last Castle"
1967 Michael Moorcock, "Behold the Man"
1968 Anne McCaffrey, "Dragonrider"
1969 Harlan Ellison, "A Boy and His Dog"
1970 Fritz Leiber, "Ill Met in Lankhmar"
1971 Katherine MacLean, "The Missing Man"
1972 Arthur C. Clarke, "A Meeting with Medusa"
1973 Gene Wolfe, "The Death of Dr. Island"
1974 Robert Silverberg, "Born with the Dead: Three Novellas about the Spirit of Man"
1975 Roger Zelazny, "Home is the Hangman"
1976 James Tiptree, Jr., "Houston, Houston, Do You Read?"
1977 Spider and Jeanne Robinson, "Stardance"

NOVELLETTE (7,500-17,550 words)

1965 Roger Zelazny, "The Doors of His Face, the Lamps of His Mouth"
1966 Gordon R. Dickson, "Call Him Lord"

1967 Fritz Leiber, "Gonna Roll Them Bones"
1968 Richard Wilson, "Mother to the World"
1969 Samuel R. Delany, "Time Considered as a Helix of Semi-Precious Stones"
1970 Theodore Sturgeon, "Slow Sculpture"
1971 Poul Anderson, "The Queen of Air and Darkness"
1972 Poul Anderson, "Goat Song"
1973 Vonda McIntyre, "Of Mist, and Grass, and Sand"
1974 Gregory Benford and Gordon Eklund, "If the Stars Are Gods"
1975 Tom Reamy, "San Diego Sue"
1976 Isaac Asimov, "The Bicentennial Man"
1977 Raccoona Sheldon, "The Screwfly Solution"

SHORT STORY (Under 7,500 words)

1965 Harlan Ellison, " 'Repent, Harlequin,' said the Ticktockman"
1966 Richard McKenna, "The Secret Place"
1967 Samuel R. Delany, "Aye, and Gomorrah"
1968 Kate Wilhelm, "The Planners"
1969 Robert Silverberg, "Passengers"
1970 No award
1971 Robert Silverberg, "Good News from the Vatican"
1972 Joanna Russ, "When It Changed"
1973 James Tiptree, Jr., "Love Is the Plan, the Plan Is Death"
1974 Ursula LeGuin, "The Day before the Revolution"
1975 Fritz Leiber, "Catch That Zeppelin"
1976 Charles L. Grant, "A Crowd of Shadows"
1977 Harlan Ellison, "Jeffty Is Five"

State Prize for Literature
State Prize for Children's and Youth's Literature
Prize of the Netherlands

NETHERLANDS MINISTRY OF CULTURE, RECREATION AND SOCIAL WELFARE
Steenvoordelaan 370, Rijwijk Z-H, Netherlands

The State Prize for Literature, known as the Hooft Prize, is given annually, alternately for important prose, poetry or essays written originally in Dutch. The prize carries a cash award of 8,000 Guilders. A jury selects the winner.

1966 W.J.M.A. Asselbergs, Essay
1967 L.J. Swaanswijk, Poetry
1968 G.K. van het Reve, Prose
1969 No award, Essay
1970 G. Kouwenaar, Poetry
1971 W.F. Hermans, Prose (Prize declined)
1972 A.J. Herzberg, Essay
1973 H. de Vries, Poetry
1974 S. Carmigglet, Prose
1975 Not available at press time, Essay
1976 Not available at press time, Poetry
1977 Not available at press time, Prose

The State Prize for Children's and Youths' Literature (Staatsprijs voor Kinder- en Jeugdliteratuur) is given every three years for an author's complete body of work for young people. The prize carries a cash award of 6,000 guilders. A jury selects the winner.

1964 A.M.G. Schmidt
1967 A. Rutgers van der Loeff

1970 M. Diekman
1973 P. Biegel
1976 Not available at press time

The Prize of the Netherlands Literature (Prijs der Nederlands Lettern) is awarded every three years for an important literary work in the Dutch language or for a complete or partial literary work of an author from the Netherlands or Belgium. The prize carries an award of 12,000 Guilders. The winner is selected by a Dutch-Belgian jury.

1956 Herman Tierlinck, Belgium
1959 A. Roland Holst, Netherlands
1962 Stijn Streuvals, Belgium
1965 Jacques C. Bloem, Netherlands
1968 Gerard Walschap, Belgium
1971 Simon Vestdijk, Netherlands
1974 Marnix Gijsen, Belgium
1977 Not available at press time

Neustadt International Prize for Literature

BOOKS ABROAD: AN INTERNATIONAL
LITERARY QUARTERLY
University of Oklahoma, Norman, Okla. 73069
(405/325-4531)

The Neustadt International Prize for Literature is awarded biennially for continuing artistic achievement in fiction, drama or poetry. An international committee of 12 judges nominates and selects the winner. Each of the dozen judges nominates one writer, and the jury as a whole votes for the winner. The award consists of a minimum of $10,000, a silver eagle feather trophy, a certificate and the dedication of one issue of *Books Abroad*.

1970 Giuseppe Ungaretti, Italy
1972 Gabriel Garcia Marquez, Colombia
1974 Francis Ponge, France
1976 Elizabeth Bishop, United States

Newbery Medal

AMERICAN LIBRARY ASSOCIATION
CHILDREN'S SERVICES DIVISION
50 E. Huron St., Chicago, Ill. 60611 (312/944-6780)

The Newbery Medal is awarded annually for the most distinguished contribution to children's literature during the preceding year. The author must be a citizen or resident of the U.S., and the work must be original, or if traditional, must be the result of original research. A 23-member committee of the Children's Services Division selects the winner.

1922 Hendrik Van Loon, *The Story of Mankind*
1923 Hugh Lofting, *The Voyages of Doctor Doolittle*
1924 Charles Boardman Hawes, *The Dark Frigate*
1925 Charles J. Finger, *Tales from Silver Lands*
1926 Arthur Bowie Chrisman, *Shen of the Sea*
1927 Will James, *Smoky, the Cowhorse*
1928 Dham Gopal Mukerji, *Gay-Neck, the Story of a Pigeon*

1929 Eric P. Kelly, *The Trumpeter of Krakow, a Tale of the Fifteenth Century*
1930 Rachel Field, *Hitty, Her First Hundred Years*
1931 Elizabeth Coatsworth, *The Cat Who Went to Heaven*
1932 Laura Adams Armer, *Waterless Mountain*
1933 Elizabeth Foreman Lewis, *Young Fu of the Upper Yangtze*
1934 Cornelia Meigs, *Invincible Louisa*
1935 Monica Shannon, *Dobry*
1936 Carol Ryrie Brink, *Caddie Woodlawn*
1937 Ruth Sawyer, *Roller Skates*
1938 Kate Seredy, *The White Stag*
1939 Elizabeth Enright, *Thimble Summer*
1940 James Daugherty, *Daniel Boone*
1941 Armstrong Sperry, *Call it Courage*
1942 Walter D. Edmonds, *The Matchlock Gun*
1943 Elizabeth Janet Gray, *Adam of the Road*
1944 Esther Forbes, *Johnny Tremain: A Novel for Old and Young*
1945 Robert Lawson, *Rabbit Hill*
1946 Lois Lenski, *Strawberry Girl*
1947 Carolyn Sherwin Bailey, *Miss Hickory*
1948 William Pene Du Bois, *The Twenty-One Balloons*
1949 Marguerite Henry, *King of the Wind*
1950 Marguerite De Angeli, *The Door in the Wall*
1951 Elizabeth Yates, *Amos Fortune, Free Man*
1952 Eleanor Estes, *Ginger Pye*
1953 Ann Nolan Clark, *Secret of the Andes*
1954 Joseph Krumgold, *. . . And Now Miguel*
1955 Meindert De Jong, *The Wheel on the School*
1956 Jean Lee Latham, *Carry on, Mr. Bowditch*
1957 Virginia Sorensen, *Miracles on Maple Hill*
1958 Harold Keith, *Rifles for Watie*
1959 Elizabeth George Speare, *The Witch of Blackbird Pond*
1960 Joseph Krumgold, *Onion John*
1961 Scott O'Dell, *Island of the Blue Dolphins*
1962 Elizabeth George Speare, *The Bronze Bow*
1963 Madeleine L'Engle, *A Wrinkle in Time*
1964 Emily Neville, *It's Like This, Cat*
1965 Maia Wojciechowska, *Shadow of a Bull*
1966 Elizabeth Borton de Trevino, *I, Juan de Pareja*
1967 Irene Hunt, *Up a Road Slowly*
1968 Elaine Konigsburg, *From the Mixed-Up Files of Mrs. Basil E. Frankweiler*
1969 Lloyd Alexander, *The High King*
1970 William H. Armstrong, *Sounder*
1971 Betsy Byars, *Summer of the Swans*
1972 Robert C. O'Brien, *Mrs. Frisby and the Rats of NIMH*
1973 Jean Craighead George, *Julie of the Wolves*
1974 Paula Fox, *The Slave Dancer*
1975 Virginia Hamilton, *M. C. Higgins, the Great*
1976 Susan Cooper, *The Grey King*
1977 Mildred D. Taylor, *Roll of Thunder, Hear My Cry*

Bourse Goncourt de la Nouvelle Silver and Gold Eagles Grand Aigle d'Or de la Ville de Nice Prix International de la Press

FESTIVAL INTERNATIONAL DU LIVRE DE NICE
Palais des Expositions, 06300 Nice, France (Tel: 55-18-55); and 5, Rue Stanislas, 75006 Paris, France (Tel: 544-20-18)

The Bourse Goncourt de la Nouvelle, which carries an honorarium of 10,000 francs, was created to support the literary form of the novella. A 10-member jury selects the winner.

1978 Henri Gougaud, *Departements et Territoires d'Outre Mort*

The Prix International de la Presse, which consists of a diploma and a medal, is given for a historical work or a document that appeared in its original language during the previous year. A seven-member jury of representatives from international news magazines, such as *Newsweek, The Observer, Le Nouvel Observateur,* selects the recipient.

1977 Jurgen Fuchs, *Gedachtnisprotokolle*

The Grand Aigle d'Or de la Ville de Nice, which carries an honorarium of 30,000 francs, is given for the work of a great French author or foreign author whose work has been translated into French. A jury of French and non-French authors and editors of literary journals and representatives of the French press select the winner.

1969 Giudo Piovene
1970 Ferreira de Castro
1971 Angus Wilson
1972 Per Olof Sundman
1973 Aldo Palazzecchi
1975 Nadine Gordimer
1976 Julio Cortazar
1977 Ernst Junger

Silver Eagles in specific categories and a Gold Eagle for overall honors are given as part of the Festival's Prix Art et Techniques Internationales du Livre to honor remarkable concepts and execution. A jury selects winners for international recognition.

1977 Golden Eagle
La Route des Incas, (Photographs by Hans Silvester; Editions du Chene; France)
Special Jury Award
Die Panoramen (Editions Orell Fussli; Switzerland)
Silver Eagles
Fine Arts: *Horst Antes: L'Oeuvre Gravee* (Office du Livre; Switzerland)
Reference Works: *Le Livre de l'Outil* (Edition Hier et Demain; France)
Practical Reference: *Universal Atlas* (George Philips; Great Britain)
Catalogues: *Andy Warhol: Das Zeichnerische Werk 1942-75* (Wurttembergischer Kunstverein; Federal Republic of Germany)
Historical Documents: *Le Voix da la Liberte - Ici Londres* (Editions Documentation Francaise/Club Francais des Bibiliophiles; France)
Illustrated Biography: *Sigmund Freud* (Suhnkamp Verlag; Federal Republic of Germany)
Youth: *The Pond Book* (Penguin Books; Great Britain)
Education: *Slabikar (Statni Pedagogicke Nakladatelstvi;* Czechoslovakia)
Science: *Atlas - SSO Technology, Medicine:* (SSO Atlas; Switzerland)
Paperback: *Alban Berg: Life and Work in Words and Pictures* (Insel Verlag; Federal Republic of Germany)

Niederdeutsche Preise:
Hans - Bottcher - Preis
Klaus - Groth - Preis
Richard - Ohnesorg - Preis
Fritz - Reuter - Preis
Fritz - Stavenhagen - Preis

STIFTUNG F.V.S.
Georgsplatz 10, 2 Hamburg I, Federal Republic of Germany
(Tel: 33-04-00 and 33-06-00)

Five literary prizes, cumulatively called the Niederdeutsche Preise, are awarded in annual rotation. A jury selects the recipient of the award, which carries a cash prize of 5,000 German marks.

HANS-BOTTCHER-PREIS (Broadcast play)

1960 Heinrich Schmidt-Barrien, Frankenburg
1962 Konrad Hansen, Bremen
1965 Hinrich Kruse, Braak bei Neumunster
1970 Ernst-Otto Schlopke, Bremen
1972 Fritz Arend, Uphusen bei Bremen
1974 Wolfgang Sieg, Offenau bei Elmshorn
1976 No award

KLAUS-GROTH-PREIS (Lyrics)

1956 Hermann Claudius Gronwohld
1958 Otto Tenne, Hamburg
1960 Carl Budich, Lubeck
1963 Norbert Johannimloh, Munster/Westf.
1966 Johann Diedrich Bellmann, Hermannsburg
1968 Hans Ehrke, Kiel
1971 Oswald Andrae, Jever
1975 Siegfried Kessemeier, Munster/Westf.

RICHARD-OHNESORG-PREIS (Acting, production, direction and recitation)

1963 Hans Mahler, Hamburg
1966 Hans Fleischer, Hamburg
1969 Walter A. Kreye, Bremen
1973 Ernst Waldau, Bremen
1976 Erwin Herzig, Lubeck

FRITZ-REUTER-PREIS (Narrative literature)

1955 Heinrich Behnken, Hamburg
1957 Hans Henning Holm, Hamburg
1959 Moritz Jahn, Gottingen
1962 Rudolf Kinau, Hamburg
1965 Thora Thyselius, Brake
1968 Heinrich Schmidt-Barrien, Frankenburg
1972 Diederich Heinrich Schmidt, Leer
1976 Christian Holsten, Bremen

FRITZ-STAVENHAGEN-PREIS (Dramatic poetry)

1959 Hans Ehrke, Kiel
1961 Hermann Otto, Hamburg
1964 Hans Heitmann, Lubeck
1967 Paul Jessen, Hockensbull
1969 Ivo Braak, Kiel
1971 Karl Bunje, Oldenburg
1973 Gunther Siegmund, Hamburg
1975 Konrad Hansen, Bremen

Nobel Prize for Literature

NOBEL FOUNDATION
Nobel House, Sturegatan 14, 11436 Stockholm, Sweden

One of six Nobel Prizes given annually, the Nobel Prize for literature is generally recognized as the highest honor that can be bestowed upon an author for his or her total body of literary work. The award, which consists of a gold medal, diploma and large honorarium, is given at a ceremony on December 10 of each year at Stockholm's City Hall. The award itself is presented and administered by the Swedish Academy, which selects the recipient. The amount of cash fluctuates; in 1977, it was approximately $145,000.

1901 Scully-Prudhomme (Rene Prudhomme), France
1902 C.M.T. Mommsen, Germany
1903 Bjornstjerne Bjornson, Norway
1904 Frederic Mistral, France
      Jose Echegaray, Spain
1905 Henryk Sienkiewicz, Poland
1906 Giosue Carducci, Italy
1907 Rudyard Kipling, Great Britain
1908 Rudolf C. Eucken, Germany
1909 Selma Lagerlof, Sweden
1910 Paul J. L. Heyse, Germany
1911 Count Maurice Maeterlinck, Belgium
1912 Gerhart Hauptmann, Germany
1913 Rabindranath Tagore, India
1914 No award
1915 Romain Rolland, France
1916 Carl G. von Heidenstam, Sweden
1917 Karl A. Gjellerup, Denmark
      Henrik Pontoppidan, Denmark
1918 No award
1919 Carl F. G. Spitteler, Switzerland
1920 Knut Hamsun, Norway
1921 Anatole France, France
1922 Jacinto Benavente, Spain
1923 William Butler Yeats, Ireland
1924 Wladyslaw S. Reymont, Poland
1925 George Bernard Shaw, Great Britain (born in Ireland)
1926 Grazia Deledda, Italy
1927 Henri Bergson, France
1928 Sigrid Undset, Norway (born in Denmark)
1929 Thomas Mann, Germany
1930 Sinclair Lewis, U.S.A.
1931 Erik A. Karlfeldt, Sweden
1932 John Galsworthy, Great Britain
1933 Ivan A. Bunin, France (born in Russia)
1934 Luigi Pirandello, Italy
1935 No award
1936 Eugene O'Neill, U.S.A.
1937 Roger Martin du Gard, France
1938 Pearl S. Buck, U.S.A.
1939 Frans E. Sillanpaa, Finland
1940 No award
1941 No award
1942 No award
1943 No award
1944 Johannes V. Jensen, Denmark
1945 Gabriela Mistral, Chile
1946 Hermann Hesse, Switzerland (born in Germany)
1947 André Gide, France
1948 T.S. Eliot, Great Britain (born in U.S.A.)
1949 William Faulkner, U.S.A.
1950 Bertrand Russell, Great Britain
1951 Par F. Lagerkvist, Sweden

1952 Francois Mauriac, France
1953 Sir Winston Churchill, Great Britain
1954 Ernest Hemingway, U.S.A.
1955 Halldor K. Laxness, Iceland
1956 Juan Ramon Jimenez, Puerto Rico (born in Spain)
1957 Albert Camus, France
1958 Boris L. Pasternak, U.S.S.R. (Prize declined)
1959 Salvatore Quasimondo, Italy
1960 Saint-John Perse, France
1961 Ivo Andric, Yugoslavia
1962 John Steinbeck, U.S.A.
1963 Giorgos Seferis, Greece
1964 Jean-Paul Sartre, France (Prize declined)
1965 Mikhail Sholokhov, U.S.S.R.
1966 Samuel Joseph Agnon, Israel (born in Austria)
      Nelly Sachs, Sweden
1967 Miguel Angel Asturias, Guatemala
1968 Yasunari Kawabata, Japan
1969 Samuel Beckett, France (born in Ireland)
1970 Aleksandr I. Solzhenitsyn, U.S.S.R.
1971 Pablo Neruda, Chile
1972 Heinrich Boll, Germany
1973 Patrick White, Australia
1974 Eyvind Johnson, Sweden
      Harry Edmund Martinson, Sweden
1975 Eugenio Montale, Italy
1976 Saul Bellow, U.S.A.
1977 Vicente Aleixandre, Spain

Nordiska Radets Litteraturpris

THE NORDIC COUNCIL
Fack, S-103, 10 Stockholm, Sweden (Tel: 14-10-00 and 20-54-02)

The Nordiska Radets Litteraturpris is awarded to a literary work of high merit written in the language of one of the Nordic countries and published during the two previous years. The award carries an honorarium of 75,000 Danish crowns and is given annually. A committee of Nordic experts makes the selection from candidates nominated by delegates of the participating countries.

1962 Eyvind Johnson (Sweden), *Hans nades tid*
1963 Vaino Linna (Finland), *Soner av ett folk*
1964 Tarjei Vesaas (Norway), *Is-slottet*
1965 William Heinesen (Faeroe Islands), *Det gode Hab*
      Olof Lagercrantz (Sweden), *Fran helvetet till paradiset*
1966 Gunnar Ekelof (Sweden), *Diwan over Fursten av Emgion*
1967 Johan Borgen (Norway), *Nye noveller*
1968 Per Olof Sundman (Sweden), *Ingenjor Andres luftfard*
1969 Per-Olof Enquist (Sweden), *Baltutlamningen*
1970 Klaus Rifbjerg (Denmark), *Anna, jeg, Anna*
1971 Thorkild Hansen (Denmark), *Slavernes oer*
1972 Karl Vennberg (Sweden), *Sju ord pa tunnelbanan*
1973 Veijo Meri (Finland), *Sergeantens pojke*
1974 Villy Sorensen (Denmark), *Uden Mal—og med*
1975 Hannu Salama (Finland), *Kommer upp i to*
1976 Olafur Sigurdsson (Iceland), *Du minns en brunn*
1977 Bo Carpelan (Finland), *I de morka rummen, i de ljusa*

William Riley Parker Prize

MODERN LANGUAGE ASSOCIATION
62 Fifth Ave., New York, N.Y. 10011 (212/741-7854)

The $500 William Riley Parker Prize is given to an MLA member for an outstanding article in *PMLA*, selected by the William Riley Parker Prize Selection Committee.

1964	David DeLaura
1965	Rene Girard
1966	Elisabeth Schneider
1967	Donald Rackin
1968	Stanley B. Greenfield
1969	Rudolf P. Gottfried
1970	E.D. Lowry
1971	Frederic R. Jameson
1972	R.A. Yoder
1973	Elisabeth Schneider
1974	George T. Wright
1975	Walter J. Ong
1976	R.G. Peterson
1977	Evelyn N. Hinz

Peace Prize of German Book Dealers

BORSENVEREIN DES DEUTSCHEN BUCHHANDELS
Grosser Hirschgraben 17-21, 6 Frankfurt-am-Main, Federal Republic of Germany

The Friedenspreis des Deutschen Buchhandels, Peace Prize of German Book Dealers, is given annually for meritorious literary contribution. The award carries a 10,000-mark honorarium.

1950	Max Tau
1951	Albert Schweitzer
1952	Romano Guardini
1953	Martin Buber
1954	Carl J. Burckhardt
1955	Hermann Hesse
1956	Reinhold Schneider
1957	Thornton Wilder
1958	Karl Jaspers
1959	Theodor Heuss
1960	Victor Gollancz
1961	Sarvepalli Radhakrishnan
1962	Paul Tillich
1963	Carl Friedrich von Weizsaecker
1964	Gabriel Marcel
1965	Nelly Sachs
1966	Augustin Bea
	Willem A. Visser't Hooft
1967	Ernst Bloch
1968	Leopold Sedar Senghor
1969	Alexander Mitscherlich
1970	Gunnar and Alva Myrdal
1971	Marion, Countess Doenhoff
1972	Janusz Korczak
1973	Club of Rome
1974	Frere Roger, Prior of Taize
1975	Alfred Grosser
1976	Max Frisch
1977	Leszek Kolakowski

Henry M. Phillips Prize

AMERICAN PHILOSOPHICAL SOCIETY
104 S. Fifth St., Philadelphia, Pa. 19106 (215/627-0706)

The Henry M. Phillips Prize, which carries an honorarium of up to $2,000, is awarded as merited for an outstanding book or essay on the science and philosophy of jurisprudence.

1895	George H. Smith, "The Theory of State"
1900	W.H. Hastings, "The Development of Law as Illustrated by the Decisions Relating to the Police Power of the State"
1912	Charles H. Burr, "The Treaty-making Power of the United States and the Methods of Its Enforcement as Affecting the Police Powers of the States"
1921	Quincy Wright, "The Relative Rights, Duties, and Responsibilities of the President, of the Senate and the House, and the Judiciary in Theory and Practice"
1935	Lon L. Fuller, "American Legal Realism"
1942	Edward S. Corwin, *The President: Office and Powers* and articles on constitutional law
1950	Philip C. Jessup, *Modern Law of Nations*
1955	Edmond Cahn, *The Sense of Injustice* and his contribution to *Supreme Court and Supreme Law*
1957	Catherine Drinker Bowen, *The Lion and the Throne*
1960	Roscoe Pound, "Jurisprudence"
1962	Karl Nickerson Llewellyn, *The Common Law Tradition: Deciding Appeals*
1974	John Rawls, *A Theory of Justice*

Pilgrim Award

SCIENCE FICTION RESEARCH ASSOCIATION
c/o Dean Arthur O. Lewis, Jr., 205 Sparks Hall, Penn State University, University Park, Pa. 16102 (814/865-1438)

A framed scroll is given to the winner of the Pilgrim Award, which annually honors an author of any nationality for scholarly contributions to science fiction and modern fantasy writing. The winner is selected by a committee.

1970	J.O. Bailey
1971	Marjorie Nicolson
1972	Julius Kagarlitski
1973	Jack Williamson
1974	I.F. Clarke
1975	Damon Knight
1976	James Gunn
1977	Thomas D. Clareson

Playboy Writing Awards

PLAYBOY MAGAZINE
919 N. Michigan Ave., Chicago, Ill. 60611 (312/PL 1-8000)

Fiction and non-fiction writers are honored annually in the Playboy Writing Awards for the year's best contributions to the magazine, as determined by the editors. The exact composition of the awards has changed over the years, but has included both major works and short pieces and has recognized the best new contributors. In addition to the $1,000 first-place winners listed here, the magazine also honors runners-up in the polling. There are occasional ties.

BEST FICTION/SHORT STORY

1956	Herbert Gold, "The Right Kind of Pride"
1957	George Langelaan, "The Fly"
1958	Richard Matheson, "The Distributor"
1959	John Wallace, "I Love You, Miss Irvine"

1960   Ken Purdy, "The Book of Tony"
1961   Harvey Jacobs, "The Lion's Share"
1962   James Jones, "The Thin Red Line"
1963   Bernard Malamud, "The Naked Nude"
1964   Romain Gary, "A Bit of A Dreamer, A Bit of A Fool"
1965   Roald Dahl, "The Visitor"
1966   Vladimir Nabokov, "Despair"
1967   Isaac Bashevis Singer, "The Lecture"
1968   John Cheever, "The Yellow Room"
1969   James Leigh, "Yes, It's Me and I'm Late Again"
       Vladimir Nabokov, "Ada"
1970   Joyce Carol Oates, "Saul Bird Says: Relate! Communicate! Liberate!"
       Irwin Shaw, Three stories that became part of novel *Rich Man, Poor Man:* "Thomas in Elysium," "Rudolph in Money Land," "Rich Man's Weather"
1971   George Axelrod, "Where Am I Now That I Need Me?"
       Sean O'Faolain, "Murder at Cobbler's Hulk"
1972   Sean O'Faolain, "Falling Rocks, Narrowing Road, Cul-de-Sac, Stop"
       Dan Jenkins, "Semi-Tough"
1973   Anthony Austin, "Where the Americans Came"
       George MacDonald Fraser, "Flashman at the Charge"
1974   Saul Bellow, "Humboldt's Gift"
       John Updike, "Nevada"
1975   George MacDonald Fraser, "Flashman in the Great Game"
1976   Norman Mailer, "The Trial of the Warlock"
       Kurt Vonnegut, "Slapstick or Lonesome No More"
       Paul Theroux, "The Autumn Dog"
1977   John Le Carre, "The Honourable Schoolboy"
       Paul Theroux, "Adulterer's Luck"

FICTION: BEST NEW WRITER/CONTRIBUTOR

1966   Tom Mayer, "The Eastern Springs"
1967   Rafael Steinberg, "Day of Good Fortune"
1968   Richard Duggin, "Gamma, Gamma, Gamma"
1969   Warner Law, "The Thousand-Dollar Cup of Crazy German Coffee"
1970   Hal Bennett, "Dotson Gerber Resurrected"
1971   William Hjortsberg, "Gray Matters"
1972   James Alan McPherson, "The Silver Bullet"
1973   Nadine Gordimer, "The Conservationist"
1974   Paul Reb, "The Legend of Step-and-a-Half"
1975   Larry McMurtry, "Dunlap Crashes In"
1976   Nicholas Meyer, "The West End Horror"
1977   Judith Johnson Sherwin, "Voyages of a Mile-High Fille de Joie"

BEST NON-FICTION/ARTICLE

1958   John Keats, "Eros and Unreason in Detroit"
1959   Ralph Ginzburg, "Cult of the Aged Leader"
1960   Charles Beaumont, "Chaplin"
1961   Ken W. Purdy, "Hypnosis"
1962   Ken W. Purdy, "Stirling Moss: A Nodding Acquaintance With Death"
1963   William Iversen, "Youth, Love, Death and the Hubby Image"
1964   John Clellon Holmes, "Revolution Below the Belt"
1965   Kenneth Tynan, "The Beatle in the Bull Ring"
1966   Nat Hentoff, "The Cold Society"
1967   John Kenneth Galbraith, "Resolving Our Vietnam Problem"
1968   Alan Watts, "Wealth Versus Money"
1969   Eric Norden, "The Paramilitary Right"
1970   Alvin Toffler, "Future Shock"
1971   John McPhee, "Centre Court"

1972   Richard Rhodes, "The Killing of the Everglades"
1973   John Clellon Holmes, "Gone in October"
1974   Robert Woodward and Carl Bernstein, "All the President's Men"
       Ed McClanahan, "Little Enis Pursues His Muse"
1975   Norman Mailer, "The Fight"
1976   Alex Haley, "Roots"
1977   Asa Baber, "The Commodities Market"

NON-FICTION: SATIRE/HUMOR

1964   Dan Greenburg, "How to be a Jewish Mother"
1965   Jean Shepherd, "Leopold Doppler and the Orpheum Gravy Boat Riot"
1966   Jean Shepherd, "Daphne Bigelow and the Spine-Chilling Saga of the Snail-Encrusted Tinfoil Noose"
1967   Jean Shepherd, "Return of the Smiling Wimpy Doll"
1968   Marvin Kitman, "How I Became a Renaissance Man in My Spare Time"
1969   Woody Allen, "Show White"
       Jean Shepherd, "Wanda Hickey's Night of Golden Memories"
1970   Marvin Kitman, "George Washington's Expense Account"
       Richard Curtis, "The Giant Chicken Eating Frog"
1971   Bruce McCall and Brock Yates, "Major Hody Bisby's Album of Forgotten Warbirds"
       Robert Morley, "Morley Meets the Frogs"
1972   G. Barry Golson, "The People—Maybe!"
       Dan Greenburg, "My First Orgy"
1973   Wayne McLoughlin and Scott Morris, "The Fallout Follies"
       Bob Ottum and William Neely, as Stroker Ace, "I Lost it in the Second Turn"
1974   Richard Curtis, "Do Plants Have Orgasms?"
       Dick Tuck, "Watergate Wasn't All My Fault"
1975   Robert S. Wieder, "Clarke Ghent's School Days"
1976   Dan Greenburg, "Dominant Writer Seeks Submissive Miss"
1977   Marshall Brickman, "The Book of Coasts"

NON-FICTION: ESSAY

1969   Martin Luther King, "Testament of Hope"
1970   David Halberstam, "The Americanization of Vietnam"
1971   John Clellon Holmes, "Thanksgiving in Florence"
1972   Herbert Gold, "In the Community of Girls and the Commerce of Culture"
1973   Germaine Greer, "Seduction Is a Four-Letter Word"
1974   Frederick Exley, "Saint Gloria and the Troll"
1975   No award
1976   Ron Kovic, "Born on the Fourth of July"
1977   D. Keith Mano, "Rocky Mountain Hype"

NON-FICTION: BEST NEW WRITER/CONTRIBUTOR

1969   Karl Hess, "The Death of Politics"
1970   Stanley Booth, "Furry's Blues"
1971   Arthur Hadley, "Goodbye to the Blind Flash"
1972   Ed McClanahan, "Grateful Dead I Have Known"
1973   Roger Rapoport, "It's Enough to Make You Sick"
1974   O'Connell Driscoll, "Jerry Lewis, Birthday Boy"
1975   Harry Crews, "Going Down in Valdeez"
       Jay Cronley, "Houston"
1976   Jim Davidson, "Punch Out the IRS"
1977   Roy Blount, Jr., "Chairman Billy"

SPECIAL AWARD

1976   Robert Scheer, Jimmy Carter interview and accompanying article: "Jimmy, We Hardly Know Y'all"

Edgar Allan Poe Awards

MYSTERY WRITERS OF AMERICA
105 E. 19th St., New York, N.Y. 10003

The Edgar Allan Poe Awards, informally known as the Edgars, are given annually for outstanding achievement in mystery writing for the year. A scroll is awarded to the winner.

BEST NOVEL

1954 Charlotte Jay, *Beat Not the Bones*
1955 Raymond Chandler, *The Long Goodbye*
1956 Margaret Millar, *Beast in View*
1957 Charlotte Armstrong, *A Dram of Poison*
1958 Ed Lacy, *Room to Swing*
1959 Stanley Ellin, *The Eighth Circle*
1960 Celia Fremlin, *The Hours Before Dawn*
1961 Julian Symons, *The Progress of a Crime*
1962 J. J. Marric, *Gideon's Fire*
1963 Ellis Peters, *Death and the Joyful Woman*
1964 Eric Ambler, *The Light of Day*
1965 John Le Carre, *The Spy Who Came in from the Cold*
1966 Adam Hall, *The Quiller Memorandum*
1967 Donald Westlake, *God Save the Mark*
1968 Jeffrey Hudson, *A Case of Need*
1969 Dick Francis, *Forfeit*
1970 Maj Sjowall and Per Wahloo, *The Laughing Policeman*
1971 Frederick Forsyth, *Day of the Jackal*
1972 Warren Kiefer, *The Lingala Code*
1973 Tony Hillerman, *The Dance of the Dead*
1974 Jon Cleary, *Peter's Pence*
1975 Brian Garfield, *Hopscotch*
1976 Robert Parker, *Promised Land*
1977 Not available at press time

BEST FIRST NOVEL

1946 Julius Fast, *Watchful at Night*
1947 Helen Eustis, *The Horizontal Man*
1948 Frederic Brown, *The Fabulous Clipjoint*
1949 Mildred Davis, *The Room Upstairs*
1950 Alan Green, *What a Body*
1951 Thomas Walsh, *Nightmare in Manhattan*
1952 Mary McMullen, *Strangle Hold*
1953 William Campbell Gault, *Don't Cry for Me*
1954 Ira Levin, *A Kiss before Dying*
1955 Jean Potts, *Go, Lovely Rose*
1956 Lane Kauffmann, *The Perfectionist*
1957 Douglas McNutt Douglas, *Rebecca's Pride*
1958 William R. Weeks, *Knock and Wait a While*
1959 Richard Martin Stern, *The Bright Road to Fear*
1960 Henry Slesar, *The Grey Flannel Shroud*
1961 John Holbrooke Vance, *The Man in the Cage*
1962 Suzanne Blanc, *The Green Stone*
1963 Robert L. Fish, *The Fugitive*
1964 Cornelius Hirschberg, *Florentine Finish*
1965 Harry Kemelman, *Friday the Rabbi Slept Late*
1966 John Ball, *In the Heat of the Night*
1967 Ross Thomas, *The Cold War Swap*
1968 Michael Collins, *Act of Fear*
1969 Joe Gores, *A Time of Predators*
1970 Lawrence Sanders, *The Anderson Tapes*
1971 A. H. Z. Carr, *Finding Maubee*
1972 R. H. Shimer, *Squaw Point*
1973 Paul E. Erdman, *The Billion Dollar Sure Thing*
1974 Gregory MacDonald, *Fletch*
1975 Rex Burns, *Alvarez Journal*
1976 James Patterson, *The Thomas Berryman Number*
1977 Not available at press time

Political Book Award

WASHINGTON MONTHLY
1028 Connecticut Ave. NW, Washington, D.C. 20036
(202/659-4866)

The annual Political Book Award is given for the best book(s) of the preceding year on politics and government. The magazine features the winning book in a major review in the March issue. A panel of editors selects the winner.

1970 Chester L. Cooper, *The Lost Crusade*
      George R. Reedy, *The Twilight of the Presidency*
1971 Ronald J. Glasser, *365 Days*
      Julian K. Prescott, *A History of the Modern Age*
1972 Daniel Ellsberg, *Papers on the War*
      Frances FitzGerald, *Fire in the Lake*
1973 John Newhouse, *Cold Dawn: The Story of SALT*
      Ward Just, *The Congressman Who Loved Flaubert and Other Political Stories*
1974 Robert A. Caro, *The Power Broker: Robert Moses and the Fall of New York*
1975 Martha Derthick, *Uncontrollable Spending for Social Service Grants*
1976 John Morton Blum, *V Was for Victory*
      John Dean, *Blind Ambition*
      John Hollander, *Reflections on Espionage*
1977 Simon Leys, *Chinese Shadows*
      Morris P. Fiorina, *Congress: Keystone of the Washington Establishment*

Poses Creative Arts Award

BRANDEIS UNIVERSITY
Brandeis University Commission Office, 12 E. 77th St., New York, N.Y. 10021 (212/472-1501)

One of a series of awards in the creative arts, The Jack I. and Lillian L. Poses Brandeis University Creative Arts Award is given annually to recognize talent in mid-career in literature. The award, which may not be applied for, carries an honorarium of $1,000 and a medal or citation. Professional juries chosen by the commission select the winners.

MEDAL AWARD

1957 William C. Williams, Poetry
1958 John Crowe Ransom, Poetry
1959 "H.D." (Hilda Doolittle), Poetry
1960 Yvor Winters, Poetry
1961 Allen Tate, Poetry
1962 Louise Bogan, Poetry
1963 Marianne Moore, Poetry
1964 Vladimir Nabokov, Fiction
1965 Stanley Kunitz, Poetry
1966 Eudora Welty, Fiction
1967 Conrad Aiken, Poetry
1968 Lionel Trilling, Non-fiction
1969 Leonie Adams, Poetry
1970 Isaac Bashevis Singer, Fiction
1971 Richard Wilbur, Poetry
1972 Katherine Anne Porter, Fiction
1973 Alfred Kazin, Non-fiction
1974 Robert Francis, Poetry
1975 Christopher Isherwood, Fiction
1976 Irving Howe, Non-fiction
1977 Robert Lowell, Poetry

CITATION

1957 Katherine Hoskins, Poetry
1958 Barbara Howes, Poetry
1959 Hayden Carruth, Poetry
1960 John Berryman, Poetry
1961 Louis O. Coxe, Poetry
1962 Ben Belitt, Poetry
1963 Howard Nemerov, Poetry
1964 Richard Yates, Fiction
1965 Anthony Hecht, Poetry
1966 John Barth, Fiction
1967 May Swenson, Poetry
1968 Elizabeth M. Thomas, Non-fiction
1969 Galway Kinnell, Poetry
1970 Robert Coover, Fiction
1971 James Wright, Poetry
1972 Edward Hoagland, Fiction
1973 Theodore Solotaroff, Non-fiction
1974 John Frederick Nims, Poetry
1975 Harold Brodkey, Fiction
1976 Susan Sontag, Non-fiction
1977 Theodore Weiss, Poetry

Pulitzer Prize

COLUMBIA UNIVERSITY
Graduate School of Journalism, New York, N.Y. 10027
(212/280-3828) (Pulitzer Prizes: 212/280-3841)

Endowed by the will of Joseph Pulitzer, founder of the *St. Louis Post Dispatch* and administered by Columbia University, the annual Pulitzer Prizes include $1,000 awards in fiction, general nonfiction, history and biography, as well as journalism, drama, music and public service, found elsewhere in this volume. Four copies of each book nominated must be sent to the Advisory Committee on Pulitzer Prizes for consideration.

FICTION (Called novel until 1947)

1917 No award
1918 Ernest Poole, *His Family*
1919 Booth Tarkington, *The Magnificent Ambersons*
1920 No award
1921 Edith Wharton, *The Age of Innocence*
1922 Booth Tarkington, *Alice Adams*
1923 Willa Cather, *One of Ours*
1924 Margaret Wilson, *The Able McLaughlins*
1925 Edna Ferber, *So Big*
1926 Sinclair Lewis, *Arrowsmith*
1927 Louis Bromfield, *Early Autumn*
1928 Thornton Wilder, *The Bridge of San Luis Rey*
1929 Julia Peterkin, *Scarlet Sister Mary*
1930 Oliver LaFarge, *Laughing Boy*
1931 Margaret Ayer Barnes, *Years of Grace*
1932 Pearl S. Buck, *The Good Earth*
1933 T. S. Stribling, *The Store*
1934 Caroline Miller, *Lamb in His Bosom*
1935 Josephine Winslow Johnson, *Now in November*
1936 Harold L. Davis, *Honey in the Horn*
1937 Margaret Mitchell, *Gone With the Wind*
1938 John Phillips Marquand, *The Late George Apley*
1939 Marjorie Kinnan Rawlings, *The Yearling*
1940 John Steinbeck, *The Grapes of Wrath*
1941 No award
1942 Ellen Glasgow, *In This Our Life*
1943 Upton Sinclair, *Dragon's Teeth*
1944 Martin Flavin, *Journey in the Dark*
1945 John Hersey, *A Bell for Adano*

1946 No award
1947 Robert Penn Warren, *All the King's Men*
1948 James Michener, *Tales of the South Pacific*
1949 James Gould Cozzens, *Guard of Honor*
1950 A. B. Guthrie, Jr., *The Way West*
1951 Conrad Richter, *The Town*
1952 Herman Wouk, *The Caine Mutiny*
1953 Ernest Hemingway, *The Old Man and the Sea*
1954 No award
1955 William Faulkner, *A Fable*
1956 MacKinlay Kantor, *Andersonville*
1957 No award
1958 James Agee, *A Death in the Family*
1959 Robert Lewis Taylor, *The Travels of Jaimie McPheeters*
1960 Allen Drury, *Advise and Consent*
1961 Harper Lee, *To Kill a Mockingbird*
1962 Edwin O'Connor, *The Edge of Sadness*
1963 William Faulkner, *The Reivers*
1964 No award
1965 Shirley Ann Grau, *The Keepers of the House*
1966 Katherine Anne Porter, *The Collected Stories of Katherine Anne Porter*
1967 Bernard Malamud, *The Fixer*
1968 William Styron, *The Confessions of Nat Turner*
1969 N. Scott Momaday, *House Made of Dawn*
1970 Jean Stafford, *Collected Stories*
1971 No award
1972 Wallace Stegner, *Angle of Repose*
1973 Eudora Welty, *The Optimist's Daughter*
1974 No award
1975 Michael Shaara, *The Killer Angels*
1976 Saul Bellow, *Humboldt's Gift*
1977 No award

HISTORY

1917 J. J. Jusserand, *With Americans of Past and Present Days*
1918 James Ford Rhodes, *A History of the Civil War, 1861-65*
1919 No award
1920 Justin H. Smith, *The War with Mexico* (2 vols.)
1921 William Sowden Sims and Burton J. Hendrick, *The Victory at Sea*
1922 James Truslow Adams, *The Founding of New England*
1923 Charles Warren, *The Supreme Court in United States History*
1924 Charles McIlwain, *The American Revolution—A Constitutional Interpretation*
1925 Frederic L. Paxson, *A History of the American Frontier*
1926 Edward Channing, *The History of the United States*
1927 Samuel Flagg Bemis, *Pinckney's Treaty*
1928 Vernon Louis Parrington, *Main Currents in American Thought* (2 vols.)
1929 Fred Albert Shannon, *The Organization and Administration of the Union Army, 1861-1865*
1930 Claude H. Van Tyne, *The War of Independence*
1931 Bernadotte E. Schmitt, *The Coming of the War: 1914*
1932 John J. Pershing, *My Experiences in the World War*
1933 Frederick J. Turner, *The Significance of Sections in American History*
1934 Herbert Agar, *The People's Choice*
1935 Charles McLean Andrews, *The Colonial Period of American History*
1936 Andrew C. McLaughlin, *The Constitutional History of the United States*
1937 Van Wyck Brooks, *The Flowering of New England*

1938 **Paul Herman Buck,** *The Road to Reunion, 1865-1900*
1939 **Frank Luther Mott,** *A History of American Magazines*
1940 **Carl Sandburg,** *Abraham Lincoln: The War Years*
1941 **Marcus Lee Hansen,** *The Atlantic Migration, 1607-1860*
1942 **Margaret Leech,** *Reveille in Washington*
1943 **Esther Forbes,** *Paul Revere and the World He Lived In*
1944 **Merle Curti,** *The Growth of American Thought*
1945 **Stephen Bonsal,** *Unfinished Business*
1946 **Arthur M. Schlesinger Jr.,** *The Age of Jackson*
1947 **James Phinney Baxter III,** *Scientists Against Time*
1948 **Bernard DeVoto,** *Across the Wide Missouri*
1949 **Roy Franklin Nichols,** *The Disruption of American Democracy*
1950 **Oliver W. Larkin,** *Art and Life in America*
1951 **R. Carlyle Buley,** *The Old Northwest: Pioneer Period, 1815-1840*
1952 **Oscar Handlin,** *The Uprooted*
1953 **George Dangerfield,** *The Era of Good Feelings*
1954 **Bruce Catton,** *A Stillness at Appomattox*
1955 **Paul Horgan,** *Great River: The Rio Grande in North American History*
1956 **Richard Hofstadter,** *Age of Reform*
1957 **George F. Kennan,** *Russia Leaves the War: Soviet-American Relations, 1917-1920*
1958 **Bray Hammond,** *Banks and Politics in America—From the Revolution to the Civil War*
1959 **Leonard D. White,** assisted by Jean Schneider, *The Republican Era: 1869-1901*
1960 **Margaret Leech,** *In the Days of McKinley*
1961 **Herbert Feis,** *Between War and Peace: The Potsdam Conference*
1962 **Lawrence H. Gipson,** *The Triumphant Empire: Thunder-Clouds Gather in the West*
1963 **Constance McLaughlin Green,** *Washington: Village and Capital, 1800-1878*
1964 **Sumner Chilton Powell,** *Puritan Village: The Formation of a New England Town*
1965 **Irwin Unger,** *The Greenback Era*
1966 **Perry Miller,** *Life of the Mind in America: From the Revolution to the Civil War*
1967 **William H. Goetzmann,** *Exploration and Empire: The Explorer and Scientist in the Winning of the American West*
1968 **Bernard Bailyn,** *The Ideological Origins of the American Revolution*
1969 **Leonard Levy,** *Origins of the Fifth Amendment*
1970 **Dean G. Acheson,** *Present at the Creation: My Years in the State Department*
1971 **James MacGregor Burns,** *Roosevelt: The Soldier of Freedom, 1940-1945*
1972 **C. N. Degler,** *Neither Black Nor White*
1973 **Michael Kammen,** *People of Paradox: An Inquiry Concerning the Origin of American Civilization*
1974 **Daniel J. Boorstin,** *The Americans: The Democratic Experience*
1975 **Dumas Malone,** *Jefferson and His Time*
1976 **Paul Horgan,** *Lamy of Sante Fe*
1977 **David M. Potter,** *The Impending Crisis 1841-1846* (a posthumous publication; manuscript finished by Don E. Fehrenbacher)

BIOGRAPHY OR AUTOBIOGRAPHY

1917 **Laura E. Richards, Maude Howe Elliott and Florence Howe Hall,** *Julia Ward Howe*
1918 **William Cabell Bruce,** *Benjamin Franklin, Self-Revealed*
1919 **Henry Adams,** *The Education of Henry Adams*

1920 **Albert J. Beveridge,** *The Life of John Marshall* (4 vols.)
1921 **Edward Bok,** *The Americanization of Edward Bok*
1922 **Hamlin Garland,** *A Daughter of the Middle Border*
1923 **Burton J. Hendrick,** *The Life and Letters of Walter H. Page*
1924 **Michael Idvorsky Pupin,** *From Immigrant to Inventor*
1925 **M. A. DeWolfe Howe,** *Barrett Wendell and His Letters*
1926 **Harvey Cushing,** *The Life of Sir William Osler* (2 vols.)
1927 **Emory Holloway,** *Whitman*
1928 **Charles Edward Russell,** *The American Orchestra and Theodore Thomas*
1929 **Burton J. Hendrick,** *The Training of an American: The Earlier Life and Letters of Walter H. Page*
1930 **Marquis James,** *The Raven*
1931 **Henry James,** *Charles W. Eliot*
1932 **Henry F. Pringle,** *Theodore Roosevelt*
1933 **Allan Nevins,** *Grover Cleveland*
1934 **Tyler Dennett,** *John Hay*
1935 **Douglas Southall Freeman,** *R. E. Lee*
1936 **Ralph Barton Perry,** *The Thought and Character of William James*
1937 **Allan Nevins,** *Hamilton Fish*
1938 **Odell Shepard,** *Pedlar's Progress*
     Marquis James, *Andrew Jackson*
1939 **Carl Van Doren,** *Benjamin Franklin*
1940 **Ray Stannard Baker,** *Woodrow Wilson, Life and Letters,* Volumes VII and VIII
1941 **Ola E. Winslow,** *Jonathan Edwards*
1942 **Forrest Wilson,** *Crusader in Crinoline*
1943 **Samuel Eliot Morison,** *Admiral of the Ocean Sea*
1944 **Carleton Mabee,** *The American Leonardo: The Life of Samuel F. B. Morse*
1945 **Russell Blaine Nye,** *George Bancroft: Brahmin Rebel*
1946 **Linnie M. Wolfe,** *Son of the Wilderness*
1947 **William Allen White,** *The Autobiography of William Allen White*
1948 **Margaret Clapp,** *Forgotten First Citizen: John Bigelow*
1949 **Robert E. Sherwood,** *Roosevelt and Hopkins*
1950 **Samuel Bemis,** *John Quincy Adams and the Foundations of American Foreign Policy*
1951 **Margaret Louise Coit,** *John C. Calhoun: American Portrait*
1952 **Merlo J. Pusey,** *Charles Evans Hughes*
1953 **David J. Mays,** *Edmund Pendleton 1721-1803*
1954 **Charles A. Lindbergh,** *The Spirit of St. Louis*
1955 **William S. White,** *The Taft Story*
1956 **T. F. Hamlin,** *Benjamin Henry Latrobe*
1957 **John F. Kennedy,** *Profiles in Courage*
1958 **Douglas Southall Freeman,** *George Washington,* Volumes I-VI
     Mary Ashworth and John Carroll, *George Washington,* Volume VII
1959 **Arthur Walworth,** *Woodrow Wilson, American Prophet*
1960 **Samuel Eliot Morison,** *John Paul Jones*
1961 **David Donald,** *Charles Sumner and the Coming of the Civil War*
1962 No award
1963 **Leon Edel,** *Henry James*
1964 **Walter Jackson Bate,** *John Keats*
1965 **Ernest Samuels,** *Henry Adams*
1966 **Arthur Schlesinger, Jr.,** *A Thousand Days*
1967 **Justin Kaplan,** *Mr. Clemens and Mark Twain*
1968 **George F. Kennan,** *Memoirs (1925-1950)*
1969 **Benjamin Reid,** *The Man from New York: George Quinn and His Friends*

1970 T. Harry Williams, *Huey Long*
1971 Lawrance R. Thompson, *Robert Frost: The Years of Triumph, 1915-1938*
1972 J. P. Lash, *Eleanor and Franklin*
1973 W. A. Swanberg, *Luce and His Empire*
1974 Louis Sheaffer, *O'Neill, Son and Artist*
1975 Robert A. Caro, *The Power Broker: Robert Moses and the Fall of New York*
1976 Richard Warrington Baldwin Lewis, *Edith Wharton: A Biography*
1977 John E. Mack, *A Prince of Our Disorder: The Life of T. E. Lawrence*

GENERAL NON-FICTION

1962 Theodore H. White, *The Making of the President 1960*
1963 Barbara Tuchman, *The Guns of August*
1964 Richard Hofstadter, *Anti-intellectualism in American Life*
1965 Howard Mumford Jones, *O Strange New World*
1966 Edwin Way Teale, *Wandering Through Winter*
1967 David Brion Davis, *The Problem of Slavery in Western Culture*
1968 Will and Ariel Durant, *Rousseau and Revolution*
1969 Rene Dubos, *So Human an Animal: How We Are Shaped by Surroundings and Events*
      Norman Mailer, *The Armies of the Night*
1970 Erik H. Erikson, *Gandhi's Truth*
1971 John Toland, *The Rising Sun*
1972 Barbara W. Tuchman, *Stilwell and the American Experience in China, 1911-1945*
1973 Frances FitzGerald, *Fire in the Lake*
      Robert Coles, *Children of Crisis*
1974 Ernest Becker, *The Denial of Death*
1975 Annie Dillard, *Pilgrim at Tinker Creek*
1976 Robert N. Butler, *Why Survive? Being Old in America*
1977 William W. Warner, *Beautiful Summers*

SPECIAL CITATIONS AND AWARDS

1957 Kenneth Roberts, *Historical novels*
1960 Garrett Mattingly, *The Armada*
1961 *American Heritage Picture History of the Civil War*
1973 James Thomas Flexner, *George Washington*, Vol. I-IV
1977 Alex Haley, *Roots*

Remembrance Award
BERGEN-BELSEN ASSOCIATIONS
Box 333, Lenox Hill Station, New York. N.Y. 10021

The Remembrance Award, which carries a $2,500 honorarium, recognizes the author of a novel, drama, poetry, essay or memoir of high literary merit inspired by the Nazi Holocaust that uses the experiences to present a humanistic and enlightened vision of the contemporary world to the present and future generations. A jury of writers selects the winner.

1965 Elie Wiesel (United States), *Town Beyond the Wall* and writings
1966 Manes Sperber (France), *Than a Tear in the Sea*
1967 Jean Cayrol (France), collected poems
1968 Jacob Presser (Holland), *The Destruction of the Dutch Jews*
      Yehoshua Vigodsky (Israel), *Collected Works*

1969 Arthur Morse (United States), *While the Six Million Died*
      Chaim Grade (United States), *Seven Little Lanes*
      Joshua Wygodski (Israel), *Collected Works*
1970 *The City of Jerusalem*
1971 Abba Kovner (Israel), *Little Sister of Mine*
1972 Uri Zvi Greenberg (Israel), *Poems from the Holocaust*
1973 Jacob Robinson (United States), Historical research
      Itzhak Meras (Israel), *Stalemate With Death*
      Daniel Stern (United States), *Who Shall Live and Who Shall Die*
      Mendel Mann (France), *Holocaust Trilogy*
      Leon Eitinger (Norway), *Psychological Studies of Survivors of the Holocaust*
      Abraham Sutzkever (Israel), *Poems from the Sea of Death*
      Leon Leneman (France), *The Tragedy of Russian Jewry*
      Mordecai Tzanim (Israel), *Collected Works of Eastern European Jewry*
      Michel Borwicz (France), *Jewish Resistance*
      S. L. Schneiderman (United States), *When the Vistula Spoke Yiddish*
      Leib Rochman (Israel), *In Your Blood You Shall Live*
1974 George Steiner (Great Britain), *In Bluebird's Castle*
1975 Andre Ne'her (France), *Collected Philosophical Works*
1976 No award
1977 No award

Renaudot Prize
THEOPHRASTE RENAUDOT SECRETARIAT
c/o Etienne Labou, 5 Villa Halle, Paris 14, France

The Theophraste Renaudot Prize annually honors the author of an original novel published during the preceeding year. While the 50-franc honorarium is an insignificant sum, the prize is important in the French literary world. A seven-member jury selects the winner.

1926 Armand Lunel, *Niccolo Peccavi*
1927 Bernard Nabonne, *Mallena*
1928 Andre Obey, *Le Joueur de triangle*
1929 Marcel Ayme, *La Table aux Creves*
1930 Germaine Beaumont, *Piege*
1931 Philippe Heriat, *L'innocent*
1932 Louis-Ferdinand Celine, *Voyage au bout de la nuit*
1933 Charles Braibant, *Le Roi dort*
1934 Louis Francis, *Blanc*
1935 Francois de Roux, *Jours sans gloire*
1936 Louis Aragon, *Les Beaux Quartiers*
1937 Jean Rogessart, *Mervale*
1938 Pierre-Jean Launay, *Leonie la bienheureuse*
1939 Jean Malaquais, *Les Javanais*
1940 David Rousset, *L'Univers Concentrationnaire*
1941 Paul Mousset, *Quand le temps travaillait pour nous*
1942 Robert Gaillard, *Les Liens de chaine*
1943 Andre Soubiban, *J'etais medecin avec les chars*
1944 Rogert Peyrepitte, *Les Amities particulieres*
1945 Henri Bosco, *Le Mas Theotime*
1946 Jules Roy, *La Vallee heureuse*
1947 Jean Cayrol, *Je vivrai l'amour des autres*
1948 Pierre Fisson, *Voyage aux horizons*
1949 Louis Guilloux, *Le Jeu de patience*
1950 Pierre Molaine, *Les Orgues de l'enfer*
1951 Robert Margerit, *Le Dieu un*
1952 Jacques Perry, *L'amour de rien*

1953 Celia Bertin, *La Derniere Innocence*
1954 Jean Reverzy, *Le Passage*
1955 Georges Govy, *Le Moissonneur d'epines*
1956 Andre Perrin, *La Pere*
1957 Michel Butor, *La Modification*
1958 Edouard Glissant, *La Lezarde*
1959 Albert Palle, *L'Experience*
1960 Alfred Kern, *Le Bonheur fragile*
1961 Roger Bordier, *Les Bles*
1962 Simone Jacquemard, *Le Veilleur de nuit*
1963 Jean-Marie Le Clezio, *Le Proces verbal*
1964 Jean-Pierre Faye, *L'Ecluse*
1965 Georges Perec, *Les Choses*
1966 Jose Cabanis, *La Bataille de Toulouse*
1967 Salvat Etchart, *Le Monde tel qu'il est*
1968 Yambo Ouologuem, *Le Devoir de violence*
1969 Max Olivier-Lacamp, *Les Feux de la Colere*
1970 Jean Freustier, *Isabelle ou l'Arriere-saison*
1971 Pierre-Jean Remy, *Le Sac du palais d'Ete*
1972 Christopher Frank, *La Nuit Americaine*
1973 Suzanne Prou, *La Terrasse des Bernardini*
1974 Georges Borgeaud, *Voyage a l'etranger*
1975 Jean Joubert, *L'homme de sable*
1976 Michel Henry, *L'amour les yeux fermes*
1977 Alphonse Boudard, *Les Combattants du Petit Bonheur*

John Llewelyn Rhys Memorial Prize
NATIONAL BOOK LEAGUE
7 Albemarle St., London W1X 4BB, United Kingdom (Tel: 01-493-9001)

The John Llewelyn Rhys Memorial Prize is given annually for a book by an author under 30 years who is a citizen of Great Britain or the Commonwealth. A panel of judges selects the winner of the £300 award.

1942 Michael Richey, *Sunk by a Mine*
1943 Morwenna Donelly, *Beauty for Ashes*
1944 Alun Lewis, *The Last Inspection*
1945 James Aldridge, *The Sea Eagle*
1946 Oriel Malet, *My Bird Sings*
1947 Anne-Marie Walters, *Moondrop to Gascony*
1948 Richard Mason, *The Wind Cannot Read*
1949 Emma Smith, *Maidens' Trip*
1950 Kenneth Allsop, *Adventure Lit Their Star*
1951 E.J. Howard, *The Beautiful Visit*
1952 No award
1953 Rachel Trickett, *The Return Home*
1954 Tom Stacey, *The Hostile Sun*
1955 John Wiles, *The Moon to Play With*
1956 John Hearne, *Voices under the Window*
1957 Ruskin Bond, *The Room on the Roof*
1958 V. S. Naipaul, *The Mystic Masseur*
1959 Dan Jacobson, *A Long Way from London*
1960 David Caute, *At Fever Pitch*
1961 David Storey, *Flight into Camden*
1962 Robert Rhodes James, *An Introduction to the House of Commons*
     Edward Lucie-Smith, *A Tropical Childhood and Other Poems*
1963 Peter Marshall, *Two Lives*
1964 Nell Dunn, *Up the Junction*
1965 Julian Mitchell, *The White Father*
1966 Margaret Drabble, *The Millstone*
1967 Anthony Masters, *The Seahorse*
1968 Angela Carter, *The Magic Toyshop*
1969 Melvyn Bragg, *Without a City Wall*
1970 Angus Calder, *The People's War*

1971 Shiva Naipaul, *Fireflies*
1972 Susan Hill, *The Albatross*
1973 Peter Smalley, *A Warm Gun*
1974 Hugh Fleetwood, *The Girl Who Passed for Normal*
1975 David Hare, *Knuckle*
     Tim Jeal, *Cushing's Crusade*
1976 No award
1977 Richard Cork, *Vorticism and Abstract Art in the First Machine Age,* Vol. I and II

Richard and Hinda Rosenthal Foundation Award
AMERICAN ACADEMY AND INSTITUTE OF ARTS AND LETTERS
633 W. 155th St., New York, N.Y. 10032 (212/286-1480)

One of a pair of awards established under the same endowment (the other being for painting), the Richard and Hinda Rosenthal Foundation Award of $2,000 annually goes for a work of fiction published during the preceding 12 months which, although not a commercial success, was "a considerable literary achievement."

1957 Elizabeth Spencer, *The Voice At The Back Door*
1958 Bernard Malamud, *The Assistant*
1959 Frederick Buechner, *The Return Of Ansel Gibbs*
1960 John Updike, *The Poorhouse Fair*
1961 John Knowles, *A Separate Peace*
1962 Paule Marshall, *Soul Clap Hands And Sing*
1963 William Melvin Kelley, *A Different Drummer*
1964 Ivan Gold, *Nickel Miseries*
1965 Thomas Berger, *Little Big Man*
1966 Tom Cole, *An End To Chivalry*
1967 Thomas Pynchon, *The Crying Of Lot 49*
1968 Joyce Carol Oates, *A Garden Of Earthly Delights*
1969 Frederick Exley, *A Fan's Notes*
1970 Jonathan Strong, *Tike And Five Stories*
1971 Christoper Brookhouse, *Running Out*
1972 Thomas McGuane, *The Bushwhacked Piano*
1973 Thomas Rogers, *The Confession Of A Child Of The Century*
1974 Alice Walker, *In Love & Trouble*
1975 Ishmael Reed, *The Last Days Of Louisiana Red*
1976 Richard Yates, *Disturbing The Peace*
1977 Spencer Holst, *Spencer Holst Stories*

W. H. Smith Literary Award
W. H. SMITH LTD.
Strand House, 10 New Fetter Lane, London EC4A 1AD, United Kingdom (Tel: 01-353-0277)

The W.H. Smith Literary Award, which carries an honorarium of £1,000, is given annually to a Commonwealth author for an outstanding contribution to literature originally published during the previous year in the United Kingdom and written originally in English. A three-judge panel selects the winner.

1959 Patrick White, *Voss*
1960 Laurie Lee, *Cider With Rosie*
1961 Nadine Gordimer, *Friday's Footprint*
1962 J.R. Ackerley, *We Think the World of You*
1963 Gabriel Fielding, *The Birthday King*
1964 E.H. Gombrich, *Meditations On A Hobby Horse*
1965 Leonard Woolf, *Beginning Again*
1966 R.C. Hitchinson, *A Child Possessed*

1967 Jean Rhys, *Wild Sargasso Sea*
1968 V.S. Naipaul, *The Mimic Men*
1969 Robert Gittings, *John Keats*
1970 John Fowles, *The French Lieutenant's Woman*
1971 Nan Fairbrother, *New Lives, New Landscapes*
1972 Kathleen Raine, *The Lost Country*
1973 Brian Moore, *Catholics*
1974 Anthony Powell, *Temporary Kings*
1975 Jon Stallworth, *Wilfred Owen: A Biography*
1976 Seamus Heaney, *North*
1977 Ronald Lewin, *Slim: The Standardbearer*

Stephen Black Prize for Drama
Jochem van Bruggen-pris vir Prosa
Roy Campbell Prize for Poetry
G.W.F. Grosskopf-prys vir Drama
C. Louis Leipoldt-prys vir Poesie
Pauline Smith Prize for Prose
DEPT. OF NATIONAL EDUCATION
Private Bag X122, Pretoria 0001, Republic of South Africa
(Tel: 29971)

A series of English and Afrikaans prizes in drama, prose and poetry is held annually, with any one of the categories judged every three years by a panel appointed by the Minister of National Education. A top prize of 750 Rand is given for the best entry in each language. The author must be a South African citizen or resident for at least a year. There are no age or religious restrictions.

STEPHEN BLACK PRIZE FOR DRAMA
1965 May Thomas, *The Unrecorded Days*
1968 J. Lodge, *In a Man's Shadow*
1971 J.A. Brown, *Travels with a Collapsible Woman*
1974 S.J. Curtis, *Steadman's Folly*

G.W.F. GROSSKOPF-PRYS VIR DRAMA
1968 C. Seymore, *Mag is n Vandaal*

PAULINE SMITH PRIZE FOR PROSE
To date, this award has not been given.

JOCHEM VAN BRUGGEN-PRYS VIR PROSA
1972 P. Pistorius, *n Spyker vir Slypsteenkop*

ROY CAMPBELL PRIZE FOR POETRY
1959 A. Delius, *A Corner of the World*
      A. Curry, *Of Africa and the East*
1963 P.R.C. Adams, *The Hand at My Door*
1967 R. Dederick, *A Low Trajectory*

C. LUIS LEIPOLDT-PRYS VIR POESIE
1973 D. Sleigh, *Bundel Gedigte*

Jesse H. Jones Award
TEXAS INSTITUTE OF LETTERS
Box 7219, Austin, Tex. 78712 (512/741-1833)

The Jesse H. Jones Award, which carries a $1,000 honorarium, is given annually for the best fictional book about Texas or by a Texas author. Until 1959,

when the Houston Endowment funded this award, it was known as the McMurray Bookshop Award.

1948 David Westheimer, *Summer on the Water*
1949 Fred Gipson, *Hound-Dog Man*
1950 William Goyan, *The House of Breath*
1951 Dillon Anderson, *I and Claudie*
1952 George Williams, *The Blind Bull*
1953 Madison Cooper, *Sironia, Texas*
1954 William A. Owens, *Walking on Borrowed Land*
1955 Fred Gipson, *Recollection Creek*
1956 Curt Anders, *The Price of Courage*
1957 Sikes Johnson, *The Hope of Refuge*
1958 William Humphrey, *Home from the Hill*
1959 Hamilton (Tex) Maule, *Jeremy Todd*
      Walter Clemons, *The Poison Tree*
1960 Bill Casey, *A Shroud for a Journey*
1961 Larry McMurtry, *Horseman, Pass By*
1962 Katherine Anne Porter, *Ship of Fools*
1963 J. Y. Bryan, *Come to the Bower*
1964 Tom Lea, *The Hands of Cantu*
1965 William Humphrey, *The Ordways*
1966 Larry McMurtry, *The Last Picture Show*
      Tom Pendleton, *The Iron Orchard*
1967 Robert Flynn, *North to Yesterday*
1968 Marshall Terry, *Tom Northway*
      Tom Horn, *The Shallow Grass*
1969 Willard Marsh, *Beachhead in Bohemia*
1970 Paul Horgan, *Whitewater*
1971 Nolan Porterfield, *A Way of Knowing*
1972 John Williams, *Augustus*
1973 Shelby Reed Hearon, *The Second Dune*
      Chester L. Sullivan, *Alligator Gar*
1974 Charles W. Smith, *Thin Men of Haddam*
1975 Donald Barthelme, *The Dead Father*
1976 Max Apple, *The Oranging of America*
1977 R. G. Vliet, *Solitudes*

Friends of the Dallas Public Library Award
TEXAS INSTITUTE OF LETTERS
Box 7219, Austin, Tex. 78712 (512/741-1833)

The Friends of the Dallas Public Library Award, which carries a $500 honorarium, is given annually for a book about Texas which contributes most to general knowledge about the state.

1959 David L. Miller, *Modern Science and Human Freedom*
1960 Robert Vines, *Trees, Shrubs, and Woody Vines*
1961 W. W. Newcomb, Jr., *Indians of Texas*
1962 Joseph Stephen Gallegly, *Footlights on the Border*
1963 Joseph Milton Nance, *After San Jacinto*
1964 Ramon Adams, *Burrs under the Saddle*
1965 Lois Wood Burkhalter, *Gideon Lincecum*
1966 William H. Goetzmann, *Exploration and Empire*
1967 W. W. Newcomb, Jr., *Rock Art of Texas Indians*
1968 C. L. Sonnichsen, *Pass of the North*
1969 Bill C. Malone, *Country Music, USA*
1970 Richard B. Henderson, *Maury Maverick*
1971 Thomas Parke Hughes, *Elmer Sperry, Inventor and Engineer*
1972 A. C. Greene, *The Last Captive*
1973 Donald E. Green, *Land of the Underground Rain, Irrigation on the Texas High Plains, 1910-1970*
1974 Harry C. Oberholser, *The Bird Life of Texas*
1975 Elizabeth A. H. John, *Storms Brewed in Other Men's Worlds*
1976 Lawrence Goodwyn, *Democratic Promise*

1977 **Frank E. Vandiver,** *Black Jack: The Life and Times of John J. Pershing*

Alexander Gode Medal

AMERICAN TRANSLATORS ASSOCIATION
Box 129, Croton-on-Hudson, N.Y. 10520 (914/271-3260)

The Alexander Gode Medal is given annually on recommendations to the ATA Honors and Awards Committee for winners of the medallion, which honors distinguished service in the field.

    1964 **Alexander Gode**
    1965 **Kurt Gingold**
    1966 **Richard and Clara Winston**
    1967 **National Translation Center (University of Texas)**
    1968 **Pierre-Francois Caille**
    1969 **Henry Fischbach**
    1970 **Carl V. Bertsche**
    1971 **Lewis Bertrand**
    1972 **Lewis Galantiere**
    1973 **Jean-Paul Vinay**
    1974 **Eliot F. Beach**
    1975 **Frederick Ungar**
    1976 **No award**
    1977 **Eugene Nida**

Goethe House-P.E.N. Translation Prize

P.E.N. AMERICAN CENTER
156 Fifth Ave., New York, N.Y. 10010 (212/255-1977)

The $500 Goethe House-P.E.N. Translation Prize is given annually for the best book translated from German into English during the year.

1973 **Sophie Wilkins,** *The Lime Works,* by Thomas Bernhard
1974 **Peter Sander,** *Ice Age,* by Tancred Dorst
1975 **Ralph Manheim,** *A Sorrow Beyond Dreams,* by Peter Handke
1976 **Douglas Parmee,** *An Exemplary Life,* by Siegfried Lenz
1977 **Not available at press time**

P.E.N. Translation Prize

P.E.N. AMERICAN CENTER
156 Fifth Ave., New York, N.Y. 10010 (212/255-1977)

The $1,000 P.E.N. Translation Prize, donated by the Book-of-the-Month Club, honors the best book-length translation from any language into English.

1962 **Archibald Colquhoun,** *The Viceroys* by Federico de Roberto
1963 **Ralph Manheim,** *The Tin Drum,* by Gunter Grass
1964 **Joseph Barnes,** *Story Of A Life,* by Konstantin Paustovsky
1965 **Geoffrey Skelton and Adrian Mitchell,** *Marat/-Sade,* by Peter Weiss
1966 **Harriet de Onis,** *Sagarana,* by J. Guimaraes Rosa
1967 **Vladimir Markov and Merrill Sparks,** *Modern Russian Poetry*
1968 **W. S. Merwin,** *Selected Translations 1948-1968*

1969 **Sidney Alexander,** *The History Of Italy,* by Francesco Guicciardini
1970 **Max Hayward,** *Hope Against Hope,* by Nadezhda Mandelstam
1971 **Richard and Clara Winston,** *Letters of Thomas Mann*
1972 **J. P. McCulloch,** *Poems Of Sextus Propertius*
1973 **Hardie St. Martin and Leonard Mades,** *Obscene Bird Of Night,* by Jose Donoso
1974 **Helen R. Lane,** *Count Julian,* by Juan Goytisolo
1975 **Richard Howard,** *A Short History Of Decay,* by E. M. Cioran
1976 **Gregory Rabassa,** *The Autumn of the Patriarch,* by Gabriel Garcia Marquez
1977 **Not available at press time**

David D. Lloyd Prize

THE HARRY S. TRUMAN LIBRARY
Independence, Mo. (816/833-1400)

Award Correspondence: c/o Professor Thomas C. Blaisdell, Jr., Dept. of Political Science, 210 Barrows Hall, University of California, Berkeley, Calif. 94720

The $1,000 David D. Lloyd Prize is awarded biennially by the Harry S. Truman Library Institute for National and International Affairs for a book published during the preceding two years that deals primarily and substantially with some aspect of political, economic and social development in the United States, principally during the Truman presidency or with the public career of Harry S. Truman.

1967 **Earl Latham,** *The Communist Conspiracy in Washington from the New Deal to McCarthy*
1969 **Irwin Ross,** *The Loneliest Campaign: The Truman Victory of 1948*
1970 **Dean G. Acheson,** *Present at the Creation: My Years in the State Department*
      Richard G. Hewlett, and Francis Duncan, *Atomic Shield, 1948-1952; My Years in the State Department*
1972 **Susan M. Hartmann,** *Truman and the 80th Congress*
1974 **Alonzo L. Hamby,** *Beyond the New Deal: Harry S. Truman and American Liberalism*
1976 **Lynn Estheridge Davis,** *The Cold War Begins: Soviet-American Conflict Over Eastern Europe*

Ulisse Prize

RIVISTA ULISSE
Sezione Premio Cortina Ulisse, Via Po 11, 00198-Rome, Italy

The European Cortina *Ulisse* Prize, which carries a 1-million lire cash award, is given annually for a book which encourages that notion that "culture ought to be a common instrument of civilization and not the privilege of the few." The winner is selected by a jury, whose members are representatives of the Accademia Nazionale dei Lincei.

1949 **John Read,** (United Kingdom), *A Direct Entry to Organic Chemistry*
1950 **Carlo Morandi,** (Italy), *L'Idea dell'Unita Politica d'Europa nel XIX e XX secolo*
      Pierre Belperron, (France), *La Guerre de Secession*
1951 **Lionello Venturi,** (Italy), *Come Si Comprende la Pittura*

1952 Ernest Baldwin, (United Kingdom), *Dynamic Aspects of Biochemistry*
1953 No award
1954 Graham Hutton, (United Kingdom), *We Too Can Prosper*
1955 Edward Spranger, (Germany), *Padagogische Perspektiven*
1956 Luigi Preti, (Italy), *Le Lotte Agrarie nella Valle Padana*
1957 No award
1958 G. Lowenthal and J. Hausen, (Germany), *Wir Werden durch Atome Leben*
1959 George Elgozy, (France), *La France devant le Marche Commun*
1960 No award
1961 Felice Ippolito, (Italy), *L'Italia e l'Energia Nucleare*
1962 Werner Holzer, (Germany), *Das Nackte Antlitz Africas*
1963 No award
1964 Hans Herbert Goetz, (Germany), *Weil Alle Besser Leben Wollen*
1965 Ladislao Mittner, (Italy), *Storia Della Letteratura Tedesca dal Pietismo al Romanticismo*
1966 No award
1967 Giulio Carlo Argan, (Italy), *Progetto e Destino*
1968 Andre Martinet, (France), *La Consideration Fonctionelle du Langage*
1969 No award
1970 Edouard Bonnefous, (France), *Le Monde Est-Il Surpeuple?*
1971 Max Nicholson, (United Kingdom), *The Environmental Revolution*
1972 No award
1973 George Stainer, (United Kingdom), *Language and Silence*
      Ezio Raimondi, (Italy), *Tecniche delle Critica Letteraria*
1974 Andrew Shonfield, (United Kingdom), *Europe: Journey to an Unknown Destination*
1975 No award
1976 Paul Bairoch, (France), *Le Tiers-Monde dans l'impasse*
1977 No award

Whitbread Award

BOOKSELLERS' ASSOCIATION
154 Buckingham Palace Rd., London SW1W 9TZ, United Kingdom (Tel: 01-730-8214)

The £1,000 Whitbread Award, which is administered by the Association and supported by Whitbread & Co., Ltd., the brewers, annually honors outstanding books in several categories published during the past year and written by authors who have lived in the United Kingdom for at least five years. A panel of judges chosen by the brewery and the Booksellers' Association of Great Britain and Northern Ireland selects the recipients.

FICTION

1971 Gerda Charles, *The Destiny Waltz*
1972 Susan Hill, *The Bird of Night*
1973 Shiva Naipaul, *The Chip Chip Gatherers*
1974 Iris Murdoch, *The Sacred and Profane Love Machine*
1975 William McIlvanney, *Docherty*
1976 William Treavor, *The Children of Dynmouth*
1977 Beryl Bainbridge, *Injury Time*

BEST FIRST BOOK

1974 Clair Tomalin, *The Life and Death of Mary Wollstonecraft*
1975 Ruth Spalding, *The Improbable Puritan: A Life of Bulstrode Whitelocke*
1976 No award
1977 No award

BEST CHILDREN'S BOOK

1972 Rumer Godden, *The Diddakoi*
1973 Alan Aldridge and William Plomer, *Grasshopper's Feast*
1974 Russell Hoban and Quentin Blake, *How Tom Beat Captain Najork and His Hired Sportsmen*
      Jill Paton Walsh, *The Emperor's Winding Sheet*
1975 No award
1976 Penelope Lively, *A Stitch in Time*
1977 Shelagh Macdonald, *No End to Yesterday*

BIOGRAPHY

1971 Michael Meyer, *Henrik Ibsen*
1972 James Pope-Hennesy, *Trollope*
1973 John Wilson, *C.B.: The Life of Sir Henry Campbell-Bannerman*
1974 Andrew Boyle, *Poor Dear Brendan*
1975 Helen Corke, *In Our Infancy: An Autobiography, 1882-1912*
1976 Winifred Gerin, *Elizabeth Gaskell*
1977 Nigel Nicolson, *No End to Yesterday*

William Allen White Children's Book Award

WILLIAM ALLEN WHITE LIBRARY
Kansas State Teachers College, Emporia, Kan. 66801

The William Allen White Children's Book Award, which consists of a bronze medal, is given annually for an outstanding children's book, as selected by a panel of Kansas youngsters from the fourth through the eighth grades from books chosen by specialists in children's literature.

1953 Elizabeth Yates, *Amos Fortune: Free Man*
1954 Doris Gates, *Little Vic*
1955 Jean Bailey, *Cherokee Bill*
1956 Marguerite Henry, *Brighty of the Grand Canyon*
1957 Phoebe Erickson, *Daniel Coon*
1958 Elliott Arnold, *White Falcon*
1959 Fred Gipson, *Old Yeller*
1960 William O. Steele, *Flaming Arrows*
1961 Keith Robertson, *Henry Reed, Inc.*
1962 Catherine O. Peare, *The Helen Keller Story*
1963 Scott O'Dell, *Island of the Blue Dolphins*
1964 Sheila Burnford, *The Incredible Journey*
1965 Zachary Ball, *Bristle Face*
1966 Sterling North, *Rascal*
1967 Annabel and Edgar Johnson, *The Grizzly*
1968 Beverly Cleary, *The Mouse and the Motorcycle*
1969 Keith Robertson, *Henry Reed's Baby-Sitting Service*
1970 E. L. Konigsburg, *From the Mixed-Up Files of Mrs. Basil E. Frankweiler*
1971 Walt Morey, *Kavik, the Wolf Dog*
1972 Barbara Corcoran, *Sasha, My Friend*
1973 E. B. White, *The Trumpet of the Swan*
1974 Robert O'Brien, *Mrs. Frisby and the Rats of NIMH*
      Zilpha K. Snyder, *The Headless Cupid*
1975 William Steig, *Dominic*

1976 Beverly Cleary, *Socks*
1977 George Selden, *Harry Cat's Pet Puppy*

Laura Ingalls Wilder Medal

AMERICAN LIBRARY ASSOCIATION
CHILDREN'S SERVICES DIVISION
50 E. Huron St., Chicago, Ill. 60611 (312/944-6780)

The Laura Ingalls Wilder Medal is given every five years to an author or illustrator whose books, published in the U.S., have made a substantial and lasting contribution to children's literature. A committee of Children's Services Division members make nominations, and the winner is selected by a mail vote of the membership.

1954 Laura Ingalls Wilder
1960 Clara Ingram Judson
1965 Ruth Sawyer Durand
1970 E.B. White
1975 Beverly Cleary

Morton Dauwen Zabel Award

AMERICAN ACADEMY AND INSTITUTE OF
ARTS AND LETTERS
633 W. 155th St., New York, N.Y. 10032 (212/286-1480)

The Morton Dauwen Zabel Award, which carries a $2,500 honorarium, is given each year to an American poet, writer of fiction or critic in rotation for "progressive, original and experimental tendencies rather than academic and conservative tendencies," as determined by a jury or by the institute's board of trustees.

1970 George Steiner (criticism)
1971 Charles Reznikoff (poetry)
1972 Donald Barthelme (fiction)
1973 Marjorie Hope Nicolson (criticism)
1974 John Logan (poetry)
1975 Charles Newman (fiction)
1976 Harold Rosenberg (criticism)
1977 David Shapiro (poetry)

Fellowship of the Academy of American Poets
Copernicus Award
Lamont Poetry Selection
Harold Morton Landon Award
Edgar Allan Poe Award
Walt Whitman Award

ACADEMY OF AMERICAN POETS
1078 Madison Ave., New York, N.Y. 10028 (212/988-6783)

The Fellowship of the Academy of American Poets "for distinguished poetic achievement," awarded annually to a living American poet, consists of a certificate and $10,000. At times, two awards are given. The Academy's twelve chancellors, who are themselves distinguished poets, nominate and elect the fellow. The fellowships may not be applied for, and chancellors may not be Academy fellows. Edwin Markham received the distinction in a special prefatory award.

1937 Edwin Markham
1946 Edgar Lee Masters
1947 Ridgely Torrence
1948 Percy MacKaye
1950 e.e. cummings
1952 Padraic Colum
1953 Robert Frost
1954 Louise Townsend Nicholl
1954 Oliver St. George Gogarty
1955 Rolfe Humphries
1956 William Carlos Williams
1957 Conrad Aiken
1958 Robinson Jeffers
1959 Leonie Adams
       Louise Bogan
1960 Jesse Stuart
1961 Horace Gregory
1962 John Crowe Ransom
1963 Ezra Pound
1964 Elizabeth Bishop
1965 Marianne Moore
1966 John Berryman
       Archibald MacLeish
1967 Mark Van Doren
1968 Stanley Kunitz
1969 Richard Eberhart
       Anthony Hecht
1970 Howard Nemerov
1971 James Wright
1972 W.D. Snodgrass
1973 W.S. Merwin
1974 Leonie Adams
1975 Robert Hayden
1976 J.V. Cunningham
1977 Louis Cox

The Copernicus Award, comprised of a certificate and $10,000, recognizes a poet's "lifetime achievement and contribution to poetry as a cultural force." It is given annually to a living citizen of the United States over 45 years of age who preferably has published a book of poems or about poetry during the two previous years. An annually changing panel of three poets selects the winner. The award may not be applied for.

1974 Robert Lowell
1975 Kenneth Rexroth
1976 Robert Penn Warren
1977 Muriel Rukeyser

The Lamont Poetry Selection honors a living American poet's second book of poems. (Prior to 1975 the award was given for a poet's first book.) A three-poet panel judges manuscripts submitted by publishers. The Academy assures publication by purchasing from the publisher 1,000 copies of the winning book for distribution to contributors and friends.

1954 Constance Carrier, *The Middle Voice*
1955 Donald Hall, *Exiles and Marriages*
1956 Philip Booth, *Letter from a Distant Land*
1957 Daniel Berrigan, S.J., *Time Without Number*
1958 Ned O'Gorman, *The Night of the Hammer*
1959 Donald Justice, *The Summer Anniversaries*
1960 Robert Mezey, *The Lovemaker*
1961 X.J. Kennedy, *Nude Descending a Staircase*

1962 Edward Field, *Stand Up, Friend, With Me*
1963 No award
1964 Adrien Stoutenberg, *Heroes Advise Us*
1965 Henri Coulette, *The War of the Secret Agents*
1966 Kenneth O. Hanson, *The Distance Anywhere*
1967 James Scully, *The Marches*
1968 Jane Cooper, *The Weather of Six Mornings*
1969 Marvin Bell, *A Probable Volume of Dreams*
1970 William Harmon, *Treasury Holiday*
1971 Stephen Dobyns, *Concurring Beasts*
1972 Peter Everwine, *Collecting the Animals*
1973 Marilyn Hacker, *Presentation Piece*
1974 John Balaban, *After Our War*
1975 Lisel Mueller, *The Private Life*
1976 Larry Levis, *The Afterlife*
1977 Gerald Stern, *Lucky Life*

The $1,000 Harold Morton Landon Award is given annually for a published translation of poetry from any language into English. One poet serves as judge, and winners must be living citizens of the United States. Published books may be sent to the Academy for judging.

1976 Robert Fitzgerald for *The Iliad* of Homer
1977 Galway Kinnell for *The Poems of Francois Villon*
     Howard Norman for *The Wishing Bone Cycle*

The Edgar Allan Poe Award comprised of a certificate and $5,000 is given annually to a living citizen of the United States who is under 45 years of age. It is awarded for the "continuing development of a younger poet's art on the occasion of a newly published book of poems." An annually changing panel of three poets chooses the winner from among books published during the previous year. The award may not be applied for.

1974 Mark Strand, *The Story of Our Lives*
1975 Charles Simic, *Return to a Place Lit by a Glass of Milk*
1976 Charles Wright, *Bloodlines*
1977 Stan Rice, *Whiteboy*

The Walt Whitman Award consisting of $1,000 and publication by a major publisher of a manuscript is given to a poet who has never published a book of poems, except in a small edition. The winner must be a living citizen of the United States, and the book-length poetry manuscript is selected from submitted works in open competition.

1975 Reg Saner, *Climbing into the Roots*, (Harper & Row)
1976 Laura Gilpin, *The Hocus-Pocus of the Universe*, (Doubleday)
1977 Lauren Shakely, *Guilty Bystander*, (Random House)

Bollingen Prize

YALE UNIVERSITY LIBRARY
New Haven, Conn. 06520 (203/436-0236)

The $5,000 Bollingen Prize is awarded biennially to an American citizen for a distinguished book of poetry published during the preceding two years, as selected by a jury, or in recognition of a poet's total achievements. This award was once given annually with a smaller monetary prize. Two poets occasionally share the prize.

1949 Wallace Stevens
1950 John Crowe Ransom
1951 Marianne Moore, *Collected Poems*
1952 Archibald MacLeish, *Collected Poems: 1917-1952*
     William Carlos Williams
1953 W.H. Auden
1954 Leonie Adams, *Poems: A Selection*
     Louis Bogan, *Collected Poems: 1922-1953*
1955 Conrad Aiken, *A Letter from Li Po*
1956 Allen Tate
1957 e.e. cummings
1958 Theodore Roethke, *Words for the Wine*
1959 Delmore Schwartz, *Summer Knowledge*
1960 Yvor Winters, *Collected Poems*
1961 John Hall Wheelock, *The Gardener*
     Richard Eberhart
1962 Robert Frost, *In the Clearing*
1964 Horace Gregory, *Collected Poems*
1966 Robert Penn Warren, *Selected Poems, New & Old, 1923-1966*
1968 John Berryman, *His Toy, His Dream, His Rest*
     Mona Van Duyn, *To See, To Take*
1972 James Merrill, *Braving the Elements*
1974 A.R. Ammons, *Sphere*
1976 David Ignatow

Kovner Memorial

NATIONAL JEWISH WELFARE BOARD
15 E. 26th St., New York, N.Y. 10010 (212/532-4949)

The $500 Harry and Florence Kovner Memorial awards now are given alternately to honor books of poetry in Yiddish, English or Hebrew written by citizens or residents of the United States or Canada. Volumes translated from another language into English are eligible if they are of Jewish interest. The book must have been published during the three previous years. Three judges' committees—one for each language—select the winners.

ENGLISH POETRY

1951 Judah Stampfer, *Jerusalem Has Many Faces*
1952 A. M. Klein, Cumulative contributions to English-Jewish poetry
1953 Isidore Goldstick, For translation of *Poems of Yehoash*
1954 Harry H. Fein, Cumulative contributions to English-Jewish poetry
1955-58 No awards
1959 Grace Goldin, *Come Under the Wings: A Midrash on Ruth*
1960 Amy K. Blank, *The Spoken Choice*
1961 No award
1962 Irving Feldman, *Work and Days and Other Poems*
1963 Charles Reznikoff, *By the Waters of Manhattan*
1964-65 No awards
1966 Ruth Finer Mintz, *The Darkening Green*
1967-68 No awards
1969 Ruth Whitman, *The Marriage Wig and Other Poems*
1971 Ruth Finer Mintz, *Traveler through Time*
1974 Harold Schimmel, trans., *Songs of Jerusalem and Myself* by Yehuda Amichai
1977 T. Carmi *El Eretz Aheretz*

HEBREW POETRY

1951 Aaron Zeitlin, *Shirim U'Poemot*
1952 Hillel Bavli, Cumulative contributions to Hebrew poetry
1953 A. S. Schwartz, Cumulative contributions to Hebrew poetry
1954 Ephraim E. Lisitzky, *Be-Ohalei Kush (In Negro Tents)*
1955 Gabriel Preil, *Ner Mul Kochavin (Candle under the Stars)*
1956 Hillel Bavli, *Aderet Ha-Shanim (Mantle of Years)*
1957 Moshe Feinstein, *Avraham Abulafia*
1958 Aaron Zeitlin, *Bein Ha-Esh Veha-Yesha*
1959 Moshe Ben Meir, *Tzlil va Tzel*
1960 Eisig Silberschlag, *Kimron Yamai*
1961 Ephraim E. Lisitzky, *K'Mo Hayom Rad*
1962 Gabriel Preil, *Mapat Erev*
1963 Arnold Band, *Ha-Rei Boer ha-Esh*
1964 No award
1965 No award
1966 Simon Halkin, *Crossing the Jabbok*
1967 Leonard D. Friedland, *Shirim be-Sulam Minor*
1968 No award
1969 Reuven Ben-Yosef, *Derech Eretz*
1972 Eisig Silberschlag, *Igrotai El Dorot Aherim (Letters to Other Generations)*
1975 Reuven Ben-Yosef, *Metim ve-Ohavim*

YIDDISH POETRY

1951 Ber Lapin, *Der Fuller Krug (The Brimming Jug)*
1952 Mordicai Jaffe, Editing and translating *Anthology of Hebrew Poetry*
1953 Mark Schwaid, Collected poems
1954 Eliezer Greenberg, *Banachtiger Dialog (Night Dialogue)*
1955 Alter Esselin, *Lider fun a Midbarnik (Poems of a Hermit)*
1956 Naphtali Gross, Cumulative contributions to Yiddish poetry
1957 Jacob Glatstein, *Fun Mein Gantzer Mei*
1958 I. J. Schwartz, Cumulative contributions to Yiddish poetry
1959 Benjamin Bialostotzky, *Lid Tzu Lid*
1960 Ephraim Auerbach, *Gildene Shekiah*
1961 Joseph Rubinstein, *Megilath Russland*
1962 Israel Emiot, *In Nigun Eingehert*
1963 Chaim Grade, *Det Mentsh fun Fier*
1964 Aaron Glanz-Leyeles, *Amerika Un Ich*
1965 Aleph Katz, *Di Emesse Hasunah*
1966 Kadia Molodowsky, *Licht fun Dorenboim*
1967 Jacob Glatstein, *A Yid fun Lublin*
1968 Aaron Zeitlin, *Lider fun Hurban un Lider fun Gloiben*
1969 Rachel H. Korn, *Di Gnod fun Vort*
1970 Eliezer Greenberg, *Eibiker Dorsht (Eternal Thirst)*
1973 Meir Sticker, *Yidishe Landshaft*
1976 M. Husid, *A Shotn Tragt Main Kroin*

Juniper Prize

UNIVERSITY OF MASSACHUSETTS PRESS
Box 429, Amherst, Mass. 01002 (413/545-2217)

The Juniper Prize, which consists of $1,000 and publication of a manuscript, is given annually for an original, book-length manuscript of poetry in English.

1975 Eleanor Lerman, *Come the Sweet By and By*
1976 David Dwyer, *Ariana Olisvos: Her Last Works and Days*
1977 Jane Shore, *Eye Level*

Edwin Markham Poetry Prize

EUGENE V. DEBS FOUNDATION
Box 843, Terre Haute, Ind. 47808 (812/232-2163)

The Edwin Markham Poetry Prize, which carries an honorarium of $1,000, is given annually for an unpublished poem in the English language of 100 lines or less dealing with social protest or social justice. A panel of three professors from the University of Indiana selects the winner. The award will be discontinued.

1976 Dan Bogen, "Lamento"
1977 No award

Lenore Marshall Poetry Prize

NEW HOPE FOUNDATION
430 Park Ave., New York, N.Y. 10022 (212/421-7200)

The Lenore Marshall Poetry Prize, which carries a $5,000 honorarium, is given annually to a living American author for the best book of poems published in the United States in the previous year, including new editions of selected and collected peoms. The winner is selected by one or more poets appointed as judges by the Foundation, which cosponsors the award with *The Saturday Review*.

1974 Cid Corman, $\frac{Q}{I}$
1975 Denise Levertov, *The Freeing of the Dust*
1976 Philip Levine, *The Names of the Lost*
1977 Not available at press time

National Book Award

ASSOCIATION OF AMERICAN PUBLISHERS
One Park Ave., New York, N.Y. 10016 (212/689-8920)

The $1,000 National Book Award in poetry is one of seven awarded annually for works by U.S. citizens "that have contributed most significantly to human awareness, to the vitality of our national culture and to the spirit of excellence." The other six awards are for prose and can be found on pp. 40-41.

1950 William Carlos Williams, *Paterson III and Selected Poems*
1951 Wallace Stevens, *The Auroras of Autumn*
1952 Marianne Moore, *Collected Poems*
1953 Archibald MacLeish, *Collected Poems: 1917-1952*
1954 Conrad Aiken, *Collected Poems*
1955 Wallace Stevens, *Collected Poems of Wallace Stevens*
  e. e. cummings, *Poems: 1923-1954* (Special citation)
1956 W. H. Auden, *The Shield of Achilles*
1957 Richard Wilbur, *Things of This World*
1958 Robert Penn Warren, *Promises: Poems, 1954-1956*
1959 Theodore Roethke, *Words for the Wind*
1960 Robert Lowell, *Life Studies*
1961 Randall Jarrell, *The Woman at the Washington Zoo*
1962 Alan Dugan, *Poems*
1963 William Stafford, *Traveling Through the Dark*
1964 John Crowe Ransom, *Selected Poems*
1965 Theodore Roethke, *The Far Field*
1966 James Dickey, *Buckdancer's Choice*
1967 James Merrill, *Nights and Days*
1968 Robert Bly, *The Light Around the Body*
1969 John Berryman, *His Toy, His Dream, His Rest*
1970 Elizabeth Bishop, *The Complete Poems*

1971 Mona Van Duyn, *To See, To Take*
1972 Howard Moss, *Selected Poems*
      Frank O'Hara, *The Collected Poems*
1973 A. R. Ammons, *Collected Poems: 1951-1971*
1974 Allen Ginsberg, *The Fall of America: Poems of These States, 1965-1971*
      Adrienne Rich, *Diving into the Wreck*
1975 Marilyn Hacker, *Presentation Piece*
1976 John Ashbery, *Self-Portrait in a Convex Mirror*
1977 Richard Eberhart, *Collected Poems: 1930-1976*

Oscar Blumenthal Prize
Jacob Glatstein Memorial Prize
Bess Hokin Prize
Levinson Prize
Eunice Tietjens Memorial Award

POETRY MAGAZINE
1228 N. Dearborn Pkwy., Chicago, Ill. 60610 (312/787-1328)

The Oscar Blumenthal Prize, which until 1975 was known as the Oscar Blumenthal-Charles Leviton Prize, awards $200 for poetry published in the two previous volumes (one year) of the magazine. The editors select the winner.

1936 Marion Strobel
1937 Thomas Hornsby Ferril
1938 Dylan Thomas
1939 Maxwell Bodenheim
1940 Muriel Rukeyser
1941 Stanley Kunitz
1942 E. L. Mayo
1943 John Ciardi
1944 P. K. Page
1945 Yvor Winters
1946 George Moor
1947 James Merrill
1948 Weldon Kees
1949 Barbara Gibbs
1950 Richard Wilbur
1951 Randall Jarrell
1952 Roy Marz
1953 William Meredith
1954 Anne Ridler
1955 William Carlos Williams
1956 Sydney Goodsir Smith
1957 Ben Belitt
1958 Howard Nemerov
1959 Josephine Miles
1960 Charles Tomlinson
1961 Kathleen Raine
1962 e. e. cummings
1963 Karl Shapiro
1964 Robert Creeley
1965 Charles Olson
1966 Louis Zukofsky
1967 Guy Davenport
1968 James Wright
1969 Turner Cassity
1970 Jon Anderson
1971 Geoffrey Grigson
1972 Douglas Le Pan
1973 Brewster Ghiselin
1974 David Wagoner
1975 Sandra McPherson
1976 David Bromwich
1977 Alfred Corn

The Jacob Glatstein Memorial Prize, which carries a $100 honorarium, is given for poetry published in the two previous volumes of the magazine. The editors select the winner.

1972 Rae Dalven
1973 Marya Zaturenska
1974 Raphael Rudnik
1975 Jayanta Mahapatra
1976 Martha Hollander
1977 Robert Siegel

The Bess Hokin Prize, which carries a $100 honorarium, is given for poetry published in the two previous volumes of the magazine. The editors select the winner.

1948 William Abrahams
1949 Barbara Howes
1950 Lloyd Frankenberg
1951 M. B. Tolson
1952 L. E. Hudgins
1953 Ruth Stone
1954 Hayden Carruth
1955 Philip Booth
1956 Charles Tomlinson
1957 Sylvia Plath
1958 Alan Neame
1959 Jean Clower
1960 Denise Levertov
1961 X. J. Kennedy
1962 W. S. Merwin
1963 Adrienne Rich
1964 Gary Snyder
1965 Galway Kinnell
1966 Thomas Clark
1967 Wendell Berry
1968 Michael Benedikt
1969 Marvin Bell
1970 Charles Martin
1971 Erica Jong
1972 Sandra McPherson
1973 Jane Shore
1974 Margaret Atwood
1975 Charles O. Hartman
1976 Norman Dubie
1977 Bess Hoskin

The Levinson Prize, which carries a $300 honorarium, is awarded for poetry published in the two previous volumes of the magazine. The editors select the winner.

1914 Carl Sandburg
1915 Vachel Lindsay
1916 Edgar Lee Masters
1917 Cloyd Head
1918 O. C. Underwood
1919 H. L. Davis
1920 Wallace Stevens
1921 Lew Sarett
1922 Robert Frost
1923 Edwin Arlington Robinson
1924 Amy Lowell
1925 Ralph Cheever Dunning
1926 Mark Turbyfill
1927 Maurice Lesemann
1928 Elinor Wylie
1929 Marjorie Seiffert

1930	Hart Crane
1931	Edna St. Vincent Millay
1932	No award
1933	Marianne Moore
1934	Horace Gregory
1935	Mary Barnard
1936	Robert Penn Warren
1937	Louise Bogan
1938	H. D.
1939	e. e. cummings
1940	Robinson Jeffers
1941	Archibald MacLeish
1942	Karl J. Shapiro
1943	John Malcolm Brinnin
1944	John Frederick Nims
1945	Dylan Thomas
1946	John Ciardi
1947	Muriel Rukeyser
1948	Randall Jarrell
1949	James Merrill
1950	John Berryman
1951	Theodore Roethke
1952	St.-John Perse
1953	Vernon Watkins
1954	William Carlos Williams
1955	Thom Gunn
1956	Stanley Kunitz
1957	Jay MacPherson
1958	Hayden Carruth
1959	Delmore Schwartz
1960	Robert Creeley
1961	David Jones
1962	Anne Sexton
1963	Robert Lowell
1964	Robert Duncan
1965	George Barker
1966	Basil Bunting
1967	Alan Dugan
1968	Gary Snyder
1969	A.D. Hope
1970	A.R. Ammons
1971	Turner Cassity
1972	Michael Hamburger
1973	Richard Howard
1974	John Hollander
1975	Howard Nemerov
1976	Judith Moffett
1977	John Ashbery

The Eunice Tietjens Memorial Award, which carries a $200 honorarium, is given for poems published in the previous two volumes of the magazine. The editors select the winner.

1944	John Ciardi
1945	Marie Borroff
1946	Alfred Hayes
1947	Theodore Roethke
1948	Peter Viereck
1949	Gwendolyn Brooks
1950	Andrew Glaze
1951	Robinson Jeffers
1952	e. e. cummings
1953	Elder Olson
1954	Reuel Denney
1955	James Wright
1956	Mona Van Duyn
1957	Kenneth Rexroth
1958	James Merrill
1959	Barbara Howes

1960	Marie Ponsot
1961	Karl Shapiro
1962	Muriel Rukeyser
1963	Helen Singer
1964	Hayden Carruth
1965	Pauline Hanson
1966	Galway Kinnell
1967	Robert Duncan
1968	Adrienne Rich
1969	Charles Wright
1970	Jean Malley
1971	Louise Gluck
1972	Maxine Kumin
1973	Judith Moffett
1974	Judith Minty
1975	James McMichael
1976	Richard Kenney
1977	David Wagoner

Melville Cane Award
Alice Fay di Castagnola Award
Gertrude R. Claytor Memorial Award
Gustav Davidson Memorial Award
Mary Carolyn Davies Memorial Award
Emily Dickinson Award
Consuelo Ford Memorial Award
Gold Medal
Cecil Hemley Award
Alfred Kreymborg Memorial Award
Elias Lieberman Memorial Award
John Masefield Memorial Award
Lucille Medwick Memorial Award
Christopher Morley Memorial Award
Poetry Society of America Awards
Shelley Memorial Award
Cecelia B. Wagner Award

POETRY SOCIETY OF AMERICA
15 Grammercy Park, New York, N.Y. 10003 (212/254-9628)

The $500 Melville Cane Award annually honors the best book of poems by an American in odd-numbered years and the best book about poetry or a poet in even-numbered years. A jury selects the winner.

1968 Jean Garrigue, *Poems*
1969 Ruth Miller, *The Poetry of Emily Dickinson*
1970 Rolfe Humphries, *Poems*
1971 Harold Bloom, *Yeats*
1972 James Wright, *Poems*
1973 Jerome J. McGann, *Swinburne: An Experiment in Criticism*
1974 William Stafford, *Poems*
1975 Richard B. Small, *The Life of Emily Dickinson*
1976 Charles Wright, *Blood Lines*
1977 Donald Howard, *The Idea of the Canterbury Tales*

The $2,000 Alice Fay di Castagnola Award is given annually for a work in progress, poetry or work about a poet or poetry by a member in the Poetry Society. A jury selects the winner.

1968   Joseph Tusiani and Ruth Whitman, Books of poems
1969   Wade Van Dore, A book on Robert Frost
1970   Jenny Lind Porter and Wallace Winchell, Books of poems
1971   Cornel Lengyel and Marcia Masters, Books of poems
1972   Erica Jong and Myra Sklarew, Books of poems
1973   George Keithley and Mary Oliver, Books of poems
1974   Charles Eaton, *The Man in the Green Chair: Poems*
1975   Philip Appleman, *In Mediterranean Air: Poems*
1976   Ann Stanford, *In Mediterranean Air: Poems*
1977   Naomi Lazard and Linda Pastan, Four books of poems

The $250 Gertrude R. Claytor Memorial Award is given annually to a member of the Poetry Society for a poem on an American scene or character. A jury selects the winner.

1975   Charles A. Wagner
1976   Ulrich Troubetzkoy
1977   Gary Miranda

The $500 Gustav Davidson Memorial Award is given annually to a member of the Poetry Society for a sonnet or sonnet sequence. A jury selects the winner.

1972   Lisa Grenelle
1973   Sallie Nixon
1974   Sarah Singer
1975   Florence Jacobs
1976   Peter Meinke
1977   Ulrich Troubetzkoy

The $250 Mary Carolyn Davies Memorial Award is given annually to a member of the Poetry Society for a lyric that can be set to music. A jury selects the winner.

1976   Catherine Hayden Jacobs
1977   Diana Der Hovanessian

The $100 Emily Dickinson Award is given annually to a member of the Poetry Society for a poem "in the spirit of the New England poet." A jury selects the winner.

1971   Olga Cabral
        Ree Dragonette
1972   Harold Whitt
1973   Sandra McPherson
1974   No award
1975   Marjorie Hawksworth
1976   Floyd Skloot
1977   Siv Cedering Fox

The $250 Consuelo Ford Memorial Award is given annually to a member of the Poetry Society for a lyric poem. A jury selects the winner.

1972   Frances Minturn Howard
1973   Sarah Singer
1974   Mary Anne Coleman
        James Reiss
1975   Ruth Whitman
        Florence Trefethen
1976   Nina Nyhart
        Gary Miranda

1977   Joan LaBombard

The Society's Gold Medal is awarded as merited for distinguished overall contributions to and achievements in poetry.

1930   Jessie Rittenhouse
        Clinton Scollard
        George Edward Woodberry
        Bliss Carman
1941   Robert Frost
1942   Edgar Lee Masters
1943   Edna St. Vincent Millay
1947   Gustav Davidson
1951   Wallace Stevens
1952   Carl Sandburg
1955   Leonora Speyer
1967   Marianne Moore
1974   John Hall Wheelock
1976   A. M. Sullivan

The $300 Cecil Hemley Award is given annually to a member of the Poetry Society for a poem based on a humanitarian theme. A jury selects the winner.

1969   Willis Barnstone
1970   Charles A. Brady
1971   Bernice Ames
1972   Ann Jonas
1973   Helen Sorrells
1974   Anne Marx
1975   Ruth Lisa Schechter
1976   No award
1977   Isabel Nathaniel

The $100 Alfred Kreymborg Memorial Award is given annually to a member of the Poetry Society for "a poem worthy of the name." A jury selects the winner.

1975   Madeline Bass
1976   Colette Inez
1977   Geraldine C. Little

The Elias Lieberman Memorial Award is given annually for a poem by an American secondary school student. A jury selects the winner.

1971   Lyn Kelly
1972   Alan Farago
1973   Heidi Schmitt
1974   Jean Sherrard
1975   Psyche Anne Pascual
1976   Edward Gaillard
1977   Paul J. Davis

The $500 John Masefield Memorial Award is given annually for a narrative poem. A jury selects the winner.

1969   Siv Cedering Fox
1970   Alvin K. Reiss
1971   Sallie W. Nixon
1972   Donald Junkins
1973   No award
1974   Penelope Schott Starkey
1975   Gail Trebbe
1976   Burt Blume, Ruth Whitman and Jack Zucker
1977   Lynn Sukenick and Fred Fierstein

The $500 Lucille Medwick Memorial Award is given

annually to a member of the Poetry Society for a poem on a humanitarian theme. A jury selects the winner.

1974 Joan LaBombard
1975 Violette Newton
1976 Olga Cabral
1977 Peter Klappert

The $500 Christopher Morley Memorial Award is given annually to a member of the Poetry Society for light verse. A jury selects the winner.

1969 David Ross
1970 Philip Appleman
1971 Sarah Lockwood
1972 R.F. Armknecht and Vinnie Marie D'Ambrosio
1973 Norma Farber
1974 Milton Kaplan and Gary Miranda
1975 Philip Appleman
1976 S. Gordden Link and Ralph Robin
1977 Darcy Gottlieb

The $200 and $300 Poetry Society of America Awards are given annually to recognize the best poetry of the year by members. The membership is balloted to select the winner.

1968 Charles A. Brady
      Hyacinthe Hill
      Mary Oliver
1969 Beren Van Slyke
      Kinereth Gensler
      Naomi Lazard
1970 Hamilton Warren
      Hannah Kahn
      Edsel Ford
1971 Charles A. Wagner
      Dorothy Richardson
      Carol Ann Pearce
1972 Frances Minturn Howard
      William Childress
      Ruth Feldman
1973 Larry Rubin
      Margaret Rockwell
      Helen Bryant
1974 Louise Gunn
      Milton Kaplan
      Gary Miranda
      Harriet Blackwell
1975 Sarah Singer
      Lawrence Spingarn
      Elizavietta Ritchie
1976 Ryah Goodman
      Colette Inez
1977 Helen Adam
      Darrell Bartee

The $1,500-$1,750 Shelley Memorial Award is given annually to a published poet on the basis of "need" and accomplishment. A jury selects the recipient.

1968 Mary Swenson
1969 Ann Stanford
1970 Mary Oliver and X.J. Kennedy
1971 Adrienne Rich and Louis Townsend Nicholl
1972 Galway Kinnell
1973 John Ashbery and Richard Wilbur
1974 W.S. Merwin
1975 Edward Field

1976 Gwendolyn Brooks
1977 Muriel Rukeyser

The $250 Cecelia B. Wagner Award is given annually for "a poem worthy of the art." A jury selects the winner

1976 Sarah Singer
1977 Joan LaBombard

Pulitzer Prize

COLUMBIA UNIVERSITY
Graduate School of Journalism, New York, N.Y. 10027
(212/280-3828) (Pulitzer Prizes: 212/280-3841)

Endowed by the will of Joseph Pulitzer, founder of the *St. Louis Post Dispatch,* and administered by Columbia University, the annual Pulitzer Prizes include a $1,000 award for poetry. Four copies of each work must be submitted to the 15-member Advisory Committee on Pulitzer Prizes for consideration.

1918 Sara Teasdale, *Love Songs*
1919 Carl Sandburg, *Corn Huskers*
      Margaret Widdemer, *Old Road to Paradise*
1920 No award
1921 No award
1922 Edwin Arlington Robinson, *Collected Poems*
1923 Edna St. Vincent Millay, *The Ballad of the Harp-Weaver; A Few Figs from Thistles;* eight sonnets in *American Poetry, 1922, A Miscellany*
1924 Robert Frost, *New Hampshire: A Poem with Notes and Grace Notes*
1925 Edwin Arlington Robinson, *The Man Who Died Twice*
1926 Amy Lowell, *What's O'Clock*
1927 Leonora Speyer, *Fiddler's Farewell*
1928 Edwin Arlington Robinson, *Tristram*
1929 Stephen V. Benet, *John Brown's Body*
1930 Conrad Aiken, *Selected Poems*
1931 Robert Frost, *Collected Poems*
1932 George Dillon, *The Flowering Stone*
1933 Archibald MacLeish, *Conquistador*
1934 Robert Hillyer, *Collected Verse*
1935 Audrey Wurdemann, *Bright Ambush*
1936 R. P. Tristram Coffin, *Strange Holiness*
1937 Robert Frost, *A Further Range*
1938 Marya Zaturenska, *Cold Morning Sky*
1939 John Gould Fletcher, *Selected Poems*
1940 Mark Van Doren, *Collected Poems*
1941 Leonard Bacon, *Sunderland Capture*
1942 William Benet, *The Dust Which Is God*
1943 Robert Frost, *A Witness Tree*
1944 Stephen Vincent Benet, *Western Star*
1945 Karl Shapiro, *V-Letter and Other Poems*
1946 No award
1947 Robert Lowell, *Lord Weary's Castle*
1948 W. H. Auden, *The Age of Anxiety*
1949 Peter Viereck, *Terror and Decorum*
1950 Gwendolyn Brooks, *Annie Allen*
1951 Carl Sandburg, *Complete Poems*
1952 Marianne Moore, *Collected Poems*
1953 Archibald MacLeish, *Collected Poems 1917-1952*
1954 Theodore Roethke, *The Waking*
1955 Wallace Stevens, *Collected Poems*
1956 Elizabeth Bishop, *Poems—North & South*
1957 Richard Wilbur, *Things of This World*
1958 Robert Penn Warren, *Promises: Poems 1954-56*

1959 Stanley Kunitz, *Selected Poems 1928-1958*
1960 W. D. Snodgrass, *Heart's Needle*
1961 Phyllis McGinley, *Times Three: Selected Verse from Three Decades*
1962 Alan Dugan, *Poems*
1963 William Carlos Williams, *Pictures from Breughel*
1964 Louis Simpson, *At the End of the Open Road*
1965 John Berryman, *77 Dream Songs*
1966 Richard Eberhart, *Selected Poems*
1967 Anne Sexton, *Live or Die*
1968 Anthony Hecht, *The Hard Hours*
1969 George Oppen, *Of Being Numerous*
1970 Richard Howard, *Untitled Subjects*
1971 W. S. Merwin, *The Carrier of Ladders*
1972 James Wright, *Collected Poems*
1973 Maxine Winokur Kumin, *Up Country*
1974 Robert Lowell, *The Dolphin*
1975 Gary Snyder, *Turtle Island*
1976 John Ashbery, *Self-Portrait in a Convex Mirror*
1977 James Merrill, *Divine Comedies*

Voertman's Poetry Award

TEXAS INSTITUTE OF LETTERS
Box 7219, Austin, Tex. 78712 (512/471-1833)

The Voertman's Poetry Award, which carries a $200 honorarium, is given annually for a volume of poetry by a Texan or on a Texas subject. (The award was known as the Daedalian Poetry Award until 1965.)

1945 David Russell, *Sing With Me Now*
1946 Whitney Montgomery, *Joseph's Coat*

1947 Arthur M. Sampley, *Of the Strong and the Fleet*
1948 Vaida S. Montgomery, *Hail for Rain*
1949 Frances Alexander, *Time at the Window*
1950 Mary Poole, *Being in Night*
1951 Arthur M. Sampley, *Furrow with Blackbirds*
1952 William D. Barney, *Kneel to the Stone*
1953 Robert Lee Brothers, *The Hidden Harp*
1954 William Burford, *Man Now*
1955 William D. Barney, *Permitted Proof*
1956 Vassar Miller, *Adam's Footprint*
1957 Eloise Roach, *Platero and I*, translated from the Spanish of Juan Ramon Jimenez
1958 No award
1959 Ramsey Yelvington, *A Cloud of Witnesses*
1960 Vassar Miller, *Wage War on Silence*
1961 Walter E. Kidd, *Time Turns West*
1962 Frederick Will, *A Wedge of Words*
1963 Vassar Miller, *My Bones Being Wiser*
1964 Thomas Whitbread, *Four Infinitives*
1965 Roger Shattuck, *Half Tame*
1966 R. G. Vliet, *Events and Celebrations*
1967 Frederic Will, *Planets*
1968 Edgar Simmons, *Driving to Biloxi*
1969 No award
1970 R. G. Vliet, *The Man with the Black Mouth*
1971 Arthur M. Sampley, *Selected Poems 1937-1971*
1972 Gene Shuford, *Selected Poems, 1933-1971*
1973 Fania Kruger, *Selected Poems*
1974 Michael Ryan, *Threats Instead of Trees*
1975 Kurth Sprague, *The Promise Kept*
1976 Walt McDonald, *Caliban in Blue*
1977 Glenn Hardin, *Giants*
      Jack Myers, *The Family War*

Journalism

Contents

Related Awards

Fourth Estate Award
AMERICAN LEGION
700 N. Pennsylvania St., Indianapolis, Ind. 46204

The American Legion Fourth Estate Award is a bronze plaque given annually in appreciation of public relations efforts to the press, radio, television or other communications media or to owners or personnel of the media, for support of Legion policies or programs. The National Public Relations Commission is empowered by the National Executive Committee to make this award, which was originally known as the American Legion Mercury Award.

1958   Jim Lucas
1959   Advertising Council, Inc.
1959   *Chicago Tribune*
1959   *U.S. News & World Report*
1960   Hearst Newspapers
1961   Scripps-Howard Newspapers
1961   Jack L. Warner, Warner Brothers Pictures
1962   Fulton Lewis, Jr.
1963   The Copley Press, Inc.
1963   *This Week* Magazine
1964   *Chicago Tribune*
1964   Mississippi Publishers Corp.
1965   Clark Mollenhoff, Cowles Publications
1965   Paul Harvey, American Broadcasting Co.
1965   Golden West Broadcasters
1966   Mutual Broadcasting System
1966   The Booth Newspapers
1966   *Columbus Dispatch*
1967   *St. Louis Globe-Democrat*
1968   William S. White
1969   George W. Healy, Jr.
1969   Raymond J. McHugh
1970   James Geddes Stahlman, *The Banner,* (Nashville, Tenn.)
1970   Jenkin Lloyd Jones, *The Tribune* (Tulsa, Okla.)
1971   Anheuser Busch, Inc.
1971   John Wayne
1972   Augustin Edwards, *El Mercurio,* Santiago, Chile
1973   Clare Boothe Luce
1974   James J. Kilpatrick, Jr.
1975   Jim Bishop
1976   Vic Cantone
        Thomas P. Chisman, Bicentennial Radio Network, Ltd.
1977   *Columbus Dispatch*
        Jess Gorkin, *Parade*

AWA Writing Awards
Lauren D. Lyman Award
James J. Strebig Award
Robert S. Ball Memorial Award
Earl D. Osborn Award
AVIATION/SPACE WRITERS ASSOCIATION
Cliffwood Rd., Chester, N.J. 07930 (201/879-5635)

AWA Writing Awards are given for outstanding aviation and space writing and reporting in various categories of newspapers and magazines. A $100 honorarium and scroll are now given each year for aviation and space writing in six categories, for a total of twelve annual awards.

NEWSPAPERS OVER 50,000 CIRCULATION
1961   Don Dwiggins
1962   Edwin G. Pipp
1963   Jack Foisie
1964   Howard Simons
1965   David H. Hoffman
1966   William Hines
1967   Howard S. Benedict
1968   Evert B. Clark

NEWSPAPERS OVER 200,000 CIRCULATION
1969   Howard Benedict
1970   Robert H. Lindsey (Aviation)
        Peter Reich (Space)
1971   Charles L. Tracy (Aviation)
        Jim Maloney (Space)
1972   Stephen M. Aug (Aviation)
        Edwin G. Pipp (Space)
1973   Edwin G. Pipp (Aviation)
        Robert C. Cowen (Space)
1974   John Finley (Aviation)
        Jim Maloney (Space)
1975   Jerry Hulse (Aviation
        Howard S. Benedict (Space)
1976   Lawrence S. Kramer (*San Francisco Examiner*), (Aviation)
        Joel J. Shurkin (*Philadelphia Inquirer*), (Space)
1977   Peter Reich (*Chicago Tribune*), (Aviation)
        Edwin G. Pipp (*Detroit News*), (Space)

NEWSPAPERS UNDER 50,000 CIRCULATION
1962   Tony Page
1963   James E. Cahill
1964   Dean Todd
1965   Dorothy M. Horzempa
1966   Harold Gold
1967   Sanders H. LaMont
1968   Sue Butler

NEWSPAPERS UNDER 200,000 CIRCULATION
1969   Sue Butler
1970   Arnold Lewis (Aviation)
        Sanders H. LaMont and Staff of *Today* (Space)
1971   Jon R. Donnelly (Aviation)
        Everett Hosking (Space)
1972   Jon R. Donnelly (Aviation)
        Ross Mackenzie (Space)
1973   Eric Filson, Stacey J. Bridges, Linda Miklowitz, Skip Perez and Dave Reddick (Aviation)
        Sanders H. LaMont and staff of *Today* (Space)
1974   Jon R. Donnelly (Aviation)
        Ed Arnone and Staff (Space)
1975   Steve Sellers (Aviation)
        Sanders H. LaMont (Space)
1976   Alan Goldsand (*Journal of Commerce*), (Aviation)
        Robert B. Robinson (*Today*, Cocoa, Fla.), (Space)
1977   David Shugarts (*Flight Line Times*), (Aviation)
        Grant Fjermedal (*Washington Daily News*), (Space)

AVIATION/SPACE MAGAZINES
1961   Claude Witze
1962   Don Downie

1963 Claude Witze
1964 William Leavitt
1965 David A. Anderton
1966 Claude Witze
1967 Jesse Samuel Butz, Jr.
1968 C. W. Borklund
1969 Capt. Robert P. Everett, USAF and Allan R. Scholin
1970 Edgar E. Ulsamer (Aviation)
     Michael Getler (Space)
1971 John F. Judge (Aviation)
     Frank A. Burnham (Space
1972 Stephen Wilkinson (Aviation)
     Edgar E. Ulsamer (Space)

GENERAL MAGAZINES

1961 Devon Francis
1962 Kenneth F. Weaver
1963 Joseph A. Walker, USAF
1964 Albert Rosenfeld
1965 Arthur C. Clarke
1966 Keith Wheeler
1967 James H. Winchester
1968 Ray Bradbury
1969 Edwin Diamond, George Alexander, Evert Clark and Henry T. Simmons
1970 No award (Aviation)
     Kenneth F. Weaver (Space)
1971 Clell Bryant & Jerry Hannifin (Aviation)
     Kenneth F. Weaver (Space)
1972 David Butler (Aviation)
     C.V. Glines (Space)

MAGAZINES (one category only, not subdivided into Aviation/Space Magazines and General Magazines)

1973 Dee Mosteller (Aviation)
     Henry S. F. Cooper, Jr. (Space)
1974 James H. Winchester (Aviation)
     Peter Gwynne (Space)
1975 Allan R. Scholin (Aviation)
     Thomas Y. Canby (Space)
1976 Robert Hotz, Herb Coleman and Robert Ropelewski, (Aviation Week and Space Technology), (Aviation)
     Gene Bylinsky Fortune (Space)
1977 C.A. Robinson and Staff, Aviation Week and Space Technology
     Willian Gregory and Staff, Aviation Week and Space Technology
     David Alpern (Newsweek)
     James J. Haggerty (Penthouse)
     Peter Stoler, (Time)

TELEVISION AND RADIO

1963 Jules Bergman
1964 Jules Bergman
1965 Frank Hall
1966 John N. Davenport
1967 No award
1968 Jerome Kuehl, Chet Huntley and George Vicas
1969 Jim Kitchell and Frank McGee
1970 George H. Rhodes and WKYC-TV, Cleveland (Aviation)
     CBS News: Robert Wussler and Walter Cronkite (Space)
1971 Charles Spence (Aviation)
     Leonard Reiffel (Space)
1972 Gary Robinson (Aviation)
     James Quigley (Space)
1973 Brad Sherman (Aviation)

Jules Bergman (Space)
1974 Charles Spence and Fletcher Cox (Aviation)
     Mark Levinson (Space)
1975 Steve Neuman (Aviation)
     John Lyons, Christine Lyons, Mark Knoller (Space)
1976 Ed Turney and Paul Fine (WMAL-TV, Washington), (Aviation)
     Jules Bergman, (ABC), (Space)
1977 Bill Neil (KOCE-TV)
     Jules Bergman (ABC News)

PHOTOJOURNALISM

1963 James Yarnell
1964 Ralph Morse
1965 Howard Sochurek
1966 Charles Moore & Charles Bonnay
1967 Anthony E. Linck
1968 No award
1969 Col. Frank Borman, USAF; Capt. James A. Lovell, Jr., USN and Lt. Col. William Anders, USAF
1970 Charles E. Rotkin (Aviation)
     Jeff Bremer, NASA (Space)
1971 Fred Hartman, Robert Murray, Joseph Sommers and Frank J. Delear (Aviation)
     Goddard Space Flight Center/National Oceanic and Atmospheric Administration (Space)
1972 Lou Davis (Aviation)
     No award (Space)
1973 Russell Munson and Stephan Wilkinson (Aviation)
     Tony Linck (Space)
1974 James Gilbert (Aviation)
1975 Richard P. Benjamin (Aviation)
     James R. Blair (Space)
1976 Robert Holt, Jr. (St. Louis Post Dispatch), (Aviation)

BOOKS (non-fiction)

1961 Martin Caidin
1962 Mel J. Hunter
1963 Maj. Gene Guerny, USAF
1964 Robert J. Serling
1965 Martin Caidin and Edward Hymoff
1966 James J. Haggerty, Jr. and H. G. Stever
1967 C. W. Borklund
1968 Don Dwiggins
1969 William R. Shelton
1970 Robert J. Serling (Aviation)
     John Noble Wilford (Space)
1971 Joe Christy and Page Schamburger (Aviation)
     Davis Thomas (Space)
1972 Ann Holtgren Pellegreno (Aviation)
     No award (Space)
1973 James A. Arey (Aviation)
     Gene and Clare Gurney (Space)
1974 Devon Francis (Aviation)
     No award (Space)
1975 Robert J. Serling (Aviation)
     Philip J. Klass (Space)
1976 Lloyd S. Jones, (U.S. Fighters), (Aviation)
1977 David Anderton (Strategic Air Command)
     William Wagner (Rueben Fleet)

BOOKS (fiction)

1967 Robert J. Serling
1968 Martin Caidin

MANUALS

1964 S. F. (Sandy) MacDonald

1965 Lt. Col. Gene Guerny, USAF and Capt. Joseph A.
      Skiera, USAF
1966 John Dohm
1967 John Smith
1968 Maj. James C. Elliott and Lt. Col. Gene Guerny

The Lauren D. Lyman Award goes annually to an individual for a long and distinguished career in aviation writing and/or public relations, exemplifying integrity, accuracy and excellence in reporting and writing. The trophy is sponsored by United Technologies.

1973 Wayne Parrish
1974 Robert Hotz
1975 Willis Player

The $500 James J. Strebig Award, sponsored by Teledyne Continental Motors Co., is given for outstanding aviation reporting or writing in any media.

1952 Arthur A. Riley
1953 Albert M. Skea
1954 Frank L. Harvey
1955 Frank Ellis and Marvin G. Miles
1956 Allan C. Fisher, Jr. and Marvin G. Miles
1957 James J. Haggerty, Jr. and Ansel E. Talbert
1958 Martin Caidin and Jean H. Pearson
1959 Marvin Miles and William G. Osmun
1960 George A. Carroll and Allan C. Fisher, Jr.
1961 Martin Caidin
1962 Tony Page
1963 Claude Witze
1964 Robert J. Serling
1965 David H. Hoffman
1966 Keith Wheeler
1967 James H. Winchester
1968 Warren R. Young
1969 John Saar and Ronald Bailey
1970 Edgar E. Ulsamer
1971 Charles L. Tracy
1972 Cecil Brownlow, Robert Hotz and Barry Miller
1973 Ronald A. Keith
1974 Dave McElhatton
1975 Donald S. Riggs
1976 Thomas G. Foxworth
1977 Peter Reich

The $500 Robert S. Ball Memorial Award, sponsored by the Chrysler Corp., is given annually for outstanding space reporting or writing in any medium.

1962 Edwin G. Pipp
1963 Jesse Samuel Butz, Jr.
1964 William Leavitt
1965 Arthur C. Clarke
1966 William Hines
1967 Howard S. Benedict
1968 Ray Bradbury
1969 Howard S. Benedict
1970 Sanders H. LaMont and Staff of *Today*
1971 Kenneth F. Weaver
1972 Cecil Brownlow, Robert Hotz and Barry Miller
1973 Henry S. F. Cooper, Jr.
1974 Kenneth F. Weaver
1975 Kenneth F. Weaver
1976 Jim Maloney
1977 William H. Gregory

The $500 Earl D. Osborn Award, sponsored by EDO Corp., is given annually for outstanding reporting or writing on general aviation in any medium.

1970 George H. Rhodes and WKYC-TV, Cleveland
1971 Charles Spence

1972 Stephan Wilkinson
1973 Lawrence W. Reithmaier
1974 Lew Townsend
1975 Richard L. Taylor
1976 Archie Trammel, Robert Stangarone, and Gordon
      Gilbert
1977 Archie Trammell

Mike Berger Memorial Award

COLUMBIA UNIVERSITY
Graduate School of Journalism, New York, N.Y. 10027
(212/280-3828)

The Mike Berger Memorial Award is not part of the Pulitzer Prize structure but is presented in honor of Pulitzer Prize-winning reporter and feature writer Meyer (Mike) Berger. The Awards are open to all New York reporters and out-of-town reporters with New York assignments. Nominations are generally made by editors of the city's daily newspapers and New York bureaus of Associated Press and United Press International. Selection of the winners is by a panel of judges, who are journalists. The winners share a $1,500 prize, and each receives a certificate.

1961 Helen Dudar, *New York Post*
      David Miller, *New York Herald Tribune*
      McCandlish Phillips, *New York Times*
1962 Pete Hamill, *New York Post*
      Lewis Lapham, *New York Herald Tribune*
1963 Newton H. Fullbright, *New York Herald Tribune*
      Peter Kihss, *New York Times*
1964 Jimmy Breslin, *New York Herald Tribune*
      Charles Grutzner, *New York Times*
1965 Homer Bigart, *New York Times*
      Bernard Gavzer, *Associated Press*
1966 Robert Lipsyte, *New York Times*
      William E. Blundell, *Wall Street Journal*
1967 Murray Schumach, *New York Times*
      Leonard Victor, *Long Island Press*
1968 Felix Kessler, *Wall Street Journal*
      J. Anthony Lukas, *New York Times*
1969 Robert Mayer, *Newsday*
      Sy Safransky and Archie Waters, *Long Island Press*
1970 Art Sears, Jr. and Donald Moffitt, *Wall Street Journal*
1971 Robert Mayer, *Newsday*
1972 Frank Faso, Joseph Martin and Paul Meskil, *New York Daily News*
1973 John Hess, *New York Times*
      Barry Cunningham, *New York Post*
1974 Penelope McMillan, *New York Sunday News*
      N. (Sonny) Kleineld, *Wall Street Journal*
1975 Deirdre Carmody, *New York Times*
      Peter Coutros, *Daily News*
1976 Israel Shenker, *New York Times*
      Howard Blum, *Village Voice*
1977 Denis Hamill, *Village Voice*
      Richard Severo, *New York Times*

SPECIAL RECOGNITION
1970 Richard Savero, *New York Times*
      Peter Coutros, *New York Daily News*
1971 Jack Newfield, *Village Voice*
      Joseph Lelyveld, *New York Times*
1972 Ray Kestenbaum, *Newsday*
      Diane Zimmerman, *New York Daily News*

Heywood Broun Award

THE NEWSPAPER GUILD
1125 15th St. NW, Washington, D.C. 20005 (202/296-2990)

Outstanding journalistic achievement, "in the spirit of Heywood Broun," is honored annually with the $1,000 Heywood Broun Award. Employees of Newspaper Guild jurisdiction newspapers, news services, news magazines, radio stations and television stations in the United States, Puerto Rico and Canada are eligible. A panel of journalists selects the winner from material submitted by the creator or another individual on righting a wrong or showing concern for the underdog.

1941 Tom O'Connor, *PM* (Revealing hazardous mine conditions)

1942 Dillard Stokes, *Washington Post* (Uncovering Nazi propaganda network in the U.S.)

1943 Milton J. Lapine, I.L Kenen, William M. Davy and E. George Green, *Cleveland Union Leader* (Series of wartime ads)

1944 Nathan Robertson, *PM* (Distinguished Washington coverage)

1945 Larry Guerin, *New Orleans Item* (Local and state coverage)

1946 James McGuire, Jack McPhaul and Karin Walsh, *Chicago Times* (For helping free a prisoner unjustly accused of murder)

1947 Bert Andrews, *New York Herald Tribune* (Exposed disregard for civil rights in State Department security dismissals)

1948 Elias A. McQuaid, *Manchester (N.H.) News* (Uncovered fraud in state contracts awards)

1949 Herbert L. Block, *Washington Post* (Editorial cartoons)
Ted Poston, *New York Post* (Courageous coverage of Flordia rape trial)

1950 Leonard Jackson, *Bay City* (Mich.) *Times* (Exposed exploitation of migrant farm workers)

1951 Jack Steele, *New York Herald Tribune* (Exposed corruption in federal government bureaus)

1952 Wallace Turner, *Portland Oregonian* (Exposed fraud in sale of Indian timberlands)

1953 Ralph S. O'Leary, *Houston Post* (Expose of the Minute Women of Texas)

1954 Anthony Lewis, *Washington Daily News* (Helped reinstate federal employee wrongly fired as security risk)

1955 Clark R. Mollenhoff, Cowles Newspapers (Stories leading to reinstatement of security "risk" and new security rules)

1956 Wallace Turner and William Lambert, *Portland Oregonian* (Stories leading to racket indictments of union, police and city officials)

1957 Aaron Epstein, *Daytona Beach* (Fla.) *Journal News* (Stories leading to slum redevelopment)
Arthur W. Geiselman, Jr., *York* (Pa.) *Gazette & Daily* (Stories leading to community reforms)

1958 George N. Allen, *New York World-Telegram & Sun* (On-scene investigation of delinquencies in city schools)

1959 William Haddad and Joseph Kahn, *New York Post* (Exposed graft and mismanagement in slum clearance)

1960 Harry Allen and Frank Drea, *Toronto Telegram* (Exposed exploitation of Italian immigrant workers)

1961 Michael Mok, *New York World-Telegram & Sun* (Exposed conditions in mental hospital)
Dale Wright, *New York World-Telegram & Sun* (Disclosed exploitation of migrant workers)

1962 Morton Mintz, *Washington Post* (Report on thalidomide leading to protective legislation)

1963 Arthur W. Geiselman, Jr., *York* (Pa.) *Gazette & Daily* (Stories leading to prosecution of housing code violations)
Samuel Stafford, Washington Daily News (Expose of abuses in surplus food distribution)

1964 Gene Goltz, *Houston Post* (Stories leading to indictment of local officials for theft and conspiracy involving public funds)

1965 John Frasca, *Tampa Tribune* (Stories leading to release of innocent man convicted and imprisoned for robbery)

1966 Gene Miller, *Miami Herald* (Stories leading to release of two persons unjustly convicted of murder)

1967 Robert Wyrick, *Cocoa* (Fla.) *Today* (Stories exposing county government corruption, leading to indictments and conviction)

1968 Mike Royko, *Chicago Daily News* (Columns pleading the cause of the underdog, leading to redress for the abused)

1969 William Lambert, *Life* (Article resulting in Justice Abe Fortas's resignation and reexamination of ethics in public life)

1970 Donald Singleton, *New York Daily News* (Series spotlighting problems of crime in New York City)

1971 Aaron Latham, *Washington Post* (Examined failures of Junior Village, the capital's home for homeless children)

1972 Carl Bernstein and Bob Woodward, *Washington Post* (Series exposing political ramifications of the Watergate Affair)

1973 Donald L. Barlett and James B. Steele, *Philadelphia Inquirer* (Series exposing uneven sentencing and discrimination by judges and prosecutors)

1974 Selwyn Raab, *New York Times* (Revealed new evidence calling into question convictions of two men for triple murder)

1975 Kent Pollock, *Philadelphia Inquirer* (Documented spread of police brutality in Philadelphia)

1976 Acel Moore and Wendell Rawls, Jr., *Philadelphia Inquirer* (Series exposing brutality, corruption and murder at Pennsylvania's Fairview State Hospital for the criminally insane)

1977 Fredric N. Tulsky and David Phelps, *Jackson* (Miss.) *Clarion Ledger* (Exposing police brutality and maladministration of justice by the city's police and court system)

John Hancock Awards for Excellence

JOHN HANCOCK MUTUAL LIFE INSURANCE CO.
John Hancock Pl., Box 111, Boston, Mass. 02117
(617/421-6000)

The John Hancock Awards for Excellence are $1,000 annual prizes for writers judged to have contributed significantly to consumer understanding of business and finance. Writers may submit material in six categories for consideration by a panel of experts in business and business journalism.

1967 Leonard Downie, Jr., *Washington Post*
Robert A. Foster, *Worcester* (Mass.) *Telegram*
Joseph L. Goodrich, *Providence Journal-Bulletin*
John K. Jessup, *Life*
David A. Jewell, *Washington Post*

J.A. Livingston, *Philadelphia Bulletin* and Publishers-Hall Syndicate

1968 Thomas G. Hartley, *Elmira* (N.Y.) *Star Gazette*
Edward S. Kerstein, *Milwaukee Journal*
J.A. Livingston, *Philadelphia Bulletin* and Publishers-Hall Syndicate
Carol J. Loomis, *Fortune*
Hobart Rowen, *Washington Post*
Max Shapiro, *Barron's Weekly*

1969 Robert Metz, *New York Times*
Theodore Levitt, *Harvard Business Review*
H. Erich Heinemann, *New York Times*
George H. Arris, *Providence Sunday Journal*
David L. Beal, *Binghamton Evening Press*
Charles E. Connelly, Jr., *Rapid City* (S.D.) *Guide*

1970 John F. Lawrence and Paul E. Steiger, *Los Angeles Times*
Richard A. Nenneman, *Christian Science Monitor*
George Church, *Time*
Fred Bleakley, *Institutional Investor*
Robert S. Rosefsky, Newsday Specials
John Hanchette, *Niagara Falls* (N.Y.) *Gazette*

1971 Laurance F. Stuntz, Associated Press
Frank Morgan, *Newsweek*
Frank Lalli, *Forbes*
Robert E. Dallos, *Los Angeles Times*
Harold Chucker, *Minneapolis Star*
George Chaplin, *Honolulu Advertiser*

1972 John T. Cunniff, Associated Press
George Church, *Time*
Philip B. Osborne, *Business Week*
Rudy Maxa, *Washington Post*
Al F. Ehrbar and Steve Petranek, *Rochester* (N.Y.) *Democrat and Chronicle*
Investigating Team, Sun Newspapers of Omaha (Neb.)

1973 J.A. Livingston, Publishers-Hall Syndicate
John Brooks, *The New Yorker*
Michael Demarest, Peter Swerdloff and William B. Mead, *Money*
Donald L. Barlett and James B. Steele, *Philadelphia Inquirer*
Richard A. Nenneman, *Christian Science Monitor*
George Chaplin, *Honolulu Advertiser*

1974 Louise Cook, Associated Press
Marshall Loeb, *Time*
Gordon L. Williams, *Business Week*
Donald L. Barlett and James B. Steele, *Philadelphia Inquirer*
Dick Youngblood, *Minneapolis Tribune*
Tom D. Miller, *Huntington* (W.Va.) *Herald-Advertiser*

1975 Jane Bryant Quinn, Washington Post Writers Group
William McWhirter, *Time*
Carol J. Loomis, *Fortune*
William S. Randall and Stephen D. Solomon, *Philadelphia Inquirer*
John Cranfill and Earl Golz, *Dallas Morning News*
Editorial Staff, *Eugene* (Ore.) *Register-Guard*

1976-77 Lee Mitgang, Associated Press
Steven Brill, *New York Magazine*
William Wolman and Philip B. Osborne, *Business Week*
Susan Trausch and Laurence Collins, *Boston Globe*
James Asher and Paul Schweizer, *Louisville Courier-Post*
Judd Cohen, *Yonkers* (N.Y.) *Herald-Statesman*

Media Award

AMOS TUCK SCHOOL OF BUSINESS ADMINISTRATION
Dartmouth College, Hanover, N.H. 03755 (603/646-2084)

The Media Award for the Advancement of Economic Understanding, which is sponsored by Champion International Corporation and administered by the Tuck school, honors outstanding economic reporting and journalism in the general media. Original works published, broadcast or telecast during the preceding year can be entered for consideration by a panel of judges. Seven top prizes of $5,000 are awarded. In addition to these first-place winners listed below, a $2,500 second prize is given in each category.

1977 Fred McGunagle, *Cleveland Press*
David Bartel, *Wichita Eagle*
Selby McCash, *Macon* (Ga.) *Telegraph*
Calvin Gatch, *Dubuque* (Iowa) *Telegraph Herald*
J.A. Livingston, *Philadelphia Inquirer* and Field Newspapers
John Riley and Seth Rothbein, *Yarmouth* (Mass.) *Post*
John T. Cunniff, Associated Press

By-Line Award

MARQUETTE UNIVERSITY COLLEGE OF JOURNALISM
1131 W. Wisconsin Ave., Milwaukee, Wisc. 53233 (414/224-7309)

The By-Line Award, which consists of a plaque, is given annually to an alumnus or alumna for competent journalism over the years and fulfillment of professional responsibility in newspaper or broadcast journalism, film, advertising, public relations or management. Alumni, students, faculty and others may make nominations for final selection by the journalism faculty and approval by the University Awards Committee.

1946 Walter J. Abel, *Catholic Herald Citizen*
Walter Belson, American Trucking Associations
Muriel Brechler, Ed Schuster & Co.
John Clifford, *Watertown* (Wisc.) *Times*
Maurice Early, *Indianapolis Star*
Joseph Helfert, *Beaver Dam* (Wisc.) *Citizen*
Don McNeill, *ABC Radio Breakfast Club*
Rev. D. F. Miller, *Liguorian Magazine* (Redemptorist Fathers)
Hugh A. Reading, J. Walter Thompson, Detroit
Aileen Ryan, *Milwaukee Journal*
John J. Shinners, *Hartford* (Wisc.) *Times-Press*
Alvin Steinkopf, Associated Press, Prague, Czechoslovakia
Raymond Welch, *National Geographic*

1947 James Strebig, Associated Press

1948 Albert Schimberg, *Catholic Herald Citizen* and author, *Story of Therese Neumann* and *The Larks of Umbria*

1949 Walter Fitzmaurice, *Newsweek* (formerly with International News Service, *Milwaukee Sentinel* and *Chicago Journal*)

1950 L. Carroll Arimond, Associated Press, Chicago
Marvin L. Tonkin, Associated Press, Chicago

1951 Leo James Bormann, WMT - Radio, Cedar Rapids, Iowa

1952 Robert C. LaBlonde, Foote, Cone and Belding International, New York

1953 Donald E. Huth, Associated Press, Manila, Philippines

1954 Edward G. Gerbic, Johnson and Johnson, New Brunswick, N.J.

1955 Albert T. Rumbach, *DuBois County Daily Herald* (Jasper, Ind.)

1956 Athlyn Deshais Faulkner, *Chicago Daily News*
Gordon R. Lewis, *South Milwaukee Voice-Journal*
William P. McCahill, President's Committee on Employment of the Physically Handicapped
Paul M. McMahon, *Milwaukee Journal*
Robert J. Riordan, *Milwaukee Sentinel*

1957 Donald F. Daubel, *Fremont (Ohio) News-Messenger*

1958 Waldo E. McNaught, Buick Motor Division, General Motors Corp.

1959 Thomas E. Moore, *Iron River* (Mich.) *Reporter*

1960 Oliver E. Kuechle, *Milwaukee Journal*
Gerald J. Liska, Associated Press Chicago
Amos T. Thisted, *Milwaukee Sentinel*

1961 Thomas P. Coleman, Associated Press
John J. Ducas, Gaylor and Ducas, Inc.
Edward S. Kerstein, *Milwaukee Journal*
H. Leo Kissel, *Milwaukee Sentinel*
Joseph I. Pettit, International Harvester Co.
Eldon H. Roesler, Business Press & Editorial Service
Clarence M. Zens, *Catholic Standard*, (Washington, D.C.)

1962 Thaddeus L. Knap, *Indianapolis Times*
John F. Loosbrock, *Air Force & Space Digest*
Joseph P. Wright, Prince & Co.

1963 Loretta J. Fox, Falk Corporation

1964 Robert E. Gilka, *National Geographic*

1965 James E. Rasmusen, *Gary* (Ind.) *Post-Tribune*

1966 Marshall W. Berges, Time-Life News Service, Los Angeles,
Edmund S. Carpenter, Marquette University
Charles H. Harbutt, Jr., Magnum Photos, Inc., New York
Newell G. Meyer, *Milwaukee Journal*
Leonard J. Scheller, *Milwaukee Journal*

1967 George E. Lardner, Jr., *Washington Post*

1968 Edwin A. Shanke, Associated Press Scandinavian Services

1969 J. Wallace Carroll, Journal and Sentinel Winston-Salem (N.C.)

1970 Daniel L. Satran and Robert L. Satran, *Vilas County News-Review* and *Three Lakes News* (Eagle River, Wisc.)

1971 John R. Springer, John Springer Associates, Inc., New York, Los Angeles, Paris, London, Rome

1972 David L. Bowen, Associated Press

1973 William R. Burleigh, *Evansville* (Ind.) *Press*

1974 Harold A. Schwartz, *Milwaukee Journal and Sentinel*

1975 Mary Lou Beatty, *Washington Post*

1976 James P. Gannon, *Wall Street Journal*, Washington, D.C. Bureau

1977 Paul Wilkes, Freelance writer

Maria Moors Cabot Prize

COLUMBIA UNIVERSITY
Graduate School of Journalism, New York, N.Y. 10027
(212/280-3828)

The Maria Moors Cabot Prize is awarded by the trustees of the university on recommendation by the dean of the Graduate School of Journalism, assisted by an advisory committee of experts in inter-American affairs, for distinguished journalism by one United States and one Latin American journalist. In addition to the individual gold medal winners listed below, most of their and other notable newspapers are honored with a plaque. Winners share a $1,500 cash prize. (* Honors for international scope.)

1939 Jose Santos Gollan, *La Prensa* (Buenos Aires, Argentina)
Luis Miro Quesada, *El Comercio* (Lima, Peru)

1940 Augustin E. Edwards, *El Mercurio* (Santiago, Chile)
Enrique Santos, *El Tiempo* (Bogota, Colombia)
Rafael Heliodoro Valle, Correspondent in Mexico City (Honduras)
James I. Miller, United Press Assns. (U.S.A.)

1941 Paulo Bittencourt, *Correio de Manha* (Rio de Janeiro, Brazil)
Silvia Bittencourt, *Correio de Manha* (Rio de Janeiro, Brazil)
Carlos Davila, Editors Press Service (Chile)
Jose Ignacio Rivero, *Diario de la Marina* (Havana, Cuba)

1942 Luis Mitre, *La Nacion* (Buenos Aires, Argentina)
Lorenzo Batlle Pacheo, *El Dia* (Montevideo, Uruguay)

1943 Pedro Cue, *El Mundo* (Havana, Cuba)
Rodrigo de Llano, *Excelsior* (Mexico City, Mexico)
Edward Tomlinson, National Broadcasting Co. (U.S.A.)

1944 Carlos Mantilla Ortega, *El Comercio* (Quito, Ecuador)
Jorge Pinto, *Diario Latino* (San Salvador, El Salvador)
Albert Victor McGeachy, *Star and Herald* (Panama City, Panama)

1945 Francisco de Assis Chateaubriand, *Diarios Associados* (Rio de Janeiro, Brazil)
Tom Wallace, *Louisville Times* (Louisville, Ky.)
Luis Teofilo Nunez, *El Universal* (Carcas, Venezuela)

1946 Grant Dexter, *Winnipeg Free Press* (Winnipeg, Man., Canada)
Miguel Lanz Duret, *El Universal* (Mexico City, Mexico)
Lee Hills, *Miami Herald* (Miami, Fla.)

1947 Carlos Victor Aramayo, *La Razon* (La Paz, Bolivia)
David Vela, *El Imparcial* (Guatemala City, Guatemala)
Alberto Lleras Camargo*, Pan American Union (Washington, D.C.)

1948 Orlando Riberio Dantas, *Diario da Noite* (Rio de Janeiro, Brazil)
Alfredo Silva-Carvallo, *La Union* (Valpariso, Chile)
Manuel Cisneros Sanchez, *La Cronica* (Lima, Peru)
Joseph L. Jones, United Press Assns. (U.S.A.)

1949 Jose Santiago Castillo, *El Telegraf* (Guayaquil, Ecuador)
Milton Bracker, *New York Times* (New York, N.Y.)
Eduardo Rodriguez Larretta, *El Pais* (Montevideo, Uruguay)

1950 Maria Constanza Huergo, *La Prensa* (Buenos Aires, Argentina)
John A. Brogan, King Features Syndicate (U.S.A.)
Joshua B. Powers, Editors Press Service, Inc. (New York, N.Y.)
Angel Ramos, *El Mundo* (San Juan, Puerto Rico)

Mons. **Jesus Maria Pellin,** *La Religion* (Caracas, Venezuela)

1951 **Elmano Cardim,** *Jornal Do Comercio* (Rio de Janeiro, Brazil)

Francisco Maria Nunez, *El Diario de Costa Rica* (San Jose, Costa Rica)

Julio Garzon, *La Prensa* (New York, N.Y.)

Ramon David Leon, *La Esfera* (Caracas, Venezuela)

1952 **Belarmino Austregesilo de Athayde,** *Diario da Noite* (Rio de Janeiro, Brazil)

Jorge Delano, *Topaze* (Santiago, Chile)

Juan B. Fernandez, *El Heraldo* (Barranquilla, Colombia)

Antonio Arias Bernal, *Hoy* (Mexico City, Mexico)

Jules Dubois, *Chicago Tribune* (Chicago, Ill.)

1953 **Carlos Lacerda,** *Tribuna da Imprensa* (Rio de Janeiro, Brazil)

Ismael Perez Castro, *El Universo* (Guayaquil, Ecuador)

Arturo Schaerer, *La Tribuno* (Ascuncion, Paraguay)

Crede H. Calhoun, *New York Times* (New York, N.Y.)

1954 **Danton Jobim,** *Diario Carioca* (Rio de Janeiro, Brazil)

Gabriel Cano, *El Espectador* (Bogota, Colombia)

Sidney Gerald Fletcher, *The Daily Gleaner* (Kingston, Jamaica)

Lloyd Stratton, Associated Press (New York, N.Y.)

Carlos Ramirez MacGregor, *Panorama* (Maracaibo, Venezuela)

1955 **Roberto Jorge Noble,** *Clarin* (Buenos Aires, Argentina)

Breno Caldas, *Correio do Povo* (Porto Alegre, Brazil)

Pedro G. Beltran, *La Prensa* (Lima, Peru)

John Oliver LaGorce, *National Geographic* (Washington, D.C.)

A.T. Steele, *New York Herald Tribune* (U.S.A.)

1956 **David Michel Torino,** *El Intransigente* (Salta, Argentina)

Roberto Garcia Pena, *El Tiempo* (Bogota, Colombia)

Jesus Alvarez del Castillo, *El Informador* (Guadalajara, Mexico)

Carl W. Ackerman, Graduate School of Journalism, Columbia University (New York, N.Y.)

Herbert L. Matthews, *New York Times* (New York, N.Y.)

1957 **Herbert Moses,** *O Globo* and president, Brazilian Press Assn. (Rio de Janeiro, Brazil)

Rene Silva Espejo, *El Mercurio* (Santiago, Chile)

Harry W. Frantz, United Press Assns. (U.S.A.)

1958 **Miguel Angel Quevedo** *Bohemia* (Havana, Cuba)

Emilio Azcarraga Vidaurreta, Cadena Radiodifusora Mexicana and Telesistema Mexicana (Mexico City, Mexico)

Eduardo Cardenas, *Selecciones del Reader's Digest* (Pleasantville, N.Y.)

Pbro. Jesus Hernandez Chapellin, *La Religion* (Caracas, Venezuela)

1959 **Hernane Tavares de Sa,** *Visao* (Sao Paulo, Brazil)

Ricardo Castro Beeche, *La Nacion* (San Jose, Costa Rica)

Clement David Hellyer, *San Diego Union* (San Diego, Calif.)

Tad Szulc, *New York Times* (New York, N.Y.)

1960 **Rudolfo N. Luque,** *La Prensa* (Buenos Aires, Argentina)

Jose Dutriz, Jr., *La Prensa Grafica* (San Salvador, El Salvador)

James B. Canel, Inter American Press Assn. (New York, N.Y.)

William M. Pepper, Jr., *Gainesville Daily Sun* (Gainesville, Fla.)

1961 **Fernando Gomez Martinez,** *El Colombiano* (Medellin, Colombia)

Alejandro Carrion, *El Universo* (Guayaquil, Ecuador)

Romulo O'Farrill, Sr., *Novedades* (Mexico City, Mexico)

Rev. Albert J. Nevins, M.M., *Maryknoll* magazine (Maryknoll, N.Y.)

John T. O'Rourke, *Washington Daily News* (Washington, D.C.)

1962 **Rudolfo Junco de la Vega,** *El Norte* and *El Sol* (Monterrey, Mexico)

John R. Herbert, *Patriot Ledger* (Quincy, Mass.)

John S. Knight, Knight Newspapers and *Miami Herald* (Miami, Fla.)

Raul Fontaina, *Radio Carve (Montevideo, Uruguay)*

1963 **Juan S. Valmaggia,** *La Nacion* (Buenos Aires, Argentina)

William Barlow, *Vision* magazine (U.S.A.)

Juan de Onis, *New York Times* (New York, N.Y.)

German Arciniegas*, Syndicated columnist, *Cuadernos* (Paris, France)

Jorge Fernandez*, Centro Internacional de Estudios Superiores de Periodismo para America Latina (Quito, Ecuador)

1964 **Enrique Nores Martinez,** *Los Principios* (Cordoba, Argentina)

Bertram B. Johansson, *Christian Science Monitor* (Boston, Mass.)

Virginia Prewett, *Washington Daily News* and North American Newspaper Alliance (U.S.A.)

Hugo Fernandez Artucio, *El Dia* (Montevideo, Uruguay)

1965 **Victoria Ocampo,** *Sur* (Buenos Aires, Argentina)

Roberto Marinho, *O Globo* (Rio de Janeiro, Brazil)

Gesford F. Fine, United Press International (U.S.A.)

Paul Sanders, Associated Press (U.S.A.)

1966 **Paul Kidd,** Southam News Service (Ottawa, Ont., Canada)

Augustin E. Edwards, *Empresa El Mercurio* (Santiago, Chile)

Alberto R. Cellario, *Life en Espanol* (New York, N.Y.)

1967 **M.F. do Nascimento Brito,** *Jornal do Brasil* (Rio de Janeiro, Brazil)

Peter Aldor, *El Tiempo* (Bogota, Colombia)

James S. Copley, Copley News Service (La Jolla, Calif.)

James Nelson Goodsell, *Christian Science Monitor* (Boston, Mass.)

Ramon Jose Velasquez Mujica, *El Nacional* (Caracas, Venezuela)

1968 **Alberto Gainza Paz,** *La Prensa* (Buenos Aires, Argentina)

Argentina S. Hills, *El Mundo* (San Juan, Puerto Rico)

Robert Berrellez, Associated Press (U.S.A.)

Guillermo Guierrez V-M*, Inter American Press Assn.

1969 **Alceu Amoroso Lima,** Author, essayist and literary critic (Rio de Janeiro, Brazil)

Luis Gabriel Cano, *El Espectador* (Bogota, Colombia)

Elsa Arana Freire, *7 Dias* (Lima, Peru)

Edward W. Barrett, Academy for Educational Development (New York, N.Y.)

George H. Beebe, *Miami Herald* (Miami, Fla.)

1970 **Alberto Dines,** *Jornal do Brasil* (Rio de Janeiro, Brazil)

John D. Harbron, *Toronto Telegram* (Toronto, Ont., Canada)

John Goshko, *Washington Post* (Washington, D.C.)

1971 **Landru (Juan Carlos Colombres),** Editorial cartoonist (Buenos Aires, Argentina)

Julio Scherer Garcia, *Excelsior* (Mexico City, Mexico)

Georgie Anne Geyer, *Chicago Daily News*, (Chicago, Ill.)

1972 Tom Streithorst, NBC News (U.S.A.)

Arturo Ulsar Pietri, *El Nacional* (Caracas, Venezuela)

1973 David Belnap, *Los Angeles Times* (Los Angeles, Calif.)

Rev. Donald J. Casey, M.M., World Horizon Films and *Maryknoll* magazine (Maryknoll, N.Y.)

1974 Fernando Pedreira, *O Estado de Sao Paulo* (Sao Paulo, Brazil)

Don Bohning, *Miami Herald* (Miami, Fla.)

William D. Montalbano, *Miami Herald* (Miami, Fla.)

1975 Enrique Zileri Gibson, *Caretas* (Lima, Peru)

Sam Sumerlin, Associated Press (U.S.A.)

1976 Jorge S. Remonda Ruibal, *La Voz Del Interior* (Cordoba, Argentina)

Bernard Deiderich, Time-Life News Service (New York, N.Y.)

1977 Pedro J. Chamorro, *La Prensa* (Managua, Nicaragua)

Jonathan Kandell, *New York Times* (New York, N.Y.)

SPECIAL CITATION (*HONORS FOR INTERNATIONAL SCOPE)

1957 Roberto Marinho, *O Globo* (Brazil)
Paulo Bittencourt*
Miguel Lanz Duret*
Luis Franzini*
John S. Knight*
Carlos Mantilla*
Guillermo Martinez Marquez*
John T. O'Rourke*
James G. Stahlman*
Tom Wallace*

1959 Juan Andres Ramirez, *El Plata* (Uruguay)

1968 Mons. Jose Joaquin Salcedo G., Accion Cultural Popular Bogota (Colombia)

1960 Eduardo Santos, *El Tiempo* (Colombia)

1972 Pedro G. Beltran, *La Prensa* (Peru)

1975 David Kraiselburd, *El Dia* (Argentina)

Norman A. Ingrey, *Buenos Aires Herald* and *Christian Science Monitor* (Argentina)

Walter Everett, American Press Institute (U.S.A.)

1976 German E. Ornes, *El Caribe* (Dominican Republic)

Robert U. Brown, *Editor & Publisher* (U.S.A.)

1977 Anita von Kahler, *Agence France-Presse* (France)

Joseph A. Taylor, Latin American Communication Program, University of Texas (U.S.A.)

Reuben Award

NATIONAL CARTOONISTS SOCIETY
9 Ebony Court, Brooklyn, N.Y. 11229 (212/743-6510)

The Reuben Award, which consists of a statuette created by the late Rube Goldberg and named for him, is given to the outstanding cartoonist of the year. The winner is selected by a secret ballot of the society's members.

1946 Milton Caniff, *Steve Canyon*
1947 Al Capp, *Li'l Abner*
1948 Chic Young, *Blondie*
1949 Alex Raymond, *Rip Kirby*
1950 Roy Crane, *Buzz Sawyer*
1951 Walt Kelly, *Pogo*

1952 Hank Ketcham, *Dennis the Menace*
1953 Mort Walker, *Beetle Bailey*
1954 Willard Mullin, *Sports* cartoons
1955 Charles Schulz, *Peanuts*
1956 Herblock, Editorial cartoons
1957 Hal Foster, *Prince Valiant*
1958 Frank King, *Gasoline Alley*
1959 Chester Gould, *Dick Tracy*
1960 Ronald Searle, Illustrations
1961 Bill Mauldin, Editorial cartoons
1962 Dik Browne, *Hi & Lois*
1963 Fred Lasswell, *Barney Google and Snuffy Smith*
1964 Charles Schulz, *Peanuts*
1965 Leonard Starr, *On Stage*
1966 Otto Soglow, *The Little King*
1967 Rube Goldberg, *Humor in Sculpture*
1968 John Hart, *B.C.* and *Wizard of Id*
      Pat Oliphant, Editorial cartoons
1969 Walter Berndt, *Smitty*
1970 Alfred Andriola, *Kerry Drake*
1971 Milton Caniff, *Steve Canyon*
1972 Pat Oliphant, Editorial cartoons
1973 Dik Browne, *Hagar the Horrible*
1974 Dick Moores, *Gasoline Alley*
1975 Bob Dunn, *They'll Do It Every Time*
1976 Ernie Bushmiller, *Nancy*
1977 Chester Gould, *Dick Tracy*

CIP Award

CATHOLIC INSTITUTE OF THE PRESS
1011 First Ave., Ste. 1920, New York, NY 10022;
212/371-6100

The CIP Award, which consists of a scroll, was awarded annually for service in the communications field that exemplified Catholic principles. It has been discontinued.

1948 Bob Considine
1949 Neil MacNeil
1950 Fulton Oursler
1951 Leo McCarey
1952 James M. O'Neill
1953 H.I. Phillips
1954 Martin Quigley
1955 Gene Lockhart
1956 Jim Bishop
1957 Arthur Daley
      "Red" Smith
1958 Clare Booth Luce
1959 John La Farge, S.J.
1960 Phyllis McGinley
1961 Edwin O'Connor
1962 Barrett McGurn
1963 Paul Horgan
1964 Daniel Callahan
1965 NBC-TV and CBS-TV
1966 Gary MacEoin

Columbia Journalism Award

COLUMBIA UNIVERSITY
Graduate School of Journalism, New York, N.Y. 10027
(212/280-3828)

The Columbia Journalism Award consists of a plaque given annually for distinguished service in the field of journalism to an individual selected by a faculty-student honors committee.

1970 Walter Lippmann
1971 I.F. Stone
1972 Neil Sheehan
1973 Katharine Graham
1974 John H. Johnson
1975 William Shawn
1976 A.H. Raskin
1977 Journalists throughout the world who, through states' tyranny, have been denied their rights to free expression

Science Writers Award
AMERICAN DENTAL ASSOCIATION
211 E. Chicago Ave., Chicago, Ill. 60611 (312/440-2803)

The $1,000 Science Writers Award annually recognizes the best article in a magazine or newspaper on dental health and/or research. The Science Writers Award Committee selects the winner.

MAGAZINES

1966 Norman A. Lobsenz and A. Norman Cranin, *Redbook*
1967 The Editors *of Better Homes and Gardens*
1968 Howard L. Lewis, *Business Week*
1969 Theodore Berland, Freelance writer
1970 Edward Edelson, *Family Health*
1971 Gerald M. Knox, *Better Homes and Gardens*
1972 Elizabeth Barley and William Glavin, *Good Housekeeping*
1973 Don Schanche, *Today's Health*
1974 Melba Rabinowitz, *Children Today*
1975 Jean Butler, *Today's Health*
1976 Constance Billie, *Family Health*
1977 Annette Stec, *Exploring*

NEWSPAPERS

1966 Ronald Kotulak, *Chicago Tribune*
1967 Alton Blakeslee, Associated Press
1968 Arthur J. Snider, *Chicago Daily News*
1969 Jean Latz Griffin, *Joliet* (Ill.) *Herald News*
1970 James G. Driscoll, *National Observer*
1971 Timothy D. Schellhardt, *Wall Street Journal*
1972 William Hager, *Bradenton* (Fla.) *Herald*
1973 Pat Atkinson, *Tulsa Daily World*
1974 Anita Buie Lamont, *St. Louis Globe-Democrat*
1975 Sarah Watke, *Green Bay* (Wisc.) *Press Gazette*
1976 Patricia McCormack, United Press International
1977 Lucy Eckberg, *Winona* (Ill.) *Daily News*

Higher Education Writer Award
AMERICAN ASSOCIATION OF UNIVERSITY PROFESSORS
One DuPont Cir., Ste. 500, Washington, D.C. 20036 (202/466-8050)

The Higher Education Writer Award, which consists of a plaque, is given annually to the individual selected by a panel of judges for having done outstanding interpretative reporting on issues in higher education.

1970 Ronald Maselka, *Buffalo Evening News*
1971 John A. Crowl, *Chronicle of Higher Education*
1972 William Trombley, *Los Angeles Times*

1973 Edward R. Weidlein, *Chronicle of Higher Education*
1974 Philip Semas, *Chronicle of Higher Education*
1975 Eric Wentworth, Washington Post
1976 William Braden, *Chicago Sun-Times*
      Andrew Shaw, *Chicago Sun-Times*
1977 Larry Van Dyne, *Chronicle of Higher Education*

Henry Johnson Fisher Award
MAGAZINE PUBLISHERS ASSOCIATION
575 Lexington Ave., New York, N.Y. 10022 (212/752-0055)

The Henry Johnson Fisher Award, which consists of a $1,000 honorarium, a crystal vase and a citation, is given annually to a notable individual or individuals in magazine publishing for contributions to the advancement of the industry. The Henry Johnson Fisher Award Committee selects the winner, approved by the board of directors of the association. In addition, the National Magazine Awards are given under a grant from the Magazine Publishers Assn. These will be found on pp. 82-83.

1964 DeWitt Wallace
1965 Henry R. Luce
1966 Richard E. Berlin
1967 Edward Weeks
1968 Arnold Gingrich
1969 A.L. Cole
1970 Roy E. Larsen and Maurice R. Robinson
1971 Gibson McCabe
1972 John H. Johnson
1973 Norman Cousins
1974 Laurence W. Lane, Jr., Melvin B. Lane and Mrs. Laurence W. Lane, Sr.
1975 Richard J. Babcock and Emory O. Cunningham
1976 Stephen E. Kelly
1977 No award

Gavel Awards
AMERICAN BAR ASSOCIATION
1155 E. 60th St., Chicago, Ill. 60637 (312/947-4000)

The Gavel Awards are given annually to honor films, the media and books for their depiction of or reportage on the law and the legal profession. The Bar Association recognizes achievements which foster greater public understanding of the American legal and judicial system, disclose areas in need of improvement or correction and encourage efforts of all levels of government to update laws. Engraved gavels are given to executives of winning news organizations.

NEWSPAPERS

1958 *Cleveland Plain Dealer* (Editorials on court administration)
      Richmond (Va.) *News Leader* (Weekly legal column)
      St. Petersburg (Fla.) *Times* (Editorials and articles on law and the courts)
1959 *St. Louis Post Dispatch* (Series of articles on U.S. Supreme Court)
      Moline (Ill.) *Daily Dispatch* (Editorials and articles on modernizing Illinois court system)
1960 *Washington Post* (Editorials on constitutional role of U.S. Supreme Court)

Pittsburgh Post Gazette (Editorials and articles explaining role of judges and lawyers)
The Oregonian, Portland, Ore. (Special Law Day USA magazine section)
Lindsay-Schaub Newspapers, Decatur, Ill. (Series on first National Conference of Judicial Selection and Court Administration)

1961 *Hartford* (Conn.) *Times* (Series on newly reorganized state court system)
Christian Science Monitor (Series documenting an alien's murder trial)
Chicago Tribune (Series analyzing Chicago court congestion problems)

1962 *Christian Science Monitor* (For journalistic enterprise in support of steps to strengthen probate court system in Massachusetts)
Washington Post (Articles interpreting Supreme Court decision on major constitutional issues)

1963 *Washington Post* Distinguished interpretative reporting of Supreme Court decision of constitutional issues of great national significance)
Chicago Tribune (Series of distinguished editorials supporting adoption of Judicial Amendment of the Illinois Constitution to modernize Illinois courts)
Chicago Daily News (Articles and editorials supporting the organized bar campaign to modernize Illinois courts)

1964 *Washington Star* (Analytical reporting, under deadline pressure, of important Supreme Court decisions)
Oklahoma City Times (Series on significance of the rule by U.S. District Court reapportioning Oklahoma legislature)

1965 *Kansas City Kansan* (Eleven-part series analyzing public benefits of 1964 Code of Civil Procedures in the courts of Kansas)
Louisville (Ky.) *Times* (Series of twenty-four interpretative articles on the importance of Kentucky Court of Appeals decisions and supplementary coverage of new law)
The Blade, Toledo, Ohio (Comprehensive reporting and editorial interpretation of court decision, legislative enactments and organized bar efforts to improve the administration of justice)
Worcester (Mass.) *Daily Telegram* (Distinctive series of weekly articles interpreting developments and trends in judicial decisions and law enforcement)

1966 *Christian Science Monitor* (Distinguished ten-part series analyzing nature and impact of significant changes in the administration of criminal justice)
St. Petersburg (Fla.) *Times* (Comprehensive series of editorials urging modernization of Florida judicial system and nonpartisan selection of judges)

1967 *Washington Post* (Seven-part series by Leonard Downie, Jr., leading to reforms in Washington Court of General Session; also for articles by John P. MacKenzie interpreting Supreme Court decisions)
Daily Oklahoman and Times, Oklahoma City (Editorial leadership in initiative petition for statewide referendum on court reform; award based on editorial series by Clarke Thomas)
The Blade, Toledo, Ohio (Leadership in formulating voluntary code of fair practice in crime coverage news to guard rights of the accused)

1968 *Christian Science Monitor* ("Crisis in the Courts" series by Howard James examining strengths and weaknesses in state court systems and recommending improvements)
Los Angeles Times (Ronald J. Ostrow's distinguished series interpretating Supreme Court decisions and operations of U.S. Dept. of Justice)

St. Louis Post-Dispatch (Interpretative articles by James C. Millstone on decision-making processes of U.S. Supreme Court and related legal subjects.)
Louisville (Ky.) *Courier-Journal* (Voluntary adoption of code of fair practices to protect fair trial and free press in crime news reporting)
Philadelphia Inquirer Ten-part series by G. Warren Nutter contrasting legal, political and social institutions in the U.S. and Soviet Union)

1969 *New York Times Magazine* (Feature article by Herbert Mitgang on work of community lawyers for the disadvantaged)
Minneapolis Star (Austin Wehrwein's series of editorials and commentaries on developments in law and administration of justice)
Anchorage (Alaska) *Daily News* (Enterprising reportorial survey of administration of justice by lawyer-journalist C. Robert Zelnick)
Riverside (Calif.) *Press-Enterprise* (Distinguished series on crime and the courts)
Washington Post (For the book, *Ten Blocks from the White House,* a chronology of 1968 riots and resulting emergency measures of court administration)

1970 *Kankakee* (Ill.) *Daily Journal* (Initiating in-depth probe into conditions affecting administration of local justice)
Niagara Falls (N.Y.) *Gazette* (Series on quality of justice administration by lower courts and need for judicial reform)
Evansville (Ind.) *Courier* (Full publication of comprehensive study of local crime and law enforcement problems and editorial support of numerous recommendations of the study)
Washington Evening Star (Eleven-part series detailing serious problems besetting trial courts in Washington and suburbs)
Christian Science Monitor (Series of fifteen articles exposing brutal conditions in juvenile detention homes and offering 170 remedial suggestions)
Louisville (Ky.) *Courier-Journal* (Series describing archaic court conditions and urgent need for modernization)
New York Times (Series examining problems of free press, fair trial, self-incrimination, court challenges and law school enrollment practices)
Chicago Sun-Times (Series on legal subjects of public importance, including need for more Negro lawyers, new state income tax law and church-state relations)
Parade **Sunday supplement** ("They Learn the Law —Before It's Too Late," explaining new law program for high school students)

1971 *Record-Chronicle,* Denton, Texas (Series explaining legal steps from time of arrest to trial of the accused)
Spartanburg (S.C.) *Journal* (Two-part series on how each court in the judicial process functions)
St. Petersburg (Fla.) *Times* (Series of more than fifty articles on prison conditions in Florida)
Valley News, Van Nuys, Calif. (Series on controversial decisions expanding individual rights)
Milwaukee Journal (Series of editorials supporting efforts to update Wisconsin's judicial system and Law Day USA supplement)
Minneapolis Star ("Judging the Law," weekly column)
National Observer (Series interpreting major Supreme Court decisions affecting all segments of society)

1972 *Oregon Statesman,* Salem, Ore. (Comprehensive explanation of key laws in Oregon's new Criminal Code)

Cincinnati Enquirer (Series about problems facing correctional institutional parole officers and parolees)

Christian Science Monitor (Best national reporting as represented by series of articles on American prisons)

Kansas City Star (Best local reporting as typified by series of editorials on problems of criminal justice and penal reform)

National Observer (Series interpreting major Supreme Court decisions affecting all segments of society)

1973 *Illinois State Register* (Comprehensive eighteen-part series on facets of American criminal justice system)

Tucson Daily Citizen (Four-part series on lax administration in Pima County probate system)

St. Louis Post-Dispatch (Five-part series on new forces and ideas in legal profession today)

St. Louis Globe Democrat (Series on corruption in Municipal Court)

Detroit Free Press (Eight-part series on conditions that are weakening the ability of the legal system to function properly)

1974 *Poughkeepsie (N.Y.) Journal* (Special section by Ed Baron and Joe Tinkleman providing study of New York State's new drug law)

Kansas City Star (Three-part series by Harry Jones, Jr., and J.J. Maloney on prison systems of Missouri and Kansas and federal institutions in those states)

Philadelphia Inquirer (Seven-part series by Donald L. Barlett and James B. Steele, revealing patterns of discrimination and bias, extreme disparity in sentencing and jailing of innocent persons by some judges)

1975 *Sharon Herald*, Grove City, Pa. (Teresa Spatara's eighteen-part series on crime and criminal justice)

Albuquerque (N.M.) Journal (Scott Beaven's series on the way New Mexico handles the mentally ill and retarded)

Minneapolis Tribune (Frank Premack, Peter Vanderpoel and Doug Stone's comprehensive look at Hennepin County juvenile justice system)

Chicago Sun-Times (Roger Simon and Patrick Oster's in-depth investigation and report on Cook County criminal justice system)

1976 *Shreveport (La.) Journal* (Special edition entitled "Justice and Injustice")

Messenger-Inquirer, Owensboro, Ky. (Series of articles and editorials calling for adoption of constitutional amendment to modernize the state's court system)

Journal-Gazette, Fort Wayne, Ind. ("A Time for Appraisal," pinpointing strengths and weaknesses of new, unified Allen County Superior Court)

1976 *Chicago Sun-Times* (Series by Roger Simon on plea bargaining.)

1977 *Lakeland Ledger (Fla)* (John R. Harrison's editorial series directed toward youth and explaining the law as it applies to juveniles)

Oakland (Mich.) Press (James S. Granelli and Alan S. Lenhoff's series on day-to-day operations of local courts)

Philadelphia Inquirer (Jan Schaffer and Jonathan Neumann's series on the alleged mishandling by law enforcement officials of a racially motivated murder case)

Detroit Free Press ("Crime in Detroit: A Search for Solutions," eight-part series)

MAGAZINES

1958 *Life* ("Crime in the U.S." series)

1959 *Southern Telephone News* (Series on law in American life)

Time (Coverage of Law Day USA)

1960 **No award**

1961 **No award**

1962 *Fortune* ("The Crisis in the Courts," a definitive article on court congestion)

Boys' Life (Series of illustrated articles on historical origins of our legal system)

1963 **No award**

1964 *Look* (Series on legal issues of current interest)

1965 *Life* ("Storm Center of Justice," distinguished assessment of record of U.S. Supreme Court in the previous decade)

1966 *Time* ("The Revolution in Criminal Justice," an essay, and for distinguished reporting of legal news in its law section)

Look (Account of reform in Chicago's police department and other discerning coverage of law news)

1967 *Time* ("Moving the Constitution Into the Police Station" on the impact of the 1964 Supreme Court decision in *Escobedo vs. Illinois* and its effect on police investigation)

Look ("The Lady Fights Back" by Julius Norwitz on a three-year court struggle by Negro attorney Cora Walker to obtain a certificate of occupancy for a renovated Harlem slum dwelling, and an article by Fletcher Knebel on jury system in U.S.)

1968 *Newsweek* ("The New Law Versus Tradition" by Peter Janssen on trends toward greater curriculum flexibility and increased social responsibilities in legal education)

Saturday Evening Post (Stewart Alsop's "The Supreme Court Asks A Question: Is It Fair?", an assessment of the Court and its members)

1969 **No award**

1970 *Psychology Today* (For contribution to original research in attitudes toward the law and courts, crime and punishment, the penal system rights and freedoms)

1971 *Fortune* (Article examining role of the Supreme Court over two decades)

Newsweek ("Prisons in Turmoil," on problems confronting penal systems)

U.S. News and World Report ("Interview with Chief Justice Warren E. Burger")

1972 *Newsweek* ("Justice on Trial," a comprehensive report on the police, courts and correctional facilities)

1973 *Apartment Ideas* (Three articles explaining legal aspects of common problems to apartment renters)

Harper's ("Your Phone Is A Party Line," detailing government's expanded bugging activities)

Reader's Digest (Three-article series on juvenile courts)

Time ("Up from Coverture" on discriminatory actions taken against women since the earliest days of civilization)

1974 *Philadelphia* ("The Last Whole Justice Catalog" by John Guinther, examining practices and procedures of Philadelphia courts)

The New Yorker ("Annals of Law: Boston Criminal Courts" by Richard Harris on how and whether justice is meted out in American courts)

1975 *Philadelphia* ("The Paint Job" by James N. Riggio on how a mayor was indicted on trumped-up charges; the investigative report was used in his defense)

The New Yorker ("A Scrap of Black Cloth," two-part article by Richard Harris on the ordeal of a New York teacher who wore an armband to express opposition to the Vietnam War)

Newsweek ("All About Impeachment" by David M. Alpern)

1976 *Philadelphia* ("A Child's Garden of Horrors" by John Guinther on injustices in Philadelphia's juvenile justice system)

U.S. News and World Report("Big Change in Prisons — Punish Not Reform" by Patrick R. Oster and Donald P. Doane)

1977 *Boston* ("The Verdict" by Gwen Kincaid analyzing the effect the trial de novo system has upon the quality of justice in Massachusetts)

Newsweek (For Peter Axthelm and Anthony Marro's article on the de facto extradition process used by the U.S. Drug Enforcement Administration to obtain the release of suspected kingpins from foreign countries)

WIRE SERVICES

1965 **Gannett News Service** ("Crime and the U.S. Supreme Court," six-article series analyzing landmark decisions broadening the rights of the accused in criminal cases)
1966 **No award**
1967 **No award**
1968 **Newhouse National News Service** (Series by Jack C. Landau on American system of military justice)
1969 **No award**
1970 **No award**
1971 **No award**
1972 **No award**
1973 *Parade* **(Sunday supplement)** (Article outlining problems facing the deaf in obtaining proper legal representation)

Birmingham News (Feature by Peggy Robertson on plea bargaining in "Dimension" supplement)
1974 **Public Insights Syndicate,** (Series of weekly columns by Harry Humphreys, "Ideas, Issues and Insights")
1975 **McGraw-Hill World News,** ("Your World Tomorrow" feature by Daniel B. Moskowitz on developments in consumer law)
1976 **No award**
1977 **Gannett News Service,** (Robert L. King's four-part series on how closed adoption records cause tragic problems for adult adoptees)

Golden Pen of Freedom
INTERNATIONAL FEDERATION OF NEWSPAPER PUBLISHERS (F.I.E.J.)
6, rue Faubourg Poissonniere, 75101 Paris, France (Tel: 523 38 88).

The Golden Pen of Freedom is awarded annually to a person, group or institution for outstanding service to press freedom. The award consists of a gold pen and a plaque. The executive committee of F.I.E.J. selects the winner.

1961 **Ahmet Emin Yalman,** *Hur Vatan* (Istanbul, Turkey)
1962 **No award**
1963 **U Sein Win,** *The Guardian* (Rangoon, Burma)
1964 **Gabriel Makoso,** *Le Courreir d'Afrique* (Leopoldville, Congo)
1965 **Esmond Wickremesinghe,** Associated Newspapers of Ceylon (Colombo)
1966 **Jules Dubois,** Chicago Tribune Press Service (Chicago)
1967 **Mochtar Lubis,** *Indonesia Raya* (Djakarta)
1968 **Christos Lambrakis,** *Ta Vima* (Athens, Greece)
1969 **The Czech press striving for liberty**

1970 **Alberto Gainza Paz,** *La Prensa* (Buenos Aires, Argentina)
1971 **No award**
1972 **Hubert Beuve-Mery,** *Le Monde* (Paris, France)
1973 **Anton Betz,** *Rheinische Post* (Dusseldorf, Federal Republic of Germany)
1974 **Julio de Mesquita Neto,** *O Estado de Sao Paolo* (Brazil)
1975 **Sang-Man Kim,** *Dong-A Ilbo* (Seoul, South Korea)
1976 **Raul Rego,** *Republica* and *A Luta* (Lisbon, Portugal)
1977 **Robert Hugh Lilley,** *Belfast Telegraph* (United Kingdom)

Golden Quill
INTERNATIONAL SOCIETY OF WEEKLY NEWSPAPERS EDITORS
c/o Dept. of Journalism, Northern Illinois University, Dekalb, Ill. 60115 (815/753-1925)

The Golden Quill award annually honors the outstanding editorial writing in a weekly newspaper in the United States. A judge or panel of judges considers editorials submitted to ISWNE on the basis both of style and the "intestinal fortitude" of the writer. A plaque is given to the winner.

1961 **Hal De Cell, editor,** *Rolling Fork* (Miss.) *Deer Creek Pilot*
1962 **Don Pease, co-editor,** *Oberlin* (Ohio) *News Tribune*
1963 **Hazel Brannon Smith,** *Lexington* (Miss.) *Advertiser*
1964 **T.M.B. Hicks,** *Dallas* (Pa.) Post
1965 **Robert E. Fisher,** *Crosset* (Ark.) *News Observer*
1966 **Owen J. McNamara, editor,** *Brookline* (Mass.) *Chronicle-Citizen*
1967 **Alvin J. Remmenga, editor,** *Cloverdale* (Calif.) *Reveille*
1968 **Henry H. Null IV,** *The Abington Journal,* (Clarks Summit, Pa.)
1969 **Dan Hicks, Jr.,** *Madisonville* (Tenn.) *Monroe County Democrat*
1970 **Richard Taylor,** *Kennett Square* (Pa.) *News and Advertiser*
1971 **Edward DeCourcy,** *Newport* (N.H.) *Argus Champion*
1972 **C. Peter Jorgensen,** *Arlington* (Mass.) *Advocate*
1973 **Robert Estabrook,** *Lakeville* (Conn.) *Journal*
1974 **Phil McLaughlin,** *Miami Republican,* (Paola, Kansas)
1975 **Betsy Cox,** *Madison County Newsweek* (Richmond, Ky.)
1976 **Peter Bodley,** *Coon Rapids Herald* (Anoka, Mont.)
1977 **Rodney A. Smith,** *Gretna* (Va.) *Gazette*

Sidney Hillman Awards
SIDNEY HILLMAN FOUNDATION
15 Union Square, New York, N.Y. 10003 (212/255-7800)

Each year the foundation awards a series of $750 prizes to honor works that support the ideals of Sidney Hillman's life, including "the protection of individual civil liberties, improved race relations, a strengthened labor movement, the advancement of social welfare and economic security, greater world understanding and related problems." Contributions may be in the fields of print or broadcast journalism or published fiction or nonfiction books, submitted for consideration by a panel of judges.

DAILY PRESS

1950 Murray Kempton, *New York Post* (Labor in the South)

A.H. Raskin, *New York Times* (Labor relations)

1951 Carl T. Rowan, *Minneapolis Tribune* (Race relations in the South)

1952 W. Horace Carter, *Labor City* (N.C.) *Tribune* (Exposing the Ku Klux Klan)

Willard G. Cole, *Whiteville* (N.C.) *News & Reporter* (Exposing the Ku Klux Klan)

Jay Jenkins, *Raleigh* (N.C.) *News and Observer* (Exposing the Ku Klux Klan)

1953 Ralph S. O'Leary, *Houston Post* (Civil liberties)

1954 Vic Reinemer, *Charlotte* (N.C.) *News* (Civil liberties and civil rights)

Daniel R. Fitzpatrick, *St. Louis Post Dispatch* (Editorial cartoons)

1955 Ben H. Bagdikian, *Providence Journal-Bulletin* (Civil liberties)

Murray Marder, *Washington Post* (Government security programs)

1956 Robert H. Spiegel, *Des Moines Tribune* (Segregation in Des Moines)

New York Times (Editorials on Middle East crisis)

1957 Harry Ashmore, *Arkansas Gazette* (Editorials on civil rights)

1958 Harry L. and Gretchen Billings, *The People's Voice*, Helena, Mont. (Editorials on civil liberties and public welfare)

Ralph McGill, *Atlanta Constitution* (Editorials defending public school system)

1959 No award

1960 Sylvan Meyer, *Gainesville* (Ga.) *Daily Times* (Editorials on race relations)

1961 Patrick J. Owens, *Pine Bluff* (Ark.) *Commercial* (Editorials on current issues)

1962 Ira Harkey, *Pascaluga* (Miss.) *Chronicle* (Editorials on the crisis at the University of Mississippi)

1963 Horance C. Davis,*Gainsville* (Fla.)*Daily Sun* (Editorials on civil rights)

1964 J.O. Emmerich, *Enterprise Journal*, McComb, Miss. (Editorials on civil rights crisis)

1965 No award

1966 Robert Keveney and Douglas Walker, *Dayton* (Ohio) *Daily News* (Articles on right wing groups)

Harrison Salisbury, *New York Times* (Reporting on North Vietnam)

1967 Howard James, *Christian Science Monitor* (Crisis in the courts)

1968 James K. Batten and Dwayne Walls, *Charlotte* (N.C.) *Observer* (For "The People Left Behind")

1969 William J. Eaton, *Chicago Daily News* (For The Appearance of Impropriety)

1970 John Kifner, *New York Times* (For reporting on the Kent State tragedy)

1971 Alfred Friendly, *Washington Post* (For "Victims of the Great American Red Hunt")

Neil Sheehan, *New York Times* (For "The Pentagon Papers")

1972 Carl Bernstein and Robert Woodward, *Washington Post* (Watergate investigation)

1973 Donald L. Barlett and James B. Steele, *Philadelphia Inquirer* (Investigative reporting)

1974 Seymour M. Hersh, *New York Times* (Reporting on the Central Intelligence Agency)

Boston Globe (Coverage of school integration crisis)

1975 Willard S. Randall and Stephen D. Solomon, *Philadelphia Inquirer* (For "54 Who Died")

1976 John Seigenthaler, *The Tennesseean*, Nashville (Courage in publishing)

1977 Stan Swofford, *Greensboro* (N.C.) *Daily News* (series on Wilmington 10 defendants)

BOOKS

1950 John Hersey, *The Wall*

1951 Alan Barth, *The Loyalty of Free Men*

1952 Herbert Block, *The Herblock Book*

1953 Theodore H. White, *Fire in the Ashes*

1954 Henry Steele Commager, *Freedom, Loyalty and Dissent*

1955 John Lord O'Brian, *National Security and Individual Freedom*

1956 Walter Gellhorn, *Individual Freedom and Governmental Restraints*

1957 Wilma Dykeman and James Stokely, *Neither Black nor White*

1958 John Kenneth Galbraith, *The Affluent Society*

1959 Harold M. Hyman, *To Try Men's Souls*

1960 Davis McEntire, *Residence and Race*

William L. Shirer, *The Rise and Fall of the Third Reich*

1961 Jane Jacobs, *Death and Life of Great American Cities*

1962 Michael Harrington, *The Other America*

1963 Richard Hofstadter, *Anti-Intellectualism in American Life*

1964 James W. Silver, *Mississippi: The Closed Society*

Bernard D. Nossiter, *The Mythmakers*

1965 Kenneth B. Clark, *Dark Ghetto*

1966 Joseph P. Lyford, *The Airtight Cage*

1967 Ronald Steel, *Pax Americana*

Alan F. Westin, *Privacy and Freedom*

1968 George R. Stewart, *Not So Rich As You Think*

1969 Rep. Richard McCarthy, *The Ultimate Folly*

1970 Ramsey Clark, *Crime in America*

1971 Morton Mintz and Jerry S. Cohen, *America, Inc.*

1972 Frances FitzGerald, *Fire In The Lake*

1973 Jervis Anderson, *A. Philip Randolph: A Biographical Portrait*

Arthur M. Schlesinger, Jr., *The Imperial Presidency*

1974 Richard J. Barnet and Ronald E. Muller, *Global Reach*

Noel Mostert, *Super Ship*

1975 E.J. Kahn, Jr., *The China Hands*

1976 Richard Kluger, *Simple Justice*

1977 Philip Caputo, *A Rumor of War*

RADIO-TELEVISION

1953 Edward R. Murrow, *See It Now*, CBS Television (Civil liberties)

Gerald W. Johnson, WAAM, Baltimore (Civil liberties)

1954 Eric Sevareid, *American Week*, CBS Television (Civil rights issues)

1955 No award

1956 No award

1957 Theodore Ayers *Face the Nation*, CBS Television (Interview with Khrushchev)

George A. Vicas *Radio Beat*, CBS Radio (Debates between Soviet and American scientists)

1958 Irving Gitlin, CBS-TV unit supervision (Especially for *Who Killed Michael Farmer?* and *P.O.W.—A Study in Survival*)

1959 Edward P. Morgan, ABC Television News WNTA-TV, New York (*Play of the Week*)

1960 Walter Peters and Marshal Diskin, ABC Television (*Cast the First Stone*)

1961 Al Wasserman and Robert Young, NBC Television White Paper (*Angola: Journey to a War*)

1962 **Warren Wallace,** WCBS-TV, New York (*Superfluous People*)
John Keats, George Dessart and David E. Wilson, WCAU-TV, Philadelphia (*Conformity*)
1963 **Millard Lampell,** CBS Television (*No Hiding Place*)
1964 **Joseph Wershba,** CBS Television (*Gideon's Trumpet: The Poor Man and The Law*)
1965 **No award**
1966 **William C. Jersey,** National·Educational Television (*A Time for Burning*)
1967 **Jay L. McMullen,** CBS Television News, (*The Tenement*)
1968 **Bill Osterhous and Dick Hubert,** Westinghouse Broadcasting Co. (*One*·*Nation Indivisible*)
1969 **Fred Freed,** NBC Television (*Who Killed Lake Erie?*)
1970 **Ronn Bonn and Walter Cronkite,** CBS Television News (*Can the World Be Saved?*)
1971 **Martin Carr,** NBC Television (*This Child is Rated X*)
1972 **Lucy Jarvis,** NBC Television (*What Price Health?*)
1973 **Paul Altmeyer,** Westinghouse Broadcasting Co. (*Freedom and Security: The Uncertain Balance*)
1974 **CBS Television Network** (*The Autobiography of Miss Jane Pittman*)
1975 **CBS Television** (*Fear on Trial*)
1976 **Paul Leaf,** NBC Television (*Judge Horton and the Scottsboro Boys*)
1977 **Bill Moyers,** CBS Television, (*The Fire Next Door*)

MAGAZINES

1950 **James H. Means,** *Atlantic Monthly* for "Doctors Lobby" and "England's Public Medicine: The Facts"
1951 **Arthur D. Mores,** *McCall's* for "Who's Trying to Ruin Our Schools?"
1952 **No award**
1953 **Joseph Wechsberg,** *The New Yorker* for "The Seventeenth of June"
1954 **Charlotte Knight,** *Collier's* for "What Price Security?"
1955 **Robert Engler,** *New Republic* for "Oil and Politics"
1956 **Robert Penn Warren,** *Life* for "Divided South Searches Its Soul"
John Fischer, *Harper's Magazine* for "The Harm Good People Do"
1957 **No award**
1958 **Giorgio De Santillana,** *The Reporter* for "Galileo and J. Robert Oppenheimer"
Harvey Swados, *The Nation* for "Myth of the Powerful Worker"
1959 **Harry W. Ernst and Charles H. Drake,** *The Nation* for "Poor, Proud and Primitive: The Lost Appalachians"
1960 **Fred J. Cook,** *The Nation* for "Gambling, Inc."
1961 **Lillian Smith,** *Redbook* for "The Ordeal of Southern Woman"
1962 **Margaret Parton,** *Ladies' Home Journal* for "Sometimes Life Just Happens"
1963 **Arnold Hano,** *Saga Magazine* for "The Burned Out Americans"
1964 **J. Robert Moskin,** *Look* for "Challenge to our Doctors"
1965 **Theodore Draper,** *Commentary* for "The Dominican Crisis—A Case Study in American Policy"
1966 **Richard Harris,** *The New Yorker* for "Medicare"
1967 **No award**
1968 **Charles and Bonnie Remsberg,** *Good Housekeeping* for "America's Hungry Families"
1969 **Daniel Lang,** *The New Yorker* for "Casualties of War"

1970 **Christopher H. Pyle,** *The Washington Monthly* for articles on army surveillance of political activity
1971 **Carolyn See, Kenneth Lasson, William Serrin, Robert Coles and Richard Todd,** *Atlantic Monthly* for "Work in America"
1972 **Frank J. Donner and Eugene Cerruti,** *The Nation* for "The Grand Jury Network"
1973 **Paul Broder,** *The New Yorker* for "Annals of Industry: Casualties of the Workplace"
Richard L. Strout, *New Republic* for columns signed "TRB"
1974 **No award**
1975 **Susan Sheehan,** *The New Yorker* for "A Welfare Mother"
1976 **Guy Neal Williams,** *Philadelphia Magazine* for "The Mushroom Pickers"
1977 **Eliot Marshall,** *New Republic* for series of higher health-care costs and inferior care

SPECIAL AWARDS

1954 **WYNC,** New York (For public service programming)
The Progressive (For special issue on Sen. Joseph McCarthy)
1973 **Aleksandr Solzhenitsyn**
WNET, New York (For outstanding programming)
1976 **Henry Steele Commager** (For lifetime contributions)
1977 **ABC Television Network** (For "Roots")

Robert F. Kennedy Journalism Awards

ROBERT F. KENNEDY JOURNALISM AWARDS COMMITTEE
1035 30th St. NW, Washington, D.C. 20007 (202/338-7444)

The Robert F. Kennedy Journalism Award(s) for Outstanding Coverage of the Problems of the Disadvantaged are given annually for outstanding print, broadcast and photographic journalism. Cash prizes of $5,000 are available, $3,000 of which can go to the grand prize winner. A panel of professional journalists in all three fields selects the recipients. (Honorable mentions and citations are not listed here.) (*Special award.)

1969 **CBS Television** (*Black History: Lost, Stolen or Strayed,* Andrew A. Rooney, producer)
WMCA-Radio, New York (Continuing special coverage of the problems of poverty and discrimination in New York City and New York State)
Nick Kotz, *Des Moines Register and Tribune* (Continuing coverage of poverty in America)
David Nevin, *Life* ("These Murdered Old Mountains")
1970 **ABC Television** (*Black Fiddler: Prejudice and the Negro,* Howard Enders, producer)
NBC Television (*Between Two Rivers* from the *First Tuesday* series; Tom Pettit, reporter; Anthony Potter, producer)
WRC-TV, Washington (*Perspective: New Set of Eyes,* Bill Leonard, producer)
WJR-Radio, Detroit (*I Am Not Alone,* Phil Jones, reporter)
Linda Rockey, *Chicago Sun-Times* (Series on the problems of hunger)
Dallas Kinney and Kent Polloc, *Palm Beach* (Fla.) *Post-Times* ("Migration to Misery" series)

Fred C. Shapiro, *The New Yorker* ("The Whitmore Confessions")

1971 NBC Television (*Migrant: An NBC White Paper,* Martin Carr, producer)
Westinghouse Broadcasting Co. (*When You Reach December*)
Ralph Looney, *Albuquerque Tribune* (Series on the Navajos)
Jerome Watson and Sam Washington, *Chicago Sun-Times* (Series on Illinois state schools for the mentally retarded)
Ruben Salazar, "Los Angeles *Times* (Columns on culture and alienation of Chicanos)
The New Thing (Washington Arts Workshop*) (*This is the Home of Mrs. Levant Graham,* Topper Carew, producer)

1972 Jon Nordheimer, *New York Times* ("From Dakto to Detroit: Death of a Troubled Hero")
Patrick Zier and Joanne Wragg, *The Lakeland* (Fla.) *Ledger* ("The Battle for Dignity")
Newsweek ("Justice on Trial," by Edward Kosner, Peter Goldman and Don Holt)
Beekman Winthrop, New South ("Worms Turn People Off")
Group W (*The Suburban Wall,* Paul Altmeyer, producer)
Doug Fox, KTOK-Radio (*The Business of Being Black* series)

1973 Joan Heller, Associated Press ("The Tuskegee Syphilis Study")
WABC-TV, New York (*Willowbrook: The Last Great Disgrace,* written and reported by Geraldo Rivera)

1974 John Guinther, *Philadelphia Magazine* ("The Only Good Indian")
Bob Dotson, WKY-TV, Oklahoma City (*Through the Looking Glass Darkly*)
Dolores Katz and Jo Thomas, *Detroit Free Press* ("Psychosurgery—On Trial")

1975 Mike Masterson, *"Hot Springs* (Ark.) *Sentinal Record* (Features, editorials and columns on poverty and discrimination)
Loretta Schwartz, *Philadelphia Magazine* ("Nothing to Eat")
Martin Berman, Peter Lance and Geraldo Rivera, WABC-TV, New York (*The Willowbrook Case: The People vs. the State of New York*)
Terence Gurley, WWVA-Radio, Wheeling, W. Va. (*Back to Bloody Harlan*)

1976 Gene Miller, *Miami Herald* (Coverage of the Pitts-Lee Case)
Michael O'Brien, *Miami News* ("John Madden: His Last Days," photojournalistic coverage)
Tom Pettit, NBC-TV News (*Feeding the Poor*)
Bob Cain and Cathleen Gurley, WWVA-Radio, Wheeling, W. Va. (*Care and Feeding of America*)
The Cavalier Daily, University of Virginia (*Benign Neglect*)

1977 Acel Moore and Wendell Rawls, *Philadelphia Inquirer* (Series on Farview State Hospital)
Evan White, KGO-TV, San Francisco ("Tenderloin Old Folks")

Liebling Award

MORE MAGAZINE
40 W. 57th St., New York, N.Y. 10019 (212/757-3040)

The A.J. Liebling Award, which consists of a plaque, is given every year for career achievement in reporting or journalism over a long period. The editors of *More* select the recipient.

1972 I.F. Stone
1973 Homer Bigart, *New York Times*
1974 Morton Mintz, *Washington Post*
1975 Studs Terkel
1976 *60 Minutes,* CBS
1977 Murray Kempton *New York Post*

Lifeline Award

AMERICAN HEALTH FOUNDATION
1370 Ave. of the Americas, New York, N.Y. 10019
(212/489-8700)

The Lifeline Award, which consists of a plaque, honors the journalist whose feature article or broadcast is judged by a committee of the Public Health Action Group of the AHF to have contributed most to enhancing public awareness of the value of preventive medicine.

1977 Jane Brody, *New York Times*
Frank Field, NBC-TV

National Magazine Awards

COLUMBIA UNIVERSITY
Graduate School of Journalism, New York, N.Y. 10027
(212/280-3828)

The National Magazine Awards, which consist of a silver plaque and a reproduction of an Alexander Calder stabile Elephant annually honor editorial excellence and innovation in several categories. All regularly published magazines in the United States may enter upon payment of a $75 entry fee for consideration by a twenty-judge panel comprised of persons chosen by the university from the magazine industry and journalism educators.

NATIONAL MAGAZINE AWARD
(one award through 1969)
1966 *Look*
1967 *Life*
1968 *Newsweek*
1969 *American Machinist*

PUBLIC SERVICE
1970 *Life*
1971 *The Nation*
1972 *Philadelphia*
1973 No award
1974 *Scientific American*
1975 *Consumer Reports*
1976 *Business Week*
1977 *Philadelphia*

GENERAL EXCELLENCE
(given once)
1973 *Business Week*

SPECIALIZED JOURNALISM
1970 *Philadelphia*
1971 *Rolling Stone*
1972 *Architectural Record*
1973 *Psychology Today*

1974 *Texas Monthly*
1975 *Medical Economics*
1976 *United Mine Workers' Journal*
1977 *Architectural Record*

VISUAL EXCELLENCE
1970 *Look*
1971 *Vogue*
1972 *Esquire*
1973 *Horizon*
1974 *Newsweek*
1975 *Country Journal*
      National Lampoon
1976 *Horticulture*
1977 *Rolling Stone*

FICTION, CRITICISM AND BELLES LETTRES
1970 *Redbook*
1971 *Esquire*
1972 *Mademoiselle*
1973 *Atlantic Monthly*
1974 *The New Yorker*
1975 *Redbook*
1976 *Essence*
1977 *Mother Jones*

REPORTING EXCELLENCE
1970 *The New Yorker*
1971 *Atlantic Monthly*
1972 *Atlantic Monthly*
1973 *New York*
1974 *The New Yorker*
1975 *The New Yorker*
1976 *Audubon*
1977 *Audubon*

SERVICE TO THE INDIVIDUAL
1974 *Sports Illustrated*
1975 *Esquire*
1976 *Modern Medicine*
1977 *Harper's*

AOA Journalism Awards
AMERICAN OSTEOPATHIC ASSOCIATION
212 E. Ohio St., Chicago, Ill. 60611 (312/944-2713)

The AOA Journalism Awards, which include $500 or $1,000 cash, are given each year for the best article or broadcast on osteopathic medicine to the scientific community and the general public. Entries may be submitted for consideration by a panel of professional journalists.

1963 **Theodore Berland,** Freelance
      A.L. Schafer, Freelance
      Don Walton, *Lincoln Star*
1964 **Dominic Crolla,** *Tucson Daily Citizen*
      Jerry Flemmons, *Fort Worth Star-Telegram*
      James Koethe, *Dallas Times-Herald*
1965 **John Langone,** *Boston Herald*
      Herschel Fink, *Flint Journal*
      Armand Gebert, *Detroit News*
1966 N.A.
1967 **Virginia Turner,** *El Paso Post*
      Jean Pearson, *Detroit News*
      Joe Western, *National Observer*
1968 **Jon McConal,** *Fort Worth Star-Telegram*
      Warren Koon, *Charleston* (S.C.) *Evening Post*

1969 **Paula Gilliland,** *Newark Star Ledger*
      Sue Ann Wood, *St. Louis Globe-Democrat*
      Al Pagel, *Miami Herald*
1970 **Ruth Winter,** Freelance
      Kenneth Levy, *Newark Star-Ledger*
1971 **Lew Larkin,** *Kansas City Star*
      Frank Carey, Freelance
1972 **Judy Hamilton,** *Tampa Times*
      Jeff Holladay, *Daily Oklahoman*
      Kathleen Cochran, Freelance
1973 **Joan Osterhoudt,** *Newark Star-Ledger*
      Marilyn Drago, *Tucson Star*
1974 **Podine Schoenberger,** *New Orleans Times-Picayune*
      Patricia McCarron, *St. Louis Post-Dispatch*
      Betty Walker, Freelance
1975 **Fraser Kent,** *Miami Herald*
      Fabia Mahoney, *Camden Courier-Post*
      Lee Linder, *Associated Press*
1976 **Elinor Benedict,** *Kettering Oakwood Times* (Ohio)
      Herbert Deneberg, Freelance
      Frank Dineen, Freelance
      Carol Langston, *Daily Oklahoman*
1977 **Chuck Radis,** Freelance
      Jon McConal, *Fort Worth Star-Telegram*
      Michael McKeating, *Buffalo Evening News*

Overseas Press Club Awards:
Cartoon Award
Bache Award
Robert Capa Gold Medal
Bob Considine Award
Madeline Dane Ross Award
OVERSEAS PRESS CLUB
55 E. 42nd St., New York, N.Y. 10017 (212/687-2430)

Annual awards in news reporting from abroad in print, broadcast and photographic journalism are based on selection by a panel of judges who are experts in the field. The awards originated as an almost spontaneous gesture to honor the work of journalists covering World War II.

DAILY NEWSPAPER OR WIRE SERVICE REPORTING FROM ABROAD (Hal Boyle Award)
1940 **Leland Stowe,** *Chicago Daily News* and *New York Post*
1941 **Cyrus L. Sulzberger,** *New York Times* (Europe)
      Ottos D. Tolichus, *New York Times* (Far East)
1942 **No award**
1943 **No award**
1944 **No award**
1945 **Drew Middleton,** *New York Times* (Berlin)
      Frank Robertson, International News Service (Tokyo)
1947 **A.T. Steele,** *New York Herald Tribune*
1948 **Harold Callender,** *New York Times*
1949 **Joseph Newman,** *New York Herald Tribune*
1950 **Homer Bigart,** *New York Herald Tribune*
      Hal Boyle, AP war reporting
1951 **Cyrus L. Sulzberger,** *New York Times*
1952 **Homer Bigart,** *New York Herald Tribune*
1953 **Joseph and Stewart Alsop,** *New York Herald Tribune*
1954 *New York Times*

1955 Clifton Daniel, *New York Times*
1956 Barrett McGurn, *New York Herald Tribune*
1957 Bob Considine, Frank Coniff and William Randolph Hearst, Jr., Hearst Newspapers
1958 Bob Considine, Hearst Newspapers
1959 A.M. Rosenthal, *New York Times*
1960 Lynn Heinzerling, Associated Press
1961 Bob Considine, Hearst Newspapers
1962 Andrew C. Borowiec, Associated Press
1963 Malcolm Browne, Associated Press
1964 Saul Pett, Associated Press
1965 Richard Critchfield, *Washington Star*
1966 Hugh Mulligan, Associated Press
1967 Joe Alex Morris, Jr., *Los Angeles Times*
1968 Peter Rehak, Associated Press
1969 William K. Tuohy, *Los Angeles Times*
1970 John Hughes, *Christian Science Monitor*
1971 Sydney Schanberg, *New York Times*
1972 Charlotte Saikowski, *Christian Science Monitor*
1973 Raymond R. Coffey, *Chicago Daily News*
1974 Robert Kaiser, *Washington Post*
1975 Sydney H. Schanberg, *New York Times*
1976 Edward Cody, Associated Press
1977 Robert C. Toth, *Los Angeles Times*

PHOTOGRAPHS, DAILY NEWSPAPER OR WIRE SERVICE

1948 Jack Birns, *Life*
1949 Henri Cartier-Bresson, Magnum Photos
1950 David Douglas Duncan, *Life*
1951 Frank Noel, Associated Press
1952 David Douglas Duncan, *Life*
1953 Michael Rougier, *Life*
1954 *Life*
1955 Henri Cartier-Bresson, Magnum Photos
1956 John Sadovy, *Life*
1957 No award
1958 Andrew St. George, Freelance in *Life*
1959 Henri Cartier-Bresson, *Life*
1960 Yasushi Nagao, United Press International
1961 Peter Leibing, Associated Press
1962 Hector Rondon, Associated Press
1963 Henri Cartier-Bresson, Magnum Photos
1964 Akihiko Okamura, *Life*
1965 Kyoichi Sawada, United Press International
1966 Kyoichi Sawada, United Press International
1967 Peter Skingley, United Press International
1968 Edward T. Adams, Associated Press
1969 Horst Faas, Associated Press
1970 Dennis Cook, United Press International
1971 *New York Times*
1972 Huynh Cong Ut, Associated Press
1973 Sydney Schanberg, *New York Times*
1974 Ovie Carter, *Chicago Tribune*

BEST PHOTOGRAPHIC REPORTING FROM ABROAD

1976 K. Kenneth Paik, *Kansas City Times*
1977 James Peter Blair, *National Geographic*

PHOTOGRAPHS, IN A MAGAZINE OR BOOK

1966 Marc Riboud, Magnum
1967 Lee Lockwood, Black Star Publishing
1968 David Robison and (posthumously) Priva Ramrahka, *Life;* Romano Cagnoni *Life*
1969 Marc Riboud, *Look*
1970 Larry Burrows, *Life* (posthumously)
1971 Frank Fischbeck, *Life*
1972 Thomas J. Abercrombie, *National Geographic*

1973 *Life Special Report*
1974 Eddie Adams, *Time*
1975 Eddie Adams, *Time*
1976 Robert W. Madden and W.E. Garrett, *National Geographic*
1977 No award

OPC PRESIDENT'S AWARD

1956 Endre Marton, Associated Press
1968 The newsmen of Czechoslovakia, all media
1969 Neil A. Armstrong
1972 International Committee to Free Journalists held in Southeast Asia
1974 Lowell Thomas
1976 Don Bolles (posthumous)
1977 Donald Woods

The overseas Press Club cash award honoring the best cartoon on foreign affairs was originally a $500 prize sponsored by three organizations. Currently, it has been dropped to $150, which is donated by the *New York Daily News.*

1968 Don Wright, *Miami News*
1969 Paul F. Conrad, Register and Tribune Syndicate
1970 Tom Darcy, *Newsday*
1971 Don Wright, *Miami News*
1972 Tom Darcy, *Newsday*
1973 Warren King, *New York Daily News*
1974 Tony Auth, *Philadelphia Inquirer*
1975 Tony Auth, *Philadelphia Inquirer*
1976 Warren King, *New York Daily News*
1977 Ed Fisher, *Omaha (Neb.) World Herald*

A $500 award, called the E.W. Fairchild Award until 1969 and the Bache Award since 1970, is given each year for the best business reporting from abroad.

1959 Peter Weaver, McGraw-Hill World News
1960 Edwin L. Dale, Jr., *New York Times*
1961 Edwin L. Dale, Jr., *New York Times*
1962 Joseph A. Livingston, *Philadelphia Bulletin*
1963 Ray Vicker, *Wall Street Journal*
1964 Don C. Winston, *McGraw-Hill*
1965 Bernard D. Nossiter, *Washington Post*
1966 Lawrence Malkin, Associated Press
1967 Ray Vicker, *Wall Street Journal*
1968 Clyde Farnsworth, *New York Times*
1969 Philip W. Whitcomb, *Christian Science Monitor*
1970 Leonard S. Silk, *New York Times*
1971 Clyde Farnsworth, Hy Maidenberg, Brendan Jones, Edward Cowan, Takashi Oka, *New York Times*
1972 Bob Wicker, editor; George Eberl, Ed Reavis, Ken Loomis, Jim Cole, Regis Bossu, Peter Jaeger, *Stars and Stripes* (European Edition)
1973 Ronald Koven and David B. Ottaway, *Washington Post*
1974 Philip W. Whitcomb, *Christian Science Monitor*
1975 J.A. Livingston, McGraw Hill, *Business Week*
1976 Alfred Zanker, *U.S. News & World Report*
1977 Carey Reich, *Institutional Investor*

The Robert Capa Gold Medal, named after *Life* photographer, recognizes superlative photography requiring exceptional courage and enterprise abroad.

1955 Howard Sochurek, Magnum Photos, in *Life*
1956 John Sadovy, *Life*
1957 No award
1958 Paul Bruck, CBS

1959 Mario Biasetti, CBS
1960 Yung Su Kwon, NBC
1961 No award
1962 Peter and Klaus, Dehmel, NBC
1963 Larry Burrows, *Life*
1964 Horst Faas, AP
1965 Larry Burrows, *Life*
1966 Henri Huet, AP
1967 David Douglas Duncan, *Life* and ABC
1968 John Olson, *Life*
1969 Anonymous Czech photographer
1970 Kyoichi Sawada, UPI (posthumously)
1971 Larry Burrows, *Life* (posthumously)
1972 Clive W. Limpkin, of London (book, *Battle of Bogside*, Penguin Books)
1973 David Burnett, Raymond Depardon and Charles Gerretsen, Gamma Presse Images
1974 W. Eugene Smith, *Camera 35*
1975 Dick Halstead, *Time*
1976 Catherine Leroy, Gamma, photos in *Time*
1977 Eddie Adams, Associated Press

RADIO AND/OR TV

1941 Cecil Brown, MBS
1947 Merrill Mueller, NBC
1948 Henry Cassidy, NBC
1949 William R. Downs, CBS
1950 Howard K. Smith, CBS
1951 Howard K. Smith, CBS
1952 Howard K. Smith, CBS
1953 Howard K. Smith, CBS
1954 Columbia Broadcasting System
1955 David Schoenbrun, CBS
1956 Irving R. Levine, NBC
1957 Frank Kearns and Yussef Masraff, CBS
1958 Winston Burdett, CBS
1959 Columbia Broadcasting System

RADIO

1960 Edwin Newman, NBC
1961 Marvin Kalb, CBS
1962 Sidney Lazard, ABC
1963 George Clay, NBC
1964 Dean Brelis, NBC
1965 Richard Valeriani, NBC
1966 Sam Jaffe, ABC
1967 Don North, ABC
1968 Bernard Redmont, Group W, Westinghouse
1969 Steve Bell, ABC
1970 Lou Cioffi, ABC; and Emerson Stone, director, with Gerald Miller (posthumously), John Laurence, Ike Pappas, William Plante, John Sheahan, Richard Threlkeld, and Don Webster, CBS team
1971 Emerson Stone, director, with Thomas Fenton, John Laurence, William Plante, Bert Quint, Don Webster and Ernest Weatherall, CBS team
1972 Heywood Hale Broun, John Laurence, Dave Marash, Bruno Wessertheil, Bill McLaughlin, Mitchell Krauss, CBS team
1973 Gene Pell, director, with Jay Bushinsky, Koe Kamalick, Asher Wall, Bernard Redmont, Charles Bierbauer, Ed De Fontaine, Jim Anderson, Jerry Udwin, Group W Westinghouse team
1974 Sam Cioffi and seventeen correspondents, ABC News team
1975 Ed Bradley, Peter Collins, Bruce Dunning, Brian Ellis, Murray Fromson, Bill Plante, Bob Simon, Richard Threlked, Eric Cavaliero and Mike Snitowsky, CBS team

1976 William Blakemore, John Cooley, Charles Glass and Jerry King, ABC team
Mike Lee and Doug Tunnell, CBS team

RADIO INTERPRETATION OF FOREIGN NEWS
(Lowell Thomas Award)

1977 Clark Tood, NBC

TELEVISION REPORTING

1949 Ernest K. Lindley, Dumont
1950 Howard K. Smith, CBS
1951 Edward R. Murrow, CBS
1952 Edward R. Murrow, CBS
1953 Edward R. Murrow, CBS
1955 *See It Now*, CBS
1955 Edward R. Murrow, CBS
1956 See above: Radio or TV
1957 See above: Radio or TV
1958 See above: Radio or TV
1959 See above: Radio or TV
1960 Columbia Broadcasting System
1961 Helen Jean Rogers and William Hartigan, ABC
1962 NBC News
1963 Peter Kalischer, CBS
1964 Frank Bourgholtzer, NBC
1965 Morley Safer, CBS
1966 Morley Safer, CBS
1967 Ted Yates, NBC
1968 Liz Trotta, NBC
1969 Don Baker, ABC
1970 Kenley Jones, NBC
1971 Phil Brady, NCB
1972 Bob Simon, correspondent, Norman Lloyd, cameraman, Mai Van Duc, cameraman, CBS News team
1973 John Laurence, CBS
1974 Lou Cioffi, ABC
1975 Bruce Dunning, correspondent; Mike Marriott, cameraman; Mai Van Duc, soundman, CBS team
1976 Mike Lee, CBS

BEST RADIO DOCUMENTARY ON FOREIGN AFFAIRS

1971 John Rich, NBC
1972 Ramsey Clark, ABC Radio News
1973 Peter Wells, producer, Reid Collins, correspondent, CBS News
1974 Ted Koppel, ABC News

BEST TV DOCUMENTARY ON FOREIGN AFFAIRS

1971 George Watson and Ernest Pendrell, ABC
1972 Elmer Lower, Charles Murphy, John Sherman, ABC team
1973 Harry Reasoner, ABC
1974 Bill McLaughlin, CBS News

BEST TV INTERPRETATION
(Edward R. Murrow Award)

1977 Barbara Walters, ABC

BEST MAGAZINE REPORTING FROM ABROAD

1955 Theodore H. White, *Collier's*
1956 Flora Lewis, *New York Times Magazine*
1957 James Michener, *Reader's Digest*
1958 Joseph Kraft, in *Saturday Evening Post*
1959 George Bailey, *The Reporter*
1960 *The Reporter*
1961 Charles J. V. Murphy, *Fortune*
1962 Robert Kaiser, Time-Life News Service
1963 Laura Bergquist, *Look*
1964 *Sports Illustrated*

1965 Michael Mok and Paul Schutzer, *Life*
1966 Sybille Bedford, *Saturday Evening Post*
1967 Linda Grant Martin, *New York Times Magazine*
1968 J. Robert Moskin, *Look*
1969 Christopher Wren, *Look*
1970 Robert Shaplen, *The New Yorker*
1971 Arnaud de Borchgrave, *Newsweek*
1972 Joseph Kraft, *The New Yorker*
1973 Anthony Bailey, *The New Yorker*
1974 Frances FitzGerald, *Harper's Magazine*
1975 John J. Putnam, *National Geographic*
1976 Barry Came, Tony Clifton, Loren Jenkins and William Schmidt, *Newsweek*

BEST MAGAZINE INTERPRETATION OF FOREIGN AFFAIRS

1977 Joseph B. Treaster, *Atlantic Monthly*

MOTION PICTURES

1956 Gerhard Schwartzkopff, CBS
1957 See below: Still or Motion Pictures
1958 Joseph Oexle, NBC
1959 Henry Toluzzi, NBC
1960 Yung Su Kwon, NBC
1961 Leonard Stark and Nobuo Hoshi, NBC
1962 NBC News
1963 Columbia Broadcasting System
1964 No award

STILL OR MOTION PICTURES

1957 Lisa Larsen, Free lance, in *Life*

BEST REPORTING ORIGINATING IN U.S. OR U.N. ON WORLD AFFAIRS

1954 James Reston, *New York Times*
1955 John Daly, CBS

BEST REPORTING INVOLVING PERSONS, PLACES OR THINGS, BEYOND THE 48 STATES

1956 *Sports Illustrated*

BEST INTERPRETATION OF FOREIGN AFFAIRS DAILY NEWSPAPER OR WIRE SERVICE

1947 Anne O'Hare McCormick, *New York Times*
1948 James Reston, *New York Times*
1949 Joseph and Stewart Alsop, *New York Herald Tribune*
1950 James Reston, *New York Times*
1951 Joseph and Stewart Alsop, *New York Herald Tribune*
1952 James Reston, *New York Times*
1953 Walter Lippmann, *New York Herald Tribune*
1954 *New York Times*
1955 Walter Lippmann. *New York Herald Tribune*
1956 See below: All Media
1957 Ernest K. Lindley *Newsweek*
1958 Graham Hovey, *Minneapolis Star and Tribune*
1959 Walter Lippmann, *New York Herald Tribune*
1960 Robert Hewett, *Minneapolis Star and Tribune*
1961 Phil Newsom, United Press International
1962 Flora Lewis, *Washington Post*
1963 Louis K. Rukeyser, *Baltimore Sun*
1964 Max Frankel, *New York Times*
1965 Jack Foisie, *Los Angeles Times*
1966 Robert S. Elegant, *Los Angeles Times*
1967 Michael R. McGrady, *Newsday*
      R. W. Apple. Jr., *New York Times*
1968 Robert S. Elegant, *Los Angeles Times*
      Stanley Karnow, *Washington Post*

1969 Max Frankel, *New York Times*
1970 Harrison E. Salisbury, *New York Times*
1971 Robert S. Elegant, *Los Angeles Times*
1972 William L. Ryan, Associated Press
1973 Al Burt, *Miami Herald;*
      William Montalbano, *Miami Herald*
1974 Donald L. Barlett and James B. Steele, *Philadelphia Inquirer*
1975 Joseph C. Harsch, *Christian Science Monitor*
1976 Flora Lewis, *New York Times*
1977 Michael Robersteen, *Minneapolis Tribune*

RADIO

1947 Edward R. Murrow, CBS
1948 Elmer Davis, ABC
1949 See below: Radio or TV
1950 Edward R. Murrow, CBS
1951 Elmer Davis, ABC
1952 Elmer Davis, ABC
1953 Elmer Davis, ABC
1954 CBS World News Roundup
1955 Eric Sevareid. CBS
1956 See below: All Media
1957
1958
1959 } See below: Radio or TV
1960
1961 Howard K. Smith, CBS
1962 Alexander Kendrick, CBS
1963 Phil Clarke, MBS
1964 Bill Sheehan, ABC
1965 Edward P. Morgan, ABC
1966 NBC News
1967 Welles Hangen and James Robinson, NBC
1968 Elie Abel, NBC
1969 Alexander Kendrick, CBS
1970 Peter Burns, Kenley Jones, Bob Green, Phil Brady, Lou Davis, Robert Goralski NBC Team
1971 James Quigley, producer; Wilson Hall, anchorman NBC Team
1972 John Chancellor, NBC
1973 Dan Rather, Marvin Kalb, Bob Schieffer, CBS Team
1974 John Chancellor, NBC
1975 Charles P. Arnot, ABC Radio News; Steve Bell, ABC cameraman (posthumous); Lou Cioffi, ABC: John Grimes, American Information Radio Network; Peter Jennings, ABC; Ted Koppel, ABC; Mike Stein , executive producer, and George Watson, ABC, on ABC News
      Morton Dean, CBS News; correspondents Murray Fromson, Bill Plante and Richard Threlkeld; Marvin Kalb; John Lawrence; Ike Papps and Robert Pierpoint, White House correspondent, CBS News
1976 Charles Collingwood, anchorman; Jonathan Ward, producer, Frank Delecki and Norman Morris CBS News

BEST RADIO SPOT FROM ABROAD (Ben Graver Award)

1977 Reid Collins, Tom Fenton, Christopher Glen, Mike Lee, Bob McNamara, Burt Quint, John Sheehan, Bob Simon, Doug Tunnell and Bruno Wassertheil, CBS Team

RADIO OR TELEVISION

1949 Edward R. Murrow, CBS

1950
1951
1952 } See above: Radio
1953
1954
1955
1956 See below: All Media
1957 **Chet Huntley**, NBC
1958 **Chet Huntley**, NBC
1959 **Quincy Howe**, ABC
1960 **Chet Huntley**, NBC

TELEVISION

1961 **David Schoenbrun**, CBS
1962 **Columbia Broadcasting System**
1963 **Fred Freed**, NBC
1964 **Marvin Kalb**, CBS
1965 **Fred Freed**, NBC
1966 **Howard K. Smith**, ABC
1967 **Eric Sevareid**, CBS
1968 **Charles Collingwood**, CBS
1969 **Elie Abel, Dean Brelis, Wilson Hall, George Murray**, NBC Team
1970 **Ted Koppel**, ABC
1971 **John Hart**, CBS
1973 **Helen Marmor**, producer; **Edwin Newman**, anchorman; and seventeen correspondents, NBC team
1974 **John Palmer, Tom Streithorst, Phil Brady, Liz Trotta**, NBC Nightly News Team
1975 **Bill Seamans and Howard K. Smith**, ABC
1976 **John Chancellor**, anchorman, and **Dan O'Connor**, producer, NBC News
1977 **Barbara Walters**, ABC News

ALL MEDIA

1956 **Cecil Brown**, NBC

MAGAZINE (Mary Hemingway Award)

1964 **Norman Cousins**, *Saturday Review*
1965 **A.M. Rosenthal**, *New York Times Magazine*
1966 **Eric Sevareid**, *Look*
1967 **Frances FitzGerald**, *Atlantic Monthly*
1968 **James C. Thomson, Jr.**, *Atlantic Monthly*
1969 **Carl Rowan**, *Reader's Digest*
     Norman Cousins, *Saturday Review* and *Look*
1970 **Anthony Lewis**, *New York Times Magazine*
1971 **John L. Cobbs and Gordon L. Williams**, *Business Week*
1972 **James A. Michener**, *New York Times Magazine*
1973 **Edward R.F. Sheehan**, *New York Times Magazine*
1974 **Robert Shaplen**, *New Yorker*
1975 **Arnaud de Borchgrave**, *Newsweek*
1976 **Robert Shaplen**, *The New Yorker*
1977 **James Pringle, Elizabeth Peer, Arnaud de Bouchgarve and Kim Willenson**, *Newsweek*

BOOK (Cornelius Ryan Award)

1957 **David Schoenbrun**, *As France Goes*
1958 **John Gunther**, *Inside Russia Today*
1959 **Cornelius Ryan**, *The Longest Day*
1960 **William L. Shirer**, *The Rise and Fall of the Third Reich*
1961 **John Toland**, *But Not in Shame*
1962 **Seymour Freidin**, *The Forgotten People*
1963 **Dan Kurzman**, *Subversion of the Innocents*
1964 **Robert Trumbull**, *The Scrutable East*
1965 **Robert Shaplen**, *The Last Revolution*
1966 **Welles Hangen**, *The Muted Revolution*
1967 **George F. Kennan**, *Memoirs, 1925-1950*
1968 **George W. Ball**, *The Discipline of Power*

1969 **Townsend Hoopes**, *The Limits of Intervention*
1970 **John Toland**, *The Rising Sun*
1971 **Anthony Austin**, *The President's War*
1972 **David Halberstam**, *The Best and the Brightest*
1973 **C. L. Sulzberger**, *An Age of Mediocrity*
1974 **Cornelius Ryan**, *A Bridge Too Far*
1975 **Phillip Knightley**, *The First Casualty*
1976 **John Toland**, *Adolph Hitler*
1977 **David McCullough**, *The Path Between the Seas*

The Bob Considine Award, which carries a $1,000 stipend from King Features, is given for reporting from abroad in any medium that required exceptional courage and initiative.

1975 **Sydney Schanberg**, *New York Times*
1976 **Robin Wright**, *Christian Science Monitor*
1977 **Jim Hoagland**, *Washington Post*

SUPPLEMENTARY AWARDS

1940 **Halbert Abend**, *New York Times*
     Edward R. Murrow, CBS

SPECIAL AWARDS

1961 **Robert Fuoss**, *Saturday Evening Post;*
     John Denson, *New York Herald Tribune*, for new and original concepts in the field of communication of ideas
1964 **John Scali**, ABC News, for outstanding journalistic achievement
     Station KTLA-TV, Los Angeles, and **Baldwin Baker, Jr.** for outstanding journalistic achievement
1965 **David Sarnoff**
1966 **Henry R. Luce**

The $350 Madeline Dane Ross Award honors international reporting showing a concern for humanity.

1973 **Robert Northshield and Vo Huynh**, NBC
1974 **K. Kenneth Paik and Harry Jones, Jr.**, *Kansas City Times*
1975 **Mayo Moh**, *Time*
1976 **June Goodwin**, *Christian Science Monitor*
1977 **Reza Baraheni**

First Prize

DREW PEARSON FOUNDATION
1156 15th St. NW, Washington, D.C. 20005 (202/293-2240)

The $5,000 First Prize is awarded annually on a vote of the board of directors to recognize excellence in investigative journalism.

1971 **Neil Sheehan**, *New York Times* (Pentagon Papers)
1972 **Robert Woodward and Carl Bernstein**, *Washington Post* (Watergate)
1973 **Jerry Landauer**, *Wall Street Journal* (Vice President Spiro Agnew)
1974 **Richard E. Cady, William E. Anderson and Harley Bierce**, *Indianapolis News* (Police corruption)
1975 **No award**
1976 **Seymour Hersh**, *New York Times* (Central Intelligence Agency)
1977 **No award**

Penney-Missouri Magazine Awards
Penney-Missouri Newspaper Awards

PENNEY-MISSOURI JOURNALISM AWARDS PROGRAM
University of Missouri, 213 Walter Williams Hall, Columbia, Mo. 65201 (314/882-7771)

The Penney-Missouri Newspaper Awards are given annually for excellence in reporting and editing stories on people and lifestyles in community, daily and weekly newspapers in the United States. The first-place winners, indicated below, receive a $1,000 cash award, a medallion and a certificate. Runnerup cash prizes are also given. A screening committee narrows down entries for an eight-judge committee, which makes the final selection.

CLASS I (Small circulation)

1960 Carol Black and Ann DeLeo, *Middleton* (N.Y.) *Daily Record*
1961 Dorothy Clifford, *Tallahassee* (Fla.) *Democrat*
1962 Dorothy-Ann Flor, *Pompano Beach* (Fla.) *Sun-Sentinel*
1963 Anne Rowe, *St. Petersburg* (Fla.) *Independent*
1964 Florence Burge, *Reno* (Nev.) *Evening Gazette*
1965 Helen Cheney, *Salisbury* (N.C.) *Post*
1966 Marilyn Reynolds, *Yakima* (Wash,) *Daily Republic*
1967 Dorothy-Ann Flor, *Lakeland* (Fla.) *Ledger*
1968 Betty Danfield, *The Paper,* (Oshkosh, Wisc.)
1969 Betty Danfield, *The Paper,* (Oshkosh, Wisc.)
1970 Mary Bach, *Scottsdale* (Ariz.) *Progress*
1971 Betty Ann Raymond, *Montana Standard* (Butte)
1972 Lucille Kahn, *Melbourne* (Fla.) *Times*
1973 Lucille Kahn, *Melbourne* (Fla.) *Times*
1974 Pat Haley, *Keene* (N.H.) *Sentinel*
1975 Gloria Bledsoe, *Salem* (Ore.) *Capitol Journal*
1976 Joyce Gabriel, Westchester-Rockland (N.Y.) Newspapers
1977 Kathryn W. Foster, *Greenville* (S.C.) *Piedmont*

CLASS II (Medium circulation)

1960 Margaret W. Claiborne, *Charlotte* (N.C.) *News*
1961 Margaret W. Claiborne, *Charlotte* (N.C.) *News*
1962 Edee Green, *Fort Lauderdale* (Fla.) *News*
1963 Marj Heyduck, *Dayton* (Ohio) *Journal-Herald*
1964 Marie Saulsbury, *San Bernardino* (Calif.) *Daily Sun*
1965 William Wundram, *Davenport* (Iowa) *Times-Democrat*
1966 Gloria Briggs, *Today* (Cocoa, Fla.)
1967 Arlene Alligood, *Suffolk Sun* (Deer Park, N.Y.)
1968 Kathryn Robinette, *Palm Beach* (Fla.) *Post-Times*
1969 Beryl Ann Brownell, *Gary* (Ind.) *Post-Tribune*
1970 Gloria Biggs, *Today* (Cocoa, Fla.)
1971 Betty Danfield, *Riverside* (Calif.) *Press-Enterprise*
1972 Jan Monahan, *Pompano Beach* (Fla.) *Sentinel Sun*
1973 Mary Ann Hill, *Today* (Cocoa, Fla.)
1974 Clara Trampe, *Rockland County* (N.Y.) *Journal-News*
1975 George M. Pica, *Eugene* (Ore.) *Register-Guard*
1976 George M. Pica, *Eugene* (Ore.) *Register-Guard*
1977 William Wundram, *Quad-City Times* (Davenport, Iowa)

CLASS III (Large circulation)

1960 Marie Anderson, *Miami Herald*
1961 Marie Anderson, *Miami Herald*
1962 Nancy Taylor, *Miami News*
1963 Billie O'Day, *Miami News*
1964 Marie Anderson, *Miami Herald*
1965 Aileen Ryan, *Milwaukee Journal*
1966 Lou Schwartz, *Newsday* (Garden City, N.Y.)
1967 Madeleine McDermott, *Houston Chronicle*
1968 Marilyn Gardner, *Milwaukee Journal*
1969 Marie Anderson, *Miami Herald*
1970 Marie Anderson, *Miami Herald*
1971 Carol Sutton, *Louisville Courier-Journal*
1972 Marion Purcelli, *Chicago Tribune*
1973 Nan Trent, *Christian Science Monitor*
1974 Buddy Martin, *St. Petersburg Times*
1975 James McGuire, *Des Moines Register*
1976 Mary Mills, *Fort Lauderdale* (Fla.) *News*
1977 Joyce Gabriel, *Akron* (Ohio) *Beacon-Journal*

CLASS IV (weeklies)

1961 Rosemary Madison, *Dundee Sun* (Omaha, Neb).
1962 Ethel Taylor, *Van Nuys* (Calif.) *News*
1963 Marianne Scott, *Arlington Heights* (Ill.) *Herald*
1964 Thelma Barrios, *San Fernando Valley* (Calif.) *Sun*
1965 Ethel Taylor, *Van Nuys* (Calif.) *News*
1966 Marianne Scott, *Arlington Heights* (Ill.) *Herald*
1967 Judy Flander, *Coalinga* (Calif.) *Record*
1968 Marianne Scott, *Arlington Heights* (Ill.) *Herald*
1969 Sandra Wesley, *Boca Raton* (Fla.) *News*
1970 Ann Clevenger, *Encinitas* (Calif.) *Coast Dispatch*
1971 Anita Richwine, *Kettering-Oakwood* (Ohio) *Times*
1972 Alice Snyder, *Glenview Announcements* (Wilmette, Ill.)
1973 Kristy Montee, *Southfield* (Miss.) *Eccentric*
1974 Jennifer Frosh, *Montgomery County Sentinel* (Rockville, Md.)
1975 Peter Cox, *Maine Times*
1976 Suzanne Ashmun, *Gresham* (Ore) *Outlook*
1977 Andy Zipser, *Port Jefferson* (N.Y.) *Record*

FASHION REPORTING (no circulation limit)

1960 Eleni Epstein, *Washington Star*
1961 Jean Cameron, *Chicago American*
1962 Graydon Heartsill, *Dallas Times Herald*
1963 Yvonne Petrie, *Detroit News*
1964 Ruth Wagner, *Washington Post*
1965 Anne Lee Singletary, *Twin City Sentinel* (Winston-Salem, N.C.)
1966 Marian Christy, *Boston Globe*
1967 Vivian Kawatzky, *Milwaukee Sentinel*
1968 Marian Christy, *Boston Globe*
1969 Marji Kunz, *Detroit Free Press*
1970 Marian Christy, *Boston Globe*
1971 Ruth Hawkins, *Norfolk* (Va.) *Ledger-Star*
1972 Jo Werne, *Miami Herald*
1973 Carol Sutton, *Louisville* (Ky.) *Courier-Journal*
1974 Judy Lunn, *Houston Post*
1975 Betty Ommerman, *Newsday* (Garden City, N.Y.)
1976 Marji Kunz, *Detroit Free Press*
1977 Eva Hodges, *Denver Post*

REPORTING-WRITING (no circulation limit)

1964 Dorothy Brant Brazier, *Seattle Times*
1965 Lois Hagen Manly, *Milwaukee Journal*
1966 Pat Millard Hunter, *Honolulu Advertiser*
1967 Pat Millard Hunter, *Honolulu Advertiser*
1968 Bobbi McCallum, *Seattle Post-Intelligencer*
1969 Helen Fogel, *Detroit Free Press*
1970 Elaine Morrissey, *Dayton* (Ohio) *Daily News*
1971 Judith Anderson, *San Francisco Chronicle*

PAUL MYHRE AWARD FOR EXCELLENCE IN REPORTING — SERIES

1972 Bella Stumbo, *Los Angeles Times*
1973 Barbara Abel, *Milwaukee Journal*
1974 Sandy Flickner, *Miami Herald*
1975 Margo Huston, *Milwaukee Journal*

1976 **Rosemary J. McClure,** *San Bernardino* (Calif.) *Sun-Telegram*
1977 **Margo Huston,** *Milwaukee Journal*

PAUL MYHRE AWARD FOR EXCELLENCE IN REPORTING — SINGLE STORY

1972 **Jan Grimley,** *Davenport* (Iowa) *Times-Democrat*
1973 **Ena Naunton,** *Miami Herald*
1974 **Judy Klemesrud,** *New York Times*
1975 **Andrew Malcolm,** *New York Times*
1976 **Frances Craig,** *Des Moines* (Iowa) *Register*
1977 **Richard Severo,** *New York Times*

PHOTOGRAPHY — PICTURE LAYOUT

1965 **George Skadding,** *Pompano Beach* (Fla.) *Sun-Sentinel*
1966 **Gary Settle,** *Wilmington* (Del.) *Journal*
1967 **James Johnson,** *Wichita* (Kans.) *Eagle Beacon*
1968 **Al McLaughlin,** *Daily Oklahoman* (Oklahoma City)
1969 **John Bowden,** *Washington Star*
1970 **Barry Edmonds,** *Flint* (Mich.) *Journal*
1971 **Nathan Benn,** *Palm Beach* (Fla.) *Post-Times*

PHOTOGRAPHY — STORY-TELLING PICTURE

1965 **Bob Eighmie,** *Fort Lauderdale* (Fla.) *News*
1966 **Gary Settle,** *Wilmington* (Del.) *Journal*
1967 **Anthony Lopez,** *Today* (Cocoa, Fla.)
1968 **Judd Gunderson,** *Los Angeles Times*
1969 **Cookie Snyder,** *Twin City Sentinel* (Winston-Salem, N.C.)
1970 **Gordon Alexander,** *New London* (Conn.) *Day*
1971 **Ken Wesley,** *San Bernardino* (Calif.) *Sun-Telegram*

PHOTOGRAPHY — PERSONALITY PORTRAIT

1965 **Don Martin,** *Charlotte* (N.C.) *News*
1966 **Donald Nussbaum,** *Milwaukee Journal*
1967 **Donn Gould,** *Pompano Beach* (Fla.) *Sun Sentinel*
1968 **Perry Riddle,** *Chicago Daily News*
1969 **Lee Romero,** *Providence* (R.I.) *Journal*
1970 **Ed Stein,** *Wisconsin State Journal* (Madison)
1971 **Fred Comegys,** *Wilmington* (Del.) *News-Journal*

WOMEN'S PAGE PHOTOGRAPHER OF THE YEAR

1965 **Mary Frampton,** *Los Angeles Times*
1966 **Al McLaughlin,** *Daily Oklahoman* and *Oklahoma City Times*
1967 **David Nance,** *Houston Chronicle*
1968 **James Johnson,** *Wichita* (Kans.) *Eagle and Beacon*
1969 **Gary Settle,** *Chicago Daily News*
1970 **Bill Luster,** *Louisville* (Ky.) *Courier-Journal* and *Times*
1971 **Bob Coyle,** *Dubuque* (Iowa) *Telegraph-Herald*

CONSUMER AFFAIRS REPORTING

1974 **Phil Weck,** *Bucks County Courier Times* (Levittown, Pa.)
1975 **Pat Ravenscraft,** *Akron* (Ohio) *Beacon-Journal*
1976 **Carolyn Nolte-Watts,** *St. Petersburg* (Fla.) *Times*
1977 **Jane E. Brody,** *New York Times*

The Penney-Missouri Magazine Awards are given annually for excellent articles published the previous year on lifestyle in a magazine published in the United States, excluding company publications, fraternal magazines, alumnae publications and magazine supplements. Winners receive a $1,000 cash award and a Baccarat crystal obelisk. A screening committee narrows down entries for a four-judge panel which selects the winners.

HOME FURNISHINGS

1967 **Lois Whitcomb Bohling,** *House Beautiful*
1968 **Elizabeth Craster,** *Better Homes and Gardens*
1969 **Evan Frances,** *Ladies' Home Journal*
1970 **Dr. and Mrs. Edward Hall,** *House and Garden*
1971 **James A. Autry,** *Better Homes and Gardens*

HOUSEHOLD MANAGEMENT

1967 **Anna Fisher Rush,** *McCall's*
1968 **Peter Lindberg,** *Better Homes and Gardens*
1969 **Margaret Cousins,** *House Beautiful*
1970 **Selwyn Raab,** *McCall's*
1971 **Betty Furness,** *McCall's*

HEALTH

1967 **Matt Clark,** *Newsweek*
1968 **Gilbert Cant,** *Time*
1969 **Susanna McBee,** *Life*
1970 **Phyllis Starr,** *Glamour*
1971 **Matt Clark,** *Newsweek*
1972 **Walter McQuade,** *Fortune*
1973 **Paul J. Dolan,** *Family Health*
1974 **Charles and Bonnie Remsberg,** *Good Housekeeping*
1975 **Matt Clark,** *Newsweek*
1976 **Kathryn Livingston,** *Town and Country*
1977 **General Jonas,** *The New Yorker*

FASHION AND BEAUTY

1967 **Gloria Guiness,** *Harper's Bazaar*
1968 **Eleanor Carruth,** *Fortune*
1969 **Lawrence S. Martz, Jr.,** *Newsweek*
1970 **Mary Butler,** *Harper's Bazaar*
1971 **Harry F. Walters,** *Newsweek*

SPECIAL INTEREST

1967 **Ponchitta Pierce,** *Ebony*
1968 **Alex Poinsett,** *Ebony*
1969 **Sylvie Reice,** *McCall's*
1970 **Natalie Gittelson,** *Harper's Bazaar*
1971 **Kurt Vonnegut, Jr.,** *Vogue*

PHOTOGRAPHY

1968 **Otto Storch,** *McCall's*
1969 **Toni Frissell,** *Life*
1970 **Co Rentmeester,** *Life*
1971 **Co Rentmeester,** *Life*

SMALL CIRCULATION (under 400,000) MAGAZINES

1969 **Harriet Goslins,** *Pace*
1970 **Gloria Steinem,** *New York Magazine*
1971 **Jane O'Reilly,** *New York Magazine*
1972 **Peyton Bailey,** *Bride's Magazine*
1973 **Susan Edmiston,** *MS*
1974 **Mimi Sheraton,** *New York Magazine*
1975 **Ann Geracimos,** *womenSports*
 Barbara Baer and Glenna Matthews, *The Nation*
1976 **Prudence Mackintosh,** *Texas Monthly*
1977 **Sam Merrill,** *New Times*
 Loretta Schwartz, *Philadelphia*

CONSUMERISM

1972 **Ralph Nader,** *Ladies' Home Journal*
1973 **Joseph N. Bell,** *Good Housekeeping*
1974 **Nora Ephron,** *Esquire*
1975 **William Mead,** *Money*

1976 Maury Levy, *Philadelphia*
1977 Bil Gilbert, *Sports Illustrated*

PERSONAL LIFESTYLE
1972 Dorothy B. Seiberling, *Life*
1973 Betty Marker, *Parents' Magazine*
1974 Jean Stafford,*Vogue*
1975 Gail Sheehy, *New York Magazine*
1976 Dan Rottenberg, *Philadelphia*
1977 Judith Ramsey, *Family Circle*

EXPANDING OPPORTUNITIES
1972 Richard Boeth, Elizabeth Peer, Ann Ray Martin and Lisa Whitman, *Newsweek*
1973 Gloria Emerson, *Vogue*
1974 Judith Viorst, *Redbook*
1975 Pete Axthelm, *Newsweek*
1976 Susan Edmiston, *Redbook*
1977 William Broyles, *Texas Monthly*

CONTEMPORARY LIVING
1972 George Bush, *Better Homes and Gardens*
1973 Fredelle Maynard, *Woman's Day*
1974 Stefan Kanfer, *Time*
1975 Michael Demarest, *Time*
1976 Loretta Schwartz, *Philadelphia*
1977 Susan Edmiston, *Woman's Day*

Journalism Award
AMERICAN SOCIETY OF PLANNING OFFICIALS
1313 E. 16th St., Chicago, Ill. (312/947-2560)

The annual Journalism Award, which consists of a $50 prize and a certificate, honors efforts to support, improve or initiate planning programs, or to inform the public about issues, problems and choices that confront them in improving their communities. Any daily or weekly newspaper in the United States, its territories and possessions and Canada may submit articles for selection by a three- to five-member judges panel.

1960 *Minneapolis Star and Tribune*
1961 *Sacramento Bee*
1962 *Worcester Evening Gazette*
1963 *Gainesville Daily Times*
1964 *Honolulu Star-Bulletin*
1965 Lloyd Hollister Publications
1966 *Milwaukee Journal*
1967 *Milwaukee Journal*
1968 *Sandusky Register*
1969 *Louisville Courier-Journal*
1970 *Louisville Courier-Journal and Times*
1971 *Miami Herald* and reporter **Juanita Greene**
1972 *Detroit News* and reporter **Don Ball**
1973 *Milwaukee Journal* and urban affairs writers **Gary C. Rummler, Chris Lecos, James Parks, Michael Kirkhorn and Paul G. Hayes**
       Honolulu Advertiser and environment writer **Harold Hostetler**
       Chicago Today for series by **Michael Hirsley** and another by **Wesley Hartzell and Fred Orehek**
1974 *Arizona Daily Star*
       Hartford Times and editorial writer **Don O. Noel, Jr.**
1975 *Las Cruces Sun News* (N.M.) and reporter **Barbara Kerr Page**
       Newsday (Garden City, N.Y.) and reporters **Tom Morris, Henry Pearson and Ed Lowe**

1976 *Deseret News* (Salt Lake City) and reporter **Nick Snow**
1977 *Port Huron Times Herald* (Mich.) and reporter **Linda Heyboer**
       Quincy Patriot Ledger (Mass.) and reporter Doris M. Melville
       Tulsa World and reporter **Ann Patton**

George K. Polk Awards
LONG ISLAND UNIVERSITY
University Plaza, Brooklyn, N.Y. 11201 (212/834-6170)

The George K. Polk Awards recognize distinguished achievement in journalism. The recipients of the Polk plaque are recommended by a national panel of former award winners, deans of journalism schools and news executives in all media. The winners are selected by a committee of university alumni and faculty. While neither the number of awards nor the categories are restricted, custom has directed recognition in certain fields of journalism plus special awards.

FOREIGN REPORTING
1949 Homer Bigart, *New York Herald Tribune*
1950 Six member reporting team, *New York Herald Tribune*
1951 Homer Bigart, *New York Herald Tribune*
1952 Milton Bracker and Virginia Lee Warren, *New York Times*
1953 Marguerite Higgins, *New York Herald Tribune*
1954 Jim Lucas, Scripps-Howard Newspapers
1955 George Weller, Chicago Daily News Syndicate
1956 Barrett, McGurn, *New York Herald Tribune*
1957 Hal Lehrman,
1958 Harrison E. Salisbury, *New York Times*
1959 Chet Huntley and Reuven Frank, National Broadcasting Co.
1960 A.M. Rosenthal, *New York Times*
1960 James Morris, *The Guardian* (Manchester, England)
1962 Morris H. Rubin, *The Progressive*
1963 Dana Adams Schmidt, *New York Times*
1964 David Halberstam, *New York Times*
1965 Malcolm W. Browne, Associated Press
1966 Dan Kurzman, *Washington Post*
1967 Harrison E. Salisbury, *New York Times*
1968 R.W. Apple, Jr., *New York Times*
1969 No award
1970 Henry Kamm, *New York Times*
1971 Gloria Emerson, *New York Times*
1972 Sydney H. Schanberg, *New York Times*
1973 Jean Thoravel and Jean Leclerc du Sablon, Agence France-Presse
1974 Henry S. Bradsher, *Washington Star-News*
1975 Donald Kirk, *Chicago Tribune*
1976 No award
1977 Robert C. Toth, *Los Angeles Times*

INTERNATIONAL REPORTING
1955 Thomas J. Hamilton, *New York Times*
1956 Thomas J. Hamilton, *New York Times*
1969 David Kraslow and Stuart H. Loory, *Los Angeles Times*

METROPOLITAN REPORTING
1949 Malcolm Johnson, *New York Sun*
1950 No award
1951 Fern Marja, *New York Post*

1952 Richard Carter, *New York Compass*
1953 Edward J. Mowry, *New York World-Telegram and Sun*
1954 William Longgood, *New York World-Telegram and Sun*
1955 James McGlincy and Sydney Mirkin, *New York Daily News*
1956 Fern Marja, Peter J. McElroy and William Dufty, *New York Post*
1957 Phil Santora, *New York Daily News*
1958 Mitchel Levitas, *New York Post*
1959 William Haddad, *New York Post*
1960 William Haddad and Joseph Kahn, *New York Post*
1961 William R. Clark and Alexander Milch, *Newark News*
1962 No award
1963 No award
1964 Norman C. Miller, *Wall Street Journal*
1965 A.M. Rosenthal, *New York Times*
1966 Barry Gottehrer, *New York Herald Tribune*
1967 Cal Olson, *Fargo Forum* (Fargo, N.D.)
1968 J. Anthony Lukas, *New York Times*
1969 No award
1970 William Federici, *New York Times*
1971 Richard Oliver, *New York News*
1972 Donald L. Bartlett and James B. Steele, *Philadelphia Inquirer*
1973 Joseph Martin, Martin McLaughlin and James Ryan, *New York News*
1974 James Savage and Mike Baxter, *Miami Herald*
      Carol Talley and Joan Hayde, *Daily Advance* (Dover, N.J.)
1975 Richard Severo, *New York Times*

LOCAL REPORTING

1977 Len Ackland, *Des Moines Register*

NATIONAL REPORTING

1950 Ted Poston, *New York Post*
1951 Ira H. Freeman, *New York Times*
1952 Jay Nelson Tuck, *New York Post*
1953 A.H. Raskin, *New York Times*
1954 James Reston, *New York Times*
1955 Luther Huston, *New York Times*
1956 Milton Mayer, *The Reporter*
1957 Jack Lotto, International News Service
1958 Relman Morin, Associated Press
1959 Richard L. Strout, *Christian Science Monitor*
1960 Nathaniel Gerstenzang, *New York Times*
1961 John T. Cunniff, Associated Press
1962 Gerard Piel, *Scientific American*
1963 Mary McGrory, *Washington Star*
1964 American Broadcasting Co.
      Columbia Broadcasting System
      National Broadcasting Co.
1965 Paul Hope and John Barron, *Washington Star*
1966 No award
1967 Richard Harwood, *Washington Post*
1968 Clayton Fritchey, *Newsday* Specials
1969 Bernard D. Nossiter, *Washington Post*
1970 Walter Rugaber, *New York Times*
1971 The Knight Newspapers
1972 *New York Times*
1973 Carl Bernstein and Robert Woodward, *Washington Post*
1974 Andrew H. Malcolm, *New York Times*
1975 Seymour M. Hersh, *New York Times*
1976 No award
1977 Walter Pincus, *Washington Post*

SUBURBAN REPORTING

1949 Larry Andrews, *Nassau* (N.Y.) *Review Star*
1950 Fred Hechinger, *Bridgeport* (Conn.) *Herald*
1951 *Long Island Daily Press*
1952 *Yonkers Herald-Statesman*
1953 No award
1954 No award
1955 Thomas Finnegan, *Long Island Star-Journal*
1956 Bob Greene, *Newsday*
1957 Mel Elfin, *Long Island Press*

REGIONAL REPORTING

1969 James K. Batten and Dwayne Walls, *Charlotte Observer*

COMMUNITY SERVICE

1949 *Brooklyn Eagle*
1950 *Brooklyn Eagle*
1951 *Newsday*
1952 *New York World-Telegram and Sun*
1953 *Brooklyn Eagle*
1954 *Newsday*
1955 WNYC
1956 *Redbook*
1957 No award
1958 Edward Wakin, *New York World-Telegram and Sun*
1959 *Brooklyn Heights Press*
1960 No award
1961 *The Village Voice*
1962 Arnold Brophy and Joseph S. Glemis, *Newsday*
1963 No award
1964 No award
1965 Samuel F. Marshall, *Cleveland Plain Dealer*
1966 No award
1967 No award
1968 *Newsday*
1969 David Burnham, *New York Times*
1970 No award
1971 Karl Grossman, *Long Island Press*
1972 No award
1973 Ronald Kessler, *Washington Post*
1974 William Sherman, *New York Daily News*
1975 William E. Anderson, Harley R. Bierce and Richard E. Cady, *Indianapolis Star*
1976 No award
1977 No award

WIRE SERVICE REPORTING

1950 Kingsbury Smith, *International News Service*
1951 Don Whitehead, Associated Press
1955 Alan J. Gould, Associated Press (Team of **Don Whitehead, Saul Pett, Ben Price, Relman Morin and Jack Bell**)

EDUCATION REPORTING

1949 Benjamin Fine, *New York Times*
1950 Lester Grant, *New York Herald Tribune*
1951 Fred Hechinger and Judith Christ, *New York Herald Tribune*
1952 Kalman Siegel, *New York Times*
1953 No award
1954 No award
1955 No award
1956 Gertrude Samuels, *New York Times*
1972 Joseph Lelyveld, *New York Times*

SCIENCE REPORTING

1949 Albert Deutsch, *PM*
1950 William Laurence, *New York Times*

1951 George Keaney, *New York World-Telegram and Sun*
1952 Alton Blakeslee, Associated Press
1953-76 No awards
1977 New England Journal of Medicine

RADIO AND TELEVISION REPORTING (*Radio; **Television)

1955 Eric Sevareid, Columbia Broadcasting System
1956 National Broadcasting Co.
1957 Columbia Broadcasting System
1958 Columbia Broadcasting System
1959 Jay McMullen, Columbia Broadcasting System
1960 Av Westin and Howard K. Smith, Columbia Broadcasting System
1961 Albert Wasserman and Robert Young, National Broadcasting Co.
1962 Robert Young and Charles Dorkins, National Broadcasting Co.
1963 WNDT-TV**
1964 No award
1965 Edward P. Morgan*, American Broadcasting Co.
      Ted Yates**, National Broadcasting Co,
1966 Morley Safer**, Columbia Broadcasting Co.
1967 No award
1968 No award
1969 NBC News, CBS News, ABC News**
1970 Tom Pettit**, National Broadcasting Co. (national reporting)
      Lee Hanna, WCBS-TV (local reporting)
1971 Alan M. Levin**, National Educational Television
1972 Phil Brady**, NBC News
1973 Jim McKay**, American Broadcasting Co.
1974 Public Broadcasting Service and National Public Affairs Center for Television**
1975 No award
1976 No award
1977 Barry Lando**, *60 Minutes*, CBS News

LOCAL RADIO AND TELEVISION REPORTING

1977 John Stossel, WCBS-TV News, New York

TELEVISION DOCUMENTARY

1966 Beryl Fox, Canadian Broadcasting Corp.
1967 No award
1968 ABC News
1969 No award
1970 No award
1971 No award
1972 Peter Davis, Perry Wolff and Roger Mudd, CBS News
1973 *60 Minutes*, CBS News
      First Tuesday, NBC News
1974 Jeremy Isaacs, *The World at War*, Thames Television (London)
1975 NBC News
1976 No award
1977 No award

SPORTS REPORTING

1951 Red Smith, *New York Herald Tribune*
1952 Ben Gould, *Brooklyn Eagle*

RELIGIOUS REPORTING

1952 Ann Elizabeth Price, *New York Herald Tribune*

NEWS PHOTOGRAPHY

1953 Bob Wendlinger, *Brooklyn Eagle*
1954 Peter Stackpole, *Life*

1955 Maureice Johnson, International News Photos
1956 William Sauro, United Press Newspictures
1957 Jack Young, United Press Newspictures
1958 Jack Jenkins, United Press Newspictures
1959 Paul Schutzer, *Life*
1960 Rangaswamy Satakopan, Associated Press
1961 Yasushi Nagao, Mainichi Newspapers, Japan
1962 Anonymous, Associated Press
1963 Hector Rondon, *La Republica*, Caracas
1964 Roger Asnong, Associated Press
1965 No award
1966 James A. Bourdier, Associated Press
1967 Horst Faas, Associated Press
1968 Catherine Leroy
1969 Edward T. Adams, Associated Press
1970 Stephen Dawson Starr, Associated Press
1971 John Darnell, John Filo and Howard Ruffner, *Life*
1972 Horst Faas and Michel Laurent, Associated Press
1973 Huynh Cong Ut, Associated Press
1974 George Brich, Associated Press
1975 Werner Baum Deutsche Press-Agentur/United Press International
1976 No award
1977 Eddie Adams, Associated Press

SPECIAL PAGE

1955 *New York World-Telegram & Sun* (School Page)

MAGAZINE REPORTING

1956 William Attwood, *Look*
1957 No award
1958 Edmund Stevens and Phillip Harrington, *Look*
1959 Marya Mannes, *The Reporter*
1960 *The Times Literary Supplement* (London)
1961 No award
1962 No award
1963 James Baldwin, *The New Yorker*
1964 Gilbert A. Harrison, *New Republic*
1965 No award
1966 No award
1967 *Ramparts*
1968 *Paris Review*
1969 Norman Mailer, *Harper's Magazine*
1970 William Lambert, *Life*
1971 *The Washington Monthly*
1972 Ross Terrill, *Atlantic Monthly*
1973 Frances FitzGerald *The New Yorker*
1974 John Osborne, *New Republic*
1975 Edward M. Brecher and Robert E. Harris, *Consumer Reports*
1976 No award
1977 Daniel Lang, *The New Yorker*

CRITICISM

1964 *New York Review of Books*
1965 Robert Brustein, *New Republic*
1966 Susan Sontag
1967 Alfred Kazin
1968 Saul Maloff, *Newsweek*
1969 John Simon, *New Leader*
1970 No award
1971 Pauline Kael, *The New Yorker*
1972 Richard Harwood, *Washington Post*
1973 No award
1974 No award
1975 No award
1976 No award
1977 Peter S. Prescott, *Newsweek*

CARICATURES

1966 David Levine, *The New York Review of Books*

EDITORIAL CARTOONS

1977 Jeff MacNally, *Richmond (Va.) News Leader*

BOOKS

1967 Wilson Follet, *Modern American Usage*
1968 Alan F. Westin, *Privacy and Freedom*
1969 Charles Rembar, *The End of Obscenity*
1970 Richard Ellmann, Ed., *The Artist as Critic: The Critical Writings of Oscar Wilde*
1971 Otto Friedrich, *Decline and Fall*
1972 Erik Barnouw, *The History of Broadcasting in the United States*
1973 Sanford J. Unger, *The Papers & The Papers*
1974 David Wise, *The Politics of Lying: Government Deception, Secrecy and Power*
1975 Mary Adelaide Mendelsohn, *Tender Loving Greed*
1976 No award
1977 No award

INVESTIGATIVE REPORTING

1973 Jean Heller, Associated Press
1974 Seymour Hersh, *New York Times*
1975 No award
1976 No award
1977 No award

COMMENTARY

1977 Red Smith, *New York Times*

EDITORIAL COMMENT

1966 John B. Oakes *New York Times*
1971 James E. Clayton *Washington Post*

INTERPRETIVE REPORTING

1966 Bernard B. Fall
1967 Murray Kempton, *New York Post*

FREEDOM OF THE PRESS AWARD

1971 Walter Cronkite, *CBS Evening News*

PUBLIC SERVICE

1972 Frances Cerra, *Newsday*

SPECIAL AWARDS

1951 *New York Daily News* (Straw poll)
1952 Edward R. Murrow, Columbia Broadcasting System
       Sponsor Magazine
1953 Jack Gould, *New York Times*
       The Reporter
       Edward R. Murrow, Columbia Broadcasting System
       New York Daily News
1954 John Crosby, *New York Herald Tribune*
       Business Week
       Leonard Engel
1955 Dan Parker, *New York Mirror*
       Leo Rosten, *Look*
1956 No award
1957 Emanuel R. Freedman, *New York Times*
       Endre Marton, Associated Press
       Ilona Nyilas, United Press
1958 Richard D. Heffner, WRCA-TV
       Edmund C. Arnold
1959 Justice William O. Douglas
       Samuel G. Blackman, Associated Press
       Walter Sullivan, *New York Times*

1960 Wilbur Schramm, Institute for Communication Research, Stanford University
1961 Douglass Cater, *The Reporter*
1962 Jules Feiffer
1963 Michael Harrington, *The Other America*
       Morton Mintz, *Washington Post*
       Theodore E. Kruglak
1964 A.H. Raskin, *New York Times*
       WNEW-Radio
       Peter Lyon
1965 Oron J. Hale
1966 No award
1967 Arnold Gingrich, *Esquire*
       Time Essay, *Time*
1968 No award
1969 No award
1970 Wes Gallagher, Associated Press
       Seymour M. Hersh
1971 I.F. Stone
1972 No award
1973 Lesley Oelsner, *New York Times*
1974 Donald L. Barlett and James B. Steele, *Philadelphia Inquirer*
1975 No award
1976 No award
1977 Carey McWilliams, *The Nation*

George Polk Memorial Award

OVERSEAS PRESS CLUB
55 E. 42nd St. New York, N.Y. 10017 (212/687-2430)

The OPC George Polk Memorial Award, with a $500 honorarium, was given until 1973 for the best reporting requiring exceptional courage and enterprise abroad. (For more information on the George Polk Awards, see also the listing on pp 90-93.)

1948 Homer Bigart, *New York Herald Tribune*
1949 Wayne Richardson, Associated Press
1950 Marguerite Higgins, *New York Herald Tribune*
1951 William N. Oatis, Associated Press
1952 Homer Bigart, *New York Herald Tribune*
1953 No award
1954 Robert Capa, *Life*
1955 Gene Symonds, United Press
1956 Russell Jones, United Press
1957 Herbert Matthews, *New York Times*
1958 Joseph Taylor, UPI
1959 No award
1960 Henry N. Taylor, Scripps-Howard Newspapers
       Lionel Durant, *Newsweek*
1961 Dickey Chapelle, *Reader's Digest,* for magazine, book and photographic coverage
1962 Dana Adams Schmidt, *New York Times*
1963 Richard Tregaskis, for the book, *Vietnam Diary*
1964 George Clay, NBC
1965 Morley Safer, CBS
1966 Ron Nessen, Vo Huynh and You Young Sang, NBC
1967 Eric Pace, *New York Times*
1968 Peter Rehak, Associated Press
1969 Horst Faas and Peter Barnett, Associated Press
1970 producers **Rus Bensley, Ernest Leiser;** crew, **John Lawrence, Keith Kay, James Clevenger** CBS Team
1971 Nicholas W. Stroh, *Washington Star*
1972 No award
1973 Leon Dash, *Washington Post*

Pulitzer Prizes

COLUMBIA UNIVERSITY
Graduate School of Journalism, New York, N.Y. 10027
(212/280-3828) (Pulitzer Prizes: 212/280-3841)

The Pulitzer Prizes are the best-known American journalism prizes. Endowed by the will of Joseph Pulitzer, founder of the *St. Louis Post-Dispatch*, and administered under the trusteeship of Columbia University, each Pulitzer Prize in journalism carries a $1,000 cash award. Any individual may submit material published in an American daily, Sunday or weekly newspaper for consideration by university-appointed juries in each category. Each jury, based on collective and individual choice, must submit from three to six nominations per category for selection by the fifteen-member Advisory Board on Pulitzer Prizes.

REPORTING (Until 1952 included various areas of journalism later divided into separate categories)

1917 Herbert Bayard Swope, *The World*, (New York, N.Y.)
1918 Harold A. Littledale *New York Evening Post*
1919 No award
1920 John J. Leary Jr. *The World*, (New York, N.Y.)
1921 Louis Seibold *The World*, (New York, N.Y.)
1922 Kirke L. Simpson Associated Press
1923 Alva Johnston *New York Times*
1924 Magner White *San Diego Sun*
1925 James W. Mulroy and Alvin H. Goldstein *Chicago Daily News*
1926 William B. Miller Louisville *Courier-Journal*
1927 John T. Rogers *St. Louis Post-Dispatch*
1928 No award
1929 Paul Y. Anderson *St. Louis Post-Dispatch*
1930 Russell D. Owen *New York Times*
1931 A. B. MacDonald *Kansas City Star*
1932 W. C. Richards, D. D. Martin, J. S. Pooler, F. D. Webb and J. N. W. Sloan *Detroit Free Press*
1933 Francis A. Jamieson Associated Press
1934 Royce Brier *San Francisco Chronicle*
1935 William H. Taylor *New York Herald Tribune*
1936 Lauren D. Lyman *New York Times*
1937 John J. O'Neill *New York Herald Tribune;* William L. Laurence *New York Times;* Howard W. Blakeslee Associated Press; Gobind Behari Lal Universal Service; and David Dietz Scripps-Howard newspapers
1938 Raymond Sprigle *Pittsburgh Post-Gazette*
1939 Thomas L. Stokes, Scripps-Howard Newspaper Alliance
1940 S. Burton Heath, *New York World-Telegram*
1941 Westbrook Pegler, *New York World-Telegram*
1942 Stanton Delaplane, *San Francisco Chronicle*
1943 George Weller, *Chicago Daily News*
1944 Paul Schoenstein and associates, *New York Journal-American*
1945 Jack S. McDowell, *The Call-Bulletin* (San Francisco)
1946 William L. Laurence *New York Times*
1947 Frederick Woltman, *New York World-Telegram*
1948 George E. Goodwin, *Atlanta Journal*
1949 Malcolm Johnson, *The Sun*, (New York, N.Y.)
1950 Meyer Berger, *New York Times*
1951 Edward S. Montgomery, *San Francisco Examiner*
1952 George de Carvalho, *San Francisco Chronicle*

LOCAL INVESTIGATIVE REPORTING (Through 1963, this category was called "Reporting, No Edition Time")

1953 Edward J. Mowery, *New York World-Telegram & Sun*
1954 Alvin S. McCoy, *Kansas City Star*
1955 Roland K. Towery, *Cuero Tex. Record*
1956 Arthur Daley, *New York Times*
1957 Wallace Turner and William Lambert, *Portland Oregonian*
1958 George Beveridge, *Washington Evening Star*
1959 John Harold Brialin, *Scranton* (Pa.) *Tribune and Scrantonian*
1960 Miriam Ottenberg, *Washington Evening Star*
1961 Edgar May, *Buffalo Evening News*
1962 George Bliss, *Chicago Tribune*
1963 Oscar O'Neal Griffin Jr., *Pecos* (Tex.) *Independent and Enterprise*
1964 James V. Magee, Albert V. Gaudiosi, and Frederick A. Meyer, *Philadelphia Bulletin*
1965 Gene Goltz, *Houston Post*
1966 John A. Frasca, *Tampa* (Fla.) *Tribune*
1967 Gene Miller, *Miami Herald*
1968 J. Anthony Lukas, *New York Times*
1969 Albert Delugach and Denny Walsh, *St. Louis Globe-Democrat*
1970 Harold E. Martin, *Montgomery* (Ala.) *Advertiser*
1971 William Hugh Jones, *Chicago Tribune*
1972 Ann DeSantis, S. A. Kurkjian, T. Leland, and G. M. O'Neill, *Boston Globe*
1973 *Sun* Newspapers, (Omaha, Neb.)
1974 William Sherman, *New York Daily News*
1975 *Indianapolis Star*
1976 Staff of *Chicago Tribune*
1977 Acel Moore and Wendell Rawls, Jr., *Philadelphia Inquirer*

LOCAL GENERAL REPORTING (Through 1963, this category was called "Reporting, Edition Time")

1953 *Providence* (R.I.) Journal and Evening Bulletin
1954 *Vicksburg* (Miss.) Sunday Post-Herald
1955 Caro Brown, *Alice* (Tex.) *Daily Echo*
1956 Lee Hills, *Detroit Free Press*
1957 *Salt Lake* (Utah) *Tribune*
1958 *Fargo* (N.D.) *Forum*
1959 Mary Lou Werner, *Washington Evening Star*
1960 Jack Nelson, *Atlanta Constitution*
1961 Sanche de Gramont, *New York Herald Tribune*
1962 Robert D. Mullins, *Deseret News*, (Salt Lake City)
1963 Sylvan Fox, Anthony Shannon, and William Longgood, *New York World-Telegram & Sun*
1964 Norman C. Miller, *The Wall Street Journal*
1965 Melvin H. Ruder, *Hungry Horse* (Mo.) *News*
1966 Staff, *Los Angeles Times*
1967 Robert V. Cox, *Chambersburg* (Pa.) *Public Opinion*
1968 *Detroit* (Mich.) *Free Press*
1969 John Fretterman, *The Louisville* (Ky.) *Courier-Journal*
1970 Thomas Fitzpatrick, *Chicago Sun-Times*
1971 *Akron* (Ohio) *Beacon Journal*
1972 R. I. Cooper and J. W. Machacek, *The Rochester* (N.Y.) *Times-Union*
1973 *Chicago Tribune*
1974 Arthur M. Petacque and Hugh F. Hough, *The Chicago Sun-Times*
1975 *The Xenia* (Ohio) *Daily Gazette*
1976 Gene Miller, *The Miami Herald,*
1977 Margo Huston, *Milwaukee Journal*

CORRESPONDENCE (This category overlapped with "Telegraphic Reporting, National," and "Telegraphic Reporting, International," and all three were superseded

in 1948 by the "National Reporting and International Reporting" categories)

1929 Paul Scott Mowrer, *Chicago Daily News*
1930 Leland Stowe, *New York Herald Tribune*
1931 H.R. Knickerbocker, *Philadelphia Public Ledger* and *New York Evening Post*
1932 Walter Duranty, *New York Times*
1933 Charles G. Ross, *St. Louis Post-Dispatch*
    Edgar Ansel Mowrer, *Chicago Daily News*
1934 Frederick R. Birchall, *New York Times*
1935 Arthur Krock, *New York Times*
1936 Wilfred C. Barber, *Chicago Tribune*
1937 Anne O'Hare McCormick, *New York Times*
1938 Arthur Krock, *New York Times*
1939 Louis P. Lochner, Associated Press
1940 Otto D. Tolichus, *New York Times*
1941 Group Award to news reporters in the war zones of Europe, Africa and Asia from the beginning of the war
1942 Carlos P. Romulo, *Philippines Herald*
1943 Hanson W. Baldwin, *New York Times*
1944 Ernest Taylor Pyle, Scripps-Howard Newspaper Alliance
1945 Harold V. "Hal" Boyle, Associated Press
1946 Arnaldo Cortesi, *New York Times*
1947 Brooks Atkinson, *New York Times*

NATIONAL REPORTING (Through 1947, this category was called "Telegraphic Reporting (National)")

1942 Louis Stark, *New York Times*
1943 No award
1944 Dewey L. Fleming, *Baltimore Sun*
1945 James B. Reston, *New York Times*
1946 Edward A. Harris, *St. Louis Post-Dispatch*
1947 Edward T. Folliard, *Washington Post*
1948 Bert Andrews, *New York Herald Tribune*
    Nat S. Finney, *Minneapolis Tribune*
1949 Charles P. Trussell, *New York Times*
1950 Edwin O. Guthman, *Seattle Times*
1951 No award
1952 Anthony Leviero, *New York Times*
1953 Don Whitehead, Associated Press
1954 Richard Wilson, Cowles Newspapers
1955 Anthony Lewis, *Washington Daily News*
1956 Charles Bartlett, *Chattanooga Times*
1957 James Reston, *New York Times*
1958 Relman Morin, Associated Press
1959 Howard Van Smith, *Miami News*
1960 Vance Trimble, Scripps-Howard
1961 Edward R. Cony, *Wall Street Journal*
1962 Nathan G. Caldwell and Gene S. Graham, *Nashville Tennessean*
1963 Anthony Lewis, *New York Times*
1964 Merriman Smith, United Press International
1965 Louis Kohlmeier, *Wall Street Journal*
1966 Hayes Johnson, *Washington Evening Star*
1967 Monroe W. Karmin and Stanley W. Penn, *Wall Street Journal*
1968 Howard James, *Christian Science Monitor*
    Nathan Kotz, *Des Moines Register*
1969 Robert Cahn, *Christian Science Monitor*
1970 William J. Seton, *Chicago Daily News*
1971 Lucinda Franks and Thomas Powers, United Press International
1972 Jack Anderson, syndicated columnist
1973 Robert Boyd and Clark Hoyt, Knight Newspapers
1974 James R. Polk, *Washington Star-News*
    Jack White, *Providence* (R.I.) *Journal-Bulletin*
1975 Donald L. Barlett and James B. Steele, *Philadelphia Inquirer*

1976 James Risser, *Des Moines Register*
1977 Walter Mears, Associated Press

INTERNATIONAL CORRESPONDENCE

1942 Laurence E. Allen, Associated Press
1943 Ira Wolfert, North American Newspaper Alliance
1944 Daniel DeLuce, Associated Press
1945 Mark S. Watson, *Baltimore Sun*
1946 Homer W. Bigart, *New York Herald Tribune*
1947 Eddy Gilmore, Associated Press
1948 Paul W. Ward, *Baltimore Sun*
1949 Price Day, *Baltimore Sun*
1950 Edmund Stevens, *Christian Science Monitor*
1951 Keyes Beech and Fred Sparks, *Chicago Daily News*, Homer Bigart and Marguerite Higgins, *New York Herald Tribune*, Relman Morin and Don Whitehead, Associated Press
1952 John M. Hightower, Associated Press
1953 Austin Wehrwein, *Milwaukee Journal*
1954 Jim G. Lucas, Scripps-Howard Newspapers
1955 Harrison Salisbury, *New York Times*
1956 William Randolph Hearst Jr., Kingsbury Smith, and Frank Conniff, International News Service
1957 Russell Jones, United Press
1958 *New York Times*
1959 Joseph Martin and Philip Santora, *New York Daily News*
1960 A. M. Rosenthal, *New York Times*
1961 Lynn Heinzerling, Associated Press
1962 Walter Lippmann, New York Herald Tribune Syndicate
1963 Hal Hendrix, *Miami News*
1964 Malcolm W. Browne, Associated Press
    David Halberstam, *New York Times*
1965 J. A. Livingston, *Philadelphia Bulletin*
1966 Peter Arnett, Associated Press
1967 R. J. Hughes, *Christian Science Monitor*
1968 Alfred Friendly, *Washington Post*
1969 William Tuohy, *Los Angeles Times*
1970 Seymour M. Hersh, Dispatch News Service
1971 Jimmie Lee Hoagland, *Washington Post*
1972 Peter R. Kann, *Wall Street Journal*
1973 Max Frankel, *New York Times*
1974 Hedrick Smith, *New York Times*
1975 William Mullen and Ovie Carter, *Chicago Tribune*
1976 Sydney H. Schanberg, *New York Times*
1977 No award

EDITORIAL WRITING

1917 *New York Tribune*
1918 *The Louisville Courier-Journal*
1919 No award
1920 Harvey E. Newbranch, *Omaha Evening World-Herald*
1921 No award
1922 Frank M. O'Brien, *New York Herald*
1923 William Allen White, *Emporia* (Kans.) *Gazette*
1924 *Boston Herald*
    Special award: Frank I. Cobb, *New York World*
1925 *Charleston* (S.C.) *News and Courier*
1926 Edward M. Kingsbury, *New York Times*
1927 F. L. Bullard, *Boston Herald*
1928 Grover Cleveland Hall, *Montgomery* (Ala.) *Advertiser*
1929 Louis I. Jaffe, *Norfolk* (Va.) *Virginian-Pilot*
1930 No award
1931 Charles S. Ryckman, *Fremont* (Neb.) *Tribune*
1932 No award
1933 *Kansas City Star*
1934 E. P. Chase, *Atlantic* (Iowa) *News-Telegraph*

1935 No award
1936 Felix Morley, *Washington Post*
     George B. Parker, Scripps-Howard
1937 John W. Owens, *Baltimore Sun*
1938 W. W. Waymack, Des Moines, *Register and Tribune*
1939 Ronald G. Callvert, Portland *Oregonian*
1940 Bart Howard, *St. Louis Post-Dispatch*
1941 Reuben Maury, *New York Daily News*
1942 Geoffrey Parsons, *New York Herald Tribune*
1943 Forrest W. Seymour, *Des Moines Register and Tribune*
1944 Henry J. Haskell, *Kansas City Star*
1945 George W. Potter, *Providence* (R.I.) *Journal-Bulletin*
1946 Hodding Carter, *Delta Democrat-Times*, (Greenville, Miss.)
1947 William Grimes, *Wall Street Journal*
1948 Virginius Dabney, *Richmond Times-Dispatch*
1949 John H. Crider, *Boston Herald*
1950 Carl M. Saunders, *Jackson Citizen Patriot*
1951 William Fitzpatrick, *New Orleans States*
1952 Louis LaCoss, *St. Louis Globe-Democrat*
1953 Vermont Royster, *Wall Street Journal*
1954 Don Murray, *Boston Herald*
1955 Royce Howes, *Detroit Free Press*
1956 Lauren K. Soth, *Des Moines Register and Tribune*
1957 Buford Boone, *Tuscaloosa* (Ala.) *News*
1958 Harry S. Ashmore, *Arkansas Gazette*, (Little Rock, Ark.)
1959 Ralph McGill, *Atlanta Constitution*
1960 Lenoir Chambers, *Norfolk Virginian-Pilot*
1961 William J. Dorvillier, *San Juan* (P.R.) *Star*
1962 Thomas M. Storke, *Santa Barbara* (Calif.) *News-Press*
1963 Ira B. Harkey Jr., *Pascagoula* (Miss.) *Chronicle*
1964 Hazel Smith, *Lexington* (Miss.) *Advertiser*
1965 John R. Harrison, *Gainesville Sun*
1966 Robert Lasch, *St. Louis Post-Dispatch*
1967 Eugene C. Patterson, *Atlanta Constitution*
1968 John S. Knight, Knight Newspapers
1969 Paul Greenberg, *Pine Bluff* (Ark.) *Commercial*
1970 Philip Geyelin, *Washington Post*
1971 Horance G. Davis Jr., *Gainesville* (Fla.) *Sun*
1972 John Strohmeyer, *Bethlehem* (Pa.) *Globe-Times*
1973 Roger B. Linscott, *The Berkshire Eagle*, (Pittsfield, Mass.)
1974 F. Gilman Spencer, *The Trenton* (N.J.) *Trentonian*
1975 John Daniell Maurice, *The Charleston* (W. Va.) *Daily Mail*
1976 Philip P. Kerby, *Los Angeles Times*
1977 Warren L. Lerude, Foster Church and Norman Cardoza, *Reno Evening Gazette* and *Nevada State Journal*

CARTOONS

1922 Rollin Kirby, *New York World*
1923 No award
1924 Jay Norwood Darling, *New York Tribune*
1925 Rollin Kirby, *New York World*
1926 D. R. Fitzpatrick, *St. Louis Post-Dispatch*
1927 Nelson Harding, *Brooklyn* (N.Y.) *Daily Eagle*
1928 Nelson Harding, *Brooklyn* (N.Y.) *Daily Eagle*
1929 Rollin Kirby, *New York World*
1930 Charles R. Macauley, *Brooklyn* (N.Y.) *Daily Eagle*
1931 Edmund Duffy, *Baltimore Sun*
1932 John McCutcheon, *Chicago Tribune*
1933 Harold Morton Talburt, *Washington Daily News*
1934 Edmund Duffy, *Baltimore Sun*
1935 Ross A. Lewis, *Milwaukee Journal*
1936 No award
1937 Clarence Daniel Batchelor, *New York Daily News*
1938 Vaughn Shoemaker, *Chicago Daily News*

1939 Charles G. Werner, *Daily Oklahoman*, (Oklahoma City)
1940 Edmond Duffy, *Baltimore Sun*
1941 Jacob Burck, *Chicago Times*
1942 Herbert L. Block (Herblock), Newspaper Enterprise Association Service
1943 Jay Norwood Darling, *New York Herald Tribune*
1944 Clifford K. Berryman, *Washington Evening Star*
1945 William (Bill) Mauldin, United Features Syndicate
1946 Bruce Russell, *Los Angeles Times*
1947 V. Shoemaker, *Chicago Daily News*
1948 Reuben L. (Rube) Goldberg, *New York Sun*
1949 Lute Pease, *Newark* (N.J.) *Evening News*
1950 James T. Berryman, *Washington Evening Star*
1951 Reginald W. Manning, *Arizona Republic* (Phoenix, Ariz.)
1952 Fred L. Packer, *New York Mirror*
1953 Edward D. Kuekes, *Cleveland Plain Dealer*
1954 Herbert L. Block (Herblock), *Washington Post & Times-Herald*
1955 Daniel R. Fitzpatrick, *St. Louis Post-Dispatch*
1956 Robert York, *Louisville* (Ky.) *Times*
1957 Tom Little, *Nashville Tennessean*
1958 Bruce M. Shanks, *Buffalo Evening News*
1959 William (Bill) Mauldin, *St. Louis Post-Dispatch*
1960 No award
1961 Carey Orr, *Chicago Tribune*
1962 E. S. Valtman, *Hartford* (Conn.) *Times*
1963 Frank Miller, *Des Moines* (Iowa) *Register*
1964 Paul Conrad, *Denver Post*
1965 No award
1966 Don Wright, *Miami News*
1967 Patrick B. Oliphant, *Denver Post*
1968 E. G. Payne, *Charlotte* (N.C.) *Observer*
1969 John Fischetti, *Chicago Daily News*
1970 Thomas Darcy, *Newsday* (Garden City, N.Y.)
1971 Paul Conrad, *Los Angeles Times*
1972 J. K. MacNelly, *Richmond* (Va.) *News Leader*
1973 No award
1974 Paul Szep, *The Boston Globe*
1975 Garry Trudeau, creator of "Doonesbury" comic strip
1976 Tony Auth, *Philadelphia Inquirer*
1977 Paul Szep, *Boston Globe*

PHOTOGRAPHY (in 1968 divided into separate spot news and feature categories)

1942 Milton Brooks, *Detroit News*
1943 Frank Noel, Associated Press
1944 Frank Filan, Associated Press
1945 Joe Rosenthal, Associated Press
1946 No award
1947 Arnold Hardy, Amateur photographer
1948 Frank Cushing, *Boston Traveler*
1949 Nathaniel Fein, *New York Herald Tribune*
1950 Bill Crouch, *Oakland* (Calif.) *Tribune*
1951 Max Desfor, Associated Press
1952 John Robinson and Don Ultang, *Des Moines Register and Tribune*
1953 William M. Gallagher, *Flint* (Mich.) *Journal*
1954 Mrs. Walter M. Schau, Photographer
1955 John L. Gaunt Jr., *Los Angeles Times*
1956 *New York Daily News*
1957 Harry A. Trask, *Boston Traveler*
1958 William C. Beall, *Washington Daily News*
1959 William Seaman, *Minneapolis Star*
1960 Andrew Lopez, United Press International
1961 Yasushi Nagao, Mainichi Newspapers, Tokyo, Japan
1962 Paul Vathis, Associated Press
1963 Hector Rondon, *La Republica* (Caracas, Venezuela)
1964 Robert H. Jackson, *Dallas Times Herald*

1965 **Horst Faas,** Associated Press
1966 **Kyoichi Sawada,** United Press International
1967 **Jack R. Thornell,** Associated Press

SPOT NEWS PHOTOGRAPHY

1968 **Rocco Morabito,** *Jacksonville* (Fla.) *Journal*
1969 **Edward T. Adams,** Associated Press
1970 **Steve Starr,** Associated Press
1971 **John Paul Filo,** Amateur photographer
1972 **H. Faas, M. Laurent,** Associated Press
1973 **Huynh Cong Ut,** Associated Press
1974 **Anthony K. Roberts,** (Freelancer)
1975 **Gerald H. Gay,** *Seattle Times*
1976 **Stanley Forman,** *Boston Herald-American*
1977 **Neal Ulevich,** Associated Press
     Stanley Forman, *Boston Herald American*

FEATURE PHOTOGRAPHY

1968 **Toshio Sakai,** United Press International
1969 **Moneta Sleet Jr.,** *Ebony* magazine
1970 **Dallas Kinney,** *Palm Beach Post*
1971 **Jack Dykinga,** *Chicago Sun-Times*
1972 **Dave Kennerly,** United Press International
1973 **B. Lanker,** *Topeka* (KS) *Capital-Journal*
1974 **Slava Veder,** Associated Press
1975 **Matthew Lewis,** *Washington Post*
1976 **Photographic staff of,** *Louisville* (Ky.) *Courier-Journal and Times*
1977 **Robin Hood,** *Chattanooga* (Tenn.) *Free Press*

CRITICISM

1970 **Ada Louise Huxtable,** *New York Times*
1971 **Harold C. Schonberg,** *New York Times*
1972 **Frank L. Peters Jr.,** *St. Louis Post-Dispatch*
1973 **Ronald Powers,** *Chicago Sun-Times*
1974 **Emily Genauer,** *Newsday* syndicate
1975 **Roger Ebert,** *Chicago Sun-Times*
1976 **Alan M. Kriegsman,** *Washington Post*
1977 **William McPherson,** *Washington Post*

COMMENTARY

1970 **Marquis Childs,** *St. Louis Post-Dispatch*
1971 **William A. Caldwell,** *The Record* (Hackensack, N.J.)
1972 **Mike Royko,** *Chicago Daily News*
1973 **David S. Broder,** *Washington Post*
1974 **Edwin A. Roberts Jr.,** *The National Observer*
1975 **Mary McGrory,** *Washington Star*
1976 **Walter W. (Red) Smith,** sports columnist, *New York Times*
1977 **George F. Will,** *Washington Post*

NEWSPAPER HISTORY (given only once)

1918 **Minna Lewinson and Henry Beetle Hough,** History of services rendered to the public by the American press during 1917.

SPECIAL CITATIONS (Awarded as merited)

1930 **William O. Dapping,** *Auburn* (N.Y.) *Citizen* for reportorial coverage of breakout at Auburn Prison.
1938 *Edmonton Journal,* For defending freedom of the press in Alberta, Canada
1941 *New York Times,* Public educational value of foreign news reporting
1944 **Mrs. William Allen White,** For interest in and service to the advisory board during previous seven years
     Byron Price, Director, Office of Censorship, for creation of newspaper and radio codes

1945 **Cartographers of the American press,** For maps that increased public knowledge on progress of armies and navies in World War II
1947 **Columbia University and the Graduate School of Journalism,** For efforts to maintain and advance the high standards of the Pulitzer Prizes, given in Pulitzer Centennial Year
1948 **Dr. Frank Diehl Fackenthal,** A scroll recognizing interest and service over the years
1951 **Cyrus L. Sulzberger,** *New York Times,* for exclusive interview with Aloysius Stepinac, Roman Catholic Primate of Yugoslavia
1952 *Kansas City Star,* News coverage of 1951 regional flood
     Max Case, *New York Journal-American,* for exposures of corruption in basketball
1953 *New York Times,* For its Review of the Week section
1958 **Walter Lippmann,** Nationally syndicated *New York Herald Tribune* columnist for wisdom, perception and high sense of responsibility in commenting on international and national news
1964 **Gannett Newspapers, Rochester, N.Y.,** for "The Road to Integration," as an example of a newspaper group's resources to complement work of individual newspapers
1976 **John Hohenberg,** For twenty-two years of service as administrator of the Pulitzer Prizes

PUBLIC SERVICE AWARD

1917 **No award**
1918 *New York Times*
1919 *Milwaukee Journal*
1920 **No award**
1921 *Boston Post*
1922 *The World,* (New York, N.Y.)
1923 *Memphis Commercial Appeal*
1924 *The World,* (New York, N.Y.)
1925 **No award**
1926 *Enquirer Sun,* (Columbus, Ga.)
1927 *Canton* (Ohio) *Daily News*
1928 *Indianapolis Times*
1929 *Evening World* (New York, N.Y.)
1930 **No award**
1031 *Atlanta Constitution*
1932 *Indianapolis News*
1933 *New York World-Telegram*
1934 *Medford* (Ore.) *Mail Tribune*
1935 *Sacramento* (Calif.) *Bee*
1936 *Cedar Rapids* (Iowa) *Gazette*
1937 *St. Louis Post-Dispatch*
1938 *Bismarck* (N.D.) *Tribune*
1939 *Miami Daily News*
1940 *Waterbury* (Conn.) *Republican and American*
1941 *St. Louis Post-Dispatch*
1942 *Los Angeles Times*
1943 *World-Herald,* (Omaha, Neb.)
1944 *New York Times*
1945 *Detroit Free Press*
1946 *Scranton* (Pa.) *Times*
1947 *Baltimore Sun*
1948 *St. Louis Post-Dispatch*
1949 *Nebraska State Journal*
1950 *Chicago Daily News*
     St. Louis Post-Dispatch
1951 *Miami Herald*
     Brooklyn (N.Y.) *Eagle*
1952 *St. Louis Post-Dispatch*
1953 *News Reporter,* (Whiteville, N.C.)
     Tabor City (N.C.) *Tribune*
1954 *Newsday,* (Garden City, N.Y.)

1955 *Columbus (Ga.) Ledger and Sunday Ledger-Enquirer*
1956 *Watsonville (Calif.) Register-Pajaronian*
1957 *Chicago Daily News*
1958 *Arkansas Gazette, (Little Rock, Ark.)*
1959 *Utica (N.Y.) Observer-Dispatch*
Utica (N.Y.) Daily Press
1960 *Los Angeles Times*
1961 *Amarillo (Tex.) Globe-Times*
1962 *Panama City (Fla.) News-Herald*
1963 *Chicago Daily News*
1964 *St. Petersburg (Fla.) Times*
1965 *Hutchinson (Kans.) News*
1966 *Boston Globe*
1967 *Louisville (Ky.) Courier-Journal*
Milwaukee Journal
1968 *The Riverside (Calif.) Press*
1969 *Los Angeles Times*
1970 *Newsday (Garden City, N.Y.)*
1971 *Winston-Salem (N.C.) Journal and Sentinel*
1972 *New York Times*
1973 *Washington Post*
1974 *Newsday, (Garden City, N.Y.)*
1975 *Boston Globe*
1976 *Anchorage (Alaska) Daily News*
1977 *Lufkin (Tex.) News*

Murray Kramer Scarlet Quill Award

BOSTON UNIVERSITY
285 Babcock St, Boston, Mass. 02215 (617/353-2872)

The Murray Kramer Scarlet Quill Award, which consists of a plaque, is given annually to honor outstanding coverage of intercollegiate sports by a journalist, columnist, broadcaster or cartoonist. A Hall of Fame Awards Committee selects the recipient from nominees.

1965 Arthur Sampson, *Boston Herald-Traveler*
1966 Don Gillis, WHDH-TV Boston
1967 Murray Kramer, *Boston Record-American*
1968 Cliff Sundberg, *Boston Herald-Traveler*
1969 Roy Mumpton, *Worcester Telegram & Gazette*
1970 Jerry Nason, *Boston Globe*
1971 Dick Dew, United Press International
1972 Walter "Red" Smith, Nationally syndicated columnist
1973 Joe Concannon, *Boston Globe*
1974 Bob Monahan, *Boston Globe*
1975 Joe Giuliotti, *Boston Herald-American*
1976 Phil Bissell, *Boston Herald-American*
1977 Francis Rosa, *Boston Globe*

Claude Bernard Science Journalism Awards

NATIONAL SOCIETY FOR MEDICAL RESEARCH
1000 Vermont Ave. NW, Ste. 1100, Washington, D.C. 20005 (202/347-9565)

The Claude Bernard Science Journalism Awards are given annually for science reporting that has contributed significantly to public understanding of basic research in the life sciences, including but not limited to experimental medicine. A $1,000 prize is given to winners in each category. Entries are judged by a panel of journalists and scientists on the basis of scientific accuracy, clarity, significance of the subject and public interest. Honorable mentions are also made. (1969 was the last year when the award was broken into circulation categories.)

NEWSPAPER OVER 100,000 CIRCULATION

1967 Irving S. Bengelsdorf, *Los Angeles Times* ("Of Atoms and Men")
1968 Ray Bruner, *Toledo Blade* ("Has Life Been Created By Science: The Answer Depends on Definitions")
1969 Judith Randal, *Washington Evening Star* ("A Study in Immunity: Real Step Forward")
1970 Lawrence K. Altman, *New York Times* ("Twelve Dogs Develop Lung Cancer in Group of 86 Taught to Smoke")
1971 Ronald Kotulak, *Chicago Tribune* ("Is a Cure for Cancer Around the Corner?")
1972 William A. Rice, *New York Times* ("Medicine Closes in on an Elusive Killer")
1973 Arthur J. Snider, *Chicago Daily News* ("Miracle of the Brain")
1974 Lawrence K. Altman, *New York Times* ("Baboon Experiment Shows Alcohol Damages Liver, Even With Good Diet")
1975 Alton Blakeslee, Associated Press ("The Stalled Diseases")
1976 Christine Russell, *Washington Star* ("Just How Reliable Are Tests in Animals?")
1977 Donald C. Drake, *Philadelphia Inquirer* ("The Breath of Life")

NEWSPAPER UNDER 100,000 CIRCULATION

1967 Jerry Lochbaum, San Antonio Express ("The Man Who Talks With Chimpanzees")
1968 Marilyn Drago, *Arizona Daily Star* ("Lowly Hamster Plays Key Role Into Birth Defects")
1969 Jill Southworth, *Columbia (Mo.) Daily Tribune* ("Mystromys: Diabetes Researcher")

MAGAZINE

1967 Judith Marcus and Gerald Cohen, *Harper's* ("The Riddle of the Dangerous Bean")
1968 C.P. Gilmore, *New York Times Magazine* ("Instead of a Heart, a Man-Made Pump")
1969 Robert Stock, *New York Times Magazine* ("The Mouse State of the New Biology")
1970 Morton Hunt, *Playboy* ("Man and Beast")
1971 Matt Clark, *Newsweek* ("Probing the Brain")
1972 Gene Bylinsky, *Fortune* ("Upjohn Puts the Cell's Own Message to Work")
1973 No award
1974 Gene Bylinsky, *Fortune* ("What Science Can Do About Hereditary Disease")
1975 Albert Rosenfeld et al., *Saturday Review* ("Inside the Brain: The Last Great Frontier")
1976 No award
1977 Arthur Fisher, Time-Life Nature/Science Annual ("Slow Viruses: Biological Time Bombs")

AIP-USSF Science Writing Awards

AMERICAN INSTITUTE OF PHYSICS
335 E. 45th St., New York, N.Y. 10017 (212/661-9404)

The American Institute of Physics-United States Steel Foundation Science-Writing Award is given annually to a journalist for excellence in writing on physics or astronomy for the general public. The prize, which consists of a Moebius Strip and $1,500, is given to a citizen or permanent resident of the United States, Canada or Mexico, selected by a panel of judges.

1968 William J. Perkinson, *Baltimore Evening Sun* ("ABM Primer: Physics for Defense")
1969 Walter Sullivan, *New York Times* ("Flight of Apollo 8")
1970 Clarence P. Gilmore, Metromedia Television ("Can We Stop Earthquakes from Happening?")
1971 Kenneth Weaver, "Voyage to the Planets" (*National Geographic*)
1972 Jerry E. Bishop, "Celestial Clue" (*Wall Street Journal*)
1973 Edward Edelson, "The Mystery of Space" (*New York Daily News*)
1974 Patrick Young, "A Quake is Due at . . . " (*National Observer*)
1975 Tom Alexander, "Ominous Changes in the World's Weather" (*Fortune*)
1976 Frederic Golden, "Forecast: Earthquake" (*Time*)
1977 William D. Metz, "Fusion Research" (*Science Magazine*)

A second AIP-USSF Science-Writing Award, also carrying a $1,500 cash prize and a Moebius Strip, is given for excellence in writing for the general public by a scientist. The selection is made from entrants who reside in or are citizens of the United States, Canada or Mexico by a panel of judges.

1969 Kip S. Thorne, California Institute of Technology, ("The Death of a Star")
1970 Jeremy Bernstein, Stevens Institute of Technology, ("The Elusive Neutrino")
1971 Robert M. March, University of Wisconsin, ("Physics for Poets")
1972 Dietrich Schroeer, University of North Carolina/-Chapel Hill, ("Physics and Its Fifth Dimension: Society")
1973 Banesh Hoffman, Queens College, CUNY, ("Albert Einstein: Creator and Rebel")
1974 Robert D. Chapman, NASA, Goddard Space Flight Center, ("Comet Kohoutek")
1975 Robert H. March, University of Wisconsin, ("The Quandary Over Quarks")
1976 Jeremy Bernstein, Stevens Institute of Technology, ("Physicist I.I. Rabi")
1977 Steven Weinberg, Harvard University, ("The First Three Minutes: A Modern View of the Origin of the Universe")

Sigma Delta Chi Awards
SOCIETY OF PROFESSIONAL
JOURNALISTS/SIGMA DELTA CHI
35 E. Wacker Dr., Chicago, Ill. 60601 (312/236-6577)

Sigma Delta Chi Awards for Distinguished Service in Journalism annually honor noteworthy performance in print and broadcast journalism. Bronze medallions and plaques are presented to the winners. Society chapters nominate individuals and media for final selection. (Broadcast journalism awards will be found on pp. 154-155.)

GENERAL REPORTING
1939 Meigs O. Frost

1940 Basil Brewer
1941 No award
1942 Jack Vincent
1943 Julius M. Klein
  Ralph S. O'Leary
1944 Edward J. Doherty
1945 James P. McGuire
  John J. McPhaul
1946 John M. McCullough
1947 George Goodwin
1948 Richard C. Looman
1949 Bob Considine
1950 Edward B. Simmons
1951 Victor Cohn
1952 Chalmers M. Roberts
1953 Carl T. Rowan
1954 Richard Hyer
  William P. Walsh
1955 Victor Cohn
1956 Alfred Kuettner
1957 Pierre J. Huss
1958 Victor Cohn
1959 Saul Pett
1960 Robert Colby Nelson
1961 Joseph Newman
1962 Oscar Griffin
1963 Jimmy Breslin
1964 J. Harold Brislin
1965 Alton Blakeslee
1966 Stanley W. Penn
  Monroe W. Karmin
1967 Charles Nicodemus
1968 Haynes Johnson
1969 Seymour M. Hersh
1970 *Washington Post* **staff writers**
1971 James B. Steele
  Donald L. Barlett
1972 William F. Reed, Jr.
  James M. Bolus
1973 James R. Polk
1974 Frank Sutherland
1975 *Detroit Free Press* **reporters**
  William Mitchell
  Billy Bowles
  Kirk Cheyfitz
  Julie Morris
  Tom Hennessey
  James Harper
  Jim Neubacher
1976 George Reasons and Mike Goodman, *Los Angeles Times*
1977 Fredric Tulsky and David Phelps, *Jackson* (Miss.) *Clarion-Ledger*

EDITORIAL WRITING
1939 W. W. Waymack
1940 Allen Drury
1941 No award
1942 Alexander Kendrick
1943 Milton Lehman
1944 Felix R. McKnight
1945 Francis P. Locke
1946 John W. Hillman
1947 Alan Barth
1948 Virginius Dabney
1949 John Crider
1950 Bradley L. Morison
1951 Robert M. White II
1952 Virginius Dabney
1953 John N. Reddin

1954 Robert Estabrook
1955 James Jackson Kilpatrick
1956 Sylvan Meyer
1957 Vermont Royster
1958 J. D. Maurice
1959 Cecil Prince
1960 Hodding Carter III
1961 James A. Clendinen
1962 Karl E. Meyer
1963 H. G. Davis, Jr.
1964 J. O. Emmerich
1965 Alfred G. Dickson
1966 Duane Croft
1967 Robert E. Fisher
1968 Robert M. White II
1969 Albert Cawood
1970 John R. Harrison
1972 Joanna Wragg
1972 John R. Harrison
1973 Frank W. Corrigan
1974 Michael Pakenham
1975 William Duncliffe
1976 George W. Wilson
1977 Desmond Stone

WASHINGTON CORRESPONDENCE

1942 Drew Pearson
       Robert S. Allen
1943 Sam O'Neal
1944 Marquis W. Childs
1945 Peter Edson
1946 Wallace R. Deuel
1947 Bert Andrews
1948 W. McNeil Lowry
1949 Jack Steele
1950 William K. Hutchinson
1951 John Hightower
1952 Clark R. Mollenhoff
1953 Richard L. Wilson
1954 Clark R. Mollenhoff
1955 Joseph and Stewart Alsop
1956 Ben Price
1957 Robert T. Hartmann
1958 James Reston
1959 Vance Trimble
1960 James Clayton
       Julius Duscha
       Murrey Marder
       Bernard Nossiter
1961 James Marlow
1962 Jules Witcover
1963 Jerry Landauer
1964 Louis M. Kohlmeier
1965 Nick Kotz
1966 Richard Harwood
1967 Jack C. Landau
1968 Joe Western
1969 Ronald J. Ostrow
       Robert Jackson
1970 Jared D. Stout
1971 Neil Sheehan
       New York Times
1972 Carl Bernstein
       Robert Woodward
1973 James M. Naughton
       John M. Crewdson
       Ben A. Franklin
       Christopher Lydon
       Agis Salpukas
1974 Seth Kantor

1975 James Risser
1976 Maxine Cheshire and Scott Armstrong
1977 Gaylord Shaw

FOREIGN CORRESPONDENCE

1939 Kenneth T. Downs
1940 Leland Stowe
1941 No award
1942 Keith Wheeler
1943 Frederick Kuh
1944 Frederick Kuh
1945 Arnaldo Cortesi
1946 Charles Gratke
1947 Daniel DeLuce
1948 Nat Barrows
1949 Kingsbury Smith
1950 Keyes Beech
       Dan Whitehead
1951 Ferdinand Kuhn
1952 Ernest S. Pisko
1953 Alexander Campbell
1954 Carl T. Rowan
1955 Carl T. Rowan
1956 Russell Jones
1957 Harrison E. Salisbury
1958 John Strohm
1959 William H. Stringer
1960 Smith Hempstone, Jr.
1961 Gaston Coblentz
1962 William J. Woestendiek
1963 Malcolm W. Browne
1964 Henry Shapiro
1965 James Nelson Goodsell
1966 Robert S. Elegant
1967 Peter Arnett
1968 Clyde H. Farnesworth
       Henry Kamm
       Tad Szulc
1969 Anatole Shub
1970 Hugh Mulligan
1971 Peter Arnett
       Bernard Gavzer
1972 Charlotte Saikowski
1973 Jacques Leslie
1974 Donald L. Barlett
       James B. Steele
1975 Sydney H. Schanberg
1976 Joe Rigert
1977 Robert Toth

NEWS PHOTOGRAPHY

1946 Frank Q. Brown
1947 Paul Calvert
1948 Frank Jurkoski
1949 *Chicago Daily News*
1950 David Douglas Duncan
1951 Edward DeLuga
       Roger Wrenn
1952 Robert I. Wendlinger
1953 Bill Wilson
1954 Leslie Dodds
1955 Richard B. Yager
1956 Dan Tompkins
1957 Eldred C. Reaney
1958 Andrew St. George
1959 Andrew Lopez
1960 J. Parke Randall
1961 Peter Leibing
1962 Cliff DeBear

1963 Bob Jackson
1964 Dom Ligato
1965 Henry Herr Gill
1966 Ray Mews
1967 Catherine Leroy
1968 Edward T. Adams
1969 Horst Faas
1970 John P. Filo
1971 Dong Jun Kim
1972 Huynh Cong "Nick" Ut
1973 Anthony K. Roberts
1974 Werner Baum
1975 Stanley J. Forman
1976 Bruce Fritz
1977 Eddie Adams

EDITORIAL CARTOONING

1942 Jacob Burck
1943 Charles Werner
1944 Henry Barrow
1945 Reuben L. Goldberg
1946 Dorman H. Smith
1947 Bruce Russell
1948 Herbert Block
1949 Herbert Block
1950 Bruce Russell
1952 Herbert Block
     Bruce Russell
1952 Cecil Jensen
1953 John Fischetti
1954 Calvin Allev
1955 John Fischetti
1956 Herbert Block
1957 Scott Long
1958 Clifford H. Baldowski
1959 Charles Gordon Brooks
1960 Dan Dowling
1961 Frank Interlandi
1962 Paul F. Conrad
1963 William H. "Bill" Mauldin
1964 Charles O. Bissell
1965 Roy Justus
1966 Patrick B. Oliphant
1967 Eugene C. Payne
1968 Paul F. Conrad
1969 Bill Mauldin
1970 Paul Conrad
1971 Hugh Haynie
1972 Bill Mauldin
1973 Paul Szep
1974 Mike Peters
1975 Tony Auth
1976 Paul Szep
1977 Don Wright

PUBLIC SERVICE IN NEWSPAPER JOURNALISM

1949 *Star-Gazette,* Moose Lake, Minn.
1950 *Atlanta* (Ga.) *Journal*
1951 *Chicago Sun-Times*
1952 *Wall Street Journal*
1953 *Chicago Daily News*
     Houston Post
1954 *Cleveland Plain Dealer*
1955 *The Register-Pajaronian,* (Watsonville, Calif.)
1956 *The Oregonian,* (Portland, Ore.)
1957 *Des Moines Register* and *Tribune*
     Minneapolis (Minn.) *Star* and *Tribune*
1958 *Tampa* (Fla.) *Tribune*
1959 *Atlanta* (Ga.) *Constitution*

1960 *The Daily Commercial,* (Leesburg, Fla.)
1961 *San Gabriel Valley Daily Tribune,* (West Covina, Calif.)
1962 *Pascagoula* (Miss.) *Chronicle*
1963 *Chicago Daily News*
1964 *McComb* (Miss.) *Enterprise-Journal*
1965 *Miami Herald*
1966 *Los Angeles Times*
     Long Island Press
1967 *Newsday,* (Garden City, N.Y.)
1968 *St. Louis Globe-Democrat*
1969 *Chicago Daily News*
1970 *Newsday,* (Garden City, N.Y.)
1971 *Boston Globe*
1972 Sun Newspapers, (Omaha, Neb.)
1973 *Newsday,* (Garden City, N.Y.)
1974 *Indianapolis Star*
1975 *Louisville Courier-Journal*
1976 *Wall Street Journal*
1977 *Philadelphia Inquirer*

MAGAZINE REPORTING

1949 Lester Velie
1950 Gordon Schendel
1951 Bill Davidson
1952 Bill Davidson
1953 James P. O'Donnell
1954 Marshall MacDuffie
1955 Fletcher Knebel
1956 John Bartlow Martin
1957 Harold H. Martin
1958 John L. Cobbs
1959 John Robert Coughlan
1960 Hobart Rowen
1961 Joseph Morschauser
1962 Peter Goldman
1963 Theodore H. White
1964 Sam Castan
1965 Ben H. Bagdikian
1966 John G. Hubbell
1967 William Lambert
1968 Kristin Hunter
1969 William Lambert
1970 David L. Chandler
1971 Arthur Hadley
1972 Thomas Thompson
1973 Floyd Miller
1974 John Guinther
1975 Mike Mallowe
1976 Mary DuBois and Laurence Gonzales
1977 John Conroy

PUBLIC SERVICE IN MAGAZINE JOURNALISM

1949 *Collier's*
1950 *Collier's*
1951 *McCall's*
1952 *Look*
1953 *Look*
1954 *Saturday Evening Post*
1955 *Look*
1956 *Life*
1957 *The Reporter*
1958 *Life*
1959 *Saturday Evening Post*
1960 *Saturday Review*
1961 *Look*
1962 *Look*
1963 *Look*
1964 *Look*

1965 *Reader's Digest*
1966 *Life*
1967 *Philadelphia Magazine*
1968 *Life*
1969 *Philadelphia Magazine*
1970 *The Washingtonian Magazine*
1971 *New Orleans Magazine*
1972 *Philadelphia Magazine*
1973 *Philadelphia Magazine*
1974 *Philadelphia Magazine*
1975 *Philadelphia Magazine*
1976 *Philadelphia Magazine*
1977 *Mother Jones*

RESEARCH ABOUT JOURNALISM

1935 Oscar W. Riegel
1936 Ralph O. Nafziger
1937 Alfred McClung Lee
1938 Frank Luther Mott
1939 Norval Neil Luxon
1940 Paul F. Lazarsfeld
1941 No award
1942 No award
1943 No award
1944 Earl English
1945 Frank Thayer
1946 Ralph D. Casey
    Bruce Lannes Smith
    Harold D. Lasswell
1947 James E. Pollard
1948 J. Edward Gerald
1949 Edwin Emery
1950 Robert S. Harper
1951 No award
1952 Curtis D. MacDougall
1953 Harold L. Cross
1954 Edwin Emery
    Henry Ladd Smith
1956 Theodore B. Peterson
1957 Frank Luther Mott
1958 L. John Martin
1959 Warren C. Price
1960 Leonard W. Levy
1961 Burton Paulu
1962 Theodore E. Kruglak
1963 David P. Forsyth
1964 John Hohenberg
1965 William L. Rivers
1966 Kenneth E. Olson
1967 John Hohenberg
1968 William A. Hachten
1969 Ronald T. Farrar
1970 William Small
1971 John C. Merrill
    Ralph L. Lowenstein
1972 William Small
1973 Philip Meyer
1974 Loren Ghiglione
1975 Marvin Barrett
1976 No award
1977 Peter Braestrup

Silver Lady

KING FEATURES / THE BANSHEES
235 E. 45th St., New York, N.Y. 10017 (212/682-5600)

The Silver Lady is a statue given annually to honor excellence in journalism or cartooning and occasion-ally to a well-known entertainer. A Banshees committee and a board of newspaper editors select the winner from nominations.

1946 **Milton Caniff,** Cartoonist, *Steve Canyon*
1947 **Walt Disney,** Cartoonist, *Mickey Mouse* and others
1948 **Chic Young,** Cartoonist, *Blondie*
1949 **Arthur "Bugs" Baer,** Humor columnist
1950 **Jimmy Hatlo,** Cartoonist, *They'll Do It Every Time*
1951 **George McManus,** Cartoonist, *Bringing Up Father*
1952 **Hal Foster,** Cartoonist, *Prince Valiant*
1953 **Bob Considine,** Columnist, "On the Line"
1954 **Westbrook Pegler,** Columnist
1955 **Mort Walker,** Cartoonist, *Beetle Bailey*
1956 **George Sokolsky,** Columnist, "These Days"
1957 **Burris Jenkins,** Editorial Cartoonist
1958 **Jim Bishop,** Columnist "Jim Bishop: Reporter"
1959 **Rube Goldberg,** Cartoonist
1960 **Milton Caniff,** Cartoonist, *Steve Canyon*
1961 **Roy Crane,** Cartoonist, *Buz Sawyer*
1962 **Fred Lasswell,** Cartoonist, *Barney Google and Snuffy Smith*
1963 **Dik Browne,** Cartoonist, *Hi & Lois*
1964 **Heloise,** Columnist, "Hints From Heloise"
1965 **John Chamberlain,** Columnist, "These Days"
1966 **Bob Hope,** "American" (inscription)
1967 **William F. Buckley,** Columnist, "On The Right"
1968 No award
1969 No award
1970 No award
1971 No award
1972 No award
1973 No award
1974 **Jimmy Durante,** "The Greatest" (inscription)
1975 No award
1976 No award
1977 No award

Harold S. Hirsch Trophy

U.S. SKI WRITERS ASSOCIATION
7 Kensington Rd., Glens Falls, N.Y. 12801 (518/793-1201)

The Harold S. Hirsch Trophy, which consits of a silver-plated typewriter, is given to the ski writer who submits a portfolio of writing deemed to consist of major contributions and to be evidence of excellent reporting on the sport of skiing.

1963 **Bill Berry,** *Sacramento Bee*
1964 **Tom Place,** *Cleveland Plain Dealer*
1965 **Mike Beatrice,** *Boston Globe*
1966 **Bill Kattermann,** *Newark Star-Ledger*
1967 **Burt Sims,** *Los Angeles Herald-Examiner*
1968 **Luanne Pfeifer,** *Santa Monica* (Calif.) *Evening Outlook*
1969 **Dave Knickerbocker,** *Newsday* (Garden City, N.Y.)
1970 **Burt Sims,** *Los Angeles Herald Examiner*
1971 **L. Dana Gatlin,** *Christian Science Monitor*
1972 **Bill Hibbard,** *Milwaukee Journal*
1973 **Ralph Thornton,** *Minneapolis Star*
1974 **Joe Van Zandt,** *Skisport/Chicago*
1975 **Mike Madigan,** *Rocky Mountain News* (Denver, Colo.)
1976 **I. William Berry,** *Long Island* (N.Y.) *Press*
1977 **Charlie Meyers,** *Denver Post*

Lincoln Steffens Award

INTERNATIONAL PLATFORM ASSOCIATION
2564 Berkshire Rd., Cleveland Hts., Ohio 44106
(216/932-0505)

The Lincoln Steffens Award, which consists of a bronze sculpture, is given periodically to the individual judged by the IPA Committee to be an outstanding investigative journalist for exercising great influence through newspapers.

1975 Jack Anderson
1976 Jack Anderson
1977 No award

Stanley Walker Journalism Award

TEXAS INSTITUTE OF LETTERS
Box 7219, Austin, Tex. 78712 (512/471-1833)

The Stanley Walker Journalism Award, which carries a $500 honorarium, is given annually for the best example of journalistic writhing about the state in newspaper, magazine or book form.

1962 Anita Brewer, *Austin American-Statesman* ("Death Takes Noted Author")
1963 A. C. Greene, *Dallas Times-Herald* ("No Life is Lived without Influence")
Larry Grove, *Dallas Morning News* ("Rain, and a Day of Reflection")
1964 Bill Porterfield, *Houston Chronicle* ("The President's Homeland")
1965 Paul Crume, *Dallas Morning News* ("A Newsman Looks at the World's Week")
1966 Jim Berry and Glen Castlebury, *Austin American-Statesman* ("Sniper in U. T. Tower")
1967 John Tackett, *Fort Worth Star-Telegram* ("Time Stands Still")
1968 Bill Porterfield, *Houston Chronicle* ("The Archbishop and the Rebel Priests")
1969 Greg Olds, *The Texas Observer* (McCroklin Stories)
1970 Elroy Bode, *The Texas Observer* ("Requiem for a WASP School")
1971 Charles Evans, *Houston Chronicle* ("The Howard Hughes Series")
1972 Larry L. King, *Life* ("The Last Frontier")
1973 Elroy Bode, *The Texas Observer* ("The Making of a Legend")
1974 Griffin Smith, Jr., *The Texas Monthly* ("Forgotten Places")
1975 Archer Fullingim, *Heidleberg Press* ("A Country Editor's View of Life")
1976 Griffin Smith, *The Texas Monthly* ("Why Does Dolph Briscoe Want to be Governor?")
1977 Gary Cartwright, *The Texas Monthly* ("The Endless Odyssey of Patrick Henry Polk")

Paul Tobenkin Memorial Award

COLUMBIA UNIVERSITY
Graduate School of Journalism, New York, N.Y. 10027 (212/280-3828)

The Paul Tobenkin Memorial Award recognizes achievement in the field of newspaper writing "in the fight against racial and religious hatred, intolerance, discrimination and every form of bigotry, reflecting the spirit of Paul Tobenkin," who was for twenty-five years a reporter with the *New York Herald Tribune*. Nominations are generally made by editors. Winners, who share $250 and receive a certificate, are selected by a jury of educators and journalists

1961 Bonnie Angelo, *Newsday*
1962 Dale Wright, *World Telegram and Sun*
1963 James K. Batten, *Charlotte* (N.C.) *Observer*
1964 Robert S. Bird, *New York Herald Tribune*
1965 No award
1966 No award
1967 Cal Olson, *Fargo* (N.D.) *Forum*
1968 Bill Burrus, *New York Post*
1969 Bernie Bookbinder and five colleagues, *Newsday*
1970 Kent Pollock, *Palm Beach* (Fla.) *Post*
1971 Richard Oliver, *New York Post*
1972 Jon Nordheimer *New York Times*
1973 Howard Kohn *Detroit Free Press*
1974 Tom Stundza, *Gary* (Ind.) *Post-Tribune*
1975 Mike Masterson, *Hot Springs* (Ark.) *National Park Sentinel-Record*
1976 Joe Stroud, *Detroit Free Press*
1977 Barry Siegel, *Los Angeles Times*

Walter Hight Award

NATIONAL TURF WRITERS ASSOCIATION
6000 Executive Blvd., Ste. 317, Rockville, Md. 20852

The Walter Haight Award is given annually for meritorious achievement in turf writing and the coverage of horse racing by a vote of the membership.

1972 Jimmy Doyle
1973 George Ryall
1974 Raleigh Burroughs
1975 Don Fair
1976 Saul Rosen
1977 Red Smith

Carr Van Anda Award

OHIO UNIVERSITY
School of Journalism, Athens, Ohio 45701 (614/594-5511)

The Carr Van Anda Award, which consists of a plaque and a citation, is given annually to honor enduring contributions to journalism. The faculty selects the winners.

1968 Turner Catledge, *New York Times*
Edward W. Barrett, Columbia University School of Journalism
Walter Cronkite, CBS News
1969 Wes Gallagher, Associated Press
Margaret Bourke-White, photojournalist
Osborne Elliott, *Newsweek*
1970 John S. Knight, Knight Newspapers
Gordon Parks, *Life*
Howard K. Smith, ABC News
1971 James Reston, *New York Times*
Norman Cousins, *Saturday Review*
1972 Pauline Frederick, NBC News
Richard Leonard, *Milwaukee Journal*
1973 William Attwood, *Newsday*
Harry Reasoner, ABC News
1974 Otis Chandler, *Los Angeles Times*
Shana Alexander, *Newsweek*
1975 Katharine Graham, *Washington Post*
Philip Meyer, Knight Newspapers
Eric Sevareid, CBS News
1976 A. M. Rosenthal, *New York Times*

Patricia Carbine, *Ms.*
1977 Mike Wallace, CBS-TV
Helen Thomas, United Press International

Award of Journalistic Merit
WILLIAM ALLEN WHITE FOUNDATION
105 Flint Hall, University of Kansas, Lawrence, Kansas. 55405 (913/864-2700)

The Award of Journalistic Merit, which carries a $500 honorarium, is given annually for journalistic effort that exemplifies service both to the profession and to the community.

1950 James B. Reston
1951 Ernest K. Lindley
1952 Erwin D. Canham
1953 Palmer Hoyt
1954 Grove Patterson
1955 Norman E. Isaacs
1956 Roy A. Roberts
1957 Irving Dilliard
1958 Jenkin Lloyd Jones
1959 Ben Hibbs
1960 Jules Dubios
1961 Hodding Carter
1962 Bernard Kilgore
1963 Paul Miller
1964 Clark R. Mollenhoff
1965 Earl J. Johnson
1966 Gardner Cowles
1967 Wes Gallagher
1968 Mark Ethridge
1969 Walter Cronkite
1970 Eugene Pulliam
1971 Vermont Royster
1972 John S. Knight
1973 Barry Bingham, Sr.
1974 Arthur O. Sulzberger
1975 Otis Chandler
1976 Peter Lisagor
1977 Sylvia Porter

John Peter Zenger Award
UNIVERSITY OF ARIZONA
Dept. of Journalism, Tucson, Ariz. 85721 (602/884-2561)

The John Peter Zenger Award, which carries a $500 honorarium, annually honors distinguished service on behalf of freedom of the press and the public's right to know. Previous winners and the head of the Department of Journalism submit nominations, which appear on a ballot sent to approximately 400 newspapers for selection.

1954 Palmer Hoyt, *Denver Post*
1955 Basil L. Walters, *Chicago Daily News*
1956 James S. Pope, *Louisville* (Ky.) *Courier Journal*
1957 James R. Wiggins, *Washington Post* and *Times Herald*
1958 John E. Moss, Chairman, House Government Information Subcommittee
1959 Herbert Brucker, *Hartford Courant*
1960 Virgil M. Newton, Jr., *Tampa* (Fla.) *Tribune*
1961 Clark R. Mollenhoff, Cowles Publications
1962 John H. Colburn, *Richmond* (Va.) *Times-Dispatch*
1963 James B. Reston, *New York Times*
1964 John N. Heiskell, *Arkansas Gazette*
1965 Eugene C. Pulliam, *Arizona Republic* and *Phoenix Gazette*
1966 Arthur Krock, *New York Times*
1967 John S. Knight, Knight Newspapers
1968 Wes Gallagher, Associated Press
1969 J. Edward Murray, *Arizona Republic* (Phoenix)
1970 Erwin D. Canham, *Christian Science Monitor*
1971 *New York Times*
1972 Dan Hicks, Jr., *Monroe County Observer* (Madisonville, Tenn.)
1973 Katharine M. Graham, *Washington Post*
1974 Thomas E. Gish, *The Berkshire Eagle* (Pittsfield, Mass.)
1975 Seymour M. Hersh, *New York Times*
1976 Donald F. Bolles, *Arizona Republic* (Phoenix)
1977 Robert W. Greene, *Newsday* (Garden City, N.Y.)

Radio & Television

Contents

Related Awards

Robert Eunson Award

ASSOCIATED PRESS BROADCASTERS
50 Rockefeller Plaza, New York, N.Y. 10020 (212/262-8122)

The Robert Eunson Award, which consists of a plaque, is given annually on selection by the AP Broadcasters' board of directors to honor distinguished service to the broadcast industry.

1976 Lawrence E. Spivak
1977 Robert Trout

Radio Programming Award
Deejay of the Year Awards

BILLBOARD
9000 Sunset Blvd., Los Angeles, Calif. 90069 (213/273-7040)

The Radio Programming Award, which consists of a plaque or scroll, annually honors outstanding achievements in programming, as based on votes of regional judges (in the case of deejay honors) and coupons in *Billboard* sent in by record and radio industry people.

1976 **Stan Monteiro** (Columbia), Vice-president in Charge of National Promotion
      Bob Sherwood (Columbia), National Promotion Man
      Mike Atkinson (Columbia, Los Angeles), Regional Promotion Man: West
      Paul Ellis (Capricorn) Cincinnati), Regional Promotion Man: East
      John Parker (Casablanca, Atlanta), Regional Promotion Man: South
      Dick Lemke (Elektra/Asylum, Chicago), Regional Promotion Man: Midwest
      Jerry Ross (Chrysalis, New York), Local Promotion Man: East
      Barry Freeman (Atlantic, Los Angeles), Local Promotion Man: West
      Lenny Zee (All South, New Orleans), Local Promotion Man: South
      Dick Ware (Columbia, Kansas City), Local Promotion Man: Midwest
      Paul Gallis, Independent Promotion Men
      KFRC (San Francisco), Radio Station of the Year-Top 40 (Major Market)
      WSGA (Savannah, Ga.), Radio Station of the Year-Top 40 (Small Market)
      KEX (Portland, Ore.), Radio Station of the Year-MOR (Major Market)
      WBT (Charlotte, N.C.), Radio Station of the Year-MOR (Small Market)
      WHN (New York), Radio Station of the Year-Country (Major Market)
      KCUB (Tucson, Ariz.), Radio Station of the Year-Country (Small Market)
      KSAN (San Francisco), Radio Station of the Year-Progressive (Major Market)
      KZEL (Eugene, Ore.), Radio Station of the Year-Progressive (Small Market)
      WDIA (Memphis, Tenn.) Radio Station of the Year-R&B (Major Market)
      WTMI (Miami), Radio Station of the Year-R&B (Small Market)
      Bill Garcia (WRBQ, Tampa, Fla.), Program Director of the Year-Top 40 (Major Market)
      Bill St. James (WBCQ, Roswell, N.M.), Program Director of the Year-Top 40 (Small Market)

Bob Hughes (WASH, Washington, D.C.), Program Director of the Year-MOR (Major Market)
Andy Bickel (WBT, Charlotte, N.C.), Program Director of the Year-MOR (Small Market)
Bill Robinson (WIRE, Indianapolis, Ind.), Program Director of the Year-Country (Major Market)
Cyril Brennan (WBAM, Montgomery, Ala.), Program Director of the Year-Country (Small Market)
Rick Liebert (KGB, San Diego, Calif.), Program Director of the Year-Progressive (Major Market)
Stan Garrett (KZEL, Eugene, Ore.), Program Director of the Year-Progressive (Small Market)
Jim Maddox (KDIA, Oakland, Calif.), Program Director of the Year-R&B (Major Markets)
Shotgun Tom Kelly (KFMB, San Diego, Calif.), Air Personalities of the Year-Top 40 (Major Markets)
Terry Tyler (WIRK, W. Palm Beach, Fla.), Air Personalities of The Year-Top 40 (Small Markets)
Gene Klavan (WNEW, New York), Air Personalities of the Year-MOR (Major Markets)
Peter Hunn (WNLC, New London, Conn.), Air Personalities of the Year-MOR (Small Markets)
Alison Steele (WNEW-FM, New York), Air Personalities of the Year-Progressive (Major Markets)
Barry Grant (WPLR, New Haven, Conn.), Air Personalities of the Year-Progressive (Small Markets)
Deano Day (WDEE, Detroit), Air Personalities of the Year-Country (Major Markets)
Bob Barwick (WWVA, Wheeling, W.Va.), Air Personalities of the Year-Country (Small Markets)
J.J. Johnson (KDAY, Los Angeles), Air Personalities of the Year-R&B
TSgt. Bill Billingsley (TUSLOG Detachment 124, Incirlik CDI, Turkey), Military Air Personalities of the Year

1977 **Bill Robinson** (WIRE, Indianapolis, Ind.), Grand International Program Director of the Year
      Gary Owens (KMPC, Los Angeles), Grand International Air Personality of the Year
      Nat Stevens (KOY, Phoenix, Ariz.), Program Director of the Year-Adult Contemporary (Major Markets)
      Bill Parris (WLPL, Baltimore), Program Director of the Year-Top 40 (Major Markets)
      Bob Pittman (WKQX, Chicago), Program Director of the Year-Album Rock (Major Markets)
      Bill Robinson (WIRE, Indianapolis, Ind.), Program Director of the Year-Country Music (Major Markets)
      J.J. Johnson (KDAY, Los Angeles), Program Director of the Year-R&B (Major Markets)
      Michael O'Shea (WFTL, Ft. Lauderdale, Fla.), Program Director of the Year-Adult Contemporary (Under a million population)
      Dave Hamilton (WROK, Rockford, Ill.), Program Director of the Year-Country (Under a million population)
      Tom Edwards (KEED, Eugene, Ore.), Program Director of the Year-Country (Under a million population)
      Barry Grant (WPLR, New Haven, Conn.), Program Director of the Year-AlbumRock (Under a million population)
      American Top 40 (Los Angeles), Best Regularly Scheduled Syndicated Program
      The Evolution of Rock (CHUM, Toronto, Ont.), Syndicated Special of the Year
      John Records Landecker (WLS, Chicago) and **Dan Ingram** (WABC, New York), Tie for Air Personality of the Year-Top 40 (Major Markets)
      Lee Arnold (WHN, New York), Air Personality of the Year-Country (Major Markets)

Gary Owens (KMPC, Los Angeles), Air Personality of the Year-Adult Contemporary (Major Markets)

Ken Noble (KLOL, Houston), Air Personality of the Year-Album Rock (Major Markets)

Bobby Jay (WWRL, New York), Air Personality of the Year-Black Music (Major Markets)

Nick O'Neil (WGH, Norfolk, Va.), Air Personality of the Year-Top 40 (Under a million population)

Charlie Cook (WWVA, Wheeling, W.Va.), Air Personality of the Year-Country (Under a million population)

John Young (WSM, Nashville, Tenn.), Air Personality of the Year-Adult Contemporary (Under a million population)

Bernie Bernard (WBAB, Babylon, N.Y.), Air Personality of the Year-Album Rock (Under a million population)

Melvin Jones (WLOK, Memphis, Tenn.), Air Personality of the Year-Black Music (Under a million population)

Jose Mauro, (Radio TUPI, Rio de Janeiro, Brazil), International Program Director of the Year

Frank Jeffcoast (2ue, Sydney, Australia), International General Manager of the Year

WGR (Buffalo, N.Y.), Radio Station of the Year-Adult Contemporary (Major Markets)

KFRC (San Francisco), Radio Station of the Year-Top 40 (Major Markets)

KMET (Los Angeles), Radio Station of the Year-Album Rock (Major Markets)

WIRE (Indianapolis, Ind.), Radio Station of the Year-Country (Major Markets)

WDIA (Memphis, Tenn.), Radio Station of the Year-Black Music (Major Markets)

WFMT (Chicago), Radio Station of the Year- Classical Music (Major Markets)

WKZO (Kalamazoo, Mich.), Radio Station of the Year-Adult Contemporary (Under a million population)

WROK (Rockford, Ill.), Radio Station of the Year-Top 40 (Under a million population)

WPLR (New Haven, Conn.), Radio Station of the Year-Country (Under a million population)

KEED (Eugene, Ore.), Radio Station of the Year-Country (Under a million population)

John O'Day (WGAR, Cleveland), Newsperson of the Year (Major Markets)

Ray Carney (KPNW, Eugene, Ore.), Newsperson of the Year (Under a million population)

Bob Levy (AFNT, Taipei, Formosa), Best Military Personality of the Year

The Abby Drover Story (CFTR, Toronto, Ont.) Public Service Program Award

An Evening with Gordon Lightfoot (KNX-FM, Los Angeles), Entertainment Special of the Year

Car Tune (WHWH, Princeton, N.J.), Commercial of the Year

Water Safety (CFTR, Toronto, Ont.), Public Service Announcement of the Year

Ed Buterbaugh (CKLW, Detroit), Engineer of the Year

Bruce Wendell (Capitol Records), Chief Promotion Executive

Steve Meyer (Capitol Records), National Promotion Executive

Tim Kehr (20th Century Records), Regional Promotion Executive

Gene Denonovich (Columbia records), Local Promotion Executive

Doug Lee (Midwest Promotions, Minneapolis, Minn.), Independent Promotion Executive

DEEJAY OF THE YEAR—LOCAL

Jim Burgess, Atlanta

John Luongo, Boston

Howard Metz, Dallas

Sam Meyer, Houston

Bob Vitteriti, Miami Area

Bobby DJ and Tom Sevarese, New York

Jim Weatherly, Phoenix

Wes Bradley, San Francisco

Bill Owens, Baltimore/Washington, D.C.

Mike Graber, Chicago

Joel Levin, Detroit

Paul Dougan, Los Angeles

Stu Neal, New Orleans

Kurt Borusiewicz, Philadelphia

Gary Larkin, Pittsburgh

John Bush, Seattle

DEEJAY OF THE YEAR (Individual and Disco)

Tom Sevarese; The Sandpiper, New York

Paul Dougan; Studio One, Los Angeles

John Hedges; The City, San Francisco

Kurt Borusiewicz; D.C.A., Philadelphia

Marty Ross; Menjo's, Detroit

Artie Feldman; Sunday's, Chicago

Jim Stuard; 1270 Disco, Boston

Jim Burgess; The Casbah, Atlanta

Ram Rocha; Old Plantation, Houston

Bill Owens; Lost & Found, Washington, D.C. Baltimore/Washington

Gary Larkin; The Giraffe, Pittsburgh

Jack Wetherby; Maggie's Back Door Disco, Phoenix

Tom Neff; Sportspage, Denver

David Lowe; Windward Resort, Miami

Victor Ocasio; Puerto Rico

Paul Werth; Boren Street Disco, Seattle

1977 DISCO FORUM AWARD *

Don't Leave Me This Way (Thelma Houston), Single of the Year (Heavy Disco/Heavy Radio Combined Play)

I Don't Wanna Lose Your Love (Emotions), Single of the Year (Heavy Disco/Light Radio Combined Play)

I Feel Love (Donna Summer), Disco Single/LP Cut of the Year

Disco Inferno (Trammps and Dr. Buzzards Original Savannah Band), Tie for Disco Album of the Year

Georgio Moroder and Peter Bellotti, Best Producers of a Disco Record

Donna Summer, Georgio Moroder and Peter Bellotti, Disco Composer of the Year

Donna Summer, Disco Artist of the Year

Grace Jones, Most Promising New Disco Artist of the year

Elton Ahi, for *Uptown Festival,* Disco DJ Mix of the Year

Uptown Festival (Shalamar), Disco DJ's Favorite 12-inch disc

Casablanca and TK Records, Tie for Disco Record Label of the Year

Ray Caviano, Disco Record Promotion Person of the Year (in-house)

Marc Simon, Disco Record Promotion Person of the Year (independent)

Salsoul Orchestra, Disco Orchestra of the Year

GLI Mixer 3880, Best New Audio Product of the Year

Meteor Sonalight (lighting controllers), Best New Disco Lighting Product of the Year

---

* This award appears here by error. It should appear with the other Disco awards on p. 260.

Norby Walters, Disco Concert Promoter
2001 Clubs, Disco Club Franchiser of the Year
Michael O'Harro, Disco Club Consultant of the Year
Ralph McDonald and Dennis Coffey, Tie for Disco Instrumentalist of the Year
Vince Montana, Disco Music Arranger of the Year
Bobby DJ and Tom Sevarese, Disco Deejay of the Year

Poses Brandeis University Creative Arts Award

BRANDEIS UNIVERSITY
Brandeis University Commission Office, 12 E. 77th St., New York, N.Y. 10021 (212/472-1501)

One of a series of awards in the creative arts, the Jack I. and Lillian L. Poses Brandeis University Creative Arts Award is given annually to recognize talent in mid-career in theatre arts and film. The award, which may not be applied for, carries an honorarium of $1,000 and a medal or citation. Professional juries chosen by the commission select the winners.

MEDAL AWARD

1957 Hallie Flanagan Davis (Theatre arts)
1958 Stark Young (Theatre arts)
1959 George Kelly (Theatre arts)
1960 Thornton Wilder (Theatre arts)
1961 Lillian Hellman (Theatre arts)
1962 Samuel N. Behrman (Theatre arts)
1963 Jo Mielziner (Theatre arts)
1964 Cheryl Crawford (Theatre arts)
1965 Tennessee Williams (Theatre arts)
1966 Eva Le Gallienne (Theatre arts)
1967 Jerome Robbins (Theatre arts)
1968 Richard Rodgers (Theatre arts)
1969 Boris Aronson (Theatre arts)
1970 Arthur Miller (Theatre arts)
1971 Charles Chaplin (Film)
1972 Alfred Lunt and Lynn Fontanne (Theatre arts)
1973 John Ford (Film)
1974 Helen Hayes (Theatre arts)
1975 King Vidor (Film)
1976 Harold Clurman (Theatre arts)
1977 Howard Hawks (Film)

CITATION

1957 The Shakespearewrights (Theatre arts)
1958 Paul Shyre (Theatre arts)
1959 Richard Hayes (Theatre arts)
1960 William Alfred (Theatre arts)
1961 Julian Bech and Judith Malina (Theatre arts)
1962 James P. Donleavy (Theatre arts)
1963 Joseph Papp (Theatre arts)
1964 Jack Richardson (Theatre arts)
1965 Michael Smith (Theatre arts)
1966 Alvin Epstein (Theatre arts)
1967 Ellen Stewart (Theatre arts)
1968 Tom O'Horgan (Theatre arts)
1969 The Negro Ensemble Company (Theatre arts)
1970 The Open Theater (Theater arts)
1971 Bruce Baillie (Film)
1972 The New Dramatists (Theatre arts)
1973 Stanley Brakhage (Film)
1974 Arena Stage (Theatre arts)
1975 Jordan Belson (Film)
1976 Sam Sheppard (Theatre arts)
1977 John Hancock (Film)

Larry Boggs Award
Robert Beisswenger Memorial Award
Idell Kaitz Memorial Award

NATIONAL CABLE TELEVISION ASSOCIATION
918 16th St. NW, Washington, D.C. 20006 (202/457-6765)

The Larry Boggs Award is given annually to an active member of the cable-television industry on recommendation of association members and selection by an awards committee.

1965 Bill Daniels
1966 Benjamin Conroy
1967 George Barco
1968 Fred Stevenson
1969 Martin Malarkey
1970 Irving B. Kahn
1971 Milton J. Shapp
1972 John Gwin
1973 E. Stratford Smith
1974 Frank Thompson
1975 Amos B. Hostetter, Jr.
1976 Alfred Stern
1977 Sam Haddock

The Robert Beisswenger Memorial Award goes annually to a member whose efforts on behalf of the association are judged as outstanding by the awards committee.

1975 NCTA Associate Members
1976 Ray Schneider
1977 Richard Jackson

The Idell Kaitz Memorial Award annually honors the significant contributions of a woman in the industry, as nominated from the membership and judged by an awards committee.

1973 Yolanda Barco
1974 Polly Dunn
1975 Beverly Murphy
1976 Beverly Land
1977 No award

John J. Gillin Jr. Award

CANADIAN ASSOCIATION OF BROADCASTERS
85 Sparks St., Ste. 909, Ottawa, Ont. K1P 5S2, Canada (613/233-4035)

The John J. Gillin Jr. Award is given to the AM Station of the Year for making the greatest public service or charitable contribution to its community. Stations may submit tape cassettes no longer than ten minutes for evaluation by a panel of judges. The winning station receives an engraved clock/barometer, and the winner's name is engraved on a permanent trophy.

1951 CJOB (Winnipeg)
1952 CJOC (Lethbridge, Alb.)
1953 CKNW (New Westminster, B.C.)
1954 CJVI (Victoria, B.C.)
1955 CFAR (Flin Flon, Man.)
1956 CHAB (Moose Jaw, Sask.)
1957 CJVI (Victoria, B.C.)
1958 CJON (St. John's, Nfld.)
1959 CHAB (Moose Jaw, Sask.)
1960 Radio Nord (Rouyn, Que.)

1961	CHUM (Toronto)
1962	CKPR (Thunder Bay [Fort William], Ont.)
1963	CJBQ (Belleville, Que.)
1964	CHUM (Toronto)
1965	CFMB (Montreal)
1966	CKAC (Montreal)
1967	CJAD and CJMS (Montreal)
1968	No award
1969	CKLG (Vancouver)
1970	CHUM (Toronto)
1971	CKLG (Vancouver)
1972	CKXL (Calgary)
1973	CJCH (Halifax)
1974	CKDH (Amherst, N.S.)
1975	CHLN (Trois-Rivieres, Que.)
1976	CKBI (Prince Albert, Sask.)
1977	CHRC (Quebec City)
	CHML (Hamilton, Ont.)

H. Gordon Love News Trophy

CANADIAN ASSOCIATION OF BROADCASTERS
85 Sparks St., Ste 909, Ottawa, Ont. K1P 5S2, Canada
(613/233-4035)

The H. Gordon Love News Trophy is awarded annually for a significant contribution to the improvement or increased availability of news material used by broadcasting stations in Canada and for making the public more conscious of the value of broadcast news. A committee of judges selects the winner, which receives a trophy that is a replica of an early microphone.

1968	CFPL-TV (London)
1969	CJCH (Halifax)
1970	CJCH-TV (Halifax)
1971	CJCI (Prince George, B.C.)
1972	CKLG (Vancouver)
1973	CKNW (New Westminster, B.C.)
1974	CFRB (Toronto)
1975	CJCB (Sydney)
1976	CKY-TV (Winnipeg)
1977	CKY-TV (Winnipeg)

Ted Rogers, Sr./Velma Rogers Graham Award

CANADIAN ASSOCIATION OF BROADCASTERS
85 Sparks St., Ste 909, Ottawa, Ont. K1P 5S2, Canada
(613/233-4035)

The Ted Rogers, Sr./Velma Rogers Graham Award honors an individual for significant single or continuing contributions to Canadian broadcasting or for exceptional community service. The award consists of an original oil painting. A committee of judges selects the winner.

1975	A.A. Brunner, Global TV
1976	G.R.A. Rice, CFRM-AM, -FM and -TV (Edmonton)
1977	Alan F. Waters, CHUM Ltd. (Toronto)

Colonel Keith S. Rogers Engineering Award

CANADIAN ASSOCIATION OF BROADCASTERS

85 Sparks St., Ste. 909, Ottawa, Ont. K1P 5S2, Canada
(613/233-4035)

The Colonel Keith S. Rogers Engineering Award recognizes significant engineering accomplishments by a station or individual for the successful development of technical ideas, approaches or methods. A panel of judges selects the winner, who receives a trophy.

1950	J. O. Blick, CJOB (Winnipeg)
1951	CJOB, CKRC and CKY (Winnipeg)
1952	George Chandler, CJOR (Vancouver)
1953	Glen Robitaille, CFPL (London, Ont.)
1954	William Forst, CKOM (Saskatoon)
1955	CFJB (Brampton) and CHUM (Toronto)
1956	No award
1957	CJON (St. John's, Nfld.)
1958	W.E. Jeynes, CHCH-TV (Hamilton, Ont.)
1959	No award
1960	No award
1961	Glen Robitaille, CFPL (London, Ont.)
1962	Clive Eastwood, CFRB (Toronto)
1963	W.B. Smith, Dept. of Transport (Ottawa)
1964	No award
1965	No award
1966	No award
1967	Ron Turnpenny, CHFI (Toronto)
1968	No award
1969	No award
1970	CFAM-CHSM (Altona-Steinbach, Man.)
1971	Conrad Lavigne, CFCL-TV (Timmins, Ont.)
1972	Western Broadcasting (Vancouver)
1973	Ernie Rose, CHAN-TV (Vancouver)
1974	No award
1975	CKXL (Calgary)
1976	No award
1977	Radiomutuel (Montreal)

Lloyd L. Moffat Award

CANADIAN ASSOCIATION OF BROADCASTERS
85 Sparks St., Ste. 909, Ottawa, Ont. K1P 5S2, Canada
(613/233-4035)

The Lloyd L. Moffat Award goes annually to the FM Station of the Year for making the greatest contribution to the community. Stations may submit tapes up to ten minutes long for evaluation by a panel of judges. The winner receives a trophy.

1968	CJMS-FM (CKMF-FM) (Montreal)
1969	CHRC-FM (Quebec)
1970	CFPL-FM (London)
1971	CFPL-FM (London)
1972	CKLG-FM (Vancouver)
1973	CFMI-FM (New Westminster, B.C.)
1974	CFFM-FM (Kamloops, B.C.)
1975	CHSC-FM (St. Catharines, Ont.)
1976	CKFM-FM (Toronto)
1977	CHQM-FM (Vancouver)

ACT Achievement in Children's Television Award

ACTION FOR CHILDREN'S TELEVISION
46 Austin St., Newtonville, Mass. 02160 (617/527-7870)

The ACT Achievement in Children's Television Award is presented annually to broadcasters who have made a significant achievement toward improving children's television. Individuals, stations, networks and companies or organizations that provide funding for exceptional programs or set meritorious advertising policies may be honored.

1972 Post-Newsweek television stations in Washington, D.C., and Florida for seeking quality programs and clustering commercials on such programs
Hallmark Cards, for sponsoring *The Snow Goose,* NBC
Health-tex, for institutional advertising on *Babar Comes to America,* NBC
Children's Television Workshop, for conceiving a creative unit devoted to producing children's shows and experimenting in television education for young children
Fred Rogers, for pioneering efforts to meet the emotional needs of young children through television
Robert Keeshan, for sixteen years of creative children's television on *Captain Kangaroo*
The Kids' Thing, WHDH-TV, Boston, for noncommercial school vacation week programs
Public broadcasting stations, for *Misterogers' Neighborhood, Sesame Street, Electric Company, Masquerade, ZOOM, Hodge Podge Lodge* and *What's New*
1973 Sears-Roebuck Foundation, for *Misterogers' Neighborhood*
Xerox Corp., for Spanish and Portuguese versions of *Sesame Street*
Mobil Oil Corp., for *Electric Company*
IBM, for *Sleeping Beauty* ballet, aired when many children were watching
Miles Laboratories, Sauter Labs/Hoffmann-La Roche and Bristol-Myers, for withdrawing vitamin pill advertising from children's programs
Avco and Meredith Broadcasting Corp., for combining resources to produce meaningful children's programs
ABC-TV, for *Afterschool Specials,* one hour monthly
CBS News, for *What's An Election All About* and *What's A Convention All About,* news specials for children
NBC-TV, for *Watch Your Child,* an attempt at a daily half-hour program with limited commercialism
Westinghouse Broadcasting, for continued commitment to science for children, specifically *Earth Lab*
WCVB-TV, Boston, for commitment to needs of community's children, specifically *Jabberwocky* and *Young Reporters*
WMAL-TV, Washington, for daily children's program with clustered commercials, *The Magic Door*
WPIX-TV, New York, for two local children's programs with clustered commercials, *Magic Garden* and *Joya's Fun School*
The 350,000 children who contributed creative material and ideas to *Zoom*
Forty-eight commercial stations who aired *Vision On,* the first children's program designed for both deaf and hearing children
Forty-four commercial stations, for airing *Sesame Street* without commercials
1974 ABC-TV stations, for *Over 7,* magazine format for family viewing
Alphaventure, for creating *Big Blue Marble* with ITT noncommercial backing and teacher materials to supplement the program
CBS-TV News, for *In the News,* brief Saturday morning reports

Chinese Committee for Affirmative Action, San Francisco, for *Yut, Yee, Sahm (Here We Come)*
Exxon USA Foundation, for supporting *Villa Alegre* on PBS
Prime Time School Television, Chicago, for developing and distributing educational materials for classroom use about televised prime-time specials and documentaries
WBZ-TV, Boston, for *Something Else,* featuring local children in a constructive alternative to Saturday morning viewing
WNET, New York, for two-week festival of quality daytime programming
1975 CBS-TV, for *The CBS Children's Film Festival*
CBS-TV News, for *Marshall Efron's Illustrated, Simplified and Painless Sunday School*
Children's Television Workshop, for *The Electric Company*
Robert Keeshan Associates, producers of *Captain Kangaroo*
KLRN-TV, Austin, Tex., for *Carrascolendas,* bilingual program
NBC-TV, for *GO-USA,* a series of historical dramas
Post-Newsweek stations, for *The Reading Show,* combining broadcast and published materials
Taft Broadcasting Co., for *Max B. Nimble*
Martin Tahse Productions, for bringing back *Kukla, Fran and Ollie*
Westinghouse Broadcasting Co, for *Call it Macaroni,* adventure series
WGBH, Boston, for *The Spider's Web,* daily radio storybook
WXYZ-TV, Detroit, for *Hot Fudge,* contributing to preventive medicine in mental health
1976 ABC-TV, for *ABC Afterschool Specials,* dramatic series
ABC-TV News, for *Animals Animals Animals*
Behrens Co., Miami, for *Kidsworld,* national news magazine for children with contributions for participating stations
Educational Development Center, Newton, Mass., for *Infinity Factory*
KETC-TV, St. Louis, for *Common Cents*
KOMO-TV, Seattle, for *Boomerang*
KRON-TV, San Francisco, for *Kidswatch*
NBC-TV, for *Muggsy*
NBC-TV, for *Special Treat*
WGBH-TV, Boston, for *Rebop*
WMAQ-TV, Chicago, for *Bubblegum Digest*
WQED-TV, Pittsburgh, for *Once Upon a Classic*
WSB-TV, Atlanta, for *Operation Education*
Sears Roebuck Foundation for *Misterogers' Neighborhood*
1977 ABC, *Weekend Specials*
CBS, *Fat Albert*
Corporation for Entertainment and Learning Inc.
Field Communications for *Snipets*
South Carolina ETV, for *Studio See*
Walt Disney Productions, for *The New Mickey Mouse Club*
WGBH, (Boston) for *Captioned Zoom*
WIIC-TV, (Pittsburgh) for *Catercousins*
WRC-TV, (Washington, D.C.) for *Beth and Bower Half Hour*
WSB-TB, (Atlanta) for *Super 2*
WTTW-TV, (Chicago) *As *We* See* It*

OTHER AWARDS

1972 Commendations (for children's programming which were cited but did not meet ACT's criteria for limitation or absence of commercialism):
Earth Lab
Children's Film Festival
In the News
You Are There
Jackson Five
Curiosity Shop
Make A Wish
Take A Giant Step
Mr. Wizard
1973 Special Mention:
The Waltons
National Geographic Society Specials
Jacques Cousteau's Specials
1975 Special Award:
Agency for Instructional Television for informational and informative classroom programs
1976 Special Award:
Public Broadcasting Service
1977 Special Award:
Westinghouse Broadcasting Co.

Morgan Cox Award

WRITERS GUILD OF AMERICA, WEST
8955 Beverly Blvd., Los Angeles, Cal. 90048 (213/550-1000)

The Morgan Cox Award, which consists of a silver medallion, is a service award granted annually for perpetuation of the ideals represented by the life of Morgan Cox, including idealism, effort and personal sacrifice.

1970 Barry Trivers
1971 Leonard Spigelgass
1972 Allen Rivkin
1973 David Harmon
1974 James R. Webb
1975 Edmund H. North
1976 William Ludwig
1977 Herbert Baker

DuPont-Columbia Awards

COLUMBIA UNIVERSITY
Graduate School of Journalism, New York, N.Y. 10027
(212/280-5047)

The Alfred I. DuPont-Columbia University Awards annually honor excellence in local and national broadcasting. The awards are based on research done in conjunction with the annual DuPont-Columbia Survey of Broadcast Journalism of news and public affairs broadcasting. Nominations may be made to the Survey and Awards Director for consideration by the jury. Until 1965 this award was known as the DuPont Award. No fixed categories exist.

1942 KGEI Radio (San Francisco)
Fulton Lewis, Jr.
1943 WLW Radio (Cincinnati)
WMAZ Radio (Macon, Ga.)
Raymond Gram Swing
1944 WJR Radio (Detroit)
WTAG Radio (Worcester, Mass.)
H.V. Kaltenborn
1945 KDKA Radio (Pittsburgh)
WNAX Radio (Yanktown, S.D.)

Lowell Thomas
1946 WHO Radio (Des Moines)
WKY Radio (Oklahoma City)
Elmer Davis
1947 WBBM Radio (Chicago)
WFIL Radio (Philadelphia)
Edward R. Murrow
1948 WLS Radio (Chicago)
KLZ Radio (Denver)
Henry J. Taylor
1949 WNOX Radio (Knoxville, Tenn.)
WWJ Radio (Detroit)
WPIX Television (New York)
American Broadcasting Co.
1950 WFIL Television (Philadelphia)
WAVZ Radio (New Haven, Conn.)
John Cameron Swayze
1951 WCAU and WCAU-TV (Philadelphia)
WEEI Radio (Boston)
Joseph C. Harsch
1952 WBNS-TV (Columbus, Ohio)
WMT-Radio (Cedar Rapids, Iowa)
Gerald W. Johnson
1953 WBZ and WBZ-TV (Boston)
WOI-TV (Ames, Iowa)
Pauline Frederick
1954 WHAS Radio (Louisville, Ky.)
KGAK Radio (Gallup, N.M.)
Eric Sevareid
1955 WTIC Radio (Hartford, Conn.)
WICC Radio (Bridgeport, Conn.)
Howard K. Smith
1956 KNXT-TV (Los Angeles)
WFMT Radio (Chicago)
Chet Huntley
1957 KRON-TV (San Francisco)
KARD Radio (Wichita, Kan.)
Clifton Utley
1958 KLZ-TV (Denver)
WSNY Radio (Schenectady, N.Y.)
David Brinkley
1959 WNTA-TV (Newark, N.J.)
KOLN-TV (Lincoln, Neb.)
David Schoenbrun
1960 KDKA-TV (Pittsburgh)
WAVZ Radio (New Haven, Conn.)
Edward P. Morgan
1961 KING Radio (Seattle)
KPFP Radio (Los Angeles)
Martin Agronsky
1962 WFMT Radio (Chicago)
KVOA-TV (Tucson, Ariz.)
Howard K. Smith
1963 WFBM (Indianapolis, Ind.)
WJZ-TV (Baltimore)
Louis M. Lyons
1964 WFTV Radio (Orlando, Fla.)
WRCV-TV (Philadelphia)
1965 WBBM-TV (Chicago)
KTWO-TV (Casper, Wyo.)
WCCO (Minneapolis)
WHCU (Ithaca, N.Y.)
WRVR (New York)
Cecil Brown
WFBM-TV (Indianapolis)
1966 No awards
1967 No awards
1968-69 Everett Parker
WRKL-Radio (Mount Ivy-New City, N.Y.)
KQED-TV (San Francisco)

NBC and *First Tuesday,* for "CBW—The Secrets of Secrecy"

Al Levin and Public Broadcast Library, for *Defense and Domestic Needs: The Contest for Tomorrow*

Don Widener and KNBC-TV (Los Angeles), for *The Slow Guillotine*

WSB-TV (Atlanta), for continuing coverage of organized crime in the community

1969-70 Kenneth A. Cox, Frederick Wiseman and National Education Television, for *Hospital*

John Laurence and *CBS Evening News* for "Charlie Company" series of reports

WCCO-TV (Minneapolis), for *Grunt's Little War*

Fred Freed and National Broadcasting Co., for *Pollution is a Matter of Choice*

WOOD-TV (Grand Rapids, Mich.) for *Our Poisoned World*

1970-71 John Sharnik and CBS News, for "Justice in America"

First Tuesday and NBC News, for "The Man from Uncle (Sam)—the FBI"

Martin Carr and NBC News, for "This Child is Rated X—Migrant"

Susan Garfield and Group W, for "All the Kids Like That"

Geraldo Rivera and WABC-TV (New York), for "Drug Crisis in East Harlem"

Diane Orr and KUTV-TV (Salt Lake City, Utah), for *Warrior Without a Weapon*

1971-72 Fred Freed and NBC News, for "The Blue Collar Trap"

Robert Markowitz and CBS News, for " . . . but what if the dream comes true?"

Group W, for *The Search for Quality Education*

John Drimmer and WNJT (Trenton, N.J.), for *Towers of Frustration*

MTVJ (Miami) for, *A Seed of Hope* and *The Swift Justice of Europe*

Tony Batten, *The 51st State,* WNET/13 (New York), for "Youth Gangs in the South Bronx"

Richard Thurston Watkins, *Like It Is* and WABC-TV (New York), for "Attica: The Unanswered Questions"

Mike Wallace, for outstanding reporting on *60 Minutes*

NPACT and KERA (Dallas, Tex.), for outstanding coverage of the 1972 political campaigns

1972-73 Arthur Holch and ABC News

Irv Drasnin and CBS News

Robert Northshield and NBC News

Dick Hubert and Group W

WBBM-TV, Chicago

WTIC-TV, Hartford, Conn.

KGW-TV, Portland, Ore.

Elizabeth Drew and NPACT

1973-74 Av Westin and ABC News, for *Close-Up*

Don Hewitt and CBS News, for *60 Minutes*

Fred Freed and NBC News, for *The Energy Crisis*

National Public Affairs Center for Television, for Watergate coverage

National Public Affairs Center for Television, for *Washington Week in Review*

KFWB Radio (Los Angeles), for *SLA 54th Street Shootout*

KNXT-TV (Los Angeles), for *Why Me?*

WKY-TV (Oklahoma City), for *Through the Looking Glass Darkly*

TVTV and WNET/13 (New York), for *The Lord of the Universe*

Frederick Wiseman and WNET/13 (New York), for *Juvenile Court*

WPVI-TV (Philadelphia), for *Public Bridges and Private Riches*

1974-75 National Public Radio, for *All Things Considered*

Tom Pettit and *NBC Nightly News,* for a series of reports on feeding the poor

Don Harris and KNBC-TV (Burbank, Calif.), for *Prison Gangs*

WBTV (Charlotte, N.C.), for news and documentary programming

WCCO-Radio (Minneapolis), for news and documentary programming

David Moore and WCCO-TV (Minneapolis), for *Moore on Sunday*

WGBH-TV (Boston), for *Arabs and Israelis*

Warren Doremus and WHEC-TV (Rochester, N.Y.), for *The Riots Plus 10 Years*

Clarence Jones and WPLG-TV (Miami), for crime reporting

1975-76 No awards

1976-77 Group W, for *Six American Families*

WBBM-TV (Chicago), for *Once A Priest*

WNET (New York) and WEDA (Washington), for *MacNeil/Lehrer Report* (PBS)

KCET-TV (Los Angeles), for *28 Tonight*

KGW-TV (Portland, Ore.), for *The Timber Farmers*

WSAA-TV (Dallas), for outstanding programming

WNBC News, for *Human Rights: A Soviet-American Debate* and *The Struggle for Freedom*

WNET (New York), for *The Police Tapes*

CBS News, for *Walter Cronkite and the CBS Evening News*

Emmy Awards

ACADEMY OF TELEVISION ARTS AND SCIENCES
6363 Sunset Blvd., Hollywood, Calif. 90028 (213/465-1131)

The Emmy Award, which consists of a statuette, is presented annually for outstanding programs, performers and behind-the-scenes talent in television broadcasting, as well as for exceptional service or contributions to the industry. The first Emmys were given at a time when there were sixteen television stations and 190,000 sets across the country. Today, the award ceremony itself is an extravaganza telecast into tens of millions of homes. Winners are selected by "blue-ribbon panels" from nominees chosen by Academy members. Through the 1975-76 season, the Emmy was given by the National Academy of Television Arts and Sciences, which no longer exists. In addition to the national awards listed here, Emmys are made for local programming in various cities. Because the categories in the national Emmy awards procedure change to a greater or lesser extent every year, winners are listed year by year rather than by category.

1948 Shirley Dinsdale and her puppet Judy Splinters, Most Outstanding Television Personality

Pantomime Quiz Time, "Most Popular Television Program"

The Necklace, "Best Film Made for Television"

KTLA (Los Angeles), "Station Award for Outstanding Overall Achievement"

Charles Mesak, "Technical Award" (for the Phase-fader)

Louis McManus, "Special Award" (for original design of the Emmy statuette)

1949 **Ed Wynn, KTTV**, "Best Live Show"
Texaco Star Theatre, "Best Kinescope Show"
Time for Beany, "Best Children's Show"
Ed Wynn, "Most Outstanding Live Personality"
Life of Riley, "Best Film Made for and Viewed on Television"
Milton Berle, "Most Outstanding Kinescoped Personality"
Crusade in Europe, "Best Public Service, Cultural or Educational Program"
Wrestling, "Best Sports Coverage"
KTLA (Los Angeles), "Station Achievement"
Lucky Strike/N.W. Ayer, "Best Commercial Made for Television"
Harold W. Jury, "Technical Award"

1950 **Alan Young**, "Best Actor"
Gertrude Berg, "Best Actress"
Groucho Marx, "Most Outstanding Personality"
City at Night, "Best Public Service"
Campus Chorus and Orchestra, "Best Cultural Show"
Departure of Marines for Korea, "Special Events"
Rams Football, "Best Sports Program"
The Alan Young Show, "Best Variety Show"
KFI-TV University, "Best Educational Show"
Time for Beany, "Best Children's Show"
Pulitzer Prize Playhouse, "Best Dramatic Show"
KTLA Newsreel, "Best News Program"
Truth or Consequences, "Best Game and Audience Participation Show"
KTLA (Los Angeles), "Station Achievement"
KNBH/NBC, "Technical Achievement for Orthogram TV"

1951 *Studio One* (CBS), "Best Dramatic Show"
Red Skelton Show (NBC), "Best Comedy Show"
Your Show of Shows (NBC), "Best Variety Show"
Sid Caesar, "Best Actor"
Imogene Coca, "Best Actress"
Red Skelton, "Best Comedian or Comedienne"
U.S. Sen. Estes Kefauver, "Special Achievement Award"

1952 *Robert Montgomery Presents* (NBC), "Best Dramatic Program"
Your Show of Shows (NBC), "Best Variety Program"
See It Now (CBS), "Best Public Affairs Program"
Dragnet (NBC), "Best Mystery, Action or Adventure Program"
I Love Lucy (CBS), "Best Situation Comedy"
What's My Line? (CBS), "Best Audience Participation, Quiz or Panel Program"
Time for Beany (KTLA), "Best Children's Program"
Thomas Mitchell, "Best Actor"
Helen Hayes, "Best Actress"
Jimmy Durante, "Best Comedian"
Lucille Ball, "Best Comedienne"
Bishop Fulton J. Sheen, "Most Outstanding Personality"

1953 *U.S. Steel Hour* (ABC), "Best Dramatic Show"
I Love Lucy (CBS), "Best Situation Comedy"
Omnibus (CBS), "Best Variety Program"
See It Now (CBS), "Best Program of News or Sports"
Victory at Sea (NBC), "Best Public Affairs Program"
Kukla, Fran and Ollie (NBC), "Best Children's Program"

Make Room for Daddy (ABC) and *U.S. Steel Hour* (ABC), "Best New Programs" (tie)
Donald O'Connor (*Colgate Comedy Hour*, NBC), "Best Male Star of Regular Series"
Eve Arden (*Our Miss Brooks*, CBS), "Best Female Star of Regular Series"
Art Carney (*The Jackie Gleason Show*, CBS), "Best Series Supporting Actor"
Vivian Vance (*I Love Lucy*, CBS), "Best Series Supporting Actress"
Dragnet (NBC), "Best Mystery, Action or Adventure Program"
This Is Your Life (NBC) and *What's My Line?* (CBS), "Best Audience Participation, Quiz or Panel Programs" (tie)
Edward R. Murrow (CBS), "Most Outstanding Personality"

1954 **George Gobel** (NBC), "Most Outstanding New Personality"
Omnibus (CBS), "Best Cultural, Religious or Educational Program"
Gillette Cavalcade of Sports (NBC), "Best Sports Program"
Lassie (CBS), "Best Children's Program"
Art Linkletter's House Party (CBS), "Best Daytime Program"
Stories of the Century (syndicated), "Best Western or Adventure Series"
John Daly (ABC), "Best News Reporter or Commentator"
This Is Your Life (NBC), "Best Audience, Guest Participation or Panel Program"
Robert Cummings (*Twelve Angry Men*, CBS), "Best Actor in a Single Performance"
Judith Anderson, on *Macbeth*, on *Hallmark Hall of Fame*, NBC), "Best Actress in a Single Performance"
Perry Como (CBS), "Best Male Singer"
Dinah Shore (NBC), "Best Female Singer"
Art Carney (*The Jackie Gleason Show*, CBS), "Best Supporting Actor in a Regular Series"
Audrey Meadows (*The Jackie Gleason Show*, CBS), "Best Supporting Actress in a Regular Series"
Danny Thomas (*Make Room for Daddy*, ABC), "Best Actor Starring in a Regular Series"
Loretta Young (*The Loretta Young Show*, NBC), "Best Actress Starring in a Regular Series"
Dragnet (NBC), "Best Mystery or Intrigue Series"
Disneyland (ABC), "Best Variety Series Including Musical Varieties"
Make Room for Daddy (ABC), "Best Situation Comedy Series"
United States Steel Hour (ABC), "Best Dramatic Series"
Operation Undersea (Disneyland, ABC), "Best Individual Program of the Year"
Bob Markell (*Mallory's Tragedy on Mt. Everest*, CBS), "Best Art Direction of a Live Show"
Ralph Berger and Albert Pyke ("A Christmas Carol" on *Shower of Stars*, CBS) "Best Art Direction of a Filmed Show"
Lester Schorr ("I Climb the Stairs" on *Medic*, NBC), "Best Direction of Photography"
Reginald Rose (*Twelve Angry Men* on *Studio One*, NBC), "Best Written Dramatic Material"
James Allardice, Jack Douglas, Hal Kanter and Harry Winkler (*The George Gobel Show*, NBC), "Best Written Comedy Material"
Four Quadrant Screen (NBC for 1954 National Election Coverage/Robert Shelby), "Best Engineering Effects"

NBC and John West, "Best Technical Achievements for Color TV Policy"

George Nicholson (*Dragnet,* NBC), "Best Television Sound Editing"

Grant Smith and Lynn Harrison ("Operation Undersea" on *Disneyland,* ABC), "Best Television Film Editing"

Franklin Schaffner (*Twelve Angry Men* on *Studio One,* CBS), "Best Direction"

Walter Schumann (*Dragnet,* NBC), "Best Original Music Composed for TV"

Victor Young (*Diamond Jubilee of Lights,* four networks), "Best Scoring of a Dramatic or Variety Program"

June Taylor (*The Jackie Gleason Show,* CBS), "Best Choreographer"

1955 *Lassie* (CBS), "Best Children's Series"

Matinee Theatre, (NBC), "Best Contribution to Daytime Programming"

A-Bomb Coverage, (CBS), "Best Special Event or News Program"

Omnibus (CBS), "Best Documentary Program"

$64,000 Question (CBS), "Best Audience Participation Series"

Disneyland (ABC, especially for "Davy Crockett" series), "Best Action or Adventure Series"

Phil Silvers, *You'll Never Get Rich* (CBS), "Best Comedy Series"

Ed Sullivan Show (CBS), "Best Variety Series"

Your Hit Parade (NBC), "Best Music Series"

Producers' Showcase (NBC), "Best Dramatic Series"

Peter Pan with Mary Martin (*Producers' Showcase,* NBC), "Best Single Program of the Year"

Lloyd Nolan (*Caine Mutiny Court Martial* on *Ford Star Jubilee,* CBS), "Best Actor—Single Performance"

Mary Martin ("Peter Pan" on *Producers' Showcase,* NBC), "Best Actress—Single Performance"

Phil Silvers (*You'll Never Get Rich,* CBS), "Best Actor —Continuing Performance"

Lucille Ball (*I Love Lucy,* CBS), "Best Actress—Continuing Performance"

Art Carney (*The Honeymooners,* CBS), "Best Actor in a Supporting Role"

Nanette Fabray (*Caesar's Hour,* CBS), "Best Actress in a Supporting Role"

Phil Silvers (CBS), "Best Comedian"

Nanette Fabray (NBC), "Best Comedienne"

Perry Como (NBC), "Best Male Singer"

Dinah Shore, "Best Female Singer"

Perry Como (NBC), "Best M.C. or Program Host—Male or Female"

Edward R. Murrow (CBS), "Best News Commentator or Reporter"

Marcel Marceau (NBC), "Best Specialty Act—Single or Group"

Nat Hiken, Barry Blitser, Arnold Auerbach, Harvey Orkin, Vincent Bogert, Arnold Rosen, Coleman Jacoby, Tony Webster and Terry Ryan (*You'll Never Get Rich,* NBC), "Best Comedy Writing"

Rod Serling (*Kraft TV Theatre,* NBC), "Best Original Teleplay Writing"

Paul Gregory and Franklin Schaffner ("Caine Mutiny Court Martial" on *Ford Star Jubilee,* CBS), "Best Television Adaptation"

Love and Marriage from **"Our Town"** (*Producers' Showcase,* NBC), "Best Musical Contribution"

Fred Coe (*Producers' Showcase,* NBC), "Best Producer —Live Series"

Walt Disney (*Disneyland,* ABC), "Best Producer—Film Series"

Franklin Schaffner ("Caine Mutiny Court Martial" on *Ford Star Jubilee,* CBS), "Best Director—Live Series"

Nat Hiken (*You'll Never Get Rich,* CBS), "Best Director—Film Series"

Otis Riggs ("Playwrights '56" and *Producers' Showcase,* NBC), "Best Art Direction—Live Series"

William Ferrari (*You Are There,* CBS) "Best Art Direction—Film Series"

William Scikner ("Black Friday" on *Medic,* NBC), "Best Cinematography for Television"

T. Miller (*Studio One,* CBS), "Best Camera Work—Live Show"

Edward Williams ("Breakdown" on *Alfred Hitchcock Presents,* CBS), "Best Editing of a Television Film"

Tony Charmoli ("Show Biz" on *Your Hit Parade,* NBC), "Best Choreographer"

RCA Tricolor Picture Tube, "Best Technical Achievement"

Ford, "Best Commercial Campaign"

President Dwight D. Eisenhower, "Governor's Award" (for his use and encouragement of television)

1956 **"Requiem for a Heavyweight"** (*Playhouse 90,* CBS), "Best Single Program of the Year"

Playhouse 90 (CBS), "Best New Program Series"

Phil Silvers Show (CBS), "Best Series—Half Hour or Less"

Caesar's Hour (NBC), "Best Series—One Hour or More"

See It Now (CBS), "Best Public Service Series"

Years of Crisis, year-end report with Edward R. Murrow and correspondents (CBS), "Best Coverage of a Newsworthy Event"

Robert Young (*Father Knows Best,* NBC), "Best Continuing Performance By an Actor in a Dramatic Series"

Loretta Young (*The Loretta Young Show,* NBC), "Best Continuing Performance By an Actress in a Dramatic Series"

Sid Caesar (*Caesar's Hour,* NBC), "Best Continuing Performance By a Comedian in a Series"

Nanette Fabray (*Caesar's Hour,* NBC), "Best Continuing Performance By a Commedienne in a Series"

Jack Palance ("Requiem for a Heavyweight" on *Playhouse 90,* CBS), "Best Single Performance by an Actor"

Claire Trevor ("Dodsworth" on *Producers' Showcase,* NBC), "Best Single Performance by an Actress"

Carl Reiner (*Caesar's Hour,* NBC), "Best Supporting Performance by an Actor"

Pat Carroll (*Caesar's Hour,* NBC), "Best Supporting Performance by an Actress"

Perry Como (NBC), "Best Male Personality—Continuing Performance"

Dinah Shore (NBC), "Best Female Personality—Continuing Performance"

Edward R. Murrow (CBS), "Best News Commentator"

James P. Cavanaugh ("Fog Closing In" on *Alfred Hitchcock Presents,* CBS), "Best Teleplay Writing—Half Hour or Less"

Rod Serling ("Requiem for a Heavyweight" on *Playhouse 90,* CBS), "Best Teleplay Writing—One Hour or More"

Nat Hiken, Billy Friedberg, Tony Webster, Leonard Stern, Arnold Rosen and Coleman Jacoby (*The Phil Silvers Show,* CBS), "Best Comedy Writing—Variety or Situation Comedy

Sheldon Leonard ("Danny's Comeback" on *The Danny Thomas Show,* ABC), "Best Direction—Half Hour or Less"

Ralph Nelson ("Requiem for a Heavyweight" on *Playhouse 90*, CBS), "Best Direction—One Hour or More"

Paul Barnes (*Your Hit Parade*, NBC), "Best Art Direction—Half Hour or Less"

Albert Heschong ("Requiem for a Heavyweight" on *Playhouse 90*, CBS), "Best Art Direction—One Hour or More"

Norbert Brodine ("The Pearl" on *The Loretta Young Show*, NBC), "Best Cinematography for Television"

Frank Keller ("Our Mr. Sun" on *AT&T Science Series*, CBS), "Best Editing of a Film for Television"

Leonard Bernstein (composing and conducting for *Omnibus*, CBS), "Best Musical Contribution for Television"

"A Night to Remember" (*Kraft Television Theatre*, NBC), "Best Live Camera Work"

Development of videotape by Ampex and further development of practical applications by CBS, "Best Engineering or Technical Development"

1957 **"The Comedian"** (*Playhouse 90*, CBS), "Best Single Program of the Year"

Seven Lively Arts (CBS), "Best New Program Series of the Year"

Playhouse 90 (CBS), "Best Dramatic Anthology Series"

Gunsmoke (CBS), "Best Dramatic Series with Continuing Characters"

Phil Silvers Show (CBS), "Best Comedy Series"

Dinah Shore — Chevy Show (NBC), "Best Musical, Variety, Audience Participation or Quiz Series"

Omnibus (ABC and NBC), "Best Public Service Program or Series"

Coverage of Riker's Island (New York) **plane crash** on *World News Roundup* (CBS), "Best Coverage of an Unscheduled Newsworthy Event"

Robert Young (*Father Knows Best*, NBC), "Best Continuing Performance by an Actor in a Leading Role in a Dramatic or Comedy Series"

Jane Wyatt (*Father Knows Best*, NBC), "Best Continuing Performance by an Actress in a Leading Role in a Dramatic or Comedy Series"

Jack Benny (*The Jack Benny Show*, CBS), "Best Continuing Performance (Male) in a Series by a Comedian, Singer, Host, Dancer, M.C., Narrator, Panelist or Any Person Who Essentially Plays Himself"

Dinah Shore (*Dinah Shore — Chevy Show*, NBC), "Best Continuing Performance (Female) in a Series by a Comedienne, Singer, Hostess, Dancer, M.C., Narrator, Panelist or Any Person Who Essentially Plays Herself"

Peter Ustinov ("The Life of Samuel Johnson" on *Omnibus*, NBC), "Actor — Best Single Performance — Lead or Support"

Polly Bergen ("Helen Morgan Story" on *Playhouse 90*, CBS), "Actress — Best Single Performance — Lead or Support"

Carl Reiner (*Caesar's Hour*, NBC), "Best Continuing Support Performance by an Actor in a Dramatic or Comedy Series"

Ann B. Davis (*Bob Cummings Show*, CBS and NBC), "Best Continuing Support Performance by an Actress in a Dramatic or Comedy Series"

Edward R. Murrow (*See It Now*, CBS), "Best News Commentary"

Paul Monash ("The Lonely Wizard" on *Schlitz Playhouse of Stars*, CBS), "Best Teleplay Writing — Half Hour or Less"

Rod Serling ("The Comedian" on *Playhouse 90*, CBS), "Best Teleplay Writing — One Hour or More"

Nat Hiken, Billy Friedberg, Phil Sharp, Terry Ryan, Coleman Jacoby and Tony Webster (*The Phil Silvers Show*, CBS), "Best Comedy Writing"

Robert Stevens ("The Glass Eye" on *Alfred Hitchcock Presents*, CBS), "Best Direction — Half Hour or Less"

Bob Banner (*Dinah Shore — Chevy Show*, NBC), "Best Direction — One Hour or More"

Rouben ter-Arutunian (*Twelfth Night* on *Hallmark Hall of Fame*, NBC), "Best Art Direction"

Harold E. Wellman ("Hemo the Magnificent" on *Bell Telephone Science Series*, CBS), "Best Cinematography for Television"

Playhouse 90 (CBS), "Best Live Camera Work"

Mike Pozen ("How to Kill a Woman" on *Gunsmoke*, CBS), "Best Editing of a Film for Television"

Leonard Bernstein (Conducting and Analyzing Music of Johann Sebastian Bach on *Omnibus*, ABC), "Best Musical Contribution for Television"

Engineering and camera techniques (*Wide Wide World*, NBC), "Best Engineering or Technical Achievement"

Jack Benny, "Trustees' Award"

1958-59 *An Evening With Fred Astaire* (NBC), "Most Outstanding Single Program of the Year"

Playhouse 90 (CBS), "Best Dramatic Series — One Hour or Longer"

Alcoa-Goodyear Theatre (NBC), "Best Dramatic Series — Less Than One Hour"

Jack Benny Show (CBS), "Best Comedy Series"

Dinah Shore — Chevy Show (NBC), "Best Musical or Variety Series"

Maverick (ABC), "Best Western Series"

Omnibus (NBC), "Best Public Service Program or Series"

Huntley-Brinkley Report (NBC), "Best News Reporting Series"

What's My Line? (CBS), "Best Panel, Quiz or Audience Participation Series"

"Little Moon of Alban" (*Hallmark Hall of Fame*, NBC), "Best Dramatic Program — One Hour or Longer"

An Evening With Fred Astaire (NBC), "Best Special Musical or Variety Program — One Hour or Longer"

Face of Red China (CBS), "Best Special News Program"

Raymond Burr (*Perry Mason*, CBS), "Best Actor in a Leading Role in a Dramatic Series (Continuing Character)"

Loretta Young (*The Loretta Young Show*, NBC), "Best Actress in a Leading Role in a Dramatic Series (Continuing Character — Hostess)"

Jack Benny (*The Jack Benny Show*, CBS), "Best Actor in a Leading Role in a Comedy Series (Continuing Character)"

Jane Wyatt (*Father Knows Best*, CBS and NBC), "Best Actress in a Leading Role in a Comedy Series (Continuing Character)"

Dennis Weaver (*Gunsmoke*, CBS), "Best Supporting Actor in a Dramatic Series (Continuing Character)"

Barbara Hale (*Perry Mason*, CBS), "Best Supporting Actress in a Dramatic Series (Continuing Character)"

Tom Poston (*Steve Allen Show*, NBC), "Best Supporting Actor in a Comedy Series (Continuing Character)"

Ann B. Davis (*Bob Cummings Show*, NBC), "Best Supporting Actress in a Comedy Series (Continuing Character)"

Perry Como (*Perry Como Show*, CBS), "Best Performance by an Actor in a Musical or Variety Series (Continuing Character)"

Dinah Shore (*Dinah Shore — Chevy Show*, NBC), "Best Performance by an Actress in a Musical or Variety Series (Continuing Character)"

Fred Astaire (*An Evening With Fred Astaire*, NBC), "Best Single Performance by an Actor"

Julie Harris ("Little Moon of Alban" on *Hallmark Hall of Fame*, NBC), "Best Single Performance by an Actress"

Edward R. Murrow (CBS), "Best News Commentator or Analyst"

Jack Smight ("Eddie" on *Alcoa-Goodyear Theatre*, NBC), "Best Direction of a Single Program of a Dramatic Series — Less than One Hour"

George Schaefer ("Little Moon of Alban" on *Hallmark Hall of Fame*, NBC), "Best Direction of a Single Program of a Dramatic Series — One Hour or Longer"

Peter Tewksbury ("Medal for Margaret" on *Father Knows Best*, CBS), "Best Direction of a Single Program of a Comedy Series"

Bud Yorkin (*An Evening With Fred Astaire*, NBC), "Best Direction of a Single Musical or Variety Program"

Alfred Brenner and Ken Hughes ("Eddie" on *Alcoa —Goodyear Theatre*, NBC), "Best Writing of a Single Program of a Dramatic Series—Less Than an Hour"

James Costigan ("Little Moon of Alban" on *Hallmark Hall of Fame*, NBC), "Best Writing of a Single Dramatic Program—One Hour or Longer"

Sam Perrin, George Balzer, Hal Goldman and Al Gordon (*Jack Benny Show*, "With Ernie Kovacs," CBS), "Best Writing of a Single Program of a Comedy Series"

Ellis W. Carter ("Alphabet Conspiracy" on *Bell Telephone Special*, NBC), "Best Cinematography for Television"

An Evening With Fred Astaire (NBC), "Best Live Camera Work"

Claudio Guzman ("Bernadette" on *Westinghouse Desilu Playhouse*, CBS), "Best Art Direction in a Television Film"

Edward Stephenson (*An Evening With Fred Astaire* NBC), "Best Art Direction in a Live Television Program"

Silvio d'Alisera ("Meet Mr. Lincoln" on *Project 20*, NBC), "Best Editing of a Film for Television"

David Rose (Musical direction of *An Evening With Fred Astaire*, NBC), "Best Musical Contribution to a Television Program"

Hermes Pan (*An Evening With Fred Astaire*, NBC), "Best Choreography for Television"

Industry-wide improvement of editing of videotape as exemplified by ABC, CBS and NBC, "Best Engineering or Technical Achievement"

Cuban Revolution coverage by CBS,"Best On-the-Spot Coverage of a News Event — Any Length"

Bob Hope "for bringing the gift of laughter to all peoples, for selflessly entertaining American troops throughout the world for many years and for making television finer by these deeds and by the consistently high quality of his television programs," "Trustees' Award"

1959-60 *Art Carney Special* (NBC), "Outstanding Program Achievement in the Field of Humor"

Playhouse 90 (CBS), "Outstanding Program Achievement in the Field of Drama"

Fabulous Fifties (CBS), "Outstanding Program Achievement in the Field of Variety"

Huntley-Brinkley Report (NBC), "Outstanding Program Achievement in the Field of News"

Twentieth Century (CBS), "Outstanding Program Achievement in the Field of Public Affairs and Education"

Huckleberry Hound (syndicated), "Outstanding Achievement in the Field of Children's Programming"

Leonard Bernstein and the New York Philharmonic (CBS), "Outstanding Achievement in the Field of Music"

Laurence Olivier (*The Moon and Sixpence*, NBC), "Outstanding Single Performance by an Actor (Lead or Support)"

Ingrid Bergman (*The Turn of the Screw* on *Ford Startime*, NBC), "Outstanding Single Performance by an Actress (Lead or Support)"

Robert Stack (*The Untouchables*, ABC), "Outstanding Performance by an Actor in a Series (Lead or Support)"

Jane Wyatt (*Father Knows Best*, CBS), "Outstanding Performance by an Actress in a Series (Lead or Support)"

Harry Belafonte ("Tonight With Belafonte," on *Revlon Revue*, CBS), "Outstanding Performance in a Variety or Musical Program Series"

Rod Serling (*Twilight Zone*, CBS), "Outstanding Writing Achievement in Drama"

Sam Perrin, George Balzer, Al Gordon and Hal Goldman (*Jack Benny Show*, CBS), "Outstanding Writing Achievement in Comedy"

Howard K. Smith and Av Westin (*The Population Explosion*, CBS), "Outstanding Writing Achievement in the Documentary Field"

Robert Mulligan (*The Moon and Sixpence*, NBC), "Outstanding Directorial Achievement in Drama"

Ralph Levy and Bud Yorkin (*Jack Benny Hour Specials*, CBS), "Outstanding Directorial Achievement in Comedy"

Ralph Berger and Frank Smith (*"Untouchables" on "Westinghouse Desilu Playhouse,"* CBS), "Outstanding Achievement in Art Direction and Scenic Design"

Charles Straumer ("Untouchables" on *Westinghouse Desilu Playhouse*, CBS), "Outstanding Achievement in Cinematography for Television"

Ben H. Ray and Robert L. Swanson (*"Untouchables"* CBS), "Outstanding Achievement in Film Editing for Television"

Winter Olympics (CBS), "Outstanding Achievement in Electronic Camera Work"

General Electric super-sensitive camera tube for colorcasting with no more light than is needed for black and white, "Best Engineering or Technical Achievement"

Frank Stanton (Columbia Broadcasting System), for advancing television as an arm of the free press), "Trustees' Award"

Ampex Corp., Radio Corp. of America, Michael R. Gargiulo and Richard Gillaspy (for capturing on videotape the Nixon-Khrushchev debate in Moscow), "Trustees' Citation"

1960-61 *Jack Benny Show* (CBS) "Outstanding Program Achievement in the Field of Humor"

Macbeth (*Hallmark Hall of Fame*, NBC), "Outstanding Program Achievement in the Field of Drama"

Astaire Time (NBC) "Outstanding Program Achievement in the Field of Variety"

Huntley-Brinkley Report (NBC), "Outstanding Program Achievement in the Field of News"

The Twentieth Century (CBS) "Outstanding Program Achievement in the Field of Public Affairs and Education"

Young People's Concert ("Aaron Copland's Birthday Party," CBS), "Outstanding Achievement in the Field of Children's Programming"

Maurice Evans (*Macbeth* on *Hallmark Hall of Fame*, NBC), "Outstanding Single Performance by an Actor in a Leading Role"

Judith Anderson (*Macbeth* on *Hallmark Hall of Fame*, NBC), "Outstanding Single Performance by an Actress in a Leading Role"

Raymond Burr (*Perry Mason*, CBS), "Outstanding Performance by an Actor in a Series (Lead)"

Barbara Stanwyck (*Barbara Stanwyck Show*, NBC), "Outstanding Performance by an Actress in a Series (Lead)"

Roddy McDowall ("Not Without Honor" on *Equitable's American Heritage*, NBC), "Outstanding Performance by an Actor or an Actress in a Supporting Role"

Don Knotts (*Andy Griffith Show*, CBS), "Outstanding Performance in a Supporting Role by an Actor or Actress in a Series"

Fred Astaire (*Astaire Time*, NBC), "Outstanding Performance in a Variety or Musical Program or Series"

Macbeth (*Hallmark Hall of Fame*, NBC), "The Program of the Year"

Leonard Bernstein (*Leonard Bernstein and the Philharmonic*, CBS), "Outstanding Achievement in the Field of Music for Television"

Rod Serling (*Twilight Zone*, CBS), "Outstanding Writing Achievement in Drama"

Sherwood Schwartz, Dave O'Brien, Al Schwartz, Martin Ragaway and Red Skelton (*Red Skelton Show*, CBS), "Outstanding Writing Achievement in Comedy"

Victor Wolfson (*Winston Churchill, The Valiant Years*, ABC), "Outstanding Writing Achievement in the Documentary Field"

George Schaeffer (*Macbeth* on *Hallmark Hall of Fame*, NBC), "Outstanding Directorial Achievement in Drama"

Sheldon Leonard (*The Danny Thomas Show*, CBS), "Outstanding Directorial Achievement in Comedy"

John J. Lloyd (*Checkmate*, CBS), "Outstanding Achievement in Art Direction and Scenic Design"

George Clemens (*Twilight Zone*, CBS), "Outstanding Achievement in Cinematography for Television"

"Sounds of America" (*Bell Telephone Hour*, Red-eo-Tape mobile unit for NBC), "Outstanding Achievement in Electronic Camera Work"

Harry Coswick, Aaron Nibley and Milton Shifman (*Naked City*, ABC), "Outstanding Achievement in Film Editing for Television"

Radio Corp. of America and Marconi's Wireless Telegraph Co. (for independent development of 4½-in. image orthicon tube and cameras), "Outstanding Engineering or Technical Achievement"

National Educational Television and Radio Center and its affiliated stations, (for foresight and perseverence in developing educational television in the U.S.), "Trustees' Award"

Joyce C. Hall (Hallmark Cards), ("for his personal interest in uplifting the standards of television"), "Trustees' Award"

1961-62 *Bob Newhart Show* (NBC), "Outstanding Program Achievement in the Field of Humor"

The Defenders (CBS), "Outstanding Program Achievement in the Field of Drama"

Garry Moore Show (CBS), "Outstanding Program Achievement in the Fields of Variety or Music"

Leonard Bernstein and the New York Philharmonic in Japan (CBS), "Outstanding Program Achievement in the Field of Music"

Huntley-Brinkley Report (NBC), "Outstanding Program Achievement in the Field of News"

David Brinkley's Journal (NBC), "Outstanding Program Achievement in the Field of Education and Public Affairs"

New York Philharmonic Young People's Concerts with Leonard Bernstein (CBS), "Outstanding Achievement in the Field of Children's Programming"

Peter Falk ("The Price of Tomatoes" on *The Dick Powell Show*, NBC), "Outstanding Single Performance by an Actor in a Leading Role"

Julie Harris ("Victoria Regina" on *Hallmark Hall of Fame*, NBC), "Outstanding Single Performance by an Actress in a Leading Role"

E.G. Marshall (*The Defenders*, CBS), "Outstanding Performance by an Actor in a Series (Lead)"

Shirley Booth (*Hazel*, NBC), "Outstanding Performance by an Actress in a Series (Lead)"

Don Knotts (*Andy Griffith Show*, CBS), "Outstanding Performance in a Supporting Role by an Actor"

Pamela Brown ("Victoria Regina" on *Hallmark Hall of Fame*, NBC), "Outstanding Performance in a Supporting Role by an Actress"

Carol Burnett (*Garry Moore Show*, CBS), "Outstanding Performance in a Variety or Musical Program or Series"

Purex Specials for Women (NBC), "Outstanding Daytime Program (Program Specifically Created for Daytime Television)"

"Victoria Regina" (*Hallmark Hall of Fame*, NBC), "The Program of the Year"

Richard Rodgers (*Winston Churchill, the Valiant Years*, ABC), "Outstanding Achievement in Original Music Composed for Television"

Reginald Rose (*The Defenders*, CBS), "Outstanding Writing Achievement in Drama"

Carl Reiner (*Dick Van Dyke Show*, CBS), "Outstanding Writing Achievement in Comedy"

Lou Hazam ("Vincent Van Gogh: A Self-Portrait," NBC), "Outstanding Writing Achievement in the Documentary Field"

Franklin Schaffner (*The Defenders*, CBS), "Outstanding Directorial Achievement in Drama"

Nat Hiken (*Car 54, Where Are You?*, NBC), "Outstanding Directorial Achievement in Comedy"

Gary Smith (*Perry Como's Kraft Music Hall*, NBC), "Outstanding Achievement in Art Direction and Scenic Design"

John S. Priestley (*Naked City*, ABC), "Outstanding Achievement in Cinematography for Television"

Ernie Kovacs (*Ernie Kovacs Show*, ABC), "Outstanding Achievement in Electronic Camera Work"

Hugh Chaloupka, Aaron Nibley and Charles L. Freeman (*Naked City*, ABC), "Outstanding Achievement in Film Editing for Television"

ABC Videotape Expander (VTX), slow-motion tape developed under Albert Malang of Video Facilities, "Outstanding Engineering or Technical Achievement"

CBS News, (for "A Tour of the White House" special) "Trustees' Award"

Jacqueline Kennedy, (for "A Tour of the White House" special) "Trustees' Award"

ABC, CBS and NBC News Department heads, "Trustees' Award" (for upholding country's policy of open reporting)

Brig. Gen. David Sarnoff, "Trustees' Award" (in recognition of his being "an illustrious statesman of our industry")

1962-63 *The Tunnel* (NBC) "Best Program of the Year"

The Dick Van Dyke Show (CBS), "Outstanding Program Achievement in the Field of Humor"

The Defenders (CBS), "Outstanding Program Achievement in the Field of Drama"

Julie and Carol at Carnegie Hall (CBS), "Outstanding Program Achievement in the Field of Music"

The Andy Williams Show (NBC), "Outstanding Program Achievement in the Field of Variety"

G-E College Bowl (CBS), "Outstanding Program Achievement in the Field of Panel, Quiz or Audience Participation"

Walt Disney's Wonderful World of Color (NBC), "Outstanding Achievement in the Field of Children's Programming"

The Tunnel (NBC), "Outstanding Achievement in the Field of Documentary Programs"

Huntley-Brinkley Report (NBC), "Outstanding Program Achievement in the Field of News"

David Brinkley's Journal (NBC), "Outstanding Program Achievement in the Field of News Commentary or Public Affairs"

Piers Anderton (NBC's Berlin correspondent for *The Tunnel*), "Outstanding Achievement in International Reporting or Commentary"

Trevor Howard in "The Invincible Mr. Disraeli" (*Hallmark Hall of Fame,* NBC), "Outstanding Single Performance by an Actor in a Leading Role"

Kim Stanley ("A Cardinal Act of Mercy" on *Ben Casey,* ABC), "Outstanding Single Performance by an Actress in a Leading Role"

E.G. Marshall (*The Defenders,* CBS), "Outstanding Continued Performance by an Actor in a Series (Lead)"

Shirley Booth (*Hazel,* NBC), "Outstanding Continued Performance by an Actress in a Series (Lead)"

Don Knotts (*The Andy Griffith Show,* CBS), "Outstanding Performance in a Supporting Role by an Actor"

Glenda Farrell ("A Cardinal Act of Mercy" on *Ben Casey,* ABC), "Outstanding Performance in a Supporting Role by an Actress"

Carol Burnett (*Julie and Carol at Carnegie Hall,* CBS), "Outstanding Performance in a variety or Musical Program or Series"

Robert Russell Bennett ("He is Risen" on *Project 20,* NBC), "Outstanding Achievement in Composing Original Music for Television"

Carroll Clark and Marvin Aubrey Davis (*Walt Disney's Wonderful World of Color,* NBC), "Outstanding Achievement in Art Direction and Scenic Design"

Robert Thom and Reginald Rose ("The Madman" on *The Defenders,* CBS), "Outstanding Writing Achievement in Drama"

Carl Reiner (*The Dick Van Dyke Show,* CBS), "Outstanding Writing Achievement in Comedy"

Stuart Rosenberg ("The Madman" on *The Defenders,* CBS), "Outstanding Directional Achievement in Drama"

John Rich (*The Dick Van Dyke Show,* CBS), "Outstanding Directorial Achievement in Comedy"

John S. Priestley (*Naked City,* ABC), "Outstanding Achievement in Cinematography for Television"

"The Invincible Mr. Disraeli" (on *Hallmark Hall of Fame,* NBC), "Outstanding Achievement in Electronic Camera Work"

Sid Katz (*The Defenders,* CBS), "Outstanding Achievement in Film Editing for Television"

War and Peace (Granada TV Network of England), "The International Award"

Superfluous People (WCBS-TV, New York), "The Station Award"

American Telephone and Telegraph Co., "Trustees' Award"

Dick Powell, "Trustees' Award"

President John F. Kennedy, (for making news conferences available to television and for participating in the program, *Conversation with the President*), "Trustees' Citation"

1963-64 *The Making of the President 1960* (ABC), "Program of the Year"

The Dick Van Dyke Show (CBS), "Outstanding Program Achievement in the Field of Comedy"

The Defenders (CBS), "Outstanding Program Achievement in the Field of Drama"

Bell Telephone Hour (NBC), "Outstanding Program Achievement in the Field of Music"

The Danny Kaye Show (CBS), "Outstanding Program Achievement in the Field of Variety"

Discovery '63-'64 (ABC), "Outstanding Program Achievement in the Field of Children's Programming"

The Making of the President 1960 (ABC), "Outstanding Achievement in the Field of Documentary Programs"

Huntley-Brinkley Report (NBC), "Outstanding Program Achievement in the Field of News Reports"

Cuba Parts I & II—"The Bay of Pigs" and "The Missile Crisis" (NBC), "Outstanding Program Achievement in the Field of News Commentary or Public Affairs"

Jack Klugman ("Blacklist" on *The Defenders,* CBS), "Outstanding Single Performance by an Actor in a Leading Role"

Shelley Winters ("Two Is The Number" on *Bob Hope Presents the Chrysler Theatre,* NBC), "Outstanding Single Performance by an Actress in a Leading Role"

Dick Van Dyke (*The Dick Van Dyke Show,* CBS), "Outstanding Continued Performance by an Actor in a Series (Lead)"

Mary Tyler Moore (*The Dick Van Dyke Show,* CBS), "Outstanding Continued Performance by an Actress in a Series (Lead)"

Albert Paulsen ("One Day in the Life of Ivan Denisovich" on *Bob Hope Presents the Chrysler Theatre,* NBC), "Outstanding Performance by an Actor in A Supporting Role"

Ruth White ("Little Moon of Alban" on *Hallmark Hall of Fame,* NBC), "Outstanding Performance by an Actress in a Supporting Role"

Danny Kaye (*The Danny Kaye Show,* CBS), "Outstanding Performance in a Variety or Musical Program or Series"

Elmer Bernstein (*The Making of the President 1960,* ABC), "Outstanding Achievement in Composing Original Music for Television"

Warren Clymer (*Hallmark Hall of Fame,* NBC), "Outstanding Achievement in Art Direction and Scenic Design"

Rod Serling ("It's Mental Work" on *Bob Hope Presents The Chrysler Theatre,* NBC), "Outstanding Writing Achievement in Drama—Adaptation"

Ernest Kinoy ("Blacklist" on *The Defenders,* CBS), "Outstanding Writing Achievement in Drama—Original"

Carl Reiner, Sam Denoff and Bill Persky (*The Dick Van Dyke Show,* CBS), "Outstanding Writing Achievement in Comedy or Variety"

Tom Gries ("Who Do You Kill?" on *East Side/West Side*, CBS), "Outstanding Directorial Achievement in Drama"

Jerry Paris (*The Dick Van Dyke Show*, CBS), "Outstanding Directorial Achievement in Comedy"

Robert Scheerer (*The Danny Kaye Show*, CBS), "Outstanding Directorial Achievement in Variety or Music"

J. Baxter Peters (*The Kremlin*, NBC), "Outstanding Achievement in Cinematography for Television"

The Danny Kaye Show (CBS), "Outstanding Achievement in Electronic Photography"

William T. Cartwright (*The Making of the President 1960*, ABC), "Outstanding Achievement in Film Editing for Television"

Les Raisins Verts (Radiodiffusion Television Francais), "The International Award"

Operation Challenge — A Study in Hope (KPIX, San Francisco), "The Station Award"

1964-65 *The Dick Van Dyke Show* (CBS), "Outstanding Program Achievement in Entertainment"

"The Magnificent Yankee" (*Hallmark Hall of Fame*, NBC), "Outstanding Program Achievement in Entertainment"

My Name Is Barbra CBS), "Outstanding Program Achievement in Entertainment"

"What Is Sonata Form" (*New York Philharmonic Young People's Concerts With Leonard Bernstein*, CBS), "Outstanding Program Achievement in Entertainment"

Leonard Bernstein (*New York Philharmonic Young People's Concerts with Leonard Bernstein*, CBS), "Outstanding Individual Achievement in Entertainment: Actors and Performers"

Lynn Fontanne ("The Magnificent Yankee" on *Hallmark Hall of Fame*, NBC), "Outstanding Individual Achievement in Entertainment: Actors and Performers"

Alfred Lunt ("The Magnificent Yankee" on *Hallmark Hall of Fame*, NBC), "Outstanding Individual Achievement in Entertainment: Actors and Performers"

Barbra Streisand (*My Name Is Barbra*, CBS), "Outstanding Individual Achievement in Entertainment: Actors and Performers"

Dick Van Dyke (*The Dick Van Dyke Show*, CBS), "Outstanding Individual Achievement in Entertainment: Actors and Performers"

David Karp ("The 700 Year Old Gang" on *The Defenders*, CBS), "Outstanding Individual Achievement in Entertainment: Writer"

Paul Bogart ("The 700 Year Old Gang" on *The Defenders*, CBS), "Outstanding Individual Achievement in Entertainment: Director"

Joe Layton (*My Name Is Barbra*, CBS), "Outstanding Individual Achievement in Entertainment: Conception, Choreography and Staging"

Warren Clymer ("The Holy Terror" on *Hallmark Hall of Fame*, NBC), "Outstanding Individual Achievement in Entertainment: Art Directors and Set Decorators"

Noel Taylor ("The Magnificent Yankee" on *Hallmark Hall of Fame*, NBC), "Outstanding Individual Achievement in Entertainment: Costume Design"

Tom John (art) **and Bill Harp** (sets) (*My Name Is Barbra*, CBS), "Outstanding Individual Achievement in Entertainment: Art Directors and Set Decorators"

Robert O'Bradovich ("The Magnificent Yankee" on *Hallmark Hall of Fame*, NBC), "Outstanding Individual Achievement in Entertainment: Make-Up Artist"

Peter Matz (*My Name Is Barbra*, CBS), "Outstanding Individual Achievement in Entertainment: Musician"

William Spencer (*Twelve O'Clock High*, ABC), "Outstanding Individual Achievement in Entertainment: Cinematographer"

Henry Berman, Joseph Dervin and Will Glock, (*The Man from U.N.C.L.E.*, NBC), "Outstanding Individual Achievement in Entertainment: Lighting Direction"

Phil Hymes ("The Magnificent Yankee" on *Hallmark Hall of Fame*, NBC), "Outstanding Individual Achievement in Entertainment: Lighting Direction"

L.B. Abbott (*Voyage to the Bottom of the Sea*, ABC), "Outstanding Individual Achievement in Entertainment: Special Photographic Effects"

Production team (*Man From U.N.C.L.E.*, NBC), "Outstanding Individual Achievement in Entertainment: Special Effects"

Edward Ancona (*Bonanza*, NBC), "Outstanding Individual Achievement in Entertainment: Color Consultant"

Clair McCoy (*The Wonderful World of Burlesque*, NBC), "Outstanding Individual Achievement in Entertainment: Technical Director"

"I, Leonardo da Vinci" (*Saga of Western Man*, ABC), "Outstanding Program Achievement in News, Documentaries and Sports"

The Louvre (NBC), "Outstanding Program Achievement in News, Documentaries or Sports "

Richard Basehart (*Let My People Go*, syndicated), "Outstanding Individual Achievement in News, Documentary or Sports"

John J. Sughrue (*The Louvre*, NBC), "Outstanding Individual Achievement in News, Documentaries or Sports: Director"

Sidney Carroll (*The Louvre*, NBC), "Outstanding Individual Achievement in News, Documentaries or Sports: Writer"

Aram Boyajian (*The Louvre*, NBC), "Outstanding Individual Achievement in News, Documentaries or Sports: Film Editor"

Tom Priestley (*The Louvre*, NBC), "Outstanding Individual Achievement in News, Documentaries or Sports: Cinematographer"

Norman Dello Joio (*The Louvre*, NBC), "Outstanding Individual Achievement in News, Documentaries or Sports: Musician"

Le Barbier de Seville (Canadian Broadcasting Co.), "The International Award"

Ku Klux Klan (WDSU-TV, New Orleans), "The Station Award"

1965-66 *The Dick Van Dyke Show* (CBS), "Outstanding Comedy Series"

The Andy Williams Show (NBC), "Outstanding Variety Series"

Chrysler Presents the Bob Hope Christmas Special (NBC), "Outstanding Variety Special"

The Fugitive (ABC), "Outstanding Dramatic Series"

Ages of Man (CBS), "Outstanding Dramatic Program"

Frank Sinatra: A Man and His Music (NBC), "Outstanding Musical Program"

A Charlie Brown Christmas (CBS), "Outstanding Children's Program"

Cliff Robertson ("The Game" on *Bob Hope Presents the Chrysler Theatre*, NBC), "Outstanding Single Performance by an Actor in a Leading Role in a Drama"

Simone Signoret ("A Small Rebellion" on *Bob Hope Presents the Chrysler Theatre*, NBC), "Outstanding Single Performance by an Actress in a Leading Role in a Drama"

Bill Cosby (*I Spy*, NBC), "Outstanding Continued Performance by an Actor in a Leading Role in a Dramatic Series"

Barbara Stanwyck (*The Big Valley*, ABC), "Outstanding Continued Performance by an Actress in a Leading Role in a Dramatic Series"

Dick Van Dyke (*The Dick Van Dyke Show*, CBS), "Outstanding Continued Performance by an Actor in a Leading Role in a Comedy Series"

Mary Tyler Moore (*The Dick Van Dyke Show*, CBS), "Outstanding Continued Performance by an Actress in a Leading Role in a Comedy Series"

James Daly ("Eagle in a Cage" on *Hallmark Hall of Fame*, NBC), "Outstanding Performance by an Actor in a Supporting Role in a Drama"

Lee Grant (*Peyton Place*, ABC), "Outstanding Performance by an Actress in a Supporting Role in a Drama"

Don Knotts (*The Andy Griffith Show*, CBS), "Outstanding Performance by an Actor in a Supporting Role in a Comedy"

Alice Pearce (*Bewitched*, ABC), "Outstanding Performance by an Actress in a Supporting Role in a Comedy"

Millard Lampell ("Eagle in a Cage" on *Hallmark Hall of Fame*, NBC), "Outstanding Writing Achievement in Drama"

Bill Persky and Sam Denoff ("Coast to Coast Big Mouth" on *The Dick Van Dyke Show*, CBS), "Outstanding Writing Achievement in Comedy"

Al Gordon, Hal Goodman and Sheldon Keller (*An Evening With Carol Channing*, CBS), "Outstanding Writing Achievement in Variety"

Sidney Pollack ("The Game" on *Bob Hope Presents the Chrysler Theatre*, NBC), "Outstanding Directorial Achievement in Drama"

William Asher (*Bewitched*, ABC), "Outstanding Directorial Achievement in Comedy"

Alan Handley (*The Julie Andrews Show*, NBC), "Outstanding Directorial Achievement in Variety or Music"

American White Paper: United States Foreign Policy (NBC), "Achievement in News and Documentaries: Programs"

KKK—The Invisible Empire, (CBS), "Achievement in News and Documentaries: Programs"

"Senate Hearings on Vietnam" (NBC), "Achievement in News and Documentaries: Programs"

Camera Three (CBS), "Achievement in Daytime Programming: Programs"

Mutual of Omaha's Wild Kingdom (NBC), "Achievement in Daytime Programming: Programs"

ABC Wide World of Sports (ABC), "Achievement in Sports: Programs"

CBS Golf Classic (CBS), "Achievement in Sports: Programs"

Shell's Wonderful World of Golf (NBC), "Achievement in Sports: Programs"

Julia Child (*The French Chef*, NET), "Achievements in Educational Television: Individual"

Laurence Rosenthal (*Michelangelo: The Last Giant*, NBC), "Individual Achievements in Music: Composition"

James Trittipo (*The Hollywood Palace*, ABC), "Individual Achievements in Art Direction"

Winston C. Hoch (*Voyage to the Bottom of the Sea*, ABC), "Individual Achievement in Cinematography"

L.B. Abbott and Howard Lydecker ("Voyage to the Bottom of the Sea," ABC), "Individual Achievement in Special Photographic Effects"

David Blewitt and William R. Cartwright (*The Making of the President 1964*, CBS), "Individual Achievement in Film Editing"

Marvin Coil, Everett Douglas and Ellsworth Hoagland (*Bonanza*, NBC), "Individual Achievement in Film Editing"

Laurence Schneider ("Seventh Annual Young Performers Program" on *The New York Philharmonic With Leonard Bernstein*, CBS), "Individual Achievement in Audio Engineering"

Craig Curtis and Art Schneider (*The Julie Andrews Show*, NBC), "Individual Achievement in Video Tape Editing"

Lon Stucky (*Frank Sinatra: A Man and His Music*, NBC), "Individual Achievement in Lighting"

O. Tamburri ("Inherit the Wind" on *The Hallmark Hall of Fame*, NBC), "Individual Achievement: Technical Director"

MVR Corporation and CBS for Stop Action Playback, "Individual Achievement in Engineering Development"

Hughes Aircraft Corporation and Communications Satellite Corporation for Early Bird Satellite, "Individual Achievement in Engineering Development"

Burr Tillstrom ("Berlin Wall" hand ballot on *That Was The Week That Was*, NBC), "Special Award for Engineering Development"

"Wyvern at War—No. 2," "Breakout" (Westward Television Ltd., Plymouth, England), "The International Award"

I See Chicago (WBBM, Chicago), "The Station Award"

Edward R. Murrow (for forty years in broadcasting and the journalistic standards he adhered to), "Trustees' Award"

Xerox Corporation (for being the rare sponsor who has subordinated its interest in television as an advertising medium to its capacity to inform, enlighten and entertain at its highest level), "Trustees' Award"

1966-67 *The Monkees* (NBC), "Outstanding Comedy Series"

The Andy Williams Show (NBC), "Outstanding Variety Series"

The Sid Caesar, Imogene Coca, Carl Reiner, Howard Morris Special (CBS), "Outstanding Variety Special"

Mission: Impossible (CBS), "Outstanding Dramatic Series"

Death of a Salesman (CBS), "Outstanding Dramatic Program"

Brigadoon (ABC), "Outstanding Musical Program"

Jack and the Beanstalk, (NBC), "Outstanding Children's Program"

Peter Ustinov ("Barefoot in Athens" on *Hallmark Hall of Fame*, NBC), "Outstanding Single Performance by an Actor in a Leading Role in a Drama"

Geraldine Page ("A Christmas Memory" on *ABC Stage 67*, ABC), "Outstanding Single Performance by an Actress in a Leading Role in a Drama"

Bill Cosby (*I Spy*, NBC), "Outstanding Continued Performance by an Actor in a Dramatic Series"

Barbara Bain (*Mission: Impossible*, CBS), "Outstanding Continuing Performance by an Actress in a Dramatic Series"

Don Adams (*Get Smart*, NBC), "Outstanding Continued Performance by an Actor in a Comedy Series"
Lucille Ball (*The Lucy Show*, CBS), "Outstanding Continued Performance by an Actress in a Comedy Series"
Eli Wallach ("The Poppy Is Also a Flower" on *Xerox Special*, ABC), "Outstanding Performance by an Actor in a Supporting Role in a Drama"
Agnes Moorehead ("Night of the Vicious Valentine" on *Wild, Wild West*, CBS), "Outstanding Performance by an Actress in a Supporting Role in a Drama"
Don Knotts (*The Andy Griffith Show*, CBS), "Outstanding Performance by an Actor in a Supporting Role in a Comedy"
Frances Bavier (*The Andy Griffith Show*, CBS), "Outstanding Performance by an Actress in a Supporting Role in a Comedy"
Bruce Geller (*Mission: Impossible*, CBS), "Outstanding Writing Achievement in Drama"
Buck Henry and Leonard Stern ("Ship of Spies" on *Get Smart*, NBC), "Outstanding Writing Achievement in Comedy"
Mel Brooks, Sam Denoff, Bill Persky, Carl Reiner and Mel Tolkin (*The Sid Caesar, Imogene Coca, Carl Reiner, Howard Morris Special*, CBS), "Outstanding Writing Achievement in Variety"
Alex Segal (*Death of a Salesman*, CBS), "Outstanding Directorial Achievement in Drama"
James Frawley ("Royal Flush" on *The Monkees*, NBC), "Outstanding Directorial Achievement in Comedy"
Fielder Cook ("Brigadoon," ABC), "Outstanding Directorial Achievement in Variety or Music"
China: The Roots of Madness, (syndicated), "Achievement in News and Documentaries: Programs"
Hall of Kings (ABC), "Achievement in News and Documentaries: Programs"
The Italians (CBS), "Achievement in News and Documentaries: Programs"
Theodore H. White (*China: The Roots of Madness*, syndicated), "Achievement in News and Documentaries: Individual"
Ray Aghayan and Bob Mackie (*Alice Through the Looking Glass*, NBC), "Individual Achievement in Costume Design"
Dick Smith (*Mark Twain Tonight!*, CBS), "Individual Achievement in Make-Up"
L.B. Abbott (*The Time Tunnel*, ABC), "Individual Achievement in Photographic Special Effects"
Paul Krasny and Robert Watts (*Mission: Impossible*, CBS), "Individual Achievement in Film Editing"
Don Hall, Dick Legrand, Daniel Mandell and John Mills (*Voyage to the Bottom of the Sea*, ABC), "Individual Achievement in Sound Editing"
A.J. Cunningham (*Brigadoon*, ABC), "Individual Achievement in Electronic Production: Technical Director"
Leard Davis (*Brigadoon*, ABC), "Individual Achievement in Lighting Direction"
Bill Cole (*Frank Sinatra: A Man and His Music, Part II*, CBS), "Individual Achievement in Audio Engineering"
Robert Dunn, Gorm Erickson, Ben Wolf and Nick Demos (*Brigadoon*, ABC), "Individual Achievement in Electronic Production: Electronic Cameramen"
A.C. Philips Gloeilampenfabrieken for Plumbicon Tube, "Individual Achievement in Engineering Development"

Ampex Company for High-Band Video Tape Recorder, "Individual Achievement in Engineering Development"
Art Carney (*The Jackie Gleason Show*, CBS), "Special Award"
Truman Capote and Eleanor Perry (adaptation of "A Christmas Memory" on *ABC Stage 67*, ABC), "Special Award"
Arthur Miller (adaptation of "Death of a Salesman," CBS), "Special Award"
Mutual of Omaha's Wild Kingdom, (NBC), "Achievement in Daytime Programming: Program"
Mike Douglas (*The Mike Douglas Show*, syndicated), "Achievement in Daytime Programming: Individual"
ABC's Wide World of Sports (ABC), "Achievement in Sports: Program"
Big Deal at Gothenburg (Tyne Tees Television Ltd., Newcastle-upon-Tyne, England), "International Award"
The Road to Nowhere (KLZ-TV, Denver), "Station Award"
Sylvester L. "Pat" Weaver, Jr., "Trustees' Award" (for his constant conviction that the American public deserves better than it gets on the television screen, for introducing the "special," for providing us with the *Today* and *Tonight* shows, programs which have long demonstrated their validity and for imagination, courage, leadership and integrity for eighteen years in our medium")

1967-68 *Crisis in the Cities* (NET), "Achievement in News and Documentaries: Program"
John Laurence and Keith Kay (CBS News Correspondent and Cameraman for "1st Cavalry," "Con Thien" and other segments on *CBS Evening News With Walter Cronkite*, CBS), "Achievement in News and Documentaries: Individual"
Frank McGee (commentary on satellite coverage of Konrad Adenauer's funeral, NBC), "Outstanding Individual Achievement in Coverage of Special Events"
Africa (ABC), "Outstanding Program Achievement in News Documentaries"
Summer '67: What We Learned (NBC), "Outstanding Program Achievement in News Documentaries"
Harry Reasoner (writer of *CBS Reports* "What About Ronald Reagan?"), "Outstanding Individual Achievement in News and Documentaries"
Vo Huynh (Cameraman on "Same Mud, Same Blood," NBC), "Outstanding Individual Achievement in News and Documentaries"
"Eric Hoffer, The Passionate State of Mind" (*CBS News Special*), "Outstanding Program Achievement in Cultural Documentaries"
"Gauguin in Tahiti, The Search for Paradise" (*CBS News Special*), "Outstanding Program Achievement in Cultural Documentaries"
"John Steinbeck's America and Americans" (NBC), "Outstanding Program Achievement in Cultural Documentaries"
"Dylan Thomas: The World I Breathe" (NET), "Outstanding Program Achievement in Cultural Documentaries"
Nathaniel Dorsky (art photographer on "Gauguin in Tahiti, The Passionate State of Mind," CBS), "Outstanding Individual Achievement in Cultural Documentaries"
Harry Morgan (writer for the Wyeth phenomenon on "Who, What, When, Where, Why With Harry Reasoner," CBS), "Outstanding Individual Achievement in Cultural Documentaries"

Thomas A. Priestley and Robert Loweree (director of photography and film editor of *John Steinbeck's America and Americans*, NBC), "Outstanding Achievement in Cultural Documentaries"

The 21st Century (CBS), "Other News and Documentary Program Achievement"

Science and Religion: Who Will Play God? (CBS), "Other News and Documentary Program Achievement"

Georges Delerue (composer for *Our World*, Global Telecast, NET), "Other News and Documentary Individual Achievement"

Get Smart (NBC), "Outstanding Comedy Series"

Mission: Impossible (CBS), "Outstanding Dramatic Series"

"Elizabeth the Queen" (*Hallmark Hall of Fame*, NBC), "Outstanding Dramatic Program"

Rowan and Martin's Laugh-In (NBC), "Outstanding Musical or Variety Series"

Rowan and Martin's Laugh-In Special (NBC), "Outstanding Musical or Variety Program"

Melvyn Douglas ("Do Not Go Gentle Into That Good Night" on *CBS Playhouse*, CBS), "Outstanding Single Performance by an Actor in a Leading Role in a Drama"

Maureen Stapleton ("Among the Paths to Eden" on *Xerox Special*, ABC), "Outstanding Single Performance by an Actress in a Leading Role in a Drama"

Bill Cosby (*I Spy*, NBC), "Outstanding Continued Performance by an Actor in a Leading Role in a Dramatic Series"

Barbara Bain (*Mission: Impossible*, CBS), "Outstanding Continued Performance by an Actress in a Leading Role in a Dramatic Series"

Don Adams (*Get Smart*, NBC), "Outstanding Continued Performance by an Actor in a Leading Role in a Comedy Series"

Lucille Ball (*The Lucy Show*, CBS), "Outstanding Continued Performance by an Actress in a Leading Role in a Comedy Series"

Milburn Stone (*Gunsmoke*, CBS), "Outstanding Performance by an Actor in a Supporting Role in a Drama"

Barbara Anderson (*Ironside*, NBC), "Outstanding Performance by an Actress in a Supporting Role in a Drama"

Werner Klemperer (*Hogan's Heroes*, CBS), "Outstanding Performance by an Actor in a Supporting Role in a Comedy"

Marion Lorne (*Bewitched*, ABC), "Outstanding Performance by an Actress in a Supporting Role in a Comedy"

Loring Mandel ("Do Not Go Gentle Into that Good Night" on *CBS Playhouse*, CBS), "Outstanding Writing Achievement in Drama"

Allan Burns and Chris Hayward ("The Coming Out Party" on *He and She*, CBS), "Outstanding Writing Achievement in Comedy"

Chris Beard, Phil Hahn, Jack Hanrahan, Coslough Johnson, Paul Keyes, Marc London, Allan Mannings, David Panich, Hugh Wedlock and Digby Wolf (*Rowan and Martin's Laugh-In*, NBC), "Outstanding Writing Achievement in *Music* or Variety"

Paul Bogart ("Dear Friends" on *CBS Playhouse*, CBS), "Outstanding Directorial Achievement in Drama"

Bruce Bilson ("Maxwell Smart, Private Eye" on *Get Smart*, NBC), "Outstanding Directorial Achievement in Comedy"

Jack Haley, Jr. (*Movin' With Nancy*, NBC) "Outstanding Directorial Achievement in Music or Variety"

Earle Hagen ("Laya" on *I Spy*, NBC), "Outstanding Achievement in Musical Composition"

James W. Trittipo (*The Fred Astaire Show*, NBC), "Outstanding Achievement in Art Direction and Scenic Design"

Ralph Woolsey ("A Thief is a Thief" on *It Takes a Thief*, ABC), "Outstanding Achievement in Cinematography"

A.J. Cunningham (technical director) **and Edward Chaney, Robert Fonorow, Harry Tatarian and Ben Wolf** (cameramen), ("Do Not Go Gentle Into That Good Night" on *CBS Playhouse*, CBS), "Outstanding Achievement in Electronic Camerawork"

Peter Johnson ("The Sounds and Sights of Chicago" on *Bell Telephone Hour*, NBC), "Outstanding Achievement in Film Editing"

Today (NBC), "Outstanding Program Achievement in Day Time Programming"

ABC's Wide World of Sports (ABC), "Outstanding Program Achievement in Sports Programming"

Jim McKay (sports commentator on *ABC's Wide World of Sports*, ABC), "Outstanding Individual Achievement in Sports Programming"

Art Carney (*The Jackie Gleason Show*, CBS), "Special Classification of Individual Achievement"

Pat Paulsen (*The Smothers Brothers Comedy Hour*, CBS), "Special Classification of Individual Achievement"

Arthur Schneider (tape editor of *Rowan and Martin's Laugh-In Special*, NBC), "Outstanding Individual Achievement in Electronic Production"

Donald McGannon (President and Chairman of the Board, Westinghouse Broadcasting Company, Group W), "Trustees' Award" (for creative leadership of a dynamic radio and television group)

British Broadcasting Corporation, (for Electronic Field — Store Colour Television Standards Converter) "Outstanding Achievement in Engineering Development"

Now Is the Time (WCAU-TV, Philadelphia), "The Station Award"

The Other Side of the Shadow (WWL-TV, New Orleans), "Special Citation"

The Other Washington (WRC-TV, Washington), "Special Citation"

La Section Anderson (*The Anderson Platoon*) (Office de Radiodiffusion Television Francais, O.R.T.F., Paris), "The International Award (Documentary)"

"Call Me Daddy" (*Armchair Theatre* on ABC Television Ltd., Middlesex, G.B.), "The International Award (Entertainment)"

1968-69 Coverage of Hunger in the United States on *The Huntley-Brinkley Report* (NBC), "Outstanding Program Achievement Within Regularly Scheduled News Programs"

Charles Kuralt, James Wilson and Robert Funk (correspondent, cameraman and soundman), "On The Road" on *CBS Evening News* (CBS), "Outstanding Individual Achievement Within Regularly Scheduled Broadcasts"

CBS for coverage of Martin Luther King's assassination and its aftermath, "Outstanding Program Achievement in Coverage of Special Events"

CBS Reports: Hunger in America (CBS), "Outstanding News Documentary Program Achievement"

Law and Order (NET), "Outstanding News Documentary Program Achievement"

Perry Wolff and Andy Rooney (writers of "Black History: Lost, Stolen or Strayed — Of Black America," on *CBS News Hour*, CBS), "Outstanding News Documentary Individual Achievement"

"Don't Count the Candles" (*CBS News Hour*, CBS), "Outstanding Cultural Documentary and 'Magazine-Type' Program or Series Achievement (Program)"

"Justice Black and The Bill of Rights" (*CBS News Hour*, CBS), "Outstanding Cultural Documentary and 'Magazine-Type' Program or Series Achievement (Program)"

"Man Who Dances: Edward Villella" (*Bell Telephone Hour*, NBC) "Outstanding Cultural Documentary and 'Magazine-Type' Program or Series Achievement (Program)"

"The Great American Novel" (*CBS News Hour*, (CBS), "Outstanding Cultural Documentary and 'Magazine-Type' Program or Series Achievement (Program)"

Walter Dombrow and Jerry Sims (cinematographers of "The Great American Novel" on *CBS News Hour*, CBS), "Outstanding Cultural Documentary and 'Magazine-Type' Program or Series Achievement (Individual)"

Tom Pettit (producer of "CBW: The Secrets of Secrecy" on *First Tuesday*, NBC), "Outstanding Cultural Documentary and 'Magazine-Type' Program or Series Achievement (Individual)"

Lord Snowdon (cinematographer for "Don't Count the Candles" on *CBS News Hour*, NBC), "Outstanding Cultural Documentary and 'Magazine-Type' Program or Series Achievement (Individual)"

Get Smart (NBC), "Outstanding Comedy Series"

NET Playhouse (NET), "Outstanding Dramatic Series"

"Teacher, Teacher" on *Hallmark Hall of Fame* (NBC), "Outstanding Dramatic Program"

Rowan and Martin's Laugh-In, (NBC), "Outstanding Variety or Musical Series"

"The Bill Cosby Special" (NBC), "Outstanding Variety or Musical Program"

Paul Scofield ("Male of the Species" on *Prudential's On-Stage*, NBC), "Outstanding Single Performance by an Actor in a Leading Role"

Geraldine Page (*The Thanksgiving Visitor*, ABC), "Outstanding Single Performance by an Actress in a Leading Role"

Carl Betz (*Judd for the Defense*, ABC), "Outstanding Continued Performance by an Actor in a Leading Role in a Dramatic Series"

Barbara Bain (*Mission: Impossible*, CBS) "Outstanding Continued Performance by an Actress in a Leading Role in a Dramatic Series"

Don Adams (*Get Smart*, NBC), "Outstanding Continued Performance by an Actor in a Leading Role in a Comedy Series"

Hope Lange (*The Ghost and Mrs. Muir*, NBC), "Outstanding Continued Performance by an Actress in a Leading Role in a Comedy Series"

Anna Calder-Marshall ("The Male of the Species" on *Prudential's On-Stage*, NBC), "Outstanding Single Performance by an Actress in a Supporting Role"

Werner Klemperer (*Hogan's Heroes*, CBS) "Outstanding Continued Performance by an Actor in a Supporting Role"

Susan Saint James (*The Name of the Game*, NBC) "Outstanding Continued Performance by an Actress in a Supporting Role"

J.P. Miller ("The People Next Door" on *CBS Playhouse*, CBS), "Outstanding Writing Achievement in Drama"

Allan Blye, Bob Einstein, Murray Roman, Carl Gottlieb, Jerry Music, Steve Martin, Cecil Tuck, Paul Wayne, Cy Howard and Mason Williams (*The Smothers Brothers Comedy Hour*, CBS), "Outstanding Writing Achievement in Comedy"

David Green ("The People Next Door" on *CBS Playhouse*, CBS) "Outstanding Directorial Achievement in Drama"

John T. Williams (*Heidi*, NBC), "Outstanding Achievement in Musical Composition"

William P. Ross and Lou Hafley (art director and set decorator, "The Bunker" on *Mission: Impossible*, CBS), "Outstanding Achievement in Art Direction and Scenic Design"

George Folsey (*Here's Peggy Fleming*, NBC) "Outstanding Achievement in Cinematography"

A.J. Cunningham (technical director) **and Nick DeMos, Bob Fonarow, Fred Gough, Jack Jennings, Dick Nelson, Rick Tanzi and Ben Wolf** (cameramen), ("The People Next Door" on *CBS Playhouse*, CBS), "Outstanding Achievement in Electronic Camerawork"

Bill Mosher ("An Elephant in a Cigarbox" on *Judd for the Defense*, ABC), "Outstanding Achievement in Film Editing"

The Dick Cavett Show (ABC), "Outstanding Program Achievement in Daytime Programming"

19th Summer Olympic Games (ABC), "Outstanding Program Achievement in Sports Programming"

Bill Bennington, Mike Freedman, Mac Memion, Robert Riger, Marv Schenkler, Andy Sidaris, Lou Volpicelli and Doug Wilson (*19th Summer Olympic Games*, ABC), "Outstanding Individual Achievement in Sports Programming"

Firing Line With William F. Buckley, Jr. (syndicated), "Special Classification Program Achievement"

Mutual of Omaha's Wild Kingdom (NBC), "Special Classification Program Achievement"

Arte Johnson (*Rowan and Martin's Laugh-In*, NBC), "Special Classification Individual Achievement (Variety Performances)"

Harvey Korman (*The Carol Burnett Show*, CBS), "Special Classification Individual Achievements (Variety Performances)"

Mort Lindsey (*Barbra Streisand: A Happening in Central Park*, CBS), "Outstanding Individual Achievement in Music"

Billy Schulman, "A Citation" (for extraordinary achievement for "Teacher, Teacher" on *The Hallmark Hall of Fame* for demonstrating a mentally retarded person can compete and accomplish as much or more than any youngsters of the same age)

William R. McAndrew, "Trustees' Award" (for his role in shaping television news as his permanent memorial)

Apollo VII, VIII, IX and X astronauts, "Trustees' Awards" (for sharing with the American public and the world the mysteries of outer space and the surface of the moon on live television)

Columbia Broadcasting System, "Citation" (for development of the Digital Control Technique used in the Mincam miniaturized color television cameras)

Pretty Soon Runs Out (WHA-TV, Madison, Wisc.), "The Station Award"

Assignment: The Young Greats (WFIL-TV, Philadelphia, Pa.), "Special Citation"

The Last Campaign of Robert Kennedy (Swiss Broadcasting and Television, Zurich), "International Award (Documentary)"

A Scent of Flowers (Canadian Broadcasting Corporation, Ontario), "International Award (Entertainment)"

1969-70 "An Investigation of Teenage Drug Addiction—Odyssey House" on *The Huntley-Brinkley Report* (NBC), "Outstanding Program Achievements Within Regularly Scheduled News Programs"

"Can the World Be Saved?" on *CBS Evening News With Walter Cronkite* (CBS), "Outstanding Program Achievement Within Regularly Scheduled News Programs"

Apollo: A Journey to the Moon (Apollo X, XI and XII) (NBC), "Outstanding Program Achievement in Coverage of Special Events"

Solar Eclipse: A Darkness at Noon (NBC), "Outstanding Program Achievement in Coverage of Special Events"

Walter Cronkite (reporter for *Man On the Moon: The Epic Journey of Apollo XI*, CBS), "Outstanding Individual Achievement in Coverage of Special Events"

Hospital (NET), "Oustanding Program Achievement in News Documentary Programming"

Frederick Wiseman (director of *Hospital*, NET), "Outstanding Individual Achievement in News Documentary Programming"

Black Journal (NET), "Outstanding Program Achievement in Magazine-Type Programming"

Tom Pettit (reporter-writer for "Some Footnotes to 25 Nuclear Years" on *First Tuesday*, NBC), "Outstanding Individual Achievement in Magazine-Type Programming"

Arthur Rubinstein (NBC), "Outstanding Program Achievement in Cultural Documentary Programming"

"Fathers and Sons" on *CBS News Hour* (CBS) "Outstanding Program Achievement in Cultural Documentary Programming"

"The Japanese" on *CBS News Hour* (CBS), "Outstanding Program Achievement in Cultural Documentary Programming"

Edwin O. Reischauer (commentator for "The Japanese" on *CBS News Hour*, CBS), "Outstanding Individual Achievement in Cultural Documentary Programming"

Arthur Rubinstein (*Arthur Rubinstein*, NBC) "Outstanding Individual Achievement in Cultural Documentary Programming"

My World and Welcome to It (NBC), "Outstanding Comedy Series"

Marcus Welby, M.D. (ABC), "Outstanding Dramatic Series"

"A Storm in Summer" on *Hallmark Hall of Fame* (NBC),"Outstanding Dramatic Program"

The David Frost Show (syndicated), "Outstanding Variety or Musical Series"

Annie, The Women in the Life of a Man(CBS),"Outstanding Variety or Musical Program (Variety or Popular)"

Cinderella (National Ballet of Canada, NET), "Outstanding Variety or Musical Program (Classical)"

Room 222 (ABC), "Outstanding New Series"

Peter Ustinov ("A Storm in Summer" on *Hallmark Hall of Fame*, NBC), "Outstanding Single Performance by an Actor in a Leading Role"

Patty Duke ("My Sweet Charlie" on *World Premier*, NBC), "Outstanding Single Performance by an Actress in a Leading Role"

Robert Young (*Marcus Welby, M.D.*, ABC), "Outstanding Continued Performance by an Actor in a Leading Role in a Dramatic Series"

Susan Hampshire (*The Forsyte Saga*, NET), "Outstanding Continued Performance by an Actress in a Leading Role in a Dramatic Series"

William Windom (*My World and Welcome to It*, NBC), "Oustanding Continued Performance by an Actor in a Leading Role in a Comedy Series"

Hope Lange (*The Ghost and Mrs. Muir*, ABC), "Outstanding Continued Performance by an Actress in a Leading Role in a Comedy Series"

James Brolin (*Marcus Welby, M.D.*, ABC), "Outstanding Performance by an Actor in a Supporting Role in Drama"

Gail Fisher (*Mannix*, CBS), "Outstanding Performance by an Actress in a Supporting Role in Drama"

Michael Constantine (*Room 222*, ABC), "Outstanding Performance by an Actor in a Supporting Role in Comedy"

Karen Valentine (*Room 222*, ABC), "Outstanding Performance by an Actress in a Supporting Role in Comedy"

Richard Levinson and William Link ("My Sweet Charlie" on *World Premiere*, NBC), "Outstanding Writing Achievement in Drama"

Gary Belkin, Peter Bellwood, Herb Sargent, Thomas Meehan and Judith Viorst (*Annie, The Women in the Life of a Man*, CBS), "Outstanding Writing Achievement in Comedy, Variety or Music"

Paul Bogart ("Shadow Game" on *CBS Playhouse*, CBS), "Outstanding Directorial Achievement in Drama"

Dwight A. Hemion ("The Sound of Burt Bacharach," on *Kraft Music Hall*, NBC), "Outstanding Directorial Achievement in Comedy, Variety or Music"

Norman Maen (*This Is Tom Jones*, ABC), "Outstanding Achievement in Choreography"

Morton Stevens ("A Thousand Pardons, You're Dead" on *Hawaii Five-O*, CBS), "Outstanding Achievement in Music Composition (for a series in first year of use)"

Pete Rugolo ("The Challengers" on *CBS Friday Night Movies*, CBS), "Outstanding Achievement in Music Composition (for special program)"

Peter Matz ("The Sound of Burt Bacharach" on *Kraft Music Hall*, NBC), "Outstanding Achievement in Music Direction of a Variety, Musical or Dramatic Program"

Arnold Margolin and Charles Fox (*Love American Style*, ABC), "Outstanding Achievement in Music, Lyrics and Special Materials"

Jan Scott and Earl Carlson (art director and set decorator of "Shadow Game" on *CBS Playhouse*, CBS), "Outstanding Achievement in Art Direction or Scenic Design (dramatic program)"

E. Jay Krause (*Mitzi's 2nd Special*, NBC), "Outstanding Achievement in Art Direction or Scenic Design (musical or variety)"

Leard Davis and Ed Hill (video: Richard Scovel and Clive Bassett), ("Appalachian Autumn" on *CBS Playhouse*, CBS), "Outstanding Achievement in Lighting Direction"

Bob Mackie (*Diana Ross and The Supremes and the Temptations on Broadway*, NBC), "Outstanding Achievement in Costume Design"

Ray Sebastian and Louis A. Phillippi (*The Don Adams Special: Hooray for Hollywood*, CBS), "Outstanding Achievement in Make-Up"

Walter Strenge ("Hello, Goodbye, Hello" on *Marcus Welby, M.D.*, ABC), "Outstanding Achievement in Cinematography for Entertainment Programming (series or single program of a series)"

Lionel Lindon ("Ritual of Evil" on *NBC Monday Night Movies*, NBC), "Outstanding Achievement in Cinematography for Entertainment Programming (special or feature-length program made for television)"

Edward Winkle ("Model Hippie" on *The Huntley-Brinkley Report*, NBC), "Outstanding Achievement in Cinematography for News and Documentary Programming (regularly scheduled news programs and coverage of special events)"

Thomas B. Priestley ("Sahara: La Caravanne du Sel," NBC), "Outstanding Achievement in Cinematography for News and Documentary Programming (documentary, magazine-type or mini-documentary programs)"

Bill Mosher ("Sweet Smell of Failure" on *Bracken's Word*, NBC), "Outstanding Achievement in Film Editing for Entertainment Programming (series or single program of a series)"

Edward R. Abroms ("My Sweet Charlie" on *World Premiere*, NBC), "Outstanding Achievement in Film Editing for Entertainment Programming (special or feature-length program made for television)"

Michael C. Shugrue ("The High School Profile" on *The Huntley-Brinkley Report*, NBC), "Outstanding Achievement in Film Editing for News and Documentary Programming (series, single program, special program, program segment or elements within)"

John Soh ("The Desert Whales" on *The Undersea World of Jacques Cousteau*, ABC), "Outstanding Achievement in Film Editing for News and Documentary Programming (documentary, magazine-type or mini-documentary program)"

Douglas H. Grindstaff, Alex Bamattre, Michael Colgan, Bill Lee, Joe Kavigan and Josef von Stroheim ("The Immortal" on *Movie of the Week*, ABC), "Outstanding Achievement in Film/Sound Editing"

Richard E. Raderman and Norman Karlin ("Charlie Noon" on *Gunsmoke*, CBS), "Outstanding Achievement in Film/Sound Editing"

Gordon L. Day and Dominick Gaffney ("The Submarine" on *Mission: Impossible*, CBS), "Outstanding Achievement in Film/Sound Mixing"

Bill Cole and Dave Williams ("The Switched-On Symphony," NBC), "Outstanding Achievement in Live or Tape Sound Mixing"

John Shultis ("The Sound of Burt Bacharach" on *Kraft Music Hall*, NBC), "Outstanding Achievement in Video Tape Editing"

Heino Ripp (technical director) with **Al Camoin, Gene Martin, Donald Mulvaney and Cal Shadwell** (cameramen) ("The Sound of Burt Bacharach" on *Kraft Music Hall*, NBC), "Outstanding Achievement in Technical Direction and Electronic Camerawork"

Sesame Street (NET), "Outstanding Program Achievement in Children's Programming"

Joe Raposo and Jeffrey Moss (music and lyrics for *This Way to Sesame Street*, NBC), "Outstanding Individual Achievement in Children's Programming"

Jon Stone, Jeffrey Moss, Ray Sipherd, Jerry Juhl, Dan Wilcox, Dave Connell, Bruce Hart, Carole Hart and Virginia Schone ("Sally Sees Sesame Street" on *Sesame Street*, NET), "Outstanding Individual Achievement in Children's Programming"

Today (NBC), "Outstanding Program Achievement in Daytime Programming"

The NFL Games, (CBS), "Outstanding Program Achievement in Sports Programming"

ABC's Wide World of Sports (ABC), "Outstanding Program Achievement in Sports Programming"

Robert R. Forte (film editing for *Pre Game Program,* CBS), "Outstanding Individual Achievement in Sports Programming"

Mutual of Omaha's Wild Kingdom (NBC), "Special Classification of Outstanding Program Achievement"

Video Communications Division, NASA, and Westinghouse Corporation, "Outstanding Achievement in Engineering Development" for Apollo Color Television from Space

Ampex Corporation, "Citation" for HS-200 color television production system

The Slow Guillotine KNBC-TV, Los Angeles), "Station Award"

The Other Americans (WJZ-TV, Baltimore), "Special Citation"

The Presidents of the three network news divisions, NASA and the 3M Company, "The Trustees' Awards"

1970-71 Five-Part Investigation of Welfare (*NBC Nightly News*, NBC), "Outstanding Program Achievement Within Regularly Scheduled News Programs"

Bruce Morton (correspondent for "Reports From the Lt. Calley Trial" on *CBS Evening News With Walter Cronkite*, CBS), "Outstanding Individual Achievement Within Regularly Scheduled News Programs"

"CBS News Space Coverage for 1970-71" (CBS), "Outstanding Program Achievement in Coverage of Special Events"

Walter Cronkite (correspondent for "CBS News Space Coverage for 1970-71," CBS), "Outstanding Individual Achievement in Coverage of Special Events"

"The Selling of the Pentagon" (*CBS News*, CBS), "Outstanding Program Achievement in News Documentary Programming"

"The World of Charlie Company" (*CBS News*, CBS), "Outstanding Program Achievement in News Documentary Programming"

NBC White Paper: Pollution is a Matter of Choice (NBC), "Outstanding Program Achievement in News Documentary Programming"

John Laurence (correspondent for "The World of Charlie Company," CBS), "Outstanding Individual Achievement in News Documentary Programming"

Fred Freed (writer for *NBC White Paper: Pollution is a Matter of Choice*, NBC), "Outstanding Individual Achievement in News Documentary Programming"

Gulf of Tonkin segment on *60 Minutes* (CBS), "Outstanding Program Achievement in Magazine-Type Programming"

"The Great American Dream Machine" (PBS), "Outstanding Program Achievement in Magazine-Type Programming"

Mike Wallace (correspondent, *60 Minutes*, CBS), "Outstanding Individual Achievement in Magazine-Type Programming"

The Everglades (NBC), "Outstanding Program Achievement in Cultural Documentary Programming"

The Making of "Butch Cassidy & The Sundance Kid" (NBC), "Outstanding Program Achievement in Cultural Documentary Programming"

Arthur Penn 1922—Themes and Variants (PBS), "Outstanding Program Achievement in Cultural Documentary Programming"

Nana Mahomo (narrator for *A Black View of South Africa*, CBS), "Outstanding Individual Achievement in Cultural Documentary Programming"

Robert Guenette and Theodore H. Strauss (writers of *They've Killed President Lincoln*, NBC), "Outstanding Individual Achievement in Cultural Documentary Programming"

Robert Young (director of *The Eskimo: Fight for Life*, CBS), "Outstanding Individual Achievement in Cultural Documentary Programming"

All in the Family (CBS), "Outstanding Series—Comedy"

The Senator—The Bold Ones (NBC), "Outstanding Series—Drama"

The Andersonville Trial (PBS), "Outstanding Single Program—Drama or Comedy"

The Flip Wilson Show (NBC), "Outstanding Variety Series—Musical"

The David Frost Show (syndicated), "Outstanding Variety Series—Talk"

Singer presents Burt Bacharach (CBS), "Outstanding Single Program—Variety or Musical (variety and popular music)"

Leopold Stokowski (PBS), "Outstanding Single Program—Variety or Musical (classical)"

All in the Family (CBS), "Outstanding New Series"

George C. Scott ("The Price" on *Hallmark Hall of Fame*, NBC), "Outstanding Single Performance by an Actor in a Leading Role"

Lee Grant ("The Neon Ceiling" on *World Premiere NBC Monday Night at the Movies*, NBC), "Outstanding Single Performance by an Actress in a Leading Role"

Hal Holbrook (*The Senator—The Bold Ones*, NBC), "Outstanding Continued Performance by an Actor in a Leading Role in a Dramatic Series"

Susan Hampshire ("The First Churchills" on *Masterpiece Theatre*, PBS), "Outstanding Continued Performance by an Actress in a Leading Role in a Dramatic Series"

Jack Klugman (*The Odd Couple*, ABC), "Outstanding Continued Performance by an Actor in a Leading Role in a Comedy Series"

Jean Stapleton (*All in the Family*, CBS), "Outstanding Continued Performance by an Actress in a Leading Role in a Comedy Series"

David Burns ("The Price" on *Hallmark Hall of Fame*, NBC), "Outstanding Performance by an Actor in a Supporting Role in Drama"

Margaret Leighton ("Hamlet" on *Hallmark Hall of Fame*, NBC), "Outstanding Performance by an Actress in a Supporting Role in Drama"

Edward Asner (*The Mary Tyler Moore Show*, CBS), "Outstanding Performance by an Actor in a Supporting Role in Comedy"

Valerie Harper (*The Mary Tyler Moore Show*, CBS), "Outstanding Performance by an Actress in a Supporting Role in Comedy"

Daryl Duke ("The Day the Lion Died" on *The Bold Ones—The Senator*, NBC), "Outstanding Directorial Achievement in Drama (single program of a series)"

Fielder Cook ("The Price" on *Hallmark Hall of Fame*, NBC), "Outstanding Directorial Achievement in Drama (single program)"

Jay Sandrich ("Toulouse Lautrec is One of My Favorite Artists" on *The Mary Tyler Moore Show*, CBS), "Outstanding Directorial Achievement in Comedy (single program of a series)"

Mark Warren (*Rowan and Martin's Laugh-In*, NBC), "Outstanding Directorial Achievement in Variety or Music (single program of a series)"

Sterling Johnson (*Timex Presents Peggy Fleming at Sun Valley*, NBC) "Outstanding Directorial Achievement in Comedy, Variety or Music (special program)"

Ernest O. Flatt (*The Carol Burnett Show*, CBS) "Outstanding Achievement in Choreography"

Joel Oliansky ("To Taste of Death But Once" on *The Bold Ones—The Senator*, NBC), "Outstanding Writing Achievement in Drama (single program of a series)"

Tracy Keenan Wynn and Marvin Schwartz ("Tribes" on *Movie of the Week*, ABC), "Outstanding Writing Achievement in Drama, Original Teleplay"

Saul Levitt ("The Andersonville Trial" on *Hollywood Television Theatre*, PBS), "Outstanding Writing Achievement in Drama, Adaptation"

James L. Brooks and Allan Burns ("Support Your Local Mother" on *The Mary Tyler Moore Show*, CBS), "Outstanding Writing Achievement in Comedy (single program of a series)"

Herbert Baker, Hal Goodman, Larry Klein, Bob Weiskopf, Bob Schiller, Norman Steinberg and Flip Wilson (*The Flip Wilson Show*, NBC), "Outstanding Writing Achievement in Variety or Music (single program of a series)"

Bob Ellison and Marty Farrell (*Singer Presents Burt Bacharach*, CBS), "Outstanding Writing Achievement in Comedy, Variety or Music (special program)"

David Rose ("The Love Child" on *Bonanza*, NBC), "Outstanding Achievement in Music Composition (for a series in the first year of use)"

Walter Scharf ("The Tragedy of the Red Salmon" on *The Undersea World of Jacques Cousteau*, ABC), "Outstanding Achievement in Music Composition (special program)"

Dominic Frontiere ("Swing Out, Sweet Land," NBC), "Outstanding Achievement in Music Direction of a Variety, Musical or Dramatic Program"

Ray Charles (*The First Nine Months Are the Hardest*, NBC), "Outstanding Achievement in Music, Lyrics and Special Material"

Jack Marta ("Cynthia Is Alive and Living in Avalon" on *The Name of the Game*, NBC), "Outstanding Achievement in Cinematography for Entertainment Programming (series or single program of a series)"

Lionel Lindon ("Vanished," Parts I and II, on *Movie of the Week*, ABC), "Outstanding Achievement in Cinematography for Entertainment Program (special program)"

Bob Collins (*Timex Presents Peggy Fleming at Sun Valley*, NBC), "Outstanding Achievement in Cinematography for Entertainment Program (special program)"

Larry Travis ("Los Angeles—Earthquake" on *CBS Evening News With Walter Cronkite*, CBS), "Outstanding Achievement in Cinematography for News and Documentary Programming (regularly scheduled news and coverage of special events)"

Jacques Renoir ("The Tragedy of the Red Salmon" on *The Undersea World of Jacques Cousteau*, ABC), "Outstanding Achievement in Cinematography for News and Documentary Programming (documentary, mini-documentary or magazine-type programs)"

Peter Roden ("Hamlet" on *Hallmark Hall of Fame*, NBC), "Outstanding Achievement in Art Direction or Scenic Design (dramatic program or feature-length film)"

James W. Trittipo and George Gaines (*Robert Young and The Family,* CBS), "Outstanding Achievement in Art Direction or Scenic Design (musical or variety)"

Martin Baugh and David Walker ("Hamlet" on *Hallmark Hall of Fame,* NBC), "Outstanding Achievement in Costume Design"

Robert Dawn ("Catafalque" on *Mission: Impossible,* CBS), "Outstanding Achievement in Make-Up"

Michael Economou ("A Continual Roar of Musketry," Parts I and II, on *The Bold Ones—The Senator,* NBC), "Outstanding Achievement in Film Editing for Entertainment Programming (series or single program of a series)"

George J. Nicholson ("Longstreet" on *Movie of the Week,* ABC), "Outstanding Achievement in Film Editing for Entertainment Programming (special or feature-length program made for television)"

George L. Johnson ("Prisons," Parts I-IV, on *NBC Nightly News,* NBC), "Outstanding Achievement in Film Editing for News and Documentary Programming (series, single program of a series or segment)"

Robert B. Loweree and Henry J. Grennon (*Cry Help! An NBC White Paper On Mentally Disturbed Youth,* NBC), "Outstanding Achievement in Film Editing for News and Documentary Programming (documentary, magazine-type or mini-documentary program)"

Don Hall, Jack Jackson, Bob Weatherford and Dick Jensen ("Tribes" on *Movie of the Week,* ABC), "Outstanding Achievement in Film Sound Editing"

Theodore Sonderberg ("Tribes" on *Movie of the Week,* ABC), "Outstanding Achievement in Film Sound Mixing"

John Rook ("Hamlet" on *Hallmark Hall of Fame,* NBC), "Outstanding Achievement in Lighting Direction"

Henry Bird ("Hamlet" on *Hallmark Hall of Fame,* NBC), "Outstanding Achievement in Live or Tape Sound Mixing"

Marco Zappia (*Hee-Haw,* CBS), "Outstanding Achievement in Video Tape Editing"

Gordon Baird, Tom Ancell, Rick Bennewitz, Larry Bentley and Jack Reader ("The Andersonville Trial" on *Hollywood Television Theatre,* PBS), "Outstanding Achievement in Technical Direction and Electronic Camerawork"

Sesame Street (PBS), "Outstanding Program Achievement in Children's Programming"

Burr Tillstrom (performer on *Kukla, Fran and Ollie,* PBS), "Outstanding Individual Achievement in Children's Programming"

Today (NBC), "Outstanding Program Achievement in Daytime Programming"

ABC's Wide World of Sports (ABC), "Outstanding Program Achievement in Sports Programming"

Jim McKay (commentator on *ABC's Wide World of Sports*), "Outstanding Individual Achievement in Sports Programming"

Don Meredith (commentator on *NFL Monday Night Football,* ABC), "Outstanding Individual Achievement in Sports Programming"

Harvey Korman (*The Carol Burnett Show,* CBS), "Special Classification of Individual Achievement"

Lenwood B. Abbott and John C. Caldwell (photographic effects on "City Beneath the Sea" on *World Premiere NBC Monday Night at the Movies,* NBC), "Outstanding Achievement in Any Area of Creative Technical Crafts"

Gene Widhoff (courtroom sketches at the Manson trial on *The Huntley-Brinkley Report—NBC Nightly News,* NBC), " Outstanding Achievement in Any Area of Creative Technical Crafts"

Ed Sullivan, "Trustees' Award" (for serving as founder and first President of the Academy and for pioneering the variety format)

Columbia Broadcasting System, "Outstanding Achievement in Engineering Development" for the Color Corrector

American Broadcasting Co., "Outstanding Achievement in Engineering Development" for open-loop synchronizing system

General Electric, "Citation" for Portable Earth Station Transmitter

Stefan Kudelski, "Citation" for design of NAGRA IV Recorder

If You Turn On (KNXT, Los Angeles), "Station Award"

1971-72 **"Defeat of Dacca"** (*NBC Nightly News,* NBC), "Outstanding Program Achievement Within Regularly Scheduled News Programs"

Phil Brady (reporter on "Defeat of Dacca," on *NBC Nightly News,* NBC), "Outstanding Individual Achievement Within Regularly Scheduled News"

Bob Schieffer, Phil Jones, Don Webster and Bill Plante (correspondents covering "The Air War" on *CBS Evening News With Walter Cronkite,* CBS), "Outstanding Individual Achievement Within Regularly Scheduled News"

Chronolog (NBC), "Outstanding Program Achievement for Regularly Scheduled Magazine-Type Programs"

The Great American Dream Machine (PBS), "Outstanding Program Achievement for Regularly Scheduled Magazine-Type Programs"

Mike Wallace (correspondent on *60 Minutes,* CBS), "Outstanding Individual Achievement for Regularly Scheduled Magazine-Type Programming"

The China Trip (ABC), "Outstanding Program Achievement in Coverage of Special Events"

June 30, 1971, A Day for History: The Supreme Court and the Pentagon Papers (NBC), "Outstanding Program Achievement in Coverage of Special Events"

A Ride on the Moon: The Flight of Apollo 15 (CBS), "Outstanding Program Achievement in Coverage of Special Events"

"A Night in Jail, A Day in Court" (*CBS Reports*), "Outstanding Documentary Program Achievement (programs—current signficance)"

This Child is Rated X: An NBC News White Paper on Juvenile Justice (NBC), "Outstanding Documentary Program Achievement (programs—current signficance)"

"Hollywood: The Dream Factory" (*The Monday Night Special,* ABC), The "Outstanding Documentary Program Achievement (cultural)"

"A Sound of Dolphins" (*The Undersea World of Jacques Cousteau,* (ABC), "Outstanding Documentary Program Achievement (cultural)"

"The Unsinkable Sea Otter" (*The Undersea World of Jacques Cousteau,* ABC), " Outstanding Documentary Program Achievement (cultural)"

Louis J. Hazam (writer of *Venice Be Damned,* NBC), "Outstanding Documentary Program Achievement (individual)"

Robert Northshield (writer on *Suffer the Little Children—An NBC News White Paper on Northern Ireland*, NBC), "Outstanding Documentary Program Achievement (individual)"

All In the Family (CBS), "Outstanding Series—Comedy"

Elizabeth R (PBS), "Outstanding Series—Drama"

"Brian's Song" (*ABC's Movie of the Week*, ABC), "Outstanding Single Program—Drama or Comedy"

The Carol Burnett Show (CBS), "Outstanding Variety Series—Musical"

The Dick Cavett Show (ABC), "Outstanding Variety Series—Talk"

"Jack Lemmon in 'S Wonderful, 'S Mavelous, 'S Gershwin" (*Bell System Family Theatre*, NBC), "Outstanding Single Program — Variety or Musical (variety and popular music)"

Beethoven's Birthday: A Celebration in Vienna With Leonard Bernstein (CBS), "Outstanding Single Program — Variety or Musical (classical)"

Elizabeth R (PBS), "Outstanding New Series"

Keith Michell ("Catherine Howard" on *Six Wives of Henry VIII*, CBS), "Outstanding Single Performance by an Actor in a Leading Role (one-time appearance in a series or special program)"

Glenda Jackson ("Shadow In The Sun" on *Elizabeth R, Masterpiece Theatre*, PBS), "Outstanding Single Performance by an Actress in a Leading Role (one-time appearance in a series or special program)"

Peter Falk (*Columbo* on *NBC Mystery Movie*, NBC), "Outstanding Continued Performance by an Actor in a Leading Role in a Dramatic Series"

Glenda Jackson (*Elizabeth R* on *Masterpiece Theatre*, PBS), "Outstanding Continued Performance by an Actress in a Leading Role in a Dramatic Series"

Carroll O'Connor (*All in the Family*, CBS), "Outstanding Continued Performance by an Actor in a Leading Role in a Comedy Series"

Jean Stapleton (*All in the Family*, CBS), "Outstanding Continued Performance by an Actress in a Leading Role in a Comedy Series"

Jack Warden ("Brian's Song" on *Movie of the Week*, ABC), "Outstanding Performance by an Actor in a Supporting Role in Drama"

Jenny Agutter ("The Snow Goose" on *Hallmark Hall of Fame*, NBC), "Outstanding Performance by an Actress in Supporting Role in Drama"

Edward Asner (*The Mary Tyler Moore Show*, CBS), "Outstanding Performance by an Actor in a Supporting Role in Comedy"

Valerie Harper (*The Mary Tyler Moore Show*, CBS), "Outstanding Performance by an Actress in a Supporting Role in Comedy"

Sally Struthers (*All in the Family* CBS), "Outstanding Performance by an Actress in a Supporting Role in Comedy"

Harvey Korman (*The Carol Burnett Show*, CBS), "Outstanding Achievement by a Performer in Music or Variety"

Alexander Singer ("The Invasion of Kevin Ireland" on *The Bold Ones—The Lawyers*, NBC), "Outstanding Directorial Achievement in Drama (single program of a series)"

Tom Gries ("The Glass House" on *The New CBS Friday Night Movies*, CBS), "Outstanding Directorial Achievement in Drama (single program)"

John Rich ("Sammy's Visit" on *All In the Family*, CBS), "Outstanding Directorial Achievement in Comedy (series)"

Art Fisher (*The Sonny & Cher Comedy Hour*, CBS), "Outstanding Directorial Achievement in Variety or Music (series)"

Walter C. Miller and Marvin Charnin ("Jack Lemmon in 'S Wonderful, 'S Marvelous, 'S Gershwin" on *Bell System Family Theatre*, NBC), "Outstanding Directorial Achievement in Comedy, Variety or Music (special)"

Alan Johnson ("Jack Lemmon in 'S Wonderful, S' Marvelous, S' Gershwin," on *Bell System Family Theatre*, NBC), "Outstanding Achievement in Choreography"

Richard L. Levinson and William Link ("Death Lends a Hand" on *Columbo*, NBC), "Outstanding Writing Achievement in Drama (single program of a series)"

Allan Sloane (*To All My Friends on Shore*, CBS), "Outstanding Writing Achievement in Drama, Original Teleplay"

William Blinn ("Brian's Song" on *Movie of the Week*, ABC), "Outstanding Writing Achievement in Drama, Adaptation"

Burt Styler ("Edith's Problem" on *All in the Family*, CBS), "Outstanding Writing Achievement in Comedy"

Don Hinkley, Stan Hart, Larry Siegel, Woody Kling, Rober Beatty, Art Baer, Ben Joelson, Stan Burns, Mike Marmer and Arnie Rosen (*The Carol Burnett Show*, CBS), "Outstanding Writing Achievement in Variety or Music"

Anne Howard Bailey ("The Trial of Mary Lincoln" on *NET Opera Theatre*, PBS), "Outstanding Writing Achievement in Comedy, Variety or Music (special program)"

Peter Rugolo ("In Defense of Ellen McKay" on *The Bold Ones—The Lawyers*, NBC), "Outstanding Achievement in Music Composition (series or single program of a series)"

John T. Williams ("Jane Eyre" on *Bell System Family Theatre*, NBC), "Outstanding Achievement in Music Composition (special program)"

Elliot Lawrence ("Jack Lemmon in 'S Wonderful, 'S Marvelous, 'S Gershwin" on *Bell System Family Theatre*, NBC), "Outstanding Achievement in Music Direction of a Variety, Musical or Dramatic Program"

Ray Charles ("The Funny Side of Marriage," NBC), "Outstanding Achievement in Music, Lyrics and Special Material"

Jan Scott ("The Scarecrow" on *Hollywood Television Theatre*, PBS), "Outstanding Achievement in Art Direction or Scenic Design (dramatic program or feature-length film made for television)"

E. Jay Krause (*Diana!*, ABC), "Outstanding Achievement in Art Direction or Scenic Design (musical or variety program)"

Elizabeth Waller ("The Lion's Cub," *Elizabeth R* on *Masterpiece Theatre*, PBS), "Outstanding Achievement in Costume Design"

Frank Westmore ("Kung Fu" on *Movie of the Week*, ABC) "Outstanding Achievement in Make-Up"

Lloyd Ahern ("Blue Print for Murder" on *Columbo*, NBC), "Outstanding Achievement in Cinematography for Entertainment Programming (series or single program of a series)"

Joseph Biroc ("Brian's Song" on *Movie of the Week*, ABC) "Outstanding Achievement in Cinematography for Entertainment Programming (special or feature-length program made for television)"

Peter McIntyre and Lim Youn Choul ("Dacca" on *NBC Nightly News*, NBC), "Outstanding Achievement in Cinematography for News and Documentary Programming (regularly scheduled news programs and coverage of special events)"

Thomas Priestley (*Venice Be Damned*, NBC), "Outstanding Achievement in Cinematography for News and Documentary Programming (documentary, magazine-type of mini-documentary programs)"

Edward R. Abroms ("Death Lends a Hand" on *Columbo*, NBC), "Outstanding Achievement in Film Editing for Entertainment Programming (series or single program of a series)

Bud S. Isaacs ("Brian's Song" on *Movie of the Week*, ABC), "Outstanding Achievement in Film Editing for Entertainment Programming (special or feature-length program made for television)"

Darold Murray ("War Song" on *NBC Nightly News*, NBC), "Outstanding Achievement in Film Editing for News and Documentary Programming (regularly scheduled news programs and coverage of special events)"

Spencer David Saxon ("Monkeys, Apes and Man" on *National Geographic Society*, CBS), "Outstanding Achievement in Film Editing for News and Documentary Programming (documentary, magazine-type and mini-documentary programs)"

Jerry Christian, James Troutman, Ronald La-Vine, Sidney Lubow, Richard Raderman, Dale Johnston, Sam Caylor, John Stacy and Jack Kirschner ("Duel" on *Movie of the Weekend*, ABC), "Outstanding Achievement in Film Sound Editing"

Theodore Soderberg and Richard Overton ("Fireball Forward" on *The ABC Sunday Night Movie*, ABC), "Outstanding Achievement in Film Sound Mixing"

Heino Ripp (technical director) and Albert Camoin, Frank Gaeta, Gene Martin and Donald Mulvaney (cameramen), ("Jack Lemmon in 'S Wonderful, 'S Marvelous, 'S Gershwin," NBC), "Outstanding Achievement in Technical Direction and Electronic Camerawork"

John Freschi ("Gideon" on *Hallmark Hall of Fame*, NBC), "Outstanding Achievement in Lighting Direction"

Pat McKenna ("Hogan's Goat" on *Special of the Week*, PBS), "Outstanding Achievement in Video Tape Editing"

Norman H. Dewes ("The Elevator Story" on *All in the Family*, CBS), "Outstanding Achievement in Live or Tape Sound Mixing"

"The Pentagon Papers" (*PBS Special*), "Special Classification of Outstanding Achievement—General Programming"

The Search for the Nile, Parts I-VI (NBC), "Special Classification of Outstanding Achievement—Docu-Drama Programming"

Michael Hastings and Derek Marlow (writers on *The Search for the Nile*, Parts I-VI, NBC), "Special Classfication of Outstanding Achievement—Individual"

ABC's Wide World of Sports (ABC), "Outstanding Program Achievement in Sports Programming"

William P. Kelley (technical director) and Jim Culley, Jack Bennett, Buddy Joseph, Mario Ciarlo, Frank Manfredi, Corey Leible, Gene Martin, Cal Shadwell, Billy Barnes and Ron Charbonneau (cameramen), (*AFC Championship Game*, NBC), "Outstanding Individual Achievement in Sports Programming"

Sesame Street (PBS), "Outstanding Program Achievement in Children's Programming"

The Doctors (NBC), "Outstanding Program Achievement in Daytime Drama"

Alfredo Antonini (music director of *And David Wept*, CBS), "Outstanding Individual Achievement in Religious Programming"

Lon Stucky (lighting director for *A City of the King*, syndicated), "Outstanding Individual Achievement in Religious Programming"

Pierre Goupil, Michael Deloire and Yves Omer (underwater cameramen for "Secrets of the Sunken Caves" on *The Undersea World of Jacques Cousteau*, ABC), "Outstanding Achievement in Any Area of Creative Technical Crafts"

Bill Lawrence, National Affairs Editor, ABC News, "Trustees' Award" for dedicating four decades of his life to reporting the news

Frank Stanton, President, CBS, "Trustees' Award" for selfless leadership and unwavering principle in defense of the industry

Lee Harrison, "Outstanding Achievement in Engineering Development" for Scanimate, electronic means of picture animation

Richard E. Hill and Electronic Engineering Company of California, "Citation" for time code and equipment to facilitate editing of magnetic video tape

National Broadcasting Company, "Citation" for Hum Bucker, practical means of correcting picture transmission defect common in remote pickups

Sickle Cell Disease: Paradox of Neglect (WZZM-TV, Grand Rapids, Mich.), "Station Award"

1972-73 *All in the Family* (CBS), "Outstanding Comedy Series"

The Waltons (CBS), "Outstanding Drama Series—Continuing"

Tom Brown's Schooldays, Parts I-V (PBS) "Outstanding Drama Series—Limited Episodes"

The Julie Andrews Hour (ABC), "Outstanding Variety Musical Series"

"A War of Children" on *The New CBS Tuesday Night Movies*, (CBS), "Outstanding Single Program—Drama or Comedy"

Singer Presents Liza With a 'Z' (NBC), "Outstanding Single Program—Variety or Popular Music"

The Sleeping Beauty (PBS), "Outstanding Single Program—Classical Music"

America (NBC), "Outstanding New Series"

The Edge of Night (CBS), "Outstanding Program Achievement in Daytime Drama"

Dinah's Place (NBC), "Outstanding Program Achievement in Daytime Programming"

Laurence Olivier (*Long Day's Journey Into Night*, ABC), "Outstanding Single Performance by an Actor in a Leading Role"

Cloris Leachman ("A Brand New Life" on *Tuesday Movie of the Week*, ABC), "Outstanding Single Performance by an Actress in a Leading Role"

Richard Thomas (*The Waltons*, CBS), "Outstanding Continued Performance by an Actor in a Leading Role (drama series—continuing)"

Anthony Murphy (*Tom Brown's Schooldays*, PBS), "Outstanding Continued Performance by an Actor in a Leading role (drama/comedy—limited episodes)"

Michael Learned (*The Waltons*, CBS), "Outstanding, Continued Performance by an Actress in a Leading Role (drama series-continuing)"

Susan Hampshire (*Vanity Fair*, Parts I-V, on *Masterpiece Theatre*, PBS) "Outstanding Continued Performance by an Actress in a Leading Role (drama/comedy—limited episodes)"

Jack Klugman (*The Odd Couple*, ABC), "Outstanding Continued Performance by an Actor in a Leading Role in a Comedy Series"

Mary Tyler Moore (*The Mary Tyler Moore Show*, CBS), "Outstanding Continued Performance by an Actress in a Leading Role in a Comedy Series"

Scott Jacoby ("That Certain Summer" on *Wednesday Night Movie of the Week*, ABC), "Outstanding Performance by an Actor in a Supporting Role in Drama"

Ellen Corby (*The Waltons*, CBS), "Outstanding Performance by an Actress in a Supporting Role in Drama"

Ted Knight (*The Mary Tyler Moore Show*, CBS), "Outstanding Performance by an Actor in a Supporting Role in Comedy"

Valerie Harper (*The Mary Tyler Moore Show*, CBS), "Outstanding Performance by an Actress in a Supporting Role in Comedy"

Tim Conway (*The Carol Burnett Show*, CBS), "Outstanding Achievement by a Supporting Performer in Music or Variety"

Jerry Thorpe ("An Eye for an Eye" on *Kung Fu*, ABC), "Outstanding Directorial Achievement in Drama (single program of a series)"

Joseph Sargent ("The Marcus-Nelson Murders" on *The CBS Thursday Night Movies*, CBS), "Outstanding Directorial Achievement in Drama (single program)"

Jay Sandrich ("It's Whether You Win or Lose" on *The Mary Tyler Moore Show*, CBS), "Outstanding Directorial Achievement in Comedy (single program of a series)"

Bill Davis (*The Julie Andrews Hour*, ABC), "Outstanding Directorial Achievement in Variety or Music (single program of a series)"

Bob Fosse (*Singer Presents Liza With a "Z,"* NBC), "Outstanding Directorial Achievement in Comedy, Variety or Music (single program)"

Abby Mann ("The Marcus-Nelson Murders" on *The CBS Thursday Night Movies*, CBS), "Outstanding Writing Achievement in Drama, Original Teleplay"

Eleanor Perry (*The House Without a Christmas Tree*, CBS), "Outstanding Writing Achievement in Drama, Adaptation"

Michael Ross, Bernie West and Lee Kalcheim ("The Bunkers and The Swingers" on *All in the Family*, CBS), "Outstanding Writing Achievement in Comedy (single program of a series)"

Stan Hart, Larry Siegel, Gail Parent, Woody Kling, Roger Beatty, Tom Patchett, Jay Tarses, Robert Hilliard, Arnie Kogen, Bill Angelos and Buz Kohan (*The Carol Burnett Show*, CBS), "Outstanding Writing Achievement in Variety or Music (single program of a series)"

Renee Taylor and Joseph Bologna (*Acts of Love—And Other Comedies*, ABC), "Outstanding Writing Achievement in Comedy, Variety or Music (special program)"

Bob Fosse (*Singer Presents Liza With a "Z,"* NBC), "Outstanding Achievement in Choreography

Charles Fox (*Love, American Style*, ABC), "Outstanding Achievement in Music Composition (for a series or single program of a series in first year of use)"

Jerry Goldsmith ("The Red Pony" on *Bell System Family Theatre*, NBC), "Outstanding Achievement in Music Composition (special program)"

Peter Matz (*The Carol Burnett Show*, CBS), "Outstanding Achievement in Music Direction of a Variety, Musical or Dramatic Program"

Fred Ebb and John Kander (*Singer Presents Liza With a 'Z',* NBC), "Outstanding Achievement in Music, Lyrics and Special Material"

Tom John (*Much Ado About Nothing*, CBS), "Outstanding Achievement for Art Direction or Scenic Design (dramatic program or feature-length film made for television)"

Brian Bartholomew and Keaton S. Walker (*The Julie Andrews Hour*, ABC), "Outstanding Achievement in Art Direction or Scenic Design (musical or variety series or Special program)"

John Freschi and John Casagrande (*44th Oscar Awards*, NBC), "Outstanding Achievement in Lighting Direction"

Truck Krone (*The Julie Andrews Hour Christmas Show*, ABC), "Outstanding Achievement in Lighting Direction"

Jack Bear (*The Julie Andrews Hour*, ABC) "Outstanding Achievement in Costume Design"

Del Armstrong, Ellis Burman and Stan Winston ("Jayoupes" on *New CBS Tuesday Night Movies*, CBS) "Outstanding Achievement in Make-up"

Jack Woolf ("Eye for an Eye" on *Kung Fu*, ABC), "Outstanding Achievement in Cinematography for Entertainment Programming (series or single program of a series)"

Howard Schwartz ("Night of Terror" on *Tuesday Movie of the Week*, ABC), "Outstanding Achievement in Cinematography for Entertainment Programming (special or feature-length film made for television)"

Gene Fowler, Jr., Marjorie Fowler and Anthony Wollner ("The Literary Man" on *The Waltons*, CBS), "Outstanding Achievement in Film Editing for Entertainment Programming (series or single program of a series)"

Peter C. Johnson and Ed Spiegel (*Surrender at Appomattox; Appointment With Destiny*, CBS), "Outstanding Achievement in Film Editing for Entertainment Programming (special or feature-length film made for television)"

Ross Taylor, Fred Brown and David Marshall ("The Red Pony" on *Bell System Family Theatre*, NBC), "Outstanding Achievement in Film Sound Editing"

Richard Wagner, George E. Porter, Eddie Nelson and Fred Leroy Granville (*Surrender at Appomattox; Appointment With Destiny*, CBS), "Outstanding Achievement in Film Sound Mixing"

Al Gramaglia and Mahlon Fox (*Much Ado About Nothing*, CBS), "Outstanding Achievement in Live or Tape Sound Mixing"

Nick Giordano and Arthur Schneider (*The Julie Andrews Hour*, ABC), "Outstanding Achievement in Video Tape Editing"

Ernie Buttelman (technical director) and **Robert A. Kemp, James Angel, James Balden and David Hilmer** (cameramen), (*The Julie Andrews Hour*, ABC), "Outstanding Achievement in Technical Direction and Electronic Camerawork"

Mary Fickett (performer in *All My Children*, ABC), "Outstanding Achievement by an Individual in Daytime Drama"

Sesame Street (PBS), "Outstanding Achievement in Children's Programming (entertainment/fictional)"

Zoom (PBS), "Outstanding Achievement in Children's Programming (entertainment/fictional)"

Tom Whedon, John Boni, Sara Compton, Tom Dunsmuir, Thad Mumford, Jeremy Stevens and Jim Thurman (writers on *The Electric Company*, PBS), "Outstanding Achievement in Children's Programming (entertainment/fictional)"

"Last of the Curlews" (*The ABC Afterschool Special*, ABC), "Outstanding Achievement in Children's Programming (informational/factual)"

Shari Lewis (performer on "A Picture of Us," on *NBC Children's Theatre*, NBC), "Outstanding Achievement in Children's Programming (informational/factual)"

ABC's Wide World of Sports (ABC), "Outstanding Achievement in Sports Programming"

1972 Summer Olympic Games (ABC), "Outstanding Achievement in Sports Programming"

John Croak, Charles Gardner, Jakob Hierl, Conrad Kraus, Edward McCarthy, Nick Mazur, Alex Moskovic, James Parker, Louis Rende, Ross Skipper, Robert Steinback, John de Lisa, George Boettscher, Merrit Roesser, Leo Scharf, Randy Cohen, Vito Gerardi, Harold Byers, Winfield Gross, Paul Scoskie, Peter Fritz, Leo Stephan, Gerber McBeath, Louis Torino, Michael Wenig, Tom Wight and James Kelley (video tape editors on *1972 Summer Olympic Games*, (ABC), "Outstanding Achievement in Sports Programming"

Sony, "Outstanding Achievement in Engineering Development" for development of Trinitron picture tube

CMX Systems (CBS Memorex), "Outstanding Achievement in Engineering Development" for video tape editing system utilizing a computer

Take Des Moines . . . Please (KDIN-TV, Des Moines, Iowa), "National Award for Community Service"

"The U.S./Soviet Wheat Deal: Is There a Scandal?" (*CBS Evening News With Walter Cronkite*, CBS), "Outstanding Achievement Within Regularly Scheduled News Programs (award for program segments)"

Walter Cronkite, Dan Rather, Daniel Schorr and Joel Blocker, (correspondents on "The Watergate Affair," on *CBS Evening News With Walter Cronkite*, CBS), "Outstanding Achievement Within Regularly Scheduled News Programs (award to individuals contributing to program segments)"

David Dick, Dan Rather, Roger Mudd and Walter Cronkite, correspondents covering the shooting of Gov. George Wallace (*CBS Evening News With Walter Cronkite*, CBS), "Outstanding Achievement Within Regularly Scheduled News Programs (award to individuals contributing to program segments)"

Eric Sevareid, correspondent ("L.B.J. The Man and the President" on *CBS Evening News With Walter Cronkite*, CBS), "Outstanding Achievement Within Regularly Scheduled News Programs (award to individuals contributing to program segments)"

"The Poppy Fields of Turkey—The Heroin Labs of Marseilles—The N.Y. Connection" (*60 Minutes*, CBS), "Outstanding Achievement for Regularly Scheduled Magazine-Type Programs (award for programs or segments)"

"The Selling of Colonel Herbert" (*60 Minutes*, CBS), "Outstanding Achievement for Regularly Scheduled Magazine-Type Programs (award for programs or segments)"

60 Minutes (CBS), "Outstanding Achievement for Regularly Scheduled Magazine-Type Programs (award for programs or segments)"

Mike Wallace (correspondent on "The Selling of Colonel Herbert," on *60 Minutes*, CBS), "Outstanding Achievement for Regularly Scheduled Magazine-Type Programs (award to individuals contributing to program or segment)"

Mike Wallace (correspondent, *60 Minutes*, CBS), "Outstanding Achievement for Regularly Scheduled Magazine-Type Programs (award to individuals contributing to program or segment)"

ABC for coverage of the Munich Olympic tragedy, "Outstanding Achievement to the Coverage of Special Events (program achievement)"

Jim McKay (commentator on the Munich Olympic tragedy, ABC), "Outstanding Achievement to the Coverage of Special Events (program achievement)"

The Blue Collar Trap (*NBC News White Paper*, NBC), "Outstanding Documentary Program Achievement (for documentaries dealing with events or matters of current significance)"

"The Mexican Connection" (*CBS Reports*, CBS), "Outstanding Documentary Program Achievement (for documentaries dealing with events or matters of current significance)"

One Billion Dollar Weapon; And Now the War Is Over—, The American Military in the '70s (NBC), "Outstanding Documentary Program Achievement (for documentaries dealing with events or matters of current significance)"

America (NBC), "Outstanding Documentary Program Achievement (for programs dealing with artistic, historic or cultural subjects)"

Jane Goodall and the World of Animal Behavior (ABC), "Outstanding Documentary Program Achievement (for programs dealing with artistic, historic or cultural subjects)"

Alistair Cooke (narrator, *America*, NBC), "Outstanding Documentary Program Achievement (to individuals contributing to documentary programs)"

Alistair Cooke (writer, "A Fireball in the Night" on *America*, NBC), "Outstanding Documentary Program Achievement (to individuals contributing to documentary programs)"

Hugo van Lawick (director of *Jane Goodall and the World of Animal Behavior*, ABC), "Outstanding Documentary Program Achievement (to individuals contributing to documentary programs)"

The Advocates (PBS), "Special Classification of Outstanding Program and Individual Achievement"

VD Blues (PBS), "Special Classification of Outstanding Program and Individual Achievement"

Duty Bound (NBC), "Outstanding Achievement in Religious Programming"

Donald Feldstein, Robert Fontana and Joe Zuckerman (animation layout of Da Vinci's art for *Leonardo: To Know How to See*, NBC), "Outstanding Achievement in Any Area of Creative Technical Crafts"

Laurens Pierce (coverage of the shooting of Gov. George Wallace on *CBS Evening News With Walter Cronkite*, CBS), "Outstanding Achievement in Cinematography for News and Documentary Programming (regularly scheduled news programs and coverage of special events)"

Des and Jen Bartlett (*The Incredible Flight of the Snow Geese*, NBC), "Outstanding Achievement in Cinematography for News and Documentary Programming (documentary, mini-documentary or magazine-type programs)"

Patrick Minerva, Martin Sheppard, George Johnson, William J. Freeda, Miguel E. Portillo, Albert J. Helias, Irwin Graf, Jean Venable, Rick Hessel, Loren Berry, Nick Wilkins, Gerry Breese, Michael Shugrue, K. Su, Edwin Einarsen, Thomas Dunphy, Russell Moore and Albert Mole (*NBC Nightly News,* NBC), "Outstanding Achievement in Film Editing for News and Documentary Programming (regularly scheduled news or coverage of special events)"

Les Parry (*The Incredible Flight of the Snow Geese,* NBC) "Outstanding Achievement in Film Editing for News and Documentary Programming (documentary, magazine-type or mini-documentary programs)"

1973-74 *M*A*S*H** (CBS), "Outstanding Comedy Series"

Upstairs, Downstairs (*Masterpiece Theatre,* PBS), "Outstanding Drama Series"

The Carol Burnett Show (CBS), "Outstanding Music/Variety Series"

Columbo (NBC), "Oustanding Limited Series"

The Autobiography of Miss Jane Pittman (CBS), "Oustanding Special—Comedy or Drama"

Lily (CBS), "Outstanding Comedy/Variety, Variety or Music Special"

Marlo Thomas and Friends in Free to Be . . . You and Me (ABC), "Oustanding Children's Special"

Alan Alda, (*M*A*S*H*,* CBS), "Best Lead Actor in Comedy Series"

Telly Savalas (*Kojak,* CBS), "Best Lead Actor in a Drama Series"

William Holden (*The Blue Knight,* NBC), "Best Lead Actor in a Limited Series"

Hal Holbrook ("Pueblo" on *ABC Theatre,* ABC), "Best Lead Actor in a Drama (special program or single appearance in a series)"

Alan Alda (*M*A*S*H*,* CBS) "Actor of the Year—Series"

Hal Holbrook ("Pueblo" on *ABC Theatre,* ABC), "Actor of the Year—Special"

Mary Tyler Moore (*The Mary Tyler Moore Show,* CBS) "Best Lead Actress in a Comedy Series"

Michael Learned (*The Waltons,* CBS), "Best Lead Actress in a Drama Series"

Mildred Natwick ("The Snoop Sisters" on *NBC Tuesday Night Mystery Movie,* NBC), "Best Lead Actress in a Limited Series"

Cicely Tyson (*The Autobiography of Miss Jane Pittman,* CBS), "Best Lead Actress in a Drama (special program or single appearance in a series)"

Mary Tyler Moore (*The Mary Tyler Moore Show,* CBS), "Actress of the Year—Series"

Cicely Tyson ("The Autobiography of Miss Jane Pittman," CBS), "Actress of the Year—Special"

Bob Reiner (*All in the Family,* CBS), "Best Supporting Actor in Comedy"

Michael Moriarty (*The Glass Menagerie,* ABC), "Best Supporting Actor in Drama"

Harvey Korman (*The Carol Burnett Show,* CBS), "Best Supporting Actor in Comedy-Variety, Variety or Music"

Michael Moriarty (*The Glass Menagerie,* ABC), "Supporting Actor of the Year"

Cloris Leachman ("The Lars Affair" on *The Mary Tyler Moore Show,* CBS), "Best Supporting Actress in Comedy"

Joanna Miles (*The Glass Menagerie,* ABC), "Best Supporting Actress in Drama"

Brenda Vaccaro (*The Shape of Things,* CBS), "Best Supporting Actress in Comedy-Variety, Variety or Music"

Joanna Miles (*The Glass Menagerie,* ABC), "Supporting Actress of the Year"

Robert Butler (*The Blue Knight,* Part III, NBC), "Best Directing in Drama (single program of a series)"

John Korty (*The Autobiography of Miss Jane Pittman,* CBS), "Best Directing in Drama (single program)"

Jackie Cooper ("Carry On, Hawkeye" on *M*A*S*H*,* CBS), "Best Directing in Comedy"

Dave Powers ("The Australia Show" on *The Carol Burnett Show,* CBS), "Best Directing in Variety or Music (single program of a series)"

Dwight Hemion (*Barbra Streisand . . . and Other Musical Instruments,* CBS), "Best Directing in Comedy-Variety, Variety or Music (special program)"

Robert Butler (*The Blue Knight,* Part III, NBC), "Director of the Year—Series"

Dwight Hemion (*Barbra Streisand . . . and Other Musical Instruments,* CBS), "Director of the Year—Special"

Joanna Lee ("The Thanksgiving Story" on *The Waltons,* CBS), "Best Writing in Drama (single program of a series)"

Fay Kanin ("Tell Me Where It Hurts" on *GE Theater,* CBS), "Best Writing in Drama, Original Teleplay"

Tracy Keenan Wynn (*The Autobiography of Miss Jane Pittman,* CBS), "Best Writing in Drama, Adaptation"

Treva Silverman ("The Lou and Edie Story" on *The Mary Tyler Moore Show,* CBS), "Best Writing in Comedy (single program of a series)"

Ed Simmons, Gary Belkin, Roger Beatty, Arnie Kogen, Bill Richmond, Gene Perret, Rudy de Luca, Barry Levinson, Dick Clair, Jenna McMahon and Barry Harman (*The Carol Burnett Show,* CBS), "Best Writing in Variety or Music (single program of a series)"

Herb Sargent, Rosalyn Drexler, Lorne Michaels, Richard Pryor, Jim Rusk, James R. Stein, Robert Illes, Lily Tomlin, George Yanok, Jane Wagner, Rod Warren, Ann Elder and Karyl Geld (*Lily,* CBS), "Best Writing in Comedy-Variety, Variety or Music (special program)"

Treva Silverman (*The Mary Tyler Moore Show,* CBS), "Writer of the Year—Series"

Fay Kanin ("Tell Me Where It Hurts" on *GE Theater,* CBS), "Writer of the Year—Special"

Tony Charmoli (*Mitzi . . . A Tribute to the American Housewife,* CBS), "Outstanding Achievement in Choreography"

Morton Stevens ("Hookman" on *Hawaii Five-O,* CBS), "Best Music Composition (for a series in first year of use)"

Fred Karlin (*The Autobiography of Miss Jane Pittman,* CBS), "Best Music Composition (special program)"

Marty Paich and David Paich ("Light the Way" on *Ironside,* NBC), "Best Song or Theme"

Jack Parnell, Ken Welch and Mitzie Welch (*Barbra Streisand . . . and Other Musical Instruments,* CBS), "Best Music Direction of a Variety, Dramatic or Musical Program"

Gerry Bucci (technical director) and Kenneth Tamburri, Dave Hilmer, Dave Smith, Jim Balden and Ron Brooks (cameramen), "In Concert (With Cat Stevens)" on *ABC Wide World of Entertainment* (ABC), "Outstanding Achievement in Technical Direction and Electronic Camerawork"

William M. Klages ("The Lie" on *CBS Playhouse 90*, CBS), "Outstanding Achievement in Lighting Direction"

Charles M. Schulz(writer), *A Charlie Brown Thanksgiving* (CBS), "Outstanding Individual Achievement in Children's Programming"

William Zaharuk (art director) and **Peter Razmofski** (set decorator), ("The Borrowers" on *Hallmark Hall of Fame*, NBC), "Outstanding Individual Achievement in Children's Programming"

The Dick Cavett Show (ABC), "Special Classification of Outstanding Program and Individual Achievement"

Tom Snyder (*Tomorrow*, NBC), "Special Classification of Outstanding Program and Individual Achievement"

ABC's Wide World of Sports (ABC) "Outstanding Achievement in Sports Programming"

Jim McKay (host, *ABC's Wide World of Sports*, ABC), "Outstanding Achievement in Sports Programming"

Jack Parnell, Ken Welch and Mitzie Welch (*Barbra Streisand . . . and Other Musical Instruments*, CBS), "Musician of the Year"

Jan Scott (art director) and **Charles Kreiner** (set decorator), ("The Lie" on *CBS Playhouse 90*, CBS), "Best Art Direction or Scenic Design (dramatic program or feature-length film made for television, single program of a series or special)"

Brian C. Bartholomew (*Barbra Streisand . . . and Other Musical Instruments*, CBS), "Best Art Direction or Scenic Design (musical or variety single program of a series or special)"

Jan Scott (art director) and **Charles Kreiner** (set decorator), ("The Lie" on *CBS Playhouse 90*, CBS), "Art Director and Set Decorator of the Year"

Bruce Walkup and Sandy Stewart (*The Autobiography of Miss Jane Pittman*, CBS), "Outstanding Achievement in Costume Design"

Stan Winston and Rick Baker (*The Autobiography of Miss Jane Pittman*, CBS), "Outstanding Achievement in Make-Up"

Harry Wolf ("Any Old Port in a Storm" on *Columbo*, NBC), "Best Cinematography for Entertainment Programming (series or single program of a series)"

Ted Voigtlander ("It's Good to Be Alive" on *GE Theater*, CBS), "Best Cinematography for Entertainment Programming (special or feature-length program made for television)"

Ted Voigtlander ("It's Good to Be Alive" on *GE Theater*, CBS), "Cinematographer of the Year"

Gene Fowler, Jr., Marjorie Fowler and Samuel E. Beetley (*The Blue Knight*, NBC), "Best Film Editing for Entertainment Programming (series or single program of a series)"

Frank Morriss ("The Execution of Private Slovik" on *NBC Wednesday Night At The Movies*, NBC), "Best Film Editing for Entertainment Programming (special or feature-length program made for television)"

Frank Morriss ("The Execution of Private Slovik" on *NBC Wednesday Night At the Movies*, NBC), "Film Editor of the Year"

Bud Nolan ("Pueblo" on *ABC Theatre*, ABC), "Outstanding Achievement in Film Sound Editing"

Albert A. Gramaglia and Michael Shindler ("Pueblo" on *ABC Theatre*, ABC), "Outstanding Achievement in Film or Tape Sound Mixing"

Alfred Muller ("Pueblo" on *ABC Theatre*, ABC), "Outstanding Achievement in Video Tape Editing"

Lynda Gurasich (hairstylist on *The Autobiography of Miss Jane Pittman*, CBS), "Outstanding Achievement in Any Area of Creative Technical Crafts"

Consolidated Video Systems, Inc. "Outstanding Achievement in Engineering Development" for application of digital video control to Time Base Corrector for lighter, more portable video tape equipment

RCA, "Outstanding Achievement in Engineering Development" for quadraplex video tape cartridge equipment

Horizon: The Making of a Natural History Film, British Broadcasting Corp., London, "International Award—Non-fiction"

La Cabina, Television Espanola, Madrid, "International Award—Fiction"

Charles Curran, President, European Broadcasting Union, and Director General, British Broadcasting Corporation, "International Directorate Emmy Award"

Through the Looking Glass Darkly (WKY-TV, Oklahoma City), "National Award for Community Service"

The Doctors (NBC), "Outstanding Drama Series"

The Other Woman (ABC), "Outstanding Drama Special"

Password (ABC), "Outstanding Game Show"

The Merv Griffin Show (syndicated) "Outstanding Talk, Service or Variety Series"

Zoom (PBS), "Outstanding Entertainment Children's Series"

"Rookie of the Year" on *The ABC Afterschool Special* (ABC), "Outstanding Entertainment Children's Special"

MacDonald Carey (*Days of Our Lives*, NBC), "Best Actor in Daytime Drama—Series"

Pat O'Brien ("The Other Woman," ABC), "Best Actor in Daytime Drama—Special"

Pat O'Brien ("The Other Woman" on *ABC Matinee Today*, ABC), "Daytime Actor of the Year"

Elizabeth Hubbard (*The Doctors*, NBC), "Best Actress in Daytime Drama—Series"

Cathleen Nesbitt ("The Mask of Love" on *ABC Matinee Today*, ABC), "Best Actress in Daytime Drama—Special"

Cathleen Nesbitt ("The Mask of Love" on *ABC Matinee Today*, ABC), "Daytime Actress of the Year"

Peter Marshall (*The Hollywood Squares*, NBC), "Best Host or Hostess in a Game Show"

Dinah Shore (*Dinah's Place*, NBC), "Best Host or Hostess in a Talk, Service or Variety Show"

Peter Marshall (*The Hollywood Squares*, NBC), "Daytime Host of the Year"

H. Wesley Kenney (*Days of Our Lives*, NBC), "Best Individual Director for a Drama Series"

H. Wesley Kenney ("Miss Kline, We Love You" on *ABC Afternoon Playbreak*, ABC), "Best Individual Director for a Special Program"

Mike Gargiulo (*Jackpot!*, NBC), "Best Individual Director for a Game Show"

Dick Carson (*The Merv Griffin Show*, syndicated), "Best Individual Director for a Talk, Service or Variety Program"

H. Wesley Kenney ("Miss Kline, We Love You" on *ABC Playbreak*, ABC), "Daytime Director of the Year"

Henry Slesar (*The Edge of Night*, CBS) "Best Writing for a Drama Series"

Lila Garrett and Sandy Krinski ("Mother of the Bride" on *ABC Afternoon Playbreak*, ABC), "Best Writing for a Special Program"

Jay Reack, Harry Friedman, Harold Schneider, Gary Johnson, Steve Levitch, Rick Kellard and Rowby Goren (*The Hollywood Squares*, NBC), "Best Writing for a Game Show"

Tony Grafalo, Bob Murphy and Merv Griffin (*The Merv Griffin Show*, syndicated), "Best Writing for a Talk, Service or Variety Program"

Lila Garrett and Sandy Krinski ("Mother of the Bride" on *ABC Playbreak*, ABC), "Daytime Writer of the Year"

Richard Clements ("A Special Act of Love" on *ABC Afternoon Playbreak*, ABC), "Outstanding Musical Direction"

Tom Trimble (art director) and Brock Broughton (set decorator), *The Young and The Restless*, CBS), "Outstanding Art Direction or Scenic Design"

Bill Jobe ("The Mark of Love" on *ABC Matinee Today*, ABC), "Outstanding Costume Design"

Douglas C. Kelly (*The Mask of Love* on *ABC Matinee Today*, *ABC*), "Outstanding Make-Up"

Lou Marchand (technical director) and Gerald M. Dowd, Frank Melchiorre and John Morris (cameraman), (*One Life to Live*, ABC), "Outstanding Technical Direction and Electronic Camerawork"

Richard Holbrook (*The Young and The Restless*, CBS), "Outstanding Lighting Direction"

Ernest Dellutri (*Days of Our Lives*, NBC), "Outstanding Sound Mixing"

Gary Anderson ("Miss Kline, We Love You," ABC), "Outstanding Editing"

Coverage of the October War from Israel's Northern Front (*CBS Evening News With Walter Cronkite*, CBS), "Outstanding Achievement Within Regularly Scheduled News Programs (for program segments)"

The Agnew Resignation (*CBS Evening News With Walter Cronkite*, CBS), "Outstanding Achievement Within Regularly Scheduled News Programs (for program segments)"

The Key Biscayne Bank Charter Struggle (*CBS Evening News With Walter Cronkite*, CBS), "Outstanding Achievement Within Regularly Scheduled News Programs (for program segments)"

Reports on World Hunger (*NBC Nightly News*, NBC), "Outstanding Achievement Within Regularly Scheduled News Programs (for program segments)"

"America's Nerve Gas Arsenal" (*First Tuesday*, NBC), "Outstanding Achievement for Regularly Scheduled Magazine-Type Programs"

"The Adversaries" (*Behind the Lines*, PBS), "Outstanding Achievement for Regularly Scheduled Magazine-Type Programs"

"A Question of Impeachment" (*Bill Moyers' Journal*, PBS), "Outstanding Achievement for Regularly Scheduled Magazine-Type Programs"

Watergate: The White House Transcripts (CBS), "Outstanding Achievement in Coverage of Special Events"

Watergate Coverage (PBS), "Outstanding Achievement in Coverage of Special Events"

"Fire!" (*ABC News Closeup*, ABC), "Outstanding Documentary Program Achievement (documentary programs dealing with events of current interest)

CBS News Special Report: The Senate and the Watergate Affair (CBS), "Outstanding Documentary Program Achievement (documentary programs dealing with events of current interest)"

"Journey to the Outer Limits," (*National Geographic Society*, ABC), "Outstanding Documentary Program Achievements (programs dealing with artistic, historical or cultural subjects)"

The World at War (syndicated), "Outstanding Documentary Program Achievements (programs dealing with artistic, historical or cultural subjects)"

CBS Reports: The Rockefellers, (CBS), "Outstanding Documentary Program Achievement (programs dealing with artistic, historical or cultural subjects)"

"Solzhenitsyn" (*CBS News Special*, CBS), "Outstanding Interview Program"

Henry Steele Commager (*Bill Moyers' Journal*, PBS), "Outstanding Interview Program"

Harry Reasoner (*ABC News*, ABC), "Outstanding Television News Broadcaster"

Bill Moyers ("Essay on Watergate," on *Bill Moyers' Journal*, PBS), "Outstanding Television News Broadcaster"

Ronald Baldwin (art director) and Nat Mongioi (set decorator), (*The Electric Company*, PBS), "Outstanding Individual Achievement in Children's Programming"

The Muppets (Jim Henson, Frank Oz, Carroll Spinney, Jerry Nelson, Richard Hunt and Fran Brill (performers on *Sesame Street*, PBS), "Outstanding Achievement in Children's Programming"

Jon Stone, Joseph A. Bailey, Jerry Juhl, Emily Perl, Kingsley, Jeffrey Moss, Ray Sipherd and Norman Stiles (writers on *Sesame Street*, PBS), "Outstanding Achievement in Children's Programming"

Kan Lamkin (technical director) and Sam Drummy, Garry Stanton and Robert Hatfield (cameramen), ("Gift of Tears" on *This Is The Life*, syndicated), "Outstanding Achievement in Religious Programming"

Pamela Hill ("Fire!", *ABC News Closeup*, ABC), "Outstanding Achievement in News and Documentary Directing"

Philippe Cousteau (Under ice photography in "Beneath the Frozen World" for *The Undersea World of Jacques Cousteau*, ABC), "Outstanding Achievement in Any Area of Creative Technical Crafts"

John Chambers and Tom Burman (make-up for "Struggle for Survival: Primal Man," ABC), "Outstanding Achievement in Any Area of Creative Technical Crafts"

Aggie Whelan (courtroom drawings for the Mitchell-Stans trial on *CBS Evening News With Walter Cronkite*, CBS), "Outstanding Achievement in Any Area of Creative Technical Crafts"

Make a Wish (ABC), "Outstanding Informational Children's Series"

The Runaways (ABC), "Outstanding Informational Children's Special"

Inside/Out (syndicated), "Outstanding Instructional Children's Programming"

Delos Hall ("Clanking Savannah Blacksmith" on "On the Road With Charles Kuralt," for *CBS Evening News With Walter Cronkite*, CBS), "Best Cinematography for News and Documentary Programming (regularly scheduled news program and coverage of special events)"

Walter Dumbrow ("Ballerina" on *60 Minutes*, CBS), "Best Cinematography for News and Documentary Programming (documentary, magazine-type or mini-documentary program)"

Walter Scharf ("Beneath the Frozen World" on *The Undersea World of Jacques Cousteau*, ABC), "Best Music Composition"

William Sunshine (*60 Minutes*, CBS), "Best Art Direction or Scenic Design"

William J. Freeda ("Profile of Poverty in Appalachia" on *NBC Nightly News*, NBC), "Best Film Editing for News and Documentary Programming (regularly scheduled news program)"

Ann Chegwidden ("The Baboons of Gombe" on *Jane Goodall and the World of Animal Behavior*, ABC), "Best Film Editing for News and Documentary Programming (documentary, magazine-type or mini-documentary program)"

Peter Pilafian, George R. Porter, Eddie J. Nelson and Robert L. Harman ("Journey to the Outer Limits" on *National Geographic Society*, ABC), "Best Film or Tape Sound Mixing"

Charles L. Campbell, Robert Cornett, Larry Caron, Larry Kaufman, Colin Moria, Don Warner and Frank R. White ("The Baboons of Gombe" on *Jane Goodall and the World of Animal Behavior*, ABC), "Best Film or Tape Sound Editing"

Gary Anderson (*Paramount Presents . . . ABC Wide World of Entertainment*, ABC), "Best Video Tape Editing"

Carl Schutzman (technical director) and **Joseph Schwartz and William Bell** (cameramen), (*60 Minutes*, CBS), "Best Technical Direction and Electronic Camerawork"

1974-75 *The Mary Tyler Moore Show* (CBS), "Outstanding Comedy Series"

Upstairs, Downstairs, (*Masterpiece Theatre*, PBS), "Outstanding Drama Series"

The Carol Burnett Show (CBS), "Outstanding Comedy/Variety or Music Series"

Benjamin Franklin (CBS), "Outstanding Limited Series"

"The Law" (*NBC World Premiere Movie*, NBC), "Outstanding Special—Drama or Comedy"

An Evening With John Denver (ABC), "Outstanding Special—Comedy/Variety or Music"

Profile in Music: Beverly Sills (PBS), "Outstanding Classical Music Program"

Tony Randall (*The Odd Couple*, ABC), "Outstanding Lead Actor in a Comedy Series"

Robert Blake (*Baretta*, ABC), "Outstanding Lead Actor in a Drama Series"

Peter Falk (*Columbo* on *NBC Saturday Night Mystery Movie*, NBC), "Outstanding Lead Actor in a Limited Series"

Laurence Olivier ("Love Among the Ruins" on *ABC Theatre*, ABC), "Outstanding Lead Actor in A Special Program—Drama or Comedy"

Valerie Harper (*Rhoda*, CBS), "Outstanding Lead Actress in a Comedy Series"

Jean Marsh (*Upstairs, Downstairs* on *Masterpiece Theatre*, PBS), "Outstanding Lead Actress in a Drama Series"

Jessica Walter (*Amy Prentiss* on *NBC Sunday Mystery Movie*, NBC), "Outstanding Lead Actress in a Limited Series"

Katharine Hepburn (*Love Among the Ruins* on *ABC Theatre*, ABC), "Outstanding Lead Actress in a Special Program—Drama or Comedy"

Ed Asner (*The Mary Tyler Moore Show*, CBS), "Outstanding Continued Performance by a Supporting Actor in a Drama Series"

Will Geer (*The Waltons*, CBS), "Outstanding Continuing Performance by a Supporting Actor in a Drama Series"

Jack Albertson (*Cher*, CBS), "Outstanding Continuing or Single Performance by a Supporting Actor in a Comedy or Drama Special"

Anthony Quayle (*QB VII*, Parts 1 and 2, *ABC Movie Special*, ABC), "Outstanding Single Performance by a Supporting Actor in a Comedy or Drama"

Patrick McGoohan ("By Dawn's Early Light" on *Columbo*, *NBC Sunday Mystery Movie*, NBC), "Outstanding Single Performance by a Supporting Actor in a Comedy or Drama Series"

Betty White (*The Mary Tyler Moore Show*, CBS), "Outstanding Continuing Performance by a Supporting Actress in a Comedy Series"

Ellen Corby (*The Waltons*, CBS), "Outstanding Continuing Performance by a Supporting Actress in a Drama Series"

Cloris Leachman (*Cher*, CBS), "Outstanding Continuing or Single Performance by a Supporting Actress in Variety or Music"

Juliet Mills (*QB VII*, Parts 1 & 2, *ABC Movie Special*, ABC), "Outstanding Single Performance by a Supporting Actress in a Comedy or Drama"

Cloris Leachman ("Phyllis Whips Inflation" on *The Mary Tyler Moore Show*, CBS), "Outstanding Single Performance by a Supporting Actress in a Comedy or Drama Series"

Zohra Lampert ("Queen of the Gypsies" on *Kojak*, CBS), "Outstanding Single Performance by a Supporting Actress in a Comedy or Drama Series"

Bill Bain (*Upstairs, Downstairs*, PBS), "Outstanding Directing in a Drama Series"

Gene Reynolds (*M*A*S*H*, CBS), "Outstanding Directing in a Comedy Series"

Dave Powers (*The Carol Burnett Show*, CBS), "Outstanding Directing in a Comedy/Variety or Music Series"

Bill Davis (*An Evening With John Denver*, ABC), "Outstanding Directing in a Comedy/Variety or Music Special"

George Cukor ("Love Among the Ruins" on *ABC Theatre*, ABC), "Outstanding Directing in a Special Program—Drama or Comedy"

Howard Fast ("The Ambassador" on *Benjamin Franklin*, CBS), "Outstanding Writing in a Drama Series"

Ed Weinberger and Stan Daniels ("Mary Richards Goes to Jail" on *The Mary Tyler Moore Show*, CBS), "Outstanding Writing in a Comedy Series"

Ed Simmons, Gary Belkin, Roger Beatty, Arnie Kogen, Bill Richmond, Gene Perret, Rudy De Luca, Barry Levinson, Dick Clair and Jenna McMahon (*The Carol Burnett Show*, CBS), "Outstanding Writing in a Comedy/Variety or Music Series"

Bob Wells, John Bradford and Cy Coleman (*Shirley MacLaine: If They Could See Me Now*, CBS), "Outstanding Writing in a Comedy/Variety or Music Special"

James Costigan ("Love Among the Ruins" on *ABC Theatre*, ABC), "Outstanding Writing in a Special Program—Drama or Comedy—Original Teleplay"

David W. Rintels (*IBM Presents Clarence Darrow*, NBC), "Outstanding Writing in a Special Program—Drama or Comedy—Adaptation"

Marge Champion (*Queen of the Stardust Ballroom*, CBS), "Outstanding Achievement in Choreography"

Billy Goldenberg ("The Rebel" on *Benjamin Franklin*, CBS), "Outstanding Achievement in Music Composition for a Series"

Jerry Goldsmith (*QB-VII*, Parts 1 and 2, on *ABC Movie Special*, ABC), "Outstanding Achievement in Music Composition for a Special"

Charles Lisanby (art director) and **Robert Checchi** (set Decorator), ("The Ambassador" on *Benjamin Franklin*, CBS), "Outstanding Achievement in Art Direction or Scenic Design (single episode of a comedy or drama series)"

Robert Kelly (art director) and **Robert Checchi** (set decorator), (*Cher*, CBS), "Outstanding Achievement in Art Direction or Scenic Design (single episode or comedy/variety or music series)"

Carmen Dillon (art director) and **Tess Davis** (set decorator) ("Love Among the Ruins" on *ABC Theatre*, ABC), "Outstanding Achievement in Art Direction or Scenic Design (dramatic special or feature-length program made for television)"

Phil Norman (*QB-VII*, Parts 1 and 2, on *ABC Movie Special*, ABC), "Outstanding Achievement in Graphic Design and Title Sequences"

Richard Glouner (*Columbo*, NBC), "Outstanding Achievement in Cinematography for Entertainment Programming for a Series"

David M. Walsh (*Queen of the Stardust Ballroom*, CBS), "Outstanding Achievement in Cinematography for Entertainment Programming for a Special"

Douglas Hines ("An Affair to Forget" on *The Mary Tyler Moore Show*, CBS), "Outstanding Film Editing for Entertainment Programming for a Series (comedy)"

Donald R. Rode ("Mirror, Mirror On the Wall" on *Petrocelli*, NBC), "Outstanding Film Editing for Entertainment Programming for a Series (drama)"

John A. Martinelli ("The Legend of Lizzie Borden" on *ABC Monday Night Movie*, ABC), "Outstanding Film Editing for Entertainment Programming for a Special"

Marvin I. Kosberg, Richard Burrow, Milton C. Burrow, Jack Milner, Ronald Ashcroft, James Ballas, Josef von Stroheim, Jerry Rosenthal, William Andrews, Edward Sandlin, David Horton, Alvin Kajita, Tony Garber and **Jeremy Hoenack** (*QB-VII*, Parts 1 and 2, on *ABC Movie Special*, ABC), "Outstanding Achievement in Film Sound Editing"

Marshall King (*The American Film Institute Salute to James Cagney*, CBS), "Outstanding Achievement in Film or Tape Sound Mixing"

Gary Anderson and **Jim McElroy** (*Judgment: The Court-Martial of Lt. William Calley*, ABC), "Outstanding Achievement in Video Tape Editing"

Ernie Buttelman (technical director) and **Jim Angel, Jim Balden, Ron Brooks** and **Art LaCombe** (cameramen), ("The Missiles of October" on *ABC Theatre*, ABC), "Outstanding Achievement in Technical Direction and Electronic Camerawork"

John Freschi (*The Perry Como Christmas Show*, CBS), "Outstanding Achievement in Lighting Direction"

Yes, Virginia, There Is a Santa Claus (ABC), "Outstanding Children's Special"

Jimmy Connors vs. Rod Laver Tennis Challenge (CBS), "Outstanding Sports Event"

Wide World of Sports (ABC), "Outstanding Sports Program"

Jim McKay (*Wide World of Sports*, ABC), "Outstanding Sports Broadcaster"

American Film Institute Salute to James Cagney (CBS), "Special Classification of Outstanding Program Achievement"

Alistair Cooke (*Masterpiece Theatre*, PBS), "Special Classification of Outstanding Individual Achievement"

Guy Verhille ("The Legend of Lizzie Borden" on *ABC Monday Night Movie*, ABC), "Outstanding Achievement in Costume Design"

Margaret Furse ("Love Among the Ruins" on *ABC Theatre*, ABC), "Outstanding Achievement in Costume Design"

Edie Panda (hairstylist), ("The Ambassador" on *Benjamin Franklin*, CBS), "Outstanding Achievement in Any Area of Creative Television Crafts"

Doug Nelson and **Norm Schwartz**, (double-system sound editing and synchronization for stereo broadcasting, *Wide World in Concert*, ABC), "Outstanding Achievement in Any Area of Creative Television Crafts"

Gene Schwarz (technical director), *1974 World Series*, NBC), "Outstanding Individual Achievement in Sports Programming"

Herb Altman (film editor), (*The Baseball World of Joe Garagiola*, NBC), "Outstanding Individual Achievement in Sports Programming"

Corey Leible, Len Basile, Jack Bennett, Lou Gerard and **Ray Figelski** (electronic cameramen), (*1974 Stanley Cup Playoffs*, NBC), "Outstanding Individual Achievement in Sports Programming"

John Pumo, Charles D'Onofrio, Frank Florio (technical directors) and **George Klimcsak, Robert Kania, Harold Hoffmann, Herman Lang, George Drago, Walt Deniear, Stan Gould, Al Diamond, Charles Armstrong, Al Brantley, Sig Meyers, Frank McSpedon, George F. Naeder, Gordon Sweeney, Jo Sidlo, William Hathaway, Gene Pescalek** and **Curly Fonorow** (cameramen), (*Masters Tournament*, CBS), "Outstanding Individual Achievement in Sports Programming"

Columbia Broadcasting System, "Outstanding Achievement in Engineering Development" for spearheading Electronic News Gathering System

Nippon Electric Company, "Outstanding Achievement in Engineering Development" for digital television frame synchronizers

Elmer Lower, American Broadcasting Company, "Trustees' Award"

Peter Goldmark, Goldmark Laboratories, "Trustees' Award"

The Willowbrook Case: The People vs. the State of New York, (WABC-TV, New York), "National Award for Community Service"

Mr. Axelford's Angel, Yorkshire Television Ltd., London, "International Award—fiction"

Aquarius: Hello Dali!, London Weekend Television, London, "International Award—non-fiction"

The Evacuees, British Broadcasting Corporation, London, "International Award—fiction"

Inside Story: Marek, British Broadcasting Corporation, London, "International Award—non-fiction"

Junzo Imamichi, Chairman of the Board, Tokyo Broadcasting System, "International Directorate Award"

The Young and the Restless (CBS), "Outstanding Daytime Drama Series"

The Girl Who Couldn't Lose (ABC), "Outstanding Daytime Drama Special"

Hollywood Squares (NBC), "Outstanding Game or Audience Participation Show"

Dinah! (syndicated), "Outstanding Talk, Service or Variety Show"

"Harlequin" on *The CBS Festival of Lively Arts for Young People*, (CBS), "Outstanding Entertainment Children's Special"

Star Trek (NBC), "Outstanding Entertainment Children's Series"

MacDonald Carey (*Days of Our Lives*, NBC), "Outstanding Actor in a Daytime Drama Series"

Bradford Dillman ("The Last Bride of Salem" on *ABC Afternoon Playbreak*, ABC), "Outstanding Actor in a Daytime Drama Special"

Susan Flannery (*Days of Our Lives*, NBC), "Outstanding Actress in a Daytime Drama Series"

Kay Lenz ("Heart in Hiding" on *ABC Afternoon Playbreak*, ABC), "Outstanding Actress in a Daytime Drama Special"

Peter Marshall (*The Hollywood Squares*, NBC), "Outstanding Host in a Game or Audience Participation Show"

Barbara Walters (*Today*, NBC), "Outstanding Host or Hostess in a Talk, Service or Variety Series"

Richard Dunlap (*The Young and the Restless*, CBS), "Outstanding Individual Director for a Daytime Drama Series"

Mort Lachman (*The Girl Who Couldn't Lose*, ABC), "Outstanding Individual Director for a Daytime Special Program"

Jerome Shaw (*The Hollywood Squares*, NBC), "Outstanding Individual Director for a Game or Audience Participation Show"

Glen Swanson ("Dinah Salutes Broadway" on *Dinah!*, syndicated), "Outstanding Individual Director for a Daytime Variety Program"

Harding Lemay, Tom King, Charles Kozloff, Jan Merlin and Douglas Marland (*Another World*, NBC), "Outstanding Writing for a Daytime Drama Series"

Audrey Davis Levin ("Heart in Hiding" on *ABC Afternoon Playbreak*, ABC), "Outstanding Writing for a Daytime Special Program"

Elinor Bunin (graphic design and title sequences for *Funshine Saturday & Sunday;* umbrella title animations, ABC), "Outstanding Individual Achievement in Children's Programming"

1975-76 *The Mary Tyler Moore Show* (CBS), "Outstanding Comedy Series"

Police Story (NBC), "Outstanding Drama Series"

NBC's Saturday Night (NBC), "Outstanding Comedy/Variety or Music Series"

Upstairs, Downstairs (*Masterpiece Theatre*, PBS), "Outstanding Limited Series"

"Eleanor and Franklin" (*ABC Theatre*, ABC), "Outstanding Special—Drama or Comedy"

Gypsy in My Soul (CBS), "Outstanding Special—Comedy-Variety or Music"

Bernstein and the New York Philharmonic (PBS), "Outstanding Classical Music Program"

Jack Albertson (*Chico and the Man*, NBC), "Outstanding Lead Actor in a Comedy Series"

Peter Falk (*Columbo*, NBC), "Outstanding Lead Actor in a Drama Series"

Hal Holbrook (*Sandburg's Lincoln*, NBC), "Outstanding Lead Actor in a Limited Series"

Anthony Hopkins ("The Lindbergh Kidnapping Case" on *NBC World Premiere Movie*, NBC), "Outstanding Lead Actor in a Drama or Comedy Special"

Edward Asner (*Rich Man, Poor Man*, ABC), "Outstanding Lead Actor for a Single Appearance in a Drama or Comedy Series"

Mary Tyler Moore (*The Mary Tyler Moore Show*, CBS), "Outstanding Lead Actress in a Comedy Series"

Michael Learned (*The Waltons*, CBS), "Outstanding Lead Actress in a Drama Series"

Rosemary Harris ("Notorious Woman" on *Masterpiece Theatre*, PBS), "Outstanding Lead Actress in a Limited Series"

Susan Clark (*Babe*, CBS), "Outstanding Lead Actress in a Drama or Comedy Special"

Kathryn Walker ("John Adams, Lawyer" on *The Adams Chronicles*, PBS), "Outstanding Lead Actress in a Single Appearance in a Drama or Comedy Series"

Ted Knight (*The Mary Tyler Moore Show*, CBS), "Outstanding Continued Performance by a Supporting Actor in a Comedy Series"

Anthony Zerbe (*Harry O*, ABC), "Outstanding Continued Performance by a Supporting Actor in a Drama Series"

Chevy Chase (*NBC's Saturday Night*, NBC), "Outstanding Continuing or Single Performance by a Supporting Actor in Variety or Music"

Ed Flanders (*A Moon for the Misbegotten*, ABC), "Outstanding Single Performance by a Supporting Actor in a Comedy or Drama Special"

Betty White (*The Mary Tyler Moore Show*, CBS), "Outstanding Continuing Performance by a Supporting Actress in a Comedy Series"

Ellen Corby (*The Waltons*, CBS), "Outstanding Continuing Performance by a Supporting Actress in a Drama Series"

Vicki Lawrence (*The Carol Burnett Show*, CBS), "Outstanding Continuing or Single Performance by a Supporting Actress in Variety or Music"

Rosemary Murphy ("Eleanor and Franklin" on *ABC Theatre*, ABC), "Outstanding Single Performance by a Supporting Actress in a Comedy or Drama Special"

Fionnuala Flanagan (*Rich Man, Poor Man*, ABC), "Outstanding Single Performance by a Supporting Actress in a Comedy or Drama Series"

David Greene (*Rich Man, Poor Man*, ABC), "Outstanding Directing in a Drama Series"

Gene Reynolds (*M*A*S*H**, CBS), "Outstanding Directing in a Comedy Series"

Dave Wilson (*NBC's Saturday Night*, NBC), "Outstanding Directing in a Comedy/Variety or Music Series"

Dwight Hemion (*Steve and Eydie: Our Love is Here to Stay*, CBS), "Outstanding Directing in a Comedy/Variety or Music Special"

Daniel Petrie ("Eleanor and Franklin" on *ABC Theatre*, ABC), "Outstanding Directing in a Special Program—Drama or Comedy"

Sherman Yellen (*The Adams Chronicles*, PBS), "Outstanding Writing in a Drama Series"

David Lloyd (*The Mary Tyler Moore Show*, CBS), "Outstanding Writing in a Comedy Series"

Anne Beatts, Chevy Chase, Al Franken, Tom Davis, Lorne Michaels, Suzanne Miller, Michael O'Donoghue, Herb Sargent, Tom Schiller, Rosie Schuster and Alan Zweibel (*NBC's Saturday Night*, NBC), "Outstanding Writing in a Comedy/Variety or Music Series"

Jane Wagner, Lorne Michaels, Ann Elder, Christopher Guest, Earl Pomerantz, Jim Rusk, Lily Tomlin, Rod Warren and George Yanok (*Lily Tomlin*, ABC), "Outstanding Writing in a Comedy/Variety of Music Special"

James Costigan ("Eleanor and Franklin" on *ABC Theatre*, ABC), "Outstanding Writing in a Special Program—Drama or Comedy—Original Teleplay"

David W. Rintels (*Fear on Trial*, CBS), "Outstanding Writing in a Special Program—Drama or Comedy—Adaptation"

You're a Good Sport, Charlie Brown (CBS), "Outstanding Children's Special"

1975 World Series (NBC), "Outstanding Live Sports Special"

NFL Monday Night Football (ABC), "Outstanding Live Sports Series"

XII Winter Olympic Games (ABC), "Outstanding Edited Sports Special"

ABC's Wide World of Sports (ABC), "Outstanding Edited Sports Series"

Jim McKay (*ABC's Wide World of Sports,* ABC), "Outstanding Sports Personality"

Forgotten Children (WBBM-TV, Chicago), "National Award for Community Service"

Bicentennial Minutes (CBS), "Special Classification of Outstanding Program Achievement"

The Tonight Show Staring Johnny Carson (NBC), "Special Classification of Outstanding Program Achievement"

Ann Marcus, Jerry Adelman and Daniel Gregory Browne (writers), (*Mary Hartman, Mary Hartman,* syndicated), "Special Classification of Outstanding Program Achievement"

Andy Sidaris, Don Ohlmeyer, Roger Goodman, Larry Kamm, Ronnie Hawkins, and Ralph Mellanby (directors), (*XII Winter Olympic Games,* ABC), "Outstanding Individual Achievement in Sports Programming"

Tony Charmoli (*Gypsy in My Soul,* CBS), "Outstanding Achievement in Choreography"

Alex North (*Rich Man, Poor Man,* ABC), "Outstanding Achievement in Music Composition for a Series"

Jerry Goldsmith (*Babe, CBS),* "Outstanding Achievement in Music Composition for a Special"

Seiji Ozawa ("Central Park in the Dark/A Hero's Life" on *Evening at Symphony,* PBS), "Outstanding Achievement in Music Direction"

Tom John (art director) and **John Wendell and Wes Laws** (set decorators) for pilot of *Beacon Hill* (CBS), "Outstanding Achievement in Art Direction or Scenic Design (comedy or drama)"

Raymond Klausen (art director) and **Robert Checchi** (set decorator), (*Cher,* CBS), "Outstanding Achievement in Art Direction or Scenic Design (comedy-variety or music)"

Jan Scott (art director) and **Anthony Mondello** (set decorator), ("Eleanor and Franklin," ABC), "Outstanding Achievement in Art Direction or Scenic Design (dramatic special or feature-length film made for television)"

Norman Sunshine (*Addie and the King of Hearts,* CBS), "Outstanding Achievement in Graphic Design and Title Sequences"

Joe I. Tompkins ("Eleanor and Franklin," ABC), "Outstanding Achievement in Costume Design for a Drama Special"

Bob Mackie (*Mitzi . . . Roarin' In The '20s,* CBS), "Outstanding Achievement in Costume Design for Music and Variety"

Jane Robinson and Jill Silverside ("Recover," "Jenny" and "Lady Randolph Churchill" on *Great Performances,* PBS), "Outstanding Achievement in Costume Design for a Drama or Comedy Series"

Del Armstrong and Mike Westmore ("Eleanor and Franklin," ABC), "Outstanding Achievement in Make-up"

Harry L. Wolf ("Keep Your Eye on the Sparrow" on *Baretta,* ABC), "Outstanding Achievement in Cinematography for Entertainment Programming for a Series"

Paul Lohmann and Edward R. Brown ("Eleanor and Franklin," ABC), "Outstanding Achievement in Cinematography for Entertainment Programming for a Special"

Stanford Tischler and Fred W. Berger ("Welcome to Korea" on *M*A*S*H*,* CBS), "Outstanding Film Editing for Entertainment Programming for a Series (single episode of a comedy series)"

Samuel Beetley and Ken Zemke ("The Quality of Mercy" on *Medical Story,* NBC), "Outstanding Film Editing for Entertainment Programming for a Series (single sipsode of a dramatic or limited series)"

Michael Kahn ("Eleanor and Franklin" on *ABC Theatre,* ABC), "Outstanding Film Editing for Entertainment Programming for a Special"

Douglas H. Grindstaff, Al Kajita, Marvin I. Kosberg, Hans Newman, Leon Selditz, Dick Friedman, Stan Gilbert, Hank Salerno, Larry Singer and William Andrews ("The Quality of Mercy" on *Medical Story,* NBC), "Outstanding Achievement in Film Sound Editing"

Don Bassman and Don Johnson ("Eleanor and Franklin" on *ABC Theatre,* ABC) "Outstanding Achievement in Film Sound Mixing"

Dave Williams (*Tonight Show Starring Johnny Carson,* anniversary show, NBC) "Outstanding Achievement in Tape Sound Mixing"

Grish Bhargava and Manfred Schorn, (*The Adams Chronicles,* PBS) "Outstanding Achievement in Video Tape Editing for a Series"

Nick V. Giordano ("Alice Cooper—The Nightmare" on *Wide World: In Concert,* ABC) "Outstanding Achievement in Video Tape Editing for a Special"

Leonard Chumbley (technical director) and **Walter Edel, John Fehler and Steve Zink** (Cameramen), (*The Adams Chronicles,* PBS) "Outstanding Achievement in Technical Direction and Electronic Camerawork "

William Krages and Don Stuckey (*Mitzi and the Hundred Guys,* CBS) "Outstanding Achievement in Lighting Direction"

John Freschi (*Mitzi . . . Roarin' in the 20's,* CBS), "Outstanding Achievement in Lighting Direction"

Ken Welch, Mitzie Welch and Artie Malvin (*The Carol Burnett Show,* CBS) "Outstanding Achievement in Special Musical Material"

Jean Burt Reilly and Billie Laughridge (hairstylists), ("Eleanor and Franklin" on *ABC Theatre,* ABC), "Outstanding Achievement in Any Area of Creative Technical Crafts"

Donald Sahlin, Kermit Love, Caroly Wilcox, John Lovelady and Rollie Krewson (costumes and props for The Muppets), (*Sesame Street,* PBS), "Outstanding Achievement in Any Area of Creative Technical Crafts"

Rene Lagler (art director) and **Richard Harvey** (set decorator), (*Dinah!,* syndicated) "Outstanding Individual Achievement in Daytime Programming"

Jeff Cohan, Joe Aceti, John Delisa, Lou Frederick, Jack Gallivan, Jim Jennett, Carol Lehti, Howard Shapiro, Katsumi Aseada, John Fernandez, Peter Fritz, Eddie C. Joseph, Ken Klingbeil, Leo Stephan, Ted Summers, Michael Wenig, Ron Ackerman, Michael Bonifazio, Barbara Bowman, Charlie Burnham, John Croak, Charles Gardner, Marvin Gench, Victor Gonzales, Jakob Hierl, Nick Mazur, Ed McCarthy, Alex Moskovic, Arthur Nace, Lou Rende, Erskin Roberts, Merritt Roesser, Arthur Volk, Roger Haenelt, Curt Brand, Phil Mollica, George Boettcher and Herb Ohlandt (tape editors), *XII Winter Olympic Games* (ABC), "Outstanding Individual Achievement in Sports Programming"

Dick Roes, Jack Kelly, Bill Sandreuter, Frank Bailey and Jack Kestenbaum (tape sound mixers), (*XII Winter Olympic Games,* ABC), "Outstanding Individual Achievement in Sports Programming"

Joseph J.H. Vadala (cinematographer on *A Determining Force,* NBC), "Outstanding Achievement in Religious Programming"

Bud Nolan and Jim Cookman (film sound editors on *Sound for Freedom,* NBC), "Outstanding Individual Achievement in Children's Programming"

Sony Corporation, "Outstanding Achievement in Engineering Development" for U-matic video cassette concept

Eastman Kodak, "Outstanding Achievement in Engineering Development" for Eastman Ektachrome Video News Film

Another World (NBC), "Outstanding Daytime Drama Series"

First Ladies' Diaries: Edith Wilson (NBC), "Outstanding Daytime Drama Special"

The $20,000 Pyramid (ABC), "Outstanding Daytime Game or Audience Participation Show"

Dinah! (syndicated), "Outstanding Daytime Talk, Service or Variety Series"

Big Blue Marble (syndicated), "Outstanding Entertainment Children's Series"

"Danny Kaye's Look-In at the Metropolitan Opera" on *The CBS Festival of Lively Arts for Young People,* CBS), "Outstanding Entertainment Children's Special"

Go (NBC), "Outstanding Informational Children's Series"

Happy Anniversary, Charlie Brown (CBS), "Outstanding Informational Children's Special"

Grammar Rock (ABC), "Outstanding Instructional Children's Programming—Series and Specials"

Larry Haines (*Search for Tomorrow,* CBS), "Outstanding Actor in a Daytime Drama Series"

Gerald Gordon (*First Ladies' Diaries: Rachel Jackson,* NBC), "Outstanding Actor in a Daytime Drama Special"

James Luisi (*First Ladies' Diaries: Martha Washington,* NBC), "Outstanding Actor in a Daytime Drama Special"

Helen Gallagher (*Ryan's Hope,* ABC), "Outstanding Actress in a Daytime Drama Series"

Elizabeth Hubbard (*First Ladies' Diaries: Edith Wilson,* NBC), "Outstanding Actress in a Daytime Drama Special"

Allen Ludden (*Password,* ABC), "Outstanding Host or Hostess in a Game or Audience Participation Show"

Dinah Shore (*Dinah!,* syndicated), "Outstanding Host or Hostess in a Talk, Service or Variety Show"

David Pressman (*One Life to Live,* ABC), "Outstanding Individual Director for Daytime Drama Series"

Nicholas Havinga (*First Ladies' Diaries: Edith Wilson,* NBC), "Outstanding Individual Director for a Daytime Special Program"

Mike Gargiulo (*The $20,000 Pyramid,* ABC), "Outstanding Individual Director for a Game or Audience Participation Show"

Glen Swanson (*Dinah!,* syndicated), "Outstanding Individual Director for a Daytime Variety Program"

William J. Bell, Kay Lenard, Pat Falken Smith, Bill Rega, Margaret Stewart, Sheri Anderson and Wanda Coleman (*Days of Our Lives,* NBC), "Outstanding Writing for a Daytime Drama Series"

Audrey Davis Levin (*First Ladies' Diaries: Edith Wilson,* NBC), "Outstanding Writing for a Daytime Special Program"

The Muppets (Jim Hensen, Jack Oz, Jerry Nelson, Carroll Spinney and Richard Hunt), (*Sesame Street,* PBS) "Outstanding Individual Achievement in Children's Programming"

1976-77 Gary Burghoff (*M*A*S*H*,* CBS), "Outstanding Continuing Performance by a Supporting Actor in a Comedy Series"

Mary Kay Place (*Mary Hartman, Mary Hartman,* syndicated), "Outstanding Continuing Performance by a Supporting Actress in a Comedy Series"

Gary Frank (*Family,* ABC), "Outstanding Continuing Performance by a Supporting Actor in a Drama Series"

Kristy McNichol (*Family,* ABC), "Outstanding Continuing Performance by a Supporting Actress in a Drama Series"

"Ballet Shoes," Parts I and II (*Piccadilly Circus,* PBS), "Outstanding Children's Special"

Allan Burns, James L. Brooks, Ed Weinberger, Stan Daniels, David Lloyd and Bob Ellison (*Mary Tyler Moore Show,* CBS), "Outstanding Writing in a Comedy Series"

Alan Alda (*M*A*S*H*,* CBS), "Outstanding Directing in a Comedy Series"

Louis Gossett, Jr. (*Roots,* Part 2, ABC), "Outstanding Lead Actor for a Single Appearance in a Drama or Comedy Series"

Beulah Bondi ("The Pony Cart" on *The Waltons,* CBS), "Outstanding Lead Actress for a Single Appearance in a Drama or Comedy Series"

Anne Beatts, Dan Aykroyd, Al Franken, Tom Davis, James Downey, Lorne Michaels, Marilyn Suzanne Miller, Michael O'Donoghue, Herb Sargent, Tom Schiller, Rosie Schuster, Alan Zweibel, John Belushi and Bill Murray (*NBC's Saturday Night,* NBC), "Outstanding Writing in a Comedy/Variety or Music Series"

Tim Conway (*The Carol Burnett Show,* CBS) "Outstanding Continuing or Single Performance by a Supporting Actor in Variety or Music"

Rita Moreno (*The Muppet Show,* syndicated), "Outstanding Continuing or Single Performance by a Supporting Actress in Variety or Music"

"American Ballet Theatre: Swan Lake" (*Live from Lincoln Center/Great Performances,* PBS), "Outstanding Classical Program in the Performing Arts"

Burgess Meredith ("Tail Gunner Joe" on *The Big Event,* NBC), "Outstanding Performance by a Supporting Actor in a Comedy or Drama Special"

Diana Hyland ("The Boy in the Plastic Bubble" on *The ABC Friday Night Movie,* ABC), "Outstanding Performance by a Supporting Actress in a Comedy or Drama Special"

Daniel Petrie ("Eleanor and Franklin: The White House Years" on *ABC Theatre,* ABC), "Outstanding Directing in a Special Program/Drama or Comedy"

Stewart Stern ("Sybil" on *The Big Event,* NBC), "Outstanding Writing in a Special Program/Drama or Comedy/Adaptation"

Lane Slate ("Tail Gunner Joe"on *The Big Event,* NBC), "Outstanding Writing in a Special Program/Drama or Comedy/Original Teleplay"

Ed Flanders (*Harry S. Truman: Plain Speaking,* PBS), "Outstanding Lead Actor in a Drama or Comedy Special"

Sally Field ("Sybil" on *The Big Event,* NBC), "Outstanding Lead Actress in a Drama or Comedy Special"

Ernest Kinoy and William Blinn (*Roots,* Part 2, ABC), "Outstanding Writing in a Drama Series"

David Green (*Roots*, Part 1, ABC), "Outstanding Directing in a Drama Series"

Edward Asner (*Roots*, Part 1, ABC), "Outstanding Single Performance by a Supporting Actor in a Comedy or Drama Series"

Olivia Cole (*Roots*, Part 8, ABC), "Outstanding Single Performance by a Supporting Actress in a Comedy or Drama Series"

The Tonight Show Starring Johnny Carson (NBC), "Special Classification of Outstanding Program Achievement"

John C. Moffitt, (director *The 28th Annual Emmy Awards*, ABC), "Outstanding Individual Achievement in Coverage of Special Events"

Carroll O'Connor (*All in the Family*, CBS), "Outstanding Lead Actor in a Comedy Series"

Beatrice Arthur (*Maude*, CBS), "Outstanding Lead Actress in a Comedy Series"

The Mary Tyler Moore Show (CBS), "Outstanding Comedy Series"

Alan Buz Kohan and Ted Strauss (*America Salutes Richard Rodgers: The Sound of His Music*, CBS), "Outstanding Writing in a Comedy/Variety or Music Special"

Dwight Hemion (*American Salutes Richard Rodgers: The Sound of His Music*, CBS), "Outstanding Directing in a Comedy/Variety or Music Special"

The Barry Manilow Special (ABC), "Outstanding Special/Comedy/Variety or Music"

Dave Powers (*The Carol Burnett Show*, CBS), "Outstanding Directing in a Comedy/Variety or Music Series"

Dick Van Dyke and Company (NBC) "Outstanding Comedy/Variety or Music Series"

Christopher Plummer ("The Moneychangers" on *NBC World Premiere: The Big Event*, NBC), "Outstanding Lead Actor in a Limited Series"

Patty Duke Astin (*Captains and the Kings* on *NBC's Best Seller*, NBC), "Outstanding Lead Actress in a Limited Series"

Roots (ABC), "Outstanding Limited Series"

James Garner (*The Rockford Files*, NBC), "Outstanding Lead Actor in a Drama Series"

Lindsay Wagner (*The Bionic Woman*, ABC), "Outstanding Lead Actress in a Drama Series"

Upstairs, Downstairs (*Masterpiece Theatre*, PBS), "Outstanding Drama Series"

"Eleanor and Franklin: The White House Years" (*ABC Theatre*, ABC), "Outstanding Special/Drama or Comedy"

"Sybil" (*NBC World Premiere Movie: The Big Event*, NBC), "Outstanding Special/Drama or Comedy"

Quincy Jones and Gerald Fried (*Roots*, Part 1, ABC), "Outstanding Achievement in Music Composition for a Series (Dramatic Underscore)"

Leonard Rosenman, Alan Bergman and Marilyn Bergman ("Sybil" on *The Big Event*, NBC), "Outstanding Achievement in Music Composition for a Special (Dramatic Underscore)"

Ian Fraser (*America Salutes Richard Rodgers: The Sound and His Music*, CBS), "Outstanding Achievement in Music Direction"

Ric Waite (*Captains and the Kings*, Chapter 1, on *NBC's Best Seller*, NBC), "Outstanding Cinematography in Entertainment Programming for a Series"

William Butler ("Raid on Entebbe" on *The Big Event*, NBC), "Outstanding Cinematography in Entertainment Programming for a Special"

Douglas Hines (*The Mary Tyler Moore Show*, CBS), "Outstanding Film Editing in a Comedy Series"

Neil Travis (*Roots*, Part 1, ABC), "Outstanding Film Editing in a Drama Series"

Rita Roland and Michael S. McLean ("Eleanor and Franklin: The White House Years" on *ABC Theater*, ABC), "Outstanding Film Editing for a Special"

Larry Carow, Larry Neiman, Don Warner, Colin Mouat, George Fredrick, Dave Pettijohn and Paul Bruce Richardson (*Roots*, Part 2, ABC), "Outstanding Achievement in Film Sound Editing for a Series"

Bernard F. Pincus, Milton C. Burrow, Gene Eliot, Don Ernst, Tony Garber, Don V. Isaacs, Larry Kaufman, William L. Manger, A. David Marshall, Richard Oswald, Edward L. Sandlin and Russ Tinsley ("Raid on Entebbe" on *The Big Event*, NBC), "Outstanding Achievement in Film Sound Editing for a Special"

Alan Bernard, George E. Porter, Eddie J. Nelson and Robert L. Harman ("The Savage Bees" on *NBC Monday Night at the Movies*, NBC), "Outstanding Achievement in Film Sound Mixing"

Thomas E. Azzari (art director), (*Fish*, ABC), "Outstanding Art Direction or Scenic Design for a Comedy Series"

Tim Harvey (scenic designer), (*The Pallisers*, Episode 1, PBS), "Outstanding Art Direction or Scenic Design for a Drama Series"

Romain Johnston (art director), (*The Mac Davis Show*, NBC), "Outstanding Art Direction or Scenic Design for a Comedy/Variety or Music Series"

Jan Scott (art director) and **Anne D. McCulley** (set decorator) ("Eleanor and Franklin: The White House Years," on *ABC Theatre*, ABC), "Outstanding Art Direction or Scenic Design for a Dramatic Special"

Robert Kelly (art director), (*America Salutes Richard Rodgers: The Sound of His Music*, CBS), "Outstanding Art Direction or Scenic Design for a Comedy/Variety or Music Special"

Eytan Keller and Stu Bernstein (*Bell Telephone Jubilee*, NBC), "Outstanding Achievement in Graphic Design and Title Sequences"

Joe I. Tompkins ("Eleanor and Franklin: The White House Years," on *ABC Theatre*, ABC), "Outstanding Achievement in Costume Design for a Drama Special"

Jan Skalicky ("The Barber of Seville" on *Live From Lincoln Center: Great Performances*, PBS), "Outstanding Achievement in Costume Design for Music/Variety"

Raymond Hughes (*The Pallisers*, Episode 1, PBS), "Outstanding Achievement in Costume Design for a Drama or Comedy Series"

Ken Chase (make-up design) and **Joe DiBella** (make-up artist), ("Eleanor and Franklin: The White House Years," on *ABC Theatre*, ABC) "Outstanding Achievement in Make-Up"

Ron Field (*America Salutes Richard Rodgers: The Sound of His Music*, CBS), "Outstanding Achievement in Choreography"

William M. Klages and Peter Edwards (*The Dorothy Hamill Special*, ABC), "Outstanding Achievement in Lighting Direction"

Doug Nelson (*John Denver and Friend*, ABC), "Outstanding Achievement in Tape Sound Mixing"

Roy Stewart ("The War Window" on *Visions*, PBS), "Outstanding Achievement in Video Tape Editing for a Series"

Gary H. Anderson (*American Bandstand's 25th Anniversary*, ABC), "Outstanding Achievement in Video Tape Editing for a Special"

Karl Messerschmidt (technical director) and **Jon Olson, Bruce Gray, John Gutierrez, Jim Dodge** and **Wayne McDonald** (cameramen), (*Doug Henning's World of Magic*, NBC), "Outstanding Achievement in Technical Direction and Electronic Camerawork"
Jean de Joux and **Elizabeth Savel** (videoanimation), **Bill Hargate** (costume design) and **Jerry Greene** (videotape editor) ("Peter Pan" on *Hallmark Hall of Fame: The Big Event*, NBC), "Outstanding Individual Achievement in Children's Programing"
Emma di Vittorio and Vivienne Walker (hairstylists), ("Eleanor and Franklin: The White House Years" on *ABC Theatre*, ABC), "Outstanding Achievement in Any Area of Creative Technical Crafts"
Allen Brewster, Bob Roethle, William Lorenz, Manuel Martinez, Ron Fleury, Mike Welch, Jerry Burling, Walter Balderson and Chuck Droege (videotape editing), ("The First Fifty Years" on *The Big Event*, NBC), "Special Classification of Outstanding Individual Achievement"
Brian C. Bartholomew and Keaton S. Walker (art directors) (*The 28th Annual Emmy Awards*, ABC), "Outstanding Individual Achievement in Coverage of Special Events"
American Broadcasting Company, "Special Award" for leadership in establishing Circularly Polarized Transmission to improve television reception
Varian Associates "Special Citation" for improving the efficiency of UHF Klystrons

Gavel Awards
AMERICAN BAR ASSOCIATION
1155 E. 60th St., Chicago, Ill. 60637 (312/974-4000)

The Gavel Awards are given annually to honor films, the media and books for their depiction of or reportage on the law and the legal profession. The Bar Association recognizes achievements which foster greater public understanding of the American legal and judicial system, disclose areas in need of improvement or correction and encourage efforts of all levels of government to update laws. Engraved gavels are presented to executives of the honored stations and networks.

RADIO

1960 WRCV (Philadelphia) for "Law in Action"
WHAS (Louisville, Ky.) for "It's the Law"
1961 KMOX (St. Louis) for "A Case In Point"
1962 WRFB (Tallahassee, Fla.) for "So Highly We Value"
1963 WMAQ (Chicago) for "A Look at the Law" and contributions to public understanding through this public service series
KYW (Cleveland) for "A Look at the Law," Lawyer/layman interview series
1964 KMPC (Los Angeles) for "Heritage" series
1965 WIBG (Philadelphia) for "Government of Man by Law"
1966 KMPC (Los Angeles) for "The Second Civil War" on causes of the Watts riots
WMAL (Washington) for "The Abused Witness"
1967 Group W, Westinghouse Broadcasting Co. for "Crime and Punishment in the 60's," twenty-one-part documentary series

1968 WMAL (Washington) for "Perspective D.C. Crime Report" on the import of the recommendations of the President's Crime Commission
WEEI (Boston) for "Benzaquin's Notepad," series of background reports on developments in the law, bar and courts
1969 NBC Radio News for "The Cop and the Court"
WJR (Detroit) for "The Rule of Law," scholarly educational series
KLAC (Los Angeles) for "Law for Laymen," educational series
1970 KFWB (Los Angeles) for "Ignorance and the Law," educational editorial series urging teaching of fundamental and basic statute law to children
1971 NBC Radio Network-NBC News for "The Prison System: Accomplice After the Fact"
WMAL (Washington) for "Streets of Fear," "Franklin Moyler and the Question of Bail" and "Congress and the Crime Bill," three-part documentary
KGO (San Francisco) for "Quality of Justice," editorial broadcasts
KEAR (San Francisco) for "Joe Bleakley," documentary
1972 WNBC (New York) for series of educational documentary programs explaining operations of New York City court system
KXYZ (Houston) for "Old Fashioned Citizenship," six-part series segment
KEEL (Shreveport, La.) for "Angola: The Crime of Louisiana Punishment," documentary on prison conditions
1973 KTOK (Oklahoma City) for "Poverty in the Courtroom" and "Behind the Walls of Big Mac"
WCCO (Minneapolis/St. Paul) for "You the Jury: Law Day 1972," presenting a factual court procedure and a jury composed of the station's audience
1974 KNX Newsradio (Los Angeles) for "Is Our Flag Still There?", documentary on Bill of Rights
WMAL (Washington) for "The Legend of Lenient Justice," testing the performance of the new District of Columbia Superior Court
National Public Radio for "All Things Considered" and "Every Tenth American: A New Look at our Public Mental Health System"
1975 CBS News Radio for "A Hearing for American Justice," thirty-part series
NBC News Radio for "Capital Punishment: Dead or Alive," documentary on "Second Sunday"
WWVA (Wheeling, W. Va.) for coverage by Jerry Kelanic of investigation, indictment and trial of United Mine Workers President Tony Boyle for the murder of Joseph Yablonski
WCBS/Newsradio (New York) for "Rape: The Law and You," a WCBS Progress Report, twenty-part series
WHLO (Akron, Ohio) for "Inside the Grand Jury," five-part series
American Forces Network (Europe) for "High Crimes and Misdemeanors," exploring two impeachment proceedings of the 19th century
1976 KMOX (St. Louis) for six programs calling upon community resources for a summit conference on crime
WRFM (New York) for crime in the streets exploration in thirty-two miniprograms
WBRU-FM (Providence R.I.) for "Brutality at the Children's Center"
KOB (Albuquerque N.M.) for six special investigative reports on misuse of authority in the Bernalillo County Sheriff's Department.

1977 **WCBS** (New York) for "Criminal Justice System: A WCBS News Radio 88 Status Report," a thirty-part weekly series examining different aspects of the system

KFWB (Los Angeles) for "John Swaney's Report on the Law," three programs on integration, small claims court and reform of the tort system, and a special series on California property tax laws

WWVA (Wheeling, W.Va.) for "Don't Hit That Lady, She's Your Wife," examining the increase in family physical violence, expecially against wives

TELEVISION

1958 **Columbia Broadcasting System** for *The Greeg Case* and *The Verdict is Yours*
National Broadcasting Company for *An Act of Law* and *American Trial by Jury*

1959 **American Broadcasting Company** for *Day in Court*
Columbia University Press for *The Constitution: Whose Interpretation?*

1960 **KPIX** (San Francisco) for *A Life in the Balance*
WRC-TV (Washington) for series on the role of juvenile court
Piasano Productions for *Perry Mason* series, dramatizing basic legal safeguards afforded the accused
Tulane University for "With Justice for All" from *Closeup*

1961 **Armstrong Circle Theatre** for dramatization of the work of the Legal Aid Society
University of Michigan Television Center for *Blessings of Liberty* series dramatizing constitutional rights
CBS Reports for "A Real Case of Murder," documentary

1962 **CBS Television Network,** for "Iron Man" segment, of *The Defenders*

1963 **National Broadcasting Company** for *The Judge,* as a contribution to public understanding of judicial role and ethical principles
Columbia Broadcasting System, for *CBS Reports'* two-part documentary, "Storm Over the Supreme Court"

1964 **Columbia Broadcasting System** for *CBS Reports* documentary, "The Crisis of Presidential Succession"
University of Michigan Television Center for *A Quest of Certainty,* twenty-part educational series
Plautus Productions, for "The Blacklist" segment of *The Defenders*

1965 **Columbia Broadcasting System** for *Gideon's Trumpet: The Poor Man and the Law,* documentary on the 1963 Supreme Court decision clarifying the right of the accused to legal counsel
National Broadcasting Company for *The Magnificent Yankee,* documentary of the thirty-year career of U.S. Supreme Court Justice Oliver Wendall Holmes
Robert Saudek Associates for *Profiles in Courage* drama of Charles Evans Hughes' struggle against ouster of New York state legislators accused of radicalism

1966 **Columbia Broadcasting System** for *Abortion and the Law* documentary
WCAU-TV (Philadelphia) for *Girard College: The Will and the Wall,* documentary on the law as adjudicator

1967 **National Broadcasting Company,** for *Meet the Press* documentary on the report of the President's Commission on Law Enforcement and *The Statesman,* historical drama on the efforts of a little-known minister for a Bill of Rights
WTVN-TV (Columbus, Ohio) for *View From the High Bench,* interview with Supreme Court Justice Potter Stewart

WNBC-TV (New York), *Due Process for the Accused,* for segments of ten-part series on arrest and search, eavesdropping and fair trials, etc.

1968 **National Broadcasting Company,** for *Justice For All?,* documentary on legal problems of the nation's poor
American Broadcasting Company for *A Case of Libel,* drama on fundamental principles of American justice through recreation of a famous trial
20th Century Fox, for "Commitment," segment of *Judd for the Defense*

1969 **Columbia Broadcasting System,** for *Justice Black and the Bill of Rights,* interview on role of Supreme Court
WMAQ-TV (Chicago), for "The Quality of Justice," documentary on Illinois reform program

1970 **National Broadcasting Company** for *Voices on the Inside* and *Between Two Rivers,* documentaries on prison conditions and plight of Indians
Universal City Studios for *The D.A.: Murder One,* on the role of the district attorney in prosecuting a murder case
American Broadcasting Company for *The Young Lawyers,* drama
National Educational Television for *The Warren Years,* documentary
WNED-TV (Buffalo) for *Are Campus Disorders Out of Hand?*

1971 **CBS News Division,** for *Bill of Rights,* survey and examination of public attitudes on constitutional rights
National Broadcasting Company for "A Continual Roar of Musketry," segment of *The Bold Ones*
WCAU-TV (Philadelphia), for *Case of Reform,* examining prisoner rehabilitation in Bucks County Prison

1972 **CBS News** for *CBS Reports'* documentary, "Justice in America, Part I," "Some are More Equal than Others"
NBC News, for *This Child is Rated X: An NBC White Paper on Juvenile Justice*
Midwestern Educational Television for "The Baseball Glove," produced by KTCA-TV for children on why rules and laws are necessary
WGBH-TV (Boston) and KCET-TV (Los Angeles) for "Jail with No Bail," from *The Advocates* series

1973 **NBC, BBC, Time-Life Films,** for "Inventing A Nation," from *America* series, examining opinions of leading members of the Constitutional Convention
NBC News for "Guilty By Reason of Race," on plight of 110,000 Japanese-Americans detained in camps throughout World War II
KNXT-TV (Los Angeles) for *Rape,* a news special
WKBF-TV (Cleveland) for *The Crime of Our Courts,* public service program
KING-TV (Seattle) for *Are Prisons for People?* on juvenile and adult incarceration methods
WMAR-TV (Baltimore) for *Bars to Progress,* on Maryland's correctional system and possible changes
New Hampshire Network/WENH-TV (Durham) for *Society's Child,* documentary on juvenile reformatory

1974 **ABC News** for *The First and Essential Freedom,* a three-part documentary
CBS News for four part series on Supreme Court decisions by Fred Graham on *CBS Evening News*
NBC News for *Watergate: The President Speaks* and *How Watergate Changed Government*
WRC-TV (Washington), for *News 4 Washington Probe: By Reason of Insanity* on discharge policies of potentially dangerous mental patients

KPIX-TV (San Francisco) for *A Case of Arson*, a children's educational program and primer on the judicial process
WMAR-TV (Baltimore) for *There Ought to be a Law*, documenting how a new law is enacted in Maryland
WTIC-TV (Hartford, Conn.), for *The Nine-Year-Old in Norfolk Prison*, documentary on trial and conviction of mentally retarded individual
KYTV (Springfield, Mo.) for *Start Inmates: Experimental Man*, documenting plight of inmates in the Medical Center for Federal Prisoners in Springfield, Mo.
WNET-TV (New York) for *Bill Moyers' Journal: An Essay on Watergate*

1975 **American television industry and ABC News Television,** for pool coverage and broadcast of the House Judiciary Committee impeachment proceedings
American television industry and CBS News, for broadcast of House Judiciary Committee impeachment proceedings
American television industry and NBC, for broadcast of House Judiciary Committee impeachment proceedings
American Television industry and Public Broadcasting Service, for broadcast of House Judiciary Committee impeachment proceedings
CBS News, for *What's It All About* explaining functions of Supreme Court, House of Representatives and processes of impeachment
National Broadcasting Company for *A Case of Rape*
WNBC-TV (New York) for *Legal Ethics: What's Happening?*
KATU-TV (Portland, Ore.) for *Is It Justice?*
WCCO-TV News (Minneapolis) for *The Time Machine,* documentary
WTTW-TV (Chicago) for *Criminal Court*
Indiana University Radio & Television Service for *The Role of the Lawyer*
Complete Channel TV (Madison, Wisc.), for *Halfway to Somewhere*

1976 **CBS News** for *The Case Against Milligan,* historical drama about suspension of habeas corpus during Civil War
WMAQ-TV (Chicago) for *"When Is Justice Coming,"* Part I on *The Overloaded Criminal Courts* and *Code 39*
WCVB-TV (Needham, Mass.) for *Crime: The War We're Losing*
WCCO-TV (Minneapolis) for *Home Sweet Prison*
WNET/13 (New York) for *OURSTORY—The Peach Gang,* the first of nine re-enactments of a 1638 trial
National Public Affairs Center for Television, WETA/26 (Washington), for *Levi and the Law: A Colloquy with the Attorney General*
WGBH-TV (Boston) for *Edelin Conviction,* dramatic re-enactment of the manslaughter trial of Dr. Kenneth Edelin

1977 **ABC News** for *Gun Control: Pro and Con,* documentary
WKYC-TV (Cleveland) for *Both Sides of Busing* and *The Trouble With Kids*
WFAA-TV (Dallas) for *A Time To Die,* documentary on the death penalty
KPRC-TV (Houston), for *Inside the FBI* and *What is Your Citizenship, Please?,* documentaries on the agency's attempt to catch criminals and solve crimes and on illegal aliens in the Southwest
Maryland Center for Public Broadcasting, for *See You In Court,* about small claims courts
Hampton Roads Educational Telecommunications Association. (Norfolk, Va.) for *Rights and Responsibilities: Sign Here, 11-part series* on citizenship

International Media Laboratory, University of Wisconsin (Milwaukee), for *Civil Commitment Hearings,* dramatization of six involuntarily civil commitment hearings from Wisconsin court records

Golden Globe Awards
HOLLYWOOD FOREIGN PRESS ASSOCIATION
8732 Sunset Blvd., Suite 210, Los Angeles, Calif. 90069
(213/657-1707 and 657-1731)

After more than two decades of honoring achievements in motion picture making (see pp. 226-232), the association in 1956 expanded its Golden Globe Awards to honor outstanding television productions of the previous year as well. Selection is by secret ballot of the membership.

BEST TELEVISION SHOWS (To individuals or for specific programs)

1956 Dinah Shore
Lucy & Desi
The American Comedy
Davy Crockett
1957 *Cheyenne*
Mickey Mouse Club
Playhouse 90
Theatre Matinee
This Is Your Life
1958 Eddie Fisher
Alfred Hitchcock
Jack Benny
Mike Wallace
1959 Paul Oates
Ann Sothern
Loretta Young
Red Skelton
Ed Sullivan
William Orr
1960 David Susskind
Chuck Connors
Pat Boone
77 Sunset Strip
Dinah Shore
Ed Sullivan
Edward R. Murrow
1961 *Hanna-Barbera Presents*
Perry Mason
Bell Telephone Hour
Hong Kong
Walter Cronkite
1962 *What's My Line?*
My Three Sons
1963 *The Dick Powell Show*
The Defenders
Mister Ed
Telstar
1964 *The Richard Boone Show*
The Danny Kaye Show
The Dick Van Dyke Show
1965 *The Rogues*
Burke's Law
1966 *The Man from U.N.C.L.E.*
1967 *I Spy*
1968 *Mission: Impossible*
1969 *Laugh-In*

BEST DRAMA SHOW

1970 *Marcus Welby M.D.*
1971 *Medical Center*
1972 *Mannix*
1973 *Columbo*
1974 *The Waltons*
1975 *Upstairs, Downstairs*
1976 *Kojak*
1977 *Rich Man Poor Man,* Book I

BEST MUSICAL OR COMEDY SHOW

1970 *The Governor and J.J.*
1971 *The Carol Burnett Show*
1972 *All in the Family*
1973 *All in the Family*
1974 *All in the Family*
1975 *Rhoda*
1976 *Barney Miller*
1977 *Barney Miller*

BEST MALE TELEVISION STAR (Dramatic only, after 1970)

1962 Bob Newhart
     John Daly
1963 Richard Chamberlain
     Rod Serling
1964 Mickey Rooney
1965 Gene Barry
1966 David Janssen
1967 Dean Martin
1968 Martin Landau
1969 Carl Betz, *Judd for the Defense*
1970 Mike Connors, *Mannix*
1971 Peter Graves, *Mission: Impossible*
1972 Robert Young, *Marcus Welby M.D.*
1973 Peter Falk, *Columbo*
1974 James Stewart, *Hawkins*
1975 Telly Savalas, *Kojak*
1976 Robert Blake, *Baretta*
     Telly Savalas, *Kojak*
1977 Richard Jordan, *Captains and the Kings*

BEST FEMALE TELEVISION STAR (Dramatic only, after 1970)

1962 Pauline Fredericks
1963 Donna Reed
1964 Inger Stevens
1965 Mary Tyler Moore
1966 Anne Francis
1967 Marlo Thomas
1968 Carol Burnett
1969 Diahann Carroll, *Julia*
1970 Linda Cristal, *High Chaparral*
1971 Peggy Lipton, *Mod Squad*
1972 Patricia Neal, *The Homecoming*
1973 Gail Fisher, *Mannix*
1974 Lee Remick, *The Blue Knight*
1975 Angie Dickinson, *Police Woman*
1976 Lee Remick *Jennie*
1977 Susan Blakely, *Rich Man, Poor Man,* Book I

BEST ACTOR (Musical or Comedy)

1970 Dan Dailey, *The Governor and J.J.*
1971 Flip Wilson
1972 Carroll O'Connor, *All in the Family*
1973 Redd Foxx, *Sanford and Son*
1974 Jack Klugman, *The Odd Couple*
1975 Alan Alda, *M.A.S.H.*
1976 Alan Alda, *M.A.S.H.*
1977 Henry Winkler, *Happy Days*

BEST ACTRESS (Musical or Comedy)

1970 Carol Burnett
     Julie Sommers
1971 Mary Tyler Moore
1972 Carol Burnett, *The Carol Burnett Show*
1973 Jean Stapleton, *All in the Family*
1974 Jean Stapleton, *All in the Family*
     Cher Bono, *Sonny and Cher*
1975 Valerie Harper, *Rhoda*
1976 Cloris Leachman, *Phyllis*
1977 Carol Burnett, *The Carol Burnett Show*

BEST SUPPORTING ACTOR IN A TELEVISION SHOW

1972 Edward Asner, *The Mary Tyler Moore Show*
1973 James Brolin, *Marcus Welby M.D.*
1974 McLean Stevenson, *M.A.S.H.*
1975 Harvey Korman, *The Carol Burnett Show*
1976 Edward Asner, *The Mary Tyler Moore Show*
     Tim Conway, *The Carol Burnett Show*
1977 Edward Asner, *Rich Man, Poor Man,* Book I

BEST SUPPORTING ACTRESS IN A TELEVISION SHOW

1972 Sue Ann Langdon, *Arnie*
1973 Ruth Buzzi, *Laugh-In*
1974 Ellen Corby *The Waltons*
1975 Betty Garrett, *All in the Family*
1976 Hermione Baddeley, *Maude*
1977 Josette Banzet, *Rich Man, Poor Man,* Book I

BEST MOVIE MADE FOR TELEVISION

1973 *That Certain Summer*
1974 No award
1975 No award
1976 *Babe*
1977 *Eleanor and Franklin*

Patsy Award

AMERICAN HUMANE ASSOCIATION
4351 S. Roslyn, Engelwood, Colo. 80110 (303/779-1400)

In 1958 the Patsy Award was extended to honor animals who were outstanding in television performances. For more details on this award, see the Patsy listing in the CINEMA section.

1958 Lassie (collie), *Lassie*
     Cleo (bassett hound), *The People's Choice*
     Rin Tin Tin (German shepherd), *Rin Tin Tin*
1959 Lassie (collie), *Lassie*
     Asta (dog), *The Thin Man*
     Rin Tin Tin (German shepherd), *Rin Tin Tin*
1960 Asta (dog) *The Thin Man*
     Lassie (collie), *Lassie*
     Fury (horse), *Bachelor Father*
     Jasper (N.A.), *Bachelor Father*
1961 Tramp (old English sheepdog), *My Three Sons*
     Lassie (collie), *Lassie*
     Fury (horse), *Bachelor Father*
1962 Mister Ed (horse), *Mister Ed*
     Lassie (collie), *Lassie*
     Tramp (old English sheepdog), *My Three Sons*
1963 Mister Ed (horse), *Mister Ed*
     Lassie (collie), *Lassie*
     Tramp (Old English sheepdog), *My Three Sons*
1964 Lassie (collie), *Lassie*
     Mister Ed (horse), *Mister Ed*
     Tramp (old English sheepdog), *My Three Sons*
1965 Flipper (porpoise), *Flipper*

Lassie (collie), *Lassie*
Mister Ed (horse), *Mister Ed*
1966 Flipper (porpoise), *Flipper*
Lord Nelson (dog), *Please Don't Eat the Daisies*
Higgins (dog), *Petticoat Junction*
1967 Judy (chimpanzee), *Daktari*
Flipper (porpoise), *Flipper*
Arnold (pig), *Green Acres*
1968 Arnold (pig), *Green Acres*
Gentle Ben (bear), *Gentle Ben*
Judy (chimpanzee), *Daktari*
1969 Arnold (pig), *Green Acres* (series)
Timmy (chimpanzee), *Beverly Hillbillies* (single performance)
1970 Scruffy (dog), *The Ghost and Mrs. Muir* (series)
Algae (seal), *The Ghost and Mrs. Muir* (single performance)
1971 Arnold (pig) *Green Acres* (series)
Lassie's three puppies, *Lassie* (single performance)
Margie (elephant), *Wonderful World of Disney* (grand award)
1972 Pax (dog), *Longstreet* (series)
Ott (horse), *Lassie* (single performance)
1973 Farouk (German shepherd), *Ironside*
1974 Midnight (cat), *Mannix* and *Barnaby Jones* (series)
Caesar (Doberman Pinscher), *Trapped* (single performance)
1975 Elsa (lion), *Born Free* (series)
Ginger and cubs (coyotes), *The Indestructible Outcasts* (single performance)
1976 Fred (cockatoo), *Baretta* (series)
17 (cat), *Dr. Shrinker* (single performance)
JoJo (raven), *Duffy Moon* (single performance)
Sled team and Kodiak (dogs), *Call of the Wild* (single performance)
Bourbon (dog), *Call of the Wild* (single performance)
YoYo (horse), *Banjo Hackett* (single performance)
Neal (lion), *The Bionic Woman* (series)
Heller (cougar), *Shazam* (Series)

TELEVISION COMMERCIAL

1968 Samba, Jr. (African lion), Dreyfus Fund
1969 Chauncey (cougar), Ford Motor Co.
1973 Morris (cat), Nine Lives (cat food)
1974 Scruffy (dog), Chuckwagon (dog food)
1975 Lawrence (red deer elk), Hartford Insurance
1976 Lawrence (red deer elk), Hartford Insurance
Unnamed horse, Top Dog

George Foster Peabody Broadcasting Award

HENRY W. GRADY SCHOOL OF JOURNALISM
University of Georgia, Athens, Ga. 30602 (404/542-3785)

The George Foster Peabody Broadcasting Award is given annually for outstanding service in broadcasting, either for programs broadcast during the calendar year for which the awards are made or to individuals for special achievements. Entries are screened by the university faculty committee, and the final selections are made by the Peabody Awards National Advisory Board. The awards categories have changed radically since the inception of the award in 1940, growing in complexity as television joined radio as a significant medium and as the Peabody organization chose to honor more types of programming and a greater number of stations and individuals. This listing, therefore, is chronological rather than by category. (In some years the awards were not assigned categories.)

1940 CBS, Network public service
WLW-Radio (Cincinnati), Public service by a large station
WGAR-Radio (Cleveland), Public service by a medium-sized station
KRFU (Columbia, Mo.), Public service by a small station
Elmer Davis, News reporting
1941 Cecil Brown (CBS), News reporting
Sandra Michael and John Gibbs, "Against the Storm," and Norman Corwin, "The Bill of Rights," Drama entertainment
Alfred Wallenstein (Mutual), Music entertainment
Chicago Roundtable of the Air (NBC), Educational program
The International Short Wave Broadcasters, Public service
1942 Charles Collingwood (CBS), News reporting
The Man Behind the Gun (CBS), Drama entertainment
"The Standard Symphony" (NBC Pacific Coast Network), Music entertainment
"Afield With Ranger Mac" (WHA-Radio, Madison, Wisc.), Educational program
"Our Hidden Enemy-Venereal Disease" (KOAC-Radio, Corvallis, Ore.), Public service by a local station
"The Home Front" (WCHS-Radio, Charleston, W.Va.), Public service by a regional station
1943 "These Are Americans" (KNX-Radio, Los Angeles), Public service by a regional station
"Calling Longshoremen" (KYA-Radio, San Francisco), Community service by a local station
Edward R. Murrow (CBS), News reporting
Lux Radio Theatre (CBS) and *An Open Letter to the American People (CBS)*, Drama entertainment
"Music and the Spoken Word" (KSL-Radio, Salt Lake City), Music entertainment
American Town Meeting (The Blue Network), Educational program
Let's Pretend (CBS), Children's program
Bob Hope, Special citation
1944 Raymond Gram Swing (Blue Network — ABC), News commentary
WLW (Cincinnati), News reporting
Cavalcade of America (NBC), Drama entertainment
Fred Allen (CBS), Special award for comedy
Telephone Hour (NBC), Entertainment in music
Human Adventure (Mutual), Educational program
Philharmonic Young Artists Series (KFI-Radio, Los Angeles), Program for youth
Col. Edward M. Kirby (War Dept. Radio Branch), Special award for adaptation of radio to the requirements of the armed forces and on the home front
Worcester and the World (WTAG-Radio, Worcester, Mass.), Public service by a regional station
WNYC-Radio and Mayor Fiorello LaGuardia, and *Cross-Roads* (WIBN-Radio, Utica, N.Y.), Public service by a local station
Song of the Columbia (KOIN-Radio, Portland, Ore.); *Syracuse on Trial* (WFBL-Radio, Syracuse, N.Y.); *Southwest Forum,* (KVOO-Radio, Tulsa, Okla.) and *St. Louis Speaks,* (KMOX-Radio, St. Louis), Regional awards
1945 CBS and Paul White, News reporting

KRNT-Radio (Des Moines, Iowa), News reporting, special citation

Edgar Bergen (NBC) and **Arch Oboler** (Mutual), Drama entertainment

The NBC Symphony of the Air and **Howard Hanson,** Eastman School of Music and WHAM-Radio, (Rochester, N.Y.), Music entertainment

America's Town Meeting of the Air (ABC) and **George V. Denney, Jr.,** Educational program

We March With Faith (KUWH-Radio, Omaha, Neb.), Children's Program

Toward A Better World (KFWB-Radio, Hollywood, Calif.), Special citation, regional public service

Mr. Colombo Discovers America (WOV-Radio, New York) and *Arnold Hartley* and *Wake Up Kentucky* (WHAS-Radio, Louisville, Ky.), Regional public service

Save A Life (KOMA-Radio, Oklahoma City), Local public service

1946 *Operation Big Muddy* (WOW-Radio, Omaha), Public service by a regional station

The Harbor We Seek (WSB-Radio, Atlanta), Special citation, regional public service

Our Town (WELL-Radio, Battle Creek, Mich.), Public service by local station

The Radio Edition of the Weekly Press (WHCU-Radio, Ithaca, N.Y.), Special citation, local public service

William L. Shirer (CBS), News reporting and interpretation

Meet the Press (Mutual), Special news citation

The Columbia Workshop, Drama entertainment

Henry Morgan (ABC) and *Suspense* (CBS), Special drama citations

Orchestras of the Nation (NBC), Music entertainment

Invitation to Music (CBS), Special citation, music entertainment

WMCA-Radio (New York), Education program

Hiroshima (Robert Saudek, ABC), Special education citation

Books Bring Adventure (Junior League of America), Special children's program citation

John Crosby (*The New York Herald Tribune*), Special award for contribution to radio through writing

1947 *Report Uncensored* (WBBM-Radio, Chicago), Public service by regional station

As the Twig Is Bent (WCCO-Radio, Minneapolis), Special citation, regional public service

"Disaster Broadcast From Cotton Valley" (KXAR-Radio, Hope, Ark.), Public service by local station

CBS Views the Press and **Elmer Davis** (ABC), News reporting and interpretation

The Boston Symphony Orchestra (ABC), Music entertainment

Theatre Guild on the Air (ABC), Drama entertainment

Studio One (CBS), Special drama citation

CBS Documentary Unit Series, Educational programs

The Children's Hour (WQQW, Washington, D.C.), Children's program

United Nations Today (United Nations Network), Special citation

1948 *Forests Aflame* (KNBC-Radio, San Francisco), Public service by regional station

You and Youth (WDAR-Radio, Savannah, Ga.), Public service by local station

Edward R. Murrow (CBS), News reporting and interpretation

The NBC University Theatre and *The Groucho Marx Show* (ABC), Drama entertainment

NBC for overall contributions of broadcasting good music, Music entertainment

Communism — U.S. Brand (ABC), Education program

Rocky Mountain Radio Council and **Lowell Institute Broadcasting Council,** Special education citations

Howdy Doody (NBC), Children's program

CBS for overall contributions, especially for Larry Le-Seur's broadcasts, Promotion of international understanding

"Little Songs About U.N." (WNEW, New York), Special citation

Actor's Studio (ABC), Contribution to television art

1949 RADIO

WWJ-Radio (NBC, Detroit), Public service by regional station

KXLJ-Radio (NBC, Helena, Mont.), Public service by local station

Eric Sevareid (CBS), News reporting and interpretation

WMAZ-Radio (CBS, Macon, Ga.) and **Erwin Canham,** *The Monitor Views the News* (ABC), Special news citations

Jack Benny (CBS), Drama entertainment

The Greatest Story Ever Told (ABC), Special citation

WQXR (New York), Music entertainment

Author Meets the Critics (ABC), Educational program

Mind Your Manners (WTIC, NBC, Hartford, Conn.), Children's program

United Nations Project (NBC), Contribution to international understanding

TELEVISION

The Ed Wynn Show (CBS), Entertainment

Crusade in Europe (ABC), Education

United Nations in Action (CBS), News reporting and interpretation

Kukla, Fran and Ollie (NBC), Children's program

SPECIAL CITATIONS

H.T. Webster, cartoon, *Unseen Audience* **United Nations and American broadcasters generally, Harold W. Ross,** *The New Yorker*

1950 RADIO

The Quiet Answer (WBBM, CBS, Chicago), Public service by regional station

WEPL-FM (Louisville Free Public Library, Ky.), Public service by local station

Elmer Davis (ABC), News reporting and interpretation

Hear It Now (CBS), Special news citation

Halls of Ivy (NBC), Drama entertainment

Metropolitan Opera (ABC), Music entertainment

Ira Hirschman (WABF-FM, New York), Special music citation

The Quick and the Dead (NBC), Education

Radio Free Europe, Contribution to international understanding

WNYC (New York) and *Pursuit of Peace* (Mutual and United Nations Radio), Special citations for contributions to international understanding

TELEVISION

Jimmy Durante (NBC), Entertainment

The Johns Hopkins Science Review (WAAM-TV, DuMont, Baltimore), Education

Zoo Parade (NBC) and *Saturday at the Zoo* (ABC), Children's programs

SPECIAL AWARDS

ABC, specifically to **President Robert E. Kitner** and his associates, **Robert Saudek and Joseph McDonald**

Providence Journal, specifically to editor **Sevellon Brown** and reporter **Ben Bagdikian**

1951 *The Nation's Nightmare,* (CBS), Radio educational program

The New York Times Youth Forums (WQXR, New York), Radio youth program

Bob and Ray (NBC), Nonmusical radio entertainment

Letter From America (Alistair Cooke, British Broadcasting Corporation), Radio's contribution to international understanding

What in the World (WCAU, CBS, Philadelphia), Television educational program

Amahl and the Night Visitors (NBC), Television musical entertainment

Celanese Theatre (ABC), Television nonmusical entertainment

Edward R. Murrow (*See It Now,* CBS), Television news and interpretation

Careers Unlimited (KPOJ, Mutual, Portland, Ore.), Local public service by radio

WSB (NBC, Atlanta), Regional public service by radio and television

1952 **Martin Agronsky** (ABC), Radio news

The New York Philharmonic Symphony Ochestra (CBS) and *The Standard Symphony* (NBC), Radio music

The Johns Hopkins Science Review (WAAM-TV, DuMont, Baltimore), Television education

Meet the Press (NBC), Television news

Mister Peepers (NBC), and *Your Hit Parade* (NBC), Television entertainment

Ding Dong School (NBC), Youth and children's program

Victory at Sea (NBC), Television special award

WIS-Radio (NBC, Columbia, S.C.), Regional public service including promotion of international understanding

WEWS-TV (ABC) and **CSB** (Cleveland), Local public service

1953 **Chet Huntley** (KABC, ABC, Los Angeles), Radio news

Gerald W. Johnson (WAAM-TV, Baltimore), Television news

NBC Television Opera Theatre, Television music

Television Playhouse (NBC), and *Imogene Coca* (NBC), Television entertainment

Cavalcade of Books (KNXT, CBS, Los Angeles) and *Camera Three* (WCBS-TV, New York), Television education

Mr. Wizard (NBC), Television youth and children's program

Coverage of the Coronation (British Broadcasting Company), Promotion of international understanding through television

WSB-AM-FM-TV (NBC, Atlanta), Public service by regional radio-TV station

WBAW (Barnwell, S.C.), Public service by local station

Edward R. Murrow (CBS), Special award

1954 **John Daly** (ABC), Radio-television news

George Gobel (NBC), Television entertainment

Adventure (CBS), Television education

Omnibus (CBS) and *The Search* (CBS), Television special awards

Disneyland (ABC), Youth and children's programs

Industry on Parade (National Association of Manufacturers), Television national public service

"Hurricane Carol" (WJAR-TV, Providence), Television regional public service

Conversation (NBC), Radio entertainment

Man's Right to Knowledge (CBS), Radio education

Pauline Frederick at the U.N. (NBC), Radio contribution to international understanding

The Navajo Hour (KGAK, Gallup, N.M.), Radio local public service

Boris Goldovsky, Metropolitan Opera (NBC), Radio music special citation

1955 **Douglas Edwards** (CBS), Television news

Perry Como (NBC) and **Jackie Gleason** (CBS), Television entertainment

Producers' Showcase (NBC), Television dramatic entertainment

Lassie (CBS), Television youth and children's program

Frank Baxter (KNXT, CBS), Television education

Omnibus and *Adams Family Series* (CBS), Special television education citation

Voice of Firestone (ABC), Radio-television music

Sylvester L. Weaver, Jr. (NBC) for pioneering programing concepts, Radio-television public service

Quincy Howe (ABC), Radio-television promotion of international understanding

Assignment: India (NBC-TV), Special citation for promotion of international understanding

Biographies in Sound (NBC), Radio education

KIRO (CBS, Seattle), Local radio public service

KFYO (CBS, Lubbock, Tex.), Special citation, radio public service

WMT-TV (CBS, Cedar Rapids, Iowa) and **KQED** (San Francisco), Special citations, local radio public service

1956 **John Charles Daly and associates** (ABC convention coverage), Television news

The Ed Sullivan Show (CBS), Television entertainment

You Are There (CBS), Television education

Youth Wants to Know (NBC), Television children's and/or youth program

World in Crisis (CBS), Television public service

The Secret Life of Danny Kaye (UNICEF), Television promotion of international understanding

Rod Serling, Television writing

Edward P. Morgan and the News (ABC), Radio news

Bob and Ray (Mutual and NBC), Radio entertainment

Books in Profile (WNYC, New York), Radio education

Little Orchestra Society Concerts (WNYC, New York), Radio youth and/or children's program

Regimented Raindrops, (WOW, Omaha, Neb.), Radio/television local-regional public service

United Nations Radio and Television, Special award for promotion of international understanding

Jack Gould, *The New York Times,* Special award for contributions to radio and television through writing

1957 **CBS NEWS** for depth and range, Radio and television news

John Charles Daly and associates, "Prologue '58" (ABC), Television news

Louis M. Lyons (WGBH, Boston), Local radio-television news

The Dinah Shore Chevy Show (NBC), Musical television entertainment

Hallmark Hall of Fame (NBC), Nonmusical television entertainment

The Heritage Series (WQED, Pittsburgh), Television education

You Are the Jury (WKAR, E. Lansing, Mich.), Local radio education

Captain Kangaroo (CBS), Television youth and children's program

Wunda, Wunda (KING-TV, ABC, Seattle), Local television youth and children's program

Panorama (KLZ-TV, CBS, Denver), Local television public service

The Last Word (CBS), Television public service

KPFA-FM (Berkeley, Calif.), Local radio public service

Bob Hope (NBC), Television contribution to international understanding

Education programs fed to educatial stations and *Know Your Schools,* (NBC stations) and **Westinghouse Broadcasting Co. Boston Conference,** Special radio-television awards

1958 *NBC News—The Huntley-Brinkley Report,* Television news

Playhouse 90 (CBS), Television dramatic entertainment

Lincoln Presents Leonard Bernstein and the New York Philharmonic (CBS), Television musical entertainment

The Steve Allen Show (NBC), Television entertainment with humor

Continental Classroom (NBC), Television education

College News Conference (ABC), Television program for youth

The Blue Fairy (WGN, Chicago), Television program for children

M.D. International (NBC), Television contribution to international understanding

CBS-TV, Television public service

James Costigan, "Little Moon of Alban," on *Hallmark Hall of Fame* (NBC), Television writing

An Evening With Fred Astaire (NBC) and **Orson Welles,** "Fountain of Youth," (*Colgate Theatre,* NBC), Television special awards

WNEW (New York), Radio news

"The Hidden Revolution" (CBS), Radio public service

Standard School Broadcast (Standard Oil Company of California), Radio education

Easy as ABC (ABC-UNESCO), Radio contribution to international understanding

1959 **"Khrushchev Abroad"** (ABC), Television news

The Play of the Week (WNTA-TV, Newark, NJ.) and **David Susskind,** *The Moon and Sixpence* (NBC), Nonmusical television entertainment

The Bell Telephone Hour (NBC) and **Great Music From Chicago** (WGN-TV, Chicago), Television musical entertainment

The Population Explosion (CBS) and *Decisions* (WGBH, Boston and the World Affairs Council), Television education

The Ed Sullivan Show (CBS) and *Small World* (CBS), Television contribution to international understanding

WDSU-TV (New Orleans), Local television public service

Frank Stanton (CBS) and *The Lost Class of '59* (CBS), Television special awards

The World Tonight (CBS), Radio news

Family Living '59 (NBC), Radio public service

WCCO (Minneapolis), Local radio public service

1960 *The Texaco Huntley-Brinkley Report* (NBC), Television news

The Fabulous Fifties (CBS), Television entertainment

NBC White Paper Series, Television education

GE College Bowl (CBS), Television youth program

The Shari Lewis Show, (NBC), Television children's program

CBS 1960 Olympic coverage, Television contribution to international understanding

CBS Reports, Television public service

Musical Spectaculars (WQXR, New York), Radio entertainment

Ireene Wicker (WNYC, New York), Radio children's program

Texaco-Metropolitan Opera Network, Radio public service

Broadcasting and Film Commission, National Council of Churches of Christ in the U.S.A., for various programs on different networks and local stations, Radio-television education

WOOD and WOOD-TV (Grand Rapids, Mich.), **KPFK** (Los Angeles), **WCKT** (Miami) and **WCCO-TV** (Minneapolis), Locally produced radio-television

Frank Stanton (CBS), Special award

1961 *David Brinkley's Journal* (NBC), Television news

The Bob Newhart Show (NBC), Television entertainment

An Age of Kings (BBC) and *Vincent Van Gogh: A Self-Portrait* (NBC), Television education

Expedition! (ABC), Television youth and children's program

Walter Lippmann and CBS, Television contribution to international understanding

Let Freedom Ring (KSL-TV, CBS, Salt Lake City), Television public service

Fine Arts Entertainment (WFMT, Chicago), Radio entertainment

The Reader's Almanac and *Teen Age Book Talk* (WNYC, New York), Radio education

WRUL (Worldwide Broadcasting, New York) for coverage of U.N. General Assembly proceedings in English and Spanish, Radio contribution to international understanding

Fred Friendly (CBS), **Capital Cities Broadcasting Corporation,** "Verdict for Tomorrow: The Eichmann Trial on Television," and **Newton N. Minow,** Chairman, Federal Communications Commission, Special awards

1962 **Walter Cronkite** (CBS), Television news

Du Pont Show of the Week (NBC) and **Carol Burnett** (CBS), Television entertainment

Biography (Official Films, Inc.), Television education

Exploring (NBC) and **Walt Disney** (NBC), Television youth and children's programming

Adlai Stevenson Reports (ABC), Television contribution to international understanding

A Tour of the White House With Mrs. John F. Kennedy (CBS), Television public service

Elliot Norton Reviews (WGBH-TV Boston), *Books for Our Time* (WNDT, New York) and *San Francisco Pageant* (KPIX-TV, WBC), Locally produced television

WQXR (New York), Radio news

Adventures in Good Music (WJR, Detroit) and *The Eternal Light* (NBC), Radio entertainment

Science Editor (KNX, CBS, Los Angeles), Radio education

Carnival of Books (WMAQ, NBC, Chicago), Radio youth and children's program

William R. MacAndrew and NBC News and NAB for study on television's effects on the young viewer, Special awards

1963 Eric Sevareid (CBS), Television news commentary
The Danny Kaye Show (CBS) and *Mr. Novak* (NBC), Television entertainment
American Revolution '63 (NBC) and *The Saga of Western Man* (ABC), Television education
The Dorothy Gordon Forum (WNBC-TV and Radio, New York), Television youth program
Treetop House (WGN, Chicago), Television children's program
Town Meeting of the World (CBS) and **Frank Stanton,** Television contribution to international understanding
CBS Reports: Storm Over the Supreme Court, Television public service
Sunday Night Monitor (NBC), Radio news
WLW (Cincinnati), Radio education
Voice of America and Edward R. Murrow, Radio contribution to international understanding
KSTP (Minneapolis), Radio public service
Broadcasting industry of the U.S.A. for coverage of the assassination of President Kennedy and related events, Special award

1964 *CBS Reports*
Profiles in Courage (NBC)
William H. (Bill) Lawrence (ABC)
Joyce Hall, *Hallmark Hall of Fame* (NBC)
Julia Child, *The French Chef* (WGBH-TV, Boston, and NET)
INTERTEL: International Television Federation
Off the Cuff (WBKB, ABC, Chicago)
Riverside Radio (WRVR-FM, New York)
The Louvre (NBC)
Burr Tillstrom
The networks and the broadcasting industry for confronting the American public with the realities of racial discontent

1965 **Frank McGee** (NBC), **Morley Safer** (CBS) and **KTLA,** Television news
The Julie Andrews Show (NBC), *My Name is Barbra* (CBS), and *Frank Sinatra — A Man and His Music* (NBC), Television entertainment
National Educational Television, Television education
A Charlie Brown Christmas (CBS), Television youth and children's program
CBS Reports: KKK—The Invisible Empire, Television public service
The National Driver's Test (CBS), Television innovation
The Mystery of Stonehenge (CBS), Television's most inventive art documentary
A Visit to Washington with Mrs. Lyndon B. Johnson — On Behalf of a More Beautiful America (ABC), Television special award
Xerox Corporation Television contribution to international understanding
"Music 'til Dawn" (CBS), Radio entertainment
WCCO-Radio (Minneapolis), Radio public

1966 **Harry Reasoner** (CBS), Television news
A Christmas Memory: ABC Stage 67, Television entertainment
National Geographic Specials (CBS) and *American White Paper: Organized Crime in the United States* (NBC), Television education
The World of Stuart Little (NBC), Television youth and children's program
The Wide World of Sports (ABC) and *Siberia: A Day in Irkutsk* (NBC), Television promotion of international understanding

Bell Telephone Hour (NBC), **Tom John** (CBS), **National Educational Television, and "CBS Reports: The Poisoned Air,"** Television special awards
"The Dorothy Gordon Youth Forum: Youth and Narcotics—Who Has the Answer?" (WNBC-TV and WNBC-Radio), Television-radio public service
Kup's Show (WBKB-TV, Chicago), Television local news-entertainment
Artists' Showcase (WGN-TV, Chicago) and **"A Polish Millennium Concert"** (WTMJ-TV, Milwaukee), Television local music
Assignment Four (KRON-TV, San Francisco), Television local public service
Edwin Newman (NBC), Radio news
Elmo Ellis (WSB, Atlanta), Radio local public service
Community Opinion (WLIB, New York), Radio local education

1967 **Elie Abel,** *The World and Washington* (NBC), Radio news
The Eternal Light (NBC), Radio education
Eric Sevareid (CBS), Radio-television news analysis and commentary
CBS Playhouse and *An Evening at Tanglewood* (NBC), Television entertainment
The Children's Film Festival (CBS), and *Mr. Knozit* (WIS-TV), Television youth or children's program
"Africa" (ABC), Television promotion of international understanding
The Opportunity Line (WBBM-TV), Television public service
Meet the Press and **Bob Hope** (NBC), Radio-television special awards
The Ed Sullivan Show (CBS), Television special award
James H. Killiam, Jr., Chairman, Massachusetts Institute of Technology, Special broadcasting education award

1968 *Second Sunday* (NBC), Radio news
Leonard Reiffel, *The World Tomorrow* (WEEI, CBS, Boston), Radio education
Steinway Hall (WQXR, New York), Radio entertainment
Kaleidoscope (WJR, CBS, Detroit), Radio public service
Charles Kuralt, "On the Road" (CBS), Television news
Robert Cromie, *Book Beat* (WTTW, Chicago) and **ABC** for its creative 1968 documentaries, Television education
Playhouse (NET), Television entertainment
Misterogers' Neighborhood (NET), Television youth or children's program
1968 Olympic Games (ABC), Television promotion of international understanding
One Nation Indivisible (Westinghouse Broadcasting), Television public service
"CBS Reports: Hunger in America," Television special award

1969 **"When Will It End?"** (WRNG, Atlanta), Radio news
"On Trial: The Man in the Middle" (NBC, New York), Radio education
Voice of America (Washington), Radio promotion of international understanding
Higher Horizons (WLIB, New York), Radio public service
Newsroom (KQED, San Francisco) and **Frank Reynolds** (ABC-TV, New York), Television news
The Advocates (WGBH-TV, Boston) and **KCET** Los Angeles) and *Who Killed Lake Erie?* (NBC-TV), Television education

Experiment in Television (NBC) and **Curt Gowdy,** Television entertainment
Sesame Street (Children's Television Workshop, New York), Television youth or children's program
"The Japanese" (CBS), Television promotion of international understanding
Tom Pettit (Investigative reporting for NBC), Network television public service
The Negro in Indianapolis (WFBM-TV, Indianapolis), Local television public service
J.T. (CBS-TV), Special television writing award
Chet Huntley, Television special award
Bing Crosby, Special individual award

1970 **Douglas Kiker,** "Jordan Reports" (NBC), Radio news
"The Danger Within: A Study of Disunity in America" (NBC), Radio education
Voice of America and **Garry Moore,** Radio promotion of international understanding
Listening/4 (WFBE-FM, Flint, Mich.), Radio youth or children's programs
"Medical Viewpoint" and **"Pearl Harbor, Lest We Forget"** (WAHT, Lebanon, Pa.), Radio public service
60 Minutes (CBS) and **"Politithon '70"** (WPBT, Miami), Television news
Flip Wilson Show (NBC), *Evening at Pops* (PBS), and *The Andersonville Trial* (PBS and KCET, Los Angeles), Television entertainment
Eye of the Storm (ABC), Television education
The Dr. Seuss Programs (CBS) and *Hot Dog* (NBC-TV), Television youth and children's program
Civilisation (BBC) and *This New Frontier* (WWL-TV, New Orleans), Television promotion of international understanding
Peace . . . On Our Time and *The Death of Rueben Salazar* (KMEX-TV, Los Angeles) and *Migrant: An NBC White Paper,* Television public service
The Selling of the Pentagon (CBS), Television special award

1971 **John Rich** (NBC Radio and Television), Broadcast news
Wisconsin on the Move (WHA, Madison, Wisc.), Radio education
Junior Town Meeting of the Air (WWVA, Wheeling, W. Va.), Radio youth or children's program
Voice of America (Washington), Radio promotion of international understanding
Second Sunday (NBC), Radio public service
The Heart of the Matter (WCCO, Minneapolis), and **Arthur Godfrey** (CBS), Radio special awards
NBC-TV dramatic programing; *The American Revolution: 1770-1783, A Conversation with Lord North* (CBS) and *Brian's Song* (ABC), Television entertainment
Make A Wish (ABC-TV News), Television youth or children's program
"The Turned On Crisis" (WQED, Pittsburgh), Television education
Mississippi Authority for Educational Television, Special television education
United Nations Day Concert with Pablo Casals (United Nations Television, New York), Television promotion of international understanding
"This Child is Rated X" (NBC), Television public service
George Heinemann (NBC-TV), Special television award
Frank Stanton (CBS), Special award

1972 **RADIO**
NBC Monitor (NBC Radio Network)

"Conversations With Will Shakespeare and Certain of His Friends" (KOAC, Corvallis, Ore.)
The Noise Show (Washington, D.C., Schools Radio Project)
Open Door (KGW, Portland, Ore.)
Broadcasting Foundation of America (New York)
Voice of America
Breakdown (Group W, New York)
No Fault Insurance—Right Road or Wrong? and *Second Sunday,* NBC and NBC owned and -operated stations)
All Things Considered (National Public Radio, Washington)

TELEVISION
Bill Monroe (*Today,* NBC) for news reporting
The Waltons (CBS-TV)
NBC/TV for three special programs devoted to twentieth century American music
WHRO-TV (Norfolk, Va.) for overall classroom programing
"The Search for the Nile" (BBC and NBC)
ABC Afterschool Specials (ABC-TV)
"The Restless Earth" (WNET, New York, and BBC)
Captain Kangaroo (CBS-TV)
"China '72: A Hole in the Bamboo Curtain" (WWL-TV, New Orleans)
"Pensions: The Broken Promise" (NBC)
"Willowbrook: The Last Great Disgrace" (WABC-TV, New York)
XX Olympiad (ABC)
Alistair Cooke

1973 **RADIO**
Lowell Thomas, News broadcast
Lyric Opera Live Broadcasts and *Music in Chicago,* (WFMT, Chicago) and *"Project Experiment* (NBC Radio, live concerts), Entertainment
WFMT (Chicago) and "Project Experiment (NBC Radio, live concerts), Entertainment
Second Sunday (NBC Radio) and *The American Past: Introduction* (KANU-FM, Lawrence, Kans.), Education
"From 18th Street: Destination Peking" (WIND, Chicago), Promotion of international understanding
"Marijuana and the Law," (KNOW, Austin, Tex.), Public service

TELEVISION
Close-Up (ABC News), News
Peter Lisagor (Chicago Daily News), Special news award
"Myshkin" (WTIU, Bloomington, Ind.) and *Red Pony* (NBC), *Pueblo* and *The Glass Menagerie,* (ABC) and *The Catholics,* (CBS Playhouse 90),Entertainment
The First and Essential Freedom (ABC), *Learning Can Be Fun,* and *Dusty's Treehouse* (KNXT, Los Angeles), Education
The Borrowers and *Street of the Flower Boxes* (NBC), Youth and children's program
Overture to Friendship: The Philadelphia Orchestra in China (WCAU), Promotion of international understanding
"Home Rule Campaign" (WRC, NBC), Public service
Pamela Ilott for *Lamp Unto My Feet* and *Look Up and Live* (CBS News), Personal public service award
"The Energy Crisis . . . An American White Paper" (NBC), Television special award
Joe Garagiola, *The Baseball World of Joe Garagiola* (NBC-TV), Special sports award

1974 **"The Hit and Run Players"** (KTW-Radio, Seattle)

The CBS Radio Mystery Theatre (CBS Radio Network)
The Second Sunday (NBC Radio Network)
Through the Looking Glass (KFAC-Radio, Los Angeles)
Conversations From Wingspread (The Johnson Foundation, Racine, Wisc.)
WSB-Radio (Atlanta), for public and community service
Battles Just Begun (WMAL-Radio, Washington)
Pledge A Job (WNBC-Radio, New York)
WCKT-TV (Miami), for investigative reporting
The Execution of Private Slovik, The Law, and *IBM Presents Clarence Darrow* (NBC Television Network)
Benjamin Franklin CBS Television Network
Theatre in America, (WNET and The Public Broadcasting Service)
Nova (WGBH-TV, Boston)
Free to Be . . . You and Me (ABC Television Network)
Go! (NBC Television Network)
How Come? (KING-TV, Seattle)
From Belfast With Love (WCCO-TV, Minneapolis)
Sadat: Action Biography (ABC Television Network)
"Tornado! 4:40 P.M., Xenia, Ohio" (NBC Television Network)
NPACT (National Public Affairs Center for Television), Washington
"The Right Man" (KPRC, Houston)
Carl Stern (NBC News)
Fred Graham (CBS News)
Marilyn Baker formerly of KQED-TV San Francisco)
Julian Goodman (Chairman, NBC)

RADIO

1975 Jim Laurie (NBC News)
"Sleeping Watchdogs," (KMOX-Radio, St. Louis)
The Collector's Shelf and *200 Years of Music in America* (WGMS, Bethesda, Md., WGMS-FM, Washington)
Standard School of Broadcast (San Francisco)
Music in Chicago: Stravinsky '75 (WFMT, Chicago)
"Land of Poetry" (WSOU-FM, S. Orange, N.J.)
"The Battle of Lexington" (Voice of America)
"A Life to Share" (WCBS-Radio, New York)
KDKB (Mesa, Ariz.) for community service
"Suffer the Little Children" and "The Legend of the Bermuda Triangle" (WMAL-Radio, Washington)

SPECIAL POSTHUMOUS AWARD

Paul Porter, member, Peabody Awards National Advisory Board

TELEVISION

"Harambee: For My People" and "Everywoman: the Hidden World" (WTOP, Washington)
WCKT-TV (Miami) for investigative reporting
Charles Kuralt (CBS News) for "On the Road to '76"
"The Dale Car: A Dream or A Nightmare" (KABC-TV, Los Angeles)
M.A.S.H. (CBS-TV)
ABC Theatre: Love Among the Ruins (ABC-TV)
Weekend (NBC-TV)
WCVB-TV (Boston)
Call It Macaroni (Group W, New York)
The ABC Afterschool Specials (ABC-TV)
Snipets (Kaiser Broadcastong, San Francisco)
Big Blue Marble (Alphaventure, New York)
Mr. Rooney Goes to Washington (CBS News)

A Sunday Journal (WWL-TV, New Orleans)
The American Assassins (CBS News)
"Las Rosas Blancas," (WAPA-TV, San Juan, P.R.)
James Killian, Boston

1976 *American Popular Song With Alec Wilder and Friends* (South Carolina Educational Radio Network, Columbia, S.C.)
"Flashback 1976" (WGIR-AM-FM, Manchester, N.H.)
"The Garden Plot: Food As a Weapon" (Associated Press Radio, Washington)
"Power Politics in Mississippi" (WLBT-TV, Jackson, Miss.)
Primary Colors, An Artist on the Campaign Trail (Franklin McMahon, WBBM-TV, Chicago)
Charles Barthold (WHO-TV, Des Moines) for filming tornado
The CBS Morning News (Hughes Rudd and Bruce Morton)
Weekend's "Sawyer Brothers" segment (NBC-TV, Sy Pearlman)
Visions (KCET/28, Los Angeles)
Sybil (NBC-TV)
Eleanor and Franklin (ABC-TV)
Animals Animals Animals (ABC News)
1976 Winter Olympic Games and 1976 Summer Olympic Games (ABC Sports)
Judge Horton and the Scottsboro Boys (Tomorrow Entertainment, Inc., New York)
In Performance at Wolf Trap (WETA-TV Washington)
Perry Como's Christmas in Austria (NBC-TV)
In the News (CBS News)
"A Thirst in the Garden" (KERA-TV, Dallas)
'76 Presidential Debates (Jim Karayn and The League of Women Voters)
The Adams Chronicles (WNET/13, New York)
In Celebration of US (CBS News)
Suddenly An Eagle (ABC News)
A Conversation With Jimmy Carter (WETA-TV, Washington and WNET/13, New York)
60 Minutes (CBS News)

1977 Not announced at press time

Gold Medal Awards
PHOTOPLAY
205 E. 42nd St., New York, N.Y. 10017 (212/983-5600)

The Photoplay Gold Medal Awards are made annually for the most popular television program and performers. The most recent awards were based on ballots of more than 60,000 readers of the magazine.

TV SHOW

1966 *The Big Valley*
1967 *Star Trek*
1968 *Mod Squad*
1969 *Marcus Welby, M.D.*
1970 *The Partridge Family*
1971 *All In the Family*
1972 *The Waltons*
1973 *The Waltons*
1974 *Rhoda*
1975 *Starsky & Hutch* (evening)
     The Young and The Restless (daytime)
1976 *Starsky & Hutch* (evening)
     Days of Our Lives (daytime)
     I Love Lucy (all-time favorite)
1977 Not announced at press time

COMEDY STAR

1967   Carol Burnett
1968   Carol Burnett
1969   Carol Burnett
1970   Carol Burnett
1971   Carol Burnett
1972   Paul Lynde
1973   No award
1974   Jack Oakie (Award renamed the Joakie)
1975   Henry Winkler
1976   Henry Winkler
1977   Not announced at press time

VARIETY STAR

1973   Sammy Davis
1974   Elvis Presley
1975   Elvis Presley
1976   Elvis Presley
1977   Not announced at press time

FAVORITE MALE TV STAR

1976   Michael Glaser, *Starsky and Hutch*
1977   Not announced at press time

FAVORITE FEMALE TV STAR

1977   Farrah Fawcett-Majors, *Charlie's Angels*
1977   Not announced at press time

FAVORITE MALE DAYTIME TV STAR

1976   Bill Hayes, *Days of Our Lives*
1977   Not announced at press time

FAVORITE FEMALE DAYTIME TV STAR

1976   Susan Seaforth Hayes, *Days of Our Lives*
1977   Not announced at press time

FAVORITE YOUNG STAR

1976   Kristy McNichol, *Family*
1977   Not announced at press time

FAVORITE LIVE ANIMAL STAR

1976   Fred (cockatoo), *Baretta*
1977   Not announced at press time

Photoplay also gives awards for the most popular male and female newcomers, which include (in fact, in recent years have been dominated by) television personalities.

Sigma Delta Chi Awards

SOCIETY OF PROFESSIONAL JOURNALISTS/SIGMA DELTA CHI

35 E. Wacker Dr., Chicago, Ill. 60601 (312/236-6577)

Sigma Delta Chi Awards for Distinguished Service in Journalism annually honor noteworthy performance in broadcast and print journalism. Bronze medallions and plaques are presented to the winners. Society chapters nominate individuals and stations for final selection. (See pp. 99-102 for winners of Sigma Delta Chi Awards in the print media).

RADIO REPORTING

1946   Allen Stout
1947   James C. McNamara
1948   George J. O'Connor
1949   Sid Pletzsch

1950   Jack E. Krueger
1951   Jim Monroe
1952   Charles and Eugene Jones
1953   Gordon Gammack
1954   Richard Chapman
1955   John Chancellor
1956   Edward J. Green
1957   Dave Muhlstein
1958   Winston Burdett
1959   Donald H. Weston
1960   Frederick A. Goerner
1961   KDKA News Staff (Pittsburgh, Pa.)
       Wip Robinson and Frank O'Roark, WSVA (Harrisonburg, Va.)
1962   WINS News Staff, (New York)
1963   WINS News Staff (New York)
1964   WNEW News (New York)
1965   WNEW News (New York)
1966   KTBC Radio News (Austin, Tex.)
1967   WJR News (Detroit, Mich.)
1968   KFWB News (Los Angeles, Calif.)
1969   Ed Joyce, WCBS (New York)
1970   Bob White, KRLD (Dallas, Tex.)
1971   John Rich, NBC Radio
1972   Val Hymes, WTOP Radio (Washington)
1973   Eric Engberg, Group W/Westinghouse Broadcasting
1974   Jim Mitchell, Gary Franklin, Herb Humphries and Hank Allison, KFWB Radio (Los Angeles)
1975   WHBF AM-FM Radio News Team (Rock Island, Ill.)
1976   Mike Lee and Doug Tunnell (CBS News)
1977   Paul McGonigle (KOY Radio, Phoenix)

PUBLIC SERVICE IN RADIO JOURNALISM

1949   WTTS (Bloomington, Ind.)
1950   WAVZ (New Haven, Conn.)
1951   WMAQ (Chicago)
1952   WMT (Cedar Rapids, Iowa)
1953   CBS Radio Network
1954   CBS Radio Network
1955   WMAQ (Chicago)
1956   CBS Radio Network
1957   KNX (Los Angeles)
1958   CBS Radio Network
1959   WIP (Philadelphia)
1960   WBT (Charlotte, N.C.)
1961   KNUZ (Houston Tex.)
1962   WBZ (Boston)
1963   WSB (Atlanta)
1964   KSEN (Shelby, Mont.)
1965   WCCO (Minneapolis-St. Paul)
1966   WIBW (Topeka, Kans.)
1967   Westinghouse Broadcasting Co., Inc.
1968   WBZ (Boston)
1969   WHN (New York)
1970   WWDC (Washington)
1971   WBZ (Boston)
1972   WGAR (Cleveland)
1973   WMAL (Washington)
1974   WIND (Chicago)
1975   WRVA Radio (Richmond, Va.)
1976   WCAU-AM Radio News (Philadelphia)
1977   WSGN-AM (Birmingham, Ala.)

EDITORIALIZING ON RADIO

1963   WRTA (Altoona, Pa.)
1964   WXYZ (Detroit)

1965 KDKA (Pittsburgh)
1966 W-A-I-T (Chicago)
1967 WSBA (York-Lancaster-Harrisburg, Pa.)
1968 Theodore Jones, WCRB (Waltham, Mass.)
1969 WWDC (Washington)
1970 WLPR (Mobile, Ala.)
1971 WSOC-AM (Charlotte, N.C.)
1972 Frank Reynolds, ABC News (New York)
1973 WGRC (Pittsfield, Mass.)
1974 Jim Branch, WRFM (New York)
1975 Charles B. Cleveland, (WIND Chicago)
1976 Ed Hinshaw, WTMJ (Milwaukee)
1977 Jay Lewis, Alabama Information Network

TELEVISION REPORTING

1952 Charles and Eugene Jones
1953 No award
1954 Spencer Allen
1955 Paul Alexander
      Gael Boden
1956 Ernest Leiser
      Jerry Schwartzkopff
      Julian B. Hoshal
      Dick Hance
1957 Jim Bennett
1958 WBBM-TV News (Chicago)
1959 WGN-TV News (Chicago)
1960 WTVJ-TV News (Miami)
1961 WKY-TV (Oklahoma City,)
1962 KWTV News (Oklahoma City)
1963 WBAP-TV (Fort Worth, Tex.)
1964 WFGA-TV (Jacksonville, Fla.)
1965 Morley Safer, CBS News
1966 WSB-TV News (Atlanta)
1967 John Laurence, CBS News
1968 Station KNXT (Los Angeles)
1969 WCCO News (Minneapolis)
1970 KBTV (Denver)
1971 Robert Schakne, CBS News
1972 Laurens Pierce, CBS News
1973 Steve Young and Roger Sims, CBS News
1974 Lee Louis, KGTV10 (San Diego)
1975 WHAS-TV News (Louisville, Ky.)
1976 KMJ-TV (Fresno, Calif.)
1977 KPIX-TV Eyewitness News Team (San Francisco)

PUBLIC SERVICE IN TV JOURNALISM

1952 WBNS-TV (Columbus, Ohio)
1953 WHAS-TV (Louisville, Ky.)
1954 Dumont Television Network
      American Broadcasting Co.
1955 KAKE-TV (Wichita, Kans.)
1956 KPIX (San Francisco)
1957 WBZ-TV (Boston)
1958 KNXT (Hollywood, Calif.)
1959 WBZ-TV (Boston)
1960 NBC Television Network
1961 Station KHOU-TV (Houston, Tex.)
1962 KGW-TV (Portland, Ore.)
1963 KDKA-TV (Pittsburgh)
      National Broadcasting Co.
1964 Columbia Broadcasting System
1965 WABC-TV (New York)
1966 KLZ-TV (Denver)
1967 National Broadcasting Co.
1968 WIBW-TV (Topeka, Kans.)
1969 WDSU-TV (New Orleans)
1970 KING-TV (Seattle)

1971 Columbia Broadcasting System
1972 WABC-TV (New York)
1973 WSOC-TV News (Charlotte, N.C.)
1974 ABC News
1975 WCKT-TV (Miami)
1976 KNXT-TV (Los Angeles)
1977 KOOL-TV (Phoenix)

EDITORIALIZING ON TELEVISION

1963 Tom Martin, KFDA-TV (Amarillo, Tex.)
1964 KDKA-TV (Pittsburgh)
1965 WTOP-TV (Washington)
1966 WFBM-TV (Indianapolis, Ind.)
1967 KWTV (Oklahoma City)
1968 WOOD-TV (Grand Rapids, Mich.)
1969 KCPX Television (Salt Lake City)
1970 WCCO-TV (Minneapolis)
1971 Robert Schulman, WHAS-TV (Louisville, Ky.)
1972 WCKT-TV (Miami)
1973 KRON-TV (San Francisco)
1974 Jay Lewis, WSFA-TV (Montgomery, Ala.)
1975 Don McGaffin and Charles Royer, KING-TV (Seattle)
1976 WCVB-TV (Boston)
1977 Rich Adams, WTOP-TV (Washington, D.C.)

RADIO OR TV COMMENTARY

1961 KDKA-TV (Pittsburgh)
1962 Harold Keen, WFMB-TV (San Diego, Calif.)

RADIO OR TV NEWSWRITING

1939 Albert Warner
1940 Cecil Brown
1942 Fulton Lewis, Jr.
1943 No award
1944 No award
1945 No award
1946 Harry M. Cochran
1947 Alex Dreier
1948 Merrill Mueller
1949 Elmer Davis
1950 Leo O'Brien
      Howard Maschmeier
1951 William E. Griffith, Jr.
1952 Clifton Utley
1953 Charles J. Chatfield
1954 Reuven Frank
1955 Charles Shaw
1956 Howard K. Smith
1957 Jerry Rosholt
1958 Harold R. Meier
1959 Gene Marine
1960 David Brinkley

Lowell Thomas Award

INTERNATIONAL PLATFORM ASSOCIATION
2564 Berkshire Rd., Cleveland Hts., Ohio 44106
(216/932-0505)

The Lowell Thomas Award, which consists of an engraved bowl, is given annually to the individual judged by the IPA Committee, Lowell Thomas and Dan T. Moore, to be the outstanding broadcast journalist of the year.

1974 Lowell Thomas
1975 Eric Sevareid
1976 Howard K. Smith
1977 Barbara Walters

Television-Radio Awards
Laurel Award for Television

WRITERS GUILD OF AMERICA, WEST
8955 Beverly Blvd., Los Angeles, Calif. 90048
(213/550-1000)

The annual Television-Radio Awards honor outstanding scripts, which are submitted to a three-judge panel for evaluation and selection. Awards are made in several categories. The early awards are listed by year. Later awards, when the categories became consistent, are listed by category and year.

1956 Donald S. Sandforc (teleplay) and **John Nesbitt**, ("The Golden Junkman" on *Telephone Time*), One-Half Hour TV Anthology Drama
Kenneth Kolb ("She Walks in Beauty" on *Medic*), One-Half Hour TV Episodic Drama
Leonard Stern and Sydney Zelinka ("The $99,000 Answer" on *The Jackie Gleason Show*), One-Half Hour TV Situation Comedy
Hal Kanter, Howard Leeds, Harry Winkler and Everett Greenbaum, (*The George Gobel Show*), Comedy-Variety Certificate of Excellence
Rod Serling ("Requiem for a Heavyweight" on *Playhouse 90*), One Hour or More TV Drama
J. Harvey Howells ("Goodbye, Grey Flannel" on *Robert Montgomery Presents*), One Hour TV Comedy
John Whedon and George Roy Hill ("A Night to Remember" on *Kraft TV Theatre*), TV Documentary
Thelma Robinson (teleplay) and **Warren Wilson** and **Claire Kennedy** (story) ("The Visitor" on *Lassie*), Children's Program
1957 Joseph Mindel ("Degree of Freedom"), One Half-Hour TV Anthology Drama
Everett DeBaun ("Pearls of Talimeco" on *Jim Bowie*), One-Half Hour TV Episodic Drama
Jerry McNeely ("The Staring Match" on *Studio One*), One Hour Anthology Drama
Gene Roddenberry ("Helen of Abajinian" on *Have Gun, Will Travel*), Television Western, Any Length
Kenneth Enochs ("Elmer the Rainmaker" on *Circus Boy*), Children's Program
Erick Moll ("The Fabulous Irishman" on *Playhouse 90*), Any Program More Than One Hour in Length
Sydney Zelinka and A.J. Russell ("Papa Bilko" on *The Phil Silvers Show*), One-Half Hour or Less TV Comedy and Sketches
Irwin Rosten ("The Human Explosion"), TV Documentary
Devery Freeman ("The Great American Hoax"), One Hour TV Comedy
1958 Valentine Davies and Kurt Vonnegut, Jr. ("Auf Wiedersehan" on *The GE Theatre*), Best Script, 30 Minutes or Less Program Length
Shimon Wincelberg ("The Sea is Boiling Hot" on *Kraft Television Theatre*), Best Script, 60 Minutes or Less, But More Than 30 Minutes Program Length
Rod Serling ("A Town Has Turned to Dust" on *Playhouse 90*), Best Script, More Than 60 Minutes Program Length
Steven Fleishman ("Face of Crime" on *20th Century*), TV Documentary-News Analysis or News in Depth
Sherwood Schwartz, Jesse Goldstein and Dave O'Brien ("Freddie's Thanksgiving" on *The Red Skelton Show*), Best Comedy/Variety or Variety, Any Length

1959 Christopher Knopf ("Interrogation" on *Zane Grey Theater*), One-Half Hour TV Anthology Drama
Richard Matheson ("Yawkey" on *Lawman*), One-Half Hour TV Episodic Drama
Tony Webster ("Call Me Back" on *The Art Carney Show*), TV Anthology, More Than One-Half Hour
William Spier ("The Assassination of Cermak" on *The Untouchables*), Television Episodic, More Than One-Half Hour
Irving G. Nieman ("Child of Our Times" on *Playhouse 90*), Television Adaptation, Any Length
Dorothy Cooper ("Margaret's Old Flame" on *Father Knows Best*), TV Episodic Comedy, Any Length
Max Wilk and A.J. Russell ("The Fabulous Fifties"), TV Variety, Any Length
Richard Hanser ("Mark Twain's America" on *Project 20*), TV Documentary, Any Length
Earle Luby ("Down Range" on *20th Century*), TV Documentary, Any Length

ANTHOLOGY DRAMA, ANY LENGTH/TV ANTHOLOGY, ANY LENGTH/BEST ANTHOLOGY/BEST ORIGINAL ANTHOLOGY

1961 Christopher Knopf ("Death of the Temple Bay" on *The June Allyson Show*)
1962 Richard Alan Simmons ("The Price of Tomatoes" on *The Dick Powell Show*)
1963 Richard Alan Simmons ("The Last of the Big Spenders" on *The Dick Powell Show*)
1964 Howard Rodman ("The Game With Glass Pieces" on *Chrysler Theater*)
1965 Harlan Ellison ("Demon With a Glass Hand" on *Outer Limits*)
1966 S. Lee Pogostin ("The Game" on *Chrysler Theatre*)
1967 S. Lee Pogostin ("Crazier Than Cotton" on *Chrysler Theatre*)
1968 Earl Hamner ("Heidi")
1969 George Bellak ("Sadbird" on *CBS Playhouse*)
1970 Tracy Keenan Wynn and Marvin Schwartz ("Tribes" on *ABC Movie of the Week*)
1971 Carol Sobieski and Howard Rodman ("The Neon Ceiling" on *NBC World Premiere*)
1972 Richard Levinson and William Link ("That Certain Summer" on *ABC Movie of the Week*)
1973 Abby Mann ("The Marcus-Nelson Murders" on *CBS Movie of the Week*)
1974 Joel Oliansky, story by William Sackhein and Joel Oliansky ("The Law" on *NBC World Premiere*)
1975 Jerome Kass (*Queen of the Stardust Ballroom*)
1976 Robert Collins ("The Quality of Mercy" on *NBC Thursday Night Movie*)
1977 Carol Sobieski ("Christmas Sunshine" on *NBC World Premiere*)

EPISODIC DRAMA, ANY LENGTH/TV EPISODIC, ANY LENGTH/BEST DRAMATIC EPISODIC

1961 Barry Trivers ("The Fault in Our Stars" on *Naked City*)
1962 Kenneth Rosen and Howard Rodman ("Today the Man Who Kills the Ants is Coming" on *Naked City*)
1963 Lawrence B. Marcus ("Man Out of Time" on *Route 66*)
1964 Arnold Perl ("Who Do You Kill?" on *East Side/West Side*)
1965 John D.F. Black ("With a Hammer in His Hand, Lord, Lord!" on *Mr. Novak*)

1966 David Ellis ("No Justice for the Judge" on *Trials of O'Brien*)
1967 Harlan Ellison ("The City on the Edge of Forever" on *Star Trek*)
1968 Robert Lewin ("To Kill a Madman" on *Judd for the Defense*)
1969 Robert Lewin ("An Elephant in a Cigar Box" on *Judd for the Defense*)
1970 David Rintels ("A Continual Roar of Musketry" on *The Bold Ones*)
1971 Thomas Y. Drake, Herb Bermann, Jerrold Freedman and Bo May ("Par for the Course" on *The Psychiatrist*)
1972 Herman Miller ("King of the Mountain" on *Kung Fu*)
1973 Harlan Ellison ("Phoenix Without Ashes" on *The Starlost*)
1974 Jim Byrnes ("Thirty a Month and Found" on *Gunsmoke*)
1975 Arthur Ross (teleplay) and Stephen Kandel (story) ("Prior Consent" on *The Law*)
1976 Loring Mandel ("Crossing the River" on *Sandburg's Lincoln*)
1977 Mark Rodgers ("Pressure Point" on *Police Story*)

TV COMEDY-VARIETY, ANY LENGTH

1962 Gary Belkin and Nat Hiken ("I Won't Go!" on *Car 54, Where Are You?*)
1963 Everett Greenbaum and Jim Fritzell ("Barney's First Car" on *The Andy Griffith Show*)

BEST COMEDY, EPISODIC

1964 Bill Idelson and Sam Bobrick ("The Shoplifters" on *The Andy Griffith Show*)
Martin Ragaway ("My Husband is the Best One" on *The Dick Van Dyke Show*)
1965 Dale McRaven and Carl Kleinschmitt ("Br-room Br-room" on *The Dick Van Dyke Show*)
1966 Jack Winter ("You Ought to Be in Pictures" on *The Dick Van Dyke Show*)
1967 Marvin Marx, Walter Stone and Gordon Rod Parker ("Movies Are Better Than Ever" on *The Jackie Gleason Show*)
1968 Bill Idelson and Sam Bobrick ("Viva Smart" on *Get Smart*)
1969 Allan Burns ("Funny Boy" on *Room 222*)
1970 Richard DeRoy ("The Valediction" on *Room 222*)
1971 Martin Cohan ("Thoroughly Unmilitant Milly" on *The Mary Tyler Moore Show*)
1972 Larry Gelbart ("Chief Surgeon Who" on *M*A*S*H**)
1973 Bob Weiskopf and Bob Schiller ("Walter's Problem," Part II, on *Maude*)
1974 Larry Gelbart and Laurence Marks ("O.R." on *M*A*S*H**)
1975 Everett Greenbaum, Jim Fritzell and Larry Gelbart ("Welcome to Korea" on *M*A*S*H**)
1976 Alan Alda ("Dear Sigmund" on *M*A*S*H**)
1977 Larry Rhine and Mel Tolkin ("Archie Gets the Business" on *All in the Family*)

BEST COMEDY VARIETY

1964 Herbert Baker, Sheldon Keller, Saul Ilson, Ernest Chambers, Gary Belkin, Paul Mazursky, Larry Tucker and Mel Tolkin (*The Danny Kaye Show*)
1965 Sheldon Keller, Gary Belkin, Ernest Chambers, Larry Tucker, Paul Mazursky, Billy Barnes, Ron Friedman and Mel Tolkin (*The Danny Kaye Show*)

1966 Garry Marshall and Jerry Belson ("The Road to Lebanon" on *The Danny Thomas Special*)

BEST COMEDY, NON-EPISODIC

1967 Mel Brooks, Sam Denoff, Bill Persky, Carl Reiner and Mel Tolkin (*The Sid Caesar, Imogene Coca, Carl Reiner, Howard Morris Special*)
1968 Sam Bobrick, Ron Clark, Danny Simon, Marty Farrell and Martin Ragaway (*Alan King's Wonderful World of Aggravation*)

BEST VARIETY

1969 Herbert Baker and Treva Silverman (*Norman Rockwell's America*)
1970 Gary Belkin, Peter Bellwood, Thomas Meehan, Herb Sargent and Judith Viorst (*Annie, the Women in the Life of a Man*)
1971 Don Hinkley, Jack Mendelsohn, Stan Hart, Larry Siegel, Woody Kling, Roger Beatty, Arnie Rosen, Kenny Solms and Gail Parent (writing supervised by Arthur Julian) (*The Carol Burnett Show*)
1972 Neil Simon (*The Trouble With People*)
1973 Norman Barasch, Jack Burns, Avery Schreiber, Bob Ellison, Bob Garland, Carroll Moore and George Yanok (*The Burns & Schreiber Comedy Hour*)
1974 Ed Simons, Gary Belkin, Roger Beatty, Arnie Kogen, Bill Richmond, Gene Perret, Rudy DeLuca, Barry Levinson, Dick Clair and Jenna McMahon (*The Carol Burnett Show*)
1975 Sybil Adelman, Barbara Gallagher, Gloria Banta, Pat Nardo, Stuart Birnbaum, Matt Neuman, Lorne Michaels, Marilyn Miller, Earl Pomerantz, Rosie Ruthchild, Lily Tomlin and Jane Wagner (*Lily*)
1976 Anne Beatts, Chevy Chase, Al Franken, Tom Davis, Lorne Michaels, Marilyn Suzanne Miller, Michael O'Donoghue, Herb Sargent, Tom Schiller, Rosie Schuster and Alan Zweibel (*NBC Saturday Night Live*)
1977 Elon Packard, Fred S. Fox and Seaman Jacob (*The George Burns One-Man Show*)

BEST VARIETY SPECIAL

1974 Norman Steinberg, Alan Uger, Howard Albrecht, Sol Weinstein, John Boni, Thad Mumford, Chevy Chase, Herb Sargent and Alan King (*Alan King's Energy Crisis, Rising Prices and Assorted Vices Comedy Hour*)

ADAPTATION FROM MATERIAL NOT ORIGINALLY WRITTEN FOR TELEVISION /BEST ADAPTATION BEST ANTHOLOGY (ADAPTATION)

1961 Bernard C. Schoenfeld ("The Little Mermaid" on *The Shirley Temple Show*)
1962 Gordon Russell ("The Forgery" on *DuPont Show of the Month*)
1963 Richard DeRoy and Iris Dornfeld ("Jeeney Ray" on *Alcoa Premiere*)
1964 Mark Rodgers, Russel Crouse and Clarence Greene ("One Day in the Life of Ivan Denisovich" on *Chrysler Theatre*)
1965 Robert Hartung ("The Magnificent Yankee" on *Hallmark Hall of Fame*)
1966 Robert Hartung ("Lamp at Midnight" on *Hallmark Hall of Fame*)
1967 Category not voted on; included in "Best Anthology" above.

1968 Category not voted on; included in "Best Anthology" above.
1969 Category not voted on; included in "Best Anthology" above.
1970 Category not voted on; included in "Best Anthology" above.
1971 William Blinn ("Brian's Song" on *ABC Movie of the Week*)
1972 Richard Matheson ("The Night Stalker" on *ABC Movie of the Week*)
1973 Carol Sobieski ("Sunshine" on *CBS Movie of the Week*)
1974 Tracy Keenan Wynn ("The Autobiography of Miss Jane Pittman" on *CBS Movie of the Week*)
1975 Fay Kanin ("Hustling" on *ABC Movie of the Week*)
David W. Rintels ("Fear on Trial" on *CBS Movie of the Week*)
1976 Stewart Stern ("Sybil" on *NBC Movie*)
1977 Steven Gethers ("A Circle of Children" on *CBS Movie*)

TV DOCUMENTARY (Any Length)

1961 Philip H. Reisman, Jr. ("The Real West" on *NBC Project 20*)
1962 Arthur Holch ("Walk in My Shoes" on *Bell & Howell Close-Up*)
1963 Frank DeFelitta and Robert Northshield ("Chosen Child")
1964 Albert Waller ("In the American Grain: William Carlos Williams" on *Eye on New York*)
1965 Robert Rogers ("Vietnam: It's a Mad War")
1966 Andrew A. Rooney and Richard Ellison ("The Great Love Affair")

BEST DOCUMENTARY (Features) /BEST DOCUMENTARY (Other Than Current Events) /BEST DOCUMENTARY FEATURE/BEST FEATURE DOCUMENTARY

1967 Theodore Strauss and Terry Sanders ("The Legend of Marilyn Monroe")
1968 James Fleming, Blaine Littell and Richard F. Siemanowski ("Africa")
Perry Wolff and Andrew Rooney ("Black History—Lost, Stolen or Strayed" on *Of Black America*)
1969 David Davidson ("The Ship That Wouldn't Die: U.S.S. Franklin")
Shimon Wincelberg ("Max Brod: Portrait of the Artist in His Own Right")
1970 Marianna Norris ("Gertrude Stein: A Biography")
1971 Andrew A. Rooney ("An Essay on War")
1972 Robert Northshield ("Guilty by Reason of Race")
1973 Marc Siegel ("Rendezvous With Freedom")
1974 Marlene Sanders ("The Right to Die")
1975 Irv Drasnin ("The Guns of Autumn")
1976 Paul W. Greenberg ("Friends, Romans, Communists")
1977 George Crile, III ("The CIA's Secret Army")

BEST DOCUMENTARY (Current Events)

1967 Robert Rogers ("The Battle for Asia," Part I, "Thailand, The New Front" on *NBC News*)
1967 Peter Davis and Martin Carr ("Hunger in America" on *CBS Reports*)
1969 Harry E. Morgan ("Fathers and Sons")
1970 Craig B. Fisher ("Survival on the Prairie")
1971 Peter Davis ("Vietnam Hindsight," Parts I and II)
1972 Robert Northshield ("Suffer the Little Children")
1973 James Fleming ("The First and Essential Freedom")
1974 Howard Stringer ("The Palestinians")

1975 Andrew Rooney ("Mr. Rooney Goes to Washington")
1976 Andrew Rooney ("Mr. Rooney Goes to Dinner")
1977 Marc Siegel ("The Panama Canal—A Test of Conscience")

BEST TV NEWSWRITING

1972 Charles West, Rabun Matthews, Gary Gates and John Merriman (*CBS Evening News with Walter Cronkite*)
Richard Cannon ("Land Fury" on *Six O'Clock Report*, WCBS-TV)
1973 Charles West, Rabun Matthews and Carol Ross (*CBS Evening News with Walter Cronkite*)
1974 Charles West ("Two Presidents: Transition in the White House")
1975 Sandor Polster, William H. Moran and Carol Ross (*CBS Evening News with Walter Cronkite*)
1976 William Moran, Ray Gandolf and Charles L. West ("In Celebration of US, July 4, 1976")
1977 Lee Townsend, Sandor M. Polster, Charles West, Allison Owings and Mary Earle (*CBS Evening News with Walter Cronkite*)

BEST DAYTIME SERIAL

1972 Loring Mandel, Nancy Ford, Kim Louis Ringwald and Max McClellan (*Love of Life*)
1973 Ralph Ellis and Eugene Hunt with Bibi Wein and Jane Chambers (*Search for Tomorrow*)
1974 Ann Marcus, Joyce Perry, Pamela Wylie and Ray Goldstone (*Search for Tomorrow*)
1975 Claire Labine, Paul Mayer, Mary Munisteri and Allan Leicht (*Ryan's Hope*)
1976 Claire Labine, Paul Avila Mayer and Mary Munisteri (*Ryan's Hope*)
1977 Claire Labine, Paul Avila Mayer, Judith Pinsker and Mary Munisteri (*Ryan's Hope*)

BEST CHILDREN'S SHOW SCRIPT

1975 Yanna Brandt (*The Superlative Horse*)
1976 Arthur Barron (*Blind Sunday*)
1977 Art Wallace (*Little Vic*)

RADIO DRAMA, ANY LENGTH

1956 Allan Sloane ("Bring On The Angela")
1957 Thomas F. Hanley, Jr. ("Misfire" on *Suspense*)

RADIO COMEDY, ANY LENGTH

1956 Si Rose (*The Edgar Bergen Show*)
1957 Stan Freberg and Pete Barnum ("Incident at Los Voraces" on *The Stan Freberg Show*)

RADIO SERIES OR SERIAL EPISODE, ANY LENGTH

1956 Stanley Niss (*The Penny*)

RADIO DOCUMENTARY

1956 Robert S. Greene ("Decision For Freedom")
1957 Jules Maitland ("Judgment")

BEST RADIO SCRIPT (Any Type, Any Length) /BEST RADIO/RADIO DOCUMENTARY

1959 Jay McMullen ("Who Killed Michael Farmer" on *Unit One Series*)
1960 George E. Lord and Ivan E. Ladizinsky ("One Deadly Drink")
1961 Robert S. Greene ("The Lincoln Story")
1962 Joseph Mindel ("The Hand of Esau" on *The Eternal Light*)
1963 Marlene Sanders ("Battle of the Warsaw Ghetto")

1964   Sol Panitz ("The Long Silence")
1965   Sol Panitz ("The Profit of Change")
1966   Sol Panitz ("The Legend of LeMans")
1967   Peter Woititz ("A Deadly Mistake")
1968   Susan A. Meyer ("The Problem Children")
1969   Robert Juhren ("No Matter Where You Are")
1970   Michael Hirsh ("Guerilla Warfare in Cairo, Illinois: There Are Three Sides to Every Story")
1971   Sol Panitz ("A Walk With Two Shadows")
Edward Hanna ("America the Violent" on *Second Sunday*)
1972   Sol Panitz ("The Firebrand")
1973   Norman S. Morris and Joan M. Burke ("The American Woman")
1974   Harvey Jacobs ("Summer on a Mountain of Spices")
1975   Norman Morris and Dale Minor ("The American Inheritance")
1976   Roberta Hollander and Phil Chin ("Prologue to the Democratic Convention: Issues and Attitudes")
1977   Martin Burke and Joseph Williams ("The American Man")

BEST RADIO NEWS

1972   Paul Glynn ("Flashback, 1972")

Joe Cook ("The Reasoner Report: A Maddened Minority")
1973   Alfred E. Downs (Newscript for Harry Birrell)
1974   Gil Longin (*Voices in the Headlines*)
1975   Hill Edell (*Voices in the Headlines*)
1976   Gil Longin (*Voices in the Headlines*)
1977   Gil Longin (*Voices in the Headlines*)

BEST RADIO DRAMATIC

1975   Sam Dann (*Goodbye, Karl Eric*)
1976   Sam Dann (*The Midas Touch*)
1977   Allan Sloane (*A Very Special Place*)

SPECIAL AWARD

1966   Shimon Wincelberg (*The Long, Long Curfew*)

The Laurel Award for Television is given annually to a member of the Guild who, in the opinion of the board of directors, has advanced the literature of television or made outstanding contributions to the television writing profession.

1976   Rod Serling
1977   Everett Greenbaum and James Fritzell

Cultural Life

& Entertainment

Contents

Related Awards

Award of Merit

AMERICAN ACADEMY OF ARTS AND LETTERS
633 W. 155th St., New York, N.Y. 10032 (212/368-5900)

The Academy's Award of Merit, which consists of a medal and $1,000, is given annually to an individual who is not a member of the academy for outstanding achievement in painting, sculpture, fiction, poetry or drama. The academy has merged with the National Institute of Arts and Letters, and awards made for specific achievements in those individual fields will be found elsewhere in this volume.

1942 Charles E. Burchfield
1943 Carl Milles
1944 Theodore Dreiser
1945 Wystan Hugh Auden
1946 John van Druten
1947 Andrew Wyeth
1948 Donal Hord
1949 Thomas Mann
1950 St. John Perse
1951 Sidney Kingsley
1952 Rico Lebrun
1953 Ivan Mestrovic
1954 Ernest Hemingway
1955 Jorge Guillen
1956 Enid Bagnold
1957 Raphael Soyer
1958 Jean de Marco
1959 Aldous Huxley
1960 Hilda Doolittle
1961 Clifford Odets
1962 Charles Sheeler
1963 Chaim Gross
1964 John O'Hara
1965 No award
1966 No award
1967 John Heliker
1968 Joseph Cornell
1969 Vladimir Nabokov
1970 Reed Whittemore
1971 No award
1972 Clyfford Still
1973 Reuben Nakian
1974 Nelson Algren
1975 Galway Kinnell
1976 No award
1977 No award

Poses Brandeis University Creative Arts Award

BRANDEIS UNIVERSITY
Brandeis University Commission Office, 12 E. 77th St., New York, N.Y. 10021 (212/472-1501)

One of a series of awards, the Jack I. and Lillian L. Poses Brandeis University Creative Arts Award is given annually to recognize notable achievement in the creative arts. A professional jury chosen by the commission selects the winner, who receives an honorarium of $1,000.

1964 R. Buckminster Fuller
1965 Alfred H. Barr, Jr.
1966 Meyer Schapiro
1967 Kenneth Burke
1968 Martha Graham

1969 Lewis Mumford
1970 Lloyd Goodrich
1971 George Balanchine
1972 I. A. Richards
1973 Leonard Bernstein
1974 No award
1975 Aaron Copland
1976 Isaac Stern
1977 Alfred A. Knopf

Entertainer of the Year Awards

SULLIVAN PRODUCTIONS, INC.
950 Third Ave., New York, N.Y. 10022 (212/758-9103)

The Entertainer of the Year Awards are given annually in a ceremony videotaped for broadcast from Caesar's Palace in Las Vegas for achievements in music, comedy and other fields of entertainment. The winners received statues of George M. Cohan, which are better known as Georgies. Selection is made by a mail vote of the membership of the American Guild of Variety Artists.

ENTERTAINER OF THE YEAR
1970 Bob Hope
1971 Bob Hope
1972 Liza Minnelli
1973 Sammy Davis, Jr.
1974 No award
1975 Ben Vereen
1976 Johnny Carson
1977 Totie Fields

MALE SINGING STAR OF THE YEAR/MALE VOCALIST OF THE YEAR
1970 Tom Jones
1971 Tom Jones
1972 Neil Diamond
1973 Sammy Davis, Jr.
1974 No award
1975 John Denver
1976 Barry Manilow
1977 Engelbert Humperdinck

FEMALE SINGING STAR OF THE YEAR/FEMALE VOCALIST OF THE YEAR
1970 Barbra Streisand
1971 Barbra Streisand
1972 Vikki Carr
1973 Roberta Flack
1974 Helen Reddy
1975 Shirley Bassey
1976 Eydie Gorme
1977 Barbra Streisand

MALE COMEDY STAR OF THE YEAR
1970 Flip Wilson
1971 Flip Wilson
1972 Carroll O'Connor
1973 Redd Foxx
1974 Rich Little
1975 Paul Lynde
1976 David Brenner
1977 Steve Martin

FEMALE COMEDY STAR OF THE YEAR
1970 Carol Burnett

1971 Carol Burnett
1972 Carol Burnett
1973 Carol Burnett
1974 Carol Burnett
1975 Joan Rivers
1976 Nancy Walker
1977 Totie Fields

MUSICAL GROUP OF THE YEAR/MUSICAL ACT OF THE YEAR/VOCAL ACT OF THE YEAR/VOCAL GROUP OF THE YEAR

1970 Blood, Sweat and Tears
1971 Richard and Karen Carpenter
1972 Sonny and Cher
1973 No award
1974 Chicago
       Gladys Knight and the Pips
1975 Tony Orlando and Dawn
1976 Captain and Tennille
1977 Donny and Marie

INSTRUMENTAL ACT OF THE YEAR

1975 Liberace
1976 Lawrence Welk
1977 Chicago

RISING STAR OF THE YEAR/MOST PROMISING NEWCOMER OF THE YEAR

1970 Melba Moore
1971 Lily Tomlin
1972 Lorna Luft
1973 No award
1974 Olivia Newton-John
1975 Ben Vereen
1976 Natalie Cole
1977 Shields and Yarnell

OUTSTANDING ANIMAL OF THE YEAR/ANIMAL ACT OF THE YEAR

1970 Tanya the Elephant
1971 Tanya the Elephant
1972 No Award
1973 Tanya the Elephant
1974 Mr. Jiggs
1975 Tony the Wonder Horse
1976 Benji
1977 Fred the Bird

COUNTRY AND WESTERN STAR OF THE YEAR/COUNTRY STAR OF THE YEAR

1972 Jimmy Dean
1973 Roy Clark
1974 Charlie Rich
1975 Linda Ronstadt
1976 John Denver
1977 Dolly Parton

SONG AND DANCE STAR OF THE YEAR

1974 Joel Grey
1975 Ben Vereen
1976 Lola Falana
1977 Shirley MacLaine

GOLDEN AWARD

1970 Jimmy Durante
1971 Jack Benny
1972 Duke Ellington
1973 Kate Smith

1974 George Burns
1975 Lucille Ball
1976 Edgar Bergen
1977 Milton Berle

OTHER AWARDS

1970 Radio City Music Hall, Outstanding Production Number of the Year
       Flying Alexanders, Novelty or Circus Act of the Year
1972 Tanya the Elephant, Circus Act of the Year
1973 Gunther Gebel-Williams, Circus Award
       Thomas H. Scallen, Ice Follies, Special Award
1974 Peggy Fleming, Special Attractions Award
1975 Cathy Rigby, Special Attraction of the Year
1976 Jim Hensen's Muppets, Novelty Act and Special Attraction of the Year
1977 Shields and Yarnell, Novelty Act and Special Attraction of the Year

Europe Prize for Folk Art
Hanseatic Goethe Prize
Gottfried von Herder Prizes
Shakespeare Prize
Henrik Steffens Prize
Joost van den Vondel Prize

STIFTUNG F.V.S.
Georgsplatz 10, 2 Hamburg 1, Federal Republic of Germany
(Tel: 33 04 00 and 33 06 00)

The Europe Prize for Folk Art, which carries a 20,000-mark honorarium, recognizes accomplishments in folk art, music and dance.

1973 Folk dance troupe of the Marie Curie Sklodowska University (Lublin, Poland)
       Popular Alsatian Art Group (Berstett, France)
       Finkwarder Speeldeel (Hamburg, Germany)
1974 France Marolt Folklore Academy (Lubljana, Yugoslavia)
       Folksong group (Plana, Bulgaria)
       Leksands troupe (Leksand, Sweden)
       Siamsa Tire, Irish Folk Theatre (Kerry, Ireland)
       Alois Senti (Bern, Switzerland)
1975 Bela Bartok Folkdance Ensemble (Budapest, Hungary)
       Calusul Folk Art Ensemble (Scornicesti-Olt, Rumania)
       Renaat Veremanskoor (Bruges, Belgium)
       Tarvon Troupe (Helsinki, Finland)
       Alfred Cammann, education commissioner (Bremen, Germany)
1976 Not available at press time
1977 Not available at press time

The Hanseatic Goethe Prize, which carries a 31,000-mark cash award, is given biennially to honor intellectual and humanitarian works which transcend national boundaries, The cash consists of a 25,000-mark prize and a 6,000-mark stipend.

1950 Carl Jacob Burckhardt (Switzerland)
1951 Martin Buber (Israel)
1952 Eduard Spranger (Tubingen, Germany)
1953 Bishop Eivind Berggrav (Norway)
1954 Thomas Stearns Eliot (Great Britain)
1955 Gabriel Marcel (France)
1956 Walter Gropius (U.S.A.)

1957 Alfred Weber (Heidelberg, Germany)
1958 Paul Tillich (U.S.A.)
1959 Theodor Heuss (Bonn, Germany)
1961 Benjamin Britten (Great Britain)
1963 Wilhelm Flitner (Hamburg, Germany)
1965 Hans Arp (France)
1967 Salvador de Madariaga (Spain and Great Britain)
1969 Robert Minder (France)
1971 Giorgio Strehler (Italy)
1972 Albin Lesky (Austria)
1973 Manes Sperber (France)
1975 Carlo Schmid (Bonn, Germany)
1977 Willem A. Vissert't Hooft (Geneva, Switzerland)

The Gottfried von Herder Prizes, which carry 20,000-mark honoraria, are given annually to seven individuals for the preservation of cultural life in eastern and southeastern Europe. Art, city planning, conservation, folklore and philosophy are among the fields in which such achievement is recognized. A jury selects the winners of the prizes, which are administered by the University of Vienna.

1964 Jan Kott (Poland)
Stanislaw Lorentz (Poland)
Otto Bihalji-Merin (Yugoslavia)
Lucijan Maria Skerjanc (Yugoslavia)
1965 Emanuel Hruska (Czechoslovakia)
Hugo Rokyta (Czechoslovakia)
Zoltan Kodaly (Hungary)
Laszlo Nemeth (Hungary)
Tudor Arghezi (Rumania)
Christo Vakareski (Bulgaria)
Manolis Chatzidakis (Greece)
1966 Aleksander Kobzdej (Poland)
Jan Cikker (Czechoslovakia)
Zlatko Gorjan (Yugoslavia)
Niko Kuret (Yugoslavia)
Dezso Dercsenyi (Hungary)
Dimiter Statkow (Bulgaria)
Anton Kriesis (Greece)
1967 Witold Lutoslawski (Poland)
Vladimir Kompanek (Czechoslovakia)
Svetozar Radojcic (Yugoslavia)
Ivan Fenyo (Hungary)
Alexandru Philippide (Rumania)
Mihai Pop (Rumania)
Spyridon Marinatos (Greece)
1968 Roman Ingarden (Poland)
Ludvik Kunz (Czechoslovakia)
Miroslav Krleza (Yugoslavia)
Lajos Vayer (Hungary)
Constantin Daicoviciu (Rumania)
Pantscho Wladigeroff (Bulgaria)
Anastasios Orlandos (Greece)
1969 Ksawery Piwocki (Poland)
Albin Brunovsky (Czechoslovakia)
Bohuslav Fuchs (Czechoslovakia)
Marijan Matkovic (Yugoslavia)
France Stele (Yugoslavia)
Jolan Balogh (Hungary)
Mihail Jora (Rumania)
1970 Jan Bialostocki (Poland)
Jan Filip (Czechoslovakia)
Milovan Gavazzi (Yugoslavia)
Gyula Illyes (Hungary)
Zoltan Franyo (Rumania)
Zeko Torbov (Bulgaria)
Yannis A. Papaioannou (Greece)
1971 Kazimierz Michalowski (Bulgaria)

Jiri Kolar (Czechoslovakia)
Blaze Koneski (Yugoslavia)
Bence Szabolsci (Hungary)
Zaharia Stancu (Rumania)
Michael Sokolovski (Bulgaria)
Georgios A. Megas (Greece)
1972 Henryk Stazewski (Poland)
Jaroslav Pesina (Czechoslovakia)
Dragotin Cvetko (Yugoslavia)
Branko Maksimovic (Yugoslavia)
Gyula Ortutay (Hungary)
Virgil Vatasianu (Rumania)
Atanas Dalcev (Bulgaria)
1973 Zbigniew Herbert (Czechoslovakia)
Jan Racek (Czechoslovakia)
Peter Lubarda (Yugoslavia)
Janos Harmatta (Hungary)
Eugen Jebeleanu (Rumania)
Veselin Besevliev (Bulgaria)
Stylianos Charkianakis (Greece)
1974 Wladyslaw Czerny (Poland)
Jan Podolak (Czechoslovakia)
Ivo Franges (Yugoslavia)
Laszlo Gero (Hungary)
Zeno Vancea (Rumania)
Ivan Dujcev (Bulgaria)
Stylianos Pelekanidis (Greece)
1975 Jozef Burszta (Poland)
Stanislav Libensky (Czechoslovakia)
Stanojlo Rajicic (Yugoslavia)
Gabor Preisich (Hungary)
Maria A. Musicescu (Rumania)
Christo M. Danov (Bulgaria)
Pandelis Prevelakis (Greece)
1976 Jagoda Buic (Yugoslavia)
Marin Goleminov (Bulgaria)
Joannes Theoph (Greece)
Deszo Keresztury (Hungary)
Nichita Stanescu (Rumania)
Rudolf Turek (Czechoslovakia)
Kazimierz Wejchert (Poland)
1977 Riko Debenjak, (Yugoslavia)
Emmanuel Kriaras, (Greece)
Albert Kutal, (Czechoslovakia)
Mate Major, (Hungary)
Krzysztof Penderecki, (Poland)
Anastas Petrov, (Bulgaria)
Ion Vladutiu, (Rumania)

The Shakespeare Prize, which carries a 25,000-mark cash award and a 6,000-mark stipend, is given for accomplishments in the arts, architecture, archeology, folklore or music stemming from Europe's English-speaking countries. The award was given briefly in the 1930s, dropped, and has been renewed as an annual honor.

1937 R.C. Williams, Composer
1938 John Masefield, Poet
1967 Peter Hall, Producer and director
1968 Graham Greene, Author
1969 Roy Pascal, German professor
1970 Harold Pinter, Playwright, actor and producer
1971 Janet Baker, Singer
1972 Paul Scofield, Actor
1973 Peter Brook, Producer and director
1974 Graham Sutherland, Artist
1975 John Pritchard, Director
1976 Philip A. Larkin, Poet
1977 John Dexter, Producer

The Henrik Steffens Prize, which carries a 25,000-mark cash award and a 6,000-mark stipend, is given annually for accomplishments in the arts, archeology, folklore or music stemming from Scandinavia. The award is administered by the University of Kiel.

1966 Rolf Herman Nevanlinna (Finland)
1967 Johannes Edfelt (Sweden)
1968 Asbjorn E. Herteig (Norway)
1969 Carl-Henning Pederson (Denmark)
1970 Magnus Mar Larusson (Iceland)
1971 Arvi Kivimaa (Finland)
1972 Harry Martinson (Sweden)
1973 Rolf Nesch (Norway)
1974 Villy Sorensen (Denmark)
1975 Hannes Petursson (Iceland)
1976 Bjorn Landstrom (Finland)
1977 Not available at press time

The Joost van den Vondel Prize, which carries a 20,000 Swiss franc cash award, annually honors achievements in Low German, Flemish or Dutch culture. A jury selects the recipients of the prize, which is administered by Munster University.

1960 Antoon Coolen (Netherlands)
  Max Lamberty (Belgium)
1961 Rev. Christian Boeck (Germany)
1962 Frans Masereel (Belgium, Flemish)
1963 Albert van Balsum (Netherlands)
1964 Hermann Teuchert (Germany)
1965 Monsg. Honore von Waeyenbergh (Belgium)
1966 Jef Last (Netherlands)
1967 Hans M. Ruwoldt (Germany)
1968 Maurits de Meyer (Belgium, Flemish)
1969 Klaas Hanzen Heeroma (Netherlands)
1970 Franz Petri (Germany)
1971 Fernand Jozef Maria Collin (Belgium, Flemish)
1972 Horst Gerson (Netherlands)
1973 Peter Elster (Germany)
1974 Leo Cappuyns (Belgium)
1975 Hebe Kohlbrugge (Netherlands)
1976 Not available at press time
1977 Not available at press time

Charles Lang Freer Medal

SMITHSONIAN INSTITUTION
1000 Jefferson Dr. SW, Washington, D.C. 20560
(202/628-4422)

The Charles Lang Freer Medal, which is of bronze, is awarded as merited for distinguished contribution to the knowledge and understanding of Oriental civilizations as reflected in their arts.

1956 Osvald Siren (Stockholm), Chinese art
1960 Ernst Kuhnel, Islamic art
1965 Yukio Yashiro (Osio, Japan) Japanese scholarship
1973 Tanaka Ichimatsu, Japanese painting

Golden Apple Trophy

CUE MAGAZINE
545 Madison Ave., New York, N.Y. 10022 (212/371-6900)

The Golden Apple Trophy is given annually for service to New York in the fields of entertainment or leisure. The editors select the receipients of this honor in a changing series of categories.

1976 Abraham Beame, Special award for contributions to New York City
  All the President's Men, Best motion picture
  Robert Redford, *All the President's Men,* Best motion picture performance by an actor
  For Colored Girls Who Have Considered Suicide / When the Rainbow is Enuf, Best play
  Jack Weston, *California Suite,* Best performance by an actor in a play
  Rita Moreno, *The Ritz,* Best motion picture performance by an actress
  Preston Jones, *A Texas Trilogy,* Playwright award
  Jane Oliver, Cabaret award
  James Levine, Metropolitan Opera, Conducting award
  Clamma Dale, Opera award
  Martine van Hamel, American Ballet Theatre, Dance award
  Rich Man, Poor Man, Television award
  WNYC-FM, Radio award
  George Benson, *Breezin',* Best record album
  WNEW-TV, Community service programming
  Thurman Munson, Sports award
  Tavern on the Green, Best restaurant
1977 Market Square, World Trade Center, Best restaurant
  Annie, Best Musical
  The Gin Game, Best play
  The Fantasticks, Special award
  Al Pacino, *The Private War of Pavlo Hummel,* Best performance by an actor in a play
  Estelle Parsons, *Miss Margerita's Way,* Best performance by an actress in a play
  Mike Nichols, *The Gin Game,* Best director
  Mike Ashford and Valerie Simpson, *Send It,* Best single
  James Taylor, *J.T.,* Best album
  Shirley MacLaine, Special award
  Commissioner Arlene Wolf, Public service award
  Annie Hall, Best movie
  Richard Burton, *Equus,* Best motion picture performance by an actor
  Jane Fonda, *Julia,* Best motion picture performance by an actress
  Erich Leinsdorf, Conducting award
  Alice Tully, Special award
  New York Yankees, Sports award
  Shirley Verrett, Opera award
  Cy Coleman, *I Love My Wife,* Composing award
  WNCN-Radio, Radio award
  WNET/13, Television award

Handel Medallion

CITY OF NEW YORK
Office of the Mayor, City Hall, New York, N.Y. 10007
(212/566-1520)

The Handel Medallion is the City of New York's highest cultural award and is given as merited to outstanding figures in the arts who have contributed to the cultural life of the city. The Mayor's staff selects the recipients

1959 John Celebre
  Hon. John M. Conway
  Thea Dispeker
  Hon. Ruggero Ferace di Villeforesta
  Robert W. Dowling

John Effrat
Equitable Choral Club
Georg Federer
Virginia Innes-Brown
Newel Jenkins
Antoine T. Koppers
John E. McCarthy
John McKeen
James F. Oates
Charles Pappas
Richard C. Patterson, Jr.
James J. Rorimer
Rose M. Singer
Hon. Sir Hugh Stephenson
William Zeckendorf
1960 Elizabeth Barry
Sara Baum
Stuart Canin
Joan Davis
Malcolm Frager
Jaime Laredo
Isaac Stern
1961 No award
1962 No award
1963 Rudolf Bing
Leopold Stokowski
Earl Wrightson
1964 S. Arthur Keith-Swenson
Sidney Poitier
John D. Rockefeller III
George Seuffert
Paul Taubman
1965 Band of the Fiji Military Forces
Joseph B. Martinson
Henry Moore
Carlos Moseley
Julius Rudel
1966 Pablo Casals
Justino Diaz
Benny Goodman
Lionel Hampton
Jane Marsh
Jan Peerce
David Sarnoff
1967 Robert Russell Bennett
Marc Chagall
George T. Delacorte
Rebekah Harkness
Richard Rodgers
William Schuman
Richard Tucker
1968 Charles Beetz
Janet Schenck
1969 Milton Cross
Helen Hull
Claire Reis
Peter Wilhousky
1970 George Balanchine
Ben Chancy
Martha Graham
Hall Johnson
Robert Merrill
John L. Motley
Alice Tully
William Warfield
1971 Aaron Copland
Dorothy Kirsten
Joseph Papp
1972 Charles Chaplin
Dizzy Gillespie

Francis Robinson
Virgil Thomson
1973 Harold Arlen
Louis Armstrong
Duke Ellington
Geraldine Fitzgerald
Gary Graffman
Melissa Hayden
Sol Hurok
Louise Nevelson
Arthur Rubinstein
1974 Oratorio Society of New York
1975 Lucia Chase
Joshua Logan
The Metropolitan Opera
Oliver Smith
1976 George Abbott
Agnes de Mille
Dame Margot Fonteyn
Eva Le Gallienne
Yehudi Menuhin
Jerome Robbins
1977 Leonard Bernstein

Man of the Year Award
Woman of the Year Award

HASTY PUDDING INSTITUTE OF 1770
12 Holyoke St., Cambridge, Mass. 02138 (617/547-6360)

The Woman of the Year Award is given annually, almost always to a woman in the theatre or entertainment world. The elaborate award presentation consists of a parade, banquet, presentation of gifts, plaques and other recognition as organized by the Harvard University students who belong to Hasty Pudding. The nomination and balloting procedure of members of Hasty Pudding Theatricals is secret.

1951 Gertrude Lawrence
1952 Barbara Bel Geddes
1953 Mamie Eisenhower
1954 Shirley Booth
1955 Debbie Reynolds
1956 Peggy Ann Garner
1957 Carroll Baker
1958 Katharine Hepburn
1959 Joanne Woodward
1960 Carol Lawrence
1961 Jane Fonda
1962 Piper Laurie
1963 Shirley MacLaine
1964 Rosalind Russell
1965 Lee Remick
1966 Ethel Merman
1967 Lauren Bacall
1968 Angela Lansbury
1970 Dionne Warwicke
1971 Carol Channing
1972 Ruby Keeler
1973 Liza Minnelli
1974 Faye Dunaway
1975 Valerie Harper
1976 Bette Midler
1977 Elizabeth Taylor

More recently, a Man of the Year selection has also been added. The selection and awards procedure is similar but does not include a parade.

1967 Bob Hope
1968 Paul Newman
1969 Bill Cosby
1970 Robert Redford
1971 James Stewart
1972 Dustin Hoffman
1973 Jack Lemmon
1974 Peter Falk
1975 Warren Beatty
1976 Robert Blake
1977 Johnny Carson

Ramon Magsaysay Award

RAMON MAGSAYSAY AWARD FOUNDATION
1680 Roxas Blvd., Manila, Philippines (Tel: 59-19-59 and 59-17-20)

The Ramon Magsaysay Award is given annually in each of five areas of achievement to individuals who exemplify the ideals of Ramon Magsaysay. Accomplishments of the previous five years in government service; public service; community leadership; journalism, literature and communication arts, and international understanding are honored. On August 31, the birthday of Ramon Magsaysay, the five awards are made in Manila to Asians regardless of race, creed, sex or nationality. The award consists of $10,000, a gold medal and a certificate.

1958 Mochtar Lubis (Indonesia), "Promotion of free and courageous press"
R. McCulloch Dick (Scot, Philippines), "Effective publishing as a power for the public good"
1959 Edward Michael Law Yone (Burma) and Tarzie Vittachi (Ceylon), "Responsible editorship"
1960 No award
1961 Amitabha Chowdhury (India), "Upholding high ethical standards"
1962 Chang Chun-Ha (Korea), "Editorial integrity in encouraging creative non-partisan intellectual discourse"
1963 No award
1964 Richard Garrett Wilson (British) and Kayser Sung (Chinese-born British), "Accurate, impartial, probing economic journalism"
1965 Akira Kurosawa (Japan), "Perceptive use of film"
1966 No award
1967 Satyajit Ray (India), "Uncompromising use of film to depict true image of India"
1968 Ton That Thien (Vietnam), "Enduring commitment to free inquiry and debate"
1969 Mitoji Nishimoto (Japan), "Design of Japan's superior educational radio and television broadcast system"
1970 No award
1971 Prayoon Chanyavongs (Thailand), "Pictorial satire and humor in unswerving defence of the public interest"
1972 Yasuji Hanamori (Japan), "Consumer advocacy"
1973 Michiko Ishimure (Japan), "Environmentalist against industrial pollution"
1974 Zacarias B. Sarian (Philippines), "Editing and publishing standards of farm news"
1975 B. George Verghese (India), "Superior developmental reporting of Indian society"
1976 Sombhu Mitra (India), Dramatist
1977 Not available at press time

Gold Medals
Award for Distinguished Service to the Arts
Marjorie Peabody Waite Award
Blashfield Foundation Address

NATIONAL INSTITUTE OF ARTS AND LETTERS
633 W. 155th St., New York, N.Y. 10032 (212/AU 6-1480)

Each year the institute awards two Gold Medals for distinguished achievement in various fields of the arts: words, music and fine arts rotating according to a complicated formula. The award, in all cases, is based on the recipient's entire body of work and consists of a medal designed by Adolph A. Weinman.

1909 Augustus Saint-Gaudens, Sculpture
1910 James Ford Rhodes, History
1911 James Whitcomb Riley, Poetry
1912 W. Rutherford Mead, Architecture
1913 Augustus Thomas, Drama
1914 John Singer Sargent, Painting
1915 William D. Howells, Fiction
1916 John Burroughs, Essays and belles-lettres
1917 Daniel Chester French, Sculpture
1918 William R. Thayer, History and biography
1919 Charles M. Loeffler, Music
1921 Cass Gilbert, Architecture
1922 Eugene G. O'Neill, Drama
1923 Edwin H. Blashfield, Painting
1924 Edith Wharton, Fiction
1925 William C. Brownell, Essays and belles-lettres
1926 Herbert Adams, Sculpture
1927 William M. Sloane, History and biography
1928 George W. Chadwick, Music
1929 Edwin A. Robinson, Poetry
1930 Charles Adams Platt, Architecture
1931 William Gillette, Drama
1932 Gari Melchers, Painting
1933 Booth Tarkington, Fiction
1935 Agnes Repplier, Essays and belles-lettres
1936 George G. Barnard, Sculpture
1937 Charles M. Andrews, History and biography
1938 Walter Damrosch, Music
1939 Robert Frost, Poetry
1940 Williams Adams Delano, Architecture
1941 Robert E. Sherwood, Drama
1942 Cecilia Beaux, Painting
1943 Stephen Vincent Benet, Literature
1944 Willa Cather, Fiction
1945 Paul Manship, Sculpture
1946 Van Wyck Brooks, Essays and criticism
1947 John Alden Carpenter, Music
1948 Charles Austin Beard, History and biography
1949 Frederick Law Olmsted, Architecture
1950 John Sloan, Painting
     Henry L. Mencken, Essays and criticism
1951 James Earle Fraser, Sculpture
     Igor Stravinsky, Music
1952 Thornton Wilder, Fiction
     Carl Sandburg, History and biography
1953 Marianne Craig Moore, Poetry
     Frank Lloyd Wright, Architecture
1954 Maxwell Anderson, Drama
     Reginald Marsh, Graphic Art
1955 Edward Hopper, Painting
     Edmund Wilson, Essays and Criticism
1956 Ivan Mestrovic, Sculpture
     Aaron Copland, Music

1957 **John Dos Passos** Fiction
      Allan Nevins, History and biography
1958 **Conrad Aiken,** Poetry
      Henry R. Shepley, Architecture
1959 **Arthur Miller,** Drama
      George Grosz, Graphic Art
1960 **Charles E. Burchfield,** Painting
      E.B. White, Essays and criticism
1961 **William Zorach,** Sculpture
      Roger Sessions, Music
1962 **William Faulkner,** Fiction
      Samuel Eliot Morison, History and biography
1963 **William Carlos Williams,** Poetry
      Ludwig Mies Van Der Rohe, Architecture
1964 **Lillian Hellman,** Drama
      Ben Shahn, Graphic Art
1965 **Andrew Wyeth,** Painting
      Walter Lippmann, Essays and criticism
1966 **Jacques Lipchitz,** Sculpture
      Virgil Thomson, Music
1967 **Katherine Anne Porter,** Fiction
      Arthur Schlesinger, Jr., History and Biography
1968 **R. Buckminster Fuller,** Architecture
      Wystan Hugh Auden, Poetry
1969 **Tennessee Williams,** Drama
      Leonard Baskin, Graphic Art
1970 **Lewis Mumford,** Belles-lettres
      Georgia O'Keeffe, Painting
1971 **Elliott C. Carter,** Music
      Alexander Calder, Sculpture
1972 **Eudora Welty,** Novels
      Henry Steele Commager, History
1973 **Louis T. Kahn,** Architecture
      John Crowe Ransom, Poetry
1974 **Saul Steinberg,** Graphic Art
1975 **Kenneth Burke,** Belles-lettres and criticism
      Willem de Kooning, Painting
1976 **Leon Edel,** Biography
      Samuel Barber, Music
1977 **Saul Bellow,** Novels
      Isamu Noguchi, Sculpture

The Award for Distinguished Service to the Arts is made as merited to an American citizen who is not a member of the Institute but to whom the world of the arts ows a special debt.

1941 **Robert Moses**
1944 **Samuel S. McClure**
1949 **Mrs. Edward MacDowell**
1952 **Mrs. Simon Guggenheim**
1954 **Sen. J. William Fulbright**
1955 **Henry Allen Moe**
1957 **Francis Henry Taylor**
1958 **Lincoln Kirstein**
1959 **Elizabeth Ames**
1962 **Paul Mellon**
1963 **Mrs. Hugh Bullock**
1965 **Frances Steloff**
1968 **Alfred H. Barr, Jr.**
1969 **Leopold Stokowski**
1970 **Martha Graham**
1973 **Felicia Geffen**
1974 **Walker Evans**
1975 **George Balanchine**
1977 **James Laughlin**

The $1,500 Marjorie Peabody Waite Award is conferred annually on an older person for continuing achievement and integrity in his or her art and is given in rotation to an artist, a composer and a writer.

1956 **Fred Nagler**
1957 **Theodore Ward Chanler**
1958 **Dorothy Parker**
1959 **Leon Hartl**
1960 **Louise Talma**
1961 **Edward McSorley**
1962 **Abraham Walkowitz**
1963 **Richard Donovan**
1964 **Dawn Powell**
1965 **Paul Burlin**
1966 **Harry Partch**
1967 **Stringfellow Barr**
1968 **Abraham Harriton**
1969 **Herbert Elwell**
1970 **Ramon Guthrie**
1971 **Ben Benn**
1972 **Vittorio Rieti**
1973 **A. Hyatt Mayor**
1974 **Ray Prohaska**
1975 **Leo Ornstein**
1976 **Rene Wellek**
1977 **Kenzo Okada**

The Evangeline Wilbour Blashfield Foundation Address was established "to assist . . . in an effort in . . . both the preservation of the English language in its beauty and integrity, and its cautious enrichment by such terms as grown out of modern conditions." The income of the fund is devoted to an annual address on some aspect of the arts or letters by a distinguished speaker.

1917 **Paul Elmer More,** "English and Englistic"
      William Milligan Sloane, "The American Academy and the English Language"
      William Crary Brownell, "The Academy and the Language"
1918 **Brander Matthews,** "The English Language and the American Academy"
1919 **Bliss Perry,** "The Academy and the Language"
1920 **Paul Shorey,** "The American Language
1921 No address
1922 **Henry Van Dyke,** "The Fringe of Words"
1923 **William Crary Brownell,** "Style"
1924 No address
1925 **Robert Underwood Johnson,** "The Glory of Words"
1928 **Wilbur L. Cross,** "The Modern English Novel"
1929 **George Pierce Baker,** "Speech in Drama"
1930 **John H. Finley,** "Virgil's Two Thousand Years"
1931 No address
1932 **Irving Babbitt,** "The Problem of Style in a Democracy"
1933 **Chauncey Brewster Tinker,** "Stedman as a Poet"
1934 **William Lyon Phelps,** "Two American Novels"
1935 No address
1936 No address
1937 **Owen Wister,** "William Dean Howells"
1938 **Hamlin Garland,** "Literary Fashions Old and New"
1939 No address
1940 **Stephen Vincent Benet,** "The Power of the Written Word"
1941 No address
1942 **Lewis Mumford,** "The Salvation of Letters"
1943 **Van Wyck Brooks,** "Thomas Jefferson, Man of Letters"
1944 **Archibald MacLeish,** "The Power of the Spoken Word"
1945 **Walter Lippmann,** "American Destiny"
1946 **J. William Fulbright,** "Our Foreign Policy"
1947 **Helen Keller,** "Power of the Spoken Word"

1948 Thornton Wilder, "A Time of Troubles"
1949 E.M. Forster, "Art for Art's Sake"
1950 Robert Frost, "How Hard It Is to Keep from Being King When It's in You and in the Situation"
1951 Mark Van Doren, "The Artist in the Changing World"
1952 Aaron Copland, "Creativity in America"
1953 Elizabeth Bowen, "Subject and the Time"
1954 Robert E. Sherwood, "Benjamin Franklin's Country"
1955 E.N. Van Kleffens, "The Spoken Word"
1956 Joseph Wood Krutch, "Geometry and Morals"
1957 Salvador de Madariaga, "Meditations on Leonardo's St. Anne"
1958 A. Whitney Griswold, "Further Obsequies for the Grammarian"
1959 Meyer Schapiro, "On the Humanity of Abstract Painting"
1960 Virgil Thomson, "Music Now"
1961 Robert Graves, "The Word Baraka"
1962 Aldous Leonard Huxley, "Utopias, Positive and Negative"
1963 Loren Eiseley, "The Divine Animal"
1964 Sir Kenneth Clark, "Popular Art"
1965 Julian Parks Boyd, "Thomas Jefferson and the Republic of Letters"
1966 Jacob Bronowski, "The Reach of Imagination"
1967 Sir Maurice Bowra, "Useless Knowledge"
1968 Kenneth Burke, "I Just Don't Know: Thoughts on the Problem of Style"
1969 Richard Hughes, "Fiction as Truth"
1970 Muriel Spark, "The Desegregation of Art"
1971 Kurt Vonnegut, Jr., "The Happiest Day in the Life of My Father"
1972 Iris Murdoch, "Salvation by Words"
1973 Victoria Ocampo, "The Nights of Ithaca"
1974 Arthur Schlesinger, Jr., "Language and Politics"
1975 Stephen Spender, "Are We Decadent?"
1976 Henry Steele Commager, "Recreating the Community of Culture"
1977 No address

In addition to these awards in the arts, generally, honors bestowed by the National Institute of Arts and Letters in specific arts will be found elsewhere in this volume.

New York State Award
NEW YORK STATE COUNCIL ON THE ARTS
80 Center St., New York, N.Y. 10013 (212/488-3846)

The New York State Award, which consists of a sculpture, was given until 1975 to honor contributions to the cultural or artistic life of New York State. Individuals and groups were eligible for selection.

1966 Binghamton Commission on Architecture and Urban Design
Buffalo Festival of the Arts Today
Citizens Advisory Committee for the Town and Village of Cazenovia
Corning Community College
Judson Memorial Church, New York
New York State Racing Association, Jamaica
New York Shakespeare Festival, New York
St. James Community Center, New York
Stockade Association, Schenectady
Syracuse Savings Bank
Mrs. Albert D. Lasker

1967 American Craftsmen's Council, New York
Carborundum Co., Niagara Falls
First Unitarian Church of Rochester
Historic Pittsford, Inc.
The Jacob Riis Houses Plaza, New York
Jazzmobile, Inc., New York
Kleinhans Music Hall, Buffalo
Lake George Opera Festival, Glens Falls
New York City Department of Parks
Olana Preservation, Inc., Hudson
Saratoga Performing Arts Center, Saratoga Springs
Whitney Museum of American Art, New York
Ada Louise Huxtable
1968 Albright-Knox Art Gallery, Buffalo
Art on Tour, Scarsdale
Eastern Airlines, New York
Endo Laboratories Inc., Garden City
Ford Foundation, New York
Hudson Valley Philharmonic Society, Poughkeepsie
Lake George Park Commission, Ticonderoga
Paley Park, New York
Society for the Preservation of Landmarks in Western New York, Rochester
Waterford Historical Museum and Cultural Center
WBAI-FM, New York
Alfred H. Barr, Jr.
1969 Air Preheater Company, Inc., Wellsville
American Museum of Natural History, New York
Brooklyn Academy of Music
Committee for a Library in the Jefferson Courthouse, New York
Everson Museum of Art, Syracuse
Geneva Historical Society
Lincoln Center for the Performing Arts, New York
New York University, New York
Albert A. Lasker Foundation, New York
92nd Street Young Men's and Young Women's Hebrew Association, New York
Rochester Museum and Science Center
State University Construction Fund, Albany
Xerox Corporation, Rochester
1970 Adirondack Museum, Blue Mountain Lake
Alice Tully Hall, New York
The Asia Society, New York
Bedford Lincoln Neighborhood Museum (MUSE), Brooklyn
Children's Television Workshop, New York
City Center of Music and Drama, New York
Erie County and the City of Buffalo
Metropolitan Museum of Art, New York
New York State Conservation Bill of Rights
Scriven Foundation and the Citizens of Cooperstown
Syracuse University Press
Youtheatre, Rochester
John B. Hightower
1971 Abraham & Straus, Brooklyn
Center of the Creative and Performing Arts in the State University of New York at Buffalo
James Prendergast Library Association, Jamestown
Lithopinion, New York
South Mall Riverfront Pumping Station, Albany
Temple Beth Zion, Buffalo
Valley Development Foundation, Binghamton
Carl Carmer
Henry Allen Moe
1972 Hudson River Museum, Yonkers

Madison County Historical Society, Oneida
New York City Landmarks Preservation Commission
New York State Bar Association, Albany
Six Nations Indian Museum, Onchiota
Three Village Reconstruction at Stony Brook, Setauket and Old Field, and Ward and Dorothy Melville
George Balanchine
Joseph Papp
1973 Alvin Ailey City Center Dance Theater, New York
County of Orange
Kenan Center, Lockport
La Mama Experimental Theatre Club, New York, and Ellen Stewart
New York Zoological Society (Bronx Zoo), New York
Theatre Development Fund, New York
Martha Graham
1974 Chautauqua Institution
City of Albany and Albany Board of Education
Dance Theatre of Harlem, New York, and Arthur Mitchell
International Arts Relations (INTAR), New York
Municipal Art Society of New York, New York
The New Yorker, New York, and William Shawn
Paper Bag Players, New York
F. & M. Schaefer Brewing Co., Brooklyn
Tri-Cities Opera, Binghamton
Nelson A. Rockefeller
Kenneth Dewey and Donald Harper
1975 Cayuga County Homesite Development Corporation, Auburn
Cooper Union for the Advancement of Science and Art, New York
Corning Glass Works Foundation
Cunningham Dance Foundation, New York
Gotham Book Mart, New York, and Frances Steloff
Negro Ensemble Company, New York
Rensselaer County Junior Museum, Troy
South Street Seaport Museum, New York
Young Filmaker's Foundation, New York
Aaron Copland
Sheldon and Caroline Keck
Seymour H. Knox, Special Citation
1976 No award
1977 No award

Gold Medal Awards

PHOTOPLAY
205 E. 42nd St., New York, N.Y. 10017 (212/983-5600)

In addition to awards specifically in the fields of motion pictures, television and music, *Photoplay* annually gives a Gold Medal to the most popular newcomer entertainers of the year, as voted by readers of the publication.

MALE

1961 Warren Beatty
1962 Gary Clarke
1963 Robert Walker
1964 Robert Goulet
1965 Chris Connelly
1966 Noel Harrison
1967 Henry Darrow
1968 Glen Campbell
1969 Jim Brolin

1970 David Cassidy
1971 Chris Mitchum
1972 David Birney
1973 Tony Musante
1974 Freddie Prinze
1975 Gabe Kaplan
1976 Gregg Henry
1977 Not announced at press time

FEMALE

1961 Deborah Walley
       Paula Prentiss
1962 Suzanne Pleshette
1963 Tippi Hedren
1964 Barbara Parkins
1965 Pat Morrow
1966 Marlo Thomas
1967 Tina Cole
1968 Peggy Lipton
1969 Karen Valentine
1970 Susan Dey
1971 Sandy Duncan
1972 Diana Ross
1973 Michelle Phillips
1974 Julie Kavner
1975 Pamela Hensley
1976 Jaclyn Smith
1977 Not announced at press time

Paul Robeson Citation

ACTORS' EQUITY ASSOCIATION
1500 Broadway, New York, N.Y. 10036 (212/869-8530)

The Paul Robeson Citation Award annually honors the entertainer whose life and career, in the opinion of the awards committee, fill the concepts and fit the example of Paul Robeson himself in terms of concern for his or her fellows and in his or her contributions to the performing arts. A plaque is presented to the winner.

1974 Paul Robeson
1975 Ruby Dee and Ossie Davis
1976 Lillian Hellman
1977 Pete Seeger

Theodore Roosevelt Award

INTERNATIONAL PLATFORM ASSOCIATION
2564 Berkshire Rd., Cleveland Hts., Ohio 44106
(216/932-0505)

The Theodore Roosevelt Award, which consists of an engraved bowl, is given annually for excellence in public speaking.

1973 Henry Kissinger
1974 No award
1975 Gov. Reuben Askew
1976 No award
1977 James Schlesinger

Ruby Award

AFTER DARK
10 Columbus Circle, New York, N.Y. 10019 (212/399-2400)

The Ruby Award named in honor of Ruby Keeler is given annually for outstanding achievements in entertainment and arts. A silver bowl is awarded by a decision of *After Dark* magazine's editors.

1971 Ruby Keeler
1972 Dorothy Collins
1973 Bette Midler
1974 Lucille Ball
1975 Ann-Margret
1976 Barry Manilow
1977 Mae West

Mark Twain Award
INTERNATIONAL PLATFORM ASSOCIATION
2564 Berkshire Rd., Cleveland Hts., Ohio 44106
(216/932-0505)

The Mark Twain Award, which consists of an engraved bowl, is given annually to the individual judged by the IPA Committee as "Mark Twain's successor as America's most delightful entertainer, gentle depictor of the virtues and weaknesses of humanity with humor's paintbrush."

1970 Hal Holbrook
1971 No award
1972 Bob Hope
1973 Erma Bombeck
1974 Victor Borge
1975 Art Buchwald
1976 Jean Shepherd
1977 Norman Lear

Theater

Contents

Related Awards

St. Clair Bayfield Award

ACTORS' EQUITY ASSOCIATION
1500 Broadway, New York, N.Y. 10036 (212/869-8530)

The St. Clair Bayfield Award, which consists of a changing cash prize and a scroll, is given annually to an unfeatured actor or actress in a Shakespearean production staged within fifty miles of New York during the previous season. The panel which selects the winner includes drama critics, Mrs. Bayfield and the President of Actors' Equity.

1973 Barnard Hughes, *Much Ado About Nothing* (Shakespeare in the Park and the Winter Garden Theatre)
1974 Randall Duc Kim, *The Tempest* (Mitzi Newhouse Theatre at Lincoln Center)
1975 John Glover, *The Winter's Tale* (American Shakespeare Festival, Stratford, Conn.)
1976 Caroline McWilliams, *Measure for Measure* (Shakespeare in the Park)
1977 No award

Clarence Derwent Awards

ACTORS' EQUITY ASSOCIATION
1500 Broadway, New York, N.Y. 10036 (212/869-8530)

The Clarence Derwent Awards, which each carry a $1,000 cash prize and an engraved crystal egg, annually honor the most promising male and female actors on the New York metropolitan scene. The award honors a meritorious performance in a supporting part in a Broadway or off-Broadway play. Stars and featured performers are ineligible for consideration by a committee of drama critics.

1945 Frederick O'Neal, *Anna Lucasta*
Judy Holliday, *Kiss Them for Me*
1946 Paul Douglas, *Born Yesterday*
Barbara Bel Geddes, *Deep are the Roots*
1947 Tom Ewell, *John Loves Mary*
Margaret Phillips, *Another Part of The Forest*
1948 Lou Gilbert, *Hope is a Thing With Feathers*
Catherine Ayers, *Moon of the Caribbean* and *Long Way From Home*
1949 Ray Watson, *Summer & Smoke*
Leora Dana, *Mad Woman of Chaillot*
1950 Douglas Watson, *Wisteria Trees*
Gloria Lane, *The Consul*
1951 Logan Ramsey, *High Ground*
Frederic Warriner, *Getting Married*
Phyllis Love, *Rose Tattoo*
1952 Iggie Wolfington, *Mrs. McThing*
Anne Meacham, *The Long Watch*
1953 David J. Stewart, *Camino Real*
Jenny Egan, *The Crucible*
1954 David Lewis, *King of Hearts*
Vilma Murer, *The Winner*
1955 Fritz Weaver, *The White Devil*
Vivian Nathan, *Anastasia*
1956 Gerald Hiken, *Uncle Vanya*
Frances Sternhagen, *The Admiral Bashville*
1957 Ellis Rabb, *The Misanthrope*
Joan Croydon, *The Potting Shed*
1958 George C. Scott, *Richard III*
Colin Wilcox, *The Day the Money Stopped*
1959 David Hurst, *Look After Lulu*
Lois Nettleton, *God & Kate Murphy*
1960 Rochelle Oliver, *Toys in the Attic*

William Daniels, *The Zoo Story*
1961 Rosemary Murphy, *Period of Adjustment*
Eric Christmas, *Little Moon of Alban*
1962 Rebecca Darke, *Who'll Save the Plowboy?*
Gene Wilder, *Complaisant Lover*
1963 Jessica Walter, *Photo Finish*
Gene Hackman, *Children From Their Games*
1964 Joyce Ebert, *The Trojan Women*
Richard McMurray, *A Case of Libel*
1965 Elizabeth Hubbard, *The Physicist*
Jame Sanchez, *Conerico Was Here to Stay*
1966 Jean Hepple, *Sgt. Musgrave's Dance*
Christopher Walken, *The Lion in Winter*
1967 Reva Rose, *You're A Good Man, Charlie Brown*
Austin Pendleton, *The Alchemist*
1968 Catherine Burns, *The Prime of Miss Jean Brodie*
David Birney, *Summertree*
1969 Marlene Warfield, *Great White Hope*
Ron O'Neal, *No Place to Be Somebody*
1970 Pamela Payton-Wright, *The Effect of Gamma Rays on Man in the Moon Marigolds*
Jeremiah Sullivan, *A Scent of Flower*
1971 Katherine Helmond, *The House of Blue Leaves*
James Woods, *Saved*
1972 Pamela Bellwood, *Butterflies are Free*
Richard Backus, *Promenade All*
1973 Mari Gorman, *Hot L Baltimore*
Christopher Murney, *Tricks*
1974 Ann Reinking, *Over Here*
Thom Christopher, *Noel Coward in 2 Keys*
1975 Marybeth Hurt, *Love For Love*
Reyno, *The First Breeze of Summer*
1976 Nancy Snyder, *Knock, Knock*
Peter Evans, *Streamers*
1977 Rose Gregorio, *The Shadow Box*
Barry Preston, *Bubbling Brown Sugar*

SPECIAL CITATION:

1966 Tom Ahearne, *Hogan's Goat*
1967 Philio Bosco, *Hal Scrawdyke*

Actors' Fund Medal Award of Merit

ACTORS' FUND OF AMERICA
1501 Broadway, Suite 2600, New York, N.Y. 10036 (212/221-7300)

The Actors' Fund Medal With Citation is awarded as merited for service to the theatre. The medal was given once, retired and reactivated in 1958. The board of trustees selects the winners.

1910 President William Howard Taft, Opening of Actors' Fund Fair
1958 Walter Vincent
Charles Dow Clark
Helen Hayes
Actors' Equity Association
League of New York Theatres
J. J. Shubert
Fact Finding Committee of Entertainment Unions in New York City
1959 Council of Resident Stock Theatres
Council of Stock Theatres
Musical Arena Theatre Association
Stephen P. Kennedy
Ralph Bellamy
Mary Martin

1960 Music Fair Enterprise
Nanette Fabray
Sam Levene
1962 American Shakespeare Festival
Hon. Robert F. Wagner
1963 Newbold Morris
League of Off-Broadway Theatres
Lawrence Shubert Lawrence, Jr.
1964 Angus Duncan
Floyd W. Stoker
Zero Mostel
1966 Warren A. Schenck
1967 Ed Sullivan
1968 Angela Lansbury
1969 Hon. John V. Lindsay
1970 Katharine Hepburn
Brooks Atkinson
Ethel Merman
1971 Danny Kaye
Richard Rodgers
Warren P. Munsell
1972 Alfred Lunt and Lynn Fontanne
Harold Prince for *Fiddler On The Roof*
Neil Simon
1973 Clive Barnes
Harry Hershfield
1974 Debbie Reynolds
Jacob I. Goodstein
1975 Robert Preston
Vincent Sardi
Ellen Burstyn
Charles Grodin
1976 Louis A. Lotito
1977 Joseph Papp, New York Shakespeare Festival

The Actors' Fund Award of Merit is given as warranted for service to the Actors' Fund both on and off the stage. The board of trustees selects the winners, of whom there have been too many to list—more than a thousand in the past twenty years.

Richard Craven Award
AMERICAN HUMANE ASSOCIATION,
5351 S. Roslyn, Engelwood, Colo. 80110 (303/779-1400)

The Richard Craven Award, which consists of a trophy, is given annually (or as merited) for an outstanding feat performed by an animal before a live audience, either in theatre, rodeo or other entertainment. Animal performances for television and films are not eligible for this award. However, for details on the selection procedure, see the Patsy listing on p. 242 in the CINEMA Section.

1951 Tamba Tamba (chimpanzee)
1952 Smoky (fighting stallion)
1953 Brackett (jumping horse)
1954 Cocaine (falling horse)
1955 Flash (falling and lying-down horse)
1956 Flame (German shepherd)
1957 King Cotton (white stallion)
1958 Roy Rogers and Trigger (25th anniversary in show business)
1959 Baldy (rearing horse)
1960 Sharkey, Dempsey, Choctaw and Joker (four-up horse team)
1961 No award
1962 No Award

1963 Mickey O'Boyle (fighting horse)
1964 No award
1965 Little Buck (falling and lying-down horse)
1966 Smoky (trick horse)
1967 No award
1968 No award
1969 No award
1970 No award
1971 Kilroy (falling horse)
1972 Cocaine (falling horse)
1973 No award
1974 No award
1975 No award
1976 No award
1977 No award

Delia Austrian Medal
DRAMA LEAGUE OF NEW YORK
c/o Mrs. Edward A. Hansen, 555 Park Ave., New York, N.Y. 10028 (212/838-5859)

The Delia Austrian Medal, which is of bronze, is presented annually for the most outstanding performance of the season on the New York stage. It may be awarded to an actor or an actress, but performances in one-man shows are not considered. The winner is chosen by a vote of the membership.

1935 Katharine Cornell, *Romeo and Juliet*
1936 Helen Hayes, *Victoria Regina*
1937 Maurice Evans, *Richard III*
1938 Cedric Hardwicke, *Shadow and Substance*
1939 Raymond Massey, *Abe Lincoln in Illinois*
1940 Paul Muni, *Key Largo*
1941 Paul Lukas, *Watch on the Rhine*
1942 Judith Evelyn, *Angel Street*
1943 Alfred Lunt and Lynn Fontanne, *The Pirate*
1944 Elisabeth Bergner, *The Two Mrs. Carrolls*
1945 Mady Christians, *I Remember Mama*
1946 Louis Calhern, *The Magnificent Yankee*
1947 Ingrid Bergman, *Joan of Lorraine*
1948 Judith Anderson, *Medea*
1949 Robert Morley, *Edward My Son*
1950 Grace George, *The Velvet Glove*
1951 Claude Rains, *Darkness at Noon*
1952 Julie Harris, *I Am A Camera*
1953 Shirley Booth, *Time of the Cuckoo*
1954 Josephine Hull, *The Solid Gold Cadillac*
1955 Viveca Lindfors, *Anastasia*
1956 David Wayne, *The Ponder Heart*
1957 Eli Wallach, *Major Barbara*
1958 Ralph Bellamy, *Sunrise at Campobello*
1959 Cyril Ritchard, *The Pleasure of His Company*
1960 Jessica Tandy, *Five Finger Exercise*
1961 Hume Cronyn, *Big Fish, Little Fish*
1962 Paul Scofield, *A Man For All Seasons*
1963 Charles Boyer, *Lord Pengo*
1964 Alec Guinness, *Dylan*
1965 John Gielgud, *Tiny Alice*
1966 Richard Kiley, *Man of La Mancha*
1967 Rosemary Harris, *The Wild Duck*
1968 Zoe Caldwell, *The Prime of Miss Jean Brodie*
1969 Alec McCowen, *Hadrian The Seventh*
1970 James Stewart, *Harvey*
1971 Anthony Quayle, *Sleuth*
1972 Eileen Atkins, Claire Bloom, *Vivat! Vivat! Regina*
1973 Alan Bates, *Butley*
1974 Christopher Plummer, *The Good Doctor*

1975 John Wood, *Sherlock Holmes*
1976 Eva Le Gallienne, *The Royal Family*
1977 Tom Courtney, *Otherwise Engaged*

George Jean Nathan Award

GEORGE JEAN NATHAN TRUST
c/o Manufacturers Hanover Trust, 600 Fifth Ave., New York, N.Y. 10020 (212/350-4469)

The George Jean Nathan Award for Dramatic Criticism, which consists of $5,000, a citation and a silver medallion, is given annually for outstanding writings on the legitimate theater or drama criticism. Authors, critics and reviewers who are United States citizens and whose work is published in U.S. newspapers, magazines, books or other periodicals or is broadcast on television or radio programs originating in the U.S. are eligible. Authors or publishers may submit work published during the theatrical year for evaluation by the selection committee, which consists of the heads of the English Departments at Cornell, Princeton and Yale universities.

1959 **Harold Clurman,** Drama critic (*The Nation*) and author of reviews and essays ("Lies Like Truth")
1960 **C.L. Barber,** Amherst College, author (*Shakespeare's Festive Comedy*)
1961 **Jerry Tallmer,** drama critic (*The Village Voice*), for reviews, particularly of the off-Broadway theater
1962 **Robert Brustein,** theater critic (*The New Republic*) for articles and reviews
1963 **Walter Kerr,** drama critic (*New York Herald-Tribune*)
1964 **Elliot Norton,** drama critic (*Boston Record American* and *Sunday Advertiser*) for newspaper and television reviews
1965 **Gerald Weales,** University of Pennsylvania, for reviews in *Drama Survey*
1966 **Eric Russell Bentley,** Columbia University, for articles, two of which appeared in the *Tulane Drama Review*
1967 **Elizabeth Hardwick,** advisory editor (*New York Review of Books*) for reviews and discussions
1968 **Martin Gottfried,** drama critic (*Women's Wear Daily*) for book (*A Theater Divided: The Postwar American Stage*)
1969 **John Lahr,** drama critic (*Evergreen Review* and *The Village Voice*) and for essays
1970 **John Simon,** drama critic (*Hudson Review* and *New York Magazine*) for reviews
1971 **Richard Gilman,** Yale University, author (*Common and Uncommon Masks: Writings on Theatre, 1961-1970*)
1972 **Jay Carr,** theater and music critic (*Detroit News*) for selected drama reviews
1973 **Stanley Kauffmann,** film and theater critic (*New Republic*) for selected drama reviews
1974 **Albert Bermel,** City University of New York, for selected drama reviews
1976 **Michael Goldman,** Princeton University, author (*The Actor's Freedom: Toward a Theory of Drama*)
1977 **Bernard Knox,** Center for Hellenic Studies, Washington, D.C., review of *Agamemnon* published in The *New York Review of Books*

NETC Annual Award
NETC Community Theatre Drama Festival Award
NETC Special Award
John Gassner Memorial Playwriting Award
Moss Hart Memorial Award

NEW ENGLAND THEATRE CONFERENCE
50 Exchange St., Waltham, Mass. 02154 (617/893-3120)

The NETC Annual Award honors significant creative achievement by individuals, groups or organizations in the performing arts. A Revere bowl is awarded to the prize winner, who is selected by nominations from the NETC membership, board of directors and advisory council and chosen by the board and council.

1957 Jo Mielziner
1958 Joshua Logan
1959 Richard Rodgers and Oscar Hammerstein II
1960 Moss Hart
1961 Howard Lindsay and Russel Crouse
1962 Lawrence Langner
1963 Joseph Papp
1964 Repertory Theater of Lincoln Center (Harold Clurman, Elia Kazan and Robert Whitehead)
1965 Morris Carnovsky
1966 William Gibson
1967 David Hays
1968 David Merrick
1969 Arthur Miller
1970 Harold Prince
1971 The Open Theatre
1972 John Houseman
1973 Lillian Hellman
1974 Elliot Norton
1975 Eva Le Gallienne
1976 Adrian Hall
1977 Cheryl Crawford

The winner of the NETC Community Theatre Drama Festival Award receives a trophy honoring the best production of a New England community theatre production. A professional adjudicator sees all productions and offers a public critique of each to select the recipient.

1954 Natick Footlighters (Natick, Mass.), *Fumed Oak*
1955 Quannapowitt Players (Reading, Mass.), *The Old Lady Shows Her Medals*
1956 Linden Players (Needham, Mass.), *The Full House*
1957 Civic League Players (Framingham, Mass.), *Fumed Oak*
1958 M.I.T. Community Players (Cambridge, Mass.), *A Phoenix Too Frequent*
1959 Concord Players (Concord, Mass.), *A Trap Is a Small Place*
1960 Norwood Curtain-Timers (Norwood, Mass.), *Cat On a Hot Tin Roof*
1961 Shrewsbury Players Guild (Shrewsbury, Mass.), *No Exit*
1962 Community Players (Framingham, Mass.), *Waltz of the Toreadors*
1963 Concord Players, (Concord, Mass.), *The Browning Version*
1964 Drama Workshop (Worcester Community Center, Worcester, Mass.), *The Death of Bessie Smith*

1965 Entr' Actors Guild (Worcester, Mass.), *The Bald Soprano*
1966 Hovey Players (Waltham, Mass.), *Snowangel*
1967 Concord Players (Concord, Mass.), *A Taste of Honey*
1968 Entr'Actors Guild (Worcester, Mass.), *Chamber Music*
1969 Winthrop Playmakers (Winthrop, Mass.), *Crawling Arnold*
1970 Entr'Actors Guild (Worcester, Mass.), *Interview*
1971 Center Players (Springfield, Mass.), *The Lion in Winter*
1972 Entr'Actors Guild (Worcester, Mass.), *Brecht on Brecht*
1973 Sudbury Players (Sudbury, Mass.), *Schubert's Last Serenade*
1974 Garrett Players (Lawrence, Mass.), *Endgame*
1975 Newton Country Players (Newton, Mass.), *The Real Inspector Hound*
1976 Garrett Players (Lawrence, Mass.), *1776*
1977 Marblehead Little Theatre (Marblehead, Mass.), *The Love Course*

The NETC Special Award annually recognizes national achievement, contribution or innovation in the interest, support and advancement of theatre on a national level. A plaque is awarded to the winner, who is nominated by the NETC membership, board of directors and advisory council and selected by the board and council.

1957 Hill and Wang
1958 Norris Houghton
1959 *Playhouse 90*
1960 David Susskind
1961 Grove Press and National Thespian Society
1962 The Living Theatre
1963 Frederick O'Neal
1964 Richard Boone, Jewish Theological Seminary of America and Raymond Sovey
1965 Alvin Ailey, Free Southern Theatre, John Gassner and Adrienne Kennedy
1966 American Place Theatre and Viola Spolin
1967 Horace Armistead, Theodore Fuchs, Earle Hyman and Stanley McCandless
1968 Orlin and Irene Corey, Lyn Ely and Tom O'Horgan
1969 Karl Malden, Julius L. Novick, The Playwrights' Unit and Budd Schulberg and the Watts Writers' Workshop and Edwin Sherin
1970 Boris Aronson, Michael Butler, Joe Layton and Peter Stone
1971 Merce Cunningham and The Chelsea Theater Center
1972 American Playwrights' Theatre and Harold Scott
1973 Alexander H. Cohen and Patricia Zipprodt
1974 Brooks Atkinson, Zelda Fichandler and Louis Sheaffer
1975 Theatre Development Fund and *The Village Voice*
1976 Alois Nagler, *Theater in America* and Theatre Communications Group
1977 Lehman Engel and Manhattan Theatre Club

Regional Citations annually honor accomplishments of New England regional theatre. The honors listed for all of the years below are separate, not joint, awards.

1957 Community Players of Concord, N.H., and **Massachusetts** High School Drama Guild
1958 Herschel L. Bricker, F. Curtis Canfield, Harlan F. Grant and WGBH, Boston

1959 The Council for a TV Course in the Humanities in the Secondary School, Gregory Falls, Newton High School and Poet's Theatre
1960 Marston Balch, The Charles Playhouse, WBZ-TV and Barbara Wellington
1961 Boston Arts Festival, Boston Children's Theatre, Mrs. Howard J. Chidley, Elliot Norton and Edwin Burr Pettet
1962 Joseph D. Batcheller, *Boston Globe*, Harold L. Cail, Marie L. Phillips, Portland Children's Theatre, Provincetown Playhouse and Weston Community Club, Inc. and The Townspeople of Weston, Vt.
1963 Warner Bentley, Boston College, Premiere Performance Company and Elsi Rowland
1964 Lucy Barton, Sarah Caldwell, Ruth St. Denis and Ted Shawn
1965 The Boston Herald Traveler Corporation, Connecticut College, Edward Finnegan, Hartford Stage Company, Theatre by the Sea (Portsmouth, N.H.) and Trinity Square Repertory Company
1966 Boston University School of Fine and Applied Arts, Francis Grover Cleveland, Richard Eberhart, Long Wharf Theatre and Theatre Company of Boston
1967 Arlington Friends of the Drama, Edward C. Cole, Elma Lewis and Project TRY
1968 Boston Herald Traveler Corporation, Harvey Grossman, Robert J. Guest, Northeastern University and George C. White, Jr.
1969 *Boston After Dark*, Brandeis University Theatre Arts Department, Entr' Actors Guild, Looking Glass Theatre and Jack Stein
1970 Emerson College Musical Theatre Society, !Improvise!, *Maine Times*, The Proposition and James Spruill
1971 Maxine Klein, Stage I Drama Workshop, Theatre Workshop Boston, Inc., and Rhode Island Festival: Theatre '71 (Brown University, Providence College, Rhode Island College, Rhode Island Junior College, Rhode Island School of Design, Roger Williams College, the University of Rhode Island, and the Rhode Island State Council on the Arts)
1972 Sarah Minchin Baker, Fisherman's Players of Cape Cod/Richard Waters, Sen. Claiborne Pell, Summerthing and E. Virginia Williams
1973 Richard Kneeland, Metropolitan Cultural Alliance, William H. Rough and Theatre Association of Maine
1974 Tony Montanaro and the Celebration Mime Theatre, Eugene O'Neill Memorial Theater Center and Gerald Roberts
1975 Harvard Theatre Collection and Stage/West
1976 Bread and Puppet Theatre, Michael P. Price/-Goodspeed Opera House, Ralf Coleman and Gustave Johnson
1977 Norman H. Leger, Evangeline Machlin and Pilobolus Dance Theatre

The John Gassner Memorial Playwriting Award, which consists of a cash stipend of to $150 plus script-in-hand showcase performance with critique, is offered for the best new, original, one-act play by a U.S. playwright. The play must be commercially unpublished, unproduced and of a twenty-minute to one-hour duration. A screening committee reads all entered plays and selects about two dozen which are submitted to the judging committee, which chooses the winner. Runnerup cash awards are also made.

1963 George Hickenlooper, *Caviar For the General*
       Robert Lehan, *A Matter of Character*
       Jack Murphy, *Benjamin*
       Brice Weisman, *Beamlight With the Red Flasher*
1964 Robert Lehan, *The Waiting Room*
       Jack Murphy, *Golden Days*
1965 No award
1966 Gerald Kean, *Immediate Occupancy*
1967 Tim Kelly, *The Natives Are Restless*
1968 No award
1969 Eric Meredith Lord, *Lions Four, Christians Nothing*
1970 Craig Clinton, *The Lunch Hours*
1971 Burt French, *Thank You, Mrs. Garrigan; It Was Nothing Mr. God*
1972 Burt French, *Chowder and Cherries*
1973 L.E. Preston, *It's Your Move*
1974 Rome Kingson, *Love in Little Wotting*
1975 Richard Barron, *National Pastime*
1976 Robert Lehan, *Lovesong*
1977 John C. Cox, *The Waverly Local*

The Moss Hart Memorial Award is a trophy given annually for superior production of a play, demonstrating human courage and taking a positive attitude toward the human condition. The play must be full-length and produced in the previous year by a theatre company resident in New England.

1962 **Drama Club of the State College at Fitchburg, Mass.,** *The Diary of Anne Frank*
1963 **Scitamard Players** (Providence, R.I.) *A Raisin in the Sun*
1964 **Community Players** (Concord, N.H.), *Inherit the Wind*
1965 **The People's Theater** (Cambridge, Mass.), *Noah*
1966 **Wheelock College Drama Club** (Boston, Mass.), *Jacobowsky and the Colonel*
1967 **Arlington Friends of the Drama** (Arlington, Mass.), *The Crucible*
1968 **Staples High School Players** (Westport, Conn.), *War and Pieces*
1969 No award
1970 **Staples High School Players** (Westport, Conn.), *Soldier, Soldier*
1971 **University of Hartford Players** (Hartford, Conn.), *The Ceremony of Innocence*
1972 **Arlington Friends of the Drama** (Arlington, Mass.), *Fiddler on the Roof*
1973 **Reagle Players,** Waltham Summer Theatre (Waltham, Mass.), *1776*
1974 **Harwich Winter Theatre** (W. Harwich, Mass.), *Uncle Vanya*
1975 **Concord Players** (Concord, Mass.), *A Flurry of Birds*
1976 **Roger Ludlowe High School,** (Fairfield, Conn.), *The Miracle Worker*
1977 **Dartmouth Players** (Dartmouth College, Hanover, N.H.), *Blood Wedding*

New York Drama Critics Circle Award

NEW YORK DRAMA CRITICS CIRCLE
29 W. 46th St., New York, N.Y. 10036 (212/246-4314)

Members of the Circle annually vote for the best play of the year, best American/foreign play and best musical. If the best play is by an American author, another award is frequently given to the author of the best foreign play. The top award carries a $1,000 cash prize, while scrolls are presented to other honored play-

wrights. New plays produced in New York during the season are eligible for these honors.

AMERICAN PLAY

1936 Maxwell Anderson, *Winterset*
1937 Maxwell Andersen, *High Tor*
1938 John Steinbeck, *Of Mice and Men*
1939 No award
1940 William Saroyan, *The Time of Your Life*
1941 Lillian Hellman, *The Watch on the Rhine*
1942 No award
1943 Sidney Kingsley, *The Patriots*
1944 No award
1945 Tennessee Williams, *The Glass Menagerie*
1946 No award
1947 Arthur Miller, *All My Sons*
1948 Tennessee Williams, *Streetcar Named Desire*
1949 Arthur Miller, *Death of a Salesman*
1950 Carson McCullers, *The Member of the Wedding*
1951 Sidney Kingsley, *Darkness at Noon*
1952 John Van Druten, *I Am a Camera*
1953 William Inge, *Picnic*
1954 John Patrick, *The Teahouse of the August Moon*
1955 Tennessee Williams, *Cat on a Hot Tin Roof*
1956 Frances Goodrich and Albert Hackett, *The Diary of Anne Frank*
1957 Eugene O'Neill, *Long Day's Journey into Night*
1958 Ketti Frings, *Look Homeward, Angel*
1959 Lorraine Hansberry, *A Raisin in the Sun*
1960 Lillian Hellman, *Toys in the Attic*
1961 Tad Mosel, *All the Way Home*
1962 Tennessee Williams, *The Night of the Iguana*
1963-68 No awards in this category
1969 Paul Zindel, *The Effect of Gamma Rays on Man-in-the-Moon Marigolds*
1970 No award
1971 John Guare, *The House of Blue Leaves*
1972 No award
1973 Lanford Wilson, *Hot L Baltimore*
1974 Miguel Pinero, *Short Eyes*
1975 Ed Bullins, *The Taking of Miss Janie*
1976 David Rabe, *Streamers*
1977 David Mamet, *American Buffalo*

FOREIGN PLAY

1938 Paul Vincent Carroll, *Shadow and Substance*
1939 Paul Vincent Carroll, *The White Steed*
1940 No award
1941 Emlyn Williams, *The Corn is Green*
1942 Noel Coward, *Blithe Spirit*
1943 No award
1944 Franz Werfel and S. N. Behrman, *Jacobowsky and the Colonel*
1945 No award
1946 No award
1947 Jean-Paul Sartre, *No Exit*
1948 Terence Rattigan, *The Winslow Boy*
1949 Maurice Valency, *The Madwoman of Chaillot*
1950 T.S. Eliot, *The Cocktail Party*
1951 Christopher Fry, *The Lady's Not for Burning*
1952 Christopher Fry, *Venus Observed*
1953 Peter Ustinov, *The Love of Four Colonels*
1954 Maurice Valency, *Ondine*
1955 Agatha Christie, *Witness for the Prosecution*
1956 Christopher Fry, *Tiger at the Gates*
1957 Jean Anouilh, *Waltz of the Toreadors*
1958 John Osborne, *Look Back in Anger*
1959 Friederich Duerrenmatt, *The Visit*
1960 Peter Shaffer, *Five Finger Exercise*

1961 Shelagh Delaney, *A Taste of Honey*
1962 Robert Bolt, *A Man for All Seasons*

BEST PLAY

1963 Edward Albee, *Who's Afraid of Virginia Woolf?*
1964 Frank Gilroy, *The Subject Was Roses*
1965 John Osborne, *Luther*
1966 Peter Weiss, *Marat/Sade*
1967 Harold Pinter, *The Homecoming*
1968 Tom Stoppard, *Rosencrantz and Guildenstern Are Dead*
1969 Howard Sackler, *The Great White Hope*
1970 Frank McMahon, *Borstal Boy*
1971 David Storey, *Home*
1972 Jason Miller, *That Championship Season*
1973 David Storey, *The Changing Room*
1974 David Storey, *The Contractor*
1975 Peter Shaffer, *Equus*
1976 Tom Stoppard, *Travesties*
1977 Simon Gray, *Otherwise Engaged*

MUSICAL

1946 *Carousel*
1947 *Brigadoon*
1948 No award
1949 *South Pacific*
1950 *The Consul*
1951 *Guys and Dolls*
1952 *Pal Joey*
1953 *Wonderful Town*
1954 John Latouche and Jerome Moross, *The Golden Apple*
1955 *The Saint of Bleecker Street*
1956 Alan Jay Lerner, *My Fair Lady*
1957 *The Most Happy Fella*
1958 Meredith Willson, *The Music Man*
1959 *La Plume de Ma Tante*
1960 George Abbott, Jerome Weidman, Sheldon Harnick, and Jerry Bock, *Fiorello!*
1961 Michael Stewart and Bob Merrill, *Carnival!*
1962 Abe Burrows, Jack Weinstock, Willie Gilbert and Frank Loesser, *How to Succeed in Business Without Really Trying*
1963 No award
1964 *Hello, Dolly!*
1965 *Fiddler on the Roof*
1966 Dale Wasserman, Mitch Leigh and Joe Darion, *Man of La Mancha*
1967 F. Ebb et al., *Cabaret*
1968 *Your Own Thing*
1969 S. Edwards and P. Stone, *1776*
1970 Stephen Sondheim and George Furth, *Company*
1971 Stephen Sondheim and James Goldman, *Follies*
1972 Galt MacDermot and John Guare, *Two Gentlemen of Verona*
1973 Hugh Wheeler and Stephen Sondheim, *A Little Night Music*
1974 *Candide*
1975 Michael Bennett, choreographer and director; James Kirkwood and Nicholas Dante, book; Marvin Hamlisch, music; Edward Kleban, lyrics, *A Chorus Line*
1976 Stephen Sondheim, music and lyrics; John Weidman, book; and Hugh Wheeler, additional material, *Pacific Overtures*
1977 Charles Strouse, music; Martin Charnin, lyrics; Thomas Meehan, book; Mike Nichols, producer, *Annie*

Obie Award
VILLAGE VOICE
80 University Place, New York, N.Y. 10003 (212/741-0030)

The Obie Award, which consists of a plaque and sometimes a monetary prize as well, is given annually for excellence and creative achievement in off-Broadway theatre. A panel of expert judges in the field selects the winners from the season's productions. The names of the categories have been changed over the years.

BEST PLAY/BEST NEW AMERICAN PLAY

1956 *Absalom* (Lionel Abel)
1957 *A House Remembered* (Louis A. Lippe)
1958 *Endgame* (Samuel Beckett)
1959 *The Quare Fellow* (Brendan Behan)
1960 *The Connection* (Jack Gelber)
1961 *The Blacks* (Jean Genet)
1962 *Who'll Save the Plowboy?* (Frank D. Gilroy)
1963 No award
1964 *Play* (Samuel Beckett)
       Dutchman (LeRoi Jones)
1965 *The Old Glory* (Robert Lowell)
1966 *The Journey of the Fifth Horse* (Ronald Ribman)
1967 No award
1968 No award
1969 See separate 1969 Obie listing below
1970 *The Effect of Gamma Rays on Man-in-the-Moon Marigolds* (Paul Zindel)
       Approaching Simone (Megan Terry)
1971 *House of Blue Leaves* (John Guare)
1972 No award
1973 *Hot L Baltimore* (Lanford Wilson)
       The River Niger (Joseph A. Walker)
1974 *Short Eyes* (Miguel Pinero)
1975 *The First Breeze of Summer* (Leslie Lee)
1976 No award
1977 *Curse of the Starving Class* (Sam Shepard)

BEST FOREIGN PLAY

1950 *The Balcony* (Jean Genet)
1962 *Happy Days* (Samuel Beckett)
1968 *The Memorandum* (Vaclav Havel)
1969 See separate 1969 Obie listing below
1970 *What the Butler Saw* (Joe Orton)
1974 *The Contractor* (David Storey)

BEST ADAPTATION

1958 *The Brothers Karamazov* (Boris Tumarin and Jack Sydow)

BEST REVIVAL

1958 *The Crucible* (Arthur Miller, directed by World Baker)

BEST COMEDY

1958 *Comic Strip* (George Panetta)

BEST ONE-ACT PLAY

1958 *Guest of the Nation* (Neil McKenzie)

BEST MUSICAL

1956 *Three Penny Opera* (Bertolt Brecht and Kurt Weill; adapted by Marc Blitzstein)
1959 *A Party With Betty Comden and Adolph Green*
1962 *Fly Blackbird* (C. Jackson, James Hatch and Jerome Eskow)

1968   *In Circles* (Gertrude Stein and Al Carmines)
1969   See separate 1969 Obie listing below
1970   *The Last Sweet Days of Isaac* (Gretchen Cryer and Nancy Ford)
       The Me Nobody Knows (Robert Livingston, Gary William Friedman and Will Holt)

BEST REVUE
1959   *Diversions* (Steven Vinaver)

BEST OFF—OFF-BROADWAY PRODUCTION
1961   *The Premise* (Produced and directed by Theodore Flicker)

DISTINGUISHED PLAY
1960   *Krapp's Last Tape* (Samuel Beckett)
       The Prodigal (Jack Richardson)
       The Zoo Story (Edward Albee)
1964   *Home Movies* (Rosalyn Drexler)
       Funny House of a Negro (Adrienne Kennedy)
1965   *Promenade* and *The Successful Life of Three* (Maria Irene Fornes)
1966   *Good Day* (Emmanuel Peluso)
       Chicago, *Icarus's Mother* and *Red Cross* (Sam Shepard)
1967   *Futz* (Rochelle Owens)
       La Turista (Sam Shepard)
1968   *Muzeeka* (John Guare)
       The Indian Wants the Bronx (Israel Horovitz)
       Melodrama Play (Sam Shepard)
1969   See separate 1969 Obie listing below
1970   *The Deer Kill* (Murray Mednick)
       The Increased Difficulty of Concentration (Vaclav Havle)
1973   *The Tooth of Crime* (Sam Shepard)
       Big Foot (Ronald Tavel)
       What If I Had Turned Up Heads? (J.E. Gaines)
1974   *Bad Habits* (Terrence McNally)
       When You Comin' Back, Red Ryder? (Mark Medoff)
       The Great MacDaddy (Paul Carter Harrison)

DISTINGUISHED PLAYWRITING
1971   Ed Bullins, *The Fabulous Miss Marie* and *In New England Winter*
       David Rabe, *Basic Training of Pavlo Hummel*

DISTINGUISHED FOREIGN PLAY
1971   *Boesman and Lena* (Athol Fugard)
       AC/DC (Heathcote Williams)
       Dream on Monkey Mountain (Derek Walcott)
1973   *Not I* (Samuel Beckett)
       Kasper (Peter Handke)

BEST PRODUCTION
1956   *Uncle Vanya* (Fourth Street Theatre)
1957   No award
1958   No award
1959   *Exiles* (Renata Theatre)
1960   *The Connection* (Living Theatre)
1961   *Hedda Gabler* (Fourth Street Theatre)
1962   No award
1963   *Six Characters in Search of an Author* (Martinique Theatre)
       The Boys From Syracuse (Theatre Four)
1964   *The Brig* (Living Theatre)
       What Happened (Judson Poets Theatre)
1965   *The Cradle Will Rock* (Theatre Four)

DISTINGUISHED PRODUCTION
1971   *The Trial of the Catonsville Nine*
1977   *The Club*
       For Colored Girls Who Have Considered Suicide/When the Rainbow is Enuf
       Dressed Like an Egg

BEST THEATRE PIECE
1972   *The Mutation Show* (The Open Theatre)

BEST ACTRESS
1956   Julie Bovasso, *The Maids*
1957   Colleen Dewhurst, *The Taming of the Shrew*, *The Eagle Has Two Heads* and *Camille*
1958   Anne Meacham, *Suddenly Last Summer* (*Garden District*)
1959   Kathleen Maguire, *The Time of the Cuckoo*
1960   Eileen Breenan, *Little Mary Sunshine*
1961   Anne Meacham, *Hedda Gabler*
1962   Barbara Harris, *Oh Dad, Poor Dad, Momma's Hung You in the Closet and I'm Feelin' So Sad*
1963   Colleen Dewhurst, *Desire Under the Elms*
1964   No award
1965   See Distinguished Performances below
1966   Jane White, *Coriolanus* and *Love's Labours Lost*
1967   No award
1968   Billie Dixon, *The Beard*

BEST ACTOR
1956   Jason Robards Jr., *The Iceman Cometh*
       George Voskovec, *Uncle Vanya*
1957   No award
1958   George C. Scott, *Richard III*, *As You Like It* and *Children of Darkness*
1959   Alfredo Ryder, *I Rise in Flame, Cried the Phoenix*
1960   Warren Finnerty, *The Connection*
1961   Khigh Dhiegh, *In the Jungle of Cities*
1962   James Earl Jones, *Clandestine on the Morning Line*, *The Apple* and *Moon on a Rainbow Shawl*
1963   George C. Scott, *Desire Under the Elms*
1964   No award
1965   See Distinguished Performances below
1966   Dustin Hoffman, *The Journey of the Fifth Horse*
1967   Seth Allen, *Futz*
1968   Al Pacino, *The Indian Wants the Bronx*
1969   No award
1970   No award
1971   Jack MacGowran, *Beckett*

DISTINGUISHED PERFORMANCES (Male and Female)
1964   Gloria Foster, *In White America*
1965   Roscoe Lee Browne, Frank Langella and Lester Rawlins, *The Old Glory*
1970   Sada Thompson, *The Effect of Gamma Rays on Man-in-the-Moon Marigolds*
1974   Barbara Barrie, *The Killdeer*
       Joseph Buloff, *Hard to Be a Jew*
       Kevin Conway, *When You Comin' Back, Red Ryder?*
       Conchata Ferrell, *The Sea Horse*
       Loretta Greene, *The Sirens*
       Barbara Montgomery, *My Sister, My Sister*
       Zipora Spaizman, *Stepnyu*
       Elizabeth Sturges, *When You Comin' Back, Red Ryder?*
1975   Reyno, *The First Breeze of Summer*
       Moses Gunn, *The First Breeze of Summer*
       Dick Latessa, *Philemon*
       Kevin McCarthy, *Harry Outside*
       Stephen D. Newman, *Polly*
       Christopher Walken, *Kid Champion*

Ian Trigger, *The True History of Squire Jonathan*
Cara Duff-McCormick, *Craig's Wife*
Priscilla Smith, *Trilogy*
Tanya Berezin, *The Mound Builders*
Tovah Feldshuh, *Yentl the Yeshiva Boy*
1976   Robert Christian, *Blood Knot*
Pamela Payton-Wright, *Jesse and the Bandit Queen*
Priscilla Smith, *The Good Woman of Setzuan*
David Warrilow, *The Lost Ones*
June Gable, *Comedy of Errors*
Sammy Williams, *A Chorus Line*
Priscilla Lopez, *A Chorus Line*
Joyce Aaron, *Acrobatics*
Mike Kellin, *American Buffalo*
Roberts Blossom, *Ice Age*
Crystal Field, *Day Old Bread*
Tony LoBianco, *Yankees 3, Detroit 0*
T. Miratti, *The Shortchanged Revue*
Kate Manheim, *Rhoda In Potatoland*
1977   Danny Aiello, *Gemini*
Martin Balsam, *Cold Storage*
Lucinda Childs, *Einstein on the Beach*
James Coco, *The Transfiguration of Benno Blimpie*
Anne DeSalvo, *Gemini*
John Heard, *G. R. Point*
Jo Henderson, *Ladyhouse Blues*
William Hurt, *My Life*
Joseph Maher, *Savages*
Roberta Maxwell, *Ashes*
Brian Murray, *Ashes*
Lola Pashalinski, *Der Ring Gott Farblonjet*
Marian Seldes, *Isadora Duncan Sleeps with the Russian Navy*
Margaret Wright, *A Manoir*

DISTINGUISHED PERFORMANCES (Actresses)

1956   Peggy McKay
Shirlee Emmons
Frances Sternhagen
Nancy Wickwire
1957   Marguerite Lenert
Betty Miller
Jutta Wolf
1958   Tammy Grimes
Grania O'Malley
Nydia Westman
1959   Rosina Fernhoff
Anne Fielding
Nancy Wickwire
1960   Patricia Falkenhain
Alisa Loti
Nancy Marchand
1961   Joan Hackett
Gerry Jedd
Surya Kumari
1962   Sudie Bond
Vinnette Carrol
Rosemary Harris
Ruth White
1963   Jacqueline Brooks
Olympia Dukakis
Anne Jackson
Madeline Sherwood
1964   Joyce Ebert
Lee Grant
Estelle Parsons
Diana Sands
Marian Seldes
1965   Margaret De Priest
Rosemary Harris

Frances Sternhagen
Sada Thompson
1966   Clarice Blackburn
Marie-Claire Charba
Gloria Foster
Sharon Gains
Florence Tarlow
1967   Bette Henritze
1968   Jean David
Mari Gorman
Peggy Pope
1969   See separate 1969 Obie listing below
1970   Rue McClanahan
Roberta Maxwell
Fredericka Weber
Pamela Payton-Wright
1971   Susan Batson
Margaret Braidwood
Joan Macintosh
1972   Salome Bey
Marilyn Chris
Jeanne Hepple
Marilyn Sokol
Kathleen Widdoes
Elizabeth Wilson
1973   Mari Gorman
Lola Pashalinski
Alice Playten
Roxie Roker
Jessica Tandy
1974   Barbara Barrie
Conchata Ferrell
Loretta Greene
Barbara Montgomery
Zipora Spaizman
Elizabeth Sturges

DISTINGUISHED PERFORMANCES (Actors)

1956   Gerald Hiken
Alan Ansara
Roberts Blossom
Addison Powell
1957   Thayer David
Michael Kane
Arthur Maiet
1958   Leonardo Cimino
Jack Cannon
Robert Geiringer
Michael Higgins
1959   Zero Mostel
Lester Rawlins
Harold Scott
1960   William Daniels
Donald Davis
Vincent Gardenia
John Heffernan
Jack Linvingston
1961   Godfrey M. Cambridge
James Coco
Lester Rawlins
1962   Clayton Corzatte
Geoff Garland
Gerald O'Laughlin
Paul Roebling
1963   Joseph Chalkin
Michael O'Sullivan
James Patterson
Eli Wallach
1964   Philip Bruns
David Hurst

Taylor Mead
Hack Warden
Ronald Weyand
1965 Brian Bedford
Roberts Blossom
Dean Dittman
Robert Duvall
James Earl Jones
1966 Frank Langella
Michael Lipton
Kevin O'Connor
Jess Osuna
Douglas Turner
1967 Tom Aldredge
Robert Bonnard
Alvin Epstein
Neil Flanagan
Stacy Keach
Terry Kiser
Eddie McCarty
Robert Salvio
Rip Torn
1968 John Cazale
James Coco
Cliff Gorman
Moses Gunn
Roy R. Schneider
1969 See separate 1969 Obie listing below
1970 Beeson Carroll
Vincent Gardenia
Harold Gould
Anthony Holland
Lee Kissman
Ron Liebman
Austin Pendleton
1971 Hector Elizondo
Donald Ewer
Sonny Jimm
Stacy Keach
Harris Laskawy
William Schallert
James Woods
1972 Maurice Blanc
Alex Bradford
Ron Faber
Danny Sewall
Ed Zang
1973 Hume Cronyn
James Hilbrant
Stacy Keach
Christopher Lloyd
Charles Ludlam
Douglas Turner Ward
Sam Waterston
1974 Joseph Buloff
Kevin Conway

BEST DIRECTOR

1956 Jose Quintero, *The Iceman Cometh*
1957 Gene Frankel, *Volpone*
1958 Stuart Vaughan, New York Shakespeare Festival
1959 William Ball, *Ivanov* (foreign play)
Jack Ragotzy, Arthur Laurents cycle (American plays)
1960 Gene Frankel, *Machinal*
1961 Gerald A. Freedman, *The Taming of the Shrew*
1962 John Wulp, *Red Eye of Love*
1963 Alan Schneider, Pinter plays
1964 Judith Malina, *The Brig*
1965 Ulu Grosbard, *A View from the Bridge*

1966 No award
1967 Tom O'Horgan, *Futz*
1968 Michael A. Schultz, *Song for the Lusitanian Bogey*
1969 See separate 1969 Obie listing below

DISTINGUISHED DIRECTION

1964 Lawrence Kornfeld
1966 Remy Charlip
Jacques Levy
1968 John Hancock
Rip Torn
1969 See separate 1969 Obie listing below
1970 Alan Arkin
Melvin Bernhardt
Maxine Klein
Gilbert Moses
1971 John Berry
Jeff Bleckner
Gordon Davidson
John Hirsch
Larry Kornfeld
1972 Wilford Leach and John Braswell
Mel Shapiro
Michael Smith
Tom Sydorick
1973 Jack Gelber
William E. Lathan
Marshall W. Mason
1974 Marvin Felix Camillo
Robert Drivas
David Licht
John Pasquin
Harold Prince
1975 Lawrence Kornfeld, *Listen to Me*
Marshall W. Mason, *Battle of Angels* and *The Mound Builders*
Gilbert Moses, *The Taking of Miss Janie*
1976 Marshall W. Mason, *Knock Knock* and *Serenading Louie*
JoAnne Akalaitis, *Cascando*
1977 Melvin Bernhardt, *Children*
Gordon Davidson, *Savages*

SETS, LIGHTING OR COSTUMES

1956 Klaus Holm
Alvin Colt
1957 No award
1958 David Hays
Will Steven Armstrong
Nikola Cernovich
1960 David Hays
1961 No award
1962 Norris Houghton
1963 No award
1964 Julian Beck
1965 Willa Kim
1966 Lindsey Decker
Ed Wittstein
1967 John Dodd
1968 Robert La Vigna
1969 See separate 1969 Obie listing below
1970 No award
1971 No award
1972 Video Free America (visual effects)
1973 No award
1974 Theoni Aldredge
Holmes Easley
Christopher Thomas

DISTINGUISHED SET DESIGN

1975 Robert U. Taylor, *Polly*
John Lee Beatty, *Down by the River . . . , Battle of Angels* and *The Mound Builders*
1976 Donald Brooks, *The Tempest*
1977 No award

MUSIC

1958 David Amram
1961 Teiji Ito
1964 Al Carmines
1972 Micki Grant
Liz Swados
1974 Bill Elliott
1976 Philip Glass

1969 AWARDS

An altered format resulted in awards for distinguished achievement rather than citations for specific categories of accomplishment. The winners:

The Living Theatre, *Frankenstein*
Jeff Weiss, *The International Wrestling Match*
Julie Bovasso, *Gloria and Esperanza*
Judith Malina and Julian Beck, *Antigone*
Israel Horovitz, *The Honest-to-Goodness Schnozzola*
Jules Feiffer, *Little Murders*
Ronald Tavel, *The Boy on the Straight Back Chair*
Nathan George and Ron O'Neal, *No Place to be Somebody*
Arlene Rothlein, *The Poor Little Match Girl*
Theatre Genesis, Sustained excellence
The Open Theatre, *The Serpent*
Om Theatre, *Riol*
The Performance Group, *Dionysus in '69*

SPECIAL CITATIONS AND AWARDS WHICH DO NOT FIT INTO OTHER CATEGORIES

1956 The Phoenix Theatre
The Shakespearean Workshop Theatre (later, The New York Shakespeare Festival)
The Tempo Playhouse
1957 Paul Shyre
1958 The Phoenix Theatre
The Theatre Club
Lucille Lortel
1959 Hal Holbrook
1960 Brooks Atkinson
1961 Bernard Frechtman
1962 Ellis Rabb for *The Hostage*
1963 Jean Erdman
The Second City
1964 Judson Memorial Church
1965 The Paper Bag Players
Caffe Cino and Cafe La Mama
1966 Joseph H. Dunn
H.M. Koutakas
Peter Schumann
Theatre for Ideas
Theatre in the Street
1967 La Mama Troupe
The Open Theatre
Tom Sankey
The Second Story Players
Jeff Weiss
1968 The Fortune Society
The Negro Ensemble Company
San Francisco Mime Troupe
El Teatro Campesino

1969 See separate 1969 Obie listing above
1970 Chelsea Theatre Center
Gardner Compton and Emile Ardolino for *Elephant Steps*
Andre Gregory
The Ridiculous Theatrical Company
Theatre of the Ridiculous
1971 *Orlando Furioso*
Kirk Kirksey
1972 Charles Stanley
Meredith Monk
Theatre of Latin America
Free the Army
1973 Richard Foreman
San Francisco Mime Troupe
City Center Acting Company
Workshop of the Player's Art
1974 Bread and Puppet Theatre
Brooklyn Academy of Music
CSC Repertory Company
Robert Wilson
1975 Andrei Serban for *Trilogy*
The Royal Shakespeare Company for *Summerfolk*
Charles Ludlam for *Professor Bedlam's Punch and Judy Show*
The Henry Street Settlement
Charles Pierce
Mabou Mines
Special 20-Year Obies to:
Judith Malina and Julian Beck
Ted Mann and the Circle in the Square
Joseph Papp
Ellen Stewart
The Fantasticks
1976 Richard Foreman, *Rhoda in Potatoland*
David Mamet, *American Buffalo* and *Sexual Perversity in Chicago*
Ralph Lee, *The Halloween Parade*
Morton Lichter and Gordon Rogoff, *Old-Timers' Sexual Symphony*
Santo Loquasto, sets and costumes of *Comedy of Errors*
Meredith Monk, *Quarry*
Edward Bond, *Bingo* at the Yale Repertory Theatre
Neil Flanagan for outstanding contribution to off-off-Broadway
Chile! Chile! (special documentary theatre award)
Creators of *A Chorus Line*
1977 Barbara Garson, *The Dinosaur Door*
Manhattan Theatre Club for sustained excellence
New York Street Theatre Caravan for sustained excellence
Theatre for the New City for sustained excellence
Philip Glass, the music for *Einstein on the Beach*
Ping Chong, *Humboldt's Current*
The creators of *Night Club Cantata*
Charles Ludlam, the design of *Der Ring Gott Farblonjet*
Carole Oditz for costumes, Douglas Schmidt for set, and Burl Hass for lighting for *Crazy Locomotive*
Henry Millman for set and Edward M. Greenberg for lighting for *Domino Courts*

Antoinette Perry Award

AMERICAN THEATRE WING
681 Fifth Ave., New York, N.Y. 10022 (212/759-5001)

The Antoinette Perry Award, known as the Tony, honors distinguished achievement in American theatre. Occasionally, multiple awards in individual categories have been given. Now, some 450 theatre people vote for the recipients of Tonys in various categories from a publicized list of nominees. These categories have changed over the years. The award, which was designed by Herman Rosse, depicts the masks of comedy and tragedy on one side and the profile of actress Antoinette Perry on the other. The awards are presented annually on nationwide television for a production at one of forty-one eligible Broadway theatres.

ACTOR (Dramatic)

1947   Jose Ferrer, *Cyrano de Bergerac*
       Fredric March, *Years Ago*
1948   Henry Fonda, *Mister Roberts*
       Paul Kelly, *Command Decision*
       Basil Rathbone, *The Heiress*
1949   Rex Harrison, *Anne of the Thousand Days*
1950   Sidney Blackmer, *Come Back, Little Sheba*
1951   Claude Rains, *Darkness at Noon*
1952   Jose Ferrer, *The Shrike*
1953   Tom Ewell, *The Seven Year Itch*
1954   David Wayne, *The Teahouse of the August Moon*
1955   Alfred Lunt, *Quadrille*
1956   Paul Muni, *Inherit the Wind*
1957   Fredric March, *Long Day's Journey Into Night*
1958   Ralph Bellamy, *Sunrise at Campobello*
1959   Jason Robards, Jr., *The Disenchanted*
1960   Melvyn Douglas, *The Best Man*
1961   Zero Mostel, *Rhinoceros*
1962   Paul Scofield, *A Man for All Seasons*
1963   Arthur Hill, *Who's Afraid of Virginia Woolf?*
1964   Alec Guinness, *Dylan*
1965   Walter Matthau, *The Odd Couple*
1966   Hal Holbrook, *Mark Twain Tonight*
1967   Paul Rogers, *The Homecoming*
1968   Martin Balsam, *You Know I Can't Hear You When the Water's Running*
1969   James Earl Jones, *The Great White Hope*
1970   Fritz Weaver, *Child's Play*
1971   Brian Bedford, *The School for Wives*
1972   Cliff Gorman, *Lenny*
1973   Alan Bates, *Butley*
1974   Michael Moriarty, *Find Your Way Home*
1975   John Kani, *Sizwe Banzi*
       Winston Ntshona, *The Island*
1976   John Wood, *Travesties*
1977   Al Pacino, *The Basic Training of Pavlo Hummel*

ACTRESS (Dramatic)

1947   Ingrid Bergman, *Joan of Lorraine*
       Helen Hayes, *Happy Birthday*
1948   Judith Anderson, *Medea*
       Katharine Cornell, *Antony and Cleopatra*
       Jessica Tandy, *A Streetcar Named Desire*
1949   Martitia Hunt, *The Madwoman of Chaillot*
1950   Shirley Booth, *Come Back, Little Sheba*
1951   Uta Hagen, *The Country Girl*
1952   Julie Harris, *I Am a Camera*
1953   Shirley Booth, *Time of the Cuckoo*
1954   Audrey Hepburn, *Ondine*
1955   Nancy Kelly, *The Bad Seed*
1956   Julie Harris, *The Lark*
1957   Margaret Leighton, *Separate Tables*
1958   Helen Hayes, *Time Remembered*
1959   Gertrude Berg, *A Majority of One*
1960   Anne Bancroft, *The Miracle Worker*

1961   Joan Plowright, *A Taste of Honey*
1962   Margaret Leighton, *Night of the Iguana*
1963   Uta Hagen, *Who's Afraid of Virginia Woolf?*
1964   Sandy Dennis, *Any Wednesday*
1965   Irene Worth, *Tiny Alice*
1966   Rosemary Harris, *The Lion in Winter*
1967   Beryl Reid, *The Killing of Sister George*
1968   Zoe Caldwell, *The Prime of Miss Jean Brodie*
1969   Julie Harris, *Forty Carats*
1970   Tammy Grimes, *Private Lives*
1971   Maureen Stapleton, *Gingerbread Lady*
1972   Sada Thompson, *Twigs*
1973   Julie Harris, *The Last of Mrs. Lincoln*
1974   Colleen Dewhurst, *A Moon for the Misbegotten*
1975   Ellen Burstyn, *Same Time, Next Year*
1976   Irene Worth, *Sweet Bird of Youth*
1977   Julie Harris, *The Belle of Amherst*

ACTOR, SUPPORTING OR FEATURED (Dramatic)

1949   Arthur Kennedy, *Death of a Salesman*
1950   No award
1951   Eli Wallach, *The Rose Tattoo*
1952   John Cromwell, *Point of No Return*
1953   John Williams, *Dial M for Murder*
1954   John Kerr, *Tea and Sympathy*
1955   Francis L. Sullivan, *Witness for the Prosecution*
1956   Ed Begley, *Inherit the Wind*
1957   Frank Conroy, *The Potting Shed*
1958   Henry Jones, *Sunrise at Campobello*
1959   Charlie Ruggles, *The Pleasure of His Company*
1960   Roddy McDowall, *The Fighting Cock*
1961   Martin Gabel, *Big Fish, Little Fish*
1962   Walter Matthau, *A Shot in the Dark*
1963   Alan Arkin, *Enter Laughing*
1964   Hume Cronyn, *Hamlet*
1965   Jack Albertson, *The Subject Was Roses*
1966   Patrick Magee, *Marat/Sade*
1967   Ian Holm, *The Homecoming*
1968   James Patterson, *The Birthday Party*
1969   Al Pacino, *Does a Tiger Wear a Necktie?*
1970   Ken Howard, *Child's Play*
1971   Paul Sand, *Story Theatre*
1972   Vincent Gardenia, *The Prisoner of Second Avenue*
1973   John Lithgow, *The Changing Room*
1974   Ed Flanders, *A Moon for the Misbegotten*
1975   Frank Langella, *Seascape*
1976   Edward Herrmann, *Mrs. Warren's Profession*
1977   Jonathan Price, *Comedians*

ACTRESS, SUPPORTING OR FEATURED (Dramatic)

1947   Patricia Neal, *Another Part of the Forest*
1948   No award
1949   Shirley Booth, *Goodbye, My Fancy*
1950   No award
1951   Maureen Stapleton, *The Rose Tattoo*
1952   Marian Winters, *I Am a Camera*
1953   Beatrice Straight, *The Crucible*
1954   Jo Van Fleet, *The Trip to Bountiful*
1955   Patricia Jessel, *Witness for the Prosecution*
1956   Una Merkel, *The Ponder Heart*
1957   Peggy Cass, *Auntie Mame*
1958   Anne Bancroft, *Two For The Seasaw*
1959   Julie Newmar, *The Marriage-Go-Round*
1960   Anne Revere, *Toys in the Attic*
1961   Colleen Dewhurst, *All the Way Home*
1962   Elizabeth Ashley, *Take Her, She's Mine*
1963   Sandy Dennis, *A Thousand Clowns*
1964   Barbara Loden, *After the Fall*

1965 Alice Ghostley, *The Sign in Sidney Brustein's Window*
1966 Zoe Caldwell, *Slapstick Tragedy*
1967 Marian Seldes, *A Delicate Balance*
1968 Zena Walker, *Joe Egg*
1969 Jane Alexander, *The Great White Hope*
1970 Blythe Danner, *Butterflies Are Free*
1971 Rae Allen, *And Miss Reardon Drinks A Little*
1972 Elizabeth Wilson, *Sticks and Bones*
1973 Leora Dana, *The Last of Mrs. Lincoln*
1974 Frances Sternhagen, *The Good Doctor*
1975 Rita Moreno, *The Ritz*
1976 Shirley Knight, *Kennedy's Children*
1977 Trazana Beverley, *For Colored Girls Who Have Considered Suicide/When the Rainbow is Enuf*

ACTOR (Musical)

1948 Paul Hartman, *Angel in the Wings*
1949 Ray Bolger, *Where's Charley?*
1950 Ezio Pinza, *South Pacific*
1951 Robert Alda, *Guys and Dolls*
1952 Phil Silvers, *Top Banana*
1953 Thomas Mitchell, *Hazel Flagg*
1954 Alfred Drake, *Kismet*
1955 Walter Slezak, *Fanny*
1956 Ray Walston, *Damn Yankees*
1957 Rex Harrison, *My Fair Lady*
1958 Robert Preston, *The Music Man*
1959 Richard Kiley, *Redhead*
1960 Jackie Gleason, *Take Me Along*
1961 Richard Burton, *Camelot*
1962 Robert Morse, *How to Succeed in Business Without Really Trying*
1963 Zero Mostel, *A Funny Thing Happened on the Way to the Forum*
1964 Bert Lahr, *Foxy*
1965 Zero Mostel, *Fiddler on the Roof*
1966 Richard Kiley, *Man of La Mancha*
1967 Robert Preston, *I Do! I Do!*
1968 Robert Goulet, *The Happy Time*
1969 Jerry Orbach, *Promises, Promises*
1970 Cleavon Little, *Purlie*
1971 Hal Linden, *The Rothschilds*
1972 Phil Silvers, *A Funny Thing Happened on the Way to the Forum*
1973 Ben Vereen, *Pippin*
1974 Christopher Plummer, *Cyrano*
1975 John Cullum, *Shenandoah*
1976 George Rose, *My Fair Lady*
1977 Barry Bostwick, *The Robber Bridegroom*

ACTRESS (Musical)

1948 Grace Hartman, *Angel With Wings*
1949 Nanette Fabray, *Love Life*
1950 Mary Martin, *South Pacific*
1951 Ethel Merman, *Call Me Madam*
1952 Gertrude Lawrence, *The King & I*
1953 Rosalind Russell, *Wonderful Town*
1954 Dolores Gray, *Carnival in Flanders*
1955 Mary Martin, *Peter Pan*
1956 Gwen Verdon, *Damn Yankees*
1957 Judy Holliday, *Bells Are Ringing*
1958 Thelma Ritter, *New Girl In Town*
      Gwen Verdon, *New Girl In Town*
1959 Gwen Verdon, *Redhead*
1960 Mary Martin, *The Sound of Music*
1961 Elizabeth Seal, *Irma la Douce*
1962 Anna Maria Alberghetti, *Carnival*
      Diahann Carroll, *No Strings*
1963 Vivien Leigh, *Tovarich*

1964 Carol Channing, *Hello, Dolly!*
1965 Liza Minnelli, *Flora, the Red Menace*
1966 Angela Lansbury, *Mame*
1967 Barbara Harris, *The Apple Tree*
1968 Patricia Routledge, *Darling of the Day*
      Leslie Uggams, *Hallelujah, Baby!*
1969 Angela Lansbury, *Dear World*
1970 Lauren Bacall, *Applause*
1971 Helen Gallagher, *No, No, Nanette*
1972 Alexis Smith, *Follies*
1973 Glynis Johns, *A Little Night Music*
1974 Virginia Capers, *Raisin*
1975 Angela Lansbury, *Gypsy*
1976 Donna McKechnie, *A Chorus Line*
1977 Dorothy Loudon, *Annie*

ACTOR SUPPORTING OR FEATURED (Musical)

1947 David Wayne, *Finian's Rainbow*
1948 No award
1949 No award
1950 Myron McCormick, *South Pacific*
1951 Russell Nype, *Call Me Madam*
1952 Yul Brynner, *The King & I*
1953 Hiram Sherman, *Two's Company*
1954 Harry Belafonte, *John Murray Anderson's Almanac*
1955 Cyril Ritchard, *Peter Pan*
1956 Russ Brown, *Damn Yankees*
1957 Sydney Chaplin, *Bells Are Ringing*
1958 David Burns, *The Music Man*
1959 Russell Nype, *Goldilocks*
      Cast, *La Plume de Ma Tante*
1960 Tom Bosley, *Fiorello!*
1961 Dick Van Dyke, *Bye, Bye Birdie*
1962 Charles Nelson Reilly, *How to Succeed in Business Without Really Trying*
1963 David Burns, *A Funny Thing Happened on the Way to the Forum*
1964 Jack Cassidy, *She Loves Me*
1965 Victor Spinetti, *Oh, What A Lovely War*
1966 Frankie Michaels, *Mame*
1967 Joel Grey, *Cabaret*
1968 Hiram Sherman, *How Now, Dow Jones*
1969 Ronald Holgate, *1776*
1970 Rene Auberjonois, *Coco*
1971 Keene Curtis, *The Rothschilds*
1972 Larry Blyden, *A Funny Thing Happened on the Way to the Forum*
1973 George S. Irving, *Irene*
1974 Tommy Tune, *Seesaw*
1975 Ted Rose, *The Wiz*
1976 Sammy Williams, *A Chorus Line*
1977 Lenny Baker, *I Love My Wife*

ACTRESS, SUPPORTING OR FEATURED (Musical)

1950 Juanita Hall, *South Pacific*
1951 Isabel Bigley, *Guys and Dolls*
1952 Helen Gallagher, *Pal Joey*
1953 Sheila Bond, *Wish You Were Here*
1954 Gwen Verdon, *Can-Can*
1955 Carol Haney, *The Pajama Game*
1956 Lotte Lenya, *The Threepenny Opera*
1957 Edith Adams, *Li'l Abner*
1958 Barbara Cook, *The Music Man*
1959 Pat Stanley, *Goldilocks*
      Cast, *La Plume de Ma Tante*
1960 Patricia Neway, *The Sound of Music*
1961 Tammy Grimes, *The Unsinkable Molly Brown*
1962 Phyllis Newman, *Subways Are for Sleeping*
1963 Anna Quayle, *Stop the World — I Want to Get Off*

1964 Tessie O'Shea, *The Girl Who Came to Supper*
1965 Maria Karnilova, *Fiddler on the Roof*
1966 Beatrice Arthur, *Mame*
1967 Peg Murray, *Cabaret*
1968 Lillian Hayman, *Hallelujah, Baby!*
1969 Marian Mercer, *Promises, Promises*
1970 Melba Moore, *Purlie*
1971 Patsy Kelly, *No, No Nanette*
1972 Linda Hopkins, *Inner City*
1973 Patricia Elliot, *A Little Night Music*
1974 Janie Sell, *Over Here!*
1975 Dee Dee Bridgewater, *The Wiz*
1976 Carole Bishop, *A Chorus Line*
1977 Delores Hall, *Your Arm's Too Short to Box with God*

PLAY (and Playwright)

1948 *Mister Roberts,* Thomas Heggen and Joshua Logan based on novel by Thomas Heggen
1949 *Death of a Salesman,* Arthur Miller
1950 *The Cocktail Party,* T.S. Eliot
1951 *The Rose Tattoo,* Tennessee Williams
1952 *The Fourposter,* Jan de Hartog
1953 *The Crucible,* Arthur Miller
1954 *The Teahouse of the August Moon,* John Patrick
1955 *The Desperate Hours,* Joseph Hayes
1956 *The Diary of Anne Frank,* Frances Goodrich and Albert Hackett
1957 *Long Day's Journey Into Night,* Eugene O'Neill
1958 *Sunrise at Campobello,* Dore Schary
1959 *J.B.,* Archibald MacLeish
1960 *The Miracle Worker,* William Gibson
1961 *Becket,* Jean Anouilh, translated by Lucienne Hill
1962 *A Man for All Seasons,* Robert Bolt
1963 *Who's Afraid of Virginia Woolf?,* Edward Albee
1964 *Luther,* John Osborne
1965 *The Subject Was Roses,* Frank Gilroy
1966 *Marat/Sade,* Peter Weiss, English version by Geoffrey Skelton
1967 *The Homecoming,* Harold Pinter
1968 *Rosencrantz and Guildenstern Are Dead,* Tom Stoppard
1969 *The Great White Hope,* Howard Sackler
1970 *Borstal Boy,* Frank McMahon
1971 *Sleuth,* Anthony Shaffer
1972 *Sticks and Bones,* David Rabe
1973 *The Championship Season,* Jason Miller
1974 *The River Niger,* Joseph A. Walker
1975 *Equus,* Peter Shaffer
1976 *Travesties,* Tom Stoppard
1977 *The Shadow Box,* Michael Cristofer

AUTHOR (Dramatic)

1948 Thomas Heggen and Joshua Logan, *Mister Roberts*
1949 Arthur Miller, *Death of a Salesman*
1950 T.S. Eliot, *The Cocktail Party*
1951 Tennessee Williams, *The Rose Tattoo*
1952 No award
1953 Arthur Miller, *The Crucible*
1954 John Patrick, *The Teahouse of the August Moon*
1955 Joseph Hayes, *The Desperate Hours*
1956 Frances Goodrich and Albert Hackett, *The Diary of Anne Frank*
1957 Eugene O'Neill, *Long Day's Journey Into Night*
1958 Dore Schary, *Sunrise at Campobello*
1959 Archibald MacLeish, *J.B.*
1960 William Gibson, *The Miracle Worker*
1961 Jean Anouilh, *Becket*
1962 Robert Bolt, *A Man for All Seasons*
1963 No award

1964 John Osborne, *Luther*
1965 Neil Simon, *The Odd Couple*

PRODUCER (Dramatic)

1948 Leland Hayward, *Mister Roberts*
1949 Kermit Bloomgarden and Walter Fried, *Death of a Salesman*
1950 Gilbert Miller, *The Cocktail Party*
1951 Cheryl Crawford, *The Rose Tattoo*
1952 No award
1953 Kermit Bloomgarden, *The Crucible*
1954 Maurice Evans and George Schaefer, *The Teahouse of the August Moon*
1955 Howard Erskine and Joseph Hayes, *The Desperate Hours*
1956 Kermit Bloomgarden, *The Diary of Anne Frank*
1957 Leigh Connell, Theodore Mann and Jose Quintero, *Long Day's Journey Into Night*
1958 Lawrence Langner, Theresa Helburn, Armina Marshall and Dore Schary, *Sunrise at Campobello*
1959 Alfred de Liagre, Jr., *J.B.*
1960 Fred Coe, *The Miracle Worker*
1961 David Merrick, *Becket*
1962 Robert Whitehead and Roger L. Stevens, *A Man for All Seasons*
1963 Richard Barr and Clinton Wilder, *Who's Afraid of Virginia Woolf?*
1964 Herman Shumlin, *The Deputy*
1965 Claire Nichtern, *Luv*
1966 No award
1967 No award
1968 David Merrick Arts Foundation, *Rosencrantz and Guildenstern Are Dead*
1969 No award
1970 No award
1971 Helen Bonfils, Morton Gottlieb and Michael White, *Sleuth*

DIRECTOR

1947 Elia Kazan, *All My Sons*
1948 No award
1949 Elia Kazan, *Death of a Salesman*
1950 Joshua Logan, *South Pacific*
1951 George S. Kaufman, *Guys and Dolls*
1952 Jose Ferrer, *The Shrike, The Fourposter* and *Stalag 17*
1953 Joshua Logan, *Picnic*
1954 Alfred Lunt, *Ondine*
1955 Robert Montgomery, *The Desperate Hours*
1956 Tyrone Guthrie, *The Matchmaker*
1957 Moss Hart, *My Fair Lady*
1958 No award
1959 Elia Kazan, *J.B.*

DIRECTOR (Dramatic)

1958 Vincent J. Donehue, *Sunrise at Campobello*
1959 No award
1960 Arthur Penn, *The Miracle Worker*
1961 Sir John Gielgud, *Big Fish, Little Fish*
1962 Noel Willman, *A Man for All Seasons*
1963 Alan Schneider, *Who's Afraid of Virginia Woolf?*
1964 Mike Nichols, *Barefoot in the Park*
1965 Mike Nichols, *Luv* and *The Odd Couple*
1966 Peter Brook, *Marat/Sade*
1967 Peter Hall, *The Homecoming*
1968 Mike Nichols, *Plaza Suite*
1969 Peter Dews, *Hadrian VII*
1970 Joseph Hardy, *Child's Play*
1971 Peter Brook, *Midsummer Night's Dream*
1972 Mike Nichols, *The Prisoner of Second Avenue*

1973 A.J. Antoon, *The Championship Season*
1974 Jose Quintero, *A Moon for the Misbegotten*
1975 John Dexter, *Equus*
1976 Ellis Rabb, *The Royal Family*
1977 Gordon Davidson, *The Shadow Box*

MUSICAL (M-music; L-lyrics; B-book; P-produced)

1949 *Kiss Me Kate* (M&L by Cole Porter, B by Bella and Samuel Spewack)
1950 *South Pacific* (M by Richard Rodgers, L by Oscar Hammerstein II, B by Oscar Hammerstein II and Joshua Logan)
1951 *Guys and Dolls* (M&L by Frank Loesser, B by Jo Swerling and Abe Burrows)
1952 *The King and I* (B&L by Oscar Hammerstein II, M by Richard Rodgers)
1953 *Wonderful Town* (B by Joseph Fields and Jerome Chodorov, M by Leonard Bernstein, L by Betty Comden and Adolph Green)
1954 *Kismet* (B by Charles Lederer and Luther Davis, M by Alexander Borodin, adapted by and with L by Robert Wright and George Forrest)
1955 *The Pajama Game* (B by George Abbott and Richard Bissell, M&L by Richard Adler and Jerry Ross)
1956 *Damn Yankees* (B by George Abbott and Douglass Wallop, M by Richard Adler and Jerry Ross, P by Frederick Brisson, Robert Griffith, Harold S. Prince in assn. with Albert B. Taylor)
1957 *My Fair Lady* (B&L by Alan Jay Lerner, M by Frederick Loewe, P by Herman Levin)
1958 *The Music Man* (B by Meredith Willson and Franklin Lacey, M&L by Meredith Willson)
1959 *Redhead* (B by Herbert and Dorothy Fields, Sidney Sheldon and David Shaw, M by Albert Hague, L by Dorothy Fields)
1960 *Fiorello!* (B by Jerome Weidman and George Abbott, L by Sheldon Harnick, M by Jerry Bock, P by Robert E. Griffith and Harold S. Prince)
1961 *Bye, Bye Birdie* (B by Michael Stewart, M by Charles Strouse, L by Lee Adams, P by Edward Padula in assn. with L. Slade Brown)
1962 *How to Succeed in Business Without Really Trying* (B by Abe Burrows, Jack Weinstock and Willie Gilbert, M&L by Frank Loesser P by Cy Feuer and Ernest Martin)
1963 *A Funny Thing Happened on the Way to the Forum* (B by Burt Shrevelove and Larry Gelbart, M&L by Stephen Sondheim, P by Harold Prince)
1964 *Hello, Dolly!* (B by Michael Stewart, M&L by Jerry Herman, P by David Merrick)
1965 *Fiddler on the Roof* (B by Joseph Stein, M by Jerry Bock, L by Sheldon Harnick, P by Harold Prince)
1966 *Man of La Mancha* (B by Dale Wasserman, M by Mitch Leigh, L by Joe Darion, P by Albert W. Selden and Hal James)
1967 *Cabaret* (B by Joseph Masteroff, M by John Kander, L by Fred Ebb, P by Harold Prince in assn. with Ruth Mitchell)
1968 *Hallelujah, Baby!* (B by Arthur Laurents, M by Jule Styne, L by Betty Comden and Adolph Green, P by Albert W. Selden, Hal James, Jane C. Nussbaum and Harry Rigby)
1969 *1776* (B by Peter Stone, M&L by Sherman Edwards, P by Stuart Ostro)
1970 *Applause* (B by Betty Comden and Adolph Green, M by Charles Strouse, L by Lee Adams, P by Joseph Kipness and Lawrence Kasha)
1971 *Company* (P by Harold Prince)
1972 *Two Gentlemen of Verona* (P by the New York Shakespeare Festival, Joseph Papp)

1973 *A Little Night Music* (P by Harold Prince)
1974 *Raisin* (P by Robert Nemiroff)
1975 *The Wiz* (P by Ken Harper)
1976 *A Chorus Line* (P by Ken Harper)
1977 *Annie* (P by Mike Nichols)

AUTHOR (Musical)

1949 Bella and Samuel Spewack, *Kiss Me Kate*
1950 Oscar Hammerstein II and Joshua Logan, *South Pacific*
1951 Jo Swerling and Abe Burrows, *Guys and Dolls*
1952 No award
1953 Joseph Fields and Jerome Chodorov, *Wonderful Town*
1954 Charles Lederer and Luther Davis, *Kismet*
1955 George Abbott and Richard Bissell, *The Pajama Game*
1956 George Abbott and Douglass Wallop, *Damn Yankees*
1957 Alan Jay Lerner, *My Fair Lady*
1958 Meredith Willson and Franklin Lacey, *The Music Man*
1959 Herbert and Dorothy Fields, Sidney Sheldon and David Shaw, *Redhead*
1960 Jerome Weidman and George Abbott, *Fiorello!* Howard Lindsay and Russel Crouse, *The Sound of Music*
1961 Michael Stewart, *Bye, Bye Birdie*
1962 Abe Burrows, Jack Weinstock and Willie Gilbert, *How to Succeed in Business Without Really Trying*
1963 Burt Shrevelove and Larry Gelbart, *A Funny Thing Happened on the Way to the Forum*
1964 Michael Stewart, *Hello, Dolly!*
1965 Joseph Stein, *Fiddler on the Roof*

PRODUCER (Musical)

1949 Saint-Subber and Lemuel Ayers, *Kiss Me Kate*
1950 Richard Rodgers, Oscar Hammerstein II and Joshua Logan, *South Pacific*
1951 Cy Feuer and Ernest Martin, *Guys and Dolls*
1952 No award
1953 Robert Fryer, *Wonderful Town*
1954 Charles Lederer, *Kismet*
1955 Frederick Brisson, Robert Griffith and Harold S. Prince, *The Pajama Game*
1956 Frederick Brisson, Robert Griffith and Harold S. Prince in assn. with Albert B. Taylor, *Damn Yankees*
1957 Herman Levin, *My Fair Lady*
1958 Kermit Bloomgarden, Herbert Greene, Frank Productions, *The Music Man*
1959 Robert Fryer and Lawrence Carr, *Redhead*
1960 Leland Hayward and Richard Halliday, *The Sound of Music* Robert Griffith and Harold Prince, *Fiorello!*
1961 Edward Padula, *Bye, Bye Birdie*
1962 Cy Feuer and Ernest Martin, *How to Succeed in Business Without Really Trying*
1963 Harold Prince, *A Funny Thing Happened on the Way to the Forum*
1964 David Merrick, *Hello, Dolly!*
1965 Harold Prince, *Fiddler on the Roof*
1966 No award
1967 No award
1968 Albert Selden, Hal James, Jane C. Nussbaum and Harry Rigby, *Hallelujah, Baby!*
1969 No award
1970 No award
1971 Harold Prince, *Company*

DIRECTOR (Musical)

1960 George Abbott, *Fiorello!*
1961 Gower Champion, *Bye, Bye Birdie*
1962 Abe Burrows, *How to Succeed in Business Without Really Trying*
1963 George Abbott, *A Funny Thing Happened on the Way to the Forum*
1964 Gower Champion, *Hello, Dolly!*
1965 Jerome Robbins, *Fiddler on the Roof*
1966 Albert Marre, *Man of La Mancha*
1967 Harold Prince, *Cabaret*
1968 Gower Champion, *The Happy Time*
1969 Peter Hunt, *1776*
1970 Ron Field, *Applause*
1971 Harold Prince, *Company*
1972 Harold Prince and Michael Bennett, *Follies*
1973 Bob Fosse, *Pippin*
1974 Harold Prince, *Candide*
1975 Geoffrey Holder, *The Wiz*
1976 Michael Bennett, *A Chorus Line*
1977 Gene Saks, *I Love My Wife*

COMPOSER & LYRICIST

1949 Cole Porter, *Kiss Me Kate*
1950 Richard Rodgers (C), *South Pacific*
1951 Frank Loesser, *Guys and Dolls*
1952 No award
1953 Leonard Bernstein (C), *Wonderful Town*
1954 Alexander Borodin (C), *Kismet*
1955 Richard Adler and Jerry Ross *The Pajama Game*
1956 Richard Adler and Jerry Ross, *Damn Yankees*
1957 Frederick Loewe (C), *My Fair Lady*
1958 Meredith Willson, *The Music Man*
1959 Albert Hague (C), *Redhead*
1960 Jerry Bock (C), *Fiorello!*
      Richard Rodgers (C), *The Sound of Music*
1961 No award
1962 Richard Rodgers, *No Strings*
1963 Lionel Bart, *Oliver!*
1964 Jerry Herman, *Hello, Dolly!*
1965 Jerry Bock and Sheldon Harnick, *Fiddler on the Roof*
1966 Mitch Leigh and Joe Darion, *Man of La Mancha*
1967 John Kander and Fred Ebb, *Cabaret*
1968 Jule Styne, Betty Comden and Adolph Green, *Hallelujah, Baby!*
1969 No award
1970 No award
1971 Stephen Sondheim, *Company*
1972 Stephen Sondheim, *Follies*
1973 Stephen Sondheim, *A Little Night Music*
1974 Frederick Loewe (C) and Alan Jay Lerner (L), *Gigi*
1975 Charlie Smalls, *The Wiz*
1976 Ed Kleban (L) and Marvin Hamlisch (C), *A Chorus Line*
1977 Charles Strouse and Martin Charnin, *Annie*

CONDUCTOR AND MUSICAL DIRECTOR

1949 Max Meth, *As the Girls Go*
1950 Maurice Abravanel, *Regina*
1951 Lehman Engel, *The Consul*
1952 Max Meth, *Pal Joey*
1953 Lehman Engel, *Wonderful Town*
1954 Louis Adrian, *Kismet*
1955 Thomas Schippers, *The Saint of Bleecker Street*
1956 Hal Hastings, *Damn Yankees*
1957 Franz Allers, *My Fair Lady*
1958 Herbert Greene, *The Music Man*
1959 Salvatore Dell'Isola, *Flower Drum Song*
1960 Frederick Dvonch, *The Sound of Music*

1961 Franz Allers, *Camelot*
1962 Elliot Lawrence, *How to Succeed in Business Without Really Trying*
1963 Donald Pippin, *Oliver!*
1964 Shepard Coleman, *Hello, Dolly!*

SCENIC DESIGNER

1948 Horace Armistead, *The Medium*
1949 Jo Mielziner, *Sleepy Hollow, Summer and Smoke, Anne of the Thousand Days, Death of a Salesman* and *South Pacific*
1950 Jo Mielziner, *The Innocents*
1951 Boris Aronson, *The Rose Tattoo, The Country Girl* and *Season in the Sun*
1952 Jo Mielziner, *The King & I*
1953 Raoul Pene du Bois, *Wonderful Town*
1954 Peter Larkin, *Ondine* and *The Teahouse of the August Moon*
1955 Oliver Messel, *House of Flowers*
1956 Peter Larkin, *Inherit the Wind* and *No Time for Sergeants*
1957 Oliver Smith, *A Clearing in the Woods, Candide, Auntie Mame, My Fair Lady, Eugenia* and *A Visit to a Small Planet*
1958 Oliver Smith, *West Side Story*
1959 Donald Oenslager, *A Majority of One*
1960 Oliver Smith, *The Sound of Music*
      Howard Bam, *Toys in the Attic*
1961 Oliver Smith, *Camelot* and *Becket*
1962 Will Steven Armstrong, *Carnival*
1963 Sean Kenny, *Oliver!*
1964 Oliver Smith, *Hello, Dolly!*
1965 Oliver Smith, *Baker Street*
1966 Howard Bay, *Man of La Mancha*
1967 Boris Aronson, *Cabaret*
1968 Desmond Heeley, *Rosencrantz and Guildenstern Are Dead*
1969 Boris Aronson, *Zorba*
1970 Jo Mielziner, *Child's Play*
1971 Boris Aronson, *Company*
1972 Boris Aronson, *Follies*
1973 Tony Walton, *Pippin*
1974 Franne and Eugene Lee, *Candide*
1975 Carl Toms, *Sherlock Holmes*
1976 Boris Aronson, *Pacific Overtures*
1977 David Mitchell, *Annie*

COSTUME DESIGNER

1947 Lucinda Ballard, *Happy Birthday, Another Part of the Forest, Street Scene, John Loves Mary* and *The Chocolate Soldier*
      David Ffolkes, *Henry VIII*
1948 Mary Percy Schenck, *The Heiress*
1949 Lemuel Ayers, *Kiss Me Kate*
1950 Aline Bernstein, *Regina*
1951 Miles White, *Bless You All*
1952 Irene Sharaff, *The King & I*
1953 Miles White, *Hazel Flagg*
1954 Richard Whorf, *Ondine*
1955 Cecil Beaton, *Quadrille*
1956 Alvin Colt, *Pipe Dream*
1957 Cecil Beaton, *My Fair Lady*
1958 Motley, *The First Gentleman*
1959 Rouben Ter-Arutunian, *Redhead*
1960 Cecil Beaton, *Saratoga*
1961 Adrian, and Tony Duquette, *Camelot*
1962 Lucinda Ballard, *The Gay Life*
1963 Anthony Powell, *The School for Scandal*
1964 Freddy Wittop, *Hello, Dolly!*

1965 Patricia Zipprodt, *Fiddler on the Roof*
1966 Gunilla Palmstierna-Weiss, *Marat/Sade*
1967 Patricia Zipprodt, *Cabaret*
1968 Desmond Heeley, *Rosencrantz and Guildenstern Are Dead*
1969 Loudon Sainthill, *Canterbury Tales*
1970 Cecil Beaton, *Coco*
1971 Raoul Pene Du Bois, *No, No Nanette*
1972 Florence Klotz, *Follies*
1973 Florence Klotz, *A Little Night Music*
1974 Franne Lee, *Candide*
1975 Geoffrey Holder, *The Wiz*
1976 Florence Klotz, *Pacific Overtures*
1977 Theoni V. Aldredge, *Annie*
        Santo Loquasto, *The Cherry Orchard*

CHOREOGRAPHER

1947 Agnes de Mille, *Brigadoon*
        Michael Kidd, *Finian's Rainbow*
1948 Jerome Robbins, *High Button Shoes*
1949 Gower Champion, *Lend an Ear*
1950 Helen Tamiris, *Touch and Go*
1951 Michael Kidd, *Guys and Dolls*
1952 Robert Alton, *Pal Joey*
1953 Donald Saddler, *Wonderful Town*
1954 Michael Kidd, *Can-Can*
1955 Bob Fosse, *The Pajama Game*
1956 Bob Fosse, *Damn Yankees*
1957 Michael Kidd, *Li'l Abner*
1958 Jerome Robbins, *West Side Story*
1959 Bob Fosse, *Redhead*
1960 Michael Kidd, *Destry Rides Again*
1961 Gower Champion, *Bye, Bye Birdie*
1962 Agnes de Mille, *Kwamina*
        Joe Layton, *No Strings*
1963 Bob Fosse, *Little Me*
1964 Gower Champion, *Hello, Dolly!*
1965 Jerome Robbins, *Fiddler on the Roof*
1966 Bob Fosse, *Sweet Charity*
1967 Ronald Field, *Cabaret*
1968 Gower Champion, *The Happy Time*
1969 Joe Layton, *George M*
1970 Ron Field, *Applause*
1971 Donald Saddler, *No, No Nanette*
1972 Michael Bennett, *Follies*
1973 Bob Fosse, *Pippin*
1974 Michael Bennett, *Seesaw*
1975 George Faison, *The Wiz*
1976 Michael Bennett and Bob Avian, *A Chorus Line*
1977 Peter Gennaro, *Annie*

LIGHTING DESIGN

1970 Jo Mielziner, *Child's Play*
1971 H.R. Poindexter, *Story Theater*
1972 Tharon Musser, *Follies*
1973 Jules Fisher, *Pippin*
1974 Jules Fisher, *Ulysses in Nighttown*
1975 Neil Patrick Jampolis, *Sherlock Holmes*
1976 Tharon Musser, *A Chorus Line*
1977 Jennifer Tipton, *The Cherry Orchard*

STAGE TECHNICIAN

1948 George Gebhardt
        George Pierce
1949 No award
1950 Joe Lynn, *Miss Liberty*
1951 Richard Raven, *The Autumn Garden*
1952 Peter Feller, *Call Me Madam*
1953 Abe Kurnit, *Wish You Were Here*

1954 John Davis, *Picnic*
1955 Richard Rodda, *Peter Pan*
1956 Harry Green, *Middle of the Night* and *Damn Yankees*
1957 Howard McDonald, *Major Barbara*
1958 Harry Romar, *Time Remembered*
1959 Sam Knapp, *The Music Man*
1960 John Walters, *The Miracle Worker*
1961 Teddy Van Bemmel, *Becket*
1962 Michael Burns, *A Man for All Seasons*
1963 Solly Pernick, *Mr. President*
        Milton Smith, *Beyond the Fringe*

SPECIAL AWARDS

1947 Dora Chamberlain
        Mr. and Mrs. Ira Katzenberg
        Jules Leventhal
        Burns Mantle
        P.A. MacDonald
        Arthur Miller
        Vincent Sardi, Sr.
        Kurt Weill
1948 Vera Allen
        Paul Beisman
        Joe E. Brown
        Robert Dowling
        Experimental Theatre, Inc.
        Rosamond Gilder
        June Lockhart
        Mary Martin
        Robert Porterfield
        James Whitmore
1949 No award
1950 Maurice Evans
        Eleanor Roosevelt
1951 Ruth Green
1952 Edward Kook
        Judy Garland
        Charles Boyer
1953 Beatrice Lillie
        Danny Kaye
        Equity Community Theatre
1954 No award
1955 Proscenium Productions
1956 *The Threepenny Opera*
        The Theatre Collection of the New York Public Library
1957 American Shakespeare Festival
        Jean-Louis Barrault, French Repertory
        Robert Russell Bennett
        William Hammerstein
        Paul Shyre
1958 New York Shakespeare Festival
        Mrs. Martin Beck
1959 John Gielgud
        Howard Lindsay and Russel Crouse
1960 John D. Rockefeller 3rd
        James Thurber and Burgess Meredith, *A Thurber Carnival*
1961 David Merrick
        The Theatre Guild
1962 Brooks Atkinson
        Franco Zeffirelli
        Richard Rodgers
1963 W. McNeil Lowry
        Irving Berlin
        Alan Bennett
        Peter Cook
        Jonathan Miller
        Dudley Moore
1964 Eva Le Gallienne

1965 Gilbert Miller
Oliver Smith
1966 Helen Menken
1967 No award
1968 Audrey Hepburn
Carol Channing
Pearl Bailey
David Merrick
Maurice Chevalier
APA-Phoenix Theatre
Marlene Dietrich
1969 The National Theatre Company of Great Britain
The Negro Ensemble Company
Rex Harrison
Leonard Bernstein
Carol Burnett
1970 Noel Coward
Alfred Lunt and Lynn Fontanne
New York Shakespeare Festival
Barbra Streisand
1971 Elliot Norton
Ingram Ash
Playbill
Roger L. Stevens
1972 The Theatre Guild-American Theatre Society
Richard Rodgers
Fiddler on the Roof
Ethel Merman
1973 John Lindsay
Actors' Fund of America
Shubert Organization
1974 Liza Minnelli
Bette Midler
Peter Cook and Dudley Moore, *Good Evening*
A Moon for the Misbegotten
Candide
Actors' Equity Assn.
Theatre Development Fund
John F. Wharton
Harold Friedlander
1975 Neil Simon
Al Hirschfield
1976 Mathilde Pincus
Circle in the Square
Thomas H. Fitzgerald
The Arena Stage
1977 National Theatre for the Deaf
Diana Ross
Lily Tomlin
Barry Manilow
Actors' Equity Library Theatre, New York
Mark Taper Forum Theatre, Los Angeles

Pulitzer Prize

COLUMBIA UNIVERSITY
Graduate School of Journalism, New York, N.Y. 10027;
212/280-3828 (Pulitzer Prizes: 212/280-3841)

Endowed by the will of Joseph Pulitzer, founder of the *St. Louis Post Dispatch,* and administered by Columbia University, the annual Pulitzer Prizes include a $1,000 award for drama. The award is made for a distinguished play by an American playwright, preferably dealing with American life and original in source. Entry must be made to the fifteen-member advisory board

on Pulitzer Prizes while the work is being performed, together with copies of the manuscript.

1917 No award
1918 *Why Marry?* Jesse L. Williams
1919 No award
1920 *Beyond the Horizon,* Eugene O'Neill
1921 *Miss Lulu Bett,* Zona Gale
1922 *Anna Christie,* Eugene O'Neill
1923 *Icebound,* Owen Davis
1924 *Hell-Bent for Heaven,* Hatcher Hughes
1925 *They Knew What They Wanted,* Sidney Howard
1926 *Craig's Wife,* George Kelly
1927 *In Abraham's Bosom,* Paul Green
1928 *Strange Interlude,* Eugene O'Neill
1929 *Street Scene,* Elmer L. Rice
1930 *The Green Pastures,* Marc Connelly
1931 *Alison's House,* Susan Glaspell
1932 *Of Thee I Sing,* George S. Kaufman, Ira Gershwin and Morris Ryskind
1933 *Both Your Houses,* Maxwell Anderson
1934 *Men in White,* Sidney Kingsley
1935 *The Old Maid,* Zoe Akins
1936 *Idiot's Delight,* Robert E. Sherwood
1937 *You Can't Take It With You,* Moss Hart and George S. Kaufman
1938 *Our Town,* Thornton Wilder
1939 *Abe Lincoln in Illinois,* Robert E. Sherwood
1940 *The Time of Your Life,* William Saroyan
1941 *There Shall Be No Night,* Robert E. Sherwood
1942 No award
1943 *The Skin of Our Teeth,* Thornton Wilder
1944 No award
1945 *Harvey,* Mary Chase
1946 *State of the Union,* Russel Crouse and Howard Lindsay
1947 No award
1948 *A Streetcar Named Desire,* Tennessee Williams
1949 *Death of a Salesman,* Arthur Miller
1950 *South Pacific,* Richard Rodgers, Oscar Hammerstein II and Joshua Logan
1951 No award
1952 *The Shrike,* Joseph Kramm
1953 *Picnic,* William Inge
1954 *The Teahouse of the August Moon,* John Patrick
1955 *Cat on a Hot Tin Roof,* Tennessee Williams
1956 *Diary of Anne Frank,* Albert Hackett and Frances Goodrich
1957 *Long Day's Journey Into Night,* Eugene O'Neill
1958 *Look Homeward, Angel,* Ketti Frings
1959 *J.B.,* Archibald MacLeish
1960 *Fiorello!,* Jerome Weidman and George Abbott
1961 *All the Way Home,* Tad Mosel
1962 *How to Succeed in Business Without Really Trying,* Frank Loesser and Abe Burrows
1963 No award
1964 No award
1965 *The Subject Was Roses,* Frank Gilroy
1966 No award
1967 *A Delicate Balance,* Edward Albee
1968 No award
1969 *The Great White Hope,* Howard Sackler
1970 *No Place to Be Somebody,* Charles Gordone
1971 *The Effect of Gamma Rays on Man-in-the-Moon Marigolds,* Paul Zindel
1972 No award
1973 *That Championship Season,* Jason Miller
1974 No award
1975 *Seascape,* Edward Albee

1976 *A Chorus Line,* musical; conceived, choreographed and directed by Michael Bennett; book by James Kirkwood and Nicholas Dante; music by Marvin Hamlisch; lyrics by Edward Kleban

1977 *The Shadow Box,* Michael Cristofer

SPECIAL AWARD

1944 **Richard Rodgers and Oscar Hammerstein II,** *Oklahoma!*

George Spelvin Award
THE MASQUERS
1765 N. Sycamore Ave., Hollywood, Calif. 90028
(213/874-0840)

The George Spelvin Award, which consits of a statuette, is given annually for outstanding dedication to the field of acting and devotion to theatre and community. A committee selects the one or two annual winners.

1972 **Debbie Reynolds**
1973 **Edith Head**
1974 **Mae West**
1975 **Liza Minnelli**
     Lee Strasberg
1976 **Groucho Marx**
     Carroll O'Connor
1977 **Lois Nettleton**
     J. Pasternak

Other Spelvin Awards winners are as follows: Dorothy Malone, John Huston, Lucille Ball, Desi Arnaz, Humphrey Bogart, Ronald Reagan, Karl Malden. The years in which they (and others) were honored are not available.

Stanley Drama Award
WAGNER COLLEGE
Staten Island, N.Y. 10301 (212/390-3256)

The Stanley Drama Award, which carries a cash honorarium of $800, is given annually for playwriting. Any theatre professional (producer, director, playwright, actor, agent, etc.) may nominate a play that has not yet been produced commercially or published by a trade publisher. Preliminary readers select finalists, from which a winner is selected by a panel of judges.

1962 **Terrence McNally,** *This Side of the Door*
1963 **Adrienne Kennedy,** *Funnyhouse of a Negro* and *The Owl Answers*
1964 **Megan Terry,** *Hothouse*
     Joseph Baldwin, *Thompson*
1965 **Lonne Elder III,** *Ceremonies in Dark Old Men*
1966 **Albert Zuckerman,** *To Become a Man*
1967 **William Parchman,** *The Prize in the Crackerjack Box*
1968 **Venable Herndon,** *Bag of Flies*
1969 **Bernard Sabath,** *A Happy New Year to the Whole World Except Alexander Graham Bell*
     Yale Udoff, *The Club*
1970 **Richard Lortz,** *Three Sons (of Sons and Brothers)*
1971 **Ben Rosa,** *Obtuse Triangle*
1972 **Marvin Denicoff,** *Fortune Teller Man*
1973 **C. Richard Gillespie,** *Carnivori*
1974 **Gus Weill,** *Son of the Last Mule Dealer*
1975 **Alan Riefe and Robert Haymes,** *Jonathan (A Musical)*
1976 **Carol Mack,** *A Safe Place*
1977 **Jack Zeman,** *Past Tense*

Cinema

Contents

Related Awards

Academy Awards

ACADEMY OF MOTION PICTURE ARTS AND SCIENCES
8948 Wilshire Blvd., Beverly Hills, Calif. 90211
(213/278-8990)

The Academy Award, a statuette known as the Oscar, is given annually for excellence in some twenty categories of motion picture achievement for films released in Los Angeles during the calendar year, plus special honors for contributions to cinema, which are given as merited. Academy members in each field of endeavor may make nominees in their own category. Up to five nominees per category are submitted for secret ballot by the entire membership. Special honors for overall achievement are conferred by the Academy's board of governors. The presentation of the Academy Award has developed from a small dinner for 250 persons in 1928 to a gala spectacle telecast to an audience estimated at more than 150-million viewers. The Oscar is the motion picture industry's best known American honor, and one of the most coveted in the world.

BEST PICTURE

1928 *Wings*
1929 *The Broadway Melody*
1930 *All Quiet on the Western Front*
1931 *Cimarron*
1932 *Grand Hotel*
1933 *Cavalcade*
1934 *It Happened One Night*
1935 *Mutiny on the Bounty*
1936 *The Great Ziegfeld*
1937 *The Life of Emile Zola*
1938 *You Can't Take It with You*
1939 *Gone With the Wind*
1940 *Rebecca*
1941 *How Green Was My Valley*
1942 *Mrs. Miniver*
1943 *Casablanca*
1944 *Going My Way*
1945 *The Lost Weekend*
1946 *The Best Years of Our Lives*
1947 *Gentleman's Agreement*
1948 *Hamlet*
1949 *All the King's Men*
1950 *All About Eve*
1951 *An American in Paris*
1952 *The Greatest Show on Earth*
1953 *From Here to Eternity*
1954 *On the Waterfront*
1955 *Marty*
1956 *Around the World in 80 Days*
1957 *The Bridge on the River Kwai*
1958 *Gigi*
1959 *Ben-Hur*
1960 *The Apartment*
1961 *West Side Story*
1962 *Lawrence of Arabia*
1963 *Tom Jones*
1964 *My Fair Lady*
1965 *The Sound of Music*
1966 *A Man for All Seasons*
1967 *In the Heat of the Night*
1968 *Oliver!*
1969 *Midnight Cowboy*
1970 *Patton*
1971 *The French Connection*
1972 *The Godfather*
1973 *The Sting*
1974 *The Godfather, Part II*
1975 *One Flew Over the Cuckoo's Nest*
1976 *Rocky*
1977 *Annie Hall*

BEST ACTOR

1928 **Emil Jannings,** *The Way of All Flesh* and *The Last Command*
1929 **Warner Baxter,** *In Old Arizona*
1930 **George Arliss,** *Disraeli*
1931 **Lionel Barrymore,** *A Free Soul*
1932 **Fredric March,** *Dr. Jekyll and Mr. Hyde,*
Wallace Beery, *The Champ*
1933 **Charles Laughton,** *The Private Life of Henry VIII*
1934 **Clark Gable,** *It Happened One Night*
1935 **Victor McLaglen,** *The Informer*
1936 **Paul Muni,** *The Story of Louis Pasteur*
1937 **Spencer Tracy,** *Captains Courageous*
1938 **Spencer Tracy,** *Boys Town*
1939 **Robert Donat,** *Goodbye, Mr. Chips*
1940 **James Stewart,** *The Philadelphia Story*
1941 **Gary Cooper,** *Sergeant York*
1942 **James Cagney,** *Yankee Doodle Dandy*
1943 **Paul Lukas,** *Watch on the Rhine*
1944 **Bing Crosby,** *Going My Way*
1945 **Ray Milland,** *The Lost Weekend*
1946 **Fredric March,** *The Best Years of Our Lives*
1947 **Ronald Colman,** *A Double Life*
1948 **Laurence Olivier,** *Hamlet*
1949 **Broderick Crawford,** *All the King's Men*
1950 **Jose Ferrer,** *Cyrano de Bergerac*
1951 **Humphrey Bogart,** *The African Queen*
1952 **Gary Cooper,** *High Noon*
1953 **William Holden,** *Stalag 17*
1954 **Marlon Brando,** *On the Waterfront*
1955 **Ernest Borgnine,** *Marty*
1956 **Yul Brynner,** *The King and I*
1957 **Alec Guinness,** *The Bridge on the River Kwai*
1958 **David Niven,** *Separate Tables*
1959 **Charlton Heston,** *Ben-Hur*
1960 **Burt Lancaster,** *Elmer Gantry*
1961 **Maximilian Schell,** *Judgment at Nuremberg*
1962 **Gregory Peck,** *To Kill a Mockingbird*
1963 **Sidney Poitier,** *Lilies of the Field*
1964 **Rex Harrison,** *My Fair Lady*
1965 **Lee Marvin,** *Cat Ballou*
1966 **Paul Scofield,** *A Man for All Seasons*
1967 **Rod Steiger,** *In the Heat of the Night*
1968 **Cliff Robertson,** *Charly*
1969 **John Wayne,** *True Grit*
1970 **George C. Scott,** *Patton*
1971 **Gene Hackman,** *The French Connection*
1972 **Marlon Brando,** *The Godfather*
1973 **Jack Lemmon,** *Save the Tiger*
1974 **Art Carney,** *Harry and Tonto*
1975 **Jack Nicholson,** *One Flew Over the Cuckoo's Nest*
1976 **Peter Finch,** *Network*
1977 **Richard Dreyfuss,** *The Goodbye Girl*

BEST ACTRESS

1928 **Janet Gaynor,** *Seventh Heaven, Street Angel* and *Sunrise*
1929 **Mary Pickford,** *Coquette*
1930 **Norma Shearer,** *The Divorcee*
1931 **Marie Dressler,** *Min and Bill*
1932 **Helen Hayes,** *The Sin of Madelon Claudet*

1933 Katharine Hepburn, *Morning Glory*
1934 Claudette Colbert, *It Happened One Night*
1935 Bette Davis, *Dangerous*
1936 Luise Rainer, *The Great Ziegfeld*
1937 Luise Rainer, *The Good Earth*
1938 Bette Davis, *Jezebel*
1939 Vivien Leigh, *Gone With the Wind*
1940 Ginger Rogers, *Kitty Foyle*
1941 Joan Fontaine, *Suspicion*
1942 Greer Garson, *Mrs. Miniver*
1943 Jennifer Jones, *The Song of Bernadette*
1944 Ingrid Bergman, *Gaslight*
1945 Joan Crawford, *Mildred Pierce*
1946 Olivia de Havilland, *To Each His Own*
1947 Loretta Young, *The Farmer's Daughter*
1948 Jane Wyman, *Johnny Belinda*
1949 Olivia de Havilland, *The Heiress*
1950 Judy Holliday, *Born Yesterday*
1951 Vivien Leigh, *A Streetcar Named Desire*
1952 Shirley Booth, *Come Back Little Sheba*
1953 Audrey Hepburn, *Roman Holiday*
1954 Grace Kelly, *The Country Girl*
1955 Anna Magnani, *The Rose Tattoo*
1956 Ingrid Bergman, *Anastasia*
1957 Joanne Woodward, *The Three Faces of Eve*
1958 Susan Hayward, *I Want to Live!*
1959 Simone Signoret, *Room at the Top*
1960 Elizabeth Taylor, *Butterfield 8*
1961 Sophia Loren, *Two Women*
1962 Anne Bancroft, *The Miracle Worker*
1963 Patricia Neal, *Hud*
1964 Julie Andrews, *Mary Poppins*
1965 Julie Christie, *Darling*
1966 Elizabeth Taylor, *Who's Afraid of Virginia Woolf?*
1967 Katharine Hepburn, *Guess Who's Coming to Dinner*
1968 Katharine Hepburn, *The Lion in Winter*
  Barbra Streisand, *Funny Girl*
1969 Maggie Smith, *The Prime of Miss Jean Brodie*
1970 Glenda Jackson, *Women in Love*
1971 Jane Fonda, *Klute*
1972 Liza Minnelli, *Cabaret*
1973 Glenda Jackson, *A Touch of Class*
1974 Ellen Burstyn, *Alice Doesn't Live Here Anymore*
1975 Louise Fletcher, *One Flew Over the Cuckoo's Nest*
1976 Faye Dunaway, *Network*
1977 Diane Keaton, *Annie Hall*

BEST DIRECTOR

1928 Frank Borzage, *Seventh Heaven*
  Lewis Milestone, *Two Arabian Nights*
1929 Frank Lloyd, *The Divine Lady*
1930 Lewis Milestone, *All Quiet on the Western Front*
1931 Norman Taurog, *Skippy*
1932 Frank Borzage, *Bad Girl*
1933 Frank Lloyd, *Cavalcade*
1934 Frank Capra, *It Happened One Night*
1935 John Ford, *The Informer*
1936 Frank Capra, *Mr. Deeds Goes to Town*
1937 Leo McCarey, *The Awful Truth*
1938 Frank Capra, *You Can't Take It with You*
1939 Victor Fleming, *Gone With the Wind*
1940 John Ford, *The Grapes of Wrath*
1941 John Ford, *How Green Was My Valley*
1942 William Wyler, *Mrs. Miniver*
1943 Michael Curtiz, *Casablanca*
1944 Leo McCarey, *Going My Way*
1945 Billy Wilder, *The Lost Weekend*
1946 William Wyler, *The Best Years of Our Lives*
1947 Elia Kazan, *Gentleman's Agreement*
1948 John Huston, *Treasure of Sierra Madre*

1949 Joseph L. Mankiewicz, *A Letter to Three Wives*
1950 Joseph L. Mankiewicz, *All About Eve*
1951 George Stevens, *A Place in the Sun*
1952 John Ford, *The Quiet Man*
1953 Fred Zinnemann, *From Here to Eternity*
1954 Elia Kazan, *On the Waterfront*
1955 Delbert Mann, *Marty*
1956 George Stevens, *Giant*
1957 David Lean, *The Bridge on the River Kwai*
1958 Vincente Minnelli, *Gigi*
1959 William Wyler, *Ben-Hur*
1960 Billy Wilder, *The Apartment*
1961 Robert Wise and Jerome Robbins, *West Side Story*
1962 David Lean, *Lawrence of Arabia*
1963 Tony Richardson, *Tom Jones*
1964 George Cukor, *My Fair Lady*
1965 Robert Wise, *The Sound of Music*
1966 Fred Zinnemann, *A Man for All Seasons*
1967 Mike Nichols, *The Graduate*
1968 Sir Carol Reed, *Oliver!*
1969 John Schlesinger, *Midnight Cowboy*
1970 Franklin J. Schaffner, *Patton*
1971 William Friedkin, *The French Connection*
1972 Bob Fosse, *Cabaret*
1973 George Roy Hill, *The Sting*
1974 Francis Ford Coppola, *The Godfather, Part II*
1975 Milos Forman, *One Flew Over the Cuckoo's Nest*
1976 John G. Avildsen, *Rocky*
1977 Woody Allen, *Annie Hall*

BEST SUPPORTING ACTOR

1936 Walter Brennan, *Come and Get It*
1937 Joseph Schildkraut, *The Life of Emile Zola*
1938 Walter Brennan, *Kentucky*
1939 Thomas Mitchell, *Stagecoach*
1940 Walter Brennan, *The Westerner*
1941 Donald Crisp, *How Green Was My Valley*
1942 Van Heflin, *Johnny Eager*
1943 Charles Coburn, *The More the Merrier*
1944 Barry Fitzgerald, *Going My Way*
1945 James Dunn, *A Tree Grows in Brooklyn*
1946 Harold Russell, *The Best Years of Our Lives*
1947 Edmund Gwenn, *Miracle on 34th Street*
1948 Walter Huston, *Treasure of Sierra Madre*
1949 Dean Jagger, *Twelve O'Clock High*
1950 George Sanders, *All About Eve*
1951 Karl Malden, *A Streetcar Named Desire*
1952 Anthony Quinn, *Viva Zapata!*
1953 Frank Sinatra, *From Here to Eternity*
1954 Edmond O'Brien, *The Barefoot Contessa*
1955 Jack Lemmon, *Mister Roberts*
1956 Anthony Quinn, *Lust for Life*
1957 Red Buttons, *Sayonara*
1958 Burl Ives, *The Big Country*
1959 Hugh Griffith, *Ben-Hur*
1960 Peter Ustinov, *Spartacus*
1961 George Chakiris, *West Side Story*
1962 Ed Begley, *Sweet Bird of Youth*
1963 Melvyn Douglas, *Hud*
1964 Peter Ustinov, *Topkapi*
1965 Martin Balsam, *A Thousand Clowns*
1966 Walter Matthau, *The Fortune Cookie*
1967 George Kennedy, *Cool Hand Luke*
1968 Jack Albertson, *The Subject Was Roses*
1969 Gig Young, *They Shoot Horses, Don't They?*
1970 John Mills, *Ryan's Daughter*
1971 Ben Johnson, *The Last Picture Show*
1972 Joel Grey, *Cabaret*
1973 John Houseman, *The Paper Chase*
1974 Robert De Niro, *The Godfather, Part II*

1975 George Burns, *The Sunshine Boys*
1976 Jason Robards, *All The President's Men*
1977 Jason Robards, *Julia*

BEST SUPPORTING ACTRESS

1936 Gale Sondergaard, *Anthony Adverse*
1937 Alice Brady, *In Old Chicago*
1938 Fay Bainter, *Jezebel*
1939 Hattie McDaniel, *Gone With the Wind*
1940 Jane Darwell, *The Grapes of Wrath*
1941 Mary Astor, *The Great Lie*
1942 Teresa Wright, *Mrs. Miniver*
1943 Katina Paxinou, *For Whom the Bell Tolls*
1944 Ethel Barrymore, *None But the Lonely Heart*
1945 Anne Revere, *National Velvet*
1946 Anne Baxter, *The Razor's Edge*
1947 Celeste Holm, *Gentleman's Agreement*
1948 Claire Trevor, *Key Largo*
1949 Mercedes McCambridge, *All the King's Men*
1950 Josephine Hull, *Harvey*
1951 Kim Hunter, *A Streetcar Named Desire*
1952 Gloria Grahame, *The Bad and the Beautiful*
1953 Donna Reed, *From Here to Eternity*
1954 Eva Marie Saint, *On the Waterfront*
1955 Jo Van Fleet, *East of Eden*
1956 Dorothy Malone, *Written on the Wind*
1957 Miyoshi Umeki, *Sayonara*
1958 Wendy Hiller, *Separate Tables*
1959 Shelley Winters, *The Diary of Anne Frank*
1960 Shirley Jones, *Elmer Gantry*
1961 Rita Moreno, *West Side Story*
1962 Patty Duke, *The Miracle Worker*
1963 Margaret Rutherford, *The V.I.P.'s*
1964 Lila Kedrova, *Zorba the Greek*
1965 Shelley Winters, *A Patch of Blue*
1966 Sandy Dennis, *Who's Afraid of Virginia Woolf?*
1967 Estelle Parsons, *Bonnie and Clyde*
1968 Ruth Gordon, *Rosemary's Baby*
1969 Goldie Hawn, *Cactus Flower*
1970 Helen Hayes, *Airport*
1971 Cloris Leachman, *The Last Picture Show*
1972 Eileen Heckart, *Butterflies Are Free*
1973 Tatum O'Neal, *Paper Moon*
1974 Ingrid Bergman, *Murder on the Orient Express*
1975 Lee Grant, *Shampoo*
1976 Beatrice Straight, *Network*
1977 Vanessa Redgrave, *Julia*

ART DIRECTION

1928 William Menzies, *The Dove* and *The Tempest*
1929 Cedric Gibbons, *The Bridge of San Luis Rey*
1930 Herman Rosse, *King of Jazz*
1931 Max Ree, *Cimarron*
1932 Gordon Wiles, *Transatlantic*
1933 William S. Darling, *Cavalcade*
1934 Cedric Gibbons and Frederic Hope, *The Merry Widow*
1935 Richard Day, *The Dark Angel*
1936 Richard Day, *Dodsworth*
1937 Stephen Goosson, *Lost Horizon*
1938 Carl Weyl, *The Adventures of Robin Hood*
1939 Lyle Wheeler, *Gone With The Wind*

ART DIRECTION/COLOR

1940 Vincent Korda, *The Thief of Bagdad*
1941 Cedric Gibbons and Urie McCleary, *Blossoms In the Dust*
1942 Richard Day and Joseph Wright, *My Gal Sal*

1943 Alexander Golitzen and John B. Goodman, *The Phantom of the Opera*
1944 Wiard Ihnen, *Wilson*
1945 Hans Dreier and Ernst Fegte, *Frenchman's Creek*
1946 Cedric Gibbons and Paul Groesse, *The Yearling*
1947 Alfred Junge, *Black Narcissus*
1948 Hein Heckroth, *The Red Shoes*
1949 Cedric Gibbons and Paul Groesse, *Little Women*
1950 Hans Dreier and Walter Tyler, *Samson and Delilah*
1951 Cedric Gibbons and Preston Ames, *An American in Paris*
1952 Paul Sheriff, *Moulin Rouge*
1953 Lyle Wheeler and George W. Davis, *The Robe*
1954 John Meehan, *20,000 Leagues Under the Sea*
1955 William Flannery and Jo Mielziner, *Picnic*
1956 Lyle R. Wheeler and John de Cuir, *The King and I*

ART DIRECTION/BLACK AND WHITE

1940 Cedric Gibbons and Paul Groesse, *Pride and Pejudice*
1941 Richard Day and Nathan Juran, *How Green Was My Valley*
1942 Richard Day and Joseph Wright, *This Above All*
1943 James Basevi and William Darling, *The Song of Bernadette*
1944 Cedric Gibbons and William Ferrari, *Gaslight*
1945 Wiard Ihnen, *Blood On the Sun*
1946 Lyle Wheeler and William Darling, *Anna and the King of Siam*
1947 John Bryan, *Great Expectations*
1948 Roger K. Furse, *Hamlet*
1949 Harry Horner and John Meehan, *The Heiress*
1950 Hans Dreier and John Meehan, *Sunset Boulevard*
1951 Richard Day, *A Streetcar Named Desire*
1952 Cedric Gibbons and Edward Carfagno, *The Bad And The Beautiful*
1953 Cedric Gibbons and Edward Carfagno, *Julius Caesar*
1954 Richard Day, *On the Waterfront*
1955 Hal Pereira and Tambi Larsen, *The Rose Tattoo*
1956 Cedric Gibbons and Malcolm F. Brown, *Somebody Up There Likes Me*

ART DIRECTION

1957 Ted Haworth, *Sayonara*
1958 William A. Horning and Preston Ames, *Gigi*

ART DIRECTION/COLOR

1959 William A. Horning and Edward Carfagno, *Ben-Hur*
1960 Alexander Golitzen and Eric Orbom, *Spartacus*
1961 Boris Leven, *West Side Story*
1962 John Box and John Stoll, *Lawrence of Arabia*
1963 John De Cuir, Jack Martin Smith, Hilyard Brown, Herman Blumental, Elven Webb, Maurice Pelling and Boris Juraga, *Cleopatra*
1964 Gene Allen and Cecil Beaton, *My Fair Lady*
1965 John Box and Terry Marsh, *Dr. Zhivago*
1966 Jack Martin Smith and Dale Hennesy, *Fantastic Voyage*

ART DIRECTION/BLACK AND WHITE

1959 Lyle R. Wheeler and George W. Davis, *The Diary of Anne Frank*
1960 Alexander Trauner, *The Apartment*
1961 Harry Horner, *The Hustler*
1962 Alexander Goltizen and Henry Bumstead, *To Kill A Mockingbird*
1963 Gene Callahan, *America, America*

1964 Vassilis Fotopoulos, *Zorba The Greek*
1965 Robert Clatworthy, *Ship of Fools*
1966 Richard Sylbert, *Who's Afraid of Virginia Woolf?*

ART DIRECTION

1967 John Truscott and Edward Carrere, *Camelot*
1968 John Box and Terence Marsh, *Oliver!*
1969 John De Cuir, Jack Martin Smith and Herman Blumenthal, *Hello, Dolly!*
1970 Urie McCleary and Gil Parrondo, *Patton*
1971 John Box, Ernest Archer, Jack Maxsted and Gil Parrondo, *Nicholas and Alexandra*
1972 Rolf Zehetbauer and Jurgen Kiebach, *Cabaret*
1973 Henry Bumstead, *The Sting*
1974 Dean Tavoularis and Angelo Graham, *The Godfather, Part II*
1975 Ken Adam and Roy Walker, *Barry Lyndon*
1976 George Jenkins, *All The President's Men*
1977 John Barry, Norman Reynolds and Leslie Dilley, *Star Wars*

CINEMATOGRAPHY

1928 Charles Rosher and Karl Struss, *Sunrise*
1929 Clyde De Vinna, *White Shadows In The South Seas*
1930 Joseph T. Rucker and Willard Van Der Veer, *With Byrd At The South Pole*
1931 Floyd Crosby, *Tabu*
1932 Lee Garmes, *Shanghai Express*
1933 Charles Bryant Lang, Jr., *A Farewell To Arms*
1934 Victor Milner, *Cleopatra*
1935 Hal Mohr, *A Midsummer Night's Dream*
1936 Tony Gaudio, *Anthony Adverse*
1937 Karl Freund, *The Good Earth*
1938 Joseph Ruttenberg, *The Great Waltz*

CINEMATOGRAPHY/COLOR

1939 Ernest Haller and Ray Rennahan, *Gone With the Wind*
1940 George Perrinal, *The Thief of Bagdad*
1941 Ernest Palmer and Ray Rennahan, *Blood And Sand*
1942 Leon Shamroy, *The Black Swan*
1943 Hal Mohr and W. Howard Greene, *The Phantom Of The Opera*
1944 Leon Shamroy, *Wilson*
1945 Leon Shamroy, *Leave Her To Heaven*
1946 Charles Rosher, Leonard Smith and Arthur Arling, *The Yearling*
1947 Jack Cardiff, *Black Narcissus*
1948 Joseph Valentine, William V. Skall and Winton Hoch, *Joan Of Arc*
1949 Winton Hoch, *She Wore A Yellow Ribbon*
1950 Robert Surtees, *King Solomon's Mines*
1951 Alfred Gilks and John Alton, *An American in Paris*
1952 Winton C. Hoch and Archie Stout, *The Quiet Man*
1953 Loyal Griggs, *Shane*
1954 Milton Krasner, *Three Coins In The Fountain*
1955 Robert Burks, *To Catch A Thief*
1956 Lionel Lindon, *Around The World In 80 Days*
1957 Jack Hildyard, *The Bridge On The River Kwai*
1958 Joseph Ruttenberg, *Gigi*
1959 Robert L. Surtees, *Ben-Hur*
1960 Russell Metty, *Spartacus*
1961 Daniel L. Fapp, *West Side Story*
1962 Fred A. Young, *Lawrence of Arabia*
1963 Leon Shamroy, *Cleopatra*
1964 Harry Stradling, *My Fair Lady*
1965 Freddie Young, *Dr. Zhivago*
1966 Ted Moore, *A Man For All Seasons*

CINEMATOGRAPHY/BLACK AND WHITE

1939 Gregg Toland, *Wuthering Heights*
1940 George Barnes, *Rebecca*
1941 Arthur Miller, *How Green Was My Valley*
1942 Joseph Ruttenberg, *Mrs. Miniver*
1943 Arthur Miller, *The Song of Bernadette*
1944 Joseph LaShelle, *Laura*
1945 Harry Stradling, *The Picture of Dorian Gray*
1946 Arthur Miller, *Anna And The King Of Siam*
1947 Guy Green, *Great Expectations*
1948 William Daniels, *The Naked City*
1949 Paul C. Vogel, *Battleground*
1950 Robert Krasker, *The Third Man*
1951 William C. Mellor, *A Place In The Sun*
1952 Robert Surtees, *The Bad And The Beautiful*
1953 Burnett Guffey, *From Here To Eternity*
1954 Boris Kaufman, *On The Waterfront*
1955 James Wong Howe, *The Rose Tattoo*
1956 Joseph Ruttenberg, *Somebody Up There Likes Me*
1957 No award
1958 Sam Leavitt, *The Defiant Ones*
1959 William C. Mellor, *The Diary Of Anne Frank*
1960 Freddie Francis, *Sons and Lovers*
1961 Eugen Shuftan, *The Hustler*
1962 Jean Bourgoin and and Walter Wottitz, *The Longest Day*
1963 James Wong Howe, *Hud*
1964 Walter Lassally, *Zorba The Greek*
1965 Ernest Laszlo, *Ship Of Fools*
1966 Haskell Wexler, *Who's Afraid of Virginia Woolf?*

CINEMATOGRAPHY

1967 Burnett Guffey, *Bonnie and Clyde*
1968 Pasqualino De Santis, *Romeo & Juliet*
1969 Conrad Hall, *Butch Cassidy and The Sundance Kid*
1970 Freddie Young, *Ryan's Daughter*
1971 Oswald Morris, *Fiddler On The Roof*
1972 Geoffrey Unsworth, *Cabaret*
1973 Sven Nykvist, *Cries and Whispers*
1974 Fred Koenekamp and Joseph Biroc, *The Towering Inferno*
1975 John Alcott, *Barry Lyndon*
1976 Haskell Wexler, *Bound for Glory*
1977 Wilmos Zsigmond, *Close Encounters of the Third Kind*

WRITING/ACHIEVEMENT

1929 Hans Kraly, *The Patriot*
1930 Frances Marion, *The Big House*

WRITING/ORIGINAL STORY

1928 Ben Hecht, *Underworld*
1929 No award
1930 No award
1931 John Monk Saunders, *The Dawn Patrol*
1932 Frances Marion, *The Champ*
1933 Robert Lord, *One Way Passage*
1934 Arthur Caesar, *Manhattan Melodrama*
1935 Ben Hecht and Charles MacArthur, *The Scoundrel*
1936 Pierre Collings and Sheridan Gibney, *The Story of Louis Pasteur*
1937 Robert Carson and William A. Wellman, *A Star Is Born*
1938 Dore Schary and Eleanore Griffin, *Boys Town*
1939 Lewis R. Foster, *Mr. Smith Goes to Washington*
1940 Benjamin Glazer and John S. Toddy, *Arise, My Love*
1941 Harry Segall, *Here Comes Mr. Jordan*
1942 Emeric Pressburger, *The Invaders*
1943 William Saroyan, *The Human Comedy*

1944 Leo McCarey, *Going My Way*
1945 Charles G. Booth, *The House on 92nd Street*
1946 Clemence Dane, *Vacation From Marriage*
1947 Valentine Davies, *Miracle on 34th Street*

WRITING/MOTION PICTURE STORY
1948 Richard Schweizer and David Wechsler, *The Search*
1949 Douglas Marrow, *The Stratton Story*
1950 Edna Anhalt and Edward Anhalt, *Panic in the Streets*
1951 Paul Dehn and James Bernard, *Seven Days to Noon*
1952 Fredric M. Frank, Theodore St. John and Frank Cavett, *The Greatest Show on Earth*
1953 Ian McLellan Hunter, *Roman Holiday*
1954 Philip Yordan, *Broken Lance*
1955 Daniel Fuchs, *Love Me or Leave Me*
1956 Dalton Trumbo, *The Brave One*

WRITING/TITLE
1928 Joseph Farnham, *The Fair Co-Ed, Laugh, Clown, Laugh* and *Telling The World*

WRITING/ADAPTATION
1928 Benjamin Glazer, *Seventh Heaven*
1929 No award
1930 No award
1930 Howard Estabrook, *Cimarron*
1932 Edwin Burke, *Bad Girl*
1933 Sarah Y. Mason and Victor Heerman, *Little Women*
1934 Robert Riskin, *It Happened One Night*
1935 No award
1936 No award
1937 No award
1938 W.P. Lipscomb, Cecil Lewis and Ian Dalrymple, *Pygmalion*

WRITING/BEST WRITTEN SCREENPLAY
1935 Dudley Nichols, *The Informer*
1936 Pierre Collings and Sheridan Gibney, *The Story of Louis Pasteur*
1937 Norman Reilly Raine, Heinz Herald and Geza Herzceg, *The Life of Emile Zola*
1938 George Bernard Shaw, *Pygmalion*
1939 Sidney Howard, *Gone With the Wind*
1940 Donald Ogden Stewart, *The Philadelphia Story*
1941 Sidney Buchman and Seton I. Miller, *Here Comes Mr. Jordan*
1942 Arthur Wimperis, George Froeschell, James Hilton and Claudine West, *Mrs. Miniver*
1943 Julius J. Epstein, Philip C. Epstein and Howard Koch, *Casablanca*
1944 Frank Butler and Frank Cavett, *Going My Way*
1945 Charles Brackett and Billy Wilder, *The Lost Weekend*
1946 Robert E. Sherwood, *The Best Years of Our Lives*
1947 George Seaton, *Miracle on 34th Street*
1948 John Juston, *Treasure of Sierre Madre*
1949 Joseph L. Mankiewicz, *A Letter to Three Wives*

WRITING/ORIGINAL SCREENPLAY
1940 Preston Sturges, *The Great McGinty*
1941 Herman J. Mankiewicz and Orson Welles, *Citizen Kane*
1942 Ring Lardner, Jr., and Michael Kanin, *Woman of the Year*
1943 Norman Krasna, *Princess O'Rourke*
1944 Lamar Trotti, *Wilson*
1945 Richard Schweizer, *Marie-Louise*

1946 Muriel Box and Sidney Box, *The Seventh Veil*
1947 Sidney Sheldon, *The Bachelor and the Bobbysoxer*

WRITING/STORY AND SCREENPLAY
1949 Robert Pirosh, *Battleground*
1950 Charles Brackett, Billy Wilder and D.M. Marshman, Jr., *Sunset Boulevard*
1951 Alan Jay Lerner, *An American in Paris*
1952 T.E.B. Clarke, *The Lavender Hill Mob*
1953 Charles Brackett, Walter Reisch and Richard Breen, *Titanic*
1954 Budd Schulberg, *On The Waterfront*
1955 William Ludwig and Sonya Levien, *Interrupted Melody*
1956 James Poe, John Farrow and S.J. Perelman, *Around the World in 80 Days* (adapted)
     Albert Lamorisse, *The Red Balloon* (original)
1957 George Wells, *Designing Woman*
1958 Nathan E. Douglas and Harold Jacob Smith, *The Defiant Ones*
1959 Russell Rouse and Clarence Greene (story) and Stanley Shapiro and Maurice Richlin (screenplay), *Pillow Talk*
1960 Billy Wilder and I.A.L. Diamond, *The Apartment*
1961 William Inge, *Splendor in the Grass*
1962 Ennio de Concini, Alfredo Giannetti and Pietro Germi, *Divorce—Italian Style*
1963 James R. Webb, *How the West Was Won*
1964 S.H. Barnett (story) and Peter Stone and Frank Tarloff (screenplay), *Father Goose*
1965 Frederick Raphael, *Darling*
1966 Claude Lelouch (story) and Pierre Uytterhoeven and Claude Lelouch (screenplay), *A Man and A Woman*
1967 William Rose, *Guess Who's Coming to Dinner*
1968 Mel Brooks, *The Producers*
1969 William Goldman, *Butch Cassidy and The Sundance Kid*
1970 Francis Ford Coppola and Edmund H. North, *Patton*
1971 Paddy Chayefsky, *The Hospital*
1972 Jeremy Larner, *The Candidate*
1973 Davis S. Ward, *The Sting*

WRITING/ORIGINAL SCREENPLAY
1974 Robert Towne, *Chinatown*
1975 Frank Pierson, *Dog Day Afternoon*
1976 Paddy Chayefsky, *Network*
1977 Woody Allen and Marshall Brickman, *Annie Hall*

WRITING/SCREENPLAY BASED ON MATERIAL FROM ANOTHER MEDIUM
1957 Pierre Boulle, *The Bridge on the River Kwai*
1958 Alan Jay Lerner, *Gigi*
1959 Neil Paterson, *Room at the Top*
1960 Richard Brooks, *Elmer Gantry*
1961 Abby Mann, *Judgment at Nuremberg*
1962 Horton Foote, *To Kill a Mockingbird*
1963 John Osborne, *Tom Jones*
1964 Edward Anhalt, *Becket*
1965 Robert Bolt, *Dr. Zhivago*
1966 Robert Bolt, *A Man for All Seasons*
1967 Stirling Silliphant, *In the Heat of the Night*
1968 James Goldman, *The Lion in Winter*
1969 Waldo Salt, *Midnight Cowboy*
1970 Ring Lardner, Jr., *M*A*S*H**
1971 Ernest Tidyman, *The French Connection*

1972 Mario Puzo and Francis Ford Coppola, *The Godfather*
1973 William Peter Blatty, *The Exorcist*

WRITING/SCREENPLAY ADAPTED FROM OTHER MATERIAL

1974 Francis Ford Coppola and Mario Puzo, *The Godfather, Part II*
1975 Lawrence Hauben and Bo Goldman, *One Flew Over the Cuckoo's Nest*
1976 William Goldman, *All The President's Men*
1977 Alvin Sargent, *Julia*

ASSISTANT DIRECTOR

1933 William Tummel, 20th Century Fox
    Charles Dorian, Metro-Goldwyn-Mayer
    Charles Barton, Paramount
    Dowey Starkey, RKO Radio
    Fred Fox, United Artists
    Scott Beal, Universal
    Gordon Hollingshead, Warner Bros.
1934 John Waters, *Viva Villa*
1935 Clen Beauchamp and Paul Wing, *Lives of a Bengal Lancer*
1936 Jack Sullivan, *The Charge of the Light Brigade*
1937 Robert Webb, *In Old Chicago*

COSTUME DESIGN/BLACK AND WHITE

1948 Roger K. Furse, *Hamlet*
1949 Edith Head and Gile Steele, *The Heiress*
1950 Edith Head and Charles Le Maire, *All About Eve*
1951 Edith Head, *A Place in the Sun*
1952 Helen Rose, *The Bad and the Beautiful*
1953 Edith Head, *Roman Holiday*
1954 Edith Head, *Sabrina*
1955 Helen Rose, *I'll Cry Tomorrow*
1956 Jean Louis, *The Solid Gold Cadillac*
1957 No award
1958 No award
1959 Orry-Kelly, *Some Like It Hot*
1960 Edith Head and Howard Stevenson, *The Facts of Life*
1961 Piero Gherardi, *La Dolce Vita*
1962 Norma Koch, *Whatever Happened to Baby Jane?*
1963 Piero Gherardi, *Federico Fellini's 8½*
1964 Dorothy Jeakins, *The Night of the Iguana*
1965 Julie Harris, *Darling*
1966 Irene Sharaff, *Who's Afraid of Virginia Woolf?*

COSTUME DESIGN/COLOR

1948 Dorothy Jeakins and Karinska, *Joan of Arc*
1949 Leah Rhodes, Travilla and Marjorie Best, *Adventures of Don Juan*
1950 Edith Head, Dorothy Jeakins, Elois Jenssen, Gile Steele and Gwen Wakeling, *Samson and Delilah*
1951 Orry-Kelly, Walter Plunkett and Irene Sharaff, *An American in Paris*
1952 Marcel Vertes, *Moulin Rouge*
1953 Charles Le Maire and Emile Santiago, *The Robe*
1954 Sanzo Wada, *Gate of Hell*
1955 Charles Le Maire, *Love is a Many-Splendored Thing*
1956 Irene Sharaff, *The King and I*
1957 Orry-Kelly, *Les Girls*
1958 Cecil Beaton, *Gigi*
1959 Elizabeth Haffenden, *Ben-Hur*
1960 Valles and Bill Thomas, *Spartacus*
1961 Irene Sharaff, *West Side Story*

1962 Mary Wills, *The Wonderful World of the Brothers Grimm*
1963 Irene Sharaff, Vittorio Nino Novarese and Renie, *Cleopatra*
1964 Cecil Beaton, *My Fair Lady*
1965 Phillis Dalton, *Dr. Zhivago*
1966 Elizabeth Haffenden and Joan Bridge, *A Man For All Seasons*

COSTUME DESIGN

1967 John Truscott, *Camelot*
1968 Danilo Donati, *Romeo and Juliet*
1969 Margaret Furse, *Anne of the Thousand Days*
1970 Nino Novarese, *Cromwell*
1971 Yvonne Blake and Antonio Castillo, *Nicholas and Alexandra*
1972 Anthony Powell, *Travels with My Aunt*
1973 Edith Head, *The Sting*
1974 Theoni V. Aldredge, *The Great Gatsby*
1975 Ulla-Britt Soderlund and Milena Cananero, *Barry Lyndon*
1976 Danilo Donati, *Fellini's Casanova*
1977 John Mollo, *Star Wars*

MUSIC/SCORE

1934 Columbia Studio Music Dept. (Louis Silvers, dept. head; thematic music by Victor Schertzinger and Gus Kahn), *One Night of Love*
1935 RKO Studio Music Dept. (Max Steiner, dept. head and composer of winning score), *The Informer*
1936 Warner Bros. Studio Music Dept. (Leo Forbstein, dept. head; Erich Wolfgang Korngold, composer), *Anthony Adverse*
1937 Universal Studio Music Dept. (Charles Previn, dept. head), *One Hundred Men and a Girl*
1938 Alfred Newman, *Alexander's Ragtime Band*

MUSIC/BEST SCORE

1939 Richard Hageman, Franke Harling, John Leipold and Leo Shuken, *Stagecoach*
1940 Alfred Newman, *Tin Pan Alley*

MUSIC/ORIGINAL SCORE

1939 Herbert Sothart, *The Wizard of Oz*
1940 Leigh Harline, Paul J. Smith and Ned Washington, *Pinocchio*

MUSIC/SCORE OF A MUSICAL PICTURE

1941 Frank Churchill and Oliver Wallace, *Dumbo*
1942 Ray Heindorf and Heinz Roemheld, *Yankee Doodle Dandy*
1943 Ray Heindorf, *This is the Army*
1944 Morris Stoloff and Carmen Dragon, *Cover Girl*
1945 Georgie Stoll, *Anchors Aweigh*
1946 Morris Stoloff, *The Jolson Story*
1947 Alfred Newman, *Mother Wore Tights*
1948 Johnny Green and Roger Edens, *Easter Parade*
1949 Roger Edens and Lennie Hayton, *On The Town*
1950 Adolph Deutsch and Roger Edens, *Annie Get Your Gun*
1951 Johnny Green and Saul Chaplin, *An American in Paris*
1952 Alfred Newman, *With a Song in My Heart*
1953 Alfred Newman, *Call Me Madam*
1954 Adolph Deutsch and Saul Chaplin, *Seven Brides for Seven Brothers*
1955 Robert Russell Bennett, Jay Blackton and Adolph Deutsch, *Oklahoma!*
1956 Alfred Newman and Ken Darby, *The King and I*

1957 No award
1958 Andre Previn, *Gigi*
1959 Andre Previn and Ken Darby, *Porgy and Bess*
1960 Morris Stoloff and Harry Sukman, *Song Without End*
1961 Saul Chaplin, Johnny Green, Sid Ramin and Irwin Kostal, *West Side Story*

MUSIC/SCORE OF A DRAMATIC OR COMEDY PICTURE

1941 Bernard Herrmann, *All That Money Can Buy*
1942 Max Steiner, *Now, Voyager*
1943 Alfred Newman, *The Song of Bernadette*
1944 Max Steiner, *Since You Went Away*
1945 Miklos Rozsa, *Spellbound*
1946 Hugo Friedhofer, *The Best Years of Our Lives*
1947 Miklos Rozsa, *A Double Life*
1948 Brian Easdale, *The Red Shoes*
1949 Aaron Copland, *The Heiress*
1950 Franz Waxman, *Sunset Boulevard*
1951 Franz Waxman, *A Place in the Sun*
1952 Dmitri Tiomkin, *High Noon*
1953 Bronislau Kaper, *Lili*
1954 Dmitri Tiomkin, *The High and The Mighty*
1955 Alfred Newman, *Love is a Many-Splendored Thing*
1956 Victor Young, *Around the World in 80 Days*
1957 Malcolm Arnold, *The Bridge on the River Kwai*
1958 Dmitri Tiomkin, *The Old Man and The Sea*
1959 Miklos Rozsa, *Ben-Hur*
1960 Ernest Gold, *Exodus*
1961 Henry Mancini, *Breakfast at Tiffany's*

MUSIC/SCORE SUBSTANTIALLY ORIGINAL/ORIGINAL MUSIC SCORE

1962 Maurice Jarre, *Lawrence of Arabia*
1963 John Addison, *Tom Jones*
1964 Richard M. Sherman and Robert B. Sherman, *Mary Poppins*
1965 Maurice Jarre, *Dr. Zhivago*
1966 John Barry, *Born Free*
1967 Elmer Bernstein, *Thoroughly Modern Millie*

MUSIC/ADAPTATION OR TREATMENT

1962 Ray Heindorf, *The Music Man*
1963 Andre Previn, *Irma La Douce*
1964 Andre Previn, *My Fair Lady*
1965 Irwin Kostal *The Sound of Music*
1966 Ken Thorne, *A Funny Thing Happened on the Way to the Forum*
1967 Alfred Newman and Ken Darby, *Camelot*

MUSIC/ORIGINAL SCORE FOR A MOTION PICTURE (NOT A MUSICAL)

1968 John Barry, *The Lion in Winter*
1969 Burt Bacharach, *Butch Cassidy and The Sundance Kid*
1970 Francis Lai, *Love Story*
1971 Michael Legrand, *Summer of '42*
1972 Charles Chaplin, Raymond Rasch and Larry Russell, *Limelight*
1973 Marvin Hamlisch, *The Way We Were*
1974 Nino Rota and Carmine Coppola, *The Godfather, Part II*
1975 John Williams, *Jaws*
1976 Jerry Goldsmith, *The Omen*
1977 John Williams, *Star Wars*

MUSIC/SCORE FOR A MUSICAL (ORIGINAL OR ADAPTATION)

1968 John Green, *Oliver!*

1969 Lenny Hayton and Lionel Newman, *Hello, Dolly!*
1970 The Beatles, *Let It Be*
1971 John Williams, *Fiddler on the Roof*
1972 Ralph Burns, *Cabaret*

MUSIC/ORIGINAL SONG SCORE AND ADAPTATION SCORING: ADAPTATION

1973 Marvin Hamlisch, *The Sting*
1974 Nelson Riddle, *The Great Gatsby*
1975 Leonard Rosenman, *Barry Lyndon*
1976 Leonard Rosenman, *Bound for Glory*
1977 Jonathan Tunick, *A Little Night Music*

MUSIC/BEST SONG

1934 Con Conrad (music) and Herb Magidson (lyrics), *Continental* from *The Gay Divorcee*
1935 Harry Warren (music) and Al Dubin (lyrics), *Lullaby of Broadway* from *Gold Diggers of 1935*
1936 Jerome Kern (music) and Dorothy Fields (lyrics), *The Way You Look Tonight* from *Swingtime*
1937 Harry Owens, *Sweet Leilani* from *Waikiki Wedding*
1938 Ralph Raininger (music) and Leo Robin (lyrics), *Thanks for the Memory* from *The Big Broadcast of 1938*
1939 Harold Arlen (music) and E.Y. Harbug (lyrics), *Over the Rainbow* from *The Wizard of Oz*
1940 Leigh Harline (music) and Ned Washington (lyrics), *When You Wish Upon a Star* from *Pinocchio*
1941 Jerome Kern (music) and Oscar Hammerstein II (lyrics), *The Last Time I Saw Paris* from *Lady Be Good*
1942 Irving Berlin, *White Christmas* from *Holiday Inn*
1943 Harry Warren (music) and Mack Gordon (lyrics), *You'll Never Know* from *Hello, Frisco, Hello*
1944 James Van Heusen (music) and Johnny Burke (lyrics), *Swinging on a Star* from *Going My Way*
1945 Richard Rodgers (music) and Oscar Hammerstein II (lyrics), *It Might As Well Be Spring* from *State Fair*
1946 Harry Warren (music) and Johnny Mercer (lyrics), *On The Atchison, Topeka and Santa Fe* from *The Harvey Girls*
1947 Allie Wrubel (music) and Ray Gilbert (lyrics), *Zip-A-Dee-Doo-Dah* from *Song of the South*
1948 Jay Livingston and Ray Evans (music and lyrics), *Buttons and Bows* from *The Paleface*
1949 Frank Loesser, *Baby It's Cold Outside,* from *Neptune's Daughter*
1950 Ray Evans and Jay Livingston (music and lyrics), *Mona Lisa* from *Captain Carey, USA*
1951 Hoagy Carmichael (music) and Johnny Mercer (lyrics), *In the Cool, Cool, Cool of the Evening* from *Here Comes the Groom*
1952 Dmitri Tiomkin (music) and Ned Washington (lyrics), *High Noon (Do Not Forsake Me, Oh My Darlin)* from *High Noon*
1953 Sammy Fain (music) and Paul Francis Webster (lyrics), *Secret Love* from *Calamity Jane*
1954 Jule Styne (music) and Sammy Cahn (lyrics), *Three Coins in the Fountain* from *Three Coins in the Fountain*
1955 Sammy Fain (music) and Paul Francis Webster (lyrics), *Love Is a Many-Splendored Thing* from *Love Is a Many-Splendored Thing*
1956 Ray Evans and Jay Livingston (music and lyrics), *Whatever Will Be, Will Be (Que Sera, Sera)* from *The Man Who Knew Too Much*
1957 James Van Heusen (music) and Sammy Cahn (lyrics), *All the Way* from *The Joker Is Wild*

1958 Frederick Lowe (music) and Alan Jay Lerner (lyrics), *Gigi* from *Gigi*
1959 James Van Heusen (music) and Sammy Cahn (lyrics), *High Hopes* from *A Hole in the Head*
1960 Manos Hadjidakis, *Never on Sunday* from *Never on Sunday*
1961 Henry Mancini (music) and Johnny Mercer (lyrics), *Moon River* from *Breakfast at Tiffany's*
1962 Henry Mancini (music) and Johnny Mercer (lyrics), *Days of Wine and Roses* from *Days of Wine and Roses*
1963 James Van Heusen (music) and Sammy Cahn (lyrics), *Call Me Irresponsible* from *Papa's Delicate Condition*
1964 Richard M. Sherman and Robert B. Sherman (music and lyrics), *Chim Chim Cher-ee* from *Mary Poppins*
1965 Johnny Mandel (music) and Paul Francis Webster (lyrics), *The Shadow of Your Smile* from *The Sandpiper*
1966 John Barry (music) and Don Black (lyrics), *Born Free* from *Born Free*
1967 Leslie Bricusse, *Talk to the Animals* from *Doctor Doolittle*
1968 Michael Legrand (music) and Alan and Marilyn Bergman (lyrics), *The Windmills of Your Mind* from *The Thomas Crown Affair*
1969 Burt Bacharach (music) and Hal David (lyrics), *Raindrops Keep Fallin' on My Head* from *Butch Cassidy and The Sundance Kid*
1970 Fred Karlin (music) and Robb Royer and James Griffin a.k.a. Robb Wilson and Arthur James (lyrics), *For All We Know* from *Lovers and Other Strangers*
1971 Isaac Hayes, Theme from *Shaft*
1972 Al Kasha and Joel Hirschhorn (music and lyrics), *The Morning After* from *The Poseidon Adventure*
1973 Marvin Hamlisch (music) and Alan and Marilyn Bergman (lyrics), *The Way We Were* from *The Way We Were*
1974 Al Kasha and Joel Hirschhorn (music and lyrics), *We May Never Love Like This Again* from *The Towering Inferno*
1975 Keith Carradine, *I'm Easy* from *Nashville*
1976 Barbra Streisand (music) and Paul Williams (lyrics), *Evergreen* from *A Star Is Born*
1977 Joseph Brooks (music and lyrics), *You Light Up My Life*

DANCE DIRECTION

1935 Dave Gould, *I've Got a Feeling You're Fooling* from *Broadway Melody of 1936* and *Straw Hat* from *Folies Bergere*
1936 Seymour Felix, *A Pretty Girl Is Like a Melody* from *The Great Ziegfeld*
1937 Hermes Pan, *Fun House* from *Damsel in Distress*

SET DECORATION OR INTERIOR DECORATION BLACK AND WHITE

1941 Thomas Little, *How Green Was My Valley*
1942 Thomas Little, *This Above All*
1943 Thomas Little, *The Song of Bernadette*
1944 Edwin B. Willis and Paul Huldschinsky, *Gaslight*
1945 A. Roland Fields, *Blood on the Sun*
1946 Thomas Little and Frank E. Hughes, *Anna and the King of Siam*
1947 Wilfred Shingleton, *Great Expectations*
1948 Carmen Dillon, *Hamlet*
1949 Emile Kuri, *The Heiress*
1950 Sam Comer and Ray Moyer, *Sunset Boulevard*
1951 George James Hopkins, *A Streetcar Named Desire*

1952 Edwin B. Willis and Keogh Gleason, *The Bad and The Beautiful*
1953 Edwin B. Willis and Hugh Hunt, *Julius Caesar*
1954 No award
1955 Sam Comer and Arthur Krams, *The Rose Tattoo*
1956 Edwin S. Willis and Keogh Gleason, *Somebody Up There Likes Me*
1957 No award
1958 No award
1959 Walter M. Scott and Stuart A. Reiss, *The Diary of Anne Frank*
1960 Edward G. Boyle, *The Apartment*
1961 Gene Callahan, *The Hustler*
1962 Oliver Emert, *To Kill a Mockingbird*
1963 No award
1964 No award
1965 Joseph Kish, *Ship of Fools*
1966 George James Hopkins, *Who's Afraid of Virginia Woolf?*

SET DIRECTION OR INTERIOR DECORATION/COLOR

1941 Edwin B. Willis, *Blossoms in the Dust*
1942 Thomas Little, *My Gal Sal*
1943 Russell A. Gausman and Ira S. Webb, *The Phantom of the Opera*
1944 Thomas Little, *Wilson*
1945 Sam Comer, *Frenchman's Creek*
1946 Edwin B. Willis, *The Yearling*
1947 Alfred Junge, *Black Narcissus*
1948 Arthur Lawson, *The Red Shoes*
1949 Edwin B. Willis and Jack D. Moore, *Little Women*
1950 Sam Comer and Ray Moyer, *Samson and Delilah*
1951 Edwin B. Willis and Keogh Gleason, *An American in Paris*
1952 Marcel Vertes, *Moulin Rouge*
1953 Walter M. Scott and Paul S. Fox, *The Robe*
1954 Emile Kuri, *20,000 Leagues Under the Sea*
1955 Robert Priestley, *Picnic*
1956 Walter M. Scott and Paul S. Fox, *The King and I*
1957 Robert Priestley, *Sayonara*
1958 Henry Grace and Keogh Gleason, *Gigi*
1959 Hugh Hunt, *Ben-Hur*
1960 Russell A. Gausman and Julia Heron, *Spartacus*
1961 Victor A. Gangelin, *West Side Story*
1962 Dario Simoni, *Lawrence of Arabia*
1963 Walter M. Scott, Paul S. Fox and Ray Moyer, *Cleopatra*
1964 George James Hopkins, *My Fair Lady*
1965 Dario Simoni, *Doctor Zhivago*
1966 Walter M. Scott and Stuart A. Reiss, *Fantastic Voyage*

SET DECORATION

1967 John W. Brown, *Camelot*
1968 Vernon Dixon and Ken Muggleston, *Oliver!*
1969 Walter M. Scott, George Hopkins and Raphael Bretton, *Hello, Dolly!*
1970 Antonio Mateos and Pierre-Louis Thevenet, *Patton*
1971 Vernon Dixon, *Nicholas and Alexandra*
1972 Herbert Strabel, *Carabet*
1973 James Payne, *The Sting*
1974 George R. Nelson, *The Godfather, Part II*
1975 Vernon Dixon, *Barry Lyndon*
1976 George Gaines, *All the President's Men*
1977 Roger Christian, *Star Wars*

SOUND RECORDING OR SOUND

1931 Paramount Studio Sound Dept.

1932 Paramount Studio Sound Dept.
1933 Paramount Studio Sound Dept. (Franklin Hansen, sound dir.), *A Farewell to Arms*
1934 Columbia Studio Sound Dept. (John Livadary, sound dir.), *One Night of Love*
1935 Metro-Goldwyn-Mayer Sound Dept. (Douglas Shearer, sound dir.), *Naughty Marietta*
1936 Metro-Goldwyn-Mayer Sound Dept. (Douglas Shearer, sound dir.), *San Francisco*
1937 Samuel Goldwyn Studio Sound Dept. (Thomas T. Moulton, sound dir.), *The Hurricane*
1938 Samuel Goldwyn Studio Sound Dept. (Thomas T. Moulton, sound dir.), *The Cowboy and the Lady*
1939 Universal Studio Sound Dept. (Bernard B. Brown, sound dir.), *When Tomorrow Comes*
1940 Metro-Goldwyn-Mayer Sound Dept. (Douglas Shearer, sound dir.), *Strike Up the Band*
1941 Alexander Korda, United Artists; General Service Studio Sound Dept. (Jack Whitney, sound dir.), *That Hamilton Woman*
1942 Warner Bros. Studio Sound Dept. (Nathan Levinson, sound dir.), *Yankee Doodle Dandy*
1943 RKO Radio Studio Sound Dept. (Stephen Dunn, sound dir.), *This Land is Mine*
1944 20th Century-Fox Studio Sound Dept. (E.H. Hansen, sound dir.), *Wilson*
1945 RKO Radio Studio Sound Dept. (Stephen Dunn, sound dir.), *The Bells of St. Mary's*
1946 Columbia Studio Sound Dept. (John Livadary, sound dir.), *The Jolson Story*
1947 Samuel Goldwyn Studio Sound Dept. (Gordon Sawyer, sound dir.), *The Bishop's Wife*
1948 20th Century-Fox Studio Sound Dept. (Thomas T. Moulton, sound dir.), *The Snake Pit*
1949 20th Century-Fox Studio Sound Dept. (Thomas T. Moulton, sound dir.), *Twelve O'Clock High*
1950 20th Century-Fox Studio Sound Dept. (Thomas T. Moulton, sound dir.), *All About Eve*
1951 Metro-Goldwyn-Mayer Studio Sound Dept. (Douglas Shearer, sound dir.), *The Great Caruso*
1952 London Films Studio Sound Dept., *Breaking the Sound Barrier*
1953 Columbia Studio Sound Dept. (John Livadary, sound dir.), *From Here to Eternity*
1954 Universal-International Studio Sound Dept. (Leslie I. Carey, sound dir.), *The Glenn Miller Story*
1955 Todd-AO Sound Dept. (Fred Hynes, sound dir.), *Oklahoma!*
1956 20th Century-Fox Studio Sound Dept. (Carl Faulkner, sound dir.), *The King and I*
1957 Warner Bros. Studio Sound Dept. (George R. Groves, sound dir.), *Sayonara*
1958 Todd-AO Sound Dept. (Fred Hynes, sound dir.), *South Pacific*
1959 Metro-Goldwyn-Mayer Studio Sound Dept. (Franklin E. Milton, sound dir.), *Ben-Hur*
1960 Samuel Goldwyn Studio Sound Dept. (Gordon E. Sawyer, sound dir.) and Todd-AO Sound Dept. (Fred Hynes, sound dir.), *The Alamo*
1961 Todd-AO Sound Dept. (Fred Hynes, sound dir.) and Samuel Goldwyn Studio Sound Dept. (Gordon E. Sawyer, sound dir.), *West Side Story*
1962 Shepperton Studio Sound Dept. (John Cox, sound dir.), *Lawrence of Arabia*
1963 Metro-Goldwyn-Mayer Studio Sound Dept. (Franklin E. Milton, sound dir.), *How the West Was Won*
1964 Warner Bros. Studio Sound Dept. (George E. Groves, sound dir.), *My Fair Lady*
1965 20th Century-Fox Studio Sound Dept. (James P. Corcoran, sound dir.) and Todd-AO Sound Dept. (Fred Hynes, sound dir.), *The Sound of Music*
1966 Metro-Goldwyn-Mayer Studio Sound Dept. (Franklin E. Milton, sound dir.), *Grand Prix*
1967 Samuel Goldwyn Studio Sound Dept., *In the Heat of the Night*
1968 Shepperton Studio Sound Dept., *Oliver!*
1969 Jack Solomon and Murray Sivack, Chenault Productions, 20th Century-Fox, *Hello Dolly!*
1970 Douglas Williams and Don Bassman, 20th Century-Fox, *Patton*
1971 Gordon McCallum and David Hildyard, Mirisch-Cartier Productions, United Artists, *Fiddler on the Roof*
1972 Robert Knudson and David Hildyard, ABC Pictures, Allied Artists, *Cabaret*
1973 Robert Knudson and Chris Newman, Hoya Productions, Warner Bros., *The Exorcist*
1974 Ronald Pierce and Melvin Metcalfe, Sr., Universal-Mark Robson-Filmakers Group Production, Universal, *Earthquake*
1975 Robert L. Hoyt, Roger Heman, Earl Madery and John Carter, Universal Zanuck/Brown Production, Universal, *Jaws*
1976 Arthur Piantadosi, Les Fresholtz, Dick Alexander and Jim Webb, Wildwood Enterprises Production, Warner Bros., *All the President's Men*
1977 Don MacDouglass, Ray West, Bob Minkler and Derek Ball, *Star Wars*

ENGINEERING EFFECTS
1928 Roy Pomeroy, *Wings*

SPECIAL EFFECTS
1940 Lawrence Butler (photographic) and Jack Whitney (sound), *The Thief of Bagdad*
1941 Farciot Edouart and Gordon Jennings (photographic) and Louis Mesenkop (sound), *I Wanted Wings*
1942 Gordon Jennings, Farciot Edouart and William L. Pereira (photographic) and Louis Mesenkop (sound), *Reap the Wild Wind*
1943 Fred Sersen (photographic) and Roger Heman (sound), *Crash Dive*
1944 A. Arnold Gillespie, Donald Jahraus and Warren Newcombe (photographic) and Douglas Shearer (sound), *Thirty Seconds Over Tokyo*
1945 John Fulton (photographic) and Arthur W. Johns (sound), *Wonder Man*
1946 Thomas Howard (photographic), *Blithe Spirit*
1947 A. Arnold Gillespie and Warren Newcombe (visual) and Douglas Shearer and Michael Steinore (audible), *Green Dolphin Street*
1948 Paul Eagler, J. McMillan Johnson, Russell Shearman and Clarence Slifer (visual) and Charles Freeman and James G. Stewart (audible), *Portrait of Jennie*
1949 ARKO Productions, *Mighty Joe Young*
1950 George Pal (producer), *Destination Moon*
1951 No award
1952 No award
1953 No award
1954 Walt Disney Studios, *20,000 Leagues Under the Sea*
1955 Paramount Studio, *The Bridges at Toko-Ri*
1956 John Fulton, *The Ten Commandments*
1957 Walter Rossi (audible), *The Enemy Below*
1958 Tom Howard (visual), *tom thumb*

1959 A. Arnold Gillespie and Robert MacDonald (visual) and Milo Lory (audible), *Ben-Hur*
1960 Gene Warren and Tim Baar (visual), *The Time Machine*
1961 Bill Warrington (visual) and Vivian C. Greenham (audible), *The Guns of Navarone*
1962 Robert MacDonald (visual) and Jacques Maumont (audible), *The Longest Day*
1963 Emil Kosa, Jr., *Cleopatra*

SPECIAL VISUAL EFFECTS

1964 Peter Ellenshaw, Hamilton Luske and Eustace Lycett, *Mary Poppins*
1965 John Stears, *Thunderball*
1966 Art Cruickshank, *Fantastic Voyage*
1967 L.B. Abbott, *Doctor Doolittle*
1968 Stanley Kubrick, *2001: A Space Odyssey*
1969 Robbie Robertson, *Marooned*
1970 A.D. Flowers and L.B. Abbott, *Tora! Tora! Tora!*
1971 Alan Maley, Eustace Lycett and Danny Lee, *Bedknobs and Broomsticks*

BEST VISUAL EFFECTS

1977 John Stears, John Dykstra, Richard Edlund, Grant McCune and Robert Blalack, *Star Wars*

FILM EDITING

1934 Conrad Nervig, *Eskimo*
1935 Ralph Dawson, *A Midsummer Night's Dream*
1936 Ralph Dawson, *Anthony Adverse*
1937 Gene Milford and Gene Havlick, *Lost Horizon*
1938 Ralph Dawson, *The Adventures of Robin Hood*
1939 Hal C. Kern and James E. Newcom, *Gone With the Wind*
1940 Anne Bauchens, *North West Mounted Police*
1941 William Holmes, *Sergeant York*
1942 Daniel Mandell, *The Pride of the Yankees*
1943 George Amy, *Air Force*
1944 Barbara McLean, *Wilson*
1945 Robert J. Kern, *National Velvet*
1946 Daniel Mandell, *The Best Years of Our Lives*
1947 Francis Lyon and Robert Parrish, *Body and Soul*
1948 Paul Weatherwax, *The Naked City*
1949 Harry Gerstad, *Champion*
1950 Ralph E. Winters and Conrad A. Nervig, *King Solomon's Mines*
1951 William Hornbeck, *A Place in the Sun*
1952 Elmo Williams and Harry Gerstad, *High Noon*
1953 William Lyon, *From Here to Eternity*
1954 Gene Milford, *On the Waterfront*
1955 Charles Nelson and William A. Lyon, *Picnic*
1956 Gene Ruggiero and Paul Weatherwax, *Around the World in 80 Days*
1957 Peter Taylor, *The Bridge on the River Kwai*
1958 Adrienne Fazan, *Gigi*
1959 Ralph E. Winters and John D. Dunning, *Ben-Hur*
1960 Daniel Mandell, *The Apartment*
1961 Thomas Stanford, *West Side Story*
1962 Anne Coates, *Lawrence of Arabia*
1963 Harold F. Kress, *How the West Was Won*
1964 Cotton Warburton, *Mary Poppins*
1965 William Reynolds, *The Sound of Music*
1966 Fredric Steinkamp, Henry Berman, Steward Linder and Frank Santillo, *Grand Prix*
1967 Hal Ashby, *In the Heat of the Night*
1968 Frank P. Keller, *Bullitt*
1969 Francoise Bonnot, *Z*
1970 Hugh S. Fowler, *Patton*
1971 Jerry Greenberg, *The French Connection*

1972 David Bretherton, *Cabaret*
1973 William Reynolds, *The Sting*
1974 Harold F. Kress and Carl Kress, *The Towering Inferno*
1975 Verna Fields, *Jaws*
1976 Richard Halsey and Scott Conrad, *Rocky*
1977 Paul Hirsch, Marcia Lucas and Richard Chew, *Star Wars*

FOREIGN LANGUAGE FILM

1956 *La Strada*
1957 *The Nights of Cabiria*
1958 *My Uncle*
1959 *Black Orpheus*
1960 *The Virgin Spring*
1961 *Through A Glass Darkly*
1962 *Sundays and Cybele*
1963 *Federico Fellini's 8½*
1964 *Yesterday, Today and Tomorrow*
1965 *The Shop on Main Street*
1966 *A Man and A Woman*
1967 *Closely Watched Trains*
1968 *War and Peace*
1969 *Z*
1970 *Investigation of a Citizen Above Suspicion*
1971 *The Garden of the Finzi-Continis*
1972 *The Discreet Charm of the Bourgeoisie*
1973 *Day for Night*
1974 *Amarcord*
1975 *Dersu Uzala*
1976 *Black and White in Color*
1977 *Madame Rosa*

DOCUMENTARY/FEATURE

1963 *Robert Frost: A Lover's Quarrel with the World*
1964 *Jacques-Yves Cousteau's World Without Sun*
1965 *The Eleanor Roosevelt Story*
1966 *The War Game*
1967 *The Anderson Platoon*
1968 *Journey Into Self*
1969 *Arthur Rubinstein—The Love of Life*
1970 *Woodstock*
1971 *The Hellstrom Chronicle*
1972 *Marjoe*
1973 *The Great American Cowboy*
1974 *Hearts and Minds*
1975 *The Man Who Skied Down Everest*
1976 *Harlan County, U.S.A.*
1977 *Who Are the DeBolts? And Where Did They Get Nineteen Kids?*

DOCUMENTARY/SHORT SUBJECT

1963 *Chagall*
1964 *Nine from Little Rock*
1965 *To Be Alive!*
1966 *A Year Toward Tomorrow*
1967 *The Redwoods*
1968 *Why Man Creates*
1969 *Czechoslovakia 1968*
1970 *Interviews with My Lai Veterans*
1971 *Sentinels of Silence*
1972 *This Tiny World*
1973 *Princeton: A Search for Answers*
1974 *Don't*
1975 *The End of the Game*
1976 *Number Our Days*
1977 *Gravity Is My Enemy*

SHORT SUBJECTS/CARTOON

1932 *Flowers and Trees*
1933 *Three Little Pigs*
1934 *The Tortoise and the Hare*
1935 *Three Orphan Kittens*
1936 *Country Cousin*
1937 *The Old Mill*
1938 *Ferdinand the Bull*
1939 *The Ugly Duckling*
1940 *Milky Way*
1941 *Lend a Paw*
1942 *Der Fuehrer's Face*
1943 *Yankee Doodle Mouse*
1944 *Mouse Trouble*
1945 *Quiet, Please*
1946 *The Cat Concerto*
1947 *Tweetie Pie*
1948 *The Little Orphans*
1949 *For Scent-Imental Reasons*
1950 *Gerald McBoing-Boing*
1951 *Two Mouseketeers*
1952 *Johann Mouse*
1953 *Toot, Whistle, Plunk and Boom*
1954 *When Magoo Flew*
1955 *Speedy Gonzales*
1956 *Mister Magoo's Puddle Jumper*
1957 *Birds Anonymous*
1958 *Knighty Knight Bugs*
1959 *Moonbird*
1960 *Munro*
1961 *Ersatz*
1962 *The Hole*
1963 *The Critic*
1964 *The Pink Phink*
1965 *The Dot and The Line*
1966 *Herb Alpert and the Tijuana Brass Double Feature*
1967 *A Place to Stand*
1968 *Winnie the Pooh and the Blustery Day*
1969 *It's Tough to Be a Bird*
1970 *Is It Always Right to Be Right?*
1971 *The Crunch Bird*
1972 *A Christmas Carol*
1973 *Frank Film*
1974 *Closed Mondays*
1975 *Great*
1976 *Leisure*
1977 *Sand Castle*

SHORT SUBJECTS/COMEDY

1932 *The Music Box*
1933 *So This is Harris*
1934 *La Cucaracha*
1935 *How to Sleep*

SHORT SUBJECTS/NOVELTY

1932 *Wrestling Swordfish*
1933 *Krakatoa*
1934 *City of Wax*
1935 *Wings Over Mt. Everest*

SHORT SUBJECTS/COLOR

1935 *Give Me Liberty*
1937 *Penny Wisdom*

SHORT SUBJECTS/ONE REEL

1936 *Bored of Education*
1937 *Private Life of the Gannets*
1938 *That Mothers Might Live*
1939 *Busy Little Bears*

1940 *Quicker 'n a Wink*
1941 *Of Pups and Puzzles*
1942 *Speaking of Animals and Their Families*
1943 *Amphibious Fighters*
1944 *Who's Who in Animal Land*
1945 *Stairway to Light*
1946 *Facing Your Danger*
1947 *Goodbye, Miss Turlock*
1948 *Symphony of a City*
1949 *Aquatic House-Party*
1950 *Grandad of Races*
1951 *World of Kids*
1952 *Light in the Window*
1953 *The Merry Wives of Windsor Overture*
1954 *This Mechanical Age*
1955 *Survival City*
1956 *Crashing the Water Barrier*

SHORT SUBJECTS/TWO REEL

1936 *The Public Pays*
1937 *Torture Money*
1938 *Declaration of Independence*
1939 *Sons of Liberty*
1940 *Teddy, The Rough Rider*
1941 *Main Street on the March*
1942 *Beyond the Line of Duty*
1943 *Heavenly Music*
1944 *Won't Play*
1945 *Star in the Night*
1946 *A Boy and His Dog*
1947 *Climbing the Matterhorn*
1948 *Seal Island*
1949 *Van Gogh*
1950 *In Beaver Valley*
1951 *Nature's Half Acre*
1952 *Water Birds*
1953 *Bear Country*
1954 *A Time Out of War*
1955 *The Face of Lincoln*
1956 *The Bespoke Overcoat*

SHORT SUBJECTS/LIVE ACTION

1957 *The Wetback Hound*
1958 *Grand Canyon*
1959 *The Golden Fish*
1960 *Day of the Painter*
1961 *Seawards the Great Ships*
1962 *Heureux Anniversaire*
1963 *An Occurrence at Owl Creek Bridge*
1964 *Casals Conducts: 1964*
1965 *The Chicken*
1966 *Wild Wings*
1967 *A Place to Stand*
1968 *Robert Kennedy Remembered*
1969 *The Magic Machines*
1970 *The Resurrection of Broncho Billy*
1971 *Sentinels of Silence*
1972 *Norman Rockwell's World ... An American Dream*
1973 *The Bolero*
1974 *One-Eyed Men Are Kings*
1975 *Angel and Big Joe*
1976 *In the Region of Ice*
1977 *I'll Find A Way*

DOCUMENTARY/FEATURE

1942 *Battle of Midway*
       Kokoda Front Line
       Moscow Strikes Back

Prelude to War
1943 Desert Victory
1944 The Fighting Lady
1945 The True Glory
1946 No award
1947 Design for Death
1948 The Secret Land
1949 Daybreak in Udi
1950 The Titan: The Story of Michelangelo
1951 Kon-Tiki
1952 The Sea Around Us
1953 The Living Desert
1954 The Vanishing Prairie
1955 Helen Keller in Her Story
1956 The Silent World
1957 Albert Schweitzer
1958 White Wilderness
1959 Serengeti Shall Not Die
1960 The Horse With the Flying Tail
1961 Le Ciel et La Boue (Sky Above and Mud Beneath)
1962 Black Fox

DOCUMENTARY/SHORT SUBJECT

1943 December 7th
1944 With The Marines at Tarawa
1945 Hitler Lives?
1946 Seeds of Destiny
1947 First Steps
1948 Toward Independence
1949 A Chance to Live
So Much for So Little
1950 Why Korea?
1951 Benjy
1952 Neighbours
1953 The Alaskan Eskimo
1954 Thursday's Children
1955 Men Against the Arctic
1956 The True Story of the Civil War
1957 No award
1958 Ama Girls
1959 Glass
1960 Guiseppina
1961 Project Hope
1962 Dylan Thomas

SCIENTIFIC OR TECHNICAL/CLASS I
(ACADEMY STATUETTE)

1931 Electrical Research Products, Inc., RCA-Photophone, Inc. and RKO Radio Pictures, Inc., For noise-reduction recording equipment
DuPont Film Manufacturing Corp. and Eastman Kodak Co., For supersensitive panchromatic film
1936 Douglas Shearer and the Metro-Goldwyn-Mayer Studio Sound Dept., For developing practical two-way horn system and a biased Class A push-pull recording system
1937 AGFA Ansco Corp., For AGFA Supreme and AGFA Ultra Speed pan motion picture negatives
1940 20th Century-Fox Film Corp. and Daniel Clark, Grover Laube, Charles Miller and Robert W. Stevens, For design and construction of silenced camera
1949 Eastman Kodak Co., For development and introduction of improved safety-base motion picture film
1952 Eastman Kodak Co., For introduction of Eastman color negative and color print films
Ansco Div., General Aniline and Film Corp., For introduction of Ansco color negative and color print films

1953 Henri Chretien and Earl Sponable, Sol Halprin, Lorin Grignon, Herbert Bragg and Carl Faulkner of 20th Century-Fox Studios, For creating, developing and engineering the equipment, processes and techniques of Cinerama
Fred Waller, For designing and developing the multiple photographic and projection systems for Cinerama
1957 Todd-AO Corp. and Westrex Corp., For developing method of producing and exhibiting wide-film motion pictures
Motion Picture Research Council, For design and development of high-efficiency projection screen for drive-in theatres
1964 Petro Vlahos, Wadsworth E. Pohl and Ub Iwerks, For conception and perfection of Color Traveling Matte Composition Cinematography
1968 Philip V. Palmquist of Minnesota Mining and Mfg. Co., Herbert Meyer of Motion Picture and Television Research Center and Charles D. Staffell of Rank Organization, For developing the successful embodiment of the reflex background projection system for composite cinematography
Eastman Kodak Co., For developing and introducing a color reversal intermediate film for motion pictures
1977 Frank Warner, for sound effects editing, Star Wars
Benjamin Burtt, J., for creation of alien creature and robot voices, Star Wars
Cinema Procucts, for development of Steadycam

SCIENTIFIC OR TECHNICAL/CLASS II
(CERTIFICATE UNTIL 1937; ACADEMY PLAQUE SINCE 1938)

1931 Fox Film Corp., For effective use of synchro-projection composite photography
1932 Technicolor Motion Picture Corp., For color cartoon process
1933 Electrical Research Products, Inc., For their recording and reproducing equipment
RCA-Victor Co., For high-fidelity recording and reproducing system
1934 Electrical Research Products, Inc., For development of vertical cut disco method of sound recording (hill and dale recording)
1935 AGFA Ansco Corp., For AGFA infra-red film
Eastman Kodak Co., For Eastman Pola-Screen
1936 E.C. Wente and Bell Telephone Laboratories, For multi-cellular high-frequency horn and receiver
RCA Mfg. Co., For rotary stabilizer sound head
1937 Walt Disney Productions, Inc., For design and application of multi-plane camera
Eastman Kodak Co., For two fine-grain duplicating film stocks
Farciot Edouart and Paramount Pictures, Inc., For dual screen transparency camera set-up
Douglas Shearer and Metro-Goldwyn-Mayer Studio Sound Dept., For a method of varying the scanning width of variable density sound tracks (squeeze tracks) to obtain increased noise reduction
1938 No award
1939 No award
1940 No award
1941 Electrical Research Products Div., Western Electric Co., For development of the precision integrating sphere densitometer
RCA Mfg. Co., For design and development of MI-3043 uni-directional microphone
1942 Carroll Clark, F. Thomas Thompson and RKO Studio Art and Miniature Depts., For design and construction of moving cloud and horizon machine

Daniel B. Clark and 20th Century-Fox Film Corp., For developing a lens calibration system and the application of this system to exposure control in cinematography

1943 Farciot Edouart, Earle Morgan, Barton Thompson and Paramount Studio and Engineering Dept., For development and application of method of duplicating and enlarging natural color photographs, transferring the image emulsions to glass plates and projecting these slides by especially designed stereopticon equipment

Photo Products Dept., E.I. duPont de Nemours & Co., Inc., For development of fine-grain motion picture films

1944 Stephen Dunn and RKO Radio Studio Sound Dept. and Radio Corp. of America, For design and development of electronic compressor-limiter

1945 No award

1946 No award

1947 C.C. Davis and Electrical Research Products Div., Western Electric Co., For development and application of improved film drive filter mechanism

C.R. Daily and Paramount Studio Film Laboratory, Still and Engineering Depts., For development and first practical application to motion picture and still photography of a method of increasing film speed as first suggested to the industry by du Pont

1948 Victor Caccialanza, Maurice Ayers and Paramount Studio Set Construction Dept., For development and application of Paralite, new lightweight plaster process for set construction

Nick Kalten, Louis J. Witti and 20th Century-Fox Studio Mechanical Effects Dept., For process of preserving and flame-proofing foliage

1949 No award

1950 James B. Gordon and 20th Century Fox Studio Camera Dept., For design and development of multiple image film viewer

John Paul Livadary, Floyd Campbell, L.W. Russell and Columbia Studio Sound Dept., For development of multi-track magnetic re-recording system

Loren L. Ryder and Paramount Studio Sound Dept., For studio-wide application of magnetic sound recording to motion picture production

1951 Gordon Jennings, S.L. Stancliffe and Paramount Studio Special Photographic and Engineering Depts., For design, construction and application of servo-operated recording and repeating device

Olin L. Dupy of Metro-Goldwyn-Mayer Studio., For design, construction and application of motion picture reproducing system

Radio Corp. of America, Victor Div., For pioneering direct positive recording with anticipatory noise reduction

1952 Technicolor Motion Picture Corp., For improved method of color photography under incandescent light

1953 Reeves Soundcraft Co., For developing a process of applying stripes of magnetic oxide to motion picture film for sound recording and reproduction

1954 No award

1955 Eastman Kodak Co., For Eastman Tri-X panchromatic negative film

Farciot Edouart, Hal Corl and Paramount Studio Transparency Dept., For engineering and developing double-frame, triple-head background projector

1956 No award

1957 Societe d'Optiques et de Mecanique de Haute Precision, For developing high-speed vari-focal photographic lens

Harlan L. Baumbach, Lorand Wargo, Howard M. Little and Unicorn Engineering Corp., For developing an automatic printer light selector

1958 Don W. Prideaux, LeRoy G. Leighton and Lamp Div., General Electric Co., Development and production of improved 10-kilowatt lamp for set lighting

Panavision, Inc., For design and development of Auto Panatar anamorphic lens for 35mm CinemaScope photography

1959 Douglas Shearer of Metro-Goldwyn-Mayer, Inc., and Robert E. Gottschalk and John R. Moore of Panavision, Inc., For developing a system of producing and exhibiting wide-film motion pictures known as Camera 65

Wadsworth E. Pohl, William Evans, Werner Hopf, S.E. Howse, Thomas P. Dixon, Stanford Research Institute and Technicolor Corp., For design and development of Technicolor electronic printing timer

Wadsworth E. Pohl, Jack Alford, Henry Imus, Joseph Schmit, Paul Fassnacht, Al Lofquist and Technicolor Corp., For development and application of equipment for wet printing

Howard S. Coleman, A. Francis Turner, Harold H. Schroeder, James R. Benford and Harold E. Rosenberger of Bausch and Lomb Optical Co., For developing the Bacold projection mirror

Robert P. Gutterman of General Kinetics, Inc., and Lipsner Smith Corp., For design and developing of the CF-2 Ultra-Sonic Film Cleaner

1960 Ampex Professional Products Co., For producing a well-engineered, multi-purpose sound system combining high quality, convenience of control, dependability and simple emergency provisions

1961 Sylvania Electric Products, Inc., For developing a hand-held high-power lighting unit known as the Sun Gun Professional

James Dale, S. Wilson, H.E. Rice, John Rude, Laurie Atkin, Wadsworth E. Pohl, H. Peasgood and Technicolor Corp., For automatic selective printing process

20th Century-Fox Research Dept. under E.I. Sponable and Herbert E. Bragg, De Luxe Laboratories, Inc., with the assistance of F.D. Leslie, R.D. Whitmore, A.A. Alden, Endel Pool and James B. Gordon, For system of decompressing and recomposing CinemaScope pictures for conventional aspect ratios

1962 Ralph Chapman, For design and development of advanced motion picture camera crane

Albert S. Pratt, James L. Wassell and Hans C. Wohlrab of Professional Div., Bell & Howell Co., For design and development of improved motion picture additive color printer

North American Philips, Inc., For developing Norelco 70/35mm projector

Charles E. Sutter, William Bryson Smith and Louis C. Kennell of Paramount Pictures Corp., For engineering and application of new system of electric power distribution

1963 No award

1964 Sidney P. Solow, Edward H. Reichard, Carl W. Hauge and Job Sanderson of Consolidated Film Industries, For design and development of versatile Automatic 35mm Composite Color Printer

Pierre Angenieux, For developing 10-to-1 zoom lens for cinematography

1965 Arthur J. Hatch of Strong Electric Corp., For developing Air Blown Carbon Arc Projection Lamp

Stefan Kudelski, For developing the Nagra portable ¼-in. tape recording system for sound recording

1966 Mitchell Camera Corp., For Mitchell Mark II 35mm portable reflex camera

Arnold & Ritcher KG, For developing Arriflex portable 35mm reflex camera

1967 No award

1968 Donald W. Norwood, For development of Norwood Photographic Exposure Meter

Eastman Kodak Co. and Producers Service Co., For development of high-speed step-optical reduction printer

Edmund M. DiGiulio, Neils G. Petersen and Norman S. Hughes of Cinema Product Development Co., For design and application of a conversion which makes available reflex viewing system for motion picture cameras

Optical Coating Laboratory, Inc., For developing an improved anti-reflection coating for photographic and projection lens systems

Eastman Kodak Co., For introduction of high-speed motion picture color negative film

Panavision Inc., For conception, design and introduction of a 65mm hand-held motion picture camera

Todd-AO Co. and Mitchell Camera Co., For design and development of Todd-AO hand-held motion picture camera

1969 Hazeltine Corp., For developing Hazeltine Color Film Analyzer

Fouad Said, For design and introduction of Cinemobile equipment trucks for location production

Juan de la Cierva and Dynasciences Corp., For development of Dynalens optical image motion compensator

1970 Leonard Sokolow and Edward H. Reichard of Consolidated Film Industries, For concept and engineering of Color Proofing Printer

1971 John A. Wilkinson of Optical Radiation Corp., For development and engineering of a system of xenon arc lamphouses for motion picture production

1972 Joseph E. Bluth, For research and development in electronic photography and transfer of video tape to film

Edward E. Reichard and Howard T. La Zare of Consolidated Film Industries and Edward Efron of IBM, For engineering of a computerized light valve monitoring system for motion picture printing

Panavision Inc., For development and engineering of Panaflex camera

1973 Joachim Gerb and Erich Kastner of Arnold & Richter Co., For developing and engineering Arriflex 35BL camera

Magna-Tech Electronic Co., For engineering and developing a high-speed re-recording system

William W. Valliant of PSC Technology, Inc., Howard F. Ott of Eastman Kodak Co. and Gerry Diebold of Richmark Camera Service, Inc., For developing liquid-gate system for motion picture printers

Harold A. Scheib, Clifford Ellis and Roger W. Banks of Research Products, Inc., For concept and engineering of Model 2101 optical printer for motion picture optical effects

1974 Joseph E. Kelly of Glen Glenn Sound, For new audio control consoles which advanced state of sound recording and re-recording

Burbank Studios Sound Dept., For new audio control consoles engineered and constructed by Quad-Eight Sound Corp.

Samuel Goldwyn Studios Sound Dept., For design of a new audio control console engineered and constructed by Quad-Eight Sound Corp.

Quad-Eight Sound Corp., For engineering and constructing new audio control consoles designed by the Burbank and Goldwyn Sound Depts.

Waldon O. Watson, Richard J. Stumpf, Robert J. Leonard and Universal City Studios Sound Dept., For developing and engineering Sensurround System for motion picture presentation

1975 Chadwell O'Connor of O'Connor Engineering Laboratories, For concept and engineering of fluid-damped camera head

William F. Miner of Universal City Studios and Westinghouse Electric Corp., For development of solid-state, 500-kilowatt direct-current static rectifier for motion picture lighting

1976 Consolidated Film Industries and Barneby-Cheney Co., For development of system for recovery film-cleaning solvent vapors in a laboratory

William L. Graham, Manfred G. Michelson, Geoffrey F. Norman and Siegfried Seibert of Technicolor, For development and engineering of continuous, high-speed, color motion picture printing system

1977 Glen Glenn Sound for concept and development of post-production audio processing system

Panavision, Inc., for concept and engineering of an improvement incorporated in the Panaflex motion picture camera

N. Paul Kenworthy, Jr., and William R. Laterdy for invention and development of the Kenworth snorkel camera system

John. C. Dykstra for development of facility oriented toward visual-effects photography

Alva J. Miller and Jerry Jeffress for engineering of electronic motion control system

Eastman Kodak Co. for development and introduction of new duplicating film

Stefan Kudelski of Nagra Magnetic Recorders, Inc., for engineering of improvement incorporated in Nagra 4.2L sound recorder

SCIENTIFIC OR TECHNICAL/CLASS III (CERTIFICATE OF HONORABLE MENTION)

1931 Electrical Research Products, Inc., For moving coil microphone transmission

RKO Radio Pictures, Inc., For reflex-type microphone concentrators

RCA-Photophone Pictures, Inc., For ribbon microphone transmitters

1932 Eastman Kodak Co., For Type-II-B Sensitometer

1933 Fox Film Corp., Fred Jackman and Warner Bros. Pictures, Inc., and Sidney Sanders of RKO Studios, Inc., For developing translucent cellulose screen for composite photography

1934 Columbia Pictures Corp., For the application of the vertical-cut disc method of recording sound for motion pictures (hill and dale recording)

Bell & Howell Co., For developing fully automatic sound and picture printer

1935 Metro-Goldwyn-Mayer Studio, For anti-directional negative and positive development by jet turbulation and its application to all negative and print processing to the producing company's entire product

William A. Mueller of Warner Bros.-First National Studio Sound Dept., For method of dubbing, in which level of dialogue automatically controls level of accompanying music and sound effects

Mole-Richardson Co., For development of Solar-Spot lamps

Douglas Shearer and Metro-Goldwyn-Mayer Studio Sound Dept., For automatic control system for cameras and sound recording machines and auxiliary stage equipment

Electrical Research Products, Inc., For design and construction of Paramount transparency air turbine developing machine

Nathan Levinson of Warner Bros.-First National Studio, For method of intercutting variable-density and variable-area soundtracks to secure increased effective range of sound

1936 RCA Mfg. Co., Inc., For method of recording and printing sound records utilizing restricted spectrum (ultra-violet light recording)

Electrical Research Products, Inc., For ERPI Type Q portable recording channel

RCA Mfg. Co., Inc., For practical design and specifications for non-slip printer

United Artists Studio Corp., For developing practical, efficient and quiet wind machine

1937 John Arnold and Metro-Goldwyn-Mayer Studio Camera Dept., For improved semi-automatic focus device and its application to all studio's cameras

John Livadary of Columbia Pictures Corp., For application of bi-planar light valve to motion-picture sound recording

Thomas T. Moulton and the United Artists Studio Sound Dept., For application of volume indicator with peak reading response and linear db scales to motion picture sound recording

RCA Mfg. Co., Inc., For introduction of modulated high-frequency method of determining optimum photographic processing conditions for variable-sound-tracks

Joseph E. Robbins and Paramount Pictures, Inc., For exceptional application of acoustic principles to sound-proofing of gasoline generators and water pumps

Douglas Shearer and Metro-Goldwyn-Mayer Studio Sound Dept., For design of film-drive mechanism in ERPI 1010 reproducer

1938 John Aalberg and RKO Radio Studio Sound Dept. For application of compression to variable-area recording

Byron Haskin and Special Effects Dept. of Warner Bros. Studio, For pioneering triple-head background projector

1939 George Anderson of Warner Bros. Studio, For improved positive head for sun arcs

John Arnold of Metro-Goldwyn-Mayer Studio, For mobile camera crane

Thomas T. Moulton, Fred Albin and Sound Dept. of Samuel Goldwyn Studio, For origination and application of Delta db test to sound recording in motion pictures

Farciot Edouart, Joseph E. Robbins, William Rudolph and Paramount Pictures, Inc., For design and construction of quiet portable treadmill

Emery Huse and Ralph B. Atkinson of Eastman Kodak Co., For specifications for chemical analysis of photographic developers and fixing baths

Harold Nye of Warner Bros. Studio, For miniature incandescent spot lamp

A.J. Tondreau of Warner Bros. Studio, For improved soundtrack printer

Multiple Award for contributions to development of new improved process projection equipment:
F.R. Abbott, Haller Belt, Alan Cook and Bausch & Lomb Optical Co., For faster projection lens

Mitchell Camera Co., For new-type process projection head

Mole-Richardson Co., For new-type automatically controlled projection arc lamp

Charles Handley, David Joy and National Carbon Co., For improved and more stable high-intensity carbons

Winton Hoch and Technicolor Motion Picture Corp., For auxiliary optical system

Don Musgrave and Selznick International Pictures, Inc., For pioneering in the use of coordinated equipment in the production of Gone With the Wind

1940 Warner Bros. Studio Art Dept. and Anton Grot, For design and perfection of water ripple and wave illusion machine

1941 Ray Wilkinson and Paramount Studio Laboratory, For pioneering use of fine-grain positive stock

Charles Lootens and the Republic Studio Sound Dept., For pioneering use of Class-B push/pull variable-area recording

Wilbur Silvertooth and the Paramount Studio Engineering Dept., For the design and computation of a relay condenser system applicable to transparency process projection

Paramount Pictures, Inc., and 20th Century-Fox, Inc., For automatic scene-slating device

Douglas Shearer and Metro-Goldwyn-Mayer Studio Sound Dept. and Loren Ryder and Paramount Studio Sound Dept., For development of fine-grain emulsions for variable-density original sound recording in studio production

1942 Robert Henderson and Paramount Studio Engineering and Transparency Depts., For design and construction of adjustable light bridges and frames for transparency process photography

Daniel J. Bloomberg and Republic Studio Sound Dept., For device for marking action negative for pre-selection purposes

1943 Daniel J. Bloomberg and Republic Studio Sound Dept., For design and development of inexpensive conversion of Moviolas to Class B push-pull reproduction

Charles Galloway Clarke and 20th Century-Fox Studio Camera Dept., For development and application of device for composing artificial clouds into motion picture scenes during production photography

Farciot Edouart and Paramount Studio Transparency Dept., For automatic electric transparency cueing timer

Willard H. Turner and RKO Studio Sound Dept., For design and construction of phono-cue starter

1944 Linwood Dunn, Cecil Love and Acme Tool Mfg., For Acme-Dunn Optical Printer

Grover Laube and 20th Century-Fox Studio Camera Dept., For continuous-loop projection device

Western Electric Co., For 1126A Limiting Amplifier for variable-density sound recording

Russell Brown, Ray Hinsdale and Joseph E. Robbins, For floating hydraulic boat rocker

Gordon Jennings, For nodal-point tripod

Radio Corp. of America and RKO Radio Studio Sound Dept., For reverberation chamber

Daniel J. Bloomberg and Republic Studio Sound Dept., for design and development of multi-interlock selector switch

Bernard B. Brown and John Livadary, For separate soloist and chorus recording room

Paul Zeff, S.J. Twining and George Seid of Columbia Studio Laboratory, For formula and application of simplified variable-area sound negative developer

Paul Lerpae, For traveling matte projection and photographing device

1945 Loren L. Ryder, Charles R. Daily and Paramount Studio Sound Dept., For first dial-controlled, step-by-step sound channel line-up and test circuit

Michael S. Leshing, Benjamin Robinson, Arthur B. Chatelain and Robert C. Stevens of 20th Century-Fox Studio and John G. Capstaff of Eastman Kodak Co., For film-processing machine

1946 Harlan L. Baumbach and Paramount West Coast Laboratory, For improved method for quantitative determination of hydroquinone and metal in photographic development baths

Herbert E. Britt, For formulas and equipment for producing cloud and smoke effects

Burton F. Miller and Warner Bros. Studio Sound and Electrical Depts., For motion picture arc-lighting generator filter

Carl Faulkner of 20th Century-Fox Studio Sound Dept., For reversed bias method, including double bias method, for light value and galvonometer desnity recording

Mole-Richardson Co., For Type 450 super high-intensity carbon arc lamp

Arthur F. Blinn, Robert O. Cook, C.O. Slyfield and Walt Disney Studio Sound Dept., For audio finder and track viewer for checking and locating noise in soundtracks

Burton F. Miller and Warner Bros. Studio Sound Dept., For equalizer to eliminate relative spectral-energy distortion in electronic compressors

Marty Martin and Hal Adkins of RKO Radio Studio Miniature Dept., For equipment producing visual bullet effects

Harold Nye and Warner Bros. Studio Electric Dept., For electronically controlled fire and gaslight effect

1947 Nathan Levinson and Warner Bros. Studio Sound Dept., For constant-speed sound editing machine

Farciot Edouart, C.R. Daily, Hal Corl, H.G. Cartwright and Paramount Studio Transparency and Engineering Depts., For first application of special anti-solarizing glass to high-intensity background and spot arc projections

Fred Ponedel of Warner Bros. Studio, For pioneering fabrication and application of large translucent photographic backgrounds

Kurt Singer and RCA-Victor Div., Radio Corp. of America, For continuously variable band elimination filter

James Gibbons of Warner Bros. Studio, For large dyed plastic filters

1948 Marty Martin, Jack Lannon, Russell Shearman and RKO Radio Studio Special Effects Dept., For new method of simulating falling snow on motion picture sets

A.J. Moran and Warner Bros Studio Electrical Dept., For a method of remote control for shutters on arc lighting equipment

1949 Loren L. Ryder, Bruce H. Denney, Robert Carr and Paramount Studio Sound Dept., For supersonic playback and public address system

M.B. Paul, For first successful large-area seamless translucent backgrounds

Herbert Britt, For formulas and equipment producing artificial snow and ice for motion picture sets

Andre Coutant and Jacques Mathot, For design of Eclair Camerette

Charles R. Daily, Steve Csillag and Paramount Studio Engineering Dept., For precision method of computing variable tempo-click tracks

International Projector Corp., For simplified, self-adjusting take-up device for projection machines

Alexander Velcoff, For application of infra-red photographic evaluator

1950 No award

1951 Richard M. Haff, Frank P. Herrnfeld, Garland C. Misener and Ansco Div., General Aniline and Film Corp., For Ansco color scene tester

Fred Ponedel, Ralph Ayres and George Brown of Warner Bros. Studio, For air-driven water motor to provide flow, wake and white water for marine sequences

Glen Robinson and Metro-Goldwyn-Mayer Studio Construction Dept., For development of balsa falling snow

1952 Carlos Rivas of Metro-Goldwyn-Mayer Studio, For automatic magnetic film splicer

Projection, Still Photographic and Development Engineering Depts. of Metro-Goldwyn-Mayer Studio, For improved method of projecting photographic backgrounds

John G. Frayne and R.R. Scoville and Westrex Corp., For method of measuring distortion in sound reproduction

Photo Research Corp., For creating Spectra color temperature meter

Gustav Jirouch, For Robot automatic film splicer

Carlos Rivas of Metro-Goldwyn-Mayer Studio, For sound reproducer for magnetic film

1953 Westrex Corp., For new film editing machine

1954 David S. Horsley and Universal International Studio Special Photographic Dept., For portable remote-control device for process projectors

Karl Freund and Frank Crandell of Photo Research Corp., For direct-reading brightness meter

Wesley C. Miller, J.W. Stafford, K.N. Frierson and Metro-Goldwyn-Mayer Studio Sound Dept., For electronic sound printing comparison device

John P. Livadary, Lloyd Russell and Columbia Studio Sound Dept., For improved limiting amplifier as applied to sound-level comparison devices

Carlos Rivas, G.M. Sprague and Metro-Goldwyn-Mayer Studio Sound Dept., For magnetic sound editing machine

Fred Wilson of Samuel Goldwyn Studio Sound Dept., For variable multiple-band equalizer

P.C. Young of Metro-Goldwyn-Mayer Studio Projection Dept., For practical application of variable focal length attachment to projection lenses

Fred Knoth and Orien Ernest of Universal-International Studio Technical Dept., For hand-portable, electric, dry oil-fog machine

1955 20th Century-Fox Studio and Bausch & Lomb Co., For new combination lenses for CinemaScope photography

Walter Jolley, Maurice Larson and R.H. Spies of 20th Century-Fox Studio, For a spraying process creating simulated metal surfaces

Steve Krilanovich, For improved camera dolly incorporating multi-directional steering

Dave Anderson of 20th Century-Fox Studio, For improved spotlight capable of maintaining fixed circle of light at constant intensity over varied distances

Loren L. Ryder, Charles West, Henry Fracker and Paramount Studio, For projection film index to establish proper framing for various aspect ratios

Farciot Edouart, Hal Corl and Paramount Studio Transparency Dept., For improved dual stereopticon background projector

1956 Richard Ranger of Rangertone, Inc., For synchronous recording and reproducing system for ¼-in. magnetic tape

Ted Hirsch, Carl Hauge and Edward Reichard of Consolidated Film Industries, For automatic scene counter for laboratory projection rooms

Technical Depts. of Paramount Pictures Corp., For light-weight, horizontal-movement Vista-Vision cameras

Roy C. Stewart and Sons of Stewart-Trans Lux Corp., C.R. Daily and Transparency Dept. of Paramount Pictures Corp., For HiTrans and Para-HiTrans rear projection screens

Construction Dept. of Metro-Goldwyn-Mayer Studio, For new hand-portable fog machine

Daniel J. Bloomberg, John Pond, William Wade and Engineering and Camera Depts. of Republic Studio, For Naturama adpatation to the Mitchell camera

1957 Charles E. Sutter, William B. Smith, Paramount Pictures Corp. and General Cable Corp., For application of aluminum light-weight electrical cable and connectors to studio use

1958 Willy Borberg and General Precision Laboratory, Inc., For high-speed intermittent movement for 35mm theatre projection equipment

Fred Ponedel, George Brown and Conrad Boye of Warner Bros. Special Effects Dept., For new rapid-fire marble gun

1959 Ub Iwerks of Walt Disney Productions, For improved optical printer for special effects and matte shots

E.L. Stones, Glen Robinson, Winfield Hubbard and Luther Newman of Metro-Goldwyn-Mayer Construction Dept., For multiple cable remote-controlled winch

1960 Arthur Holcomb, Petro Vlahos and Columbia Studio Camera Dept., For camera flicker-indicating device

Anthony Paglia and 20th Century-Fox Studio Mechanical Effects Dept., For miniature flak gun and ammunition

Carl Hauge, Robert Grubel and Edward Reichard of Consolidated Film Laboratories, For automatic developer-replenisher system

1961 Hurletron, Inc., Electric Eye Equipment Div., For automatic light-changing system for printers

Wadsworth E. Pohl and Technicolor Corp., For integrated sound and picture transfer process

1962 Electro-Voice, Inc., For highly directional dynamic line microphone

Louis G. MacKenzie, For selective sound effects repeater

1963 Douglas A. Shearer and A. Arnold Gillespie of Metro-Goldwyn-Mayer Studios, For improved Background Process Projection System

1964 Milton Forman, Richard B. Glickman and Daniel J. Pearlman of ColorTran Industries, For advances in lighting units using quartz iodine lamps

Stewart Filmscreen Corp., For seamless translucent Blue Screen for Traveling Matte Color Cinematography

Anthony Paglia and 20th Century-Fox Studio Mechanical Effects Dept., For improved method of processing explosion flash effects

Edward H. Reichard and Carl W. Hauge of Consolidated Film Industries, For Proximity Cue Detector and its application to motion picture printers

Edward H. Reichard, Leonard L. Sokolow and Carl W. Hauge of Consolidated Film Industries, For design and application of stroboscopic scene tester for color and black-and-white film

Nelson Tyler, For improved helicopter camera system

1965 No award

1966 Panavision, Inc., For Panatron Power Inverter and its application to camera operation

Carroll Knudson, For production of composers' manual for motion picture music synchronization

Ruby Raksin, For production of composers' manual for motion picture music synchronization

1967 Electro-Optical Div., Kollmorgen Corp., For series of projection lenses

Panavision, Inc., For variable-speed motor for cameras

Fred R. Wilson of Samuel Goldwyn Studio Sound Dept., For audio level clamper

Walden O. Watson and Universal City Studio Sound Dept., For new concepts in design of music scoring stage

1968 Carl W. Hauge and Edward Reichard of Consolidated Film Laboratories and E. Michael Meahl and Roy J. Ridenour of Ramtronics, For automatic exposure control for printing machine lamps

Eastman Kodak Co., and Consolidated Film Industries, For new direct positive film and for the application of this film to post-production work prints

1969 Otto Popelka of Magna-Tech Electronics Co., Inc., For electronically controlled looping system

Fenton Hamilton of Metro-Goldwyn-Mayer Studios, For mobile battery-power unit for location lighting

Panavision, Inc., For Panaspeed motion picture camera motor

Robert M. Flynn and Russell Hessy of Universal City Studios, For machine-gun modification for motion picture photography

1970 Sylvania Electric Products, Inc., For series of compact tungsten halogen lamps

B.J. Losmandy, For concept, design and application of micro-miniature solid-state amplifier modules in recording equipment

Eastman Kodak Co. and Photo Electronics Corp., For improved video color analyzer for laboratories

Electro-Sound, Inc., For Series 8000 sound system for theatres

1971 Thomas Jefferson Hutchinson, James R. Rochester and Fenton Hamilton, For Sunbrute system of xenon arc lamps for location lighting

Photo Research Div., Kollmorgen Corp., For film/lens-balanced three-color meter

Robert D. Auguste and Cinema Products Co., For new crystal-controlled lightweight motor for 35mm Arriflex cameras

Producers Service Corp. and Consolidated Film Industries, and Cinema Research Corp. and Research Products, Inc., For engineering and implementation of fully automatic blow-up printing systems

Cinema Products Co., For control motor to actuate zoom lenses on cameras

1972 Photo Research Div. of Kollmorgen Corp., and PSC Technology, Inc., Acme Products Div., For Spectra Gate Photometer for printers

Carter Equipment Co. and Ramtronics, For light-valve photometer for printers

David Degenkolb, Harry Larson, Manfred Michelson and Fred Scobey of DeLuxe General Inc., For development of computerized printer and process control system

Jiro Mukai and Ryusho Hirose of Canon, Inc., and Wilton R. Holm of AMPTP Motion Picture and Television Research Center, For Canon Macro Zoom Lens

Philip V. Palmquist and Leonard L. Olson of 3M Co. and Frank P. Clark of AMPTP Motion Picture and Television Research Center, For Nextel simulated blood for color photography

E.H. Geissler and G.M. Berggren of Wil-Kin, Inc., For Ultra-Vision theatre projection system

1973 Rosco Laboratories, Inc., For technical advances and development of complete system of light-control materials for photography

Richard H. Vetter of Todd-AO Corp., For improved anamorphic focusing system

1974 Elemack Co., For Spyder camera dolly

Louis Ami of Universal City Studios, For reciprocating camera platform for special visual effects photography

1975 Lawrence W. Butler and Roger Banks, For concept of applying low-inertia and stepping electric motors to film transport systems and optical printers

David J. Degenkolb and Fred Scobey of DeLuxe General Inc., and John C. Dolan and Richard DuBois of Akwaklame Co., For technique of silver recovery from photographic wash waters by ion exchange

Joseph Westheimer, For a device to obtain shadowed titles on film

Carter Equipment Co. and RAMtronics, For computerized tape-punching system for programming laboratory printing machines

Hollywood Film Co., For computerized tape-punching system for programming laboratory printing machines

Bell & Howell Co., For computerized tape-punching system for programming laboratory printing machines

Fredrick Schlyter, For computerized tape-punching system for programming laboratory printing machines

1976 Fred Bartscher of Kollmorgen Corp. and Glenn Berggren of Schneider Corp., For single-lens magnifier for projection lenses

Panavision, Inc., For super-speed lenses for photography

Hiroshi Suzukawa of Canon and Wilton R. Holm of AMPTP Motion Picture and Television Research Center, For super-speed lenses for photography

Carl Zeiss Co., For super-speed lenses for photography

Photo Research Div., Kollmorgen Corp., For Spectra Tri-Color Meter

1977 Ernst Nettman of Astrovision Div., Continental Camera Systems, Inc., For engineering of periscope aerial camera system

Electronic Engineering Co. of California, For developing method of interlocking non-sprocketed film and tape media used in motion picture production

Bernhard Kuhl and Werner Block of OSRAM GmBH, For development of mercury-medium iodide, high-efficiency discharge lamp

Panavision, Inc., For design of Panalite, camera-mounted controllable light

Panavision, Inc., For engineering of Panahead gear head for motion picture cameras

Piclear, Inc., For developing a projector attachment to improve screen image quality

SOUND EFFECTS

1964 Norman Wantsall, *Goldfinger*
1965 Tregoweth Brown, *The Great Race*
1966 Gordon Daniel, *Grand Prix*
1967 John Poyner, *The Dirty Dozen*

SPECIAL EFFECTS

1951 *When Worlds Collide*
1952 *Plymouth Adventure*
1953 *War of the Worlds*

SPECIAL ACHIEVEMENT AWARD FOR VISUAL EFFECTS

1972 *The Poseidon Adventure*
1976 *King Kong*
     Logan's Run

JEAN HERSHOLT HUMANITARIAN AWARD

1956 Y. Frank Freeman
1957 Samuel Goldwyn
1958 No award
1959 Bob Hope
1960 Sol Lesser
1961 George Seaton
1962 Steve Broidy
1963 No award
1964 No award
1965 Edmond L. DePatie
1966 George Bagnall
1967 Gregory Peck
1968 Martha Raye
1969 George Jessel
1970 Frank Sinatra
1971 No award
1972 Rosalind Russell
1973 Lew Wasserman
1974 Arthur B. Krim
1975 Jules Stein
1976 No award
1977 Charlton Heston

IRVING G. THALBERG MEMORIAL AWARD

1937 Darryl F. Zanuck
1938 Hal B. Wallis
1939 David O. Selznick
1940 No award
1941 Walter E. Disney
1942 Sidney Franklin
1943 Hal B. Wallis
1944 Darryl F. Zanuck
1945 No award
1946 Samuel Goldwyn
1947 No award
1948 Jerry Wald
1949 No award
1950 Darryl F. Zanuck
1951 Arthur Freed
1952 Cecil B. DeMille
1953 George Stevens
1954 No award
1955 No award
1956 Buddy Adler
1957 No award
1958 Jack L. Warner
1959 No award

1960 No award
1961 Stanley Kramer
1962 No award
1963 Sam Spiegel
1964 No award
1965 William Wyler
1966 Robert Wise
1967 Alfred Hitchcock
1968 No award
1969 No award
1970 Ingmar Bergman
1971 No award
1972 No award
1973 Lawrence Weingarten
1974 No award
1975 Mervyn LeRoy
1976 Pandro S. Berman
1977 Walter Mirisch

HONORARY AWARDS

FOREIGN LANGUAGE FILM AWARD

1948 *Monsieur Vincent* (France)
1949 *The Bicycle Thief* (Italy)
1950 *The Walls of Malapaga* (France/Italy)
1951 *Rashomon* (Japan)
1952 *Forbidden Games* (France)
1953 No award
1954 *Gate of Hell* (Japan)
1955 *Samurai* (Japan)

SPECIAL AWARDS

1928 **Warner Bros.,** For producing *The Jazz Singer*
      Charles Chaplin, For his versatility and genius in writing, acting, directing and producing *The Circus*
1932 **Walt Disney,** For creating Mickey Mouse
1934 **Shirley Temple,** In recognition of her outstanding contribution to screen entertainment during 1934
1935 **David Wark Griffith,** For distinguished creative achievements as director and producer and lasting contributions to the progress of the motion picture arts
1935 *The March of Time,* For its significance to motion pictures for revolutionizing an important branch of the industry, the newsreel
1936 **W. Howard Greene and Harold Rosen,** For color cinematography of *The Garden of Allah*
1937 **Mack Sennett,** For lasting contributions to comedy technique on the screen
      Edgar Bergen, For creating Charlie McCarthy
      Museum of Modern Art Film Library, For its significant work collecting films dating from 1895 and making study of them available to the public
      W. Howard Greene, For color photography of *A Star Is Born*
1938 **Deanna Durbin and Mickey Rooney,** For significant contribution to bringing to the screen the spirit and personification of youth and setting a high standard of ability and achievement for juvenile players
      Harry M. Warner, In recognition of patriotic service in the production of historical short subjects
      Walt Disney, For *Snow White and The Seven Dwarfs,* a significant screen innovation and pioneering field for the motion picture cartoon
      Oliver Marsh and Allen Davey, For color photography of *Sweethearts*

Gordon Jennings assisted by **Jan Domela, Dev Jennings, Irmin Roberts and Art Smith** (special effects), **Farciot Edouart** assisted by **Loyal Griggs** (transparencies) and **Loren Ryder** assisted by **Harry Mills, Louis Mesenkop and Walter Oberst** (sound effects), For outstanding special photographic and sound effects in *Spawn of the North*
J. Arthur Ball, For outstanding contributions to the advancement of color in motion picture photography
Douglas Fairbanks, A commemorative award for his unique contribution as the Academy's first president
Motion Picture Relief Fund and Jean Hersholt (president), **Ralph Morgan** (chairman, Executive Committee), **Ralph Block** (first vice president) and **Conrad Nagel,** For services to the industry and progressive leadership
Technicolor Co., For contributions for successfully bringing the three-color feature to the screen
Judy Garland, For outstanding performance as a screen juvenile during the previous year
William Cameron Menzies, For outstanding achievement in use of color for enhancement of the dramatic mood in *Gone With the Wind*
1940 **Bob Hope,** For his unselfish services to the motion picture industry
      Col. Nathan Levinson, For outstanding service to the industry and the Army during the past nine years, making possible the efficient mobilization of the motion picture industry for the production of Army training films
1941 *Churchill's Island,* Canadian National Film Board, Citation for distinctive achievement in short documentary subjects
      Rey Scott, For extraordinary achievement in producing *Kukan,* a film record of China's struggle, with a 16mm camera under the most difficult and dangerous conditions
      British Ministry of Information, For vivid and dramatic presentation of the Royal Air Force in its documentary *Target for Tonight*
      Walt Disney, William Garity, John N.A. Hawkins and RCA Mfg. Co., For outstanding contribution to advancement of sound in motion pictures through the production of *Fantasia*
      Leopold Stokowski and associates, For unique achievement in creating a new form of visualized music in *Fantasia,* thereby widening the scope of the motion picture as entertainment and art form
1942 **Charles Boyer,** For progressive cultural achievement in establishing French Research Foundation in Los Angeles as a source of reference for the industry
      Noel Coward, For outstanding production achievement for *In Which We Serve*
      Metro-Goldwyn-Mayer Studio, For presenting the American way of life in the production of the Andy Hardy series of films
1943 **George Pal,** For developing novel methods and techniques in production of Puppetoons short subjects
1944 **Margaret O'Brien,** As the outstanding child actress of 1944
      Bob Hope, For his many services to the Academy, a Life Membership
1945 **Walter Wanger,** For his six years as president of the Academy
      Peggy Ann Garner, As the outstanding child actress of 1945
      Fran Ross and Mervyn LeRoy (producers), **Albert Maltz** (screenplay) **Earl Robinson and Lewis Allen** (title song) and **Frank Sinatra** (star), For *The House I Live In,* a short subject promoting tolerance

Republic Studios, Daniel J. Bloomberg and the Republic Studio Sound Dept., For building an outstanding musical scoring auditorium

1946 Laurence Olivier, For outstanding achievement as actor, producer and director in bringing *Henry V* to the screen

Harold Russell, For bringing hope and courage to fellow veterans through his appearance in *The Best Years of Our Lives*

Ernst Lubitsch, For distinguished contributions to the art of the motion picture

Claude Jarman, Jr., As the outstanding child star of 1946

1947 *Bill and Coo,* A novel and entertaining use of the motion picture medium

Shoe-Shine, An Italian production of superlative quality made under adverse circumstances

Col. William N. Selig, Albert E. Smith, George K. Spoor and Thomas Armat, For their contributions as motion picture pioneers to the development of the film industry

James Baskett, For his characterization of Uncle Remus in *Song of the South*

1948 Ivan Jandl, For outstanding juvenile performance of 1948 in *The Search*

Sid Grauman, Master showman who raised the standard of exhibition of motion pictures

Adolph Zukor, For 40 years of service to the industry

Walter Wanger, For distinguished service to the industry in adding to its moral stature in the world community through the production of *Joan of Arc*

1949 Bobby Driscoll, As the outstanding juvenile actor of 1949

Fred Astaire, For unique artistry and contributions to musical motion pictures

Cecil B. DeMille, Distinguished pioneer for 37 years of brilliant showmanship

Jean Hersholt, For distinguished service to the industry

HONORARY AWARDS

1950 George Murphy, For services to the film industry and the country at large

Louis B. Mayer, For distinguished service to the industry

1951 Gene Kelly, In appreciation of his versatility as an actor, singer, director and dancer, and specifically for his brilliant achievements in film choreography

1952 George Alfred Mitchell, For the design and development of the camera which bears his name for his continued and dominant presence in cinematography

Joseph M. Schenck, For long and distinguished service to the industry

Merian C. Cooper, For many innovations and contributions to the art of motion pictures.

Harold Lloyd, Master comedian and good citizen

Bob Hope, For contributions to the laughter of the world, service to the industry and devotion to the American promise

1953 Pete Smith, For witty and pungent observations of the American scene in his series *Pete Smith Specialties*

20th Century-Fox Film Corp., In recognition of imagination, showmanship and foresight in introducing the revolutionary process, CinemaScope

Joseph I. Breen, For conscientious, open-minded and dignified management of the Motion Picture Production Code

Bell & Howell Co., For pioneering and basic achievements in the advancement of the industry

1954 Bausch & Lomb Optical Co., For contributions to the advancement of the industry

Kemp R. Niver, For development of the Renovare Process, making possible the restoration of the Library of Congress Film Collection

Greta Garbo, For her unforgettable film performances

Danny Kaye, For his unique talents, service to the Academy, the industry and the American people

Jon Whitely, For outstanding juvenile performance in *The Little Kidnappers*

Vincent Winter, For outstanding juvenile performance in *The Little Kidnappers*

1955 No award

1956 Eddie Cantor, For distinguished service to the industry

1957 Charles Brackett, For distinguished service to the Academy

B.B. Kahane, For distinguished service to the industry

Gilbert M. "Broncho Billy" Anderson, For his contributions as a motion picture pioneer to the development of film as entertainment

Society of Motion Picture and Television Engineers, For contributions to the advancement of the industry

1958 Maurice Chevalier, For contributions to the world of entertainment for more than half a century

1959 Lee de Forest, For pioneering inventions that brought sound to motion pictures

Buster Keaton, For unique talents which brought immortal comedies to the screen

1960 Gary Cooper, For his many memorable screen performances and international recognition he gained for the industry

Stan Laurel, For creative pioneering in cinema comedy

Hayley Mills, For the most outstanding juvenile performance of 1960 in *Pollyanna*

1961 William L. Hendricks, For outstanding patriotic service in conception, writing and production of Marine Corps film, *A Force in Readiness*

Jerome Robbins, For brilliant achievements in choreography on film

Fred L. Metzler, For dedication and service to the Academy

1962 No award

1963 No award

1964 William Tuttle, For outstanding make-up achievement in *7 Faces of Dr. Lao*

1965 Bob Hope, For unique and distinguished service to the industry and Academy

1966 Y. Frank Freeman, For unusual and outstanding service to the Academy during 30 years in Hollywood

Yakima Canutt, For achievements as a stunt man and for developing safety devices to protect stunt men everywhere

1967 Arthur Freed, For distinguished service to the Academy and the production of six awards telecasts

1968 John Chambers, For outstanding make-up achievement in *Planet of the Apes*

Onna White, For outstanding choreography in *Oliver!*

1969 Cary Grant, For unique mastery of the art of screen acting with the respect and affection of his colleagues

1970 Lillian Gish, For superlative artistry and distinguished contribution to motion picture progress

Orson Welles, For superlative artistry and versatility in the creation of motion pictures

1971 **Charles Chaplin,** For the incaculable effect he has had in making motion pictures the art form of this century

1972 **Charles S. Boren,** A leader for 38 years of the industry's enlightened labor relations and architect of its policy of non-discrimination, with respect and affection of all who work in films

Edward G. Robinson, As a great player, patron of the arts and dedicated citizen—"a Renaissance man"

1973 **Henri Langlois,** For his devotion to the art of film, massive contributions to preserving its past and unswerving faith in its future

Groucho Marx, In recognition of his brilliant creativity and the unequalled achievements of the Marx Brothers in the art of motion picture comedy

1974 **Howard Hawks,** Master American filmmaker, whose creative efforts hold a distinguished place in world cinema

Jean Renoir, A genius who with grace, responsibility and devotion through silent and sound film, documentary, feature film and television has won the world's admiration

1975 **Mary Pickford,** In recognition of her unique contributions to the industry and the development of film as an artistic medium

1976 **No award**

1977 **Maggie Booth,** In honor of years a film editor

Life Achievement Award
AMERICAN FILM INSTITUTE
Kennedy Center, Washington, D.C. 20566 (202/833-9300)

The Life Achievement Award, which consists of a statuette presented annually at a nationally televised banquet, is given to an individual who "in a fundamental way contributed to the filmmaking art; whose accomplishments have been acknowledged by scholars, critics, professional peers and the general public; and whose work has stood the test of time." The institute's board of trustees selects the winner.

1973 **John Ford,** Director
1974 **James Cagney,** Actor
1975 **Orson Welles,** Actor and director
1976 **William Wyler,** Director
1977 **Bette Davis,** Actress

Golden Berlin Bear
BERLIN INTERNATIONAL FILM FESTIVAL
1000 Berlin 15, Bundesalle 1-12, Federal Republic of Germany (Tel: 030-882 20 81)

The Berlin International Film Festival is held each summer for films from all countries which have been released not more than one year prior to the festival year. A nine-member jury selects prize winners in various categories. The Grand Prize winner in each category receives a Golden Bear Statuette. Additionally, up to eight Silver Bears and several Bronze Bears are awarded for other film aspects, and Honorable or Special Mentions are frequently made. These are not listed here. Further, the Festival is the framework in which other special honors are made. Film titles not in their original language below are translated or transliterated into German.

FEATURE FILM—GRAND PRIZE—GOLDEN BERLIN BEAR

1951 *Sans Laisser d'adresse,* France
Justice Est Faite, France
Die Vier im Jeep, Switzerland
Cinderella, U.S.A.
1952 *Hon Dansade en Sommar,* Sweden
1953 No award
1954 *Hobson's Choice,* Great Britain
1955 *Die Ratten,* Federal Republic of Germany
1956 *Vor Sonnenuntergang,* Federal Republic of Germany
Invitation to the Dance, U.S.A.
1957 *Twelve Angry Men,* U.S.A.
1958 *Smultronstallet (Wild Strawberries),* Sweden
1959 *Les Cousins,* France
1960 *El Lazarillo de Tormes,* Spain
1961 *La Notte,* Italy
1962 *A Kind of Loving,* Great Britain
1963 *La Diavolo,* Italy
Bushino Zankoku Monogatari, Japan
1964 *Susuz Yaz,* Turkey
1965 *Alphaville,* France
1966 *Cul-de-Sac,* Great Britain
1967 *Le Depart,* Belgium
1968 *Ole Dole Doff,* Sweden
1969 *Rani Radovi,* Yugoslavia
1970 No award
1971 *Il Giardino dei Finzi-Contini,* Italy
1972 *Canterbury Tales,* Italy
1973 *Ashani Sanket,* India
1974 *The Apprenticeship of Duddy Kravitz,* Canada
1975 *Orokbefogadas,* Hungary
1976 *Buffalo Bill and the Indians,* U.S.A.
1977 *Woschozdenie,* U.S.S.R.

SHORT FILM—GRAND PRIZE—GOLDEN BERLIN BEAR

1951 *Der Film Entdeckte Kunstwerke Indianischer Vorzeit,* Federal Republic of Germany
Kleine Nachtgespenster, Federal Republic of Germany
The Story of Time, Great Britain
1952 No award
1953 No award
1954 No award
1955 *Zimmerleute des Waldes,* Federal Republic of Germany
1956 *Paris La Nuit,* France
1957 *Gente Lontana,* Italy
1958 *La Lunga Raccolta,* Italy
1959 *Prijs de Zee,* Netherlands
1960 *Le Songe des Chevaux Sauvages,* France
1961 *Gesicht von der Stange,* Federal Republic of Germany
1962 *De Werkelijkheid von Karel Appel,* Netherlands
1963 *Bouwspelment,* Netherlands
1964 *Kirdi,* Austria
1965 *Yeats Country,* Ireland
1966 *KNUD,* Denmark
1967 *Through the Eyes of a Painter,* India
1968 *Portrait Orson Welles,* France
1969 *To See or Not to See,* Canada
1970 No award
1971 *1501½ (The Apartment),* U.S.A.
1972 *Flyaway,* Great Britain
1973 *Colter's Hell,* Great Britain
1974 *The Convert,* Great Britain
1975 No award
1976 No award

1977 *Ortsfremd . . . Wohnhaft Vormals Mainzerland-strasse,* Federal Republic of Germany

LONG DOCUMENTARY—GRAND PRIZE—GOLDEN BERLIN BEAR
1951 *Beaver Valley,* U.S.A.
1952 No award
1953 No award
1954 *The Living Desert,* U.S.A.
1955 *The Vanishing Prairie,* U.S.A.
1956 *Kein Platz Fur Wilde Tiere,* Federal Republic of Germany
1957 *Man Against the Arctic,* U.S.A.
 Secrets of Life, U.S.A.
1958 *Perri,* U.S.A.
1959 *White Wilderness,* U.S.A.
1960 *Faja Lobbi,* Netherlands
1961 *Description d'un Combat,* Israel
1962 No award
1963 No award
1964 *Alleman,* Netherlands

Cannes Honors
FESTIVAL INTERNATIONAL DU FILM
71 Rue du Faubourg-Saint-Honore, 75008 Paris, France
(Tel: 266-92-20)

The Grand Prize, the Gold Palm and other awards and mentions made to international filmmakers by a jury of international filmmakers has changed from year to year in the three decades of the festival now known as the Cannes Film Festival. Therefore, in a departure from the system used elsewhere in this volume, Cannes honors are listed year by year, with notations indicating the specific categories set up for that particular year and the winners. The film titles are given as they appear in the Festival; that is, normally in their original language or in French; some foreign names will have been transliterated into French.

1946 GRAND PRIZE OF THE INTERNATIONAL FILM FESTIVAL (by country)
Czechoslovakia: *Les Hommes Sans Ailes,* produced by M. Cap
Denmark: *La Terre Sera Rouge,* produced by Bodil Ipsen and L. Lauritzen
France: *La Symphonie Pastorale,* produced by Jean Delannoy
Great Britain: *Brief Encounter,* produced by David Lean
India: *Neecha Nagar,* produced by Chetan Anand
Italy: *Roma Citta Aperta,* produced by Roberto Rossellini
Mexico: *Maria Candelaria,* produced by Emilio Fernandez
Sweden: *L'Epreuve,* produced by Alf Sjoberg
Switzerland: *La Derniere Chance,* produced by Leopold Lindtberg
U.S.A.: *The Lost Weekend,* produced by Billy Wilder
U.S.S.R.: *Le Tournant Decisif,* produced by Frederic Ermler

PRIX DU JURY INTERNATIONAL (International Jury Prize)
Rene Clement, producer, *La Bataille du Rail* (France)

GRANDS PRIX INTERNATIONALS (International Grand Prizes)
Rene Clement, director, *La Bataille du Rail* (France)
Michele Morgan, actress, *La Symphonie Pastorale* (France)
Ray Milland, actor, *The Lost Weekend* (U.S.A.)

OTHER JURY PRIZES FOR SHORT FILMS
Tchirkov, screenplay, *Le Tournant Decisif* (U.S.S.R.)
Romm, producer, *Matricule 217* (U.S.S.R.)
Georges Auric, music, (France)
Figueroa, *Maria Candelaria* and *Les Trois Mousquetaires* (Mexico)
A. Ptouchko, color, *Fleur de Pierre* (U.S.S.R.)
 Berlin (U.S.S.R.)
Walt Disney, animation, *Make Mine Music* (U.S.A.)

PRIX INTERNATIONAL DE LA PAIX (International Peace Prize)
Leopold Lindtberg, producer, *La Derniere Chance* (Switzerland)

PRIX DU CIDALC (Prize of the International Committee for the Furtherance of Arts and Letters by Film)
Y. Cousteau, *Epaves* (France)

SHORT SUBJECTS: GRAND PRIX INTERNATIONAL (International Grand Prize)
Documentary: *Ombres sur la Neige* (Sweden)
Scientific film: *La Cite des Abeilles* (U.S.S.R.)
Educational film: *Wieliczka* (Poland)
Newsfilm: *Jeunesse de Notre Pays* (U.S.S.R.)
Animated film: *Les Brigands et les Animaux* (Czechoslovakia)
Scenario: *Reve de Noel* (Czechoslovakia)
Peace prize: *Jeunesse de Notre Pays* (U.S.S.R.)

1947 **Psychology and love story:** *Antoine et Antoinette,* produced by Jacques Becker (France)
Adventure or police story: *Les Maudits,* produced by Rene Clement (France)
Sociological film: *Cross Fire,* produced by Edward Dmytryk (U.S.A.)
Musical comedy: *Ziegfeld Follies,* produced by Vincente Minnelli (U.S.A.)
Animation: *Dumbo,* produced by Walt Disney (U.S.A.)
Documentary: *Inondations en Pologne* (Poland)
Special Mention: *Mine Own Executioner,* produced by Anthony Kimmins (Great Britain)
Special Mention: *Skeep Tiel Induland,* produced by Ingmar Bergman (Sweden)

1948 No festival

1949 FEATURE FILMS
Grand Prix du Festival (Grand Prize of the Festival): *The Third Man,* produced by Carol Reed, (Great Britain)
Direction: Rene Clement, for *La Mura di Malapaga* (Italy)
Actress: Isa Miranda, for *La Mura di Malapaga* (Italy)
Actor: Edward G. Robinson for *House of Strangers* (U.S.A.)
Screenplay: *Lost Boundaries* produced by V. Shaler (U.S.A.)
Music: *Pueblerina* produced by Emilio Fernandez (Mexico)
Sets: *Occupe-toi d'Amelie,* produced by Claude Autan Lara (France)

Subject: *Palle Seul au Monde,* produced by A. Henning-Jensen (Denmark)
Montage: *Pacific 231,* produced by Jean Mitry (France)
Photography: *Paturages,* produced by S. Mizdzenski (Poland)
Color: *Images Medievales,* produced by William Novick (France)
Newsfilm: *Seal Island,* produced by Walt Disney (U.S.A.)

1950 No festival

1951 GRAND PRIX DU FESTIVAL INTERNATIONAL DU FILM (Grand Prize of the International Film Festival-Cannes)
Feature film: *Miracolo A Milano* produced by Vittorio De Sica (Italy)
Froken Julie produced by Alf Sjoberg (Sweden)

OTHER JURY PRIZES FOR FEATURE FILMS
Special Prize: *All About Eve,* produced by Joseph L. Mankiewicz (U.S.A.)
Direction: Luis Bunuel for *Los Olvidados* (Mexico)
Actress: Bette Davis for *All About Eve* (U.S.A.)
Actor: Michael Redgrave, for *The Browning Version* (Great Britain)
Screenplay: Terence Rattigan for *The Browning Version* (Great Britain)
Music: Joseph Kosma for *Juliette ou La Clef des Songes* (France)
Photography: *La Caravelle Isabel Partira ce Soir,* produced by Luis-Maria Beltran (Venezuela)
Sets: *Moussorgsky,* produced by Souvorov A. Veksler (U.S.S.R.)
Prix Exceptionnel: *Les Contes d'Hoffman,* produced by Michael Powell and Emeric Pressburger (Great Britain)
Diplome Special: The country of Italy for having presented the best selection

GRAND PRIX DU FESTIVAL INTERNATIONAL DU FILM (Grand Prize of the International Film Festival-Cannes)
Short film: *Miroirs de Hollande,* produced by Bert Haanstra (Netherlands)
Scientific or Educational Film: *L'Eruption de l'Etna,* produced by Domenico Paolella (Italy)
Prix Special du Jury: *La Voie est Ouest,* produced by K. Gordon (Poland)
Distinguished Films from One Country, a Special Jury Prize: U.S.S.R. for *Ukraine en Fleurs* (M. Sloutzky, producer), *Lettonie Sovietique* (F. Kissiliov, producer), *Esthonie Sovietique* (V. Tomber and I. Guidine, producers), and *Azerbaidjan Sovietique* (F. Kissiliov and M. Dadachev, producers)

1952 GRAND PRIX DU FESTIVAL INTERNATIONAL (Grand Prize of the International Festival-Cannes)
Feature Films: *Due Soldi di Speranza,* produced by Renato Castellani (Italy)
Othello, produced by Orson Welles (Morocco)

OTHER JURY PRIZES FOR FEATURE FILMS
Prix Special du Jury: *Nous Sommes Tous des Assasins,* produced by Andre Cayatte (France)
Lyrical Film: *Le Medium,* produced by Gian Carlo Menotti (U.S.A.)
Direction: Christian-Jaque for *Fanfan la Tulip* (France)

Screenplay: Piero Fellini for *Gendarmes et Voleurs* (Italy)
Actress: Lee Grant for *Detective Story* (U.S.A.)
Actor: Marlon Brando for *Viva Zapata* (U.S.A.)
Music: Sven Skold for *Hon Dansade en Sommar* (Sweden)
Photography: Kohei Sugiyama for *Genji Monogatari* (Japan)

GRAND PRIX DU FESTIVAL INTERNATIONAL (Grand Prix of the International Festival-Cannes)
Short film: *Het Schot is the Boord,* produced by Herman van der Horst (Netherlands)

OTHER JURY PRIZES FOR SHORT FILMS
Prix Special du Jury: *Indisk By,* produced by Arne Sucksdorff (Sweden)
Color *Animated Genesis,* produced by Joan and Peter Foldes (Great Britain)
Scientific or Educational Film: *Groenland,* produced by Marcel Ichac (France)
Diplome Special: The country of Italy for having presented the best selection
Hommage Special: The continuing efforts of the Netherlands in documentary film-making
Alexandre Astruc, a young producer, for *Le Rideau Cramoisi* (France)

1953 GRAND PRIX DU FESTIVAL INTERNATIONAL DU FILM (Grand Prix of the International Film Festival)
Feature Film: *Le Salaire de la Peur,* produced by Georges Clouzot (France)
Special Mention Charles Vanel as best male actor, for *Le Salaire de la Peur* (France)

PRIX INTERNATIONAUX (International Prizes)
Adventure Film with Special Mention for Music: *O Cangacerio,* produced by L. Barreto (Brazil)
Best Humor Film with Special Mention for Screenplay: *Bienvenudo, Mister Marshall,* produced by Luis C. Berlanga (Spain)
Best Light Film with Special Mention for Charming Interpretation: *Lili,* produced by Charles Walters (U.S.A.)
Dramatic Film: *Come Back, Little Sheba,* Daniel Mann, producer, with Special Mention for the Best Female Actor: Shirley Booth, (U.S.A.)
Best Legendary Film: *Valkoinen Peura,* produced by Erik Blomberg (Finland)
Best Exploration Film: *Magia Verde,* produced by Gian Gaspare Napolitano with Special Mention for Color (Italy)
Best Image: *La Red,* produced by Emilio Fernandez (Mexico)
Special Award: *Duende y Misterio del Flamenco,* produced by Edgar Neville (Spain)

GRAND PRIX DU FESTIVAL INTERNATIONAL DU FILM (Grand Prize of the International Film Festival)
Short Film: *Crin Blanc,* produced by Albert Lamorisse (France)

OTHER PRIZES FOR SHORT FILMS
Documentary: *Houen Zo,* Herman van der Horst, producer (Netherlands)
Fiction: *The Stranger Left No Card,* Wendy Toye, producer (Great Britain)
Art film: *Doderhultarn* Olle Hellbom, producer (Sweden)

Animated film: *Sports et Transports,* Colin Low, producer (Canada)

1954 Special award for a Film Classified as Out of the Competition: *From Here to Eternity,* produced by Fred Zinnemann (U.S.A.)

GRAND PRIX DU FESTIVAL INTERNATIONAL DU FILM (Grand Prize of the International Film Festival)
Feature Film: *Jigoku-Mon,* produced by Teinosuke Kinugasa (Japan)
Prix Special du Jury (Special Jury Prize): *Knave of Hearts,* produced by Rene Clement (Great Britain)

PRIX INTERNATIONAUX (International Prizes)
Die Letzte Brucke, produced by Helmuth Kautner, with Special Mention for Actress Maria Schell (Austria)
The Living Desert, produced by Walt Disney with Special Mention for the Cameramen (U.S.A.)
Avant Le Deluge, produced by Andre Cayatte and Charles Spaak with Special Mention for the Cast (France)
Do Bighazamin, produced by Bimal Roy (India)
Carosello Napoletano, produced by Ettore Giannini (Italy)
Crinache di Peveri Amanti, produced by Carlo Lizzani (Italy)
Piatka z Ulicy Barskiej, directed by Aleksander Ford with Special Mention for Direction (Poland)
Det Stora Aventyret, with Special Mention for Arne Sucksdorff (Sweden)
Veliky Voine Albany, Scander-Beg, with Special Mention for Production Work, produced by Serge Youtkevitch (U.S.S.R.)

OTHER PRIZES FOR FEATURE FILMS
Entertainment: *Toot-Whistle Plunk and Boom,* produced by Walt Disney (U.S.A.)
Marionettes: *O Sklenicku Vic,* produced by Bretislov Pojar (Czechoslovakia)
Documentary with Special Mention for the Quality of the Subject: *Stare Miasto,* produced by Jerzy Bossak (Poland)
Poetic Fantasy: *The Pleasure Garden,* produced by James Broughton (Great Britain)
Nature Film: *Aptenodytes Foresteri,* produced by Mario Marret (France)
Special Mention: The constant high quality of the films of the **Netherlands**
Special Mention Television Film: *Leriche, Chirurgien de la Douleur,* produced by Rene Lucot (France)

1955 PALME D'OR DU FESTIVAL INTERNATIONAL DU FILM (Gold Palm of the International Film Festival)
Feature Film, with Special Recognition of the Entire Cast: *Marty,* Paddy Chayefsky, screenplay, Delbert Mann, director, Ernest Borgnine and Betsy Blair, actors (U.S.A.)

PRIX SPECIAL DU JURY (Special Jury Prize)
With Special Mention for the Poetic Images and Utilization of Sound: *Continente Perduto,* Leonardo Bonzi, Matio Craveri, Enrico Gras, F. Lavagnino, G. Moser (Italy)

PRIX INTERNATIONAUX (International Prizes)
Direction: Serge Vassiliev for *Gueroite Na Chipka* (Bulgaria)

Jules Dassin for *Du Rififi chez Les Hommes* (France)
Acting: Spencer Tracy, actor, for *Bad Day at Black Rock* (U.S.A.)
Cast Honors: *Bolchaia Semia,* produced by Joseph Heifitz (U.S.S.R.)

OTHER PRIZES FOR FEATURE FILMS
Dramatic Film: *East of Eden,* produced by Elia Kazan (U.S.A.)
Lyric Film: *Romeo and Juliette,* L. Arnchtam and L. Lavrovsky, producers, with Special Mention of the Dancer, Gabila Oulanova (U.S.S.R.)
Special Mention, Children: *Boot Polish,* "Baby" Naaz (India)
Marcelino Pan y Vino, produced by Ladislao Vajda (Spain)
Special Recognition: *Hill 24 Doesn't Answer,* produced by Haya Hararit (Israel)

PALME D'OR DU FESTIVAL INTERNATIONAL DU FILM (Gold Palm of the International Film Festival)
Short Film: *Blinkity Blank,* produced by Norman McLaren (Canada)

PRIX INTERNATIONAUX (International Prizes)
Documentary: *Isola di Fuoco,* produced by V. Deseta (Italy)
Newsfilm: *La Grande Peche,* produced by Henri Fabiani (France)
Special Mention for Animation: *Zolataia Antilopa,* produced by L. Atamanov (U.S.S.R.)

1956 PALME D'OR DU FESIVAL INTERNATIONAL DU FILM (Gold Palm of the International Film Festival)
Le Monde du Silence, produced by Jacques Yves Cousteau and Louis Malle (France)

PRIX SPECIAL DU JURY (Special Jury Prize)
Feature Film: *Le Mystere Picasso,* produced by Henri Georges Clouzot (France)

PRIX INTERNATIONAUX (International Prizes)
Production: *Othello,* produced by Serge Youtkevitch (U.S.S.R.)
Acting: Susan Hayward for *I'll Cry Tomorrow* (U.S.A.)
Poetic Humor: *Sommarnattens Leende,* produced by Ingmar Bergman (Sweden)
Human Document: *Pather Panchali,* produced by Satyajit Ray (India)

PALME D'OR DU FESTIVAL INTERNATIONAL DU FILM (Gold Palm of the International Film Festival)
Short Film: *Le Ballon Rouge,* produced by Albert Lamorisse (France)

OTHER PRIZES FOR SHORT FILMS
Documentary: *La Corsa Delle Roche,* produced by Gian Luigi Polidori (Italy)
Andre Modeste Gretry, produced by Lucien Deroisy (Belgium)
Fiction: *Lourdja Magdany,* produced by T. Abouladze and R. Tchkheidze (U.S.S.R.)
Special Mention: *Loutky Jiriho Trnky,* Jiri Trnka, marionettes, Bruno Sefranek, producer (Czechoslovakia)
Research: *Together,* produced by Lorenza Mazzetti (Great Britain)

Tant qu'il y Aura des Betes, produced by Brassai (France)

1957 PALME D'OR DU FESTIVAL INTERNATIONAL DU FILM (Gold Palm of the International Film Festival)

Feature Film: *Friendly Persuasion,* produced by William Wyler (U.S.A.)

Prix Special du Jury (Special Jury Prize): *Kanal,* produced by Andrzej Wajda (Poland)

Det Sjunde Inseglet, produced by Ingmar Bergman (Sweden)

PRIX SPECIAL (Special Prize)

For its Original Screenplay, Humane Quality and Romantic Grandeur: *Sorok Pervyi,* produced by Grigori Tchoukhrai (U.S.S.R.)

OTHER PRIZES FOR FEATURE FILMS

Direction: Robert Bresson for *Un Condamne a Mort s'est Echappe* (France)

Actress: Giulietta Masina for *Le Notti de Cabiria* with Hommage to Frederico Fellini (Italy)

Actor: John Kitzmiller for *Dolina Miru* (Yugoslavia)

Romantic Documentary: *Shiroi Sammyaku,* produced by Sadao Imamura (Japan)

Qivitoq, produced by Erik Balling (Denmark)

Exceptional Mention: *Gotoma the Buddha,* produced by Rajbans Khanna (India)

Best selection: *Celui qui Doit Mourir,* produced by Jules Dassin (France)

Un Condamne a Mort s'est Echappe, produced by Robert Bresson (France)

Niok, produced by Edmond Sechan (France)

Toute la Memoire du Monde, produced by Alain Resnais (France)

PALME D'OR DU FESTIVAL INTERNATIONAL DU FILM (Gold Palm of the International Film Festival)

Short Film: *Courte Histoire,* produced by Ion Pepesco Gopo (Rumania)

OTHER PRIZES FOR SHORT FILMS

Documentary: *Capitale de l'Or,* produced by Colin Low and Wolf Koenig (Canada)

Nature Film: *Wiesensommer,* produced by Heinz Sielmann (Federal Republic of Germany)

Special Mention: *Les Chaseurs des Mers du Sud,* produced by S. Kogan (U.S.S.R.)

1958 PALME D'OR DU FESTIVAL INTERNATIONAL DU FILM (Gold Palm of the International Film Festival)

Feature Film: *Letiat Jouravly,* produced by Michel Kalatozov (U.S.S.R.)

Special Recognition: *Tatiana Samoilova,* actress, for *Letiat Jouravly* (U.S.S.R.)

PRIX SPECIAL DU JURY (Special Jury Prize)

Feature Film: *Mon Oncle,* Jacques Tati (France)

PRIX INTERNATIONAUX (International Prizes)

Direction: *Ingmar Bergman* for *Nara Livet* (Sweden)

Original screenplay: *Giovani Mariti,* P.P. Pasolini, Massimo Franciosa, P. Festa Campanile; Mauro Bolinini, producer (Italy)

Collective Acting Award, Female: *Bibi Andersson, Eva Dahlbeck, Barbro Hiort-af-Ornas, Ingrid Thulin, Nara Livet* (Sweden)

Acting, Male: Paul Newman for *The Long Hot Summer* (U.S.A.)

Poetic Originality and Exceptional Quality and Dialogue: *Goha,* produced by Jacques Baratier and written by Georges Schehade (Tunisia)

Veracity and Authenticity and for the Simple Beauty of its Images: *Visages de Bronze,* Bernard Taisant (Switzerland)

PALME D'OR DU FESTIVAL INTERNATIONAL DU FILM (Gold Palm of the International Film Festival)

Short Films: *La Seine a Rencontre Paris,* Joris Ivens (France)

La Joconde, Henri Gruel and Jean Suyeux (France)

PRIX SPECIAL (Special Prize)

Scientific Interest and Poetic Vision of the World: $C_{12}H_{22}O_{11}$ *Auf den Spuren des Lebens,* Fritz Heydenreich (Federal Republic of Germany)

Ingenious Use of Photography and Animation: *Nez Nam Narostla Kridla,* Jiri Brdecka (Czechoslovakia)

1959 PALME D'OR DU FESTIVAL INTERNATIONAL DU FILM (Gold Palm of the International Film Festival)

Feature Film: *Orfeu Negro,* produced by Marcel Camus (France)

SPECIAL PRIX DU JURY (Special Jury Prize)

Feature Film: *Sterne,* produced by Konrad Wolf (Bulgaria)

Prix International (International Prize): *Nazarin,* written by Luis Bunuel (Mexico)

OTHER PRIZES FOR FEATURE FILMS:

Direction: Francois Truffaut for *Les Quatre Cents Coups* (France)

Actress: Simone Signoret for *Room at the Top* (Great Britain)

Actor: Dean Stockwell, Bradford Dillman and Orson Welles for *Compulsion* (U.S.A.)

Comedy: *Policarpo dei Tappeti,* Mario Soldati (Italy)

Special Mention: *Shirasagi,* Teinosuke Kinugasa (Japan)

PALME D'OR DU FESTIVAL INTERNATIONAL (Gold Palm of the International Film Festival)

Short Film: *Motyli Zde Neziji,* Miro Bernat (Czechoslovakia)

PRIX SPECIAL DU JURY (Special Jury Prize)

Poetic Humor and Rich Inventiveness: *Histoire d'un Poisson Rouge,* Edmond Sechan (France)

OTHER PRIZES FOR SHORT FILMS:

Prizes: *N.Y.-N.Y.,* Francis Thompson (U.S.A.)

Zmisna Warty, Halina Bielinska and Wodzimierz Haupe (Poland)

Mention: *Le Petit Pecheur de la Mer de Chine,* Serge Hanin (Vietnam)

Best Selection: *Sen Noci Svatojanskue,* Jiri Trnka (Czechoslovakia)

Touha, Vojtech Jasny (Czechoslovakia)

Motyli Zde Neziji, Miro Bernat (Czechoslovakia)

1960 SPECIAL HOMMAGE

Jungfrukallen, produced by Ingmar Bergman (Sweden)
Luis Bunuel for *The Young One* (Mexico)

PALME D'OR DU FESTIVAL INTERNATIONAL DU FILM (Gold Palm of the International Film Festival)

Feature Film: *La Dolce Vita,* produced by Federico Fellini (Italy)

OTHER PRIZES FOR FEATURE FILMS

Best Participation: *Ballada O Soldatie,* produced by Grigori Tchoukhrai (U.S.S.R.)
Dama S Sobatchkoi, produced by Joseph Heifitz (U.S.S.R.)
For Contributions to a New Cinematic Language: **Michelangelo Antonioni** for *L'Avventura* (Italy)
For Courage of Its Approach: *Kagi,* produced by Kon Ichikawa (Japan)
Actress: **Melina Mercouri** for *Jamais le Dimanche* (Greece)
Jeanne Moreau for *Moderato Cantabile* (France)

PALME D'OR DE FESTIVAL INTERNATIONAL DU FILM (Gold Palm of the International Film Festival)

Short Film: *Le Sourire,* produced by Serge Bourguignon (France)

OTHER PRIZES FOR SHORT FILMS

For its Plastic Quality and Originality of Production: *Paris La Belle,* produced by Pierre Prevert (France)
For the New Form Used in Describing the Life of a City: *Une Ville Nommee Copenhague,* produced by Jorgen Roos (Denmark)
For its Perfection in Exposing and Illustrating a Great Scientific Theme: *Notre Universe,* produced by Roman Kroitor (Canada)
Honorable Mention: *Jours de Mes Annees,* produced by Max de Haas (Netherlands)
Best Selection: *Enfants des Courants d'Air,* Edouard Luntz (France)
Le Journal d'un Certain David, Pierre and Sylvie Jallaud (France)
Paris La Belle, Pierre Prevert (France)
Le Sourire, Serge Bourguingon (France)

1961 PALME D'OR DU FESTIVAL INTERNATIONAL DU FILM (gold palm of the international film festival)

Feature Films: *Viridiana,* produced by Luis Bunuel (Spain)
Une Aussi Longue Absence, produced by Henri Colpi (France)

PRIX SPECIAL DU JURY (special jury film)

Feature film: *Matka Joahna od Aniotow,* produced by Jerzy Kawalerowicz (Poland)

OTHER PRIZES FOR FEATURE FILMS

Direction: **Yultia Sontzeva** for *Povest Plamennykh Let* (U.S.S.R.)
Actress: **Sophia Loren** for *La Ciociara* (Italy)
Actor: **Anthony Perkins** for *Aimez-vous Brahms* (U.S.A.)
Best Selection: Italy
Gary Cooper Prize in Recognition of Humanity in Subject Treatment: *A Raisin in the Sun,* produced by Daniel Petrie (U.S.A.)

PALME D'OR DU FESTIVAL INTERNATIONAL DU FILM (Gold Palm of the International Film Festival)

Short Film: *La Petite Cuillere,* produced by Carlos Villardebo (France)

PRIX SPECIAL (special prize)

For Pleading with Humor for Peaceful Use of the Atom: *Parbaj,* produced by Gyula Maeskassy, (Hungary)

1962 PALME D'OR DU FESTIVAL INTERNATIONAL DU FILM (Gold Palm of the International Film Festival)

Feature Film: *O Pagador de Promessas,* Anselmo Duarte (Brazil)

PRIX SPECIAL DU JURY (special jury prize)

Feature Films: *Proces de Jeanne d'Arc,* Robert Bresson (France)
L'Eclisse, Michelangelo Antonioni (Italy)
Principal Players: **Katharine Hepburn, Ralph Richardson, Jason Robards, Jr., and Dean Stockwell,** actors; Sidney Lumet, producer, for *Long Day's Journey Into Night* (U.S.A.)
Principal Players: **Rita Tushingham and Murray Melvin,** actors; Tony Richardson, producer, for *A Taste of Honey* (Great Britain)

OTHER PRIZES FOR FEATURE FILMS

Cinematography: *Electra,* Michael Cacoyannis (Greece)
Best Comedy: *Divorz all'Italiana,* Pietro Germi (Italy)

PALME D'OR DU FESTIVAL INTERNATIONAL DU FILM (Gold Palm of the International Film Festival)

Short Film: *La Riviere du Hibou,* Robert Enrico (France)

PRIX SPECIAUX DU JURY (Special Jury Prizes)

For Originality, Poetry and Impeccable Technique of Animation: *Oczekiwanie,* produced by Witold Giersz and Ludwik Perski (Poland)
For Profound Love of Nature and Eminent Qualities of Visual and Sound Technique: *Pan,* Herman van der Horst (Netherlands)

1963 PALME D'OR DU FESTIVAL INTERNATIONAL DU FILM (Gold Palm of the International Film Festival)

Feature Film: *Il Gattopardo,* Luchino Visconti (Italy)

PRIX SPECIAL DU JURY (Special Jury Prize)

Feature Film: *Seppuku,* Masaki Kobayashi (Japan)
Runner-up: *Az Prijde Kocour,* Vojtech Jasny (Czechoslovakia)

OTHER PRIZES FOR FEATURE FILMS

Actress: **Marina Vlady** for *Ape Regina* (Italy)
Actor: **Richard Harris** for *This Sporting Life* (Great Britain)
Best Evocation of a Revolutionary Theme: *Optimistitcheskaia Traguedia,* produced by S. Samsonov (U.S.S.R.)
Screenplay: **Henri Colpi** for *Condine* (Rumania)
Gary Cooper Prize: *To Kill a Mockingbird,* Robert Mulligan (U.S.A.)

PALME D'OR DU FESTIVAL INTERNATIONAL DU FILM (Gold Palm of the International Film Festival)

Short Film: *A Fleur d'Eau,* Alex J. Seiler (Switzerland)
Le Haricot, Edmond Sechan (France)

PRIX SPECIAL DU JURY (Special Jury Prize)

Short Film: *Moj Stan,* Zvonimir Berkovic (Yugoslavia)
Special Mention for the Solemnity with Which it Treats the Subject of Solitude: *Di Domenica,* produced by Luigi Bazzoni, (Italy)
Special Mention for the Finesse of its Interpretation of the Eternal Subject of Love: *Toi,* produced by Istvan Szabo (Hungary)

1964 GRAND PRIX DU FESTIVAL INTERNATIONAL DU FILM CANNES (Grand Prize of the Cannes International Film Festival)

Feature Film: *Les Parapluies de Cherbourg,* Jacques Demy (France)

PRIX SPECIAL DU JURY (Special Jury Prize)

Feature Film: *Suna no Onna,* Hiroshi Teshigahara (Japan)

OTHER PRIZES FOR FEATURE FILMS

Actress: Anne Bancroft for *The Pumpkin Eater* (Great Britain)
Barbara Barrie for *One Potato-Two Potato* (U.S.A.)
Actor: Antal Pager for *Pacsirta* (Hungary)
Saro Urzi for *Sedotta e Abbandonata* (Italy)

SPECIAL PRIZES

Hommage for Film Left Incomplete Due to the Death of its Creator: *La Passagere,* Andrzej Munk
Special Mention to Young Producers: *Le Premier Cri,* Jaromil Jires (Czechoslovakia)
Romance a Moscou, Georgui Danelia (USSR)
La Jeune Fille en Deuil, Manuel Summers (Spain)

GRAND PRIX DU FESTIVAL INTERNATIONAL DU FILM CANNES (Grand Prize of the Cannes International Film Festival

Short Film: *La Douceur du Village,* Francois Reichinbach (France)
Le Prix de la Victoire, Nobulo Shibuya (Japan)

PRIX SPECIAL DU JURY DES FILMS DE COURT METRAGE (Special Jury Prize for Short Subjects)

For Brilliant Writing and Experimental Character Accessible to All: *Help! My Snowman's Burning Down,* Carson Davidson (U.S.A.)
For the Authenticity with which it Suggests the Secret Affinities of Countrymen: *Sillages,* Serge Roullet (France)

1965 GRAND PRIX DU FESTIVAL INTERNATIONAL DU FILM CANNES (Grand Prize of the Cannes International Film Festival)

Feature Film: *The Knack . . . and How to Get It,* Richard Lester (Great Britain)

PRIX SPECIAL DU JURY (Special Jury Prize)

Feature Film: *Kwaidan,* Masaki Kobayashi (Japan)

OTHER PRIZES FOR FEATURE FILMS

Acting: Samantha Eggar and Terence Stamp for *The Collector* (U.S.A.)
Directing: Liviu Ciulei for *Padurea Spinzuratilor* (Rumania)
Screenplay: *The Hill,* Sidney Lumet (Great Britain)
317eme Section, Pierre Schoendoerffer (France)
Mentions: Jozef Kroner (Czechoslovakia)
Ida Kaminska (Czechoslovakia)
Vera Kouznetsova (USSR)

GRAND PRIX DU FESTIVAL INTERNATIONAL DU FILM CANNES (Grand Prize of the Cannes International Film Festival)

Short Film: *Nyitany,* Janos Vadasz (Hungary)

PRIX SPECIAL DU JURY (Special Jury Prize)

Short Film: *Monsieur Plateau,* Jean Brismee (Belgium)
For Research Qualities: *Johann Sebastian Bach: Fantasie G Moll,* Jan Svanmajer (Czechoslovakia)
For Writing: *Evariste Gallois,* Alexandre Astruc (France)

1966 PRIX DU XXEME ANNIVERSAIRE DU FESTIVAL INTERNATIONAL DU FILM CANNES (20th Anniversary Prize of the Cannes International Film Festival)

Special Honor for contributions to world cinema: Orson Welles

GRAND PRIX DU XXEME ANNIVERSAIRE DU FESTIVAL INTERNATIONAL DU FILM CANNES (20th Anniversary Grand Prize of the Cannes International Film Festival)

Feature Films: *Un Homme et Une Femme,* Claude Lelouch (France)
Signore e Signori, Pietro Germi (Italy)

PRIX SPECIAL DU JURY (Special Jury Prize)

Feature Film: *Alfie,* Lewis Gilbert (Great Britain)

OTHER PRIZES FOR FEATURE FILMS

Actress: Vanessa Redgrave for *Morgan — A Suitable Case for Treatment* (Great Britain)
Actor: Per Oscarsson for *Sult* (Denmark)
Special Mention: Toto
Direction: Serge Youtkevitch for *Lenine en Pologne* (U.S.S.R.)
First Work: *Rascoala,* Mircea Muresan (Rumania)

GRAND PRIX DU XXEME ANNIVERSAIRE DU FESTIVAL INTERNATIONAL DU FILM CANNES (20th Anniversary Grand Prize of the Cannes International Film Festival)

Short Film: *Skater Dater,* Noel Black (U.S.A.)

1967 Special Honor: The Works of Robert Bresson

GRAND PRIX INTERNATIONAL DU FESTIVAL CANNES (Grand Prize of the Cannes International Festival)

Feature Film: *Blow Up,* Michelangelo Antonioni (Great Britain)

GRAND SPECIAL PRIX DU JURY (Special Jury Grand Prize)

Feature Films: *Accident,* Joseph Losey (Great Britain)
Skulpjaci Perja, Aleksandr Petrovic (Yugoslavia)

OTHER PRIZES FOR FEATURE FILMS

Actress: Pia Degermark for *Elvira Madigan* (Sweden)

Actor: **Odded Kotler** for *Trois Jours et un Enfant* (Israel)
Director: **Ferenc Kosa** for *Tizezer Nap* (Hungary)
Screenplay: *Jeu de Massacre*, Alain Jessua (France)
A Ciascuno Il Suo, Elio Petri and Ugo Pierro (Italy)
First Work: *Le Vent des Aures*, Mohammed Lakhdar Hamina (Algeria)

GRAND PRIX DU FESTIVAL CANNES (Grand Prize of the Cannes Festival)

Short Film: *Ciels de Hollande*, John Ferno Fernhout (Netherlands)

PRIX SPECIAL DU JURY (Special Jury Prize)

Short Film: *Jedan Plus Jedan Jeste Tri*, Branko Ratinovic and Zdenko Gasparovic (Yugoslavia)
Special Mention: *L'Emploi du Temps*, produced by Bernard Lemoine (France)

1968 GRAND PRIX INTERNATIONAL DU FESTIVAL CANNES (Grand Prize of the Cannes Festival)

If, produced by Lindsay Anderson (Great Britain)

GRAND PRIX SPECIAL DU JURY (Special Jury Grand Prize)

Adalen 31, produced by Bo Widerberg (Sweden)

OTHER PRIZES FOR FEATURE FILMS

Actress: **Vanessa Redgrave** for *Isadora* (Great Britain)
Actor: **Jean-Louis Trintignant** for *Z* (France)
Jury Prize: *Z*, produced by Costa-Gavras (France)
Director: **Glauber Rocha** for *Antonio-Das-Mortes* (Brazil)
Vojtech Jasny for *Vsichni Dobri Rodaci* (Czechoslovakia)
First Work: *Easy Rider*, Dennis Hopper (U.S.A.)

GRAND PRIX INTERNATIONAL DU FESTIVAL CANNES (Grand Prize of the Cannes International Festival)

Short Film: *Cintecele Renasterii*, Mirel Iliesu (Rumania)

PRIX SPECIAL DU JURY (Special Jury Prize)

Short Film: *La Prince a Ongles*, Jean-Claude Carriere (France)

1970 GRAND PRIX INTERNATIONAL DU FESTIVAL CANNES (Grand Prize of the Cannes International Festival

Feature Film: *M*A*S*H**, produced by Robert Altman **(U.S.A.)**

GRAND PRIX SPECIAL DU JURY (Special Jury Grand Prize)

Feature Film: *Indagine su un Cittadino al di Sopra di Ogni Sospetto*, Elio Petri (Italy)

OTHER PRIZES FOR FEATURE FILMS

Actress: **Ottavia Piccolo** for *Metello* (Italy)
Actor: **Marcello Mastroianni** for *Dramma Della Gelosia . . . Tutti I Particolari in Cronaca* (Italy)
Director: **John Boorman** for *Leo the Last* (Great Britain)
Jury Prize: *Magasiskola*, Istvan Gal (Hungary)
The Strawberry Statement, Stuart Hagman (U.S.A.)
First Work: *Hoa-Binh*, Raoul Coutard (France)

GRAND PRIX (Grand Prize)

Short Film: No award

PRIZES FOR SHORT FILMS

For Poetic Candor and Joy: *Magic Machines*, Bob Curtis (U.S.A.)
Mention for the Emotional Value from this Evocation of the Past: *Et Salammbo?*, Jean-Pierre Richard (Tunisia)

1971 PRIX DU XXVEME ANNIVERSAIRE DU FESTIVAL INTERNATIONAL DU FILM (25th Anniversary Prize of the International Film Festival)

For One Film and a Body of Work: Luchino Visconti for *Morte A Venezia* (Italy)

GRAND PRIX INTERNATIONAL DU FESTIVAL CANNES (Grand Prize of the Cannes International Film Festival)

Feature Film: *The Go-Between*, Joseph Losey (Great Britain)

GRAND PRIX SPECIAL DU JURY (Special Jury Grand Prize)

Feature Films: *Taking Off*, Milos Forman (U.S.A.)
Johnny Got His Gun, Dalton Trumbo (U.S.A.)

OTHER PRIZES FOR FEATURE FILMS

Actress: **Kitty Winn** for *Panic in Needle Park* (U.S.A.)
Actor: **Piccardo Cucciolla** for *Sacco e Vanzetti* (Italy)
Prix du Jury (Jury Prize) With Special Mention: *Szerelem*, Karoly Makk, producer, Lili Darvas and Mari Torocsik, actresses (Hungary)
Prix du Jury (Jury Prize): *Joe Hill*, Bo Widerberg (Sweden)
First Work: *Per Grazia Ricevuta*, Nino Menfredi (Italy)

GRAND PRIX (Grand Prize)

Short Film: No award

PRIX SPECIAL DU JURY (Special Jury Prize)

Short Film: *Star Spangled Banner*, Roger Flint (U.S.A.)
Mentions: *Stuiter*, de Jan Oonk (Netherlands)
Une Statuette, Carlos Vilardebo (France)

1972 GRAND PRIX INTERNATIONAL DU FESTIVAL CANNES (Grand Prize of the Cannes International Festival)

Feature Film: *La Classe Operaia Va in Paradiso*, Elio Petri (Italy)
Il Caso Mettei, Francesco Rosi, producer, with Recognition for actor **Gian-Maria Volonte** (Italy)

GRAND PRIX SPECIAL DU JURY (Special Jury Grand Prize)

Feature Film: *Solaris*, Andrei Tarkovsky **(USSR)**

OTHER PRIZES FOR FEATURE FILMS

Actress: **Susannah York** for *Images* (Ireland)
Actor: **Jean Yanne** for *Nous ne Vieillirons pas Ensemble* (France)
Direction: **Miklos Jancso** for *Meg Ker A Nep* (Hungary)
Prix du Jury (Jury Prize): *Slaughterhouse Five*, George Roy Hill (U.S.A.)

GRAND PRIX INTERNATIONAL DU FESTIVAL CANNES (International Grand Prize of the Cannes Festival)

Short Film: *Le Fusil a Lunette*, J. Chapot (France)

PRIX SPECIAL DU JURY (Special Jury Prize)

Operation X-70, Raoul Servais (Belgium)

1973 GRAND PRIX INTERNATIONAL DU FESTIVAL CANNES (International Grand Prize of the Cannes Festival)

Feature Films: *Scarecrow*, Jerry Schatzberg, producer, Al Pacino and Gene Hackman, actors (U.S.A.) *The Hireling*, Alan Bridges, producer, Sarah Miles, actress (Great Britain)

GRAND PRIX SPECIAL DU JURY (Special Jury Grand Prize)

Feature Film: *La Maman et la Putain*, Jean Eustache (France)

OTHER PRIZES FOR FEATURE FILMS

Actress: **Joanne Woodward** for *The Effect of Gamma Rays on Man-in-the-Moon Marigolds* (U.S.A.) Actor: Actors for *Film d'Amore et d'Amarchia* (**Italy**) Special Prize: *La Planet Sauvage*, Rene Lamoux (France) Prix du Jury (**Jury Prize**): *Sanatorium Pod Klepsydra*, Wojciech Has (Poland) *L'Invitation*, Claude Goretta (Switzerland) First Work: *Jeremy*, Arthur Barron (U.S.A.)

GRAND PRIX INTERNATIONAL DU FESTIVAL CANNES (International Grand Prize of the Cannes Festival)

Short Film: *Balablok*, Bretislav Pojar (Canada)

PRIX SPECIAL DU JURY (Special Jury Prize)

1812, Sandor Reisenbuckler (Hungary)

1974 GRAND PRIX INTERNATIONAL DU FESTIVAL CANNES (International Grand Prix of the Cannes Festival)

Feature Film: *The Conversation*, Francis Ford Coppola (U.S.A.)

GRAND PRIX SPECIAL DU JURY (Special Jury Grand Prize)

Feature Film: *Il Fiore Mille e Une Notte*, Pier Paolo Pasolini (Italy)

OTHER PRIZES FOR FEATURE FILMS

Special Hommage: **Charles Boyer**, actor, for *Stavisky*, Actress: **Marie-Jose Nat** for *Les Violons du Bal* (France) Actor: **Jack Nicholson** for *The Last Detail* (U.S.A.)

PRIX DU JURY (Jury Prize)

Screenplay: *Sugarland Express* (U.S.A.) Carlos Saura Spain

GRAND PRIX INTERNATIONAL DU FESTIVAL CANNES (International Grand Prize of the Cannes Festival)

Short Film: *Ostrov*, V. Zuikov and E. Nazarov (U.S.S.R.) Prix du Jury (**Jury Prize**): *La Faim*, Peter Foldes (Canada)

1975 PALME D'OR DU FESTIVAL INTRERNATIONAL DU FILM CANNES (Gold Palm of the Cannes International Film Festival)

Feature Film: *Chronique des Annees de Braise*, M. Lakhdar Hamina (Algeria)

GRAND PRIX SPECIAL DU JURY (Special Jury Grand Prize)

Feature Film: *Jeder Fur Sich und Gott gegen Alle*, Werner Herzog (Federal Republic of Germany)

OTHER PRIZES FOR FEATURE FILMS

Actress: **Valerie Perrine** for *Lenny* (U.S.A.) Actor: **Vittorio Gassman** for *Profumo di Donna* (Italy) Production: *Les Ordres*, Michel Brault (Canada) *Section speciale*, Costa-Gavras (France) Recognition: **Delphine Seyrig**

PALME D'OR DU FESTIVAL INTERNATIONAL DU FILM CANNES (Gold Palm of the Cannes International Film Festival)

Short Film: *Lautrec*, Geoff Dunbar (Great Britain)

PRIX SPECIAL DU JURY (Special Jury Prize)

Short Film: *Dariou Tebe Zvezdou*, Fedor Hitrouk (U.S.S.R.)

1976 PALME D'OR DU FESTIVAL INTERNATIONAL DU FILM (Gold Palm of the Cannes International Film Festival)

Feature Film: *Taxi Driver*, Martin Scorcese (U.S.A.)

GRAND PRIX SPECIAL DU JURY (Special Jury Grand Prize)

Feature Film: *Cria Cuervos*, Carlos Saura (Spain) *Die Marquise von 'O'*, Eric Rohmer

OTHER PRIZES FOR FEATURE FILMS

Actress: **Mari Torocsik** for *Deryne, Hol Van?* **Dominique Sanda** for *L'eredita Ferramonti* Actor: **Jose Luis Gomez** for *Pascal Duarte* Direction: **Ettore Scola** for *Brutti, Sporchi, Cattivi*

PALME D'OR DU FESTIVAL INTERNATIONAL DU FILM (Gold Palm of the International Film Festival)

Short Film: *Metamorphosis*, Barry Greenwald First Jury Prize: *Agulana*, Gerald Frydman Second Jury Prize: *Nightlife*, Robin Lehman

1977 PALME D'OR DU FESTIVAL INTERNATIONAL DU FILM (Gold Palm of the International Film Festival)

Feature Film: *Padre Padrone*, Paolo and Vittorio Taviani (Italy)

OTHER PRIZES FOR FEATURE FILMS

Actress: **Shelley Duvall** for *3 Women* (U.S.A.) **Monique Mercure** for *J.A. Martin Photographe* (Canada) Actor: **Fernando Rey** for *Eliza, Vida Mia* (Spain) Jury Prize for a First Work: **Ridley Scott** for *The Duellists* (Great Britain) Music: **Norman Whitfield** for *Car Wash* (U.S.A.)

PALME D'OR DU FESTIVAL INTERANTIONAL DU FILM (Gold Palm of the International Film Festival)

Short Film: *Kuzdok*, Marcel Jankovics (Hungary)

PRIX SPECIAL DU JURY (Special Jury Prize)
Short Film: *Di Cavalcanti,* Glauber Rocha (Brazil)
Hommage for Animation: Peter Foldes (Canada)

Cindy Award

INFORMATION FILM PRODUCERS OF AMERICA
3518 Cahuenga Blvd. W., Suite 313, Hollywood, Calif. 90068
(213/874-2266)

The Cindy Award, which consists of a trophy and certificate, is given annually for excellence in film, videotape, filmstrip or slidefilm production in categories
ranging from Government/Industry/Business to Environment and Ecology, plus special awards. Entries are
judged by IFPA chapters throughout the U.S., and a
Blue Ribbon Panel selects the winners from the finalists. In addition to the winners of gold Cindys indicated
here, silver and bronze trophies are also given.

FILM AND VIDEOTAPE

1976 Arthur H. Wolf, *The American Phoenix*
Bruce McGee and Ron Phillips, *Prowler—the Lone Trailer Story*
Patricia Brose, *The Intrusion Conspiracy*
Bill Buffinger, *Trans-Alaska Pipeline—Fluor Report No. 2*
Bruce Cummings, *Team Kawasaki*
Yanna Kroyt Brandt, *The Superlative Horse*
John J. Hennessy, *Symbol B. Numbers*
The Creative Works, Inc. *The Legacy of Currier and Ives*
Chuck Braverman, *The Television Newsman*
Chuck Braverman, *Trader Vic*
Randall Hood, *A Walk in the Forest*
Potter, Orchard and Petrie, Inc., *Lonely Times—Happy Times*
The Filmakers, Inc., *Nosocomial Infections and Critical Care*
John P. Breeden, Jr., *Renaissance Center*
Mike Lubow, *Learn Not to Burn*
Julian Krainin, *To Communicate in the Beginning . . .*
Irwin Rosten, *The Incredible Machine*
Lawrence Winter, *Multiple Choice*
Ray Jewell, *Fire Solution*
Warren Miller, *Free Ride*
MPI Productions Ltd., *Come in from Away*
USC, Div. of Cinema, *The Preparatory*
1977 Nick Bosutow, Dick Olson and Irv Millgate, *I've Got a Woman Boss*
Los Angeles County Sheriff's Dept., *Officer Survival III*
Arthur H. Wolf, *A Day Under Sea*
Bob Crook, *Lunar Geology*
Richard A. Miner and H. Saunders, *Get It Together*
Dick Young, *Firewood—The Other Energy Crisis*
Louis Mucciolo, *Anta-Scanners*
Filmakers, Inc., *The March of 7Up*
Grania Gurievitch, *Speaking for Ourselves: The Challenge of Being Deaf*
Jamil D. Simon, *Help Yourself to Better Health*
Burson-Marstellar, *A Day at the Fair*
Gordon Films, *Lloyd Todd's Southern Ocean*
Paul Buck and Art Ciocco, *Equality*
Veriation Films, *Ocean Thermal Energy Conversion*
Jim Freeman and Greg MacGillivary, *The Magic Rolling Board*

Crawley Films and Film Counselors, *Indonesia—The Changing Face*
Tom Thayer, *Alcatraz*

FILMSTRIP AND SLIDEFILM

1976 Philip Werber, *What Is Journalism?*
Sara Maxwell, *Adventures in Science: The Body*
Worris D. Wertenberger, *When I Get to Be 18*
Ed Schultz, *The Future*
Nahum Zilberberg, *The Secret is You*
Donald E. Miller, *Physical Assessment: Heart and Lungs*
Morris D. Wertenberger, *Fry Your Way to Fame and Fortune*
Universal Training Systems, *When It Leaves Your Hands*
Michael J. Enzer, *A Step Ahead: The Congoleum Theory*
Robert Intrater, ACI Media, Inc., *The Art—Composition and Light*
1977 Lyceum Productions, *Inscape: The Realm of Haiku*
Carole Coleman, *To Save a Living Sea*
M.D. Wertenberger, Jr., *You and Communication*
Cliff Braggins, *The Credit Squeeze*
Donna Lawrence, *A Newspaper Story*
M.D. Wertenberger, Jr., *Altec 1628 Microphone Mixer*

SPECIAL ACHIEVEMENT AWARDS

1976 *A Walk in the Forest,* Best of Show
The Incredible Machine, Special Technical Achievement
The Preparatory, Best Direction
A Walk in the Forest, Best Writing
A Walk in the Forest, Best Photography
A Walk in the Forest, Best Editing
A Walk in the Forest, Best Music
The Owl Who Married a Goose, Best Animated Subject
1977 Paul Buck and Art Ciocco, *Equality,* Best of Show, Film and Videotape
Donna Lawrence, *The Newspaper Story,* Best of Show, Filmstrip and Slidefilm
Kingsmill on the James, Cinematography
Jim Freeman and Greg MacGillivary, *The Magic Rolling Board,* Special Photographic Achievement
Art Ciocco, *Equality,* Editing
Marshall Harvey, *A Sport Suite,* Editing
Frank Dobbs and Gary Carr, *A Thread of Hope,* Writing
Michael J. Seebeck, *Replere,* Special Achievement by a Student for Optical Effects

Eddie Award

AMERICAN CINEMA EDITORS
422 S. Western Ave., Los Angeles, Calif. 90020
(213/386-1946)

The Eddie Award, which consists of a statue, is given
annually by a vote of ACE membership for the best
editing in four categories for films and television shows.

FEATURES

1962 Philip W. Anderson, *The Parent Trap*
1963 Samuel E. Beetley, *The Longest Day*
1964 Harold Kress, *How the West Was Won*

1965 Cotton Warburton, *Mary Poppins*
1966 William Reynolds, *The Sound of Music*
1967 William B. Murphy, *Fantastic Voyage*
1968 Michael Luciano, *The Dirty Dozen*
1969 Frank Keller, *Bullitt*
1970 Warren Low, *True Grit*
1971 Hugh Fowler, *Patton*
1972 Folmar Blangsted, *Summer of '42*
1973 David Bretherton, *Cabaret*
1974 William Reynolds, *The Sting*
1975 Michael Luciano, *The Longest Yard*
1976 Verna Fields, *Jaws*
1977 Richard E. Halsey and Scott Conrad, *Rocky*

TELEVISION EPISODE

1962 Desmond Marquette, "Ricochet" segment, *The Dick Powell Show*
1963 Desmond Marquette, "The Court Marshall of Captain Wycliff" segment," *Dick Powell Theater*
1964 Joseph Dervin, "Four Feet in the Morning" segment, *Dr. Kildare*
1965 Gene Fowler, "No Dogs or Drovers" segment, *Rawhide*
1966 Harry Coswick, *A Slice of Sunday*
1967 Jodie Copelan, "The All-American" segment, *Twelve O'Clock High*
1968 Desmond Marquette, "The Disappearance" segment, *The Big Valley*
1969 Norman Colbert, *The Bob Hope Christmas Special*
1970 Gene Palmer, *Marcus Welby, M.D.* (pilot)
1971 Richard Cahoon, "Death Grip" segment, *Medical Center*
1972 Richard Cahoon, "The Imposter" segment, *Medical Center*
1973 Fred W. Berger, "Bananas, Crackers and Nuts" segment, *M*A*S*H**
1974 Fred W. Berger and Stanford Tischler, "The Trial of Henry Blake" segment, *M*A*S*H**
1975 Red W. Berger and Stanford Tischler, "A Full Rich Day" segment, *M*A*S*H**
1976 Bob Bring, "The Sky's The Limit," Parts I/II, *Wonderful World of Disney*
Howard Kunin, "Web of Lies" segment, *The Streets of San Francisco*
1977 Howard Kunin, "Dead or Alive" segment, *The Streets of San Francisco*

TELEVISION SPECIAL

1973 Ira Heymann, "Visions," *Tuesday Night at the Movies*
1974 Richard Wray, *Portrait of a Man Whose Name Was John*
1975 Frank E. Morriss, *The Execution of Private Slovik*
1976 Henry Berman, *Babe*
1977 Michael Kahn, *Eleanor and Franklin*

DOCUMENTARY

1973 John Soh, "Forgotten Mermaids," *Undersea World of Jacques Cousteau*
Axel Hubert, *The Bengal Tiger*
1974 Leslie Parry, *The Incredible Flight of the Snow Geese*
1975 Bud Friedgen and David Blewitt, *That's Entertainment*
1976 David Saxon, *Search for the Great Apes*
1977 Robert K. Lambert and Peter Johnson, *Life Goes to the Movies*

SPECIAL AWARDS

1963 Russell Tinsley, *The Cadillac*

1964 William T. Cartwright, *The Making of the President,* A Wolper TV Special

Emily Trophy
John Grierson Award
EDUCATION FILM LIBRARY ASSOCIATION
43 W. 61st St., New York, N.Y. 10023 (212/246-4533)

The John Grierson Award, endowed by the National Film Board of Canada and Films Incorporated, is a plaque and a cash prize of $500 presented annually to a new filmmaker in the social documentary field. The winning film is selected by a special jury at the American Film Festival.

1973 Martha Coolidge, *David: Off and On*
1974 Jerry Bruck, Jr., *I.F. Stone's Weekly*
Cinda Firestone, *Attica*
1975 Pacific Street Film Collective, *Frame-Up! The Imprisonment of Martin Sostre*
1976 Richard Brick, *Last Stand Farmer*
Richard Keller, *Lovejoy's Nuclear War*
1977 Barbara Kopple, *Harlan County, U.S.A.*

Based on the ratings of two juries evaluating preliminary and final screenings of the American Film Festival, the Emily Trophy is presented annually to the non-theatrical film which receives the highest numerical rating. Blue Ribbons are awarded to films judged best in each of several categories The Emily listed here is a "best in show" award.

1969 *Ski the Outer Limits*
1970 *Pas de Deux*
1971 *Sad Song of Yellow Skin*
1972 *Rock-a-Bye Baby*
1973 *The Three Robbers*
1974 *I.F. Stone's Weekly*
1975 *Antonia*
1976 *The Gentleman Tramp*
1977 *Harlan County, U.S.A.*

Gavel Awards
AMERICAN BAR ASSOCIATION
1155 E. 60th St., Chicago, Ill. 60637 (312/974-4000)

The Gavel Awards are given annually to honor films, the media and books for their depiction of, or reportage on, the law and the legal profession. The Bar Association recognizes achievements which foster greater public understanding of the American legal and judicial system, disclose areas in need of improvement or correction and encourage efforts of all levels of government to update laws. Engraved gavels are given to the winners.

1958 *Twelve Angry Men,* United Artists Corp.
1959 No award
1960 No award
1961 No award
1962 *Judgment at Nuremberg,* Stanley Kramer Corp.
1963 No award
1964 *The Great Rights,* Brandon Films
1965 No award
1966 No award
1967 No award

1968 No award
1969 No award
1970 No award
1971 *The D.A.: Conspiracy to Kill,* Universal Television
and Mark VII Ltd.
1972 Motion picture for television release which launched
Owen Marshall, Counsellor at Law series on the
ABC-TV Network, Groverton Production and Universal Television
1973 *"Heat of Anger"* for *CBS Friday Night Movies,*
Berg-Metromedia Production
1974 No award
1975 No award
1976 *Fear on Trial, the Life of John Henry Faulk,* Aland
Landsburg Productions
1977 *Judge Horton and the Scottsboro Boys,* Tomorrow
Entertainment

OTHER AWARDS

1975 Dome Productions (theatre), one-man play, *Clarence
Darrow*

Golden Apple Awards
Louella O. Parsons Award

HOLLYWOOD WOMEN'S PRESS CLUB
4446 Ledge Ave., N. Hollywood, Calif. 91602 (213/769-2506)

The Golden Apple Awards were originally established
to "thank" the "most cooperative" stars at a time when
the Hollywood Women's Press Association had a membership largely of correspondents and reporters. In
1967, when more press agents who might favor their
own clients had joined the Association, the criteria
changed to honor a "Star of the Year" and a "New Star
of the Year." The former honors contributions to the
motion picture industry, while the latter recognizes a
new personality for his or her impact on the public
during the year. A committee nominates and the membership votes on the recipients, who are given jewelry
with a golden apple motif.

GOLDEN APPLE/MOST COOPERATIVE MALE STAR

1941 Bob Hope
1942 Cary Grant
1943 Bob Hope
1944 Alan Ladd
1945 Gregory Peck
1946 Dana Andrews
1947 Gregory Peck
1948 Glenn Ford
1949 Kirk Douglas
1950 Alan Ladd
1951 John Derek
     William Holden
1952 Tony Curtis
1953 Roy Rogers
1954 Dean Martin and Jerry Lewis
1955 William Holden
1956 Charlton Heston
1957 Glenn Ford
1958 Tony Curtis
1959 David Niven
1960 Jack Lemmon
1961 No award
1962 Richard Chamberlain
1963 Dick Van Dyke

1964 Lorne Greene
1965 John Wayne
1966 Bill Cosby

GOLDEN APPLE/MALE STAR OF THE YEAR

1967 Sidney Poitier
1968 Fred Astaire
1969 Gregory Peck
1970 James Stewart
     Robert Young
1971 Hal Holbrook
1972 Peter Falk
1973 Robert Redford
1974 Alan Alda
1975 George Burns
1976 John Wayne
1977 Frank Sinatra

GOLDEN APPLE/MOST COOPERATIVE FEMALE STAR

1941 Bette Davis
1942 Rosalind Russell
1943 Ann Sheridan
1944 Betty Hutton
1945 Joan Crawford
1946 Joan Crawford
1947 Joan Fontaine
1948 Dorothy Lamour
1949 June Haver
1950 Loretta Young
1951 Anne Baxter
1952 Janet Leigh
1953 Dale Evans
1954 Debbie Reynolds
1955 Jane Russell
1956 Deborah Kerr
1957 Kim Novak
1958 Dinah Shore
1959 Shirley MacLaine
1960 Nanette Fabray
     Janet Leigh
1961 Barbara Stanwyck
1962 Connie Stevens
1963 Bette Davis
1964 Donna Reed
1965 Dorothy Malone
1966 Phyllis Diller

GOLDEN APPLE/FEMALE STAR OF THE YEAR

1967 Carol Channing
1968 Barbra Streisand
1969 Mae West
1970 Carol Burnett
1971 Mary Tyler Moore
1972 Liza Minnelli
1973 Lucille Ball
1974 Valerie Harper
1975 Katharine Hepburn
1976 Joanne Woodward
1977 Jane Fonda

GOLDEN APPLE/NEW MALE STAR OF THE YEAR

1967 Tommy Steele
1968 Robert Brown
     Glen Campbell
1969 Elliott Gould
1970 Flip Wilson
1971 David Cassidy
1972 Richard Thomas
1973 John Davidson
1974 Freddie Prinze

1975   Jeff Bridges
1976   Nick Nolte
1977   John Denver

GOLDEN APPLE/NEW FEMALE STAR OF THE YEAR

1967   Faye Dunaway
1968   Diahann Carroll
1969   Goldie Hawn
1970   Carrie Snodgress
1971   Sandy Duncan
1972   Diana Ross
1973   Tatum O'Neal
1974   Kate Jackson
1975   Susan Clark
1976   Susan Blakely
1977   Kathleen Quinlan

The Louella O. Parsons Award is given annually to the person who, in the opinion of the membership, gives the best image of Hollywood to the world.

1970   Danny Thomas
1971   Gregory Peck
1972   Ross Hunter
1973   Rosalind Russell
1974   Jack Benny
1975   Bob Hope
1976   Shirley Temple Black
1977   Jack L. Warner

Golden Globe Awards

HOLLYWOOD FOREIGN PRESS ASSOCIATION
8732 Sunset Blvd., Ste. 210, Los Angeles, Calif. 90069
(213/657-1707 and 657-1731)

The Golden Globe Awards, which consist of statuettes, are awarded annually to motion pictures and television films of the previous calendar year that have been shown to the Association membership. Selection is by secret ballot of the membership. (For television awards see pp. 145–147.)

BEST MOTION PICTURE

1944   *The Song of Bernadette*
1945   *Going My Way*
1946   *Lost Weekend*
1947   *The Best Years of Our Lives*
1948   *Gentleman's Agreement*
1949   *Treasure of Sierra Madre*
       Johnny Belinda
1950   *All the King's Men*
1951   *Sunset Boulevard*

BEST DRAMATIC MOTION PICTURE

1952   *A Place in the Sun*
1953   *The Greatest Show on Earth*
1954   *The Robe*
1955   *On the Waterfront*
1956   *East of Eden*
1957   *Around the World in 80 Days*
1958   *The Bridge on the River Kwai*
1959   *The Defiant Ones*
1960   *Ben Hur*
1961   *Spartacus*
1962   *The Guns of Navarone*
1963   *Lawrence of Arabia*
1964   *The Cardinal*
1965   *Becket*

1966   *Dr. Zhivago*
1967   *A Man for All Seasons*
1968   *In the Heat of the Night*
1969   *The Lion in Winter*
1970   *Anne of the Thousand Days*
1971   *Love Story*
1972   *The French Connection*
1973   *The Godfather*
1974   *The Exorcist*
1975   *Chinatown*
1976   *One Flew Over the Cuckoo's Nest*
1977   *Rocky*

BEST MUSCIAL MOTION PICTURE

1952   *An American in Paris*
1953   *With A Song in My Heart*
1954   No award
1955   *Carmen Jones*
1956   *Guys & Dolls*
1957   *The King and I*
1958   *Les Girls*
1959   *Gigi*
1960   *Porgy and Bess*
1961   *Song Without End*
1962   *West Side Story*
1963   *The Music Man*
1964   No award
1965   *My Fair Lady*
1966   *The Sound of Music*
1967   No award
1968   No award
1969   *Oliver!*
1970   No award
1971   No award
1972   *Fiddler on the Roof*
1973   *Cabaret*
1974   No award
1975   No award
1976   No award
1977   *A Star Is Born*

BEST COMEDY MOTION PICTURE

1959   *Auntie Mame*
1960   *Some Like It Hot*
1961   *The Apartment*
1962   *A Majority of One*
1963   *That Touch of Mink*
1964   *Tom Jones*
1965   No award
1966   No award
1967   *The Russians Are Coming*
1968   *The Graduate*
1969   No award
1970   *The Secret of Santa Vittoria*
1971   *M*A*S*H**
1972   No award
1973   No award
1974   *American Graffiti*
1975   *The Longest Yard*
1976   *The Sunshine Boys*
1977   No award

BEST FOREIGN FILM

In some years, separate awards were given for different language categories. In those years, films indicated by one asterisk (*) are English language films, while those indicated by two asterisks (**) are foreign language films. The countries are not always given, but most of the English language films were made in Great Britain. Films denoted by three asterisks (***) won the Silver Globe Award.

1950   *The Bicycle Thief* (Italy)
1951   No award
1952   No award
1953   No award
1954   No award
1955   *Genevieve* (Great Britain)
       No Way Back (Germany)
       Twenty-Four Eyes (Japan)
       La Mujer de la Camelias (Argentina)
1956   *Ordet* (Denmark
       Stella (Greece))
       Eyes of Children (Japan)
       Sons, Mothers and A General (Germany)
       Dangerous Curves (Brazil)
1957   *Richard III**
       The White Reindeer** (Finland)
       Before Sundown** (Germany)
       The Girls in Black** (Greece)
       Rose on the Arm** (Japan)
       War & Peace** (Italy)
1958   *Woman In A Dressing Gown**
       The Confessions of Felix Krull** (Germany)
       Yellow Crow** (Japan)
       Tizok** (Mexico)
1959   *Night to Remember**
       The Road A Year Long** (Yugoslavia)
       The Girl and the River** (France)
       The Girl Rosemarie** (Germany)
1960   *Black Orpheus* (France)
       Odd Obsession (Japan)
       The Bridge (Germany)
       Wild Strawberries (Sweden)
       Aren't We Wonderful (Germany)
1961   *The Man With the Green Carnation**
       La Verite** (France)
       Virgin Spring** (Sweden)
1962   *Two Women* (Italy)
       Animas Trujano*** (Mexico)
       Good Soldier Schweik*** (Germany)
1963   *Divorce Italian Style* (Italy)
       Best of Enemies (Italy)
1964   *Tom Jones**
       Any Number Can Win**
1965   *Marriage Italian Style** (Italy)
       Shallah** (Israel)
       The Girl With the Green Eyes (England)
1966   *Darling**
       Giulietta of the Spirits** (Italy)
1967   *Alfie**
       A Man and a Woman** (France)
1968   *The Fox** (Canada)
       Live for Life** (France)
1969   *Romeo & Juliet**
       War & Peace** (U.S.S.R.)
1970   *Oh! What A Lovely War!**
       Z** (Algeria)
1971   *Women in Love**
       Rider on the Rain**
1972   *Sunday, Bloody Sunday**
       The Policeman**
1973   *Young Winston**
       The Emigrants (Part I)** and *The New Land* (Part II)** (Sweden)
1974   *The Pedestrian*
1975   *Scenes From a Marriage* (Sweden)
1976   *Lies My Father Told Me*

1977   *Face to Face*

BEST FILM PROMOTING INTERNATIONAL UNDERSTANDING

1947   *The Last Change*
1948   No award
1949   *The Search*
1950   *The Hasty Heart*
1951   *Broken Arrow*
1952   *The Day the Earth Stood Still*
1953   *Anything Can Happen*
1954   *Little Boy Lost*
1955   *Broken Lance*
1956   *Love Is a Many-Splendored Thing*
1957   *Battle Hymn*
1958   *The Happy Road*
1959   *Inn of the Sixth Happiness*
1960   *Diary of Anne Frank*
1961   *Hand In Hand*
1963   *A Majority of One*
1964   *To Kill A Mockingbird*
1965   *Lilies of the Field*

BEST MOTION PICTURE ACTOR

1944   Paul Lukas, *Watch on the Rhine*
1945   Alexander Knox, *Wilson*
1946   Ray Milland, *Lost Weekend*
1947   Gregory Peck, *The Yearling*
1948   Ronald Colman, *Mourning Becomes Electra*
1949   Laurence Olivier, *Hamlet*
1950   Broderick Crawford, *All the King's Men*
1951   Jose Ferrer, *Cyrano de Bergerac*
1952   Fredric March, *Death of a Salesman*
1953   Gary Cooper, *High Noon*
1954   Spencer Tracy, *The Actress*
1955   Marlon Brando, *On The Waterfront*
1956   Ernest Borgnine, *Marty*
1957   Kirk Douglas, *Lust for Life*
1958   Alec Guinness, *The Bridge on the River Kwai*
1959   David Niven, *Separate Tables*
1960   Anthony Franciosa, *Career*
1961   Burt Lancaster, *Elmer Gantry*
1962   Maximilian Schell, *Judgment at Nuremberg*
1963   Gregory Peck, *To Kill A Mockingbird*
1964   Sidney Poitier, *Lilies of the Field*
1965   Peter O'Toole, *Becket*
1966   Omar Sharif, *Dr. Zhivago*
1967   Paul Scofield, *A Man for All Seasons*
1968   Rod Steiger, *In the Heat of the Night*
1969   Peter O'Toole, *The Lion in Winter*
1970   John Wayne, *True Grit*
1971   George C. Scott, *Patton*
1972   Gene Hackman, *The French Connection*
1973   Marlon Brando, *The Godfather*
1974   Al Pacino, *Serpico*
1975   Jack Nicholson, *Chinatown*
1976   Jack Nicholson, *One Flew Over the Cuckoo's Nest*
1977   Peter Finch, *Network*

BEST ACTOR (Musical/Comedy)

1951   Fred Astaire, *Three Little Words*
1952   Danny Kaye, *On the Riviera*
1953   Donald O'Connor, *Singing in the Rain*
1954   David Niven, *The Moon is Blue*
1955   James Mason, *A Star is Born*
1956   Tom Ewell, *Seven-Year Itch*
1957   Cantinflas, *Around the World in 80 Days*
1958   Frank Sinatra, *Pal Joey*
1959   Danny Kaye, *Me and the Colonel*

1960 Jack Lemmon, *Some Like It Hot*
1961 Jack Lemmon, *The Apartment*
1962 Glenn Ford, *Pocket Full of Miracles*
1963 Marcello Mastroianni, *Divorce Italian Style*
1964 Alberto Sordi, *To Bed or Not to Bed*
1965 Rex Harrison, *My Fair Lady*
1966 Lee Marvin, *Cat Ballou*
1967 Alan Arkin, *The Russians Are Coming*
1968 Richard Harris, *Camelot*
1969 Ron Moody, *Oliver!*
1970 Peter O'Toole, *Goodbye, Mr. Chips*
1971 Albert Finney, *Scrooge*
1972 Topol, *Fiddler on the Roof*
1973 Jack Lemmon, *Avanti*
1974 George Segal, *A Touch of Class*
1975 Art Carney, *Harry and Tonto*
1976 Walter Matthau, *The Sunshine Boys*
1977 Kris Kristofferson, *A Star is Born*

BEST MOTION PICTURE ACTRESS

1944 Jennifer Jones, *The Song of Bernadette*
1945 Ingrid Bergman, *Bells of St. Mary*
1946 Ingrid Bergman, *Gaslight*
1947 Rosalind Russell, *Sister Kenny*
1948 Rosalind Russell, *Mourning Becomes Electra*
1949 Jane Wyman, *Johnny Belinda*
1950 Olivia de Havilland, *The Heiress*
1951 Gloria Swanson, *Sunset Boulevard*
1952 Jane Wyman, *The Blue Veil*
1953 Shirley Booth, *Come Back, Little Sheba*
1954 Audrey Hepburn, *Roman Holiday*
1955 Grace Kelly, *The Country Girl*
1956 Anna Magnani, *The Rose Tattoo*
1957 Ingrid Bergman, *Anastasia*
1958 Joanne Woodward, *Three Faces of Eve*
1959 Susan Hayward, *I Want to Live*
1960 Elizabeth Taylor, *Suddenly Last Summer*
1961 Greer Garson, *Sunrise at Campobello*
1962 Geraldine Page, *Summer & Smoke*
1963 Geraldine Page, *Sweet Bird of Youth*
1964 Leslie Caron, *The L-Shaped Room*
1965 Anne Bancroft, *The Pumpkin Eater*
1966 Samantha Eggar, *The Collector*
1967 Anouk Aimee, *A Man and a Woman*
1968 Dame Edith Evans, *The Whisperers*
1969 Joanne Woodward, *Rachel, Rachel*
1970 Genevieve Bujold, *Anne of the Thousand Days*
1971 Ali MacGraw, *Love Story*
1972 Jane Fonda, *Klute*
1973 Liv Ullmann, *The Emigrants*
1974 Marsha Mason, *Cinderella Liberty*
1975 Gena Rowlands, *A Woman Under the Influence*
1976 Louise Fletcher, *One Flew Over the Cuckoo's Nest*
1977 Faye Dunaway, *Network*

BEST ACTRESS (Comedy/Drama)

1951 Judy Holliday, *Born Yesterday*
1952 June Allyson, *Too Young to Kiss*
1953 Susan Hayward, *With a Song in My Heart*
1954 Ethel Merman, *Call Me Madam*
1955 Judy Garland, *A Star Is Born*
1956 Jean Simmons, *Guys & Dolls*
1957 Deborah Kerr, *The King & I*
1958 Kay Kendall, *Les Girls*
1959 Rosalind Russell, *Auntie Mame*
1960 Marilyn Monroe, *Some Like It Hot*
1961 Shirley MacLaine, *The Apartment*
1962 Rosalind Russell, *A Majority of One*
1963 Rosalind Russell, *Gypsy*

1964 Shirley MacLaine, *Irma La Douce*
1965 Julie Andrews, *Mary Poppins*
1966 Julie Andrews, *The Sound of Music*
1967 Lynn Redgrave, *Georgy Girl*
1968 Anne Bancroft, *The Graduate*
1969 Barbra Streisand, *Funny Girl*
1970 Patty Duke, *Me, Natalie*
1971 Carrie Snodgress, *Diary of a Mad Housewife*
1972 Twiggy, *The Boy Friend*
1973 Liza Minnelli, *Cabaret*
1974 Glenda Jackson, *A Touch of Class*
1975 Raquel Welch, *The Three Musketeers*
1976 Ann-Margret, *Tommy*
1977 Barbra Streisand, *A Star Is Born*

BEST ACTOR IN SUPPORTING ROLE IN A MOTION PICTURE

1946 J. Carrol Naish, *Gaslight*
1947 Clifton Webb, *The Razor's Edge*
1948 Edmund Gwenn, *Miracle on 34th Street*
1949 Walter Huston, *Treasure of Sierra Madre*
1950 James Whitmore, *Battleground*
1951 Edmund Gwenn, *Mister 880*
1952 Peter Ustinov, *Quo Vadis*
1953 Millard Mitchell, *My Six Convicts*
1954 Frank Sinatra, *From Here to Eternity*
1955 Edmond O'Brien, *The Barefoot Contessa*
1956 Arthur Kennedy, *The Trial*
1957 Earl Holliman, *The Rainmaker*
1958 Red Buttons, *Sayonara*
1959 Burl Ives, *The Big Country*
1960 Stephen Boyd, *Ben Hur*
1961 Sal Mineo, *Exodus*
1962 George Chakiris, *West Side Story*
1963 Omar Sharif, *Lawrence of Arabia*
1964 John Huston, *The Cardinal*
1965 Edmond O'Brien, *Seven Days in May*
1966 Oskar Werner, *The Spy Who Came in From the Cold*
1967 Richard Attenborough, *The Sand Pebbles*
1968 Richard Attenborough, *Dr. Doolittle*
1969 Daniel Massey, *Star*
1970 Gig Young, *They Shoot Horses, Don't They?*
1971 John Mills, *Ryan's Daughter*
1972 Ben Johnson, *The Last Picture Show*
1973 Joel Grey, *Cabaret*
1974 John Houseman, *Paper Chase*
1975 Fred Astaire, *The Towering Inferno*
1976 Richard Benjamin, *The Sunshine Boys*
1977 Laurence Olivier, *Marathon Man*

BEST ACTRESS IN SUPPORTING ROLE IN A MOTION PICTURE

1946 Angela Lansbury, *Gaslight*
1947 Anne Baxter, *The Razor's Edge*
1948 Celeste Holm, *Gentleman's Agreement*
1949 Ellen Corby, *I Remember Mama*
1950 Mercedes McCambridge, *All the King's Men*
1951 Josephine Hull, *Harvey*
1952 Kim Hunter, *Streetcar Named Desire*
1953 Katy Jurado, *High Noon*
1954 Grace Kelly, *Mogambo*
1955 Jan Sterling, *The High and the Mighty*
1956 Marisa Pavan, *The Rose Tattoo*
1957 Eileen Heckart, *Bad Seed*
1958 Elsa Lancaster, *Witness for the Prosecution*
1959 Hermione Gingold, *Gigi*
1960 Susan Kohner, *Imitation of Life*
1961 Janet Leigh, *Psycho*
1962 Rita Moreno, *West Side Story*

1963 Angela Lansbury, *The Manchurian Candidate*
1964 Margaret Rutherford, *VIP*
1965 Agnes Moorehead, *Hush, Hush Sweet Charlotte*
1966 Ruth Gordon, *Inside Daisy Clover*
1967 Jocelyn La Garde, *Hawaii*
1968 Carol Channing, *Thoroughly Modern Millie*
1969 Ruth Gordon, *Rosemary's Baby*
1970 Goldie Hawn, *Cactus Flower*
1971 Karen Black, *Five Easy Pieces*
     Maureen Stapleton, *Airport*
1972 Ann-Margret, *Carnal Knowledge*
1973 Shelley Winters, *The Poseidon Adventure*
1974 Linda Blair, *The Exorcist*
1975 Karen Black, *The Great Gatsby*
1976 Brenda Vaccaro, *Once is Not Enough*
1977 Katharine Ross, *Voyage of the Damned*

MOST PROMISING NEWCOMERS/MALE (Called "Best Acting Debut" since 1976)

1950 Richard Todd, *The Hasty Heart*
1951 Gene Nelson, *Tea for Two*
1952 Kevin McCarthy, *Death of a Salesman*
1953 Richard Burton, *My Cousin Rachel*
1954 Hugh O'Brian
     Steve Forrest
     Richard Egan
1955 Joe Adams
     George Nader
     Jeff Richards
1956 Ray Danton
     Russ Tamblyn
1957 John Kerr
     Paul Newman
     Tony Perkins
     Jacques Bergerac (foreign)
1958 James Garner
     John Saxon
     Pat Wayne
1959 Bradford Dillman
     John Gavin
     Efrem Zimbalist Jr.
1960 James Shigeta
     Barry Coe
     Troy Donahue
     George Hamilton
1961 Michael Callan
     Mark Damon
     Brett Halsey
1962 Richard Beymer
     Bobby Darin
     Warren Beatty
1963 Keir Dullea
     Omar Sharif
     Terence Stamp
1964 Albert Finney
     Robert Walker
     Stathis Giallelis
1965 Harv Presnell
     George Segal
     Chaim Topol
1966 Robert Redford, *Inside Daisy Clover*
1967 James Farentino, *The Pad*
1968 Dustin Hoffman, *The Graduate*
1969 Leonard Whiting, *Romeo & Juliet*
1970 Jon Voight, *Midnight Cowboy*
1971 James Earl Jones, *The Great White Hope*
1972 Desi Arnaz, Jr., *Red Sky at Morning*
1973 Edward Albert, *Butterflies Are Free*
1974 Paul Le Mat, *American Graffiti*
1975 Joseph Bottoms, *The Dove*

1976 Brad Dourif, *One Flew Over the Cuckoo's Nest*
1977 Arnold Schwarzenegger, *Stay Hungry*

MOST PROMISING NEWCOMER/FEMALE (Called Best Acting Debut Since 1976)

1950 Mercedes McCambridge, *All The King's Men*
1951 No award
1952 Pier Angeli, *Teresa*
1953 Collette Marchand, *Moulin Rouge*
1954 Pat Crowley
     Bella Darvi
     Barbara Rush
1955 Shirley MacLaine
     Kim Novak
     Karen Sharpe
1956 Anita Ekberg
     Virginia Shaw
     Dana Wynter
1957 Carroll Baker
     Jayne Mansfield
     Natalie Wood
     Taina Elg (foreign)
1958 Sandra Dee
     Carolyn Jones
     Diane Varsi
1959 Linda Cristal
     Susan Kohner
     Tina Louise
1960 Tuesday Weld
     Angie Dickinson
     Janet Munro
     Stella Stevens
1961 Ina Balin
     Nancy Kwan
     Hayley Mills
1962 Christine Kaufmann
     Ann-Margret
     Jane Fonda
1963 Patty Duke
     Sue Lyon
     Rita Tushingham
1964 Ursula Andress
     Tippi Hedren
     Elke Sommer
1965 Mia Farrow
     Celia Kaye
     Mary Ann Mobley
1966 Elizabeth Hartman, *A Patch of Blue*
1967 Camilla Sparv, *Dead Heat on a Merry Go Round*
1968 Katharine Ross, *The Graduate*
1969 Olivia Hussey, *Romeo & Juliet*
1970 Ali MacGraw, *Goodbye, Columbus*
1971 Carrie Snodgress, *Diary of a Mad Housewife*
1972 Twiggy, *The Boy Friend*
1973 Diana Ross, *Lady Sings the Blues*
1974 Tatum O'Neal, *Paper Moon*
1975 Susan Flannery, *The Towering Inferno*
1976 Marilyn Hassett, *The Other Side of the Mountain*
1977 Jessica Lange, *King Kong*

BEST MOTION PICTURE DIRECTOR

1947 Frank Capra, *It's A Wonderful Life*
1948 Elia Kazan, *Gentleman's Agreement*
1949 John Huston, *Treasure of Sierra Madre*
1950 Robert Rossen, *All the King's Men*
1951 Billy Wilder, *Sunset Boulevard*
1952 Laslo Benedek, *Death of a Salesman*
1953 Cecil B. DeMille, *The Greatest Show on Earth*
1954 Fred Zinnemann, *From Here to Eternity*

1955 Elia Kazan, *On the Waterfront*
1956 Joshua Logan, *Picnic*
1957 Elia Kazan, *Baby Doll*
1958 David Lean, *Bridge On the River Kwai*
1959 Vincente Minnelli, *Gigi*
1960 William Wyler, *Ben Hur*
1961 Jack Cardiff, *Sons and Lovers*
1962 Stanley Kramer, *Judgment at Nuremberg*
1963 David Lean, *Lawrence of Arabia*
1964 Elia Kazan, *America, America*
1965 George Cukor, *My Fair Lady*
1966 David Lean, *Dr. Zhivago*
1967 Fred Zinnemann, *A Man for All Seasons*
1968 Mike Nichols, *The Graduate*
1969 Paul Newman, *Rachel, Rachel*
1970 Charles Jarrott, *Anne of the Thousand Days*
1971 Arthur Hiller, *Love Story*
1972 William Friedkin, *The French Connection*
1973 Francis Ford Coppola, *The Godfather*
1974 William Friedkin, *The Exorcist*
1975 Roman Polanski, *Chinatown*
1976 Milos Forman, *One Flew Over the Cuckoo's Nest*
1977 Sidney Lumet, *Network*

BEST MOTION PICTURE SCREENPLAY

1948 George Seaton, *The Miracle on 34th Street*
1949 Richard Schweizer, *The Search*
1950 Robert Pirosh, *Battleground*
1951 Joseph Mankiewicz, *All About Eve*
1952 Robert Buckner, *Bright Victory*
1953 Michael Wilson, *Five Fingers*
1954 Helen Deutsch, *Lili*
1955 Billy Wilder, Samuel Taylor and Ernest Lehman, *Sabrina*
1956 No award
1957 No award
1958 No award
1959 No award
1960 No award
1961 No award
1962 No award
1963 No award
1964 No award
1965 No award
1966 Robert Bolt, *Dr. Zhivago*
1967 Robert Bolt, *A Man for All Seasons*
1968 Sterling Silliphant, *In the Heat of the Night*
1969 Sterling Silliphant, *Charly*
1970 John Hale, Bridget Boland and Richard Sokolove, *Anne of the Thousand Days*
1971 Erich Segal, *Love Story*
1972 Paddy Chayefsky, *The Hospital*
1973 Francis Ford Coppola and Mario Puzo, *The Godfather*
1974 William Peter Blatty, *The Exorcist*
1975 Robert Towne, *Chinatown*
1976 Laurence Hauben and Bo Goldman, *One Flew Over the Cuckoo's Nest*
1977 Paddy Chayefsky, *Network*

BEST ORIGINAL MOTION PICTURE SCORE

1948 Max Steiner, *Life With Father*
1949 Brian Easdale, *The Red Shoes*
1950 Johnny Green, *The Inspector General*
1951 Franz Waxman, *Sunset Boulevard*
1952 Victor Young, *September Affair*
1953 Dmitri Tiomkin, *High Noon*
1954 No award
1955 No award

1956 No award
1957 No award
1958 No award
1959 No award
1960 Ernest Gold, *On the Beach*
1961 Dmitri Tiomkin, *Alamo*
1962 Dmitri Tiomkin, *The Guns of Navarone*
1963 Elmer Bernstein, *To Kill A Mockingbird*
1964 No award
1965 Dmitri Tiomkin, *The Fall of the Roman Empire*
1966 Maurice Jarre, *Dr. Zhivago*
1967 Elmer Bernstein, *Hawaii*
1968 Frederick Loewe, *Camelot*
1969 Alex North, *The Shoes of the Fisherman*
1970 Burt Bacharach, *Butch Cassidy and the Sundance Kid*
1971 Francis Lai, *Love Story*
1972 Isaac Hayes, *Shaft*
1973 Nino Rota, *The Godfather*
1974 Neil Diamond, *Jonathan Livingston Seagull*
1975 Alan Jay Lerner and Frederick Loewe, *The Little Prince*
1976 John Williams, *Jaws*
1977 Paul Williams and Kenny Ascher, *A Star is Born*

BEST ORIGINAL SONG FROM A MOTION PICTURE

1962 Dmitri Tiomkin and Ned Washington, *Town Without Pity* title song
1963 No award
1964 No award
1965 Dmitri Tiomkin and Ned Washington, *Circus World*
1966 *Forget Domani* from *Yellow Rolls Royce*
1967 *Strangers in the Night* from *A Man Could Get Killed*
1968 *If Ever I Should Leave You* from *Camelot*
1969 *The Windmills of Your Mind* from *The Thomas Crown Affair*
1970 *Jean* from *The Prime of Miss Jean Brodie*
1971 *Whistling Away the Dark* from *Darling Lili*
1972 *Life Is What You Make It* from *Kotch*
1973 Walter Scharf and Don Black, *Ben* title song
1974 Marvin Hamlisch and M. and A. Bergman, *The Way We Were* title song
1975 Euel and Betty Box, *I Feel Love* from *Benji*
1976 Keith Carradine, *I'm Easy* from *Nashville*
1977 Paul Williams and Kenny Ascher, *Evergreen* from *A Star is Born*

BEST CINEMATOGRAPHY

1948 Jack Cardiff, *Black Narcissus*
1949 Gabriel Figueroa, *The Pearl*
1950 Frank Planer, *Champion* (black and white)
      Walt Disney Studios, *Ichabod and Mr. Toad* (color)
1951 Frank Planer, *Cyrano de Bergerac* (black and white)
      Robert Surtees, *King Solomon's Mines* (color)
1952 Frank Planer, *Death of a Salesman* (black and white)
      Robert Surtees and William V. Skall, *Quo Vadis* (color)
1953 Floyd Crosby, *High Noon* (black and white)
      George Barnes and Peverell Marley, *The Greatest Show on Earth* (color)
1954 No award
1955 Boris Kaufman, *On the Waterfront* (black and white)
      Joseph Ruttenberg, *Brigadoon* (color)
1963 *The Longest Day* (black and white)
      Lawrence of Arabia (color)

CECIL B. DEMILLE AWARD

1952 Cecil B. DeMille
1953 Walt Disney

Golden Globe Awards 231

1954 Darryl Zanuck
1955 Jean Hersholt
1956 Jack Warner
1957 Mervyn LeRoy
1958 Buddy Adler
1959 Maurice Chevalier
1960 Bing Crosby
1961 Fred Astaire
1962 Judy Garland
1963 Bob Hope
1964 Joseph E. Levine
1965 James Stewart
1966 John Wayne
1967 Charlton Heston
1968 Kirk Douglas
1969 Gregory Peck
1970 Joan Crawford
1971 Frank Sinatra
1972 Alfred Hitchcock
1973 Samuel Goldwyn
1974 Bette Davis
1975 Hal D. Wallis
1976 No award
1977 Walter Mirsch

WORLD FILM FAVORITE (MALE)
1951 Gregory Peck
1952 No award
1953 John Wayne
1954 Robert Taylor
     Alan Ladd
1955 Gregory Peck
1956 Marlon Brando
1957 James Dean
1958 Tony Curtis
1959 Rock Hudson
1960 Rock Hudson
1961 Rock Hudson
     Tony Curtis
1962 Charlton Heston
1963 Rock Hudson
1964 Paul Newman
1965 Marcello Mastroianni
1966 Paul Newman
1967 Steve McQueen
1968 Paul Newman
1969 Sidney Poitier
1970 Steve McQueen
1971 Clint Eastwood
1972 Charles Bronson
     Sean Connery
1973 Marlon Brando
1974 Marlon Brando
1975 Robert Redford
1976 No award
1977 Robert Redford

WORLD FILM FAVORITE (FEMALE)
1951 Jane Wyman
1952 No award
1953 Susan Hayward
1954 Marilyn Monroe
1955 Audrey Hepburn
1956 Grace Kelly
1957 Kim Novak
1958 Doris Day
1959 Deborah Kerr
1960 Doris Day

1961 Gina Lollobrigida
1962 Marilyn Monroe
1963 Doris Day
1964 Inger Stevens
1965 Sophia Loren
1966 Natalie Wood
1967 Julie Andrews
1968 Julie Andrews
1969 Sophia Loren
1970 Barbra Streisand
1971 Barbra Streisand
1972 Ali MacGraw
1973 Jane Fonda
1974 Elizabeth Taylor
1975 Barbra Streisand
1976 No award
1977 Sophia Loren

In addition to the awards in consistent categories, the Association confers Special Awards, Merit Awards and other citations as warranted each year. By year, they are as follows:

1947 Award for Best Non-Professional Acting: **Harold Russell**, *The Best Years of Our Lives*
1948 Special Award to Best Juvenile Actor: **Dean Stockwell**, *Gentleman's Agreement*
     Special Award for Furthering the Influence on the Screen: **Walt Disney**
1949 Special Award to Best Juvenile Actor: **Ivan Yandl**, *The Search*
1950 **No award**
1951 **No award**
1952 **No award**
1953 Special Award to Best Juvenile Actors: **Brandon de Wilde**, *Member of the Wedding*
     Francis Kee Teller, *Navajo*
1954 Best Documentary of Historical Interest: **Walt Disney**, *Living Desert*
     Best Western Star: **Guy Madison**
     Honor Award: **Jack Cummings**, producer for 30 years at MGM
1955 Pioneer Award in the Motion Picture Industry: **John Ford**
     Pioneer Award for Color on the Screen: **Herbert Kalmus**
     Special Award for Creative Musical Contribution: **Dmitri Tiomkin**
     Special Award for Experimental Film: *Anywhere in Our Time*
1956 Hollywood Citizenship Award: **Esther Williams**
     Best Outdoor Drama: *Wichita*
     Posthumous Award for Best Dramatic Actor: **James Dean**
1957 Recognition Award for Music in Motion Pictures: **Dmitri Tiomkin**
     Special Award for Advancing Film Industry: **Edwin Schallert**
     Hollywood Citizenship Award: **Ronald Reagan**
     Award for Consistent Performance: **Elizabeth Taylor**
1958 Best Film Choreography: **Le Roy Prinz**
     Best World Entertainment Through Musical Films: **George Sidney**
     Special Award for Bettering the Standard of Motion Picture Music: **Hugo Friedhofer**
     Most Versatile Actress: **Jean Simmons**
     Most Glamorous Actress: **Zsa Zsa Gabor**
     Ambassador of Good Will: **Bob Hope**
1959 Special Award to Best Juvenile: **David Ladd**
     Special Award to Most Versatile Actress: **Shirley MacLaine**

1960 Special Award for Directing Chariot Race in Film *Ben Hur:* **Andrew Morton**
Outstanding Merit: *The Nun's Story*
Journalistic Merit Awards: **Hedda Hopper** and **Louella H. Parsons**
Special Awards to Famous Silent Film Stars: **Francis X. Bushman** and **Ramon Navarro**
1961 Special Award for Comedy: **Cantinflas**
Special Award for Artistic Integrity: **Stanley Kramer**
Merit Award: *The Sundowners*
1962 Special Merit Award: **Samuel Bronston,** *El Cid*
Special Journalistic Merit Awards: **Army Archerd** and **Mike Connolly**
1963 Special Award for International Contribution to Recording World: **Nat "King" Cole**
Samuel Goldwyn Award: *Sunday and Cybele*
1964 Samuel Goldwyn Award: *Yesterday, Today and Tomorrow*
International Contribution to the Recording World: **Connie Francis**
1965 No award
1966 No award
1967 No award
1968 No award
1969 No award
1970 No award
1971 No award
1972 No award
1973 Best Documentary Film: *Elvis on Tour* and *Walls of Fire*
1974 Best Documentary Film: *Visions of Eight*
1975 Best Documentary Film: *Beautiful People*
1976 Best Documentary: *Youthquake*
1977 Best Documentary: *Altars of the World*

Hugo Award

WORLD SCIENCE FICTION SOCIETY
c/o Howard DeVore, 4705 Weddel St., Dearborn Heights, Mich. 48125 (313/565-4157)

The Hugo Award is given annually for an outstanding science fiction film or television program, as determined by a vote of the people who attend the Science Fiction Convention. The award is a rocket ship-shaped trophy, whose official name is the Science Fiction Achievement Award.

1960 *Twilight Zone* (Television)
1961 *Twilight Zone* (Television)
1962 *Twilight Zone* (Television)
1963 No award
1964 No award
1965 *Dr. Strangelove* (Film)
1966 No award
1967 "The Menagerie" on *Star Trek* (Television)
1968 "City on the Edge of Forever" on *Star Trek* (Television)
1969 *2001: A Space Odyssey* (Film)
1970 Apollo XI coverage (Television)
1971 No award
1972 *A Clockwork Orange* (Film)
1973 *Slaughterhouse Five* (Film)
1974 *Sleeper* (Film)
1975 *Young Frankenstein* (Film)
1976 *A Boy and His Dog* (Film)
1977 No award

Dan T. Moore Award

INTERNATIONAL PLATFORM ASSOCIATION
2564 Berkshire Rd., Cleveland Hts., Ohio 44106 (216/932-0505)

The Dan T. Moore Award, which consists of an engraved gavel, is given annually on the decision of the IPA Committee, to the best film lecturer.

1975 Dan Tyler Moore
1976 No award
1977 No award

"Ten Best"

NATIONAL BOARD OF REVIEW OF MOTION PICTURES
Box 589, Lenox Hill Station, New York, N.Y. 10021 (212/535-2528)

The film board annually selects the "Ten Best" films and recognizes exceptional displays of talent by cast and crew. The Board's review committee of about a hundred "public spirited men and women with an interest in the motion picture and a mature sense of social responsibility" votes on films recommended by the Board's committee on exceptional films. Though the Board started selecting and individuals the "Ten Best" in 1919, the present list of pictures and individuals begins with the first full year of sound motion pictures and includes selections of top films cited by the Board in other specific categories.

AMERICAN

1930 *All Quiet on the Western Front*
Holiday
Laughter
The Man from Blankley's
Men Without Women
Morocco
Outward Bound
Romance
The Street of Chance
Tol'able David
1931 *Cimarron*
City Lights
City Streets
Dishonored
The Front Page
The Guardsman
Quick Millions
Rango
Surrender
Tabu
1932 *I Am a Fugitive from a Chain Gang*
As You Desire Me
A Bill of Divorcement
A Farewell to Arms
Madame Racketeer
Payment Deferred
Scarface
Tarzan
Trouble in Paradise
Two Seconds
1933 *Topaze*
Berkeley Square
Cavalcade
Little Women
Mama Loves Papa

The Piped Piper (cartoon)
She Done Him Wrong
State Fair
Three Cornered Moon
Zoo in Budapest
1934 It Happened One Night
The Count of Monte Cristo
Crime Without Passion
Eskimo
The First World War
The Lost Patrol
Lost in Sodom (non-theatrical short)
No Greater Glory
The Thin Man
Viva Villa
1935 The Informer
Alice Adams
Anna Karenina
David Copperfield
The Gilded Lily
Les Miserables
The Lives of the Bengal Lancers
Mutiny on the Bounty
Ruggles of Red Gap
Who Killed Cock Robin (cartoon)
1936 Mr. Deeds Goes to Town
The Story of Louis Pasteur
Modern Times
Fury
Winterset
The Devil Is a Sissy
Ceiling Zero
Romeo and Juliet
The Prisoner of Shark Island
The Green Pastures
1937 Night Must Fall
The Life of Emile Zola
Black Legion
Camille
Make Way for Tomorrow
The Good Earth
They Won't Forget
Captains Courageous
A Star Is Born
Stage Door
1938 The Citadel
Snow White and the Seven Dwarfs
The Beachcomber
To the Victor
Sing You Sinners
The Edge of the World
Of Human Hearts
Jezebel
South Riding
Three Comrades
1939 Confessions of a Nazi Spy
Wuthering Heights
Stagecoach
Ninotchka
Young Mr. Lincoln
Crisis
Goodbye, Mr. Chips
Mr. Smith Goes to Washington
The Roaring Twenties
U-Boat 29
1940 The Grapes of Wrath
The Great Dictator
Of Mice and Men
Our Town
Fantasia

The Long Voyage Home
Foreign Correspondent
The Biscuit Eater
Gone With the Wind
Rebecca
1941 Citizen Kane
How Green Was My Valley
The Little Foxes
The Stars Look Down
Dumbo
High Sierra
Here Comes Mr. Jordan
Tom, Dick and Harry
The Road to Zanzibar
The Lady Eve
1942 In Which We Serve
One of Our Aircraft Is Missing
Mrs. Miniver
Journey for Margaret
Wake Island
The Male Animal
The Major and the Minor
Sullivan's Travels
The Moon and Sixpence
The Pied Piper
1943 The Ox-Bow Incident
Watch on the Rhine
Air Force
Holy Matrimony
The Hard Way
Casablanca
Lassie Come Home
Bataan
The Moon is Down
The Next of Kin
1944 None But the Lonely Heart
Going My Way
The Miracle of Morgan's Creek
Hail the Conquering Hero
The Song of Bernadette
Wilson
Meet Me in St. Louis
Thirty Seconds Over Tokyo
Thunder Rock
Lifeboat

FOREIGN
1930 High Treason
Old and New
Soil
Storm Over Asia
Zwei Herzen in 3/4 Takt
1931 Die Dreigroschenoper
Das Lied vom Leben
Le Million
Sous Les Toits de Paris
Vier von der Infantrie
1932 A Nous la Liberte
Der Andere
The Battle of Gallipoli
Golden Mountains
Kameradschaft
Madchen in Uniform
Der Raub der Mona Lisa
Reserved for Ladies
Road to Life
Zwei Menschen
1933 Hertha's Erwachen
Ivan
M

Morgenrot
Niemandsland (Hell on Earth)
Poil de Carotte
The Private Life of Henry VIII
Quatorze Juliette
Rome Express
Le Sang d'un Poete
1934　*Man of Aran*
The Blue Light
Catherine the Great
The Constant Nymph
Madame Bovary
1935　*Chapayev*
Crime et Chatiment
Le Dernier Milliardaire
The Man Who Knew Too Much
Marie Chapdelaine
La Maternelle
The New Gulliver
Peasants
Thunder in the East
The Youth of Maxim
1936　*Le Kermesse Heroique*
The New Earth
Rembrandt
The Ghost Goes West
Nine Days a Queen
We Are From Kronstadt
Son of Mongolia
The Yellow Cruise
Les Miserables
The Secret Agent
1937　*The Eternal Mask*
The Lower Depths
Baltic Deputy
Mayerling
The Spanish Earth
Golgotha
Elephant Boy
Rembrandt
Janosik
The Wedding of Palo
1938　*La Grande Illusion*
Ballerina
Un Carnet de Bal
Generals Without Buttons
Peter the First
1939　*Port of Shadows*
Harvest
Alexander Nevsky
The End of a Day
Robert Koch
1940　*The Baker's Wife*
1941　*Pepe Le Moko*
1942　None cited
1943　None cited
1944　None cited

DOCUMENTARY

1940　*The Flight for Life*
1941　*Target for Tonight*
1942　*Moscow Strikes Back*
1943　*Desert Victory*
Battle of Russia
Prelude to War
Saludos Amigos
The Silent Village
1944　*The Memphis Belle*
Attack! (The Battle for New Britain)
With the Marines at Tarawa

Battle for the Marianas
Tunisian Victory

THE TEN BEST (Including documentaries)

1945　*The True Glory*
The Lost Weekend
The Southerner
The Story of G.I. Joe
The Last Chance
Colonel Blimp
A Tree Grows in Brooklyn
The Fighting Lady
The Way Ahead
The Clock
1946　*Henry V*
Open City
The Best Years of Our Lives
Brief Encounters
A Walk in the Sun
It Happened at the Inn
My Darling Clementine
The Diary of a Chambermaid
The Killers
Anna and the King of Siam
1947　*Monsieur Verdoux*
Great Expectations
Shoe-shine
Crossfire
Boomerang!
Odd Man Out
Gentleman's Agreement
To Live in Peace
It's a Wonderful Life
The Overlanders
1948　*Paisan*
Day of Wrath
The Search
Treasure of Sierra Madre
Louisiana Story
Hamlet
The Snake Pit
Johnny Belinda
Joan of Arc
The Red Shoes
1949　*The Bicycle Thief*
The Quiet One
Intruder in the Dust
The Heiress
Devil in the Flesh
Quartet
Germany, Year Zero
Home of the Brave
A Letter to Three Wives
The Fallen Idol

AMERICAN FILMS

1950　*Sunset Boulevard*
All About Eve
The Asphalt Jungle
The Men
Edge of Doom
Twelve O'Clock High
Panic in the Streets
Cyrano de Bergerac
No Way Out
Stage Fright
1951　*A Place in the Sun*
The Red Badge of Courage
An American In Paris

Death of a Salesman
Detective Story
A Streetcar Named Desire
Decision Before Dawn
Strangers On a Train
Quo Vadis
Fourteen Hours
1952 The Quiet Man
High Noon
Limelight
Five Fingers
The Snows of Kilimanjaro
The Thief
The Bad and the Beautiful
Singin' in the Rain
Above and Beyond
My Son John
1953 Julius Caesar
Shane
From Here to Eternity
Martin Luther
Lili
Roman Holiday
Stalag 17
Little Fugitive
Mogambo
The Robe
1954 On the Waterfront
Seven Brides for Seven Brothers
The Country Girl
A Star is Born
Executive Suite
The Vanishing Prairie
Sabrina
20,000 Leagues Under the Sea
The Unconquered
Beat the Devil
1955 Marty
East of Eden
Mister Roberts
Bad Day at Black Rock
Summertime
The Rose Tattoo
A Man Called Peter
Not As a Stranger
Picnic
The African Lion
1956 Around the World in 80 Days
Moby Dick
The King and I
Lust for Life
Friendly Persuasion
Somebody Up There Likes Me
The Catered Affair
Anastasia
The Man Who Never Was
Bus Stop
1957 The Bridge on the River Kwai
Twelve Angry Men
The Spirit of St. Louis
The Rising of the Moon
Albert Schweitzer
Funny Face
The Bachelor Party
The Enemy Below
A Hatful of Rain
A Farewell to Arms
1958 The Old Man and the Sea
Separate Tables
The Last Hurrah

The Long Hot Summer
Windjammer
Cat on a Hot Tin Roof
The Goddess
The Brothers Karamazov
Me and the Colonel
Gigi
1959 The Nun's Story
Ben-Hur
Anatomy of a Murder
The Diary of Anne Frank
Middle of the Night
The Man Who Understood Women
Some Like It Hot
Suddenly, Last Summer
On the Beach
North by Northwest
1960 Sons and Lovers
The Alamo
The Sundowners
Inherit the Wind
Sunrise at Campobello
Elmer Gantry
Home from the Hill
The Apartment
Wild River
The Dark at the Top of the Stairs
1961 Question
The Hustler
West Side Story
The Innocents
The Hoodlum Priest
Summer and Smoke
The Young Doctors
Judgment at Nuremberg
One, Two, Three
Fanny
1962 The Longest Day
Billy Budd
The Miracle Worker
Lawrence of Arabia
Long Day's Journey Into Night
Whistle Down the Wind
Requiem for a Heavyweight
A Taste of Honey
Birdman of Alcatraz
War Hunt
1963 Tom Jones
Lilies of the Field
All the Way Home
Hud
This Sporting Life
Lord of the Flies
The L-Shaped Room
The Great Escape
How the West Was Won
The Cardinal
1964 Becket
My Fair Lady
Girl With Green Eyes
The World of Henry Orient
Zorba the Greek
Topkapi
The Chalk Garden
The Finest Hours
Four Days in November
Seance on a Wet Afternoon
1965 The Eleanor Roosevelt Story
The Agony and the Ecstasy
Doctor Zhivago

Ship of Fools
The Spy Who Came in from the Cold
Darling
The Greatest Story Ever Told
A Thousand Clowns
The Sound of Music
The Train
1966 A Man for All Seasons
Born Free
Alfie
Who's Afraid of Virginia Woolf?
The Bible
Georgy Girl
Years of Lightning, Day of Drums
It Happened Here
The Russians Are Coming, The Russians Are Coming
Shakespeare Wallah
1967 Far From the Madding Crowd
The Whisperers
Ulysses
In Cold Blood
The Family Way
The Taming of the Shrew
Doctor Doolittle
The Graduate
The Comedians
Accident
1968 The Shoes of the Fisherman
Romeo and Juliet
The Yellow Submarine
Charly
Rachel, Rachel
The Subject Was Roses
The Lion in Winter
Planet of the Apes
Oliver!
2001: A Space Odyssey
1969 They Shoot Horses, Don't They?
Ring of Bright Water
Topaz
Goodbye, Mr. Chips
Battle of Britain
The Loves of Isadora
The Prime of Miss Jean Brodie
Support Your Local Sheriff
True Grit
Midnight Cowboy
1970 Patton
Kes
Women in Love
Five Easy Pieces
Ryan's Daughter
I Never Sang for my Father
Diary of a Mad Housewife
Love Story
The Virgin and the Gypsy
Tora, Tora, Tora
1971 Macbeth
The Boy Friend
One Day in the Life of Ivan Denisovich
The French Connection
The Last Picture Show
Nicholas and Alexandra
The Go-Between
King Lear
Peter Rabbit and Tales of Beatrix Potter
Death in Venice
1972 Cabaret
Man of La Mancha
The Godfather

Sounder
1776
The Effect of Gamma Rays on Man-in-the-Moon Marigolds
Deliverance
The Ruling Class
The Candidate
Frenzy
1973 The Sting
Paper Moon
The Homecoming
Bang the Drum Slowly
Serpico
O Lucky Man
The Last American Hero
The Hireling
The Day of the Dolphin
The Way We Were
1974 The Converstion
Murder on the Orient Express
Chinatown
The Last Detail
Harry and Tonto
A Woman Under the Influence
Thieves Like Us
Lenny
Daisy Miller
The Three Musketeers
1975 Barry Lyndon/Nashville
Conduct Unbecoming
One Flew Over the Cuckoo's Nest
Lies My Father Told Me
Dog Day Afternoon
Day of the Locust
The Passenger
Hearts of the West
Farewell, My Lovely
Alice Doesn't Live Here Anymore
1976 All the President's Men
Network
Rocky
The Last Tycoon
The Seven-Per-Cent Solution
The Front
The Shootist
Family Plot
Silent Movie
Obsession
1977 The Turning Point
Annie Hall
Star Wars
Julia
Close Encounters of the Third Kind
The Late Show
Saturday Night Fever
Equus
The Picture Show Man
Harlan County, U.S.A.

FOREIGN FILMS
1950 The Titan
Tight Little Island
The Third Man
Kind Hearts and Coronets
Paris 1900
1951 Rashomon
The River
Miracle in Milan
Kon Tiki
The Browning Version
1952 Breaking the Sound Barrier

The Man in the White Suit
Forbidden Games
Beauty and the Devil
Ivory Hunter
1953 *A Queen is Crowned*
Moulin Rouge
The Little World of Don Camillo
Strange Deception
Conquest of Everest
1954 *Romeo and Juliet*
The Heart of the Matter
Gate of Hell
The Diary of a Country Priest
The Little Kidnappers
Genevieve
Beauties of the Night
Mr. Hulot's Holiday
The Detective
Bread, Love and Dreams
1955 *The Prisoner*
The Great Adventure
The Divided Heart
Diabolique
The End of the Affair
1956 *The Silent World*
War and Peace
Richard III
La Strada
Rififi
1957 *Ordet*
Gervaise
Torero!
The Red Balloon
A Man Escaped
1958 *Pather Panchali*
Rouge et Noir
The Horse's Mouth
My Uncle
A Night to Remember
1959 *Wild Strawberries*
Room at the Top
Aparajito
The Roof
Look Back in Anger
1960 *The World of Apu*
General Della Rovere
The Angry Silence
I'm All Right, Jack
Hiroshima, Mon Amour
1961 *The Bridge*
La Dolce Vita
Two Women
Saturday Night and Sunday Morning
A Summer to Remember
1962 *Sundays and Cybele*
Barabbas
Divorce, Italian Style
The Island
Through a Glass Darkly
1963 *8½*
The Four Days of Naples
Winter Light
The Leopard
Any Number Can Win
1964 *World Without Sun*
The Organizer
Anatomy of a Marriage
Seduced and Abandoned
Yesterday, Today and Tomorrow
1965 *Juliet of the Spirits*
The Overcoat

La Boheme
La Tia Tula
Gertrud
1966 *The Sleeping Car Murder*
The Gospel According to St. Matthew
The Shameless Old Lady
A Man and a Woman
Hamlet
1967 *Elvira Madigan*
The Hunt
Africa Addio
Persona
The Great Train Robbery
1968 *War and Peace*
Hagbard and Signe ("The Red Mantle")
Hunger
The Two of Us
The Bride Wore Black
1969 *Shame*
Stolen Kisses
The Damned
La Femme Infidele
Adalen '31
1970 *The Wild Child*
My Night at Maud's
The Passion of Anna
The Confession
This Man Must Die
1971 *Claire's Knee*
Bed and Board
The Clowns
The Garden of the Finzi-Continis
The Conformist
1972 *The Sorrow and the Pity*
The Emigrants
The Discreet Charm of the Bourgeoisie
Chloe in the Afternoon
Uncle Vanya
1973 *Cries and Whispers*
Day for Night
The New Land
The Tall Blond Man with One Brown Shoe
Alfredo
Traffic
1974 *Amarcord*
Lacombe, Lucien
Scenes from a Marriage
The Phantom of Liberte
The Pedestrian
1975 *Story of Adele H*
Brief Vacation
Special Section
Stavisky
Swept Away
1976 *Marquise of O*
Face to Face
Small Change
Cousin Cousine
The Clockmaker
1977 *That Obscure Object of Desire*
The Man Who Loved Women
A Special Day
Cria
The American Friend

BEST ACTING
1937 Harry Baur, *The Golem*
Humphrey Bogart, *Black Legion*
Charles Boyer, *Conquest*
Nikolai Cherkassov, *Baltic Deputy*
Danielle Darrieux, *Mayerling*

Greta Garbo, *Camille*
Robert Montgomery, *Night Must Fall*
Maria Ouspenskaya, *Conquest*
Luise Rainer, *The Good Earth*
Joseph Schildkraut, *The Life of Emile Zola*
Mathias Wieman, *The Eternal Mask*
Dame May Whitty, *Night Must Fall*
1938 Lew Ayres, *Holiday*
Pierre Blanchar, *Un Carnet de Bal*
Harry Baur, *Un Carnet de Bal*
Louis Jouvet, *Un Carnet de Bal*
Raim, *Un Carnet de Bal*
James Cagney, *Angels With Dirty Faces*
Joseph Calleia, *Algiers*
Chico, *The Adventure of Chico*
Robert Donat, *The Citadel*
Will Fyffe, *To The Victor*
Pierre Fresnay, *La Grande Illusion*
Jean John, *La Grande Illusion*
Dita Parlo, *La Grande Illusion*
Eric Von Stroheim, *La Grande Illusion*
John Garfield, *Four Daughters*
Wendy Hiller, *Pygmalion*
Charles Laughton, *The Beachcomber*
Elsa Lanchester, *The Beachcomber*
Robert Morley, *Marie Antoinette*
Ralph Richardson, *South Riding* and *The Citadel*
Margaret Sullavan, *Three Comrades*
Spencer Tracy, *Boys Town*
1939 James Cagney, *Roaring Twenties*
Bette Davis, *Dark Victory* and *The Old Maid*
Geraldine Fitzgerald, *Wuthering Heights* and *Dark Victory*
Henry Fonda, *Young Mr. Lincoln*
Jean Gabin, *Port of Shadows*
Greta Garbo, *Ninotchka*
Francis Lederer, *Confessions of a Nazi Spy*
Paul Lukas, *Confessions of a Nazi Spy*
Thomas Mitchell, *Stagecoach*
Laurence Olivier, *Wuthering Heights*
Flora Robson, *We Are Not Alone*
Michel Simon, *Port of Shadows* and *End of Day*
1940 Jane Bryan, *We Are Not Alone*
Charles Chaplin, *The Great Dictator*
Jane Darwell, *The Grapes of Wrath*
Betty Field, *Of Mice and Men*
Henry Fonda, *The Grapes of Wrath* and *Return of Frank James*
Joan Fontaine, *Rebecca*
Greer Garson, *Pride and Prejudice*
William Holden, *Our Town*
Vivien Leigh, *Gone With the Wind* and *Waterloo Bridge*
Thomas Mitchell, *The Long Voyage Home*
Raimu, *The Baker's Wife*
Ralph Richardson, *The Fugitives*
Ginger Rogers, *The Primrose Path*
George Sanders, *Rebecca*
Martha Scott, *Our Town*
James Stewart, *The Shop Around the Corner*
Conrad Veidt, *Escape*
1941 Sara Allgood, *How Green Was My Valley*
Mary Astor, *The Great Lie* and *The Maltese Falcon*
Ingrid Bergman, *Rage in Heaven*
Humphrey Bogart, *High Sierra* and *The Maltese Falcon*
Gary Cooper, *Sergeant York*
Donald Crisp, *How Green Was My Valley*
Bing Crosby, *The Road to Zanzibar* and *Birth of the Blues*
George Coulouris, *Citizen Kane*

Patricia Collinge, *The Little Foxes*
Bette Davis, *The Little Foxes*
Isobel Elsom, *Ladies in Retirement*
Joan Fontaine, *Suspicion*
Greta Garbo, *Two-Faced Woman*
James Gleason, *Meet John Doe* and *Here Comes Mr. Jordan*
Walter Huston, *All That Money Can Buy*
Ida Lupino, *High Sierra* and *Ladies in Retirement*
Roddy McDowall, *How Green Was My Valley*
Robert Montgomery, *Rage in Heaven* and *Here Comes Mr. Jordan*
Ginger Rogers, *Kitty Foyle* and *Tom, Dick and Harry*
James Stephenson, *The Letter* and *Shining Victory*
Orson Welles, *Citizen Kane*
1942 Ernest Anderson, *In This Our Life*
Florence Bates, *The Moon and Sixpence*
James Cagney, *Yankee Doodle Dandy*
Charles Coburn, *H.M. Pulham, Esq.*, *In This Our Life* and *Kings Row*
Jack Carson, *The Male Animal*
Greer Garson, *Mrs. Miniver* and *Random Harvest*
Sidney Greenstreet, *Across the Pacific*
William Holden, *The Remarkable Andrew*
Tim Holt, *The Magnificent Ambersons*
Glynis Johns, *The Invaders*
Gene Kelly, *For Me and My Gal*
Diana Lynn, *The Major and the Minor*
Ida Lupino, *Moontide*
Bernard Miles, *In Which We Serve*
John Mills, *In Which We Serve*
Agnes Moorehead, *The Magnificent Ambersons*
Hattie McDaniel, *In This Our Life*
Thomas Mitchell, *Moontide*
Margaret O'Brien, *Journey for Margaret*
Susan Peters, *Random Harvest*
Edward G. Robinson, *Tales of Manhattan*
Ginger Rogers, *Roxy Hart* and *The Major and the Minor*
George Sanders, *The Moon and Sixpence*
Ann Sheridan, *Kings Row*
William Severn, *Journey for Margaret*
Rudy Vallee, *The Palm Beach Story*
Anton Walbrook, *The Invaders*
Googie Withers, *One of Our Aircraft is Missing*
Monty Woolley, *The Pied Piper*
Teresa Wright, *Mrs. Miniver*
Robert Young, *H.M. Pulham, Esq.*, *Joe Smith American* and *Journey for Margaret*
1943 Gracie Fields, *Holy Matrimony*
Katina Paxinou, *For Whom the Bell Tolls*
Teresa Wright, *Shadow of a Doubt*
Paul Lukas, *Watch on the Rhine*
Henry Morgan, *The Ox-Bow Incident* and *Happy Land*
Cedric Hardwicke, *The Moon is Down* and *The Cross of Lorraine*
1944 Ethel Barrymore, *None But the Lonely Heart*
Ingrid Bergman, *Gaslight*
Eddie Bracken, *Hail the Conquering Hero*
Humphrey Bogart, *To Have and Have Not*
Bing Crosby, *Going My Way*
June Duprez, *None But the Lonely Heart*
Barry Fitzgerald, *Going My Way*
Betty Hutton, *The Miracle of Morgan's Creek*
Jennifer Jones, *The Song of Bernadette*
Margaret O'Brien, *Meet Me in St. Louis*
Franklin Pangborn, *Hail the Conquering Hero*

BEST ACTRESS
1945 Joan Crawford, *Mildred Pierce*

1946 Anna Magnani, *Open City*
1947 Celia Johnson, *This Happy Breed*
1948 Olivia de Havilland, *The Snake Pit*
1949 None cited
1950 Gloria Swanson, *Sunset Boulevard*
1951 Jan Sterling, *The Big Carnival*
1952 Shirley Booth, *Come Back, Little Sheba*
1953 Jean Simmons, *Young Bess, The Robe* and *The Actress*
1954 Grace Kelly, *The Country Girl*
1955 Anna Magnani, *The Rose Tattoo*
1956 Dorothy McGuire, *Friendly Persuasion*
1957 Joanne Woodward, *The Three Faces of Eve* and *No Down Payment*
1958 Ingrid Bergman, *The Inn of the Sixth Happiness*
1959 Simone Signoret, *Room at the Top*
1960 Greer Garson, *Sunrise at Campobello*
1961 Geraldine Page, *Summer and Smoke*
1962 Anne Bancroft, *The Miracle Worker*
1963 Patricia Neal, *Hud*
1964 Kim Stanley, *Seance on a Wet Afternoon*
1965 Julie Christie, *Darling* and *Doctor Zhivago*
1966 Elizabeth Taylor, *Who's Afraid of Virginia Woolf?*
1967 Edith Evans, *The Whisperers*
1968 Liv Ullmann, *Hour of the Wolf* and *Shame*
1969 Geraldine Page, *Trilogy*
1970 Glenda Jackson, *Women in Love*
1971 Irene Pappas, *The Trojan Women*
1972 Cicely Tyson, *Sounder*
1973 Liv Ullmann, *The New Land*
1974 Gena Rowlands, *A Woman Under the Influence*
1975 Isabelle Adjani, *The Story of Adele H*
1976 Liv Ullmann, *Face to Face*
1977 Anne Bancroft, *The Turning Point*

BEST ACTOR

1945 Ray Milland, *The Lost Weekend*
1946 Laurence Olivier, *Henry V*
1947 Michael Redgrave, *Mourning Becomes Elektra*
1948 Walter Huston, *The Treasure of the Sierra Madre*
1949 Ralph Richardson, *The Heiress* and *The Fallen Idol*
1950 Alec Guinness, *Kind Hearts and Coronets*
1951 Richard Basehart, *Fourteen Hours*
1952 Ralph Richardson, *Breaking the Sound Barrier*
1953 James Mason, *Face to Face, Desert Rats, The Man Between* and *Julius Caesar*
1954 Bing Crosby, *The Country Girl*
1955 Ernest Borgnine, *Marty*
1956 Yul Brynner, *The King and I, Anastasia* and *The Ten Commandments*
1957 Alec Guinness, *The Bridge on the River Kwai*
1958 Spencer Tracy, *The Old Man and the Sea* and *The Last Hurrah*
1959 Victor Seastrom, *Wild Strawberries*
1960 Robert Mitchum, *Home from the Hill* and *The Sundowners*
1961 Albert Finney, *Saturday Night and Sunday Morning*
1962 Jason Robards, Jr., *Long Day's Journey Into Night*
1963 Rex Harrison, *Cleopatra*
1964 Anthony Quinn, *Zorba the Greek*
1965 Lee Marvin, *Cat Ballou* and *Ship of Fools*
1966 Paul Scofield, *A Man for All Seasons*
1967 Peter Finch, *Far From the Madding Crowd*
1968 Cliff Robertson, *Charly*
1969 Peter O'Toole, *Goodbye, Mr. Chips*
1970 George C. Scott, *Patton*
1971 Gene Hackman, *The French Connection*
1972 Peter O'Toole, *The Ruling Class* and *Man of La Mancha*
1973 Al Pacino, *Serpico*
       Robert Ryan, *The Iceman Cometh*
1974 Gene Hackman, *The Conversation*

1975 Jack Nicholson, *One Flew Over the Cuckoo's Nest*
1976 David Carradine, *Bound For Glory*
1977 John Travolta, *Saturday Night Fever*

BEST SUPPORTING ACTRESS

1954 Nina Foch, *Executive Suite*
1955 Marjorie Rambeau, *A Man Called Peter* and *The View from Pompey's Head*
1956 Debbie Reynolds, *The Catered Affair*
1957 Dame Sybil Thorndyke, *The Prince and the Showgirl*
1958 Kay Walsh, *The Horse's Mouth*
1959 Dame Edith Evans, *The Nun's Story*
1960 Shirley Jones, *Elmer Gantry*
1961 Ruby Dee, *A Raisin in the Sun*
1962 Angela Lansbury, *The Manchurian Candidate* and *All Fall Down*
1963 Margaret Rutherford, *The V.I.P.s*
1964 Dame Edith Evans, *The Chalk Garden*
1965 Joan Blondell, *The Cincinnati Kid*
1966 Vivien Merchant, *Alfie*
1967 Marjorie Rhondes, *The Family Way*
1968 Virginia Maskell, *Interlude*
1969 Pamela Franklin, *The Prime of Miss Jean Brodie*
1970 Karen Black, *Five Easy Pieces*
1971 Cloris Leachman, *The Last Picture Show*
1972 Marisa Berenson, *Cabaret*
1973 Sylvia Sidney, *Summer Wishes, Winter Dreams*
1974 Valerie Perrine, *Lenny*
1975 Ronee Blakely, *Nashville*
1976 Talia Shire, *Rocky*
1977 Diane Keaton, *Annie Hall*

BEST SUPPORTING ACTOR

1954 John Williams, *Sabrina* and *Dial M for Murder*
1955 Charles Bickford, *Not as a Stranger*
1956 Richard Basehart, *Moby Dick*
1957 Sessue Hayakawa, *The Bridge on the River Kwai*
1958 Albert Salmi, *The Brothers Karamazov* and *The Bravados*
1959 Hugh Griffith, *Ben-Hur*
1960 George Peppard, *Home from the Hill*
1961 Jackie Gleason, *The Hustler*
1962 Burgess Meredith, *Advise and Consent*
1963 Melvyn Douglas, *Hud*
1964 Martin Balsam, *The Carpetbaggers*
1965 Harry Andrews, *The Agony and the Ecstasy* and *The Hill*
1966 Robert Shaw, *A Man for All Seasons*
1967 Paul Ford, *The Comedians*
1968 Leo McKern, *The Shoes of the Fisherman*
1969 Philippe Noiret, *Topaz*
1970 Frank Langella, *Diary of a Mad Housewife* and *The Twelve Chairs*
1971 Ben Johnson, *The Last Picture Show*
1972 Al Pacino, *The Godfather*
       Joel Grey, *Cabaret*
1973 John Houseman, *Paper Chase*
1974 Holger Lowenadler, *Lacombe, Lucien*
1975 Charles Durning, *Dog Day Afternoon*
1976 Jason Robards, *All the President's Men*
1977 Tom Skerritt, *The Turning Point*

BEST DIRECTION

1943 William Wellman, *The Ox-Bow Incident*
       Tay Garnett, *Bataan* and *The Cross of Lorraine*
       Michael Curtiz, *Casablanca* and *This Is the Army*
1944 No citation
1945 Jean Renoir, *The Southerner*
1946 William Wyler, *The Best Years of Our Lives*
1947 Elia Kazan, *Boomerang!* and *Gentleman's Agreement*

1948 Roberto Rossellini, *Paisan*
1949 Vittorio de Sica, *The Bicycle Thief*
1950 John Huston, *The Asphalt Jungle*
1951 Akira Kurosawa, *Rashomon*
1952 David Lean, *Breaking the Sound Barrier*
1953 George Stevens, *Shane*
1954 Renato Castellani, *Romeo and Juliet*
1955 William Wyler, *The Desparate Hours*
1956 John Huston, *Moby Dick*
1957 David Lean, *The Bridge on the River Kwai*
1958 John Ford, *The Last Hurrah*
1959 Fred Zinnemann, *The Nun's Story*
1960 Jack Cardiff, *Sons and Lovers*
1961 Jack Clayton, *The Innocents*
1962 David Lean, *Lawrence of Arabia*
1963 Tony Richardson, *Tom Jones*
1964 Desmond Davies, *Girl With Green Eyes*
1965 John Schlesinger, *Darling*
1966 Fred Zinnemann, *A Man For All Seasons*
1967 Richard Brooks, *In Cold Blood*
1968 Franco Zeffirelli, *Romeo and Juliet*
1969 Alfred Hitchcock, *Topaz*
1970 Francois Truffaut, *The Wild Child*
1971 Ken Russell, *The Devils* and *The Boy Friend*
1972 Bob Fosse, *Cabaret*
1973 Ingmar Bergman, *Cries and Whispers*
1974 Francis Ford Coppola, *The Conversation*
1975 Stanley Kubrick, *Barry Lyndon*
     Robert Altman, *Nashville*
1976 Alan Pakula, *All the President's Men*
1977 Luis Bunuel, *That Obscure Object of Desire*

BEST SCRIPT

1948 John Huston, *Treasure of Sierra Madre*
1949 Graham Greene, *The Fallen Idol*
1950 None cited
1951 T.E.B. Clarke, *The Lavender Hill Mob*

SPECIAL CITATIONS

1954 Michael Kidd, Choreography for *Seven Brides for Seven Brothers*
     Machiko Kyo, Modernization of traditional acting in *Gate of Hell* and *Ugetsu*
     Puppetry, *Hansel and Gretel*
1955 Aerial Photography, *Strategic Air Command*
1957 Photographic innovations, *Funny Face*
1958 Robert Donat, Valor of his last performance in *The Inn of the Sixth Happiness*
1959 Ingmar Bergman, Body of work
     Andrew Marton and Yakima Canutt, Direction of the chariot race in *Ben-Hur*
1974 Robert G. Youngson, Pioneer work in compilation films, notably *The Golden Age of Comedy* and *When Comedy Was King*
     Special effects department of 20th Century Fox and Warner Brothers, *The Towering Inferno*
     Special effects department of Universal Pictures, *Earthquake*
     Ray Harryhausen, For special effect in *The Golden Voyage of Sinbad*
1977 Walt Disney Studios, for animation, *The Rescuers*
     Close Encounters of the Third Kind

Interreligious Film Awards

NATIONAL COUNCIL OF THE CHURCHES OF CHRIST
475 Riverside Dr., New York, N.Y. 10027 (212/870-2567)

Until 1971, annual Interreligious Film Awards were made to honor meritorious films released to the public. The selections were made by the broadcasting and film commission of the Council, the Committee on Films of the Synagogue Council of America and the Division for Film and Broadcasting of the U.S. Catholic Conference. Although the Council has discontinued the awards, it issues a film newsletter citing noteworthy cinematic achievements.

1965 *Darling*
     The Eleanor Roosevelt Story
     Juliet of the Spirits
     Nobody Waved Goodbye
     Nothing But A Man
     A Patch of Blue
     The Pawnbroker
     The Sound of Music
     World Without Sun
1966 *And Now Miguel*
     Born Free
     Georgy Girl
     The Gospel According to St. Matthew
     A Man for All Seasons
     The Russians Are Coming
     The Sand Pebbles
     The Shop on Main Street
     Who's Afraid of Virginia Woolf?
1967 *The Battle of Algiers*
     Bonnie and Clyde
     Elvira Madigan
     In Cold Blood
     In the Heat of the Night
     Up the Down Staircase
     The War Game
     The Whisperers
1968 *Faces*
     The Heart Is A Lonely Hunter
     Nazarin
     Oliver
     Rachel, Rachel
     2001: A Space Odyssey
     Yellow Submarine
1969 *Oh! What A Lovely War*
     The Reivers
     Z
1970 *I Never Sang for My Father*
     Kes
     My Night at Maud's
     The Wild Child
1971 *Fiddler on the Roof*
     One Day in the Life of Ivan Denisovich
     The Garden of the Finzi-Continis

SPECIAL AWARDS

1965 Universal Pictures, Inc.
1966 Buena Vista Distributing Co., Inc.
1969 Robert Radnitz
1970 John Korty
1971 Corp. for Public Broadcasting

New York Film Critics Circle Awards

NEW YORK FILM CRITICS CIRCLE
c/o William Wolf, *Cue* Magazine, 545 Madison Ave., New York, N.Y. 10022 (212/371-6900)

The New York Film Critics Circle Awards are presented annually for excellence in the creation and performance of films released commercially during the calendar year. Members of the Circle select the winners, who are presented with plaques.

BEST PICTURE

1935   *The Informer*
1936   *Mr. Deeds Goes to Town*
1937   *The Life of Emile Zola*
1938   *The Citadel*
1939   *Wuthering Heights*
1940   *The Grapes of Wrath*
1941   *Citizen Kane*
1942   *In Which We Serve*
1943   *Watch on the Rhine*
1944   *Going My Way*
1945   *The Lost Weekend*
1946   *The Best Years of Our Lives*
1947   *Gentleman's Agreement*
1948   *Treasure of Sierra Madre*
1949   *All the King's Men*
1950   *All About Eve*
1951   *A Streetcar Named Desire*
1952   *High Noon*
1953   *From Here to Eternity*
1954   *On the Waterfront*
1955   *Marty*
1956   *Around the World in 80 Days*
1957   *The Bridge on the River Kwai*
1958   *The Defiant Ones*
1959   *Ben-Hur*
1960   *The Apartment*
       Sons and Lovers
1961   *West Side Story*
1962   No award
1963   *Tom Jones*
1964   *My Fair Lady*
1965   *Darling*
1966   *A Man for All Seasons*
1967   *In the Heat of the Night*
1968   *The Lion in Winter*
1969   *Z*
1970   *Five Easy Pieces*
1971   *A Clockwork Orange*
1972   *Cries and Whispers*
1973   *Day for Night*
1974   *Amarcord*
1975   *Nashville*
1976   *All the President's Men*
1977   *Annie Hall*

BEST ACTOR

1935   Charles Laughton, *Mutiny on the Bounty* and *Ruggles of Red Gap*
1936   Walter Huston, *Dodsworth*
1937   Paul Muni, *The Life of Emile Zola*
1938   James Cagney, *Angels With Dirty Faces*
1939   James Stewart, *Mr. Smith Goes to Washington*
1940   Charles Chaplin, *The Great Dictator*
1941   Gary Cooper, *Sergeant York*
1942   James Cagney, *Yankee Doodle Dandy*
1943   Paul Lukas, *Watch on the Rhine*
1944   Barry Fitzgerald, *Going My Way*
1945   Ray Milland, *The Lost Weekend*
1946   Laurence Olivier, *Henry V*
1947   William Powell, *Life with Father* and *The Senator was Indiscreet*
1948   Laurence Olivier, *Hamlet*
1949   Broderick Crawford, *All the King's Men*
1950   Gregory Peck, *Twelve O'Clock High*
1951   Arthur Kennedy, *Bright Victory*
1952   Ralph Richardson, *Breaking the Sound Barrier*

1953   Burt Lancaster, *From Here to Eternity*
1954   Marlon Brando, *On the Waterfront*
1955   Ernest Borgnine, *Marty*
1956   Kirk Douglas, *Lust for Life*
1957   Alec Guinness, *The Bridge on the River Kwai*
1958   David Niven, *Separate Tables*
1959   James Stewart, *Anatomy of a Murder*
1960   Burt Lancaster, *Elmer Gantry*
1961   Maximilian Schell, *Judgment at Nuremberg*
1962   No award
1963   Albert Finney, *Tom Jones*
1964   Rex Harrison, *My Fair Lady*
1965   Oskar Werner, *Ship of Fools*
1966   Paul Scofield, *A Man for All Seasons*
1967   Rod Steiger, *In the Heat of the Night*
1968   Alan Arkin, *The Heart is a Lonely Hunter*
1969   Jon Voight, *Midnight Cowboy*
1970   George C. Scott, *Patton*
1971   Gene Hackman, *French Connection*
1972   Laurence Olivier, *Sleuth*
1973   Marlon Brando, *The Godfather*
1974   Jack Nicholson, *Chinatown*
1975   Jack Nicholson, *One Flew Over the Cuckoo's Nest*
1976   Robert De Niro, *Taxi Driver*
1977   Sir John Geilgud, *Providence*

BEST ACTRESS

1935   Greta Garbo, *Anna Karenina*
1936   Luise Rainer, *The Great Ziegfeld*
1937   Greta Garbo, *Camille*
1938   Margaret Sullavan, *Three Comrades*
1939   Vivien Leigh, *Gone With the Wind*
1940   Katharine Hepburn, *The Philadelphia Story*
1941   Joan Fontaine, *Suspicion*
1942   Agnes Moorehead, *The Magnificent Ambersons*
1943   Ida Lupino, *The Hard Way*
1944   Tallulah Bankhead, *Lifeboat*
1945   Ingrid Bergman, *Spellbound* and *The Bells of St. Mary's*
1946   Celia Johnson, *Brief Encounter*
1947   Deborah Kerr, *Black Narcissus* and *The Adventuress*
1948   Olivia de Havilland, *The Snake Pit*
1949   Olivia de Havilland, *The Heiress*
1950   Bette Davis, *All About Eve*
1951   Vivien Leigh, *A Streetcar Named Desire*
1952   Shirley Booth, *Come Back, Little Sheba*
1953   Audrey Hepburn, *Roman Holiday*
1954   Grace Kelly, *The Country Girl, Rear Window* and *Dial M for Murder*
1955   Anna Magnani, *The Rose Tattoo*
1956   Ingrid Bergman, *Anastasia*
1957   Deborah Kerr, *Heaven Knows, Mr. Allison*
1958   Susan Hayward, *I Want to Live!*
1959   Audrey Hepburn, *The Nun's Story*
1960   Deborah Kerr, *The Sundowners*
1961   Sophia Loren, *Two Women*
1962   No award
1963   Patricia Neal, *Hud*
1964   Kim Stanley, *Seance on a Wet Afternnon*
1965   Julie Christie, *Darling*
1966   Elizabeth Taylor, *Who's Afraid of Virginia Woolf?*
       Lynn Redgrave, *Georgy Girl*
1967   Dame Edith Evans, *The Whisperers*
1968   Joanne Woodward, *Rachel, Rachel*
1969   Jane Fonda, *They Shoot Horses, Don't They?*
1970   Glenda Jackson, *Women in Love*
1971   Jane Fonda, *Klute*
1972   Liv Ullmann, *Cries and Whispers*
1973   Joanne Woodward, *Summer Wishes, Winter Dreams*
1974   Liv Ullmann, *Scenes from a Marriage*
1975   Isabelle Adjani, *The Story of Adele H*

1976 Liv Ullmann, *Face to Face*
1977 Diane Keaton, *Annie Hall*

BEST DIRECTION

1935 John Ford, *The Informer*
1936 Rouben Mamoulian, *The Gay Desperado*
1937 Gregory La Cava, *Stage Door*
1938 Alfred Hitchcock, *The Lady Vanishes*
1939 John Ford, *Stagecoach*
1940 John Ford, *The Grapes of Wrath* and *The Long Voyage Home*
1941 John Ford, *How Green Was My Valley*
1942 John Farrow, *Wake Island*
1943 George Stevens, *The More the Merrier*
1944 Leo McCarey, *Going My Way*
1945 Billy Wilder, *The Lost Weekend*
1946 William Wyler, *The Best Years of Our Lives*
1947 Elia Kazan, *Gentleman's Agreement* and *Boomerang*
1948 John Huston, *Treasure of Sierra Madre*
1949 Carol Reed, *The Fallen Idol*
1950 Joseph L. Mankiewicz, *All About Eve*
1951 Elia Kazan, *A Streetcar Named Desire*
1952 Fred Zinnemann, *High Noon*
1953 Fred Zinnemann, *From Here to Eternity*
1954 Elia Kazan, *On the Waterfront*
1955 David Lean, *Summertime*
1956 John Huston, *Moby Dick*
1957 David Lean, *The Bridge on the River Kwai*
1958 Stanley Kramer, *The Defiant Ones*
1959 Fred Zinnemann, *The Nun's Story*
1960 Billy Wilder, *The Apartment*
     Jack Cardiff, *Sons and Lovers*
1961 Robert Rossen, *The Hustler*
1962 No award
1963 Tony Richardson, *Tom Jones*
1964 Stanley Kubrick, *Dr. Strangelove*
1965 John Schlesinger, *Darling*
1966 Fred Zinnemann, *A Man for All Seasons*
1967 Mike Nichols, *The Graduate*
1968 Paul Newman, *Rachel, Rachel*
1969 Costa-Gavras, *Z*
1970 Bob Rafelson, *Five Easy Pieces*
1971 Stanley Kubrick, *A Clockwork Orange*
1972 Ingmar Bergman, *Cries and Whispers*
1973 Francois Truffaut, *Day for Night*
1974 Federico Fellini, *Amarcord*
1975 Robert Altman, *Nashville*
1976 Alan J. Pakula, *All the President's Men*
1977 Woody Allen, *Annie Hall*

BEST FOREIGN-LANGUAGE FILM

1936 *La Kermesse Heroique* (French)
1937 *Mayerling* (French)
1938 *Grande Illusion* (French)
1939 *Harvest* (French)
1940 *The Baker's Wife* (French)
1941 No award
1946 *Open City* (Italian)
1947 *To Live in Peace* (Italian)
1948 *Paisan* (Italian)
1949 *The Bicycle Thief* (Italian)
1950 *Ways of Love* (Franco-Italian)
1951 *Miracle in Milan* (Italian)
1952 *Forbidden Games* (French)
1953 *Justice Is Done* (French)
1954 *Gate of Hell* (Japanese)
1955 *Diabolique* (French)
     Umberto D. (Italian)
1956 *La Strada* (Italian)
1957 *Gervaise* (French)

1958 *Mon Oncle* (French)
1959 *The 400 Blows* (French)
1960 *Hiroshima, Mon Amour* (French)
1961 *La Dolce Vita* (Italian)
1962 No award
1963 *8½* (Italian)
1964 *That Man From Rio* (French)
1965 *Juliet of the Spirits* (Italian)
1966 *The Shop on Main Street* (Czech)
1967 *La Guerre est Finie* (French)
1968 *War and Peace* (Russian)

SCREENPLAY WRITING

1958 Nathan E. Douglas and Harold J. Smith, *The Defiant Ones*
1959 Wendell Mayes, *Anatomy of a Murder*
1960 Billy Wilder and I.A.L. Diamond, *The Apartment*
1961 Abby Mann, *Judgment at Nuremberg*
1962 No award
1963 Irving Ravetch and Harriet Frank, Jr., *Hud*
1964 Harold Pinter, *The Servant*
1965 No award
1966 Robert Bolt, *A Man for All Seasons*
1967 David Newman and Robert Benton, *Bonnie and Clyde*
1968 Lorenzo Semple, Jr., *Pretty Poison*
1969 Paul Mazursky and Larry Tucker, *Bob & Carol & Ted & Alice*
1970 Eric Rohmer, *Ma Nuit Chez Maude*
1971 Penelope Gilliatt, *Sunday Bloody Sunday*
     Larry McMurtry and Peter Bogdanovich, *The Last Picture Show*
1972 Ingmar Bergman, *Cries and Whispers*
1973 George Lucas, Gloria Katz and Willard Huyck, *American Graffiti*
1974 Ingmar Bergman, *Scenes from a Marriage*
1975 Francois Truffaut, Jean Gruault and Suzanne Schiffman, *The Story of Adele H*
1976 Paddy Chayefsky, *Network*
1977 Woody Allen and Marshall Brickman, *Annie Hall*

BEST SUPPORTING ACTOR

1972 Robert Duvall, *The Godfather*
1973 Robert De Niro, *Mean Streets*
1974 Charles Boyer, *Stavisky*
1975 Alan Arkin, *Hearts of the West*
1976 Jason Robards, *All the President's Men*
1977 Maximilian Schell, *Julia*

BEST SUPPORTING ACTRESS

1972 Jeannie Berlin, *The Heartbreak Kid*
1973 Valentina Cortese, *Day for Night*
1974 Valerie Perrine, *Lenny*
1975 Lily Tomlin, *Nashville*
1976 Talia Shire, *Rocky*
1977 Sissy Spacek, *Three Women*

SPECIAL AWARDS

1964 *To Be Alive,* New York World's Fair (Johnson Wax pavilion)
1972 *The Sorrow and the Pity* (French documentary)

Patsy Award
AMERICAN HUMANE ASSOCIATION
5351 S. Roslyn, Engelwood, Colo. 80110 (303/779-1400)

The Patsy Award, which consists of a trophy, is presented annually for outstanding film appearances by animals. The Humane Association receives nominations from producers and directors, its own field officers and animal trainers. A Patsy Committee narrows these to a field of nominees for selection by a blue-ribbon panel of prominent people. (see pp. 146-147 for television Patsy Awards.)

1951 **Francis** (talking mule), *Francis*
California (Palomino horse), *The Palomino*
Pierre (chimpanzee), *My Friend Irma Goes West*
1952 **Rhubarb** (cat), *Rhubarb*
Francis (talking mule), *Francis Goes to the Races*
Cheta (chimpanzee), *Tarzan's Peril*
1953 **Jackie** (African lion), *Fearless Fagin*
Bonzo (chimpanzee), *Bonzo Goes to College*
Trigger (horse), *Son of Paleface*
1954 **Laddie** (collie), *Hondo*
Francis (talking mule), *Francis Covers the Big Town*
Jackie (African lion), *Androcles and the Lion*
1955 **Gypsy** (black stallion), *Gypsy Colt*
Francis (talking mule), *Francis Joins the WACS*
Esmeralda (seal), *20,000 Leagues Under the Sea*
1956 **Wildfire** (bull terrier), *It's a Dog's Life*
Francis (talking mule), *Francis Joins the Navy*
Faro (dog), *The Kentuckian*
1957 **Samantha** (goose), *Friendly Persuasion*
War Winds (black stallion), *Giant*
Francis (talking mule), *Francis in the Haunted House*
1958 **Spike** (dog), *Old Yeller*
Beauty (horse), *Wild is the Wind*
Kelly (dog), *Kelly and Me*
1959 **Pyewacket** (cat), *Bell, Book and Candle*
Tonka (horse), *Tonka*
Harry (hare), *Geisha Boy*
1960 **Shaggy** (old English sheepdog), *The Shaggy Dog*
Herman (pigeon), *The Gazebo*
North Wind (horse), *The Sad Horse*
1961 **Cotton** (horse), *Pepe*
Spike (dog), *A Dog of Flanders*
Mr. Stubbs (chimpanzee), *Visit to a Small Planet*
Skip (N.A.), *Visit to a Small Planet*
1962 **Cat** (cat), *Breakfast at Tiffany's*
Pete (dog), *The Silent Call*
Flame (horse), *The Clown and the Kid*
1963 **Big Red** (dog), *Big Red*
Sydney (elephant), *Jumbo*
Zamba (Afican lion), *The Lion*
1964 **Tom Dooley** (dog), *Savage Sam*
Pluto (dog), *My Six Loves*
Raunchy (jaguar), *Rampage*
1965 **Patrina** (tiger), *A Tiger Walks*
Storm (dog), *Goodbye Charlie*
Junior (dog), *Island of the Blue Dolphins*
1966 **Syn** (siamese cat), *That Darn Cat*
Clarence (African lion), *Clarence, the Cross-Eyed Lion*
Judy (chimpanzee), *The Monkey's Uncle*
1967 **Elsa** (African lioness), *Born Free*
Duke (dog), *The Ugly Dachshund*
Vindicator (bull), *The Rare Breed*
1968 **Gentle Ben** (bear), *Gentle Giant*
Sir Tom (mountain lion), *The Cat*
Sophie (sea lion), *Dr. Doolittle*
1969 **Albarado** (horse), *Horse in the Gray Flannel Suit*
1970 **Rascal** (raccoon), *Rascal*
1971 **Sancho** (wolf), *The Wild Country*
1972 **Ben** (rat), *Willard*
1973 **Ben** (rat), *Ben*
1974 **Alpha** (dolphin), *The Day of the Dolphin*
1975 **Tonto** (cat), *Harry and Tonto*
1976 **Valentine** (camel), *Hawmps*
Five dobermans (dogs), *The Amazing Dobermans*

Gus (dog), *Won Ton Ton, The Dog Who Saved Hollywood*
Gus (mule), *Gus*
Shoshone (horse), *Mustang Country*
Ollie (dog), *The Shaggy D.A.*
Bandit (raccoon), *Guardian of the Wilderness*
Bruno (bear), *Guardian of the Wilderness*
1977 **Not available at press time**

Gold Medal Awards
PHOTOPLAY
205 E. 42nd St., New York, N.Y. 10017 (212/983-5600)

The *Photoplay* Gold Medal Awards are made for popular motion pictures, performers and occasionally for individuals' special achievements in the entertainment industry. The most recent awards were based on ballots of more than 60,000 readers of the magazine. (*Photoplay* also gives other awards for popular entertainment personalities, which can be found on pp. 153-154, 170.)

FILMS

1920 *Humoresque*
1921 *Tol'Able David*
1922 *Robin Hood*
1923 *Covered Wagon*
1924 *Abraham Lincoln*
1925 *The Big Parade*
1926 *Beau Geste*
1927 *Seventh Heaven*
1928 *Four Sons*
1929 *Disraeli*
1930 *All Quiet On The Western Front*
1931 *Cimarron*
1932 *Smilin' Through*
1933 *Little Women*
1934 *Barretts of Wimpole Street*
1935 *Naughty Marietta*
1936 *San Francisco*
1937 *Captains Courageous*
1938 *Sweethearts*
1939 *Gone With the Wind*
1940 No award
1941 No award
1942 No award
1943 No award
1944 *Going My Way*
1945 *The Valley of Decision*
1946 *The Bells of St. Mary's*
1947 *The Jolson Story*
1948 *Sitting Pretty*
1949 *The Stratton Story*
1950 *Battleground*
1951 *Showboat*
1952 *With A Song In My Heart*
1953 *From Here to Eternity*
1954 *Magnificent Obsession*
1955 *Love Is A Many-Splendored Thing*
1956 *Giant*
1957 *An Affair to Remember*
1958 *Gigi*
1959 *Pillow Talk*
1960 No award
1961 *Splendor in the Grass*
1962 *The Miracle Worker*
1963 *How the West Was Won*
1964 *The Unsinkable Molly Brown*
1965 *The Sound of Music*

1966 *The Russians Are Coming, The Russians Are Coming*
1967 *The Dirty Dozen*
1968 *Rosemary's Baby*
1969 *True Grit*
1970 *Love Story*
1971 *Summer of '42*
1972 *The Godfather*
1973 *Walking Tall*
1974 *Towering Inferno*
1975 *Jaws*
1976 *Gone With the Wind* (Voted all-time favorite movie)
      A Star Is Born
1977 Not available at press time

ACTOR

1944 Bing Crosby
1945 Bing Crosby
1946 Bing Crosby
1947 Bing Crosby
1948 Bing Crosby
1949 James Stewart
1950 John Wayne
1951 Mario Lanza
1952 Gary Cooper
1953 Burt Lancaster
      Frank Sinatra
1954 William Holden
1955 William Holden
1956 Rock Hudson
1957 Rock Hudson
1958 Tony Curtis
1959 Rock Hudson
1960 No award
1961 Troy Donahue
1962 Richard Chamberlain
1963 Richard Chamberlain
1964 Richard Chamberlain
1965 Robert Vaughn
1966 David Janssen
1967 Paul Newman
1968 Steve McQueen
1969 John Wayne
1970 Ryan O'Neal
1971 John Wayne
1972 Chad Everett
1973 Burt Reynolds
1974 Robert Redford
1975 Robert Redford
1976 John Wayne (Voted All-time favorite star)
1977 Not available at press time

ACTRESS

1944 Greer Garson
1945 Greer Garson
1946 Ingrid Bergman
1947 Ingrid Bergman
1948 Ingrid Bergman
1949 Jane Wyman
1950 Betty Hutton
1951 Doris Day
1952 Susan Hayward
1953 Deborah Kerr
1954 June Allyson
1955 Jennifer Jones
1956 Kim Novak
1957 Deborah Kerr
1958 Debbie Reynolds
1959 Doris Day
1960 No award

1961 Connie Stevens
1962 Bette Davis
1963 Connie Stevens
1964 Ann-Margret
1965 Dorothy Malone
1966 Barbara Stanwyck
1967 Barbara Stanwyck
1968 Diahann Carroll
1969 Marlo Thomas
1970 Ali MacGraw
1971 Ann-Margret
1972 Ann-Margret
1973 Elizabeth Taylor
1974 Valerie Harper
1975 Angie Dickinson
1976 Barbra Streisand
1977 Not available at press time

SPECIAL AWARD (Citation)

1952 **Marilyn Monroe,** For "her sensational rise to stardom"
      Dean Martin and Jerry Lewis, "As a team whose pictures are constant winners at the box office"
      William Goetz, Universal International, "For his efforts in the development of new talents in the fields of acting, writing and directing"
1954 **Y. Frank Freeman** (Paramount), "Magnificent contribution to motion pictures with the introduction . . . of Vistavision"
      Otto Preminger, "For giving the film-going public a rare treat of translating the classic film of the opera *Carmen* into a distinguished American movie, *Carmen Jones*"
      Van Johnson, Who "emerged during 1954 as an actor of real scope and force"
1955 **Columbia,** For "a delightful screen reflection of Americana in *Picnic*"
      James Dean, "Outstanding dramatic appearances"
      Glenn Ford and Eleanor Powell Ford, "For their magnificent contributions to the establishment of better relationships among boys and girls of their community"
      Otto Preminger, "For his courage and great talent [in producing] *The Man With the Golden Arm*"
1956 **Cecil B. DeMille,** "For the creation of one of the screen's greatest emotional and religious experiences, *The Ten Commandments*"
      Barbara Stanwyck, "For meeting with simplicity, honesty and superb craftsmanship the challenges of leading roles in 75 films"
      Michael Todd, For the development of Todd-AO
1957 No award
1958 **Maurice Chevalier,** Year's Best Foreign Star
      David Ladd, Youngest Hit

SPECIAL EDITOR'S AWARD

1964 Bob Hope (Public Service Award)
1965 John Wayne
1966 Ginger Rogers
1967 Bob Hope
      Joey Bishop
      Glenn Ford
1968 James Stewart
1969 Danny Thomas
1970 Debbie Reynolds
1971 Johnny Carson
1972 Elvis Presley
1973 Andy Williams
1977 Alfred Hitchcock
      Joan Crawford (tribute)

Grand Prize

SAN REMO FILM FESTIVAL

Rotonda dei Mille, 24100 Bergamo, Italy (Tel: 243.566 or 243.162)

The Grand Prize of the San Remo Film Festival is given annually to the author of the best 16mm or 35mm prior to its release. A jury selects the winner on the basis of cultural and artistic considerations. The Grand Prize winner receives a cash award of 5,000,000 lire. The list below indicates the winners beginning with the Ninth Annual San Remo Film Festival; earlier winners are not available.

1966 *Bariera,* Poland (Jerzy Skolimowski, director)
1967 *Sedmikrasky,* Czechoslovakia (Vera Chytilova)
1968 *O Slavnosti a Hostech,* Czechoslovakia (Jan Nemec)
1969 No award
1970 *Valerie a Tyden Divu,* Czechoslovakia (Jaromil Jires)
1971 *Sho o Suteyo, Machi e Deyo,* Japan (Shuji Terayama)
  Za Sciana, Poland (Kryzysztof Zanussi)
1972 *Pilvilinna,* Finland (Sakari Rimmiwen)
1973 *Laukaus Tehtaalla,* Finland (Erkko Kivikoski)
1974 *Harmadik Nekifutas,* Hungary (Peter Bacso)
  Molba, U.S.S.R. (Tenghis Abuladse)
1975 *Takiji Kobayashi,* Japan (Tadashi Imai)
1976 *Zofia,* Poland (Ryszard Czekala)
1977 *The Naked Civil Servant,* Great Britain (Jack Gold)
  La Vocation Suspendue, France (Paul Ruiz)

Valentine Davies Award

WRITERS GUILD OF AMERICA, WEST

8955 Beverly Blvd., Los Angeles, Calif. 90048 (213/550-1000)

The Valentine Davies Award honors contributions to the motion picture community through the work and achievements of a professional writer. A silver medallion is presented to the winner.

1962 Mary McCall, Jr.
1963 Allen Rivkin
1964 Morgan Cox
1965 James R. Webb
1966 Leonard Spigelgass
1967 Edmund H. North
1968 George Seaton
1969 Dore Schary
1970 Richard Murphy
1971 Daniel Taradash
1972 Michael Blankfort
  Norman Corwin
1973 William Ludwig
1974 Ray Bradbury
  Philip Dunne
1975 Fay Kanin
1976 Winston Miller
1977 Carl Foreman

Screen Awards

WRITERS GUILD OF AMERICA, WEST

8955 Beverly Blvd., Los Angeles, Calif. 90048 (213/550-1000)

The Screen Awards, which consist of bronze plaques,

annually honor excellence in screenwriting by Guild members in various motion picture categories.

COMEDY
1948 F. Hugh Herbert, *Sitting Pretty*
1949 Joseph L. Mankiewicz, *A Letter to Three Wives*
1950 Joseph L. Mankiewicz, *All About Eve*
1951 Frances Goodrich and Albert Hackett, *Father's Little Dividend*
1952 Frank S. Nugent, *The Quiet Man*
1953 Ian McLellan Hunter and John Dighton, *Roman Holiday*
1954 Billy Wilder, Samuel Taylor and John Dighton, *Sabrina*
1955 Frank Nugent and Joshua Logan, *Mr. Roberts*
1956 James Poe, John Farrow and S.J. Perelman, *Around the World in 80 Days*
1957 Billy Wilder and I.A.L. Diamond, *Love in the Afternoon*
1958 S.N. Behrman and George Froeschel, *Jacobowsky and the Colonel*
1959 Billy Wilder and I.A.L. Diamond, *Some Like It Hot*
1960 Billy Wilder and I.A.L. Diamond, *The Apartment*
1961 George Axelrod, *Breakfast at Tiffany's*
1962 Stanley Shapiro and Nate Monaster, *That Touch of Mink*
1963 James Poe, *Lilies of the Field*
1964 Stanley Kubrick, Peter George and Terry Southern, *Dr. Strangelove; Or How I Learned to Stop Worrying and Love the Bomb*
1965 Herb Gardner, *A Thousand Clowns*
1966 William Rose, *The Russians Are Coming, The Russians Are Coming*
1967 Calder Willingham and Buck Henry, *The Graduate*
1968 Neil Simon, *The Odd Couple*
1969 Paul Mazursky and Larry Tucker, *Bob & Carol & Ted & Alice*

BEST COMEDY WRITTEN DIRECTLY FOR THE SCREEN
1970 Neil Simon, *The Out-of-Towners*
1971 Paddy Chayefsky, *The Hospital*
1972 Buck Henry, David Newman and Robert Benton, *What's Up, Doc?*
1973 Melvin Frank and Jack Rose, *A Touch of Class*
1974 Mel Brooks, Norman Steinberg, Andrew Bergman, Richard Pryor and Alan Uger, *Blazing Saddles*
1975 Robert Towne and Warren Beatty, *Shampoo*
1976 Bill Lancaster, *The Bad News Bears*
1977 Woody Allen and Marshall Brickman, *Annie Hall*

BEST COMEDY ADAPTED FROM ANOTHER MEDIUM
1969 Arnold Schulman, *Goodbye, Columbus*
1970 Ring Lardner, Jr., *M*A*S*H*
1971 John Paxton, *Kotch*
1972 Jay Presson Allen, *Cabaret*
1973 Alvin Sargent, *Paper Moon*
1974 Mordecai Richler, *The Apprenticeship of Duddy Kravitz*
1975 Neil Simon, *Sunshine Boys*
1976 Frank Waldman and Blake Edwards, *The Pink Panther Strikes Again*
1977 Larry Gelbart, *Oh, God!*

BEST DRAMA
1948 Frank Partos and Millen Brand, *The Snake Pit*
1949 Robert Rossen, *All the King's Men*
1950 Charles Brackett, Billy Wilder and D.M. Marshman, Jr., *Sunset Boulevard*

1951 Michael Wilson and Harry Brown, *A Place in the Sun*
1952 Carl Foreman, *High Noon*
1953 Daniel Taradash, *From Here to Eternity*
1954 Budd Schulberg, *On the Waterfront*
1955 Paddy Chayefsky, *Marty*
1956 Michael Wilson, *Friendly Persuasion*
1957 Reginald Rose, *Twelve Angry Men*
1958 Harold Jacob Smith and Nathan E. Douglas, *The Defiant Ones*
1959 Frances Goodrich and Albert Hackett, *The Diary of Anne Frank*
1960 Richard Brooks, *Elmer Gantry*
1961 Sidney Carroll and Robert Rossen, *The Hustler*
1962 Horton Foote, *To Kill a Mockingbird*
1963 Harriet Frank, Jr., and Irving Ravetch, *Hud*
1964 Edward Anhalt, *Becket*
1965 Morton Fine and David Friedkin, *The Pawnbroker*
1966 Ernest Lehman, *Who's Afraid of Virginia Woolf?*
1967 David Newman and Robert Benton, *Bonnie and Clyde*
1968 James Goldman, *The Lion in Winter*

BEST DRAMA WRITTEN DIRECTLY FOR THE SCREEN
1969 William Goldman, *Butch Cassidy and The Sundance Kid*
1970 Francis Ford Coppola and Edmund H. North, *Patton*
1971 Penelope Gilliatt, *Sunday Bloody Sunday*
1972 Jeremy Larner, *The Candidate*
1973 Steve Shagan, *Save the Tiger*
1974 Robert Towne, *Chinatown*
1975 Frank Pierson, *Dog Day Afternoon*
1976 Paddy Chayefsky, *Network*
1977 Arthur Laurents, *The Turning Point*

BEST DRAMA ADAPTED FROM ANOTHER MEDIUM
1969 Waldo Salt, *Midnight Cowboy*
1970 Robert Anderson, *I Never Sang for My Father*
1971 Ernest Tidyman, *The French Connection*
1972 Mario Puzo and Francis Ford Coppola, *The Godfather*
1973 Waldo Salt and Norman Wexler, *Serpico*
1974 Francis Ford Coppola and Mario Puzo, *The Godfather, Part II*
1975 Lawrence Hauben and Bo Goldman, *One Flew Over the Cuckoo's Nest*
1976 William Goldman, *All the President's Men*
1977 Alvin Sargent, *Julia*

BEST MUSICAL
1948 Sidney Sheldon, Frances Goodrich and Albert Hackett, *Easter Parade*
1949 Betty Comden and Adolph Green, *On the Town*
1950 Sidney Sheldon, *Annie Get Your Gun*
1951 Alan Jay Lerner, *An American in Paris*
1952 Betty Comden and Adolph Green, *Singin' in the Rain*
1953 Helen Deutsch, *Lili*
1954 Albert Hackett, Frances Goodrich and Ernest Lehman, *Seven Brides for Seven Brothers*

1955 Daniel Fuchs and Isobel Lennart, *Love Me or Leave Me*
1956 Ernest Lehman, *The King and I*
1957 John Patrick, *Les Girls*
1958 Alan Jay Lerner, *Gigi*
1959 Melville Savelson and Jack Rose, *The Five Pennies*
1960 Betty Comden and Adolph Green, *Bells Are Ringing*
1961 Ernest Lehman, *West Side Story*
1962 Marion Hargrove, *The Music Man*
1963 No Award
1964 Bill Walsh and Don Da Gradi, *Mary Poppins*
1965 Ernest Lehman, *The Sound of Music*

SCREENPLAY DEALING MOST ABLY WITH PROBLEMS OF THE AMERICAN SCENE (The Robert Meltzer Award)
1948 Frank Partos and Millen Brand, *The Snake Pit*
1949 Robert Rossen, *All the King's Men*
1950 Carl Foreman, *The Men*
1951 Robert Bruckner, *Bright Victory*

Laurel Award
WRITERS GUILD OF AMERICA, WEST
8955 Beverly Blvd., Los Angeles, Calif. 90048
(213/550-1000)

The Laurel Award, which is represented by a silver medallion, annually recognizes contributions of note to the screenwriting profession. Only members of the Guild are eligible for this honor.

1953 Sonya Levien
1954 Dudley Nichols
1955 Robert Riskin
1956 Julius and Philip Epstein
       Albert Hackett
       Frances Goodrich
1957 Charles Brackett
       Billy Wilder
1958 John Lee Mahin
1959 Nunnally Johnson
1960 Norman Krasna
1961 George Seaton
1962 Philip Dunne
1963 Joseph L. Mankiewicz
1964 John Huston
1965 Sidney Buchman
1966 Isobel Lennart
1967 Richard Brooks
1968 Casey Robinson
1969 Carl Foreman
1970 Dalton Trumbo
1971 James Poe
1972 Ernest Lehman
1973 William Rose
1974 Paddy Chayefsky
1975 Preston Sturges
1976 Michael Wilson
1977 Samson Raphaelson

Music & Dance

Contents

Related Awards

AWAPA Statuette

ACADEMY OF WIND AND PERCUSSION ARTS
National Band Assn., W. Lafayette, Ind. 47907
(317/494-8476)

The nine-inch silver AWAPA statuette is awarded as merited to honor an individual for significant and outstanding contributions to bands and band music. A three-member commission appointed by the Academy's president selects the winner.

1961 **William Revelli**, Ann Arbor, Mich.
1962 **Karl L. King**
1963 No award
1964 No award
1965 **Harold D. Bachman**
     Glenn Cliffe Bainum
1966 No award
1967 No award
1968 **Merle Evans**, Sarasota, Fla.
1969 **Harry Guggenheim**
     Al G. Wright, W. Lafayette, Ind.
     Paul V. Yoder, Fort Lauderdale, Fla.
1970 **Toshio Akiyama**, Tokyo, Japan
1971 **Richard Franko Goldman**, Baltimore, Md.
1972 **Richard M. Nixon**, Washington, D.C., and San Clemente, Calif.
     John Paynter, Evanston, Ill.
1973 **Sir Vivian Dunn**, Sussex, U.K.
     Traugott Rohner, Evanston, Ill.
1974 **Jan Molenaar**, Wormerveer, Netherlands
1975 **Frederick Fennell**, Miami, Fla.
1976 **George S. Howard**, San Antonio, Tex.
     Harry Mortimer, United Kingdom
1977 **Mark Hindsley**, Champaign, Ill.

Gran Premio Alfredo Casella
Daniela Napolitano Prize

ACCADEMIA MUSICALE NAPOLETANA
Via S. Pasquale 62, 80121 Naples, Italy (Tel. 415-292 and 397-708)

The Gran Premio Alfredo Casella is given to the winner of the biennial Alfredo Casella Piano Competition. Entrants between the ages of eighteen and thirty-two undergo a three-step elimination and judging process, the last being a public performance. The total cash award is 1.5-million lire, and a silver cup is given.

1952 **George Solchany**, Hungary
1954 **Esteban Sanchez Herrero**, Spain
     Walter Blankentheim, Germany
1956 **Gabriel Tacchino**, "Italian-French"
1958 **Ivan Davis**, U.S.A.
1960 **Pierre Ives le Roux**, France
1962 **Richard Siracuse**, "Italian-American"
1964 **Sergio Varella Cid**, Portugal
1966 **Michele Campanella**, Italy
1968 **Franco Medori**, Italy (tied for second place; no first)
     Ewa Anna Osinska, Poland (tied for second place; no first)
1970 **Alain Pierre Neveux**, France
1972 **Michel Krist**, Germany
1974 **Christian Blakschaw**, Great Britain
1976 **Sandro de Palma**, Italy
     Gerald Oppitz, Germany

The Daniela Napolitano Prize is given to the winner of the biennial Alfredo Casella Competition of Composition. An international jury selects the winner, who receives a gold medal and has his/her composition published.

1960 **Filip Pires**, Portugal
1962 No award
1964 **Carlo Cammarota**, Italy
     Jose Soproni, Hungary
1966 No award
1968 **Mauro Bortolotti**, Italy
1970 **Teresa Procaccini**, Italy
1972 No award
1974 No award
1976 **David Saperstein**, U.S.A.

American Dance Guild Award

AMERICAN DANCE GUILD
1619 Broadway, Rm. 603, New York, N.Y. 10019
(212/245-4833)

The American Dance Guild Annual Award, which consists of a statuette and a plaque, is given annually for outstanding service to dance. The winner is selected by the awards committee, with approval of the board of directors.

1970 **Genevieve Oswald**, Established Dance Collection at Library of Performing Arts,
1971 **Marion Van Tuyl**, Educator at Mills College and editor of *Impulse*
1972 **Irmgard Bartenieff**, Pioneer in effort/shape and dance therapy
1973 **Ruth Lovell Murray**, Educator in dance in elementary education.
1974 **Martha Hill Davies**, Pioneer in college education
1975 **Katherine Dunham**, For work as a performer and in community-related work.
1976 **Selma Jeanne Cohen**, Dance scholar and historian
1977 **Antony Tudor**, Choreographer

American Music Conference Award

NATIONAL NEWSPAPER ASSOCIATION
491 National Press Bldg., 14th and F Sts. NW, Washington, D.C. 20045 (202/783-1651)

Plaques are awarded annually to the three newspapers judged to do the most creative and effective job of reporting on the amateur musical scene in communities and local schools. Interviews, features and news stories are considered, but reviews are not. The winners of this award, which is sponsored by the American Music Conference and administered by the National Newspaper Association, receive plaques. A panel of newspaper editors and reporters selects the recipients. (Since 1974 awards have not been broken down into circulation categories.)

1973 OVER 4,000 CIRCULATION
Meridien (Miss.) *Towne Courier*
Birmingham (Ala.) *Shades Valley Sun*
McMinnville (Ohio) *News Register*

UNDER 4,000 CIRCULATION
Orville (Ohio) *Courier-Crescent*

Mountain View (Ark.) ***Stone County Ledger***
Cornwall (N.Y.) ***Local***

1974 OVER 4,000 CIRCULATION
    North Platte (N.D.) ***Telegraph***
    Graham (N.C.) ***Alamace News***
    Morehead (N.C.) ***Press Times***

    UNDER 4,000 CIRCULATION
    Monticello (Minn.) ***Times***
    Selma (Calif.) ***Enterprise***
    Ulysses (Kans.) ***News***
1975 *Kettering-Oakwood* (Ohio) ***Times***
    Visalia (Calif.) ***Times-Delta***
    Birmingham (Ala.) ***Shades Valley Sun***
1976 *Fairbury* (Ill.) ***Blade***
    Selma (Calif.) ***Enterprise***
    Birmingham (Ala.) ***Shades Valley Sun***
1977 *Columbia* (Md.) ***Flier***
    Columbia (Mo.) ***News Sun***
    Monticello (Minn.) ***Times***

ASCAP-Deems Taylor Awards
AMERICAN SOCIETY OF COMPOSERS, AUTHORS AND PUBLISHERS
1 Lincoln Plaza, New York, N.Y. 10023 (212/595-3050)

The ASCAP-Deems Taylor Awards, which consist of $500 honorariums to writers and plaques to publishers, are given annually for the best nonfiction books and articles in magazines or newspapers published in the United States on the subject of music or its creators. Six ASCAP judges—three each in popular and symphonic music—select the winners. The awards, though annual, are not given out regularly. In the list below, the awards are assigned to the year in which most of the work under consideration was completed and published.

BOOKS

1968 George T. Simon, *The Big Bands* (Macmillan Co.)
Sidney Shemel and M. William Krasilovsky, *More About this Business of Music* (Billboard)
George Eells, *The Life That Late He Led* (G.P. Putnam's Sons)
1969 Gunther Schuller, *Early Jazz* (Oxford University Press)
Ravi Shankar, *My Music, My Life* (Simon & Schuster)
Otto Deri, *Exploring Twentieth-Century Music* (Holt, Rinehart and Winston)
1970 Alan Rich, *Music: Mirror of the Arts* (Praeger Publishers and Ridge Press)
Irving Kolodin, *The Continuity of Music* (Alfred A. Knopf)
Milton Goldin, *The Music Merchants* (Macmillan Co.)
1971 Lee Elliot Berk, *Legal Protection for the Creative Musician* (Berklee Press)
Ned Rorem, *Critical Affairs—A Composer's Journal* (George Braziller)
Aksel Schiotz, *The Singer and His Art* (Harper & Row)
1972 Charles Rosen, *The Classical Style: Haydn, Mozart, Beethoven* (Viking Press)
Eileen Southern, *The Music of Black Americans, A History* (W. W. Norton and Co.)

Tom Stoddard, *Pops Foster—The Autobiography of a New Orleans Jazzman* (University of California Press)
Martin Williams, *The Jazz Tradition* (Oxford University Press)
1973 Lillian Libman, *And Music At The Close: Stravinsky's Last Years* (W. W. Norton & Co.)
Alec Wilder, *American Popular Song—The Great Innovators, 1900-1950* (Oxford University Press)
Richard A. Peterson and R. Serge Denisoff, *Sounds of Social Change* (Rand McNally)
Boris Schwarz, *Music and Musical Life In Soviet Russia 1917-1970* (W. W. Norton & Co.)
Lehman Engel, *Words With Music* (Macmillan Co.)
1974 Henry-Louis de La Grange, *Mahler* (Doubleday & Co.)
Max Wilk, *They're Playing Our Song* (Atheneum)
Myra Friedman, *Buried Alive* (Wm. Morrow & Co.)
Duke Ellington, *Music Is My Mistress* (Doubleday & Co.)
Philip Hart and Claire Brook, *Orpheus In The New World* (W.W. Norton & Co.)
1975 J. H. Kwabena Nketia, *The Music Of Africa* (W. W. Norton & Co.)
Ned Rorem, *The Final Diary* (Holt, Rinehart and Winston)
Edward T. Cone, *The Composer's Voice* (University of California Press)
Howard Dietz, *Dancing In The Dark* (Quadrangle)
Hampton Hawes and Don Asher, *Raise Up Off Me* (Coward, McCann & Geoghegan)
1976 Vera Brodsky Lawrence, *Music for Patriots, Politicians, and Presidents* (Macmillan)
Philip S. Foner, *American Labor Songs of the Nineteenth Century* (University of Illinois Press)
Frank R. Rossiter, *Charles Ives & His America* (Liveright Publishing)
Leonard Stein, *Style and Idea* (St. Martin's Press)
Charles Rosen, *Arnold Schoenberg* (Viking Press)
1977 Dan Morgenstern, *Jazz People* (Harry N. Abrams)
Albert Murray, *Stomping The Blues* (McGraw Hill)
Larry Sandberg and Dick Weissman, *The Folk Music Sourcebook* (Alfred A. Knopf)
Geoffrey Stokes, *Starmaking Machinery* (Bobbs-Merrill Co.)
Leo Kraft, *Gradus* (W. W. Norton & Co.)

ARTICLES

1968 James Ringo, five reviews (*The American Record Guide*)
Arnold Shaw, articles (*Cavalier*)
Joan Peyser, article (*Columbia University Forum*)
1969 Joan Peyser, article (*New York Times*)
James Ringo, article (*American Record Guide*)
James Lyons, notes (*Boston Symphony Orchestra Program*)
1970 Ralph J. Gleason, article (*Lithopinion*)
Alan Rich, article (*New York Magazine*)
Issachar Miron, article (*New York Times*)
1971 Boris E. Nelson, 19 articles (*Toledo Blade*)
Paul Glass, "A Hiatus in American Music History" (*Afro-American Studies*)
Louis Carp, "Mozart: His Tragic Life and Controversial Death" (*Bulletin*, N.Y. Academy of Medicine)
1972 Elliott W. Galkin, articles (*Baltimore Sun*)
George Perle, "Webern's Twelve-Tone Sketches" (*The Musical Quarterly*)
Ralph J. Gleason, "God Bless Louis Armstrong" (*Rolling Stone*)
Irving Lowens, articles (*Washington Star*)
1973 Martin Bernheimer, article (*Los Angeles Times*)

Alan Rich, article (*New York Magazine*)
Robert Finn, article (*Cleveland Plain Dealer*)
Bruce Pollock, article (*Rock Magazine*)
1974 Jack O'Brien, syndicated columns
Hubert Saal, (*Newsweek*)
Ben Fong Torres, (*Rolling Stone*)
Alan Rich, (*New York Magazine*)
1975 Richard Franko Goldman, "American Music: 1918-1960" chapter in *The New Oxford History of Music* (Oxford University Press)
Ralph J. Gleason, "Farewell to the Duke" (*Rolling Stone*)
Elliott W. Galkin, articles (*Baltimore Sun*)
Andrew Porter, articles (*The New Yorker*)
David Hamilton, articles (*The New Yorker*)
1976 Robert Commanday, (*San Francisco Chronicle*)
Richard Dyer, (*Boston Globe*)
Jack O'Brien, syndicated columns (King Features Syndicate)
Gary Giddins, articles (*Village Voice*)
1977 Paul Baratta, (*Songwriter Magazine*)
Gary Giddins, (*Village Voice*)
Maureen Orth, (*Newsweek*)
Samuel Lipman, (*Commentary*)
Karen Monson, (*Chicago Daily News*)
Irving Lowens, (*Washington Star*)
Richard Dyer, (*Boston Globe*)
John Ardoin, (*Dallas Morning News*)

Bach International Competitions Awards

AMERICAN BACH FOUNDATION
1211 Potomac St. NW, Washington, D.C. 20007
(202/338-1111)

The Johann Sebastian Bach International Competitions are held almost every year at Washington's George Washington University under the sponsorship of the Eugene and Agnes E. Meyer Foundation, organized by the American Bach Foundation. The winners receive a number of performance options plus various cash awards, now including the $500 H.E. Berndt von Staden Award presented by the Ambassador of the Federal Republic of Germany, the $1,000 Mr. and Mrs. David Lloyd Kreeger first prize for violinists and the $1,000 Youth Concerts Foundation Award for first place in the cello competition. Additionally, cash prizes are given to the second- and third-place winners. Starting in 1978, violinists and cellists between seventeen and thirty-five years of age may enter the competition, which is judged by a three-person panel. Previously, the contest was for pianists, who received prizes similar to those offered to string musicians in 1978.

PIANISTS
1960 Zola Shaulis, U.S.A.
1961 Tasker Polk, U.S.A.
1962 Bonnie Boggle, U.S.A.
1963 No award
1964 Michele Levin, U.S.A.
1965 Pamela Le Nevez, Australia
1966 Paul Posnak, U.S.A.
Sontraud Speidel, Germany
1967 No award
1968 Mari-Elizabeth Morgen, Canada
1969 Marilyn Engle, Canada

1970 No award
1971 Peter Vinograde, U.S.A.
1972 No award
1973 Hans Carl Boepple, U.S.A.
1974 No award
1975 Bronislawa Kawalla, Poland
1976 Michael Landrum, U.S.A.
1977 No award

BMI Awards

BROADCAST MUSIC INCORPORATED
49 W. 57th St., New York, N.Y. 10019 (212/586-2000)

The annual BMI Awards to Student Composers total $15,000 and range from $300 to $2,500 per recipient, awarded at the discretion of a judges' panel, which selects winners from manuscripts or recorded works. Applicants must be citizens or permanent residents of a Western Hemisphere country, be under twenty-six years of age and be enrolled in an accredited secondary or postsecondary school or study music privately with established teachers. Only one original composition, created during the previous year, may be entered.

1952 Elnora Case
Eugene Cramer
Alvin L. Epstein
Robert Gauldin
Virginia Gittens
Barrie W. Heitkamp
Donald Jenni
Donald Martino
Earl K. Scott, Jr
Hale Smith, Jr.
Rodger D. Vaughan
Jean Winters
1953 Dominick Argento
William Bolcom
Ramiro Cortes
Higo H. Harada
Frederick Heutte
Michael Kassler
Teo Macero
Donald Martino
Donald Scavarda
David Ward-Steinman
1954 Genevieve Chinn
Ramiro Cortes
David M. Epstein
Edwin A. Freeman
Jack S. Gottlieb
John Harbison
Donald Jenni
Russell J. Peck
Arno Safran
Roland Trogan
David Ward-Steinman
1955 Donald Jenni
Michael Kassler
1956 Bruce Archibald
Jan Bach
Robert Bernat
Allen Brings
Richmond Browne
George H. Crumb
George C. Forest
Samuel Gale
Michael Kassler

Robert Lombardo
Leon Clayton Nedbalek
Michael Sahl
Jose Serenbrier
1957 Seymour Altucher
Richmond Browne
Frank Philip Campo
William Bayard Carlin
Ramiro Cortes
Paul Glass
Michael Kassler
Jack Normain Kimmel
Robert Lombardo
Donal R. Michalsky
Henry Onderdonk
1958 David S. Bates
Jed Curtis
Marjorie Greif
Michael M. Horvit
Gerald Humel
Alan Kemler
J. Theodore Prochazka
Thomas R. Putsche
William Wilder
1959 Mario Davidovsky
Philip M. Glass
Ellen Glickman
David Serrendero Proust
David Ward-Steinman
Charles Wuorinen
1960 Stephen J. Albert
Mark Bernard DeVoto
Stephen D. Fisher
William Hibbard
Arthur Murphy
Fredric Myrow
Robert Sheff
David Ward-Steinman
1961 William H. Albright
Michael Fink
Robert Fraser Glover
Arthur B. Hunkins
Marlos Nobre
David Saperstein
Robert Suderburg
Charles Wuorinen
1962 Conal Boyce
Charles M. Dodge
Alan Leichtling
William McKinley
Arthur Murphy
Richard Toensing
Charles Wuorinen
1963 Alvin S. Curran
Charles M. Dodge
Humphrey Evans III
Steve Gellman
Steven Gilbert
Peter F. Huse
Dennis K.M. Kam
Ellene S. Levenson
Fredric Myrow
John Earl Rogers
David Saperstein
Hal Tamblyn
Richard Toensing
Charles Wuorinen
1964 Luis Arias
Harley Gaber
John Heineman

Russell J. Peck
Phillip C. Rhodes
David Saperstein
1965 William Benjamin
Robert S.W. Buckley
Peter M. Dickey
Charles M. Dodge
Steven Gilbert
Robert Henderson
Roger O. Johnson
Judith Lang
Richard Manners
Frank L. McCarty
Joan Panetti
Phillip C. Rhodes
Joseph C. Schwantner
David N. Stewart
1966 William H. Albright
Charles M. Dodge
Humphrey Evans III
Daniel Foley
David Foley
Clare Franco
Steven Gilbert
Hugh Hartwell
Brian M. Israel
John M. Mills-Cockell
Lawrence Morton
Peter Ness
Joan Panetti
Russell J. Peck
Dennis D. Riley
Eric N. Robertson
Joseph C. Schwantner
Luis Maria Serra
Richard T. Trifan
Alice Webber
1967 Richard S. Ames
Stephen S. Dankner
Stephen Dickman
Primous Fountain III
Harley Gaber
Dennis K.M. Kam
Howard Lubin
William David Noon
Eugene O'Brien
Dennis D. Riley
Joseph C. Schwantner
Daria Semegen
Kathleen Solose
Greg A. Steinke
1968 Bruce M. Adolphe
William H. Albright
Kurt Carpenter
Stephen Dickman
Dennis J. Eberhard
Paul H. Epstein
David Foley
Clare Franco
Peter Griffith
John Hawkins
Brian M. Israel
Terrence T. Kincaid
Howard Lubin
Robert Morris
Russell J. Peck
John Rea
Walter B. Saul
Ryan L. Whitney
Hugh M. Wolff

1969 Robert Boury
      Humphrey Evans III
      Daniel Foley
      Andrew Frank
      Stephen Hartke
      Jeffrey Jones
      Daniel Kessner
      Jeffrey Kresky
      Gerald Levinson
      Denis Lorrain
      Howard Lubin
      John M. Mann
      Peter Salemi
      Walter B. Saul
      Daria Semegen
      Donald A. Steven
      Preston Trombly
      Hugh M. Wolff
1970 John Adams
      William Eric Benson
      Mickey Cohen
      Daniel Foley
      Andrew Frank
      Joan Harkness
      Daniel Kessner
      David Koblitz
      Gerald Levinson
      Philip Magnuson
      Robert P. Mounsey
      William David Noon
      Eugene O'Brien
      Steven Sandberg
      Michael Seyfrit
      Michael Udow
      Hugh M. Wolff
1971 Kurt Carpenter
      John A. Celona
      John Stepehn Dydo
      Guy Hallman
      Stephen Hartke
      Joel Hoffman
      David Koblitz
      Matthias Kriesberg
      Michel Longtin
      Stephen L. Mosko
      John Sarracco
      Ira Taxin
      David Winkler
1972 Donald Crockett
      Sydney Goodwin
      Gary Hardie
      Denis Lorrain
      William Matthews
      Christopher Rouse
      Brian Schober
      Charles Sepos
      Philip Stoll
      Bruce J. Taub
      Wayne A. Walker
      Mark E. Wilson
1973 W. Claude Baker, Jr.
      Larry Bell
      Ronald Braunstein
      Stephen Chatman
      Robert Dick
      Eric Ewazen
      David Koblitz
      Rachel Kutten
      Gerald Levinson
      William Matthews

      Stephen L. Mosko
      Jay Reise
      Christopher Rouse
      Helge Skjeveland
      Ira Taxin
1974 Stephen Chatman
      Stephen Dembski
      Richard Derby
      Hal Freedman
      Margaret Ann Griebling
      Murray Gross
      Stephen A. Jaffe
      Carson Kievman
      William Matthews
      Jay Reise
      Rodney I. Rogers
      Christopher Roze
1975 Todd Brief
      Alexander Cardona
      Stephen Chatman
      Theodore Dollarhide
      Jonathan Drexler
      Burton Goldstein
      Dan Gutwin
      Carson Kievman
      Stephen Lano
      William Maiben
      Daniel Plante
      Rodney I. Rogers
      David Shuler
      Jeffrey Wood
      Lenard Yen
1976 Allen Anderson
      Alexander Xavier Cardona
      Thomas Crawford
      William C. Heinrichs
      Joseph A. Hudson
      Ralph N. Jackson
      Aaron Kernis
      David Moser McKay
      Cindy McTee
      Rodney Rogers
      Philip Rosenberg
      Mark Howard Steidel
      Randall Edgar Stokes
1977 Tobias Picker
      Lenard Yen
      David Snow
      Ralph N. Jackson
      Edgardo J. Simone
      Mindy Lee
      Michael H. Kurek
      Scott M. Fessler

Busoni Prize

CONCORSO BUSONI
Conservatorio Statale di Musica, C. Monteverdi, Piazza
Domenicani 19, I-39100, Bolzano, Italy (Tel. 23-5-79)

The Busoni Prize is given periodically in conjunction
with the International Piano Competition run by various city and state agencies. A jury hears applicants
perform a twenty- to thirty-minute musical program,
which conforms to a proscribed set of requirements. A
million-lire contract for a concert and recital series is
offered to the winner.

1952 **Sergio Perticaroli,** Italy

1953 Ella Goldstein, U.S.A.
1954 Aldo Mancinelli, U.S.A.
1956 Joerg Demus, Austria
1957 Martha Argerich, Argentina
1961 Jerome Rose, U.S.A.
1964 Michael Ponti, U.S.A.
1966 Garrick Ohlsson, U.S.A.
1968 Vladimir Selivochin, U.S.S.R.
1969 Ursula Oppens, U.S.A.
1972 Arnaldo Cohen, Brazil
1974 Robert Benz, Germany
1976 Roberto Cappello, Italy

Capezio Dance Award

CAPEZIO FOUNDATION
543 W. 43rd St., New York, N.Y. 10036 (212/564-7060)

The Capezio Dance Award is given annually for a lifetime contribution to dance by artists and devotees of dance. An award committee selects the winner, who receives $1,000 and a plaque.

1952 Zachary Solov
1953 Lincoln Kirstein
1954 Doris Humphrey
1955 Louis Horst
1956 Genevieve Oswald
1957 Ted Shawn
1958 Alexandra Danilova
1959 Sol Hurok
1960 Martha Graham
1961 Ruth St. Denis
1962 Barbara Karinska
1963 Donald McKayle
1964 Jose Limon
1965 Maria Tallchief
1966 Agnes De Mille
1967 Paul Taylor
1968 Lucia Chase
1969 John Martin
1970 William Kolodney
1971 Arthur Mitchell
1972 The Laubins
     La Meri
1973 Isadora Bennett
1974 Robert Joffrey
1975 Robert Irving
1976 Jerome Robbins
1977 Merce Cunningham

Concert Artists Guild Awards

CONCERT ARTISTS GUILD
154 W. 57th St., New York, N.Y. 10019 (212/757-8344)

A maximum of 10 awards a year are available to instrumentalists thirty years old or younger, singers thirty-five or younger and ensembles averaging thirty or younger who have not made a formal New York debut. Awards, based on preliminary and final auditions, are made at the Carnegie Recital Hall. The Guild assumes the recital cost and gives a cash award of $250 for soloists and $500 for ensembles.

1951 Anita Katchen
     Frank Martori
     Robin Allardice
     Richard Leshin
     Ira Shur

Nathan Goldstein
Elizabeth Devlin
Barbara Berkman
Kenneth Chertok
Alan Grishman
Sandra Propp
Laurence Watson
Otis Wilensky
Sally Allen
Angela Pistelli
Thaddeus Brys
Ruth Brall
Roger Kamien
Yvette Rudin
Vincent Sperando
Rosalie Adagna
Pasquale Verduce
Thea Glussman
Mme. Simon Barere
Harriet Emerson
Helen Rice
Samuel Sanders
1952 Catalina Zandueta
     Leah Mellman
     Gabriel Banat
     Esther Fernandez
     Ara Charles Adrian
     Eleanor Mandel
     Olanda Drewery
     Virginia-Gene Shankel
     Shirley Bardin
     Byron Goode
     Helen Spina
     Mary-Louise Brown
     Robert Natkoff
     Valerie Lamoree
     Samuel Sanders
     Militades Siadimas
     Charlotte Bloecher
     Harry Wimmer
     Allen Rogers
     Dina Soresi
     Daniel Abrams
     Louis F. Simon
     Joseph Plon
     Andrew Frierson
1953 Ellen Alexander
     Paul Gurevich
     David Wells
     Robert Hearn
     Leyna Gabriele
     Leonor Umstead
     Barbara Allen
     Beverly Somach
     Anita Katchen
     Muriel Kirby
     Oliver Colbentson
     Ruth Lakeway
     Allen Brown
     Norma Ferris
     Uzi Wiesel
     William deValentine
     Stephen Manes
     Arabella Honig
     Stanley Babin
     Dorothy Phillips
     Christina C. Cardillo
1954 Evelyn Lear
     Isador Lateiner
     Sheila Minzer

Gertrude Prinzi
Martin Canin
Nancy Cirillo
Thomas Stewart
Bruce Stegg
Martin Eshelman
Mara Shorr
Mitchell Andrews
Charles Dunn
Bernard Kreger
Shirley Givins
Sosio Manzo
Marvin Morgenstern
Eileen DiTullio
Donald Betts
Robert Menga
Emilia Cundari
1955 Betty Allen
Erick Friedman
Dorothy Happel
Andrew Heath
Ellen Pahl
Zelda Gilgore
Alexander Horvath
Sara Jane Fleming
Frances Bartley
Ramy Shevelov
Joan Marie Moynagh
Emilio Rosario
Elaine Bonazzi
John Browning
William Metcalf
Ralph Feinstein
Clifford Snyder
Audrey Kooper
Harry Wimmer
Donna Pegors
Eugenia Hyman
Lorraine Wollnik
John Pidgeon
1956 Charles Castleman
Daniel Pollack
Ada Pinchuk
Madelyn Vose
Nancy Hall
Manuel Maramba
Lynn Rasmussen
Harold Jones
Margarita Zambrana
Deanne Garcy
Denver Oldham
Sophia Steffan
Mary Freeman
Angelica Lozada
Morey Ritt
Thomas Carey
1957 Shirley Verrett
Reri Grist
Tana Bawden
Donn Alexander-Feder
Richard Syracuse
Eva Marie Wolff
Grant Williams
Clifton Matthews
Mary Hensley
Charles Engel
Annina Celli
Olegna Fuschi
Jeanette Scovotti
Joseph Schwartz

Hyman Bress
Sheila Henig
1958 Judith Raskin
Howard Aibel
Joy Pottle
Harold S. Johnson
Margaret Kalil
Victoria Markowski
Francesco Cedrone
Mayne Miller
Judith Basch
Hugh Matheny
Herbert Chatzky
Howard Lebow
Raymond Michalski
Ramon Gilbert
Lois Carole Pachucki
Georgia Davis
Agustin Anievas
Martina Arroyo
1959 Alexander Fiorello
Dan Marek
Richard Kuelling
Doris Allen
Helen Cox Raab
Marilyn Anne Laughlin
Rita Schoen
Andre De La Varre
Enid Dale
Beatrice Rippy
Lois Carole Pachucki
Deborah Reeder
Maris-Stella Bonell
Phyllis Frankel
Jack Dane Litten
1960 George Shirley
Michael Rogers
Joan Wall
Carol Wilder
Charles Haupt
Catherine Wallace
Arline Billings
Mark Bellfort Chalat
Dolores Holtz
Patricia MacDonald
Naomi Weiss
Joanne Cohen
Albertine Baumgartner
Charles Wendt
Ronald Rogers
Ilana Vered
Laurel Miller
Toby Saks
1961 Vera Graf
Thomas S. Vasiloff
Maria Luisa Lopez-Vito
Rama Jucker
Malka Silberberg
Miguel Pinto
Harriet Lawyer
Marcia Heller
Alpha Brawner
David Rosenstein
Kenneth Goldsmith
Jesse Levine
Edgar Fischer
Edward Zolas
Gene Boucher
1962 Daniel Domb
Bonnie Bogle

Ernest Chang
Madeline Stevenson
Donald Walker
Isabel Berg
Donna Precht
Sanford Margolis
Masako Fujii
Evangelin Marko
Alan Finell
Marilyn Dubow
David Kaiserman
Marie Traficante
James Stafford
Alexandra Hunt
Wanda Maximillian
1963 Edward Aldwell
Nina Kaleska
Lee Dougherty
David Yeomans
Jung-ja Kim
Nan Gullo
Glen Jacobson
Evelyn Watson
Neal O'Doan
Grace Di Battista
Verica Fassel
Helen Merritt
Jamesetta Holliman
William Steck
Leonidas Lipovetsky
Mary Beck
Janet Goodman
1964 Richard Syracuse
William Cheadle
Jean Kraft
Stephen Flamberg
Winifred Dettore
Takaho Nishizaki
Shirley Love
Constance C. Douglass
Fernando Illanes
Louis Nagel
William Greene
Matithahu Braun
Sheila Schonbrun
Findlay Cockrell
Nancy Wyner
1965 Robert Preston
Phyllis Mailing
Roe Van Boskirk
Joan Summers
Ruth Glasser
Judith Allen
Sheldon Shkolnik
Clyde Tipton
David Garlock
Ruth McCoy Gatto
James Stroud
Mertine Johns
Karen Shaw
Sylvia Chambless Patrick
John Large
Richard Allen
1966 Richard Anderson
Gisela Depkat
Richard Allen
Sheila Schonbrun
Grayson Hirst
Jerome Rosen
Eleanor Edwards

LaVergne Monette
Ellen Hassman
Virginia Marks
Almita Hyman-Vamos
Judith Davidoff
Lanoue Davenport
Bruce Prince-Joseph
Ronald Roseman
1967 Christine Edinger
Yehuda Hanani
Odette Noslier
John Cerminaro
Romauld Tecco
Peter Basquin
Sivia Serrlya
Jody Lasky
Arthur Ozolins
Masako Yanagita
Donald Green
1968 Jerome Bunke
Barbara Chenault
Daniel Epstein
Diane Walsh
Michael Haran
Carmen Alvarez
Nathan Brand
Judith Hubbell
Hidemitsu Hayashi
Shari Anderson
1969 Yolanda Roman
Paul Posnak
Ivan Oak
Sandra Darling
Edith Kraft
Li-Ping Hsieh
Noelle Rogers
Betty Jones
1970 Gabriel Chodos
Elaine Comparone
Larry Graham
Irene Gubrud
Alan Marks
Yoko Nozaki
Gerardo Ribeiro
Idith Zvi
Justin Blasdale
James Kreger
Marsha Heller
Interaction:
    Yuval Waldman
    Paul Posnak
    Jonathan Abramowitz
    Daniel Epstein
    James Kreger
    William Henry
1971 Ani Kavafian
Robert Christesen
David Stern
Marioara Trifan
Daniel Waitzman
Etsuko Tazaki
1972 Susan Davenny Wyner
Pawel Checinski
Donald Green
Richard Fredrickson
Paul Tobias
Pamela Mia Paul
Davi Oei
Carol Wincenc
Sung-Kil Kim

David Stern
1973 Harvey Pittel
Susan Salm
Andrew Rangell
Sandra Miller
Nancy Evers
Marian Hahn
Jane Hamborsky
David Shifrin
Amanza Trio:
Ida Bieler
Eugene Moye, Jr.
Mary Louise Vetrano
1974 Manuel Barrueco
Emanuel Gruber
Karen Johnson
David Northington
Gary Steigerwalt
Robin McCabe
Alan Weiss
Arisos Woodwind Quintet:
Nadine Asin
Anne Leek
Gary McGee
Daniel Worley
David Wakefield
1975 Peter Corey
Annette Parker
Laufman Duo
Nancy Green
Raphael Trio:
Daniel Epstein
Susan Salm
Charles Castleman
1976 Eugene Drucker
Elizabethan Enterprise:
Lucy Cross
Mary Springfels
Wendy Gillespie
David Hart
Peter Becker
William Grubb
Mary Elizabeth Stephenson
Jacob Krichaf
Stewart Newbold
Stephanie Jutt
Katherine Ciesinski
William Black
Pamela Guidetti
1977 Chang/Kogan Duo (Lynn Chang and Richard Kogan)
Lois Shapiro
Quintet di Legno:
Eric Thomas
Gail Gillespie
Ronald Haroutunian
Thomas Haunton
Claudia Wann
Michael Thomopoulos
Karen Buranskas
Daisietta Kim
William Hoyt
Franck Avril

Country Music Award

COUNTRY MUSIC ASSOCIATION
7 Music Circle N., Nashville, Tenn. 37203 (615/244-2840)

Nominations for the Country Music Award, which is a bullet-shaped trophy, are submitted by members of the Association and subjected to a vote. Winners are announced on a national television show.

ENTERTAINER OF THE YEAR
1967 Eddy Arnold
1968 Glen Campbell
1969 Johnny Cash
1970 Merle Haggard
1971 Charley Pride
1972 Loretta Lynn
1973 Roy Clark
1974 Charlie Rich
1975 John Denver
1976 Mel Tillis
1977 Ronnie Milsap

SINGLE OF THE YEAR
1967 *There Goes My Everything,* Jack Greene, Decca
1968 *Harper Valley P.T.A.,* Jeannie C. Riley, Plantation
1969 *A Boy Named Sue,* Johnny Cash, Columbia
1970 *Okie From Muskogee,* Merle Haggard, Capitol
1971 *Help Me Make It Through The Night,* Sammi Smith, Mega
1972 *Happiest Girl In The Whole U.S.A.,* Donna Fargo, Dot
1973 *Behind Closed Doors,* Charlie Rich, Epic
1974 *Country Bumpkin,* Cal Smith, MCA
1975 *Before The Next Teardrop Falls,* Freddy Fender, ABC/Dot
1976 *Good Hearted Woman,* Waylon Jennings and Willie Nelson, RCA
1977 *Lucille,* Kenny Rogers, United Artists Records

ALBUM OF THE YEAR
1967 *There Goes My Everything,* Jack Greene, Decca
1968 *Johnny Cash At Folsom Prison,* Johnny Cash, Columbia
1969 *Johnny Cash At San Quentin Prison,* Johnny Cash, Columbia
1970 *Okie From Muskogee,* Merle Haggard, Capitol
1971 *I Won't Mention It Again,* Ray Price, Columbia
1972 *Let Me Tell You About A Song,* Merle Haggard, Capitol
1973 *Behind Closed Doors,* Charlie Rich, Epic
1974 *A Very Special Love Song,* Charlie Rich, Epic
1975 *A Legend In My Time,* Ronnie Milsap, RCA
1976 *Wanted — The Outlaws,* Waylon Jennings, Jessi Colter, Tompall Glaser and Willie Nelson, RCA
1977 *Ronnie Milsap Live,* Ronnie Milsap, RCA

SONG OF THE YEAR
1967 *There Goes My Everything,* Dallas Frazier
1968 *Honey,* Bobby Russell
1969 *Carroll County Accident,* Bob Ferguson
1970 *Sunday Morning Coming Down,* Kris Kristofferson
1971 *Easy Loving,* Freddie Hart
1972 *Easy Loving,* Freddie Hart
1973 *Behind Closed Doors,* Kenny O'Dell
1974 *Country Bumpkin,* Don Wayne
1975 *Back Home Again,* John Denver
1976 *Rhinestone Cowboy,* Larry Weiss
1977 *Lucille,* Roger Bowling and Hal Bynum

FEMALE VOCALIST OF THE YEAR
1967 Loretta Lynn
1968 Tammy Wynette

1969 Tammy Wynette
1970 Tammy Wynette
1971 Lynn Anderson
1972 Loretta Lynn
1973 Loretta Lynn
1974 Olivia Newton-John
1975 Dolly Parton
1976 Dolly Parton
1977 Crystal Gayle

MALE VOCALIST OF THE YEAR

1967 Jack Greene
1968 Glen Campbell
1969 Johnny Cash
1970 Merle Haggard
1971 Charley Pride
1972 Charley Pride
1973 Charlie Rich
1974 Ronnie Milsap
1975 Waylon Jennings
1976 Ronnie Milsap
1977 Ronnie Milsap

VOCAL GROUP OF THE YEAR

1967 The Stoneman Family
1968 Porter Wagoner and Dolly Parton
1969 Johnny Cash and June Carter
1970 The Glaser Brothers
1971 The Osborne Brothers
1972 The Statler Brothers
1973 The Statler Brothers
1974 The Statler Brothers
1975 The Statler Brothers
1976 The Statler Brothers
1977 The Statler Brothers

VOCAL DUO OF THE YEAR

1970 Porter Wagoner and Dolly Parton
1971 Porter Wagoner and Dolly Parton
1972 Conway Twitty and Loretta Lynn
1973 Conway Twitty and Loretta Lynn
1974 Conway Twitty and Loretta Lynn
1975 Conway Twitty and Loretta Lynn
1976 Waylon Jennings and Willie Nelson
1977 Jim Ed Brown and Helen Cornelius

INSTRUMENTAL GROUP OR BAND OF THE YEAR

1967 The Buckaroos
1968 The Buckaroos
1969 Danny Davis and the Nashville Brass
1970 Danny Davis and the Nashville Brass
1971 Danny Davis and the Nashville Brass
1972 Danny Davis and the Nashville Brass
1973 Danny Davis and the Nashville Brass
1974 Danny Davis and the Nashville Brass
1975 Roy Clark and Buck Trent
1976 Roy Clark and Buck Trent
1977 Original Playboys

INSTRUMENTALIST OF THE YEAR

1967 Chet Atkins
1968 Chet Atkins
1969 Chet Atkins
1970 Jerry Reed
1971 Jerry Reed
1972 Charlie McCoy
1973 Charlie McCoy
1974 Don Rich
1975 Johnny Gimble

1976 Hargus "Pig" Robbins
1977 Roy Clark

COMEDIAN OF THE YEAR (Eliminated in 1971)

1967 Don Bowman
1968 Ben Colder
1969 Archie Campbell
1970 Roy Clark

HALL OF FAME

1977 Merle Travis

Silver Bowl

DANCE MAGAZINE

10 Columbus Circle, New York, N.Y. 10019 (212/399-2410)

The recipients of the Silver Bowl, which represents the *Dance Magazine* Award, are honored annually for outstanding achievements and contributions to the dance world. Selections are made by the magazine's editorial staff.

1954 Max Liebman
      Omnibus
      Tony Charmoli
      Adventure
1955 Moira Shearer
      Jack Cole
      Gene Nelson
1956 Martha Graham
      Agnes de Mille
1957 Alicia Markova
      Lucia Chase
      Jerome Robbins
      Jose Limon
1958 Doris Humphrey
      Gene Kelly
      Igor Youskevitch
      Alicia Alonso
1959 Dorothy Alexander
      Fred Astaire
      George Balanchine
1960 Merce Cunningham
      Igor Moiseyev
      Maria Tallchief
1961 Melissa Hayden
      Gwen Verdon
      Anna Sokolow
1962 Margot Fonteyn
      Bob Fosse
      Isadora Bennett
1963 Gower Champion
      Robert Joffrey
      Pauline Koner
1964 Edward Villella
      John Butler
      Peter Gennaro
1965 Margaret H'Doubler
      Edwin Denby
      Maya Plisetskaya
1966 Sol Hurok
      Carmen de Lavallade
      Wesleyan University Press
1967 Alwin Nikolais
      Violette Verdy
      Eugene Loring
1968 Carla Fracci
      Erik Bruhn

Katherine Dunham
1969 Sir Frederick Ashton
Carolyn Brown
Ted Shawn
1970 No award
1971 No award
1972 Judith Jamison
Anthony Dowell
1973 The Christensen Brothers (Lew, Harold, and William)
Rudolf Nureyev
1974 Gerald Arpino
Maurice Bejart
Antony Tudor
1975 Cynthia Gregory
Arthur Mitchell
Alvin Ailey
1976 Michael Bennett
Suzanne Farrell
E. Virginia Williams
1977 Peter Martins
Natalia Makarova
Murray Louis

Dent Medal

ROYAL MUSICAL ASSOCIATION
British Library, Great Russell St., London WCl, U.K. (Tel: 01-636 1544)

The Dent Medal, which is of gold, is given annually for a specific work or group of works published in the field of musicology. Usually, the winner is forty years of age or older and is honored for works of the previous three to five years. The Directorium of the International Musicological Society submits a list of nominees to the council of the Royal Musical Assocation. The council then selects the winner from this list and from any other musicologists it adds to that list.

1961 Gilbert Reany, Great Britain
1962 Solange Corbin, France
1963 Denes Bartha, Hungary
1964 Pierre Pidoux, Switzerland
1965 Barry S. Brook, U.S.A.
1966 Alberto Gallo, Italy
1967 William W. Austin, U.S.A.
1968 Heinrich Huschen, Federal Republic of Germany
1969 Willem Elders, Holland
1970 Daniel Heartz, U.S.A.
1971 Klaus Wolfgang Niemoller, Federal Republic of Germany
1972 Jozef Robijns, Belgium
1973 Max Lutolf, Switzerland
1974 Andrew McCredie, Australia
1975 Martin Stachelin, Federal Republic of Germany
1976 No award
1977 Reinhard Strohm, Great Britain

Disco Forum Awards

BILLBOARD
9000 Sunset Blvd., Los Angeles, Calif. 90069 (213/273-7040)

The Disco Forum Awards, which consist of plaques, are awarded for various achievements in the discotheque field, as determined by a vote by more than 2,000 disco disc jockeys and others in the field.

1975 *The Hustle,* Disco Record of the Year

KC and the Sunshine Band, TK Productions, Disco Album of the Year
Atlantic Records, Disco Company of the Year
Donna Summer, Casablanca Records, Most Promising New Artist of the Year
Casey & Finch, TK Productions, Producer of the Year
Labelle, Epic Records, Disco Artist of the Year
Salsoul Orchestra, Disco Orchestra of the Year
Richard Nader, Disco Concert Promoter of the Year
Disco Sound Associates, Specialist Company of the Year
Dimples, Consumer Publication of the Year
Michael O'Harro, Disco Consultant of the Year
2001 Clubs, Disco Franchise of the Year
Earl Young, The Trammps, Drummer of the Year
Johnny Walker, London's BBC Radio-1 Deejay, U.K. DJ of the Year
1976 **The Trammps,** Atlantic Records, Disco Artist of the Year
Disco Party, The Trammps, Atlantic Records, Disco Cut of the Year
That's Where The Happy People Go, The Trammps, Alantic Records, Disco Album of the Year
Van McCoy, H&L Records, Disco Arranger
Van McCoy, H&L Records, Disco Instrumentalist
Love Hangover, Diana Ross, Disco/Radio Single
Vicki Sue Robinson, RCA Records, Most Promising New Disco Artist
Jesse Green, Disco Single Award
Salsoul Orchestra, Disco Orchestra
Dave Crawford, Disco Composer
Casablanca Records, Tied for Disco Label of Year
Salsoul Records, Tied for Disco Label of the Year
Salsoul Records, Most Important New Disco Software Product
Salsoul Records, Innovative 12-inch Disco Disk for Consumers
Tom Sevarese, Tied for Disco Deejay of the Year
Bobby D.J., Tied for Disco Deejay of the Year
Burma East Music Tied for Disco Music Publisher
Bull Pen Music/Perren-Vibes Music, Tied for Disco Music Publisher
Michael O'Harro, Tramps Discotheque, Washington, D.C., Disco Consultant of the Year
Michael O'Harro, Tramps Discotheque, Washington, D.C., Disco Club Owner of the Year
Tom Moulton, Disco Mixing Award
Freddie Perren, Disco Producer
Norby Walters, Disco Concert Promoter of the Year
Sigma Sound, Philadelphia, Disco Recording Studio of the Year
2001 Clubs, Disco Franchiser of the Year
Dave Todd, RCA Records, Disco Promotion Person of the Year
Cerwin Vega's, "Earthquake" Speaker, Best New Disco Audio Product
Digital Lighting's 6×9 Modular Programmable Dimming System, Best New Disco Lighting Product
1977 Because of an error, the 1977 Disco Forum Awards appear on pp. 109-110.

Alfred Einstein Award

AMERICAN MUSICOLOGICAL SOCIETY
201 S. 34th St., Philadelphia, Pa. 19104 (215/243-5000)

The annual Alfred Einstein Award, carrying a cash prize of $400, is awarded for a musicological article published by a young scholar during the previous year.

1967 Richard L. Crocker, "The Troping Hypothesis" (*Musical Quarterly*)

1968 Ursula Kirkendale, "The Ruspoli Documents on Handel" (*Journal of the American Musicological Society*)

1969 Philip Gossett, "Rossini in Naples: some major works recovered" (*Musical Quarterly*)

1970 Lawrence Gushee, "New Sources for the Biography of Johannes de Muris" (*Journal of the American Musicological Society*)

1971 Lewis Lockwood, "The Autograph of the first movement of Beethoven's Sonata for Violoncello and Pianforte, opus 69" (*Music Forum*)

1972 Sarah Fuller, "Hidden Polyphony—a Reappraisal" (*Journal of the American Musicological Society*)

1973 Rebecca A. Baltzer, "Thirteenth-Century Illuminated Miniatures and the date of the Florence Manuscript" (*Journal of the American Musicological Society*)

1974 Lawrence F. Bernstein, "La Courone et fleur des chansons a troys: A Mirror of the French Chanson in Italy in the Years between Ottaviano Petrucci and Antonio Gardano" (*Journal of the American Musicological Society*)

1975 Eugene K. Wolf and Jean K. Wolf, "A Newly Identified Complex of Manuscripts from Mannheim" (*Journal of the American Musicological Society*)

1976 Craig Wright, "Dufay at Cambrai: Discoveries and Revisions" (*Journal of the American Musicological Society*)

1977 James Webster, "Violoncello and Double Bass in the Chamber Music of Haydn and his Viennese Contemporaries, 1750-1780" (*Journal of the American Musicological Society*)

Avery Fisher Awards
Avery Fisher Prize
LINCOLN CENTER FOR THE PERFORMING ARTS
Attn.: Avery Fisher Artist Program, New York, N.Y. 10023 (212/580-8700)

The Avery Fisher Artist Program began with one presentation of the Avery Fisher Awards, which went to two outstanding young instrumentalists who established major reputations and had already given proof of their abilities as solo performers. The Award consisted of a $5,000 honorarium and numerous performance engagements with the New York Philharmonic and other leading musical organizations.

1975 Lynn Harrell, Cellist
Murray Perahia, Pianist

Subsequently, the Avery Fisher Artists Program was restructured as the Avery Fisher Prize, which goes annually to exceptionally talented, younger American instrumentalists who have demonstrated to experts in the musical field that they deserve wider attention. This is not a playing competition but a system whereby nominations are made by a board of nationally known conductors, instrumentalists, educators and others for selection by an executive committee. Each winner receives a $2,500 honorarium, plus a debut engagement with the New York Philharmonic and engagements

with other Lincoln Center musical organizations and about six others outside New York.

1976 Ani Kavafian, Violinist
Heidi Lehwader, Harpist
Ursula Oppens, Pianist
Paul Schenly, Pianist

1977 Andre-Michel Schub, Pianist
Richard Stoltzman, Clarinetist

Gold Baton
AMERICAN SYMPHONY ORCHESTRA LEAGUE
Box 669, Vienna, Va. 22180 (703/281-1230)

The Gold Baton annually honors service by individuals, organizations or corporations to music in particular and the arts in general. Plaques are given to the winner(s), selected by the board of directors upon recommendation of a special awards committee.

1948 Ernest La Prade, *NBC Orchestras of the Nations*

1952 John B. Ford, President, Detroit Sympathy Orchestra

1956 Marjorie Merriweather Post, Vice President, Washington National Symphony

1958 Samuel Rosenbaum, Henry B. Cabot, Dudley T. Easby, Jr., Charles Garside and Henry Allen Moe, The Study Committee on Orchestra Legal Documents

1959 Leonard Bernstein, conductor, New York Philharmonic

1960 Association of Junior Leagues of America, Charles Farnsley, former Mayor, Louisville, Ky.

1961 Arthur Judson, former manager, New York Philharmonic

1962 The Women's Association of Symphony Orchestras

1963 John D. Rockefeller, 3rd
Officers and directors of Lincoln Center for the Performing Arts

1964 Richard Lert, music director, Pasadena Symphony
Paul Mellon, A. W. Mellon Educational and Charitable Trusts, Richard King Mellon Charitable Trusts, Howard Heinz Endowment

1965 American Federation of Musicians

1966 Ford Foundation

1967 American Telephone and Telegraph Co.

1968 Leopold Stokowski
Jouett Shouse

1969 New York State Council on the Arts

1970 Helen M. Thompson

1971 Martha Baird Rockefeller

1972 Amyas Ames

1973 Danny Kaye

1974 Nancy Hanks and National Council on the Arts

1975 John S. Edwards, manager, Chicago Symphony

1976 Arthur Fiedler

1977 Avery Fisher
Alcoa Foundation

Grammy Awards
NATIONAL ACADEMY OF RECORDING ARTS AND SCIENCES
4444 Riverside Dr., Ste. 202, Burbank, Calif. 91505 (213/843-8233)

The Grammy statuette, which depicts an early gramophone, is presented annually in nationally telecast ceremonies to honor oustanding creativity in artistic and technical areas of recording. Academy members and recording companies recommend recordings of merit released during the specified year. Special committees and the local governors and national trustees of the Academy select finalists (usually five) in each category for a second round of balloting, which determines the winners. Members are limited to voting in their area of expertise. Unless otherwise specified, singles and albums are considered for Grammys in the same categories.

RECORD OF THE YEAR

1958 *Nel Blu Dipinto di Blu* (*Volare*) Domenico Modugno
1959 *Mack the Knife,* Bobby Darin
1960 *Theme from 'A Summer Place,'* Percy Faith
1961 *Moon River,* Henry Mancini
1962 *I Left My Heart in San Francisco,* Tony Bennett
1963 *The Days of Wine and Roses,* Henry Mancini
1964 *The Girl from Ipanema,* Stan Getz and Astrud Gilberto
1965 *A Taste of Honey,* Herb Alpert & the Tijuana Brass (prod. by Herb Alpert and Jerry Moss)
1966 *Strangers in the Night,* Frank Sinatra (prod. by Jimmy Bowen)
1967 *Up, Up and Away,* 5th Dimension (prod. by Marc Gordon and Johnny Rivers)
1968 *Mrs. Robinson,* Simon & Garfunkel (prod. by Paul Simon, Art Garfunkel and Roy Halee)
1969 *Aquarius, Let the Sunshine In,* 5th Dimension (prod. by Bones Howe)
1970 *Bridge Over Troubled Water,* Simon & Garfunkel (prod. by Paul Simon, Art Garfunkel and Roy Halee)
1971 *It's Too Late,* Carole King (prod. by Lou Adler)
1972 *The First Time Ever I Saw Your Face,* Roberta Flack (prod. by Joel Dorn)
1973 *Killing Me Softly With His Song,* Roberta Flack (prod. by Joel Dorn)
1974 *I Honestly Love You,* Olivia Newton-John (prod. by John Farrar)
1975 *Love Will Keep Us Together,* Captain & Tennille (prod. by Daryl Dragon)
1976 *This Masquerade,* George Benson (prod. by Tommy Lipuma)
1977 *Hotel California,* The Eagles (prod. by Bill Szymczyk)

ALBUM OF THE YEAR

1958 *The Music From Peter Gunn,* Henry Mancini
1959 *Come Dance With Me,* Frank Sinatra
1960 *Button Down Mind,* Bob Newhart
1961 *Judy at Carnegie Hall,* Judy Garland
1962 *The First Family,* Vaughn Meader
1963 *The Barbra Streisand Album,* Barbra Streisand
1964 *Getz/Gilberto,* Stan Getz and Joao Gilberto
1965 *September of My Years,* Frank Sinatra (prod. by Sonny Burke)
1966 *Sinatra: A Man and His Music,* Frank Sinatra (prod. by Sonny Burke)
1967 *Sgt. Pepper's Lonely Hearts Club Band,* The Beatles (prod. by George Martin)
1968 *By the Time I Get to Phoenix,* Glen Campbell (prod. by Al de Lory)
1969 *Blood, Sweat & Tears,* Blood, Sweat & Tears (prod. by James Guerico)
1970 *Bridge Over Troubled Water,* Simon & Garfunkel (prod. by Paul Simon, Art Garfunkel and Roy Halee)
1971 *Tapestry,* Carole King (prod. by Lou Adler)
1972 *The Concert for Bangla Desh,* George Harrison, Ravi Shankar, Bob Dylan, Leon Russell, Ringo Starr, Billy Preston, Eric Clapton and Klaus Voormann (prod. by George Harrison and Phil Spector)
1973 *Innervisions,* Stevie Wonder (prod. by Stevie Wonder)
1974 *Fulfillingness' First Finale,* Stevie Wonder (prod. by Stevie Wonder)
1975 *Still Crazy After All these Years,* Paul Simon (prod. by Paul Simon and Phil Ramone)
1976 *Songs in the Key of Life,* Stevie Wonder (prod. by Stevie Wonder
1977 *Rumors,* Fleetwood Mac (prod. by Richard Pashut and Ken Caillat)

SONG OF THE YEAR (Award to Songwriter)

1958 Domenico Modugno, for *Nel Blu Dipinto di Blu*
1959 Jimmy Driftwood, for *The Battle of New Orleans*
1960 Ernest Gold, for Theme from *Exodus*
1961 Henry Mancini and Johnny Mercer, for *Moon River*
1962 Leslie Bricusse and Anthony Newley, for *What Kind of Fool Am I*
1963 Henry Mancini and Johnny Mercer, for *The Days of Wine and Roses*
1964 Jerry Herman, for *Hello, Dolly!*
1965 Paul Francis Webster and Johnny Mandel, *For The Shadow of Your Smile*
1966 John Lennon and Paul McCartney, for *Michelle*
1967 Jim Webb, for *Up, Up and Away*
1968 Bobby Russell, for *Little Green Apples*
1969 Joe South, for *Games People Play*
1970 Paul Simon, for *Bridge Over Troubled Water*
1971 Carole King, for *You've Got a Friend*
1972 Ewan MacColl, for *The First Time Ever I Saw Your Face*
1973 Norman Gimbel and Charles Fox, for *Killing Me Softly With His Song*
1974 Marilyn and Alan Bergman and Marvin Hamlisch, for *The Way We Were*
1975 Stephen Sondheim, for *Send in the Clowns*
1976 Bruce Johnson, for *I Write the Songs*
1977 Barbra Streisand and Paul Williams, for *Evergreen* Joe Brooks, for *You Light Up My Life*

BEST NEW ARTIST OF THE YEAR

1959 Bobby Darin
1960 Bob Newhart
1961 Peter Nero
1962 Robert Goulet
1963 Swingle Singers
1964 The Beatles
1965 Tom Jones
1966 Category not voted on
1967 Bobbie Gentry
1968 Jose Feliciano
1969 Crosby, Stills and Nash
1970 The Carpenters
1971 Carly Simon
1972 America
1973 Bette Midler
1974 Marvin Hamlisch
1975 Natalie Cole
1976 Starland Vocal Band
1977 Debby Boone

BEST VOCAL PERFORMANCE/BEST SOLO VOCAL PERFORMANCE/BEST CONTEMPORARY POP VOCAL PERFORMANCE (Female)

1958 Ella Fitzgerald, *Ella Fitzgerald Sings the Irving Berlin Song Book*

1959 Ella Fitzgerald, *But Not for Me*
1960 Ella Fitzgerald, *Mack the Knife* (single)
Ella Fitzgerald, *Mack the Knife—Ella in Berlin* (album)
1961 Judy Garland, *Judy at Carnegie Hall* (album)
1962 Ella Fitzgerald, *Ella Swings Brightly With Nelson Riddle* (album)
1963 Barbra Streisand, *The Barbra Streisand Album* (album)
1964 Barbra Streisand, *People* (single)
1965 Barbra Streisand, *My Name Is Barbra* (album)
1966 Eydie Gorme, *If He Walked Into My Life* (single)
1967 Bobbie Gentry, *Ode to Billy Joe* (single
1968 Dionne Warwicke, *Do You Know the Way to San Jose?* (single)
1969 Peggy Lee, *Is That All There Is* (single)
1970 Dionne Warwicke, *I'll Never Fall in Love Again* (album)
1971 Carole King, *Tapestry* (album)
1972 Helen Reddy, *I Am Woman* (single)
1973 Roberta Flack, *Killing Me Softly With His Song* (single)
1974 Olivia Newton-John, *I Honestly Love You* (single)
1975 Janis Ian, *At Seventeen* (single)
1976 Linda Ronstadt *Hasten Down the Wind* (album)
1977 Barbra Streisand *Evergreen* (single)

BEST VOCAL PERFORMANCE/BEST SOLO VOCAL PERFORMANCE/BEST CONTEMPORARY POP VOCAL PERFORMANCE (male)
1958 Perry Como, *Catch a Falling Star*
1959 Frank Sinatra, *Come Dance With Me*
1960 Ray Charles, *Georgia On My Mind* (single)
Ray Charles, *Genius of Ray Charles* (album)
1961 Jack Jones, *Lollipops and Roses* (single)
1962 Tony Bennett, *I Left My Heart in San Francisco* (album)
1963 Jack Jones, *Wives and Lovers* (single)
1964 Louis Armstrong, *Hello, Dolly!* (single)
1965 Frank Sinatra, *It Was a Very Good Year* (single)
1966 Frank Sinatra, *Strangers in the Night* (single)
1967 Glen Campbell, *By the Time I Get to Phoenix* (single)
1968 Jose Feliciano, *Light My Fire* (single)
1969 Harry Nilsson, *Everybody's Talkin*
1970 Ray Stevens, *Everything Is Beautiful* (single)
1971 James Taylor, *You've Got a Friend* (single)
1972 Harry Nilsson, *Without You* (single)
1973 Stevie Wonder, *You Are The Sunshine of My Life* (single)
1974 Stevie Wonder, *Fulfillingness' First Finale* (album)
1975 Paul Simon, *Still Crazy After All These Years* (album)
1976 Stevie Wonder, *Songs in the Key of Life* (album)
1977 James Taylor, *Handy Man* (album)

BEST PERFORMANCE BY AN ORCHESTRA/BEST INSTRUMENTAL PERFORMANCE/POP INSTRUMENTAL PERFORMANCE
1958 Billy May, *Billy May's Big Fat Brass*
1959 David Rose and his Orchestra with Andre Previn, *Like Young*
1960 Henry Mancini, *Mr. Lucky*
1961 Henry Mancini, *Breakfast at Tiffany's*
1962 Peter Nero, *The Colorful Peter Nero*
1963 Al Hirt, *Java*
1964 Henry Mancini, *Pink Panther*
1965 Herb Alpert & the Tijuana Brass, *A Taste of Honey*

1966 Herb Alpert & the Tijuana Brass, *What Now My Love*
1967 Chet Atkins, *Chet Atkins Picks the Best*
1968 Mason Williams, *Classical Gas*
1969 Blood, Sweat and Tears, *Variations on a Theme by Eric Satie*
1970 Henry Mancini, *Theme from 'Z' and Other Film Music*
1971 Quincy Jones, *Smackwater Jack*
1972 Billy Preston, *Outa-Space*
Isaac Hayes, *Black Moses*
1973 Eumir Deodato, *Also Sprach Zarathustra* (theme from *2001: A Space Odyssey*)
1974 Marvin Hamlisch, *The Entertainer*
1975 Van McCoy and the Soul City Symphony, *The Hustle*
1976 George Benson, *Breezin'*
1977 John Williams conducting the London Symphony Orchestra, *Star Wars*

BEST PERFORMANCE BY A DANCE BAND/BEST PERFORMANCE OF A BAND FOR DANCING/BEST PERFORMANCE BY AN ORCHESTRA FOR DANCING
1958 Count Basie, *Basie*
1959 Duke Ellington, *Anatomy of a Murder*
1960 Count Basie, *Dance With Basie*
1961 Si Zentner, *Up a Lazy River*
1962 Joe Harnell, *Fly Me to the Moon Bossa Nova*
1963 Count Basie, *This Time by Basie! Hits of the 50s and 60s*

BEST ARRANGEMENT/BEST INSTRUMENTAL ARRANGEMENT
1958 Henry Mancini, *The Music from 'Peter Gunn'*
1959 Billy May, *Come Dance With Me*
1960 Henry Mancini, *Mr. Lucky*
1961 Henry Mancini, *Moon River*
1962 Henry Mancini, *Baby Elephant Walk*
1963 Quincy Jones, *I Can't Stop Loving You*
1964 Henry Mancini, *Pink Panther*
1965 Herb Alpert, *A Taste of Honey*
1966 Herb Alpert, *What Now My Love*
1967 Burt Bacharach, *Alfie*
1968 Mike Post, *Classical Gas*
1969 Henry Mancini, Love Theme from *Romeo and Juliet*
1970 Henry Mancini, Theme from *Z*
1971 Isaac Hayes and Johnny Allen, Theme from *Shaft*
1972 Don Ellis, Theme from *The French Connection*
1973 Quincy Jones, *Summer in the City*
1974 Pat Williams, *Threshold*
1975 Mike Post and Pete Carpenter, *The Rockford Files*
1976 Chick Corea, *Leprechaun's Dream*
1977 Harry Betts, Perry Botkin, Jr., and Barry de Vorzan, *Nadia's Theme*

BEST INSTRUMENTAL THEME/BEST INSTRUMENTAL COMPOSITION (Excluding Jazz) (Award to Composer)
1961 Galt McDermott, *African Waltz*
1962 Bobby Scott and Ric Marlow, *A Taste of Honey*
1963 Norman Newell, Nino Oliviero and Riz Ortolani, *More* (theme from *Mondo Cane*)
1964 Henry Mancini, *The Pink Panther Theme*
1965 Category not voted on
1966 Neal Hefti, *Batman* theme
1967 Lalo Shifrin, *Mission: Impossible*
1968 Mason Williams, *Classical Gas*
1969 John Barry, *Midnight Cowboy*
1970 Alfred Newman, *Airport Love Theme*
1971 Michel Legrand, Theme from *Summer of '42*

1972 Michel Legrand, *Brian's Song*
1973 Gato Barbieri, *Last Tango in Paris*
1974 Mike Oldfield, *Tubular Bells* (from *The Exorcist*)
1975 Michel Legrand, *Images*
1976 Chuck Mangione, *Bellavia*
1977 John Williams, Main title theme from *Star Wars*

BEST BACKGROUND ARRANGEMENT/BEST ACCOMPANIMENT ARRANGEMENT FOR VOCALIST(S) OR INSTRUMENTALISTS/BEST ARRANGEMENT ACCOMPANYING VOCALISTS

1962 Marty Manning, *I Left My Heart in San Francisco*
1963 Henry Mancini, *The Days of Wine and Roses*
1964 Peter Matz, *People*
1965 Gordon Jenkins, *It Was a Very Good Year*
1966 Ernie Freeman, *Strangers in the Night*
1967 Jimmie Haskell, *Ode to Billie Joe*
1968 Jim Webb, *MacArthur Park*
1969 Fred Lipsius, *Spinning Wheel*
1970 Paul Simon, Art Garfunkel, Jimmie Haskell, Ernie Freeman and Larry Knechtel, *Bridge Over Troubled Waters*
1971 Paul McCartney, *Uncle Albert/Admiral Halsey*
1972 Michel Legrand, *What Are You Doing the Rest of Your Life?*
1973 George Martin, *Live and Let Die*
1974 Joni Mitchell and Tom Scott, *Down to You*
1975 Ray Stevens, *Misty*
1976 Jimmie Haskell and James William Guerico, *If You Leave Me Now*
1977 Ian Freebairn-Smith, *Evergreen*

BEST ARRANGEMENT FOR VOICES (Duo, Group or Chorus)

1976 Starland Vocal Band, *Afternoon Delight*
1977 Eagles, *New Kid in Town*

BEST PERFORMANCE BY A VOCAL GROUP OR CHORUS

1958 Louis Prima and Keely Smith, *That Old Black Magic*

BEST PERFORMANCE BY A CHORUS/BEST CONTEMPORARY POP CHORUS PERFORMANCE

1959 Mormon Tabernacle Choir (Richard Condie, conductor), *Battle Hymn of the Republic*
1960 Norman Luboff Choir, *Songs of the Cowboy*
1961 Johnny Mann Singers, *Great Band with Great Voices*
1962 New Christy Minstrels, *Presenting the New Christy Minstrels*
1963 Swingle Singers, *Bach's Greatest Hits*
1964 Swingle Singers, *The Swingle Singers Going Baroque*
1965 Swingle Singers, *Anyone for Mozart?*
1966 Ray Conniff & Singers, *Somewhere My Love*
1967 5th Dimension, *Up, Up and Away*
1968 Alan Copeland Singers, *Mission Impossible/Norwegian Wood*
1969 Percy Faith Orchestra & Chorus, *Romeo and Juliet* love theme

BEST ROCK AND ROLL RECORDING

1961 Chubby Checker, *Let's Twist Again*
1962 Bent Fabric, *Alley Cat*
1963 Nino Tempo and April Stevens, *Deep Purple*
1964 Petula Clark, *Downtown*

BEST CONTEMPORARY R & R SINGLE

1965 Roger Miller, *King of the Road*
1966 New Vaudeville Band, *Winchester Cathedral*

BEST CONTEMPORARY SOLO VOCAL PERFORMANCE (Male or Female)

1965 Petula Clark (female), *I Know A Place*
     Roger Miller (male), *King of the Road*
1966 Paul McCartney, *Eleanor Rigby*

BEST CONTEMPORARY R&R PERFORMANCE GROUP (Vocal or Instrumental)

1965 Statler Brothers, *Flowers on the Wall*
1966 Mamas & Papas, *Monday, Monday*

BEST CONTEMPORARY SINGLE

1967 5th Dimension (prod. by Marc Gordon and Carlie Rivers), *Up, Up and Away*

BEST CONTEMPORARY SONG (Award to Songwriter)

1969 Joe South, *Games People Play*
1970 Paul Simon, *Bridge Over Troubled Water*

BEST CONTEMPORARY ALBUM

1967 The Beatles (prod. by George Martin), *Sgt. Pepper's Lonely Hearts Club Band*

BEST PERFORMANCE BY A VOCAL GROUP/BEST CONTEMPORARY VOCAL DUO OR GROUP PERFORMANCE/BEST POP VOCAL PERFORMANCE BY A DUO, GROUP OR CHORUS

1960 Steve Lawrence and Eydie Gorme, *We Got Us*
1961 Lambert, Hendricks and Ross, *High Flying*
1962 Peter, Paul and Mary, *If I Had A Hammer*
1963 Peter, Paul and Mary, *Blowin' in the Wind*
1964 The Beatles, *A Hard Day's Night*
1965 Anita Kerr Singers, *We Dig Mancini*
1966 Anita Kerr Singers, *A Man and A Woman*
1967 5th Dimension, *Up, Up and Away*
1968 Simon & Garfunkel, *Mrs. Robinson*
1969 5th Dimension, *Aquarius/Let the Sunshine In*
1970 Carpenters, *Close to You*
1971 Carpenters, *Carpenters*
1972 Roberta Flack and Donny Hathaway, *Where Is the Love*
1973 Gladys Knight & The Pips, *Neither One of Us (Wants to Be the First to Say Goodbye)*
1974 Paul McCartney & Wings, *Band on the Run*
1975 Eagles, *Lyin' Eyes*
1976 Chicago, *If You Leave Me Now*
1977 Bee Gees, *How Deep is Your Love?*

BEST JAZZ PERFORMANCE/SOLO/SOLO OR SMALL GROUP/SMALL GROUP OR SOLOIST WITH (SMALL) GROUP

1958 Ella Fitzgerald, *Ella Sings the Duke Ellington Song Book*
1959 Ella Fitzgerald, *Ella Swings Lightly*
1960 Andre Previn, *West Side Story*
1961 Andre Previn, *Andre Previn Plays Harold Arlen*
1962 Stan Getz, *Desafinado*
1963 Bill Evans, *Conversations with Myself*
1964 Stan Getz, *Getz/Gilberto*
1965 Ramsey Lewis Trio, *The 'In' Crowd*
1966 Wes Montgomery, *Goin' Out of My Head*
1967 Cannonball Adderly Quintet, *Mercy, Mercy, Mercy*
1968 Bill Evans Trio, *Bill Evans Trio at the Montreux Jazz Festival*
1969 Wes Montgomery, *Willow Weep for Me*
1970 Bill Evans, *Alone*
1971 Bill Evans, *The Bill Evans Album*
1972 Gary Burton, *Alone at Last*

BEST JAZZ PERFORMANCE BY A SOLOIST

1973 Art Tatum, *God Is in the House*
1974 Charlie Parker, *First Recordings*
1975 Dizzy Gillespie, *Oscar Peterson and Dizzy Gillespie*
1976 Ella Fitzgerald, *Ella & Pass . . . Again* (vocalist)
       Count Basie, *Basie and Zoot* (instrumentalist)
1977 Al Jarreau, *Look to the Rainbow* (vocalist)
       Oscar Peterson, *The Giants* (instrumentalist)

BEST JAZZ PERFORMANCE, GROUP

1958 Count Basie, *Basie*
1959 Jonah Jones, *I Dig Chicks*

**BEST JAZZ PERFORMANCE BY A LARGE
GROUP/INSTRUMENTAL/LARGE GROUP OR SOLOIST
WITH LARGE GROUP**

1960 Henry Mancini, *Blues and the Beat*
1961 Stan Kenton, *West Side Story*
1962 Stan Kenton, *Adventures in Jazz*
1963 Woody Herman Band, *Encore Woody Herman, 1963*
1964 Laurindo Almeida, *Guitar from Ipanema*
1965 Duke Ellington Orchestra, *Ellington '66*
1966 Category not voted on
1967 Duke Ellington, *Far East Suite*
1968 Duke Ellington, *And His Mother Called Him Bill*
1969 Quincy Jones, *Walking in Space*
1970 Miles Davis, *Bitches Brew*

BEST JAZZ PERFORMANCE BY A GROUP

1971 Bill Evans Trio, *The Bill Evans Album*
1972 Freddie Hubbard, *First Light*
1973 Supersax, *Supersax Plays Bird*
1974 Oscar Peterson, Joe Pass and Neils Pedersen, *The Trio*
1975 Chick Corea and Return to Favor, *No Mystery*
1976 Chick Corea, *The Leprechaun*
1977 Phil Woods, *The Phil Woods Six, Live from the Showboat*

BEST JAZZ PERFORMANCE BY A BIG BAND

1971 Duke Ellington, *New Orleans Suite*
1972 Duke Ellington, *Toga Brava Suite*
1973 Woody Herman, *Giant Steps*
1974 Woody Herman, *Thundering Herd*
1975 Phil Woods with Michel Legrand and His Orchestra, *Images*
1976 Duke Ellington, *The Ellington Suites*
1977 Count Basie, *Prime Time*

BEST ORIGINAL JAZZ COMPOSITION

1961 Galt MacDermott, *African Waltz*
1962 Vince Guaraldi, *Cast Your Fate to the Winds*
1963 Steve Allen and Ray Brown, *Gravy Waltz*
1964 Lalo Shifrin, *The Cat*
1965 Lalo Shifrin, *Jazz Suite on the Mass Texts*
1966 Duke Ellington, *In the Beginning God*

BEST COMEDY PERFORMANCE

1958 David Seville, *The Chipmunk Song*
1959 Shelley Berman, *Inside Shelley Berman*
       Homer and Jethro, *The Battle of Kookamonga*
1960 Bob Newhart, *Button Down Strikes Back*
       Jonathan and Darlene Edwards, *Jonathan and Darlene Edwards in Paris*
1961 Mike Nichols and Elaine May, *An Evening With Mike Nichols and Elaine May*
1962 Vaughn Meader, *The First Family*
1963 Allan Sherman, *Hello Muddah, Hello Faddah*

1964 Bill Cosby, *I Started Out As a Child*
1965 Bill Cosby, *Why Is There Air?*
1966 Bill Cosby, *Wonderfulness*
1967 Bill Cosby, *Revenge*
1968 Bill Cosby, *To Russell, My Brother, Whom I Slept With*
1969 Bill Cosby, *Bill Cosby*
1970 Flip Wilson, *The Devil Made Me Buy This Dress*
1971 Lily Tomlin, *This Is a Recording*
1972 George Carlin, *FM & AM*
1973 Cheech and Chong, *Los Cochinos*
1974 Richard Pryor, *That Nigger's Crazy*
1975 Richard Pryor, *Is It Something I Said?*
1976 Richard Pryor, *Bicentennial Nigger*
1977 Steve Martin, *Let's Get Small*

**BEST PERFORMANCE, FOLK/BEST FOLK
PERFORMANCE**

1959 Kingston Trio, *The Kingston Trio at Large*
1960 Harry Belafonte, *Swing Dat Hammer*
1961 Belafonte Folk Singers, *Belafonte Folksingers at Home and Abroad*
1962 Peter, Paul and Mary, *If I Had a Hammer*
1963 Peter, Paul and Mary, *Blowin' in the Wind*
1964 Gale Garnett, *We'll Sing in the Sunshine*
1965 Harry Belafonte and Miriam Makeba, *An Evening With Belafonte/Makeba*
1966 Cortelia Clark, *Blues in the Street*
1967 John Hartford, *Gentle on My Mind*
1968 Judy Collins, *Both Sides Now*
1969 Joni Mitchell, *Clouds*

BEST ETHNIC OR TRADITIONAL RECORDING

1970 T-Bone Walker, *Good Feelin'*
1971 Muddy Waters, *They Call Me Muddy Waters*
1972 Muddy Waters, *The London Muddy Waters Session*
1973 Doc Watson, *Then and Now*
1974 Doc and Merle Watson, *Two Days in November*
1975 Muddy Waters, *The Muddy Waters Woodstock Album*
1976 John Hartford, *Mark Twang*
1977 Muddy Waters, *Hard Again*

BEST LATIN RECORDING

1975 Eddie Palmieri, *Sun of Latin Music*
1976 Eddie Palmieri, *Unfinished Masterpiece*
1977 Mongo Santamaria, *Dawn*

**BEST COUNTRY AND WESTERN PERFORMANCE/BEST
COUNTRY AND WESTERN RECORDING**

1958 Kingston Trio, *Tom Dooley*
1959 Johnny Horton, *Battle of New Orleans*
1960 Marty Robbins, *El Paso*
1961 Jimmy Dean, *Big Bad John*
1962 Burl Ives, *Funny Way of Laughin'*
1963 Bobby Bare, *Detroit City*
1964 Roger Miller, *Dang Me* (single)
       Roger Miller, *Dang Me/Chug-a-Lug* (album)
1965 Roger Miller, *King of the Road* (single)
       Roger Miller, *The Return of Roger Miller* (album)
1966 David Houston, *Almost Persuaded*
1967 Glen Campbell (produced by Al DeLory), *Gentle on My Mind*

**BEST COUNTRY (and Western) VOCAL PERFORMANCE
(Female)**

1964 Dottie West, *Here Comes My Baby*
1965 Jody Miller, *Queen of the House*
1966 Jeannie Seely, *Harper Valley P.T.A.*
1967 Tammy Wynette, *I Don't Wanna Play House*

1968 Jeannie C. Riley, *Harper Valley P.T.A.*
1969 Tammy Wynette, *Stand By Your Man*
1970 Lynn Anderson, *Rose Garden*
1971 Sammi Smith, *Help Me Make It Through the Night*
1972 Donna Fargo, *Happiest Girl in the Whole USA*
1973 Olivia Newton-John, *Let Me Be There*
1974 Anne Murray, *Love Song*
1975 Linda Ronstadt, *I Can't Help It (If I'm Still in Love with You)*
1976 Emmylou Harris, *Elite Hotel*
1977 Crystal Gale, *Don't It Make My Brown Eyes Blue*

BEST COUNTRY (and Western) VOCAL PERFORMANCE (Male)

1964 Roger Miller, *Dang Me*
1965 Roger Miller, *King of the Road*
1966 David Houston, *Almost Persuaded*
1967 Glen Campbell, *Gentle on My Mind*
1968 Johnny Cash, *Folsom Prison Blues*
1969 Johnny Cash, *A Boy Named Sue*
1970 Ray Price, *For the Good Times*
1971 Jerry Reed, *When You're Hot, You're Hot*
1972 Charley Pride, *Charley Pride Sings Heart Songs*
1973 Charlie Rich, *Behind Closed Doors*
1974 Ronnie Milsap, *Please Don't Tell Me How the Story Ends*
1975 Willie Nelson, *Blue Eyes Cryin' in the Rain*
1976 Ronnie Milsap, *(I'm a) Stand By My Woman Man*
1977 Kenny Rogers, *Lucille*

BEST COUNTRY AND WESTERN DUET, TRIO OR GROUP (Vocal or Instrumental)

1967 Johnny Cash and June Carter, *Jackson*
1968 Flatt & Scruggs, *Foggy Mountain Breakdown*

BEST COUNTRY PERFORMANCE BY A DUO OR GROUP/BEST COUNTRY VOCAL PERFORMANCE BY A DUO OR GROUP

1969 Waylon Jennings and the Kimberlys, *MacArthur Park*
1970 Johnny Cash and June Carter, *If I Were a Carpenter*
1971 Conway Twitty and Loretta Lynn, *After the Fire Is Gone*
1972 Statler Brothers, *Class of '57*
1973 Kris Kristofferson and Rita Coolidge, *From the Bottle to the Bottom*
1974 Pointer Sisters, *Fairytale*
1975 Kris Kristofferson and Rita Coolidge, *Lover Please*
1976 Amazing Rhythm Aces, *The End Is Not in Sight* (The Cowboy Tune)
1977 The Kendalls, *Heaven's Just a Sin Away*

BEST COUNTRY INSTRUMENTAL PERFORMANCE

1969 Danny Davis and the Nashville Brass, *The Nashville Brass Featuring Danny Davis Play More Nashville Sounds*
1970 Chet Atkins and Jerry Reed, *Me & Jerry*
1971 Chet Atkins, *Snowbird*
1972 Charlie McCoy, *Charlie McCoy/The Real McCoy*
1973 Eric Weissberg and Steven Mandell, *Dueling Banjos*
1974 Chet Atkins and Merle Travis, *The Atkins-Travis Traveling Show*
1975 Chet Atkins, *The Entertainer*
1976 Chet Atkins and Les Paul, *Chester & Lester*
1977 Hargus "Pig" Robbins, *Hargus 'Pig' Robbins*

BEST COUNTRY (and Western) Song (Award to Songwriter)

1964 Roger Miller, *Dang Me*

1965 Roger Miller, *King of the Road*
1966 Billy Sherrill and Glenn Sutton, *Almost Persuaded*
1967 John Hartford, *Gentle on My Mind*
1968 Bobby Russell, *Little Green Apples*
1969 Shel Silverstein, *A Boy Named Sue*
1970 Marty Robbins, *My Woman, My Woman, My Wife*
1971 Kris Kristofferson, *Help Me Make It Through the Night*
1972 Ben Peters, *Kiss an Angel Good Morning*
1973 Kenny O'Dell, *Behind Closed Doors*
1974 Norris Wilson and Billy Sherrill, *A Very Special Love Song*
1975 Chips Moman and Larry Butler, *(Hey, Won't You Play) Another Somebody Done Somebody Wrong Song*
1976 Larry Gatlin, *Broken Lady*
1977 Richard Leigh, *Don't It Make My Brown Eyes Blue*

BEST RHYTHM AND BLUES PERFORMANCE

1958 The Champs, *Tequila*
1959 Dinah Washington, *What a Difference a Day Makes*
1960 Ray Charles, *Let the Good Times Roll*
1961 Ray Charles, *Hit the Road Jack*
1962 Ray Charles, *I Can't Stop Loving You*
1963 Ray Charles, *Busted*
1964 Nancy Wilson, *How Glad I Am*
1965 James Brown, *Papa's Got a Brand New Bag*
1966 Ray Charles, *Crying Time*

BEST RHYTHM AND BLUES RECORDING, SOLO VOCAL

1966 Ray Charles, *Crying Time*
1967 Aretha Franklin, *Respect* (prod. by Jerry Wexler)

BEST RHYTHM AND BLUES VOCAL PERFORMANCE (Female)

1967 Aretha Franklin, *Respect*
1968 Aretha Franklin, *Chain of Fools*
1969 Aretha Franklin, *Share Your Love With Me*
1970 Aretha Franklin, *Don't Play That Song*
1971 Aretha Franklin, *Bridge Over Troubled Water*
1972 Aretha Franklin, *Young, Gifted and Black*
1973 Aretha Franklin, *Master of Eyes*
1974 Aretha Franklin, *Ain't Nothing Like the Real Thing*
1975 Natalie Cole, *This Will Be*
1976 Natalie Cole, *Sophisticated Lady (She's a Different Lady)*
1977 Thelma Houston, *Don't Leave Me This Way*

BEST RHYTHM AND BLUES VOCAL PERFORMANCE (Male)

1967 Lou Rawls, *Dead End Street*
1968 Otis Redding, *(Sittin' on) The Dock of the Bay*
1969 Joe Simon, *The Chokin' Kind*
1970 B.B. King, *The Thrill Is Gone*
1971 Lou Rawls, *A Natural Man*
1972 Billy Paul, *Me and Mrs. Jones*
1973 Stevie Wonder, *Superstitition*
1974 Stevie Wonder, *Boogie on Reggae Woman*
1975 Ray Charles, *Living for the City*
1976 Stevie Wonder, *I Wish*
1977 Lou Rawls, *Unmistakably Lou*

BEST RHYTHM AND BLUES GROUP PERFORMANCE (Two or More), VOCAL OR INSTRUMENTAL

1966 Ramsey Lewis, *Hold It Right There*
1967 Sam & Dave, *Soul Man*
1968 The Temptations, *Cloud Nine*

BEST RHYTHM AND BLUES VOCAL PERFORMANCE BY A GROUP OR DUO/DUO, GROUP OR CHORUS

1969 Isley Brothers, *It's Your Thing*
1970 The Delfonics, *Didn't I (Blow Your Mind This Time)?*
1971 Ike & Tina Turner, *Proud Mary*
1972 The Temptations, *Papa Was A Rolling Stone*
1973 Gladys Knight & The Pips, *Midnight Train to Georgia*
1974 Rufus, *Tell Me Something Good*
1975 Earth, Wind & Fire, *Shining Star*
1976 Marilyn McCoo and Billy Davis, Jr., *You Don't Have to be a Star (to Be in My Show)*
1977 Emotions, *Best of My Love*

BEST RHYTHM AND BLUES INSTRUMENTAL PERFORMANCE

1969 King Curtis, *Games People Play*
1970 Category not voted on
1971 Category not voted on
1972 The Temptations (Paul Riser, cond.), *Papa Was A Rolling Stone*
1973 Ramsey Lewis, *Hang On Sloopy*
1974 MFSB, *TSOP (The Sound of Philadelphia)*
1975 Silver Convention, *Fly, Robin, Fly*
1976 George Benson, *Theme from Good King Bad*
1977 Brothers Johnson, *Q*

BEST RHYTHM AND BLUES SONG (Award to Songwriter)

1968 Otis Redding and Steve Cropper, *(Sittin' on) The Dock of the Bay*
1969 Richard Spencer, *Color Him Father*
1970 Ronald Dunbar and General Johnson, *Patches*
1971 Bill Withers, *Ain't No Sunshine*
1972 Barrett Strong and Norman Whitfield, *Papa Was a Rolling Stone*
1973 Stevie Wonder, *Superstitition*
1974 Stevie Wonder, *Living for the City*
1975 Harry Wayne Casey, Richard Finch, Willie Clarke and Betty Wright, *Where Is the Love?*
1976 Boz Scaggs and David Paich, *Lowdown*
1977 Lou Sayer and Vini Poncia, *You Make Me Feel Like Dancing*

BEST GOSPEL OR OTHER RELIGIOUS RECORDING

1961 Mahalia Jackson *Everytime I Feel the Spirit*
1962 Mahalia Jackson *Great Songs of Love and Faith*
1963 Soeur Sourire, *Dominique*
1964 Tennessee Ernie Ford, *Great Gospel Songs*
1965 George Beverly Shea and the Anita Kerr Singers, *Southland Favorites*

BEST INSPIRATIONAL PERFORMANCE

1977 B.J. Thomas, *Home Where I Belong*

BEST SACRED RECORDING/BEST SACRED PERFORMANCE/BEST INSPIRATIONAL PERFORMANCE/BEST GOSPEL PERFORMANCE, CONTEMPORARY OR INSPIRATIONAL

1966 Porter Wagoner and the Blackwood Brothers, *Grand Old Gospel*
1967 Elvis Presley, *How Great Thou Art*
1968 Jake Hess, *Beautiful Isle of Somewhere*
1969 Jake Hess, *Ain't That Beautiful Singing*
1970 Jake Hess, *Everything Is Beautiful*
1971 Charley Pride, *Did You Think to Pray?*
1972 Elvis Presley, *He Touched Me*
1973 Bill Gaither Trio, *Let's Just Praise the Lord*
1974 Elvis Presley, *How Great Thou Art*

1975 Bill Gaither Trio, *Jesus, We Just Want to Thank You*
1976 Gary S. Paxton, *The Astonishing, Outrageous, Amazing, Incredible, Unbelievable, Different World of Gary S. Paxton*
1977 Imperials, *Sail On*

BEST SOUL GOSPEL PERFORMANCE, CONTEMPORARY

1977 Eddie Hawkins and the Eddie Hawkins Singers, *Wonderful*

BEST GOSPEL PERFORMANCE (Other than Soul Gospel)/BEST GOSPEL PERFORMANCE, TRADITIONAL

1967 Porter Wagoner and the Blackwood Brothers, *More Grand Old Gospel*
1968 Happy Goodman Family, *The Happy Gospel of the Happy Goodmans*
1969 Porter Wagoner and the Blackwood Brothers, *In Gospel Country*
1970 Oak Ridge Boys, *Talk About the Good Times*
1971 Charley Pride, *Let Me Live*
1972 Blackwood Brothers, *Love*
1973 Blackwood Brothers, *Release Me (from My Sin)*
1974 Oak Ridge Boys, *The Baptism of Jesse Taylor*
1975 Imperials, *No Shortage*
1976 Oak Ridge Boys, *Where the Soul Never Dies*
1977 Oak Ridge Boys, *Just a Little Talk with Jesus*

BEST SOUL GOSPEL PERFORMANCE

1968 Dottie Rambo, *The Soul of Me*
1969 Edwin Hawkins Singers, *Oh, Happy Day*
1970 Edwin Hawkins Singers, *Every Man Wants to Be Free*
1971 Shirley Caesar, *Put Your Hand in the Hand of the Man from Galilee*
1972 Aretha Franklin, *Amazing Grace*
1973 Dixie Hummingbirds, *Love Me Like a Rock*
1974 James Cleveland and the Southern California Community Choir, *In the Ghetto*
1975 Andrae Crouch and the Disciples, *Take Me Back*
1976 Mahalia Jackson, *How I Got Over*
1977 James Cleveland, *James Cleveland at Carnegie Hall*

BEST ORIGINAL CAST ALBUM, BROADWAY OR TV

1958 Meredith Willson, *The Music Man*

BEST BROADWAY SHOW ALBUM/BEST SHOW ALBUM (Original Cast)/BEST SCORE FROM ORIGINAL CAST SHOW ALBUM/BEST CAST SHOW ALBUM (beginning in 1961, Grammy to composer; since 1967, also to producer)

1959 Ethel Merman, *Gypsy*
     Gwen Verdon, *Redhead*
1960 Mary Martin (composed by Richard Rodgers and Oscar Hammerstein II), *The Sound of Music*
1961 Frank Loesser, *How to Succeed in Business Without Really Trying*
1962 Richard Rodgers, *No Strings*
1963 Jerry Block and Sheldon Harnick, *She Loves Me*
1964 Jule Styne and Bob Merrill, *Funny Girl*
1965 Alan Lerner and Burton Lane, *On a Clear Day*
1966 Jerry Herman, *Mame*
1967 Fred Ebb and John Kander (prod. by Goddard Lieberson), *Cabaret*
1968 Gerome Ragni, James Rado and Galt MacDermott (prod. by Andy Wiswell), *Hair*
1969 Burt Bacharach and Hal David (prod. by Henry Jerome and Phil Ramone), *Promises, Promises*
1970 Stephen Sondheim (prod. by Thomas Z. Shepard), *Company*

1971 **Stephen Schwartz** (prod. by Stephen Schwartz), *Godspell*
1972 **Micki Grant** (prod. by Jerry Ragnvoy), *Don't Bother Me, I Can't Cope*
1973 **Stephen Sondheim** (prod. by Goddard Lieberson), *A Little Night Music*
1974 **Judd Woldin and John Brittan** (prod. by Thomas Z. Shepard), *Raisin*
1975 **Charlie Smalls** (prod. by Jerry Wexler), *The Wiz*
1976 **Hugo & Luigi** (prod.), *Bubbling Brown Sugar*
1977 **Charles Strouse and Martin Charnin** (prod. by Larry Morton and Charles Strouse), *Annie*

BEST SOUNDTRACK ALBUM, DRAMATIC PICTURE SCORE OR ORIGINAL CAST

1958 Andre Previn, *Gigi*

BEST SOUNDTRACK ALBUM OR RECORDING OF MUSIC SCORE FROM MOTION PICTURE OR TELEVISION (Award to Composer)

1959 **Duke Ellington**, *Anatomy of A Murder*
1960 **Ernest Gold**, *Exodus*
1961 **Henry Mancini**, *Breakfast at Tiffany's*
1962 **Category not voted on**
1963 **John Addison**, *Tom Jones*
1964 **Richard M. and Roger B. Sherman**, *Mary Poppins*
1965 **Johnny Mandel**, *The Sandpiper*
1966 **Maurice Jarre**, *Dr. Zhivago*
1967 **Lalo Shifrin**, *Mission: Impossible*
1968 **Paul Simon** (additional music by David Grusin), *The Graduate*
1969 **Burt Bacharach**, *Butch Cassidy & The Sundance Kid*
1970 **John Lennon, Paul McCartney, George Harrison and Ringo Starr**, *Let It Be*
1971 **Isaac Hayes**, *Shaft*
1972 **Nino Rota**, *The Godfather*
1973 **Neil Diamond**, *Jonathan Livingston Seagull*
1974 **Marvin Hamlisch, Alan and Marilyn Bergman**, *The Way We Were*
1975 **John Williams**, *Jaws*
1976 **Norman Whitfield**, *Car Wash*
1977 **John Williams**, *Star Wars*

BEST SOUNDTRACK ALBUM, ORIGNAL CAST, MOTION PICTURE OR TELEVISION

1959 **Andre Previn and Ken Darby**, *Porgy and Bess*
1960 **Cole Porter** (composer), *Can Can*
1961 **Johnny Green, Saul Chaplin, Sid Ramin and Irwin Kostal** (collaborators), *West Side Story*

BEST RECORDING FOR CHILDREN

1958 **David Seville**, *The Chipmunk Song*
1959 **Peter Ustinov** (narrator) and **Herbert von Karajan** (conductor), *Peter and the Wolf*
1960 **David Seville**, *Let's All Sing with the Chipmunks*
1961 **Leonard Bernstein** conducting the New York Philharmonic, *Peter and the Wolf*
1962 **Leonard Bernstein**, *Saint Saens: Carnival of the Animals/Britten: Young Person's Guide to the Orchestra*
1963 **Leonard Bernstein**, *Bernstein Conducts for Young People*
1964 **Julie Andrews and Dick Van Dyke**, *Mary Poppins*
1965 **Marvin Miller**, *Dr. Seuss Presents "Fox in Sox" and "Green Eggs and Ham"*
1966 **Marvin Miller**, *Dr. Seuss Presents "If I Ran the Zoo" and "Sleep Book"*
1967 **Boris Karloff**, *Dr. Seuss Presents "How the Grinch Stole Christmas"*
1968 **Category not voted on**

1969 **Peter, Paul and Mary**, *Peter Paul and Mary*
1970 **Joan Cooney** (producer), *Sesame Street*
1971 **Bill Cosby**, *Bill Cosby Talks to Kids About Drugs*
1972 **Christopher Cerf** (proj. dir.), **Lee Chamberlain, Bill Cosby, Rita Moreno and Joe Raposa** (producer), *The Electric Company*
1973 ***Sesame Street* cast and Joe Raposa** (producer), *Sesame Street Live*
1974 **Sebastian Cabot, Sterling Holloway and Paul Winchell**, *Winnie the Pooh & Tigger Too*
1975 **Richard Burton**, *The Little Prince*
1976 **Hermione Gingold and Karl Bohm**, *Prokofiev: Peter and the Wolf/Saint Saens: Carnival of the Animals*
1977 **Christopher Cerf and Jimmy Timmens**, *Aren't You Glad You're You*

BEST PERFORMANCE, DOCUMENTARY OR SPOKEN WORD/BEST SPOKEN WORK OR DRAMA RECORDING

1958 **Stan Freberg**, *The Best of the Stan Freberg Show*
1959 **Carl Sandburg**, *A Lincoln Portrait*
1960 **Robert Bialek** (producer), *F.D.R. Speaks*
1961 **Leonard Bernstein**, *Humor in Music*
1962 **Charles Laughton**, *The Story-Teller: A Session with Charles Laughton*
1963 **Edward Albee**, *Who's Afraid of Virginia Woolf?*
1964 ***That Was the Week That Was* cast**, *BBC Tribute to John F. Kennedy*
1965 **Goddard Lieberson** (producer), *John F. Kennedy—As We Remember Him*
1966 **Edward R. Murrow**, *Edward R. Murrow—A Reporter Remembers, Vol. I, The War Years*
1967 **Sen. Everett M. Dirksen**, *Gallant Men*
1968 **Rod McKuen**, *Lonesome Cities*
1969 **Art Linkletter and Diane**, *We Love You, Call Collect*
1970 **Martin Luther King, Jr.**, *Why I Oppose the War in Vietnam*
1971 **Les Crane**, *Desiderata*
1972 **Bruce Botnick** (producer), *Lenny*
1973 **Richard Harris**, *Jonathan Livingston Seagull*
1974 **Peter Cook and Dudley Moore**, *Good Evening*
1975 **James Whitmore**, *Give 'Em Hell, Harry*
1976 **Orson Welles, Henry Fonda, Helen Hayes and James Earl Jones**, *Great American Documents*
1977 **Julie Harris**, *The Belle of Amherst*

ALBUM OF THE YEAR, CLASSICAL

1961 **Igor Stravinsky** conducting the Columbia Symphony, *Stravinsky Conducts, 1960: Le Sacre du Printemps; Petrouchka*
1962 **Vladimir Horowitz**, *Columbia Records Presents Vladimir Horowitz*
1963 **Benjamin Britten** conducting the London Symphony Orchestra and Chorus, *Britten: War Requiem*
1964 **Leonard Bernstein** conducting the New York Philharmonic, *Bernstein Symphony No. 3 (Kaddish)*
1965 **Vladimir Horowitz** (prod. by Thomas Frost), *Horowitz at Carnegie Hall (An Historic Return)*
1966 **Morton Gould** conducting the Chicago Symphony (prod. by Howard Scott), *Ives: Symphony No. 1 in D Minor*
1967 **Pierre Boulez and the Paris National Opera** (prod. by Thomas Z. Shepard), *Berg: Wozzeck*
 Leonard Bernstein and the London Symphony Orchestra (prod. by John McClure), *Mahler: Symphony No. 8 in E Flat Major (Symphony of a Thousand)*
1968 **Category not voted on**
1969 **Walter Carlos** (prod. by Rachel Elkind), *Switched-on Bach*

1970 **Colin Davis and the Royal Opera House Orchestra** (prod. by Erik Smith), *Berlioz: Les Troyens*

1971 **Vladimir Horowitz** (prod. by Richard Killough and Thomas Frost), *Horowitz Plays Rachmaninoff*

1972 **Georg Solti conducting the Chicago Symphony Orchestra, Vienna Boys' Choir, Vienna State Opera Chorus and Vienna Sangerverein chorus and soloists** (prod. by David Harvey), *Mahler: Symphony No. 8*

1973 **Pierre Boulez conducting the New York Philharmonic** (prod. by Thomas Z. Shepard), *Bartok: Concerto for Orchestra*

1974 **Georg Solti conducting the Chicago Symphony Orchestra** (prod. by David Harvey), *Berlioz: Symphonie Fantastique*

1975 **Sir Georg Solti conducting the Chicago Symphony Orchestra** (prod. by Ray Minshull), *Beethoven: Symphonies (9) Complete*

1976 **Artur Rubinstein and Daniel Barenboim conducting the London Philharmonic** (prod. by Max Wilcox), *Beethoven: The Five Piano Concertos*

1977 **Leonard Bernstein, Vladimir Horowitz, Isaac Stern, Mstislav Rostropovich, Dietrich Fischer-Dieskau, Yehudi Menuhin and Lyndon Woodside** (prod. by Thomas Fronts), *Concert of the Century*

BEST CLASSICAL PERFORMANCE, ORCHESTRAL

1958 **Felix Slatkin and the Hollywood Bowl Symphony Orchestra**, *Gaite Parisienne*

1959 **Charles Munch conducting the Boston Symphony Orchestra**, *Debussy: Images for Orchestra*

1960 **Fritz Reiner conducting the Chicago Symphony Orchestra**, *Bartok: Music for Strings, Percussion and Celeste*

1961 **Charles Munch conducting the Boston Symphony Orchestra**, *Ravel: Daphnis and Chloe*

1962 **Igor Stravinsky conducting the Columbia Symphony**, *Stravinsky: The Firebird Ballet*

1963 **Erich Leinsdorf conducting the Boston Symphony Orchestra**, *Bartok: Concerto for Orchestra*

1964 **Erich Leinsdorf conducting the Boston Symphony Orchestra**, *Mahler: Symphony in C Sharp Minor/Berg: 'Wozzeck' Excerpts*

1965 **Leopold Stokowski conducting the American Symphony Orchestra**, *Ives: Symphony No. 4*

1966 **Erich Leinsdorf conducting the Boston Symphony Orchestra**, *Mahler: Symphony No. 6 in A Minor*

1967 **Igor Stravinsky conducting the Columbia Symphony**, *Stravinsky: Firebird & Petrouchka Suites*

1968 **Pierre Boulez conducting the New Philharmonic Orchestra**, *Boulez Conducts Debussy*

1969 **Pierre Boulez conducting the Cleveland Orchestra**, *Boulez Conducts Debussy, Vol. 2, Images Pour Orchestre*

1970 **Pierre Boulez conducting the Cleveland Orchestra**, *Stravinsky: Le Sacre du Printemps*

1971 **Carlo Maria Giulini conducting the Chicago Symphony Orchestra**, *Mahler: Symphony No. 1 in D Major*

1972 **Georg Solti conducting the Chicago Symphony Orchestra**, *Mahler: Symphony No. 7*

1973 **Pierre Boulez conducting the New York Philharmonic**, *Bartok: Concerto for Orchestra*

1974 **Georg Solti conducting the Chicago Symphony**, *Berlioz: Symphonie Fantastique*

1975 **Pierre Boulez conducting the New York Philharmonic**, *Ravel: Daphnis and Chloe*

1976 **Sir Georg Solti conducting the Chicago Symphony** (prod. by Ray Minshull), *Strauss: Also Sprach Zarathustra*

1977 **Carlo Maria Giulini conducting the Chicago Symphony Orchestra** (prod. by Gunther Breest), *Mahler: Symphony No. 9*

BEST CLASSICAL PERFORMANCE, INSTRUMENTAL, CONCERTO OR INSTRUMENTAL SOLOIST (Concerto Scale)

1958 **Van Cliburn, pianist, and Kiril Kondrashin and his Symphony Orchestra**, *Tchaikovsky: Concerto No. 1 in B Flat Minor, Op. 23*

1959 **Van Cliburn, pianist, and Kiril Kondrashin conducting the Symphony of the Air**, *Rachmaninoff: Piano Concerto No. 3*

1960 **Sviatoslav Ritcher with Erich Leinsdorf conducting the Chicago Symphony Orchestra**, *Brahms: Piano Concerto No. 2 in B Flat*

1961 **Isaac Stern, violinist, with Eugene Ormandy conducting the Philadelphia Orchestra**, *Bartok: Concerto No. 1 for Violin and Orchestra*

1962 **Isaac Stern with Igor Stravinsky conducting the Columbia Symphony**, *Stravinsky: Concerto in D for Violin*

1963 **Artur Rubinstein with Erich Leinsdorf conducting the Boston Symphony Orchestra**, *Tchaikovsky: Concerto No. 1 in B Flat Minor for Piano and Orchestra*

1964 **Isaac Stern with Eugene Ormandy conducting the Philadelphia Orchestra**, *Prokofieff: Concerto No. 1 in D Major for Violin*

1965 **Artur Rubinstein with Erich Leinsdorf conducting the Boston Symphony Orchestra**, *Beethoven: Concerto No. 4 in G Major for Piano and Orchestra*

BEST CLASSICAL PERFORMANCE, INSTRUMENTALIST (Other Than Concerto Scale)

1958 **Andres Segovia**, *Segovia Golden Jubilee*

BEST CLASSICAL PERFORMANCE — INSTRUMENTAL SOLOIST (Other than Full Orchestral Accompaniment)

1959 **Artur Rubinstein**, *Beethoven: Sonata No. 21 in C, Op. 53; Sonata No. 18 in E Flat, Op. 31, No. 3*

1960 **Laurindo Almeida**, *The Spanish Guitars of Laurindo Almeida*

BEST PERFORMANCE — INSTRUMENTAL SOLOIST(S) (With or Without Orchestra)

1966 **Julian Bream**, *Baroque Guitar*

1967 **Vladimir Horowitz**, *Horowitz in Concert*

1968 **Vladimir Horowitz**, *Horowitz on Television*

1969 **Walter Carlos**, *Switched-On Bach*

1970 **David Oistrakh and Mstislav Rostropovich**, *Brahms: Double Concerto (Concerto in A Minor for Violin and Cello)*

BEST CLASSICAL PERFORMANCE — INSTRUMENTAL SOLOIST OR DUO WITHOUT ORCHESTRA

1961 **Laurindo Almeida**, *Reverie for Spanish Guitars*

1962 **Vladimir Horowitz**, *Columbia Records Presents Vladimir Horowitz*

1963 **Vladimir Horowitz**, *The Sound of Horowitz*

1964 **Vladimir Horowitz**, *Vladimir Horowitz Plays Beethoven, Debussy, Chopin*

1965 **Vladimir Horowitz**, *Horowitz at Carnegie Hall — An Historic Return*

BEST INSTRUMENTAL SOLOIST PERFORMANCE (Without Orchestra)

1971 **Vladimir Horowitz**, *Horowitz Plays Rachmaninoff*

1972 **Vladimir Horowitz**, *Horowitz Plays Chopin*

1973 **Vladimir Horowitz**, *Horowitz Plays Scriabin*

1974 Alicia de Larrocha, *Albeniz: Iberia*
1975 Nathan Milstein, *Bach: Sonatas and Partitas for Violin Unaccompanied*
1976 Vladimir Horowitz, *Horowitz Concerts 1975/76*
1977 Artur Rubinstein, *Beethoven: Sonata for Piano No. 18/Schumann: Fantasiestucke*

BEST INSTRUMENTAL SOLOIST PERFORMANCE (With Orchestra)

1971 Julian Bream, *Villa Lobos: Concerto for Guitar*
1972 Artur Rubinstein, *Brahms: Concerto No. 2*
1973 Vladimir Ashkenazy with Georg Solti conducting the Chicago Symphony Orchestra, *Beethoven: Concerti (5) for Piano and Orchestra*
1974 David Oistrakh, *Shostakovich: Violin Concerto No. 1*
1975 Alicia de Larrocha with De Burgos and Foster conducting the London Philharmonic, *Ravel: Concerto for Left Hand and Concerto for Piano in G Major/Faure: Fantasie for Piano and Orchestra*
1976 Artur Rubinstein with Daniel Barenboim conducting the London Philharmonic, *Beethoven: The Five Piano Concertos*
1977 Itzhak Perlman with the London Philharmonic Orchestra, *Vivaldi: The Four Seasons*

BEST CLASSICAL PERFORMANCE, CHAMBER MUSIC/VOCAL OR INSTRUMENTAL CHAMBER MUSIC

1958 Hollywood String Quartet, *Beethoven Quartet 130*
1959 Artur Rubinstein, *Beethoven: Sonata No. 21 in C, Op. 53; Sonata No. 18 in E Flat, Op. 31, No. 3*
1960 Laurindo Almeida, *Conversations with the Guitar*
1961 Jascha Heifetz, Gregor Piatigorsky and William Primrose, *Beethoven: Serenade, Op. 8/Kodaly: Duo for Violin and Cello, Op. 7*
1962 Jascha Heifetz, Gregor Piatigorsky and William Primrose, *The Heifetz-Piatigorsky Concerts with Primrose, Pennario and Guests*
1963 Julian Bream Consort, *Evening of Elizabethan Music*
1964 Jascha Heifetz and Gregor Piatigorsky (with Jacob Lateiner, pianist), *Beethoven: Trio No. 1 in E Flat, Op. 1, No. 1*
New York Pro Musica, cond. by Noah Greenberg, *It Was A Lover and His Lass (Morley, Bird and Others)*
1965 Juilliard String Quartet, *Bartok: The Six String Quartets*
1966 Boston Symphony Chamber Players, *Boston Symphony Chamber Players*
1967 Ravi Shankar and Yehudi Menuhin, *West Meets East*
1968 E. Power Biggs with Edward Tarr Ensemble and Gabrieli Consort cond. by Victor Negri, *Gabrieli: Canzoni for Brass, Winds, Strings and Organ*
1969 Philadelphia, Cleveland and Chicago Brass Ensembles, *Gabrieli: Antiphonal Music of Gabrieli (Canzoni for Brass Choirs)*
1970 Eugene Istomin, Isaac Stern and Leonard Rose, *Beethoven: The Complete Piano Trios*
1971 Juilliard Quartet, *Debussy: Quartet in G Minor/Ravel: Quartet in F Major*
1972 Julian Bream and John Williams, *Julian and John*
1973 Gunther Schuller and the New England Conservatory Ragtime Ensemble, *Joplin: The Red Back Book*
1974 Artur Rubinstein, Henryk Szeryng and Pierre Fournier, *Brahms and Schumann Trios*
1975 Artur Rubinstein, Henryk Szeryng and Pierre Fournier, *Schubert: Trios Nos. 1 in B Flat Major, Op. 99 and 2 in E Flat Major, Op. 100 (The Piano Trios)*

1976 David Munrow conducting Early Music Consort of London, *The Art of Courtly Love*
1977 Juilliard Quartet, *Schoenberg: Quartets for Strings*

BEST CLASSICAL PERFORMANCE—VOCAL SOLOIST (With or Without Orchestra)/BEST VOCAL SOLOIST PERFORMANCE, CLASSICAL/BEST CLASSICAL VOCAL SOLOIST PERFORMANCE

1958 Renata Tebaldi, *Operatic Recital*
1959 Jussi Bjoerling, *Bjoerling in Opera*
1960 Leontyne Price, *A Program of Song*
1961 Joan Sutherland, *The Art of the Prima Donna*
1962 Eileen Farrell, *Wagner: Gotterdammerung—Brunnhilde's Immolation Scene/Wesendonck Songs*
1963 Leontyne Price, *Great Scenes from Gershwin's Porgy and Bess*
1964 Leontyne Price, *Berlioz: Nuits d'Ete (Song Cycle)/Falla: El Amor Brujo*
1965 Leontyne Price, *Strauss: Salome (Dance of the Seven Veils, Interlude, Final Scene); The Egyptian Helen (Awakening Scene)*
1966 Leontyne Price, *Prima Donna*
1967 Leontyne Price, *Prima Donna, Vol. 2*
1968 Montserrat Caballe, *Rossini Rarities*
1969 Leontyne Price, *Barber: Two Scenes from "Antony and Cleopatra"/Knoxville: Summer of 1915*
1970 Dietrich Fischer-Dieskau, *Schubert: Lieder*
1971 Leontyne Price, *Leontyne Price Sings Robert Schumann*
1972 Dietrich Fischer-Dieskau, *Brahms: Die Schone Magelone*
1973 Leontyne Price, *Puccini: Heroines (La Boheme, La Rondine, Tosca, Manon Lescaut)*
1974 Leontyne Price, *Leontyne Sings Richard Strauss*
1975 Janet Baker, *Mahler: Kindertotenlieder*
1976 Beverly Sills, *Music of Victor Herbert*
1977 Janet Baker, *Bach Arias*

BEST CLASSICAL PERFORMANCE — OPERATIC OR CHORAL

1958 Roger Wagner Chorale, *Virtuoso*
1959 Erich Leinsdorf conducting the Vienna Philharmonic Orchestra, *Mozart: The Marriage of Figaro*

BEST CLASSICAL OPERA PRODUCTION/BEST OPERA RECORDING

1960 Renata Tebaldi, Birgit Nilsson, Jussi Bjoerling and Giorgio Tozzi with Erich Leinsdorf conducting the Rome Opera House Chorus and Orchestra, *Puccini: Turandot*
1961 Gabriele Santini conducting the Rome Opera House Chorus and Orchestra, *Puccini: Madama Butterfly*
1962 Georg Solti conducting the Rome Opera House Chorus and Orchestra and Leontyne Price, Jon Vickers, Rita Gorr, Robert Merrill and Giorgio Tozzi, *Verdi: Aida*
1963 Erich Leinsdorf conducting the RCA Italiana Opera Orchestra with Leontyne Price, Richard Tucker and Rosalind Elias, *Puccini: Madama Butterfly*
1964 Herbert von Karajan conducting the Vienna Philharmonic Orchestra and Chorus with Leontyne Price, Franco Corelli, Robert Merrill and Mirella Freni, *Bizet: Carmen*
1965 Karl Bohm conducting the Orchestra of the German Opera with Dietrich Fischer-Dieskau, Evelyn Lear and Fritz Wunderlich, *Berg: Wozzeck*

1966 Georg Solti conducting the Vienna Philharmonic with Birgit Nilsson, Regine Crespin, Christa Ludwig, James King and Hans Hotter, *Wagner: Die Walkure*

1967 Pierre Boulez conducting the Paris National Opera with Walter Berry, Strauss, Fritz Uhl and Karl Doench, *Berg: Wozzeck*

1968 Erich Leinsdorf conducting the New Philharmonia Orchestra and Ambrosian Opera Chorus with Leontyne Price, Judith Raskin, Madelena Troyanos, Sherill Milnes, Shirley and Ezio Flagello, *Mozart: Cosi Fan Tutti*

1969 Herbert von Karajan conducting the Berlin Philharmonic with Jess Thomas, Thomas Stewart, Gerhard Stolze, Helga Dernesch, Zoltan Keleman, Oralia Dominguez, Catherine Goyer and Karl Ridderbusch, *Wagner: Siegfried*

1970 Colin Davis conducting the Royal Opera House Orchestra and Chorus with Jon Vickers, Josephine Veasey and Berret Lindholm, *Berlioz: Les Troyens*

1971 Erich Leinsdorf conducting the London Philharmonic with Leontyne Price, Placido Domingo, Sherrill Milnes, Grace Bumbry and Ruggerro Raimondi, *Verdi: Aida*

1972 Colin Davis conducting the BBC Symphony Orchestra and Chorus of Covent Garden, *Berlioz: Benvenuto Cellini*

1973 Leonard Bernstein conducting the Metropolitan Opera Orchestra and Manhattan Opera Chorus with Marilyn Horne, James McCracken, Adriana Maliponte and Tom Krause, *Bizet: Carmen*

1974 Georg Solti (conductor), *Puccini: La Boheme*

1975 Colin Davis conducting the Royal Opera House Orchestra with Montserrat Caballe, Janet Baker, Nicolai Gedda, Vladimiro Ganzarolli, Richard Van Allen and Ileana Cotrubas, *Mozart: Cosi Fan Tutti*

1976 Lorin Maazel conducting the Cleveland Orchestra and Chorus, *Gershwin: Porgy and Bess*

1977 John De Main conducting Sherwin M. Goldman/Houston Grand Orchestra, *Gershwin: Porgy and Bess*

BEST CLASSICAL PERFORMANCE, CHORAL (including Oratorio)/BEST CLASSICAL CHORAL PERFORMANCE

1960 Sir Thomas Beecham conducting the Royal Philharmonic Orchestra and Chorus, *Handel: The Messiah*

1961 Robert Shaw Chorale, *Bach: B Minor Mass*

1962 Philharmonia Choir with William Pitz, choral dir., and Otto Klemperer conducting the Philharmonia Orchestra, *Bach: St. Matthew Passion*

1963 Bach Choir and Highgate School Choir dir. by Edward Chapman and Benjamin Britten conducting the London Symphony Orchestra, *Britten: War Requiem*

1964 Robert Shaw Chorale, *Britten: A Ceremony of Carols*

1965 Robert Shaw Chorale, *Stravinsky: Symphony of Psalms/Poulenc: Gloria*

1966 Robert Shaw Chorale, *Handel: Messiah*
Gregg Smith conducting the Columbia Chamber Orchestra, Gregg Smith Singers and Ithaca College Concert Choir and George Bragg conducting the Texas Boys Choir, *Ives: Music for Chorus*

1967 Leonard Bernstein conducting the London Symphony Orchestra, *Mahler: Symphony in E Flat Major*
Robert Page conducting the Temple University Chorus and Eugene Ormandy conducting the Philadelphia Orchestra, *Orff: Catulli Carmina*

1968 Vittorio Negri, conductor; Gregg Smith Singers, Texas Choir Boys, Edward Tarr Ensemble (George Bragg, dir.) and E. Power Biggs, *The Glory of Gabrieli*

1969 Swingle Singers and Luciano Berio conducting the New York Philharmonic, *Berio: Sinfonia*

1970 Gregg Smith Singers and Columbia Chamber Ensemble, *(Ives) New Music of Charles Ives*

1971 Colin Davis conducting the London Symphony Orchestra, Russell Burgess conducting the Wandsworth School Boys Choir and Arthur Oldham conducting the London Symphony Chorus, *Berlioz: Requiem*

1972 Georg Solti conducting Chicago Symphony Orchestra, Vienna Boys Choir, Vienna State Opera Chorus and Vienna Sangerverein chorus and soloists, *Mahler: Symphony No. 8*

1973 Andre Previn conducting the London Symphony Orchestra and Arthur Oldham conducting the London Symphony Orchestra Chorus, *Walton: Belshazzar's Feast*

1974 Colin Davis (conductor), *Berlioz: The Damnation of Faust*

1975 Robert Page directing the Cleveland Orchestra Chorus and Boys Choir and Michael Tilson Thomas conducting the Cleveland Orchestra, *Orff: Carmina Burana*

1976 Arthur Oldham (chorus master) of the London Symphony Chorus and Andre Previn conducting the London Symphony Orchestra, *Rachmaninoff: The Bells*

1977 Margaret Hillis (choral dir.) and the Chicago Symphony Chorus with Sir Georg Solti conducting the Chicago Symphony Orchestra, *Verdi: Requiem*

BEST COMPOSITION FIRST RECORDED AND RELEASED DURING YEAR/BEST CONTEMPORARY CLASSICAL COMPOSITION/BEST CLASSICAL COMPOSITION BY A CONTEMPORARY COMPOSER

1958 Nelson Riddle, *Cross Country Suite*

1959 Duke Ellington, *Anatomy of a Murder*

1960 Aaron Copland, *Orchestral Suite from Tender Land Suite*

1961 Laurindo Almeida, *Discantus*
Igor Stravinsky, *Movements for Piano and Orchestra*

1962 Igor Stravinsky, *The Flood*

1963 Benjamin Britten, *War Requiem*

1964 Samuel Barber, *Piano Concerto*

1965 Charles Ives, *Symphony No. 4*

BEST ENGINEERED RECORD, OTHER THAN CLASSICAL/BEST ENGINEERING CONTRIBUTION/BEST ENGINEERED RECORDING OTHER THAN CLASSICAL

1958 Ted Keep, *The Chipmunk Song*

1959 Robert Simpson, *Belafonte at Carnegie Hall*

1960 Luis P. Valentin, *Ella Fitzgerald Sings the George and Ira Gershwin Song Book*

1961 Robert Arnold, *Judy at Carnegie Hall*

1962 Al Schmitt, *Hatari!*

1963 James Malloy, *Charade*

1964 Phil Ramone, *Getz/Gilberto*

1965 Larry Levine, *A Taste of Honey*

1966 Eddie Brackett and Lee Herschberg, *Strangers in the Night*

1967 Geoff Emerick, *Sgt. Pepper's Lonely Hearts Club Band*

1968 Joe Polito and Hugh Davies, *Wichita Lineman*

1969 Geoff Emerick and Phillip McDonald, *Abbey Road*

1970 Roy Halee, *Bridge Over Troubled Water*

1971   Dave Purple, Ron Capone and Henry Bush, *Theme from Shaft*
1972   Armin Steiner, *Moods*
1973   Robert Margouleff and Malcolm Cecil, *Innervisions*
1974   Geoff Emerick, *Band on the Run*
1975   Brooks Arthur, Larry Alexander and Russ Payne, *Between the Lines*
1976   Al Schmitt, *Breezin'*
1977   Roger Nichols, Elliot Scheiner, Bill Schnee and Al Schmitt, *AJA*

BEST ENGINEERING CONTRIBUTION, NOVELTY/NOVELTY OR SPECIAL EFFECTS

1959   Ted Keep, *Alvin's Harmonica*
1960   John Kraus, *The Old Payola Roll Blues*
1961   John Kraus, *Stan Freberg Presents the United States of America*
1962   Robert Fine, *The Civil War*, Vol. 1
1963   Robert Fine, *The Civil War*, Vol. 2
1964   Dave Hassinger, *The Chipmunks Sing the Beatles*

BEST ALBUM COVER/BEST ALBUM COVER, GRAPHIC ARTS/BEST ALBUM PACKAGE (Award to Art Director)

1959   Robert M. Jones, *Shostakovitch Symphony No. 5*
1960   Marvin Schwartz, *Latin a la Lee*
1961   Jim Silke, *Judy at Carnegie Hall*
1962   Robert M. Jones, *Lena . . . Lovely and Alive*
1963   John Berg, *The Barbra Streisand Album*
1964   Robert Cato (art. dir.) and Don Bronstein (photographer), *People*
1965   See cover photography category below; no separate graphics category for non-classical
1966   Klaus Voormann, *Revolver*
1967   Peter Blake and Jann Haworth, *Sgt. Pepper's Lonely Hearts Club Band*
1968   John Berg and Richard Mantel (art dirs.) and Horn/Griner Studio (photography), *Underground*
1969   Evelyn J. Kelbish (painting) and David Stahlberg (graphics), *America the Beautiful*
1970   Robert Lochart (design) and Ivan Nagy (photography), *Indianola Mississippi Seeds*
1971   Dean O. Torrance (album design) and Gene Browell (art dir.), *Pollution*
1972   Acy Lehman (art dir.) and Harvey Dinerstein (artist), *The Siegel Schwall Band*
1973   Wilkes and Braun, Inc. (art dir.), *Tommy*
1974   Ed Thrasher and Christopher Whorf, *Come & Gone*
1975   Jim Ladwig, *Honey*
1976   John Berg, *Chicago X*
1977   Kosh, *Simple Dreams*

BEST ALBUM COVER PHOTOGRAPHY

1965   Robert Jones (art dir.) and Ken Whitmore (photographer), *Jazz Suite on the Mass Texts*
1966   Robert Jones (art dir.) and Les Leverette (photographer), *Confessions of a Broken Man*
1967   John Carto (art dir.) and Roland Scherman (photographer), *Bob Dylan's Greatest Hits*

BEST ALBUM NOTES (Award to Annotator)

1963   Stanley Dance and Leonard Feather, *The Ellington Era*
1964   Stanton Catlin and Carleton Beals, *Mexico (Legacy Collection)*
1965   Stan Cornyn, *September of My Years*
1966   Stan Cornyn, *Sinatra at the Sands*
1967   John D. Loudermilk, *Suburban Attitudes in Country Verse*
1968   Johnny Cash, *Johnny Cash at Folsom Prison*

1969   Johnny Cash, *Nashville Skyline*
1970   Chris Albertson, *The World's Greatest Blues Singer*
1971   Sam Samudio, *Sam, Hard and Heavy*
1972   Tom T. Hall, *Tom T. Hall's Greatest Hitts*
1973   Dan Morgenstern, *God is in the House*
1974   Charles R. Townsend, *For the Last Time*
         Dan Morgenstern, *The Hawk Flies*
1975   Pete Hamill, *Blood on the Tracks*
1976   Dan Morgenstern, *The Changing Face of Harlem*
1977   George T. Simon, *Bing Crosby: A Legendary Performer*

BEST PRODUCER OF THE YEAR

1974   Thom Bell
1975   Arif Mardin
1976   Stevie Wonder, *Songs in the Key of Life*
1977   Peter Asher

BEST ENGINEERED RECORD, CLASSICAL/BEST ENGINEERING CONTRIBUTION, CLASSICAL RECORDING/BEST ENGINEERED RECORDING, CLASSICAL

1958   Sherwood Hall III, *Duets with a Spanish Guitar*
1959   Lewis W. Layton, *Victory at Sea*, Vol. 1
1960   Hugh Davies, *Spanish Guitars of Laurindo Almeida*
1961   Lewis W. Layton, *Ravel: Daphnis and Chloe*
1962   Lewis W. Layton, *Strauss: Also Sprach Zarathustra, Op. 30*
1963   Lewis W. Layton, *Madama Butterfly*
1964   Douglas Larter, *Britten: Young Person's Guide to the Orchestra*
1965   Fred Plaut, *Horowitz at Carnegie Hall*
1966   Anthony Salvatore, *Wagner: Lohengrin*
1967   Edward T. Graham, *The Glorious Sound of Brass*
1968   Gordon Parry, *Mahler: Symphony No. 9 in D Major*
1969   Walter Carlos, *Switched-On Bach*
1970   Fred Plaut, Ray Moore and Arthur Kendy, *Stravinsky: Le Sacre du Printemps*
1971   Vittorio Negri, *Berlioz: Requiem*
1972   Gordon Parry and Kenneth Wilkinson, *Mahler: Symphony No. 8*
1973   Edward T. Graham and Raymond Moore, *Bartok: Concerto for Orchestra*   •
1974   Kenneth Wilkinson, *Berlioz: Symphonie Fantastique*
1975   Edward T. "Bud" Graham, Ray Moore and Milton Cherin, *Ravel: Daphnis and Chloe*
1976   Edward T. Graham, Ray Moore and Milton Cherin, *Gershwin: Rhapsody in Blue*
1977   Kenneth Wilkinson, *Ravel: Bolero*

BEST ALBUM COVER

1959   See Best Album Cover category above; only category one for classical and non-classical
1961   Marvin Schwartz, *Puccini: Madama Butterfly*
1962   Marvin Schwartz, *The Intimate Bach*
1963   Robert Jones, *Puccini: Madama Butterfly*
1964   Robert Jones (art dir.) and Jan Balet (graphic artist), *Saint-Saens: Carnival of the Animals/Britten: Young Person's Guide to the Orchestra*
1965   George Estes (art dir.) and James Alexander (graphic arts), *Bartok: Concerto No. 2 for Violin/Stravinsky: Concerto for Violin*

BEST ALBUM NOTES, CLASSICAL (to Annotator)

1972   James Lyons, *Vaughn Williams: Symphony No. 2*
1973   Glenn Gould, *Hindemith: Sonatas for Piano (Complete)*
1974   Rory Guy, *The Classic Erich Wolfgang Korngold*
1975   Gunther Schuller, *Footlifters*

SPECIAL NATIONAL TRUSTEES' AWARD FOR ARTISTS AND REPERTOIRE CONTRIBUTION

1959 Bobby Darin (prod. by Ahmet Ertegun), *Mack the Knife* (Record of the Year)
Frank Sinatra (prod. by Dave Cavanaugh), *Come Dance With Me* (Album of the Year)

1960 Ernest Altschuler (producer), *Theme from "A Summer Place"* (Record of the Year)
George Avakian (producer), *Button Down Mind* (Album of the Year)

SPECIAL TRUSTEES' AWARD

1967 Greg Culshaw (producer) and Georg Solti (conductor), *Wagner: Der Ring Des Niebelungen*

1968 Krzysztof Penderecki (composer), *The Passion According to St. Luke*
Billy Strayhorn and Duke Ellington, for overall contributions and for composing *The Far East Suite*

1970 Robert Moog, for the Moog Synthesizer

1971 John Hammond and Chris Albertson (co-producers) and Larry Hiller (engineer), *Bessie Smith Reissue Series*
Paul Weston, founding father and first national president of the Academy, for years of dedication

1972 The Beatles, for revolutionizing music and recordings with talent, originality and musical creativity

MISCELLANEOUS AWARDS

1959 Nat "King" Cole, *Midnight Flyer*, Best Performance by a "Top 40" Artist

1960 Ray Charles, *Georgia on My Mind*, Best Performance by a Pop Single Artist
Miles Davis and Gil Evans, *Sketches of Spain*, Best Jazz Composition of More Than Five Minutes Duration

1963 Andre Watts, Most Promising New Recording Artist

1964 Marilyn Horne, Most Promising New Recording Artist
Roger Miller, Best New Country and Western Artist of 1964

1965 Peter Serkin, Most Promising New Recording Artist
Statler Brothers, Best New Country and Western Artist

The Bing Crosby Award, which consists of a plaque rather than a Grammy statuette, is presented periodically to members of the industry for creative contributions of outstanding artistic or scientific significance of the field of phonograph records. The trustees select the winner.

1963 Bing Crosby, "Thirty years of making records of outstanding musicianship, uncompromising dignity and never-failing enthusiasm"

1965 Frank Sinatra, "Continuing dedication to the highest standards both as a performer and as a recording artist"

1966 Duke Ellington, "Tremendously high standards of musicianship and creativity through a career as a composer, pianist, arranger and conductor"

1967 Ella Fitzgerald, "Superb musicianship and consistent musical integrity"

1968 Irving Berlin, "More than half a century of composing so many songs, seemingly simple yet filled with warmth"

1971 Elvis Presley, "Artistic creativity and influence in the field of recorded music upon a generation of performers and listeners"

1972 Mahalia Jackson, "World's Greatest Gospel Singer, whose voice and lifelong commitment to God have epitomized the ennobling role of music"

1972 Louis Armstrong, "America's Good Will Ambassador, for outstanding contributions to music and for leading the way for millions of jazz musicians of all horns and colors, and for hundreds of brilliant recordings"

Hot 100 Awards

BILLBOARD
9000 Sunset Blvd., Los Angeles, Calif. 90069 (213/273-7040)

The Hot 100 Award, which consists of a plaque, is given to the record that achieves the top position on the *Billboard* record chart.

1977 *You Don't Have to be a Star,* Marilyn McCoo/Billy Davis
You Make Me Feel Like Dancin', Leo Sayer
I Wish, Rose Royce
Car Wash, Rose Royce
Torn Between Two Lovers, Mary MacGregor
Blinded by the Light, Manfred Mann's Earth Band
New Kid in Town, Eagles
Love Theme from "A Star Is Born," Barbra Streisand
Rich Girl, Daryl Hall/John Oates
Dancing Queen, Abba
Don't Give up on Us, David Soul
Don't Leave Me This Way, Thelma Houston
Southern Nights, Glen Campbell
Hotel California, Eagles
When I Need You, Leo Sayer
Sir Duke, Stevie Wonder
I'm Your Boogie Man, K C & Sunshine Band
Dreams, Fleetwood Mac
Got to Give It Up, Marvin Gaye
Gonna Fly Now (Theme from "Rocky"), Bill Conti
Undercover Angel, Alan O'Day
Da Doo Ron Ron, Shaun Cassidy
Looks Like We Made It, Barry Manilow
I Just Want to be Your Everything, Andy Gibb
Best of My Love, Emotions
Star Wars Title Theme, Meco
You Light Up My Life, Debby Boone
How Deep Is Your Love, Bee Gees

Jeunesses Musicales Prizes

INTERNATIONAL COMPETITION OF YOUNG MUSICIANS (JEUNESSES MUSICALES)
Terazije 26, 1100e-Belgrade, Yugoslavia (Tel: 326-485)

The competition is held annually to give young musicians at the start of their careers opportunities to win cash prizes and performance opportunities. A panel of judges selects winners from the instrumentalists and vocalists eligible in any given year. In 1978, for instance, the competition will be for cellists and string quartets. The individual first-place winner will receive 17,000 dinars, while the quartet will share 34,000 dinars. Second- and third-place winners also receive a monetary award. Solo musicians must be thirty years of age or under, while no member of a group may be older than thirty-five.

1971 James Campbell (Canada), Clarinette
Gotfried Schneider (Federal Republic of Germany), Violin
String quartet (U.S.S.R.)

1972 Elena Kuznethova (U.S.S.R.), Piano
Mosconcert Trio (U.S.S.R.)
1973 Ivan Konsulov (Bulgaria), Male voice
Jolanta Omiljanowitz (Poland), Female voice
Agneza Miteva and Philippe Pavlov (Bulgaria), Violin and piano duo
1974 Irena Grafenauer (Yugoslavia), Flute
Dusan Bogdanvic (Yugoslavia), Guitar
Paul Taffanel (France), Wind Quintet
1975 Mineo Hayashi (Japan), Cello
Academica (Rumania), String quartet
1976 Kim Seung Ho (Democratic Peoples' Republic of Korea), Violin
New Prague Trio (Czechoslovakia), Piano trio
1977 Philippe Bianconi (France), Piano
Camillo and Umberto Bertetti (Italy), Piano duo

International Singing Contest Medals
SOCIEDADE BRASILEIRA DE RALIZACNOES
Av. F. Roosevelt 23, S/310-Rio de Janeiro, Brazil
(Tel: 3-920681)

Gold medals are now awarded to the four young singers who win the International Singing Contest held every two years in Rio de Janeiro. In addition, $6,000 in prizes are given, as are silver medals, diplomas and recital bookings to runners-up.

1963 Vera Soukupova (Czechoslovakia)
Halina Slonicka (Poland)
Alfonz Bartha (Hungary)
1965 Ludwig Spiess (Rumania)
Teresa Tourne (Spain)
1967 Irina Bogachova (U.S.S.R.), Mezzo
Taru Valjjaka (Finland), Soprano
Rimma Volkova (U.S.S.R.), Soprano
1969 Angela Beale (Great Britain), Soprano
Helja Angervo (Finland), Mezzo
Marcos Bakker (Holland) Bass
1971 Ana Toumowa (Bulgaria), Soprano
Wolfgang Schone (Germany), Baritone
Lucien Marinescu (Rumania), Baritone
1973 Kloos Kovacs (Hungary), Bass
Christina Gorantcheva (Bulgaria), Coloratura soprano
Hariana Branisteanu (Rumania), Soprano
1975 Ruth Falcon (U.S.A.), Soprano and Olga Basistiuk (U.S.S.R.), Soprano
Anatole Ponomarenko (U.S.S.R.), Baritone
Istvan Gati (Hungary), Bass baritone
La Verne Williams (U.S.A.), Soprano
1977 Akeshi Wakamoto (Japan), Tenor
Ludmila Chemchouk (U.S.S.R.), Mezzo
Tatiana Novikova (U.S.S.R.), Soprano
Betty Lane (U.S.A.), Soprano

International Voice Competition
CONCOURS INTERNATIONAL DE CHANT
Theatre du Capitole, 3100 Toulouse, France (Tel: 21.20.78 and 21-80-41)

The City of Toulouse awards the winners of the International Voice Competition 10,000 francs, diplomas and bookings to perform. The competition is open to male and female vocalists between the ages of eighteen and thirty-five of any nationality. A panel of judges selects the winners.

WOMEN
1954 Francoise Ogeas, France
1955 Enriquetta Tarres-Rabassa, Spain
1956 Janine Panis, France
1957 Galina Olenitchenko, U.S.S.R.
1958 Dories Mayes, U.S.A.
1959 Nadyda Kniplova, Czechoslovakia
1960 Hanna Rumowska, Poland
1961 Julia Buciuceanu, Rumania
1962 Galina Kovalieva, U.S.S.R.
1963 Margaret Sun, China
1964 Viorica Cortez, Rumania
1965 Anna-Maria Higueras-Rodriguez, Spain
1966 Alexandrina Miltcheva, Bulgaria
1967 Zdzislawa Donat, Poland
1968 Stefka Popangelova, Bulgaria
1969 Magdalena Cononovici, Rumania
1970 Eugenia Moldoveanu, Rumania
1971 Nina Fomina, U.S.S.R.
1972 Nadaja Krasnaya, U.S.S.R.
1973 No competition
1974 Bozena Porznyska, Poland
1975 No award
1976 Not available at press time
1977 Not available at press time

MEN
1954 Jullen Haas, Belgium
1955 No award
1956 Krsta B. Krstic, Yugoslavia
1957 Ladislau Konya, Rumania
1958 Antonin Svorc, Czechoslovakia
1959 Remy Corazza, France
1960 Takao Okamura, Japan
1961 Jose van Damm, Belgium
1962 Ramon Calzadilla, Cuba
1963 No award
1964 Ludovico Spiess, Rumania
1965 Kazimierz Myrlak, Poland
1966 George Pappas, Greece
1967 Louis Hagen-William, U.S.A.
1968 No award
1969 Lucian Marinescu, Rumania
1970 William Parker, U.S.A.
1971 Vatslovas Daounoras, U.S.S.R.
1972 Robert Christensen, U.S.A.
1973 No competition
1974 Pietr Gluboky, U.S.S.R.
1975 No award
1976 Not available at press time
1977 Not available at press time

Koussevitzky International Recording Award
AMERICAN INTERNATIONAL MUSIC FUND
30 W. 60th St., New York N.Y. 10023 (212/CO 5-0277)

The Koussevitzky International Recording Award, which carries a $1,000 honorarium, is made annually to the living composer of an outstanding symphonic work or a chamber music work for a minimum of sixteen players released on commercial recordings during the previous year. A jury selects the winner.

1963 Edgard Varese, Arcana, CBS
1964 Witold Lutoslawski, Trois Poemes d'Henri Michaux, Polski Nagrania in connection with the Festival of Contemporary Music, Zagreb, 1963

1965 Ingvar Lidholm, *Poesies per Orchestra,* Columbia in cooperation with the Naumberg Foundation
1966 Peter Maxwell Davies, *Leopardi Fragments,* EMI as part of the Gulbenkian Foundation's Music Today series
1967 Olivier Messiaen, *Trios Petites Liturgies de la Presence Divine,* Erato (Music Guild in the U.S.A.)
1968 Carlos Chavez, *Six Symphonies,* Columbia
1969 Roberto Gerhard, *Concerto for Orchestra,* Argo
1970 Stefan Wolpe, *Chamber Piece No. 1,* Nonesuch
Seymour Shifrin, *Satires of Circumstance,* Nonesuch
1971 George Crumb, *Ancient Voices of Children,* Nonesuch
1972 Seymour Shifrin, *Three Pieces for Orchestra,* CRI
1974 Roque Cordero, *Concerto for Violin and Orchestra,* Columbia
1975 No award
1976 Henri Dutilleux, *Tout un Monde Lointain,* EMI
1977 Not available at press time

Laurel Leaf Award

AMERICAN COMPOSERS ALLIANCE
170 W. 74th St., New York, N.Y. 10023 (212/873-1250)

The Laurel Leaf Award is a parchment scroll given annually to an individual or organization for encouraging American music

1951 Radio station WGBH, Boston
1952 Maro and Anahid Ajemian
1953 Herman Neuman Green Bay (Wisc.) Symphonette
1955 George Szell
1956 Robert Whitney
1957 Howard Hanson
Juilliard String Quartet
1958 Thor Johnson
1959 Martha Graham
Jack Benny
1960 Howard Mitchell
Oliver Daniel
1961 Helen Thompson
William Stickland
1962 Bethany Beardslee
Hugh Ross
Samuel Rosenbaum
1963 Clair Reis
Carl Haverlin
1964 Walter Hinrichsen
Margaret L. Crofts
Max Pollikoff
1965 Henry Cowell
Avery Claflin
Elizabeth Ames
1966 Henry A. Moe
Lawrence Morton
1967 Radio station WBAI, New York Fromm Foundation
Composers' Forum
1968 Aaron Copland
1969 Group for Contemporary Music
1970 Otto Luening
Harris Danziger
1971 Alice M. Ditson Fund
1972 Leopold Stokowski
1973 MacDowell Colony
1974 Theresa Sterne
1975 Nelson Rockefeller
1976 Gunther Schuller
1977 Arthur Weisberg

Leeds International Pianoforte Competition

UNIVERSITY OF LEEDS
Leeds LS2 9JT, U.K. (Tel: Bradford-0274 33321)

The winner of the Leeds International Pianoforte Competition receives a gold medal and £2,850 and more than fifty engagements. Eligible pianists may be of any nationality but must be under thirty years of age. An international panel selects the winner of this triennial award.

1963 Michael Roll
1966 Raphael Orozco
1969 Radu Lupu
1972 Murray Perahia
1975 Dimitry Alexeev

Musician of the Year

MUSICAL AMERICA
130 E. 59th St., New York, N.Y. 10022 (212/826-8360)

A Musician of the Year is named annually by *Musical America,* a classical music publication, generally for contributions in vocal, instrumental or orchestral performances and recording

1960 Leonard Bernstein
1961 Leontyne Price
1962 Igor Stravinsky
1963 Erich Leinsdorf
1964 Benjamin Britten
1965 Vladimir Horowitz
1966 Yehudi Menuhin
1967 Leopold Stokowski
1968/9 Birgit Nilsson
1970 Beverly Sills
1971 Michael Tilson Thomas
1972 Pierre Boulez
1973 George Balanchine
1974 Sarah Caldwell
1975 Eugene Ormandy
1976 Arthur Rubinstein
1977 Placido Domingo

Otto Kinkeldy Award

AMERICAN MUSICOLOGICAL SOCIETY
201 S. 34th St., Philadelphia, Pa. 19104 (215/243-5000)

The Otto Kinkeldy Award, which consists of $400 and a scroll, is given annually to an American or Canadian author for a notable full-length study in any branch of musicology. A special committe selects the recipient.

1967 William W. Austin, *Music in the Twentieth Century*
1968 Rulan Chao Pian, *Song Dynasty Musical Sources and their Interpretation*
1969 Edward Lowinsky, *The Medici Codex of 1518*
1970 Nino Pirrotta, *Li due Orfei, da Poliziano a Monteverdi*
1971 Daniel Heartz, *Pierre d'Attaignant, Royal Printer of Music*
Joseph Kerman, *Ludwig van Beethoven, Autograph Miscellany from ca. 1786 to 1799*
1972 Albert Seay, *Jacobus Arcadelt, Opera Omnia.,* Vol. II
1973 H. Colin Slim, *A Gift of Madrigals and Motets*
1974 Robert L. Marshall, *The Compositional Process of J.S. Bach*

1975 Vivian Perlis, *Charles Ives Remembered, an Oral History*
1976 David P. McKay & Richard Crawford, *William Billings of Boston: Eighteenth-Century Composer*
1977 H. C. Robbins Landon, Hayden: *Chronicle and Works, Vol. 3; Hayden in London 1791-1795*

Arts and Letters Awards
Marc Blitzstein Award
Charles Ives Award
Ives Grant Award

NATIONAL INSTITUTE OF ARTS AND LETTERS
633 W. 155th St., New York, N.Y. 10023 (212/AU 6-1480)

To encourage qualified writers and help them continue their creative work, the Institute annually gives $3,000 in awards to non-members. These Arts and Letters Awards may not be applied for.

1941 Frederick Woltmann
1942 Bernard Hermann
      Edward Margetson
      Robert McBride
1943 Paul Creston
      William Schuman
1944 Nicolai Berezowsky
      David Diamond
      Burrill Phillips
1945 William Bergsma
      Jerzy Fitelberg
      Gian Carlo Menotti
1946 Marc Blitzstein
      Norman Dello Joio
      Otto Luening
      Peter Mennin
      Robert Palmer
      Robert Ward
1947 Alexei Haieff
      Ulysses Kay
      Norman Lockwood
1948 Henry Cowell
      Lou Harrison
      Vincent Persichetti
1949 John Cage
      Louis Mennini
      Stefan Wolpe
1950 Elliott C. Carter
      Andrew Imbrie
      Ben Weber
1951 Alan Hovhaness
      Leon Kirchner
      Frank Wigglesworth
1952 Robert Kurka
      John Lessard
      Howard Swanson
1953 Peggy Glanville-Hicks
      Roger Goeb
      Nikolai Lopatnikoff
1954 Ingolf Dahl
      Colin McPhee
      Hugo Weisgall
1955 Henry Brant
      Irving Fine
      Adolph Weiss
1956 Ross Lee Finney
      Robert Moevs
      Jacques Louis Monod

1957 Lukas Foss
      Lee Hoiby
      Seymour Shifrin
1958 Arnold Franchetti
      Hunter Johnson
      Billy Jim Layton
1959 Milton Babbitt
      John Bavicchi
      Mark Bucci
      Noel Lee
1960 Arthur Berger
      Easley Blackwood
      Salvatore Martirano
      Gunther Schuller
1961 Ramiro Cortes
      Halsey Stevens
      Lester Trimble
      Yehudi Wyner
1962 Ernst Bacon
      John LaMontaine
      George Rochberg
      William Sydeman
1963 Chou Wen-chung
      Mel Powell
      Russell Smith
      Vladimir Ussachevsky
1964 Leslie Bassett
      Gordon Binkerd
      Hall Overton
      Julia Perry
1965 Mario Davidovsky
      Gerald Humel
      Earl Kim
      Harvey Sollberger
1966 Walter Aschaffenburg
      Richard Hoffman
      John MacIvor Perkins
      Ralph Shapey
1967 George H. Crumb
      Donald Martino
      Julian Orbon
      Charles Wuorinen
1968 David Del Tredici
      William Flanagan
      Ned Rorem
      Francis Thorne
1969 Michael Brozen
      Jacob R. Druckman
      Nicolas Roussakis
      Claudio Spies
1970 William Albright
      Arnold Elston
      Morton Feldman
      George Bach Wilson
1971 Sydney Hodkinson
      Fred Lerdahl
      Roger Reynolds
      Loren Rush
1972 Earle Brown
      John Eaton
      John Harbison
      William Overton Smith
1973 John C. Heiss
      Betsy Jolas
      Barbara Kolb
      Curry Tison Street
1974 Richard Felciano
      Raoul Pleskow
      Phillip Rhodes
      Olly W. Wilson

1975 Marc Antonio Consoli
Charles Dodge
Daniel Perlongo
Christian Wolff
1976 Dominick Argento
Robert Helps
Robert Hall Lewis
Richard Wernick
1977 Harold Blumenfeld
Paul Cooper
Paul Lansky
George Perle

The $2,500 Marc Blitzstein Award for the Musical Theater is given periodically to encourage the creation of works of merit for the musical theatre by a composer, lyricist or librettist.

1965 William Bolcom
1968 Jack Beeson
1976 John Olon-Scrymgeour

The Charles Ives Award consists of $5,000 in scholarships to young composers for further study in composition.

1970 Joseph C. Schwantner
1971 Louis Smith Weingarden
1972 Thomas Janson
Robert J. Krupnick
Michael Seyfrit
1973 Philip Caldwell Carlsen
Robert Gerster
Peter Lieberson
1974 Paul Alan Levi
Allen Shearer
Ira Taxin
1975 Chester Biscardi
Stephen Chatman
David Koblitz
1976 Michael Eckert
Joseph A. Hudson
Tod Machover
Robert E. Martin
William Matthews
Bruce Saylor
1977 Gregory Ballard
Larry Thomas Bell
John Halvor Benson
Matthias Kriesberg
John Anthony Lennon
Maurice Wright

The $5,000 Ives Grant is awarded to further the publication and performances of the music of Charles E. Ives.

1970 John Kirkpatrick
1971 Vivian Perlis
1972 Harold Farberman
1973 The Charles E. Ives Society
1975 Music Library, Yale University

National Music Awards

AMERICAN MUSIC CONFERENCE
1000 Skokie Blvd., Wilmette, Ill. 60091 (312/251-1600)

The National Music Awards were instituted in 1976 to honor performers, lyricists and composers who have contributed significantly to music in America. The winners need not be native Americans, but the bulk of their work must relate to the U.S. The initial awards list recognized musicians active between 1776 and 1956. It is anticipated that in the future, three to six recipients will be named every three to five years. In order to eliminate fad music, only contributions twenty or more years in the past are considered. Living winners receive a trophy, which depicts abstractly the continuation of music. Three panels of judges with expertise in classical, popular (including country and show) and jazz (including blues) select the winners.

1976 Harold Arlen
Louis "Satchmo" Armstrong
Milton Babbitt
Samuel Barber
William "Count" Basie
Mrs. H. H. A. Beach
Leon Bismarck "Bix" Beiderbecke
Irving Berlin
Leonard Bernstein
Charles Edward Anderson "Chuck" Berry
William Billings
Jimmy Blanton
Clifford Brown
John Cage
Hoagland Howard "Hoagy" Carmichael
Benjamin Carr
Bennett Lester "Benny" Carter
Elliott Carter
George Whitefield Chadwick
Ray Charles (Ray Charles Robinson)
Charles "Charlie" Christian
George M. Cohan
Nat "King" Cole (Nathaniel Adams Coles)
Aaron Copland
Henry Cowell
Miles Davis, Jr.
Norman Dello Joio
B. G. "George Gard" "Buddy" DeSylva
Robert Nathaniel Dett
Warren "Baby" Dodds
Walter Donaldson
Thomas A. "Tommy" Dorsey
Paul Dresser
Edward Kennedy "Duke" Ellington
Daniel Decatur Emmett
Ian Ernest Gilmore Green "Gil" Evans
Arthur Farwell
Ella Fitzgerald
Stephen Collins Foster
William Henry Fry
George Gershwin
Ira Gershwin
Stanley "Stan" Getz
Henry Franklin Belknap Gilbert
John Birks "Dizzy" Gillespie
Benjamin David "Benny" Goodman
Louis Moreau Gottschalk
Charles Tomlinson Griffes
Woody Guthrie
Oscar Hammerstein II
William Christopher "W.C." Handy
Howard Harold Hanson
Roy Harris
Lorenz Hart
Coleman Hawkins
Anthony Philip Heinrich
Fletcher Henderson
Victor Herbert

Woodrow Charles "Woody" Herman
James Hewitt
John Hill Hewitt
Earl "Fatha" Hines
Billie Holiday
Francis Hopkinson
Charles Ives
Mahalia Jackson
Milton "Milt" Jackson
James "J.J." Johnson
James Price Johnson
Robert Johnson
Scott Joplin
Stanley Newcomb "Stan" Kenton
Jerome Kern
Leon Kirchner
Gene Krupa
Eddie Lang
James Melvin "Jimmie" Lunceford
James Lyon
Edward MacDowell
Daniel Gregory Mason
Lowell Mason
Gian-Carlo Menotti
John H. "Johnny" Mercer
Thelonius Monk
Douglas Stuart Moore
John Knowles Paine
Charles Christopher "Charlie Bird" or
"Yardbird" Parker
Horatio Parker
Cole Porter
Earl "Bud" Powell
Chano Pozo (Luciano Pozo Gonzales)
Donald Matthew "Don" Redman
Alexander Reinagle
Wallingford Riegger
Maxwell "Max" Roach
James Charles "Jimmie" Rodgers
Richard Rodgers
George Frederick Root
George Russell
Henry Russell
William Howard Schuman
Roger Sessions
Bessie Smith
John Philip Sousa
Arthur "Art" Tatum
Deems Taylor
Weldon John "Jack" Teagarden
Virgil Thomson
Leonard Joseph "Lennie" Tristano
Edgard Varese
Sarah Vaughan
Giuseppe "Joe" Venuti
Harry Von Tilzer
Thomas "Fats" Waller
Harry Warren
Richard A. Whiting
Hank Williams
Bob Wills
Henry Clay Work
Vincent Youmans
Lester "Pres" Young

Naumburg Awards

WALTER W. NAUMBURG FOUNDATION
144 W. 66th St., New York, N.Y. 10023 (212/874-1150)

Begun as a way for young chamber musicians to gain performance experience and critical review, the Naumburg Foundation's annual awards program has been altered and expanded to honor other instrumentalists, vocalists, recording artists and composers. The awards, originally known as the Naumburg Auditions, have undergone many changes over the years. Now, three traditional categories of piano, strings and voice rotate on a triannual basis. The winners receive a cash award and several recital appearances, including ones at New York's Alice Tully Hall and at the summer Aspen Music Festival. Recently, two chamber music groups have been chosen annually and awarded with a commission and an appearance contract, in a cooperative venture by the Foundation and the National Endowment for the Arts.

1925 Catherine Wade Smith, violin
       Adeline Masino, violin
       Bernard Ocko, violin
1926 Phyllis Kraeuter, cello
       Margaret Hamilton, piano
       Sonia Skalka, piano
1927 Dorothy Kendrick, piano
       William Sauber, piano
       Sadah Stuchari, violin
       Daniel Saidenberg, cello
       Julian Kahn, cello
       Sadie Schwartz, violin
1928 Adele Marcus, piano
       Helen Berlin, violin
       Louis Kaufman, violin
       Olga Zundel, cello
       George Rasely, tenor
       August Werner, baritone
1929 No winners
1930 Helen McGraw, piano
       Ruth Culbertson, piano
       Mila Wellerson, cello
       Louise Bernhardt, contralto
1931 Lillian Rehberg Goodman, cello
       Marguerite Hawkins, soprano
       Edwina Eustis, contralto
       Kurtis Brownell, tenor
1932 Milo Miloradovich, soprano
       Foster Miller, bass-baritone
       Dalies Frantz, piano
       Huddie Johnson, violin
       Inez Lauritano, violin
1933 Catherine Carver, piano
       Harry Katzman, violin
1934 Joseph Knitzer, violin
       Ruby Mercer, soprano
1935 Benjamin deLoache, baritone
       Judith Sidorsky, piano
       Aniceta Shea, soprano
       Harvey Shapiro, cello
       Florence Vickland, soprano
       Marshall Moss, violin
1936 Frederick Buldrini, violin
1937 Jorge Bolet, piano
       Ida Krehm, piano
       Pauline Pierce, mezzo-soprano
       Maurice Bialkin, cello
1938 Carroll Glenn, violin
1939 Mara Sebriansky, violin
       William Horne, tenor
       Zadel Skolovsky, piano
       Gertrude Gibson, soprano

1940 Abbey Simon, piano
Harry Cykman, violin
Thomas Richner, piano
1941 William Kappell, piano
Robert Mann, violin
Lura Stover, soprano
1942 Jane Rogers, contralto
Annette Elkanova, piano
David Sarser, violin
1943 Dolores Miller, violin
Constance Keene, piano
Ruth Geiger, piano
1944 Jeanne Therrien, piano
Jean Carlton, soprano
Carol Brice, contralto
1945 Jane Boedeker, mezzo-soprano
Paula Lenchner, soprano
1946 Leonid Hambro, piano
Jeanne Rosenblum, piano
Anahid Ajemian, violin
1947 Berl Senofsky, violin
Abba Bogin, piano
Jane Carlson, piano
1948 Sidney Harth, violin
Paul Olefsky, cello
Theodore Lettvin, piano
1949 Lorne Munroe, cello
1950 Angelene Collins, soprano
Esther Glazer, violinist
Betty Jean Hagen, violin
Margaret Barthel, piano
1951 June Kovach, piano
Laurel Hurley, soprano
Joyce Flissler, violin
1952 Diana Steiner, violin
Yoko Matsuo, violin
Lois Marshall, soprano
1953 Gilda Muhlbauer, violin
Lee Cass, bass-baritone
Georgia Laster, soprano
1954 William Doppmann, piano
Jean Wentworth, piano
Jules Eskin, cello
Martha Flowers, soprano
1955 Ronald Leonard, cello
Mary MacKenzie, contralto
Nancy Cirillo, violin
1956 Donald McCall, cello
Wayne Connor, tenor
George Katz, piano
1957 Regina Sarfaty, mezzo-soprano
Angelica Lozada, soprano
Michael Grebanier, cello
1958 Joseph Schwartz, piano
Shirley Verrett, mezzo-soprano
Elaine Lee, violin
1959 Howard Aibel, piano
Sophia Steffan, voice
Ralph Votapek, piano
1960 Joseph Silverstein, violin (Recording: Bach: Sonata
in G Minor/Bartok: Violin Solo Sonata)
1961 Werner Torkanowsky, conductor (Recording: Rochberg: Chamber Concerto)
1964 Elizabeth Mosher, soprano
1968 Jorge Mester, conductor
1971 Kun-Woo Paik, piano
Zola Shaulis, piano (Recording: Barber: Excursions
Gruenberg: Polychroma/Bloch: Sonata)
1972 Robert Davidovici, violin
1973 Edmund LeRoy, baritone

Barbara Hendricks, soprano
Susan Davenny Wyner, soprano
1974 Andre-Michel Schub, piano
Edith Kraft, piano
Richard Atamian, piano
1975 Dickran Atamian, piano
Elmar Oliveira, violin
Clamma Dale, soprano
Joy Simpson, soprano
1976 No winners
1977 Nathaniel Rosen, cello

NAUMBURG CHAMBER MUSIC AWARDS (CHAMBER
GROUP AND BELOW EACH, COMPOSER
COMMISSIONED FOR A WORK)

1965 Beaux Arts String Quartet
Leon Kirchner: *Quartet No. 3 for Strings and Elec-
tronic Tape* (composition)
1971 The Contemporary Group (University of Washing-
ton)
University of Michigan Contemporary Ensemble
1972 Speculum Musicae
Donald Martino: *Notturno* (composition)
Charles Wuorinen: *Speculum Speculi* (composition)
Concord String Quartet
George Rochberg: *String Quartet No. 3* (composition)
1973 Cambridge Consort
Seymour Shifrin (composition)
John Harbison (composition)
Da Capo Chamber Players
Milton Babbitt: *Arie da Capo* (composition)
Harvey Sollberger: *Riding the Wind* (composition)
1974 American String Quartet
Claus Adam (composition)
Francesco Trio
Earl Kim (composition)
1975 New York Renaissance Band
Alvin Brehm (composition)
1976 Empire Brass Quintet
Stanley Silverman (composition)
Sequoia String Quartet
Thomas McKinley (composition)
1977 Jubal Trio
Joseph Schwanter (composition)
Primavera String Quartet
Paul Chihara (composition)

NAUMBURG RECORDING AWARDS

1949 Roger Sessions: *Symphony No. 2* (New York Philharmonic, Dimitri Mitropoulos, cond.)
1950 William Schuman: *Symphony No. 3* (Philadelphia Orchestra, Eugene Ormandy, cond.)
1951 Wallingford Riegger: *Symphony No. 3* (Eastman-
Rochester Symphony Orchestra, Howard Hanson,
cond.)
1952 Peter Mennin: *Symphony No. 3* (New York Philharmonic, Dimitri Mitropoulos, cond.)
1953 Walter Piston: *Symphony No. 4* (Philadelphia Orchestra, Eugene Ormandy, cond.)
1954 Leon Kirchner, piano; Leon Kirchner: *Concerto for
Piano and Orchestra* (New York Philharmonic, Dimitri Mitropoulos, cond.)
Harold Shapero: *String Quartet No. 1* (Robert Koff,
Paul Bellam, Walter Trampler, Charles McCracken)
1955 Roy Harris: *Symphony No. 7* (Philadelphia Orchestra,
Eugene Ormandy, cond.)
1956 Jacob Avshalomov: *Sinfonietta* (Columbia Symphony Orchestra, Jacob Avshalomov, cond.)

280 Music & Dance

Elliott Carter: *Sonata for Flute, Oboe, Violoncello, and Harpsichord* (Annabelle Brieff, Josef Marx, Loren Bernsohn, Robert Conant)

1957 Lukas Foss: *The Song of Songs* (Jennie Tourel, mezzo-soprano; New York Philharmonic, Leonard Bernstein, cond.)

1958 Robert Helps: *Symphony No. 1* (Columbia Symphony Orchestra, Zoltan Rozsnyai, cond.)

1959 George Barati *Chamber Concerto* (Members of the Philadelphia Orchestra, Eugene Ormandy, cond.)
Cecil Effinger: *Little Symphony No. 1* (Columbia Symphony Orchestra, Zoltan Rozsnyai, cond.)

1960 Andrew Imbrie: *Violin Concerto* (Carroll Glenn, violin; Columbia Symphony Orchestra, Zoltan Rozsnyai, cond.)

1961 George Rochberg: *Symphony No. 2* (New York Philharmonic, Werner Torkanowsky, cond.)

1962 Richard Donovan: *Music for Six; Five Elizabethan Lyrics* (Columbia Chamber Ensemble, Gunther Schuller, cond.; Adele Addison, soprano; Galimir String Quartet)

1963 Carl Ruggles: *Sun Treader* (Columbia Symphony Orchestra, Zoltan Rozsnyai, cond.)

1964 Arthur Berger: *Chamber Music for Thirteen Players; Three Pieces for Two Pianos* (Columbia Chamber Ensemble, Gunther Schuller, cond.; Paul Jacobs and Gilbert Kalish, pianos)

1966 Ralph Shapey: *Rituals for Symphony Orchestra; String Quartet No. 6* (London Sinfonietta, Ralph Shapey, cond.; Lexington Quartet of the Contemporary Chamber Players of the University of Chicago)

1967 Henry Weinberg: *String Quartet No. 2* (Composers Quartet)

1970 Seymour Shifrin: *Three Pieces for Orchestra* (London Sinfonietta, Jacques Monod, cond.)

1972 David Diamond: *String Quartet No. 9; Nonet* (Composers Quartet String Ensemble cond. by Charles Wuorinen)
David del Tredici: *I Hear an Army; Scherzo* (Phyllis Bryn-Julson, soprano; Composers Quartet; Robert Helps and David del Tredici, pianos)

1973 Mario Davidovsky: *Inflexions; Chacona* (Ensemble cond. by David Gilbert; Jeanne Benjamin, violin; Joel Krosnick, cello; Robert Miller, piano)
Tison Street: *String Quartet* (Concord String Quartet)
Richard Trythall: *Coincidences* (Richard Trythall, piano)

1974 Donald Erb: *Three Pieces for Brass Quintet and Piano* New York Brass Quintet; James Smolko, piano; Matthias Bamert, cond.)
Leslie Bassett: *Sextet for Piano and Strings* (Concord String Quartet; John Graham, viola; Gilbert Kalish, piano)
George Edwards: *Kreuz und Quer* (Boston Musica Viva, Richard Pittman, cond.)
Robert MacDougall: *Anacoluthon: A Confluence* (Contemporary Chamber Ensemble, Arthur Weisberg, cond.)

1975 Walter Mays: *Six Invocations to the Svara Mandala for Percussion Orchestra;* **Richard Wernick:** *A Prayer for Jerusalem* (Jan DeGaetani, mezzo-soprano; Glenn Steele, percussion)

1976 No awards

1977 Edwin Dugger, *Intemezzi* and *Abwesenheiten und wiedersehen*
Fred Lerdahl, *Eros*

Nordiska Radets Musikpris

THE NORDIC COUNCIL
Fack, S-103, 10-Stockholm, Sweden (Tel: 14 10 00 and 20 54 02)

The Nordiska Radets Musikpris, which carries a cash honorarium of 50,000 Danish crowns, is awarded biennially to a living composer for a recent composition which meets the highest artistic standards. A committee of Nordic experts makes the selection from candidates nominated by delegates of participating countries.

1965 Karl Birger Blomdahl (Sweden), *Aniara* (opera)
1968 Joonas Kokkonen (Finland), *Symfoni nr 3*
1970 Lars Johan Werle (Sweden), *Drommen om Therese* (opera)
1972 Arne Nordheim (Norway), *ECO*
1974 Per Norgard (Denmark), *Gilgamesh* (opera)
1976 Atli Heimir Sveinsson (Iceland), *Koncert for flojte og orkester*

No. 1 Awards

BILLBOARD
9000 Sunset Blvd., Los Angeles, Calif. 90069 (213/273-7040)

Billboard No. 1 Awards annually recognize top records, recording artists, producers and labels, based on a point-value structure of the publication's record charts of radio airplay and record sales. The winners of the No. 1 honors receive Lucite trophies. In addition to the top winner in each category listed here, *Billboard* annually publishes the runner-up places. The categories have changed over the years.

SINGLE OF THE YEAR-POP

1975 *Love Will Keep Us Together,* The Captain and Tennille
1976 *Silly Love Songs,* Wings
1977 *Tonight's the Night,* Rod Stewart

ALBUM OF THE YEAR-POP

1975 *Elton John's Greatest Hits,* Elton John
1976 *Frampton Comes Alive,* Peter Frampton
1977 *Rumors,* Fleetwood Mac

ARTISTS OF THE YEAR AND NO. 1 AWARDS (Pop unless indicated otherwise)

1975 John Denver, Singles Artist No. 1 Award
John Denver, Singles—Male Artist
Linda Ronstadt, Singles—Female Artist
America, Singles—Duos and Groups
Van McCoy and the Soul City Symphony, Singles—Instrumentalists
Elton John, Albums Artist No. 1 Award
Elton John, Albums—Male Artists
Olivia Newton-John, Albums—Female Artists
The Blackbyrds, Albums—Instrumentalists
Average White Band, Albums—Duos and Groups

1976 Aerosmith, Album Artists
Barry Manilow, Singles—Male Artist
Diana Ross, Singles—Female Artist
Rhythm Heritage, Singles—Instrumentalist Duos and Groups
Hagood Hardy, Singles—Instrumentalist
Bee Gees, Singles—Duos and Groups
John Denver, Albums—Male Artist

Diana Ross, Albums—Female Artists
Aerosmith, Albums—Duos and Groups
George Benson, Albums—Instrumentalist Duos and Groups
Salsoul Orchestra, Albums—Instrumentalist
1977 **Stevie Wonder,** Male Artist of the Year
Linda Ronstadt, Female Artist of the Year
Barbra Streisand, Easy Listening Artist of the Year
Fleetwood Mac, Group of the Year
Waylon Jennings, Country Artist of the Year
Stevie Wonder, Soul Artist of the Year
Foreigner, Pop New Artist of the Year
Rod Stewart, Pop Single of the Year—*Tonight's the Night (Gonna be Alright)*
Fleetwood Mac, Album of the Year—*Rumors*
Rod Stewart, Pop Singles—Male Artist
Barbra Streisand, Pop Singles—Female Artist
London Symphony Orchestra, Pop Singles—Instrumentalist Duos and Groups
Maynard Ferguson, Pop Singles—Instrumentalists
Steve Miller Band, Pop Singles—Duos and Groups
Stevie Wonder, Pop Albums—Male Artist
Linda Ronstadt, Pop Albums—Female Artist
Fleetwood Mac, Pop Albums—Duos and Groups
Salsoul Orchestra, Pop Albums—Instrumentalist Duos and Groups
Maynard Ferguson, Pop Albums—Instrumentalists

SINGLES LABLES — POP

1975 Capitol
1976 Capitol
1977 Warner Brothers

ALBUM LABELS — POP

1975 Columbia
1976 Columbia
1977 Warner Brothers

PROCUCERS — POP

1975 Gus Dudgeon
1976 Freddie Perren
1977 Richard Perry

PUBLISHERS

1975 Jobete
1976 Jobete
1977 Jobete

HONOR ROLL OF NEW ARTISTS AND NO. 1 AWARDS

1975 **Pure Prairie League,** New Album Artist
Freddy Fender, Singles — New Male Artist
Jessi Colter, Singles — New Female Artist
Captain and Tennille, Singles — New Duos and Groups
Van McCoy and the Soul City Symphony, Singles — New Instrumentalists
Freddy Fender, Albums — New Male Artist
Gloria Gaynor, Albums — New Female artist
Pure Prairie League, Albums — New Duos and Groups
Van McCoy and the Soul City Symphony, Albums — New Instrumentalists
1976 **Rhythm Heritage,** New Singles Artists
Brass Construction, New Album Artists
Dorothy Moore, Singles — New Female Artist
Gary Wright, Singles — New Male Artist
Rhythm Heritage, Singles — New Instrumentalists
Wild Cherry, Singles — New Duos and Groups

Vicki Sue Robinson, Albums — New Female Artist
John Travolta, Albums — New Male Artist
Lee Oskar, Albums — New Intrumentalist
Brass Construction, Albums — New Duos and Groups
1977 **Foreigner,** New Pop Artist
Foreigner, New Pop Album Artist
Kenny Nolan, New Pop Singles Artist
Jennifer Warnes, New Pop Singles Female Artist
Kenny Nolan, New Pop Singles Male Artist
Cerrone, New Pop Singles Instrumentalists
Foreigner, New Pop Singles Duos and Groups
Mary MacGregor, New Pop Albums Female Artist
Teddy Pendergrass, New Pop Albums Male Artist
Lonnie Liston Smith, New Pop Albums Instrumentalists
Foreigner, New Pop Albums Duos and Groups

COUNTRY SINGLES

1975 *Rhinestone Cowboy,* Glen Campbell
1976 *Convoy,* C.W. McCall
1977 *Luckenbach, Texas,* Waylon Jennings

SINGLES ARTIST — COUNTRY

1975 Joe Stampley
1976 Freddy Fender
1977 Waylon Jennings

COUNTRY ALBUM

1975 *Back Home Again,* John Denver
1976 *The Sound in Your Mind,* Willie Nelson
1977 *Ol' Waylon,* Waylon Jennings

ALBUMS ARTIST — COUNTRY

1975 Charlie Rich
1976 Willie Nelson
1977 Waylon Jennings

SINGLES NEW ARTIST — COUNTRY

1975 Freddy Fender
1976 Dave and Sugar
1977 Vern Gosdin

SINGLES LABELS — POP

1975 Columbia
1976 RCA
1977 RCA

ALBUMS LABELS — COUNTRY

1975 RCA
1976 RCA
1977 RCA

PUBLISHERS — COUNTRY

1975 Acuff-Rose
1976 Tree
1977 Tree

EASY LISTENING SINGLES

1975 *Midnight Blue,* Melissa Manchester
1976 *Paloma Blanca,* George Baker Selection
1977 *Nobody Does It Better,* Carly Simon

SINGLES ARTIST — EASY LISTENING

1975 John Denver
1976 Olivia Newton-John
1977 Barbra Streisand

LABELS — EASY LISTENING
1975 Columbia
1976 Columbia
1977 Columbia

PUBLISHERS — EASY LISTENING
1975 Warner Brothers
1976 Warner Brothers
1977 Unart

SOUL SINGLES
1975 *Fight the Power,* Isley Brothers
1976 *Disco Lady,* Johnny Taylor
1977 *Float On,* Floaters

SINGLES ARTIST — SOUL
1975 Gladys Knight and the Pips
1976 Johnny Taylor
1977 Natalie Cole

NEW ARTISTS — SOUL SINGLES
1975 Major Harris
1976 Brothers Johnson
1977 Floaters

SINGLES LABELS — SOUL
1975 Atlantic
1976 Columbia
1977 ABC

SOUL ALBUMS
1975 *That's the Way of the World,* Earth, Wind and Fire
1976 *Rufus Featuring Chaka Khan,* Rufus Featuring Chaka Kahn
1977 *Songs in the Key of Life,* Stevie Wonder

ALBUMS ARTIST — SOUL
1975 Ohio Players
1976 Rufus Featuring Chaka Kahn
1977 Stevie Wonder

ALBUMS LABELS — SOUL
1975 Atlantic
1976 Columbia
1977 Tamila

PUBLISHERS — SOUL
1975 Mighty Three
1976 Mighty Three
1977 Jobete

JAZZ ALBUMS
1975 *Pieces of Dreams,* Stanley Turrentine
1976 *Breezin',* George Benson
1977 *In Flight,* George Benson

ALBUM ARTISTS — JAZZ
1975 Stanley Turrentine
1976 George Benson
1977 George Benson

ALBUM LABELS — JAZZ
1975 Columbia
1976 Columbia
1977 Columbia

CLASSICAL ALBUMS
1975 *Snowflakes Are Dancing: The Newest Sounds of Debussy,* Isao Tomita
1976 *Pachelbel Canon,* Stuttgart Chamber Orchestra
1977 *The Great Pavarotti,* Luciano Pavarotti

ALBUM LABELS — CLASSICAL
1975 London
1976 London
1977 Columbia

GOSPEL ALBUMS
1975 *Live at Carnegie Hall,* Andrae Crouch
1976 *Jesus Is the Best Thing That Ever Happened to Me,* James Cleveland and Charles Fold Singers
1977 *Love Alive,* Walter Hawkins and the Love Center Choir

ALBUM LABELS — GOSPEL
1975 Savoy
1976 Savoy
1977 Savoy

GOSPEL ARTISTS
1977 Andrae Crouch and the Disciples

SOUNDTRACK
1975 *Tommy*
1976 *Barry Lyndon*
1977 *A Star Is Born*

COMEDY SINGLE
1975 *Mr. Jaws,* Dickie Goodman
1976 *Yes, Yes, Yes,* Bill Cosby
1977 No award

COMEDY ALBUM
1975 *Wedding Album,* Cheech and Chong
1976 *Sleeping Beauty,* Cheech and Chong
1977 No award

COMEDY ALBUM ARTIST
1977 Richard Pryor

DISCO — AUDIENCE RESPONSE
1976 *That's Where the Happy People Go,* Trammps
1977 *Anyway You Like It/Don't Leave Me This Way,* Thelma Houston

DISCO ARTIST
1976 Donna Summer
1977 Donna Summer

DISCO LABEL
1976 Motown
1977 Casablanca

LATIN POP ARTIST
1977 Julio Iglesias

LATIN SALSA ARTIST
1977 Celia, Johnny, Justo & Papo

BOX OFFICE AWARDS:

STADIUMS AND FESTIVALS (20,000 and over)
1976 Yes/Peter Frampton/Gary Wright/Pousette, J.F.K. Stadium, Philadelphia (6/12/76)

1977 Peter Frampton/Lynyrd Skynyrd/Santana/The Outlaws, Oakland (Calif.) Stadium, (7/2-4/77)

ARTIST
1976 Peter Frampton
1977 Peter Frampton

PROMOTER
1976 Bill Graham
1977 Bill Graham

FACILITY
1976 Oakland (Calif.) Stadium
1977 Oakland (Calif.) Stadium

ARENAS (6-20,000)
1976 Elton John, Madison Sq. Garden, N.Y. (8/10-17/76)
1977 Pink Floyd, Madison Sq. Garden, N.Y., (7/1-4/77)

ARTIST
1976 Elton John
1977 Elvis Presley

PROMOTER
1976 Electric Factory Concerts
1977 Bill Graham

FACILITIES
1976 Spectrum Theater, Philadelphia
1977 Spectrum Theater, Philadelphia

AUDITORIUMS (under 6,000)
1976 Ella Fitzgerald/Oscar Peterson/Count Basie Orchestra/Joe Pass, Shubert Theater, Century City, Calif. (5/4-9/76)
1977 Johnny Mathis, Avery Fisher Hall, N.Y., (4/1-3/77)

ARTIST
1976 Lynyrd Skynyrd
1977 George Benson

PROMOTER
1976 Bill Graham
1977 Electric Factory Concerts

FACILITIES
1976 Civic Auditorium, Santa Monica, Calif.
1977 Tower Theater, Philadelphia

N. Paganini International Violin Competition Prize
CITY OF GENOA
Palazzo Tursi, Via Garibaldi 9, Genoa, Italy (Tel: 010 2098)

The first-place winner of the N. Paganini International Violin Competition Prize is currently awarded 3 million lire. The three-round competition is open to musicians under thirty-five years of age. Judging is by a jury of six non-Italians and three Italians.

1956 Gerard Poulet, France
      Gyorgy Pauk, Hungary
1957 No award
1958 Salvatore Accordo, Italy
1959 Stuart Canin, U.S.A.
1960 No award

1961 Emil Kamilarow, Bulgaria
1962 Maryvonne Le Dizes, France
1963 Oleg Kryssa, U.S.S.R.
1964 Jean Jacques Kantorow, France
1965 Vittorio Pikaisen, U.S.S.R.
1966 No award
1967 Gregorio Gislin, U.S.S.R.
1968 Miriam Fries, Israel
1969 Ghidon Kremmer, U.S.S.R.
1970 No award
1971 Mose Secler, U.S.S.R.
1972 Eugene Fodor, U.S.A.
1973 Allesandro Kravarov, U.S.S.R.
1974 No award
1975 Yuri Korcinsky, U.S.S.R.
1976 Lenuta Ciulei, Rumania
1977 Ilja Groubert, U.S.S.R.

Paris International Voice Competition
CONCOURS INTERNATIONAL DE CHANT DE PARIS
14 bis, avenue du President Wilson, F-75016 Paris, France (Tel: 723 62 23)

The Paris International Voice Competition now offers three major prizes, a Grand Prize and first prizes for a man and a woman. In addition to cash awards, finalists and prize winners are offered concert and recital engagements. Singers up to the age of thirty-two years are eligible. The recipients are selected by a jury. Until now, the Competition has been held annually. After 1978, it will become a biennial event.

1967 Anna Maria Miranda, France
      Sylvia Valet, France
1968 Evelyn Brunner, Switzerland
1969 Zuinglio Faustini, Argentina
      Christiane Issartel, France
1970 Robert Dume, France
      Gerda Hartmann, South Africa
1971 William Parker, U.S.A.
      Esther Casas Coll, Spain
1972 Pavlov Raptis, Poland
      Barbara Hendricks, U.S.A.
      Edith Tremblay, Canada
1973 Robert Currier Christensen, U.S.A.
1974 Lajos Miller, Hungary
1975 No award
1976 Serge Leiferkouss, U.S.S.R.
1977 Katherine Ciesinski, U.S.A. (Grand Prize)
      John Aler, U.S.A.
      Christina Manolova, Bulgaria

Gold Medal Awards
PHOTOPLAY
205 E. 42nd St., New York, N.Y. 10017 (212/983-5600)

The Photoplay Gold Medal Awards are made for popular music performers. The most recent awards were based on ballots of more than 60,000 readers of the magazine.

FAVORITE COUNTRY MUSIC STAR
    1976 Charley Pride
    1977 Not available at press time

  1976 Barry Manilow
  1977 Not available at press time

Poses Brandeis University Creative Arts Award

BRANDEIS UNIVERSITY
Brandeis University Commission Office, 12 E. 77th St., New York, N.Y. 10021 (212/472-1501)

One of a series of awards in the creative arts, the Jack I. and Lillian L. Poses Brandeis University Creative Arts Award is given annually to recognize talent in mid-career in music or dance. The award, which may not be applied for, carries an honorarium of $1,000 and a medal or citation. Professional juries chosen by the Commission select the winners.

1957 William Schuman (Medal), Robert Kurka (Citation), Music
1958 Roger Sessions (Medal), Andrew Imbrie (Citation), Music
1959 Ernest Bloch (Medal), Seymour Shifrin (Citation), Music
1960 Aaron Copland (Medal), Gunther Schuller (Citation), Music
1961 Wallingford Riegger (Medal), Billy Jim Layton (Citation), Music
1962 Edgard Varese (Medal), Ralph Shapey (Citation), Music
1963 Walter Piston (Medal), Yehudi Wyner (Citation), Music
1964 Carl Ruggles (Medal), Donald Martino (Citation), Music
1965 Elliott Cook Carter (Medal), Salvatore Martirano (Citation), Music
1966 Stefan Wolpe (Medal), Mario Davidovsky (Citation), Music
1967 Ross Lee Finney (Medal), Claudio Spies (Citation), Music
1968 Virgil Thomson (Medal), Easley Blackwood (Citation), Music
1969 Ernst Krenek (Medal), Henry Weinberg (Citation), Music
1970 Milton Babbitt (Medal), Charles Wuorinen (Citation), Music
1971 Earl Kim (Medal), John Harbison (Citation), Music
1972 Merce Cunningham (Medal), Twyla Tharp (Citation), Dance
1973 Roy Harris (Medal), David Del Tredici (Citation), Music
1974 Anna Sokolow (Medal), William Dunas and Meredith Monk (Citation), Dance
1975 Vincent Persichetti (Medal), Jacob Druckman (Citation), Music
1976 Antony Tudor (Medal), Eliot Feld (Citation), Dance
1977 Leon Kirchner (Medal), Earle Brown (Citation), Music

Pulitzer Prize

COLUMBIA UNIVERSITY
Graduate School of Journalism, New York, N.Y. 10027
(212/280-3828) (Pulitzer Prizes: 212/280-3841)

Endowed by the will of Joseph Pulitzer, founder of the St. Louis Post Dispatch, and administered by Columbia University, the annual Pulitzer Prizes include a $1,000 award for music. Entry must be made to the fifteen-member advisory board on Pulitzer Prizes in the form or scores or recordings.

1943 William Schuman, *Secular Cantata No. 2*
1944 Howard Hanson, *Symphony No. 4, opus 34*
1945 Aaron Copland, *Appalachian Spring*
1946 Leo Sowerby, *The Canticle of the Sun*
1947 Charles Ives, *Symphony No. 3*
1948 Walter Piston, *Symphony No. 3*
1949 Virgil Thomson, *Louisiana Story*
1950 Gian-Carlo Menotti, *The Consul*
1951 Douglas S. Moore, *Giants in the Earth*
1952 Gail Kubik, *Symphony Concertante*
1953 No award
1954 Quincy Porter, *Concerto for Two Pianos and Orchestra*
1955 Gian-Carlo Menotti, *The Saint of Bleecker Street*
1956 Ernst Toch, *Symphony No. 3*
1957 Norman Dello Joio, *Meditations on Ecclesiastes*
1958 Samuel Barber, The Score of *Vanessa*
1959 John La Montaine, *Concerto for Piano and Orchestra*
1960 Elliott Cook Carter, Jr., *Second String Quartet*
1961 Walter Piston, *Symphony No. 7*
1962 Robert Ward, *The Crucible*
1963 Samuel Barber, *Piano Concerto No. 1*
1964 No award
1965 No award
1966 Leslie Bassett, *Variations for Orchestra*
1967 Leon Kirchner, *Quartet No. 3*
1968 George Crumb, *Echoes of Time and the River*
1969 Karel Husa, *String Quartet No. 3*
1970 Charles W. Wuorinen, *Time's Encomium*
1971 Mario Davidovsky, *Synchronisms No. 6*
1972 Jacob Druckman, *Windows*
1973 Elliott Carter, *String Quartet No. 3*
1974 Donald Martino, *Notturno*
1975 Dominick Argento, *From the Diary of Virginia Woolf*
1976 Ned Rorem, *Air Music*, 10 etudes for orchestra
1977 Richard Wernick, *Visions of Terror and Wonder*

SPECIAL AWARDS AND CITATIONS

1974 Roger Sessions, Life's work in composition
1976 Scott Joplin, Bicentennial honor bestowed posthumously for contributions to American music

Recording Academy Hall of Fame

NATIONAL ACADEMY OF RECORDING ARTS AND SCIENCES
4444 Riverside Dr., Suite 202, Burbank, Calif. 91505
(213/843-8233)

Admission to the Recording Academy Hall of Fame honors outstanding historical, qualitative or lasting recordings. The honor includes permanent enshrinement in the Hall of Fame and inscribed certificates to all creative participants. A ninety-person committee of musicologists and experts in the field selects the recordings to be honored. Hall of Fame winners were inducted from 1974 to 1977; the dates indicated are those of recording, not the induction. All recordings predate 1958.

1907 *Leoncavallo: Pagliacci, Act 1, "Vesti la Giubba,"* Enrico Caruso
1927 *Gershwin: Rhapsody in Blue,* Paul Whiteman with George Gershwin, RCA Victor
Singin' the Blues, Frankie Trumbauer and his Orchestra featuring Bix Beiderbecke on cornet; Okeh
1928 *West End Blues,* Louis Armstrong; Okeh
1929 *Rachmaninoff: Piano Concert No. 2 in C Minor,* Sergei Rachmaninoff (piano); Philadelphia Orchestra with Leopold Stokowski conducting; Victor
1930 *Mood Indigo,* Duke Ellington; Brunswick
1937 *I Can't Get Started,* Bunny Berigan; Victor
1938 *Begin the Beguine,* Artie Shaw; Bluebird
Beethoven Piano Sonatas, Arthur Schnabel; Beethoven Piano Society/RCA
1939 *Body and Soul,* Coleman Hawkins; Bluebird
1941 *God Bless the Child,* Billie Holiday; Okeh
Take the 'A' Train, Duke Ellington and his Orchestra; Victor
1942 *White Christmas,* Bing Crosby; Decca
1943 *Oklahoma!,* Original cast incl. Alfred Drake; orchestra and chorus directed by Jay Blackton; Decca
1949-54 *Bach: The Well-Tempered Clavier,* Wanda Landowska; RCA Victor
1950 *Carnegie Hall Jazz Concert,* Benny Goodman; Columbia
1950-53 *Beethoven: Nine Symphonies,* Arturo Toscanini conducting the NBC Symphony Orchestra; RCA Victor
1951 *Gershwin: Porgy and Bess,* Lehman Engel, conductor; cast included Lawrence, Winters, Camella, Williams; Columbia
1954 *Christmas Song,* Nat "King" Cole; Capitol
1956 *My Fair Lady,* Original Cast with Rex Harrison and Julie Andrews; Columbia

Rock Music Awards
ROCK MUSIC ASSOCIATION
Address unknown

The Rock Music Awards have been given annually since 1975 in nationally telecast ceremonies for excellence in this area of popular music. Neither details of the selection process nor 1975 and 1976 winners are available.

ROCK PERSONALITY OF THE YEAR
1977 Fleetwood Mac

BEST FEMALE VOCALIST
1977 Linda Ronstadt

BEST MALE VOCALIST
1977 Stevie Wonder

BEST GROUP
1977 Fleetwood Mac

BEST NEW FEMALE VOCALIST
1977 Yvonne Elliman

BEST NEW MALE VOCALIST
1977 Stephen Bishop

BEST NEW GROUP
1977 Boston

BEST R&B SINGLE
1977 Boz Scaggs, *Low Down*

BEST R&B ALBUM
1977 Stevie Wonder, *Songs in the Key of Life*

BEST SINGLE
1977 Boz Scaggs, *Low Down*

BEST ALBUM
1977 Fleetwood Mac, *Rumors*

BEST SONG COMPOSER
1977 Bruce Springsteen, *Blinded by the Light*

BEST PRODUCER
1977 Fleetwood Mac

PUBLIC SERVICE AWARD
1977 Joan Baez
Bee Gees
Harry Chapin
Fleetwood Mac
Kansas
Spinners

ROCK MUSIC HALL OF FAME
1977 Elvis Presley

International Jean Sibelius Violin Competition
SIBELIUS SOCIETY
P. Rautatiekatu 9, SF-00100 Helsinki, Finland (Tel: 90-492 223)

The International Jean Sibelius Violin Competition is held every five years for violinists between the ages of sixteen and thirty-three. A jury selects the winner, who is awarded a cash honorarium.

1965 Oleg Kagan, U.S.S.R.
1970 Liana Isakadze, U.S.S.R.
Pavel Kogan, U.S.S.R.
1975 Yuval Yaron, Israel

Talent Forum Award
BILLBOARD
9000 Sunset Blvd., Los Angeles, Calif. 90069 (213/273-7040)

The Talent Forum Award, which consists of a plaque, honors achievement in the live-talent field as determined by a vote of Talent Forum registrants.

1976 Bill Graham, Concert promoter
Dee Anthony, Bandana Productions, Personal manager
Frank Barsalona, Premier, Independent booking agent
Tom Ross, ICM, Staff booking agent
Magid, Bijou, Philadelphia, Nightclub operator
Chuck Morris, Ebbets Field, Denver, Nightclub operator (small clubs)
Elmer Valentine, Roxy, Los Angeles, Nightclub operator in Los Angeles or New York
Claire Rothman, Los Angeles Forum, Facility manager

Mike Klenfner, Arista, Artists relations executive
Bob Levinson, Levinson Associates, Publicist
Stuart Allen, Aladdin, Las Vegas, Talent buyer (hotels)
Sonny Anderson, Disneyland, Top talent buyer (fairs and parks)
Joff Dubin, U. of Calif. at Berkeley, Talent buyer (colleges)
Eagles, Warner Bros., Talent Attraction of the Year
1977 Dee Anthony, Personal manager
Nat Weiss, Entertainment attorney
Ron Delsener, Concert promoter
Boston, Breakout artist
Barbara Skydell, Premier, Staff booking agent
Joe Cohen, Madison Sq. Garden, Facility manager
Frank Barsalona, Premier, Independent booking agent
Susan Blond, Publicist
Allan Pepper and Stanley Sandowsky, Bottom Line, Nightclub operator
Suzanne Young, U. of Michigan, College talent buyer
Jonathan Coffino, Columbia, Artist relations Executive
James Tamer, Aladdin, Talent Buyer of the Year
Performing Arts Theatre, (hotels, fairs, parks)

International Tchaikovsky Awards

INTERNATIONAL TCHAIKOVSKY COMPETITION
15 Neglinnaya St., Moscow, U.S.S.R. (Tel: 294-64-61; 223-13-87; 294-14-20)

The International Tchaikovsky Competition takes place every four years for pianists, violinists, cellists and solo singers of any nationality between the ages of sixteen and thirty. Two preliminary and one final round of competition before the public are held, and winners are expected to participate gratis in concerts that mark the closing of the competition. Six cash awards are made in each category, with the top prize consisting of 2,500 rubles and a gold medal.

PIANO
1958 Van Cliburn (U.S.A.)
1962 John Andrew Howard Ogden (Great Britain)
1964 Grigory Sokolov (U.S.S.R.)
1970 Vladimir Krainev (U.S.S.R.)
1974 Andrei Gavrilov (U.S.S.R.)

VIOLIN
1958 Valery Klimov (U.S.S.R.)
1962 Boris Gutnikov (U.S.S.R.)
1966 Viktor Tretyakov (U.S.S.R.)
1970 Gideon Kramer (U.S.S.R.)
1974 Tied for second place; no first-prize winner:
Ruben Agaronyan (U.S.S.R.)
Eugene Fodor (U.S.A.)
Rusudan Gvasaliya (U.S.S.R.)

CELLO
1962 Natalya Shakhovskaya (U.S.S.R.)
1966 Karine Georgian (U.S.S.R.)
1970 David Geringas (U.S.S.R.)
1974 Boris Pergamentchikov (U.S.S.R.)

VOICE (Male)
1966 Vladimir Atlantov (U.S.S.R.)
1970 Evgeny Nesterenko (U.S.S.R.)

1974 Ivan Ponomorenko (U.S.S.R.)

VOICE (Female)
1966 Jane Marsh (U.S.A.)
1970 Elena Obratsova (U.S.S.R.)
1974 Tied for second place; no first-prize winner:
Stefka Evstatieva (Bulgaria)
Sylvia Sass (Hungary)
Liudmila Sergienko (U.S.S.R.)

Trendsetter Award

BILLBOARD
9000 Sunset Blvd., Los Angeles, Calif. 90069 (213/273-7040)

The Trendsetter Award, which consists of a Lucite statue, is given for outstanding achievement in the music field that represents a specific innovation or trend in the industry. The management, editors and sales staff of *Billboard* select the members of the industry who receive this annual honor.

1976 David Infante, Laser Physics, Opening disco and concert areas to laser light shows
Joe Cayre, Salsoul Records, Developing first 12-inch single for commercial sale
Don Biederman, ABC Records, Crusade to halt retailers from selling counterfeit and promotional albums
Lee Fisher, Aladdin Hotel, Las Vegas, Nev., Opened Las Vegas's first concert hall on the Strip
Tony Martell, CBS Records, Developing the country music prepack album program
Neil Bogart, Casablanca Records, Developing a program of limited edition LPS for major artists
Ernest Fleischman & the Los Angeles Philharmonic, Developing a formula with the American Federation of Musicians to allow orchestra to record without paying for a full complement of musicians.
George De Rado, TEAC, Expanding the market for semi-professional sound equipment
1977 Creed Taylor, Creating cross-over brand of jazz, appealing to pop and disco fans
Chris Blackwell and Denny Cordell, Introduction of Jamaican reggae music to U.S. market
John Denver, Musical style which draws adults into pop market
Freddy Fender and Huey Meaux, Established Tex-Mex music on national market
CBS Records and Vice President Bruce Lundvall and Jack Graigo, Promoting wide-margin price concept for catalogue LPs
Atlantic Records and Dickie Klein and Henry Allen, Series of 12-in. singles for discotheques
Andy Park, Devising adventurous programing of various sounds for Scotland's commercial station, Radio Clyde
Moffat Communications, Installing computer-assisted programing system at its Canadian radio stations
Willem van Kooten, Masterminding and guiding international impact of Dutch talent
Wonderama, Presenting top-name contemporary music acts to young children via Sunday morning TV
Exxon Corp., Leading corporate funding of classical concert music on radio, television and in concert

Varna Prize

INTERNATIONAL BALLET COMPETITION
56 Alabin St., 1000-Sofia, Bulgaria (Tel. 880853)

The International Ballet Competition for men and women currently takes place biennially in Varna and comprises three stages of contemporary and classical dance programs. Male and female dancers are evaluated separately by juries, whether they enter as soloists or duos. Class A competition is for dancers nineteen years of age or over, while Class B is for young dancers between fourteen and nineteen years of age. The first-place Class A winners receive 2000 leva, a gold medal and a diploma, while the first-place Class B dancers receive 800 leva, a diploma and a medal. In addition to the first-place winners listed here, Class A prizes are awarded down to the fifth place and Class B prizes to the third place.

1964 Vladimir Vassilev (U.S.S.R.) Grand Prize
Ala Sizova (U.S.S.R.) First Prize
Ekaterina Maximova (U.S.S.R.) First Prize
Vera Kirova (Bulgaria) First Prize
Sergei Vikulov (U.S.S.R.) First Prize
Nikita Dolgushin (U.S.S.R.) First Prize
1965 Mikhail Lavrovsky (U.S.S.R.) First Prize
Loipa Araujo (Cuba) First Prize
Vladimir Tikhonov (U.S.S.R.) First Prize
Natalia Bessmertnova (U.S.S.R.) First Prize
1966 Mikhail Baryshnikov (U.S.S.R.) Junior First Prize
Martine van Hamel (Canada) Junior First Prize
Olga Vtorushina (U.S.S.R.) Junior First Prize
Marin Stanse (Romania) Junior First Prize
Yuriy Vladimirov (U.S.S.R.) Senior First Prize
Nina Sorekina (U.S.S.R.) Senior First Prize
Aurora Bosch (Cuba) Senior First Prize
Marta Drotnerova (Czechoslovakia) Senior First Prize
1968 Jan Nuits (Belgium) Junior First Prize
Bisser Beyanou (Bulgaria) Junior First Prize
Mirta Garcia (Cuba) Junior First Prize
Villen Gastian (U.S.S.R.) Senior First Prize
1970 Rosario Suarez (Cuba) Junior First Prize
Eva Evdokimova (U.S.A.) Senior First Prize
1972 Hana Vlacilova (Czechoslovakia) Junior First Prize
Gabor Kevehazy (Hungary) Junior First Prize
Lyubov Konakova (U.S.S.R.) Senior First Prize
Vladimir Fedyanin (U.S.S.R.) Senior First Prize
1974 Yoko Morishita (Japan)
Fernando Bujones (U.S.A.), Technical Award
Mihail Civin (U.S.S.R.)
Bisser Dejanov (Bulgaria)
Galina Tessjolkina (Special Award)
Soile Hainonen (Finland)
1976 Tied for Senior Second Prize; no First Prize Awarded:
Hana Vlacilova (Czechoslovakia)
Larissa Matiuhina (U.S.S.R.)
Marin Bojeru (Romania), Senior First Prize
Alla Mihalchenko (U.S.S.R.), Junior First Prize
Ben van Kauenberg (Belgium), Junior Second Prize; no First Prize awarded

Verdi Medal of Achievement

METROPOLITAN OPERA NATIONAL COUNCIL
Metropolitan Opera, Lincoln Center for the Performing Arts, New York, N.Y. 10023 (212/799-3100)

The Verdi Medal of Achievement is awarded annually to the individual who has made the greatest contribution to opera in the previous year. The medal, which is of bronze, was sculpted by Betti Richard. A committee selects the winner.

1977 Maria F. Rich, Director, Central Opera Service, and editor, *Metropolitan Opera Bulletin*

Wihuri-Sibelius Prize

JENNY AND ANTTI WIHURI FOUNDATION
Arkadiankatu 21 B 25, 00100-Helsinki 10, Finland (Tel: 444 145)

Among the prizes, honors and scholarships awarded by this foundation and its research institute is the Wihuri-Sibelius Prize, given as warranted for merit in music.

1953 Jean Sibelius
1955 Paul Hindemith
1958 Dmitri Shostakovich
1963 Igor Stravinsky
1965 Benjamin Britten
Erik Bergman
Usko Merilainen
Einojuhani Rautavaara
1971 Olivier Messiaen
1973 Witold Lutoslawski
Joonas Kokkonen

Grand Prix

YAMAHA MUSIC FOUNDATION
3-24-22, Shimonoguro, Meguro-ku, Tokyo 153, Japan (Tel: 03/719-3101)

The Grand Prix of the World Popular Music Festival, which consists of $5,000 and a gold medallion, is given annually for the best original song unpublished—except under special circumstances—before the Festival. A panel of international judges selects the winners, one of whom is from Japan and one of whom is from a foreign country. In addition to the Grand Prix, lesser cash awards are given for excellence in performance and composition.

1970 *I Dream of Naomi,* by David Krivoshi, performed by Hedva and David (Israel)
1971 *The Song of Departure,* by Hitoshi Komuro, performed by Kamijo and Rokumonsen (Japan)
Un Jour L'Amour, by Andre Popp, performed by Martine Clemenseau (France)
1972 *Feeling,* by Peter Yellowstone and Jane Schwarz, performed by Capricorn (United Kingdom)
Life Is Just For Livin', by Ernie Smith, performed by Ernie Smith (Jamaica)
1973 *I Wish You Were Here With Me,* by Akiko Kosaka, performed by Akiko Kosaka (Japan)
If All the Kings and Castles, by Shawn Phillips, performed by Shawn Phillips (U.S.A.)
Head Over Heels, by Zack Lawrence, performed by Keeley Ford (United Kingdom)·
How Strange Paris is Sometimes, by Gino Mescoli and Alfred Ferrari, performed by Gilda Giuliani (Italy)

1974 *Someday,* by Yoshimi Hamada, performed by Yoshimi Hamada (Japan)
You Made Me Feel I Could Fly, by Kristian Lindeman, performed by Ellen Nikolaysen (Norway)

1975 *Lucky Man,* by Jorge Garcia-Castil, performed by Mr. Loco (Mexico)
Time Goes Around, by Miyuki Nakajima, performed by Miyaki Nakajima (Japan)

1976 *Goodbye Morning,* by Kaoru Nakajima, performed by Sandy (Japan)
Song (title N. A.) by Gino Mescoli, performed by Franco and Regina (Italy)

1977 Song (title N.A.) by Masanori Sera, performed by Masanori Sera and Twist (Japan)
Song (title N.A.) by Richard Gillinson and David Hayes, performed by Rags (United Kingdom)

Visual Arts

Contents

Related Awards

ASMP Awards
AMERICAN SOCIETY OF MAGAZINE
PHOTOGRAPHERS
60 E. 42nd St., New York, N.Y. 10017 (212/661-6450)

The ASMP annually confers awards on individuals in
the photographic world for contributions in the creative, technical or curatory aspects of the field. The
Awards Committee chooses the recipients, who are presented with a certificate, in areas such as Photographer
of the Year, Technical Achievement and others. Neither these areas of honor nor the number of winners is
fixed. In addition, special awards, including an Honor
Roll citation, are given as merited.

1953 Henri Cartier-Bresson
      Roland S. Potter
      Roy Stryker
1954 Ernst Haas
      Alexey Brodovitch
1955 Robert Capa
      Werner Bischof
      John A. Leermakers
      Wayne Miller
      Edward Steichen
1956 Ylla
      Roman Vishniac
1957 Richard Avedon
      Will Connell
      Allen F. Gifford
1958 Marty Forscher
      Emil Schulthess
      Wilson Hicks
1960 Gordon Parks
      Edwin Land
      Richard Simon
      David Douglas Duncan
1961 Irving Penn
      Japanese Camera Industry
      John Simon Guggenheim Foundation
1962 Brian Brake
      George Silk
      Bill Brandt
1963 Gjon Mili
1964 Art Kane
      Polaroid Corp.
      Berenice Abbott
      Charles Moore
1965 David Linton
      Ralph Baum
      Morris Gordon
      Imogen Cunningham
      Lennart Nilsson
      Harold Edgerton
1966 Andreas Feininger
      Victor Hasselblad
1967 Vietnam War photographers, living and
      dead
      Charles Wycoff
      Dennis Gabor, Emmett Leith and Juris Upat-
      nieks
1968 David Douglas Duncan
      Cornell Capa
      Lisette Model
      Homer Newell
      Leopold Godowsky and Leopold Manners
      Alexander Smakula
      Beaumont Newhall
      Grace Mayer

1969 Hiro
      Fritz Gruber
      Ben Rose
      Yoichi R. Okamoto
      Romana Javits
      Edwin L. Wisherd
      James Van Derzee
      Ott Schade
      Oscar Bernack
1970 Bruce Davidson
      Diane Arbus
      Jerry Uelsmann
      Jacob Deschin
      Walter Clark
      Peter C. Goldmark
1972 David B. Eisendrath
      Lee D. Witkin
1975 Philippe Halsman
      Arnold Newman
      Donald McCullin
      Alexander Liberman
      Edwin Land
1976 No award
1977 No award

FOUNDERS AWARD
1965 Allan Gould
      Michael Elliot
      Ewing Krainin
      Ike Vern
      Bradley Smith
      John Adam Knight

HONOR ROLL
1961 Man Ray
1962 Roy Stryker
      Alexey Brodovitch
      Edward Steichen
      Will Connell
1963 Dorothea Lange
      Walker Evans
      Cecil Beaton
      Paul Strand
      George Hoyningen-Huene
1964 Margaret Bourke-White
1965 Andre Kertesz
1966 Ansel Adams
      Brassai
1967 Roman Vishniac
      Bill Brandt
1968 Beaumont Newhall
1969 Fritz Gruber
1970 W. Eugene Smith
1971 Ernst Haas
1972 Henri Cartier-Bresson
1975 Cornell Capa
1976 No award
1977 No award

Arts and Letters Awards
Richard & Hinda Rosenthal Award
AMERICAN ACADEMY AND INSTITUTE OF
ARTS AND LETTERS
633 W. 155th St., New York, N.Y. 10032 (212/286-1480)

To encourage qualified artists, the Institute gives annual $3,000 awards to nonmembers. These Arts and

Letters Awards may not be applied for. Similar awards are given in music and literature and may be found on pp. 276 and 18 of this volume.

1941
Jon Corbino   Arthur Lee

1942
Peggy Bacon   Donal Hord
Cathal B. O'Toole

1943
Isabel Bishop   Hugh Ferris
Gertrude K. Lathrop   Bruce Moore

1944
Janet de Coux   Charles Locke
Berta Margoulies   Eleanor Platt
Charles Rudy   Esther Williams

1945
Peter Dalton   Donald De Lue
Vincent Glinsky   Edward Laning
Andree Ruellan   Raphael Soyer

1946
Richmond Barthe   Louis Gugliemi
Robert Gwathmey   Rosella Hartman
Jack Levine   Harry Rosin
Concetta Scaravaglione   Zoltan Sepeshy

1947
Peter Blume   Dorothea Greenbaum
Joseph Hirsch   Victoria Hutson Huntley
Mitchell Jamieson   Carl Schmitz

1948
Louis Bosa   Robert H. Cook, Jr.
Stephen Csoka   Philip Guston
Oronzio Maldarelli   John W. Taylor

1949
Federico Castellon   Carl Hall
Henry Kreis   John McCrady
William Pachner   Harry Wickey

1950
Jean de Marco   Lamar Dodd
Sue Fuller   Peter Hopkins
Bruno Mankowski   Sol Wilson

1951
Saul Baizerman   Lu Duble
Joseph Floch   Xavier Gonzalez
Peppino Mangravite   William Thon

1952
Clara Fasano   H.L. Kammerer
Edward Melcarth   Doris Rosenthal
Walter Stuempfig   Charles White

1953
Hyman Bloom   Albino Cavallito
Jacob Lawrence   William Palmer
Carl M. Schultheiss   Francis Speight

1954
Virginia Cuthbert   Koren Der Harootian
Edwin Dickinson   Hazard Durfee
Antonio Frasoni   David K. Rubins

1955
George Beattie   Hazel Janicki
Julian Levi   Zygmunt Menkes
Mitchell Siporin   Albert Stewart
Sahl Swarz

1956
Henry Di Spirito   Philip Evergood
Morris Graves   Chaim Gross
Barbara Lekberg   Theodoros Stamos

1957
John Heliker   Jonah Kinigstein
Kenzo Okada   Anne Poor
Hugo Robus   Polygnotos Vagis

1958
Charles H. Alston   David Aronson
Al Blaustein   Herbert Katzman
Seymour Lipton   Jack Zajac

1959
Jose de Rivera   Frank Duncan
Ruth Gikow   John Guerin
Minna Harkavy   Nathaniel Kaz
James Kearns

1960
Chen Chi   Marvin Cherney
Eugene Ludins   Rhoda Sherbell
George Tooker   Harold Tovish
Walter Williams

1961
Leonard Baskin   Paul Cadmus
Kahlil Gibran   Philip Grausman
Walter Murch   Gregorio Prestopino
Joseph Solman

1962
Robert M. Broderson   Nicolai Cikovsky
Richard Diebenkorn   Seymour Drumlevitch
Camilo Egas   Dimitri Hadzi
Bernard Reder

1963
Harold Altman   Wolfgang Behl
Elmer Bischoff   Jan Doubrava
James McGarrell   Raymond Saunders
Karl Zerbe

1964
Thomas B. Cornell   Edward J. Hill
Reuben Kramer   Michael Mazur
Bernard Perlin   Sarai Sherman
Charles Wells

1965
Sigmund Abeles   Lee Gatch
David V. Hayes   Richard Mayhew
Elliott Offner   Joyce Reopel
Thomas Stearns

1966

Romare Bearden
Carroll Cloar
Ezio Mantinelli
Richard Claude Ziemann

Lee Bontecou
Ray Johnson
Karl Schrag

1967

Byron Burford
Stephen Greene
Dennis Leon
Louis Tytell

Jared French
Leo Kenney
Hugh Townley

1968

Robert A. Birmelin
Leon Goldin
Vincent D. Smith
Charles Wilson

Kenneth Callahan
Joe Lasker
Elbert Weinberg

1969

Lennart Anderson
Frank Gallo
Red Grooms
Ben Kamihira

William Christopher
Leonel Gongora
Sidney J. Hurwitz
Alice Neel

1970

Leland Bell
Kenneth Campbell
Ralston Crawford
Harvey Weiss

Charles F. Cajori
Giorgio Cavallon
Allan D'Arcangelo

1971

Ilya Bolotowsky
Alfred Leslie
Ludwig Sander
Harold Tovish

Robert Goodnough
Norman Lewis
Hedda Sterne

1972

Richard Aakre
Lowry Burgess
Maud F. Gatewood
Anton Van Dalen

Varujan Boghosian
Mary Frank
Herman Rose

1973

Rudolf Baranik
Robert Grosvenor
Michio Ihara
Philip Pearlstein

Leon Golub
Raoul Hague
Clement Meadmore

1974

Perle Fine
Marilynn Gelfman-Pereira
Nancy Grossman
Charlotte Park

Richard Fleischner
George Griffin
Ibram Lassaw

1975

Calvin Albert
Barbara Falk
Leonid
William Talbot

Harry Bertoia
Claus Hoie
Seymour Pearlstein

1976

Judith Brown
William Kienbusch
Anthony Padovano
Joseph Wolins

Gregory Gillespie
Julio F. Larraz
Sidney Simon

1977

Nina Bohlen
Alex Markhoff
Fritz Scholder

Alan Gussow
Paul Resika
Susan Smyly

One of a pair of awards established under the same endowment (the other being for a work of fiction, see pp. 53), the Richard and Hinda Rosenthal Award in art is a $2,000 honorarium given to a young American painter of distinction who has not yet been accorded due recognition. This award may not be applied for.

1960   Ann Steinbrocker
1961   Zubel Kachadoorian
1962   Robert Andrew Parker
1963   Karen Arden
1964   Gregory Gillespie
1965   Marcia Marcus
1966   Howard Hack
1967   Robert D'Arista
1968   Elizabeth Osborne
1969   Nicholas Sperakis
1970   George Schneeman
1971   Donald Perlis
1972   Barkley L. Hendricks
1973   Jim Sullivan
1974   Julie Curtis Reed
1975   Richard Merkin
1976   Carl Nicholas Titolo
1977   Sigrid Burton

Poses Brandeis University Creative Arts Award

BRANDEIS UNIVERSITY
Brandeis University Commission Office, 12 E. 77th St., New York, N.Y. 10021 (212/472-1501)

One of a series of awards in the creative arts, the Jack I. and Lillian L. Poses Brandeis University Creative Arts Award is given annually to recognize talent in mid-career in the fine arts. The award, which may not be applied for, carries an honorarium of $1,000 and a medal or citation. Professional juries chosen by the Commission select the winner.

1957   Stuart Davis (Medal); Jimmy Ernst (citation); Painting
1958   Jacques Lipchitz (Medal); Richard Lippold (citation); Sculpture
1959   Edwin Dickinson (Medal); Theodoros Stamos (citation); Painting
1960   Naum Gabo (Medal); James Rosati (citation); Sculpture
1961   Karl Knaths (Medal); George Mueller (citation); Painting
1962   Alexander Calder (Medal); Davis Slivka (citation); Sculpture
1963   Georgia O'Keeffe (Medal); Ellsworth Kelly (citation); Painting
1964   David Smith (Medal); Peter Agostini (citation); Sculpture
1965   Mark Rothko (Medal); Kenneth Noland (citation); Painting
1966   Isamu Noguchi (Medal); Richard Stankiewicz (citation); Sculpture
1967   Ludwig Mies van der Rohe (Medal); Kevin Roche (citation); Architecture
1968   Joseph Cornell (Medal); Frank Stella (citation); Painting
1969   Jose de Rivera (Medal); Mark di Suvero (citation); Sculpture

1970 **Barnett Newman** (Medal); **Jasper Johns** (citation); Painting
1971 **Louise Nevelson** (Medal); **Claes Oldenburg** (citation); Sculpture
1972 **Louis I. Kahn** (Medal); **Ian McHarg** (citation); Architecture
1973 **Willem de Kooning** (Medal); **Joan Mitchell** (citation); Painting
1974 **Tony Smith** (Medal); **Robert Morris** (citation); Sculpture
1975 **Isabel Bishop** (Medal); **Robert Whitman** (citation); Painting & Visual Arts
1976 **Philip Johnson** (Medal); **Robert Venturi** (citation); Architecture
1977 **Rueben Nakiacio** (Medal); **Mary Frank** (citation); Sculpture

Mary Martin Award
AMERICAN NEEDLEPOINT GUILD
6342 Brolwood Rd., Charlotte, N.C. 28211 (704/366-5692)

The Mary Martin Award is given annually for excellence and creativity in needlepoint and especially for promotion of the craft. The winner, who receives a plaque, is selected by an advisory board.

1974 **Princess Grace of Monaco**, Needlepoint enthusiast
1975 **Pat Trexler**, Syndicated columnist
1976 **Erica Wilson**, Author
1977 **Maggie Lane**, Author

Herbert Adams Memorial Medal
Mrs. Louis Bennett Prize
Council of American Artists' Societies' Award
C. Percival Dietsch Sculpture Prize
Gold, Silver & Bronze Medals
John Gregory Award
Henry Hering Memorial Medal
Dr. Maurice B. Hexter Prize
Walter Lantz Youth Award
Medal of Honor of the National Sculpture Society
Lindsay Morris Memorial Prize
Therese and Edwin H. Richard Memorial Prize
John Spring Art Founder Award
Tallix Foundry Prize
NATIONAL SCULPTURE SOCIETY
777 Third Ave., New York, N.Y. 10017 (212/838-5218)

The Herbert Adams Memorial Medal, designed in 1946 by Thomas G. Lo Medico, is presented as the occasion arises for service to American sculpture or to a sculptor for outstanding achievement.

1947 **Adeline Valentine Pond Adams**
1953 **Cecil Howard**
1954 **Robert G. Eberhard**
     Avard Fairbanks

Walker Hancock
Jean de Marco
Lee Lawrie
1955 Leo Friedlander
     Leo Lentelli
1956 Sidney Waugh
1957 Ivan Mestrovic
1958 Albino Cavallito
1961 Adolph Block
1962 Paul Fjelde
     Pietro Montana
     Wheeler Williams
1963 No award
1964 Joseph Kiselewski
1965 Daniel Chester French Foundation
     Saint-Gaudens Memorial
1966 Moissaye Marans
1967 Donald De Lue
1968 Eugene F. Kennedy, Jr.
1969 J. Kellum Smith, Jr.
1970 Karel Yasko
     Irving Stone
1971 Thomas S. Carroll
1972 Bruno Mankowski
1973 Donald S. Nelson
1974 Alfred Easton Poor
     Paul A. Thiry
1975 Harry N. Abrams
     Patricia Janis Broder
1976 John Dole
     EvAngelos Frudakis
     Pennsylvania Academy of the Fine Arts
1977 Thomas Armstrong, Whitney Museum
     Hall of Fame for Great Americans

The Mrs. Louis Bennett Prize of $50 is given to a young bas-relief sculptor for a meritorious entry in the Society's annual exhibition.

1942 Albert W. Wein
1943 No award
1944 John Flanagan
1945 No award
1946 Donald De Lue
1947 Michael Lantz
1948 Jean De Marco
1949 Thomas G. Lo Medico
1950 No award
1951 John Amore
1952 Robert A. Weinman
1953 Bruno Mankowski
1954 Frank Eliscu
1955 Theodore Spicer-Simson
1956 Abram Belskie
1957 No award
1958 Ferenc Varga
1959 Dexter Jones
1960 Anthony Notaro
1961 Richard Frazier
1962 Karen Worth
1963 Laci De Gerenday
1964 Henry Berge
1965 Adlai S. Hardin
1966 Wheeler Williams
1967 Kristin C. Lothrop
1968 Donald Miller
1969 No award
1970 Frances Lamont
1971 Edward Grove
1972 Eleanor Platt
1973 George Gach

1974 Joel Rudnick
1975 Nina Winkel
1976 Theodore Barbarossa
1977 Gertrude K. Lathrop

The $100 Council of American Artists' Societies' Award is given for outstanding traditional work.

1966 Harriet Whitney Frishmuth
1967 Anthony Notaro
1968 Jean De Marco
1969 Richard Frazier
1970 Charles C. Parks
1971 Gaetano Cecere
1972 Marilyn Newmark
1973 Jane B. Armstrong
1974 Eric Parks
1975 Bunny Adelman
1976 Brian Rodden
1977 Laci de Gerenday

The $200 C. Percival Dietsch Sculpture Prize is given for sculpture in the round.

1968 Vincent Glinsky
1969 Frances Lamont
1970 Clark T. Bailey
1971 Adolph Block
1972 Christopher Parks
1973 Joan Bugbee
1974 George Gach
1975 Edward Widstrom
1976 Cleo Hartwig
1977 Marilyn Newmark

The National Sculpture Society gold, silver and bronze medals designed by Hermon MacNeil are awarded annually.

1966 Donald De Lue, Gold
       Charlotte Dunwiddie, Silver
       Adlai S. Hardin, Bronze
1967 Vincent Glinsky, Gold
       Adolph Block, Silver
       Nina Winkel, Bronze
1968 C. Paul Jennewein, Gold
       Arthur E. Lorenzani, Silver
       Terry Iles, Bronze
1969 Elizabeth B. Holbrook, Gold
       Cleo Hartwig, Silver
       Kenneth R. Bunn, Bronze
1970 George Gach, Gold
       Waylande Gregory, Silver
       Stanley Bleifeld, Bronze
1971 Charles Parks, Gold
       Harriet Frishmuth, Silver
       Nina Winkel, Bronze
1972 EvAngelos Frudakis, Gold
       Edward Widstrom, Silver
       Vincent Glinsky, Bronze
1973 Charles Rudy, Gold
       E.F. Hoffman, III, Silver
       Richardson White, Bronze
1974 No award, Gold
       Gary Leddy, Silver
       Leonda Finke, Bronze
1975 Karl Gruppe, Gold
       Margaret Boots, Silver
       Grete Schuller, Bronze
1976 Maurice B. Hexter, Gold
       Bruno Mankowski, Silver
       Jane B. Armstrong, Bronze
1977 Frank James Morgan, Gold

Richard Kislov, Silver
Moissaye Marans, Bronze

The $500 John Gregory Award is given to U.S. citizens under forty-five years of age showing originality and imagination.

1959 William M. Philips
       Mary Tilden Strebeigh
1960 Betti Richard
1961 Dexter Jones
1962 Tylden W. Street
1963 Neil Estern
       EvAngelos Frudakis
1964 Stanley Bleifeld
1965 Kahlil Gibran
       Joseph Turkaly
1966 No award
1967 Philip E. Fowler
1968-73 No awards
1974 Tom Yglesias
1975 Christopher Parks
1976 Michael Stelzer
1977 Norman Holen

The Henry Hering Memorial Medal, designed by Albino Manca, is awarded for outstanding collaboration between architect, owner and sculptor in the distinguished use of sculpture on religious, monumental, institutional and commercial sites.

1960 Religious: Voorhees, Walker, Smith and Haines (Architect)
       Loyola Seminary, Shrub Oak, N.Y. (Site)
       Society of Jesus (Owner)
       Donald De Lue, Gleb Derujinsky, Henry Kreis, Joseph Kiselewski, Oronzio Maldarelli, Carl L. Schmitz (Sculptors)
       Monumental: Harbeson, Hough, Livingston & Larson (Architect)
       St. Laurent Cemetery, France (Site)
       American Battle Monuments Commission (Owner)
       Donald De Lue (Sculptor)
       Commercial: Emery Roth & Sons (Architect)
       160 Church Street and 529 Fifth Avenue, New York City (Site)
       Erwin S. Wolfson (Owner)
       Frank Eliscu (Sculptor)
1961 Religious: Eugene F. Kennedy, Jr. of Maginnis, Walsh & Kennedy, Boston, Mass. (Architect)
       National Shrine of the Immaculate Conception, Washington, D.C. (Site)
       The Catholic Clergy and Faithful of the United States, His Eminence Francis Cardinal Spellman representing (Owner)
       John Angel, Ulysses A. Ricci, Adolph Block, Joseph C. Fleri, Lee Lawrie, Thomas G. Lo Medico, Ivan Mestrovic, Pietro Montana, George H. Snowden (Sculptors)
       Religious: Eugene F. Kennedy Jr., Boston, Mass. (Architect)
       Cathedral of Mary Our Queen, Baltimore, Md. (Site)
       The Catholic Clergy and Faithful of the United States, His Excellence Most Reverend Francis P. Keough, DD, Archbishop of Baltimore representing (Owner)
       Theodore C. Barbarossa, Arcangelo Cascieri, Joseph Coletti, Jean de Marco, Gleb Derujinsky, Adio di Biccari, Leo Friedlander, Michael Lantz, Ernest E. Morenon (Sculptors)

Monumental: Eric Gugler of Gugler, Kimball & Husted, New York City (Architect)
Sicily-Rome American Memorial at Anzio-Nettuno, Italy (Site)
American Battle Monuments Commission (Owner)
Paul Manship (Sculptor)
1962 No award
1963 Religious: Maurice Reinholt Salo (Architect)
The Community Church of New York, 40 East 35 St., New York City (Site)
The Community Church, Donald S. Harrington representing (Owner)
Moissaye Marans (Sculptor)
Monumental: Richard E. Collins (Architect)
Virginia World War II & Korean War Memorial at Richmond, Va. (Site)
State of Virginia, Senator John J. Wicker, Jr. representing (Owner)
Leo Friedlander (Sculptor)
1965 Monumental: Clark & Beauttler, San Francisco, Calif. (Architect)
West Coast World War II Memorial, San Francisco, Calif. (Site)
American Battle Monuments Commission (Owner)
Jean de Marco (Sculptor)
1966 Religious: Eugene F. Kennedy, Boston, Mass. (Architect)
Chapel of Our Mother Of Sorrow, National Shrine of the Immaculate Conception, Washington, D.C. (Site)
The Catholic Clergy and Faithful of the U.S., His Eminence Francis Cardinal Spellman, representing (Owner)
Ernest E. Morenon (Sculptor)
1968 Religious: Philip Frohmann (Architect)
Cathedral Church of St. Peter & St. Paul, Washington, D.C. (Site)
Protestant Episcopal Cathedral Foundation, Richard T. Feller, Clerk of the Works of the Cathedral representing (Owner)
Granville W. Carter (Sculptor)
Monumental: Ernest Weihe (Architect)
Honolulu Memorial, National Cemetery of the Pacific, Honolulu (Site)
American Battle Monuments Commission (Owner)
Bruce Moore (Sculptor)
1972 Religious: Cyrus Silling, West Virginia (Architect)
Many Faiths Chapel, University Hospital, W. Va. (Site)
West Virginia University, John Slack representing (Owner)
Milton Horn (Sculptor)
Monumental: William Gehron, Gilbert Seltzer, New York, N.Y. (Architect)
East Coast Memorial, New York City (Site)
American Battle Monuments Commission, Col. W.P. Jones representing (Owner)
Albino Manca (Sculptor)
Institutional: John Richards, Ohio (Architect)
Union Building (Site)
Ohio State U, Frederick Stecker representing (Owner)
Marshall Fredericks (Sculptor)
1976 Institutional: Paul A. Thiry (Architect)
Libby Dam Treaty Tower, Kootenai River, Mont. (Site)
Brig. Gen. Walter O. Bachus, representing U.S. Army Corps of Engineers (Owner)
Albert Wein (Sculptor)

The $500 Dr. Maurice B. Hexter Prize is given for creative sculpture in the round.
1972 Roger Williams
1973 Donald De Lue
1974 Barbara Lekberg
1975 Christopher Parks
1976 Richardson White
1977 Theodore C. Barbarossa

The Walter Lantz Youth Award of $250 is given to a sculptor under forty-five years of age.
1973 Jerry Luisi
1974 Lloyd Radell
1975 Don Gale
1976 Eric Parks
1977 Sherry St. Renz

The Medal of Honor of the National Sculpture Society is awarded to individuals for notable achievement in and for encouragement of American sculpture. The medal was designed by Laura Gardin Fraser.
1929 Archer M. Huntington
     Adeline Adams
     Daniel Chester French
1933 Richard Welling
1940 Dwight James Baum
     Herbert Adams
1942 Paul Manship
1943 A.F. Brinckerhoff
1945 Robert Moses
1948 Adolph Alexander Weinman
1951 Alfred Geiffert, Jr.
     James Earle Fraser
     Leo Friedlander
1952 George Lober
1953 Frederick H. Zurmuhlen
1956 John Gregory
1958 Clyde C. Trees
1959 Rudulph Evans
1964 Malvina Hoffman
     John F. Harbeson
1967 C. Paul Jennewein
1969 Frances K. Trees
1970 Gilmore D. Clarke
1971 Francis Keally
1974 Donald De Lue

The $150 Lindsay Morris Memorial Prize is given for a meritorious bas-relief sculpture.
1933 Anthony De Francisci
1934 Carl L. Schmitz
1935 Gaetano Cecere
1936 Henry Kreis
1937 Erwin Springweiler
1938 Chester Beach
1939 Richard H. Recchia
1941 Walker Hancock
1942 Donald De Lue
1943 Janet De Coux
1944 Gertrude K. Lathrop
1945 Jean De Marco
1946 Albert W. Wein
1947 Edmond Amateis
1948 Edmondo Quattrocchi
1949 Theodore C. Barbarossa
1950 Michael Lantz
1951 Abram Belskie
1952 Thomas G. Lo Medico
1953 Paul Manship

1954 Gleb Derujinsky
1955 Laci De Gerenday
1956 Adlai S. Hardin
1957 Paul Fjelde
1958 Adolph Block
1959 Pietro Montana
1960 Katharine Lane Weems
1961 No award
1962 Bryant Baker
1963 Albert T. D'Andrea
1964 Agop Agopoff
1965 John Terken
1966 Granville W. Carter
1967 Edward R. Grove
1968 Karl Gruppe
1969 Margaret C. Grigor
1970 Leonda Finke
1971 Charlotte Dunwiddie
1972 Joseph Kiselewski
1973 Roger Williams
1974 Elizabeth Weistrop
1975 Albino Manca
1976 Frieda Rosenstein
1977 Marcel Jovine

The Therese and Edwin H. Richard Memorial Prize of
$300 is awarded for outstanding portrait sculpture in
the round. The competition is open to all sculptors, and
selection is made on the basis of photographs.

1965 Eleanor Platt
     Bashka Paeff (Hon. Mention)
     Maysie Stone (Mention)
1966 Edmondo Quattrochi
1967 Vernita Haynes
1968 Donald De Lue
1969 Jose de Creeft
     Winifred Gordon (Hon. Mention)
1970 Philip Fowler
1971 Richard Frazier
1972 EvAngelos Frudakis
     Moissaye Marans
1973 Dexter Jones
1974 John Cavanaugh
1975 Agop Agopoff
1976 Ruth Nickerson
1977 Karl Gruppe

The John Spring Art Founder Award consists of a life-
size head cast in bronze by the Modern Art Foundry to
a sculptor chosen at the National Sculpture Society's
annual exhibition.

1973 Edward Widstrom
1974 Fritz Cleary
1975 Spero Anargyros
1976 Anthony Notaro
1977 Antonio Frudakis

The Tallix Foundry Prize consists of casting a life-size
head or sculpture of similar size and complexity by a
woman sculptor under thirty-five years of age.

1974 Ruth Nickerson
1975 Marilyn Newmark
1976 Jean Donner Grove
1977 Leonda Finke

Playboy Awards
PLAYBOY MAGAZINE
919 N. Michigan Ave., Chicago, Ill. 60611 (312/PL 1-8000)

As an adjunct to their long-standing Playboy Writers
Awards, the editors of *Playboy* magazine have instituted similar honors for artists and photographers
whose contributions have been published in the preceding year.

BEST NON-FICTION ILLUSTRATION
1977 Alan Magee, "Good Night, Sweet Prinze"

BEST FICTION ILLUSTRATION
1977 Kathy Calderwood, "Adulterer's Luck"

BEST PICTORIAL ESSAY
1977 Pompeo Posar, "Playmate of the Year"

BEST SERVICE PICTORIAL
1977 Mario Casilli, "Shields and Yarnell"

BEST PLAYMATE PICTORIAL
1977 Robert Scott Hooper, September Playmate, Debra
Jo Fondren

BEST BLACK-AND-WHITE PHOTOGRAPH
1977 Norman Seeff, of John Travolta

SPECIAL AWARD
1977 Brad Holland, "Ribald Classics" illustrations

Special Project: Sculpture
   Competition
Ziuta and Joseph James Akston
   Foundation Award
Owen H. Kenan Award
Atwater Kent Award
THE SOCIETY OF THE FOUR ARTS
Four Arts Plaza, Palm Beach, Fla. 33480 (305/655-7226)

The Society gives several awards, generally bearing
cash honoraria, to artists whose work is shown in the
Society's Annual Exhibition of Contemporary American Paintings, which in 1980 reaches its fortieth year.
In addition, the Society sponsored in 1974 as a special
project a major sculpture competition. The Society has
supplied the names only of recent awards winners.

SPECIAL PROJECT (Sculpture competition made
   possible by a grant from the Ziuta and Joseph James
   Akston Foundation):
1974 Robert Morris ($25,000 sculpture project grant)
     Isamu Noguchi ($10,000 sculpture project grant)
     Richard Stankiewicz ($5,000 sculpture project grant)

ANNUAL EXHIBITION OF CONTEMPORARY AMERICAN
   PAINTINGS: Ziuta and Joseph James Akston
   Foundation Award
1974 LaMonte Anderson ($1,500)

1975   Michael Klezmer ($1,000)
       Joseph Almyda ($500)
1976   Emilio Falero ($1,500)
1977   Jim Houser ($1,500)

OWEN H. KENAN AWARD

1974   Anne Minich ($1,500)
1975   Bruce L. Marsh ($1,500)
1976   Harriet Lefkowitz ($750)
1976   Walter Z. Prochownik ($750)
1977   Philip Carpenter ($500)

ATWATER KENT AWARD

1974   Judith Boodon ($2,500)
1975   Gary L. Matthews ($2,000)
1976   Jim Houser ($2,000)
1977   John H. Woodworth ($2,000)
       Elenora Chambers ($500)
       Henry C. Ransom, Jr. ($500)

Architecture &

Design

Contents

Related Awards

AIA Medals
Architectural Firm Award
Gold Medal
Edward C. Kemper Award
Reynolds Aluminum Grand Prize
R.S. Reynolds Award
R.S. Reynolds Award for Community Architecture
Twenty-Five Year Award
AMERICAN INSTITUTE OF ARCHITECTS
1735 New York Ave. NW, Washington, D.C. 20006
(202/785-7300)

AIA Medals are now awarded in one group encompassing five areas of achievement related to architecture, the architectural profession and architectural projects. These are presented to artists or craftsmen; illustrators or recorders; individuals or organizations who have influenced the profession; individuals or organizations responsible for a specific project; and individuals or groups responsible for specific interdisciplinary accomplishments related to architecture. In 1976 AIA rules were changed to provide for the presentation of ten medals a year, no more than three in any of these categories. The five categories of awards and medals consolidate the dozen separate and narrower categories used before 1975.

ARCHITECTURE CRITICS' MEDAL
1968 Lewis Mumford
1969 Ada Louise Huxtable
1970 Henry-Russell Hitchcock
1971 Sibyl Moholy-Magy
1972 Wolf Von Eckardt
1973 Robin Boyd
1974 Walter McQuade
1975 Peter Blake

ARCHITECTURE CRITICS' CITATION
1968 George McCue
1969 No award
1970 "Cosmopolis," documentary presented by American Broadcasting Companies, Inc.
1971 Perspecta, The Yale Architectural Journal
1972 Peter Collins
1973 Alan Dunn
1974 Regional Plan Association
1975 Jane Jacobs

FINE ARTS MEDAL
1921 Paul Manship, Sculpture
1922 No award
1923 Arthur F. Mathews, Decorative Painting
1924 No award
1925 John Singer Sargent, Mural Painting
1926 Leopold Stokowski, Music
1927 Lee Lawrie, Sculpture
1928 H. Siddons Mowbray, Mural Painting
1929 Diego Rivera, Painting
1930 Adolph Alexander Weinman, Sculpture
1931 Frederick Law Olmsted, Landscape Architecture
1932 No award
1933 No award

1934 James Henry Breasted, Literature
1935 No award
1936 Robert Edmond Jones, Theatre Design
1937 No award
1938 Carl Milles, Sculpture
1939-44 No awards
1945 John Taylor Arms, Etching
1946 No award
1947 Samuel Chamberlain, Etching
1948 John Marin, Painting
1949 Louis Conrad Rosenberg, Etching
1950 Edward Steichen, Photography
1951 Thomas Church, Landscape Architecture
1952 Marshall Fredericks, Sculpture
1953 Donal Hord, Sculpture
1954 Judan Hoke Harris, Sculpture
1955 Nan Mestrovic, Sculpture
1956 M. Hidreth Meiere, Painting
1957 Mark Tobey, Painting
1958 Viktor Schreckengost, Sculpture
1959 Kenneth Hedrich, Photography
1960 Thomas Hart Benton, Painting and Murals
1961 Alexander Calder, Sculpture
1962 Stuart Davis, Painting
1963 Isamu Noguchi, Sculpture
1964 Henry Moore, Sculpture
1965 Roberto Burle Marx, Landscape Architecture, Painting
1966 Ben Shahn, Artist
1967 Costantino Nivola, Sculpture
1968 Gyorgy Kepes, Art
1969 Jacques Lipchitz, Sculpture
1970 Richard Lippold, Sculpture
1971 Anthony Smith, Sculpture
1972 George Rickey, Sculpture
1973 Harry Bertoia, Sculpture
1974 Ruth Asawa Lanier, Sculpture
1975 Josef Albers, Art

COLLABORATIVE ACHIEVEMENT IN ARCHITECTURE AWARD
1964 The Seagram Building, its Plaza and the Four Seasons Restaurant, New York
1965 No award
1966 Ghirardelli Square, San Francisco
1967 No award
1972 Rochester Institute of Technology, N.Y.
1973 Bay Area Rapid Transit (BART), San Francisco and environs
1974 No award
1975 No award

HENRY BACON MEDAL FOR MEMORIAL ARCHITECTURE
1966 Gateway Arch, St. Louis, Mo.
1967 No award
1968 No award
1969 Fosse Ardeatine Caves, Rome
1970-74 No awards
1975 Le Memorial des Martyrs de la Deportation, Paris

CRAFTSMANSHIP MEDAL
1920 Samuel Yellin, Iron Work
1921 Henry C. Mercer, Ceramics
1922 No award
1923 Frederic W. Goudy, Typography
1924 No award
1925 Charles Jay Connick, Stained Glass
1926 V. F. Von Lossberg, Metal Work
1927 Frank J. Holmes, Ceramics

1928 **William D. Gates,** Ceramics
1929 **Cheney Brothers,** Textiles
1930 **John Kirchmayer,** Wood Carving
1931 **Leon V. Solon,** Terra Cotta, Faience
1932 **No award**
1933 **No award**
1934 **Walter W. Kantack,** Metal and Glass
1935 **No award**
1936 **John J. Earley,** Masonry, Concrete
1937 **No award**
1938 **J. H. Dulles Allen,** Ceramics
1939 **No award**
1940-46 **No awards**
1947 **Dorothy Wright Liebes,** Textiles
     Wilbur Herbert Burnham, Stained and Leaded Glass
1948 **No award**
1949 **No award**
1950 **Joseph Gardiner Reynolds, Jr.,** Stained Glass
1951 **No award**
1952 **George Nakashima,** Furniture
1953 **Emil Frei,** Stained Glass
1954 **Maria Montoya Martinez,** Pottery
1955 **John Howard Benson,** Calligraphy
1956 **Harry Bertoia,** Metal Design
1957 **Charles Eames,** Furniture
1958 **Francois Lorin,** Stained Glass
1959 **No award**
1960 **William L. DeMatteo,** Silversmith
1961 **Anni Albers,** Art of Weaving
1962 **Theodore Conrad,** Model Making
1963 **Paolo Soleri,** Ceramics
1964 **Jan de Swart,** Stained Glass
1965 **No award**
1966 **Harold Balazs,** Wood Sculpture
1967 **Sister Mary Remy Revor,** Fabric Design
1968 **Jack Lenor Larsen,** Fabric Design
1969 **Henry Easterwood,** Fabric Design
1970 **Trude Guermonprez,** Textiles
1971 **Wharton Esherick,** Wood Furniture
1972 **No award**
1973 **Helena Hemmarck,** Tapestries
1974 **Sheila Hicks,** Textile Sculpture
1975 **No award**

ARCHITECTURAL PHOTOGRAPHY MEDAL

1960 **Roger Sturtevant**
1961 **Ezra Stoller**
1962 **Ernst Haas**
1963 **G. E. Kidder Smith**
1964 **Balthazar Korab**
1965 **Robert Damora**
1966 **Moorley Baer**
1967 **William C. Hedrich**
1968 **Ernest Braun**
1969 **Julius Shulman**
1970 **George Cserna**
1971 **Alexandre Georges**
1972 **Robert C. Lautman**
1973 **No award**
1974 **David Hirsch**
1975 **Yukio Futagawa**

INDUSTRIAL ARTS MEDAL

1958 **Merle Armitage**
1959 **No award**
1960 **No award**
1961 **Florence Schust Knoll**
1962 **Sundberg-Ferar Inc.**

1963 **No award**
1964 **George Nelson**
1965 **Eliot Noyes**
1966 **Gideon Kramer**
1967 **Chermayeff & Geismar**
1968 **Paul Grotz**
1969 **Carl Koch**
1970 **Barbara Stauffacher Solomon**
1971 **Edith Heath**
1972 **Charles Eames**
1973 **Lella and Massimo Vignelli**
1974 **C. Olivetti & CSpA**
1975 **Gemini C.E.L.**

AIA MEDAL FOR RESEARCH

1972 **Christopher Alexander**
1973 **Harold B. Gores**
1974 **Ralph Knowles**
1975 **Environmental Research and Development Corp.**

ALLIED PROFESSIONS MEDAL

1958 **Fred N. Severud**
1959 **Robert Moses**
1960 **William Francis Gibbs,** Naval Architect
1961 **No award**
1962 **Othmar H. Ammann & Charles S. Whitney**
1963 **R. Buckminster Fuller**
1964 **Lawrence Halprin**
1965 **Leonardo Zeevaert**
1966 **Alexander Girard**
1967 **Richard Kelly**
1968 **Le Messurier Associates Inc.**
1969 **John Skilling**
1970 **Robert L. Van Nice**
1971 **Daniel U. Kiley**
1972 **Ian L. McHarg**
1973 **Hideo Sasaki**
1974 **Kevin Lynch**
1975 **Carl Sapers**

WHITNEY M. YOUNG JR. CITATION (Social Consciousness Award)

1972 **Robert J. Nash**
1973 **Architects Workshop of Philadelphia**
1974 **Stephan Cram**
1975 **Van B. Bruner, Jr.**

CITATION OF AN ORGANIZATION

1947 **Tennessee Valley Authority**
1948-50 **No awards**
1951 **Steuben Glass Inc.**
1952 **No award**
1953 **Reinhold Publishing Corp.,** Architectural Publishing
1954 **No award**
1955 **Kohler Foundation Inc.**
1956 **Society of Architectural Historians**
1957 **Office of Foreign Buildings, U.S. Dept. of State**
1958 **United States Steel Corp.**
1959 **General Services Administration**
1960 **Providence City Plan Commission**
     General Motors Corp.
     International Business Machines Corp.
1961 **Philadelphia City Planning Commission**
1962 **Museum of Modern Art, New York**
1963 **American Craftsmen's Council**
1964 **Educational Facilities Laboratories**
1965 **Architectural League of New York**
1966 **Museum of Modern Art,** New York

1967 Boston Architectural Center
1968 The Graham Foundation, Chicago
1969 State University Construction Fund, Albany, N.Y.
1970 National Park Service, U.S. Dept. of Interior
1971 San Francisco Bay Commission
1972 New York State Dormitory Authority
1973 San Francisco Planning Commission
1974 New York State Urban Development Corp.
1975 Cummins Engine Foundation

AIA MEDALS

1976 Edmund N. Bacon
      Charles A. Blessing
      Wendell J. Campbell
      Gordon Cullen
      Institute for Architecture and Urban Studies
      Robert Le Ricolais
      New York City Planning Commission and New
      York City Landmarks Preservation Commission
      Saul Steinberg
      James Marston Fitch
1977 Claes Oldenburg
      Louise Nevelson
      Arthur Drexler
      Historic American Buildings Survey
      G. Holmes Perkins
      Barbara Ward Jackson
      Walker Art Center
      City of Boston
      Pittsburgh History and Landmarks Foundation
      Montreal Metro System

SPECIAL CITATION

1936 Restoration of Colonial Williamsburg (Perry, Shaw
      and Hepburn; John A. Shurcliff; John D. Rockefeller,
      Jr., and William A. R. Goodwin)

AWARD FOR OUTSTANDING SERVICE TO
ARCHITECTURE (by Non-Architectural Group, Society,
or Business)

1956 Fortune Magazine

EXHIBITION MEDAL

1921 Betram Goodhue and Lee Lawrie, Ecclesiastical
      Reginald Johnson, Domestic
      Charles Z. Klauder, Institutional
      Howard Dwight Smith, Public Buildings
      George C. Nimmons and Co., Industrial Buildings
1925 Charles D. Maginnis and Timothy Walsh, Ec-
      clesiastical
      Edward L. Tilton and Alfred Morton Githens, Pub-
      lic Buildings
      Sproatt and Rolph, Institutional Buildings
      A. Stewart Walker and Leon N. Gillette, Domestic
      Buildings
      Arthur Loomis Harmon, Commercial Buildings

ASC/AIA AWARD FOR EXCELLENCE IN
ARCHITECTURAL EDUCATION

1976 Jean Labatut, Princeton University

CITATION OF HONOR

1956 Pearl Chase
      Nathan Haris, President, Far Eastern Society of Ar-
      chitects
1957 Milton Horn, Sculptor
1958 No award
1959 Kansas City Chapter, AIA—Field of Planning
1960 No award

1961 No award
1962 Lewis Mumford, Author-Critic
      John Fitzgerald Kennedy
1963 No award
1964 Lister Hill
      Harold H. Burton
      Marie C. McGuire
1965 Lyndon Baines Johnson
      Stewart Lee Udall

In addition to the awards and medals listed here, the
Institute recognizes exceptional architectural excellence in recently completed projects by presenting architects, engineers and other professionals with Honor
Awards. These citations were initiated to encourage
appreciation of excellence in architecture in the United
States and by American architects working abroad.

1949 Marsh, Smith and Powell Architects, for Corona
      del Mar School, Corona del Mar, Calif.
      Frederick J. Langhorst, for Dr. and Mrs. Alex J.
      Ker's residence, Marin County, Calif.
1950 A. Quincy Jones, Jr., for H.C. Hvistendahl residence,
      San Diego, Calif.
      Harold M. Heatley and Ketchum, Gina and Sharp,
      Assoc., for Davis-Paxton Company Store, Augusta,
      Ga.
1951 Thorshov and Cerney, for Clearwater County
      Memorial Hospital, Bagley, Mont.
      Stone and Pitts, for Coca Cola bottling plant, Hous-
      ton, Tex.
1952 Skidmore, Owings and Merrill Assoc., for Lever
      House, New York
      William S. Beckett, for William S. Beckett's office,
      Los Angeles
      Young and Richards, Carleton and Detlie, for Gaff-
      ney's Lake Wilderness, Maple Valley, Wisc.
1953 Saarinen, Saarinen & Assoc., and Smith, Hinch-
      man and Grylls, for Engineering Staff Bldgs., Gen-
      eral Motors Technical Center, Warren, Mich.
      Matthew Nowicki, William Henry Dietrick and
      Severud-Elstad-Kreuger, for North Carolina State
      Fair Pavilion, Raleigh N.C.
1954 Richard P. Neutra and Dion Neutra, for Moore resi-
      dence, Ojai, Calif.
      Vincent G. King, for Lankenau Hospital, Phila-
      delphia
      John P. Wiltshire and J. Herschel Fisher, for Fort
      Brown Memorial Civic Center, Brownsville, Tex.
      Curtis and Davis, for Twomy Lafon School, New Or-
      leans
      Perkins and Will and Caudill, Rowlett, Scott As-
      soc., for Norman High School, Norman, Okla.
      Marsh Smith and Powell, for Santa Monica City Col-
      lege, Calif.
1955 Ralph Rapson and John van der Meulen, for
      American Embassy, Stockholm, Sweden
      Eero Saarinen and Assoc. and Smith, Hinchman &
      Grylls, for Central Restaurant Bldg., General Motors
      Technical Center, Warren, Mich.
      Eero Saarinen and Assoc., for Women's Dormitories
      and Dining Hall, Drake University, Des Moines, Iowa.
      Ernest J. Kump, for North Hillsborough Elementary
      School, Hillsborough, Calif.
      Charles B. Genther of Pace Assoc., for General
      Telephone Co. of the Southwest, San Antonio, Tex.
1956 John Lyon Reid & Partners, for Hillsdale School,
      San Mateo, Calif.

Wurster, Bernardi & Emmons, for Center for Advanced Study in Behavioral Sciences, near Palo Alto, Calif.
Hellmuth, Yamasaki & Leinweber, for Lambert St. Louis Municipal Airport Terminal Bldg., St. Louis, Mo.
Skidmore, Owings & Merrill, for Manufacturers Trust Co., Fifth Ave. branch, New York, N.Y.
Philip C. Johnson, for Hodgson house, New Canaan, Conn.

1957 Anderson, Beckwith and Haible, for office building for Middlesex Mutual Building Trust, Waltham, Mass.
Warren H. Ashley, for Junior/Senior School, Greenburgh, N.Y.
Eliot Noyes, for house, New Canaan, Conn.
Caudill, Rowlett, Scott & Assoc., for Brazos County Court House and Jail, Brazos, Tex.
Antonin Raymond and L.L. Rado, for St. Anselm's Priory for the Benedictine Fathers, Tokyo, Japan
Anshen and Allen, for Chapel of the Holy Cross, Sedona, Ariz.

1958 Skidmore, Owings & Merrill, for home office building for Connecticut General Life Insurance Co., Bloomfield, Conn.
Edward D. Stone, for pharmaceutical headquarters for the Stuart Co., Pasadena, Calif.
Mario J. Ciampi, for elementary school, Sonoma, Calif.
Pereira and Luckman, for specialty shop, Robinson's, Palm Springs, Calif.

1959 Colbert, Lowrey & Assoc., For Dias-Simon Pediatric Clinic, New Orleans, La.
Kenneth W. Brooks and Bruce W. Walker, for Central Service Facility, Spokane, Wash.
Minoru Yamasaki & Assoc., for McGregor Memorial Community Conference Center, Detroit, Mich.
Eero Saarinen & Assoc., for Concordia Senior College, Fort Wayne, Ind.
I.M. Pei & Assoc., for Zeckendorf Plaza Development, May D&F Dept. Store, Denver, Colo.

1960 Sherwood, Mills and Smith, for Mutual Insurance Co. of Hartford, Conn.
Robert L. Geddes, Melvin Brecher, Warren W. Cunningham, partners in Geddes Brecher, Qualls, for Moore School of Electrical Engineering, University of Pennsylvania, Philadelphia
Killingsworth, Brady and Smith, for Mr. and Mrs. Richard Opdahl's residence, Long Beach, Calif.
Corbett & Kman Kitchen and Hunt, for Blyth Arena, Squaw Valley, Calif.
Eero Saarinen and Assoc., for U.S. Embassy Office Bldg., Oslo, Norway

1961 Edward Durell Stone, for United States Embassy, New Delhi, India
Mario J. Ciampi and Paul Reiter, for Fernando Rivera Elementary School, Daly City, Calif.
Philip Johnson, for Shrine, New Harmony, Ind.
Minoru Yamasaki, for Reynolds Metal Regional Sales Office Bldg., Detroit
Philip Johnson, for Nuclear reactor, Rehovot, Israel
Skidmore, Owings & Merrill, for Pepsi-Cola World Headquarters, New York
Birkerts & Straub, for Summer house, Northville, Mich.

1962 Ernest J. Kump and Masten & Hurd, for Foothill College, Los Altos, La.
Anshen and Allen, for Interational Bldg., San Francisco

1963 Eero Saarinen & Assoc., for Stiles and Morse Colleges, Yale University New Haven, Conn.

Skidmore, Owings & Merrill, for Albright-Knox Art Gallery Addition, Buffalo, N.Y.
Ralph M. Parsons Co. and Minoru Yamasaki, for Dhahran International Air Terminal, Dharran, Saudi Arabia
Joseph Salerno, for United Church House of Worship, Rowayton, Conn.

1964 Architects Collaborative, for Phillips Academy Arts and Communications Center and Science Bldg., Andover, Mass.
Skidmore, Owings & Merrill, for Ehmart Mfg. Co. headquarters bldg., Bloomfield, Conn.
Paul Rudolph, for Yale University School of Art and Architecture, New Haven, Conn.
Skidmore, Owings and Merrill, for BMA Tower, Kansas City, Mo.

1965 Reid & Tarics, for Eleanor Connelly Erdman Memorial Chapel, Pebble Beach, Calif.
Sert, Jackson and Gourley, for Francis Greenwood Peabody Terrace, Cambridge, Mass.
Eero Saarinen and Assoc., for Deere & Co. Administrative Center, Moline, Ill.
I.M. Pei & Assoc., for School of Journalism, S.I Newhouse Communications Center, Syracuse University, Syracuse, N.Y.

1966 Eero Saarinen and Assoc., for Columbia Broadcasting System Headquarters Bldg., New York, N.Y.
Eero Saarinen and Assoc.,' for Dulles International Airport Terminal Bldg., Chantilly, Va.
Keyes, Lethbridge & Condon, for Tiber Island, Washington, D.C.

1967 Fred Bassetti & Co., for Ridgeway Men's Dormintories/Phase III, Western Washington State College, Bellingham, Wash.
Caudill, Rowlett, Scott, for Jesse H. Jones Hall for the Performing Arts, Houston, Tex.
Hammel Green & Abrahamson, for St. Bede's Priory, Eau Claire, Wisc.
Vincent G. Kling, for Municipal Services Bldg., Philadelphia, Pa.
Ian MacKinley, for Boreal Ridge, Truckee, Calif.
Moore, Lyndon, Turnbull, Whitaker, for Sea Ranch Condominium I, The Sea Ranch, Calif.
I.M. Pei & Partners, for University Plaza, New York University, New York
Skidmore Owings & Merrill, for National Headquarters Bldg., American Republic Insurance Co., Des Moines, Iowa
Pomerance & Breines, for amphitheatre and plaza, Jacob Riis Houses, New York
Skidmore Owings and Merrill, for Mauna Kea Beach Hotel, Kamuela, Ha.
Skidmore Owings and Merrill, for Banque Lambert, office building and residence, Brussels, Belgium
Skidmore Owings and Merrill, for Beinecke Rare Book and Manuscript Library, Yale Univ., New Haven, Conn.
Skidmore Owings and Merrill, for Vannevar Bush Center for Materials Science and Engineering, Massachusetts Institute of Technology, Cambridge, Mass.
Smith, Hinchman & Grylls, for First Federal Office Bldg., Detroit
Neill Smith and Assoc., for Redwood National Bank, Napa, Calif.
Stickney & Hull, for Los Gatos Civic Center, Los Gatos, Calif.
Edward Durell Stone, for Museo de Arte de Ponce, Ponce, Puerto Rico

Architects Collaborative, for Dormitory and Commons Bldg. Quadrangle, Clark University, Worcester, Mass.

Architects Collaborative and Campbell, Aldrich & Nulty, for C. Thurston Chase Learning Center, Eaglebrook School, Deerfield, Mass.

Toombs, Amisano & Wells, for John Knox Presbyterian Church, Marietta, Ga.

1968 Fred Bassetti & Co., for East Pine Receiving Station, Seattle, Wash.

C.F. Murphy Assoc; Skidmore, Owings & Merrill, and Loebl, Schlossman, Bennett & Dart, for Chicago Civic Center, Chicago, Ill.

Crites and McConnell, for Covenant United Presbyterian Church, Danville, Ill.

William N. Breger, for Civic Center Synagogue, New York, N.Y.

Giorgio Cavaglieri, for Jefferson Market Branch Library, New York, N.Y.

Davis, Brody & Assoc. and Horowitz and Chun, for Humanities/Social Science Center, Long Island University, Brooklyn, N.Y.

Alfred De Vido, for Hale Matthews House, East Hampton, N.Y.

Joseph Esherick, for Adlai E. Stevenson College, University of California, Santa Cruz, Calif.

Stevenson Flemer, Eason Cross, Harry Adreon, for Washington & Lee High School Gymnasium, Montross, Va.

R. Buckminster Fuller/Fuller and Sadao Inc., Geometrics Inc, and Cambridge Seven Assoc., for U.S. Exhibition at Expo 67, Ilse Ste. Helene, Montreal, Que., Canada

Gruzen & Partners and Abraham W. Geller, for Suburban YM & YWHA, W. Orange, N.J.

Gwathmey & Henderson, for residence, Purchase, N.Y.

Hirshen/Van der Ryn, for Migrant Master Plan, Indio Camp, Indio, Calif.

Mackinley/Winnacker, for Syntex Interim Facilities, Stanford Industrial Park, Palo Alto, Calif.

MLTW/Moore Turnbull, for Sea Ranch Swim & Tennis, The Sea Ranch, Calif.

McCue Boone Tomsick, for Research Laboratory D, Richmond, Calif.

Office of Oberwarth Assoc., for classroom building, Kentucky State College, Frankfort, Ky.

Reid, Rockwell, Banwell & Taries, for Health & Sciences Instruction & Research, San Francisco Medical Center, University of California, San Francisco

Rogers, Taliaferro, Kostritsky, Lamb, for John Deere Co., Timonium, Md.

Benjamin Thompson & Assoc., for dormitories and fraternity, Colby College, Waterville, Me.

1969 Desmond-Miremont-Birks, for D.C. Reeves Elementary School, Ponchatonla, La.

Frank L. Hope Assoc., for San Diego Stadium, San Diego, Calif.

Hugh Newell Jacobsen, for Bolton Square, Baltimore, Md.

Kallman, McKinnell & Knowles and Campbell, Aldrich & Nulty, for Boston City Hall, Boston, Mass.

Vincent G. Kling & Assoc., for Monsanto Co. Cafeteria, St. Louis, Mo.

Ernest J. Kump Assoc. and the Office of Masten & Hurd, for DeAnza College, Cupertino, Calif.

Richard Meier, for Smith house, Darien, Conn.

Neill Smith & Assoc. and Dreyfuss & Blackford, for Collegetown, Phase I, Sacramento, Calif.

I.M. Pei & Partners, for Des Moines Art Center Addition, Des Moines, Iowa

I.M. Pei & Partners and Pederson, Hueber, Hares & Glavin, for Everson Museum of Art, Syracuse, N.Y.

John B. Rogers, for Girls' Dormitory, Putney School, Putney, Vt.

Skidmore, Owings & Merrill, for Tenneco Bldg., Houston, Tex.

Smotrich & Platt, for Exodus house, New York, N.Y.

Walker/McGough, Foltz and Lyerla/Peden, for Convent of the Holy Names, Spokane, Wash.

Harry Weese & Assoc., Cromlie Taylor, for Auditorium Theatre Restoration, Chicago, Ill.

Wurster, Bernardi & Emmons, for Mill Valley Library, Mill Valley, Calif.

1970 Gunnar Birkets and Assoc., for Lincoln Elementary School, Columbus, Ind.

Marcel Breuer and Hamilton Smith, Michael H. Irving, for Whitney Museum of American Art, New York, N.Y.

Cerny Associates, for pedestrian skyways, Minneapolis, Minn.

Joseph Esherick and Assoc., for The Cannery, San Francisco, Calif.

Faulkner, Stenhouse, Fryer & Faulkner, for National Collection of Fine Arts and National Portrait Gallery, Washington, D.C.

Ulrich Franzen & Assoc., for Bradfield and Emerson Halls, Cornell University, Ithaca, N.Y.

Hartman-Cox, for Phillips/Brewer residence, Chevy Chase, Md.

1971 Davis, Brody & Assoc./Richard Dattner & Assoc., for Estee Lauder Laboratories, Melville, N.Y.

Davis, Brody, Chermayeff, Geismar, DeHarak Assoc. and Ohbayashi-Bumi Ltd., for U.S. Pavilion, Japan World Exposition 1970, Osaka, Japan

Ulrich Franzen, for Christensen Hall, University of New Hampshire, Durham, N.H.

Hartman-Cox, for Florence Hollis Hand Chapel, Mount Vernon College, Washington, D.C.

Richard Meier, for Westbeth Artists' Housing, New York, N.Y.

Pierce & Pierce, for Avco Everett Research Laboratory, Everett, Mass.

Quinn & Oda, for Church of Our Divine Savior, Chico, Calif.

The Architects Collaborative, for Children's Hospital Medical Center, Boston

Benjamin Thompson & Assoc., for Design Research Bldg., Cambridge, Mass.

Wolf Assoc., for North Carolina National Bank Branch, Charlotte, N.C.

1972 Edward Larrabee Barnes, for Walker Art Center, Minneapolis, Minn.

Marcel Breuer & Herbert Beckhard, for Koerfer House, Lago Maggiore, Switzerland

Ulrich Franzen, for Alley Theatre, Houston, Tex.

John M. Johansen, for Mummers Theater, Oklahoma City, Okla.

C.F. Murphy Assoc., for McCormick Place-On-The-Lake, Chicago

James Stewart Polshek & Assoc., for New York State Bar Center, Albany, N.Y.

Claude Samton & Assoc., for YM-YWHA Camp, Mt. Olive, N.J.

Skidmore Owings & Merrill, for Weyerhaeuser Headquarters, Tacoma, Wash.

Wurster, Bernardi and Emmos, for Ice Houses I & II, San Francisco, Calif.

1973 John Anderws/Anderson/Baldwin, for Harvard Graduate School of Design George Gund Hall, Cambridge, Mass.
Marcel Breuer and Herbert Beckhard, for St. Francis de Sales College, Muskegon, Mich.
Edward Cuetara, for Woolner Residence, Chilmark, Mass.
Esherick Homsey Dodge & Davis, for Julian McPhee College Union, California Polytechnic State University, San Luis Obispo, Calif.
Ronald Gourley and Carleton R. Richmond, Jr., for faculty housing, Radcliffe College, Cambridge, Mass.
William Kessler Assoc., for public housing for the elderly, Wayne, Mich.
Loebl Schlossman Bennett and Dart, for St. Procopius Abbey, Lisle, Ill.
McCue Boone Tomsick, for vacation residence, San Mateo County, Calif.
MLTW/Moore Turnbull, for beach house, Santa Cruz County, Calif.
RTKL Inc., for Fountain Square, Cincinnati, Ohio
Skidmore Owings and Merrill, for American Can Co., Greenwich, Conn.
Harry Weese & Assoc., for Time & Life Bldg., Chicago
1974 Daniel L. Dworsky & Assoc., for multi-purpose track and field stadium, University of California, Los Angeles
Holabird and Root, for 4A Equipment Bldg., Illinois Bell Telephone Co., Northbrook, Ill.
John Carl Warnecke and Assoc. and Hugh Newell Jacobsen, for Renwick Gallery, Washington, D.C.
Richard Meier & Assoc., for Twin Parks Northeast Housing, Bronx, N.Y.
Mitchell/Giurgola Assoc., for MDRT Foundation Hall, Adult Learning Research Laboratory, Bryn Mawr, Pa.
William Morgan Architects, for Morgan residence, Atlantic Beach, Fla.
I.M. Pei & Partners, for Paul Mellon Center for the Arts, Choate School, Wallingford, Conn.
Wolf Assoc., for North Carolina National Bank, Charlotte, N.C.
1975 Louis I. Kahn, for Kimbell Art Museum, Fort Worth, Tex.
Muchow Assoc., for Park Central, Denver, Colo.
I.M. Pei & Partners, for H.F. Johnson Museum, Ithaca, N.Y.
I.M. Pei & Partners, for 88 Pine Street, New York, N.Y.
Michael Graves, for Hanselmann residence, Fort Wayne, Ind.
Mitchell/Giurgola Assoc., for Columbus East H.S., Columbus, Ind.
Skidmore Owings & Merrill, for The Republic, Columbus, Ind.
Philip Johnson/John Burgee, for I.D.S. Center, Minneapolis, Minn.
Ralph Rapson & Assoc., for Cedar Square West, Minneapolis, Minn.
1976 Anderson Notter Assoc., for Old Boston City Hall, Boston
Davis, Brody & Assoc., for Waterside, New York
Myron Goldfinger, for Marcus house, Bedford, N.Y.
Gwathmey Siegel Architects, for dormitory, dining and student union facility State University College, Purchase, N.Y.
Gwathmey Siegel Architects, for Whig Hall, Princeton University, Princeton, N.J.

Hardy Holzman Pfeiffer Assoc., for Columbus Occupational Health Center, Columbus, Ind.
William Kessler and Assoc., for Center for Creative Studies, Detroit
Richard Meier and Assoc., for Douglas house, Harbor Springs, Mich.
Miller Hanson Westerbeck Bell, for Butler Square, Minneapolis, Minn.
C.F. Murphy Assoc., for Crosby Kemper Memorial Arena, Kansas City, Mo.
1977 No awards

The annual Architectural Firm Award, which is the highest honor that can be bestowed on a firm, is given for continuing collaboration among individuals who have caused the organization to be the principal force in consistently producing distinguished architecture for at least ten years.

1962 Skidmore, Owings & Merrill
1963 No award
1964 The Architects Collaborative
1965 Wurster, Bernardi & Emmons
1966 No award
1967 Hugh Stubbins & Associate
1968 I. M. Pei & Partners
1969 Jones and Emmons Architects
1970 Ernest J. Kump, Associates
1971 Albert Kahn Associates Inc.
1972 Caudill Rowlett Scott
1973 Shepley Bulfinch Richardson and Abbott
1974 Kevin Roche John Dinkeloo & Associates
1975 David, Brody and Associates
1976 Mitchell/Giurgola, Architects
1977 Sert, Jackson and Associates

The Gold Medal is awarded annually to an individual for distinguished service to the architectural profession or to the Institute. It is the Institute's highest honor.

1907 Sir Aston Webb, London
1908 No award
1909 Charles Follen McKim, New York
1910 No award
1911 George B. Post, New York
1912 No award
1913 No award
1914 Jean Louis Pascal, Paris
1915-21 No awards
1922 Victor Laloux, Paris
1923 Henry Bacon, New York
1924 No award
1925 Sir Edwin Landseer Lutyens, London
1925 Bertram Grosvenor Goodhue, New York
1926 No award
1927 Howard Van Doren Shaw, Chicago
1928 No award
1929 Milton Bennett Médary, Philadephia
1929-33 No awards
1934 Ragnar Ostberg, Stockholm
1935-37 No awards
1938 Paul Philippe Cret, Philadelphia
1939-45 No awards
1946 Louis Henri Sullivan, Chicago
1947 Eliel Saarinen, Bloomfield Hills, Mich.
1948 Charles Donagh Maginnis, Boston
1949 Frank Lloyd Wright, Spring Green, Wisc.
1950 Sir Patrick Abercrombie, London
1951 Bernard Ralph Maybeck, San Francisco

1952 **Auguste Perret,** Paris
1953 **William Adams Delano,** New York
1954 **No award**
1955 **Willem Marinus Dudok,** Hilversum, Netherlands
1956 **Clarence S. Stein,** New York
1957 **Ralph Walker,** New York (Centennial Medal of Honor)
1957 **Luis Skidmore,** New York
1958 **John Wellborn Root,** Chicago
1959 **Walter Gropius,** Cambridge, Mass.
1960 **Ludwig Mies van der Rohe,** Chicago
1961 **"Le Corbusier" (Charles Edouard Jeanneret-Gris),** Paris
1962 **Eero Saarinen,** Bloomfield Hills, Mich.
1963 **Alvar Aalto,** Helsinki
1964 **Pier Luigi Nervi,** Rome
1965 **No award**
1966 **Kenzo Tange,** Tokyo
1967 **Wallace K. Harrison,** New York
1968 **Marcel Breuer,** New York
1969 **William W. Wurster,** San Francisco
1970 **Richard Buckminster Fuller,** Carbondale, Ill.
1971 **Louis I. Kahn,** Philadelphia
1972 **Pietro Belluschi,** Boston
1973-76 **No awards**
1977 **Richard Joseph Neutra,** Los Angeles

The Edward C. Kemper Award is given annually to an AIA member for significant contributions to the profession of architecture and to the Institute.

1950 **William Perkins**
1951 **Marshall Shaffer**
1952 **William Stanley Parker**
1953 **Gerrit J. De Gelleke**
1954 **Henry H. Saylor**
1955 **Turpin C. Bannister**
1956 **Theodore Irving Coe**
1957 **David C. Baer**
1958 **Edmund R. Purves**
1959 **Bradley P. Kidder**
1960 **Philip D. Creer**
1961 **Earl H. Reed**
1962 **Harry D. Payne**
1963 **Samuel E. Lunden**
1964 **Daniel Schwartzman**
1965 **Joseph Watterson**
1966 **William W. Eshbach**
1967 **Robert H. Levison**
1968 **E. James Gambaro**
1969 **Philip J. Meathe**
1970 **Ulysses Floyd Rible**
1971 **Gerald McCue**
1972 **David N. Yerkes**
1973 **Bernard B. Rothschild**
1974 **Jack D. Train**
1975 **F. Carter Williams**
1976 **Leo A. Daly**
1977 **Ronald A. Straka**

The Reynolds Aluminum Grand Prize for architectural students honors original design for aluminum components in building. A $5,000 honorarium is divided between the student and the school.

1961 **John L. Dewey,** University of Cincinnati
1962 **Jon H. Starnes,** University of Texas
1963 **Manual A. Fernandez,** University of New Mexico
1964 **John F. Torti,** Notre Dame University
1965 **Douglas F. Trees,** Ohio State University
1966 **William R. Mitchell,** North Carolina State University

1967 **Kent C. Underwood,** Ohio State University
1968 **Charles R. Ansell, John W. Bradford,** Virginia Polytechnic Institute
1969 **Gerald Runkel,** Ohio State University
1970 **John Ahrendes, Joe Eng,** University of California, Berkeley
1971 **Hugh L. McMillan, Rick W. Redden,** University of Arkansas
1972 **L. Wayne Barcelon, Darlene S. Jang,** University of California, Berkeley
1973 **Raymond D. Snowden, Steven Lee Kinzler,** University of Arkansas
1974 **No award**
1975 **Joseph R. Barker, Laurance P. Dickie, Harold A. Ruck, Eric Stein, David R. Wilson,** University of Tennessee
1976 **Allen Koster,** University of Minnesota
1977 **Daniel T. Dolen,** Yale University

The R.S. Reynolds Award, which carries a $25,000 honorarium and is accompanied by a sculpted emblem, recognizes the creators of a significant work of architecture in which aluminum has been used as an important contributing factor.

1957 **Cesar Oritz-Echague, Manual Barbero Rebolledo and Rafael de la Joya,** Madrid Spain
1958 **T.F. Hoet-Segers, H. Montois, R. Courtois, J. Goossens-Bara, R. Moens de Hase and A. Lipski,** Brussels, Belgium
1959 **Yuncken, Freeman Brothers, Griffiths and Simpson and Barry B. Patten,** Melbourne, Australia
1960 **Jean Tschumi,** Lausanne, Switzerland
1961 **Joseph D. Murphy and Eugene J. Mackey,** St. Louis, Mo.
1962 **Guy Lagneau, Michel Weill and Jean Dimitrijeuic,** Le Havre, France
1963 **Hans Maurer,** Munich, Germany
1964 **Skidmore, Owings and Merrill,** Chicago, Ill.
1965 **James Stirling and James Gowan,** Leicester, England
1966 **Hans Hollein,** Vienna, Austria
1967 **Victor Christ-Janer,** New Cannaan, Conn.
1968 **Eijkelenboom & Middelhoek,** Holland, and **George F. Eber,** Canada
1969 **Boyd Auger,** London, England
1970 **Marcel Lods, Paul Depondt, Henri Beauclair,** France
1971 **Walter Custer, Fred Hochstrasser and Hans Bleiker,** Switzerland
1972 **Willi Walter,** Switzerland
1973 **Hannes Westermann,** Braunschweig, Federal Republic of Germany
1974 **no award**
1975 **Gustav Peiche,** Austria
1976 **Norman Foster,** London, England
1977 **Richard Maier,** New York

The R.S. Reynolds Award for Community Architecture, which carries a $25,000 cash prize and an original aluminum sculpture, honors a community for using architectural design to solve problems of modern urban living. It is awarded approximately every three years.

1967 **Cumbemauld New Town,** Scotland, Architects and Planners of Cumbernauld
1969 **Beersheba,** Israel
1974 **Pedestrian Way,** Munich
1977 **Edmund N. Bacon, City of Philadelphia**

The Twenty-Five Year Award honors architectural design of enduring significance to a project judged to have withstood the test of time.

1969 Rockefeller Center
1970 No award
1971 Crow Island School
1972 Baldwin Hills Village
1973 Tallesin West
1974 Johnson's Wax Administration Bldg.
1975 Philip Johnson's residence
1976 860-880 North Lake Shore Drive Apartments

Distinguished Service Award
Honor Award
Merit Award
Meritorious Program Award
Chapter Achievement Award
Diana Donald Award
Special Award
Special Fiftieth Anniversary Awards
AMERICAN INSTITUTE OF PLANNERS
1776 Massachusetts Ave. NW, Washington, D.C. 20036
(202/872-0611)

The Distinguished Service Award annually honors individuals active over a period of at least 15 years for contributions to local, regional, state or national planning. AIP members are eligible for this honor, which is conferred for activities in research or education, theory or philosophy, techniques and practices, implementation or administration or advancement of planning. An awards jury selects winners from nominations by AIP members.

1953 Frederick Bigger
      Russell Van Nest Black
      Frederick Olmstead
1954 Tracy Augur
1955 Frederick J. Adams
      Harland Bartholomew
      Flavel Shurtleff
1956 Charles B. Bennett
1957 Walter H. Blucher
      Harold M. Lewis
      Ladislas Segoe
      Lawrence V. Sheridan
1958 Harold S. Buttenheim
      Clarence S. Stein
1959 Robert B. Mitchell
      Gordon Whitnall
1960 S. R. DeBoer
1961 Charles W. Eliot
      Lawrence M. Orton
1962 Henry S. Churchill
      Hugh R. Pomeroy
1963 John T. Howard
1964 Francis A. Pitkin
      Warren J. Vinton
1965 Dennis O'Harrow
      Max Wehrly
1966 Howard Menhinick
1967 No award

1968 F. Stuart Chapin, Jr.
1969 Hans Blumenfeld
1970 Charles Abrams
1971 Edmund Bacon
1972 C. McKim Norton
      Coleman Woodbury
1973-76 No awards
1977 Richard L. Steiner

The Honor Award is given as merited to communities or regional organizations for noteworthy planning efforts. An awards jury selects the winner.

1962 Fremont, Calif.
1963 Cincinnati, Ohio
1964 Rye, N.Y., (population under 50,000)
      Pomona, Calif., (population 50,000 - 500,000)
      Detroit, Mich., (population over 500,000)
1965 Rockville, Md., (under 50,000)
      New Haven, Conn., (50,000 - 500,000)
1966 Camden, N.J., (50,000 - 500,000)
      Capital Region, Conn., (over 500,000)
1968 City and County of Denver, Colo., (over 500,000)

The Merit Award honors significant works and programs in planning. An awards jury selects the winner.

1968 *Planning for Balanced Growth in Connecticut*
1969 Bay Conservation and Development Commission Plan
      Goals for Dallas Program
      Principles and Practice of Urban Planning
1971 Education Program, Philadelphia Regional Chapter
      Goals for Texas Program, State of Texas

The Meritorious Program Award is given as warrented to recognize a significant work in the areas of professional education and training, community planning, regional and state planning, urban design or social responsibility. An awards jury selects the winner.

1972 Baltimore Metro Center, Md.
      Salt River Indian Community Planning Program, Ariz.
      Twin Cities Area of Minneapolis-St. Paul and its Metropolitan Council
1973-76 No awards
1977 Lowell, Mass., Urban National Cultural Parks Plan

The Chapter Achievement Award honors AIP chapters for contributions to the planning profession and AIP through an outstanding chapter program, activities or efforts that have advanced planning policy, development or the chapter. An awards jury selects the winner from nominations submitted by the membership,

1972 *Little Magazine,* Minnesota Chapter
1973-76 No awards
1977 National Capital Area Chapter

The Diana Donald Award is given to an outstanding planner who has made substantial contributions to women's rights, as demonstrated by significant contributions to the profession, the holding of a responsible management position and the devotion of substantial effort to community service. An awards jury selects the winner from nominations made by the membership.

1977 Margaret Lotspeich

Special Awards are given upon a decision by an awards jury to honor outstanding service to AIP.

1970 Alan M. Voorhees

Harold F. Wise
1971　No award
1972　Flavel Shurtleff
1972　Frederick Aschman
1973-76　No awards
1977　Paul Opperman

SPECIAL FIFTIETH ANNIVERSARY AWARDS

American Society of Planning Officials, Citation for contribution to the public acceptance and technical effectiveness of planning as a part of the process of government in the United States

City of Philadelphia, Citation honoring a city, two of its distinguished mayors who brought it through some decisive years of change (Joseph S. Clark and Richardson Dilworth) and a planner inseparably identified with the transformation these years have wrought

National Resources Planning Board, Citation as the spiritual forerunner of contemporary planning in the United States

Regional Plan Association (New York, New Jersey and Connecticut Metropolitan Area), Citation for achievement and contribution in Metropolitan Planning

Tennessee Valley Authority, Citation for achievement in carrying through a pioneering philosophy of resource use; in recognition of an uninterrupted line of inspired leadership from its board of directors; to honor the contributions from its distinguished and innovative professionals

Frederick Johnstone Adams, Citation for achievement and contribution in planning education

Harland Bartholomew, Citation for achievement and contribution in planning practice

Alfred Bettman, Citation for achievement and contribution in planning law

Kevin Lynch, Citation for achievement and contribution in planning and design theory

Martin Meyerson, Citation for achievement and contribution in planning theory and research

Lewis Mumford, Citation for achievement and contribution in planning philosophy

Ladislas Segoe, Citation for achievement and contribution in planning practice

Clarence S. Stein, Citation for achievement and contribution in planning design principles

Catherine Bauer Wurster, Citation for achievement and contribution in planning criticism

Bard Awards

CITY CLUB OF NEW YORK
55 E. 43rd St., New York, N.Y. 10017 (212/687-3116)

The Bard Award annually honors distinguished achievement in urban architecture in New York. An awards jury of prominent architects selects the winners from entries submitted by architects or owners or of their own choosing. Certificates are given in three categories.

FIRST HONOR AWARDS
1963　No award
1964　**Skidmore, Owings & Merrill,** for Pepsi-Cola Building
1965　**I.M. Pei & Associates and S.J. Kessler & Sons,** for Kips Bay Plaza
　　　Warner, Burns, Toan, Lunde, for Warner Weaver Hall, New York University

1966　**Philip C. Johnson,** for Henry Moses Institute, Montefiore Hospital
　　　Philip C. Johnson and Zion & Breen, for Sculpture Garden, Museum of Modern Art
　　　Philip Johnson Associates; Eero Saarinen & Associates; Skidmore, Owings & Merrill; Pietro Belluschi, and Catalono & Westerman, with Dan Kiley, landscape consultant, for Lincoln Center Plaza North
1967　**I.M. Pei & Partners,** for University Plaza Apartments
　　　Kelly & Gruzen, for Chatham Towers Apartments
　　　Wallace, McHarg, Roberts & Todd and Alan M. Voorhees & Associates, for Lower Manhattan Plan
1968　**Kevin Roche, John Dinkeloo & Associates,** for Ford Foundation
　　　Marcel Breuer, Hamilton Smith and Michael Irving, consulting architect, for Whitney Museum of American Art
　　　Zion & Breen Associates and Albert Preston Moore, for Paley Park
1969　**Davis, Brody & Associates,** for Riverbend Houses
　　　Edelman & Salzman, for 9-G Cooperative
1970　**Pietro Belluschi and Catalono & Westerman,** for Concert Halls, the Juilliard School
　　　Hardy Holzman Pfeiffer Associates, for Bedford Lincoln Community Center
1971　No award
1972　**I.M. Pei & Associates,** for National Airlines Terminal
　　　Abraham W. Geller, for Henry Ittelson Center for Child Research
1973　**Gruzen & Partners,** for Bronx State Hospital Rehabilitation Center
　　　Morris Lapidus Associates, for Bedford-Stuyvesant Community Pool
　　　Davis, Brody & Associates, for East Midtown Plaza
　　　Richard Meier & Associates, for Twin Parks Northeast
　　　Prentice & Chan, Ohlhausen, for Twin Parks Northwest, Site 5 & 11
1974　No award
1975　**Caudill Rowlett Scott,** for Salanter-Akiba-Riverdale Academy
1976　**Holden/Yang/Raemsch/Terjesen,** for bus stop shelters
　　　Prentice & Chan, Ohlhausen, for Arts for Living Center
　　　Hodne/Stageberg Partners, for 1199 Plaza Cooperative Towers
1977　**Richard Meier & Associates,** for Bronx Developmental Center

AWARDS FOR MERIT
1963　No award
1964　**Marcel Breuer,** for Bergrisch Hall, New York University Heights Campus
　　　Mayer, Whittlesey & Glass, for Premier Apartment House
　　　Abraham Geller and Ben Schlanger, for Cinema I and Cinema II
1965　**Harrison & Abramovitz,** for Terminal Building, LaGuardia Airport
1966　No award
1967　**Pomerance & Breines and M. Paul Friedberg & Associates,** for Riis Amphitheatre and Plaza
1968　No award
1969　**Smotrich & Platt,** for Exodus House
　　　Morris Ketchum Jr. & Associates, for Exhibition Building for Nocturnal Animals, Bronx Zoo

1970 Perkins & Will Partnership, for Wagner College Student Union
Walker Hodgetts, Mangurian & Godard, for Creative Playthings
Bill Hoch, for Latinas
Ulrich Franzen, for Paraphernalia
Hans Hollein, for Richard Feigen Gallery
Paul K.Y. Chen and George Thiel, for Zum Zum Restaurants
Isabel Hebey and Justin Henshell, for Rive Gauche Boutique
1971 Carl J. Petrilli, for The Mall, Graduate Center, City University of New York
Marcel Breuer and Hamilton B. Smith, for Technology Building II, New York University
1972 No award
1973 No award
1974 No award
1975 Mayers & Schiff, for Times Square Theatre Center
Edelman and Salzman, for reclamation of the Graveyards, St. Marks Church-in-the-Bouwerie
Castro Blanco, Piscionieri & Feder, PC and Gruzen & Partners, for Arthur A. Schomburg Plaza Apartments
Richard D. Kaplan/Stevens, Bertin, O'Connell & Harvey, for Crown Gardens
Davis, Brody & Associates, for Waterside
Ciardullo/Ehmann, for Plaza Borinquen/Motthaven Infill Housing
1976 No award
1977 Johnson/Burgee; Giorgio Cavaglieri; Johansen & Bhavnani; Sert, Jackson & Associates; Lev Zetlin Associates; Prentice & Chan, Ohlhausen; Kallmann & McKinnell; New York State Urban Development Corp. and Roosevelt Island Development Corp., for Roosevelt Island

SPECIAL AWARDS

1965 Pomerance & Breines and M. Paul Friedberg, for Carver Houses Plaza
Marquesa de Duevas, for 680 and 684 Park Avenue
1967 Stewart L. Udall, Secretary of the Interior
1968 Giorgio Cavaglieri, for Public Theatre Center, New York Shakespeare Festival; Old Astor Library rehab
1975 Warren W. Gran & Associates, for Clinton study
1976 New York City Department of Highways, for reconstruction of the Ave. of the Americas
1977 William N. Breger Associates, for C.A.B.S. Nursing Home
Gruzen & Partners, for U.S. Courthouse and Metropolitan Correctional Center
Gwathmey Siegel, for Shezan Restaurant
Kevin Roche/John Dinkeloo Associates, for Fifth Avenue Plaza and East Front, Metropolitan Museum of Art
Helmuth, Obata & Kassabaum, for Greenwich Savings Bank
Hardy Holman Pfeiffer Assocciates, for Smithsonian's Cooper-Hewitt National Museum of Design

Arnold W. Brunner Prize

NATIONAL INSTITUTE OF ARTS AND LETTERS
633 W. 155th St., New York, N.Y. 10032 (212/AU 6-1480)

The $1,000 Arnold W. Brunner Prize in Architecture is given annually to an architect who has contributed to the field as an art. A committee of Institute members who are architects selects the winner.

1955 Gordon Bunshaft
1956 John Yeon
1957 John Carl Warnecke
1958 Paul Rudolph
1959 Edward Larrabee Barnes
1960 Louis I. Kahn
1961 Ieoh Ming Pei
1962 Ulrich Franzen
1963 Edward Charles Bassett
1964 Harry Weese
1965 Kevin Roche
1966 Romaldo Giurgola
1968 John M. Johansen
1969 Noel Michael McKinnell
1970 Charles Gwathmey
Richard Henderson
1971 John Andrews
1972 Richard Meier
1973 Robert Venturi
1974 Hugh Hardy with Norman Pfeiffer and Malcolm Holzman
1975 Lewis Davis and Samuel Brody
1976 James Frazer Stirling
1977 Henry N. Cobb

Library Building Award

AMERICAN LIBRARY ASSOCIATION
Library Administration Div.
50 E. Huron St. Chicago, Ill. 60611 (312/944-6780)

The Library Buildings Award, cosponsored by the Association and the American Institute of Architects, is given biennially for excellence in architectural design and planning of libraries. A jury of four architects and three librarian/building experts selects the winners, which are honored with a plaque and certificate. New buildings, renovations and additions of all kinds of libraries in the U.S. and elsewhere are included.

HONOR AWARDS (Plaque and Certificates)

1963 Bennington (Vt.) College Library
Undergraduate Library, University of South Carolina
Walnut Hills Branch of the Dallas (Tex.) Public Library
Skokie (Ill.) Public Library
Flossmoor (Ill.) Public Library
1964 Beinecke Rare Book Room & Manuscript Library, Yale University, New Haven, Conn.
Charles Patterson Van Pelt Library, University of Pennsylvania, Philadelphia, Pa.
Flora B. Tenzler Memorial Library, Pierce County, Tacoma, Wash.
1966 Magnolia Branch Library, Seattle (Wash.) Public Library
1968 No award
1970 Bancroft Elementary Library, Andover, Mass.
1972 Providence College Library, Providence, R.I.
Ohio Historical Center Library-Archives, Columbus, Ohio
1974 Monroe C. Gutman Library, Harvard Graduate School of Education, Cambridge, Mass.
North Branch Library, Omaha, Neb.
Southdale Hennepin Area Library, Edina, Minn.
1976 Stephen B. Luce Library, Fort Schulyer, Bronx, N.Y.
Lineberg Memorial Library, Lutheran Theological Seminary, Columbia, S.C.
Joseph Mark Lauinger Library, Georgetown University, Washington, D.C.

Nathan Marsh Pusey Library, Harvard University, Cambridge, Mass.
Randall Memorial Library, Stow, Mass
Marin County Library, Novata, Calif.
Rockford Road Branch, Hennepin County Library, Crystal, Minn.
Corning Public Library and Southern Tier Library System, Corning, N.Y.

MERIT AWARD (CERTIFICATE)

1963 Lourdes Library, Gwynedd Mercy Junior Colleges, Gwynedd Valley, Pa.
Grinnell College Burling Library, Grinnell, Iowa
Schulz Memorial Library, Concordia Theological Seminary, Springfield, Ill.
Foothill College Library, Los Altos Hills, Calif.
Douglass College Library, Rutgers University, New Brunswich, N.J.
Washington State Library, Olympia, Wash
Louisiana State Library Baton Rouge, La.
New Orleans (La.) Public Library
Santa Fe Springs (Calif.) City Library
Sequoyah Hills Branch, Knoxville (Tenn.) Public Library
Wellesley (Mass.) Free Library
West Bloomfield Township Library, Orchard Lake, (Mich.)

1964 Archbishop Alemany Library, Dominican College, San Rafael, Calif.
Leverett House Library, Harvard University, Cambridge, Mass.
Lafayette College Library, Easton, Pa.
Hollis F. Price Library, Le Moyne College, Memphis, Tenn.
Otto G. Richter Library, University of Miami, Coral Gables, Fla.
Southwest Branch, Seattle (Wash,) Public Library
Sprain Brook Branch, Yonkers (N.Y.) Public Library
Silas Bronson Library, Waterbury, Conn.
Detroit (Mich.) Public Library
Coconut Grove Branch, Miami (Fla.) Public Library
Willey Library, Seaside High School, Fort Ord, Calif.
Redwood High School Library, Larkspur, Calif.
Westtown School Library, Westtown, Chester County, Pa.

1966 University Research Library, University of California at Los Angeles
Swirbul Library, Adelphi University, Garden City, N.Y.
Countway Library of Medicine, Harvard University Medical School, Boston, Mass.
Wilmot Branch Library, Tucson (Ariz.) Public Library
South Branch of the Berkeley (Calif.) Public Library
New Jersey State Library, Trenton, N.J.
Casa View Branch, Dallas (Tex.) Public Library
W. Clarke Swanson Library, Omaha, Neb.
Salt Lake City (Utah) Public Library
McBean Library, Cate School, Carpinteria, Calif.

1968 Library Institute for Advanced Education, Princeton, N.J.
St. John's University Library, Collegeville, Minn.
Hofstra University Library, Hempstead, N.Y.
Mill Valley (Calif) Public Library
La Crosse (Wisc.) Public Library
Wichita (Kans.) Public Library
Mount Anthony Union High School Library, Bennington, Vt.

1970 Adlai Stevenson College Library, University of California at Santa Cruz
Robert Hutchings Goddard Library, Clark University, Worcester, Mass.
Anna E. Waden Branch Library, San Francisco, Calif.
Madden Hills Branch Library, Dayton, Ohio
Henry B. DuPont Library, Pomfret School, Pomfret, Conn.

1972 Bailey Library, Hendrix College, Conway, Ark.
Loomis Library, Loomis Institute, Windsor, Conn.
Joseph Regenstein Library, University of Chicago
Richardson (Tex.) Public Library
South County Library, Deale, Md.
Corte Madera Branch, Marin County Library, Corte Madera, Calif.
Tate Library of the Fieldston School, Riverdale, N.Y.

1974 Loyola-Notre Dame Library, Baltimore, Md.
Library of the Villa Angela Academy, Cleveland, Ohio.

1976 Bates College, Lewiston, Me.
Pekin Public Library and Everett McKinley Dirksen Congressional Leadership Research Center, Pekin, Ill.
Jefferson Market Branch, Library, New York, N.Y.

The Roscoe

RESOURCES COUNCIL

979 Third Ave., New York, N.Y. 10022 (212/752-9040)

The Roscoe, a crystal trophy designed by Tiffany, annually honors excellence and innovation in design and technology of household furnishings and fixtures. Entries are accepted at $75 each. A judges' panel narrows the field down from hundreds of entries for a vote by attendees at a Council designers' market, which in 1977 was a four-day event. Until the introduction of the trophy in 1977, certificates were awarded to winners in a variety of categories and by different voting procedures. Award winners are listed here, but honorable mentions are not.

1971 Wolf Bauer, "Wheels & Yves," printed textiles
Francisca Reichardt, "Omahar," printed textiles
Gretl and Leo Wollner, "Sling," printed textiles
Ulrike Rhomberg, "Slant," printed textiles
Al Marsh, "Interplay," wallcovering
James Hill, "Kaleidoscope," wool rug
Lee Rosen, "Prismatic," ceramic wall design
Fritz Haller, Haller Program, collection of office furniture
William Sklaroff and Thomas H. Janicz, Uniplane desk and credenza

1972 Frank O. Gehry, Edgeboard contour rocker
William C. Andrus, "Soft Seating Group"
Jack Lenor Larsen, "The Great Colour of China," textile collection
James Seeman Studios, "Kaleidoscope," collection of murals and super-graphics
Roger McDonald and Paul W. V'Soske, "Northern Lights" and "Strata," wool rugs
Magee Design Studios, "Glen Eagle" and "Empire Stripe," wool carpets
Herbert Bright, "Polka Dots," "Gingham" and "Houndstooth," vinyl flooring collection
Richard Ludwig, "Sang-de-Boeuf," hand-thrown stoneware lamps
Nando Vigo, "Golden Gate," arc floor lamp

Achille Castiglioni, "Parenthesis," lighting fixture
1973 Kibrel Steele Terry, Marble and steel dining table
William H.P. Tacke, "Ergo," secretarial chair
Ken Millette, "Expresso-X," indoor/outdoor folding chair
Theodore R. Meyer, "Galaxy," plexiglass desk
Margaret D. Nelson, "Botanical," crewel embroidery fabric
Schule-McCarville, "Harriet," fabric
Dorothy A. Christie, "Star and Block," upholstery fabric
Robert O. Webb, Woven aluminum window shade
Anthony W. V'Soske, "Gridola," wool rug
Allied Chemical Design Studio, "Kinder Karpet"
Monogram Design Studio, "Bandana," wool area rug
Herbert Bright, "Ultrabronze," and stainless steel flooring
Dan Hawkins, "All-Most," hand-screened wallpaper
Helen Watkins, "Xanadu," wallpaper mural
Michael Babbitts, "Berberwool," wool wallcovering
William M. Groff, "Mono-Facade," ceramic wall tile
Eric Mulvany, "Quadri," Plexiglas lamp
Brent J. Bennett, Stoneware hanging lantern
Lenox Design Dept., "Dewdrops," Temperware china
Marie Creamer, "International Set," towel and rug collection
William Sklaroff Design Associates, "Radius One," desk accessories
Don Doman Associates, "Birthday Bath," bath tub
1974 Henry A. Olko, Rattan and reed daybed in the Oriental manner
William Sklaroff, Sled-base, contour-back armchair
Linda Sparrow, "Sampler," upholstery fabric
Joseph Grusczak, "Knits for Windows and Walls," fabric
Levolor Lorentzen Design Studio, "Gingham," Riviera blinds
Monogram Design Studio, "Mountain Mist," area rug
Hamdi and Brunhild El Attar, "Country House," sisal carpet tile
Herbert Bright, "Country Plaid," vinyl floor tile
Francois Benjamin, "Roxy," handscreened wallpaper
Jack Lenor Larsen, "Muralto," wall-surfacing textile
Eric Mulvany, "Trio," table lamp
Ben Mayer Design Studio, "Envelite," illuminated ceiling system
Ena de Silva, Batik bedspread
John W. Ledford, "The Spiral," staircase
Gino Valle and Herbert Ohl, "Metrix," dining/conference table
Suzanne Hugeunin, "Sequoia," upholstery fabric
Stanley J. V'Soske, Jr., "Avenues," area rug
David Nordahl, "Clouds," lithographic wall mural
1975 Eve Frankl, "Multi," series "Z" table
Roger Kenneth Leib, Modular lounge seating
Lawrence Peabody, Bronze and Haitian Sea Grass dining chair
Albert Zellers, "Carnations," fabric
Louis M. Bromante, "King Tut," quilted fabric
V'Soske Studios, "Puntilla," wool and silk area rug
Jack Lenor Larsen, "Happiness," carpet
Henry Torreggiani, "Geometric," ceramic tile
Arthur Athas, Barry Crooks and F. Galacar, "The Jaffrey Room," wallpaper
Cindi Mufson, "Hardrock," wallcovering

Adam Tihany/Joey Mancini, Unigram, Inc., "Triangolo," lamp series
Leon Conn, Innervisions bronze mirror lighting fixture
F.V. Herr and C.A. Tucker, "Eclipse," desk accessories
Fabio Lenci, "2001," shower in the round
C.J. Corona, "Superstone," synthetic fossilized stone
1976 O.B. Solie and R.G. Sonnenleiter, "Parabola," dining table
Ray Wilkes, Modular sofa group
William Stumpf, "Ergon," chair
Everett Brown Associates, "Sweet Potata," fabric
Jack Lindsay, "Djakarta," fabric
Kirk-Brummel Studios, "Lorelei," fabric
Larsen Design Studio, "Pastorale-Sheer," fabric
Levolor Design Dept., Riviera Tiltone duo-colored blind
Nadia Stark, Rumanian Kilim rug
Walter Dorwin Teague Associates and Anthony V'Soske, "Zap," area rug
Alan Meiselman, "Quadro," Berber broadloom
Nadia Stark, "Pande," broadloom carpet
Sylvia Gold Spellos, "Barnside," vinyl flooring
Laura Ashley, "A Fine & Private Place," wallpaper
Antonio Rodbechia, "Rodbechia," ceramic wall tile
Eric Mulvany, "Capricorn," table lamp
Habitat Design Team, Habitat Designers' Fluorescent
Paul Mayen, Desk-top accessory unit
Fabio Lenci, Bath and shower in the round
Maya, Tie-dyed floor canvas
1977 Jay S. Goldsamt, Chinese altar table
Doug Bickle, Dining/conference table
Ray Wilkes, Shelf Life Unlimited
George Nelson, Daniel Lewis and David Schowalter, Office furniture system
Henry Olko, Rattan Manau chair
Craig and Saul Goldman, "Quiltessence," fabric
Kirk-Brummel Studios, "Staccato Weave," fabric
Connaissance Studio, "Grand Prix," jacquard fabric
Marella Agnelli, "Sorbiers," fabric
Federico Forquet and Gustav Zumsteg, "Tahiti," fabric
Joel Berman, Mecho-Shade for windows
Lee Rosen, Grid relief pattern ceramic floor tile
Arthur Athas, Frederic Galacar and Barry Crooks, "Birds of Paradise," wallcovering
Andre Matenciot Design Studio, "Patches," wallcovering
Eric Mulvany, "Emerald," acrylic lamp
Barbara Roth, Egyptian lamp
Rolando T. Curtis, "Mirra Dome," lighting
Enzo Mari, Bowl, Danese Ceramic Collection
William Sklaroff, Covered face clock
Yolanda Quitman, Plexiglas medicine cabinet
Maya Romanoff, "Red Sienna Rain," Palangi-dyed leather and suede
Shirley Mellinger, "Ferocious Lion," rug
Joseph Freitag, "Botanica," stencils on sisal rug
John and Steven Stark, "Agadir," Berber broadloom carpet

Fritz Schumacher Foundation Award

STIFTUNG F.V.S.
Georgsplatz 10, 2 Hamburg 1, Federal Republic of Germany
(Tel: 33 04 00 and 33 06 00)

The Fritz Schumacher Foundation Award honors achievements in city- and land-planning, architecture, environmentalism and historic preservation in Europe. Two cash prizes of 20,000 German marks each are offered. The Technical University of Hanover administers the award.

1960 **Wolfgang Bangert** (Kassel, Germany
     Alwin Seifert (Munich, Germany)
1961 **C. van Traa** (Rotterdam, Netherlands)
     Fritz Leonhardt (Stuttgart, Germany)
1962 **Heinrich Wiepking** (Munster, Germany)
     Horst Linde (Stuttgart, Germany)
1963 **Arne Jacobsen** (Copenhagen, Denmark)
     Gunther Grundmann (Hamburg, Germany)
1964 **Adolf Ciborowski** (Warsaw, Poland)
     Konstanty Gutschow (Hamburg, Germany)
1965 **Francisco Caldeira Cabral** (Lisbon, Portugal)
     Josef Umlauf (Stuttgart, Germany)
1966 **Friedrich Tamms** (Dusseldorf, Germany)
     Gerhard Ziegler (Stuttgart, Germany)
1967 **Cornelis van Leeuwen** (Bloemdedaal, Netherlands)
     Arie C. Krijn (Bussum, Netherlands)
     Jan H. van Loenen (Beverwijk, Netherlands)
     Rudolf Wurzer (Vienna, Austria)
1968 **Robert Will** (Strasbourg, France)
     Fernand Guri (Strasbourg, France)
     Javier Carvajal (Madrid, Spain)
     Ricardo Bofill (Barcelona, Spain)
1969 **Wilhelm Wortmann** (Hanover, Germany)
     Renato Bazzoni (Milan, Italy)
1970 **Sir Hubert Bennett** (London, England)
     Heikki von Hertzen (Tapiola, Finland)
1971 **Colin Douglas Buchanan** (London, England)
     Walter Rossow (Berlin, Germany)
1972 **Elisabeth Pfeil** (Hamburg, Germany)
     Harald Clauss (Nuremberg, Germany)
     Heinz Schmeissner (Nuremberg, Germany)
1973 **M. Robert Vassas** (Paris, France)

     Friedrich Cordes (Kiel, Germany)
1974 **Herman Hertzberger** (N.A.)
     Frank van Klingeren (Amsterdam, Netherlands)
     Erich Kuhn (Aachen, Germany)
1975 **Pier Luigi Cervellati** (Bologna, Italy)
     Armando Sarti (Bologna, Italy)
     Hubert Kath (Celle, Germany)
     Fritz Schmidt (Celle, Germany)
     Fred Angerer (Lochham bei Munchen, Germany)
     Eberhard Haller (Lindau, Germany)
     Horst Heidhardt (Oldenburg, Germany)
     Friedrich Hasskamp (Oldenburg, Germany)
     Hans Petzholdt (Trier, Germany)
1977 **Jon de Ranitz** (Rotterdam, Netherlands)
     Helmut Gebhard (Munich, Germany)
     Gerd Ruile (Regensburg, Germany)

UNESCO Prize for Architecture
UNITED NATIONS EDUCATIONAL, SCIENTIFIC AND CULTURAL ORGANIZATION
7 Place du Fontenoy, 75700 Paris, France (Tel: 577 16 10, Ext. 4004)

The UNESCO Prize for Architecture, which carries a $4,000 honorarium, is given every three years to a student or faculty member in architecture in UNESCO member states for a meritorious architectural project. The International Union of Architects conducts an international competition, from which the winner is selected.

1969 **Mitsuo Morozumi** (Japan), Social housing scheme
1972 **Vladimir Kirpitshev** (U.S.S.R.), Collective recreational facilities
1975 **Alka Shah and Vidyadhar Chavda** (India), Emergency habitat

Librarianship & Information

Sciences

Contents

Related Awards

Armed Forces Librarians Achievement Citation

AMERICAN LIBRARY ASSOCIATION
Armed Forces Librarians Section, 50 E. Huron St., Chicago, Ill. 60611 (312/944-6780)

The Armed Forces Librarians Achievement Citation is given annually for significant contributions to the development of armed forces library services and to organizations that encourage interest in libraries and reading. The AFLS Awards Committee selects the recipient.

1965 Helen E. Fry
1966 Harry F. Cook
1967 Ruth Sheahan Howard
1968 Agnes Crawford
1969 Mary J. Carter
1970 Frances M. O'Halloran
1971 Dorothy Fayne
1972 Lucia Gordon
1973 No award
1974 Josephine Neil
     Robert W. Severance
1975 No award
1976 Mariana J. Thurber
1977 No award

John Cotton Dana Library Public Relations Award

AMERICAN LIBRARY ASSOCIATION
Library Administration Div., 50 E. Huron, Chicago, Ill. 60611 (312/944-6780)

The John Cotton Dana Library Public Relations Award, cosponsored by the Association and the H.W. Wilson Co., recognizes effective public relations programs or projects, as documented by scrapbooks and non-print materials submitted for evaluation. A panel of library experts selects the recipients of the Dana Certificate.

1974 Orlando, Fla., Public Library
     San Mateo, Calif., Public Library
     Glendale, Calif., Public Library
     Pomona, Calif., Public Library
     Cortez, Colo., Public Library
     Denver, Colo., Public Library
     Indianapolis-Marion County, Ind., Public Library
     Northwestern Regional Library, Elkin N.C.
     Tulsa City-County Library, Okla.
     Houston, Tex., Public Library
     Vancouver Island Regional Library, Nanaimo, B.C., Canada
     Metropolitan Toronto, Ont., Central Library, Canada
     Connecticut State Library, Hartford, Conn.
     University of Colorado Libraries, Boulder, Colo.
     University of Texas at Austin Graduate School of Library Science
     Oak Park and River Forest High School Library, Ill.
     Whetstone High School Library, Columbus, Ohio
     Elizabeth Redd Primary School Library, Richmond, Va.

Floyd E. Kellam High School Library, Virginia Beach, Va.
Clark AFB Library, Philippines
Scott AFB Library, Ill.
Fort Monmouth Post Library, N.J.
Minot AFB Library, N.D.
Lackland AFB Library, Tex.
Randolph AFB Library, Tex.

1975 Greenville, S.C., County Library
     Glendale, Calif., Public Library
     Vancouver Island Regional Library, Nanaimo, B.C., Canada
     George S. Houston Memorial Library, Dothan, Ala.
     Mono County Free Library, Bridgeport, Calif.
     Pomona, Calif., Public Library
     San Francisco, Calif., Public Library
     Cortez, Colo., Public Library
     Denver, Colo., Public Library
     Hartford, Conn., Public Library
     Broward County Library, Ft. Lauderdale, Fla.
     Paducah, Ky, Public Library
     Washington County Library System, Greenville, Miss.
     East Meadow, N.Y., Public Library
     Farmingdale, N.Y., Public Library
     Troy-Miami County Public Library, Troy, Ohio
     Salt Lake County Library System, Salt Lake City, Utah
     Timberland Regional Library, Lacey, Wash.
     Laramie County Library System, Cheyenne, Wyo.
     York Regional Library, Fredricton, N.B., Canada
     West Virginia Library Commission, Wheeling, W. Va.
     South Carolina State Library, Charleston, S.C.
     State University of New York at Buffalo
     Alaska Library Assn.
     U.S. Military Academy Library, West Point, N.Y.
     Toledo, Ohio, Public Schools
     Wheeler AFB Library, Ha.
     Chanute AFB Library, Ill.
     Clark AFB Library, Philippines
     Randolph AFB Library, Tex.
     Webb AFB Library, Tex.
     Fletcher Library, U.S. Navy, Adak, Alas.

1976 Pomona, Calif., Public Library
     Sacramento, Calif., Public Library
     Cortez, Colo., Public Library
     Pueblo Regional Library District, Pueblo, Colo.
     Perry County Public Library, Hazard, Ky.
     Clark County Library District, Las Vegas, Nev.
     Buffalo & Erie County Public Library, Buffalo, N.Y.
     Public Library of Charlotte and Mecklenburg County, N.C.
     Beaver County Federated Library System, Monaca, Pa.
     Salt Lake County Library System, Salt Lake City, Utah
     Long Beach, Calif., Public Library
     Los Angeles, Calif., Public Library
     Santiago Library System, Orange, Calif.
     S. Pasadena, Calif., Public Library

Evergreen, Colo., Regional Library
Danbury, Conn., Public Library
Broward County Library System, Ft. Lauderdale, Fla.
Orlando, Fla., Public Library
Atlanta, Ga., Public Library
Scott Candler Library, Decatur, Ga.
Iberville Parish Library, Plaquemine, La.
Cambridge, Mass., Public Library
Concord, Mass., Free Public Library
Watertown, Mass., Free Public Library
Detroit, Mich., Public Library
Mideastern Michigan Library Cooperative, Flint, Mich.
Pike-Amite Library System, McComb, Miss.
Madison, N.J., Public Library
Public Library of Youngstown and Mahoning County, Ohio
Pioneer Multi-County Library, Norman, Okla.
Fulton County Library Project, McConnellsburg, Pa.
Montgomery County-Norristown Public Library, Pa.
Greenville, S.C., County Library
Fairfax County Public Library, Springfield, Va.
Timberland Regional Library, Lacy, Wash.
Brown County Library, Green Bay, Wisc.
Madison, Wisc., Public Library
Bankstown, Australia, Municipal Library
Dartmouth Regional Library, N.S., Canada
West Virginia Library Commission, Wheeling, W. Va.
State Prison of Southern Michigan, Jackson, Mich.
Orange County Law Library, Santa Ana, Calif.
Maryland State Dept. of Education, Div. of Instructional Television
Seneca County Library Council, Tiffin, Ohio.
West Point Academy Library, N.Y.
Salem State College Library, Mass.
University of Denver Library, Colo.
Allegany Community College Library, Cumberland, Md.
Hampshire College Library Center, Amherst, Mass.
University of Wisconsin-Parkside Library, Kenosha, Wisc.
Greenwich, Conn., Public Schools
Monroe Junior High School Library, Columbus, Ohio
Azalea Middle School, St. Petersburg, Fla.
Board of Education of Baltimore County, Towson, Md.
Rocky Hill Library, Knoxville, Tenn.
Yongsan Library, U.S. Army Recreation Services Agency, Korea
Barksdale AFB Library, La.
Travis AFB Library, Calif.
K.I. Sawyer AFB Library, Mich.
Columbus AFB Library, Miss.
Minot AFB Library, N.D.
1977   Public Library of Columbus and Franklin County, Columbus, Ohio
Cherokee Regional Talking Book Center, La Fayette, Ga.
University of Texas Library at Austin
Travis AFB Library, Calif.

Birmingham, Ala., Public Library
Mobile, Ala., Public Library
Altadena, Calif., Library District
Sacramento, Calif., Public Library
Orlando, Fla., Public Library
Ewa Beach Community-School Library, Haw.
Makiki Library, Honolulu, Haw.
Ames, Iowa, Public Library
Watertown, Mass., Public Library
Bad Axe, Mich., Public Library
Clark County Library District, Las Vegas, Nev.
Buffalo and Erie County Public Library, N.Y.
Public Library of Charlotte and Mecklenburg County, Charlotte, N.C.
Public Library of Cincinnati and Hamilton County, Cincinnati, Ohio
El Paso, Tex., Public Library
Metropolitan Toronto Library, Ont., Canada
State Library of North Carolina
West Virginia Library Commission
Pennsylvania Library Assn.
Metropolitan Library Service Agency, St. Paul, Minn.
Mid-Bergen Federation of Libraries, N.J.
Hickam AFB Library, Haw.
K.I. Sawyer AFB Library, Mich.
Minot AFB Library, N.D.

Dartmouth Medal

AMERICAN LIBRARY ASSOCIATION
Reference and Adult Services Division, 50 E. Huron St., Chicago, Ill. 60611 (312/944-6780)

The Dartmouth Medal, which is of bronze designed by Rudolph Ruzicka, annually recognizes the creation of reference works judged as outstanding and significant. The work involved may be writing, compilation, editing or publishing books or other reference materials during the preceding year. A Dartmouth Medal Awards Committee selects the winner.

1975   New England Board of Higher Education, Northeast Academic Science Information Center Wellsley, Mass.
1976   No award
1977   Lester J. Cappon, *Atlas of Early American History: The Revolutionary Era 1760-1790*

Melvil Dewey Award

AMERICAN LIBRARY ASSOCIATION
50 E. Huron, St., Chicago, Ill. 60611 (312/944-6780)

The Melvil Dewey Award, which consists of a medal and citation, is given annually for recent professional creative achievement in such fields as library management, training, cataloging and classification. A five-person jury appointed by the ALA Awards Committee chairperson selects the winner.

1953   Ralph R. Shaw
1954   Herman H. Fussler
1955   Maurice F. Tauber
1956   Norah Albanell MacColl
1957   Wyllis E. Wright
1958   Janet S. Dickson

1959 Benjamin A. Custer	1965 Sarah Lewis Jones
1960 Harriet E. Howe	1966 Mildred L. Batchelder
1961 Julia C. Pressey	1967 Lura E. Crawford
1962 Leon Carnovsky	1968 Augusta Baker
1963 Frank B. Rogers	1969 Anne R. Izard
1964 John W. Cronin	1970 Julia Losinski
1965 Bertha Margaret Frick	1971 Sara Siebert
1966 Lucile Morsch	1972 Ronald W. McCracken
1967 Walter Herbert Kaiser	1973 Eleanor Kidder
1968 Jesse H. Shera	1974 Regina U. Minudri
1969 William S. Dix	1975 Jane B. Wilson
1970 Joseph Treyz	1976 Virginia Haviland
1971 William J. Welsh	1977 Elizabeth Fast
1972 Jerrold Orne	
1973 Virginia Lacy Jones	
1974 Robert B. Downs	
1975 No award	
1976 Louis Round Wilson	
1977 Seymour Lubetsky	

Grolier National Library Week Grant

AMERICAN LIBRARY ASSOCIATION
50 E. Huron St., Chicago, Ill. 60611 (312/944-6780)

The Grolier National Library Week Grant of $1,000 is presented annually to the state library association submitting the best proposal to promote library services. The ALA National Library Week Committee selects the winner during the Association's mid-winter conference.

1975 **West Virginia Library Assn.,** "Information Power" (public relations program)
1976 **Illinois Library Assn.,** "Librarians to the People" (speaker's bureau project)
1977 **New Jersey Library Assn.,** "Influencing City Hall" (public relations program)

Robert B. Downs Award

UNIVERSITY OF ILLINOIS GRADUATE SCHOOL OF LIBRARY SCIENCE
Urbana, Ill. 61801 (217/333-3280)

The Robert B. Downs Award is given for outstanding contributions to the cause of intellectual freedom in libraries by vote of the school's faculty. The award is given annually and consists of $500 and a certificate.

1969 **LeRoy Charles Merritt,** Dean, School of Librarianship, University of Oregon (Eugene)
1970 **Orrin Dow,** Public Library, Farmingdale, N.Y.
1971 **President's Commission on Obscenity & Pornography**
1972 **John T. Carey,** St. Mary's College (St. Mary's City, Md.)
1973 **Alex P. Allain,** Attorney, Jeannerette, La.
1974 **Everett T. Moore,** University of California at Los Angeles
1975 **No award**
1976 **Eli Oboler,** Idaho State University (Pocatello)
1977 **Irene Turin,** Island Trees High School (Levittown, N.Y.)

Hammond Inc. Library Award

AMERICAN LIBRARY ASSOCIATION
50 E. Huron St., Chicago, Ill. 60611 (312/944-6780)

The $500 Hammond Inc. Library Award goes annually to a librarian or a library in a community or school in recognition of an unusual contribution of lasting value for effective use or increased interest in maps, atlases and globes by children and young people. The chairperson of the ALA Awards Committee appoints a five-person jury to make selections from nominations received.

1963 **Clara E. LeGear**
1964 **No award**
1965 **James M. Day**
1966 **No award**
1967 **No award**
1968 **Ellen Freeman**
1969 **No award**
1970 **No award**
1971 **University of Chicago Laboratory Schools High School Library**
1972 **Patterson Library,** Westfield, N.Y.
1973 **Betty Ryder, Pasadena Public Library, Calif.**
1974 **No award**
1975 **No award**
1976 **Gail Borden Library District, Elgin, Ill.,** for their work with the LaSalle Expedition II
1977 **Upper Hudson Library Federation,** Albany, N.Y.

Grolier Foundation Award

AMERICAN LIBRARY ASSOCIATION
50 E. Huron St., Chicago, Ill. 60611 (312/944-6780)

The $1,000 Grolier Foundation Award is given annually to a community or school librarian for unusual contributions to the stimulation and guidance of reading by children and young people. A five-person jury appointed by the ALA Awards Committee chairperson selects the winner from nominations received.

1954 Siddie Joe Johnson
1955 Charlemae Rollins
1956 Georgia Sealoff
1957 Margaret Alexander Edwards
1958 Mary Peacock Douglas
1959 Evelyn Sickels
1960 Margaret Scoggin
1961 Della Louise McGregor
1962 Alice McGuire
1963 Caroline W. Field
1964 Inger Boye

Library Research Round Table Award

LIBRARY RESEARCH ROUND TABLE
c/o American Library Assn., 50 E. Huron St., Chicago, Ill. 60611 (312/944-6780)

The $400 Library Research Round Table award is given annually for a piece of completed research in the area of library and information science, based on the decision of a selection committee which judges papers submitted to it.

1975 Robert L. Burr, "Toward a General Theory of Circulation"
Maurice P. Marchant, "University Libraries as Economic Systems" and "Patterns of Staff Involvement in University Library Management"
1976 James D. Baughman, "Toward a Structural Approach to Collection Development"
Ruth Wender, Esther Fruehauf, Marilyn Vent and Connie Wilson, "The Determination of Clinician Continuing Education Needs from a Literature Study Search"
1977 Herbert S. White and Karen Hasenjager, "Some Measurements of the Impact of the Rapid Growth of Library Doctoral Programs'
Robert W. Burns, Jr., "Library Performance Measures as Seen in the Descriptive Statistics Generated by a Computer Managed Circulation System"

Joseph W. Lippincott Award

AMERICAN LIBRARY ASSOCIATION
50 E. Huron St., Chicago, Ill. 60611 (312/944-6780)

The Joseph W. Lippincott Award, consisting of $1,000, a medal and a citation, is given annual to a librarian for outstanding participation in the activities of professional associations, notable professional writings and other significant activities. A jury appointed by the ALA chairperson selects the recipients from nominations received.

1938	Mary U. Rothrock
1939	Herbert Putnam
1940	No awards
1948	Carl H. Milam
1949	Harry M. Lydenberg
1950	Halsey W. Wilson
1951	Helen Haines
1952	Carl Vitz
1953	Marian C. Manley
1954	Jack Dalton
1955	Emerson Greenaway
1956	Ralph A. Ulveling
1957	Flora Belle Ludington
1958	Carleton B. Joeckel
1959	Essae Martha Culver
1960	Verner W. Clapp
1961	Joseph L. Wheeler
1962	David H. Clift
1963	Frances W. Henne
1964	Robert B. Downs
1965	Frances Clarke Sayers
1966	Keyes DeWitt Metcalf
1967	Edmon Low
1968	Lucile Nix
1969	Germaine Krettek
1970	Paul Howard
1971	William S. Dix
1972	Guy Lyle
1973	Jesse H. Shera
1974	Jerrold Orne
1975	Leon Carnovsky
1976	Lester Asheim
1977	Virginia Lacy Jones

Margaret Mann Citation

AMERICAN LIBRARY ASSOCIATION
Resources and Technical Services Division, 50 E. Huron St., Chicago, Ill. 60611 (312/944-6780, Ext. 228)

The Margaret Mann Citation is awarded annually for outstanding achievement in cataloging and/or classification. A jury selects the winner.

1951 Lucile M. Morsch, "Rules for Descriptive Cataloging"
1952 Marie Louise Prevost, Promotion and establishment of the *Journal of Cataloging and Classification*
1953 Maurice F. Tauber, Planning, organizing, conducting and reporting on subject analysis of library materials
1954 Pauline A. Seely, Outstanding participation in national, regional and local activities
1955 Seymour Lubetzky, Scholarly analysis and critiques that stimulated and influenced revision of cataloging rules
1956 Susan G. Akers, Author, teacher, leader of cataloging activities in Southeast and throughout U.S.
1957 David J. Haykin, Subject cataloging and classification
1958 Esther J. Piercy, Editor, *Journal of Cataloguing and Classification*, and its successor, *Library Resources & Technical Services*
1959 Andrew D. Osborn, Contributions to cataloging
1960 M. Ruth MacDonald, Distinguished service to field
1961 John W. Cronin, Centralized cataloging and bibliographic services
1962 Wyllis E. Wright, Leadership in securing wide acceptance here and abroad of cataloging principles
1963 Arthur H. Chaplin, "Draft Statement of Principles," basis for international agreement
1964 Catherine MacQuarrie, Contributions to development of mechanically produced catalog in book form
1965 Laura C. Colvin, *Cataloging Sampler*
1966 F. Bernice Field, Scholarly and practical leadership in descriptive cataloging
1967 C. Sumner Spalding, *Anglo-American Cataloging Rules*
1968 Paul S. Dunkin, Contributions to philosophy and techniques of organizing recorded human knowledge
1969 Katharine L. Ball, International activities in cataloging, teaching, publication and participation in professional associations
1970 S.R. Ranganathan, Colon classification
1971 Henriette D. Avram, Contributions to promotion of standard format for bibliographic records in machine-readable form
1972 Edmond L. Applebaum, Contribution to National Program for Acquisitions and Cataloging
1973 Doralyn J. Hickey, Contributions to all aspects of cataloging and classification
1974 Frederick G. Kilgour, Organizing and putting into operation the first practical centralized computer bibliographic center

1975   Margaret W. Ayrault, Leadership in cataloging and classification
1976   Eva Verona, *Corporate Headings*
1977   Phyllis A. Richmond, Teaching of cataloging and classification, scholarly publication and contributions to professional associations

Isidore Gilbert Mudge Citation
AMERICAN LIBRARY ASSOCIATION
Reference and Adult Services Division, 50 E. Huron St., Chicago, Ill. 60611 (312/944-6780)

The Isidore Gilbert Mudge Citation is awarded annually to an individual for distinguished contribution to reference librarianship, as evidenced by an imaginative and constructive program in a particular library, the writing of a significant book or articles in the reference field, active participation in professional associations, teaching or any other noteworthy accomplishment. The Isidore Gilbert Mudge Citation Committee selects the winner.

1959   Mary Neill Barton
1960   Constance Mabel Winchell
1961   Edith M. Coulter
1962   Frances Neel Cheney
1963   Mable Conat
1964   Ruth Walling
1965   Katharine G. Harris
1966   Frances B. Jenkins
1967   Louis Shores
1968   Thomas S. Shaw
1969   No award
1970   Theodore Besterman
1971   James Bennet Childs
1972   Thomas J. Galvin
1973   William A. Katz
1974   Florence E. Blakely
1975   Jean L. Connor
1976   John Neal Waddell
1977   Bohdan S. Wynar

Esther J. Piercy Award
AMERICAN LIBRARY ASSOCIATION
Resources and Technical Services Division, 50 E. Huron St., Chicago, Ill. 60611 (312/944-6780, Ext. 228)

The Esther J. Piercy Award is given for outstanding promise in the field of technical services by a librarian with no more than 10 years of professional experience. A jury annually selects the recipient of the citation which signifies this honor.

1969   Richard M. Dougherty, Research, teaching and administrative leadership
1970   John B. Corbin, Promise as an organizer, supervisor, consultant, author and editor
1971   John Phillip Immroth, Research, writing and teaching leadership
1972   Carol A. Nemeyer, *Scholarly Reprint Publishing in the United States*
1973   Glen A. Zimmerman, Library of Congress Cataloging in Publication (CIP) program
1974   No award
1975   John D. Byrum, Jr., Talent for understanding and developing cataloging rules

1976   Ruth L. Tighe, Leadership, innovation and expedition in bibliographic exchange
1977   No award

Herbert Putnam Honor Fund Award
AMERICAN LIBRARY ASSOCIATION
50 E. Huron St., Chicago, Ill. 60611 (312/944-6780)

The $500 Herbert Putnam Honor Fund Award is given approximately every five years to an American librarian as a grant-in-aid for travel, writing or other use that might improve his or her service to the library profession. The ALA Awards Committee selects the winner from nominations received.

1949   Carleton B. Joeckel
1954   Louis Round Wilson
1963   Mary V. Gaver
1972   Michael H. Harris
1975   Wayne A. Weigund

Ralph R. Shaw Award
AMERICAN LIBRARY ASSOCIATION
50 E. Huron St., Chicago, Ill. 60611 (312/944-6780)

The $500 Ralph R. Shaw Award for Library Literature is given to an American librarian for library literature published during the preceding three years. A jury of five appointed by the chairperson of the ALA Awards Committee makes the selection from nominations received.

1960   Marjorie Fiske Lowenthal, *Book Selection and Censorship*
1961   No award
1962   Sarah K. Vann, *Training for Librarianship Before 1923*
1963   Joseph L. Wheeler and Herbert Goldhor, *Practical Administration of Public Libraries*
1964   Edward G. Holley, *Charles Evans, American Bibliographer*
1965   Roberta Bowler, *Local Public Library Administration*
1966   Keyes DeWitt Metcalf, *Planning Academic and Research Library Buildings*
1967   No award
1968   Lester Asheim, *Librarianship in the Developing Countries*
1969   Ralph McCoy, *Freedom of the Press: An Annotated Bibliography*
1970   Lowell Martin, *Library Response to Urban Change*
1971   Irene Braden Hoadley, *The Undergraduate Library*
1972   No award
1973   No award
1974   Jesse H. Shera, *Foundations of Education for Librarianship*
1975   No award
1976   Herman Fussler, *Research Libraries and Technology*
1977   Kathleen Molz, *Federal Policy and Library Support*

Resources Scholarship Award
AMERICAN LIBRARY ASSOCIATION
Resources and Technical Services Division, 50 E. Huron St., Chicago, Ill. 60611 (312/944-6780, Ext. 228)

The Resources Scholarship Award, which carries a

$1,000 honorarium, is given for a monograph, published article or original paper on acquisitions pertaining to college and university libraries. A jury selects the winner.

1976 Hendrik Edelman, Carol Nemeyer and Sandra Paul, "The Library Market: A Special Publisher's Weekly Survey"

1977 Herbert White, "Publishers, Libraries and Costs of Journal Subscriptions in Times of Funding Retrenchment"

Trustee Citation

AMERICAN LIBRARY TRUSTEE ASSOCIATION
50 E. Huron St., Chicago, Ill. 60611 (312/944-6780)

The American Library Trustee Association administers the Trustee Citation, which is given annually by the ALA for distinguished service to library development on any level and involving libraries of any size. A five-member jury selects recipients from nominations by library boards, individual library trustees, station library extensions or various other organizations in the field.

1941 Rush Barton
     William Elder Marcus
1942 James Oliver Modisette
     Charles Whedbee
1943 Marian Doren Tomlinson
     Ora L. Wildermuth
1944 Lenore W. Smith
     B. F. Coen
1945 M. M. Harris
     Lucy Wilson Errett
1946 James J. Weadock
     Mrs. James E. Price
1947 Mary E. Frayser
     Thomas J. McKaig
1948 Emma V. Baldwin
     Thomas J. Porro
1949 Julia Brown Asplund
     Robert B. Tunstall
1950 Hasel M. Wills
     Anthony Joseph Cerrato
1951 Charles B. Farnsley
     Milton G. Farris
1952 A. J. Quigley
     Harold J. Bailey
1953 Jacob M. Lashley
     Frank A. Smith
1954 Mrs. Merlin M. Moore
     Joseph B. Fleming
1955 Mrs. George Rodney Wallace
     Ralph D. Remley
1956 Mrs. Otis G. Wilson
     Eugene A. Burdick
1957 J. N. Heiskell
     Stephen M. Pronko
1958 Mrs. J. Henry Mohr
     Cecil U. Edmonds
1959 Francis Bergan
     Alan Neil Schneider
1960 Mrs. Emil G. Bloedow
     Thomas Dreier
1961 Paul D. Brown
     Walter Varner, Jr.
1962 S. L. Townsend
     Mrs. Raymond A. Young

1963 Kenneth U. Blass
     John E. Fogarty
1964 Mrs. Weldon Lynch
     Mrs. Samuel Berg
1965 Mrs. Henry Steffens
     Jacob A. Meckstroth
1966 Mrs. Bruce "C'Ceal" Coombs
     Charles E. Reid
1967 Mrs. J. R. Sweasy
     James L. Love
1968 Raymond Holden
     John Bennett Shaw
1969 Rachel Gross
     Alex P. Allain
1970 George W. Coen
     John Veblen
1971 Jacqueline Enochs
     Jean Smith
1972 Story Birdseye
     Mrs. V. Kelsey Carlson
1973 Alice Ihrig
     Carroll K. Shakelford
1974 Eldred C. Wolzien
     R. A. Cox
1975 Marie Cole
     Dorothy E. Rosen
1976 Elizabeth F. Ruffner
     James A. Hess
1977 C. E. Campbell Beall
     Daniel W. Casey

SPECIAL CITATION:

1977 President Jimmy Carter

H.W. Wilson Co. Library Periodical Award

AMERICAN LIBRARY ASSOCIATION
50 E. Huron St., Chicago, Ill. 60611 (312/944-6780)

The $250 H.W. Wilson Co. Library Periodical Award is given annually to a periodical published by a local, state or regional library group in the U.S. or Canada which has made an outstanding contribution to librarianship. A jury selected by the chairperson of the ALA Awards Committee chooses the winner.

1961 *The California Librarian,* California Library Association, William R. Eshelman, Editor

1962 *North Country Libraries,* New Hampshire State Library and the Vermont Free Public Library Commission, Louise Hazelton, Editor

1963 *Bay State Librarian,* Massachusetts Library Association, John Berry, Editor

1964 *The California Librarian,* California Library Association, Miller Madden, Editor

1965 *PNLA Quarterly,* Pacific Northwest Library Association, Eli M. Oboler, Editor

1966 *Ohio Library Association Bulletin,* Gerald Shields, Editor

1967 *British Columbia Library Quarterly,* Alan Woodland, Editor

1968 *The California Librarian,* California Library Association, Richard D. Johnson, Editor

1969 *Missouri Library Association Quarterly,* Missouri Library Association, John Gordon Burke, Editor

1970 *Synergy,* sponsored by Bay Area Reference Center, San Francisco Public Library, Celeste West, Editor

1971 *Texas Library Journal,* Texas Library Association, Mary Pound, Editor

1972 *Synergy,* sponsored by Bay Area Reference Center, San Francisco Public Library, Celeste West, Editor

1973 *Illinois Libraries,* Illinois State Library, Springfield, Irma Bostian, Editor

1974 *Ohio Library Association Bulletin,* Robert F. Cayton, Editor

1975 *PNLA Quarterly,* Pacific Northwest Library Association, Richard Moore, Editor

1976 *Hennepin County Library Cataloging Bulletin,* Edina, Minn., Sanford Berman, Editor

1977 *Utah Libraries,* Blaine H. Hall, Editor

Humanities &

Social Sciences

Contents

Related Awards

Huxley Memorial Lecture and Medal
Curl Lecture
Henry Myers Lecture
Rivers Memorial Medal

ROYAL ANTHROPOLOGICAL INSTITUTE OF
GREAT BRITAIN AND IRELAND
56 Queen Anne St., London WI, England

The Huxley Memorial Lecture and Medal is the Institute's highest honor in the field. A special council selects the recipient of the annual medal. Part of the award is publication of the lecture.

1960 S. Lothrop
1961 A.E. Mourant
1962 A.D. Garrod
1963 E.E. Evans-Pritchard
1964 G.H.R. Von Konigswald
1965 C. Levi-Strauss
1966 J.E.S. Thompson
1967 S.L. Washburn
1968 G.H. Riviere
1969 I. Schapera
1970 C.D. Forde
1971 G.P. Murdock
1972 L.L. Cavilli-Sforza
1973 K. Wachsmann
1974 J.D. Clark
1975 G. Reichel-Dolmatoff
1976 M.N. Srinivas
1977 M. Fortes

The Curl Lecture consists of a fifty-guinea honorarium plus publication of the lecture, which is preferably in the fields of physical anthropology, archeology, material culture or linguistics. A council selects the winner of this biennial honor.

1963 D.F.B. Roberts
1965 Anthony Forge
1967 G. Ainsworth Harrison
1969 Peter Ucko
1971 Warwick Bray
1973 Caroline Humphrey
1975 A.J. Boyce
1977 Richard E. Leakey

The Henry Myers Lecture honors a noteworthy lecture on some aspect of the role of religion in society with publication. A council selects the winner of this biennial honor.

1945 A.R. Radcliffe-Brown
1948 Raymond Firth
1950 E.O. James
1952 E.D. Smith
1954 E.E. Evans-Pritchard
1956 Dorothy Emmett
1958 Isaac Schapera
1960 Meyer Fortes
1962 Claude Levi-Strauss
1964 Joseph Needham
1966 Edmund Leach
1968 Audrey Richards
1970 Louis Dumont
1972 Mary Douglas
1974 C. von Furer-Haimendorf
1976 Jean La Fontaine

The Rivers Memorial Medal is awarded annually for a recent body of published work on social, physical or cultural anthropology or archeology. A council selects the winner.

1924 A.C. Haddon
1925 C.G. Seligman
1926 Edward Westermarck
1927 Sir W. Baldwin Spencer
1928 Sidney H. Ray
1929 John Henry Hutton
1930 Bronislaw Malinowski
1931 E.W. Smith
1932 Melville William Seligman
1933 Brenda Zara Seligman
1934 Gertrude Caton-Thompson
1935 A.M. Hocart
1936 Peter H. Buck
1937 Edward Evan Evans-Pritchard
1938 Dorothy Ann Elizabeth Garrod
1939 Isaac Schapera
1940 Raymond Firth
1941 Diamond Jenness
1942 James Philip Mills
1943 Beatrice Mary Blackwood
1944 James Hornell
1945 J. Eric Thompson
1946 Ian J. Hogbin
1947 Meyer Fortes
1948 Verrier Elwin
1949 C. von Furer-Haimendorf
1950 S.F. Nadel
1951 R.F. Fortune
1952 L.S.B. Leakey
1953 Donald F. Thomson
1954 Max Gluckman
1955 M.N. Srinivas
1956 Daryll Forde
1957 Phyllis M. Kaberry
1958 E.R. Leach
1959 J.A. Barnes
1960 J.C. Mitchell
1961 Hilda Kuper
1962 H. Lehman
1963 Derek Stenning
1964 Adrian Mayer
1965 V. Turner
1966 Philip Gulliver
1967 Philip Mayer and N.A. Barnicot
1968 Eric Higgs and Mary Douglas
1969 J.S. Weiner
1970 Rodney Needham
1971 No award
1972 J. Waechter
1973 S.J. Tambiah
1974 D.F. Pocock
1975 J.R. Goody
1976 A. Strathern and M. Strathern
1977 Peter Ucko

Gold Medal
Olivia James Traveling Fellowship
Harriet Pomerance Fellowship

ARCHAEOLOGICAL INSTITUTE OF AMERICA
260 W. Broadway, New York, N.Y. 10013 (212/925-7333)

The Gold Medal for Distinguished Archaeological Achievement is presented annually to a member of the

Institute for field work, teaching, publication or a combination of these.

1965 Carl William Blegen, Professor Emeritus of Classical Archaeology, University of Cincinnati and excavator of Troy and the Palace of Nestor at Pylos
1965 Hetty Goldman, Professor Emeritus, Institute for Advanced Study in Princeton and pioneer woman excavator in Greece and Near East
1967 William Foxwell Albright, Professor Emeritus of Near Eastern Studies (Semantic Languages), Johns Hopkins University
1968 Gisela Marie Augusta Richter, scholar and curator
1969 Oscar Theodore Broncer, discoverer of the site of the Isthmian Games and the Sanctuary Poseidon at the Isthmus of Corinth
Rhys Carpenter, Professor Emeritus of Clasical Archaeology, Bryn Mawr College
William Bell Dinsmoor, author and past president of the Archaeological Institute of America
1970 George Emmanuel Mylonas, Washington University, director of archaeological excavation at Aghios, Kosmos, Eleusis and Mycenae
1971 Robert John Braidwood, archaeologist, anthropologist and author in Near Eastern prehistorical studies
1972 Homer Armstrong Thompson, expert on the topography and monuments of ancient Athens
1973 Gordon Randolph Wiley, New World archaeologist
1974 Margaret Bieber, authority on the archaeology of the Greek and Roman theater, ancient dress and the sculpture of the Hellenistic Age
1975 Eugene Vanderpool, American School of Classical Studies at Athens, authority on the antiquities and the topography of Greece
1976 Lucy Shoe Merritt, scholar, editor and teacher
1977 Edith Porada, Columbia University

The Olivia James Traveling Fellowship, carrying a maximum stipend of $7,000, is given each academic year for a proposed project or plan of study in Greece, the Aegean Islands, Sicily, southern Italy or Asia Minor for studies in classics, sculpture, architecture, archeology or history.

1975 Eric Hostetter
1976 Michal Eisman
 Trudy S. Kawami
1977 Patricia M. Bikai
 Ira S. Mark

The Harriet Pomerance Fellowship, carrying a $1,750 stipend, is given to a resident of the U.S. or Canada for an individual scholarly project relating to the Aegean Bronze Age archeology, preferably for travel to the Mediterranean to pursue the project.

1975 Livingston V. Watrous
 Robert R. Stieglitz
1976 Kenneth C. Gutwein
 Jeffrey S. Soles
1977 Halford W. Haskell
 Paul Yule

Fellow of the Athenaeum
THE ATHENAEUM OF PHILADELPHIA
219 S. Sixth St., Philadelphia, Pa. 19106 (215/WA5-2688)

The Fellow of the Athenaeum honor is bestowed annually for outstanding contribution to 19th-century stud-

ies. It consists of a scroll and lifetime membership in the Athenaeum.

1977 Henry Russell Hitchcock, Author, historian
 Nathaniel Burt, Author

Distinguished Service Award
AMERICAN ASSOCIATION OF CRIMINOLOGY
Box 1115, N. Marshfield, Mass. 02059 (617/837-0052)

The Distinguished Service Award is given annually according to a vote of the Committee on Credentials for outstanding contribution to the advancement in criminology, psychology and sociology.

1965 Chief Raymond G. Dehn, Law enforcement
1966 Jan S. Olbrycht, Forensic medicine
1970 Commissioner George Puig, Criminal identification
1971 Patrick B. Kelly, Criminal law
1972 J.H. Drose, Criminal sociology
1973 Edward Podolsky, Forensic medicine
1974 Bruce Harrison, Criminology
1975 Yvan Van Garsse, Criminalistics
1976 Harold L. Gluck, Criminal jurisprudence
1977 Judge Robert L. Pruett, Sr., Criminal jurisprudence

Edwin H. Sutherland Award
August Vollmer Award
AMERICAN SOCIETY OF CRIMINOLOGY
106 Human Development Bldg., University Park, Pa. 16802

The Edwin H. Sutherland Award, which consists of a silver plaque, is given annually to recognize outstanding contributions to research or theoretical work in criminology. The award may be for a single book or for a body of work on criminal or deviant behavior, the criminal justice system, corrections, law or justice.

1960 Thorsten Sellin, University of Pennsylvania
1961 Orlando Wilson, Chicago Police Superintendent; Professor Emeritus, University of California
1962 Negley Teeters, Temple University
1963 Herbert Wechsler, Columbia University Law School
 Walter Reckless, Ohio State University
1964 Hon J.C. McRuer, Chairman Royal Commission on Civil Rights; former Chief Justice of Ontario
1965 No award
1966 George Vold, University of Minnesota
1967 Donald R. Cressey, University of California/Santa Barbara
1968 Denis Szabo, University of Montreal
1969 Lloyd Ohlin, Harvard University Law School
1970 Alfred Lindesmith, University of Indiana
1971 Marshall Clinard, University of Wisconsin
1972 Leslie Wilkins, State University of New York at Albany
1973 Edwin Lemert, University of California
1974 Simon Dinitz, Ohio State University
1975 C. Ray Jeffery, Florida State
1976 Daniel Glaster, University of Southern California
1977 Solomon Kobrin, University of California/Los Angeles

The August Vollmer Award, which consists of a silver plaque, recognizes contributions to justice or to the control, treatment or prevention of criminal or deviant behavior. The award may be made for a single contribution or a series of contributions.

1960 **Marvin Wolfgang,** University of Pennsylvania
Paul Bohannon, Northwestern University
1961 **Sheldon and Eleanor Glueck,** Harvard University Law School
1962 **James Bennett,** Director, U.S. Bureau of Prisons
1963 **Austin MacCormick,** Executive Director, The Osborne Assn.
1964 **Hon J. Adrien Robert,** Director, Montreal Police Department; Chief, Quebec Provincial Police
1965 **No award**
1966 **Judge George Edwards,** former Justice, Supreme Court of Michigan; Police Commissioner of Detroit; Justice U.S. Circuit Court of Appeals
1967 **Howard Leary,** Police Commissioner of New York
1968 **Myrl Alexander,** Director, U.S. Bureau of Prisons
1969 **Hon, Joseph Tydings,** U.S. Senator, Maryland
1970 **Milton Rector,** Executive Director of the National Council on Crime and Delinquency
1971 **No award**
1972 **Jerome Skolnick,** University of California/Berkeley
1973 **E. Preston Sharpe,** General Secretary, American Correctional Assn.
1974 **Patrick Murphy,** President, Police Foundation
Sol Rubin, Counsel Emeritus, National Council on Crime and Delinquency
1975 **No award**
1976 **Patricia M. Wald,** Litigation Director, Mental Health Law Project, Washington, D.C.
1977 **Richard A. McGee,** President, American Justice Institute, Sacramento, Calif.

John Bates Clark Medal
Franci A. Walker Medal

AMERICAN ECONOMIC ASSOCIATION.
1313 21st Ave. S., Nashville, Tenn. 37212 (615/322-2595)

The John Bates Clark Medal, which is of bronze, is given every two years to an American economist 40 years of age or under who is a member of the Association for significant contributions to economic thought and knowledge.

1947 **Paul A. Samuelson**
1949 **Kenneth E. Boulding**
1951 **Milton Friedman**
1953 **No award**
1955 **James Tobin**
1957 **Kenneth J. Arrow**
1959 **Lawrence R. Klein**
1961 **Robert M. Solow**
1963 **Hendrik S. Houthakker**
1965 **Zvi Griliches**
1967 **Gary S. Becker**
1969 **Marc Leon Nerlove**
1971 **Dale W. Jorgenson**
1973 **Franklin M. Fisher**
1975 **Daniel McFadden**
1977 **Martin Feldstein**

The Franci A. Walker Medal, which is of silver, is awarded every five years for great contributions made to economics in the career of a living American member of the Association.

1947 **Wesley C. Mitchell**
1952 **John Maurice Clark**

1957 **Frank H. Knight**
1962 **Jacob Viner**
1967 **Alvin H. Hansen**
1972 **Theodore W. Schultz**
1977 **Simon Kuznets**

Nobel Prize for Economics

NOBEL FOUNDATION
Nobel House, Sturegatan 14, 11436-Stockholm, Sweden

One of six Nobel Prizes given annually, the Nobel Prize for Economics is generally recognized as the highest honor which can be bestowed on an economist. The award, which consists of a gold medal, diploma and large honorarium, is given at a ceremony on December 10 of each year at Stockholm's City Hall. The award itself is presented and administered by the Royal Swedish Academy of Sciences. The amount of the honorarium fluctuates; in 1977, it was approximately $145,000.

1969 **Ragnar Frisch,** (Norway), Developed mathematical models for analyzing economic activity.
Jan Tinbergen, (Netherlands), Developed mathematical models for analyzing economic activity.
1970 **Paul A. Samuelson,** (U.S.A.), Raised the level of scientific analysis in economic theory.
1971 **Simon Kuznets,** (U.S.A.), Worked out methods to determine a country's gross national product.
1972 **Kenneth J. Arrow,** (U.S.A.), Pioneered theory of general economic equilibrium.
Sir John R. Hicks, (Great Britain), Pioneered theory of general economic equilibrium.
1973 **Wassily Leontif,** (U.S.A.; born in Russia), Developed the "input-output" method of economic analysis used by most industrial nations.
1974 **Gunnar Myrdal,** (Sweden), Pioneered the theory of money and economic fluctuations.
Friedrich A. von Hayek, (Austrian), Pioneered the theory of money and economic fluctuations.
1975 **Leonid V. Kantorovich,** (Russian), Contributed to the theory of the optimum allocation of resources.
Tjalling C. Koopmans, (U.S.A., born in the Netherlands),Contributed to the theory of the optimum allocation of resources.
1976 **Milton Friedman,** (U.S.A.), Work in consumption analysis, monetary history and theory, and demonstration of the complexity of stabilization policy.
1977 **Bertil Ohlin,** (Sweden) and **James E. Meade** (Great Britain), Contributed to theory of international trade and capital movement

Herbert Baxter Adams Prize
George Louis Beer Prize
Albert Beveridge Award
Albert B. Corey Prize
John H. Dunning Prize
John K. Fairbank Prize
Leo Gershoy Award
Clarence H. Haring Prize
Howard R. Marraro Prize

Robert Livingston Schuyler Prize
Watamull Prize

AMERICAN HISTORICAL ASSOCIATION
400 A St. SE, Washington, D.C. 20003 (202/544-2422)

The $300 Herbert Baxter Adams Prize now annually honors an American citizen's book on European history. It is generally the author's first substantial published work. The winners of this and all other American Historical Association prizes are selected by expert committees in the field.

1938 Arthur McCandless Wilson, *French Foreign Policy During the Administration of Cardinal Fleury, 1726-1743*
1940 John Shelton Curtiss, *Church and State in Russia, 1900-1917*
1942 E. Harris Harbison, *Rival Ambassadors at the Court of Queen Mary*
1944 R. H. Fisher, *The Russian Fur Trade, 1550-1700*
1946 A. W. Salomone, *Italian Democracy in the Making*
1948 Raymond de Roover, *The Medici Bank: Its Organization, Management, Operations, and Decline*
1950 Hans W. Gatzke, *Germany's Drive to the West*
1952 Arthur J. May, *The Hapsburg Monarchy, 1867-1914*
1954 W. C. Richardson, *Tudor Chamber Administration, 1485-1547*
1956 Gordon Craig, *Politics of the Prussian Army, 1640-1945*
1958 Arthur Wilson, *Diderot: The Testing Years*
1960 Caroline Robbins, *The Eighteenth Century Commonwealthman*
1962 Jerome Blum, *Lord and Peasant in Russia*
1964 Archibald S. Foord, *His Majesty's Opposition, 1714-1830*
1966 Gabriel Jackson, *The Spanish Republic and the Civil War, 1931-39*
1968 Arno J. Mayer, *Politics and Diplomacy of Peacemaking: Containment and Counter-Revolution at Versailles 1918-1919*
1970 John P. McKay, *Pioneers for Profit: Foreign Entrepreneurship and Russian Industrialization, 1885-1913*
1971 Edward E. Malefakis, *Agrarian Reform and Peasant Revolution in Spain, Origins of the Civil War*
1972 Richard Hellie, *Enserfment and Military Change in Moscovy*
1973 Martin Jay, *The Dialectical Imagination: A History of the Frankfurt School and the Institute for Social Research, 1923-1950*
1974 Joan Wallach Scott, *The Glassworkers of Carmaux: French Craftsmen and Political Action in a Nineteenth-Century City*
1975 James S. Donnelly, Jr., *The Land and the People of Nineteenth-Century Cork*
1976 Frederick H. Russell, *The Just War in the Middle Ages*
1977 Charles S. Maier, *Recasting Bourgeois Europe: Stabilization in France, Germany and Italy in the Decade After World War 1*

The $300 George Louis Beer Prize annually honors the best book by an American on European history since 1895.

1930 Bernadotte Everly Schmitt, *The Coming of the War*
1931 Oran James Hale, *Germany and the Diplomatic Revolution: A Study in Diplomacy and the Press, 1904-1906*
1932 Oswald H. Wedel, *Austro-German Diplomatic Relations, 1908-1914*
1933 Robert Thomas Pollard, *China's Foreign Relations, 1917-1931*
1934 Ross J. S. Hoffman, *Great Britain and the German Trade Rivalry, 1875-1914*
1935 No award
1936 No award
1937 Charles Wesley Porter, *The Career of Theophile Delasse*
1938 Rene Albrecht-Carrie, *Italy at the Paris Peace Conference*
1939 Pauline Relyea Anderson, *Background of Anti-English Feeling in Germany, 1890-1902*
1940 Richard Heathcote Heindel, *The American Impact on Great Britain, 1898-1914*
1941 Arthur J. Marder, *The Anatomy of British Sea Power*
1942 No award
1943 Arthur Norton Cook, *British Enterprise in Nigeria*
1944-51 No awards
1952 Robert H. Ferrell, *Peace in Their Time: The Origins of the Kellogg-Briand Pact*
1953 Russell Fifield, *Woodrow Wilson and the Far East*
1954 Wayne S. Vucinich, *Serbia Between East and West: The Events of 1903-1908*
1955 Richard Pipes, *The Formation of the Soviet Union*
1956 Henry Cord Meyer, *Mitteleuropa in German Thought and Action, 1815-1945*
1957 Alexander Dallin, *German Rule in Russia, 1941-1945*
1958 Vincent Marmety, *The United States and East Central Europe*
1959 Ernest R. May, *The World War and American Isolation 1914-17*
1960 Rudolph Binion, *Defeated Leaders: The Political Fate of Caillaux, Jouvenel and Tardieu*
1961 Charles F. Delzell, *Mussolini's Enemies: The Italian Anti-Fascist Resistance*
1962 Piotr S. Wandycz, *France and Her Eastern Allies, 1919-1925*
1963 Edward W. Bennett, *Germany and the Diplomacy of the Financial Crisis, 1931*
Hans A. Schmitt, *The Path to European Union*
1964 Ivo J. Lederer, *Yugoslavia at the Paris Peace Conference*
Harold I. Nelson, *Land and Power: British and Allied Policy on Germany's Frontiers, 1916-1919*
1965 Paul Spencer Guinn, Jr., *British Strategy and Politics 1914 to 1918*
1966 No award
1967 George A. Brinkley, *The Volunteer Army and the Revolution in South Russia*
Robert Wohl, *French Communism in the Making*
1968 No award
1969 Richard H. Ullman, *Britain and the Russian Civil War, November 1918-February 1920*
1970 Samuel R. Williamson, Jr., *The Politics of Grand Strategy: Britain and France Prepare for War, 1904-1914*
1971 Gerhard L. Weinberg, *The Foreign Policy of Hitler's Germany, Diplomatic Revolution in Europe, 1933-36*
1972 Jon Jacobson, *Locarno Diplomacy: Germany and the West*
1973 No award
1974 No award
1975 No award
1976 Charles S. Maier, *Recasting Bourgeois Europe: Stabilization in France, Germany and Italy in the Decade after World War I*
1977 Stephen A. Schuker, *The End of French Predominence in Europe: The Financial Crisis of 1924 and the Adoption of the Dawes Plan*

The $5,000 Albert Beveridge Award is given annually for the best book in English on the history of the Western Hemisphere from 1492 to the present.

1939 **John T. Horton,** *James Kent: A Study in Conservatism*

1941 **Charles A. Barker,** *The Background of the Revolution in Maryland*

1943 **Harold Whitman Bradley,** *The American Frontier in Hawaii: The Pioneers, 1789-1843*

1945 **John Richard Alden,** *John Stuart and the Southern Colonial Frontier*

1946 **Arthur E. Bestor,** *Backwoods Utopias: The Sectarian and Owenite Phases of Communitarian Socialism in America, 1663-1829*

1947 **Lewis Hanke,** *The Struggle for Justice in the Spanish Conquest of America*

1948 **Donald Fleming,** *John William Draper and the Religion of Science*

1949 **Reynold M. Wik,** *Steam Power on the American Farm: A Chapter in Agricultural History, 1850-1920*

1950 **Glyndon G. Van Deusen,** *Horace Greeley: Nineteenth Century Crusader*

1951 **Robert Twymann,** *History of Marshall Field and Co., 1852-1906*

1952 **Clarence Versteeg,** *Robert Morris, Revolutionary Financier*

1953 **George R. Bentley,** *A History of the Freedman's Bureau*

1954 **Arthur M. Johnson,** *The Development of American Petroleum Pipelines: A Study in Enterprise and Public Policy*

1955 **Ian C. C. Graham,** *Colonists from Scotland: Emigration to North America, 1707-1783*

1956 **Paul Schroeder,** *The Axis Alliance and Japanese-American Relations, 1941*

1957 **David Fletcher,** *Rails, Mines, and Progress: Seven American Promoters in Mexico*

1958 **Paul Conkin,** *Tomorrow a New World: The New Deal Community Program*

1959 **Arnold M. Paul,** *Free Conservative Crisis and the Rule of Law: Attitudes of Bar and Bench, 1887-1895*

1960 **C. Clarence Clendenen,** *The United States and Pancho Villa*
   Nathan Miller, *The Enterprise of A Free People: Canals and the Canal Fund in the New York Economy, 1792-1838*

1961 **Calvin DeArmond Davis,** *The United States and the First Hague Peace Conference*

1962 **Walter LaFeber,** *The New Empire: An Interpretation of American Expansion, 1860-1898*

1963 **No award**

1964 **Linda Grant De Pauw,** *The Eleventh Pillar: New York State and the Federal Constitution*

1965 **Daniel M. Fox,** *The Discovery of Abundance*

1966 **Herman Belz,** *Reconstructing the Union: Conflict of Theory and Policy during the Civil War*

1967 **No award**

1968 **Michael Paul Rogin,** *The Intellectuals and McCarthy: The Radical Specter*

1969 **Sam Bass Warner, Jr.,** *The Private City: Philadelphia in Three Periods of Its Growth*

1970 **Sheldon Hackney,** *Populism to Progressivism in Alabama*
   Leonard L. Richards, *Gentlemen of Property and Standing: Anti-Abolition Mobs in Jacksonian America*

1971 **Carl N. Degler,** *Neither Black nor White: Slavery and Race Relations in Brazil and the United States*
   David J. Rothman, *The Discovery of the Asylum: Social Order and Disorder in the New Republic*

1972 **James T. Lemon,** *The Best Poor Man's Country*

1973 **Richard L. Slotkin,** *Regeneration through Violence: The Mythology of the American Frontier, 1600-1850*

1974 **Peter H. Wood,** *Black Majority*

1975 **David Brion Davis,** *The Problem of Slavery in the Age of Revolution, 1700-1823*

1976 **Edmund S. Morgan,** *American Slavery-American Freedom: The Ordeal of Colonial Virginia*

1977 **Henry F. May,** *The Enlightenment in America*

The $1,000 Albert B. Corey Prize in Canadian-American Relations, awarded jointly by the American and Canadian Historical Associations, biennially recognizes the best book on the history of Canadian-American relations or the history of the two countries.

1967 **Gustave Lanctot,** *Canada and the American Revolution*

1969 **Kenneth Bourne,** *Britain and the Balance of Power in North America, 1815-1908*

1971 **No award**

1972 **Charles P. Stacey,** *Arms, Men and Governments: The War Policies of Canada 1939-45*

1974 **Lester B. Pearson,** *Mike, The Memoirs of the Right Honourable Lester B. Pearson*

1976 **No award**

The $300 John H. Dunning Prize is given biennially for the best book on American history.

1929 **Haywood J. Pearce, Jr.,** *Benjamin H. Hill: Secession and Reconstruction*

1931 **Francis B. Simkins and R. H. Woody,** *South Carolina During Reconstruction*

1933 **Amos A. Ettinger,** *The Mission to Spain of Pierre Soule*

1935 **Angie Debo,** *The Rise and Fall of the Choctaw Republic*

1937 **No award**

1938 **Robert A. East,** *Business Enterprise in the American Revolutionary Era*

1940 **Richard W. Leopold,** *Robert Dale Owen*

1942 **Oscar Handlin,** *Boston's Immigrants*

1944 **Elting E. Morison,** *Admiral Sims and the Modern American Navy*

1946 **David Ellis,** *Landlords and Farmers in the Hudson Mohawk Region*

1948 **William E. Livezey,** *Mahan and Seapower*

1950 **Henry Nash Smith,** *Virgin Land: The American West as Symbol and Myth*

1952 **Louis C. and Beatrice J. Hunter,** *Steamboats on the Western Rivers: An Economic and Technological History*

1954 **Gerald Carson,** *The Old Country Store*

1956 **John Higham,** *Strangers in the Land: Patterns of American Nativitism*

1958 **Marvin Meyers,** *The Jacksonian Persuasion*

1960 **Eric McKitrick,** *Andrew Johnson and Reconstruction*

1962 **E. James Ferguson,** *The Power of the Purse: A History of American Public Finance, 1776-1790*

1964 **John H. and LaWanda Cox,** *Politics, Principle, and Prejudice, 1865-1866*

1966 **John Willard Shy,** *Toward Lexington: The Role of the British Army in the American Revolution*

1968 **Robert L. Beisner,** *Twelve Against Empire: The Anti-Imperialists, 1898-1900*

1970 **Gordon S. Wood,** *The Creation of the American Republic, 1776-1787*

1972 **John P. Diggins,** *Mussolini and Fascism: The View from America*
1974 **Paul Boyer and Stephen Nissenbaum,** *Salem Possessed: The Social Origins of Witchcraft*
1976 **Thomas S. Hines,** *Burnham of Chicago: Architect and Planner*

The $500 John K. Fairbank Prize in East Asian History is awarded every two years for a noteworthy book on the history of China, Chinese Central Asia, Japan, Korea, Manchuria, Mongolia or Vietnam from 1800 to the present.

1969 **Tetsuo Najita,** *Hara Kei in the Politics of Compromise, 1905-1915*
     Harold Schiffrin, *Sun Yat-sen and the Origins of the Chinese Revolution*
1971 **Jerome B. Greider,** *Hu Shih and the Chinese Renaissance: Liberalism in the Chinese Revolution, 1917-1937*
1973 **W. G. Beasley,** *The Meiji Restoration*
1975 **Jen Yu-wen,** *The Taiping Revolutionary Movement*
1977 **Gail Lee Bernstein,** *Japanese Marxist: A Portrait of Kawakami Hajine, 1879-1946*

The $1,000 Leo Gershoy Award is given every two years for an outstanding book on 17th- and 18th-century European history published in English.

1977 **Simon Chama,** *Patriots and Liberators: Revolution in the Netherlands, 1790-1813*

The $500 Clarence H. Haring Prize is given every five years for the best book on Latin American history written during the previous half-decade.

1966 **Daniel Cosio Villegas,** *Historia Moderna de Mexico*
1971 **Luis Gonzalez,** *Pueblo en vilo*
1976 **Tulio Halperin-Donghi,** *Politics, Economics and Society in Argentina in the Revolutionary Period*

The $500 Howard R. Marraro Prize is awarded annually for the best book or article on Italian cultural history or American-Italian relations written by a resident of the United States or Canada.

1973 **Edward R. Tannenbaum,** *The Fascist Experience: Italian Society and Culture, 1922-1945*
1974 **Benjamin F. Brown,** *The Complete Works of Sidney Sonnino*
1975 **Robert Brentano,** *Rome before Avignon: A Social History of Thirteenth Century Rome*
1976 **Richard A. Webster,** *Industrial Imperialism in Italy, 1908-1915*
1977 **Gene A. Brucker,** *The Civic World of Early Renaissance Florence*

The $500 Robert Livingston Schuyler Prize is given every five years for the most outstanding book on British history (modern, Commonwealth or Imperial) written by an American citizen. This award may be applied for.

1951 **Howard Robinson,** *Britain's Post Office*
1956 **David Harris Willson,** *King James VI and I*
1961 **Mark H. Curtis,** *Oxford and Cambridge in Transition, 1558-1642*
1966 **Philip D. Curtin,** *The Image of Africa: British Ideas and Action, 1780-1850*
1971 **W. K. Jordan,** *Edward VI: The Young King* and *The Threshold of Power,* 2 vols.
1976 **John Clive,** *Macaulay: The Shaping of the Historian*

The $1,000 Watamull Prize is awarded every two years

for the best work(s) on the history of India published in the United States.

1945 **Ernest J. H. Mackay,** *Chanhu-Daro Excavations, 1935-36*
1947 **No award**
1949 **Gertrude Emerson Sen,** *The Pageant of India History*
     Holden Furber, *John Company at Work*
1951 **T. Walter Wallbank,** *India in the New Era*
     Louis Fischer, *The Life of Mahatma Gandhi*
1954 **D. Mackenzie Brown,** *The White Umbrella: Indian Political Thought from Manu to Gandhi*
     W. Norman Brown, *The United States and India and Pakistan*
1956 **No award**
1958 **William de Bary, ed.,** *Sources of the Indian Tradition*
1960 **Michael Brecher,** *Nehru: A Political Biography*
1962 **George D. Bearce,** *British Attitudes Toward India, 1784-1858*
     Stanley A. Wolpert, *Tilak and Gokhale: Revolution and Reform in the Making of Modern India*
1964 **Charles A. Drekmeier,** *Kingship and Community in Early India*
     Charles H. Heimsath, *Indian Nationalism and Hindu Social Reform*
1966 **B. R. Nayar,** *Minority Politics in the Punjab*
     Thomas R. Metcalf, *The Aftermath of Revolt: India, 1857-1870*
1968 **John Broomfield,** *Elite Conflict in a Plural Society: Twentieth Century Bengal*
     Myron Weiner, *Party Building in a New Nation*
1970 **Stephen N. Hay,** *Asian Ideas of East and West: Tagore and His Critics in Japan, China, and India*
     David Kopt, *British Orientalism and the Bengal Renaissance: The Dynamics of Indian Modernization, 1773-1835*
     Eugene F. Irschick, *Politics and Social Conflict in South India: The Non-Brahman Movement and Tamil Separatism, 1916-1929*
1972 **Elizabeth Whitcombe,** *Agrarian Conditions in Northern India, Vol. 1: The United Provinces Under British Rule, 1860-1900*
1974 **Leonard A. Gordon,** *Bengal: The Nationalist Movement, 1876-1940*
1976 **Michael Pearson,** *Merchants and Rulers in Gujarat: The Response to the Portuguese in the Sixteenth Century*

Allan Nevins Award
Francis Parkman Award

SOCIETY OF AMERICAN HISTORIANS
610 Fayerweather Hall, Columbia University, New York, N.Y. 10027 (212/280-3568)

The $1,000 Allan Nevins Award goes annually for the best doctoral dissertation completed during the previous year in American history, which exhibits scholarly distinction and literary grace. The winner is selected by a panel of judges from entries submitted by college and university history departments.

1960 **Waldo H. Heinrichs** (Harvard University), "American Ambassador: Joseph C. Grew and the Development of the United States Diplomatic Tradition"
1961 **John L. Thomas** (Brown University), "The Liberator: William Lloyd Garrison"
1962 **Willie Lee Rose** (Johns Hopkins University), "Re-

hearsal for Reconstruction: The Port Royal Experiment"
1963 **Joanne L. Neel** (Bryn Mawr College), "Phineas Bond: A Study in Anglo American Relations, 1786-1812"
1964 **William W. Freehling** (University of California/-Berkeley), "Prelude to Conflict: The Nullification Controversy in South Carolina, 1816-1836"
1965 **Robert L. Beisner** (University of Chicago), "Twelve Against the Empire: The Anti-Imperialists, 1898-1900"
1966 **Alan Lawson** (University of Michigan), "The Failure of Independent Liberalism"
1967 **Jerome Sternstein** (Brown University), "Nelson Aldrich, The Early Years"
1968 **Steven A. Channing** (University of North Carolina), "Crisis of Fear"
1969 **Mary Beth Norton** (Harvard University), "The British-Americans"
1970 **Edward H. McKinley** (University of Wisconsin), "The Lure of Africa: The American Interest in Tropical Africa, 1919-1939"
1971 **Heath Twitchell, Jr.** (American University), "The Biography of General Henry T. Allen"
1972 **George Bernard Forgie** (Stanford University), "Father Past and Child Nation: The Romantic Imagination and the Origins of the American Civil War"
1973 **James L. Roark** (Stanford University), "Masters Without Slaves: Southern Planters in the Civil War and Reconstruction"
1974 **Gary May** (University of California/Los Angeles), "The China Service of John Carter Vincent, 1924-1953"
1975 **Robert Davidoff** (Cornell University), "The Education of Edmund Randolph"
1976 **John McCardell** (Harvard University), "The Idea of a Southern Nation"
1977 **Mark Schwen,** (Stanford University), "The Making of a Modern Consciousness: A Study of Henry Adams and William James"

The $500 Francis Parkman Award is given annually for the book published in American history which best exhibits scholarly merit and literary grace. A panel of judges selects the winner, who also receives a bronze medal.

1956 **George F. Kennan,** *Russia Leaves the War*
1957 **Arthur M. Schlesinger, Jr.,** *The Crisis of the Old Order, 1919-1933*
1958 **Ernest Samuels,** *Henry Adams: The Middle Years, 1877-1891*
1959 **Matthew Josephson,** *Edison: A Biography*
1960 **Elting E. Morison,** *Turmoil and Tradition: A Study in the Life and Times of Henry L. Stimson*
1961 **Leon Wolff,** *Little Brown Brother: How the United States Purchased and Pacified the Philippine Islands at the Century's Turn*
1962 **James Thomas Flexner,** *That Wilder Image: The Painting of America's Native School from Thomas Cole to Winslow Homer*
1963 **William E. Leuchtenberg,** *Franklin D. Roosevelt and the New Deal, 1932-1940*
1964 **Willie Lee Rose,** *Rehearsal for Reconstruction: The Port Royal Experiment*
1965 **Daniel J. Boorstin,** *The Americans: The National Experience*
1966 **William H. Goetzmann,** *Exploration and Empire*
1967 **No award**
1968 **Winthrop D. Jordan,** *White Over Black: American Attitudes Toward the Negro, 1550-1812*

1969 **Theodore A. Wilson,** *The First Summit: Roosevelt and Churchill at Placentia Bay, 1941*
1970 **James MacGregor Burns,** *Roosevelt: The Soldier of Freedom, 1940-1945*
1971 **Joseph P. Lash,** *Eleanor and Franklin*
1972 **Kenneth S. Davis,** *F.D.R.: The Beckoning of Destiny, 1882-1928*
1973 **Robert W. Johannsen,** *Stephen A. Douglas*
1974 **Robert A. Caro,** *The Power Broker: Robert Moses and the Fall of New York*
1975 **Edmund S. Morgan,** *American Slavery, American Freedom*
1976 **Irving Howe,** *The World of Our Fathers*
1977 **David McCullogh,** *The Path Between the Seas*

Stuart Bernath Book Prize
Stuart Bernath Article Prize
Stuart Bernath Lecture Prize
SOCIETY FOR HISTORIANS OF AMERICAN FOREIGN RELATIONS
c/o University of Akron, Dept. of History, Akron, Ohio 44325
(216/375-7008)

The Stuart Bernath Book Prize, which carries a $500 honorarium, is awarded annually for an author's first or second book published on an aspect of American foreign relations. Copies of books entered are submitted to a special committee for review and selection

1972 **Joan Hoff Wilson,** *American Business and Foreign Policy, 1920-1933*
1972 **Kenneth E. Shewmaker,** *American and Chinese Communists, 1927-1945.*
1973 **John Gaddis,** *The United States and the Origins of the Cold War, 1941-1947*
1974 **Michael H. Hunt,** *Frontier Defense and the Open Door: Manchuria and Chinese-American Relations, 1895-1911*
1975 **Frank D. McCann, Jr.,** *The Brazilian-American Alliance, 1937-1945*
1975 **Stephen E. Pelz,** *Race to Pearl Harbor: The Failure of the Second London Naval Conference and the Onset of World War II*
1976 **Martin Sherwin,** *A World Destroyed: The Atomic Bomb and the Grand Alliance*
1977 **Roger V. Dingman,** *Power in the Pacific: The Origins of Naval Arms Limitations, 1914-1922*

The $200 Stuart L. Bernath Article Prize is awarded annually for a published article, one of the author's first seven published scholarly works, on a topic in American foreign relations. A special committee of the Society selects the winner.

1977 **John Stagg** (University of Auckland, New Zealand), "James Madison and the 'Malcontents': The Political Origins of the War of 1812"

The Stuart L. Bernath Lecture Prize, which carries a $300 honorarium, recognizes scholars under 45 years of age for excellence in teaching and research. A special committee of the Society selects the winner.

1977 **Joan Hoff Wilson,** "Foreign Policy Trends Since the 1920s"

John Gilmary Shea Prize

AMERICAN CATHOLIC HISTORICAL
ASSOCIATION
The Catholic University of America, Washington, D.C. 20064
(202/635-5079)

The John Gilmary Shea Prize, which carries a $300 honorarium, is given annually to honor an outstanding book on Catholic history written by an American or Canadian citizen or resident. Books may be entered for consideration by a jury, which consists of Association officials plus three historians specializing in different fields of history.

1946 **Carlton J. H. Hayes,** *Wartime Mission in Spain*
1947 No award
1948 No award
1949 No award
1950 **John H. Kennedy,** *Jesuit and Savage in New France*
1951 **George Pare,** *The Catholic Church in Detroit, 1701-1888*
1952 No award
1953 No award
1954 **Philip Hughes,** *The Reformation in England*
1955 **Annabelle M. Melville,** *John Carroll of Baltimore*
1956 **John Tracy Ellis,** *American Catholicism*
1957 **Thomas T. McAvoy, C.S.C.,** *The Great Crisis in American Catholic History, 1895-1900*
1958 **John M. Daley, S.J.,** *Georgetown University: Origin and Early Years*
1959 **Robert A. Graham, S.J.,** *Vatican Diplomacy: A Study of Church and State on the International Plane*
1960 **Maynard J. Geiger, O.F.M.,** *The Life and Times of Junipero Serra*
1961 **John Courtney Murray, S.J.,** *We Hold These Truths: Catholic Reflections on the American Proposition*
1962 **Francis Dvornik,** *The Slavs in European History and Civilization*
1963 **Oscar Halecki,** *The Millennium of Europe*
1964 **Helen C. White,** *Tudor Books of Saints and Martyrs*
1965 **John T. Noonan, Jr.,** *Contraception: A History of Its Treatment by the Catholic Theologians and Canonists*
1966 **Robert Ignatius Burns, S.J.,** *The Jesuits and the Indian Wars of the Northwest*
1967 **Robert Ignatius Burns, S.J.,** *The Crusader Kingdom of Valencia: Reconstruction on a Thirteenth-Century Frontier*
1968 **Edward Surtz, S.J.,** *The Works and Days of John Fisher, 1469-1535, Bishop of Rochester, in the English Renaissance and the Reformation*
1969 **Robert Brentano,** *Two Churches: England and Italy in the Thirteenth Century*
1970 **David M. Kennedy,** *Birth Control in America: The Career of Margaret Sanger*
1971 **Jaroslav Pelikan,** *The Emergence of the Catholic Tradition (100-600)*
1972 **John T. Noonan, Jr.,** *Power to Dissolve: Lawyers and Marriages in the Courts of the Roman Curia*
1973 **Robert E. Quirk,** *The Mexican Revolution and the Catholic Church, 1910-1929*
1974 **Thomas W. Spalding,** *Martin John Spalding, American Churchman*
1975 **Jay P. Dolan,** *The Immigrant Church: New York's Irish and German Catholics, 1815-1865*
1976 **Emmett Larkin,** *The Roman Catholic Church and the Creation of the Modern Irish State, 1978-1886*
1977 **Timothy Tackett,** *Priest and Parish in 18th Century France*

Lee Max Friedman Award

AMERICAN JEWISH HISTORICAL SOCIETY
2 Thornton Rd., Waltham, Mass. 02154 (617/891-8110)

The Lee Max Friedman Award Medal, which is of gold, annually honors distinguished service and contributions to the field of American Jewish history. A committee comprised of previous medal recipients and the executive committee of the Society selects the winner.

1960 **Isidore Solomon Meyer**
1961 **Jacob Rader Marcus**
1962 **David de Sola Pool**
1963 **Salo Wittmayer Baron**
1964 **Bertram Wallace Korn**
1966 **Maurice Jacobs**
1967 **Abram Kanof**
1968 **Leon Jacob Obermayer**
1970 **Philip David Sang**
1974 **Abram Vossen Goodman**
1975 **Oscar I. Janowsky**
1976 **Abraham J. Karp**
1977 **Abram L. Sachar**

Howard R. Marraro Prize

MODERN LANGUAGE ASSOCIATION
62 Fifth Ave., New York, N.Y. 10011 (212/741-7854)

The $750 Howard R. Marraro Prize is given for outstanding achievement in Italian studies to an MLA member for scholarly study in Italian Literature or comparative literature involving Italian. It had been an annual honor through 1976, but it will be given every two years in the future. Members submit nominations which are voted on by the Howard R. Marraro Prize Selection Committee.

1973 **Bernard Weinberg,** *Trattati di poetica e retorica del Cinquecento*
1974 **Thomas G. Bergin,** Lifetime achievement
1975 **Beatrice Corrigan,** Lifetime achievement
1976 **Joseph G. Fucilla,** Lifetime achievement
1977 No award

Pitirim A. Sorokin Award
MacIver Award
Dubois-Johnson-Frazier Award
Stouffer Award

AMERICAN SOCIOLOGICAL ASSOCIATION
1722 N St. NW, Washington, D.C. 20036 (202/833-3410)

The $500 Pitirim A. Sorokin Award is given annually to an Association member to recognize a published piece which contributed "to an outstanding degree" to progress in sociology. Nominations may be made to the Sorokin Awards Committee, which chooses the recipient.

1968 **Peter Blau, Otis D. Duncan and Andrea Tyree,** *The American Occupational Structure*
1969 **William A. Gamson,** *Power and Discontent*
1970 **Arthur L. Stinchcombe,** *Constructing Social Theories*

1971   **Robert W. Friedrichs,** *A Sociology of Sociology*
       Harrison C. White, *Chains of Opportunity: Systems Models of Mobility in Organization*
1972   **Eliot Friedson,** *Profession of Medicine: A Study of the Sociology of Applied Knowledge*
1973   **No award**
1974   **Clifford Geerts,** *The Interpretation of Cultures*
       Christopher Jenks, *Inequality*
1975   **Immanuel Wallerstein,** *The Modern World System*
1976   **Robert Bellah,** *The Broken Covenant: American Civil Religion in Time of Trial*
       Jeffrey Paige, *Agrarian Revolution: Social Movements and Export Agriculture in the Underdeveloped World*
1977   **Kai T. Erikson,** *Everything in Its Path*
       Perry Anderson, *Considerations on Western Marxism*

The MacIver Award, honoring publications prior to the establishment of the Sorokin Award, is no longer given.

1956   **E. Franklin Frazier,** *The Black Bourgeoisie*
1958   **Reinhard Bendix,** *Work and Authority in Industry*
1959   **August B. Hollingshead and Frederick C. Redlich,** *Social Class and Mental Illness: A Community Study*
1960   **No award**
1961   **Erving Goffman,** *The Presentation of Self in Everyday Life*
1962   **Seymour Martin Lipset,** *Political Man: The Social Bases of Politics*
1963   **Wilbert E. Moore,** *The Conduct of the Corporation*
1964   **Shmuel N. Eisenstadt,** *The Political Systems of Empires*
1965   **William J. Goode,** *World Revolution and Family Patterns*
1966   **John Porter,** *The Vertical Mosaic: An Analysis of Social Class and Power in Canada*
1967   **Kai T. Erikson,** *Wayward Puritan*
1968   **Barrington Moore, Jr.,** *Social Origins of Dictatorship and Democracy*

The Dubois-Johnson-Frazier Award, which carries a $500 cash prize, biennially honors a member of the Association for development of scholarly efforts. When the award is made to an institution, a commemorative plaque is also given. The Dubois-Johnson-Frazier Award Committee selects the recipient

1971   **Oliver Cromwell Cox**
1973   **St. Clair Drake**
1976   **Hylan Garnett Lewis**

The Stouffer Award, which carries a $500 honorarium, is given annually for a work or a series of works published during the previous five years which notably advanced the methodology of sociological research. The Stouffer Award Committee selects the winner.

1973   **Hubert M. Blalock, Jr.**
1974   **O.C. Duncan**
       Leo A. Goodman
1975   **James S. Coleman**
       Harrison C. White
1976   **No award**
1977   **Otis Dudley Duncan**
Special Award
1973   **Paul F. Lazarsfeld**

Louis I. Dublin Award
AMERICAN ASSOCIATION OF SUICIDOLOGY
Box 3267, Houstonm Tex. 77001 (713/644-7911)

The recipient of the Louis I. Dublin Award receives a plaque in recognition of contributions to the field of suicidology and suicide prevention.

1971   **Karl Menninger**
1972   **Edwin Shneidman**
1973   **Norman Farberow**
1974   **Reverend Chad Varah**
1975   **Robert Felix**
1976   **Theodore Curphey**
1977   **Avery Weisman**

Education

Contents

Related Awards

Agronomic Education Award

AMERICAN SOCIETY OF AGRONOMY
677 S. Segoe Rd., Madison, Wisc. 53711 (608/274-1212)

The $200 Agronomic Education Award annually recognizes educational innovations developed and used successfully, with a focus on educational contributions of classroom teachers, extension agronomists, industrial agronomists and others whose primary concern is teaching of the science. A Selection Committee picks the recipient from a list of nominees.

1957	T.H. Goodding
1958	D.F. Metcalfe
1959	H.D. Foth
1960	J.K. Patterson
1961	A.R. Hilst
1962	A.A. Johnson
1963	H.W. Smith
1964	A.W. Burger
1965	S.R. Aldrich
1966	M.D. Dawson
1967	B.A. Krantz
1968	W.H. Scholtus
1969	W.L. Colville
1970	L.H. Smith
1971	W.F. Keim
1972	D.P. McGill
1973	W.O. Scott
1974	S.L. Ahlrichs
1975	E.A. Emery
1976	D.A. Miller
1977	K.L. Larson

Western Electric Fund Award
Dow Jones Award

AMERICAN ASSEMBLY OF COLLEGIATE
SCHOOLS OF BUSINESS
760 Office Parkway, Suite 50, St. Louis, Mo. 63141
(314/872-8481)

The Western Electric Fund Award honors institutions and individuals for innovations in undergraduate education in business administration. Deans or heads of business schools that are AACSB members may nominate faculty members for unique classroom programs. A selection committee choses the winner. The individual receives $1,000 and the sponsoring university or college receives $5,000.

1970 University of Oregon, John R. Wish, "Beachhead College"

1971 Indiana University, William G. Panschar, "Four-Course Integrative Core"

1972 Massachusetts Institute of Technology Sloan School of Management, John F. Rockart, "An Integrated Use of Available Resource (Student, Professor, and Technology) in the Learning Process"

1973 Washington State University, Mark Hammer and C. Obert Henderson, "A Program for Improving Large Class Instruction"

1974 University of Hawaii, Bruce M. Hass, "Time-Compressed Speech"

1975 Southern Illinois University, Edwardsville, David J. Werner, "Management Problem Laboratory Program"

1976 Carnegie Mellon University, Gerald L. Thompson, "Self-Managed Learning of Mathematics—Operations Research"

1977 Miami University, Dr. John P. Maggard, "Laws, Hall and Associates"

The Dow Jones Award, which carries a $5,000 cash grant donated to the college or university of the winner's choice, honors individuals for contributions to business education. The Assembly considers nominess irrespective of an association with the organization.

1974 Walter Hoving, Tiffany & Co. donated to The Wharton School, University of Pennsylvania

1975 E.G. Bach, Frank E. Buck Professor of Economics and Public Policy, Stanford University, donated to Stanford University and Carnegie-Mellon University

1976 Paul Garner, Dean Emeritus, College of Commerce, University of Atlanta, donated to University of Alabama and University of Texas

1977 Charles J. Dirksen, Dean of the Graduate School, University of Santa Clara, donated to University of Santa Clara

C. Albert Koob Award

NATIONAL CATHOLIC EDUCATIONAL ASSN.
One Dupont Cir. NW, Washington, D.C. 20036
(202/293/5954)

The C. Albert Koob Award is given as merited, usually annually, to any individual who has made an outstanding contribution to Catholic education in America. An award committee appointed by the chairman of the board reviews nominees and submits their names to board members for a vote.

1968	Most Rev. Ernest J. Primeau
1969	Msgr. Carl J. Ryan
	Msgr. Frank M. Schneider
	William F. Conley
	Msgr. Sylvester J. Hobel
	Msgr. James E. Hoflich
	Msgr. Felix N. Pitt
1970	Most Rev. William E. McManus
	Msgr. John T. Foudy
	Sister Mary Emil Penet, IHM
	William B. Ball
	David J. Young
	Msgr. O'Neil C. D'Amour
	Sister M. Rufina Lutz, OSF
1971	Brother Anthony Wallace, FSC
	Rev. Theodore M. Hesburgh, CSC
1972	Msgr. Eugene J. Molloy
	Sister M. Sheila Haskett, OSF
1973	No award
1974	Rev. C. W. Friedman
	Rev. C. Albert Koob
1975	Most Rev. Raymond J. Gallagher
1976	J. Lloyd Trump
	Sister M. Lillian McCormack, SSND
	Most Rev. William E. McManus
1977	Rev. Theodore M. Hesburgh, CSC
	Sister Kathleen Short, OP
	Rev. Andrew Greeley

AERA/ACT Award
American Educational Research Association Award

AMERICAN EDUCATIONAL RESEARCH ASSOCIATION
1126 16th St. NW, Washington, D.C. 20036 (202/223-9485)

The AERA/ACT (American College Testing) Award, which consists of $1,500 and a scroll, is given annually for a work of outstanding research dealing with college student growth and development. The award was instituted to encourage sophisticated work in the field and is awarded to a recipient selected by a joint committee of the two organizations.

1972 Wilbert J. McKeachie
1973 Theodore M. Newcomb
1974 Ralph Tyler
1975 William Sewell
1976 Ralph F. Berdie
1977 T. R. McConnell

The American Educational Research Association Award for Distinguished Contributions to Research in Education, which consists of $1,500 and a scroll, is awarded for meritorious achievements in and distinguished contributions to the field. It honors the overall contributions of a scholar who is selected by the Awards Committee.

1964 Arthur I. Gates
1965 Ralph W. Tyler
1966 T. R. McConnell
1967 E. F. Lindquist
1968 Jean Piaget and Barbel Inhelder
1969 Lawrence A. Cremin
1970 Benjamin S. Bloom
1971 Patrick Suppes
1972 Robert M. Gagne
1973 Robert J. Havighurst
1974 James S. Coleman
1975 Urie Bronfenbrenner
1976 Robert Glaser
1977 Lee J. Cronbach

Ruth Strang Research Award

NATIONAL ASSOCIATION FOR WOMEN DEANS, ADMINISTRATORS AND COUNSELORS
1028 Connecticut Ave. NW, Suite 922, Washington, D.C. 20036

The $500 Ruth Strang Research Award is given annually for excellence in research among individuals early in their careers in a historical, philosophical, evaluative or descriptive field deemed of timely and professional importance to NAWDAC members. Original manuscripts up to 50 pages long may be submitted to the Ruth Strang Research Award Committee for consideration.

1974 Dolores Muhich, title unknown
1975 Barbara S. Knox, "Trends in Counseling Women in Higher Education, 1957-1973"
1976 Elizabeth A. Ashburn, "Motivation, Personality and Work-Related Characteristics of Women in Male-Dominated Professions"

1977 Katherine Van Wessem Goerss, "Women Administrators in Education: A Review of Research 1960-1976"

National Teacher of the Year Award

COUNCIL OF STATE SCHOOL OFFICERS
1201 16th St. NW, Washington, D.C. 20036 (202/833-4192)

The National Teacher of the Year award is given annually by the President or the First Lady at a White House ceremony and honors a full-time career public-classroom teacher. The award consists of a tie clasp or brooch, a certificate and a Presidential appointment to the Commission on Presidential Scholars. The award was established by the Council in cooperation with the *Enclopaedia Britannica, The Ladies' Home Journal* and *Look* magazine to focus on America's best teachers and to encourage all teachers.

1952 Geraldine Jones, First grade; Hope Public School, Santa Barbara, Calif.
1953 Dorothy Hamilton, Social studies; Milford High School, Milford, Conn.
1954 Willard Widerberg, Seventh grade; DeKalb Junior High School, DeKalb, Ill.
1955 Margaret Perry, Fourth grade; Monmouth Elementary, Monmouth, Ore.
1956 Richard Nelson, Science; Flathead County High School, Kalispell, Mont.
1957 Eugene G. Bizzell, Speech, English, and debate; A. N. McCallum High School, Austin, Tex
       Mary F. Schartz, Third grade; Bristol Elementary, Kansas City, Mo.
1958 Jean Listebarger Humphrey, Second grade; Edwards Elementary, Ames, Iowa
1959 Edna Donley, Mathematics and speech; Alva High School, Alva, Okla.
1960 Hazel B. Davenport, First grade; Central Elementary, Beckley, W. Va.
1961 Helen Adams, Kindergarten, Cumberland Public School, Cumberland, Wisc.
1962 Marjorie French, Mathematics, Topeka High School, Topeka, Kans.
1963 Elmon Ousley, Speech, American government and world problems; Bellevue Senior High School, Bellevue, Wash.
1964 Lawana Trout, English; Charles Page High School, Sand Springs, Okla.
1965 Richard E. Klinck, Sixth grade; Reed Street Elementary, Wheat Ridge, Colo.
1966 Mona Dayton, First grade; Walter Douglas Elementary, Tucson, Ariz.
1967 Roger Tenney, Music; Owatonna Jr.-Sr. High, Owatonna, Minn.
1968 David E. Graf, Vocational education and industrial arts; Sandwich Community High School, Sandwich, Ill.
1969 Barbara Goleman, Language arts; Miami Jackson High School, Miami, Fla.
1970 Johnnie T. Dennis, Physics and math analysis; Walla Walla High School, Walla Walla, Wash.
1971 Martha M. Stringfellow, First grade; Lewisville Elementary, Chester County, S.C.
1972 James M. Rogers, American history and black studies; Durham High School, Durham, N.C.
1973 John A. Ensworth, Sixth grade; Kenwood School, Bend, Ore.
1974 Vivian Tom, Social studies; Lincoln High School, Yonkers, N.Y.

1975   **Robert G. Heyer,** Science; Johanna Junior High School, St. Paul, Minn.
1976   **Ruby Murchison,** Social studies; Washington Drive Junior High School, Fayetteville, N.C.
1977   **Myrra Lee,** Social living; Helix High School, La Mesa, Calif.

Mohammed Reza Pahlavi Prize
Nadezhda K. Krupskaya Prize
UNITED NATIONS EDUCATIONAL, SCIENTIFIC AND CULTURAL ORGANIZATION
7 Place du Fontenoy, 75700 Paris, France (Tel: 577 16 10, Ext. 3420)

The Mohammed Reza Pahlavi Prize, founded by His Imperial Majesty the Shahinshah of Iran, annually awards $5,000 to institutions, organizations or individuals for outstanding work in combatting illiteracy. The governments of United Nations member states, in consultation with their UNESCO National Commissions, and non-governmental international educational organizations having consultant status with UNESCO nominate candidates for selection by the Director General. In addition to the winners listed below, honorable mentions are made each year.

1967   **Girls attending the secondary school in Tabora,** Tanzania
1968   **Basic Education Movement,** Brazil
1969   **Royal National Committee for Literacy,** Cambodia
1970   **Popular-action Radio School of Sutatenza,** Colombia

1971   **General Literacy Supervisory and Coordinating Committe,** Burma
1972   **Gram Shikshan Mohim,** India
1973   **Emma Espina, Sergio Arevalo, and Arnulfo Reubilar,** authors of "Suggestions for Literacy," Chile
1974   **All-Pakistan Women's Association,** Pakistan
1975   **Paulo Freire,** Brazil
1976   **Pasteur Jacques Kofi Adzomada,** Togo
1977   **No award**

The Nadezhda K. Krupskaya Prize, Founded by the government of the U.S.S.R., carries an honorarium of 5,000 rubles and is awarded annually for outstanding work in combatting illiteracy. The governments of United Nations member states, in consultation with their UNESCO National Commissions, and non-governmental international educational organizations having consultant status with UNESCO nominate candidates for selection by the Director General. In addition to the winners listed below, honorable mentions are made each year.

1970   **Institute of Language and Literature and the Academy of Sciences,** People's Republic of Mongolia
1971   **Program for adult literacy,** Zambia
1972   **Armee du Savoir** (Army of Knowledge), Iran
1973   **Literacy project in the Western Lake region,** Tanzania
1974   **Cercle for the Development of the Shyorongi Commune (CEDECOS),** Rwanda
1975   **Abdirizak Mohamoud Abukar,** Somalia
1976   **Department of Literacy of the Ministry of Education and Culture,** Syria
1977   **No award**

Science

Contents

& Technology

Davis Research Award

STEVENS INSTITUTE OF TECHNOLOGY
Castle Point, Hoboken, N.J. 07030 (201/792-2700)

The $1,000 Davis Research Award goes annually to honor research published during the previous calendar year in pure or applied science. A faculty committee selects the winner.

1961 **George Schmidt,** Theoretical plasma physics
1962 **Everett R. Johnson,** Radiation chemistry
1963 **Earl L. Koller and Snowden Taylor,** High energy physics
1964 **Stephen J. Lukasik and Chester E. Grosch,** Wave-induced seabed pressures
1965 **Robert F. McAlevy III,** Combustion mechanisms
1965 **Daniel Savitsky,** Performance of planning hulls
1966 **Franklin Pollock,** Vortex motions in ideal fluids
1966 **John P. Breslin and Stavros Tsakonas,** Propeller induced vibrations
1967 **Winnifred Jacobs,** Stability of ships
1968 **Salvatore Stivala,** Heparin extraction techniques
1969 **Ajay K. Bose and Maghar S. Manhas,** Total synthesis of penicillin
1970 **Rodney D. Andrews Jr. and Edward A. Friedman,** Inelastic light scattering in polymers
1971 **John G. Daunt and Eugenio Lerner,** Low temperature absorption
1972 **Milton Ohring,** Electro-migration in thin films
1973 **Winston H. Bostick, Vittorio Nardi and William Prior,** Experimental plasma physics
1974 **Haruzo Eda,** Ship controllability
1974 **Hans Meissner and Robert Peters,** Low temperature physics
1975 **Gerald M. Rothberg,** Mossbauer effect studies
1976 **Cheung H. Kim,** Ship motions
1977 **No award**

Richard Hopper Day Memorial Medal

ACADEMY OF NATURAL SCIENCES OF PHILADELPHIA
19th and The Parkway, Philadelphia, Pa. 19103 (215/299-1015)

The Richard Hopper Day Memorial Medal, which is of bronze and carries an honorarium, is awarded at the discretion of the donor and the director of the Academy to honor outstanding exploration and discovery in natural sciences.

1960 **Jacques Piccard
Lt. Lawrence A. Shumaker,** USN
**Andreas B. Rechnitzer
Lt. Don Walsh,** USN
1964 **L.S.B. Leakey**
1966 **H. Bradford Washburn**
1967 **Charles A. Berry**
1969 **Ruth Patrick**
1973 **Harrison H. Schmitt**

Francqui Prize

FRANCQUI FOUNDATION
11 Egmont St., 1050 Brussels, Belgium (Tel: 02/511 81 00)

The Francqui Prize, which carries an honorarium of one million Belgian francs, is given annually to a Belgian scientists under the age of 50 for distinguished research. An international jury selects the recipient.

1933 Henri Pirenne
1934 Georges Lemaitre
1936 Franz Cumont
1938 Jacques Errera
1940 Pierre Nolf
1946 Marcel Florkin
        Francois-L. Ganshof
        Frans-H. van den Dungen
1948 Zenon-Marcel Bacq
        Jean Brachet
        Marc de Hemptinne
        Leon-H. Dupriez
        Pol Swings
1949 Leon Rosenfeld
1950 Paul Harsin
1951 Henri Koch
1952 Florent-Joseph Bureau
1953 Etienne Lamotte
        Claire Preaux
1954 Raymond Jeener
1955 Ilya Prigogine
1956 Louis Remacle
1957 Lucien Massart
1958 Leon Van Hove
1959 Gerard Garitte
1960 Christian de Duve
1961 Jules Duchesne
        Adolphe Van Tiggelen
1962 Chaim Perelman
1963 Hubert Chantrenne
1964 Paul Ledoux
1965 Roland Mortier
1966 Henri Hers
1967 Jose Fripiat
1968 Jules Horrent
1969 Isidoor Leusen
1970 Radu Balescu
1971 Georges Thines
1972 Jean-Edouard Desmedt
1973 Pierre Macq
1974 Raoul van Caenegem
1975 Rene Thomas
1976 Walter Fiers
1977 Jacques Taminiaux

Dannie Heineman Prize

AKADEMIE DER WISSENSCHAFT IN GOTTINGEN
Minna James Heineman Stiftung, Gottingen, Federal Republic of Germany (Tel: 0551/41298)

The Dannie Heineman Prize is given every two years for an outstanding work, usually in the field of natural sciences. A 30,000-mark honorarium accompanies the prize. The winner is selected by members of the Academy.

1962 **James Franck,** (University of North Carolina, Durham), Photosynthesis
1963 **Edmund Hlawka,** (University of Vienna), Mathematics
1965 **Georg Wittig,** (University of Heidelberg), Chemistry
1967 **Martin Schwarzschild,** (Princeton University), Astronomy
        H. Gobind Khorana, (University of Wisconsin), Molecular Biology

1969 Alfred Brian Pippard, (Cambridge University), Physics
1971 Neil Bartlett, (University of California, Berkeley), Chemistry
1973 Igor R. Schafarevitsch, (University of Moscow), Mathematics
1975 Philip W. Anderson, (Bell Telephone Laboratories), Physics
1977 Albert Eschenmoser (Eidgenossische Technische Hochschule, Zurich,) Organic Chemistry

Gilles Holst Medal
ROYAL NETHERLANDS ACADEMY OF ARTS AND SCIENCES
Kloveniersburgwal 29, Amsterdam, The Netherlands (Tel: 020 22 29 02)

The Gilles Holst Medal, which is of gold, is given approximately every four years for research in the field of applied physics or applied chemistry. A selection committee chooses the winner, who must be of Dutch nationality.

1963 W.G. Burgers
1967 M.C. Teves
1971 J.D. Fast
1976 P.M. de Wolff

Sarah Zinder Leedy Memorial Award
WEIZMANN INSTITUTE OF SCIENCE
Rehovot, Israel (Tel: 054-82111)

The Sarah Zinder Leedy Memorial Award alternates each year between biological sciences and physical-mathematical sciences.

1962 A. Balugrund, Nuclear physics
Haim Ginsburg, Genetics
1964 Arnon Dar, Nuclear physics
1965 Israel Shechter, Chemical immunology
1966 Haim Harari, Nuclear physics
1967 Jonathan Gressel, Plant genetics, specifically for work on photo-induction and RNA synthetics involving the mechanism of spore formation in a fungus
1968 Gabriel Veneziano, Physics, specifically for work on the properties of elementary particles
1969 No award
1970 Max Herzberg, Biological ultrastructure, specifically for contributions to the elucidation of the structural basis of the production of proteins
Adam Schwimmer, Nuclear physics, specifically for contributions to the description of the duality properties of strong interactions and the hadron spectrum
1971 No award
1972 Richard Hornreich, Electronics, for contribution in the field of magnetoelastic effect
Zelig Rabinowitz, Genetics, for work on the reversion of transformed cells by non-viral carcinogenesis
1973 Abraham Nimrod, Biodynamics, specifically for work on the biosynthesis of estrogenic hormones and metabolism of progesterone in the rat ovary in relation to ovum implantation
1974 Dorit Carmeli, For work on mathematical modeling and quantitative inheritance
1975 No award

1976 Abraham Amsterdam, Hormone research specifically for work on cell membrane cytoskeleton in information transfer between and within cells
1977 David Mukamel, Accomplishments in phase transition, critical and multi-critical behavior

Leeuwenhoek Medal
ROYAL NETHERLANDS ACADEMY OF ARTS AND SCIENCES
Kloveniersburgwal 29, Amsterdam, The Netherlands (Tel: 020 22 29 02)

The Leeuwenhoek Medal, which is of gold, is given every 10 years for outstanding research in the field of microscopical organisms. A selection committee chooses the winner of this international honor.

1875 C.G. Ehrenberg, Berlin, Germany
1885 Ferdinand Cohn, Breslau, Germany
1895 Louis Pasteur, Paris, France
1905 M.W. Beijerinck, Delft, The Netherlands
1915 Sir David Bruce, London, England
1925 Felix d'Herelle, Alexandria, Egypt
1935 Sergei Nikolaevitch Winogradsky, Brie/Comte-Robert, France
1950 Selman A. Waksman, New Brunswick, N.J.
1960 Andre Lwoff, Paris, France
1970 C.B. van Niel, Pacific Grove, Calif.

Joseph Leidy Award
ACADEMY OF NATURAL SCIENCES OF PHILADELPHIA
19th and The Parkway, Philadelphia, Pa. 19103 (215/299-1015)

The Joseph Leidy Award, which consists of a bronze medal and a $100 honorarium, is given every three years for the best publication, exploration, discovery or research in the natural sciences, as judged by a committee of Academy and non-Academy scientists.

1925 Herbert Spencer Jennings
1928 Henry A. Pilsbry
1931 William Morton Wheeler
1934 Gerrit Smith Miller, Jr.
1937 Edwin Linton
1940 Merritt Lyndon Fernald
1943 Chancey Juday
1946 Ernst Mayr
1949 Warren P. Spencer
1952 G. Evelyn Hutchinson
1955 Herbert Friedmann
1958 H.B. Hungerford
1961 Robert Evans Snodgrass
1964 Carl L. Hubbs
1967 Donn Eric Rosen
1970 Arthur Cronquist
1973 James Bond
1976 No award

Lomonosov Medal
ACADEMY OF SCIENCES
Leninsky Prospekt 14, Moscow 117901, USSR (Tel: 232-29-10)

The Lomonosov Medal, which is of gold, is the Soviet

Union's highest scientific award. Initially, one medal was awarded each year, but since 1967 one Soviet and one foreign scholar annually receive a Lomonosov Medal to honor outstanding work in the natural or social sciences.

1959 **Pyotr L. Kapista (USSR)**, Physics
1960 **No award**
1961 **No award**
1962 **A.N. Nesmeyanov (USSR)**, Chemistry
1963 **No award**
1964 **S. Tomanaga (Japan)**, Physics
1965 **G. Florie (Great Britain)**, Medicine
       N.V. Belov (USSR), Crystallography
1966 **No award**
1967 **I.E. Tamm (USSR)**, Theoretical physics
       S.F. Powell (Great Britain), Elementary-particle physics
1968 **V.A. Engelhardt (USSR)**, Biochemistry and molecular biology
       Istvan Rusnak (Hungary), Medicine
1969 **N.N. Semyonov (USSR)**, Chemical physics
       Giulio Natta (Italy), Polymer chemistry
1970 **I.M. Vinogradov (USSR)**, Mathematics
       Arnaud Danjoie (France), Mathematics
1971 **V.A. Ambartsumyan (USSR)**, Astronomy and astrophysics
       Hans Alven (Sweden), Plasma physics and astrophysics
1972 **N.I. Muskhelishvili, (USSR)**, Mathematics and mechanics
       Max Steinbeck (German Democratic Republic), Plasma physics
1973 **A.P. Vinogradov (USSR)**, Geochemistry
       Vladimir Zoubek (Czechoslovakia), Geology
1974 **A.I. Tselikov (USSR)**, Geology
       Angel Balevsky (Bulgaria), Metal technology
1975 **M.V. Keldysh (USSR)**, Mathematics, mechanics and cosmic research
       Maurice Rouault (France), Mechanics and applied mechanics
1976 **S.I. Wolfkovich (USSR)**, Chemistry and phosphorous technology; development of scientific bases for USSR agricultural chemistry
       Herman Klary (German Democratic Republic), Chemistry
1977 **M.A. Lavrentiev (USSR)**, Mathematics and mechanics
       Linus Pauling (U.S.A.), Chemistry and biochemistry

Lubell Memorial Award

WEIZMANN INSTITUTE OF SCIENCE
Rehovot, Israel (951721)

The Jeanette and Samuel L. Lubell Memorial Award is given every second year for achievement in any field of research by a Weizmann Institute scientist 40 years of age or under holding the grade of senior scientist or below.

1971 **Ada Zamir**, Biochemistry, for contribution to the study of the nature and mode of action of ribosomes
1973 **Adam Schwimmer**, Nuclear physics, specifically for contribution to understanding high energy scattering processes of elementary particles
1975 **Ruth Sperling and Michael Bustin**, Chemical physics, for work on the assembly and structure of chromosomes of higher organisms

1977 **Ada Zamir**, Biochemistry

National Academy of Sciences Award
Alexander Agassiz Gold Medal
NAS Award in Applied Mathematics and Numerical Analysis
Arctowski Medal
John J. Carty Medal
Comstock Prize
Arthur Day Award
Henry Draper Medal
Daniel Giraud Elliot Medal
NAS Award for Environmental Quality
Gibbs Brothers Medal
Benjamin Apthorp Gould Fund
NAS Public Welfare Medal
H.P. Robertson Memorial Lecture Fund
J. Lawrence Smith Medal
U.S. Steel Foundation Award in Molecular Biology
Mary Clark Thompson Medal
Selman A. Waksman Award in Microbiology
Charles Doolittle Walcott Medal
G. K. Warren Prize
James Craig Watson Medal

THE NATIONAL ACADEMY OF SCIENCES
2101 Constitution Ave. NW, Washington, D.C. 20418
(202/393-8100)

The Hunsaker Fund has endowed the National Academy of Sciences Award in Aeronautical Engineering, which consists of a $4,000 honorarium awarded every five years.

1968 **Leroy Randle Grumman**
1973 **Donald Wills Douglas, Sr.**

The Murray Fund awards the Alexander Agassiz Gold Medal, which carries an honorarium, approximately every three years for original contributions to oceanography. A two-member committee selects the winner.

1913 **Johan Hjort**
1918 **Albert I, Prince of Monaco**
1920 **Charles Dwight Sigsbee**
1924 **Otto Sven Pettersson**
1926 **Wilhelm Bjerknes**
1927 **Max Weber**
1928 **Walfrid Vagn Ekman**
1929 **Stanley J. Gardiner**
1930 **Johannes Schmidt**
1931 **Henry Bryant Bigelow**
1932 **Albert Defant**

1933	Bjorn Helland-Hansen
1934	Haakon Hasberg Gran
1935	Wayland T. Vaughan
1936	Martin Knudsen
1937	Edgar Allen Johnson
1938	Ulrik Harald Sverdrup
1939	Frank Rattray Lillie
1942	Columbus Iselin II
1946	Joseph Proudman
1947	Felix Andries Vening Meinesz
1948	Thomas Gordon Thompson
1951	Harry A. Marmer
1952	H. W. Harvey
1954	Maurice Ewing
1955	Alfred Clarence Redfield
1959	Martin Wiggo Johnson
1960	Anton Frederik Bruun
1962	George Edward Raven Deacon
1963	Roger R. Revelle
1965	Sir Edward Bullard
1966	Carl Eckart
1969	Frederick C. Fuglister
1972	Seiya Uyeda
1973	John H. Steele
1976	Walter Heinrich Munk

The NAS Award in Applied Mathematics and Numerical Analysis, which carries a $5,000 honorarium, is awarded irregularly. A four-member committee selects the winner.

1972	Kurt Otto Friedrichs
1973	Samuel Karlin
1976	Chia-Chiao Lin

The Arctowski Medal, which is of gold and carries a $5,000 honorarium, is awarded approximately every three years for studies of short- or long-duration solar activity changes and their effects on the ionosphere and the terrestrial atmosphere. A three-member committee selects the winner.

1969	Eugene Norman Parker
	Paul J. Wild
1972	Francis Severin Johnson
1975	Jacques M. Beckers

The John J. Carty Medal and Award for the Advancement of Science, consisting of a gold medal and $3,000 honorarium, is awarded approximately every three years for noteworthy and distinguished achievement in any field of science within the scope of the Academy. A three-member committee selects the winner.

1932	John J. Carty
1936	Edmund Beecher Wilson
1939	Sir William Bragg
1943	Edwin Grant Conklin
1945	William Frederick Durand
1947	Ross Granville Harrison
1950	Irving Langmuir
1953	Vannevar Bush
1961	Charles Hard Townes
1963	Maurice Ewing
1965	Alfred Henry Sturtevant
1968	Murray Gell-Mann
1971	James Dewey Watson
1975	J. Tuzo Wilson

The Comstock Prize, which carries an honorarium of $4,000, is awarded every five years for the most impor-

tant discovery or investigation in electricity, magnetism or radiant energy.

1913	Robert A. Millikan
1918	Samuel J. Barnett
1923	William Duane
1928	C. J. Davisson
1933	Percy W. Bridgman
1938	Ernest O. Lawrence
1943	Donald W. Kerst
1948	Merle A. Tuve
1953	William Shockley
1958	Charles Hard Townes
1963	Chien-Shiung Wu
1968	Leon N. Cooper
	J. Robert Schrieffer
1973	Robert H. Dicke

The Arthur Day Fund has been established to advance the study of the physics of the Earth. The recipient of the Day Award is chosen by a four-member committee.

1972	Hatten S. Yoder
1975	Drummond H. Matthews
	Fred J. Vine

The Henry Draper Medal, which is of gold and carries a $1,000 honorarium, is awarded not more often than every two years for investigations in astronomical physics.

1886	Samuel P. Langley
1888	E. C. Pickering
1890	H. A. Rowland
1893	H. K. Vogel
1899	J. E. Keeler
1901	Sir William Huggins
1904	George E. Hale
1906	W. W. Campbell
1910	C. G. Abbot
1913	H. Deslandres
1915	Joel Stebbins
1916	A. A. Michelson
1918	W. S. Adams
1919	Charles Fabry
1920	Alfred Fowler
1921	Pieter Zeeman
1922	Henry Norris Russell
1924	Sir Arthur Stanley Eddington
1926	Harlow Shapley
1928	William Hammond Wright
1931	Annie Jump Cannon
1932	V. M. Slipher
1934	John Stanley Plaskett
1936	C. E. Kenneth Mees
1940	Robert Williams Wood
1942	Ira Sprague Bowen
1945	Paul W. Merrill
1947	Hans Albrecht Bethe
1949	Otto Struve
1951	Bernard Lyot
1955	Hendrik C. van de Hulst
1957	Horace W. Babcock
1960	Martin Schwarzschild
1963	Richard Tousey
1965	Martin Ryle
1968	Bengt Edlen
1971	Subrahmanyan Chandrasekhar
1974	Lyman Spitzer Jr.
1977	Arno Penzias and Robert W. Wilson

The Daniel Giraud Elliot Medal, which carries a $1,000 honorarium, is awarded for the most meritorious work in zoology or paleontology published in a three- to five-year period. A four-member committee selects the winner.

1917	F. M. Chapman
1918	William Beebe
1919	Robert Ridgway
1920	Othenio Abel
1921	Bashford Dean
1922	William Morton Wheeler
1923	Ferdinand Canu
1924	Henri Breuil
1925	Edmund B. Wilson
1927	Erik A. Stensio, Jr.
1928	Ernest Thompson Seton
1929	Henry Fairfield Osborn
1930	George Ellett Coghill
1931	Davidson Black
1932	James P. Chapin
1933	Richard Swann Lull
1934	Theophilus Shickel Painter
1935	Edwin H. Colbert
1936	Robert Cushman Murphy
1937	George Howard Parker
1938	Malcolm Robert Irwin
1939	John Howard Northrop
1940	William Berryman Scott
1941	Theodosius Dobzhansky
1942	Sir D'Arcy W. Thompson
1943	Karl Spencer Lashley
1944	George Gaylord Simpson
1945	Sewall Green Wright
1946	Robert Broom
1947	John Thomas Patterson
1948	Henry B. Bigelow
1949	Arthur Cleveland Bent
1950	Raymond Carrol Osburn
1951	Libbie Henrietta Hyman
1952	Archie Fairly Carr
1953	Sven P. Ekman
1955	Herbert Friedmann
1956	Alfred Sherwood Rober
1957	Philip J. Darlington Jr.
1958	Donald Redfield Griffin
1965	George Gaylord Simpson
1967	Ernst Mayr
1971	Richard Alexander
1976	Howard Ensign Davis

The $5,000 NAS Award for Environmental Quality, which may be awarded annually, is given for outstanding scientific or technological contributions to improve the quality of the environment or to control its pollution. A five-member committee selects the winner.

1972	Arie Jan Haagen-Smit
1973	W. Thomas Edmonson
1974	G. Evelyn Hutchinson
1975	John T. Middleton
1976	David M. Evans
1977	Miron L. Heinselman

The Gibbs Brothers Medal, which carries a $1,000 honorarium, is awarded not more often than every two years for outstanding contributions in naval engineering or marine architecture. A four-member committee selects the winner.

1965	Frederick Henry Todd
1967	Alfred Adolph Heinrich Kiel
1971	Henry A. Schade
1974	Phillip Eisenberg

1976	John Charles Niedermaier

The Benjamin Apthorp Gould Fund, which carries a $5,000 honorarium, is given every two or three years for outstanding contributions in astronomy, the mechanics of orbits of asteroids or problems of local galactic structure. A four-member committee selects the winner

1971	Elizabeth Roemer
1973	Kenneth I. Kellermann
1975	Lodewijk Woltjer

The NAS Public Welfare Medal is awarded as merited for distinguished contributions in the application of science to the public welfare. A four-member committee comprising the Council Committee on National Science Policy selects the winner.

1914	G. W. Goethals
	W. C. Gorgas
1916	Cleveland Abbe
	Gifford Pinchot
1917	S. W. Stratton
1920	Herbert Hoover
1921	C. W. Stiles
1928	Charles V. Chapin
1930	Stephen Tyng Mather
1931	Wickliffe Rose
1932	William Hallock Park
1933	David Fairchild
1934	August Vollmer
1935	F. F. Russel
	Hugh S. Cumming
1937	Willis Rodney Whitney
1939	John Edgar Hoover
1943	John D. Rockefeller, Jr.
1945	Vannevar Bush
1947	Karl Taylor Compton
1948	George Harrison Shull
1951	David E. Lilienthal
1956	James R. Killian, Jr.
1957	Warren Weaver
1958	Henry Allen Moe
1959	James H. Doolittle
1960	Alan T. Waterman
1962	James A. Shannon
1963	J. George Harrar
1964	Detlev Wulf Bronk
1966	John W. Gardner
1969	Lister Hill
1972	Leonard Carmichael
1976	Emilio Q. Daddorio
1977	Leona Baumgartner

The H.P. Robertson Memorial Lecture Fund provides a $2,500 stipend and invites distinguished scientists from anywhere in the world to present the Robertson Memorial Lecture to the Academy. A four-member committee selects the recipient approximately every three years.

1967	John A. Wheeler
1971	Paul Doty
1975	Martin Rees

The J. Lawrence Smith Medal, which is of gold, is awarded approximately every three years for investigations in meteoric bodies. A four-member committee selects the winner.

1888	H. A. Newton
1922	George P. Merrill

1945   Stuart Hoffman Perry
1949   Fred Lawrence Whipple
1954   Peter Mackenzie Millman
1957   Mark G. Inghram
1960   Ernst J. Opik
1962   Harold Clayton Urey
1967   John Hamilton Reynolds
1970   Edward Porter Henderson
1971   Edward Anders
1973   Clair Cameron Patterson
1976   John Armstead Wood

The U.S. Steel Foundation Award in Molecular Biology, which carries a $5,000 honorarium, may be presented annually for a recent notable discovery in molecular biology by a young scientist. A four-member committee selects the winner.

1962   Marshall W. Nirenberg
1953   Matthew S. Meselson
1964   Charles Yanofsky
1965   Robert Stuart Edgar
1966   Norton D. Zinder
1967   Robert W. Holley
1968   Walter Gilbert
1969   William Barry Wood III
1970   Armin Dale Kaiser
1917   Masayasu Nomura
1972   Howard Martin Temin
1973   Donald David Brown
1974   David Baltimore
1975   Bruce M. Alberts
1976   Daniel Nathans
1977   Aaron J. Shatkin

The Mary Clark Thompson Medal, which carries a $1,000 honorarium is given not more often than every three years for the most important contributions to geology or paleontology. A five-member committee selects the winner.

1921   Charles Doolittle Walcott
1923   Emmanuel de Margerie
1925   John Mason Clarke
1928   James Perrin Smith
1930   William Berryman Scott
         Edward Oscar Ulrich
1931   David White
1932   Francis Authur Bather
1934   Charles Schuchert
1936   Amadeus William Grabua
1941   David Meredith Seares Watson
1942   Sir Arthur Smith Woodward
         Edward Wilber Berry
1943   George Gaylord Simpson
1944   William Joscelyn Arkell
1945   T. Wayland Vaughan
1946   John Bernard Reeside, Jr.
1948   Frank McLearn
1949   Lauge Koch
1952   Lloyd William Stephenson
1954   Alfred Sherwood Romer
1957   Gustav Arthur Cooper
1958   Roman Kozlowski
1961   Norman Dennis Newell
1964   Milton Nunn Bramlette
1967   Wendell Phillips Woodring
1970   Raymond Cecil Moore
1973   Hollis Dow Hedberg
1976   James Morton Schiff

The $5,000 Selman A. Waksman Award in Microbiology of the Foundation for Microbiology is awarded annually or biennially for contributions in the field. A two-member committee selects the winner.

1968   Jack L. Strominger
1970   Earl Reece Stadtman
1972   Charles Yanofsky
1974   Renato Dulbecco
1976   Wallace Prescott Rowe

The Charles Doolittle Walcott Medal, which is of bronze and carries a $1,000 honorarium, is awarded not more often than every five years to stimulate research in pre-Cambrian or Cambrian life. A four-member committee selects the winner.

1934   David White
1939   A. H. Westergaard
1947   Alexander G. Vologdin
1952   Franco Rasetti
1957   Pierre Hupe
1962   Armin Alexander Opik
1967   Allison Ralph Palmer
1972   Elso Sterrenberg Barghoorn
1977   Preston Cloud

The G.K. Warren Prize, which carries a $1,000 honorarium, is awarded approximately every four years for accomplishment in any field of science within the scope of the Academy charter, with a preference for fluviatile geology. A two-member committee selects the winner.

1969   R.A. Bagnold
1973   Luna Bergere Leopold
1976   Walter B. Langbein

The James Craig Watson Medal, which is of gold and carries an honorarium, is awarded approximately every three years for contributions to astronomy and to support astronomical research. A four-member committee selects the winner.

1887   Benjamin A. Gould
1889   Ed. Schoenfeld
1891   Arthur Auwers
1894   S. C. Chandler
1899   Sir David Gill
1913   J. C. Kapteyn
1916   A. O. Leuschner
1924   C. V. L. Charlier
1929   Willem de Sitter
1936   Ernest William Brown
1948   Samuel A. Mitchell
1951   Herbert R. Morgan
1955   Chester B. Watts
1957   George Van Biesbroeck
1960   Yusuke Hagihara
1961   Otto Heckmann
1964   Willem Jacob Luyten
1965   Paul Herget
1966   Wallace J. Eckert
1969   Jurgen Kurt Moser
1972   Andre Deprit
1975   G. M. Clemence

National Medals of Science
Alan T. Waterman Award
NATIONAL SCIENCE FOUNDATION
1800 G St. NW, Washington, D.C. 20550 (202/632-4050)

The National Medals of Science presented annually by the President of the United States honor outstanding contributions to knowledge in the physical, biological, mathematical or engineering sciences.

1962 Theodore von Karman, Professor of Aeronautical Engineering, Emeritus, California Institute of Technology

1963 Luis Walter Alvarez, Professor of Physics, University of California, Berkeley

Vannevar Bush, Administrator; Electrical engineer; former President, Carnegie Institution of Washington; Honorary Chairman, MIT Corp.

John Robinson Pierce, Executive Director, Communications Division Systems, Bell Telephone Laboratories

Cornelis B. van Niel, Professor of Microbiology, Stanford University

Norbert Wiener, Professor of Mathematics, Massachusetts Institute of Technology

1964 Roger Adams, Professor of Chemistry, Emeritus, University of Illinois

Othmar H. Ammann, Consulting Engineer, Ammann and Whitney, Rye, N.Y.

Theodosius Dobzhansky, Member, The Rockefeller Institute

Charles Stark Draper, Head, Dept. of Aeronautics and Astronautics, Massachusetts Institute of Technology

Solomon Leftschetz, Professor of Mathematics, Emeritus, Princeton University

Neal Elgar Miller, Professor of Psychology, Yale University

Harold Marston Morse, Professor of Mathematics, Institute for Advanced Studies

Marshall Warren Nirenberg, Chief, Section of Biochemical Genetics, National Institutes of Health

Julian Schwinger, Professor of Physics, Harvard University

Harold Clayton Urey, Professor of Chemistry, University of California, Berkeley

Robert Burns Woodward, Professor of Chemistry, Harvard University

1965 John Bardeen, Professor of Electrical Engineering and Physics, University of Illinois

Peter J.W. Debye, Professor of Chemistry, Emeritus, Cornell University

Hugh L. Dryden, Former Deputy Administrator, National Aeronautics and Space Administration

Clarence Leonard Johnson, Vice President for Advanced Development Projects, Lockheed Aircraft Corp.

Leon M. Lederman, Professor of Physics, Columbia University

Warren Kendall Lewis, Professor of Chemical Engineering, Emeritus, Massachusetts Institute of Technology

Francis Peyton Rous, Member, Emeritus, The Rockefeller Institute

William Walden Rubey, Professor of Geology and Geophysics, University of California, Los Angeles

George Gaylord Simpson, Professor of Vertebrate Paleontology, Harvard University

Donald D. Van Slyke, Research Chemist, Brookhaven National Laboratories

Oscar Zariski, Professor of Mathematics, Harvard University

1966 Jacob Bjerknes, Professor of Meteorology, University of California, Los Angeles

Subrahmanyan Chandrasekhar, Professor of Theoretical Astrophysics, University of Chicago

Henry Eyring, Dean, Graduate School, University of Utah

E.F. Knipling, Director, Entomology Research Div., U.S. Dept of Agriculture

Fritz A. Lipman, Professor of Biochemistry, Rockefeller University

John W. Milnor, Professor of Mathematics, Princeton University

William C. Rose, Professor of Chemistry, Emeritus, University of Illinois

Claude E. Shannon, Donner Professor of Science, Massachusetts Institute of Technology

J.H. Van Vleck, Professor of Physics, Harvard University

Sewall Wright, Professor of Genetics, Emeritus, University of Wisconsin

Vladimir Kosma Zworykin, Radio Corp. of America

1967 J.W. Beams, Professor of Physics, University of Virginia

A. Francis Birch, Professor of Geological Sciences, Harvard University

Gregory Breit, Professor of Physics, Yale University

Paul J. Cohen, Professor of Mathematics, Stanford University

Kenneth S. Cole, Senior Research Biophysicist, National Institutes of Health

Louis Plack Hammett, Professor of Chemistry, Columbia University

Harry F. Harlow, Professor of Psychology, University of Wisconsin

Michael Heidelberger, Professor of Immunochemistry, New York University

G.B. Kistiakowsky, Professor of Chemistry, Harvard University

Edwin Herbert Land, President, Polaroid Corp.

Igor I. Sikorsky, Former Engineering Manager, Sikorsky Aircraft Div. of United Aircraft Corp.

Alfred Henry Sturtevant, Professor of Biology, Emeritus, California Institute of Techonology

1968 Horace Albert Baker, Professor of Biochemistry, University of California, Berkeley

Paul D. Bartlett, Professor of Chemistry, Harvard University

Bernard B. Brodie, Chief, Laboratory of Chemical Pharmacology, National Institutes of Health

Detlev W. Bronk, President Emeritus, Rockefeller University

J. Presper Eckert, Vice President, Remington Rand Univac Div., Sperry Rand Corp.

Herbert Friedman, Superintendent, Atmosphere and Astrophysics Div., Naval Research Laboratory

Jay L. Lush, Professor of Animal Breeding, Iowa State University

N.M. Newmark, Professor of Civil Engineering, University of Illinois

Jerzy Neyman, Professor of Mathematics, University of California, Berkeley

Lars Onsager, Professor of Chemistry, Yale University

Eugene P. Wigner, Professor of Mathematical Physics, Princeton University

1969 Herbert C. Brown, Professor of Chemistry, Purdue University

William Feller, Professor of Mathematics, Princeton University

Robert Joseph Huebner, Chief, Viral Carcinogenesis Branch, National Cancer Institute, National Institutes of Health

Jack S.C. Kilby, Manager, Customer Requirements Dept., Texas Instruments

Ernst Mayr, Director and Professor, Museum of Comparative Zoology, Harvard University

W.K.H. Panofsky, Director, Stanford Linear Accelerator Center, Stanford University

1970 **Richard D. Brauer,** Professor of Mathematics, Harvard University

Robert H. Dicke, Cyrus Fogg Brackett Professor of Physics, Princeton University

Barbara McClintock, Distinguished Service Member, Carnegie Institute of Washington

George E. Mueller, Senior Vice President, General Dynamics Corp.

Albert B. Sabin, President, Weizmann Institute of Science, Rehovot, Israel

Allan R. Sandage, Staff Member, Hale Observatories, Carnegie Institute of Washington; California Institute of Technology

John C. Slater, Professor of Physics and Chemistry, University of Florida

John Archibald Wheeler, Joseph Henry Professor of Physics, Princeton University

Saul Winstein, Professor of Chemistry, University of California, Los Angeles

1971 No award

1972 No award

1973 **Daniel I. Amon,** Professor and Chairman, Dept. of Cell Physiology and Biochemist in the Agricultural Experiment Station, University of California, Berkeley

Carl Djerassi, Professor of Chemistry, Stanford University

Harold E. Edgerton, Professor Emeritus, Massachusetts Institute of Technology

William Maurice Ewing, Distinguished Professor, Electrical Engineering, Marine Institute, University of Texas, Galveston

Arie J. Haagen-Smit, Professor of Biochemistry, Emeritus, California Institute of Technology

Vladimir Haensel, Vice President for Research and Development, Universal Oil Products Corp.

Frederick Seitz, President, Rockefeller University

Earl W. Sutherland, Jr., Professor of Biochemistry, University of Miami

John W. Tukey, Professor of Statistics, Princeton University

Richard Travis Whitcomb, Aeronautical engineer, Langley Research Center

Robert R. Wilson, Director, Fermi National Accelator Laboratory, Weston, Ill.

1974 **Nicolaas Bloembergen,** Professor of Applied Physics, Harvard University

Britton Chance, Director, Johnson Research Foundation; Chairman Dept. of Physics, University of Pennsylvania

Erwin Chargaff, Professor of Biochemistry, Columbia University

Paul John Flory, Jackson Wood Professor of Chemistry, Stanford University

William A. Fowler, Professor of Physics, California Institute of Technology

Kurt Godel, Professor of Mathematics, Institute for Advanced Study

Rudolf Kompfner, Professor of Applied Physics, Stanford University

James V. Neel, Lee R. Dice Professor of Human Genetics, University of Michigan Medical School

Linus Pauling, Professor of Chemistry, Stanford University

Ralph Brazelton Peck, Consultant; Foundation Engineer; Professor Emeritus, University of Illinois

K.S. Pitzer, Professor of Chemistry, University of California, Berkeley

James A. Shannon, Special Adviser to the President; Rockefeller University

Abel Wolman, Professor Emeritus, Sanitary Engineering, Johns Hopkins University

1975 **John Backus,** IBM staff member, San Jose Research Laboratory, Calif.

Manson Benedict, Institute Professor Emeritus, Massachusetts Institute of Technology

Hans A. Bethe, Emeritus John Wendell Anderson Professor of Physics, Cornell University

Shiing-shen Chern, Professor of Mathematics, University of California, Berkeley

George Bernard Dantzig, Professor of Operations Research and Computer Science, Stanford University

Hallowell Davis, Director Emeritus of Research, Central Institute for the Deaf; Emeritus Professor of Otolaryngology, Washington University

Paul Gyorgy, Professor Emeritus of Pediatrics, University of Pennsylvania Medical School; Consultant, Philadelphia General Hospital

Sterling B. Hendricks, Formerly Chief Chemist, Beltsville Plant Industry Station, U.S. Dept of Agriculture

Joseph Oakland Hirschfelder, Homer Adkins Professor of Theoretical Chemistry, University of Wisconson, Madison

William H. Pickering, Director, Jet Propulsion Laboratory, California Institute of Technology

Lewis Hastings Sarett, President, Merck, Sharp and Dohme Research Laboratories

Frederick Emmons Terman, Provost Emeritus, Stanford University

Orville Alvin Vogel, Professor Emeritus, Dept. of Agronomy and Soils, Washington State University

E. Bright Wilson, Theodore William Richards Professor of Chemistry, Harvard University

Chien-Shiung Wu, Michael I. Pupin Professor of Chemistry, Columbia University

1976 No awards

1977 **Morris Cohen,** Massachusetts Institute of Technology

Kurt Otto Fredericks, New York University

Peter C. Goldmark, President, Goldmark Communications Corp.

Samuel A. Goudsmit, Brookhaven National Laboratory

Roger Guillemin, Salk Institute, San Diego

H.S. Gutowsky, University of Illinois

Erwin W. Mueller, Pennsylvania State University

Keith Roberts Porter, University of Colorado

Efraim Racker, Cornell University

Frederick D. Rossini, Rice University

Verner E. Suomi, University of Wisconsin

Henry Taube, Stanford University

George E. Uhlenbeck, Rockefeller University

Hassler Whitney, Institute for Advanced Studies, Princeton University

Edward O. Wilson, Harvard University

The Alan T. Waterman Award, which consists of a maximum-$50,000 grant for up to three years, is given annually to an outstanding American scientist under 35 years of age in mathematical, biological, engineering, social or other science. A. selection committee choses the winner.

1976 **Charles L. Fefferman,** Princeton; Research in Fourier analysis, partial differential equations and several complex variables which have contributed signally to the advancement of modern mathematical analysis

1977 **J. William Schopf,** UCLA; For outstanding geochemical and micropaleontological analyses of pre-Cambrian organic matter, pioneering study of delicate and ancient micro-organisms and development of techniques for their examination and identification

Pfizer Award

HISTORY OF SCIENCE SOCIETY
c/o Prof. Sally Kohlstedt, Department of History, 311 Maxwell Hall, Syracuse University, Syracuse, N.Y. 13010 (315/423-3307)

The Pfizer Award, which carries a $1,000 cash prize and a citation, is given annually for an outstanding monograph appearing on science in an American or Canadian publication, as judged by a committee.

1959 Marie Boas Hall
1960 Marshall Clagett
1961 Cyril Stanley Smith
1962 Henry Guerlac
1963 Lynn T. White
1964 Robert E. Schofield
1965 C.D. O'Malley
1966 L. Pearce Williams
1967 Howard B. Adelmann
1968 Edwin Rosen
1969 Margaret T. May
1970 Michael Ghiselin
1971 David Joravsky
1972 Richard S. Westfall
1973 Joseph S. Fruton
1974 Susan Schlee
1975 Frederic L. Holmes
1976 Otto Neugebauer
1977 Stephen Brush

Rumford Medal

AMERICAN ACADEMY OF ARTS AND SCIENCES
165 Allandale St., Jamaica Plain Station, Boston, Mass. 02130 (617/522-2400 and 522-0733)

The Rumford Medal, which is accompanied by an honorarium, is presented periodically for work with or discovery in the field of heat and light that is beneficial to mankind. The Rumford Committee selects the winner.

1839 **Robert Hare,** Philadelphia, Invented compound or oxyhydrogen blowpipe
1862 **John Ericsson,** New York, Improvements in heat management, particularly the caloric engine
1865 **Daniel Treadwell,** Cambridge, Mass., Improvements in heat management, especially involving construction of large-caliber cannons
1866 **Alvan Clark,** Cambridge, Mass., Improved manufacture of refracting telescopes
1869 **George Henry Corliss,** Providence, R.I., Improved steam engine
1871 **Joseph Harrison, Jr.,** Philadelphia, Improved steam-boiler safety through construction method

1873 **Lewis Morris Rutherford,** New York, Improved astronomical photography
1875 **John William Draper,** New York, Research on radiant energy
1880 **Josiah Willard Gibbs,** New Haven, Conn., Research on thermodynamics
1883 **Henry Augustus Rowland,** Baltimore, Research on light and heat
1886 **Samuel Pierpont Langley,** Allegheny, Pa., Research on radiant energy
1888 **Albert Abraham Michelson,** Cleveland, Determination of velocity of light, research on motion of luminiferous ether and work on absolute determination of wavelengths of light
1891 **Edward Charles Pickering,** Cambridge, Mass., Work on photometry of stars and on stellar spectra
1895 **Thomas Alva Edison,** Orange, N.J., Investigations in electric lighting
1898 **James Edward Keeler,** Allegheny, Pa., Application of spectroscope to astronomical problems, especially investigations of proper motions of nebulae and physical constitution of Saturn's rings by use of that instrument
1899 **Charles Francis Brush,** Cleveland, Practical development of electric arc lighting
1900 **Carl Barus,** Providence, R.I., Research on heat
1901 **Elihu Thomson,** Lynn, Mass., Inventions in electric welding and lighting
1902 **George Ellery Hale,** Chicago, Investigations in solar and stellar physics, especially invention and perfection of spectro-heliograph
1904 **Ernest Fox Nichols,** New York, Research on radiation, especially pressure due to radiation, star heat and infra-red spectrum
1907 **Edward Goodrich Acheson,** Niagara Falls, N.Y., Application of heat in electric furnaces to industrial production of carborundum, graphite and other substances
1909 **Robert Williams Wood,** Baltimore, Discoveries in light, especially optical properties of sodium and other metallic vapors
1910 **Charles Gordon Curtins,** New York, Improved utilization of heat as work in the steam turbine
1911 **James Mason Crafts,** Boston, Research in high-temperature thermometry and determination of new fixed points on the thermometric scale
1912 **Frederic Eugene Ives,** Woodcliff-on-Hudson, N.Y., Optical inventions, especially in color photography and photo-engraving
1913 **Joel Stebbins,** Urbana, Ill., Developed selenium photometer for application to astronomical problems
1914 **William David Coolidge,** Schenectady, N.Y., Invented ductile tungsten for application to production of radiation
1915 **Charles Greeley Abbot,** Washington, D.C., Research on solar radiation
1917 **Percy Williams Bridgman,** Cambridge, Mass., Thermodynamical research of extremely high pressure
1918 **Theodore Lyman,** Cambridge, Mass., Research on light of very short wave length
1920 **Irving Langmuir,** Schenectady, N.Y., Research in thermionic and allied phenomena
1925 **Henry Norris Russell,** Princeton, N.J., Research in stellar radiation
1926 **Arthur Holly Compton,** Chicago, Research in Rontgen rays
1928 **Edward Leamington Nichols,** Ithaca, N.Y., Research in spectrophotometry
1930 **John Stanley Plaskett,** Victoria, B.C., Canada, Stellar spectrographic research

1931 Karl Taylor Compton, Cambridge, Mass., Research in thermionics and spectroscopy

1933 Harlow Shapley, Cambridge, Mass., Research on luminosity of stars and galaxies

1937 William Weber Coblentz, Washington, D.C., Pioneer in technology and measurement of heat and light

1939 George Russell Harrison, Boston, Improved spectroscopic technique

1941 Vladimir Kosma Zworykin, Princeton, N.J., Invented iconoscope and other television devices

1943 Charles Edward Mees, Rochester, N.Y., Contributions to science of photography

1945 Edwin Herbert Land, Cambridge, Mass., New applications in polarized light and photography

1947 Edmund Newton Harvey, Princeton, N.J., Investigations into nature of bioluminescence

1949 Ira Sprague Bowen, Pasadena, Calif., Solution of the mystery of nebulium and other work in spectroscopy

1951 Herbert E. Ives, Montclair, N.J., Contributions to optics

1953 Enrico Fermi, Chicago, Ill., Studies of radiation theory and nuclear energy
Willis E. Lamb, Jr., Stanford, Calif., Studies of atomic hydrogen spectrum
Lars Onsager, New Haven, Conn., Contributions to thermodynamics of transport processes

1955 James Franck, Chicago, Ill., Fundamental studies on photosynthesis

1957 Subrahmanyan Chandrasekhar, Williams Bay, Wisc., Work on radiative transfer of energy in interior of stars

1959 George Wald, Cambridge, Mass., Studies in biochemical basis of vision

1961 Charles Hard Townes, New York, For development of the maser

1963 Hans Albrecht Bethe, Ithaca, N.Y., Theoretical studies of energy production in stars

1965 Samuel Cornette Collins, Cambridge, Mass., Invented Collins Helium Cryostat and pioneered low-temperature research
William David McElroy, Baltimore, Work on molecular basis of bioluminescence

1967 Robert Henry Dicke, Princeton, N.J., Contributions to microwave radiometry and to understanding of atomic structure
Cornelis B. Van Niel, Stanford, Calif., Contributions to understanding of photosynthesis

1968 Maarten Schmidt, Pasadena, Calif., Discoveries in spectra of quasi-stellar objects

1971 M.I.T. Group, Cambridge, Mass. **(John A. Ball, Alan H. Barrett, Bernard F. Burke, Joseph C. Carter, Patricia P. Crowther, James M. Moran, Jr., and Alan E. Rogers),** Canadian Group **(Norman W. Broten, R.M. Chisholm, John A. Galt, Herbert P. Gush, Thomas H. Legg, Jack L. Locke, Charles W. McLeish, Roger S. Richards and Jui Lin Yen)** and NRAO-Cornell Group **(C.C. Bare, Barry G. Clark, Marshall H. Cohen, David L. Jauncey and Kenneth I. Kellermann),** Work in long-baseline interferometry

1973 E. Bridge Wilson, Cambridge, Mass., Early recognition of importance of symmetry properties in polyatomic molecules and pioneering development of microwave spectroscopy

1976 Bruno Rossi, Cambridge, Mass., Discoveries in nature and origins of cosmic radiations.

Kalinga Prize for the Popularization of Science
UNESCO Science Prize
Carlos J. Finlay Prize

UNITED NATIONS EDUCATIONAL, SCIENTIFIC AND CULTURAL ORGANIZATION
Place de Fontenoy, 75700 Paris (Tel: 577 16 10, Ext. 3206, 3207)

The Kalinga Prize for the Popularization of Science, funded by the Kalinga Trust Foundation of India, annually honors individuals for popularizing science with a cash award of 1,000 British pounds and a trip to India. Nominations are submitted through National Commissions for UNESCO, which forwards them to Paris for selection by a jury and approval by the director general of UNESCO.

1952 Prince Louis de Broglie (France)
1953 Sir Julian Huxley (Great Britain)
1954 Waldemar Kaempffert (U.S.A.)
1955 Augusto Pi Suner (Venezuela)
1956 George Gamow (U.S.A.)
1957 Bertrand Russell (Great Britain)
1958 K. von Frisch (Federal Republic of Germany)
1959 Jean Rostand (France)
1960 Ritchie Calder, C.B.E. (Great Britain)
1961 Arthur C. Clarke (Great Britain)
1962 Gerard Piel (U.S.A.)
1963 Jagjit Singh (India)
1964 Warren Weaver (U.S.A.)
1965 Eugene Rabinowitch (U.S.A.)
1966 Paul Couderc (France)
1967 Fred Hoyle (Great Britain)
1968 Sir Gavin de Beer (Great Britain)
1969 Konrad Lorenz (U.S.A.)
1970 Margaret Mead (U.S.A.)
1971 Pierre Auger (France)
1972 Philip H. Abelson (U.S.A.)
Nigel Calder (Great Britain)
1973 No award
1974 Jose Reis (Brazil)
Luis Estrada (Mexico)
1975 No award
1976 No award
1977 No award

The biennial UNESCO Science Prize, which carries a $3,000 honorarium, honors outstanding contributions to the development of any United Nations member state or region through the application of science and technology. Nominations may be submitted by any individual or group through a National Committee for UNESCO, which forwards them to Paris for selection by a jury and approval by the director general of UNESCO.

1968 Robert Simpson Silver (Great Britain),Discovery of a process for the demineralalization of sea water
1970 International Maize and Wheat Improvement Center (Mexico),Improvement strains of cereals
International Rice Research Institute (Philippines),Improved strains of cereals
1972 Viktor A. Kovda (U.S.S.R.),Theory on hydromorphic origin of soils of the great plains of Asia, Africa, America and Europe

Nine Austrian research workers (Austria),Development of L-D steel production process to help small developed country compete economically and effectively with large, highly industrialized nations
1974 **No award**
1976 **Alfred Champagnat** (France),For findings on low-cost mass production of new proteins from petroleum
1977 **No award**

The Carlos J. Finlay Prize, donated by the government of Cuba, will be given for meritorious work in microbiology beginning in 1978. The $5,000 prize will be given every two years following the momination and selection procedures above.

Bradford Washburn Award
Walker Prize
MUSEUM OF SCIENCE
Science Park, Boston, Mass. 02114 (617/723-2500)

The Bradford Washburn Award, which consists of a gold medal and a $5,000 honorarium, recognizes outstanding contributions toward public understanding of science and "appreciation of the vital role it plays in all our lives."

1964 **Melville Bell Grosvenor,** Contributing to great interest in science through *The National Geographic*
1965 **Jacques-Yves Cousteau,** Undersea explorer; filmmaker
1966 **Gerard Piel,** Publisher, *Scientific American*
1967 **Donald B. MacMillan,** Arctic explorer; leader; teacher
1968 **George Wald,** Biologist and teacher
1969 **Sir George Taylor,** Director, Royal Botanic Gardens, United Kingdom
1970-71 **Walter Cronkite,** Senior CBS news correspondent, for reporting on U.S. space program
1972 **Walter Sullivan,** Science editor, *New York Times*
1973 **Rene Dubos,** Micro-biologist; author; lecturer
1974 **Jane Goodall and Hugo van Lawick,** Writer; student of primates; and photographer and film-maker
1975 **Jean Mayer,** Nutritionist; writer; lecturer
1976 **Loren Eiseley,** Anthropologist; writer
1977 **Arthur C. Clarke,** Science fiction and science writer

The Walker Prize, which carries a $5,000 honorarium, is given as merited for worthy published scientific investigation and discovery. When the prize was started in the 19th century, it was divided into several small cash awards. The winners below have been selected by the Committee of Trustees since the consolidation of the smaller prizes into one award carrying a significant amount.

1967 **Martin H. Moynihan,** Naturalist of the Tropics
1968 **Howard E. Evans,** Studies of the wasp
1969 **Robert K. Selander,** Ornithologist
1970 **Irven DeVore,** Studies of baboons and Bushmen
1971 **Ernst Mayr,** Contributions to understanding process of evolution
1973 **Alfred C. Redfield,** Oceanographer
1976 **Richard M. Eakin,** Zoologist

Shmuel Yaroslavsky Memorial Award
WEIZMANN INSTITUTE OF SCIENCE
Rehovot, Israel (Tel: 054-82111)

The Shmuel Yaroslavsky Memorial Award is given annually for biological and physical research with potential for industrial applications.

1968 **Mati Fridkin,** Use of polymers as reagents in organic synthesis
        Sara Ehrlich-Rogozinsky, Special award for completing Dr. Yaroslavsky's research and preparing his last results for publication
1969 **Haim Rosen,** Polymer research, specifically for work on dimerization and cross-dimerization of acrylic monomers
1970 **Michael Martan,** Plastics, specifically for work on oxidation in liquid phase of hydronaphthalenes
1971 **No award**
1972 **David Gabison,** Biophysics, specifically for rennin for manufacture of cheese
1973 **No award**
1974 **Stephen Daren,** Work on the industrial synthesis of bromostyrene
1975 **No award**
1976 **Moshe Shapiro,** Chemical physics, specifically for work on a theoretical study of photodissociation and exothermic chemical reactions with possible applications to photodissociation lasers and chemical lasers
1977 **Hadassah Degani,** Developed use of magnetics resonance spectroscopic to determine mechanism and kinetics of ion transport processes in the membrane system

Eunice Rockwell Oberly Memorial
Award
AMERICAN LIBRARY ASSOCIATION
ASSOCIATION OF COLLEGE AND RESEARCH
LIBRARIES
50 E. Huron St., Chicago, Ill. 60611 (312/944-6780)

The Eunice Rockwell Oberly Memorial Award, which consists of a citation and an honorarium, is awarded biennially by the Association's Agriculture and Biological Services Section for the best bibliography in the field of agriculture or related sciences. An awards committee selects the winner from nominations previously received.

1925 **Max Meisel**
1927 **Mary G. Lacy, Annie M. Hannay and Emily E. Day**
1929 **Annie M. Hannay**
1931 **Everett E. Edwards**
1933 **Louise O. Bercaw and Esther Marie Colvin**
1935 **Louise O. Bercaw, Annie M. Hannay and Esther Marie Colvin**
1937 **Victor A. Schaefer**
1939 **Louise O. Bercaw and Annie M. Hannay**
1941 **Elmer D. Merrill and Egbert H. Walker**
1943 **No award**
1945 **S.F. Blake and Alice Atwood**
        J.C. Cunningham
1947 **Burch Hart Schneider**
1949 **Ina L. Hawes and Rose Eisenberg**
1951 **Richard Weibe and Janina Nowakowska**
1953 **Dorothy B. Skau, Ralph W. Planck and Frank C. Pack**
1955 **Arthur Rose and Elizabeth Rose**
1957 **Ira J. Condit and Julius Enderud**

1959 J. Richard Blanchard and Harald Ostvold
1961 Egbert H. Walker
1963 Allan Stevenson
1965 Ida Kaplan Langman
1967 George Neville Jones
1969 No award
1971 John T. Schlebecker
1973 Olga Landvay
1975 Ann E. Kerker and Henry T. Murphy
1977 Helen Purdy Beale

Agronomic Research Award
Edward Browning Award for
Improvement of Food Sources
International Agronomy Award
Soil Science Award

AMERICAN SOCIETY OF AGRONOMY
677 S. Segoe Rd., Madison, Wisc. 53711 (608/274-1212)

The $200 Agronomic Research Award recognizes discoveries, techniques, inventions or materials that increase crop yields, improve crop quality, food products, land and water development, environmental quality or conservation. A selection committee picks the recipient from a list of nominees.

1975 A.J. Ohlrogge
1976 T.M. McCalla
1977 George Stanford

The $5,000 Edward Browning Award for Improvement of Food Sources, which consists of a bronze medal and a certificate, is given annually to an individual who has made outstanding improvement of food sources anywhere in the world within the previous 10 years. Each nominee must be sponsored by a recognized professional association and society, and the recipient is chosen by a selection committee.

1971 J.G. Harrar
1972 O.A. Gobel
1973 E.R. Burmester
1974 E.G. Mertz and O.E. Nelson
1975 G.W. Burton
1976 E.A. Black
1977 E.O. Heady

The $200 International Agronomy Award recognizes influence on the growth and development of agronomy outside the United States, with a focus on creative efforts, relevance and effectiveness of the recipient's international agronomic activities. A selection committee picks the winner from a list of nominees.

1968 N. E. Borlaug
1969 E.J. Wellhausen
1970 R.W. Cummings
1971 R.A. Olson
1972 R.F. Chandler
1973 Richard Bradfield
1974 Matthew Drosdoff
1975 Sterling Worthman
1976 J.R. Harlan
1977 H.W. Ream

The Soil Science Award, for the past two years given by the Soil Science Society of America, which is located at the same address as the American Society of Agronomy, is a $200 prize which honors demonstrated creativity, reasoning and/or technical skill or research contributions to basic or applied soil science. A selection committee picks the winner from a list of nominees.

1975 Dale Swartzendruber
1976 Max Mortland
1977 Edwin L. Schmidt

Justus von Liebig Prizes

STIFTUNG F.V.S.
Georgesplatz 10, 2 Hamburg 1, Federal Republic of Germany
(Tel: 33 04 00 and 33 06 00)

The Justus von Liebig Prizes, which each carry a 20,000-mark cash award, are given annually for the advancement of agriculture in Europe. The award is administered by the University of Kiel.

1949/50 Theodor Roemer, Halle, Germany
Carl Heinz Dencker, Bonn, Germany
1951 Emil Alfred, Neckarelz, Wurttemberg, Germany
1952 Walter Laube, Gottingen, Germany
1953 August Block, Rittergut Banteln, Germany
Richard von Flemming, Uelzen, Germany
1954 Walter Kubiena, Vienna, Austria
1955 Peter Rasmussen, Apenrade, Denmark
1956 Ernst Klapp, Bonn, Germany
1957 Wilhelm Ries, Michelstadt, Germany
1958 Walter Wittich, Hann.-Munden, Germany
1959 Hans Lembke, Rostock, Germany
Otto Bolten Rothenstein/Kreis Eckernforde, Germany
1960 Arthur Hanau, Gottingen, Germany
Roderich Plate, Stuttgart-Hohenheim, Germany
1961 Hans-Ulrich von Oertzen, Bad Godesberg, Germany
1962 P.B. de Boers, Stiens, Holland,
Count Ian D. Hamilton, Barseback, Sweden
1963 Bernard Poullain, La Queue-les-Yvelines, France
Bernhard Rademacher, Stuttgart-Hohenheim, Germany
1964 Walter Mader, Bruck a.d. Leitha, Austria
Fritz Schilke, Hambourg
1965 Giovanni Haussmann, Lodi, Italy
Constantin von Dietze, Freiburg i. Br., Germany
1966 Paul Nicolai, Gorsem, Belgium
Anton Freiherr von Herzogenberg, Salem/Baden, Germany
1967 Kutzenhausen Community, France
Dietz Freiherr von Thungen, Thungen,Unterfranken, Germany
1968 Sir Richard Trehane, Wimborne,Dorset, United Kingdom
Paul Rintelen, Munich, Germany
1969 Karl Brandt, Palo Alto, Calif.
Hans Rabe Jr., Sonke-Nissen-Koog, Germany
1970 Hjalmar Clausen, Copenhagen, Denmark,
Georg Blohm, Kiel, Germany
1971 Charles Kiss, La Menitre, France
Hermann Strehle, Reichertsweilerhof bei Donauworth, Germany
1972 Harald Skjervold Vollebekk, Norway,
Klauss Kleeberg, Eisbergen b. Minden, Germany
1973 Luigi Cavazza, Bologna, Italy
Count Heinrich Finck von Finckenstein, Winterburen/Hessen, Germany
1974 Lucijan Krivec, Ljubljana, Yugoslavia
Ulrich Dieckmann, Schaumburg, Germany

1975 Ingvar Ekesbo, Skara, Sweden
      Joachim von Wulfing, Swisttal-Heimerzheim, Germany
1976 Leopold Wiklicky, Tulln, Austria
      Philipp Kuhne, Gottingen, Germany
1977 Per Henrick Sumelius, Helsinki, Finland

Annie J. Cannon Award in Astronomy
Helen B. Warner Prize for Astronomy
Newton Lacey Pierce Prize in Astronomy
Henry Norris Russell Lectureship

AMERICAN ASTRONOMICAL SOCIETY
211 FitzRandolph Rd., Princeton, N.J. 08540 (609/452-3819)

The Annie J. Cannon Award in Astronomy is a grant given not more often than every two years to a woman under 35 years of age in support of astronomy research. The American Association of University Women makes the award to an applicant who normally has already earned her doctorate. The AAUW, assisted by the American Astronomical Society, selects the recipient.

1934 C. Payne-Gaposchkin (Harvard College Observatory), Stellar spectroscopy
1937 C. M. Sitterly (Princeton University Observatory), Atomic and solar spectra
1940 J. M. Vinter-Hansen (Royal Observatory, Copenhagen), Minor planets and comets
1943 A. C. Maury (Harvard College Observatory), Stellar spectra, Beta Lyrae
1946 E. W. Vyssotsky (Leander McCormick Observatory), Color indices, stellar spectra
1949 H. S. Hogg (David Dunlap Observatory), Globular star clusters
1952 I. Barney (Yale University Observatory), Fundamental star catalogues
1955 H. D. Prince (McMath-Hulbert Observatory), Solar investigations
1958 M. W. Mayall (AAVSO), Variable stars
1962 M. Harwood (Maria Mitchell Observatory), Variable stars
1965 E. Bohm-Vitense (Institut fur Theoretische Physik, Kiel, Germany), Theoretical astrophysics
1968 H. H. Swope (Hale Observatories), Stellar statistics
1976 Catherine Garmany (Unaffiliated), Stellar dynamics

The Helen B. Warner Prize for Astronomy, which carries a $1,000 honorarium, is awarded annually for significant contributions to astronomy during the five years preceding the award. Any member of the Society may nominate candidates who are North American residents and who are under 35 years of age for consideration by the Warner Prize Committee. The Warner Prize Committee will be combined with the Pierce Prize Committee [see below], and no individual will be eligible for both awards.

1954 A. B. Meinel, Infrared
1955 G. H. Herbig, Stellar spectroscopy
1956 H. Johnson, Photometry
1957 A. R. Sandage, Extragalactic
1958 M. F. Walker, Photometry

E. M. and G. Burbidge, Neucleosynthesis
1960 H. C. Arp, Extragalactic
1961 J. W. Chamberlain, Aurora
1962 R. P. Kraft, Stellar spectroscopy
1963 B. F. Burke, Radio observation
1964 M. Schmidt, Quasars
1965 G. W. Preston, Stellar atmospheres
1966 R. Giacconi, X-rays
1967 P. Demarque, Stellar interiors
1968 F. J. Low, Infrared observations
1969 W. L. W. Sargent, Extraglactic
1970 J. C. Bahcall, Neutrinos
1971 K. I. Kellermann, Radio interferometry
1972 J. P. Ostriker, Degenerate stars
1973 G. R. Carruthers, Instrumentation
1974 D. Mihalas, Stellar atmospheres
1975 B. Zuckerman and B. Palmer, Interstellar molecules
1976 S. Strom, Stellar structure
1977 F. Shu, Stellar dynamics

The Newton Lacey Pierce Prize in Astronomy, which consists of an honorarium and a certificate or other token determined by the Council, is awarded annually to an astronomer under 35 years of age for outstanding achievement over the previous five years in observational research based on measurements of radiation coming from any kind of astronomical object. Any member of the Society may nominate a candidate who is a resident of North America for consideration. The Pierce Prize Committee will be combined with the Warner Prize Commitee [see above], and no individual will be eligible for both awards

1973 E. Kellogg, X-ray instrumentation
1974 E. Becklin, Infrared instrumentation
1975 No award
1976 R. Angel, Polarization instrumentation
1977 D.N.B. Hall, Interferometry

The Henry Norris Russell Lectureship, which carries an honorarium of $500, is given annually for eminence in astronomical research. The candidate is selected by the Russell Lecture Committee with the approval of the Council.

1946 H. N. Russell, Structure
1947 W. S. Adams, Spectroscopy
1948 No award
1949 S. Chandrasekhar, Structure
1950 H. Shapley, Galactic structure
1951 J. H. Oort, Galactic structure
1952 No award
1953 E. Fermi, Neutrino theory
      L. Spitzer, Jr., Plasma theory
1954 No award
1955 P. W. Merrill, Spectroscopy
1956 J. Stebbins, Photometry
1957 O. Struve, Spectroscopy
1958 W. Baade, Galaxies
1959 G. P. Kuiper, Planetary
1960 M. Schwarzschild, Atmospheres
1961 W. W. Morgan, Classification
1962 G. Reber, Radio observation
1963 W. A. Fowler, Neucleosynthesis
1964 I. S. Bowen, Atomic theory
1965 B. G. Stromgren, Photometry
1966 R. Tousey, Rocket observation
1967 O. Neugebauer, Infrared
1968 J. G. Bolton, Radio observation
1969 E. N. Parker, X-ray theory
1970 J. Greenstein, Degenerate stars

1971 **F. Hoyle,** Cosmology
1972 **A. R. Sandage,** Cosmology
1972 **L. Goldberg,** Solar physics
1974 **E. Salpeter,** Stellar structure
1975 **G. Herbig,** Interstellar
1976 **C. P. Gaposchkin,** Variable stars
1977 **O. C. Wilson,** Spectroscopy

Astronomical League Award Presidential Citation

ASTRONOMICAL LEAGUE
Box 251, Papillion, Neb. 68046 (402/592-1196)

The Astronomical League Award plaque is given upon nomination and vote by the incumbent and two past presidents of the League for outstanding work in amateur astronomical societies or general astronomy.

1951 **Albert L. Ingalis,** "Father of Amateur Astronomy," author and telescope maker
1952 **Walter H. Haas,** Director, Assn. of Lunar and Planetary Observation
1953 **Charles A. Federer, Jr.,** Charter member of League; editor-in-chief, *Sky & Telescope Magazine*
1954 **H. Percy Wilkins,** English professional astronomer; author
      Armand Spitz, Lecturer; general benefactor of amateur astronomy; initiator, Moon Watch program
1955 **Carl P. Richards,** Pioneer League member; author of League history
1956 **Harlow Shapley,** Author; lecturer; head, Harvard School of Science
      Charlie M. Noble, Teacher; benefactor; involved with junior amateur astronomers
1957 **No award**
1958 **Clarence E. Johnson,** Publisher, monthly newsletter for junior astronomers; League junior chairman
1959 **Grace Scholz Spitz,** Charter member, executive secretary and president of the League; benefactor
1960 **No award**
1961 **No award**
1962 **Robert Cox,** Master telescope maker; *Sky & Telescope* columnist
1963 **Wilma A. Cherup,** League executive secretary for 23 years
1964 **Margaret W. Mayall,** Director, American Assn. of Variable Star Observers
1965 **G.R. (Bob) Wright,** League charter member
1966 **No award**
1967 **Norman Edmund,** Publisher, League Newsletter
1968 **Leslie Peltier,** Author; observer
1969 **Leonard G. Pardue,** League treasurer for 11 years
1970 **Russell C. Maag,** League officer; editor, League observer manual
1971 **Ralph K. Dakin,** League president; lecturer
1972 **Edward Halbach,** First elected League president
1973 **No award**
1974 **Walter Scott Houston,** Observer with own observatory; *Sky & Telescope* columnist
1975 **No award**
1976 **No award**
1977 **William and Cathryn DuVall** Contributions to the League

PRESIDENTIAL CITATION
1977 Wilma A. Cherup

Waterford Bio-Medical Science Award

SCRIPPS CLINIC & RESEARCH FOUNDATION
La Jolla, Calif. 92037 (714/455-9100)

The $7,500 Waterford Bio-Medical Science Award was initiated to honor significant achievements in biomedical research. Waterford Crystal supports the award, which is administered by the Scripps Foundation. A crystal trophy accompanies the honor. The recipient, who may be of any nationality, is selected by a scientists' committee of peers.

1977 **Maclyn McCarty,** Rockefeller University

Botanical Society of America Merit Awards
Darbaker Prize

BOTANICAL SOCIETY OF AMERICA
New York Botanical Garden, Bronx, N.Y. 10458
(212/220-8628)

Three Botanical Society of America Merit Award certificates are given each year for outstanding contributions in botanical science as selected by the president of the society. Previously, more than three awards a year were given.

1956 **Harry Ardell Allard**
      Edgar Anderson
      Dixon Lloyd Bailey
      Irving Widmer Bailey
      Harley Harris Bartlett
      George Wells Beadle
      Ernst Athearn Bessey
      Sidney Fay Blake
      Emma Lucy Braun
      Stanley Adair Cain
      Ralph Works Chaney
      Agnes Chase
      Jens Christian Clausen
      Ralph Erskine Cleland
      Henry Shoemaker Conard
      William Skinner Cooper
      John Nathaniel Couch
      Bernard Ogilvie Dodge
      Benjamin Minge Duggar
      Arthur Johnson Eames
      Katherine Esau
      Alexander William Evans
      Henry Allan Gleason
      Thomas H. Kearney
      George Wannamaker Keitt
      Paul Jackson Kramer
      Louis Otto Kunkel
      Daniel Trembly MacDougal
      George Willard Martin
      Maximino Martinez
      Frederick Wilson Popenoe
      William Jacob Robbins
      Andrew Denney Rodgers III
      Jacques Rousseau
      Karl Sax
      Paul Bigelow Sears
      Homer Leroy Shantz
      Edmund Ware Sinnott
      Folke Karl Skoog

Gilbert Morgan Smith
Elvin Charles Stakman
George Ledyard Stebbins, Jr.
John Albert Stevenson
Kenneth Vivian Thimann
Edgar Nelson Transeau
Cornelius Bernardus Van Niel
John Ernst Weaver
Fritz Warnolt Went
Ralph Harley Wetmore
Truman George Yuncker
1957 Donald F. Jones
Paul Mangelsdorf
Barbara McClintock
William H. Weston
1958 Harry James Fuller
Philip Alexander Munz
Lester Whyland Sharp
1959 James Bonner
Lincoln Constance
Adriance S. Foster
Bernard S. Meyer
Loren C. Petry
1960 James P. Bennett
William Dwight Billings
Walter Conrad Muenscher
Kenneth B. Raper
Reed Clark Rollins
1961 F. C. Steward
William Randolph Taylor
1962 David R. Goddard
Marcus M. Rhoades
1963 Harry A. Borthwick
Vernon I. Cheadle
John C. Walker
1964 Ralph Emerson
Sterling Hendricks
Ira Wiggins
1965 Daniel I. Arnon
Harold C. Bold
1966 Henry N. Andrews, Jr.
R. H. Burris
George F. PapenfussR. H. Burris
1967 C. J. Alexopoulos
William M. Miesey
1968 Elso S. Barghoorn
F. K. Sparrow
1969 Armin C. Braun
John R. Raper
Jacob R. Schram
Alex H. Smith
1970 Charles Drechsler
Arthur Galston
James M. Schopf
Albert C. Smith
1971 Murray F. Buell
Verne Grant
Ruth Patrick
A. Earling Porsild
1972 Charles B. Heiser, Jr.
Frank Harlan Lewis
Aaron J. Sharp
1973 Charles Stacy French
Mildred Esther Mathias
Richard Cawthon Starr
1974 Chester A. Arnold
Arthur Cronquist
Gerald W. Prescott
1975 Harlan P. Banks
F. Herbert Bormann

William C. Steere
1976 Charles M. Rick
Paul Weatherwax
Thomas W. Whitaker
1977 Sherwin Carlquist
Rogers McVaugh
Peter Raven

One Darbaker Prize of $400 is given each year to a resident of North America for meritorious work in the study of microscopical algae. Selection is made by a Botanical Society committee selected by the president.

1955 R. C. Starr
1956 R. W. Krauss
1957 No award
1958 R. A. Lewin and P. C. Silva
1959 J. Myers
1960 J. Stein
1961 Paul Green
1962 Mary B. Allen
1963 Y. Dawson
1964 R. Scagel
1965 F. R. Trainor
1966 R. D. Wood
1967 J. Lewin
1968 R. Guillard and J. S. Craigie
1969 Isabella A. Abbott and Norma J. Lang
1970 Bruce C. Parker
1971 Richard W. Eppley and Michael J. Wynne
1972 Michael Neushul
1973 John West
1974 Jeremy David Pickett-Heaps
1975 Sarah P. Gibbs and Larry R. Hoffman
1976 Kenneth Stewart and Karl Mattox
1977 Alfred Loeblich III

Mary Soper Pope Award
CRANBROOK INSTITUTE OF SCIENCE
500 Lone Pine Rd., Box 807, Bloomfield Hills, Mich. 48013
(313/645-3200)

The Mary Soper Pope Award, which consists of a medal designed by Marshall M. Fredericks, is given as warranted for accomplishment in education or research in the botanical sciences. A six-member awards committee selects the recipient.

1947 Frans Verdoorn
1948 William Vogt
1949 Charles Deam
1950 Jens C. Clausen, David D. Keck, and William M. Hiesey
1951 Martin Cardenas
1952 E. Lucy Braun
1954 Irving W. Bailey
1959 Kenneth W. Neatby
1962 Edmund H. Fulling
1964 Edgar T. Wherry
1966 Karl and Hally Jolivette Sax
1969 Stanley Adair Cain
1970 William Campbell Steere

Nobel Prize in Chemistry
NOBEL FOUNDATION
Nobel House, Sturegatan 14, 11436-Stockholm, Sweden

The Nobel Prize in Chemistry is generally recognized

as the highest honor which can be bestowed upon a chemist for an exceptionally noteworthy discovery in this scientific field. The award, which consists of a gold medal, diploma and a large honorarium, is given in a ceremony on December 10 of each year at Stockholm's City Hall. The awards are presented and administered by the Royal Swedish Academy of Sciences. The amount of the honorarium fluctuates. In 1977, it was approximately $145,000.

1901 **Jacobus H. van't Hoff** (Netherlands), Discovered chemical-dynamics laws and osmotic pressure in solutions

1902 **Hermann E. Fisher** (Germany), Research on sugar and purine syntheses

1903 **Svante E. Arrhenius** (Sweden), Electrolytic theory of dissociation

1904 **Sir William Ramsey** (Great Britain), Discovered inert gaseous elements in air and determined their place in the periodic system

1905 **Johann von Baeyer** (Germany), Work on organic dyes and hydroaromatic compounds

1906 **Henri Moissan** (France), Study and isolation of fluorine; development of an electric furnace

1907 **Eduard Buchner** (Germany), Biochemical research on cell-free fermentatation

1908 **Ernest Rutherford** (Great Britain), Work on disintegration of elements and chemistry of radioactive substances

1909 **Wilhelm Ostwald** (Germany), Research on catalysis and basic principles of chemical equilibria and rates of reaction

1910 **Otto Wallach** (Germany), Pioneering work in alicyclic compounds

1911 **Marie Curie** (France, born in Poland), Discovered radium and polonium, isolated radium and studied its nature

1912 **Victor Grignard** (France), Discovered Grignard reagent
Paul Sabatier (France), Hydrogenated organic compounds in the presence of disintegrated metals

1913 **Alfred Werner** (Switzerland, born in Germany), Linked atoms in molecules

1914 **Theodore W. Richards** (U.S.A.), Determination of atomic weight of many elements

1915 **Richard M. Willstatter** (Germany), Research on plant pigments, particularly chlorophyll

1916 **No award**

1917 **No award**

1918 **Fritz Haber** (Germany), Synthesized ammonia

1919 **No award**

1920 **Walter H. Nernst** (Germany), Research in thermochemistry

1921 **Frederick Soddy** (Great Britain), Studied radioactive substances and investigated the origin and nature of isotopes

1922 **Francis W. Alston** (Great Britain), Discovered isotopes in many non-radioactive materials

1923 **Fritz Pregl** (Austria), Invented method of microanalyzing organic substances

1924 **No award**

1925 **Richard A. Zsigmondy** (Germany), Demonstrated heterogeneous nature of colloid solutions

1926 **Theodor Svedberg** (Sweden), Dispersion-system research

1927 **Heinrich O. Wieland** (Germany), Studied bile acids and related substances

1928 **Adolf O.R. Windaus** (Germany), Research on sterols and their relation to vitamins

1929 **Arthur Harden** (Great Britain), Research on fermentation of sugar and fermentative enzymes
Hans von Euler-Chelpin (Sweden), Research on fermentation of sugar and fermentative enzymes

1930 **Hans Fischer** (Germany), Work on haemin and chlorophyll

1931 **Friedrich Bergius** (Germany), Developed chemical high-pressure methods

1932 **Irving Langmuir** (U.S.A.), Surface-chemistry research

1933 **No award**

1934 **Harold C. Urey** (U.S.A.), Discovered heavy hydrogen

1935 **Frederic Joliot-Curie and Irene Joliot-Curie** (France), Synthesized new radioactive elements

1936 **Peter J.W. Debye** (Netherlands), Work on molecular structure via studies of dipole moments and diffraction of X-rays and electrons in gases

1937 **Walter N. Haworth** (Great Britain), Work on carbohydrates and vitamin C
Paul Karrer (Switzerland, born in Russia), Work on carotenoids, flavin and vitamins A and B_2

1938 **Richard Kuhn** (Germany), Work on vitamins

1939 **Adolf F. J. Butenandt** (Germany), Work on sex hormones
Leopold Ruzicka (Switzerland), Research on polymethylenes and higher terpenes

1940 **No award**

1941 **No award**

1942 **No award**

1943 **Georg de Hevesy** (Hungary), Use of isotopes as chemical tracers

1944 **Otto Hahn** (Germany), Heavy-nuclei fission

1945 **Artturi I. Virtanen** (Finland), Agricultural and nutrition chemistry

1946 **James B. Summer** (U.S.A.), Crystallization of enzymes
John H. Northrup and Wendell M. Stanley (U.S.A.), Prepared pure form of enzymes

1947 **Sir Robert Robinson** (Great Britain), Investigated biologically important plant products

1948 **Arne W.K. Tiselius** (Sweden), Work on electrophoresis and adsorption analysis

1949 **William F. Giauque** (U.S.A.), Chemical thermodynamic research, especially on the behavior of substances at extremely low temperatures

1950 **Kurt Adler and Otto P.H. Diels** (Germany), Discovered and developed diene synthesis

1951 **Edwin M. McMillan and Glenn T. Seaborg** (U.S.A.), Research on transuranium elements

1952 **Archer J.P. Martin and Richard L.M. Synge** (Great Britain), Invented partition chromatography to analyze mixtures

1953 **Hermann Staudinger** (Germany), Macromolecular chemistry research

1954 **Linus C. Pauling** (U.S.A.), Research on nature of chemical bond and its application to the elucidation of complex substance structure

1955 **Vincent du Vigneaud** (U.S.A.), Research of biochemically significant compounds, particularly the synthesis of a polypeptide hormone

1956 **Sir Cyril N. Hinshelwood** (Great Britain) **and Nikolai N. Semenov** (U.S.S.R.) Research on chemical-reaction mechanisms

1957 **Sir Alexander R. Todd** (Great Britain), Research on nucleotides and nucleotide coenzymes

1958 **Frederick Sanger** (Great Britain), Work on protein structure, especially of insulin

1959 **Jaroslav Heyrovsky** (Czechoslovakia), Discovered and developed polarographic methods of analysis

1960 **Willard F. Libby** (U.S.A.), Used carbon 14 dating for age determination in archeology, geology, geophysics, etc.

1961 **Melvin Calvin** (U.S.A.), Research on assimilation of carbon dioxide in plants

1962 **John C. Kendrew** (Great Britain) **and Max F. Perutz** (Great Britain, born in Austria), Research on structures of globular proteins

1963 **Guilio Natta** (Italy) **and Karl Ziegler** (Germany), Research of chemistry and technology of high polymers

1964 **Dorothy Crowfoot Hodgkin** (Great Britain), Discovered structure of significant biochemical substances by X-ray

1965 **Robert B. Woodward** (U.S.A.), Synthesized complicated organic compounds

1966 **Robert S. Mulliken** (U.S.A.), Basic work on chemical bonds and electronic structure of molecules by the modular orbital method

1967 **Manfred Eigen** (Germany), **Ronald G.W. Norrish** (Great Britain) **and George Porter** (Great Britain), Work on extremely rapid chemical reactions accomplished by disturbing the equilibrium with short pulses of energy

1968 **Lars Onsager** (U.S.A., born in Norway), Discovered reciprocal relations fundamental to thermodynamics of irreversible processes

1969 **Derek H.R. Barton** (Great Britain) **and Odd Hassel** (Norway), Development and application of conformation in chemistry

1970 **Luis F. Leloir** (Argentina), Discovered sugar nucleotides

1971 **Gerhard Herzberg** (Canada, born in Germany), Research in electronic structure and geometry of molecules

1972 **Christian B. Anfinsen, Stanford Moore and William H. Stein** (U.S.A.), Work on chemical structure and biological reactions of protein, especially ribonuclease

1973 **Ernst Otto Fischer** (Germany) **and Geoffry Wilkinson** (Great Britain), Merged organic and metallic compounds as part of auto-pollution control research

1974 **Paul J. Flory** (U.S.A.), Analytical methodology for studying longchain molecules for development of synthetics

1975 **John Warcus Cornforth** (Great Britain), **and Vladimir Prelog** (Switzerland, born in Yugoslavia), Stereochemistry research involving how properties of chemical compounds are influenced by arrangement of their atoms

1976 **William N. Lipscomb** (U.S.A.), Research on structure and bonding of boranes and nature of chemical bonding

1977 **Ilya Prigogine** (U.S.A. and Belgium, born in Russia), Contributions to nonequilibrium thermodynamics, especially theory of dissipative structures

Roger Adams Award in Organic Chemistry

ACS Creative Invention Award

ACS Award for Creative Work in Synthetic Organic Chemistry

ACS Award in Chemical Education

ACS Award for Distinguished Service in the Advancement of Inorganic Chemistry

ACS Award in Colloid or Surface Chemistry

ACS Award in Nuclear Applications in Chemistry

ACS Award in Analytical Chemistry

ACS Award in Chromatography

ACS Award in Inorganic Chemistry

ACS Award in Petroleum Chemistry

ACS Award in Polymer Chemistry

ACS Award in Pure Chemistry

ACS Award in the Chemistry of Plastics and Coatings

Arthur S. Cope Award

Garvan Medal

James R. Grady Award for Interpreting Chemistry for the Public

Ernest Guenther Award in the Chemistry of Essential Oils

Ipatieff Prize

Frederick Stanley Kipping Award in Organosilicon Chemistry

Irving Langmuir Award in Chemical Physics

E. V. Murphree Award in Industrial and Engineering Chemistry

James Flack Norris Award in Inorganic Chemistry

Charles Lathrop Parsons Award

Priestley Medal

AMERICAN CHEMICAL SOCIETY
1155 Sixteenth St. NW, Washington, D.C. 20036
(202/872-4481)

American Chemical Society Awards are made through nomination by Society members and selection by a committee of experts in each field. Recipients must appear at the ACS annual meeting; each award includes a travel stipend in addition to the honorarium indicated, as well as a medal, scroll or citation.

The $10,000 Roger Adams Award in Organic Chemistry, sponsored by Organic Reactions, Inc., is presented biennially for research defined in its broadest sense. The recipient must deliver a lecture at the Biennial National Organic Chemistry Symposium.

1959 D.H.R. Barton
1961 Robert B. Woodward
1963 Paul D. Bartlett
1965 Arthur C. Cope
1967 John D. Roberts
1969 Vladimir Prelog
1971 Herbert C. Brown
1973 George Wittig
1975 Rolf Huisgen
1977 William S. Johnson

The $2,000 ACS Creative Invention Award, sponsored by the Society's Corporate Associates, honors an individual residing in the United States or Canada for successful applications of research in chemistry and/or chemical engineering that contributes "to the material prosperity or happiness of people."

1968 William G. Pfann
1969 J. Paul Hogan
1970 Gordon K. Teal
1971 S. Donald Stookey
1972 H. Tracy Hall
1973 Carl Djerassi
1974 Charles C. Price
1975 James D. Idol, Jr.
1976 Manuel M. Baizer
1977 Herman A. Bruson

The $2,000 ACS Award for Creative Work in Synthetic Organic Chemistry, sponsored by Aldrich Chemical Co., recognizes outstanding creative work in synthetic organic chemistry published by an American journal during the five preceeding years.

1957 Robert B. Woodward
1958 William S. Johnson
1959 John C. Sheehan
1960 Herbert C. Brown
1961 Melvin S. Newman
1962 Charles R. Hauser
1963 Nelson J. Leonard
1964 Lewis H. Sarett
1965 Donald J. Cram
1966 William von E. Doering
1967 Gilbert J. Stork
1968 Theodore L. Cairns
1969 H. Gobind Khorana
1970 Eugene E. van Tamelen
1971 Elias J. Corey
1972 Bruce Merrifield
1973 George Buchi
1974 Edward C. Taylor
1975 Herbert O. House
1976 Franz Sondheimer
1977 No award

The $2,000 ACS Award in Chemical Education, sponsored by Union Carbide Corp., recognizes contributions to chemical education in its broadest meaning, including the training of professional chemists, dissemination of reliable information about the field and the integration of chemistry into our educational system. The recipient's activities may lie in teaching any level, organization or administration. Preference is given to American citizens.

1952 Joel H. Hildebrand

1953 Howard J. Lucas
1954 Raymond E. Kirk
1955 Gerrit Van Zyl
1956 Otto M. Smith
1957 Norris W. Rakestraw
1958 Frank E. Brown
1959 Harry F. Lewis
1960 Arthur F. Scott
1961 John C. Bailar, Jr.
1962 William G. Young
1963 Edward L. Haenisch
1964 Alfred B. Garrett
1965 Theodore A. Ashford
1966 W. Conway Pierce
1967 Louis F. Fieser
1968 William F. Kieffer
1969 L. Carroll King
1970 Hubert N. Alyea
1971 Laurence E. Strong
1972 J. Arthur Campbell
1973 Robert C. Brasted
1974 George S. Hammond
1975 William T. Lippincott
1976 Leallyn B. Clapp
1977 Robert W. Parry

The $2,000 ACS Award to a Society member for Distinguished Service in the Advancement of Inorganic Chemistry, sponsored by Mallinckrodt, Inc., honors extensive contributions in the field, such as teaching, writing, research and administration.

1965 Robert W. Parry
1966 George H. Cady
1967 Henry Taube
1968 William N. Lipscomb, Jr.
1969 Anton B. Burg
1970 Ralph G. Pearson
1971 Joseph Chatt
1972 John C. Bailar, Jr.
1973 Ronald J. Gillespie
1974 F. Albert Cotton
1975 Fred Basolo
1976 Daryle H. Busch
1977 James L. Hoard

The $2,000 ACS Award in Colloid or Surface Chemistry, sponsored by The Kendall Co., honors the achievements of a resident of the U.S. or Canada in colloid or surface chemistry.

1954 Harry N. Holmes
1955 John W. Williams
1956 Victor K. La Mer
1957 Peter J. W. Debye
1958 Paul H. Emmett
1959 Floyd E. Bartell
1960 John D. Ferry
1961 Stephen Brunauer
1962 George Scatchard
1963 William Albert Zisman
1964 Karol J. Mysels
1965 George D. Halsey, Jr.
1966 Robert S. Hansen
1967 Stanley G. Mason
1968 Albert C. Zettlemoyer
1969 Terrell L. Hill
1970 Jerome Vinograd
1971 Milton Kerker
1972 Egon Matijevic
1973 Robert L. Burwell, Jr.

1974 W. Keith Hall
1975 Robert Gomer
1976 Robert J. Good
1977 Michel Boudart

The $2,000 ACS Award in Nuclear Applications in Chemistry, sponsored by G.D. Searle & Co., recognizes contributions to nuclear isotopic applications in the field of chemistry.

1955 Henry Taube
1956 Willard F. Libby
1957 Melvin Calvin
1958 Jacob Bigeleisen
1959 John E. Willard
1960 Charles D. Coryell
1961 Joseph J. Katz
1962 Truman P. Kohman
1963 Martin D. Kamen
1964 Isadore Perlman
1965 Stanley G. Thompson
1966 Arthur C. Wahl
1967 Gerhart Friedlander
1968 Richard L. Wolfgang
1969 George E. Boyd
1970 Paul R. Fields
1971 Alfred P. Wolf
1972 Anthony Turkevich
1973 Albert Ghiorso
1974 Lawrence E. Glendenin
1975 John R. Huizenga
1976 John O. Rasmussen
1977 Glen E. Gordon

The $2,000 ACS Award in Analytical Chemistry, sponsored by the Fisher Scientific Co., honors a resident of the U.S. or Canada for contributions in the field, with special consideration given to independence of thought and originality shown, or to the importance of the work when applied to public welfare, economics or the needs and desires of humanity.

1948 N. Howell Furman
1949 G.E.F. Lundell
1950 Isaac M. Kolthoff
1951 M. H. Willard
1952 Melvin G. Mellon
1953 Donald D. Van Slyke
1954 G. Frederick Smith
1955 Ernest H. Swift
1956 Harvey Diehl
1957 John H. Yoe
1958 James J. Lingane
1959 James I. Hoffman
1960 Philip J. Elving
1961 Herbert A. Laitinen
1962 H. A. Liebhafsky
1963 David N. Hume
1964 John Mitchell, Jr.
1965 Charles N. Reilley
1966 Lyman C. Craig
1967 Lawrence T. Hallett
1968 Lockhart B. Rogers
1969 Roger G. Bates
1970 Charles V. Banks
1971 George H. Morrison
1972 W. Wayne Meinke
1973 James D. Winefordner
1974 Philip W. West
1975 Sidney Siggia
1976 Howard V. Malmstadt

1977 George G. Guilbault

The $2,000 ACS Award in Chromatography, sponsored by SUPELCO, Inc., is given for contributions to chromography, with particular considerations to new methods.

1961 Harold H. Strain
1962 L. Zechmeister
1963 Waldo E. Cohn
1964 Stanford Moore and William H. Stein
1965 Stephen Dal Nogare
1966 Kurt A. Kraus
1967 J. Calvin Giddings
1968 Lewis G. Longsworth
1969 Morton Beroza
1970 Julian F. Johnson
1972 J.J. Kirkland
1973 Albert Zlatkis
1974 Lockhart B. Rogers
1975 Egon Stahl
1976 James S. Fritz
1977 Raymond P.W. Scott

The $2,000 ACS Award in Inorganic Chemistry, sponsored by the Monsanto Co., honors accomplishments in the preparation, properties, reactions or structure of inorganic substances.

1962 F. Albert Cotton
1963 Daryle H. Busch
1964 Fred Basolo
1965 Earl L. Muetterties
1966 Geoffrey Wilkinson
1967 John L. Margrave
1968 Jack Halpern
1969 Russell S. Drago
1970 Neil Bartlett
1971 Jack Lewis
1972 Theodore L. Brown
1973 M. F. Hawthorne
1974 Lawrence F. Dahl
1975 James P. Collman
1976 Richard H. Holm
1977 No award

The $5,000 ACS Award in Petroleum Chemistry, sponsored by the Lubrizol Corp., is given to a resident of the U.S. or Canada for outstanding research in the chemistry of petroleum or fundamental research that contributes directly and materially to the knowledge of petroleum and its products. Special consideration is given for independence of thought and originality.

1949 Bruce H. Sage
1950 Kenneth S. Pitzer
1951 Louis Schmerling
1952 Vladimir Haensel
1953 Robert W. Schiessler
1954 Arthur P. Lien
1955 Frank Ciapetta
1956 Milburn J. O'Neal, Jr.
1957 C. Gardner Swain
1958 Robert P. Eischens
1959 George C. Pimentel
1960 Robert W. Taft, Jr.
1961 George S. Hammond
1962 Harold Hart
1963 John P. McCullough
1964 George A. Olah
1965 Glen A. Russell
1966 James Wei

1967	Andrew Streitwieser, Jr.
1968	Keith U. Ingold
1969	Alan Schriesheim
1970	Lloyd R. Snyder
1971	Gerasimos J. Karabatsos
1972	Paul G. Gassman
1973	Joe W. Hightower
1976	John H. Sinfelt
1977	Sidney W. Benson

The $2,000 ACS Award in Polymer Chemistry, sponsored by Witco Chemical Corp. Foundation, recognizes achievements in the field.

1964	Carl S. Marvel
1965	Herman F. Mark
1966	Walter H. Stockmayer
1967	Frank R. Mayo
1968	Charles G. Overberger
1969	Frank A. Bovey
1970	Michael M. Szwarc
1971	Georges J. Smets
1972	Arthur V. Tobolsky
1973	Turner Alfrey, Jr.
1974	John D. Ferry
1975	Leo Mandelkern
1976	Paul W. Morgan
1977	William J. Bailey

The $2,000 ACS Award in Pure Chemistry, sponsored by the Alpha Chi Sigma Fraternity is given to an individual under 36 years of age "on the threshold of his career" for research of unusual merit, with special consideration for originality of research which must have been done in North America and for independence of thought.

1931	Linus Pauling
1932	Oscar K. Rice
1933	Frank H. Spedding
1934	C. Frederick Koelsch
1935	Raymond M. Fuoss
1936	John Gamble Kirkwood
1937	E. Bright Wilson, Jr.
1938	Paul D. Bartlett
1940	Lawrence O. Brockway
1941	Karl A. Folkers
1942	John Lawrence Oncley
1943	Kenneth S. Pitzer
1944	Arthur C. Cope
1945	Frederick T. Wall
1946	Charles C. Price, III
1947	Glenn T. Seaborg
1948	Saul Winstein
1949	Richard T. Arnold
1950	Verner Schomaker
1951	John C. Sheehan
1952	Harrison S. Brown
1953	William von E. Doering
1954	John D. Roberts
1955	Paul Delahay
1956	Paul M. Doty
1957	Gilbert J. Stork
1958	Carl Djerassi
1959	Ernest M. Grunwald
1960	Elias J. Corey
1961	Eugene E. van Tamelen
1962	Harden M. McConnell
1963	Stuart A. Rice
1964	Marshall Fixman
1965	Dudley Herschbach

1966	Ronald Breslow
1967	John D. Baldeschwieler
1968	Orville L. Chapman
1969	Roald Hoffmann
1970	Harry B. Gray
1971	R. Bruce King
1972	Roy G. Gordon
1973	John I. Brauman
1974	Nicholas J. Turro
1975	George M. Whitesides
1976	Karl F. Freed
1977	Barry M. Trost

The $2,000 ACS Award in the Chemistry of Plastics and Coatings, sponsored by the Borden Foundation, is given to a resident of the U.S. or Canada under 46 years of age for achievements in the chemistry and application of plastics and coatings to adhesives, printing and thermoplastic polymers.

1968	Harry Burrell
1969	Sylvan O. Greenlee
1970	Raymond F. Boyer
1971	Raymond R. Myers
1972	Richard S. Stein
1973	Carl S. Marvel
1974	Vivian T. Stannett
1975	Maurice L. Huggins
1976	Herman F. Mark
1977	William A. Zisman

The $10,000 Arthur S. Cope Award recognizes outstanding achievement in organic chemistry, whose significance has become apparent within the previous five years. A gold medal and bronze replica are also awarded in this biennial honor. In addition, an unrestricted grant-in-aid of $10,000 for research in organic chemistry under the direction of the Cope Award recipient may be made to a university or non-profit institution selected by the recipient

1973	Robert B. Woodward and Roald Hoffmann
1974	Donald J. Cram
1976	Elias J. Corey

The $2,000 Garvan Medal recognizes distinguished service by a woman chemist who is a citizen of the United States.

1937	Emma P. Carr
1940	Mary E. Pennington
1942	Florence B. Seibert
1946	Icie G. Macy-Hoobler
1947	Mary Laura Sherrill
1948	Gerty T. Cori
1949	Agnes Fay Morgan
1950	Pauline Beery Mack
1951	Katherine B. Blodgett
1952	Gladys A. Emerson
1953	Leonora N. Bilger
1954	Betty Sullivan
1955	Grace Medes
1956	Allene R. Jeans
1957	Lucy W. Pickett
1958	Arda A. Green
1959	Dorothy V. Nightingale
1960	Mary L. Caldwell
1961	Sarah Ratner
1962	Helen M. Dyer
1963	Mildred Cohn
1964	Birgit Vennesland
1965	Gertrude E. Perlmann

1966   Mary L. Peterman
1967   Marjorie J. Vold
1968   Gertrude B. Elion
1969   Sofia Simmonds
1970   Ruth R. Benerito
1971   Mary Fieser
1972   Jean'ne M. Shreeve
1973   Mary L. Good
1974   Joyce J. Kaufman
1975   Marjorie C. Caserio
1976   Isabella L. Karle
1977   Marjorie C. Horning

The $2,000 James R. Grady Award for Interpreting Chemistry for the Public honors noteworthy presentations through a public-communication medium to increase the American public's understanding of chemistry and chemical progress.

1957   David H. Killeffer
1958   William L. Laurence
1959   Alton L. Blakeslee
1960   Watson Davis
1961   David Dietz
1962   John F. Baxter
1963   Lawrence Lessing
1964   Nate Haseltine
1965   Isaac Asimov
1966   Frank E. Carey
1967   Irving S. Bengelsdorf
1968   Raymond A. Bruner
1969   Walter Sullivan
1970   Robert C. Cowen
1971   Victor Cohn
1972   Dan Q. Posin
1973   O. A. Battista
1974   Ronald Kotulak
1975   Jon Franklin
1976   Gene Bylinsky
1977   Patrick Young

The $2,000 Ernest Guenther Award in the Chemistry of Essential Oils and Related Products, sponsored by Fritzsche Dodge & Olcott, Inc., honors work in analysis, structure elucidation, chemical synthesis of essential oils, flavors and related substances, with special consideration for independence of thought and originality.

1949   John L. Simonsen
1950   A. J. Haagen-Smit
1951   Edgar Lederer
1952   Yves-Rene Naves
1953   Max Stoll
1954   A. R. Penfold
1955   Hans Schinz
1956   Herman Pines
1957   D.H. R. Barton
1958   George H. Buchi
1959   Frantisek Sorm
1960   Carl Djerassi
1961   C. F. Seidel
1962   E. R. H. Jones
1063   Arthur J. Birch
1964   Oskar Jeger
1965   Konrad E. Bloch
1966   Albert J. Eschenmoser
1967   George A. Sim
1968   Elias J. Corey
1969   John W. Cornforth
1970   Duilio Arigoni
1971   Ernest Wenkert

1972   Guy Ourisson
1973   William G. Dauben
1974   Gunther Ohloff
1975   S. Morris Kupchan
1976   Alastair I. Scott
1977   Robert E. Ireland

The $3,000 Ipatieff Prize is awarded every three years to an individual under 40 years of age for outstanding chemical experimental work in the field of catalysis or high pressure. While preference is given to American chemists, the work may have been carried out in any country or by scientists of any nationality. Special consideration is given for independence or thought and originality.

1947   Louis Schmerling
1950   Herman E. Ries
1953   Robert B. Anderson
1956   Harry G. Drickamer
1959   Cedomir M. Sliepcevich
1962   Charles Kemball
1965   Robert H. Wentorf, Jr.
1968   Charles R. Adams
1971   Paul B. Venuto
1974   George A. Samara
1977   Charles A. Eckert

The $2,000 Frederick Stanley Kipping Award in Organosilicon Chemistry, sponsored by the Dow Corning Corp., honors achievement in the field over the previous 10 years. The measure of this achievement is the winner's significant publications and may also include contributions in a related field.

1962   Henry Gilman
1963   Leo H. Sommer
1964   Colin Eaborn
1965   Eugene G. Rochow
1966   Gerhard Fritz
1967   Makoto Kumada
1968   Ulrich Wannagat
1969   Robert A. Benkeser
1970   Robert West
1971   Alan G. MacDiarmid
1972   Dietmar Seyferth
1973   Adrian G. Brook
1974   Hubert Schmidbaur
1975   Hans Bock
1976   Michael F. Lappert

The $5,000 Irving Langmuir Award in Chemical Physics, sponsored by the General Electric Foundation, honors a resident of the United States for achievement during the previous 10 years in chemical physics or physical chemistry. The honorarium must be used in the United States.

1965   John H. Van Vleck
1966   H. S. Gutowsky
1967   John C. Slater
1968   Henry Eyring
1969   Charles P. Slichter
1970   John A. Pople
1971   Michael E. Fisher
1972   Harden M. McConnell
1973   Peter M. Rentzepis
1974   Harry G. Drickamer
1975   Robert H. Cole
1976   John S. Waugh
1977   No award

The $2,000 E.V. Murphree Award in Industrial and Engineering Chemistry, sponsored by Exxon Research and Engineering Co., honors research of a theoretical or experimental nature in industrial chemistry or chemical engineering.

1957	Warren K. Lewis
1958	duBois Eastman
1959	Edwin R. Gilliland
1960	Neal R. Amundson
1961	Olaf A. Hougen
1962	Eugene J. Houdry
1963	Manson Benedict
1964	Bruce H. Sage
1965	Vladimir Haensel
1966	Richard H. Wilhelm
1967	Alfred Clark
1968	Melvin A. Cook
1969	Alex G. Obald
1970	Peter V. Danckwerts
1971	Heinz Heinemann
1972	Paul B. Weisz
1973	Thomas K. Sherwood
1974	Herman S. Bloch
1975	Donald L. Katz
1976	James F. Roth
1977	Alexis Voorhies, Jr.

The $2,000 James Flack Norris Award in Inorganic Chemistry, sponsored by the Northeastern Section ACS, honors contributions in physical inorganic chemistry.

1965	Christopher K. Ingold
1966	Louis P. Hammett
1967	Saul Winstein
1968	George S. Hammond
1969	Paul D. Bartlett
1970	Frank H. Westheimer
1971	Cheves Walling
1972	Stanley J. Cristol
1973	Kenneth B. Wiberg
1974	Gerhard L. Closs
1975	Kurt M. Mislow
1976	Howard E. Zimmerman
1977	Edward M. Arnett

The $2,000 Charles Lathrop Parsons Award is generally given at intervals of two years or greater to an American citizen and ACS member for outstanding public service as part of or outside the individual's field.

1952	Charles L. Parsons
1955	James B. Conant
1958	Roger Adams
1961	George B. Kistiakowsky
1964	Glenn T. Seaborg
1967	Donald F. Hornig
1970	W. Albert Noyes, Jr.
1973	Charles C. Price
1974	Russell W. Peterson
1976	William O. Baker

The Priestley Medal, which is of gold, annually honors an individual's services to chemistry.

1923	Ira Remsen
1926	Edgar F. Smith
1929	Francis P. Garvan
1932	Charles L. Parsons
1935	William A. Noyes
1938	Marston T. Bogert
1941	Thomas Midgley, Jr.

1944	James B. Conant
1945	Ian Heilbron
1946	Roger Adams
1947	Warren K. Lewis
1948	Edward R. Weidlein
1949	Arthur B. Lamb
1950	Charles A. Kraus
1951	E.J. Crane
1952	Samuel C. Lind
1953	Robert Robinson
1954	W. Albert Noyes, Jr.
1955	Charles A. Thomas
1956	Carl S. Marvel
1957	Farrington Daniels
1958	Ernest H. Volwiler
1959	H.I. Schlesinger
1960	Wallace R. Brode
1961	Louis P. Hammett
1962	Joel H. Hildebrand
1963	Peter J. W. Debye
1964	John C. Bailar, Jr.
1965	William J. Sparks
1966	William O. Baker
1967	Ralph Connor
1968	William G. Young
1969	Kenneth S. Pitzer
1970	Max Tishler
1971	Frederick D. Rossini
1972	George B. Kistiakowsky
1973	Harold C. Urey
1974	Paul J. Flory
1975	Henry Eyring
1976	George S. Hammond
1977	Henry Gilman

Chemical Pioneers Scroll Gold Medal

AMERICAN INSTITUTE OF CHEMISTS
7315 Wisconsin Ave., Washington, D.C. 20014
(301/652-2447)

The Chemical Pioneers Scroll is awarded annually to chemists whose research ideas have benefited mankind and expanded the frontiers of knowledge and technology.

1966 Carl E. Barnes, Applied chemistry
Herman A. Bruson (Olin Mathieson Corp.), Organic chemistry
C.H. Fisher (U.S. Dept. of Agriculture), Rubber chemistry
Robert M. Joyce, Inorganic chemistry
Charles C. Price (University of Notre Dame), Polymer chemistry
Eugene G. Rochow, Inorganic chemistry
1967 Vladimir Haensel, Petrochemistry
William E. Hanford (Olin Mathieson Corp.), Industrial chemistry
Henry B. Hass (Pullman Kellogg Corp.), Gas chromotopography
Carl S. Marvel (Wright Patterson AFB), Polymer chemistry
Benjamin Phillips (Union Carbine Corp.), Polymer chemistry
David W. Young (Sinclair Oil Corp.), Petrochemistry
1968 Ralph A. Connor (Rohm and Haas Co.), Industrial chemistry

James D. Idol, Jr. (Standard Oil Co. of Ohio), Petrochemistry
Percy L. Julian, Medicinal chemistry
Glenn T. Seaborg (University of California), Nuclear energy
Max Tishler (Merck and Co.), Nutrition and drug research

1969 **O.A. Battista** (FMC Corp.), Colloidal chemistry
Irving E. Levine, Industrial applications
Roy J. Plunkett (E.I. du Pont de Nemours), Industrial chemistry, "Teflon"
William G. Toland, Industrial chemistry
Harold C. Urey (Columbia University), Nuclear research
Harvey H. Voge (Shell Chemical Co.), Catalysis theory

1970 **Gerald C. Cox** (University of Pittsburgh), Fluoride research
H. Tracy Hall (General Electric Research), Diamond synthesis
Foster D. Snell, Surface chemistry, aerosols
William J. Sparks, Rubber chemistry

1971 **C. Kenneth Banks** (American Can Corp.), Molecular chemistry, "Promacetin"
Oliver W. Burke, Jr., Synthetic rubber
Sterling B. Hendricks (U.S. Dept. of Agriculture), Photoperiodism
Everett C. Hughes (Standard Oil Co. of Ohio), Petrochemistry
Joseph H. Simons, Fluorocarbons

1972 **J. Paul Hogan** (Phillips Petroleum Co.), Polymer chemistry
Herman F. Mark (Polytechnic Institute of N.Y.), Polymer chemistry
Alex G. Oblad, Petrochemistry
E. Emmet Reid, Organic chemistry
Lewis Sarett (Merck Sharp and Dohme), Medicinal chemistry, "Decadron"

1973 **Melvin A. Cook,** Explosives
Carl Djerassi (Syntex S.A.), Medicinal chemistry
Paul J. Flory, Polymer chemistry
Percival C. Keith, Atomic energy
Bartholomeus van't Riet (Medical College of Virginia), Medicinal chemistry

1974 **C.C. Hobbs** (Celanese Chemical Co.), Hydrocarbon research
Samuel E. Horne, Jr. (B.F. Goodrich Co.), Rubber chemistry
Charles J. Plank (Mobil Oil Corp.), Petrochemistry
Paul B. Weisz (Mobil Research and Development Corp.), Petrochemistry

1975 **Herbert C. Brown** (Purdue University), Borane chemistry
Rachel Brown (N.Y. State Dept. of Health), Antibiotic chemistry
Elizabeth Hazen, Medicinal chemistry, "Nystatin"
Linus C. Pauling, Body of thought
Christian Van Dijk (M.W. Kellogg Co.), Chlorine Research

1976 **Rowland C. Hansford** (Union Oil Co. of Calif.), Petrochemistry
Edwin T. Mertz (Purdue University), Nutrition research
Wilson C. Reeves, Fabric treatment
Jerome S. Spevack (Deuterium Corp.), Rubber chemistry

1977 **John Bjorksten** (Bjorksten Research Institute), Biochemistry
John Kollar (Redox Technologies), Petrochemistry
Henry McGrath (TRW), Chemical engineering
Donald Othmer (Polytechnic Institute of N.Y.), Chemical engineering

The Gold Medal is given annually to stimulate and recognize service to the science of chemistry or to the professions of chemist and chemical engineer.

1926 William Blum
1927 Lafayette B. Mendel
1929 Mr. and Mrs. Francis P. Garvan
1930 George Eastman
1931 Andrew W. and Richard B. Mellon
1932 Charles H. Herty
1933 Henry C. Sherman
1934 James Bryant Conant
1936 Marston Taylor Bogert
1937 James F. Norris
1938 Frederick G. Cottrell
1940 Gustav Egloff
1941 Henry G. Knight
1942 William Lloyd Evans
1943 Walter S. Landis
1944 Willard H. Dow
1945 John W. Thomas
1946 Robert Price Russell
1947 Moses Leverock Crossley
1948 Charles Allen Thomas
1949 Warren K. Lewis
1950 Walter J. Murphy
1951 Harry N. Holmes
1952 Fred J. Emmerich
1953 J.C. Warner
1954 William J. Sparks
1955 Carl S. Marvel
1956 Raymond Stevens
1957 Roy C. Newton
1958 Lawrence Flett
1959 Crawford H. Greenewalt
1960 Ernest H. Volwiler
1961 Alden H. Emery
1962 W. George Parks
1963 Ralph Connor
1964 Roger Adams
1965 Brig. Gen. Edwin Cox
1966 John H. Nair
1967 Wayne E. Kuhn
1968 Orville E. May
1969 Henry B. Hass
1970 Willard F. Libby
1971 Emmett B. Carmichael
1972 Harold C. Urey
1973 Glenn T. Seaborg
1974 W. E. (Butch) Hanford
1975 William O. Baker
1976 Kenneth S. Pitzer
1977 Max Tishler

Netherlands Fund for Chemistry Prize

ROYAL NETHERLANDS ACADEMY OF ARTS AND SCIENCES
Kloveniersburgwal 29, Amsterdam, the Netherlands (Tel: 020 22 29 02)

The Netherlands Fund for Chemistry Prize, which carries an honorarium, is given approximately every five years for research in chemistry. A Selection Committee chooses the winner, who must be of Dutch nationality.

1959 **J.F. Arens,** Groningen
1964 **H.J. den Hartog,** Wageningen
1969 **G.J.M. van der Kerk,** Utrecht
1975 **Th.J. de Boer,** Amsterdam

Somach Sachs Memorial Award

WEIZMANN INSTITUTE OF SCIENCE
Rehovot, Israel (Tel: 054-82111 and 83111)

The Somach Sachs Memorial Award honors outstanding work in chemistry by a scientist under 35 years of age at the Weizmann Institute. It is given every second year.

1961 **Z. Luz,** Nuclear magnetic resonance
      B. Silver, Isotope research
1964 **Raphael Mechoulam,** Organic chemistry, specifically the isolation and elucidation of the structure of the active constituent of hashish
1966 **Harry Friedmann,** Nuclear physics, specifically for "The Rotation-Translation Coupling Spectrum of Matrix-Isolated Molecules"
1968 **Rachel Goldman,** Biophysics, specifically for work on membranes having enzymatic activity
1970 **Michael Revel,** Biochemistry, specifically for the elucidation of the basic processes in the production of the protein molecule in the living cell
1972 **Michael Inbar,** Genetics, specifically for his work in the use of carbohydrate-binding protein concanavalin to measure the location of certain carbohydrate-containing sites on the surface of membrane cells
1974 **Ada Yonath,** Structural chemistry, specifically for work on the structure of biological molecules
1976 **Victor Yakhot,** Structural chemistry and chemical physics, specifically for work on geometric distortions in excited states

Harry Goode Memorial Award

AMERICAN FEDERATION OF INFORMATION PROCESSING SOCIETIES
210 Summit Ave., Montvale, N.J. 07645

The Harry Goode Memorial Award annually honors individuals for pioneering contributions to the furtherance of computer science and information processing. An awards committee selects the recipient of the bronze medal.

1964 **Howard Hathaway Aiken,** Digital computers

1965 **George Robert Stibitz and Konrad Zuse,** Automatic computing
1966 **J. Presper Eckert,** ENIAC/BINAC/UNIVAC computers
1967 **Samuel Nathan Alexander,** Computers in the federal government
1968 **Maurice Vincent Wilkes,** Computer engineering and software
1969 **Alston Scott Householder,** Numerical intelligence/programming
1970 **Grace Murray Hopper,** Computer software
1971 **Allen Newell,** Artificial intelligence/programming
1972 **Seymour R. Cray,** Digital computers and multiprocessing systems
1974 **Edsger W. Dijkstra,** Computer programming/ALGOL
1975 **Kenneth E. Iverson,** Computer programming/APL
1976 **Lawrence G. Roberts,** Computer-communication systems
1977 **Jay W. Forrester,** Core storage; Whirlwind 1; computer modeling and simulation; system dynamics

Harry Levine Prize in Computer Sciences

WEIZMANN INSTITUTE OF SCIENCE
Rehovot, Israel (Tel: 054-82111 and 83111)

The Harry Levine Prize in Computer Sciences is awarded every second year for outstanding work in the field.

1976 **Amiram Caspi and Zvi Lapidot**

ASME Engineers Medal
Ralph Coats Roe Medal
ASME Edwin F. Church Medal
Holley Medal
Charles Russ Richards Memorial Award
Gustus L. Larson Memorial Award
Pi Tau Sigma Gold Medal
Spirit of St. Louis Medal
ASME George Westinghouse Medal
Timoshenko Medal
Machine Design Award
Mayo D. Hersey Award
J. Hall Taylor Medal
Diesel and Gas Engine Power Award
Rufus Oldenburger Medal

R. Tom Sawyer Award

Melville Medal

Worcester Reed Warner Medal

Alfred Nobel Prize

Henry Hess Award

Arthur L. Williston Medal

Charles T. Main Award

"Old Guard" Prize for ASME Student Members

Blackall Machine Tool and Gauge Award

Prime Movers Committee Award

Gas Turbine Power Award

ASME Rail Transportation Award

Freeman Scholar Award

ASME Nadai Award

Heat Transfer Memorial Award

Burt L. Newkirk Tribology Award

ASME Codes and Standards Medal

AMERICAN SOCIETY OF MECHANICAL ENGINEERS
345 E. 47th St., New York, N.Y. 10017 (212/644-7722)

The ASME Engineers Medal, which carries a $1,000 honorarium, is awarded annually for "eminently distinguished engineering achievement."

1921 Hjalmar G. Carlson
1922 Frederick A. Halsey
1923 John R. Freeman
1924-25 No award
1926 R. A. Millikan
1927 Wilfred Lewis
1928 Julian Kennedy
1929 No award
1930 W. L. R. Emmet
1931 Albert Kingsbury
1932 No award
1933 Ambrose Swasey
1934 Willis H. Carrier
1935 Charles T. Main
1936 Edward Bausch
1937 Edward P. Bullard
1938 Stephen J. Pigott
1939 James E. Gleason
1940 Charles F. Kettering
1941 Theodore von Karman
1942 Ervin G. Bailey
1943 Lewis K. Sillcox
1944 Edward G. Budd
1945 William F. Durand

1946 Morris E. Leeds
1947 Paul W. Kiefer
1948 Frederick G. Keys
1949 Fred L. Dornbrook
1950 Harvey C. Knowles
1951 Glenn B. Warren
1952 Nevin E. Funk
1953 Crosby Field
1954 E. Burnley Powell
1955 Granville M. Read
1956 Harry F. Vickers
1957 L. M. K. Boelter
1958 Wilbur H. Armacost
1959 Martin Frisch
1960 C. Richard Soderberg
1961 No award
1962 Philip Sporn
1963 Igor I. Sikorsky
1964 Alan Howard
1965 Johnannes M. Burgers
1966 No award
1967 Mayo D. Hersey
1968 Samuel C. Collins
1969 Lloyd H. Donnell
1970 Robert Rowe Gilruth
1971 Horace Smart Beattie
1972 Waloddi Weibull
1973 Christopher C. Kraft, Jr.
1974 Nicholas J. Hoff
1975 Maxime A. Faget
1976 Raymond D. Mindlin
1977 Robert W. Mann

The Ralph Coats Roe Medal, which is presented annually with a $1,000 honorarium, honors contributions to public understanding of the engineering profession's worth to contemporary society.

1974 Emilio Q. Daddorio
1975 Walter Sullivan
1976 No award
1977 Robert C. Seamans, Jr.

The ASME Edwin F. Church Medal, which carries a $1,000 honorarium, annually honors mechanical engineering excellence in its broadest sense, including eminent service in increasing the value, importance and attractiveness of the mechanical engineering education, including in-house, continuing or other training programs as well as programs at universities and technical institutes.

1973 Wilbur Richard Leopold
1974 Hobart A. Weaver
1975 Harry Conn
1976 Frank W. VonFlue
1977 No award

The Holley Medal, which is of gold, honors some great and unique act of genius of an engineering nature which has accomplished a great and timely public benefit.

1924 Hjalmar G. Carlson
1928 Elmer A. Sperry
1930 Baron C. Shiba
1934 Irving Langmuir
1936 Henry Ford

1937	Frederick G. Cottrell
1938	Francis Hodgkinson
1939	Carl E. Johansson
1940	Edwin H. Armstrong
1941	John C. Garand
1942	Ernest O. Lawrence
1943	Vannevar Bush
1944	Carl L. Norden
1945	Sanford A. Moss
1946	Norman Gibson
1947	Raymond D. Johnson
1948	Edwin H. Land
1950	Charles G. Curtis
1951	George R. Fink
1952	Sanford L. Cluett
1953	Philip M. McKenna
1954	Walter A. Shewhart
1955	George J. Hood
1957	Charles S. Draper
1959	Col. Maurice J. Fletcher
1961	Thomas Elmer Moon
1963	William Shockley
1968	Chester F. Carlson
1969	Willis J. Whitfield
1973	Harold E. Edgerton
	Kenneth J. Germeshausen
1975	George M. Grover
1976	Emmett N. Leith
	Juris Upatnieks
1977	J. David Margerum

The Charles Russ Richards Memorial Award, which is now supported by the Pi Tau Sigma Honorary Mechanical Engineering Fraternity, carries a $1,000 honorarium and recognizes outstanding mid-career mechanical engineering achievement. The recipient must have graduated from a recognized college or university engineering course not more than 25 nor less than 20 years prior to the year in which the award is given.

1947	Jacob P. Den Hartog
1948	No award
1949	Arthur M. Wahl
1950	Burgess H. Jennings
1951	J. Kenneth Salisbury
1952	Jess H. Davis
1953	Thomas M. Lumly
1954	Robert H. Hughes
1955	Sylan Cromer
1956	Everett M. Barber
1957	Wayne C. Edmister
1958	Donald C. Burnham
1959	M. Eugene Merchant
1960	Ascher H. Shapiro
1961	Harrison A. Storm, Jr.
1962	Dudley D. Fuller
1963	George F. Carrier
1964	Simon Astrach
1965	Leonard J. Koch
1966	J. Lowen Shearer
1967	T. Cyril Noon
1968	Bernard W. Shaffer
1969	Robert E. Uhrig
1970	Ralph G. Nevins
1971	Howard L. Harrison
1972	Charles E. Jones
1973	Ali A. Seireg

1974	Richard J. Grosh
1975	Carl F. Zorowski
1976	Ali Suphi Argon
1977	Hassan A. Hassan

The Gustus L. Larson Memorial Award, funded by Pi Tau Sigma, carries a $1,000 honorarium and recognizes outstanding early-career achievement. The recipient must have graduated from a recognized college or university engineering course not more than 20 nor less than 10 years prior to the year in which the award is given.

1975	Chang-Lin Tien
1976	John G. Bollinger
1977	Nam P. Suh

The Pi Tau Sigma Gold Medal honors a young engineering graduate within 10 years of graduating from a recognized college or university engineering course.

1938	Wilfred E. Johnson
1939	John Yellot, Jr.
1940	George A. Hawkins
1941	R. Hosmer Norris
1942	John T. Rettaliata
1943-46	No awards
1947	David Cochrane
1948	Walter G. Vincenti
1949	Philip S. Meyers
1950	Arthur P. Adamson
1951	Warren M. Rohsenow
1952	Robert L. O'Brien
1953	Merle Baker
1954	Emmett E. Day
1955	Robert C. Dean, Jr.
1956	John A. Clark
1957	Patrick McDonald, Jr.
1958	Allison E. Simons
1959	Donald F. Hays
1960	George Hatsopoulos
1961	Ernest T. Selig
1962	E. Bruce Lee
1963	Herbert Richardson
1964	Richard L. Peskin
1965	John Bollinger
1966	Jason R. Lemon
1967	William O'Donnell
1968	Randall F. Barron
1969	Henry K. Newhall
1970	Richard Elwood Barrett
1971	James R. Rice
1972	John F. Stephens, III
1973	Christian Ernst
	Georg Przirembel
1974	Jace W. Nunziato
1975	Ted B. Belytschko
1976	John S. Walker
1977	Richard E. Lovejoy

The Spirit of St. Louis Medal, which is of gold, is awarded for meritorious service in the advancement of aeronautics and astronautics

1929	Daniel Guggenheim
1932	Paul Litchfield

1935 Will Rogers
1938 James H. Doolittle
1941 John E. Younger
1944 George W. Lewis
1947 John E. Northrup
1950 Helmut P. Kroon
1954 Arthur E. Raymond
1955 Ralph S. Damon
1958 George S. Schairer
1961 Samuel K. Hoffman
1962 Robert H. Widmer
1963 Frederick C. Crawford
1964 Robert R. Gilruth
1965 William H. Pickering
1966 Christopher C. Kraft
1967 Ira G. Hedrick
1968 George S. Moore
1969 G. Merritt Preston
1970 Clarence L. Johnson
1971 Ralph L. Creel
1972 Neil A. Armstrong
1973 John F. Yardley
1974 Abe Silverstein
1975 No award
1976 No award
1977 George D. McLean

The ASME George Westinghouse Medal, which is of gold, honors distinguished achievement of service in the power field of mechanical engineering. A second Westinghouse Medal, which is of silver, has been established to honor achievement in the field by an engineer 40 years of age or younger.

GOLD MEDAL

1953 Alexander G. Christie
1954 Walker L. Cisler
1955 Hyman G. Rickover
1956 Perry W. Pratt
1957 Alfred Iddles
1958 Frederick P. Fairchild
1960 Ernest C. Gaston
1961 Gerald V. Williamson
1962 Edwin Holmes Kreig
1963 Abbott L. Penniman, Jr.
1964 Frederick W. Argue
1965 Robert A. Bowman
1966 Robert C. Allen
1967 Robert A. Baker, Sr.
1968 Roland A. Budenholzer
1969 Ralph C. Roe
1970 Charles Aloysius Meyer
      Robert C. Spencer, Jr.
1971 Wilfred McGregor Hall
1972 William States Lee
1973 Bernard F. Langer
1974 Charles W. Elston
1975 No award
1976 John W. Simpson
1977 No award

SILVER MEDAL

1972 William Eugene Rice
1973 Michael A. Ambrose
1974 Shelby L. Owens
1975 No award
1976 Richard V. Shanklin III
1977 James C. Corman

The Timoshenko Medal, which is of bronze, recognizes

contributions to applied mechanics without restrictions on nationality or profession.

1957 Stephen P. Timoshenko
1958 Arpad L. Nadai
      Sir Geoffrey Taylor
      Theodore von Karman
1959 Sir Richard Southwell
1960 Cornelius B. Biezano
      Richard Grammel
1961 James Norman Goodier
1962 Maurice Anthony Biot
1963 Michael James Lighthill
1964 Raymond D. Mindlin
1965 Sydney Goldstein
1966 William Prager
1967 Hillel Poritsky
1968 Warner T. Koitzer
1969 Jakob Ackeret
1970 James Johnston Stoker
1971 Howard Wilson Emmons
1972 Jacob Pieter Den Hartog
1973 Eric Reissner
1974 Albert E. Green
1975 Chia-Chiao Lin
1976 Erastus Henry Lee
1977 John D. Eshelby

The Machine Design Award, which consists of a bronze plaque, is awarded to honor achievement or service in the field of machine design, including application, research, development or teaching of machine design.

1959 Charles E. Crede
1960 Rudolph E. Peterson
1961 Robert G. LeTourneau
1962 J. F. Downie Smith
1963 Colin Carmichael
1964 Rufus Oldenburger
1965 A. M. Wahl
1966 Beno Sternlicht
1967 Ernest Wildhaber
1968 C. Walton Musser
1969 Eugene L. Radzimovsky
1970 Reynold Benjamin Johnson
1971 Walter L. Starkey
1972 Ferdinand Freudenstein
1974 Allen S. Hall, Jr.
1975 No award
1976 Charles W. Radcliffe
1977 Mathew Kuts

The Mayo D. Hersey Award, which consists of a bronze plaque, recognizes distinguished contributions over a substantial period of time to the advancement of lubrication engineering and science of a pure or applied nature.

1965 Mayo D. Hersey
1966 Harmen Blok
1967 Milton C. Shaw
1968 Ragnar Holm
1969 William A. Zisman
1970 Merrell Robert Fenske
1971 Dudley Dean Fuller
1972 Sydney J. Needs
1973 Donald F. Wilcock
1974 David Tabor
1975 Arthur F. Underwood
1976 John Boyd
1977 Robert L. Johnson

The J. Hall Taylor Medal, which is of bronze, recognizes distinction in the field of codes and services in the broad areas of piping and pressure vessels. Preference is given to Society members.

1966	Frank S.G. Williams
1967	David B. Wesstrom
1968	Max B. Higgins
1969	Everett O. Waters
1970	Bernard F. Langer
1971	James M. Guy
1972	William Rolfe Gall
1973	John Dalton Mattimore
1974	Jean L. Lattan
1975	Frederic A. Hough
	Walter H. Davidson
	Joseph J. King
	Burton T. Mast
	Andrew J. Shoup
1976	No award
1977	James S. Clarke
	Raymond R. Maccary

The Diesel and Gas Engine Power Award, which consists of a bronze plaque, recognizes achievement over a substantial period of time in research, innovation or education in advancing the art of engineering in the field of internal combustion engines, or in directing the efforts of individuals so involved.

1967	Frederick P. Porter
1969	Leo T. Brinson, Jr.
1971	Melvin J. Helmich
1972	R. Rex Robinson
1973	Warren A. Rhoades
1974	Warren J. Severin
1975	William Speicher
1976	No award
1977	No award

The Rufus Oldenburger Medal, which is of bronze, recognizes contributions and achievements in automatic control, including education, research, development, innovation and service. There are no restrictions of profession, nationality or Society membership for this honor.

1968	Rufus Oldenburger
1969	Nathaniel B. Nichols
1970	John R. Ragazzini
1971	Charles Stark Draper
1972	Albert J. Williams, Jr.
1973	Clesson E. Mason
1974	Herbert W. Ziebolz
1975	Hendrick W. Bode and Harry Nyquist
1976	Rudolph Emil Kalman
1977	No award

The R. Tom Sawyer Award, which consists of a bronze plaque, honors contributions to the gas turbine industry and to the Gas Turbine Division of ASME.

1972	R. Tom Sawyer
1973	John W. Sawyer
1974	Waheed Rizk
1975	Bruce O. Buckland
1976	Curt Keller
1977	Alexander L. London

The Melville Medal, which is of bronze and carries a $1,000 honorarium, is given for the best original paper presented before the Society during the previous calendar year, or published or approved for publication by the Society. The author or authors must hold ASME membership.

1927	Leon P. Alford
1928	No award
1929	Joseph W. Roe
1930	Herman Diederichs
	William Pomeroy
1931	Arthur Grunert
1932	Alexey Stepanoff
1933	William Caldwell
1934	No award
1935	Oscar R. Wikander
1936	H. A. S. Howarth
1937	Alfred J. Buchi
1938	Alphonse Lipetz
1939	Lester Goldsmith
1940	Carl A. W. Brandt
1941	Roger V. Terry
1942	Kenneth Salisbury
1943	No award
1944	Ernest Robinson
1945	William J. King
1946	Troels Warming
1947	Raymond Martinelli
1948	Reginald Gillmor
1949	Harold B. Maynard
1950	Samuel J. Loring
1952	Neil P. Bailey
1953	Jefferson Falkner
1954	Edmund Sylvester
1955	Robert T. Knapp
1956	No award
1957	No award
1958	Thomas P. Goodman
1959	Stephen J. Kline
1960	William G. Steltz
1961	Otto Erich Balje
1962	T. P. Goodman
1963	J.S. Ausman
1964	J. K. Jakobsen
1965	W. Van Der Sluys
1966	No award
1967	Bernard Roth
1968	Yian-Nian Chen
1969	Leon R. Glicksman
1970	J. William Holl and A. L. Kornhauser
1971	Thomas Slot
1972	H. W. O'Connor
	A. S. Weinstein
1973	No award
1974	V. H. Arakerl
	Allan J. Acosta
1975	V. Turchina
	David M. Sanborn
	Ward O. Winer
1976	Bernard J. Hamrock
	Duncan Dowson
1977	E.F. Fichter and K.H. Hunt

The Worcester Reed Warner Medal, which is of gold and carries a $1,000 honorarium, is given for outstanding contributions to the permanent literature of engineering, which may be a single paper, treatise, book or series of papers dealing with progressive ideas on engineering, scientific and industrial research associated with mechnical engineering, design and operation of mechanical and association equipment, industrial engineering or management and other related subjects. The paper or treatise must be not less than five years old and may have been prepared by a member or non-member.

1933	Dexter S. Kimball
1934	Ralph E. Flanders
1935	Stephen Timoshenko
1936	Charles M. Allen
1937	Clarence Hirshfeld
1938	Lawford H. Fry
1939	Rupen Eksergian
1940	William Gregory
1941	Richard Southwell
1942	Fred H. Colvin
1943	Igor I. Sikorsky
1944	Earle Buckingham
1945	Joseph M. Juran
1946	No award
1947	Arpad L. Nadai
1948	Edward S. Cole
1949	Fred B. Seely
1950	Orlan W. Boston
1951	Jacob Den Hartog
1952	Max Jakob
1953	William McAdams
1954	Joseph Keenan
1955	Howard S. Bean
1956	J. Keith Louden
1957	William Prager
1958	Harold J. Rose
1959	Daniel Glasstone
1960	Lloyd H. Donnell
1961	C. L. W. Trinks
1962	Virgil M. Faires
1963	Frederick Morse
1964	Oscar J. Horger
1965	Ascher H. Shapiro
1966	Eric A. Farber
1967	Nicholas J. Hoff
1968	Merhyle F. Spotts
1969	Hans W. Liepmann
1970	Wilhelm Flugge
1971	Stephen H. Crandall
1972	Burgess H. Jennings
1973	Max Mark Frocht
1974	Victor L. Streeter
1975	Philip G. Hodge, Jr.
1976	Dennis C. Shepherd
1977	Joseph E. Shigley

The Alfred Nobel Prize, which carries a variable cash honorarium, is awarded to a member of ASME or one of several other engineering associations for a technical paper of exceptional excellence accepted for publication by any of the cooperating societies. The author must be thirty years of age or younger and the award is for papers published in the year of the award by an individual author (no joint authorship).

1969	Ronald Gibala (AIME)
1970	Peter W. Marshall (ASCE)
1971	Ben G. Burke (ASCE)
1972	C. L. Magee (ASCE)
1974	Viney K. Gupta (ASME)
1975	William L. Smith (ASCE)
1976	S.N. Singh (AIME)
1977	J.E. Killough (SPE)

The Henry Hess Award, which carries a $250 honorarium, is given for an original technical paper by an author or authors thirty years of age or younger.

1915	Ernest Hickstein

1916	L.B. McMillan
1917	No award
1918	No award
1919	E.D. Whalen
1920	No award
1921	S. Logan Kerr
1922	R.H. Heilman and F.L. Kallam
1923	S.S. Sanford and S. Crocker
1924	R.H. Heilman
1925	Gilbert Schaller
1926	No award
1927	William M. Frame
1928	M.D. Aisenstein
1929	Arthur M. Wahl
1930	Ed. S. Smith, Jr.
1931	Montrose Dewry
1932	Edmund M. Wagner
1933	Townsend Tinker
1934	John Yellott, Jr.
1935	Stanley Mikawa
1936	H.F. Mullikin, Jr.
1937	Leslie J. Hooper
1938	Arthur C. Stern
1939	No award
1940	Robert E. Newton
1941	John Rettaliata
1942	Winston M. Dudley
1943	Troels Warming
1944	No award
1945	Bruce Del Mar
1946	Martin Goland
1947	Gilbert T. Rowe
1948	Hunt Davis
1949	Gerhard Nothmann
1950	No award
1951	John D. Stantz
1952	Warren Rohsenow
1953	No award
1954	No award
1955	F. Freudenstein
1956	No award
1957	No award
1958	No award
1959	Victor Salesmann
1960	Gunnar Heskestad
	Duane Olberts
1961	J. E. Fleckenstein
1962	Miklos Sajben
1963	A. Thiruvengadam
1964	R. J. McGrattan
1965	J. F. Booker
1966	Jerry R. Johanson
1967	Richard Barett
1968	No award
1969	James R. Rice
1970	T. L. Geers
1971	No award
1972	D. C. Gakenheimer
1973	Hazem A. Ezzat
1974	Lambert B. Freund
1975	No award
1976	G.D. Gupta
1977	R.J. Hannemann

The Arthur L. Williston Medal, which is of bronze and carries a $500 honorarium, is given for the best paper submitted in the Williston-Main Awards Contest on a subject that challenges the engineering abilities of students and involves the supporting influence of engineering faculties.

1956 John A. Welsh
1957 Walter P. Logeman
1958 No award
1959 Rowe A. Giardinin
1960 Marc Fishbein
1961 James R. Stewart
1962 Charles H. Recht
1963 No award
1964 Kenneth E. Gawronski
1965 LaRoux K. Gillespie
1966 Eddie R. Howe
1967 L. Thomas Cooper III
1968 Frank A. Ralbovsky
1969 Arlo Fossum
1970 Steven H. Carlson
1971 James A. Willms
1972 Dennis L. Sandberg
1973 Frank H. Roubleau, Jr.
1974 James J. Calls
1975 No award
1976 Ehud David Laska
1977 Harry W. Groot

The Charles T. Main Award, which also carries a $250 honorarium, supplements the Williston Award, above.

1925 Clement R. Brown, Catholic University of America
1926 W. C. Taylor, John Hopkins University
1927 No award
1928 Robert M. Meyer, Newark College of Engineering
1929 No award
1930 Jules Podnosoff, Polytechnic Institute of Brooklyn
1931 Robert E. Klise, University of Michigan
1931 Marshall Anderson, University of Michigan
1932 No award
1933 George D. Wilkinson, Jr., Newark College of Engineering
1934 Philip P. Self, Colorado State College
1935 G. Lowell Williams, Lafayette College
1936 No award
1937 Allan P. Stern, Case School of Applied Science
1938 Edward W. Connelly, University of Detroit
1939 James H. Bright, Lehigh University
1940 Frank de Pould, Case School of Applied Science
1941 John J. Balun, University of Detroit
1942 Bernard J. Isabella, Case School of Applied Science
1943 Mitchell C. Kazen, University of Detroit
1944 Fred M. Piaskowski, University of Detroit
1945 Jack Drandell, Southern Methodist University
1946 Victor S. Rykwalder, University of Detroit
1947 Alvaro R. Boera, Stevens Institute of Technology
1948 Earle Duane Stewart, University of Pittsburgh
1949 Stanley M. Kuvacheff, University of Detroit
1950 Richard T. Johnson, University of Detroit
1951 No award
1952 Israel E. Rubin, Cooper Union School of Engineering
1953 Peter Ashurkoff, Princeton University
1954 John B. Pendergrass, Jr., Carnegie Institute of Technology
1955 Richard J. Slember, Cooper Union School of Engineering
1956 Marion J. Balcerzak, University of Detroit
1957 Joseph P. Hunter, University of Detroit
1958 Frank D. Sams, Clemson Agricultural College
1959 James L. Benson, University of Vermont
1960 John W. McDaniel, Rice Institute
1961 Lester W. Wurm, Kansas State University
1962 David W. Wieting, Lamar State College of Technology
1963 Robert Lafayette Ash, Kansas State University
1964 No award
1965 No award

1966 No award
1967 Muzzamil Niazi, Wichita State University
1968 Terry Dean Schmidt, University of Washington
1969 No award
1970 Steve H. Woodard, Arizona State University
1971 James M. Singleton, University of Alabama
1972 Harold Chapin Lowe, University of Kansas
1973 Gary Patrick Pezall, University of Wisconsin, Madison
1974 Adrian P. Villa, Clarkson College of Technology
1975 No award
1976 Scott Elliott Baker
1977 Charles S. Tamarin

The "Old Guard" Prize for ASME Student Members, which consists of $250, is given for the best presentation of a technical paper by a student member. The "Old Guard" of members, who have reached 65 years of age and are exempt from ASME dues, supports this prize for the younger members.

1956 Joseph W. Jacobson, University of Texas
1957 George M. Reynolds, Northwestern University
1958 Harry Hollinghaus, University of Utah
1959 James S. Kishi, University of Texas
1960 Joseph W. Lindsey, University of Utah
1961 Joseph J. Marino, University of Connecticut
1962 Jay S. Fein, Rutgers University
1963 Walter Clark Dean II, Lehigh University
1964 Robert J. Arnzen, Washington University of St. Louis
1965 Joseph P. Collins, University of Wisconsin
1966 John A. Leo, III, Auburn University
1967 William E. Hughes, Brigham Young University
1968 Maurice H. Bunn, Arizona State University
1969 Walter H. Peters, III, Auburn University
1970 Joseph R. Titone, Cornell University
1971 J. L. Lee, Auburn University
1972 Stanley W. Blossom, Oklahoma State University
1973 Steven H. Blossom, Oklahoma State University
     E. J. Strande, University of Washington
1974 No award
1975 Steven R. Bussolari, Union College
1976 No award
1977 No award

The Blackall Machine Tool and Gauge Award, which consists of $100 and a bronze plaque, honors the best paper or papers on the design and application of machine tools, gauges or dimensional measuring instruments submitted to the ASME for presentation and publication.

1965 Carl J. Osford, Jr. and John Cook
1966 Orland W. Boston and William W. Gilbert
1967 Bei T. Chao and Kenneth J. Trigger
1968 S.A. Tobias and Wilfred Fishwick
1960 B. Popper and David W. Pessen
1961 Joseph R. Roubik
1962 W.A. Mohn
1963 E.G. Thomsen, A.G. MacDonald and Shiro Kobayashi
1964 No award
1965 Robert S. Hahn
1966 No award
1967 J. Hopenfeld and R.R. Cole
1968 Kuo-King Wang, Shien-Ming Wu and Kazuaki Iwata
1972 No award
1973 No award
1974 S.P. Loutrel and N.H. Cook

1975   No award
1976   No award
1977   No award

The Prime Movers Committee Award consists of a certificate honoring outstanding contributions to the literature of thermal electric station practice or equipment through public presentation or publication.

1955   Louis Elliott
       Walter F. Friend
       Edward C. Duffy
       Gustaf A. Gaffert
       Fred W. Argue
       Bernhardt G. A. Skrotski
1956   Robert B. Donworth
       Walter J. Lyman
       T. Harry Mandil
       Nunzio J. Palladino
       Milton Shaw
       John W. Simpson
1957   Heinrich Hegetschweller
       Robert L. Bartlett
1958   Vivian F. Estcourt
1959   J. Kenneth Salisbury
1960   Sigmund N. Fiala
       James H. Harlow
1961   Charles Strohmeyer, Jr.
1962   No award
1963   E.F. Walsh, R.L. Jackson, Walter Sinton and
       R.E. Warner
1964   Everett P. Partridge
1965   A.E. Weller, and W.T. Reid
1966   F.J. Hanzalek and P.G. Ipson
1967   Homer F. Hatfield and Mark G. Pfeiffer
1968   G.N. Stone and A.J. Clarke
1969   Paul Goldstein and Charles L. Burton
1970   Paul Leung and Raymond E. Moore
1971   Paul Leung and Raymond E. Moore
1972   G.S. Rahoi, R.C. Scarberry, J.R. Crum and
       P.E. Morris
1974   B. Bornstein and Paul Leung
1975   Karl A. Gulbrand and Paul Leung
1976   Wolfgang Mattick, Hans-Guenter Hadden-
       horst, Otto Weber and Z. Stanley Stys
1977   H. Haneda, M. Araoka, K. Setoguchi, J.D.
       Fox and W.F. Siddall

The Gas Turbine Power Award, which consists of a turbine wheel with bronze insert, recognizes outstanding contribution to the literature of combustion gas turbines or gas turbines combined thermally with nuclear or steam power plants or any aspect of this field. Papers published anywhere in the world are eligible.

1964   A.L. London
1965   J.S. Alford
1966   No award
1967   R.O. Carta
1968   Arthur D. Bernstein, William H. Heiser and
       Charles M. Hevenor
1969   O.E. Balje
1970   No award
1971   Carlyle Reid
1972   H.A. Harmon, A.A. Mikolajczak and D. Mar-
       chent
1973   F.B. Metzger and D.B. Hanson
1974   No award
1975   John Moore
1976   G.L. Commerford and Lynn E. Snyder
1977   Edward M. Greitzer

The ASME Rail Transportation Award is a certificate given annually for an original paper on railroad mechnical engineering describing a new and basic technical discovery, or exhibiting original thinking on railway mechanical engineering beyond the routine, or describing such work in practice. The paper must have been presented during the calendar year prior to that of the award, although non-members are also eligible.

1966   W.P. Manos
       J. C. Shang
1967   F. E. King
       R. W. Radford
1968   Thomas Schur
1969   Richard T. Gray
       Samuel Levy
       James A. Bain
       Estelle J. Playdon
1970   H. C. Meacham
       R. D. Ahlbeck
1972   L. A. Peterson
       W. H. Freeman
       J. M. Wandrisco
1973   G. E. Novak
       B. J. Eck
1974   J. N. Siddall
       M. A. Dokainish
       W. Elmaraghy
1975   V. Terry Hawthorne
1976   M.R. Johnson, R.E. Welch and K.S. Yeung
1977   No award

The Freeman Scholar Award consists of a $3,000 honorarium given every two years for fluids engineering. The recipient with wide experience in the field is expected to review a coherent topic in the specialty including a comprehensive statement of "the state of the art" and suggestions for key future research needs.

1971   Jack W. Hoyt and Ronald F. Probstein
1974   Jack E. Cermak
1976   William J. McCroskey

The ASME Nadai Award is given annually for work in materials research and applications development.

1975   George M. Sinclair
1976   Evan Albert Davis
1977   George R. Irwin

The Heat Transfer Memorial Award is given annually.

1975   Simon Ostrach
       Warren H. Giedt
1976   Peter Griffith
       Raymond Viskanta
1977   Robert D. Cess
       Rolf H. Sabersky

The Burt L. Newkirk Tribology Award is presented annually jointly with the American Society of Lubrication Engineers.

1976   Francis E. Kennedy, Jr.
1977   Steve M. Rhode

The ASME Codes and Standards Medal is given annually for contributions to codes and standards.

1977   William G. McLean

IEEE Medal of Honor
Alexander Graham Bell Medal
Edison Medal
Founders Medal
Lamme Medal
IEEE Education Medal
Harry Diamond Memorial Award
William M. Habirshaw Award
Hernand and Sostheses Behn Award in International Communication
Morris E. Leeds Award
Morris N. Liebmann Memorial Award
Jack A. Morton Award
Frederik Philips Award
Emanuel R. Piore Award
David Sarnoff Award
Nikola Tesla Award
Vladimir K. Zworykin Award
W.R.G. Baker Prize
Browder J. Thompson Memorial Prize Award

INSTITUTE OF ELECTRICAL AND
ELECTRONICS ENGINEERS (IEEE)
345 E. 47th St., New York, N.Y. 10017 (212/644-7882)

The IEEE Medal of Honor, which consists of a gold medal, bronze replica and $10,000, is awarded as warranted for an exceptional addition to science and technology of concern to the Institute. Nominations are reviewed by a special committee and approved by the board of directors.

1917	E. H. Armstrong
1918	No award
1919	E. F. W. Alexanderson
1920	Guglielmo Marconi
1921	R. A. Fessenden
1922	Lee deForest
1923	John Stone-Stone
1924	M. I. Pupin
1925	No award
1926	G. W. Pickard
1927	L. W. Austin
1928	Jonathan Zenneck
1929	G. W. Pierce
1930	P. O. Pedersen
1931	G. A. Ferrie
1932	A. E. Kennelly
1933	J. A. Fleming
1934	S. C. Hooper
1935	Balth. van der Pol
1936	G. A. Campbell
1937	Melville Eastham
1938	J. H. Dellinger
1939	A. G. Lee
1940	Lloyd Espenschied
1941	A. N. Goldsmith
1942	A. H. Taylor
1943	William Wilson
1944	Haraden Pratt
1945	H. H. Beverage
1946	R. V. L. Hartley
1947	No award
1948	L. C. F. Horle
1949	Ralph Bown
1950	F. E. Terman
1951	V. K. Zworykin
1952	W. R. G. Baker
1953	J. M. Miller
1954	W. L. Everitt
1955	H. T. Friis
1956	J. V. L. Hogan
1957	J. A. Stratton
1958	A. W. Hull
1959	E. L. Chaffee
1960	Harry Nyquist
1961	Ernst A. Guillemin
1962	Edward V. Appleton
1963	John H. Hammond, Jr.
	George C. Southworth
1964	Harold A. Wheeler
1965	No award
1966	Claude E. Shannon
1967	Charles H. Townes
1968	Gordon K. Teal
1969	Edward L. Ginzton
1970	Dennis Gabor
1971	John Bardeen
1972	Jay W. Forrester
1973	Rudolf Kompfner
1974	Rudolf E. Kalman
1975	John R. Pierce
1976	No award
1977	H. Earle Vauhan

The Alexander Graham Bell Medal, which consists of a gold medal, bronze replica and $10,000, honors exceptional contributions to the advancement of telecommunications. A committee review nominations and the Board of Directors gives final approval.

1976	Amos E. Joel, Jr.
	William Keister
	Raymond W. Ketchledge
1977	Eberhart Rechtin

The Edison Medal, which consists of a gold medal, small gold replica, certificate and $10,000, honors a career of meritorious achievement in electrical science, electrical engineering or the electrical arts. A committee reviews nominations and the board of directors gives final approval.

1909	Elihu Thomson
1910	Frank J. Sprague
1911	George Westinghouse
1912	William Stanley
1913	Charles F. Brush
1914	Alexander Graham Bell
1915	No award
1916	Nikola Tesla
1917	John J. Carty
1918	Benjamin G. Lamme
1919	W. L. R. Emmet
1920	Michael I. Pupin
1921	Cummings C. Chesney
1922	Robert A. Millikan
1923	John W. Lieb
1924	John W. Howell
1925	Harris J. Ryan

1926	No award
1927	William D. Coolidge
1928	Frank B. Jewett
1929	Charles F. Scott
1930	Frank Conrad
1931	E. W. Rice, Jr.
1932	Bancroft Gherardi
1933	Arthur E. Kennelly
1934	Willis R. Whitney
1935	Lewis B. Stillwell
1936	Alex Dow
1937	Gano Dunn
1938	Dugald C. Jackson
1939	Philip Torchio
1940	George A. Campbell
1941	John B. Whitehead
1942	Edwin H. Armstrong
1943	Vannevar Bush
1944	E. F. W. Alexanderson
1945	Philip Sporn
1946	Lee deForest
1947	Joseph Slepian
1948	Morris E. Leeds
1949	Karl B. McEachron
1950	Otto B. Blackwell
1951	Charles F. Wagner
1952	Vladimir K. Zworykin
1953	John F. Peters
1954	Oliver E. Buckley
1955	Leonid A. Umansky
1956	Comfort A. Adams
1957	John K. Hodnette
1958	Charles F. Kettering
1959	James F. Fairman
1960	Harold S. Osborne
1961	William B. Kouwenhoven
1962	Alexander C. Monteith
1963	John R. Pierce
1964	No award; schedule revised
1965	Walker L. Cisler
1966	Wilmer L. Barrow
1967	George H. Brown
1968	Charles F. Avila
1969	Hendrik W. Bode
1970	Howard H. Aiken
1971	John W. Simpson
1972	William H. Pickering
1973	B. D. H. Tellegen
1974	Jan A. Rajchman
1975	Sidney Darlington
1976	Murray Joslin
1977	Henri G. Busignies

The Founders Medal, which consists of a cash award, a gold medal and bronze replica, is given periodically for major contributions in the leadership, planning and administration of "affairs of great value to the electrical and electronics engineering profession." A special committee reviews nominations, which are approved by the board of directors.

1953	David Sarnoff
1954	Alfred N. Goldsmith
1955	No award
1956	No award
1957	Raymond A. Heising
1958	W. R. G. Baker
1959	No award
1960	Haraden Pratt
1961	Ralph Bown

1962	No award
1963	Frederick E. Terman
1964	Andrew G. L. McNaughton
1965	No award
1966	Elmer W. Engstrom
1967	Harvey Fletcher
1968	Patrick E. Haggerty
1969	E. Finley Carter
1970	Morris D. Hooven
1971	Ernst Weber
1972	Masaru Ibuka
	William R. Hewlett
1973	David Packard
1974	Lawrence A. Hyland
1975	John G. Brainerd
1976	Edward W. Herold
1977	Jerome B. Wiesner

The Lamme Medal, which consists of a gold medal, bronze replica and certificate, is awarded for meritorious achievement in the development of electrical or electronic apparatus or systems.

1928	Allan Bertram Field
1929	Rudolf E. Hellmund
1930	William J. Foster
1931	Giuseppe Faccioli
1932	Edward Weston
1933	Lewis B. Stillwell
1934	Henry E. Warren
1935	Vannevar Bush
1936	Frank Conrad
1937	Robert E. Doherty
1938	Marion A. Savage
1939	Norman W. Storer
1940	Comfort A. Adams
1941	Forrest E. Ricketts
1942	Joseph Slepian
1943	A. H. Kehoe
1944	S. H. Mortensen
1945	David C. Prince
1946	J. B. MacNeill
1947	A. M. MacCutcheon
1948	V. K. Zworykin
1949	C. M. Laffoon
1950	Donald I. Bohn
1951	Arthur E. Silver
1952	I. F. Kinnard
1953	F. A. Cowan
1954	A. M. deBellis
1955	C. R. Hanna
1956	H. H. Beverage
1957	H. S. Black
1958	P. L. Alger
	S. Beckwith
1959	L. A. Kilgore
1960	John G. Trump
1961	Charles Concordia
1962	E. L. Harder
1963	Loyal V. Bewley
1964	No award; schedule revised
1965	A. Uno Lamm
1966	Rene Andre Baudry
1967	Warren P. Mason
1968	Nathan Cohn
1969	James D. Cobine
1970	Harry F. Olson
1971	Winthrop M. Leeds
1972	Yu H. Ku
	Robert H. Park
1973	Charles S. Draper

1974 Seymour B. Cohn
1975 Harold B. Law
1976 C. Kumar N. Patel
1977 Bernard M. Oliver

The IEEE Education Medal, which consists of a gold medal, bronze replica and certificate, honors excellence in teaching and the ability to inspire students, and leadership in electrical engineering education through writings and publication.

1956 F. E. Terman
1957 W. L. Everitt
1958 J. F. Calvert
1959 G. S. Brown
1960 Ernst Weber
1961 George F. Corcoran
1962 Ernst A. Guillemin
1963 William G. Dow
1964 B. R. Teare, Jr.
1965 Hugh H. Skilling
1966 William H. Huggins
1967 John R. Whinnery
1968 Edward C. Jordan
1969 Donald O. Pederson
1970 Jacob Millman
1971 Franz Ollendorff
1972 M. E. Van Valkenburg
1973 Lotfi A. Zadeh
1974 John G. Truxal
1975 Charles A. Desoer
1976 John G. Linvill
1977 Robert M. Fanow

The Harry Diamond Memorial Award, which consists of a certificate and $2,000, honors technical contributions in government service in any country, as evidenced by publication in professional journals. A special committee reviews nominations, which are approved by the board of directors.

1950 A. V. Haeff
1951 M. J. E. Golay
1952 Newbern Smith
1953 R. M. Page
1954 Harold Zahl
1955 Bernard Salzberg
1956 W. S. Hinman, Jr.
1957 Georg Goubau
1958 E. W. Allen, Jr.
1959 J. W. Herbstreit
1960 K. A. Norton
1961 H. L. Brueckmann
1962 William Culshaw
1963 Allen H. Schooley
1964 James R. Wait
1965 George J. Thaler
1966 John J. Egli
1967 Rudolf A. Stampfl
1968 Harry I. Davis
1969 Maurice Apstein
1970 Allen V. Astin
1971 Arthur H. Guenther
1972 William B. McLean
1973 Harold Jacobs
1974 Chester H. Page
1975 Louis Costrell
1976 Maxime A. Faget
1977 Jacob Rabinow

The William M. Habirshaw Award, which consists of a bronze medal and $1,000, recognizes contributions in

the field of the transmission and distribution of power. A committee nominates and the board of directors approves the recipient.

1959 William A. Del Mar
1960 Selden B. Crary
1961 Samuel B. Griscom
1962 Herman Halperin
1963 L. M. Robertson
1964 C. S. Schifreen
1965 Wilfred F. Skeats
1966 I. Birger Johnson
1967 Robert J. Wiseman
1968 Eugene C. Starr
1969 James A. Rawls
1970 Fred J. Vogel
1971 Gunnar Jancke
1972 J. J. Archambault
     Lionel Cahill
1973 Eugene W. Boehne
1974 Herbert R. Stewart
1975 Everett J. Harrington
1976 Francis J. Lane
1977 No award; schedule revised

The Hernand and Sostheses Behn Award in International Communication, which consists of a plaque, certificate and $1,000, honors outstanding contributions in the field. A committee nominates and the board of directors approves the recipient.

1966 E. Maurice Deloraine
1967 Leonard Jaffe
1968 Edward W. Allen
1969 Henri Busignies
1970 Herre Rinia
1971 Eugene F. O'Neill
     Frank deJager
1972 Johannes A. Greefkes
1973 Vladimir A. Kotelnikov
1974 Leslie H. Bedford
1975 John G. Puente
1976 Sidney Metzger
1977 No award; schedule revised

The Morris E. Leeds Award, which consists of a certificate and $1,000, honors contributions in electrical measurement, with special consideration given to an engineer under 36 years of age. A special committee nominates the candidate, who is approved by the board of directors.

1959 Herbert B. Brooks
1960 Perry A. Borden
1961 Theodore A. Rich
1962 Bernard E. Lenehan
1963 Francis B. Silsbee
1964 John G. Ferguson
1965 Harold E. Edgerton
1966 William W. Mumford
1967 Henry R. Chope
1968 Albert J. Williams, Jr.
1969 Harry W. Houck
1970 Harold I. Ewen
1971 Martin E. Packard
1972 Forest K. Harris
1973 C. Howard Vollum
1974 Norbert L. Kusters
1976 Francis L. Hermach
1977 Arthur M. Thompson

The Morris N. Liebmann Memorial Award, which consists of a certificate and $2,000, recognizes important contributions to emerging technologies during the three preceding calendar years. A special committee reviews nominations, which are approved by the board of directors.

1919   L. F. Fuller
1920   R. A. Weagant
1921   R. A. Heising
1922   C. S. Franklin
1923   H. H. Beverage
1924   J.R. Carson
1925   Frank Conrad
1926   Ralph Bown
1927   A. H. Taylor
1928   W. G. Cady
1929   E. V. Appleton
1930   A. W. Hull
1931   Stuart Ballantine
1932   Edmond Bruce
1933   Heinrich Barkhausen
1934   V. K. Zworykin
1935   F. B. Llewellyn
1936   B. J. Thompson
1937   W. H. Doherty
1938   G. C. Southworth
1939   H. T. Friis
1940   H. A. Wheeler
1941   P. T. Farnsworth
1942   S. A. Schelkunoff
1943   W. L. Barrow
1944   W. W. Hansen
1945   P. C. Goldmark
1946   Albert Rose
1947   J. R. Pierce
1948   S. W. Seeley
1949   C. E. Shannon
1950   O. H. Schade
1951   R. B. Dome
1952   William Shockley
1953   J. A. Pierce
1954   R. R. Warnecke
1955   A. V. Loughren
1956   Kenneth Bullington
1957   O. G. Villard, Jr.
1958   E. L. Ginzton
1959   Nicolaas Bloembergen
          C. H. Townes
1960   J. A. Rajchman
1961   Leo Esaki
1962   Victor H. Rumsey
1963   Ian Munro Ross
1964   Arthur L. Schawlow
1965   William R. Bennett, Jr.
1966   Paul K. Weimer
1967   No award
1968   Emmett N. Leith
1969   John B. Gunn
1970   John A. Copeland
1971   Martin Ryle
1972   Stewart E. Miller
1973   Nick Holonyak, Jr.
1974   Willard S. Boyle
          George E. Smith
1975   A. H. Bobeck
          P. C. Michaelis
          H. E. D. Scovil
1976   Herbert J. Shaw
          Horst H. Berger
1977   Siegfried K. Wiedmann

The Jack A. Morton Award, consisting of a bronze medal and $2,000, honors contributions in the field of solid state devices. The recipient is nominated by a special committee and approved by the board of directors.

1976   Robert N. Hall
1977   Morgan Sparks

The Frederik Philips Award, which consists of a gold medal, certificate and $2,000, recognizes accomplishments in research and development resulting in effective innovation in the electrical and electronics industry. The recipient is nominated by a special committee and approved by the board of directors.

1971   Frederik J. Philips
1972   William O. Baker
1973   John H. Dessauer
1974   Chauncey Guy Suits
1975   C. Lester Hogan
1976   Koji Kobayashi
1977   No award; schedule revised

The Emanuel R. Piore Award, which consists of a bronze medal, a certificate, $2,000 and a $2,500 international travel grant, honors achievements in information processing related to computer science. The recipient is nominated by a special committee and approved by the board of directors.

1977   George R. Stibitz

The David Sarnoff Award, which consists of a gold medal, bronze replica, certificate and $1,000, honors an outstanding contribution in electronics. The recipient is nominated by a special committee and approved by the board of directors.

1959   David Sarnoff
1960   Rudolf Kompfner
1961   Charles H. Townes
1962   Harry B. Smith
1963   Robert N. Hall
1964   Henri G. Busignies
1965   Jack A. Morton
1966   Jack S. Kilby
1967   James Hillier
1968   Walter P. Dyke
1969   Robert H. Rediker
1970   John B. Johnson
1971   Alan L. McWhorter
1972   Edward G. Ramberg
1973   Max V. Mathews
1974   F. L. J. Sangster
1975   Bernard C. De Loach, Jr.
1976   George H. Heilmeier
1977   Jack M. Manley
          Harrison E. Rowe

The Nikola Tesla Award, which consists of a plaque and $1,000, honors achievements in the field of electric power. The recipient is nominated by a special committee and approved by the board of directors.

1976   Leon T. Rosenberg
1977   Cyril G. Vienott

The Vladimir K. Zworykin Award, which consists of a certificate and $1,000, honors contributions in the field of electronic television. A special committee nominates and the board of directors approves the recipient.

1952   B. D. Loughlin

1953	Frank Gray
1954	A. V. Bedford
1955	H. B. Law
1956	F. J. Bingley
1957	Donald Richman
1958	C. P. Ginsburg
1959	P. K. Weimer
1960	No award
1961	P. C. Goldmark
1962	G. A. Morton
1963	P. J. Rice, Jr.
	W. E. Evans, Jr.
1964	No award
1965	Norman F. Fyler
1966	Ray D. Kell
1967	Keiji Suzuki
1968	Kurt Schlesinger
1969	Otto H. Schade
1970	Charles H. Coleman
1971	Alfred C. Schroeder
1972	Robin E. Davies
1973	Albert Macovski
1974	Senri Miyaoka
	Eugene I. Gordon
1975	Ralph E. Simon
1976	No award
1977	Dalton H. Pritchard

The W.R.G. Baker Prize, which consists of a certificate and $1,000, honors an outstanding paper in any of the *IEEE Transactions, Journals* or *Proceedings*. A special committee review authors' papers, and the board of directors approves the selection.

1957	D. R. Fewer
	R. J. Kircher
	R. L. Trent
1958	R. L. Kyhl
	H. F. Webster
1959	R. D. Thornton
1960	E. J. Nalos
1961	Manfred Clynes
1962	Marvin Chodorow
	Tore Wessel-Berg
1963	Leonard Lewin
1964	Donald L. White
1965	D. C. Youla
1966	Robert G. Gallager
1967	Dean E. McCumber
	Alan G. Chynoweth
1968	J. Andersen
	H. B. Lee
1969	Tosiro Koga
1970	George J. Friedman
	Cornelius T. Leondes
1971	Andrew H. Bobeck
	Robert F. Fischer
	Anthony J. Perneski
	J. P. Remeika
	L. G. Van Uitert
1972	Dirk J. Kuizenga
	Anthony E. Siegman
1973	Leon O. Chua
1974	David B. Large
	Lawrence Ball
	Arnold J. Farstad
1975	Stewart E. Miller
	Enrique A. J. Marcatili
	Tingye Li
1976	Robert W. Keyes
1977	Manfred Schroeder

The Browder J. Thompson Memorial Prize Award, which consists of a certificate and $1,000, recognizes an outstanding paper by an author under 30 years of age in any IEEE publication. A special committee reviews the papers, and the board of directors approves the selection.

1946	G. M. Lee
1947	C. L. Dolph
1948	W. H. Huggins
1949	R. V. Pound
1950	J. F. Hull
	A. W. Randals
1951	A. B. Macnee
1952	H. W. Welch, Jr.
1953	R. C. Booton, Jr.
1954	R. L. Petritz
1955	B. D. Smith, Jr.
1956	J. E. Bridges
1957	D. A. Buck
1958	Arthur Karp
1959	F. H. Blecher
1960	J. W. Gewartowski
1961	Eiichi Goto
1962	Henri B. Smets
1963	Chi-Tang Sah
1964	Harry B. Lee
1965	S. R. Hofstein
	F. P. Heiman
1966	Kenneth M. Johnson
1967	Leon O. Chua
	R. A. Rohrer
1968	Michael L. Dertouzos
1969	Malvin C. Teich
1970	J. David Rhodes
1971	L. J. Griffiths
1972	G. David Forney, Jr.
1973	Jerry Mar
1974	Jorn Justesen
1975	Nuggehally S. Jayant
1976	Russell M. Mersereau
	Dan E. Dudgeon
1977	Michael R. Portnoff

Founders Award

NATIONAL ACADEMY OF ENGINEERING
2101 Constitution Ave. NW, Washington, D.C. 20418
(202/389-6438)

The annual Founders Award is presented to an engineer (excluding founding members of the Academy) for "outstanding engineering accomplishments over a long period of time and of benefit to the people of the United States." The award, consisting of a gold-plated medal, bronze medal and citation, is given to a winner selected by a special awards committee appointed by the president and confirmed by the council.

1966	Vannevar Bush
1967	James Smith McDonnell
1968	Vladimir K. Zworykin
1969	Harry Nyquist
1970	Charles S. Draper
1971	Clarence L. Johnson
1972	Edwin H. Land
1973	Warren K. Lewis
1974	J. Erik Jonsson
1975	James B. Fisk

1976 Manson Benedict
1977 John R. Pierce

INDUCTION
INVENTORS HALL OF FAME
No address (Information phone: 414/273-3700)

Induction into the Inventors Hall of Fame gives public recognition to the inventor. Selection is by nomination from the general public and balloting by an independent Selection Committee.

1973 **Thomas A. Edison,** Lightbulb and other inventions
1974 **Alexander Graham Bell,** Telephone
Eli Whitney, Cotton gin
John Bardeen, Electronics innovations
Walter H. Brattain and William Shockley, Transistor
1975 **Wilbur and Orville Wright,** Airplane
Guglielmo Marconi, Radio telegraphy
Nikola Tesla, Induction motors
Samuel F. B. Morse, Telegraph
William D. Coolidge, Tungsten lamp filament and the X-ray tube
1976 **Cyrus H. McCormick,** Reaper
Charles M. Hall, Process for mfg. aluminum
Charles Goodyear, Vulcanized rubber
Enrico Fermi, Neutronic reactor
Rudolf Diesel, Internal combustion engine
Charles H. Townes, Maser and, from that, the laser
1977 **George Eastman,** Kodak camera and processes
Lee DeForest, Device for amplifying feeble electrical currents (Vacuum Tube)
Edwin H. Land, Polaroid camera
Charles P. Steinmetz, System of distribution by alternating currents
Vladimir K. Zworykin, Cathode ray tube

Axel Axison Johnson Lecture
ROYAL SWEDISH ACADEMY OF ENGINEERING SCIENCES
S-104 O5 Stockholm, Sweden

The Axel Axison Johnson Lecture is an international honor conferred every two or three years upon prominent engineering scientists in the fields of energy or power. The lecturer is selected by the Academy based on nominations from a three-member committee. A plaque is given as a tribute to the lecturer.

1955 **Pierre Ailleret,** Elektricite de France, France
1957 **Sir Christopher Hinton,** Atomic Energy Authority, Great Britain
1962 **Arthur Davenport,** New Zealand Electricity Dept., Wellington, N.Z.
1966 **Monroe E. Spaght,** Royal Dutch/Shell Group Companies, U.S.A.
1971 **A.M. Petrosyants,** Soviet Union State Committee for Atomic Energy, USSR
1974 **Dixy Lee Ray,** Atomic Energy Commission, U.S.A.

Karl Jordan Medal
THE LEPIDOPTERISTS' SOCIETY
Allyn Museum of Entomology, 712 Sarasota Bank Bldg., Sarasota, Fla. 33577 (813/355-8475) or Department of

Entomology, Los Angeles County Museum of Natural History, Los Angeles, Calif. 90007 (213/746-0410)

The Karl Jordan Medal, which carries a $1,000 honorarium, is a silver medal given annually for an outstanding original contribution in lepidopterology, especially in morphology, zoogeography and natural history. An awards committee unanimously selects the winner from nominees.

1973 **Henri Stempfer,** "The Genera of the African Lycaenidae," *Bulletin of the British Museum*
1974 **Frederick W. Stehr,** "A Revision of the Genus Malacosoma Hubner in North America," *Systematics, Biology, Immatures and Parasites*
1975 **No award**
1976 **No award**
1977 **Don R. Davis,** "A Revision of the Moths of the Subfamily Prodoxinae Lepidoptera: Incurvariidea," *Bulletin of the United States National Museums*

Award of Excellence
AMERICAN FISHERIES SOCIETY
5410 Grosvenor La., Bethesda, Md. 20014 (301/897-8616)

The annual Award of Excellence, consisting of $1,000, a medal and a certificate, honors scientists in the fields of fisheries and aquatic biology. A committee selects the winner by substantial or unanimous agreement.

1969 **William E. Ricker** (British Columbia, Canada)
1970 **Stanislas Snieszko** (West Virginia)
1971 **F.E.J. Fry** (Ontario, Canada)
1972 **Ralph Hile** (Michigan)
1973 **Carl Hubbs** (California)
1974 **Clarence Tarzwell** (Rhode Island)
1975 **Robert Rush Miller** (Michigan)
1976 **A.W.H. Needler** (New Brunswick, Canada)
1977 **Arthur D. Hoster** (Wisconsin)

Cullum Geographical Medal
Charles B. Daly Medal
David Livingstone Centenary Medal
Samuel Finley Breese Morse Medal
George Davidson Medal
O. M. Miller Cartographic Medal
Van Cleef Memorial Medal
Honorary Fellowship in the American Geographical Society
AMERICAN GEOGRAPHICAL SOCIETY
Broadway at 156th St., New York, N.Y. 10032 (212/234-8100)

The Cullum Geographical Medal, which is of gold, is awarded as merited for distinguished contributions to the science of geography or for outstanding geographical discoveries made by individuals or exploration parties of any nation.

1896 **Robert E. Peary**
1897 **Fridtjof Nansen**
1899 **Sir John Murray**
1901 **Thomas C. Mendenhall**
1902 **A. Donaldson Smith**

1903	Duke of the Abruzzi
1904	Georg von Neumayer
	Sven Hedin
1906	Robert Falcon Scott
	Robert Bell
1908	William Morris Davis
1909	Francisco P. Moreno
	Sir Ernest Shackleton
1910	Hermann Wagner
1911	Jean B. E. A. Charcot
1914	Ellen Churchill Semple
	John Scott Keltie
1917	George W. Goethals
1918	Frederick Haynes Newell
1919	Emmanuel de Margerie
	Henry Fairfield Osborn
1921	Albert I, Prince of Monaco
1922	Edward A. Reeves
1924	Jovan Cvijic
1925	Pedro C. Sanchez
	Lucien Gallois
	Harvey C. Hayes
1929	Hugh Robert Mill
	Jean Brunhes
	Alfred Hettner
	Jules de Schokalsky
1930	Curtis F. Marbut
1931	Mark Jefferson
1932	Bertram Thomas
1935	Douglas Johnson
1938	Louise Arner Boyd
1939	Emmanuel de Martonne
1940	Robert Cushman Murphy
1943	Arthur Robert Hinks
1948	Hugh Hammond Bennett
1950	Hans W:son Ahlmann
1952	Roberto Almagia
1954	British Everest Expedition
1956	J. Russell Smith
1958	Charles Warren Thornthwaite
1959	Albert Paddock Crary
1963	Rachel Louise Carson
1964	John Leighly
1965	Kirtley Fletcher Mather
1967	Peter Haggett
1968	Luna B. Leopold
1969	Neil A. Armstrong
	Edwin E. Aldrin, Jr.
	Michael Collins
1973	Bruce Heezen
1975	Rene Dubos

The Charles B. Daly Medal, which is of gold, honors distinguished service to geography.

1902	Robert E. Peary
1906	Thorvald Thoroddsen
1908	George Davidson
1909	William W. Rockhill
	Charles Chaille-Long
1910	Grove Karl Gilbert
	Roald Amundsen
1913	Alfred H. Brooks
1914	Albrecht Penck
1915	Paul Vidal de la Blache
1917	George G. Chisholm
1918	Vilhjalmur Stefansson
1920	George Otis Smith
1922	Sir Francis Younghusband
	Adolphus W. Greely
	Ernest de K. Leffingwell

1924	Claude H. Birdseye
	Knud Rasmussen
1925	Robert A. Bartlett
	David L. Brainard
1927	Alois Musil
1929	Filippo De Filippi
	Emile Feliz Gautier
1930	Joseph B. Tyrrell
	Nelson H. Darton
	Lauge Koch
1931	Gunnar Isachsen
1935	Roy Chapman Andrews
1938	Alexander Forbes
1939	Herbert John Fleure
1940	Carl Ortwin Sauer
1941	Julio Garzon Nieto
1943	Sir Halford J. Mackinder
1948	Henri Baulig
1950	Laurence Dudley Stamp
1952	J. M. Wordie
1954	John K. Wright
1956	Raoul Blanchard
1959	Richard Hartshorne
1961	Theodore Monod
1962	Osborn Maitland Miller
1963	Henry Clifford Darby
1964	Jean Gottmann
1965	William Skinner Cooper
1966	Torsten Hagerstrand
1967	Marston Bates
1968	O.H.K. Spate
1969	Paul B. Sears
	William O. Field
1971	Gilbert F. White
1973	Walter Sullivan
1974	Walter Wood

The David Livingstone Centenary Medal, which may be of gold, silver or bronze, is awarded as merited for scientific achievements in the geography of the Southern Hemisphere.

1916	Sir Douglas Mawson
1917	Theodore Roosevelt
	Manuel Vincente Ballivian
1918	Candido Rondon
1920	William Speirs Bruce
	Alexander Hamilton Rice
1923	Griffith Taylor
1924	Frank Wild
1925	Luis Riso Patron
1926	Erich von Drygalski
1929	Richard E. Byrd
1930	Jose M. Sobral
	Laurence M. Gould
1931	Hjalmar Riiser-Larsen
1935	Lars Christensen
1936	Lincoln Ellsworth
1939	John R. Rymill
1945	Isaiah Bowman
1948	Frank Debenham
1950	Robert L. Pendleton
1952	Carlos Delgado de Carvalho
1956	George McCutchen McBride
1958	Paul Allman Siple
1959	William Edward Rudolph
1965	Bassett McGuire
1966	Preston E. James
1968	William H. Phelps, Jr.
1972	Akin L. Mabogunje

The Samuel Finley Breese Morse Medal, which is of gold, is awarded as merited for the encouragement of geographical research.

1928   Sir George Hubert Wilkins
1945   Archer M. Huntington
1952   Gilbert Grosvenor
1966   Charles B. Hitchcock
1968   Wilma B. Fairchild

The George Davidson Medal, which is of gold, is given as merited for outstanding research or exploration of the Pacific Ocean or of the land masses bordering the Pacific.

1952   George B. Cressey
1972   F. Raymond Fosberg
1974   Joseph Spencer
1975   Shinzo Kiuchi

The O. M. Miller Cartographic Medal, which is of gold, honors noteworthy contributions to cartography or geodesy.

1968   Richard Edes Harrison

The Van Cleef Memorial Medal, which is of gold, honors contributions of note to applied urban geography.

1970   John R. Bochert
1974   Harold Rose

Honorary Fellowship in the American Geographical Society is conferred upon explorers and scientists for meritorious contributions to the field.

1918   E. C. Andrews
       Robert A. Bartlett
       Pierre Denis
       William Curtis Farabee
       Emmanuel de Margerie
       Emmanuel de Martonne
       Marion E. Newbigin
       Paul Walle
1919   Morton P. Porsild
       Knud Rasmussen
1922   Gunnar Andersson
       Charles Raymond Beazley
       Jose J. Bravo
       James Henry Breasted
       Jean Brunhes
       Henry Chandler Cowles
       Baron Gerard De Geer
       Albert Demangeon
       Lucien Gallois
       Guillaume Grandidier
       Adolphus Washington Greely
       David George Hogarth
       Sir Thomas Holdich
       Mark Jefferson
       Curtis Fletcher Marbut
       Olinto Marinelli
       John Linton Myers
       Charles Rabot
       Sir Aurel Stein
       Jean Tilho
       Frederick Jackson Turner
       Robert De Courcy Ward
1923   E. Deville
1924   Andre Allix
       Edwin R. Heath
       Lauge Koch
       Paul Le Cointe
       Count Byron Kuhn de Prorock

       Homer Leroy Shantz
1930   Roberto Almagia
       Henry Bryant Bigelow
       Baron Sten De Geer
       Carl Ben Eielson
       Vernor Clifford Finch
       Herbert John Fleure
       Julio Garzon Nieto
       Alfredo Jahn
       William B. Mayo
       Henri Francois Pittier
       Sir Napier Shaw
       Hussein Sirri Bey
       Harald U. Sverdrup
1931   Louise Arner Boyd
1932   Field Marshall Lord Allenby
       Harry Clifton Heaton
1935   Rafael Aguilar y Santillan
       Hans Ahlmann
       Charles Carlyle Colby
       Osbert Guy Stanhope Crawford
       Carlos M. Delgado de Carvalho
       Charles Bungay Fawcett
       Nevin M. Fenneman
       Alexander Forbes
       William Archibald Mackintosh
       Lawrence Martin
       Carl Ortwin Sauer
       Camille Vallaux
1939   Ernst Antevs
       Henri Baulig
       Giotto Danielli
       Sir Wilfred Grenfell
       Ludwig Leonhard Mecking
       William E. Rudolph
       Paul Gerhard Schott
       Laurence Dudley Stamp
1942   Albert Berthold Hoen
1943   Christovam Leite de Castro
       Manuel Medina
1948   Charles H. Behre, Jr.
       Owen Lattimore
       John Leighly
       George McCutchen McBride
       Robert Larimore Pendleton
       George H. H. Tate
       Charles Warren Thornthwaite
1949   Wofford Benjamin Camp
1952   John Foster Dulles
1956   Jean Gottmann
       Stephen B. Jones
       Rafael Pico
1958   Felix Cardona Puig
1961   Clarence Fielden Jones
       John Ewing Orchard
       Robert H. Randall
       H. Bradford Washburn
1962   F. Kenneth Hare
       Samuel Van Valkenburg
1963   John Quincy Stewart
       Gilbert Fowler White
       Georg Wust
1964   Kenneth C. Cumberland
       Arch C. Gerlach
       S. V. Kalesnik
1965   Maxwell J. Dunbar
       Peveril Meigs
1966   Waldo R. Tobler
1967   William A. Hance
1968   S. P. Chatterjee

Clara Egli Le Gear
Lionel A. Walford
J. Russell Whitaker
1969 Hans Boesch
Marvin Mikesell
1970 Charles W. M. Swithinbank
Alexander Melamid
1971 Louis O. Quam
Hans Kinzl
1972 Konstantin A. Salishchev
Richard L. Morrill
David Lowenthal
1973 Meredith F. Burrill
Sir A. Grenfell Price
1974 Marton Pecsi
Evelyn L. Pruitt
1975 Sir Laurence P. Kirwan
Andrew H. Clark

Hubbard Medal
Gold Medal
Grosvenor Medal
John Oliver La Gorce Medal
Jane McGrew Smith Award
Franklin L. Burr Prize for Science

NATIONAL GEOGRAPHIC SOCIETY
17th and M Sts. NW, Washington, D.C. 20036
(202/857-7000)

The Hubbard Medal, named for Gardiner Greene Hubbard, the first president of the Society, is given as warranted for distinction in exploration, discovery and research.

1906 **Cdr. Robert E. Peary,** Arctic explorations; farthest north 87°06'
1907 **Capt. Roald Amundsen,** First traverse of Northwest Passage in a vessel; location of North Magnetic Pole
1909 **Capt. Robert A. Bartlett,** Attaining farthest north, 87°48', with Peary's 1909 expedition
Grove Karl Gilbert, Thirty years' investigations and achievements in physiographic research
1910 **Sir Ernest H. Shackleton,** Explorations in Antarctic; farthest south 88°23'
1919 **Vilhjalmur Stefansson,** Discoveries in Canadian Arctic
1926 **Lt. Cdr. Richard E. Byrd, Jr.,** First to reach North Pole by airplane
1927 **Col. Charles A. Lindbergh,** Solo flight from New York to Paris
1931 **Roy Chapman Andrews,** Geographic discoveries in central Asia
1934 **Anne Morrow Lindbergh,** Notable flights as co-pilot on Charles A. Lindbergh aerial surveys
1935 **Capts. Albert W. Stevens and Orvil A. Anderson,** Research achieved while gaining world altitude record of 72,395 feet in Explorer II, National Geographic Society-U.S. Army Air Corps Stratosphere Expedition
1936 **Lincoln Ellsworth,** Heroic, extraordinary achievements in Arctic and Antarctic exploration
1945 **Gen. H.H. Arnold,** Contributions to the science of aviation
1953 **Comdr. Donald B. MacMillan,** Arctic explorations, 1908-52

1954 **British Everest Expedition,** Conquest of Earth's highest mountain to Sir John Hunt (leader), Sir Edmund Hillary and Tenzing Norgay
1958 **Paul A. Siple,** Scientific leadership of first group to winter at the South Pole; 30 years of Antarctic explorations
1959 **U.S. Navy Antarctic Expeditions,** Exploring South Polar regions; establishing stations for International Geophysical Year, to Secretary of the Navy Thomas S. Gates, Jr., Adm. Arleigh A. Burke and Rear Adm. George Dufek
Sir Vivian Fuchs, Leadership of British Trans-Arctic Expedition; contribution to geographic knowledge
1962 **Louis S.B. and Mary Leakey,** Unearthing fossil bones of earliest man and giant animals in East Africa
Lt. Col. John H. Glenn, Jr., Extraordinary contributions to scientific knowledge of the world and beyond as a pioneer in exploring the ocean of space
1963 **American Mount Everest Expedition,** Contributions to geography through high-altitude research; conquest of Earth's highest peak; pioneering a West Ridge route and making the first summit traverse, to Norman G. Dyhrenfurth (leader)
1967 **Juan T. Trippe,** Extraordinary contributions to geography and exploration through the development of new air routes across continents and oceans, and a lifetime of service to the art and science of aviation
1969 **Apollo 8 Astronauts,** Unique contributions to science and the exploration of space; first to break the bonds of Earth and soar in orbit around the moon to Col. Frank Borman, Capt. James A. Lovell, Jr. and Lt. Col. William F. Anders
1970 **Apollo 11 Astronauts,** Unique contributions to science and the exploration of space; first to land on the mysterious moon, set up scientific instruments and begin its exploration to Neil A. Armstrong, Col. Edwin E. Aldrin, Jr., and Lt. Col. Michael Collins
1975 **Alexander Wetmore,** Outstanding contributions to geography through pioneering explorations and biological studies in the jungles of South and Central America, islands of the central Pacific Ocean and worldwide advancement of the science of ornithology

The Society's Special Gold Medal is given as merited for extraordinary geographic achievement.

1909 **Comdr. Robert E. Peary,** Discovery of the North Pole
1913 **Capt. Roald Amundsen,** Discovery of the South Pole
1914 **Col. George W. Goethals,** Directing completion of the Panama Canal
1926 **Floyd Bennett, USN,** Flight to North Pole with Byrd
1930 **Hugo Eckener,** First global navigation of an airship
Rear Adm. Richard E. Byrd, Jr., Adding to the knowledge of Antarctica; first attainment of the South Pole by air
1932 **Amelia Earhart,** First solo Atlantic flight by a woman
1937 **Thomas C. Poulter,** Achievements, Byrd Antarctic Expedition
1955 **Mrs. Robert E. Peary,** Contributions to Adm. Peary's expeditions to Greenland and Canadian Arctic
1957 **Prince Philip, Duke of Edinburgh,** Promoting science and better understanding among the world's people
1961 **Capt. Jacques-Yves Cousteau,** Giving earthbound man the key to undersea exploration

The Grosvenor Medal is awarded as merited for outstanding service to geography.

1949 **Gilbert Grosvenor,** Outstanding service as editor of *The National Geographic,* 1899-1949

1955 John Oliver La Gorce, Outstanding service to the increase and diffusion of geographic knowledge
1974 Melville Bell Grosvenor, Outstanding service to the increase and diffusion of geographic knowledge

The John Oliver La Gorce Medal is awarded as merited for accomplishment in geographic exploration, or in the sciences, or for public service that advances international understanding.

1967 American Antarctic Mountaineering Expedition, For contributions to science and exploration through the first ascent of Antarctica's highest mountain to Nicholas B. Clinch (leader)
1968 Harold E. Edgerton, For contributions to science and exploration through invention and development of electronic photographic and geophysical equipment
Philip Van Horn Weems, Pioneering achievements in marine, air and space navigation

The Jane McGrew Smith Award medal was usually given annually from 1917 to 1964 to individuals for their contributions to scientific work, much of which was documented in *National Geographic* articles.

1917 Hiram Bingham, Historian, explorer
Alfred H. Brooks, Geologist
George Kennan, Authority on Russia
Henry Pittier, Agriculturist
1919 Frank G. Carpenter, Journalist
O.F. Cook, Plant explorer
William H. Dall, Naturalist
Robert F. Griggs, Botanist
William H. Holmes, Art curator
Stephen T. Mather, Park Service director
Edward W. Nelson, Biologist
Joseph T. Strauss, Rear Admiral, USN
Walter T. Swingle, Plant explorer
1921 Frank M. Chapman, Ornithologist
Herbert E. Gregory, Geologist
Lt. Donald B. Macmillan, USNR, Explorer
R.G. McConnell, Canadian explorer
J.B. Tyrell, Canadian explorer
1925 Robert A. Bartlett, Far north explorer
William Brooks Cabot, Author, engineer
Neil M. Judd, Archeologist
Joseph F. Rock, Agricultural explorer
Charles Sheldon, Alaska explorer
Philip Sidney Smith, Geologist
1926 Knud Rasmussen, Greenland explorer
1927 Charles A. Lindbergh, Transatlantic flight pioneer
1929 Andrew E. Douglass, Astronomer, dendrochronologist
Cornelius A. Pugsley, Banker, conservationist
Herbert Putnam, Librarian of Congress
Curtis D. Wilbur, Secretary of the Navy, ret.
1930 Sir Wilfred Grenfell, Surgeon, missionary, author
1931 Andre Citroen, Industrialist
Laurence M. Gould, Biologist
Douglas W. Johnson, Physiographer
Capt. Ashley C. McKinley, USA, Aerial photographer
Capt. Albert W. Stevens, USA, Aerial photographer
1933 William H. Hobbs, Geologist
1934 Vernon Bailey, Field naturalist
Clifford K. Berryman, Political cartoonist
Eugene Edward Buck, President, A.S.C.A.P.
Charles F. Marvin, Meteorologist
W. Coleman Nevils, S.J., President, Georgetown University
James P. Thompson, Royal Geographical Society of Australia

1935 Joseph P. Connelly, Geologist, college president
Col. William R. Pope, U.S. Army
Leonhard Stejneger, Biologist
1936 H.L. Baldwin, U.S. Geological Survey, ret.
Rogers Birnie, U.S. Army, ret.
Lawrence W. Burpee, Canadian commissioner
Samuel S. Gannett, Geographer
Herbert Hollick-Kenyon, Pilot, Canadian Airways
His Majesty King Leopold, Belgium
Robert Muldrow, U.S. Geological Survey, ret.
A.E. Murlin, U.S. Geological Survey, ret.
W.J. Peters, U.S. Geological Survey, ret.
Capt. Randolph P. Williams, U.S. Army Air Corps
1937 Web Hill, Merchant
Prince Iyesato Tokugawa, Japan
1938 Franklin Adams, Authority on Latin America
Stephen R. Capps, Geologist
1940 Maj. George W. Goddard, U.S.A.A.F., Aerial photographer
1941 J. Fred Essary, Journalist
1942 Charles Henry Deetz, Cartographer
1943 Samuel Whittemore Boggs, Geographer
Harry Warner Frantz, Journalist
Maj. Gen. Eli Helmick, U.S. Army, ret.
Mrs. William G. Paden, Author
Maj. Gen. Alexander M. Patch, U.S. Army
Edmund W. Starling, U.S. Secret Service
1944 Christova Leite de Castro, Geographer
1945 Frank B. Jewett, President, National Academy of Sciences
Frank Mace MacFarland, President, California Academy of Sciences
S.S. Visher, Geographer
1946 Salvador Massip, Geographer
Fleet Adm. Chester W. Nimitz, USN, Chief of Naval Operations
1947 Maurice Ewing, Geologist
Geoffrey T. Hellman, Essayist
Malcolm J. Proudfoot, Geographer
1948 Nicholas H. Darton, Geologist
Benjamin R. Hoffman, Geographical Society of Philadelphia
1949 George J. Miller, Editor, *Journal of Geography*
John O'Keefe, U.S. Army Map Service
Earl B. Shaw, President, Council of Geography Teachers
1950 Mrs. Albert W. Stevens, Smith life member widow
Mrs. Henry H. Arnold, Smith life member widow
1951 Hugh L. Dryden, Director, National Advisory Committee for Aeronautics
Herbert Friedmann, Curator of Birds, U.S. National Museum
Albert E. Giesecke, Government adviser, Peru
Mrs. J.R. Hildebrand, Widow of assistant editor, *National Geographic*
Ruth B. Shipley, Passport Office, U.S. Department of State
1952 Gen. Andrew George Latta McNaughton, Canadian Army, ret.
1953 Robert M. Anderson, Secretary of the Navy
Mrs. Franklin L. Fisher, Widow of illustrations editor, *National Geographic*
Col. Kenneth H. Gibson, U.S. Air Force
Maynard Owen Williams, Chief of foreign staff, *National Geographic*
1955 Ira S. Bowen, Astronomer
Ardito Desio, K-2 Expedition leader
1956 Charles P. Mountford, Anthropologist
1959 Sir Vivian Fuchs, Geologist, explorer
Sir Bruce Ingram, Editor, *London Illustrated News*

Edwin A. Link, Inventor, undersea pioneer
Albert A. Stanley, U.S. Coast and Geodetic Survey
Capt. P.V.H. Weems, USN, ret.
1960 **Adm. Arleigh A. Burke, USN,** Chief of Naval Operations
1962 **Lyndon B. Johnson,** Vice President of the United States
1964 **Calvin H. Plimpton,** President, Amherst College

The Franklin L. Burr Prize for Science is a cash award, which has ranged from $500 to $5,000 per recipient, that is given as merited to leaders in the Society's expeditions and researches for exceptionally meritorious work.

1933 **Capt. Albert W. Stevens,** Aerial phography
1936 **Capt. Albert W. Stevens,** Commanding "Explorer II" stratosphere flight, Nov. 11, 1935
Capt. Orvil A. Anderson, Piloting "Explorer II" stratosphere flight, Nov. 11, 1935
Capt. Randolph P. Williams, Ground officer and alternate pilot, "Explorer II" stratosphere flight, Nov. 11, 1935
1938 **Dr. and Mrs. William M. Mann,** Expedition to collect wild animals, 1937
1939 **Bradford Washburn,** Explorations in the Mount St. Elias region
Matthew W. Stirling, Archeological work in Veracruz State, Mexico, including discovery of world's oldest dated work
1941 **Matthew W. Stirling,** Discoveries of colossal basalt heads and carved jade, Veracruz State, Mexico
Mrs. Matthew W. Stirling, Field secretary of her husband's 1940-41 expeditions to southern Mexico
1944 **Alexander Wetmore,** Initiating, directing and participating in *National Geographic*-Smithsonian Institution's expeditions to southern Mexico
1945 **Thomas A. Jaggar,** Developing "Honukai" (Sea Turtle, forerunner of World War II amphibious Dukw [Duck])
Lyman J. Briggs, Outstanding direction of *National Geographic*-Army Air Corps stratosphere expeditions, 1934-36
1947 **George Van Biesbroeck,** Service to eclipse expedition to Brazil, 1947
1948 **Edward A. Halbach, Francis J. Heyden, Carl W. Miller, Charles H. Smiley and George Van Biesbroeck,** Achievement as participants to Society's solar eclipse expedition in Asia (Burma, China, Siam and Korea)
Arthur A. Allen, Locating and photographing Alaskan nesting place of bristle-thighed curlew
1950 **Charles P. Mountford,** Leader of expedition to Arnhem Land, northern Australia
Frank M. Setzler, Deputy leader of Arnhem Land expedition
1952 **Harold E. Edgerton,** Invention and development of high-speed photographic flash lighting equipment
1953 **George Van Biesbroeck,** Solar eclipse research in Khartoum, Sudan, with a bearing on Einstein's theory of relativity
1954 **Lyman J. Briggs,** Contributions to many fields of science and 20 years as chairman of the Committee for Research and Exploration, National Geographic Society
1955 **Neil M. Judd,** Pueblo Bonito research and monograph
Mrs. Robert E. Peary, For her notable part in her husband's early Arctic expeditions: 1891, 1893, 1897, 1900 and 1902

Marie Peary Stafford, Co-leader of 1932 expedition which built a memorial to her father at Kap York, Greenland
1956 **Robert F. Griggs,** Leader, Mount Katmai, Alaska expeditions, 1915-30
Matthew W. Stirling, Contributions to knowledge of New World pre-history as leader of 13 *National Geographic*-Smithsonian Institution expeditions
1959 **Carl F. Miller,** Leader of archeological investigation of Russell Cave, Ala.
1961 **Louis S.B. Leakey and Mary D. Leakey,** Outstanding paleontological revelations at Olduvai Gorge, Tanganyika
1962 **Jane Goodall,** Research on chimpanzees, East Africa
Lyman J. Briggs, Scientific achievement as chairman of Society's Committee for Research and Exploration for 28 years
1963 **Rear Adm. Donald B. Macmillan, USN,** Contributions from many explorations into the Arctic
Neil M. Judd, Archeological investigations at Pueblo Bonito, N.M., and series of monographs and related tree-ring studies
Barry C. Bishop, Mountaineering and scientific achievements in conquest of Mount Everest by the American Mount Everest Expedition, 1963
1964 **Jane van Lawick-Goodall,** Outstanding contributions to science through her studies of wild chimpanzees in Tanzania, unique technical achievements and dedicated and courageous pursuit of this research
Helge Ingstad and Anne Stine Ingstad, Outstanding contributions to archeological research through explorations of L'Anse aux Meadows, Newfoundland, which resulted in finding first authenticated pre-Columbian Viking settlement in North America
1965 **Richard E. Leakey,** Co-leader of Lake Natron expeditions, Kenya and Tanzania
Bradford Washburn, Contributions to geography through discovery of Mount Kennedy, Yukon Territory, Canada, 1935, and detailed mapping of the area, 1965
Norman G. Dyhrenfurth, Leader and organizer of American Mount Everest Expedition, 1963
1967 **Maynard M. Miller,** Outstanding contributions through leadership of four Alaskan Commemorative Glacier Projects and service as deputy leader of Mount Kennedy Survey Expedition 1965, and glaciologist on American Mount Everest Expedition, 1963
1973 **Dian J. Fossey,** Courageous and diligent field work in some of the most inaccessible forests of Africa and authority on behavior of the mountain gorilla
Richard E. Leakey, Studies of new, large, fossil-bearing area of East Africa and following in the footsteps of his distinguished parents
Kenan T. Erim, Classical archeologist for discoveries of world-recognized importance regarding structures and life of Aphrodiasias, once a city in what is now Turkey

Gilbert H. Cady Award
Kirk Bryan Award
E.B. Burwell, Jr. Award
O.E. Meinzer Award
Penrose Medal
Arthur L. Day Medal
GEOLOGICAL SOCIETY OF AMERICA
3300 Penrose Place, Boulder, Colo. 80301 (303/447-2020)

The Gilbert H. Cady Award, which carries a monetary prize, is awarded biennially for contributions to the field of coal geology, generally in North America. The winner's name is submitted by the Coal Geology Division to the Geological Society Society council for approval.

1973 James M. Schopf
1975 Jack A. Simon
1977 William Spackman

The Kirk Bryan Award is given annually by the Society's Quarternary Geology Geomorphology Division to the author(s) of a published paper of distinction that advances the field or a related field. The Quarternary Geology and Geomorphology Division selects the winner for the approval of the council. The award consists of a certificate and a $500 honorarium.

1958 Luna B. Leopold
      Thomas J. Maddock, Jr.
1959 Jack L. Hough
1960 John F. Nye
1961 John T. Hack
1962 Anders Rapp
1963 Arthur H. Lachenbruch
1964 Robert P. Sharp
1965 Gerald M. Richmond
1966 Charles S. Denny
1967 Clyde A. Wahrhaftig
1968 David M. Hopkins
1969 Ronald L. Shreve
1970 Harold E. Malde
1971 A. Lincoln Washburn
1972 Dwight R. Crandell
1973 John T. Andrews
1974 Robert V. Ruhe
1975 James B. Benedict
1976 Geoffrey S. Boulton
1977 M. Church

The E.B. Burwell, Jr. Award, which carries a monetary prize, is given annually for a published paper which advances knowledge about engineering geology, soil or rock mechanics or related areas. The Engineering Geology Division selects the winner with the approval of the council.

1969 Lloyd B. Underwood
1970 Glenn R. Scott
      David J. Varnes
1971 Edwin B. Eckel
1972 R.J. Proctor
1973 J.E. Hackett
      Murray R. McComas
1974 Robert F. Legget
1975 Erhard M. Winkler
1976 David J. Varnes
1977 Richard E. Goodman

The O.E. Meinzer Award, which consists of a silver bowl and a certificate, annually honors a distinguished paper published in hydrogeology or a related field. The Hydrogeology Divison selects the winner with the approval of the council.

1965 Jozsef Toth
1966 Charles L. McGuinness
1967 Robert W. Stallman
1968 Mahdi S. Hantush
1969 Hilton H. Cooper, Jr.
1970 Victor T. Stringfield

1971 George B. Maxey
1972 Joseph F. Poland
      George H. Davis
1973 William Back
      Bruce B. Hanshaw
1974 R. Allan Freeze
1975 John D. Bredehoeft
      George F. Pinder
1976 Shlomo P. Neuman
      Paul A. Witherspoon
1977 No award

The Penrose Medal, which is of gold, recognizes outstanding, original contributions or achievements which mark a "decided advance" in the science of geology. The medal is given as merited by the council of the Society.

1927 Thomas Chrowder Chamberlin
1928 Jakob Johannes Sederholm
1929 No award
1930 François Alfred Antoine Lacroix
1931 William Morris Davis
1932 Edward Oscar Ulrich
1933 Waldemar Lindgren
1934 Charles Schuchert
1935 Reginald Aldworth Daly
1936 Arthur Philemon Coleman
1937 No award
1938 Andrew Cowper Lawson
1939 William Berryman Scott
1940 Nelson Horatio Darton
1941 Norman Levi Bowen
1942 Charles Kenneth Leith
1943 No award
1944 Bailey Willis
1945 Felix Andries Vening-Meinesz
1946 T. Wayland Vaughan
1947 Arthur Louis Day
1948 Hans Cloos
1949 Wendell P. Woodring
1950 Morley Evans Wilson
1951 Pentti Eskola
1952 George Gaylord Simpson
1953 Esper S. Larsen, Jr.
1954 Arthur Francis Buddington
1955 Maurice Gignoux
1956 Arthur Holmes
1957 Bruno Sander
1958 James Gilluly
1959 Adolph Knopf
1960 Walter Herman Bucher
1961 Philip Henry Kuenen
1962 Alfred Sherwood Romer
1963 William Walden Rubey
1964 Donnel Foster Hewett
1965 Philip Burke King
1966 Harry H. Hess
1967 Herbert Harold Read
1968 J. Tuzo Wilson
1969 Francis Birch
1970 Ralph Alger Bagnold
1971 Marshall Kay
1972 Wilmot H. Bradley
1973 M. King Hubbert
1974 William Maurice Ewing
1975 Francis J. Pettijohn
1976 Preston Cloud
1977 Robert P. Sharp

The Arthur L. Day Medal, which is of gold, honors distinctive contributions to geologic knowledge through the application of physics and chemistry to the solution of geologic problems. Except in unusual situations, the candidates considered by the council are North Americans. The honor carries with it honorary fellowship in the Society.

1948 George W. Morey
1949 William Maurice Ewing
1950 Francis Birch
1951 Martin J. Buerger
1952 Sterling Hendricks
1953 John F. Schairer
1954 Marion King Hubbert
1955 Earl Ingerson
1956 Alfred O. C. Nier
1957 Hugo Benioff
1958 John Verhoogen
1959 Sir Edward C. Bullard
1960 Konrad B. Krauskopf
1961 Willard F. Libby
1962 Hatten Schuyler Yoder
1963 Keith Edward Bullen
1964 James Burleigh Thompson, Jr.
1965 Walter H. Munk
1966 Robert M. Garrels
1967 O. Frank Tuttle
1968 Frederick J. Vine
1969 Harold C. Urey
1970 Gerald J. Wasserburg
1971 Hans P. Eugster
1972 Frank Press
1973 David T. Griggs
1974 A.E. Ringwood
1975 Allan Cox
1976 Hans Ramberg
1977 Akiho Miyashiro

Hayden Memorial Geological Award
ACADEMY OF NATURAL SCIENCES OF PHILADELPHIA
19th and The Parkway, Philadelphia, Pa. 19103
(215/299-1015)

The Hayden Memorial Geological Award, which consists of a bronze medal and $300, is given every three years for the best publication, exploration, discovery or research in geology and paleontology as judged by a committee.

1890 James Hall
1891 Edward D. Cope
1892 Edward Suess
1893 Thomas H. Huxley
1894 Gabriel Augusto Daubree
1895 Karl A. von Zittel
1896 Giovanni Capellini
1897 A. Karpinski
1898 Otto Torell
1899 Gilles Joseph Gustave Dowalque
1902 Archibald Geikie
1905 Charles Doolittle Walcott
1908 John Mason Clarke
1911 John C. Branner
1914 Henry Fairfield Osborn
1917 William Morris Davis
1920 Thomas Chrowder Chamberlin

1923 Alfred Lacroix
1926 William B. Scott
1929 Charles Schuchert
1932 Reginald A. Daly
1935 Andrew C. Lawson
1938 Sir Arthur Smith Woodward
1941 Amadeus W. Grabau
1944 Joseph A. Cushman
1947 Paul Niggli
1950 George Gaylord Simpson
1953 Norman L. Bowen
1956 Raymond C. Moore
1959 Carl O. Dunbar
1962 Alfred S. Remer
1965 Normal D. Newell
1968 Elso S. Barghoorn
1971 Wilmot H. Bradley
1974 No award
1977 No award

Vetlesen Prize
COLUMBIA UNIVERSITY LAMONT-DOHERTY GEOLOGICAL OBSERVATORY
Palisades, N.Y. 10964 (914/359-2900)

The Vetlesen Prize, which consists of $50,000 and a gold medal, is awarded every two years for outstanding scientific achievement resulting in a clearer understanding of the Earth, its history and its relationship to the rest of the Universe. The winner is selected by a committee named by the Lamont-Doherty Observatory and the Georg Unger Vetlesen Foundation.

1960 Maurice Ewing
1962 Sir Harold Jeffreys
     Felix Andries Vening Meinesz
1964 Pentti Eelis Eskola
     Arthur Holmes
1966 Jan Hendrik Oort
1968 Sir Edward Bullard
     Francis Birch
1970 S. Keith Runcorn
     Allan V. Cox
     Richard D. Dolle
1972 William A. Fowler
1974 Chaim Lieb Pekaris
1977 J. Tuzo Wilson

William Bowie Medal
James B. Macelwane Award
Walter H. Bucher Medal
John Adam Fleming Medal
Robert E. Horton Medal
Maurice Ewing Award
AMERICAN GEOPHYSICAL UNION
1909 King St. NW, Washington, D.C. 20006 (202/231-0370)

The William Bowie Medal is given annually for outstanding contributions to fundamental geophysics and for unselfish cooperation in research.

1939 William Bowie
1940 Arthur Louis Day
1941 John Adam Fleming
1942 Nicholas Hunter Heck

1943 Oscar Edward Meinzer
1944 Henry Bryant Bigelow
1945 Jacob Aall Bonnevie Bjerknes
1946 Reginald Alsworth Daly
1947 Felix Andries Vening Meinesz
1948 James Bernard Macelwane
1949 Walter Davis Lambert
1950 Leason Heberling Adams
1951 Harald Ulrik Sverdrup
1952 Harold Jeffreys
1953 Beno Gutenberg
1954 Richard Montgomery Field
1955 Walter Hermann Bucher
1956 Weikko Aleksanteri Heiskanen
1957 William Maurice Ewing
1958 Johannes Theodoor Thijsse
1959 Walter M. Elsasser
1960 Francis Birch
1961 Keith Edward Bullen
1962 Sydney Chapman
1963 Merle Antony Tuve
1964 Julius Bartels
1965 Hugo Benioff
1966 Louis B. Slichter
1967 Lloyd V. Berkner
1968 Roger Revelle
1969 Walter B. Langbein
1970 Bernhard Haurwitz
1971 Inge Lehmann
1972 Carl Eckhart
1973 George P. Woollard
1974 A. E. Ringwood
1975 Edward Bullard
1976 Jules G. Charney
1977 James A. Van Allen

The James B. Macelwane Award recognizes significant contributions by a physicist less than 36 years of age. A plaque is given to the winner(s).

1962 James N. Brune
1963 Alexander J. Dessler
1964 Klaus F. Hasselmann
1965 Gordon J. K. MacDonald
1966 Don L. Anderson
1967 Manik Talwani
1968 Michael B. McElroy
1969 Richard S. Lindzen
1970 Lynn R. Sykes
1971 Carl I. Wunsch
1972 John Michael Wallace
1973 R. Allan Freeze
1974 Amos M. Nur
1975 Dan McKenzie
1975 Vytenis M. Vasyliunas
1975 Gerald Schubert
1976 John S. Lewis
1976 Kurt Lambeck
1976 Robert L. Parker
1977 Paul G. Richards
1977 Ignacio Rodriguez-Iturbe
1977 Christopher T. Russell

The Walter H. Bucher Medal is given every two years for original contributions to knowledge of the Earth's crust.

1968 J. Tuzo Wilson
1969 James Gilluly
1970 David. T. Griggs
1971 Robert S. Dietz
1972 William Jason Morgan

1974 Maurice Ewing
1975 Lynn Sykes
1977 Bruce C. Heezen

The John Adam Fleming Medel is given every two years for original research and technical leadership in geomagnetism, atmospheric electricity, aeronomy and related sciences.

1962 Lloyd V. Berkner
1963 James A. Van Allen
1964 Edward O. Hulburt
1965 Norman F. Ness
1966 Scott E. Forbush
1967 Ernest Harry Vestine
1968 Eugene N. Parker
1969 Allan Verne Cox
1970 Joseph Kaplan
1971 Walter M. Elsasser
1972 William Ian Axford
1973 Victor Vaquier
1975 Carl E. McIlwain
1977 Francis S. Johnson

The Robert E. Horton Medal is awarded for outstanding contributions to the geophysical aspects of hydrology.

1976 Walter B. Langbein

The annual Maurice Ewing Award is given jointly by the AGU and the U.S. Navy for contributions for understanding physical, geophysical and geological processes in the ocean, to engineering, technology and instrumentation and/or service to marine sciences.

1976 Walter H. Munk
1977 Henry Stommell

Bocher Memorial Prize
Frank Nelson Cole Prizes in Algebra and Number Theory
Oswald Veblen Prize in Geometry
George David Birkhoff Prize in Applied Mathematics
Norbert Wiener Prize in Applied Mathematics
LeRoy P. Steele Prizes

AMERICAN MATHEMATICAL SOCIETY
201 Charles St., Box 6248, Providence, R.I. 02940
(401/272-9500)

The Bocher Memorial Prize is given every five years for "a notable research memoir in analysis" which appeared in the previous five years. The $1,450 prize goes to a Society member or to a contributor to a recognized North American journal.

1923 G.D. Birkhoff, "Dynamical Systems with Two Degrees of Freedom"
1924 E.T. Bell, "Arithmetical Paraphrases"
1928 J.W. Alexander, "Combinatorial Analysis Situs"
1933 Marston Morse, "The Foundations of a Theory of the Calculus of Variations in the Large M-Space"
1938 John von Neumann, "Almost Periodic Functions and Groups"

1943 Jesse Douglas, "Green's Function and the Problem of Plateau"
1948 A.C. Schaeffer and D.C. Spencer, "Coefficients of Schicht Functions"
1953 Norman Levinson, Contributions to the theory of linear, non-linear, ordinary and partial differential equation in various papers.
1959 Louis Nirenberg, Work in partial differential equations
1964 Paul J. Cohen, "On a Conjecture of Littlewood and Idempotent Measures"
1969 I.M. Singer, Work on the index problem.
1974 Donald S. Ornstein, "Bernoulli Shifts with the Same Entropy are Isomorphic"

The Frank Nelson Cole Prize in Algebra and the Frank Nelson Cole Prize in Number Theory are each awarded at five-year intervals for contributions to algebra and the theory of numbers, under restrictions similar to those of the Bocher Prize. The present honorarium is $2,250.

1928 L.E. Dickson, "Algebren und Ihre Zahlentheorie"
1931 H.S. Vandiver, Papers on Fermat's last theorem
1939 A. Adrian Albert, Papers on the construction of Riemann matrices
1944 Oscar Zariski, Papers on algebraic varieties
1946 H.B. Mann, "A Proof of the Fundamental Theorem of the Density of Sums of Sets of Positive Integers"
1949 Richard Bauer, "On Artin's L-Series with General Group Characters"
1951 Paul Erdos, Papers on the theory of numbers
1954 Harish-Chandra, Papers on representations of semisimple Lie algebras and groups
1956 John T. Tate, "The Higher Dimensional Cohomology Groups of Class Field Theory"
1960 Serge Lang, "Unramified Class Field Theory over Function Fields in Several Variables"
Maxwell E. Rosenlicht, "Generalized Jacobian Varieties"
1962 Kenkichi Iwasawa, "Gamma Extensions of Number Fields"
Bernard M. Dwork, "On the Rationality on the Zeta Function of an Algebraic Variety"
1965 Walter Feit and John G. Thompson, "Solvability of Groups of Odd Order"
1967 James B. Ax and Simon B. Kochen, "Diophantine Problems over Local Fields"
1970 John R. Stallings, "On Torsion-free Groups with Infinitely Many Ends"
Robert G. Swan, "Groups of Cohomological Dimension One"
1972 Wolfgang M. Schmidt, "On Simultaneous Approximations of Two Algebraic Numbers by Rationals" and other papers
1975 Hyman Bass, "Unitary Algebraic K-Theory"
Donald G. Quillen, "Higher Algebraic K-Theories"

The Oswald Veblen Prize in Geometry is a $2,000 award, which in the future will ordinarily be made every five years under conditions similar to those of the Bocher Prize.

1964 C.D. Papakyriakopoulos, "On Solid Tori" and "On Dehn's Lemma and the Asphercity of Knots"
Raoul Bott, "The Space of Loops of a Lie Group" and "The Stable Homotopy of the Classical Groups"
1966 Stephen Smale, Contributions to differential topology
Morton Brown and Barry Mazur, Work on the generalized Schoenflies theorem

1971 Robion C. Kirby, "Stable Homeomorphisms and the Annulus Conjecture"
Dennis P. Sullivan, "On the Hauptvermutung for Manifolds"

The George David Birkhoff Prize in Applied Mathematics of $2,066 is normally awarded every five years jointly by the American Mathematical Society and the Society for Industrial and Applied Mathematics to a member of one of these societies who is a resident of the United States, Canada or Mexico.

1968 Jurgen K. Moser, Contributions to the theory of Hamiltonian dynamical systems
1973 Fritz John, Work in partial differential equations in numerical analysis
James B. Serrin, Fundamental contributions to the theory of non-linear partial differential equations

The $2,000 Norbert Wiener Prize in Applied Mathematics is made jointly by the American Mathematicl Society and the Society for Industrial and Applied Mathematics under conditions similar to the Birkhoff Prize. It is awarded every five years.

1970 Richard E. Bellman, Work in dynamic programming and for related work
1975 Peter D. Lax, Work on numerical and theoretical aspects of partial differential equations and on scattering theory

The LeRoy P. Steele Prizes, endowed by a $143,000 bequest, are awarded for outstanding published mathematical research. One or more prizes may be given each year.

1970 Solomon Lefschetz, "A Page of Mathematical Autobiography"
1971 James B. Carrell, "Invariant Theory, Old and New," written with Jean A. Dieudonne
Jean A. Dieudonne, "Algebraic Geometry"
Phillip A. Griffiths, "Periods of Integrals on Algebraic Manifolds"
1972 Edward B. Curtis, "Simplical Homotopy Theory"
William J. Ellison, "Waring's Problem"
Lawrence F. Payne, "Isoperimetric Inequalities and Their Applications"
Dana S. Scott, "A Proof of the Independence of the Continuum Hypothesis"
1975 Lipman Bers, "Uniformization Moduli, and Kleinian Groups"
Martin D. Davis, "Hilbert's Tenth Problem is Unsolvable"
Joseph L. Taylor, "Measure Algebras"
H. Blaine Lawson, "Foliations"
George W. Mackey, "Ergodic Theory and Its Significance for Statistical Mechanics and Probability Theory"

Carl-Gustaf Rossby Research Medal
Second Half Century Award
Charles Franklin Brooks Award
Cleveland Abbe Award for Distinguished Service to Atmospheric Sciences
Sverdrup Gold Medal
Clarence Leroy Meisinger Award
Award for Outstanding Service by a Weather Forecaster
Award for the Advancement of Applied Meteorology
Award for Outstanding Achievement in Bioclimatology
Award for Outstanding Services to Meteorology
Editor's Award
Special Awards
Father James W. Macelwane Awards in Meteorology

AMERICAN METEOROLOGICAL SOCIETY
45 Beacon St., Boston, Mass. 02108 (617/227-2425)

The Carl-Gustaf Rossby Research Medal, which is of gold, honors contributions to the understanding of the structure or behavior of the atmosphere. It is the Society's highest honor and is presented to an individual selected by the awards committee.

1951	Hurd Curtis Willett
1952	No award
1953	Carl-Gustaf Arvid Rossby
1954	No award
1955	Jerome Namias
1956	John von Neumann
1957	No award
1958	No award
1959	No award
1960	J. Bjerknes and Erik Palmen
1961	Victor P. Starr
1962	Bernhard Haurwitz
1963	Harry Wexler
1964	Jule G. Charney
1965	Arnt Elaissen
1966	Zdenek Sekera
1967	Dave Fultz
1968	Verner E. Suomi
1969	Edward N. Lorenz
1970	Hsiao-Lan Kuo
1971	Norman A. Phillips
1972	Joseph Smagorinsky
1973	Christian E. Junge
1974	Heinz H. Lettau
1975	Charles H.B. Priestley
1976	Hans A. Panofsky
1977	Akio Arakawa

The Second Half Century Award, which consists of a medallion, honors a Society member for contributions to geofluid sciences. No more than three awards are given annually. They are generally made to individuals about 50 years of age at the time of presentation. The honor was instituted for the Society's 50th anniversary year.

1970	Rudolph Nael
	Don T. Hilleary
	Lewis D. Kaplan
	David Q. Wark
1971	No award
1972	Richard J. Reed
1973	Douglas K. Lilly
1974	James W. Deardorff
	Tiruvalam N. Krishnamurti
1975	Louis J. Battan
1976	Roger M. Lehrmitte
1977	Syukuro Manabe

The Charles Franklin Brooks Award is given as merited to an individual for service to the Society.

1951	Henry Southworth Shaw
1953	Harry Guggenheim
1955	Charles Franklin Brooks
1956	Robert Granville Stone
1957	Carl-Gustaf Arvid Rossby
1958	Henry Garrett Houghton
1960	Horace Robert Byers
1961	Howard T. Orville
1962	Sverre Petterssen
1963	David M. Ludlum
1964	Thomas F. Malone
1965	Patrick D. McTaggart-Cowan
1966	John C. Beckman
1967	Phil E. Church
1968	Kenneth C. Spengler
1969	Alfred K. Blackadar
1970	Robert Dawson Fletcher
1971	Louis J. Batton
1972	Helmut E. Landsberg
1973	Glenn R. Hilst
1974	David F. Landrigan
1975	Werner A. Baum
1976	Earl G. Droessler
1977	Eugene Bollay

The Cleveland Abbe Award for Distinguished Service to Atmospheric Sciences, which consists of a certificate, is awarded as merited to an individual for progress in atmospheric science or its application to general social, economic or humanitarian welfare.

1963	Lloyd V. Berkner
1964	Francis W. Reichelderfer
1965	Sverre Petterssen
1966	Alan T. Waterman
1967	Arthur F. Merewether
1968	Thomas F. Malone
1969	Robert M. White
1970	Walter Orr Roberts
1971	Robert G. Fleagle
1972	Homer E. Newell
1973	Fred D. White
1974	Lester Machta
1975	George P. Cressman
1976	Patrick D. McTaggart-Cowan
1977	Richard M. Goody

The Sverdrup Gold Medal honors important research in the scientific knowledge of interactions between oceans and atmosphere. This medal is awarded as merited by the President of the Society upon the advice of an international committee in consultation with representatives of leading marine research facilities.

1964 Henry Stommel
1966 Walter H. Munk
1970 Kirk Bryan
1971 Klaus Hasselmann
1972 Vladimir Kamenkovich
1975 Owen M. Phillips
1976 Robert W. Stewart
1977 Raymond B. Montgomery

The Clarence Leroy Meisinger Award annually recognizes research achievement that is, at least in part, aerological in nature. The award consists of an honorarium and a certificate. Preference is given to scientists 35 years of age or younger.

1938 Jerome Namias
1939 No award
1940 No award
1941 Joseph J. George
1942 No award
1943 No award
1944 No award
1945 No award
1946 Morris Neiburger
1947 Herbert Riehl
1948 James E. Miller
1949 Jule G. Charney and Arnt Eliassen
1950 John Freeman, Jr., and Morris Tepper
1951 Dave Fultz
1952 No award
1953 No award
1954 No award
1955 No award
1956 Ernest J. Fawbush and Robert C. Miller
1957 David Atlas
1959 Robert G. Fleagle
1960 Philip D. Thompson and Norman A. Phillips
1961 Verner E. Suomi
1962 Louis J. Battan
Joanne Starr Malkus
1963 Edward N. Lorenz
1964 Richard J. Reed
1965 Hans A. Panofsky
1966 George W. Platzman
1967 Tetsuya Fujita, Joseph Smargorinsky, Syukuro Manabe, Yale Mintz, Akio Arakawa and Cecil E. Leith
1968 Katsuyuki Ooyama
1969 Richard S. Lindzen
1970 William L. Smith
1971 Joseph Pedlosky
1972 Francis P. Bretherton
1973 Robert E. Dickinson
James R. Holton
1974 Keith A. Browning
1975 John M. Wallace
1976 Thomas W. Flattery
1977 Roger A. Pielke

The annual Award for Outstanding Service by a Weather Forecaster honors the Society member who has provided distinguished service that is a credit to the profession, especially involving public safety and well-being.

1967 Charles L. Mitchell
1968 Gordon E. Dunn
1969 Lee George Dickinson
1970 Harlan K. Saylor

1971 Leonard W. Snellman
1972 Robert E. Clark
1973 Hilmer Crumrine
1974 W. Clyde Conner
Raymond H. Craft
1975 Robert C. Miller
1976 James F. Andrews
James F. O'Connor
1977 Capt. Charles R. Holliday, USAF

The Award for the Advancement of Applied Meteorology annually honors an individual for contributions to direct application of the science to climatological knowledge toward the fulfillment of industrial or agricultural needs or to the development of scientific knowledge which ultimately can meet those needs.

1956 Joseph J. George
1957 William J. Schaefer
1958 No award
1959 Carl-Gustaf Arvid Rossby
1960 Henry T. Harrison
1961 Robert D. Elliott
1962 Alfred H. Glenn
1963 Herbert C.S. Thom
1964 No award
1965 Loren W. Crow
1966 Eugene Bollay
1967 Charles Pennypacker Smith
1968 Wallace E. Howell
1969 E. Wendell Hewson
1970 Arthur F. Merewether
1971 George P. Cressman
1972 Vincent J. Oliver
Howard B. Kaster
1973 Harold A. Bedient
Robert E. Munn
1974 Robert A. McCormick
1975 William H. Klein
1976 Don G. Friedman
Bernard Vonnegut
1977 John E. Wallace

The Award for Outstanding Achievement in Bioclimatology is a certificate given as merited for outstanding contributions in the field. A Committee on Biometeorology submits a list of nominees to the Awards Committee for selection.

1960 Frederick Sargent II
1963 Konrad J.K. Buettner
1964 Helmut E. Landsberg
1966 Frederick A. Brooks
1967 Paul E. Waggoner
1969 William G. Wellington
1971 David M. Gates
1972 Igho J. Kornblueh
1973 Harold D. Johnson
1976 G. LeRoy Hahn
1977 No award

The annual Award for Outstanding Services to Meteorology by a Corporation honors advancement of the science or its application with a certificate.

1951 *House Beautiful* magazine
1952 No award
1953 Munitalp Foundation
1954 National Broadcasting Co.
1955 Science Service, Inc.
1956 *New York Times*
1957 Travelers Insurance Co.

1958	No award
1959	General Electric Co.
1960	American Airlines
	Eastern Airlines
	Pan American World Airways
	Trans World Airlines
	United Air Lines
1961	Pacific Gas and Electric Co.
1962	No award
1963	Radio Corp. of America
1965	*Christian Science Monitor*
1966	Industrial Laboratories of the International Telephone and Telegraph Corp.
1967	Atlantic Research Corp.
1968	Hughes Aircraft Co.
	Santa Barbara Research Center
1969	Science Associates, Inc.
1970	A.H. Glenn and Assoc.
	Murray and Trettel, Inc.
	North American Weather Consultants
	Northeast Weather Service
	Weather Corp. of America
1971	*Scientific American*
1973	WTVT Television Service, Tampa, Fla.
1974	Barnes Engineering Co.
1975	National Geographic Society
1976	Franklin Institute
1977	University Corp. for Atmospheric Research

The annual Editor's Award, which consists of a certificate, recognizes a manuscript of outstanding merit submitted to one of the Society's publications.

1969	Norman A. Phillips
1970	Charles W. Newton
1971	Peter V. Hobbs
1972	James W. Deardorff
1973	George W. Platzman
1974	Norihiko Fukuta
1975	Gabriel T. Csanady
1976	Stanley L. Barnes
	Robert E. Dickinson
1977	No award

Special awards and citations are made as merited to individuals or organizations whose accomplishments are noteworthy but which do not fit within the framework of the Society's regular awards program.

1957	KSOK Radio, Arkansas City, Kans.
	WKY-TV, Oklahoma City, Okla.
	Joseph Bartatto
	Stuart Grazier Bigler
1959	Maurice Levy
	Jean Felix Piccard
1960	U.S. Forest Service
	Charles B. Moore
	Malcolm D. Ross
	Lee Lewis
	Walter Rue
	Nicholas Brango
1961	William W. Kellogg
	Stanley M. Greenfield
	John C. Freeman
	Archie M. Kahan
1962	Werner A. Baum
1964	Dean Blake
	Rev. Adelhelm Hess, O.S.B.
1965	Gordon D. Cartwright
	Morton J. Rubin
1966	Gertrude M. Woods
1969	*Fortune* magazine

	Lawrence Lessing
	KCID, Spencer,Iowa
1970	Hydrologic Services of the ESSA Weather Bureau
	Ferdinand C. Bates
	Howard H. Hanks, Jr.
	WMAQ-TV, Chicago
1971	George L. Hammond
	Robert E. Cardinal
	National Broadcasting Co.
	WKY Television Systems, Inc., Oklahoma City, Okla.
	Raymond E. Falconer
	Raymond A. Wrightson
1972	Robert Jastrow
	Francis W. Reichelderfer
	Malcolm Rigby
1973	Agricultural (Fruit Frost) Weather Forecasters, Ariz. and Calif.
	William H. Best, Jr.
	James W. Reid
1974	Illinois State Water Survey
1975	Robert O. Reid
1974	National Weather Service Office, Huntsville, Ala. Det. 15, 15th Wea. Sq. 5th Wea. Wg., Air Weather Service, Wright-Patterson AFB, Ohio
1976	Albert W. Duckworth
1977	John F. Henz
	Vincent R. Scheetz
	Viking Meterology Flight Team
	KCOL radio, Fort Collins, Colo.
	Alan K. Betts
	Stephen K. Cox
	Edward J. Zipser

The Father James W. Macelwane Awards in Meteorology, which carry cash prizes, annually honor the winners in a student paper contest, whose purpose it is to stimulate interest in the atmospheric sciences. Undergraduate students may enter the competition. The first prize, whose winners are listed here, is $200. Two other cash awards are given.

1960	William E. Shenk, Pennsylvania State University
1961	No award
1962	No award
1963	John B. Armstrong, University of British Columbia
1964	Charles B. Pyke, University of California/Los Angeles
1965	William L. Woodley, University of California/Los Angeles
1966	Edward E. Hindman II, Colorado State University
1967	No award
1968	Peter H. Hildebrand, University of Chicago
1969	I.R. Graham, University of Toronto
1970	Andres J. Heymsfield, State University of New York/Fredonia
1971	Dean G. Duffy, Case Institute of Technology
1972	Robert M. Friedman, New York University
1973	Louis W. Uccelini, University of Wisconsin
1974	Robert M. Thompson, Jr., Florida State University
1975	Paul W. Greiman, Florida State University
1976	Stephen J. Culucci, State University of New York/Albany
1977	David Schachterle, University of Colorado

Losey Atmospheric Sciences Award

AMERICAN INSTITUTE OF AERONAUTICS AND ASTRONAUTICS
1290 Ave. of the Americas, New York, N.Y. 10019
(212/581-4300)

The Losey Atmospheric Sciences Award, originally called the Robert M. Losey Award, recognizes contributions to meteorology as applied to aeronautics. The award consists of a medal and certificate, and is made upon a decision of the honors and awards committee.

ROBERT M. LOSEY AWARD

1940 Henry G. Houghton, Jr.
1941 Horace R. Byers
1942 F.W. Riechelderfer
1943 Joseph J. George
1944 John C. Bellamy
1945 Harry Wexler
1946 Carl G. Rossby
1947 Benjamin G. Holzman
1948 Paul A. Humphrey
1949 William Lewis
1950 Roscoe R. Braham
1951 Ivan R. Tannehill
1952 Vincent J. Schaefer
1953 Henry T. Harrison, Jr.
1954 Hermann B. Wobus
1955 Robert C. Bundgaard
1956 Ross Gunn
1957 Jule G. Charney
1958 P.D. McTaggard-Cowan
1959 Herbert Riehl
1960 Thomas F. Malone
1961 Arthur F. Merewether
1962 Jacob A.B. Bjerknes
1964 Robert C. Miller
1965 George P. Cressman
1966 David Atlas
1967 Elmar R. Reiter
1969 Robert D. Fletcher
1970 Newton A. Lieurance
1971 Verner E. Suomi
1972 David Q. Wark
1973 George H. Fichtl
1974 Norman Sissenwine
1975 Paul W. Kadlec
1976 No award

LOSEY ATMOSPHERIC SCIENCES AWARD

1977 Robert Knollenberg

Buys Ballot Medal

ROYAL NETHERLANDS ACADEMY OF ARTS AND SCIENCES
Klovenniersburgwal 29, Amsterdam, Holland (020 22 29 02)

The Buys Ballot Medal, which is of gold, is awarded every 10 years for research in meteorology. A selection committee chooses the winner of this international honor.

1893 Julius Hann (Austria)
1903 R. Assmann and A. Berson (Germany)
1913 H. Hergesell (France)
1923 Sir Napier Shaw (United Kingdom)
1933 V. Bjerknes (Norway)

1948 S. Petterssen (Norway)
1953 G.J.H. Swoboda (Switzerland)
1963 E.H. Palmen (Finland)
1973 J. Smagorinsky (U.S.A.)

Matthew Fontaine Maury Medal

SMITHSONIAN INSTITUTION
1000 Jefferson Dr. SW, Washington, D.C. 20560
(202/628-4422)

The Matthew Fontaine Maury Medal, which is of gold, honors distinguished contributions in underwater ocean science. It is awarded as merited.

1971 Edwin A. Link and J. Seward Johnson, Conception and development of Johnson-Sea-Link, the first in a class of submersible research vehicles
1976 Robert M. White, For distinguished service as first administrator of the National Oceanic and Atmospheric Administration and efforts in fostering research on a national level

Nobel Prize in Physics

NOBEL FOUNDATION
Nobel House, Sturegatan 14, 11436-Stockholm, Sweden

The Nobel Prize in Physics is generally recognized as the highest honor which can be bestowed upon a physicist for an exceptionally noteworthy discovery in this scientific field. The award, which consists of a gold medal, diploma and a large honorarium, is given in a ceremony on December 10 of each year at Stockholm's City Hall. The awards are presented and administered by the Royal Swedish Academy of Sciences. The amount of the honorarium fluctuates. In 1977 it was approximately $145,000.

1901 Wilhelm C. Roentgen (Germany), Discovery of X-rays
1902 Hendrik A. Lorentz and Pieter Zeeman (Netherlands), Work on magnetic influences on radiation phenomena
1903 Antoine Henri Becquerel (France), Discovered spontaneous radioactivity
Marie Curie and Pierre Curie (France), Research on radiation phenomena discovered by Becquerel
1904 Lord Rayliegh (John W. Strutt) (Great Britain), Investigated densitites of important gases and discovered argon
1905 Philipp E. von Lenard (Germany, born in Hungary), Work on cathode rays
1906 Sir Joseph J. Thomson (Great Britain), Experimented and developed theories on conduction of electricity by gases
1907 Albert A. Michelson (U.S.A., born in Germany), Precision instruments for spectroscopic and meteorological studies
1908 Gabriel Lippmann (France), Reproduced colors photographically
1909 Guglielmo Marconi (Italy), Developed radio
1910 Johannes D. van der Waals (Netherlands), Research on equation of state for liquids and gases
1911 Wilhelm Wien (Germany), Work on laws of heat radiation
1912 Nils G. Dalen (Sweden), Invented automatic regulators for gas accumulators for lighthouse and buoy illumination

1913 Heike Kamerlingh-Onnes (Netherlands), Investigated properties of matters at low temperatures, leading to production of liquid helium
1914 Max von Laue (Germany), Discovered X-ray diffraction by crystals
1915 Sir William H. Bragg and William L. Bragg (Great Britain), Analyzed crystal structure by X-ray
1916 No award
1917 Charles G. Barkla (Great Britain), Discovered characteristic Roentgen radiation of elements
1918 Max K.E.L. Planck (Germany), Discovered energy quanta
1919 Johannes Stark (Germany), Discovered Doppler effect in canal rays and splitting of spectral lines in electric fields
1920 Charles E. Guillaume (France, born in Switzerland), Discovered anomalies in nickel-steel alloys
1921 Albert Einstein (U.S.A., born in Germany), Studies in theoretical physics, especially the law of photo-electric effect
1922 Niels Bohr (Denmark), Work on atomic structure and radiation
1923 Robert A. Millikan (U.S.A.), Research on elementary electric charge and photoelectric effect
1924 Karl M.G. Siegbahn (Sweden), Work on X-ray spectroscopy
1925 James Franck and Gustav Hertz (Germany), Discovered laws of impact of an electron on an atom
1926 Jean B. Perrin (France), Research on discontinuous structure of matter, particularly discovery of sedimentation equilibrium
1927 Arthur H. Compton (U.S.A.), Discovered Compton effect concerning increased wave length of X-rays and gamma rays scattered by electrons
1928 Owen W. Richardson (Great Britain), Thermionic research on phenomena of emission of electrically charged particles in a heated body and discovered of Richardson's Law
1929 Prince Louis-Victor de Broglie (France), Discovered wave nature of electrons
1930 Sir Chandrasekhara V. Raman (India), Research of light scattering and discovery of Raman effect
1931 No award
1932 Werner Heisenberg (Germany), Created quantum mechanics leading to discovery of allotrophic forms of hydrogen
1933 Paul A.M. Dirac (Great Britain) and **Erwin Schrodinger** (Austria), Extensions of atomic theory
1934 No award
1935 James Chadwick (Great Britain), Discovered neutrons
1936 Carl D. Anderson (U.S.A.), Discovered positron
Victor F. Hess (Austria), Discovered cosmic radiation
1937 Clinton J. Davisson (U.S.A.) and **George P. Thomson** (Great Britain), Research on diffraction of electrons by crystals
1938 Enrico Fermi (U.S.A., born in Italy), Used irradiation to demonstrate existence of new radioactive elements and discovered nuclear reactions caused by slow neutrons
1939 Ernest O. Lawrence (U.S.A.), Developed cyclotron to investigate artificial radioactive elements
1940 No award
1941 No award
1942 No award
1943 Otto Stern (U.S.A., born in Germany), Work on molecular ray method and discovered magnetic moment of proton
1944 Isidor Isaac Rabi (U.S.A.), Recorded magnetism of atomic nuclei via resonance method

1945 Wolfgang Pauli (U.S.A.), Discovered Pauli Principle, exclusion principle in quantum mechanics
1946 Percy Williams Bridgman (U.S.A.), Invented device to produce extremely high pressures, resulting in discoveries in high-pressure physics
1947 Sir Edward V. Appleton (Great Britain), Work on physics of upper atmosphere and discovery of Appleton layer of ionosphere
1948 Patrick M.S. Blackett (Great Britain), Developed Wilson cloud chamber method for research in nuclear physics and cosmic radiation
1949 Hideki Yukawa (Japan), Theoretical prediction of existences of mesons
1950 Cecil F. Powell (Great Britain), Developed photographic method for research on nuclear processes leading to discovery of mesons
1951 Sir John D. Cockroft (Great Britain) and **Ernest T.W. Walton** (Ireland), Work on atomic-nucleus transmutation by artificially accelerated atomic particles
1952 Felix Bloch (U.S.A., born in Switzerland), Developed methods of precisely measuring nuclear magnetism and related discoveries
1953 Fritz Zernike (Netherlands), Demonstrated phase-control method and invented phase-contrast microscope
1954 Max Born (Great Britain, born in Germany), Fundamental work in quantum mechanics
Walter Bothe (Germany), Coincidence method of counting
1955 Polykarp Kusch (U.S.A., born in Germany), Determined precisely the magnetic moment of the electron
Willis E. Lamb (U.S.A.), Discoveries in fine structure of the hydrogen spectrum
1956 John Bardeen, Walter H. Brattain and William Shockley (U.S.A.), Research on semi-conductors and invention of the transistor
1957 Tsung-Dao Lee and Chen Ning Yang (U.S.A., born in China), Investigations of parity laws, especially regarding elementary particles and resulting discoveries
1958 Paval A. Cherenkov, Ilya M. Frank and Igor J. Tamm (USSR), Discovery and interpretation of the Cherenkov effect
1959 Owen Chamberlain and Emilio G. Segre (U.S.A.), Discovered the antiproton
1960 Donald A. Glaser (U.S.A.), Invented bubble chamber
1961 Robert Hofstadter (U.S.A.), Research on electron scattering and discoveries on nucleon structure
Rudolf L. Mossbauer (Germany), Studied resonance absorption of gamma radition and Mossbauer effect
1962 Lev D. Landau (USSR), Theories on condensed matter, particularly liquid helium
1963 Maria Goeppert-Mayer (U.S.A.) and **J. Hans D. Jensen** (Germany), Discoveries on nuclear cell structures
Eugene P. Wigner (U.S.A.), Theories on atomic nucleus and elementary particles
1964 Nikolai G. Basov (USSR), **Aleksandr M. Prochorov** (USSR) and **Charles H. Townes** (U.S.A.), Basic research in quantum electronics and subsequent construction of maser-laser oscillators and amplifiers
1965 Richard P. Feynman (U.S.A.), **Julian S. Schwinger** (U.S.A.) and **Shinichiro Tomanaga** (Japan), Work on quantum electrodynamics, especially regarding elementary particles in high-energy physics
1966 Alfred Kastler (France), Developed optical methods for Herzian resonance atom study
1967 Hans A. Bethe (U.S.A., born in Germany), Nuclear-reaction theories, especially on energy production of stars

1968 **Luis W. Alvarez** (U.S.A.), Work of physics of subatomic particles, especially regarding many resonance states
1969 **Murray Gell-Mann** (U.S.A.), Discoveries about the classifications of elementary particles and their interactions
1970 **Hannes O.G. Alfven** (Sweden), Work in magnetohydrodynamics and its application in plasma physics
Louis E.F. Neel (France), Ferromagnetism and antiferromagnetism work with applications in solid state physics
1971 **Dennis Gabor** (Great Britain, born in Hungary), Invented holography
1972 **John Bardeen, Leon N. Cooper and John F. Schrieffer** (U.S.A.), Developed superconductivity theory for various metals at very low temperatures
1973 **Ivar Giaever and Leo Esaki** (U.S.A., born in Norway), Work in miniature electronic semiconductors and superconductors
1974 **Anthony Hewish and Martin Ryle** (Great Britain), Radiotelescopic study of the universe and discovery of pulsars
1975 **L. James Rainwater** (U.S.A.), **Aage Bohn** (Denmark) and **Ben Roy Mottelson** (Denmark, born in U.S.A.), Work on nuclei of atoms resulting in discovery that not all are spherical due to connection between collective motion and particle motion in the nucleus
1976 **Burton Richter and Samuel C.C. Ting** (U.S.A.), Discovered Psi or J particle, thought to be smallest building block of matter
1977 **Philip Anderson** (U.S.A.), **John Van Vleck** (U.S.A.) and **Nevill Mott** (Great Britain), Research in solid-state physics

Thomas Young Medal and Prize
Rutherford Medal and Prize
Simon Memorial Prize
Max Born Medal and Prize
Maxwell Medal and Prize
Holweck Medal and Prize
Guthrie Medal and Prize
Duddell Medal and Prize
Glazebrook Medal and Prize
Charles Chree Medal and Prize
Charles Vernon Boys Prize
Bragg Medal and Prize
THE INSTITUTE OF PHYSICS
47 Belgrave Sq., London SW1X 8QX, United Kingdom (Tel. 01-235 6111)

The Thomas Young Medal and Prize, originally known as The Thomas Young Oration, is awarded in odd-numbered years for an outstanding work on optics. The prize consists of £150 and a bronze medal.

ORATORS
1907 **Marius Hans Erik Tscherning**
1910 **Robert Williams Wood**
1915 **James Crichton-Browne**
1921 **Charles Sheard**
1923 **Moritz von Rohr**
1928 **G. W. Ritchey**

1931 **John H Parsons**
1933 **Herbert E. Ives**
1935 **Charles Fabry**
1937 **Richard James Lythgoe**
1939 **M. N. MacLeod**
1941 **Harold Spencer Jones**
1943 **Frederick Charles Bartlett**
1945 **Ragnar Granit**
1947 **F. Zernike**
1949 **Thomas Smith**
1951 **William David Wright**
1953 **No award**
1955 **Walter Stanley Stiles**
1957 **John Guild**
1959 **Robert William Ditchburn**
1961 **Harold Horace Hopkins**

MEDALISTS
1963 **Charles Hard Townes and Arthur Leonard Schawlow**
1965 **Andre Marechal**
1967 **Dennis Gabor**
1969 **Giuliano Toraldo di Francia**
1971 **Charles Gorrie Wynne**
1973 **Walter Thompson Welford**
1975 **Daniel Joseph Bradley**
1977 **R. Clark Jones**

The Rutherford Medal and Prize, initially known as The Rutherford Memorial Lecture, is made in even-numbered years for contributions to nuclear physics, elementary particle physics or nuclear technology. The prize consists of £150 and a bronze medal.

LECTURERS
1942 **Harold Roper Robinson**
1944 **John D. Cockcroft**
1946 **Marcus Laurence Elwin Oliphant**
1948 **Ernest Marsden**
1950 **Alexander Smith Russell**
1952 **Rudolf Ernst Peierls**
1954 **Patrick Maynard Stuart Blackett**
1956 **Philip I. Dee**
1958 **Niels Bohr**
1960 **Cecil Frank Powell**
1962 **Denys Haigh Wilkinson**
1964 **Peter H. Fowler**

MEDALISTS
1966 **Peter Kapitza**
1968 **Brian Hilton Flowers**
1970 **Samuel Devons**
1972 **Aage Bohr**
1973 **James MacDonald Cassels**
1974 **Albert Edward Litherland**
1976 **R.J. Blin Stone and Joan M. Freeman**

The Simon Memorial Prize of £ 300 is awarded approximately every three years by the Low Temperature Group of the Society for a distinguished work in experimental or theoretical low temperature physics.

1959 **H. London**
1961 **I. M. Lifschitz**
1963 **Henry Edgar Hall and William Frank Vinen**
1965 **John Charles Wheatley**
1968 **Kurt Alfred Georg Mendelssohn**
1970 **Walther Meissner**
1973 **Peter Kapitza**

The Max Born Medal and Prize is awarded alternately

by the councils of the Institute and the German Physical Society to a physicist selected from a list of nominees submitted by the other. The award, which consists of £150 and a silver medal, is given for outstanding contributions in the field.

1973   Roger Arthur Cowley
1974   Walter Greiner
1975   Trevor Simpson Moss
1976   H. Haaken
1977   W.E. Spear

The Maxwell Medal and Prize recognizes outstanding contributions in theoretical physics over a 10-year period to physicists 35 years of age or less. The prize consists of £150 and a bronze medal.

1962   Abdus Salam
1964   Walter Charles Marshall
1966   Richard Henry Dalitz
1968   Roger James Elliott and Kenneth William Harry Stevens
1970   Richard John Eden
1971   John Bryan Taylor
1972   Volker Heine
1973   David James Thouless
1974   Samuel Frederick Edwards
1975   Anthony James Leggett
1976   S.W. Hawkins
1977   E. Jakeman

The Holweck Medal and Prize, instituted jointly by the French and British Physical Societies, is made for distinguished work in experimental physics or theoretical physics if closely related to experimental work, which is either still in progress or has been carried out during the preceding 10 years. The £150 award and gold medal now goes to a French physicist in odd-numbered years and a British physicist in even-numbered years.

1946   Charles Sadron
1947   Edward Neville da Costa Andrade
1948   Yves Rocard
1949   Leslie Fleetwood Bates
1950   Pierre Jacquinot
1951   Thomas Ralph Merton
1952   Louis Neel
1953   John Ashworth Ratcliffe
1954   Alfred Kastler
1955   Nicholas Kurti
1956   Jean Paul Mathieu
1957   Denys Haigh Wilkinson
1958   Anatole Abragam
1959   Robert Hanbury Brown
1960   Jean Brossel
1961   Alfred Brian Pippard
1962   Jean-François Denisse
1963   Frederick Charles Frank
1964   Jacques Friedel
1965   Martin Ryle
1966   Raymond Castaing
1967   Heinrich Gerhard Kuhn
1968   Pierre-Gilles de Gennes
1969   Alan Howard Cottrell
1970   Pierre Connes
1971   Dennis Gabor
1972   Ionel Solomon
1973   Brian David Josephson
1974   Philippe Nozieres
        Antony Hewish
1975   Evry Schatzman

1976   Harry Elliot
1977   M. Goldman

The Guthrie Medal and Prize, original established as a lecture, consists of £250 and a silver gilt medal and is given annually to a physicist of international reputation for exceptional contributions.

LECTURERS

1914   Robert Williams Wood
1916   William B. Hardy
1917   Paul Langevin
1918   John C. McLennan
1919   No award
1920   Charles Edouarde Guillaume
1921   Albert Abraham Michelson
1922   Niels Bohr
1923   James H. Jeans
1924   Maurice le Duc de Broglie
1925   Wilhelm Wien
1926   Charles Fabry
1927   Lord Rutherford of Nelson
1928   Joseph J. Thomson
1929   Percy Williams Bridgman
1930   Peter Debye
1931   Richard T. Glazebrook
1932   Max Planck
1933   Karl Manne Georg Siegbahn
1934   Charles V. Boys
1935   Arthur Holly Compton
1936   Lord Cherwell of Oxford
1937   Clifford C. Paterson
1938   Archibald Vivian Hill
1940   Patrick Maynard Stuart Blackett
1941   Edward Neville da Costa Andrade
1942   Edward V. Appleton
1943   Edmund T. Whittaker
1944   Joel H. Hildebrand
1945   Arturo Duperier
1946   Max Jakob
1947   John Desmond Bernal
1948   George P. Thomson
1949   Alexander Oliver Rankine
1950   George Ingle Finch
1951   Nevill Francis Mott
1952   W. Lawrence Bragg
1953   Max Born
1954   Geoffrey Taylor
1955   Edmund Clifton Stoner
1956   Francis Simon
1957   Harold C. Urey
1958   Willis Eugene Lamb
1959   Harrie Stewart Wilson Massey
1960   Fred Hoyle
1961   David Shoenberg
1962   Alfred Charles Bernard Lovell
1963   Leslie Fleetwood Bates
1964   Martin Ryle
1965   John Bertram Adams

MEDALISTS

1966   William Cochran
1967   James Chadwick
1968   Rudolf Ernst Peierls
1969   Cecil Frank Powell
1970   Alfred Brian Pippard
1971   John Ashworth Ratcliffe
1972   Brian David Josephson
1973   Hermann Bondi
1974   Rudolf Ludwig Mossbauer

1975 David Tabor
1976 Abdus Salam
1977 Sir Alan Cottrell

The Duddell Medal and Prize is made annually to an individual who has contributed to the advancement of knowledge by the invention or design of scientific instruments or by the discovery of materials used in their construction or has made outstanding contributions to the application of physics. The prize is £150 and a bronze medal.

1923 Hugh Longbourne Callendar
1924 Charles V. Boys
1925 Albert Campbell
1926 Frank Twyman
1927 Frank E. Smith
1928 Charles Edouarde Guillaume
1929 Albert Abraham Michelson
1930 J. Ambrose Fleming
1931 Charles Thomson Rees Wilson
1932 Wolfgang Gaede
1933 Harold Dennis Taylor
1934 W. Ewart Williams
1935 Charles Vickery Drysdale
1936 Walter Guyton Cady
1937 Hans Geiger
1938 Robert William Paul
1940 Ernest Orlando Lawrence
1941 William David Collidge
1942 Cecil Reginald Burch
1943 John Guild
1944 Francis William Aston
1945 John Turton Randall
1946 Karl Weissenberg
1947 Robert Jemison Van de Graaff
1948 Karl Manne Georg Siegbahn
1949 Edwin Herbert Land
1950 Donald William Fry
1951 Albert Beaumont Wood
1952 Cecil Waller
1953 William Sucksmith
1954 Alfred Charles Bernard Lovell
1955 Rudolf Kompfner
1956 John Gilbert Daunt
1957 Charles Eryl Wynn-Williams
1958 Leonard Charles Jackson
1959 George William Hutchison and Gordon George Scarrott
1960 Reginald Victor Jones
1961 John Bertram Adams
1963 Bertram Neville Brockhouse
1965 Hugh Alastair Gebbie
1967 Keith Davy Froome and Robert Howard Bradsell
1969 Charles William Oatley
1971 Vernon Ellis Cosslett and Kenneth Charles Arthur Smith
1973 Albert Franks
1975 Ernst Ruska
1976 G.N. Housnfield
1977 R.F. Pearson

The Glazebrook Medal and Prize is made annually for outstanding contributions in the organization, utilization or application of science. The prize is £250 and a silver gilt medal.

1966 Christopher Hinton
1967 Charles Sykes
1968 Frank Philip Bowden

1969 William George Penney
1970 Eric Eastwood
1971 Francis Edgar Jones
1972 Gordon Brims Black McIvor Sutherland
1973 Kurt Hoselitz
1974 Basil John Mason
1975 Walter Charles Marshall
1976 Sir Montague Finniston
1977 Sir James Menter

The Charles Chree Medal and Prize is made every two years for distinguished research in terrestrial magnestism, atmospheric electricity and other aspects of geophysics. The prize is £150 pounds and a silver medal.

1941 Sydney Chapman
1943 Basil Ferdinand Jamieson Schonland
1945 John Adam Fleming
1947 Edward V. Appleton
1949 Gordon Miller Bourne Dobson
1951 George C. Simpson
1953 Julius Bartels
1955 David Forbes Martyn
1957 Edward C. Bullard
1959 Reginald Cockcroft Sutcliffe
1961 Scott Ellsworth Forbush
1963 Maurice Neville Hill
1965 Basil John Mason
1967 John Herbert Chapman
1969 Stanley Keith Runcorn
1971 Desmond George King-Hele
1973 David Robert Bates
1975 Raymond Hide
1977 D.H. Matthews and F.J. Vine

The Charles Vernon Boys Prize is made annually to a physicist 35 years of age or less for distinguished research in experimental physics which is still in progress or which has been carried out in the previous 10 years. The prize is £ 150.

1945 Athelstan Hylas Stoughton Holbourn
1946 Robert William Sutton
1947 Cecil Frank Powell
1948 Samuel Tolansky
1949 Andre Jean Guinier
1950 Guiseppe Paolo Stanislao Occhialini
1951 James Howard Eagle Griffiths
1952 Brebis Bleaney
1953 Frederick Calland Williams
1954 Jeofry Stuart Courtney-Pratt
1955 John Wesley Mitchell
1956 George Dixon Rochester and Clifford Charles Butler
1957 Louis Essen
1958 Donald A. Glaser
1959 David West
1960 Frank Llewellyn Jones
1961 Alexander Walter Merrison
1962 Peter Bernhard Hirsch
1963 Keith Davy Froome
1964 Andrew Richard Lang
1965 Archibald Howie and Michael John Whelan
1966 Peter Duncumb
1967 Alan Hugh Cook
1968 John Owen
1969 Harold Percy Rooksby
1970 Anthony Hewish
1971 Michael Hart
1972 Michael Warwick Thompson
1973 John William Charles Gates

1974 Patrick George Henry Sandars
1975 Richard Anthony Stradling
1976 S.D. Smith
1977 J. Clark

The Bragg Medal and Prize is given every two years for distinguished contributions to the teaching of physics. The prize is $150 and a bronze medal.

1967 Donald McGill
1969 John Logan Lewis
1971 George Robert Noakes
1973 Jon Michael Ogborn and Paul Joseph Black
1975 William Albert Coates
1977 W.J. Wenham

Bakhuis-Rooseboom Medal
Lorentz Medal

ROYAL NETHERLANDS ACADEMY OF ARTS AND SCIENCES
Kloveniersburgwal 29, Amsterdam, The Netherlands (Tel: 020 22 29 02)

The Bakhuis-Rooseboom Medal, which is of gold, is awarded approximately every eight years for research in the field of phase theory. Prior to 1960, the medal was given every four or five years. A selection committee chooses the winner of this international honor.

1916 F.A.H. Schreinemakers, Leiden
1923 Gustav Tammann, Gottingen
1929 J.J. van Laar, Tavel sur Clarens
1933 P.W. Bridgman, Cambridge
1939 Arthur L. Day, Maryland, U.S.A.
1950 W. Hume-Rothery, Oxford
1954 Norman L. Bowen, Washington, D.C.
1960 J.L. Meijering, Eindhoven
1969 F.P. Bundy, Schenectady, N.Y.

The Lorentz Medal, which is of gold, is given about every five years for research in the field of pure physics. A selection committee chooses the winner of this international honor.

1927 M. Planck, Berlin
1931 W. Pauli, Zurich
1935 P. Debije, Leipzig
1939 A. Sommerfeld, Munich
1947 H.A. Kramers, Leiden
1953 F. London, Durham, N.C.
1958 Lars Onsager, New Haven, Conn.
1962 R.E. Peierls, Birmingham
1966 Freeman J. Dyson, Princeton, N.J.
1970 G.E. Uhlenbeck, New York
1974 J.H. van Vleck, Cambridge, Mass.

Wolf Prize in Physics

WOLF FOUNDATION
Box 398, Herzliah-Bet, Israel

The $100,000 Wolf Prize in Physics is a new honor for an outstanding body of work in physics, as determined by a committee of judges.

1977 Chien Shiung Wu, (Columbia University), Nuclear physics, especially experiments dealing with rays emitting from a spinning atom

Honorary Membership in the Society
Outstanding Service Award

NATIONAL SPELEOLOGICAL SOCIETY
Cave Ave., Huntsville, Ala. 35810 (312/331-0011)

Honorary membership in the Society honors outstanding accomplishment in cave-oriented science, leadership or exploration. Memberships are conferred annually on recommendation of the awards committee and selection by the board of governors.

1941 Vernon O. Bailey
1942 Roy J. Holden
1943 Ralph W. Stone
1944 Allyn Coats Swinnerton
1945 Alexander Wetmore
1946 Robert deJoly
1947 Don Bloch
1948 William J. Stephenson
1949 Robert Broom
1950 Mark R. Harrington
1951 Emil W. Haury
1952 Rene G. Jeannel
1953 Charles E. Mohr
1954 J. Harlen Bretz
1955 Abbe Henri Breuil
1956 Norbert Casteret
1957 Carl F. Miller
1958 Donald R. Griffin
1959 John S. Petrie
1960 William E. Davies
1961 No award; change in award year designation
1962 Julia L. Staniland Day
1963 Thomas C. Barr, Jr.
1964 A. Vandel
1965 William R. Halliday
1966 Brig. E. Aubrey Glennie
1967 Russell H. Gurnee
1968 G. Nicholas Sullivan
1969 Walter B. Jones
1970 Donald N. Cournoyer
1971 John A. Stellmack
1972 Jack Herschend
1973 Rodger Brucker
1974 Don Sawyer
1975 Derek C. Ford
1976 Marjorie M. Sweeting
1977 Herb and Jan Conn

The Outstanding Service Award recognizes outstanding service to the Society, leadership, science and/or exploration.

1973 John Cooper
1974 Charles Larson
1975 William B. White
1976 William F. Cuddington III
1977 Roy A. Davis

M. W. Biejerinck-Virologie Medal

ROYAL NETHERLANDS ACADEMY OF ARTS AND SCIENCES
Kloveniersburgwal 29, Amsterdam, The Netherlands (Tel: 020 22 29 02)

The M.W. Biejerinck-Virologie Medal, which is of gold, is given every three years to a scientist, preferably of Dutch nationality, for research in virology, including biochemistry and biophysics. A selection committee chooses the recipient.

1966 **E. van Slogteren,** Bennebroek
1969 **R.L. Sinsheimer,** University of California/Pasadena

1972 **W. Berends,** Delft
1975 **E.M.J. Jaspars,** Leiden
A. van Kammen, Wageningen

Medicine & Health

Contents

Related Awards

Distinguished Service Award
Joseph B. Goldberger Award
Dr. Benjamin Rush Award
Arnold and Marie Schwartz Award
Scientific Achievement Award
Dr. Rodman E. Sheen and Thomas G. Sheen Award

AMERICAN MEDICAL ASSOCIATION
535 N. Dearborn St., Chicago, Ill. 60610 (312/751-6000)

The Distinguished Service Award, consisting of a gold medal and citation, honors a member of the association for meritorious service in the sciences and art of medicine. The membership nominates and the Board of Trustees selects the recipient of this annual honor. (All the award winners are M.D.s unless otherwise indicated.)

1938   Rudolph Matas, New Orleans
1939   James B. Herrick, Chicago
1940   Chevalier Jackson, Philadelphia
1941   James Ewing, New York
1942   Ludvig Hektoen, Chicago
1943   Elliott P. Joslin, Boston
1944   George Dock, Pasadena
1945   George R. Minot, Boston
1946   Anton J. Carlson, Ph. D., Chicago
1947   Henry A. Christian, Boston
1948   Isaac A. Abt, Chicago
1949   Seale Harris, Birmingham, Ala.
1950   Evarts A. Graham, St. Louis
1951   Allen C. Whipple, New York
1952   Paul Dudley White, Boston
1953   Alfred Blalock, Baltimore
1954   W. Wayne Babcock, Philadelphia
1955   Donald C. Balfour, Rochester, Minn.
1956   Walter L. Bierring, Des Moines, Iowa
1957   Tom Douglas Spies, Birmingham, Ala.
1958   Frank H. Krusen, Rochester, Minn.
1959   Michael E. De Bakey, Houston
1960   Charles Doan, Columbus, Ohio
1961   Walter H. Judd, Washington, D.C., and Minneapolis
1962   Russell L. Cecil, New York
1963   Lester R. Dragstedt, Gainesville, Fla.
1964   Irvine H. Page, Cleveland
1965   Tinsley R. Harrison, Birmingham, Ala.
1966   Warren H. Cole, Chicago
1967   E. W. Alton Ochsner, New Orleans
1968   Owen H. Wangensteen, Minneapolis
1969   Jay Arnold Bargen, Temple, Tex.
1970   Henry L. Bockus, Philadelphia
1971   George R. Herrmann, Galveston
1972   Milton Helpern, New York
1973   George Hoyt Whipple, Rochester, N.Y.
1974   William Fouts House, Los Angeles
1975   William R. Willard, Moundville, Ala.
1976   Claude E. Welch, Boston, Mass.
1977   Franz J. Ingelfinger, Boston, Mass.

The $1,000 Joseph B. Goldberger Award and commemorative plaque honors medical investigation in public and private health and physicians who have made important contributions in the knowledge of nutrition.

1949   Randolph West, New York
1951   Fuller Albright, Boston

1952   W. Henry Sebrell, Jr., New York
1953   James S. McLester, Birmingham, Ala.
1954   Russell M. Wilder, Rochester, Minn.
1957   Paul Gyorgy, Philadelphia
1958   Virgil P. Sydenstricker, Augusta, Ga.
1959   Carl V. Moore, St-Louis
1960   Richard W. Vilter, Cincinnati
1961   Fredrick J. Stare, Boston
1962   Edwards A. Park, Baltimore
1963   John B. Youmans, New York
1964   William J. Darby, Nashville
1965   Grace A. Goldsmith, New Orleans
1966   William B. Castle, Boston
1967   Cicely D. Williams, London, U.K.
1968   L. Emmett Holt, Jr., New York
1969   Nevin S. Scrimshaw, Cambridge, Mass.
1970   Jonathan E. Rhoads and Stanley J. Dudrick, Philadelphia
1971   John E. Canham, Iowa City, and Robert E. Hodges, Denver
1972   George G. Graham, Baltimore
1973   Clement A. Finch, Seattle
1974   Robert E. Olson, St-Louis
1975   Ananda S. Prasad, Detroit
1976   Charles E. Butterworth, Jr., Birmingham
1977   George F. Cahill, Jr.

The $5,000 Dr. Benjamin Rush Award honors a physician for his professional achievements and as a patriot, social reformer and citizen. It is specifically given for contributions to the community above and beyond the call of duty as a practicing physician. The AMA Committee on Awards selects the recipient.

1973   Otis R. Bowen, Governor of Indiana
1974   Charles E. Robert Parker, Montgomery, Ala.
1975   Francis E. West, San Diego, Calif.
1976   Mario E. Ramirez, Rio Grande City, Tex.
1977   Luis Martin Perez, Sanford Fla.

The Arnold and Marie Schwartz Award, consisting of $5,000 and a plaque, encourages physicians 50 years of age or younger who are U.S. citizens toward further contributions in medical research, teaching or clinical practice. The award honors a single achievement of an accumulated career of excellence.

1973   Lawrence L. Weed, Vt.
1974   Thomas E. Starzl, Colo.
1975   Stanley J. Dudrick, Tex.
1976   Alton I. Sutnick, Pa.
1977   Theodore Cooper, Md.

On recommendation of the Council of Scientific Assembly and approval by the board of trustees, the Scientific Achievement Award gold medal is given for achievement by a physician or non-physician.

1962   Donald D. Van Slyke, Ph. D., Upton, N.Y.
1963   John F. Enders, Ph. D., Boston, Mass.
1964   Rene J. Dubos, Ph. D., New York
1965   Edward C. Kendall, Ph. D., Princeton, N.J.
1966   Wendell M. Stanley, Ph. D., Berkeley, Calif.
1967   Gregory Pincus, Sc. D., Shrewsbury, Mass.
1968   Arthur Kornberg, M. D., Palo Alto, Calif.
1969   Philip Handler, Ph. D., Durham, N.C.
1970   Choh Hao Li, Ph. D., Berkeley, Calif.
1971   Robert B. Woodward, Cambridge, Mass.
1972   William Bennett Kouwenhoven, Dr. Ing., Baltimore
1973   Edith Hinkley Quimby, Sc. D., Palo Alto, Calif.
1974   Philip Abelson, Ph. D., Washington, D.C.

1975 **Rosalyn Yalow**, Ph. D., and **Solomon A. Berson**, M.D., Bronx, N.Y.
1976 **Harry Goldblatt**, M. D., Cleveland, Ohio
1977 **Helen B. Taussig**, M. D., Baltimore, Md.

The Dr. Rodman E. Sheen and Thomas G. Sheen Award, consisting of a $10,000 stipend and a plaque, honors the scientific accomplishment of a U.S. physician. The Awards Committee of the AMA Board of Trustees makes the selection.

1968 **Irvine E. Page**, Ohio
1969 **Robert E. Gross**, Mass.
1970 **Charles B. Huggins**, Ill.
1971 **Maxwell Finland**, Mass.
1972 **Paul Dudley White**, Mass.
1973 **William Bosworth Castle**, Mass.
1974 **R. Lee Clark**, Tex.
1975 **Rudolph H. Kampmeier**, Tenn.
1976 **Howard A. Rusk**, N.Y.
1977 **Robert M. Zollinger**, Ohio

Ammy Award
AMERICAN MEDICAL WRITERS ASSOCIATION
5272 River Rd., Suite 290, Bethesda, Md. 20016
(301/986-9119)

The Ammy, a commemorative cube, annually honors the creators of outstanding books and films in the field. Entries are reviewed by a panel of judges, which select the winners (listed below) plus numerous honorable mentions. It should be noted that information on the book awards prior to 1973 is not available. The book categories change almost annually. For convenience, these are grouped here into books for professional and lay audiences, plus others awarded periodically.

BEST BOOK(S) FOR PROFESSIONAL READERSHIP
1973 **Silvio Aladjem**, *Risks in the Practice of Modern Obstetrics*
Howard F. Conn, *Current Therapy*
1974 **Keith L. Moore**, *The Developing Human*
James F. Holland and Emil Frei III, *Cancer Medicine*
1975 **Sanford L. Palay and Victoria Chan-Palay**, *Cerebellar Cortex, Cytology and Organization*
David G. Nathan and Frank A. Oski, *Hematology in Infancy and Childhood*
Gilles R.G. Monif, *Infectious Diseases in Obstetrics and Gynecology*
1976 **Abraham I. Braude**, *Antimicrobial Drug Therapy*
David Malikin and Herbert Rusalem, *Contemporary Vocational Rehabilitation*
1977 **Alfred S. Evans**, *Viral Infections of Humans*
Irene Mortenson Burnside, *Nursing and the Aged*

BEST BOOK(S) FOR LAY READERSHIP
1973 **Shirley M. Linde**, *A Complete Guide to Prevention and Treatment*
**Edward M. Brecher and the Editors of *Consumer Reports*, *Licit and Illicit Drugs*
1974 **David R. Zimmerman**, *Rh*
Meyer Friedman and Ray H. Rosenman, *Type 'A' Behavior and Your Heart*
1975 **Robert Massie and Suzanne Massie**, *Journey*
Spyros Andreopoulos, *Primary Care: Where Medicine Fails*
1976 **Alfred W. Crosby, Jr.**, *Epidemic and Peace 1918*

1977 **David Hendin**, *Life Givers*

MEDICAL HISTORY BOOK
1975 **Guido Majno**, *The Healing Hand: Man and Wound in the Ancient World*

SEX EDUCATION BOOK
1976 **David S. Delvin**, *The Book of Love*

BEST FILM
1974 **Noel Nosseck**, *First Aid Quiz 1: Saving a Life*
1975 **Cinemakers, Inc./American Cancer Society**, *Nursing Management of Children With Cancer*
1976 **Wexler Film Productions**, *Minilaparotomy Technique*

BEST FILM FOR MEDICAL AUDIENCE
1974 **U.S.C. School of Medicine/Ortho Pharmaceutical Corp.**, *Teaching Breast Self Examination*
1975 **Wright Mfg. Co.**, *Smith Total Ankle*

BEST INSTRUCTIONAL FILM FOR MEDICAL AUDIENCES
1976 **University of Michigan School of Medicine**, *The Combined Collis-Belsey Operation*
Synthesis Communications, *Sex and the Heart Patient*

BEST PROMOTIONAL FILM FOR MEDICAL AUDIENCES
1976 **Teletronics Intl./American Academy of Pediatrics**, *You're Not Listening*

BEST INSTRUCTIONAL FILM FOR LAY AUDIENCES
1974 **Noel Nosseck**, *First Aid Quiz 1: Saving a Life*
1975 **Paramount Productions**, *How to Save a Choking Victim: The Heimlich Maneuver*
1976 **Professional Research, Inc.**, *Vasectomy*
1977 **American Society of Therapeutic Radiologist**, *Radiation: the Cancer Fighter*

BEST INFORMATIONAL FILM FOR LAY AUDIENCES
1974 **Lawren Productions/Coppertone Corp.**, *Sun and Your Skin*
1975 **American Dental Assn.**, *The Haunted Mouth*

BEST PROMOTIONAL FILM FOR LAY AUDIENCES
1977 **Richard S. Milbauer/American Podiatry Assn.**, *Feet: A Key to Keeping Fit*

BEST DOCUMENTARY
1974 **Macmillan Films/ABC News**, *The Right to Die*
1975 **CBS News/KNXT-TV, Los Angeles**, *Why Me?*
1976 **John Cosgrove**, *A Gift of Life*
1977 **Case Western Reserve University**, *Mild Retardation: A Family Profile*

BEST DIRECTION
1976 **Sy Wexler**, *The Human Brain*

BEST SCRIPT
1976 **Mark Orringer**, *The Combined Collis-Belsey Operation*
1977 **Lester T. Hibbard**, *Minilaparotomy Technique*

BEST EDITING
1976 **David Shapiro**, *Making A Good Impression*
1977 **Eric Johnson and Audrey Evans**, *Minilaparotomy Technique*

BEST CINEMATOGRAPHY

1976 Edgar L. Sherman, *The Combined Collis-Belsey Operation*

BEST TECHNICAL DEMONSTRATION

1976 Gregor and David Rempel, *The Human Brain*

SPECIAL RECOGNITION/MERIT/AWARD

1974 Doctors Hospital (Tucker, Ga.)/Emory University/American Podiatry Assn., *An Arthoplastic Technique for Repair of the First Metatarsophalangeal Joint*
1975 No award
1977 Richard C. Schneider, *First Aid for Neck Injuries in Football*
1976 James Hodge, *The Use of Hypnosis in Psychotherapy* American Occupational Therapy Assn., *Hand in Hand* University of Kansas College of Health Sciences and Hospital, *Colostomy and Ileostomy: Module II: What to Expect Before, During and After Surgery*

Albert Lasker Awards

ALBERT AND MARY LASKER FOUNDATION
24 E. 10th St., New York, N.Y. 10003 (212/673-0920 and 212/533-7988)

The Albert Lasker Award, which carries a $15,000 honorarium, is given annually for medical research of a pioneering nature. Individuals and groups who have made significant contributions in basic or clinical research in the diseases which are the main causes of death and disability are considered for the honor by a 22-person committee. A symbolic statuette of the Winged Victory is also presented.

BASIC RESEARCH

1962 Chou H. Li, Pituitary-hormone chemistry
1963 Lyman C. Craig, Countercurrent distribution technique to separate biologically significant compounds, and isolation and structure studies of antibiotics
1964 Renato Dulbecco and Harry Rubin, Added to knowledge of relationship between cancer and cancer-producing DNA and RNA viruses
1965 Robert W. Holley, Determined chemical structure of an amino acid transfer RNA
1966 George E. Palade, Electron microscopy of biological materials
1967 Bernard B. Brodie, Biochemical pharmacology
1968 Marshall W. Nierenberg, Contributions toward deciphering the genetic code
       H. Gobind Khorana, Contributions toward deciphering the genetic code
       William F. Windle, Basic discoveries in developmental biology
1969 Bruce Merrifield, New synthesis of polypeptides and proteins
1970 Earl W. Sutherland, Discovery of cyclic AMP, and provision of comprehension of how this key chemical mechanism regulates hormonal action
1971 Seymour Benzer, Molecular genetics
       Sydney Brenner, Molecular genetics
       Charles Yanofsky, Molecular genetics
1972 Ludwick Gross, Discovered leukemia- and cancer-causing viruses in mammals and elucidated their biology and epidemology

Howard E. Skipper, Contributions to groundwork for the chemotherapy of cancer
Sol Spiegelman, Molecular biology, including molecular hybridization and synthesis of an infectious nucleic acid
Howard M. Temin, Biology of RNA-containing cancer viruses and elucidation of the mode of action of viral genes
1975 Roger C.L. Guillemin, Added to knowledge of interplay between the hypothalmus and endocrine system
       Andrew V. Schally, Added to knowledge of interplay between hypothalmus and endocrine system
       Frank J. Dixon, Contributed to creation of new medical discipline: immunopathology
       Henry G. Kunkel, Contributed to creation of new medical discipline: immunopathology
1976 Rosalyn S. Yalow, Discovered and developed technique of radioimmunoassay
1977 K. Sune D. Bergstrom, Isolated prostaglandins and elucidated chemical structures of two types
       Bengt Samuelsson, Elucidated mechanism of biosynthesis of prostaglandins and developed method for their measurement
       John R. Vane, Discovered prostaglandin X (prostacyclin) which prevents formation of blood clots leading to heart attack and stroke

CLINICAL RESEARCH

1962 Joseph Smadel, Added to understanding, diagnosis and treatment of virus and rickettsial diseases
1963 Michael E. DeBakey, Leadership and accomplishments in cardiovascular surgery
       Charles Huggins, Incitor and catalyst to modern endocrine studies of tumor control
1964 Nathan S. Kline, Introduced iproniazid to treat severe depression
1965 Albert B. Sabin, Development of live, oral poliovirus vaccine
1966 Sidney Farber, Use of Aminopterin and methotrexate to control acute childhood leukemia and constant search for chemical agents against cancer
1967 Robert Alan Phillips (Capt. MC, USN Ret.), Contributions to conquest of cholera
1968 John H. Gibbon, Jr., Designed and developed heart-lung machine
1969 George C. Cotzias, Demonstrated effectiveness of L-DOPA to treat Parkinson's Disease
1970 Robert A. Good, Added to understanding of mechanism of immunity
1971 Edward D. Freis, Demonstrated effectiveness of drugs in treatment of hypertension
1972 Min Chiu Li, Contribution to chemotherapeutic treatment of gestational choriocarcinoma
       Roy Hertz, Contribution to the successful chemotherapeutic treatment of gestational choriocarcinoma
       Denis Burkitt, Identified Burkitt's tumor
       Joseph H. Burchenal, Recognized importance of Burkitt's tumor as a unique model
       V. Anomah Ngu, Expanded successful chemotherapeutic treatment of Burkitt's tumor
       John L. Ziegler, Contribution in increasing the cure rate of Burkitt's tumor by chemotherapy
       Edmund Klein, Treatment of premalignant and malignant cancers of the skin
       Emil Frei III, Applied concept of combination chemotherapy to lymphoma and acute adult leukemia
       Emil J. Freireich, Contributions in combination chemotherapy, and in supportive care of patients receiving combination chemotherapy for acute leukemia

James F. Holland, Contribution to the concept and application of combination therapy in the treatment of acute leukemia in children

Donald Pinkel, Advances in the concept of combination therapy in the treatment of acute leukemia in children

Paul P. Carbone, Contribution to the concept of combination therapy in the treatment of Hodgkin's disease

Vincent T. De Vita, Jr., Contribution to the concept of combination therapy in the treatment of Hodgkin's disease

Eugene J. Van Scott, Contribution to the concept of topical chemotherapy in the treatment of mycosis fungoides

Isaac Djerassi, Contribution in the supportive care, by platelet transfusion, for patients receiving intensive chemotherapy

Special Award to C. Gordon Zubrod, Leadership in expanding the frontiers of cancer chemotherapy

1973 Paul M. Zoll, Developed closed-chest defibrillator and pacemaker

William B. Kouwenhoven, Development of open- and closed-chest defibrillators and originated external cardiac massage technique

1974 John Charnley, Developed total hip-joint replacement

1975 Godfrey N. Hounsfield, Revolutionized diagnostic radiology

William Oldendorf, Envisaged revolution in diagnostic radiology through his work

1976 Raymond P. Ahlquist, Developed propranolol to treat heart disease

J.W. Black, Developed propranolol to treat heart disease

1977 Inge G. Edler, Pioneered clinical application of ultrasound to diagnosis of abnormalities of the heart

C. Helmuth Hertz, Pioneered ultrasound technology in medicine

The Foundation also presents a series of other honors to individuals and organizations for their work in and contributions to public health and disease control and cure.

SPECIAL PUBLIC SERVICE AWARDS

1963 Melvin R. Laird, U.S. House of Representatives, Recognition of new needs and challenges to legislative leadership in health

Oren Harris, U.S. House of Representatives, Dedication to congressional committee with jurisdiction over public health and safety legislation

1966 Eunice Kennedy Shriver, Encouraged national legislation to improve care of mentally retarded

President Lyndon Baines Johnson, Outstanding contributions to health of the people of the U.S.

1967 Claude Pepper, U.S. House of Representatives, Dedication to medical legislation

1968 Lister Hill, U.S. Senate, Leadership in guiding passage of over 80 major pieces of health legislation

1973 Warren Magnuson, U.S. Senate, Leadership and support of medical research

1975 Jules Stein, Contributions to preservation of vision and restoration of sight

1976 World Health Organization, Historic achievement in imminent and practical eradication of smallpox

SPECIAL PUBLIC HEALTH AWARD

1975 Research Team of Merck Sharp and Dohme Research Laboratories: Karl H. Beyer, Jr., James M. Sprague, John E. Baer and Frederick C. Novello, Creation of new spectrum of medications to control high blood pressure

ALBERT LASKER AWARDS GIVEN THROUGH THE INTERNATIONAL SOCIETY FOR THE REHABILITATION OF THE DISABLED

1954 Henry H. Kessler, Leadership in stimulating and improving services for the disabled

Juan Farill, Vision and leadership in developing international cooperation on behalf of the world's disabled

Viscount Nuffield, Services in international development of rehabilitation programs

1957 Howard A. Rusk, Eloquent spokesman and distinguished rehabilitation mentor

Fabian W.G. Langenskiold, Surgeon, educator and administrator

World Veterans Foundation, Leadership, technical assistance and support in advancing rehabilitation services

1960 Mary E. Switzer, Leadership in improving services for the world's handicapped

Gudmund Harlem, Physician, administrator and consultant for rehabilitation services in Norway

Paul W. Brand, Treatment and rehabilitation of persons disabled from leprosy

1963 Renato Da Costa Bonfim, Advanced rehabilitation services in Latin America

Kurt Jansson, Extended rehabilitation services through United Nations and World Veterans' Federation

Leonard W. Mayo, Global champion of rights of handicapped children, teacher and administrator

1966 Poul Stochholm, Brought rehabilitation trainees from all over the world to Denmark

Wiktor Dega, Advanced rehabilitation techniques in Poland

Eugene J. Taylor, Planned rehabilitation facilities for training programs and wrote on concepts and methods

1969 G. Gringras, Medical Director, Montreal Institute of Rehabilitation, who brought trainees from Latin America and Asia

Dr. and Mrs. Raden Soeharso, Founders and Directors, National Rehabilitation Center in Solo, Indonesia

Andre Trannoy, Himself a paraplegic, he founded coordination body for rehabilitation services in France

International Labour Union, Promoted vocational rehabilitation of the disabled for 50 years

1972 James F. Garrett, Assistant Administrator-Research, Development and Training, Social and Rehabilitation Service of U.S. Dept. of Health, Education and Welfare

Kamala V. Nimbkar, Editor and Founder, *Journal of Rehabilitation in Asia*

Jean Regniers, Businessman and philanthropist; Director of Belgian Assn. for Handicapped Children

ALBERT LASKER AWARDS GIVEN THROUGH THE AMERICAN PUBLIC HEALTH ASSN.—BASIC RESEARCH AWARDS

RESEARCH AWARDS

1946 Carl Ferdinand Cori, Work in carbohydrate metabolism, clarifying action of insulin in diabetes

1947 Oswald T. Avery, Studies on the chemical construction of bacteria

Thomas Francis, Jr., Influenza and development of vaccine against Types A and B

Homer Smith, Cardiovascular and renal physiology research

1948 Vincent Du Vigneaud, Basic studies of transmethylation and contributions to structure and synthesis of biotin and penicillin

Selman Waksman and Rene J. Dubos, Jointly for studies of antibiotic properties of soil bacteria; Dr. Waksman was also cited for discovery of streptomycin

1949 Andre Cournand, Work on physiology of circulation and diagnosis and treatment of heart disease

William S. Tillett and L.S. Christensen, Discovery and purification of streptokinase and streptodornase enzymes

1950 George Wells Beadle, Contributions to understanding of genetic control of metabolic processes

1951 Karl F. Meyer, Bacteriological research in parasitology

1952 Sir F. MacFarlane Burnet, Fundamentally modified knowledge of virus and inheritance of characteristics by viruses

1953 Hans A. Krebs, Discovered urea and citric acid cycles, basic to understanding of how body converts food into energy

Michael Heidelberger, Developed new subscience, the precise measuring tool of immunochemistry.

George Wald, Explained physiology of vision in man

1954 Edwin B. Astwood, Research on endocrine function, leading to control of hyperthyroidism

John Enders, Cultivation of viruses of poliomylitis, mumps and measles

1955 Karl Paul Link, Work on mechanism of blood clotting and development of methods of treatment for thromboembolic conditions

1956 Karl Meyer and Francis O. Schmitt, Pioneering studies of biochemical components of connective tissues, contributing to understanding of arthritis and rheumatic diseases

1957 No award

1958 Peyton Rous, Work on causes of cancers, the source of antibodies and mechanism of blood cell generation and destruction

Theodore Puck, Developed original methods for pure culture of living mammalian cells as basis for new research on nutrition, growth, genetics and mutation

Alfred D. Hershey, Gerhard Schramm and Heinz Fraenkel-Conrat, Jointly for Discoveries of fundamental role of nucleic acid in reproduction of viruses and transmission of inherited characterisitcs

1959 Albert Coons, Work in immunology, specifically development of fluroescent method of labeling proteins

Jules Freund, Discoveries in immunology and allergy, strengthening immunization procedures against tuberculosis, malaria, rabies and poliomylitis

1960 M.H.F. Wilkins, F.H.C. Crick and James D. Watson, Revealed structure of DNA molecule

James V. Neel and L.S. Penrose, Laid foundations for development of research in genetics, specifically to Dr. Neel for work on thalassemia and sickle cell anemia

Ernest Ruska and James Hillier, Contributed to design, construction, development and perfection of electron microscope

CLINICAL RESEARCH AWARDS

1946 John Friend Mahoney, Pioneer in treatment of syphilis with penicillin

1947 No award

1948 No award

1949 Max Theiler, Experiments leading to production of two effective vaccines against yellow fever

1950 No award

1951 Elise L'Esperance and Catherine McFarlane, Developed cancer detection clinics for discovery of early cancer or precancerous lesions

William G. Lennox and Fredric A. Gibbs, Research on epilepsy

1952 Conrad A. Elvehjem, Contributions to biochemical and nutrition research

Frederick S. McKay and H. Trendley Dean, Development of community-wide fluoridation programs

1953 No award

1954 Alfred Blalock, Helen B. Taussig and Robert Gross, Contributions to cardiovascular surgery and knowledge

1955 C. Walton Lillehei, Morley Cohen, Herbert Warden and Richard L. Varco, Advances in cardiac surgery, making possible more direct and safer approaches to the heart

Hoffman-LaRoche Research Laboratories, Squibb Institute for Medical Research: Edward H. Robitzek, Irving Selikoff, Walsh McDermott and Carl Muschenheim, Establishment of efficacy of isoniazid drugs to treat tuberculosis, meningitis and generalized miliary tuberculosis

1956 Jonas E. Salk, Developed safe and effective vaccine against poliomyelitis

V. Everett Kinsey and Arnall Patz, Discovered that excessive oxygen administration causes retrolental fibroplasia (blinding) in premature babies

1957 Rustom Jal Vakil, Nathan Kline, Robert Noce, Henri Laborit, Dr. Pierre Deniker and Heinz E. Lehmann, To Dr. Vakil for systemic studies on Rauwolfia in hypertension; to Dr. Kline for demonstrating of value of Rauwolfia derivatives, especially reserpine, in treatment of mental and nervous disorders; to Dr. Noce for studies of reserpine treatment of mentally ill and mental defectives; to Dr. Laborit for studies of surgical shock and post-operative illness resulting in use of chlorpromazine as therapeutic agent; to Dr. Deniker for introduction of chlorpromazine into psychiatry and demonstrating that a medication can influence the clinical course of major psychosis; to Dr. Lehmann for demonstrating clinical uses of chlorpromazine in treatment of mental and nervous disorders

1958 Robert W. Wilkins, Work on control of heart and blood vessel diseases through investigations in causes, diagnosis and treatment of hypertension

1959 John Holmes Dingle, Work on knowledge of and ability to control acute respiratory diseases

Gilbert Dalldorf, Demonstrated ability of one virus to modify course of infection by another and discovered Coxsackie virus by a unique and broadly applicable technique

BASIC AND CLINICAL RESEARCH AWARDS

1946 Karl Landsteiner, Alexander Wiener and Philip Levine, Discovery of RH factor in blood and its significance both as a cause of sickness and death of infants before the afterbirth and in blood transfusions

1947 No award

1948 No award

1949 Edward C. Kendall and Philip S. Hench, Chemical, physiological and clinical studies of adrenal hormones culminating in the use of cortisone in rheumatic disease therapy

1950 George Papincolaou, Early diagnosis of cancer through cytological methods

1951-56 No awards

1957 **Richard E. Shope,** Better understanding of infectious diseases in animals and humans, and discovery of new microbiological principles

SPECIAL AWARDS

1947 **Thomas Parran,** Leadership in public health administration as Surgeon General of U.S., President of International Health Conference and contributions to control of venereal diseases

1949 **Haven Emerson,** Developed national program of rural community health services

1952 **Charles-Edward Amory Winslow,** More than a half century of inspiring and inspired leadership as teacher and exponent of public health

1956 **Alan Gregg,** Vice President, Rockefeller University, and leader in public health, medical education and research

1959 **Lister Hill, U.S. Senate, and John E. Fogarty, U.S. House of Representatives,** Contributions to public health and research through leadership in Congress

PUBLIC SERVICE AWARDS

1946 **Alfred Newton Richards,** Organization and Administration of Committee on Medical Research of the Office of Scientific Research and Development; supervised wartime mass production of penicillin and search for antimalarial drug and preparation of blood plasma

Fred L. Soper, Administrative achievement in control of yellow fever and malaria through eradication of insect carriers

1947 **Alice Hamilton,** Leader in toxology and contribution to prevention of occupational diseases and betterment of workers' health

1948 **R.E. Dyer,** Microbiological research and service as Director of National Institutes of Health during war and postwar years

Martha M. Eliot, Organization and operation of Emergency Maternal and Infant Care Program of the Children's Bureau

1949 **Marion W. Sheahan,** Leadership in nursing and public health

1950 **Eugene Lindsay Bishop,** Original accomplismments in public health administration

1951 **Florence R. Sabin,** Accomplishments in public health administration as chairman of the Health Committee of the Governor of Colorado's Post-War Planning Committee

1952 **Brock Chisholm,** First director of World Health Organization, for leadership in organization of this vast public health concept

Howard A. Rusk, Work in service of physically disabled and distinguished rehabilitation mentor to the world

1953 **Felix J. Underwood,** Demonstrated how long-sustained, sound and expanding health services benefits a people

Earle B. Phelps, Lifetime of pioneering leadership in public health and sanitary sciences

1954 **Leona Baumgartner,** Public health administration leadership and strengthening of community health

1955 **Robert Defries,** Development of preventive medicine and public health in Canada

Menninger Foundation and Karl and William Menninger, Sustained and highly productive attack against mental diseases

Nursing Services of U.S. Public Health Service: Lucile Petry Leone, Pearl McIver and Margaret G. Arnstein, Distinguished contributions to advancement and well-being of the nation through public health nursing

1956 **William P. Shepard,** Pioneering as industrial health physician, educator and government advisor

1957 **Frank G. Boudreau,** Work with Milbank Memorial Fund to promote better mental health, good nutrition and healthful housing

C.J. Van Slyke, Laid foundations of national program of medical research and training

Reginald M. Atwater, Guided American Public Health Assn. to position of leadership in western world

1958 **Basil O'Connor,** Extraordinary administrative leadership on eradication of poliomyelitis through development of effective vaccine (March of Dimes)

1959 **Maurice Pate,** Service to world's children and skilled development of United Nation's Children's Fund program of improving maternal and child health

1960 **John B. Grant,** International statesman on public health, authority on problems of preventive medicine and medical care

Abel Wolman, Leader of lay and professional health groups, corporate consultant, engineer and organizer

GROUP AWARD CITATIONS

1946 **National Institutes of Health,** Contributions to prevention and control of diseases

Northern Regional Research Laboratory, U.S. Dept of Agriculture, Development of powerful penicillin-producing molds

Board for the Coordination of Malarial Studies, Comprehensive studies of anti-malarial agents

Bureau of Entomology and Plant Quarantine, U.S. Dept. of Agriculture, Solution to problems involving health and comfort of the Armed Forces, specifically regarding insect-borne diseases and the use of DDT

Army Epidemological Board, Research on influenza, mapping of its epidemiology and a vaccine

1947 **British Ministers of Food and Health,** Maintenance and even improvement of public health in Great Britain in spite of war

U.S. Committee on Joint Causes of Death, International statistical classification of diseases, injuries and causes of death

1948 **Veterans Administration,** Efficient program of medical care for millions of veterans

1949 **American Academy of Pediatrics,** Studies of personnel services and facilities for the protection of child health

Life Insurance Medical Research Fund, Initiation and support of research on main cause of cardiovascular disease

1950 **International Health Div., Rockefeller Foundation,** Control of infectious diseases and education of health personnel throughout the world

1951 **Health Insurance Plan of Greater New York,** Pioneering a combination of group medical practice and prepayments to provide comprehensive, high-quality care

Alcoholics Anonymous, Unique and highly successful approach to a public-health and social problem

1952 No award

1953 **Div. of Research Grants, National Institutes of Health,** Outstanding administration of research-grants program

University Laboratory of Physical Chemistry Related to Medicine, Harvard University, Basic protein studies leading to fundamental achievements in blood separation and gamma globulin preparation

1954 Streptococcal Disease Laboratory, Armed Forces Epidemiological Board: Frances E. Warren AFB, Charles H. Rammelkamp, Jr., Dir., Contributions to knowledge of streptococcal diseases

1955 No award

1956 Food and Drug Administration, Half-century of public service safeguarding American people against contaminated or misrepresented products

Medical Care Program, Welfare and Retirement Fund, United Mine Workers of America, Model program of health services for a million and a half workers and their families

1957 No award

1958 No award

1959 No award

1960 Crippled Children's Program of the Children's Bureau, Dept. of Health, Education and Welfare, Stimulated comprehensive services for physically handicapped children

Chronic Disease Program, California State Dept. of Public Health, Making prevention and control of heart disease a matter of public concern

ALBERT LASKER AWARDS GIVEN THROUGH THE PLANNED PARENTHOOD—WORLD POPULATION

1945 John McLeod, Research on metabolism of mobility of human sperm cells

1946 Robert Latou Dickinson, Work on human fertility and its control, as gynecologist, anatomist, educator, scholar and artist

Irl Cephas Reggin, Making planned parenthood available as part of Virginia's state public health program

1947 Alan F. Guttmacher, Leadership in marriage counseling

Abraham Stone, Leadership in marriage counseling

1948 John Rock, Treatment of childless couples and help to parents in planning their families

Richard N. Pierson, Mobilized medical profession in behalf of family planning

1949 George M. Cooper, Services in maternal and child health

Carl G. Hartman, Physiology of human reproduction work

1950 Margaret Sanger, Singular role in founding the birth control movement

Bessie L. Moses, Enlisted concern and talents of physicians and nurses in family planning

1951 Guy Irving Burch, Interpretation to lay public of world population trends and problems

William Vogt, Presentation to a world audience of the critical relationship between dwindling resources and expanding population

1952 William Roy Norton, Leadership in making birth control an integral part of North Carolina public health services

Herbert Thomas, Developed techniques of natural child bearing; medical leadership in marriage counseling

Eleanor Bellows Pillsbury, Led Planned Parenthood to position of national and international force

1953 Harry Emerson Fosdick, Contribution to safeguarding the rights of motherhood in the pattern of constructive family life

Elise Ottesen-Jensen, Leadership in developing healthy and ethical sex education program in Swedish schools

1954 Lady Dhanvanthi Rama Rau, Contributions to family planning in India and the world

M.C. Chang, Research on physiologic fertility control

Howard C. Taylor, Furthered knowledge of human fertility

1955 Warren O. Nelson, Studies of the biology of spermatogenesis

Robert Carter Cook, Unique role with Population Reference Bureau in interpretation of the world population dilemma.

1956 No award

1957 No award

1958 Harrison S. Brown, Increased awareness that conservation of resources must be coupled with world-wide family planning

1959 Sir Julian Huxley, Helped achieve world recognition of population crisis and necessity of confronting it

1960 Gregory Pincus, Developed first oral contraceptive pill

1961 John D. Rockefeller III, Leadership in enlisting support of governments in attacking global population problems

1963 Cass Canfield, Leadership in world recognition of global population problems

1965 C. Lee Buxton and Estelle T. Griswold, Advancement of cause of voluntary parenthood in Connecticut and throughout the U.S.

ALBERT LASKER AWARDS GIVEN THROUGH THE NATIONAL COMMITTEE AGAINST MENTAL ILLNESS

1944 Col. William C. Menninger, Advancement of mental health in the field of war psychiatry

1945 Maj. Gen. G. Brock Chisholm, Advancement of mental health in rehabilitation

Brig. Gen. John Rawlings Rees, Advancement of mental health in rehabilitation

1946 W. Horsley Gantt, Experimental modification and analysis of behavior

Jules H. Masserman, Investigations into neurotic behavior

Walter Lerch and D.P. Sharpe, Aroused people of Ohio to start major improvements in hospital care of mental patients

1947 Lawrence K. Frank, Contributions through adult education, particularly through parent-child relationships and child-development programs

Catherine MacKenzie, Reporter and columnist who provided campaign of education on care and emotional development of children

1948 C. Anderson Aldrich, Educated physicians in psychological aspects of pediatrics

Mike Gorman, Reporter whose contributions resulted in new mental health legislation and increased appropriations in the field

Al Ostrow, Reporter who helped give public and legislative support for programs of care for the mentally ill in California

1949 Mildred C. Scoville, Integration of mental health concepts in medical education and practice

Albert Deutsch, Advancement of mental health through books, magazine and newspaper articles

ALBERT LASKER AWARDS GIVEN THROUGH THE AMERICAN HEART ASSN.—BASIC RESEARCH

1954 Albert Szent-Gyorgyi, Research in cardiovascular diseases, including the discovery of actomyosin, the essential contractible element of muscle

1955 **Carl J. Wiggers,** Contributions to understanding of cardiovascular physiology
1956 **No award**
1957 **Isaac Starr,** Work in heart and circulation research and development of first practical ballistocardiograph
1958 **Irvine H. Page,** Contributions to knowledge of basic mechanisms of hypertension

ALBERT LASKER AWARDS GIVEN THROUGH THE AMERICAN HEART ASSN.—CLINICAL RESEARCH

1953 **Paul Dudley White,** Distinguished achievement in pathology, diagnosis and treatment of heart diseases
1954 **No award**
1955 **No award**
1956 **No award**
1957 **No award**
1958 **No award**
1959 **Robert E. Gross,** Performed first successful operation on an inborn cardiovascular defect

ALBERT LASKER AWARDS GIVEN THROUGH THE AMERICAN HEART ASSN.—BASIC AND CLINICAL RESEARCH

1956 **Louis N. Katz,** Contributions in cardiovascular research and advancement of thesis that experimental atherosclerosis is a preventable and reversible metabolic disease
1957 **No award**
1958 **No award**
1959 **No award**
1960 **Karl Paul Link, Irving S. Wright and Edgar V. Allen,** Pioneering development and use of anticoagulant drugs

Jessie Stevenson Kovalenko Medal

THE NATIONAL ACADEMY OF SCIENCES
2101 Constitution Ave. NW, Washington, D.C. 20418
(202/393-8100)

The Jessie Stevenson Kovalenko Medal, which is of gold and carries a $2,000 honorarium, is awarded approximately every three years for contributions to medical science. A four-member committee selects the winner.

1952 **Alfred Newton Richard**
1955 **Peyton Rous**
1958 **Ernest W. Goodpasture**
1959 **Eugene Lindsay Opie**
1961 **Karl Fredrich Meyer**
1962 **George Hoyt Whipple**
1966 **Rufus Cole**
1967 **Karl Paul Link**
1970 **Thomas Francis Jr.**
1973 **Seymour Solomon Kety**
1976 **Julius Hiram Comroe, Jr.**

Nobel Prize for Medicine or Physiology

NOBEL FOUNDATION
Nobel House, Sturegatan 14, 11436-Stockholm, Sweden

One of six Nobel Prizes given annually, the Nobel Prize for Medicine or Physiology is generally recognized as the highest honor which can be bestowed upon a physician or scientist for an exceptionally significant contribution in medicine or physiology. The award, which consists of a gold medal, diploma and large honorarium, is given at a ceremony on December 10 of each year in Stockholm's City Hall. The award itself is presented and administered by the Caroline Institute in Stockholm, which selects the winner. The amount of the cash honorarium fluctuates. In 1977 it was approximately $145,000.

1901 **Emil A. von Behring** (Germany), Serum therapy, specifically for diphtheria
1902 **Sir Ronald Ross** (Great Britain), Investigation on how malaria parasites enter the body
1903 **Niels R. Finsen** (Denmark), Treatment of tubercular skin diseases, such as lupus vulgaris, with concentrated light radiation
1904 **Ivan P. Pavlov** (Russia), Physiological studies on digestion
1905 **Robert Koch** (Germany), Research on tuberculosis
1906 **Camillo Golgi** (Italy) and **Santiago Roman y Cajal** (Spain), Studied structure of the nervous system
1907 **Charles A. Laveran** (France), Research on role protozoa play in cause of disease
1908 **Pau Erlich** (Germany) and **Elie Metchnikoff** (France, born in Russia), Immunity research
1909 **Emil T. Kocher** (Switzerland), Study of thyroid, including pathology, physiology and surgery
1910 **Albrecht Kossel** (Germany), Research in proteins, specifically in the area of cell chemistry
1911 **Allvar Gullstrand** (Sweden), Research on eye dioptics
1912 **Alexis Carrel** (U.S.A., born in France), Transplantation and suture of blood vessels and organs
1913 **Charles R. Richet** (France), Research on allergies and anaphylaxis
1914 **Robert Barany** (Hungary), Physiology and pathology of inner ear
1915 **No award**
1916 **No award**
1917 **No award**
1918 **No award**
1919 **Jules Bordet** (Belgium), Immunity research
1920 **Schack A.S. Krogh** (Denmark), Discovered the motor-regulation mechanism of capallaries
1921 **No award**
1922 **Archibald V. Hill** (Great Britain), Work on production of heat in muscles
Otto F. Meyerhoff (Germany), Discovered relationship between oxygen use and lactic-acid metabolism in muscle
1923 **Frederick G. Banting and John J.R. MacLeod,** (Canada), Discovered insulin
1924 **Willem Einthoven** (Netherlands), Discovered electrocardiogram mechanism
1925 **No award**
1926 **Johannes A.G. Fibiger** (Denmark), Experiments on producing cancer-like growths in rats
1927 **Julius Wagner-Jauregg** (Austria), Used inoculations against malaria to treat paralysis and mental deterioration from syphilis
1928 **Charles J.H. Nicolle** (France), Typhus research
1929 **Christiaan Eijkman** (Netherlands), Discovered effects of vitamin B deficiency
Sir Frederick G. Hopkins (Great Britain), Research on growth-stimulating vitamins
1930 **Kurt Landsteiner** (U.S.A., born in Austria), Discovered blood groups of humans

1931 Otto H. Warburg (Germany), Work in behavior of respiratory enzyme

1932 Edgar D. Adrian and Sir Charles S. Sherrington (Great Britain), Discoveries about nerve-cell functioning

1933 Thomas H. Morgan (U.S.A.), Research on role of chromosomes in heredity

1934 George R. Minot, William P. Murphy and George H. Whipple (U.S.A.), Research on liver therapy for anemia

1935 Hans Spemann (Germany), Discovered "organizer effect" of development of embryo

1936 Otto Loewi (U.S.A., born in Germany), and Sir Henry H. Dale (Great Britain), Research on chemical transmission of nerve impulses

1937 Albert Szent-Gyorgyi von Nagyrapolt (U.S.A., born in Hungary), Work in body metabolism, especially regarding vitamin C and fumaric acid

1938 Corneille J.F. Heymanns (Belgium), Discovered role of sinus and aortic mechanisms in regulation of respiration

1939 Gerhard Domagk (Germany), Work on anti-bacterial properties of prontosil

1940 No award

1941 No award

1942 No award

1943 Henrik C.P. Dam (Denmark), Discovered vitamin K
Edward A. Doisy (U.S.A.), Work in chemistry of vitamin K

1944 Joseph Erlanger (U.S.A.), and Herbert S. Gasser (U.S.A.), Discoveries on differentiated functions of single nerve fibers

1945 Sir Alexander Fleming Ernst B. Chain and Sir Howard W. Florey (Great Britain), Discovered penicillin and its effect on curing certain infectious diseases

1946 Hermann J. Muller (U.S.A.), Discovered mutations by X-ray use

1947 Carl F. Gerty T. Cori (U.S.A., born in Czechoslovakia), Research on catalytic conversion of glycogen
Bernardo A. Houssay (Argentina), Work in role of anterior pituitary lobe hormone in metabolizing sugar

1948 Paul H. Muller (Switzerland), Discovered DDT as efficient insecticide

1949 Walter R. Hess (Switzerland), Discovered role of inter-brain as a "coordinator" of internal organ activity
Antonio Moniz (Portugal), Work on treatment of some psychoses by prefrontal lobotomy

1950 Philip S. Hench (U.S.A.), Edward C. Kendall (U.S.A.) and Tadeus Reichstein (Switzerland, born in Poland), Work on adrenal cortex hormones, including their structural and biological effects

1951 Max Theiler (U.S.A., born in South Africa), Work combatting yellow fever

1952 Selman A. Waksman (U.S.A.), Discovered streptomycin for tuberculosis treatment

1953 Hans A. Krebs (Great Britain, born in Germany), Discovered cycle of citric acid
Fritz A. Lipmann (U.S.A., born in Germany), Discovered coenzyme A and its effect on intermediary metabolism

1954 John F. Enders, Frederick C. Robbins and Thomas H. Weller (U.S.A.), Discovered how poliomyelitis viruses grow in various tissue cultures

1955 Alex H.T. Theorell (Sweden), Work on oxidation enzymes

1956 Andre F. Cournand (U.S.A., born in France), Werner Forssmann (Germany) and Dickinson W. Richards, Jr. (U.S.A.), Work on heart catherization and changes in circulatory system

1957 Daniel Bovet (Italy, born in Switzerland), Work on synthetic compounds that curtail action of some body substances

1958 George W. Beadle and Edward L. Tatum (U.S.A.), Discovered that genes regulate certain chemical events
Joshua Lederburg (U.S.A.), Work in genetic recombination and organization of genetic material in bacteria

1959 Arthur Kornbert (U.S.A.) and Severo Ochoa (U.S.A., born in Spain), Discovered biological synthesis of RNA and DNA

1960 Sir F. Macfarlane Burnet (Australia) and Peter B. Medawar (Great Britain, born in Brazil), Work in acquired immunological tolerance

1961 Georg von Bekesy (U.S.A., born in Hungary), Discovered physical mechanism of stimulation of the cochlea of the inner ear

1962 Francis H.C. Crick (Great Britain), James D. Watson (U.S.A.) and Maurice H.F. Wilkins (Great Britain), Research on molecular structure of nuclear acids and its importance in information transfer in living material

1963 Sir John C. Eccles (Australia), Alan L. Hodgkin and Andrew F. Huxley (Great Britain), Work on nerve cell membrane

1964 Konrad E. Bloch (U.S.A.) and Feodor Lynen (Germany), Work on mechanism and regulation of cholesterol and metabolism of fatty acid

1965 Francois Jacob, Andre Lwoff and Jacques Monod (France), Discovered regulatory processes of body cells contributing to genetic control of enzymes and virus synthesis

1966 Charles B. Huggins (U.S.A.), Work on hormonal treatment of prostrate gland cancer
Francis Peyton Rous (U.S.A.), Discovered tumor-inducing viruses in chickens

1967 Ragnar Granit (Sweden, born in Finland), Haldan Keffer Hartine (U.S.A.) and George Wald (U.S.A.) Work on primary chemical and physiological processes in the eye

1968 Robert W. Holley (U.S.A.), Har Gobind Khorana (U.S.A., born in India) and Marshall W. Nirenberg (U.S.A), Described genetic code that determines cell functions

1969 Max Delbruck (U.S.A., born in Germany), Alfred D. Hershey (U.S.A.) and Salvador D. Luria (U.S.A., born in Italy), Work on reproduction and genetic structure of viruses

1970 Julius Axelrod (U.S.A.), Ulf von Euler (Sweden) and Bernard Katz (Great Britain), Basic research in nerve-transmission chemistry

1971 Earl W. Sutherland, Jr. (U.S.A.), Work on mechanisms of hormonal actions

1972 Gerald M. Edelman (U.S.A.) and Rodney Porter (Great Britain), Determined nature of an antibody

1973 Karl von Frisch (Austria), Konrad Lorenz (Austria) and Nikolaas Tinberger (Great Britain, born in the Netherlands), Work on individual and social behavior patterns of birds and bees, specifically related to selection and survival of the species

1974 Albert Claude (U.S.A., born in Luxembourg), Christian Rene de Duve (Belgium) and George Emil Palade (U.S.A., born in Rumania), Founded cell-biology science, pioneered use of electron microscope to study living cells and discovered certain cell parts

1975 David Baltimore (U.S.A.), Howard Martin Temin (U.S.A.) and Renato Dulbecco (U.S.A., born in Italy), Research on tumor viruses and the genetic material of the living cell

1976 **Baruch S. Blumberg** (U.S.A.), Research on the hepatitis virus in donated blood and on a hepatitis vaccine
D. Carlton Gajdusek (U.S.A.), Discovered kuru disease virus among cannibals
1977 **Rosalyn Yalow** (U.S.A.), **Roger C. L. Guillemin** (U.S.A.) and **Andrew V. Schally** (U.S.A.), Research in hormones in human body

Passano Foundation Award

PASSANO FOUNDATION
c/o Williams & Wilkens Press, 428 E. Preston St., Baltimore, Md. 21202 (301/528-4000)

The Passano Foundation Award annually honors distinguished work done in the United States in medical research, especially work with a clinical application. Originally, one award was endowed. Now there are two each year, a Senior Award with a $12,000 cash prize and a Junior Award with a $6,000 honorarium. The Board of Medical Directors of the foundation selects the recipients.

1945 **Edwin Joseph Cohn,** Harvard Medical School, Cambridge, Mass.
1946 **Ernest William Goodpasture,** Vanderbilt University, Nashville, Tenn.
1947 **Selman A. Waksman,** New Jersey Agricultural Experiment Station, Princeton, N.J.
1948 **Alfred Blalock, Johns Hopkins,** University School of Medicine, Baltimore
Helen Brooke Taussig, Johns Hopkins University School of Medicine, Baltimore
1949 **Oswald Theodore Avery,** Rockefeller Institute for Medical Research, New York
1950 **Edward Calvin Kendall,** Mayo Clinic, Rochester, Minn.
Philip Showalter Hench, Mayo Clinic, Rochester, Minn
1951 **Philip Levine,** Ortho Research Foundation, Raritan, N.J.
Alexander S. Wiener, Jewish Hospital, Brooklyn, N.Y.
1952 **Herbert McLean Evans,** University of California
1953 **John Franklin Enders,** Harvard Medical School and Children's Hospital, Boston, Mass.
1954 **Homer William Smith,** New York University College of Medicine
1955 **Vincent du Vigneaud,** Cornell University Medical College, New York
1956 **George Nicholas Papanicolaou,** Cornell University Medical College, New York
1957 **William Mansfield Clark,** Johns Hopkins University, Baltimore
1958 **George Washington Corner,** American Philosophical Society
1959 **Stanhope Bayne-Jones,** Office of the Surgeon General
1960 **Rene J. Dubos,** Rockefeller University, New York
1961 **Owen H. Wangensteen,** University of Minnesota Medical School
1962 **Albert H. Coons,** Harvard Medical School, Boston
1963 **Horace W. Magoun,** University of California School of Medicine, Los Angeles
1964 **Keith R. Porter,** Harvard University, Cambridge, Mass.
George E. Palade, Rockefeller University, New York

1965 **Charles B. Huggins,** Ben May Laboratory for Cancer Research, Chicago
1966 **John T. Edsall,** Harvard University, Cambridge, Mass.
1967 **Irvine H. Page,** Cleveland Clinic Foundation
1968 **John Eager Howard,** Johns Hopkins University School of Medicine, Baltimore
1969 **George Herbert Hitchings,** vice president in charge of research, Burroughs Wellcome & Company
1970 **Paul Charles Zamecnik,** Massachusetts General Hospital, Boston
1971 **Stephen W. Kuffler,** Harvard Medical School, Cambridge, Mass.
1972 **Kimishige Ishizaka,** Johns Hopkins University School of Medicine, Baltimore
Teruko Ishizaka, Johns Hopkins University School of Medicine, Baltimore
1973 **Roger W. Sperry,** California Institute of Technology, Pasadena
1974 **Seymour S. Cohen,** University of Colorado School of Medicine, Denver
Baruch S. Blumberg, Institute for Cancer Research, Fox Chase, Philadelphia
1975 **Henry G. Kunkel,** Rockefeller University, New York
Joan Argetsinger Steitz, Yale University, New Haven, Conn.
1976 **Roger Guillemin,** Salk Institute, San Diego, Calif.
Ralph A. Bradshaw, Universtiy of Washington School of Medicine, Seattle
1977 **Curt P. Richter,** Johns Hopkins University School of Medicine, Baltimore
Eric A. Jaffe, Cornell University Medical College, New York

Georg Michael Pfaff Medal

GEORG MICHAEL PFAFF GEDACHTNISSTIFTUNG
Eisenbahnstrasse 28-30, D-6750 Kaiserslautern, Federal Republic of Germany (Tel: 0631/64265)

The Georg Michael Pfaff Medal is given approximately every two years, on a judgment by the foundation's board of trustees, for contributions in the health field.

1971 **Artbeitskreis Gesundheitskunde,** Healthy food for children
1973 **Gottfried Gulicher and Dieter Menninger,** Televised health education
1976 **Fritz Strempfer, Emma Stoll and Hans-Gunther Schumacher,** Contributions in health education

Lewis S. Rosenstiel Award

ROSENSTEIL BASIC MEDICAL SCIENCES RESEARCH CENTER
Brandeis University, Waltham, Mass. 02154 (617/647-2431)

The Lewis S. Rosenstiel Award for Distinguished Medical Research, which consists of $5,000 and a bronze medal, is awarded annually for an outstanding accomplishment in the development of basic science as it applies to medicine. An anonymous committee of scientists from institutions in the greater Boston area selects the winner from nominees.

1972 **David H. Hubel**
Torstein N. Wiesel
1973 **Boris Ephrussi**

1974 H. Ronald Kaback
      Saul Roseman
1975 Arthur B. Pardee
      H. Edwin Umbarger
1976 Bruce N. Ames
      Elizabeth C. Miller
      James A Miller
1977 Peter D. Mitchell

T. Duckett Jones Memorial Award

HELEN HAY WHITNEY FOUNDATION
1230 York Ave., New York, N.Y. 10021 (212/861-6066)

The T. Duckett Jones Memorial Award, which includes an honorarium, is presented annually for scientific achievement in biomedical research. The foundation's scientific Committee selects the recipient.

1958 **Luis F. LeLoir,** Instituto de Investigaciones Bioquimicas Fundacion Compomar, Buenos Aires, Isolation of uridine diphosphoglucose and other derivatives
1959 **Karl Meyer,** Columbia College of Physicians and Surgeons, New York, Pioneering work in mucopolysaccharides
1960 **Rebecca C. Lancefield,** Rockefeller University, New York, Biology of hemolytic streptococci
1961 **William T. Astbury,** University of Leeds, United Kingdom, Pioneering studies on molecular structure of variety of fibrous proteins and, in particular, collagen
1962 **Albert H. Coons,** Harvard Medical College, Boston, Work on labeling of antibodies with fluorescent dyes, enhancing our knowledge of immune reactions
1963 **Francis O. Schmitt,** Massachusetts Institute of Technology, Cambridge, Mass., Contributions to knowledge of the fine structure of properties of tissue components, particularly collagen, nerve and muscle
1964 **Michael Heidelberger,** Rutgers University Institute of Microbiology, News Brunswick, N.J., Pioneer work in quantitative immunochemistry
1965 **Eugene L. Opie,** Rockefeller Institute, New York, Contributions in experimental pathology over a period of many decades
1966 **George E. Palade,** Rockefeller University, New York Contributions to knowledge of cellular structure and function
1967 **George Wald,** Harvard University, Cambridge, Mass., Contributions to biology of vision and leadership in stimulating broad interest in the biological sciences
1968 **No award**
1969 **No award**
1970 **Karl A. Piez,** National Institute of Dental Research (National Institutes of Health), Bethesda, Md., Contributions to knowledge of chemical structure of collagen
1971 **Hans J. Muller-Eberhard,** Scripps Clinic and Research Foundation, La Jolla, Calif., Chemistry and biology of complement system
1972 **Jerome Vinograd,** California Institute of Technology, Pasadena, Conceptual and technical contributions to molecular biology
1973 **Saul Roseman,** Johns Hopkins University, Baltimore, Biochemistry of carbohydrates and their biological role
1974 **Henry G. Kunkel,** Rockefeller University, New York, Studies on immunological mechanisms of disease
1975 **Seymour Benzer,** California Institute of Technology, Pasadena, Microbial genetics and molecular and genetic approach to behavior
1976 **Baruj Benacerraf,** Harvard Medical School, Boston, Work on the immune response

1977 **Daniel E. Koshland, Jr.,** University of California/-Berkeley, Pioneering work on enzyme function and structure and investigations of cell functions

Louis H. Bauer Founders Award
Walter M. Boothby Award
Howard K. Edwards Award
Mary T. Klinker Award
Eric Liljencrantz Award
Theodore C. Lyster Award
Harry G. Moseley Award
John A. Maisea Award
Arnold D. Tuttle Award
Raymond F. Longacre Award
Julian E. Ward Memorial Award

AEROSPACE MEDICAL ASSOCIATION
Washington National Airport, Washington, D.C. 20001
(202/892-2240)

The $500 Louis H. Bauer Founders Award annually honors the most significant contribution to the field of space medicine.

1961 Lt. Col. Stanley C. White, USAF, MC
1962 Don Flickinger, M.D.
1963 Col. Paul A. Campbell, USAF, MC
1964 Col. William K. Douglas, USAF, MC
1965 Hubertus Strughold, M.D.
1966 Charles A. Berry, M.D.
1967 R/Adm Frank B. Voris, USN, MC
1968 James N. Waggoner, M.D.
1969 Maj. Gen. Otis O. Benson, Jr., USAF (Ret.)
1970 Walton L. Jones, M.D.
1971 Maj. Gen. James W. Humphreys, USAF (Ret.)
1972 Capt. Ralph L. Christy, MC, USN
1973 Karl H. Houghton, M.D.
1974 Willard R. Hawkins, M.D.
1975 Col. John Pickering, USAF (Ret.)
1976 Lawrence F. Dietlein, M.D., Ph.D.
1977 Rufus R. Hessberg, M.D.

The Walter M. Boothby Award, which consists of a plaque and $1,000, is now given biennially and recognizes outstanding research in the prevention of disease and the promotion of health among airline pilots.

1961 John E. Smith
1962 Ross A. McFarland
1963 Jan H. Tillisch
1964 Louis R. Krasno
1965 Earl T. Carter
1966 Stanley R. Mohler
1967 G. Earle Wight
1968 Charles R. Harper
1969 John S. Howitt
1970 Michael T. Lategola
1971 Kenneth G. Bergin
1972 George F. Catlett
1973 Charles E. Billings
1975 Karl E. Klein
1977 Wg/Cdr. Anthony N. Nicholson, RAF, MC

The Howard K. Edwards Award, which carries a $1,000 honorarium and a plaque, is now awarded biennially alternately with the Walter M. Boothby Award for the outstanding practice of clinical medicine pertaining to airline pilots.

1961 George J. Kidera
1962 Otis B. Schreuder
1963 Ludwig G. Lederer
1964 Andre Allard
1965 John E. Smith
1966 Charles C. Gullett
1967 George F. Catlett
1968 Peter V. Siegel
1969 M. Frederick Leeds
1970 Joseph G. Constantino
1971 Heinrich Gartmann
1972 John K. Cullen
1973 Birger Hannisdahl
1974 Ian Anderson
1976 Eugine Lafontaine

The Mary T. Klinker Award, which consists of $500, a plaque and a watch, is given annually to the Flight Nurse of the Year for outstanding contributions to or achievement in service, education, research, aerospace nursing or aerospace evacuation.

1968 Maj. Virginia M. Alena, USAF, NC
1969 Maj. Helen Kopczynski, USAF, NC
1970 Lt. Col. Pearl E. Tucker, USAF, NC
1971 Capt. Gertrude M. Campbell, USAF, NC
1972 Capt. Anne R. Spurlin, USAFR, NC
1973 Capt. Mary K. Littlejohn, USAF, NC
1974 Capt. LaDonn B. Cramer, USAF, NC
1975 Lt. Col. Patricia A. Farrell, USAF, NC
1976 Lt. Col. Dorothy R. Novotny, USAF, NC
1977 Lt. Col. Mary M. Thomas, USAF, NC

The $500 Eric Liljencrantz Award is presented for basic research into the problems of acceleration and altitude as they affect the body.

1957 Col. John P. Stapp, USAF, MC
1958 Brig. Gen. Victor A. Byrnes, USAF, (Ret.)
1959 Capt. Edward L. Beckman, MC, USN
1960 James D. Hardy
1961 Capt. Ashton Graybiel, MC, USN
1962 Wilbur R. Franks
1963 Earl H. Wood
1964 Capt. Ralph L. Christy, MC, USN
1965 David M. Clark
1966 Henning von Gierke
1967 Charles F. Gell
1968 Edward J. Baldes
1969 Capt. Roger O. Ireland, MC, USN
1970 Sidney D. Leverett, Jr.
1971 Otto H. Gauer
1972 Capt. Marvin D. Courtney, MC, USN
1973 Adolf P. Gagge
1974 Cdr Donald J. Sass, MC, USN
1975 Wg./Cdr. John Ernsting, RAF, MC
1976 Ulrich C. Luft
1977 Channing L. Ewing

The annual Theodore C. Lyster Award, which consists of a plaque and $500, is given for outstanding achievement in the general field of aerospace medicine.

1947 Louis H. Bauer
1948 Wilbur R. Franks
1949 Maj. Gen. Harry G. Armstrong, USAF, MC
1950 Capt. Ashton Graybiel, MC, USN
1951 R/Adm. B. Groesbeck, Jr., MC, USN
1952 Kenneth A. Evelyn
1953 Capt. Wilbur E. Kellum, MC, USN

1954 W. R. Stovall
1955 Brig. Gen. Otis O. Benson, Jr., USAF, MC
1956 Brig. Gen. Don Flickinger, USAF, MC
1957 Capt. Charles F. Gell, MC, USN
1958 Hurbertus Strughold
1959 Capt. Clifford P. Phoebus, MC, USN
1960 Air Cdr. A. A. G. Corbet, RCAF
1961 Air Cdr. William K. Stewart, RAF
1962 Robert J. Benford
1963 Maj. Gen. M. Samuel White, USAF, MC
1964 William Randolph Lovelace, II
1965 William J. Kennard
1966 Brig. Gen. Eugen G. Reinartz, USAF, MC
1967 Brig. Gen. John M. Talbot, USAF, MC
1968 Jan H. Tillisch
1969 Ludwig G. Lederer
1970 George J. Kidera
1971 John P. Marbarger
1972 Joseph P. Pollard
1973 Andre Allard
1974 Co. Stanley C. White, USAF, MC
1975 Merrill H. Goodwin
1976 Maj. Gen. Heinz S. Fuchs, GAF, MC
1977 Maj. Gen. Spurgeon H. Neel, MC, USA

The Harry G. Moseley Award, which consists of a plaque, annually honors the year's most outstanding contribution to flight safety.

1961 Capt. Carl E. Wilbur, MC, USN
1962 Col. F. M. Townsend, USAF, MC
1963 Brig. Gen. Kenneth E. Pletcher, USAF, MC
1964 Capt. W. Harley Davidson, USAF, MC
1965 Capt. Richard E. Luehrs, MC, USN
1966 Capt. Roland A. Bosee, MSC, USN
1967 Maj. Richard M. Chubb, USAF, MC
1968 John J. Swearingen
1969 W/C David I. Fryer, M.D., OBE, RAF
1970 Ernest B. McFadden
1971 William J. Reals
1972 A. Howard Hasbrook
1973 Capt. Frank H. Austin, Jr., MC, USN
1974 Stanley R. Mohler
1975 Richard G. Snyder
1976 Harry W. Orlady
1977 Homer L. Reighard

The $100 John A. Maisea Award annually honors contributions to aviation medicine in general and its application to the aviation field.

1963 Herbert F. Fenwick
1964 Delazon S. Bostwick
1965 Neil E. Baxter
1966 George B. McNeely
1967 Howard Allen Dishongh
1968 J. Harold Brown
1969 Thomas A. Coates
1970 H. D. Vickers
1971 William Gillespie
1972 James Y. Bradfield
1973 Harold N. Brown
1974 Luis A. Amezcua G.
1975 Robert L. Wick, Jr.
1976 Harry L. Gibbons
1977 Harold V. Ellingson

The Arnold D. Tuttle Award, which consists of a plaque and $500, recognizes the most significant contribution toward the solution of a challenging problem in aerospace medicine.

1952 Edward H. Lambert

1953   James. P. Henry
1954   John P. Marbarger
1955   Fred A. Hitchcock
1956   W. H. Johnson
1957   Maj. David G. Simons, USAF, MC
1958   Siegfried J. Gerathewohl
1959   Lawrence E. Lamb
1960   Hermann J. Schaefer
1961   Lt. Col. Charles A. Berry, USAF, MC
1962   Clayton S. White
1963   Charles I. Barron
1964   Vincent M. Downey
1965   Capt. Ashton Graybiel, MC, USN
1966   Lt. Col. James F. Culver, USAF, MC
1967   Billy E. Welch
1968   Dietrich E. Beischer
1969   Randall M. Chambers
1970   Christian J. Lambertsen
1971   G. Melvill Jones
1972   Harold J. von Beckh
1973   Surg/Capt John S. P. Rawlins, RN
1974   Henning E. von Gierke
1975   Col. Malcolm C. Lancaster, USAF, MC
1976   Russell R. Burton
1977   Kent K. Gillingham

The $500 Raymond F. Longacre Award annually honors outstanding contributions to the psychological or psychiatric aspects of aerospace medicine.

1947   Ross A. McFarland
1948   Detlev W. Bronk
1949   Sir Charles P. Symonds
1950   Donald W. Hastings
1951   Col. Neeley C. Mashburn, USAF (Ret.)
1952   Sir Frederick Bartlett
1953   Walter F. Grether
1954   John C. Flanagan
1955   Roy R. Grinker
1956   Saul B. Sells
1957   Brig. Gen. Eugen G. Reinartz, USAF, MC
1958   Col. Harry G. Moseley, USAF, MC
1959   Capt. George E. Ruff, USAF, MC
1960   Brant Clark
1961   Capt. Philip B. Phillips, MC, USN
1962   George T. Hauty
1963   Henry A. Imus
1964   Frederick H. Rohles
1965   Anchard F. Zeller
1966   Richard Trumbull
1967   Col. Don E. Flinn, USAF, MC
1968   Frederick E. Guedry, Jr.
1969   Bryce O. Hartman
1970   Capt. Roger F. Reinhardt, MC, USN
1971   William E. Collins
1972   Rosalie K. Ambler
1973   Claude J. Blanc
1974   Herbert C. Haynes
1975   Alan J. Benson
1976   W. Dean Chiles
1977   Capt. Joseph A. Pursch, MC, USN

The $200 Julian E. Ward Memorial Award is given for outstanding achievement in aerospace medicine during medical residency training.

1963   Cdr. Frank H. Austin, Jr., USN, MC
1964   Maj. Samuel J. Brewer, USAF, MC
1965   Capt. Ronald E. Costin, USAF, MC
1966   Maj. Calvin Chapman, USAF, MC
1967   Capt. Kenneth W. Curtis, Jr., USAF, MC
1968   Maj. Charles R. O'Briant, USAF, MC

1969   George W. Hoffler
1970   Cdr. William W. Simmons, USN, MC
1971   Sarah Ann Nunneley
1972   Maj. William E. Barry, USAF, MC
1973   Maj. Frederic M. Brown, USAF, MC
1974   Cdr. Robert P. Caudill, USN, MC
1975   Maj. Hubert F. Bonfili, USAF, MC
1976   Maj. George K. Anderson, USAF, MC
1977   Joseph J. C. Degioanni

Jeffries Medical Research Award
AMERICAN INSTITUTE OF AERONAUTICS AND ASTRONAUTICS
1290 Ave. of the Americas, New York, N.Y. 10019
(212/581-4300)

The Jeffries Medical Research Award, originally the John Jeffries Award, honors outstanding contributions to aerospace medical research. The award consists of a medal and citation and is given by decision of an honors and awards committee.

JOHN JEFFRIES AWARD
1940   Louis H. Bauer
1941   Harry G. Armstrong
1942   Edward C. Schneider
1943   Eugen G. Reinartz
1944   Harold E. Wittingham
1945   John C. Adams
1946   Malcolm C. Grow
1947   J. Winifred Tice
1948   W. Randolph Lovelace, II
1949   A.D. Tuttle
1950   Otis O. Bensen, Jr.
1951   John R. Poppen
1952   John Stapp
1953   Charles F. Gell
1954   James P. Henry
1955   Wilbur E. Kellum
1956   Ross A. McFarland
1957   David C. Simons
1958   Hubertus Strughold
1959   Don Flickinger
1960   Joseph W. Kittinger
1961   Ashton Graybiel
1962   James L. Goddard
1964   Eugene Konecci
1965   William K. Douglas
1966   Charles A. Berry
1967   Charles I. Barron
1968   Loren D. Carlson
1969   Frank B. Voris
1970   Walton L. Jones
1971   Richard St. Johnston
1972   Roger G. Ireland
1973   Karl H. Houghton
1974   Malcolm Clayton Lancaster
1975   Lawrence F. Dietlein

JEFFRIES MEDICAL RESEARCH AWARD
1977   Harold von Beckh

Heart-of-the-Year Award
AMERICAN HEART ASSOCIATION
7320 Greenville Ave., Dallas, Tex. 75231 (214/750-5300)

The Heart-of-the-Year Award is presented annually to a distinguished American to show that cardiovascular disease is not a barrier to productivity and achievement. Winners are generally well-known public figures, and the award has been presented in White House ceremonies by Presidents of the United States from Dwight D. Eisenhower on—as well as to several Presidents and former Presidents.

1959 Lyndon Baines Johnson, Then Senate Majority Leader
1960 Mrs. Dwight D. Eisenhower, First Lady
1961 Arthur Hays Sulzberger, Editor and Publisher, *The New York Times*
1962 Clarence B. Randall, Retired Chairman of the Board, Inland Steel Co.
1963 Gen. Lauris Norstad, Former Supreme Allied Commander in Europe
1964 Vice Adm. H.G. Rickover, "Father of the Atomic Navy"
1965 George Tebbets, Manager, the Cleveland Indians
1966 John E. Fogarty, U.S. Congressman
1967 Dwight D. Eisenhower, Former President
1968 Patricia Neal, Actress
1969 Irvine H. Page, Cleveland physician
1970 Owen R. Cheatham, Founder, Georgia-Pacific Corp.
1971 Carl Albert, Speaker, U.S. House of Representatives
1972 Pearl Bailey, Entertainer
1973 Richard M. Nixon, President of the United States
1974 No award
1975 No award
1976 Donald Slayton, Astronaut
1977 Walter Matthau, Actor

Distinguished Service Award

AMERICAN COLLEGE OF CARDIOLOGY
9111 Old Georgetown Rd., Bethesda, Md. 20014
(301/897-5400)

The Distinguished Service Award is given annually to a physician, scientist or layperson for contributions to medicine and/or the delivery of health care.

1967 Pres. Lyndon Baines Johnson
1968 Sen. Lister Hill
Mrs. Albert D. Lasker
1969 No award
1970 No award
1971 William B. Walsh, Washington, D.C.
1972 Warren G. Magnuson
1973 Paul G. Rogers
1974 Professor Zednek Fejfar, Prague, Czechoslovakia
1975 Theodore Cooper, Washington, D.C.
1976 Rep. Daniel J. Flood
1977 No award

Certificates of Meritorious Achievement

AMERICAN DENTAL ASSOCIATION
211 E. Chicago Ave., Chicago, Ill. 60611 (312/440-2803)

Two Certificates of Meritorious Achievement, each accompanied by $100 for scientific equipment, are given annually for high school science projects that are finalists at the International Science and Engineering Fair with application to dental health and oral research. A judging team of dental researchers and educators selects the winners.

1973 Daniel Gallagher, Michigan City, Ind.
Michael Marks, Florence, Ala.
1974 Jewel Jurovich, Metairie, La.
Keith Zych, Bayside, Wisc.
1975 Joan Gartrell, Reno, Nev.
Glenda Dale Knox, Vicksburg, Miss.
1976 Stephen Budak, Michigan City, Ind.
Deborah Malone, Grants, N.M.
1977 Janice M. Russell, Harrisville, R.I.
Deanna L. Sieren, Thornburg, Iowa

Research Achievement Award

MENTAL HEALTH ASSOCIATION
1800 N. Kent St., Arlington, Va. 22209 (703/528-6405)

The Mental Health Assn. Research Achievement Award, known as the McAlpin Medal, is given annually for outstanding research in the causes and prevention of mental illness. The award consists of a plaque and $10,000 which may given to an individual or research team, providing the winner(s) are United States citizens. Nominations are made by professional organizations, MHA members and others, and the winner is selected by the Research Committee and National Board of the association.

1972 Seymour Kety, Biochemical research in schizophrenia
1973 Robert Coles
1974 Erik H. Erikson, Psychoanalysis and human development
1975 Alexander Leighton, Social psychiatry
1976 William E. Bunney, Biochemistry of depression
1977 Lyman Winn and Margaret Singer, Work on schizophrenia

Isaac Ray Award

AMERICAN PSYCHIATRIC ASSOCIATION
1700 18th St. NW, Washington, D.C. 20009 (202/797-4900)

The Isaac Ray Award, which carries a $1,500 cash prize, is given annually to a psychiatrist, attorney or judge for noteworthy contributions to psychiatry and the law and to close understanding between experts in the two fields. The recipient gives a series of lectures on the subject during the year.

1952 Winfred Overholser, St. Elizabeth's Hospital, Washington, D.C.
1953 Gregory Zilboorg, Professor of Psychiatry, New York State University Medical College, New York
1954 Hon. John Biggs, Jr., Chief Judge of U.S. Court of Appeals for the Third Judicial Circuit, Wilmington, Del.
1955 Henry Weihofen, Professor of Law, University of New Mexico, Albuquerque
1956 Philip Roche, Associate in Psychiatry, University of Pennsylvania Medical School, Philadelphia
1957 Manfred Guttmacher, psychiatrist and Chief Medical Officer of the Supreme Bench of Baltimore
1958 Alistair William McLeod, Assistant Professor of Psychiatry, McGill University, Montreal, Canada
1959 Maxwell Jones, Director, Social Rehabilitation Unit, Belmont Hospital, Sutton, Surrey, U.K.

1960 Judge David L. Bazelon, U.S. Court of Appeals in Washington, D.C.
1961 Sheldon Glueck, Roscoe Pound Professor of Law, Harvard University, Cambridge, Mass
1962 Karl A. Menninger, Menninger Foundation, Topeka, Kans.
1963 Judge Morris Ploscowe, Associate Professor of Law, New York University, New York
1964 Judge Justine Wise Polier, New York
1965 Georg K. Sturup, Hellerup, Denmark
1966-67 No awards
1968 Bernard Diamond, University of California, Berkeley, Calif.
1969-74 No awards
1975 Jay Katz, Professor Adjunct of Law and Psychiatry, Yale University, New Haven, Conn.
1976 Jonas Robitscher, Henry R. Luce Professor of Law and Behavioral Sciences, Emory University School of Law, Atlanta, Ga.
1977 Bruno Conier, Professor, Dept. of Psychiatry, McGill University, Montreal, Canada

Florence Nightingale Award
INTERNATIONAL COMMITTEE OF THE RED CROSS
17 Avenue de la Paix, CH-1211 Geneva, Switzerland (Tel. 34.60.01/283)

The Florence Nightingale Award, which consists of a gold medal and a diploma, is given every two years to not more than 36 nurses and voluntary aides, honoring exceptional devotion to the sick and wounded in difficult and perilous situations, such as those which often prevail in times of war, epidemics or natural disaster. National Red Cross organizations send nominees to the International Committee, which sets up a special commission to select the recipients. The first 41 recipients were honored specifically for their actions during World War I; 1947 awards recognize individuals for their World War II devotion.

1920 Martha Paula Heller, Austria
Maria Adamcycyk, Austria
Astley Campbell, Belgium (British citizen)
Kate Schandeleer, Belgium
Magdalene Tidemand, France
Helene Scott Hay, U.S.A.
Florence Merriam Johnson, U.S.A.
Martha M. Russel, U.S.A.
Linda K. Meirs, U.S.A.
Alma E. Foerster, U.S.A.
Mary E. Gladwin, U.S.A.
Marie Balli Panas, France
Louise Leclere Hugues, France
Germaine St.-Girons Legrix, France
Christine de Chevron de Villette, France
The Marquise de Clappiers (nee de Foresta), France
Marguerite Voisin, France
Renee Aline Flourens, France
Marie Elisabeth Lajusan, France
Alice Lockhart Lambert, Great Britain
Beatrice Isabel Jones, Great Britain
Gladys Laura White, Great Britain
Kate Maxey, Great Britain
Gertrude Mary Wilton Smith, Great Britain
Lucy Minchin, Great Britain
Hester MacLean, Great Britain (New Zealand)

E.R. Creagh, Great Britain (South Africa)
Helene Vassilopoulo, Greece
Baroness Gizella Apor, Hungary
Ilona Durgo, Hungary
S.A.R. Elena di Francia, Duchess of Aosta, Italy
Ina Battistella, Italy
Maria Concetta Clhudzinska, Italy
Maria Andina, Italy
Maria Natonietta Clerici, Italy
Take Hagiwara, Japan
Ya-o Yomamoto, Japan
Ume U-asa, Japan
Elonore Mihailescu, Rumania
Irene Metejickova, Czechoslavakia
Sylva Macharova, Czechoslovakia
Countess Alexandrine von Uexhall, Germany
Anni Roth, Germany
Dora Rothe, Germany
Elsbeth von Keudell, Germany
Agnes von Frankenberg und Proschlitz, Germany
Annemarie Wenzel, Germany
Christina Vateva, Bulgaria
Margaret Clotilde MacDonald, Canada
Marie Theresa Viotti, Italy
Delfia Jovanitch, Serbia

1923 Maria Douglas, Germany
Elza Haeckx, Belgium
Clara D. Noyes, U.S.A.
Laurence Pidiere des Prinveaux, France
Maud Emma McCarthy, Great Britain
Josephine Todorffy Viczian, Hungary
Rhoda de Bellegarde, Italy
Yuki Inada, Japan
Countess Marie Tarnowka (nee Princess Czetwertynska), Poland
Anka Durovic, Serbia
Alma Charlotte Brunskog, Sweden
Safie Hussein Bey (nee Ahmed Pacha), Turkey

1925 Anna von Zimmermann, Germany
Berta Hermine Schwarzott, Austria
Juliette Parmentier, Belgium
Maria del Carmen Angolotti y Mesa, Spain
Lucy Minnigerode, U.S.A.
Baroness Sophie Mannerheim, Finland
Helene Moulin, France
Marta Celmin, Latvia
Louise Sternlieb, Poland
Ljoubitza Loukovitsch, Rumania
Jindra Tilsova, Czechoslovakia

1927 Marie Viehauser (Sister Silveria), Germany
Eugenie Henry, Belgium
Idalia de Araujo Porte-Alegre, Brazil
Alice Fitzgerald, U.S.A.
Alice Krug, France
Dame Sidney Brown, Great Britain
Angelique Phikiori, Greece
Alice Abranyi, Hungary
Marquise Irene di Targiani Giunti, Italy
Tamaki-Ei, Japan
Anne Techbeltye, Lithuania
Josephine Dudajek, Poland

1929 Countess Mathilde von Horn, Germany
Jenny Lutterloh, Germany
Dame Sarah Swift, Great Britain
Sister Marie Gabrielle, Countess Lodron, Austria
Sister Josefa Weidinger, Austria
Grace Margaret Wilson, Australia
Jeanne Hellemans, Belgium
Sister Stoyanka Alexandrova, Bulgaria
Sister Anastassia Kirinkova, Bulgaria

Anne Hartley, Canada
Major Julia C. Stimson, U.S.A.
Carrie M. Hall, U.S.A.
Therese-Marie-Leonie Freminet, France
Marie-Leonie Genin, France
Alice Pezet Aubry, France
Sophie L. Deligeorges, Greece
Pauline Nahalka, Hungary
Anne Novadovsky Gasci, Hungary
Melanie Elaine Tippetts, India
Norah Beresford, India
Duchess Elisabetta Cita di Torrescuso (nee di Sambuy), Italy
Midori Kagawa, Japan
Kei Mizuno, Japan
Elza Grivans, Latvia
Rosalie Jachimovicz, Poland
Helene Nagorska, Poland
Emma Novakova, Czechoslovakia
1931 Henny Dyckerhoff, Germany
Sister Minna Weiss, Germany
Sister Leokadia Ammann, Austria
Cecile Mechelynck, Belgium
Sister Helena Radoikova, Bulgaria
Vivien Adlard Tremaine, Canada
Elizabeth Gordon Fox, U.S.A.
Henriette de Grancey de Bertier de Sauvigny, France
Marie-Eugenie Lapere, France
Dame Ann Beadsmore Smith, Great Britain
Julie Andreades, Greece
Helene Tricoupis, Greece
Baroness Marie de Fiath, Hungary
Suzanne Ferencz, Hungary
Antoinette Heyl, Hungary
Alice Rosina Lowe, India
Minnie Eda MacLean, India
Suye Otsuka, Japan
Shighe Homma, Japan
Justine Kushke, Latvia
Sister Karethe Johnsen, Norway
Stephanie Potocka-Ziembinska, Poland
Wanda Idzikowska, Poland
Marie Modrezewska, Poland
Constantza Ionescu Tarasof, Rumania
Zoe V. Iorga Georgescu, Rumania
Bossa Svet Rankovitch, Yugoslavia
1933 Pia Bauer, Germany
Juliane Husstedt, Germany
Charlotte Miller Heilman, U.S.A.
Edith Cornwell, Australia
Hermine Wadowska, Austria
Sister Rosa Jogna, Austria
Gabrielle Kaeckenbeck, Belgium
Sister Elena Pope Bojkova, Bulgaria
Felicie Marie Angele Dauch, France
Marguerite Charlotte Legros, France
Lloyd Still, Great Britain
Caroline Revay Mero, Hungary
Helene Hankiss Nyary, Hungary
Agatha Mary Phillips, India
W.E. Walters, India
E. MacFarlane, India
Sita Meyer Camperio, Italy
Yori Ono, Japan
Tomo Fujii, Japan
Elza Nulle-Siecenieks, Latvia
Rosalie Tomosiunaite, Lithuania
Ona Brazyte, Lithuania
Edwige Suffczynska, Poland

Hedwige Gronczynska, Poland
Micheline Mieleszkiewicz, Poland
Marie Benesova, Czechoslovakia
Sofia Igrochanatz, Yugoslavia
Sister Stefania Papailiolulos, Yugoslavia
1935 Elisabeth Tomitius, Germany
Elsbeth Hosig Vaughan, U.S.A.
Elsie Clare Pidgeon, Australia
Frederike Zehetner, Austria
Louise Guinotte-van der Stichelen, Belgium
Anna Sagaroska, Bulgaria
Jean Isabel Gunn, Canada
Leonie Chaptal de Chanteloup, France
Dame Ethel Hope Becher, Great Britain
Marie Negroponte, Greece
Paula Halper, Hungary
The Hon. Florence Mary MacNaughton, India
Countess Carolina Monroy di Ranchibile, Italy
Shika Morimoto, Japan
Sister Ailke Westerhof, Netherlands
Rev. Mother Sister Rosa, Peru
Sophie Szlenkierowna, Poland
Bertha Wellin, Sweden
Elisabeth von Bergen, Sweden
Josefa Andelova, Czechoslovakia
Roujitsa Helih, Yugoslavia
1937 Erna Marie Auguste Anne Wittich, Germany
Adelaide Maud Kellett, Australia
Berthe Marie Crutzen-de Vos, Belgium
Ida F. Butler, U.S.A.
Gertrude Marcelle Muzeau, France
Mrs. Maynard Linden Carter, Great Britain
Helene Paraskevopoula, Greece
Margit de Daniel, Hungary
Lorna Ellice MacKenzie, India
Mose Ono, Japan
Masayo Tabutchi, Japan
Maria Bellavita Pellizzari, Italy
Marie Elisabeth Joys, Norway
Adriana Elisabeth Schipper, Netherlands
Vera Schleimer, Yugoslavia
1939 Gerda von Freyold, Germany
Stella Mathews, U.S.A.
H.M. Queen Elisabeth of Belgium, Belgium
Agatha Mary Phillips, Great Britain
Jean Elizabeth Browne, Canada
Victoria Bianchi y Bianchi, Chile
Anette Massov, Estonia
Jeanne-Marie-Emilie-Leonie Le Pescheux Duhautbourg, France
Rennee-Anne-Berthe Blanc, France
Athena Messolora, Greece
Marie Bosnyak Gebhardt, Hungary
Dora Chadwick, India
Katherine Anne Duncan, India
Vincenza Campari, Italy
Miyo Akoyama, Japan
Tsune Numamoto, Japan
Helene Karoline Larsen, Norway
Marie Skorupska, Poland
Constance Cantacuzene, Rumania
Anna Mankova, Czechoslovakia
Zenie Berengovitch, Yugoslavia
1941 No awards
1943 No awards
1945 No awards
1947 Lt. Col. Ida W. Danielson, U.S.A.
Mrs. Walter Lippmann, U.S.A.
Col. Annie Moriah Sage, Australia
Capt. Vivian Bullwinkel, Australia

Cdr. Barbara Moriarty, Australia
Germaine Dewandre Van Hoegaerden, Belgium
Jeanne Rahier, Belgium
Jeanne Van Lier, Belgium
Zoe Helene Spilliaert, Belgium
Yvonne Cardon de Lichtbuer, Belgium
Dame Emily Mathieson Blair, Great Britain
Lyyli Ingrid Hagan, Finland
Venny Snellman, Finland
Martta Siitonen, Finland
Alice Soulange-Bodin, France
Mathilde-Marie Bernardine de Cleron D'Haussonville, France
Marcelle Barry, France
Marie-Therese Desse, France
Arriete Lambrinoudis Degleris, Greece
Marriete Velissariou, Greece
Sophie Marschalko, Hungary
Marie Radnay, Hungary
Marthe Mauks, Hungary
Etelka Endrey, Hungary
Irma Balazs, Hungary
Marie Kasics Vilmos Varnay, Hungary
Phyllis Widger, India
Winifred Grace McKenzie, India
Mercy John, India
Margaret Neal, India
S.A.I. Princess Achraf Pahlavi, Iran
Elisa Carini, Italy
Sofia Novellis di Coarazze, Italy
Antonietta Pedace, Italy
Constanza Bruno, Italy
Ermelinda Ducler, Italy
Elda Malagu, Italy
Emma Mazzolari, Italy
Etsu Kuno, Japan
Akie Higashiyama, Japan
Ai Fukui, Japan
Yoshio Tomura, Japan
Maria Adriana Anna Bloem, Netherlands
Leintje Jacoba Jobse, Netherlands
Regina M. Esser, Netherlands
Rev. Sister Stephania O.P. Netherlands
Helena Maria Verheul, Netherlands
Irene Flora Campbell, New Zealand
Wladyslawa Dyczakowska, Poland
Bronislawa Karpowicz, Poland
Wanda Peszke, Poland
Jadwiga Romanowska, Poland
Janina Tyszynska, Poland
Halina Swiatecka, Poland
Alice Wierzbicka, Poland
Maria Babicka-Zachertowa, Poland
Zofia Bittenek, Poland
Marguerite Zmudzka, Poland
Elisabet Lind, Sweden
Kerstin Nordendahl, Sweden
Sister Elsbeth Kasser, Switzerland
Zofie Lehocka, Czechoslovakia
Bozena Mandokova, Czechoslovakia
Ruzena Struzkova, Czechoslovakia
Anna Rypackova, Czechoslavakia
Bedriska Bohacova, Czechoslovakia
Anna Kralova, Czechoslovakia
Nan Mary Harper, South Africa
Margaret Ellen Stoney, South Africa
Elizabeth Jane Waugh, South Africa
Rose Millicent Vandecar, South Africa
1949 Alta Elizabeth Dines, U.S.A.
Mary M. Roberts, U.S.A.

Ruby Evelyn Storey, Australia
Maj. Alice Rose Appleford, Australia
Ingeborg Ellison-Nidlef, Austria
Maria Ultschning, Austria
Marie-Madeleine Bihet, Belgium
Irene Cotegipe de Miranda, Brazil
Dame Katherine Watt, Great Britain
Edith Kathleen Russell, Canada
Maria Fernandez Le Cappelain de Tinocco, Costa Rica
Eli Magnussen, Denmark
Rachel Edgren, Finland
Kyllikki Pohkola, Finland
Louise Bader-Gruber, France
Alice Le Sergen d'Hendecourt, France
Jeanne de Joannis, France
Thalie Lecou, Greece
Clea Vassilopoulos, Greece
Dorothy Grace Howard, India
Mariamma Thomas, India
Alice Reeves, Ireland
Sigridur Eriksdottir Thorvaldsson, Iceland
Paolo Menada, Italy
Sjoukje Hoyting, Netherlands
Eike Flikkema, Netherlands
Helen Iris Crooke, New Zealand
Bertha Helgestad, Norway
Bergljot Larsson, Norway
Gladys Ada Penhearow, Pakistan
Anna Rydel, Poland
Marie Wilkonska, Poland
Sanguanwan Fuang-Bejara, Siam
Marianne Edwaline Pfeiffer, South Africa
Elisabet Dillner, Sweden
1951 Florence A. Blanchfield, U.S.A.
Sophie C. Nelson, U.S.A.
Maria Josefina Ghiglione, Argentina
Rita Malcolm, Australia
Olive Pascke, Australia
Gretrud Finze, Austria
Anna Pia Goldschmid, Austria
Suzanne Lippens-Orban, Belgium
Rev. Mother Marie-Therese (nee Germaine Provoyeur), Belgium
Dame Doris Beale, Great Britain
Signe Jansen, Denmark
Tyyne Maria Luoma, Finland
Sister Agnes (nee Helene Hennart), France
Helly Chatzilazarou Adossides, Greece
Colliope Ghioulounda, Greece
Ethel Ellen Hutchings, India
Dorothy Davis, India
Amy Katharine Bullock, India
Linda MacWhinney, Ireland
Antonietta Colotti, Italy
Conchita Scotti Guerra, Italy
Maria Senni, Italy
Carmela Vidacovi, Italy
Yuki Ono, Japan
Myo Mizutani, Japan
Jasue Kunibe, Japan
Ritsu Sugiyama, Japan
Edna Jean House, New Zealand
Ingeborg Kolrud, Norway
Agnes Rimestad, Norway
Iris Murray, Pakistan
Mary Greta Borcherds, South Africa
Maria Amparo Larrosa Irizarry, Venezuela
Vera Lipovscak, Yugoslavia
1953 Ethel Jessie Bowe, Australia

Edith Johnson, Australia
Sarah Charlotte MacDonald, Australia
Florence H.M. Emory, Canada
Blanca Marti de David Almeida, Colombia
Beatrix Restrepo Herrera, Colombia
Ellen Marie Christensen, Denmark
Annabelle Peterson, U.S.A.
Jeanne Berlie, France
Madeleine Castan, France
Anne Chipon, France
Elisabeth Duval, France
Yvonne Foltz, France
Makie Fujimoto, Japan
Kin Kato, Japan
To Yameda, Japan
Nasra Aboudi, Jordan
Renee Araman, Lebanon
Rosa Maria Acosta Gonzalez, Mexico
Sister Karen Elise Moe, Norway
Gul Mehernosh Darrah, Pakistan
Gabriele Fries, Federal Republic of Germany
Maria Lerchl, Federal Republic of Germany
Else Weecks, Federal Republic of Germany
Beate Welschof, Federal Repulic of Germany
Daisy Caroline Bridges, United Kingdom
Gerda Hojer, Sweden
Karin Elfverson, Sweden
1955 Blanca Julia Clermont, Argentina
Sen. Sister Lucy Thelma Marshall, Australia
Sen. Sister Hermine Hansgirg, Austria
Sen. Sister Hertha Groller, Austria
Amelia Balmaceda Lazcano, Chile
Maja Edel Foget, Denmark
Ruby G. Bradley, U.S.A.
Isabel Maitland Stewart, U.S.A.
Genevieve de Galard-Terraube, France
Genevieve Ponsot, France
Jeanne Gavouyere, France
Despina Chouroglou, Greece
Nina Carakiozides, Greece
Margaretta Craig, India
Florence Taylor, India
Takeno Tanimoto, Japan
Haya Ishibashi, Japan
Ingrid Wyller, Norway
Anna Holthe, Norway
Begum Ismat Khanum Shah, Pakistan
Sister Sofie Kienzle, Federal Republic of Germany
Sister Marie Schickinger, Federal Republic of Germany
Gerda Dreiser, Federal Republic of Germnay
Sister Ella Priscilla Jorden, United Kingdom
Eva-Ulrika Beck-Friis, Sweden
Verna Hagman, Sweden
Sister Julie Fanny Lina Hofmann, Switzerland
Sister Jane McLarty, Union of South Africa
1957 Joan Abbott, Australia
Ana Maria Cermak, Bolivia
Helen G. McArthur, Canada
Maria Luisa Torres de la Cruz, Chile
Sister Eva Lyngby, Denmark
Zelna Mollerup, Denmark
Sigrid Eleonora Larsson, Finland
Anne Valette, France
Jeanne Le Camus, France
Regine Kohler, Federal Republic of Germany
Clare Port, Federal Republic of Germany
Sigridur Bachmann, Iceland
Tehmina K. Adranvala, India
Ellen Lund, India

Rosetta Sheridan, India
Mimy Rigat Macchi, Italy
Bice Enriques, Italy
Hisako Nagashima, Japan
Chiyo Mikami, Japan
Nabiha Salameh Wirr, Jordan
Sister Kuk Sin-bok, North Korea
Sister Li Myong-oo, North Korea
Hyo Chung Lee, South Korea
Marcelle Hochar, Lebanon
Eva Helou Serhal, Lebanon
Catherine Lynette Wells, New Zealand
Sister Martha Palm, Norway
Gladys Maure Hodgson, Pakistan
Dame Elizabeth Cockayne, United Kingdom
Elizabeth K. Porter, U.S.A.
Marion W. Sheahan, U.S.A.
1959 Phyllis Mary Daymon, Australia
Patricia Downes Chomley, Australia
Amanda Brieba de Lorca, Chile
Signe Henriette Vest, Denmark
Dorothea Frederikke Bengtzen, Denmark
Maria Elvira Yoder, Ecuador
Helene Rouvier, France
Emma Ruidavetz, France
Marguerite Patrimonio, France
Luise von Oertzen, Federal Republic of Germany
Louise Sophie Knigge, Federal Republic of Germany
Mary Edith McKay Buchanan, India
Aki Oku, Japan
Koto Imaru, Japan
Oshie Kinutani, Japan
Milica Zelovic, Yugoslavia
Frances Lee Whang, South Korea
A.E.W. Chr. Engelberts, Netherlands
Flora Jean Cameron, New Zealand
Borghild Kessel, Norway
Karin Louise Naess, Norway
Salma Tarin, Pakistan
Patricia E. Intenga, Philippines
Catalina Evangelista, Philippines
Effie J. Taylor, U.S.A.
Lucile Petry Leone, U.S.A.
Ruth Sleeper, U.S.A.
1961 Margaret Jean Moloney, Australia
Jean Evelyn Headberry, Australia
Paulina Perelman de Wilhelm, Chile
Blanca Luarte de Cavieres, Chile
Ellen Johanne Broe, Denmark
Anne Marie Krohn, Finland
Sen. Sister Benigna Niggl, Federal Republic of Germany
Marianne Petersen, Federal Republic of Germany
Maliese von Bechtolsheim, Federal Republic of Germany
Sister Olive Laura Colquhoun, Great Britain
Marjorie Eadon Craven, Great Britain
Mariam Korah, India
Sister Stella Diana, Italy
Sister Carolina Cresto Calvo, Italy
Sister Carolina Salvati Accolti Gil, Italy
Haru Shinozaki, Japan
Hideko Yamazaki, Japan
Yae Ibuka, Japan
Young-Jin Kim, South Korea
Sin-Eun Choi, South Korea
Doris Ogilvy Ramsay, New Zealand
Edith Mary Rudd, New Zealand
Sister Annie Margareth Skau, Norway
Amy Sajjad, Pakistan

Julita V. Sotejo, Philippines
Maria Stencel, Poland
Wanda Lorenczuk, Poland
Emma Dagmar Stenbeck, Sweden
Constance Anne Nothard, Union of South Africa
Irina Nikolaievna Levtchenko, U.S.S.R.
Lydia Philippovna Savtchenko, U.S.S.R.
Pearl McIver, U.S.A.
Sister Charles Marie (Frank), U.S.A.
Cecilia H. Haugues, U.S.A.

1963 Rose Zelma Huppatz, Australia
Maria Hafner, Austria
Sister Khin Ohn Mya, Burma
Mona Gordon Wilson, Canada
Elena Velasco de Castillo, Chile
Annemarie M.A. Van Bockhoven, Finland
Anne de Cadoudal, France
Germaine Tanguy, France
Yoland Bonnet de Paillerets, France
Sister Emmy Dorfet, German Democratic Republic
Sister Claudine Rohnisch, German Democratic
Republic
Margaret Gerhardt, Federal Republic of Germany
Berta Veeck, Federal Repbulic of Germany
Sister Ernestine Thren, Federal Republic of Ger-
many
Janet Patience Adams, Great Britain
Edith H. Paull, India
Rev. Mother Mary Martin, Ireland
Virginia Benussi, Italy
Eleonora Masini Lucceti, Italy
Yae Abe, Japan
Mitsu Yoshino, Japan
Kiyo Kawashima, Japan
Jeannette L. King, Liberia
Mary Ann Gidall, New Zealand
Maj. Margaret Caroline Bearcroft, Pakistan
Florita Loberiza Legayada, Philippines
Capt. Angelina R. Castro, Philippines
Irene M. Abelgas, Philippines
Rosario Andaya, Philippines
Ri-Kil Won, Republic of Korea (South)
Ioana Cruceanu, Rumania
Elena Zeleniuc, Rumania
Iris Irene Marwick, Union of South Africa
Ann K. Magnussen, U.S.A.
Nan L. Dorsey, U.S.A.
R. Louise McManus, U.S.A.

1963 Special Posthumous Award: Nicole Vroonen, Belgium

1965 Lucy Wise MacIntosh, Australia
Mary Dorothy Edis, Australia
Ines Yuraszeck Cantin de Schmidt, Chile
Anna Knapcokova, Czechoslovakia
Lilia de Vendeuvre, France
Gertrud Baltzer, Federal Republic of Germany
Sister Irene von Scheel, Federal Republic of Ger-
many
Mary Sheelagh Patterson McConnel Folke, Great
Britain
Irene Komarik, Hungary
Lt. Col. Florence St. Claire Watkins, India
Kikuyo Uchiyama, Japan
Kiyo Ushioda, Japan
Kise Makita, Japan
Chung-Sun Kim, South Korea
Bo-Shin Lo, South Korea
Muriel Jessie Jackson, New Zealand
Maj. Honorata P. Seraspi, Philippines
Basilia Hernando, Philippines

Maria Menez Concepcion, Philippines
Wladystawa Steffen, Poland
Luba Blum-Bielicka, Poland
Victoria May Freeman, South Africa
Maria Savelievna Chkarletova, U.S.S.R.
Marie Dmitrievna Serdiouk, U.S.S.R.
Agnia Ivanovna Khablova, U.S.S.R.
Faina Khoussainovna Tchanycheva, U.S.S.R.
Zenaida Mikhailovna Toussnolobova-Martchenko,
U.S.S.R.

1967 Betty Constance Lawson, Australia
Gabrielle Revelard, Belgium
Alice M. Girard, Canada
Joanquina Escarpenter de Segeur, Chile
Marta Anna Sindlerova, Czechoslovakia
Aino Jenny Durchman, Finland
Lucie Roques, France
Marie Loprestis, France
Toni Stemmler, Germany Democratic Republic
Henni Thiessen, Federal Republic of Germany
Jula Muller, Federal Republic of Germany
Sister Anna Kellner, Federal Republic of Geramny
Elaine Hills-Young, Great Britain
Maria D. Eleftheriou, Greece
Elizabeth Kenny, Ireland
Shizu Kaneko, Japan
Iwano Niki, Japan
Moyo Suzuki, Japan
Ahn Kuy-Boon Kim, South Korea
Eul-Ran Kim, South Korea
Socorro Salamanca Dias, Philippines
Helen Nussbaum, Switzerland
Tawinwantg Dutiyabodhi, Thailand
Eugenie Maximovna Chevtschko, U.S.S.R.
Anna Romanovna Kousnetzova, U.S.S.R.
Irene Ivanova Klykova, U.S.S.R.
Claude Vassilievna Boutova, U.S.S.R.

1969 Col. Edna Nell Doig, Australia
Jean Elsie Ferguson, Australia
Sister Kathleen Tweedy, Australia
Elisa Ripamonti de Bulnes, Chile
Helena Misurdovna, Czechoslovakia
Elisabeth H. Larsen, Denmark
Irja Pohjala, Finland
Jeanne Euverte, France
Lucile Cantan, France
Johanna Held, Federal Repbulic of Germany
Eva G. Lancaster, Great Britain
Sarolta Deme, Hungary
Ilona Laborczi Smideliusz, Hungary
R. Murtasiah Soepomo, Indonesia
Anna Maria Platter, Italy
Shizv Koyama, Japan
Sei Tozawa, Japan
Sato Takahashi, Japan
Kwon Sok-Hei Kim, South Korea
Soon-Han New, South Korea
Nabila Saab Drooby, Lebanon
Danzangin Therma, Mongolia
Lidwina M. Ch. W. Verlinden, Netherlands
Sister Moya Clare McTamney, New Zealand
Mumtaz Painda Khan, Pakistan
Elisa R. Ochoa, Philippines
Felipa T. Javalera, Philippines
Zofia Muszka, Poland
Maria Hadera, Poland
Florentyna Wronska Kaczmarska, Poland
Charlotte Searle, South Africa
Agnes Wilson Simpson, South Africa
Dean Frances Reiter, U.S.A.

1971 Gr. Off. Betty Bristow Docker, Australia
Constance Amy Fall, Australia
Evelyn Agnes Pepper, Canada
Marie Hajkova, Czechoslovakia
Sister Luz Isabel Cueva Santana, El Salvador
Rita Birgitta Berggren, Finland
Marta Strasser, Democratic Republic of Germany
Gwyneth Ceris Jones, Great Britain
Marjorie Houghton, Great Britain
Aristea Papadatou, Greece
Olinga Fikiori, Greece
Otome Mori, Japan
Matsue Kobayashi, Japan
Soyo Kurimoto, Japan
Oak Soon Hong, South Korea
Shin Young Hong, South Korea
Dolores Campos de Estrada, Mexico
Batin Dulma, Mongolia
Dambin Norovdava, Mongolia
Helga Dagsland, Norway
Elsa Caroline Semmelmann, Norway
Safdari Beg, T.Q.A., Pakistan
Annie Sand, Philippines
A. Rabina Teodorica, Philippines
Doreen Henrietta Radloff, South Africa
Majsa Andrell, Sweden
Maria Zakharovna Chtcherbatchenko, U.S.S.R.
Zinaida Ivanovna Smirnova, U.S.S.R.
Matliuba Ichankhojaeva, U.S.S.R.
Dobrila Petronijevic, Yugoslavia
Darinka Nestorovic, Yugoslavia
Joveva Ivanka Karakjozova, Yugoslavia
Milesa Stanojlovic, Yugoslavia
Razija Ajanovic, Yugolsavia
Slavijanka Vlahceva, Yugoslavia

1973 Maria de Jesus Tovar Bermeo, Colombia
Maria Bizikova, Czechoslovakia
Ilona Ryskova, Czechoslovakia
Baroness Jacqueline Mallet, France
Beatrice de Foucaud, France
Yvonne Deschamps, France
Margarete Hildebrandt, German Democratic Republic
Ilse von Troschke, Federal Republic of Germany
Sister Mathilde Verhall, Federal Republic of Germany
Virginia Zanna, Greece
Sagy Ferencne, Hungary
Schonfeld Ferencne, Hungary
Lt. Col. Yeddu Vijayamma, India
Marina Caruana, Italy
Shima Yano, Japan
Ryu Saga, Japan
Masae Yukinaga, Japan
Keum Bong Lee, South Korea
Kwi Hyang Lee, South Korea
Soon Bong Kim, South Korea
Kofoworola Abeni Pratt, Nigeria
Angelita F. Corpus, Philippines
Helena Dabrowska, Poland
Elzbieta-Klementyna Krzywicka-Kowalik, Poland
Helen Joyce Cholmeley, United Kingdom
Sonia Denie Stromwall, United Kingdom
Maria Juana Marchesi de Podesta, Uruguay
Vera Sergueevna Kachtcheeva, U.S.S.R.
Matrena Semienovna Netchiportchukova, U.S.S.R.
Maria Petrovna Smirnova, U.S.S.R.
Djulietta Vartanovna Bagdasaryan, U.S.S.R.
Salipa Koublanova, U.S.S.R.

Sister Dina Urbancic, Yugoslavia
Sister Sita Lovrencic-Bole, Yugoslavia
Sister Jugoslava Polk-Bregant, Yugoslavia
Sister Ruza Stojanova, Yugoslavia

1975 Jeanette Ouelett, Canada
Karla Petrovicova, Czechoslovakia
Anna Benesova, Czechoslovakia
Anne Marie Beauchais, France
Christiane Sery, France
Sister Ilse Giese, German Democratic Republic
Sister Isa, Duchess von der Goltz, Federal Republic of Germany
Catherine Megapanou, Greece
Roza Almassy, Hungary
Zofia Maroskozi, Hungary
Marianne Tuapattinaya-Lohonauman, Indonesia
Fumiko Hosokawa, Japan
Matsuko Takase, Japan
Toyo Oka, Japan
Margaret Kattan, Jordan
Sung Soon Yew, South Korea
Bok Eum Kim, South Korea
Catherina M. MacKenzie, South Korea
Tourin Badamlynkhur, Mongolia
Sister Ngaire Kirkpatrick Simpson, New Zealand
Mumtaz Salma Lodhi, Pakistan
Irene F. Francia, Philippines
Maria Aleksandrowicz, Poland
Irena Weiman, Poland
Krystyna Stankowska, Poland
Julia Nenko, Poland
Remone Susan Quinn, United Kingdom
Vera Ivanovna Ivanova, U.S.S.R.
Ludmila Antonovna Rodiniova, U.S.S.R.
Nadeja Andreevna Boyko, U.S.S.R.
Sophia Vassilievna Goloukhova, U.S.S.R.
Razia Chakenovna Iskakova, U.S.S.R.
Evdokia Pavlovna Vartzaba, U.S.S.R.
Ekaterina Efimovna Sirenko, U.S.S.R.

1977 Patricia G. Deal, Australia
Bartz Schultz, Australia
Dorothy M. Percy, Canada
Maria Artigas Valls, Chile
Sister Anna Sipova, Czechoslovakia
Angela Zacharova, Czechoslovakia
Ruth Saynajarvi, Finland
Sister Senta Herdam, German Democratic Republic
Hanna Stoltenhoff, Federal Republic of Germany
Cleopatre Avayianou, Greece
Gabriella Majoros, Hungary
Erzsebet Karpati, Hungary
Bjarney Samuelsdottir, Iceland
Elisabetta Tufarelli Galati, Italy
Shizu Nagashio, Japan
Hana Koga, Japan
Masu Yumaki, Japan
Fumiko Watanabe, Japan
Young Nok Lee, South Korea
Marie Lysnes, Norway
Begum Mumtaz Chughtai, Pakistan
Lt. Col. Saula R. Magdaraog, Philippines
Juana Bactat, Philippines
Halina Szczudlowska, Poland
Janina Glinowicz, Poland
Wanda Wozniak, Poland
Maria Zakrzewska, Poland
Maria Elizabeth Venter, South Africa
Concepcion Bermejo Ruiz, Spain
Yvonne Hentsch, Switzerland
Somrak Hutinda, Thailand

Helen C. Fraser, United Kingdom
Patricia M. Ash, United Kingdom
Neza Jarnovic, Yugoslavia
Sasa Javorina, Yugoslavia
Mihaela Terzic, Yugoslavia

Anna Fillmore Award
Lucille Petry Leone Award
NLN Distinguished Service Award
Mary Adelaide Nutting Award
Linda Richards Award
NATIONAL LEAGUE FOR NURSING
10 Columbus Circle, New York, N.Y. 10019 (212/582-1022)

The Anna Fillmore Award, which consists of a plaque, recognizes contributions in development and administration of community health services on a local, state or national level.

1977   Eva M. Reese

The Lucile Petry Leone Award, which carries a $500 honorarium, is given every two years to an outstanding nurse-teacher with no more than seven years of teaching experience in the last 10 years.

1967   Martha Clyde Davis
1969   Kathryn E. Barnard
1971   Ada Sue Hinshaw
1973   Rhoda B. Epstein
1975   Lillian Gatlin Stokes
1977   Gail Elaine Wiscarz Stuart

The NLN Distinguished Service Award honors an individual, groups or team with presentation of a Steuben crystal item for outstanding leadership and service in the development or implementation of one or more of the League's goals.

1967   Mildred Gaynor
        Marion Sheahan
1969   Alma B. Gault
        Frances Reiter
1971   Mary C. Rockefeller
        The Albama League for Nursing
1973   Ruth Sleeper
1975   Anna Fillmore
1977   Lulu Wolf Hassenplug

The Mary Adelaide Nutting Award, which consists of a silver medal, is given every two years to honor outstanding leadership and achievement in nursing education or nursing service.

1944   Mary Adelaide Nutting
1947   International Council of Nurses
        Isabel Maitland Stewart
1949   Annie Warburton Goodrich
        Mary M. Roberts
1951   Frances Payne Bolton
        Maternity Center Association of New York
1955   Stella Goostray
1957   Nell V. Beeby
1959   Effie J. Taylor
1961   Mary Breckenridge
1963   R. Louise MacManus
1965   Lulu Wolf Hassenplug
1967   Helen Nahm
        Ruth B. Freeman

1969   Helen Bunge
        Mildred E. Newton
1971   Jessie M. Scott
        The W.K. Kellogg Foundation
1973   Lucile Petry Leone
        Esther Lucile Brown
1975   Jo Eleanor Elliott
        Mary Kelly Mullane
1977   Virginia Henderson

The Linda Richards Award, which is a pin bearing the likeness of Linda Richards mounted on a maltese cross, honors an individual actively engaged in nursing whose contribution is unique, of a pioneering nature or of such excellence as to merit national recognition.

1963   Mildred L. Montag
1967   Signe S. Cooper
1969   Billie B. Larch
1971   No award
1973   Hildegard Peplau
        Mabel Keaton Staupers
1975   Rosemary Wood
1977   M. Lucille Kinlein

Ebert Prize
Kilmer Prize
APhA Foundation-Academy of
Pharmaceutical Sciences Research
Achievement Awards
Hugo H. Schaefer Award
Daniel B. Smith Award
Pharmacy Literary Award
Kolthoff Gold Medal
Remington Honor Medal
AMERICAN PHARMACEUTICAL ASSOCIATION
2215 Constitution Ave. NW, Washington, D.C. 20037
(202/628-4410)

The Ebert Prize, which consists of a medal and certificate, is given annually for the best original paper published during the preceding year in the *Journal of Pharmaceutical Sciences*.

1874   Charles Mitchell
1875   No award
1876   No award
1877   Frederick B. Power
1882   John Uri Lloyd
1883-85 No awards
1886   Emlen Painter
1887   Edward Kremers
1888   Joseph Geisler
1890   William T. Wenzell
1891   John Uri Lloyd
1892-96 No awards
1897   James W. T. Knox with Albert B. Prescott
1898   Virgil Coblentz
1899   Henry Kraemer
1900   Edward Kremers with Oswald Schreiner
1901   No award
1902   J. O. Schlotterbeck with H. C. Watkins
1903   Frederick B. Power
1904   No award
1905   Ernest Schmidt

1906	J. O. Schlotterbeck with H. C. Watkins
1907	Frederick B. Power with Frank Tutin
1908	A. B. Stevens with L. E. Warren
1909	Henry Kraemer
1910	Harry M. Gordin
1911	W. A. Puckner with L. E. Warren
1915	E. N. Gathercoal
1916	John Uri Lloyd
1917	No award
1918	No award
1919	Arno Viehover with C. O. Ewing and J. F. Clevenger
1920	George D. Beal
1921	Albert Schneider
1922	W. L. Scoville
1923	Paul S. Pittenger
1924	H. V. Arny and Abraham Taub
1925	H. W. Youngken
1926	J. A. Handy with L. F. Hoyt
1927	L. W. Rowe
1928	E. E. Swanson
1929	John C. Krantz Jr.
1930	M. R. Thompson
1931	H. W. Youngken
1932	Zdenek F. Klan
1933	Ewin Gillis with H. A. Langenhan
1934	No award
1935	Marvin J. Andrews
1936	Glenn L. Jenkins with Charles F. Bruening
1938	Frederick F. Johnson
1939	B. V. Christensen with L. G. Gramling
1940	Lloyd C. Miller
1941	William J. Husa
1942	Ole Gisvold
1943	No award
1944	No award
1945	Paul Jannke with Howard Jensen
1946	Lloyd W. Hazleton with Kathleen D. Talbert
1947	Walter H. Hartung
1948	Harry W. Hind with Frank M. Goyan
1949	Robertson Pratt with Jean Dufrenoy, P. T. Sah and Louis A. Strait
1950	Rudolph H. Blythe with Harlan H. Tuthill and John J. Gulesich
1951	Louis W. Busse with Takeru Higuchi
1952	Lloyd M. Parks with Arnold J. Hennig and Takeru Higuchi
1953	Ole Gisvold with Arnold J. Hennig, G. G. Krishnamurtz, W. F. White and Raymond E. Hopponen
1954	Takeru Higuchi with A. Narshima Rao and D. A. Zuck
1955	Fred W. Schueler
1956	Martin Barr with Martin Katz
1957	John E. Christian
1958	Joseph V. Swintosky with Manford J. Robinson
1959	Sidney Riegelman with W. J. Crowell
1960	S. Morris Kupchan
1961	John G. Wagner with Stuart Long and William Veldcamp
1962	Einar Brochmann-Hanssen
1963	Edward R. Garrett
1964	Bernard Randall Baker
1965	Howard J. Schaeffer
1966	Alfred N. Martin with John L. Colaizzi and Adelbert M. Knevel
1967	Gordon H. Svoboda with Gerald A. Poore
1968	William I. Higuchi
1969	Gerhard Levy

1970	William I. Higuchi with A. H. Ghanem and Anthony P. Simonelli
1971	Thomas J. Bardos with C. K. Nevada and Z. F. Chmielewicz
1972	Kenneth B. Bischoff with Robert L. Dedrick, Daniel S. Zaharko and James A. Longstreth
1973	Gordon L. Flynn with Samuel Yalkowsky
1974	Jacob L. Varsano with Seymour G. Gilbert
1975	Gordon L. Amidon with Samuel H. Yalkowsky
1976	J. T. Carstensen with Pakdee Pothisiri
1977	Michael J. Pikal, Lee Floyd Ellis and Anita L. Lukes

The Kilmer Prize, which consists of a medal and a $200 honorarium, goes to a member of a graduating class in pharmacology for a meritorious work in pharmacognosy documented in a paper on the subject.

1937	Milton Kahn
1939	Guilford G. Gross
1940	Barbara Jacobs
1941	Richard O. Vycital
1942	Charles Wendt
1946	Elaine Friedberg
1947	David Breenberg
1948	Charles R. Chase Jr.
1951	W. J. Kelleher
1952	Lionel Ward
1953	John E. Gardner
1954	Dolores Ann Strittmater
1955	Berton E. Ballard
1956	Fenna Lee Fisher
1957	Lee C. Schramm
1958	Phillip Catalfomo
1959	Edward E. Gonzalez
1960	Edward Caldwell
1961	Roger Bruce McPhail
1962	Thomas F. Burks
1963	Donna J. Drinkard
1964	Gregory T. Sinner
1965	Judy Taeko Miyata
1966	Marilyn L. Montfort
1967	Robert D. Imholte
1969	Bruce H. Mock
1970	Garre E. Blair
1971	James C. Cloyd
1972	Steven R. Adams
1973	Patrick J. Davis
1974	John DiGiovanni
1975	Gaetana Forte
1976	Christopher J. Linden

The APhA Foundation-Academy of Pharmaceutical Sciences Research Achievement Awards annually honor outstanding individual achievements in specific areas of pharmacy. The awards consists of cash grants from various pharmaceutical firms and a certificate. Not all awards are given each year.

DRUG STANDARDS AND ASSAY (Justin L. Powers Award): changed to **PHARMACEUTICAL ANALYSIS** by 1973. Sponsored by Abbott Laboratories.

1962	John E. Christian
1963	Einar Brochmann-Hanssen
1964	Takeru Higuchi
1965	Lloyd C. Miller
1966	William J. Mader
1967	Frank H. Wiley
1968	Morris E. Auerbach
1969	Albert Q. Butler

1970 Edward R. Garrett
1973 Klaus Biemann
1974 No award
1975 Ernest G. Wollish
1976 No award
1977 No award

ADVANCEMENT OF PHARMACY: Discontinued.

1962 Troy C. Daniels
1963 Linwood F. Tice
1964 No award
1965 Louis C. Zopf
1966 Lloyd M. Parks
1967 Louis W. Busse
1968 George P. Hager

PHARMACODYNAMICS: changed to **PHARMACOLOGY** in 1972. Sponsored by Eli Lilly and Co.

1962 E. Leong Way
1963 Lawrence C. Weaver
1964 Tom S. Miya
1965 Ewart A. Swinyard
1966 Joseph P. Buckley
1967 Karl H. Beyer Jr.
1968 Allan H. Conney
1969 David H. Tedeschi
1970 Sidney Riegelman
1971 No award
1972 Lewis S. Schanker
1973 No award
1974 No award
1975 Erminio Costa
1976 No award
1977 Louis S. Harris

NATURAL PRODUCTS: Sponsored by Merck Sharp and Dohme until 1970, and since then by FMC Corp., Avicel Dept.

1962 Ole Gisvold
1963 Gordon H. Svoboda
1964 Taito O. Soine
1965 S. Morris Kupchan
1966 Varro E. Tyler, Jr.
1967 John C. Craig
1968 William I. Taylor
1969 Egil Ramstad
1970 Monroe Wall
1971 No award
1972 No award
1973 No award
1974 Norman R. Farnsworth
1975 No award
1976 Heinz G. Floss
1977 No award

PHYSICAL PHARMACY: changed to **PHARMACEUTICS** in 1974; sponsored by Parke, Davis and Co. until 1970 and since then by Syntex Corp.

1962 Takeru Higuchi
1963 Edward R. Garrett
1964 Joseph V. Swintosky
1965 Dale E. Wurster
1966 Eino Nelson
1967 Alfred N. Martin
1968 Sidney Riegelman
1969 Gerhard Levy
1970 William I. Higuchi
1971 No award
1972 No award

1973 Arnold Beckett
1975 John L. Lach
1976 No award
1977 Jens T. Carstensen

STIMULATION OF RESEARCH: sponsored by Smith Kline and French Foundation.

1962 Glenn L. Jenkins
1963 Rudolph H. Blythe
1964 Arthur E. Schwarting
1965 Arthur H. Uhl
1966 W. Lewis Nobles
1967 Takru Higuchi
1968 Daniel H. Murray
1969 Walter Fred Enz
1970 No award
1971 No award
1972 Bernard B. Brodie
1973 No award
1974 No award
1975 No award
1976 Milo Gibaldi
1977 No award

PHARMACEUTICAL AND MEDICINAL CHEMISTRY: sponsored by The Upjohn Co.

1962 Joseph H. Burckhalter
1963 Bernard R. Baker
1964 James M. Sprague
1965 Edward E. Smissman
1966 John H. Biel
1967 Alfred Burger
1968 Joseph Sam
1969 Corwin H. Hansch
1970 William O. Foye
1972 Henry Rapoport
1973 No award
1974 Karl Folkers
1976 Everett May
1977 No award

The Hugo H. Schaefer Award honors contributions to the profession of pharmacy and especially to the American Pharmaceutical Assn.

1964 Hugo H. Schaefer
1965 Hubert H. Humphrey
1966 William S. Apple
1967 Wallace Werble
1969 E. Claiborne Robins
1970 No award
1971 Harry C. Shirkey
1972 No award
1973 Willard B. Simmons
1974 Gaylord A. Nelson
1975 No award
1976 Philip R. Lee
1977 No award

The Daniel B. Smith Award honors achievements in community pharmacy by a practitioner distinguished by outstanding personal and professional performance. The award is a bronze medallion.

1965 Eugene V. White
1966 Raymond L. Dunn
1967 James W. Moore
1968 Arnold Snyder
1969 David J. Krigstein
1970 William F. Appel
1971 Wallace S. Klein

1972 Paul W. Lofholm	1949 Ernest Little
1973 Martin Rein	1950 Edwin Leigh Newcomb
1974 Kenneth E. Tiemann	1951 Hugo H Schaefer
1975 Morris Boynoff	1952 Patrick Henry Costello
1976 Donald J. Wernik	1953 Hugh C. Muldoon
1977 William R. Bacon	1955 Roy Bird Cook

The Section on Pharmacy Literary Award recognizes the best contribution to pharmacy literature made by an association member during the preceeding year. It must deal with the practice of pharmacy in which factual knowledge is incorporated into patient-related service or management, or be of scientific or research nature. The award consists of a plaque.

1956 Frank W. Moudry
1957 W. Paul Briggs
1958 Eli Lilly
1959 Justin L. Powers
1960 Ivor Griffith
1962 Harry J. Anslinger
1963 Glenn L. Jenkins
1964 Robert A. Hardt
1965 K. K. Chen

1965 Lt. Cdr. Theodore W. Tober
1966 Lowell R. Pfau
1967 Jules M. Meisler
1968 Joseph F. Gallelli
1969 Capt. William J. Briner
1970 Lt. Lloyd A. Fox
1971 Capt. Glidden N. Libby
1972 Douglas G. Christian
1973 Clarence L. Fortner
1974 William A. Cornelis with Clarence L. Fortner and Douglas Christian

1967 William S. Apple
1969 George F. Archambault
1970 Donald E. Francke
1971 Linwood F. Tice
1972 Glenn Sonnedecker
1973 Grover C. Bowles
1974 Lloyd M. Parks
1975 Albert Doerr
1976 Melvin W. Green
1977 No award

The Kolthoff Gold Medal, which carries a $1,000 honorarium, is awarded every two years to a scientist who has contributed significantly to the advancement of pharmaceutical analysis. The nominee is selected by the Award Committee of the Academy's Section on Pharmaceutical Analysis and Control.

1967 I. M. Kolthoff
1969 A. J. P. Martin
1971 Lyman C. Craig
1973 Egon Stahl
1975 Sidney Siggia

The Remington Honor Medal is given each year to the individual who has done the most for American pharmacy during the year of whose contributions to the advancement of pharmacy over a period of years have been outstanding.

1919 James Hartley Beal
1920 John Uri Lloud
1922 Henry Vincome Arny
1923 Henry Hurd Rusby
1924 George Mahlon Beringer
1925 Henry Milton Whelpley
1926 Henry A. B. Dunning
1928 Charles H. LaWall
1929 Wilbur Lincoln Scoville
1930 Edward Kremers
1931 Ernest Fullerton Cook
1932 Eugene G. Eberle
1933 Evander F. Kelly
1934 Sir Henry S. Wellcome
1935 Samuel Louis Hilton
1936 Edmund Norris Gathercoal
1937 J. Leon Lascoff
1938 Henry C. Christensen
1940 Robert L. Swain
1941 George D. Beal
1942 Josiah K. Lilly
1943 Robert P. Fischelis
1944 H. Evert Kendig
1945 Joseph Rosin
1947 Rufus Ashley Lyman
1948 Andrew Grover DuMez

Award for Excellence
International Award for Excellence
Edward W. Browning Achievement Award
Sedgwick Memorial Award
Matthew Rosenhaus Lecture
AMERICAN PUBLIC HEALTH ASSOCIATION
1015 Eighteenth St. NW, Washington, D.C. 20036
(202/467-5450)

The annual Award for Excellence, which consists of $5,000 and a Steuben Glass gift, is given for a recognized contribution to an individual at a point in his/her career where further contributions can be expected in the field of public health. Nominations are solicited from experts in the field, and the recipient is selected by an awards committee.

1973 H. Jack Geiger
1974 John D. Rockefeller III
1975 Kurt W. Deuschle
1976 June Jackson Christmas
1977 Sam Shapiro

The annual International Award for Excellence, consisting of $5,000 and a Steuben Glass gift, carries the same criteria and involves the same selection process as the national award above.

1973 James Westland Wright
1974 Nevin Stewart Scrimshaw
1975 Donald A. Henderson
1976 David J. Sencer
1977 Milton I. Roemer

The Edward W. Browning Achievement Award, which carries on honorarium of $5,000 and a medal, is given for outstanding contribution to the prevention of disease. A special Awards Committee selects the recipient.

1971 B. Russell Franklin
1972 E. Cuyler Hammond

1973 Hildrus A. Poindexter
1974 Harriet L. Hardy
1975 C. Henry Kempe
1976 John W. Knutson
1977 John C. Hume

The Sedgwick Memorial Medal is given annual for distinguished service and the advancement of public health knowledge and practice.

1929 Charles V. Chapin
1930 Theobald Smith
1931 George W. McCoy
1932 William H. Park
1933 Milton J. Rosenau
1934 Edwin O. Jordan
1935 Haven Emerson
1936 Frederick F. Russell
1938 Wade H. Frost
1939 Thomas Parran
1940 Hans Zinsser
1941 Charles Armstrong
1942 C.E.A. Winslow
1943 James S. Simmons
1944 Ernest W. Goodpasture
1946 Karl F. Meyer
1947 Reginald M. Atwater
1948 Abel Wolman
1949 Henry V. Baughan
1950 Rolla Eugene Dyer
1951 Edward S. Godfrey, Jr.
1952 Kenneth F. Maxcy
1953 Carl E. Buck
1954 Willson G. Smillie
1955 Albert J. Chesley
1956 Frederick W. Jackson
1957 Lowell J. Reed
1958 Martha M. Eliot
1959 Louis I. Dublin
1960 Fred T. Foard
1961 Frank G. Boudreau
1962 Ira V. Hiscock
1963 Gaylord V. Anderson
1964 Leona Baumgartner
1965 Willimina R. Walsh
1966 Fred L. Soper
1967 George Baehr
1968 Herman E. Hilleboe
1969 Marion W. Sheahan
1970 Hugh R. Leavell
1971 Margaret G. Arnstein
1972 Paul B. Cornely
1973 Isidore S. Falk
1974 Myron E. Wegman
1975 Leroy E. Burney
1976 Malcolm H. Merrill
1977 Lester Breslow

The Matthew B. Rosenhaus Lecture is an annual honor bestowed on an individual who shares his/her views on a topic of importance and timeliness in public health. An awards committee selects the recipient, who receives a $2,000 honorarium.

1973 Gov. Raymond P. Shaefer
1974 James Haughton
1975 John Higginson
1976 Mark Lalonde
1977 Sen. Edward M. Kennedy

Francis Amory Prize
AMERICAN ACADEMY OF ARTS AND SCIENCES
154 Allendale St., Jamaica Plain Station, Boston, Mass. 02130 (617/522-2400 and 522-0733)

The Francis Amory Prize, which carries an honorarium was initially awarded every seven years for research or discoveries in human reproductive-organ diseases, particularly those of males, with several awards presented at the end of each septennium. After the 1968 awards, the requirement of a seven-year interval was removed.

1940 Ernest Laquer, Amsterdam, Netherlands
      Joseph Francis McCarthy, New York
      Carl Richard Moore, Chicago
      Hugh Hampton Young, Baltimore
1947 Alexander Benjamin Gutman, New York
      Charles Brenton Huggins, Chicago
      Willem Johan Kolff, Kampen, Netherlands
      Guy Frederic Marrian, Edinburgh, Scotland
      George Nicholas Papanicolaou, New York
      Selman Abraham Waksman, New Brunswick, N.J.
1954 Frederic E.B. Foley, St. Paul, Minn.
      Choh Hao Li, Berkeley, Calif.
      Thaddeus R.R. Mann, Cambridge, U.K.
      Terence J. Millin, London
      Warren O. Nelson, Iowa City, Iowa
      Frederick J. Wallace, New York
      Lawson Wilkins, Baltimore
1961 J. Hartwell Harrison, David M. Hume and Joseph E. Murray, Boston
      John P. Merrill, Benjamin F. Miller and George W. Thorn, Boston
      Harry Goldblatt and Eugene Poutasse, Cleveland
      Eugene M. Bricker and Justin J. Cordonnier, St. Louis
1968 Geoffrey Wingfield Harris, Oxford, U.K.
      Hans Henriksen Ussing, Copenhagen
1975 Karl Sune Detlof Bergstrom, Stockholm, Sweden
      Min-Chueh Chang, Worcester, Mass.
      Howard Guy Williams-Ashman, Chicago
1977 Mary Frances Lyon, Harwell, U.K.
      Jean D. Wilson, Dallas
      Elwood Vernon Jensen, Chicago

Aviation &

Aeronautics

Contents

Related Awards

H. H. Arnold Award

AIR FORCE ASSOCIATION
1750 Pennsylvania Ave. NW, Washington, D.C. 20006
(202/637-3300)

The H.H. Arnold Award is given annually to an individual or group to honor outstanding contributions to aerospace. The award, which consists of a plaque, is in effect a "Man of the Year" award.

1948   W. Stuart Symington, Secretary of the Air Force
1949   Maj. Gen. William H. Tunner and the men of the Berlin Airlift
1950   Airmen of the United Nations in the Far East
1951   Lt. Gen. Curtis E. LeMay and the personnel of Strategic Air Command
1952   Lyndon B. Johnson, U.S. Senator
        Joseph C. O'Mahoney, U.S. Senator
1953   Gen. Hoyt S. Vandenberg, former Chief of Staff, U.S. Air Force
1956   W. Stuart Symington, U.S. Senator
1957   Edward P. Curtis, Special Assistant to the President
1958   Maj. Gen. Bernard A. Schriever, Commander, Ballistic Missile Division, ARDC
1959   Gen. Thomas S. Power, Commander in Chief, Strategic Air Command
1960   Gen. Thomas D. White, Chief of Staff, U.S. Air Force
1961   Lyle S. Garlock, Assistant Secretary of the Air Force
1962   A. C. Dickieson, Bell Telephone Laboratories
        John R. Pierce, Bell Telephone Laboratories
1963   363d Tactical Reconnaissance Wing, TAC, 4080th Strategic Wing, Strategic Air Command
1964   Gen. Curtis E. LeMay, chief of staff, U.S. Air Force
1965   Second Air Division, PACAF, U.S. Air Force
1966   8th, 12th, 355th, 366th, and 388th Tactical Fighter Wings; 432d and 460th Tactical Reconnaissance Wings
1967   Gen. William W. Momyer, Commander, 7th Air Force, PACAF
1968   Col. Frank Borman, Capt. James Lovell, Lt. Col. William Anders, Appollo 8 Crew
1969   No award
1970   J.L. Atwood, Lt. Gen. Samuel C. Phillips, Neil Armstrong, Col. Edwin E. Aldrin, Jr. and Col. Michael Collins, Apollo 11 Team
1971   John S. Foster, Jr., Director of Defense Research and Engineering
1972   Air Units of the Allied Forces in Southeast Asia (Air Force, Navy, Army, Marine Corps, and the Vietnamese Air Force)
1973   Gen. John D. Ryan, U.S. Air Force
1974   Gen. George S. Brown, Chairman, Joint Chiefs of Staff
1975   James R. Schlesinger, Secretary of Defense
1976   Barry M. Goldwater, U.S. Senator
1977   Howard W. Cannon, U.S. Senator

Aeroacoustics Award
Aerospace Communications Award
Air Breathing Propulsion Award
Aircraft Design Award

AIAA Educational Achievement Award
Chanute Flight Award
De Florenz Training Award
Distinguished Service Award
Dryden Research Lecture
Fluid and Plasmadynamics Award
Goddard Astronautics Award
Daniel Guggenheim Medal Award
Haley Space Flight Award
History Manuscript Award
Information Systems Award
William Littlewood Memorial Lecture Award
Mechanics and Control of Flight Award
Pendray Aerospace Literature Award
Reed Aeronautics Award
Research Award in Structural Mechanics
Simulation and Ground Testing Award
Space Science Award
Space Systems Award
Lawrence Sperry Award
Structures, Structural Dynamics and Materials Award
Support Systems Award
System Effectiveness and Safety Award
Thermophysics Award
Von Karman Lectureship in Astronautics
Wright Brothers Lectureship in Aeronautics
Wyld Propulsion Award

AMERICAN INSTITUTE OF AERONAUTICS AND ASTRONAUTICS
1290 Ave. of the Americas, New York, N.Y. 10019
(212/581-4300)

The Aeroacoustics Award, which consists of a medal and certificate, is presented annually for achievement in aircraft community noise reduction upon a decision by an honors and awards committee.

1975   Michael J. Lighthill
1976   Herbert Ribner
1977   John Ffowes Williams

The Aerospace Communications Award, which consists of a medal and certificate honors the achievement in the broad field of aerospace communications and is presented biennially on a decision by an honor and awards committee.

1968   Donald D. Williams
       Harold A. Rosen
1969   Eberhardt Rechtin
1970   Edmund J. Habib
1971   Siegfried H. Reiger
1972   Wilbur Pritchard
1974   Arthur C. Clark
1976   Robert F. Garbarini

The Air Breathing Propulsion Award, which consists of a medal and certificate, honors air breathing populsion advances, including those in turbo-machinery or any other approach dependent on atmospheric air. An honors and awards committee selects the winner.

1976   Frederick T. Rall, Jr.
1977   Edward Woll

The Aircraft Design Award, which consists of a medal and certificate, recognizes advancement in aircraft design or design technology. An honors and awards committee selects the winner.

1969   Harold W. Adams
1970   Harrison A. Storms
1971   Joseph F. Sutter
1972   Ben R. Rich
1973   Herman D. Barkey
1974   Richard T. Whitcomb
1975   Walter E. Fellers
1976   Kendall Perkins
1977   Howard A. Evans

The AIAA Educational Achievement Award, presented jointly with the ASEE Aerospace Division, consists of an honorarium in recognition of improvements of lasting influence to aerospace engineering education.

1976   Barnes W. McCormick, Jr.
1977   No award

The Chanute Flight Award, originally called the Octave Chanute Award, is a medal and certificate given to a pilot or test personnel for contributions to aeronautics. Until recently the award was made annually, but beginning in 1976, its frequency was changed to once every two years.

1939   Edmund T. Allen
1940   Howard Hughes
1941   Melvin N. Gough
1942   A.L. MacClain
1943   William H. McAvoy
1944   Benjamin S. Kelsey
1945   Robert T. Lamson
       Elliott Merrill
1946   Ernest A. Cutrell
1947   Lawrence A. Clousing
1948   Herbert H. Hoover
1949   Frederick M. Trapnell
1950   Donald B. MacDiarmid

1951   Marion E. Carl
1952   John C. Seal
1953   W.T. Bridgeman
1954   George E. Cooper
1955   Albert Boyd
1956   A.M. Johnston
1957   Frank K. Everest
1958   A. Scott Crossfield
1959   John P. Reeder
1960   Joseph J. Tymczyszyn
1961   Joseph A. Walker
1962   Neil Armstrong
1963   E.J. Bechtold
1964   Fred J. Drinkwater, III
       Robert C. Innis
1965   Alvin S. White
1966   Donald F. McKusker
       John L. Swigert, Jr.
1967   Milton O. Thompson
1968   William J. Knight
1969   William C. Park
1970   Jerauld P. Gentry
1971   William M. Magruder
1972   Donald R. Segner
1973   Cecil W. Powell
1974   Charles A. Sewell
1975   Alan L. Bean
       Owen K. Garriott
       Jack R. Lousma
1976   Thomas Stafford

The De Florenz Training Award, which consists of a medal and certificate, is given annually for improvements in aerospace training. An honors and awards committee selects the winner.

1965   Lloyd L. Kelly
1966   Warren J. North
1967   Edwin H. Link
1968   Joseph La Russa
1969   Gifford Bull
1970   Harold G. Miller
1971   Walter P. Moran
1972   James W. Campbell
1973   Carroll H. Woodling
1974   Hugh Harrison Hurt, Jr.
1975   John C. Dusterberry
1977   John E. Duberg

The Distinguished Service Award, which consists of a certificate, recognizes contributions by an AIAA member to the institute over a period of years, based on selection by the president, president-elect and vice presidents.

1968   Harvey M. Cook, Jr.
1969   Peter C. Johnson
1970   H. Dana Moran
1971   Frederick H. Roever
1972   William F. Chana
1973   H. Norman Abramson
1974   Charles Appleman
1975   Warren Curry
1977   Kenneth Randle

The Dryden Research Lecture, succeeding the Research Award, recognizes achievement in basic research in the advancement of aeronautics and astronautics. The award consists of a medal and citation, and is made upon decision of an honors and awards committee with the approval of the board of directors.

RESEARCH AWARD

1961   James A. Van Allen
1962   A. Theodore Forrester
1964   Henry M. Shuey
1965   Wallace D. Hayes
1966   Shao-Chi Lin
1967   Edward W. Price

DRYDEN RESEARCH LECTURE

1968   Hans W. Liepmann
1969   Gerald P. Kuiper
1970   Bernard Budiansky
1971   Coleman D. Donaldson
1972   John C. Houbolt
1973   Herbert Friedman
1974   Herbert F. Hardrath
1975   Antonio Ferri
1976   Anatol Roshko
1977   Abraham Hertzberg

The Fluid and Plasmadynamics Award, which consists of a medal and certificate, recognizes contributions to the understanding of the behavior of liquids and gases in motion or of the physical properties and dynamical behavior of matter in the plasma state as related to aeronautics and astronautics. An honors and awards committee selects the winner.

1976   Mark Morkovin
1977   Harvard Lomax

The Goddard Astronautics Award has been broadened from the engineering science of propulsion to include the entire field of astronautics. The award consists of a medal and citation, and is given upon a decision by an honors and awards committee with the approval of the board of directors. Now the Institute's highest honor, it combines the ARS Goddard Memorial Award and Louis W. Hill Space Transportation Award.

ARS GODDARD MEMORIAL AWARD

1948   John Shesta
1949   Calvin M. Bolster
1950   Lovell Lawrence, Jr.
1951   Robert C. Traux
1952   Richard W. Porter
1953   David A. Young
1954   A.M.O. Smith
1955   E.N. Hall
1956   Chandler C. Ross
1957   Thomas F. Dixon
1958   Richard B. Canright
1959   Samuel K. Hoffman
1960   Theodore von Karman
1961   Wernher von Braun
1962   Robert R. Gilruth

GODDARD AWARD

1965   Frank Whittle
1966   Hans J.P. von Ohain
       A.W. Blackman
       George D. Lewis
1967   Robert O. Bullock
       Irving A. Johnson
       Seymour Lieblein
1968   Donald C. Berkey

       Ernest C. Simpson
       James E. Worsham
1969   Perry W. Pratt
       Stanley G. Hooker
1970   Gerhard Neumann
1972   Howard E. Schumacher
       Brian Brimelow
       Gary Plourde
1973   Edward S. Taylor
1974   Paul D. Castenholz
       Richard Mulready
       John Sloop
1975   George Rosen
       Gordon Holbrook
1976   Edward Prince

LOUIS W. HILL SPACE TRANSPORTATION AWARD

1958   Robert H. Goddard
1959   James A. Van Allen
1960   S.K. Hoffman
       Thomas F. Dixon
1961   Robert R. Gilruth
1962   C. Stark Draper
1963   Robert J. Parks
       Jack M. James
1964   Hugh L. Dryden
1965   Wernher von Braun
1966   W. Randolph Lovelace, II
1967   Abe Silverstein
1968   W.H. Pickering
1969   George M. Low
1970   Christopher C. Kraft, Jr.
1971   Hubertus Strughold
1972   David G. Hoag
       Richard H. Battin
1973   Kurt H. Debus
1974   Rocco A. Petrone
1975   Glenn Lunney

GODDARD ASTRONAUTICS AWARD

1977   James S. Martin, Jr.

The Daniel Guggenheim Medal Award honors notable achievement in the advancement of aeronautics and is presented jointly by AIAA, American Society of Mechinical Engineers and Society of Automotive Engineers. The award consists of a medal and certificate.

1929   Orville Wright
1930   Ludwig Prandtl
1931   Frederick W. Lanchester
1932   Juan de la Cierva
1933   Jerome C. Unsaker
1934   William E. Boeing
1935   William F. Durand
1936   George W. Lewis
1937   Hugh Eckener
1938   Alfred H.R. Fedden
1939   Donald W. Douglas
1940   Glenn L. Martin
1941   Juan T. Trippe
1942   James H. Doolittle
1943   Edmund Turney Allen
1944   Lawrence D. Bell
1945   Theodore P. Wright
1946   Frank Whittle
1947   Lester Durand Gardner
1948   Leroy Randle Grumman
1949   Edward Pearson Warner
1950   Hugh Latimer Dryden

1951	Igor Ivan Sikorsky
1952	Sir Geoffrey De Havilland
1953	Charles A. Lindberg
1954	Clarence Decatur Howe
1955	Theodore von Karman
1956	Frederick B. Rentschler
1957	Arthur Emmons Raymond
1958	William Littlewood
1959	Sir George R. Edwards
1960	Grover Loening
1961	Jerome Lederer
1962	James H. Kindelberger
1963	James S. McDonnell, Jr.
1964	Robert H. Goddard
1965	Sir Sydney Camm
1966	Charles Stark Draper
1967	George Schairer
1968	H.M. Horner
1969	H. Julian Allen
1970	Jakob Ackeret
1971	Sir Archibald E. Russell
1972	William C. Mentzer
1973	William McPherson Allen
1974	Floyd L. Thompson
1975	Duane Wallace
1976	Marcel Dassault
1977	No award

The Haley Space Flight Award, originally called the Astronautics Award, is given for outstanding contribution by an astronaut or flight test personnel. The award, from now on to be made every two years, is given to the winner selected by an honors and awards committee, and consists of a medal and citation.

ASTRONAUTICS AWARD

1954	Theodore von Karman
1955	Wernher von Braun
1956	Joseph Kaplan
1957	Krafft Ehricke
1958	Ivan C. Kincheloe, Jr.
1959	Walter R. Dornberger
1960	A. Scott Crossfield
1961	Alan Shepard
1962	John H. Glenn, Jr.
1963	Walter M. Schirra, Jr.
	Gordon Cooper
1964	Walter C. Williams
1965	Joseph S. Bleymaier

HALEY ASTRONAUTICS AWARD

1966	Neil A. Armstrong
	David R. Scott
1967	Edward H. White, II
1968	Virgil I. Grissom
1969	Donn F. Eisele
	R. Walter Cunningham
	Walter M. Schirra, Jr.
1970	Frank Borman
	James A. Lovell, Jr.
	William Anders
1971	John Swigert
	Fred W. Haise, Jr
	James A. Lovell, Jr.
1972	David Worden
	David Scott
	James Irwin
1973	John Young
	Thomas Mattingly, II

	Charles Duke, Jr.
1974	Paul J. Weitz
	Charles Conrad, Jr.
	Joseph P. Kerwin
1975	Gerald Carr
	William Pogue
	Edward Gibson
1976	William H. Dana
1977	No award

The History Manuscript Award, which consists of a medal and certificate, honors the winner of an annual competition for the best historical manuscript on science, technology and/or the impact of aeronautics and astronautics on society. A technical committee is responsible for selecting the winner.

1969	Milton Lomask
	Constance McLaughlin Green
1971	Richard C. Lukas
1972	Richard K. Smith
1973	William M. Leary, Jr.
1975	Richard P. Hallion
1977	Thomas Crouch

The Information Systems Award, which consists of a medal and certificate, is presented biennially for contributions to technical and/or management contributions to space and aeronautics computer-sensing aspects of information technology. An honors and awards committee selects the winner.

1977 Albert Hopkins, Jr.

The William Littlewood Memorial Lecture Award, which consists of an honorarium to be decided by a committee and a certificate, is given jointly by the AIAA and the Society of Automotive Engineers.

1971	Peter G. Masefield
1972	John Borger
1973	Richard Jackson
1974	Edward Wells
1975	Gerhard Neumann
1976	Raymond Kelly
	Franklin Kolk

The Mechanics and Control of Flight Award, which consists of a medal and certificate, honors outstanding recent technical or scientific contribution to the mechanics, guidance or control of flight. An honors and award committee selects the winner.

1967	Derek F. Lawden
1968	Robert V. Knox
1969	John P. Mayer
1970	Irving L. Ashkenas
	Duane T. McRuer
1971	George W. Cherry
	Kenneth J. Cox
	William S. Widnall
1972	John V. Breakwell
1973	Henry J. Kelley
1974	Harold Roy Vaughn
1975	Bernard Etkin
1976	Charles Murphy
1977	Joseph R. Chambers
	William P. Gilbert

The Pendray Aerospace Literature Award, formerly called the G. Edward Pendray Award, honors outstanding contributions to recent aeronautical and astronautical literature, preferably within the previous three years. High quality and the influence of the work are valued more highly than the underlying technological contributions The award consists of a medal and certificate and is the responsibility of a technical committee.

G. EDWARD PENDRAY AWARD

1951	George P. Sutton
1952	M.J. Zucrow
1953	M.S. Tsien
1954	Martin Summerfield
1955	Walter Dornberger
1956	Herman Oberth
1957	Grayson Merrill
1958	Homer E. Newell
1959	Ali B. Cambell
1960	Luigi Crocco
1961	Krafft Ehricke
1962	Howard E. Seifert
1964	Andrew G. Haley
1965	Dinsmore Alter
1966	A.K. Oppenheim
1967	Robert A. Gross
1968	Arthur E. Bryson, Jr.
1970	Wilmot N. Hess
1971	Nicholas J. Hoff
1972	Edward W. Price
1973	Marcus F. Heidmann
	Richard Priem
1974	Frederick Ordway
1975	William R. Sears
1976	Stanford S. Penner

PENDRAY AEROSPACE LITERATURE AWARD

1977	George Leitmann

The Reed Aeronautics Award, formerly the Sylvanus Albert Reed Award, honors the most notable achievement in aeronautical science and engineering. The award consists of a medal and citation, and is given upon a decision by an honors and awards committee with the approval of the board of directors.

1934	C.G. Rossby
	H.G. Willett
1935	Frank W. Caldwell
1936	Edward S. Taylor
1937	Eastman N. Jacobs
1938	Alfred Victor de Forest
1939	George J. Mead
1940	Hugh L. Dryden
1941	Theodore von Karman
1942	Igor I. Sikorsky
1943	Sanford A. Moss
1944	Fred E. Weick
1945	Charles S. Draper
1946	Robert T. Jones
1947	Galen B. Schubauer
	Harold K. Skramstad
1848	George W. Brady
1949	George S. Schairer
1950	Robert R. Gilruth
1951	E.H. Heinemann
1952	John Stack
1953	Ernest G. Stout
1954	Clark B. Millikan
1955	H. Julian Allen
1956	Clarence L. Johnson
1957	R.L. Bisplinghoff
1958	Victor E. Carbonera

1959	Karel J. Bossart
1960	John W. Becker
1961	Alfred J. Eggers, Jr.
1962	Walter C. Williams
1964	Abe Silverstein
1965	Arthur E. Raymond
1966	Clarence L. Johnson
1967	Adolph Busemann
1968	William H. Cook
1969	Rene H. Miller
1970	Richard T. Whitcomb
1971	Ira Grant Hedrick
1972	Max Munk
1973	I.E. Garrick
1974	Willis Hawkins
1975	Antonio Ferri
1976	George Spangenberg
1977	William C. Dietz

The Research Award in Structural Mechanics, given jointly by the AIAA and the Office of Naval Research, consists of a medal, certificate and full-time support at the winner's current income level, usually for one year, to honor and encourage research related closely to naval structural mechanics problems. Individuals may apply for this award. A screening committee of the AIAA reviews the applicants for final selection by the ONR.

1970	Stanley B. Dong
1971	Lawrence H.N. Lee
1972	Robert E. Nickell
1973	Robert M. Jones
1974	Dave Bushnell
1975	Edward Stanton
1976	No award
1977	No award

The Simulation and Ground Testing Award, which consists of a medal and a certificate, recognizes achievement in the development or utilization of technology procedures, facilities or model techniques for ground testing associated with astronautics or aeronautics. An honors and awards committee selects the winner.

1976	Bernhard H. Goethart
1977	No award

The Space Science Award, which consists of a medal and certificate, honors studies of the physics or atmosphere of celestial bodies or other related processes occurring in space or experienced by space vehicles. An honors and awards committee selects the winner.

1962	John R. Winkler
1963	No award
1964	Herbert Friedman
1965	Eugene N. Parker
1966	Francis S. Johnson
1967	Robert B. Leighton
1968	Kinsey A. Anderson
1969	Charles P. Sonnett
1970	Carl E. McIlwain
1971	William Ian Axford
1972	Norman F. Ness
1973	Paul W. Gast
1974	John H. Wolfe
1975	Murray Dryer
1976	Riccardo Giacconi
1977	Bruce Murray

The Space Systems Award, originally the Spacecraft

Design Award, honors achievement in systems analysis, design and implementation in spacecraft and launch vehicle technology. The award consists of a medal and certificate and is presented upon a decision of an honors and awards committee.

SPACECRAFT DESIGN AWARD

1969	Otto E. Bartoe, Jr.
1970	Maxime A. Faget
1971	Anthony J. Iorillo
1972	Thomas J. Kelly
1973	Harold A. Rosen
1974	Harold Lassen
1975	Caldwell C. Johnson, Jr.

SPACE SYSTEM AWARD

| 1977 | Walter O. Lowrie |

The Lawrence Sperry Award, which consists of a medal and certificate, honors a notable contribution by an individual 35 years of age or younger to the advancement of aeronautics or astronautics. An honors and awards committee selects the winners.

1936	William C. Rockefeller
1937	Clarence L. Johnson
1938	Russell C. Newhouse
1939	Charles M. Kearns, Jr.
1940	William B. Oswald
1941	E.G. Stout
1942	E.C. Wells
1943	William B. Bergen
1944	William H. Phillips
1945	Richard Hutton
1946	Peter R. Murray
1947	N.A.N. Gaylor
1948	Allen E. Puckett
1949	Alexander H. Flax
1950	Frank N. Piasecki
1951	R.C. Seamans, Jr.
1952	Dean R. Chapman
1953	Donald Coles
1954	A. Scott Crossfield
1955	Giles J. Strickroth
1956	George F. Jude
1957	Clarence A. Syvertson
1958	Robert G. Loewy
1959	James E. McCune
1960	Robert B. Howell
1961	Douglas G. Harvey
1962	Robert O. Pilland
1964	Daniel M. Tellep
1965	Rodney C. Wingrove
1966	Joe H. Engle
1967	Eugene F. Kranz
1968	Roy V. Harris
1969	Edgar C. Lineberry, Jr.
1970	Glenn S. Lunney
1971	Ronald L. Berry
1972	Sheila E. Widnall
1973	Dino A. Lorenzini
1974	Jan Rusby Tulinius
1975	David Bushnell
1976	No award
1977	Joseph L. Weingarten

The Structures, Structural Dynamics and Materials Award, which consists of a medal and certificate, honors scientific or technical contributions in aerospace structures, structural dynamics or materials. An honors and awards committee selects the winner.

1968	John C. Houbolt
1969	Holt Ashley
1970	Joseph D. Van Dyke, Jr.
1971	Nicholas J. Hoff
1972	M. Jonathan Turner
1973	Robert T. Schwartz
	George P. Peterson
1974	William D. Cowie
1975	Theodore H.H. Pian
1976	Charles Tiffany
1977	Walter J. Mykytow

The Support Systems Award, which consists of a medal and certificate, recognizes contributions to the over-all effectiveness of aeronautical or aerospace systems technology through improved support systems. An honors and awards committee selects the winner.

| 1976 | Gene A. Petry |
| 1977 | Thomas A. Ellison |

The System Effectiveness and Safety Award, which consists of a medal and certificate, recognizes contributions to system effectiveness or safety or related disciplines. An honors and awards committee selects the winner.

| 1977 | Thomas D. Matteson |
| | F. Stanley Nowlan |

The Thermophysics Award, which consists of a medal and certificate, honors recent technical or scientific contribution to thermophysics as related to thermal energy transfer and especially to the study of environmental effects of radiation. An honors and awards committee selects the winner.

| 1976 | Donald K. Edwards |
| 1977 | Chang-Lin Tien |

The Von Karman Lectureship in Astronautics, formerly the Von Karman Lecture, honors notable performance and technical distinction in astronautics. The award consists of a medal and citation, and is given upon a decision of an honors and awards committee with the approval of the board of directors.

VON KARMAN LECTURE

1962	Hugh L. Dryden
1964	Arthur Kantrowitz
1965	R.L. Bisplinghoff
1966	Nicholas J. Hoff
1967	Lester Lees
1968	William R. Sears
1979	Courtland D. Perkins
1970	Erik L. Mollo-Christensen
1971	Irmgard Flugge-Lotz
1972	Eugene Love
1973	Alan M. Lovelace
1974	Harrison Schurmeier
1975	I.E. Garrick

VON KARMAN LECTURESHIP IN ASTRONAUTICS

| 1977 | Joseph V. Charyk |

The Wright Brothers Lectureship in Aeronautics, formerly the Wright Brothers Lecture, recognizes leadership in aeronautics. The award consists of a medal and citation, and is given upon a decision by an honors and awards committee with the approval of the Board of Directors.

WRIGHT BROTHERS LECTURE

1937	B. Melville Jones
1938	Hugh L. Dryden
1939	Clark B. Millikan
1940	Sverte Pettersen
1941	Richard V. Southwell
1942	Edmund T. Allen
1943	W. S. Farren
1944	John Stack
1945	H. Roxbee Cox
1946	Theodore von Karman
1947	Sydney S. Goldstein
1948	Abe Silverstein
1949	A.E. Russell
1950	William Bollay
1951	P.B. Walker
1952	William Littlewood
1953	Glenn L. Martin
1954	Bo K.O. Lundberg
1955	R.L. Bisplinghoff
1956	Arnold Hall
1957	H. Julian Allen
1958	Maurice Roy
1959	Alexander H. Flax
1960	A.W. Quick
1961	Robert Jastrow
1962	M. James Lighthill
1964	George S. Schairer
1965	Gordon N. Patterson
1966	C. Stark Draper
1967	P. Poisson-Quinton
1968	Charles W. Harper
1969	Pierre Satre
1970	F.A. Cleveland
1971	Robert L. Lickley
1972	Franklin Kolk
1973	H. Schlichting
1974	A.M.O. Smith
1975	Henri Ziegler

WRIGHT BROTHERS LECTURESHIP IN AERONAUTICS

1976	J.L. Atwood
1977	Gero Madelung

The Wyld Propulsion Award, which consists of a medal and certificate, combines the former James H.Wyld Memorial Award and the Propulsion Award to honor achievement in the development or application of rocket propulsion systems. An honors and awards committee selects the winner.

PROPULSION AWARD

1948	Frank Malina
1949	James A. Van Allen
1950	Leslie Skinner
1951	William Avery
1952	A.L. Antonio
1953	Charles E. Bartley
1954	Harold W. Ritchey
1955	D.S. Miller
1956	Bruce H. Sage
1957	Levering Smith
1958	Barnet R. Adelman
1959	Ernest Roberts
1960	Ernst Stuhlinger
1961	Robert B. Young

1962	Samuel K. Hoffman
1964	David Altman

JAMES H. WYLD MEMORIAL AWARD

1954	Milton W. Rosen
1955	John P. Stapp
1956	Louis G. Dunn
1957	William H. Pickering
1958	Holger N. Toftoy
1959	K.J. Bossard
1960	Robert L. Johnson
1961	Harrison A. Storms
1962	William F. Raborn
1964	Joseph S. Bleymaier

JAMES H. WYLD PROPULSION AWARD

1965	Werner R. Kirchner
1966	Maurice J. Zucrow
1967	Adelbert O. Tischler
1968	Harold B. Finger
1969	Harold R. Kaufman
1970	Hans G. Paul
	Joseph G. Thibodaux, Jr.
1971	Luigi M. Crocco
1972	Karl Klager
1973	Gerard W. Elverum, Jr.
	Norman C. Reuel
1974	Clarence W. Schnare
1975	James Lazar
	Rodrick Spence
1976	Howard Seifert
1977	Martin Summerfield

Distinguished Public Service Award
Harry Lever Award
Special Citations
Monsanto Aviation Safety Award
Public Information Officer Awards
Public Relations Award

AVIATION/SPACE WRITERS ASSOCIATION
Cliffwood Rd., Chester N.J. 07930

AWA's Distinguished Public Service Award is a trophy presented annually to an individual who has "used the products of aviation and/or space technology to make exemplary contributions to the welfare and quality of life of fellow citizens."

1972	Frank Sinatra
1973	William G. Magruder
1974	Sen. Barry M. Goldwater
1975	Robert F. Six
1976	N.A.
1977	Michael Collins and Paul E. Garber

The Harry Lever Award annually recognizes outstanding service to AWA.

1958	LeRoy Whitman
1959	James J. Haggerty, Jr.
1960	M. L. (Bo) McLaughlin
1961	William A. Lookadoo
1962	Herbert O. Fisher
1963	Leon Shloss
1964	M. L. (Bo) McLaughlin
1965	William S. Beller
1966	E. H. Pickering

1967 Gerald J. McAllister
1968 Ronald S. Gall
1969 Lt. Col. Kenneth E. Grine, USAF
1970 Grover D. Nobles, Jr.
1971 Warren W. Kenn
1972 William F. Kaiser
1973 Warren H. Goodman and Kenneth S. Fletcher
1974 Robert G. Button and C. M. Plattner
1975 William J. McGinty
1976 Not available
1977 James R. Greenwood

The AWA annually honors individuals and organizations with special citations.

1965 Vern Haugland
     National Geographic Magazine
1967 Robert J. Serling
     Ronald S. Gall
1968 Ansel E. Talbert
1969 Wayne W. Parrish
     Maj. W. F. Gabella, USA
     Col. Mark A. Gilman, USAF
1970 Grumman Aircraft
     North American Rockwell
     Eric Burgess
     Frank J. Delear
     Louis R. Stockstill
     Jules Bergman
     Frank McGee
     Robert J. Sterling
     Robert Burkhardt
1971 Edward G. Uhl and Fairchild Industries
     Edgar E. Ulsamer
     Paul H. and Eleanore Wilkinson
     Grover Loening
1972 Brig. Gen. Thomas P. Coleman, USAF
1973 Richard L. Taylor
     Ansel E. Talbert
     Howard Benedict
     Philip J. Klass
     Dave Swaim
     Kenneth F. Weaver
     Laurence L. Doty
     Steven C. Paton
1974 James Street
     Edwin G. Pipp
     Joel N. Shurkin
     Karl Kristofferson
     Stephan Wikinson
     Richard B. Weeghman
     John T. Lyons
     Kenneth S. Fletcher
     Kenneth Hudson
     Larry Levy
     William D. Conner
     Carroll V. Glines
     Jerome Fanciulli
1975 Richard P. Benjamin
     Duane Cole
     David Crain
     Vern Haugland
     Ross MacKenzie
     John B. Meyer
     Marvin G. Miles
     Barry Schiff
     L.B. Taylor
     Charles L. Tracy
     Paul A. Turk
     John J. Nopper

Steven C. Paton
Julian R. Levine
1976 Not available
1977 Gladys E. Wise

THE MONSANTO AVIATION SAFETY AWARD, ADMINISTERED BY THE FLIGHT SAFETY FOUNDATION, WAS AWARDED ANNUALLY UNTIL 1969.

1958 Jerome Lederer
1959 Maj. Gen Joseph D. Caldara, USAF
1960 E. R. Quesada
1961 E. S. Calvert
1962 Otto E. Kirchner. Sr.
1963 Dr. William Littlewood
1964 Bo K. O. Lundbert
1965 Najeeb Halaby
1966 W. A. Patterson
1967 David D. Thomas
1968 Frank E. Christofferson
1969 Edwin A. Link

Public Information Officer Awards honor high standards in public information and effort performed by commissioned officers, enlisted personnel or civilian employees in the interest of aviation and space arms of the military and other branches of the federal government. The recipient of the award, which is sponsored by Grumman Corporation, is given a scroll and a silver tray. The various awards were restructured in 1972 into just one award.

ORVILLE WRIGHT AWARDS

1963 Maj Philip Salk, USAF
1964 Lt. Col. Stratton M. Appleman, USAF and Maj. Harold A. Susskind, USAF
1965 Maj. James C. Elliott, USAF
1966 Col. William J. McGinty, USAF
1967 Maj. Sydney Lester, USAF
1968 Lt. Col. Lawrence J. Tacker, USAF
1969 Maj. Carroll Shershun, USAF
     Lt. Col. Irving Neuwirth, USAF
1970 Capt. Robert E. Neely, USAF
1971 Maj. Peter L. Sloan, USAF
1972 Harold M. Helfman

WILBUR WRIGHT AWARD

1963 Col. William V. Schmitt, USA
1964 Col. Ben W. Legare, USA
1965 Capt. Mel R. Jones, USA
1966 Lt. Col. Thomas E. Thompson, USA
1967 Col. George R. Creel, USA
1968 Col. Roger R. Bankson, USA
1969 Brig. Gen. Winant Sidle, USA
1970 Lt. Col. Phillip H. Stevens, USA
1971 Maj. William F. Gabella, USA
1972 Maj. Joseph E. Burlas, USA

GLENN H. CURTISS AWARD

1963 Cdr. Kenneth W. Wade, USN
1964 Cdr. H. Harold Bishop, USN
1965 Capt. James S. Dowdell, USN and Cdr. Louis DiGiusto. Jr., USNR
1966 Rear Adm. William P. Mack, USN and Gy. Sgt. Clifton V. Stallings, USMC
1967 Col. Thomas M. Fields, USMC
1968 Capt. Pickett Lumpkin, USN
1969 Lt. Col. Arvid W. Realson, USMC and Capt. Kenneth Wade, USN
1970 Lt. Dan L. Davidson, USN

1971 No award
1972 Cdr. Williams S. Graves, USN

CHARLES L. LAWRENCE AWARD

1968 Edward E. Slattery, Jr.
1969 Volta Torrey
1970 John W. King
1971 Gene Kropf
1972 No award

PUBLIC INFORMATION OFFICER AWARD

1973 Capt. Arthur C. Forster, Jr., USAF
1974 Col. H. J. Dalton, Jr., USAF
1975 R/Adm. William Thompson, USN
1976 Not available
1977 Lt. Col. William F. Gabella, USAF

The Public Relations Award is presented annually to an Associate Member of AWA in recognition of outstanding contributions in publicizing, promotion or otherwise bringing aviation and/or space activities to the public's attention.

1956 Walter T. Bonney and Information Staff of NACA
1957 Air Force Ass.
1958 Willis Player and Public Relations Staff of the Air Transport Assn.
1959 No award
1960 Peggy G. Hereford and James C. Fuller
1961 Lt. Col. Kenneth E. Grine, USAF, and Lt. Col. Sid F. Spear, USAF
1962 Richard Larrick
1963 James R. Greenwood
1964 Gordon S. Williams
1965 Carl W. Dahlem
1966 Fred McClement
1967 Larry M. Hayes
1968 William G. Robinson
1969 Earl Blount
1970 No award
1971 Marvin G. Klemow
1972 Don Fairchilds
1973 Hubert K. Gagos
1974 Thomas H. Rhone
1975 Charles Gablehouse
1976 Not available
1977 Richard J. Ferris

PUBLIC RELATIONS CITATION

1977 Don Fairchild

Robert J. Collier Trophy

NATIONAL AERONAUTIC ASSOCIATION
821 15th St. W NW, Washington, D.C. 20005 (202/347-2808)

The Robert J. Collier Trophy is given annually to an individual or a group of individuals for contributions to "improving the performance, efficiency or safety of air or space vehicles, the value of which has been thoroughly demonstrated by actual use during the preceding year." The winner is selected by the Collier Trophy Committee, appointed by the president of the association, and the presentation is frequently made by the President of the United States in a White House ceremony.

1911 Glenn H. Curtiss, Hydro-aeroplane
1912 Glenn H. Curtiss, Flying boat

1913 Orville Wright, Automatic stabilizer
1914 Elmer A. Sperry, Gyroscopic control
1915 W. Sterling Burgess, Burgess-Dunner Hydro-aeroplane
1916 Elmer A. Sperry, Drift indicator
1917 No award
1918 No award
1919 No award
1920 No award
1921 Grover Loening, Aerial yacht
1922 Personnel of the U.S. Air Mail Service
1923 Personnel of the U.S. Air Mail Service
1924 U.S. Army
1925 S. Albert Reed, Metal propeller
1926 Maj. E.L. Hoffman, Practical parachute
1927 Charles L. Lawrence, Radial air-cooled engine
1928 Aeronautics Branch, U.S. Dept. of Commerce, Airways and air-navigation facilities
1929 National Advisory Committee for Aeronautics, NACA cowling
1930 Harold Pitcairn and staff, Autogiro
1931 Packard Motor Car Co., Aircraft diesel engine
1932 Glenn L. Martin, Bi-engine, high-speed, weight-carrying airplane
1933 Hamilton Standard Propeller Co. and chief engineer Frank W. Caldwell, Controllable-pitch propeller
1934 Maj. Albert F. Hegenberger, Blind-landing experimentation
1935 Donald Douglas and staff, DC-2
1936 Pan American Airways, Trans-Pacific and overwater operations
1937 Army Air Corps, Sub-stratosphere airplane
1938 Howard Hughes and crew, Round-the-world flight
1939 Airlines of the United States, Record of air-travel safety
1940 Sanford Moss and the Army Air Corps, Turbosupercharger
1941 Air Forces and airlines, Worldwide operations typified by Air Transport Command
1942 General H.H. Arnold, Organization and leadership of the "mightiest air force in the world"
1943 Capt. Luis de Florez, USNR, Synthetic training devices for flyers
1944 Gen. Carl A. Spaatz, Demonstrated air power concept through use of American aviation in war against Germany
1945 Louis W. Alvarez, Ground-controlled approach radar landing system
1946 Lewis A. Robert, Thermal ice-prevention system
1947 John Stack, Lawrence Bell and Capt. Charles E. Yaeger, Supersonic flight
1948 Radio Technical Commission for Aeronatics, System of air-traffic control to permit safe and unlimited operations under all weather conditions
1949 William P. Lear, Lear F-5 automatic pilot and automatic control coupler system
1950 Helicopter industry, military services and Coast Guard, Rotary-wing aircraft for air-rescue operations
1951 John Stack and associates at Langley Aeronautical Laboratory, Practical application of transonic wind-tunnel throat
1952 Leonard S. Hobbs of United Aircraft Corp., J-57 jet engine
1953 James H. Kindelberger and Edward H. Heinemann, Supersonic airplanes in service
1954 Richard T. Whitcomb, Verification of area rule, yielding higher speed and range with same air power

1955 William M. Allen and Boeing Co., and Gen. Nathan F. Twining and U.S. Air Force, Operational use of B-52

1956 Charles J. McCarthy and associates of Chance-Vought Aircraft, Inc., and V. Adm. James S. Russell and associates of U.S. Navy Bureau of Aeronautics, F-8U Crusader

1957 Edward P. Curtis, Report, *Aviation Facilities Planning*

1958 U.S. Air Force and industry team, F-104 interceptor Clarence L. Johnson of Lockheed Aircraft Corp., for F-104 airframe
Neil Burgess and Gerhard Neumann of General Electric Co., for F-104 J-79 turbojet engines
Maj. Howard C. Johnson, USAF, for F-104 world landplane altitude record
Capt. Walter W. Irwin USAF, for F-104 world straightaway speed record

1959 U.S. Air Force, Convair Div. of General Dynamics and Space Technology Laboratories, Inc., Atlas, American's first intercontinental ballistic missile

1960 V. Adm. William F. Raborn, Polaris, Operational Fleet Balistic Missile Weapon System

1961 Maj. Robert M. White, Joseph A. Walker, A. Scott Crossfield and Cdr. Forrest Petersen, Test pilots of the X-15

1962 Lt. Cdr. M. Scott Carpenter, USN; Maj. L. Gordon Cooper, USAF; Lt. Col. John H. Glenn, USMC; Maj. Virgil I. Grissom, USAF; Cdr. Walter M. Schirra, Jr., USN; Cdr. Alan B. Shepard, Jr., USN, and Maj. Donald K. Slayton, USAF, Pioneering manned space flight in the United States

1963 Clarence L. "Kelly" Johnson, A-11 Mach 3 aircraft

1964 Gen. Curtis E. LeMay, Great achievements toward air vehicles and national defense

1965 James E. Webb and Hugh L. Dryden, Gemini program team representatives, for contributions to human experience in space flight

1966 James S. McDonnell, F-4 Phantom aircraft and Gemini space vehicles

1967 Lawrence A. Hyland, Surveyor Program Team that "put the eyes and hands of the United States on the Moon"

1968 Col. Frank Borman, USAF; Capt. James A. Lovell, Jr., USN, and Lt. Col. William A. Anders, USAF, Crew of Apollo 8, first manned lunar orbit expedition

1969 Neil A. Armstrong, Col. Edwin E. Aldrin, Jr., USAF and Col. Michael Collins, USAF, "Epic flight of Apollo 11" and first landing of man on the surface of the Moon

1970 Boeing Co. (with special recognition to Pratt & Whitney and Pan American World Airways), Commercial introduction of 747

1971 Col. David R. Scott, USAF; Col. James B. Irwin, USAF; and Lt. Col. Alfred M. Worden, USAF and to Robert R. Gilruth, Apollo 15, "man's most prolonged and scientifically productive lunar mission"

1972 Adm. Thomas H. Moorer, USN, Representing 7th and 8th Air Forces of U.S. Air Force and Task Force 77 of U.S. Navy for Operation Linebacker II

1973 John F. Clark, NASA and Daniel J. Fink, General Electric Co., with special recognition to Hughes Aircraft Co. and RCA, NASA/industry team responsible for LANDSAT, Earth Resources Technology Satellite Program

1974 Skylab Program, with special recognition to William C. Schneider, program director, and three Skylab crews, "Proving beyond question the value of man in future explorations of space and production of data of benefit to all the people on Earth"

1975 David S. Lewis, General Dynamics Corp., and F-16 Air Force-industry team, Fighter-aircraft technology and innovations

1976 Gen. David C. Jones, USAF, and Robert Anderson, Rockwell International, Air Force-industry team responsible for B-1 strategic aircraft system

1977 Gen. Robert V. Dixon, USAF (Ret.), and Air Force Tactical Air Command, Red Flag, combat simulation flight-training program

De La Vaulx Medal
Yuri A. Gagarin Gold Medal
Gold Air Medal
Gold Space Medal
Nile Gold Medal

FEDERATION AERONAUTIQUE INTERNATIONALE
6 Rue Galilee, Paris 75782, France (Tel: 723-72-52 and 720-93-20)

The De La Vaulx Medal annually honors holders of recognized absolute world records of the previous year.

1969 Janko Lutovac (Yugoslavia)
1970 Pierre Lard (France)
1971 Nadezhda Pryakhina (U.S.S.R.)
1972 No award
1973 Pierre Lemoigne (France)
1974 Steven Snyder (U.S.A.)
1975 No award
1976 Arkadi Gouskov (U.S.S.R.)
1977 Not available at press time

The Yuri A. Gagarin Gold Medal is given in memory of the first astronaut and honors the space pilot who has accomplished the highest achievement in the conquest of space. The membership nominates candidates for a secret ballot by the federation's council.

1968 Georgy Timofeevitch Beregovoi (U.S.S.R.)
1969 Charles Conrad, Jr. (U.S.A.)
1970 A.G. Nikolayev (U.S.S.R.)
V.I. Sevastinov, (U.S.S.R.)
1971 V.A. Chatalov (U.S.S.R.)
A.S. Eliseev (U.S.S.R.)
1972 John W. Young (U.S.A.)
1973 Alan L. Bean (U.S.A.)
1974 Edward G. Gibson (U.S.A.)
1975 D.K. Slayton (U.S.A.)
V.D. Brand (U.S.A.)
V.N. Koubasov (U.S.S.R.)
1976 Not available at press time
1977 Not available at press time

The Gold Air Medal is awarded annually on a secret ballot of the Federation's Council from nominees by the membership for outstanding achievements in the development of aeronautics by activities, work, achievements, initiative or devotion to aviation.

1925 Gen. Francesco de Pinedo, Italy
1926 Sir Alan J. Cobham, Great Britain
1927 Charles A. Lindbergh, U.S.A.
1928 Bert Hinkler, Great Britain
1929 Capt. D. Costes, France
1930 Gen. Italo Balbo, Italy
1931 Dr. Eckener, Germany
1932 Don Juan La Cierva, Spain

1933 Wiley Post, U.S.A.
1934 C.W.A. Scott, Great Britain
1935 No award
1936 Jean Mermoz, France
1937 Jean Batten, Great Britain
1938-45 No awards
1946 Igor Sikorsky, U.S.A.
1947 No award
1948 Igor Sikorsky, U.S.A.
1947 No award
1948 Capt. Charles E. Yeager, U.S.A.
1949 No award
1950 Air Commodore Sir Frank Whittle, Great Britain
1951 Ed. P. Warner, U.S.A.
1952 No award
1953 Jacqueline Cochran, U.S.A.
1954 James H. Doolittle, U.S.A.
1955 Maurice Hurel, France
1956 L.P. Twiss, Great Britain
1957 Maj. David G. Simons, U.S.A.
1958 Andrey Mickolaevich Tupolev, U.S.S.R.
1959 Pierre Satre, France
1960 No award
1961 Yuri Gagarin, U.S.S.R.
1962 Sir Geoffrey de Havilland, Great Britain
1963 No award
1964 Jacqueline Auriol, France
1965 V. Kokkinaki, U.S.S.R.
1966 Col. Robert L. Stephens, U.S.A.
1967 Alexander S. Yakovlev, U.S.S.R.
1968 Joseph A. Walker, U.S.A.
1969 S.V. Iliouchine, U.S.S.R.
1970 Jose Luis Aresti, Spain
1970 M.H.T. "Dick" Merrill, U.S.A.
1971 Elgen M. Long, U.S.A.
1972 Marina L. Popovitch, U.S.S.R.
1973 Sir Donald Anderson, Australia
1974 Alexander Fedotov, U.S.S.R.
1975 Curtis H. Pitts, U.S.A.
1976 Sholto Hamilton Georgeson, New Zealand
1977 Not available at press time

The Gold Space Medal, which is of equal standing with the Gold Air Medal, annually honors an astronaut who has achieved outstanding performance in space. The membership nominates candidates for a secret ballot by the Federation's Council.

1963 A. Nikolaev, U.S.S.R.
       P. Popovitch, U.S.S.R.
1964 Valentina Teretchkova, U.S.S.R.
1965 V. Komarov, U.S.S.R.
       K. Feotistov, U.S.S.R.
       B. Egorov, U.S.S.R.
1966 A.A. Leonov, U.S.S.R.
1967 James A. Lovell, Jr., U.S.A.
1968 Frank Borman, U.S.A.
1969 Neil A. Armstrong, U.S.A.
1970 James A. Lovell, Jr., U.S.A.
1971 David R. Scott, U.S.A.
1972 Eugene A. Cernan U.S.A.
1973 Charles Conrad, Jr., U.S.A.
1974 Gerald P. Carr, U.S.A.
1975 Thomas P. Stafford, U.S.A.
       Alexei Arkhipovitch Leonov, U.S.S.R.
1976 Michael Collins, U.S.A.
1977 Not available at press time

The Nile Gold Medal is presented annually to the individual, group or organization for distinguished work in aerospace education, especially during the preceding

year. Any active member of the federation can propose one candidate each year for selection by the International Aerospace Education Committee.

1972 Aer Lingus Training Section, Ireland
1973 Olavi M. Lumes, Finland
1974 Wayne R. Matson, U.S.A.
1975 General A.A. Rafat, Iran
1976 Vyatcheslav Bashkirov, U.S.S.R.
1977 Not available at press time

Edward Warner Award
INTERNATIONAL CIVIL AVIATION ORGANIZATION
1000 Sherbrooke St. NW, Montreal, Quebec, Canada
(514/285-8219)

The Edward Warner Award is given by ICAO on behalf of its 138 member states to an individual or institution for outstanding contributions towards the furthering of civil aviation. A nominations committee recommends the recipient of the gold medal for the approval of the ICAO council.

1959 Albert Plesman (Netherlands), Founder and President of KLM Royal Dutch Airlines
1961 International Aeronautical Federation (Est. 1905, Paris), Worldwide organization of national aero clubs
1963 Max Hymans (France), Secretary General for civil aviation in France; President of Air France
1965 William Hildred (Great Britain), Director General of Civil Aviation in the United Kingdom; Director General of the International Air Transport Assn.
1968 Henri Bouche (France), Founder of the Air Transport Institute, Paris; represented France on the ICAO Council
1971 Ruben Martin Berta (Brazil), Former President of Varig Airlines
1972 Agence pour la Securite de la Navigation Aerienne en Afrique et a Madagascar, Organization of 15 French-speaking states to ensure safety and regularity of civil air service in Africa
1973 Shizuma Matsuo (Japan), President and Chairman of the Board of Japan Air Lines; 23 years in government civil aviation posts including Director General of Aeronautics Safety Board and Director General of Japan Aeronautics Agency
1974 Alex Meyer (Federal Republic of Germany), Academician, jurist and aviator; established and directed Institute of Air Law and Space Law at Cologne University
1975 Charles A. Lindbergh (U.S.A.), Aviation pioneer, who through his 1927 solo flight across the Atlantic unveiled the potential of international air transport; lifetime dedication to aviation
1976 Corporacion Centroamericana de Servicios de Navegacion Aerea (Est. 1960), Provides efficient, coordinated air service for navigation and communications in Central American region
1977 Not available at press time

Langley Medal
SMITHSONIAN INSTITUTION
1000 Jefferson Dr. SW, Washington, D.C. 20560
(202/628-4422)

The Langley Medal, which is of gold, is awarded as merited for especially significant investigations connected with the sciences of aeronautics and astronautics.

1909	Wilbur and Orville Wright
1913	Glenn H. Curtis
	Gustave Eiffel
1927	Charles A. Lindbergh
1929	Charles Matthews Manly
	Richard E. Byrd
1935	Joseph S. Ames
1955	Jerome C. Hunsaker
1960	Robert H. Goddard
1962	Hugh Latimer Dryden
1964	Alan B. Shepard, Jr.
1967	Wernher von Braun
1971	Samuel Phillips
1976	James Webb
	Grover Loening

Distinguished Achievement Award

WINGS CLUB
The Biltmore, Madison Ave. and 43rd St., New York, N.Y. 10017 (212/867-1770)

The Distinguished Achievement Award is given annually for outstanding public service "of enduring value to aviation." Members are invited to submit nominations for selection by an awards committee.

1975	Gen. James A. Doolittle
1976	Neil Armstrong
1977	Laurance S. Rockefeller

Wright Brothers Trophy

NATIONAL AERONAUTIC ASSOCIATION
821 15th St. NW, Washington, D.C. 20005 (202/347-2808)

The Wright Brothers Trophy is given annually to an American who, as a civilian, has rendered personal and direct service to American aviation. A seven-member jury appointed by the president of the association selects the winner.

1948	William F. Durand
1949	Charles A. Lindbergh
1950	Grover Loening
1951	Jerome C. Hunsaker
1952	Lt. Gen. James A. Doolittle, USAF
1953	Carl Hinshaw, U.S. Representative
1954	Theodore von Karman
1955	Hugh L. Dryden
1956	Edward P. Warner
1957	Sen. Stuart Symington
1958	John Frederick Victory
1959	William P. McCracken, Jr
1960	Frederick C. Crawford
1961	A.S. "Mike" Monroney, U.S. Representative and Senator
1962	John Stack
1963	Donald W. Douglas, Sr.
1964	Harry F. Guggenheim
1965	Jerome Lederer
1966	Juan Terry Trippe
1967	Igor I. Sikorsky
1968	Sen. Warren G. Magnuson
1969	William M. Allen
1970	C.R. Smith
1971	Sen. Howard W. Cannon
1972	John H. Shaffer
1973	Sen. Barry M. Goldwater
1974	Richard T. Whitcomb
1975	Clarence L. "Kelly" Johnson
1976	William Allan Patterson
1977	Ira C. Aker

Conservation &

Environment

Contents

Related Awards

Frank A. Chambers Award
S. Smith Griswold Award
Richard Beatty Mellon Award

AIR POLLUTION CONTROL ASSOCIATION
Box 2861, Pittsburgh, Pa. 15230 (412/621-1090)

The Frank A. Chambers Award recognizes achievement in the science and art of air pollution control on a technical level. The winner receives a plaque.

1955 Moyer D. Thomas
1956 Ward F. Davidson
1957 Walter A. Schmidt
1958 Arie Jan Haagen-Smit
1959 Robert E. Swain
1960 No award
1961 Philip A. Leighton
1962 Bert L. Richards
1963 No award
1964 Charles W. Gruber
1965 Morris A. Katz
1966 Louis C. McCabe
1967 No award
1968 Sir Oliver Graham Sutton
1969 W. C. L. Hemeon
1970 A. Paul Altshuller
1971 Harry J. White
1972 No award
1973 W. L. Faith
1974 James P. Lodge
1975 E. R. Hendrickson
1976 Richard B. Engdahl
1977 Gaylord W. Penney

The S. Smith Griswold Award honors accomplishment in the prevention and control of air pollution by an individual who is a past or present governmental agency staff member. The winner receives a plaque.

1972 Robert L. Chass
1973 William H. Megonnell
1974 John A. Maga
1975 William A. Munroe
1976 Charles M. Copley, Jr.
1977 Don Goodwin

The Richard Beatty Mellon Award goes to an individual whose contributions of a civic nature have aided the abatement of air pollution. The winner receives a plaque.

1956 Edward R. Weidlein, Sr.
1957 Raymond R. Tucker
1958 No award
1959 John F. Barkley
1960 Robert A. Kehoe
1961 No award
1962 Richard K. Mellon
1963 R. L. Ireland
1964 No award
1965 Edmund S. Muskie
1966 Leslie Silverman
1967 Arnold Marsh
1968 No award
1969 Vernon G. Mackenzie
1970 Arthur C. Stern
1971 Allen D. Brandt
1972 John T. Middleton
1973 No award
1974 W. Brad Drowley
1975 Maurice F. Strong

1976 No award
1977 No award

Audubon Medal

NATIONAL AUDUBON SOCIETY
950 Third Ave., New York, N.Y. 10022 (212/832-3200)

The Audubon Medal, which is of gold, annually honors an individual who has served the cause of conservation.

1947 Hugh Bennett
1948 No award
1949 Ira N. Gabrielson
1950 John D. Rockefeller, Jr.
1951 No award
1952 Louis Bromfield
1953 No award
1954 No award
1955 Walt Disney
1956 Ludlow Griscom
1957 No award
1958 No award
1959 Olaus J. Murie
1960 Jay N. Darling
1961 Clarence Cottam
1962 William O. Douglas
1963 Rachel Carson
1964 Laurance S. Rockefeller
1965 No award
1966 A. Starker Leopold
1967 Stewart L. Udall
1968 Fairfield Osborn
1969 Horace M. Albright
1970 No award
1971 No award
1972 Roger Tory Peterson
1973 Barbara Ward
1974 Governor Tom McCall
1975 Maurice Strong
1976 John Oakes
1977 Russell Peterson

Burroughs Medal

THE JOHN BURROUGHS MEMORIAL ASSOCIATION
American Museum of Natural History, 79th St. at Central Park West, New York, N.Y. 10024 (212/873-1300)

The Burroughs Medal honors a literary naturalist for a book published in English within the previous two years which combines literary merit and scientific worth. A five-person jury selects the winner of the bronze medal.

1926 William Beebe, *Pheasants of the World*
1927 Ernest Thompson Seton, *Lives of Game Animals*
1928 John Russell McCarthy, *Nature Poems*
1929 Frank M. Chapman, *Handbook of North American Birds*
1930 Archibald Rutledge, *Peace in the Heart*
1931 No award
1932 Frederick S. Dellenbaugh, *A Canyon Voyage*
1933 Oliver Perry Medsgar, *Spring; Summer; Fall; Winter*
1934 W.W. Christman, *Wild Pasture Pine*
1935 No award
1936 Charles Crawford Ghorst, *Recordings of Bird Calls*
1937 No award

1938 **Robert Cushman Murphy,** *Oceanic Birds of South America*
1939 **T. Gilbert Pearson,** *Adventures in Bird Protection*
1940 **Arthur Cleveland Bent,** *Life Histories of North American Birds*
1941 **Louis J. Halle, Jr.,** *Birds Against Man*
1942 **Edward Armstrong,** *Birds of the Grey Wind*
1943 **Edwin Way Teale,** *Near Horizons*
1944 No award
1945 **Rutherford Platt,** *This Green World*
1946 **Mr. and Mrs. Lee Jaques,** *Snowshoe Country*
1947 No award
1948 **Theodora Stanwell-Fletcher,** *Driftwood Valley*
1949 **Mr. and Mrs. Allan Cruickshank,** *Flight into Sunshine*
1950 **Roger Tory Peterson,** *Birds over America*
1951 No award
1952 **Rachel Carson,** *The Sea Around Us*
1953 **Gilbert Klingel,** *The Bay*
1954 **Joseph Wood Krutch,** *The Desert Year*
1955 **Wallace B. Grange,** *Those of the Forest*
1956 **Guy Murchie,** *Song of the Sky*
1957 **Archie Carr,** *The Windward Road*
1958 **Robert Porter Allen,** *On the Trail of Vanishing Birds*
1959 No award
1960 **John Kieran,** *Natural History of New York City*
1961 **Loren C. Eiseley,** *The Firmament of Time*
1962 **George Miksch Sutton,** *Iceland Summer*
1963 **Adolph Murie,** *A Naturalist in Alaska*
1964 **John Hay,** *The Great Beach*
1965 **Paul Brooks,** *Roadless Area*
1966 **Louis Darling,** *The Gull's Way*
1967 **Charlton Ogburn,** *The Winter Beach*
1968 **Hal Borland,** *Hill Country Harvest*
1969 **Louis deKiriline Lawrence,** *The Lovely and The Wild*
1970 **Victor B. Scheffer,** *The Year of The Whale*
1971 **John K. Terres,** *From Laurel Hill to Siler's Bog*
1972 **Robert Arbib,** *The Lord's Woods*
1973 **Elizabeth Barlow,** *The Forests and Wetlands of New York City*
1974 **Sigurd F. Olson,** *Wilderness Days*
1975 No award
1976 **Ann Haymond Zwinger,** *Run, River, Run*
1977 **Aldo Leopold,** *Sand County Almanac Illustrated*

Eminent Ecologist Award
ECOLOGICAL SOCIETY OF AMERICA
c/o Dr. Ed Kormondy, Provost, Evergreen State College, Olympia, Wash. 98505 (206/866-6400)

The Eminent Ecologist Award annually honors outstanding contributions to the field either in teaching or research.

1954 **H. S. Conrad,** botany, Grinnell
1955 **A. H. Wright,** zoology, Cornell
1956 **G. B. Rigg,** botany, University of Washington
1957 **D. P. Schmidt,** herpetology, Chicago
1958 **A. W. Sampson,** forestry, University of California
1959 **H. A. Gleason,** botany, New York Botanical Garden
1960 **W. P. Cottam,** botany, University of Utah
1961 **Charles Elton,** animal ecology, Oxford University
1962 **G. E. Hutchinson,** limnology, Yale
1963 **W. Cooper,** botany, Minnesota
1964 **S. R. Dice,** zoology, Michigan
1965 **Paul B. Sears,** botany, retired
1966 **A. Redfield,** marine biology, retired
1967 **A. E. Emerson,** zoology, retired
1968 **Victor Shelford,** zoology, retired

1969 **Stanley Cain,** botany, University of Michigan
1970 **Murray F. Buell,** botany, Rutgers
1971 **Thomas Park,** zoology, University of Chicago
1972 **Ruth Patrick,** limnology, Academy of Natural Sciences
1973 No award
1974 **Eugene P. Odum,** ecosystem ecology, University of Georgia
1975 **C. H. Muller,** ecology-community-allelopathy, University of California, Santa Barbara
1976 **Alton Lindsey,** plant ecologist, Purdue University
1977 Not avalable at press time

Award for Environmental Quality
NATIONAL ACADEMY OF SCIENCES
2101 Constitution Ave., Washington, D.C. 20418
(202/393-8100)

The Academy's annual Award for Environmental Quality is given to honor significant contributions to environmental quality or in the control of pollution. The award was established in honor of long-time Academy member Frederick Gardner Correll.

1972 **Arie Jan Haagen-Smit**
1973 **W. Thomas Edmondson**
1974 **G. Evelyn Hutchinson**
1975 **John T. Middleton**
1976 **David M. Evans**
1977 **Miron Heinselman**

Hodgkins Medal and Prize
SMITHSONIAN INSTITUTION
1000 Jefferson Dr. SW, Washington, D.C. 20560
(202/628-4422)

The Hodgkins Medal and Prize, which consists of a gold medal and a cash award, is given as merited to encourage and/or honor noteworthy contributions to environmental studies both from a scientific and a social standpoint. It is generally awarded annually or biennially after a lapse of several decades from the initial award.

1899 **James Dewar,** Great Britain
1902 **J.J. Thompson,** Great Britain
1965 **Sydney Chapman,** United States
     Joseph Kaplan, United States
     Marcel Nicolet, Belgium
1967 **John Grahame Douglas Clark,** Great Britain
     Fritz W. Went, United States
1969 **Jule Gregory Charney,** United States
     Arie Haagen-Smit, United States
1971 **Lewis Mumford,** Great Britain; Italy
1973 **Walter Orr Roberts,** United States
1976 **E. Cuyler Hammond,** United States

Alexander von Humboldt Medal
STIFTUNG F.V.S.
Georgsplatz 10, 2 Hamburg 1, Federal Republic of Germany
(Tel: 33 04 00 and 33 06 00)

The Alexander von Humboldt Medal, which is of gold, is given annually for achievements in conservation and nature-park work in Europe.

1961 **Theodor Sonnemann,** Limperich bei Bonn, Germany
1962 **Hubert Schmitt-Degenhardt,** Aachen, Germany
1963 **Karl Asal,** Freiburg, Germany
1964 **Renzo Videsott,** Turin, Italy
1965 **Arthur Uehlinger,** Schaffhausen, Switzerland
1966 **Justus Danckwerts,** Hannover, Germany
     Egon Selchow, Hamburg, Germany
1967 **Ludwig Seiterich,** Konstanz, Germany
1968 **Jean-Paul Harroy,** Brussels
1969 **Emil Meynen,** Bad Godesberg, Germany
     Herbert Offner, Bonn, Germany
1970 **Sir Peter Smithers,** Vico Morcote, Switzerland
     Helmut Schaefer, Hoffnungsthal, Germany
1971 **Tassilo Troscher,** Wiesbaden, Germany
1972 **Paul Hochstrasser,** Richterswil, Switzerland
     Nikolaus Freiherr von und zu Bodman, Moggingen/Bodensee, Germany
1973 **Wolfgang Engelhardt,** Munich
1974 **Jean Servat,** Paris
1975 **H.R.H. Prince Bernhard of the Netherlands**
1976 **Reinhold Tuxen,** Todenmann uber Rinteln, Germany
1977 **Hermann Kerl,** Clausthal-Zellerfeld, Germany

Award for Distinguished Service in Environmental Planning

INDUSTRIAL DEVELOPMENT RESEARCH COUNCIL
1954 Airport Rd., Peachtree Air Terminal, Atlanta, Ga. 30341
(404/458-6026)

The Council and Conway Publications, Inc., annually present the Award for Distinguished Service in Environmental Planning for the harmonizing of new industrial facilities with the environment. A selection committee of council members and Conway personnel chooses the winner.

1972 **James B. Coulter,** Secretary, Maryland Dept. of Natural Resources
     Charles Davis, Interstate Paper Co., Riceland, Ga.
     L. Jack Davis, Gulf Coast Waste Disposal Authority, Houston, Tex.
     James K. Keefe, Commissioner, Maine Dept. of Commerce and Industry
     Jack Lacy, Spirit of '76, Junction City, Kans.
     O.C. Linde, South Pacific Land Co., San Francisco
     David F. McElroy, Northern States Power Co.
     Calvin Rampton, Governor, State of Utah
     Nelson Rockefeller, Governor, State of New York
     Walt Disney World Co.
1973 **Jay D. Aldridge,** Penn's Southwest Assn., Pittsburgh
     Max Brewer, Commissioner, Alaska Dept. of Environmental Conservation
     Charles Dougherty, Union Electric Co., St. Louis
     Paul A. Duke, Duke Enterprises, Norcross, Ga.
     John J. Gilligan, Governor, State of Ohio
     Harold Jensen, Real Estate IC Industries, Chicago
     Howard T. Odum, Dept. of Environmental Engineering, University of Florida
     Roger M. Scott, City Manager, Virginia Beach, Va.
     Robert J. Worden, Executive Director, Arizona Dept. of Planning and Economic Development
1974 **Thomas W. Carmody,** SHARE, Ponce, P.R.
     Charles Fraser, Palmas del Mar Co., Palmas del Mar, P.R.
     Damon Harrison, Kentucky Commissioner of Commerce
     Wendell J. Kelly, Illinois Power Co.

J. Andrew McAlister, Georgia Kraft Co., Rome and Macon, Ga.
Muskegon County (Mich.) Planning Commission
1975 **AT&T Bedminster and Basking Ridge (N.J.) facilities**
     Joseph Baxter, City Councilman, Franklin, Ohio
     Pierre Gousseland, AMAX, Inc., Fort Madison, Iowa
     Donald Hall, Hallmark Cards, Kansas City, Mo.
     John P. Moran, Vice President for Facilities, Princeton University, N.J.
     Grant G. Simmons, Jr., Simmons Co., Norcross, Ga.
     Raymond L. Watson, The Irvine Co., Irvine, Calif.
1976 **August A. Busch III,** Anheuser-Busch, Inc., Williamsburg, Va.
     Robert F. Denig, Deere and Co., Davenport, Iowa
     Wayne S. Doran, Ford Motor Land Development Co., Detroit
     David L. Duensing, Armour & Co., Scottsdale, Ariz.
     Stanley D. Fisher, F.I.P. Corp., Farmington, Conn.
     Armand Hammer, Occidental Petroleum Corp., El Cajon, Calif.
     Charles T. Keenan, Western Environmental Trade Assn.
1977 **C.H. Barre,** Marathon Oil Co.
     Dwight F. Barger, Louisiana Refining Div., Marathon Oil Co.
     Ernest H. Bennett, Textile Fibers Co., Du Pont Co., Charleston, S.C.
     D. Scott Hudgens, Shenandoah Development Co., Inc. Park Central, Dallas
     William F. May, American Can Co., Milwaukee, Wisc.
     Harry T. Morley, St. Louis Regional Commerce and Growth Assn.
     Earl Wantland, Tektronix, Inc., Wilsonville, Ore.
     Robert K. Zimmerman, Kansas City Power & Light Co.

Wilhelm Leopold Pfeil Prize

STIFTUNG F.V.S.
Georgsplatz 10, 2 Hamburg 1, Federal Republic of Germany
(Tel. 33 04 00 and 33 06 00)

The Wilhelm Leopold Pfeil Prize, which carries a cash award of 16,000 German marks, is awarded annually for modern, futuristic forestry in Europe. The University of Freiburg administers the award.

1963 **Victor Dieterich,** Stuttgart-Vaihingen, Germany
1964 **Gustav Kraub,** Germany
1965 **Ulrich Rodenwaldt,** Villingen, Germany
1966 **Kjeld Ladefoged,** Arhus, Netherlands
1967 **Gerben Hellinga,** Wageningen, Germany
     Johannes Louis Frederic Overbeek, Zwolle, Germany
1968 **Wilhelm Hassenteufel,** Absam bei Innsbruck, Austria
     Lukas Leiber, Freiburg i. Br., Germany
1969 **Hans Leibundgut,** Zurich, Switzerland
     Hans Siebenbaum, Kitzeberg bei Kiel, Germany
1970 **Jon Popescu-Zeletin,** Bucharest, Rumania
1971 **Hermann Junack,** Gartow/Elbe, Germany
1972 **Jean Parde,** Nancy, France
     Kurt Ruppert, Frankfurt am Main, Germany
1973 **Muharrem Miraboglu,** Ankara/Istanbul, Turkey
1974 **Gerhard Petsch,** Essen, Germany
1975 **Stanislaw Kasprzyk,** Warsaw, Poland
     Josef Nikolaus Kostler, Ramsau, Germany
1976 **No award**
1977 **Carl Olof, Tamm,** Stockholm, Sweden

Louise du Pont Crowninshield Award
David E. Finley Award
Gordon Gray Award
President's Award

NATIONAL TRUST FOR HISTORIC PRESERVATION
1001 Connecticut Ave. NW, Washington D.C. (202/638-5200)
Mailing address: 740-748 Jackson Pl. NW, Washington, D.C. 20006

The Louise du Pont Crowninshield Award is given for superlative achievement in the preservation and interpretation of sites, buildings, architecture, districts and objects of national significance. The award, which consists of a trophy and a stipend, may be made to a salaried worker, volunteer, organization, individual or several entities jointly. Nominations may be submitted for this award.

1960 **Mount Vernon Ladies Association of the Union,** Va.
1961 **Henry Francis du Pont,** Winterthur, Del.
1962 **Katherine Prentis Murphy,** N.Y. and Conn.
1963 **Mrs. Robert G. Robinson,** New Orleans, La.
1964 **Mr. and Mrs. Betram K. Little,** Brookline, Mass
1965 **Charles E. Peterson,** Philadelphia, Pa.
1966 **Ima Hogg,** Houston, Tex., and **Mrs. John A. Kellenberger,** N.C.
1967 No award
1968 **Mrs. J. M. P. Wright,** Annapolis, Md.
1969 **Mr. and Mrs. Henry N. Flynt,** Greenwich, Conn.
1970 **Frank L. Horton,** Winston-Salem, N.C.
1971 **Frances Edmunds,** Charleston, S.C.
1972 **Alice Winchester,** New York
1973 **Ricardo E. Alegria,** San Juan, P.R.
1974 **Mr. and Mrs. Jacob Morrison,** New Orleans, La.
1975 No award
1976 **Mrs. George Henry Warren and The Preservation Society of Newport County,** R.I.
1977 **The San Antonio Conservation Society,** San Antonio, Tex.

The David E. Finley Award, formerly a citation that was renamed for the founder and first chairman of the Trust, is given for outstanding achievement in the preservation, restoration and interpretation of sites, buildings, architecture, districts and objects significant on a regional level. The award, which consists of a scroll, a trophy or both, may be given to a salaried worker, volunteer, organization, individual or several entities jointly. Nominations may be submitted for this award.

1971 **The Foundation for Historic Christ Church, Inc.,** Irvington, Va.
   James L. Cogar, President, Shakertown at Pleasant Hill, Ky.
   Lydia Chichester Laird, New Castle, Del.
   The Society for the Preservation of Weeksville and Bedford-Stuyvesant History of Brooklyn, N.Y.
1972 **Pittsburgh History and Landmarks Foundation of Pittsburgh,** Pa.
   The Old Santa Fe Association, of Santa Fe, N.M.
   Citizens to Preserve Overton Park of Memphis, Tenn.
1973 **Bishop Hill Heritage Association,** Bishop Hill, Ill.
   Mrs. Malcolm G. Chace, Jr., Providence, R.I.
   Pearl Chase, Santa Barbara, Calif.

   Mrs. Lawrence K. (Amy Bess Williams) Miller, president, Shaker Community, Inc., Hancock Shaker Village, Hancock, Mass.
1974 **Wilbert Hasbrouck,** Chicago
   Myra Ellen Jenkins, Santa Fe, N.M.
   H. Merrill Roenke, Jr., Geneva, N.Y.
   Mrs. Charles F. Loewer, Little Rock, Ark.
1975 **Harold Brooks,** Marshall, Mich.
   The Community Design Commission, of Medina, Ohio
   Mrs. William Fluty, Wheeling, W.Va.
   Mrs. Albert H. Powers, Oregon City, Ore.
   The Utah Heritage Foundation, Willard, Utah
1976 **Georgia Ray DeCoster and Elizabeth Musser,** St. Paul, Minn.
   Anna F. Hesse and Historic Hermann, Hermann, Mo.
   Junior League of Louisville, Ky.
   New Mexico and Colorado Railroad Authority, Santa Fe, N.M.
1977 **The Mark Twain Memorial,** Hartford, Conn.
   Frank Fetch, and the German Village Society, Inc., Columbus, Ohio
   Georgetown Society, Inc., Georgetown, Colo.
   The Pennsylvania Academy of Fine Arts, Philadelphia

The Gordon Gray Award, formerly a Special Award renamed in 1977 to honor the second chairman of the National Trust, recognizes outstanding achievement in special areas in support of historic preservation, though not necessarily in the field of preservation itself, such as banking, business, industry, communications media, scholarship, restoration architecture, traditional crafts, adaptive use of historical structures, public agencies or legislation. The award, which consists of a scroll, trophy or both, may go to an organization, individual or several entities jointly and may be applied for.

1971 **Ada Louise Huxtable,** *New York Times*
   Nancy Carson Shirk, Boston, Mass.
   Nancy Schultz, Washington D.C.
1972 **Samuel Chamberlain,** Mass.
   Senator William S. James, Md.
1973 **Virginia Daiker,** Library of Congress, Washington, D.C.
   George McCue, Arts and Urban Design Critic, *St. Louis Post Dispatch*
   A. Edwin Kendrew, Williamsburg, Va.
1974 **Peter Pastreich,** Exec. Dir., The St. Louis Symphony Orchestra
   James Marston Fitch, New York
   William M. Roth, San Francisco
1975 **College of Charleston,** Charleston, S.C.
   Frederick C. Williamson, Providence, R.I.
1976 **Childs Bertman Tseckares Associates, Inc.,** Boston, Mass.
   Muriel Dinsmore, Eureka, Calif.
   Sigma Phi Fraternity, University of Wisconsin Chapter, Madison, Wisc.
1977 **Lucille Basler,** Ste. Genevieve, Mo.
   Senator and Mrs. Robert Edington, Mobile, Ala.
   William Marlin, New York

The National Trust President's Award is given in recognition of an achievement in historic preservation of community significance. The award, which consists of a scroll may be given to an individual, organization or several entities jointly. The award may be applied for.

1977   The City Fathers of Bath, Sagadahoc Preservation Inc., Bath Area Chamber of Commerce, and Bath Maritime Museum; Bath, Me.
Franklin Savings Association, Austin, Tex.
Kahuku Sugar Mill Restoration, Hawaii

Dr. John C. Phillips Medal
INTERNATIONAL UNION FOR THE CONSERVATION OF NATURE AND NATURAL RESOURCES
CH-1110 Morges, Switzerland

The Dr. John C. Phillips Medal is given every three years for distinguished service in international conservation. The medal is cast from a design by sculptor Ralph J. Menconi.

1963   E.M. Nicholson, Great Britain
1966   E. Beltran, Mexico
1969   Salim Ali, India
1972   H.R.H. Prince Bernhard of the Netherlands
1975   Sir Frank Fraser Darling, Great Britain

Van Tienhoven Prize
STIFTUNG F.V.S.
Georgsplatz 10, 2 Hamburg 1, Federal Republic of Germany
(Tel: 33 04 00 and 33 06 00)

The Van Tienhoven Prize, which carries a cash award of 10,000 German marks, is given annually for the furthering of nature parks in Europe. The University of Bonn administers the award.

1957   Hermann Kunanz, Konradsdorf, Germany
1958   Walery Groetel, Cracow, Poland
1959   Rudi Ronge, Hannover-Munden, Germany
Johannes Wiegand, Mainz, Germany
1960   Sir Herbert Griffin, London, U.K.
1961   Otto Kraus, Munich, Germany
1962   Marinus van der Goes van Naters, Wassenaar, Netherlands
1963   Hans Krieg, Wolfratshausen, Germany
1964   Georges Wagner, Clerf, Luxemburg
Konrad Schubach, Trier, Germany
1965   Ernst Schlensker, Arnsberg/Westphalia, Germany
1966   Edgard Pisani, Paris, France
1967   Angela Piskernik, Ljubljana, Yugoslavia
1968   Ekkehard Lommel, Heppenheim, Germany
1969   Jaroslav Vesely, Prague, Czechoslovakia
1970   Meester Hans Paul Gorter, Amsterdam, Netherlands
1971   Jakob Bachtold, Berne, Switzerland
1972   Adalbert Mullmann, Brilon/Westphalia, Germany
1973   Norges Naturvernforbund, Oslo, Norway
1974   Erwin Stein, Annerod/Gieben, Germany
Per Olof Swanberg, Skara, Sweden
1975   Alexander von Mielecki, Wolfhagen, Germany
1976   Marcelin Melges Ojcow, Poland
1977   Victor Westhoff, Groesbeek, Netherlands

Tyler Ecology Award
PEPPERDINE UNIVERSITY
Malibu, Calif. 90265 (213/456-2358)

The Pepperdine University Tyler Ecology Award is given "to the individual or team of individuals working on a common project whose accomplishment has been recognized as conferring the greatest benefit on mankind in the fields of ecology and environment." The recipient(s) of the $150,000 tax-free award is (are) selected from nominations reviewed by a selection committee composed of representatives of nine universities.

1973   Arie J. Haagen-Smit, professor emeritus, California Institute of Technology who discovered photochemical smog
F. Evelyn Hutchinson, professor emeritus, Yale University, for work in the chemistry of the atmosphere
Maurice F. Strong, Former executive director of the United Nations Environment Program for communications and environmental programs
1974   Ruth Patrick, Chairman of the Board, Academy of Natural Science (Philadelphia) for limnology and water pollution work
1975   Charles Elton, professor emeritus, Oxford University (England), for animal ecology
Rene Jules Dubos, professor emeritus, Rockefeller University (New York), for experiments in pathology
Abel Wolman, professor emeritus, Johns Hopkins University (Baltimore), for sanitation and water engineering
1976   Eugene P. Odum, professor, University of Georgia (Athens), for zoology and practical approach of ecology
1977   Russel Train (World Wildlife Fund), for services to conservation and wildlife protection

International Environmental Prize
UNITED NATIONS
First Ave. & 42nd St., New York, N.Y. 10017 (212/754-1234)

The International Environmental Prize, which carries a $50,000 honorarium, is awarded annually for exceptional contributions to world environmental protection and ecology.

1976   Maurice Strong, Founding Director of the U.N. Environmental Program
1977   Jacques-Yves Cousteau, Oceanographer and underwater film-maker
Sir Peter Scott, Founder, World Wildlife Fund

"54" Founders Award
IZAAK WALTON LEAGUE OF AMERICA
1800 N. Kent St., Suite 806, Arlington, Va. 22209
(703/528-1818)

The "54" Founders Award, which consists of a plaque and citation, is presented annually to an individual, group or institution judged to have made an outstanding contribution to conservation of America's renewable natural resources during the previous year. The bronze plaque was designed by Louis Paul Jones.

1959   Seth Gordon
1960   Maytag Co.
1961   No award
1962   Laurance S. Rockefeller
1963   Rachel Carson
1964   Stewart L. Udall

1965	Congressman Wayne N. Aspinall
1966	Mrs. Lyndon B. Johnson
1967	Paul H. Douglas
1968	Vinton W. Bacon
1969	Sigurd F. Olson
1970	Congressman John P. Saylor
1971	Raymond A. Haik
1972	Joseph W. Penfold
1973	Frank B. Hubachek
1974	Thomas E. Dustin
1975	Malcolm King
1976	No award
1977	No award

National At-Large Conservation Awards
Special Conservation Award
Resources Defense Award
International Achievement Award

NATIONAL WILDLIFE FEDERATION
1412 16th St. NW, Washington, D.C. 20036 (202/797-6800)

The National At-Large Conservation Awards, consisting of Whooping Crane statuettes, recognize significant national achievement in four categories, plus special awards in fields outside these categories. The NWF Awards Committee selects winners from nominees submitted by board members, staff and affiliate officers.

CONSERVATIONIST OF THE YEAR (general achievement)

1965	Lady Bird Johnson
1966	Dorothy A. Buell
	Paul H. Douglas
1967	Alan Bible
	Thomas H. Kuchel
1968	Orville L. Freeman
1969	Victor J. Yannacone, Jr.
1970	H. James Morrison, Jr.
1971	Russell W. Peterson
1972	Jack C. Watson
1973	Tom McCall
1974	Russell E. Train
1975	Warren G. Magnuson
1976	William E. Towell
1977	Butler Derrick

COMMUNICATIONS

1965	Outdoor Writers Assn. of America
1966	National Assn. of Broadcasters
1967	NBC News
1968	*Christian Science Monitor*
1969	Bill Mauldin
	Pat Oliphant
1970	Jacques Cousteau
	Patrick R. Cullen
1972	Lupi Saldana
	Providence Journal-Bulletin
1974	Ernest B. Furguson
1975	*Detroit News*
1976	Brian Kelley, *Washington Star*
1977	*Arkansas Gazette* and George Fisher, cartoonist

ORGANIZATION

1965	General Electric Co.

1966	Ford Motor Co.
1968	League of Women Voters
1969	Save Our Bay Action Committee
1970	Douglas MacArthur High School Anti-Pollution Committee
1972	The Scouting Movement of America
1973	The United States Jaycees Environmental Improvement Program
1974	Society for the Protection of New Hampshire Forests
1975	Gulf States Paper Corporation
1976	Rachel Carson Trust for the Living Environment
1977	Wildlife Management Institute

LEGISLATIVE

1965	Frank Church
1966	Edmund S. Muskie
1967	John D. Dingell
1968	Gaylord Nelson
1969	Henry M. Jackson
1970	Philip A. Hart
1971	Henry S. Reuss
1972	Clinton P. Anderson
1973	Morris K. Udall
1974	Ernest F. Hollings
1975	Warren G. Magnuson
1976	Richard L. Ottinger
1977	Gary Hart

The Special Conservation Award honors the contributions of individuals and organizations which might otherwise be overlooked by allowing nominations to be made by persons outside the normal nomination structure for the At-Large Awards.

1965	Nelson A. Rockefeller
1968	George A. Selke
1969	Joseph W. Penfold
1972	Ralph A. MacMullan
1973	John S. Gottschalk
1974	Roger Tory Peterson
	E. Budd Marter, III
	Mrs. Lewis E. Smoot
1975	Richard H. Stroud
	William A. Butler
	Lily Peter
	Arthur R. Marshall
	Joseph M. Long
	Carl N. Crouse
1976	Barbara Blum
	Lewis E. Carpenter
	Henry E. Clipper
	William Hargis, Jr.
1977	Steve Galizioli
	Seth Gordon
	Henry Herrmann
	Laurence Pringle
	John E. Murphy

The Resources Defense Award honors special achievement in the protection of natural resources. It is given as merited or annually, and is an area the Federation especially wishes to encourage.

1976	J. Gus Speth
1977	Michael Osborne

The International Achievement Award, which consists of a peregrine falcon, honors individuals for special achievement in international conservation. It is given as merited or annually, and is an area the federation especially wishes to encourage.

1972 Maurice F. Strong
1973 No award
1974 No award
1975 No award
1976 Peter Markham Scott
     Robert M. White
1977 Ruth C. Clusen

Business, Management &

Labor

Contents

Related Awards

Horatio Alger Award

HORATIO ALGER AWARDS COMMITTEE
1 Rockefeller Plaza, Suite 1609, New York, N.Y. 10020
(212/581-6433)

The Horatio Alger Award annually honors individuals who rose to success in America from humble beginnings. The award, which was conceived of by the American Schools and Colleges Association, is designed to encourage young people to realize that success in this country can be achieved by working in the free enterprise system, which the Horatio Alger Awards Committee supports. Recipients of the award are frequently in business, although public servants, educators and entertainers are also honored.

1947 I. J. Fox
Walter S. Mack, President, C & C Super Corporation
Grover A. Whalen, New York greeter and businessman
Charles E. Wilson, President, General Electric
Robert R. Young, Chairman, New York Central Railroad
1948 Bernard Baruch, Financier
Earl Bunting, Director National Assn. of Manufacturers
George A. Hamid, Owner, Atlantic City Steel Pier
Charles Luckman, Pereira & Luckman
Dorothy Shaver, President, Lord & Taylor
1949 Allen B. Dumont, President, Allen Dumont Laboratories
Earl William Muntz, President, Muntz T.V., Inc.
Lee E. Nadeau, President, The Nestle-Le Muir Co.
Vincent Riggio, Chairman, American Tobacco Co.
Anna Rosenberg, Assistant Secretary of Defense
1950 Thomas E. Courtney, President, Northern Illinois Corp.
Alexander Harris, President, Ronson Corporation
C. N. Hilton, President, Hilton Hotels, Inc.
Alexander Milton Lewyt, Inventor, Lewyt Vacuum Cleaner
Charles Revson, Chairman and President, Revlon Corp.
1951 Frank Bailey, President, Title Guarantee & Trust Co.
James L. Kraft, Chairman, Kraft-Phoenix Cheese Corp.
Finn H. Magnus, President, The Magnus Harmonica Corp.
James J. Nance, Chairman, First Union Real Estate Investments
F. C. Russell, President, The F. C. Russell Company
Brig. Gen. David Sarnoff, Chairman, Radio Corporation of America
Harold E. Stassen, Special Assistant to the President and former Governor of Minnesota
Arthur Wiesenberger, President, Arthur Wiesenberger, Inc.
1952 Ralph Johnson Bunche, Nobel Prize winner and United Nations Delegate
Milton S. Eisenhower, President, Pennsylvania State University
James J. Kerrigan, Chairman Executive Committee, Merck & Company
Charles F. Kettering, Research Consultant, General Motors Corp.
Thomas E. Millsop, President, National Steel Corporation
Norman Vincent Peale, Minister, Marble Collegiate Church, and author

William A. Roberts, President Allis-Chalmers Manufacturing Company
1953 Gen. Sandy Beaver, Chairman and President, Riverside Military Academy, Calif.
Col. Henry Crown, President, Empire State Building and Materials Service Corp.
Walter D. Fuller, President and Chairman, Curtis Publishing Co.
Byron Alfred Gray, Chairman, International Shoe Co.
Paul Gray Hoffman, Chairman, Studebaker-Packard Corp.
Herbert Hoover, former President of the United States
John Jay Hopkins, Chairman and President, General Dynamics Corp.
J. C. Penney, Chairman, J. C. Penney Company
Harold Schaffer, President, Gold Seal Company
Thomas John Watson, Chairman, International Business Machines
Adolph Zukor, Chairman, Paramount Pictures Corporation
1954 Michael Baker, Jr., President Michael Baker, Jr. Engineering Co.
Donald R. Brann, President, Easi-Bild Pattern Corporation
John Allan Bush, Chairman, Brown Shoe Company
Clifford F. Hood, President, United States Steel Corp.
Fred A. Lawson, President, E. L. Patch Company
William P. Lear, Chairman, Lear, Inc.
Daniel A. Poling, Editor, *Christian Herald*
Andrew R. Shea, President, Pan American Grace Airlines
Harold V. Smith, President, Home Insurance Co.
Joseph Sunnen, President, Sunnen Products Co.
1955 Roger Ward Babson, President, Babson's Statistical Service
Hugh Roy Cullen, President, Quintana Petroleum Corp.
Percy J. Ebbott, Vice Chairman, Chase Manhattan Bank of New York
William E. Levis, Chairman, Owens-Illinois Glass Company
James W. McAfee, President, Union Electric Company
Frank B. Rackley, President, Jessop Steel Co.
Arthur Rubloff, Chairman, Arthur Rubloff & Co.
James C. Self, President, Greenwood Mills
Carl J. Sharp, Chairman, Acme Steel Co.
Donald S. Smith, President, Perfection Stove Co.
1956 Lester W. Carter, President, American Hotel Assn.
Armando Conti, President, Trenton Beverage Co.
G. S. Eyssell, President, Rockefeller Center, Inc.
Allen Gellman, President, Elgin-American Company
Roy T. Hurley, President, Curtiss-Wright Company
John M. Joyce, President, Seven-Up Bottling Co.
William Cords Snyder, Jr., President, Blaw-Knox Manufacturing Co.
Edward Vernon Rickenbacker, Chairman and President Eastern Air Lines
1957 Charles C. Bales, Head of C. C. Bales Agency
John Bentia, President, Alliance Manufacturing Co.
Thomas Carvel, President, The Carvel Company
Alwin F. Franz, President and Chairman, Colorado Fuel and Iron Corp.
Joyce C. Hall, President, Hallmark Greeting Card Co.
Gwilym A. Price, President and Chairman, Westinghouse Electric Corp
John J. Sheinin, President, Chicago Medical School
Harry Sugar, President, Alsco, Inc.

John H. Ware, Chairman, American Water Works Co.
Adam Young, President, Young Television Corporation
Louis Zahn, President, Zahn Drug Company
1958 **J. H. Carmichael,** Chairman, Capital Airlines
Paul Dawson Eddy, President, Adelphi College (citation)
Benjamin F. Fairless, President, American Iron & Steel Institute
Milton G. Hulme, President, Hulme, Applegate & Humphrey, Inc.
Howard K. Moore, Headmaster, Peekskill Military Academy (citation)
William Thomas Payne, President, Big Chief Drilling Company
T. Claude Ryan, President, Ryan Aeronautical Company
Raymond E. Salvati, President, Island Creek Coal Co.
William B. Tabler, Architect
Peter Volid, Chairman, King Korn Trading Stamp Co.
1959 **Albert J. Berdis,** President, Great Lakes Steel Corp.
John F. Ernsthausen, President and Founder, Norwalk Truck Lines, Inc.
Alfred C. Fuller, "The Original Fuller Brush Man"
Alfred L. Hammell, President, Railway Express Agency, Inc.
Walter L. Jacobs, President, The Hertz Corporation
James P. Mitchell, U.S. Secretary of Labor
Charles F. Noyes, President, Charles F. Noyes Co., Inc.
Eric A. Walker, President, Pennsylvania State University
Benjamin H. Wooten, President, First National Bank in Dallas
1960 **Frank Armour, Jr.,** President, H. J. Heinz Company
John W. Galbreath, Realtor and owner, John W. Galbreath & Co.
Carl S. Hallauer, President and Board Chairman, Bausch & Lomb Optical Co.
Garvice D. Kincaid, Financier, Bankers & Securities, Inc.
Ed C. Leach, President, Jack Tar Hotels chain
James A. Ryder, President, Ryder System, Inc
John H. Slater, Owner and President, Slater Food Service Management
Robert S. Solinsky, President and Board Chairman, National Can Corp.
Vernon C. Beebe, Co-Founder, Beebe Advertising Agency, Inc. (citation)
1961 **John A. Barr,** Chairman, Montgomery Ward & Company
Dwight David Eisenhower, Former President of the United States
Richard Prentice Ettinger, Chairman, Prentice-Hall, Inc.
Warren G. Grimes, Board Chairman, Grimes Manufacturing Co.
William G. Karnes, President, Beatrice Foods Company
Merl C. Kelce, President, Peabody Coal Company
John D. MacArthur, President, Bankers Life & Casualty Co.
C. R. Smith, President, American Airlines
Walter J. Tuohy, President, Chesapeake & Ohio Railway
James W. Walter, President, Jim Walter Corporation
1962 **Charles W. Anderson,** President, Ametek, Inc.
Frank G. Atkinson, President, Joseph Dixon Crucible Co.

James R. Caldwell, Chairman, Rubbermaid, Inc.
James M. Hill, Hill Enterprises
J. Patrick Lannan, Chairman, Susquehanna Corp.
James J. Ling, President, Ling-Temco Vought, Inc.
Allen Ludden, Senior Executive, CBS *and* College Bowl Moderator
Clarence R. Moll, President, Pennsylvania Military College
E. J. Thomas, Chairman and Chief Executive, Goodyear Tire & Rubber Co.
Edward A. White, President, Bowmar Instrument Corporation
1963 **Charles R. Anthony,** President and Chairman, C. R. Anthony Co.
John Bowles, President, The Rexall Drug Company
Bernard Castro, President, Castro Convertible Corp.
Albert Dorne, Artist, Illustrator and President, Famous Artists Schools
Titus Haffa, Chairman of the Board, Webcor, Inc.
Wayne A. Johnston, President, Illinois Central Railroad
Abner Vernon McCall, President, Baylor University
George O. Nodyne, President, East River Savings Bank of New York
John W. Rollins, President, Rollins Leasing Corporation
R. Perry Shorts, Chairman, Second Nat'l Bank of Saginaw, Mich.
W. Clement Stone, President, Combined Insurance Company of America
1964 **Gene Autry,** Actor, producer and businessman
Charles Bates Thornton, Chairman, Litton Industries
Pearl Buck, Author
Carr P. Collins, Chairman, Fidelity Union Life Ins. Co.
T. Jack Foster, Building and Land Development
E. Ellis Johnson, President, Chicago, Rock Island & Pacific Railroad
Nathaniel Leverone, Chairman, Automatic Canteen Co. of America
J. C. Warner, President, Carnegie Institute of Technology
Herbert J. Watt, President, Peabody Institute
Minoru Yamasaki, Architect
1965 **Elmer Bobst,** Chairman, Warner-Lambert Pharmaceutical Co.
Paul Carnahan, Chairman, National Steel Corp.
R. Carl Chandler, Chairman, Standard Packaging Co.
Rev. Billy Graham, Evangelist, author and educator
Joseph E. Maddy, National Music Corporation
William A. Patterson, President, United Air Lines
Jeno F. Paulucci, President and Chairman, Chun King Corp.
Col. Harland Sanders, Founder, Kentucky Fried Chicken Corp.
George D. Sax, Chairman, Exchange National Bank
Louis S. Vosburgh, Chairman, Lincoln Extension Institute
Harry Winokur, Chairman, Mr. Donut of America, Inc.
1966 **Roy L. Ash,** President, Litton Industries
Walter Brennan, Actor
Chester Carlson, Inventor (Xerox Corporation)
William Forrest Foster, President, Merit Clothing Co.
William E. Grace, President and Chief Executive Officer, Fruehauf Corp.
Robert W. Hawkinson, President, Belden Manufacturing Co.

George W. Jenkins, President, Publix Super Markets, Inc.

John H. Johnson, President and Editor, Johnson Publishing Co., Inc.

Samuel H. Levinson, President, Railweight, Inc.

Elmer F. Pierson, President and Chairman, The Vendo Co.

Harold Toppel, Chairman, H. C. Bohack Co., Inc.

Leslie B. Worthington, President, U.S. Steel Corp.

1967 Carl E. Anderson, Chairman and President, E. W. Bliss Co.

Max Coffman, President, Mammoth Mart, Inc.

Davre J. Davidson, Chairman, Automatic Retailers of America

Michael E. Debakey, Chairman of Surgery, Baylor University, Tex.

John A. Howard, President, Rockford College

Ewing Marion Kauffman, President, Marion Laboratories, Inc.

Robert F. McCune, President, Robert F. McCune Associates, Inc.

Lewis Phillips, President, Nedick's Stores

Lawrence Welk, Musical conductor

Elmer L. Winter, President, Manpower, Inc.

1968 Walter D. Behlen, Chairman, Behlen Manufacturing Co.

Marvin Chandler, Chairman & President, Northern Illinois Gas Co.

Arthur J. Goldberg, Permanent Representitive of the U.S. to United Nations

George S. Halas, Owner and Coach, Chicago Bears football club

Bob Hope, Entertainer

Wallace E. Johnson, President, Holiday Inns of America, Inc.

Kenneth J. King, Sr., President, Kenny King's Family Restaurants

Charles W. Lubin, Chairman, Kitchens of Sara Lee

Thomas W. Moore, Group Vice President, American Broadcasting Co., Inc.

W. Dewey Presley, President, First National Bank in Dallas

Margaret Durham Robey, President, Southern Seminary & Jr. College

Joseph Timan, President, Horizon Land Corporation

1969 Ragnar Benson, Chairman, Ragnar Benson, Inc.

Winston A. Burnett, President and Chairman, Winston A. Burnett Co.

Emmett J. Culligan, Founder, Culligan, Inc.

Charles Deaton, Architect

Erik Jonsson, Mayor, Dallas, Tex.

Herman W. Lay, Chairman, PepsiCo, Inc.

Thurgood Marshall, Justice of the U.S. Supreme Court

Gerald C. O'Brien, President and Chairman, North American Development Corp.

Michael L. Rachunis, Eye, ear, nose and throat physician

Ronald Reagan, Governor, State of California

Meshulam Riklis, Chairman, Rapid-American, McCrory, Glen Alden Corp

1970 Harry F. Chaddick, President, Chicago Industrial District, Inc.

Sam M. Fleming, President, Third National Bank & NLT Corp.

Hiram L. Fong, U. S. Senator from Hawaii

Luther H. Hodges, Chairman, Research Triangle Foundation

Harold J. Richards, Chairman, Fidelity Corporation

Riley V. Sims, Chairman, Burnup & Sims, Inc.

Carl B. Stokes, Mayor, Cleveland, Ohio

Jackie Williams, Chairman and Chief Executive Officer, AAA Enterprises, Inc.

Kemmons Wilson, Chairman, Holiday Inns, Inc.

Sam Wyly, Chairman, University Computing Co.

1971 Robert H. Abplanalp, President and Chairman, Precision Valve Corp.

Lawrence A. Appley, Chairman, American Management Assn.

Adron Doran, President, Morehead State University

Robert S. Fogarty, Jr., Founder and President, Habitation Resources, Inc.

Alexander G. Hardy, Chairman, The AVEMCO Group

Leon W. "Pete" Harman, President, Harman-Managers Investment, Inc.

Charles Stewart Mott, Director, General Motors and founder, The Mott Foundation

Howard A. Rusk, Director, Institute of Rehabilitation Medicine

Edward Durell Stone, Architect

Lowell Thomas, Commentator and author

1972 William G. Bailey, Chairman, Bestline Products, Inc.

Lee S. Bickmore, Chairman, Nabisco, Inc.

Lt. Gen. James H. Doolittle, Awarded Congressional Medal of Honor

Walter J. Hickel, Governor, State of Alaska

Ray A. Kroc, Chairman, McDonald's Corporation

Floyd Odlum, Financier

Patrick L. O'Malley, President, Canteen Corp.

H. Ross Perot, Chairman, Electronic Data Systems Corp.

James R. Price, Chairman, National Homes Corp.

James B. Reston, Vice-President, *The New York Times*

Henry G. Walter, Honorary Trustee, Illinois Masonic Medical Center

1973 No awards

1974 Andrew F. Brimmer, Board of Governors, Federal Reserve System

George P. Cullum, Sr., Founder and Chairman, Cullum Construction Co.

Robert Beverley Evans, Detroit Industrialist and Director, American Motors Corp.

Zenon C. R. Hansen, President and Chairman, Mack Trucks

Herbert C. Johnson, Chairman, Consolidated Natural Gas Co.

Clare Boothe Luce, Playwright, actress, Congresswoman, ambassador and lecturer

J. Willard Marriott, Founder and Chairman, Marriott Corp.

Arthur H. "Red" Motley, Chairman, *Parade* magazine

Harold G. Scheie, Director, Scheie Eye Institute

Norman H. Stone, Chairman and Chief Executive Officer, Stone Container Corp.

Frederic Whitaker, Founder, Audubon Artists

1975 Helen F. Boehm, Chairman, Edward Marshall Boehm, Inc.

Edward E. Carlson, Chairman of the Board, UAL, Inc.

R. J. Foresman, President and Chief Operating Officer, Michigan General Corp.

Dean W. Jeffers, General Chairman, Nationwide Insurance Companies

Ronald V. Markham, Co-Founder, Anvil Mining Corp.

Vincent G. Marotta, President, North American Systems, Inc.

Allen H. Neuharth, President and Chief Executive, Gannett Co.
Robert L. Rice, Founder and Chairman, Health Industries, Inc.
William G. Salatich, President, Gillette North America
George Shinn, President, George Shinn & Associates
Herbert J. Stiefel, President Stiefel/Raymond Advertising, Inc.
1976 **Carlos J. Arboleya,** President, Barnett Banks of Miami
Loren M. Berry, Founder, L.M. Berry & Company
Roy J. Carver, Founder and Chairman, Bandag, Inc.
William E. Dearden, Vice Chairman and Chief Executive Officer, Hershey Foods Corp.
Robert E. Farrell, President, Farrell's Ice Cream Parlour Restaurants
J. M. Haggar, Sr., Founder and Honorary Chairman, Haggar Company
Joseph H. Hirshhorn, Joseph H. Hirshhorn Museum & Sculpture Garden
Gen. Daniel James, Jr., Commander-in-Chief, North American Air Defense Command
Art Linkletter, Television and radio star, and chairman, Linkletter Enterprises
George M. Mardikian, Food consultant and owner, Omar Khayyam's Restaurant
Rod McKuen, Poet, pop composer, author, singer and classical composer
John Milano, President, Byer-Rolnick Company
Francine I. Neff, Treasurer of the United States
Ernest L. Wilkinson, President-Emeritus, Brigham Young University
1977 **Johnny Cash,** Entertainer
Robert P. Gerholz, President, Gerholz Community Homes, Inc.
J. Ira Harris, General Partner, Salomon Brothers
George J. Kneeland, Chairman, Executive Committee, St. Regis Paper Co.
David J. Mahoney, Chairman and President, Norton Simon, Inc.
Ruth Stafford Peale, Author, lecturer and publisher
Ann Person, Founder and President, Stretch & Sew, Inc.
Roger Tory Peterson, Artist, ornithologist and author
Rose Cook Small, Founder and Vice President, Bluebird, Inc.
L. Homer Surbeck, Partner, Hughes, Hubbard & Reed
Sarkes Tarzian, Founder and President, Sarkes Tarzian, Inc.
Jessie L. Ternberg, Director, Surgery, Pediatric Division, St. Louis Children's Hospital
Danny Thomas, Entertainer

Beyer Medal
President's Award
Junior Achievement Treasurer of the Year

NATIONAL ASSOCIATION OF ACCOUNTANTS
919 Third Ave., New York, N.Y. 10022 (212/754-9764)

The Beyer Medal, which is of gold, is given for the highest scores in a three-day examination for the Certificate in Management Accounting.

1972	**Robert F. Garland**
1973	**Scott G. Thompson**
1974	**Amit M. Nanavati**
1975	**Michael Duffy**
1976	**Bhaskar Bhave**
1977	**Kay A. Scheible**

The President's Award, which consists of a trophy, honors consistent performance over a five-year period as determined by year-end standing in annual incentive competitions among the 300 local chapters of the NAA.

1975	**Eugene, Ore.**
1976	**Piedmont Winston-Salem, N.C.**
1977	**Akron, Ohio**

The Junior Achievement Treasurer of the Year honors a high-school junior achiever who is judged the best treasurer of a Junior Achievement company. Judging is done first on a local level, then on a regional level and finally nationally. The winner receives $750 and a plaque.

1967	**Douglas Moore**
1968	**Charles Golay**
1969	**Michael Oslon**
1970	**Marie E. Cox**
1971	**Dennis Keenan**
1972	**Deborah Tierney**
1973	**Kay Boeskool**
1974	**Craig R. Choun**
1975	**Williams S. Simpkins**
1976	**Greg Maislin**
1977	**Kenneth Parrish**

Clio Awards

30 E. 60th St., New York., N.Y. 10022 (212/593-1900)

The Clio Award is a statue given annually to honor excellence in advertising, worldwide, in all media. Entries are judged in product and campaign categories by advertising creative executives and groups of technical specialists. Judges, who must abstain from voting on their own work, comprise a panel of 450 members who represent 16 cities in 10 countries from five continents.

1974 U.S. PRODUCT WINNERS

Old Home Bakeries, "Bread City", "Coffee Rolls", "Nice Buns" (Campaign), Bozell & Jacobs/Visual Presentations
Thom McAn Shoes, "Standing On My Foot" (Apparel), Carole Langer/Horn-Griner
Johnson & Johnson Baby Powder, "Roommates" (Bath Products), Young & Rubican/Ampersand
Malt Duck, "It Certainly is . . . " (Beers and wines), W.B. Doner/Sedelmaier
M & M Candies, "Goddess" (Confections/snacks), Ted Bates/EUE
General Electric, "Absent Mother" (Corporate/institutional), BBDO/Gomes-Loew
Eau de Love, "Oh Da Flowers" (Cosmetics/toiletries-women), Wells, Rich, Greene/Wylde
Ocean Spray Cranapple Juice, "Sweet Tart" (Dairy products), Ted Bates/Chance III
Kodak Film, "Memories" (Gift items), J. Walter Thompson/EUE/Screen Gems

Frigidaire Range, "Tech Center" (Home furnishings), Needham, Harper, Steers/Wheiner-Berman

Slurp, "The Slurp" (Household items), The Project Group/Wylde

Metropolitan Life, "Ring" (Insurance) Young & Rubicam/Wylde

Pippin Show, "Dance" (Media promotion/entertainment), Blaine-Thompson/Pucci-Stone

Purina Meow Mix, "Singing Cats" (Pet products), Della Femina, Travisano/David Langley

Scope Mouthwash, "A Day in the Life" (Pharmaceuticals/dentifrices), Benton & Bowles/Jenkins-Covington

Muscular Dystrophy Assn., "Ezzard Charles" (Public service), Benton & Bowles/EUE

Titleist Golf Balls, "Snorkel" (Recreation equipment), Humphrey Browning MacDougall/Petersen

Benihana of Tokyo, "Graduation" (Retail food stores/restaurants), Kracauer & Marvin/Rick Levine

Barney's, "1923" (Retail stores/services), Scali, McCabe, Sloves/Ampersand

Tonka Toys, "Excuses" (Toys and games), Carl Ally

United Airlines, "Friends" (Travel), Leo Burnett-/Opus III

AT&T Long Distance, "Friends" (Utilities), N.W. Ayer/Jenkins Covington

Dr. Pepper, "Pepperettes" (Soft drinks), Young & Rubicam/Ampersand

TECHNIQUE WINNERS

Sunbeam Lady Shavers, "Tricky Pair" (Animation), N.W. Ayer/Kurtz & Friends

Nat'l Institute on Alcohol Abuse, "Typical Alcoholic" (Copy), Grey-North/James Garrett

Arrow Shirts, "Garden Party" (Costume design), Young & Rubicam/Ampersand

Eastern Air Lines, "Vacation Islands" (Editing), Young & Rubicam/Summit/Murffitt

U.S. Travel Bureau, "Ice Block" (Film effects), Young & Rubicam/Canadian Cinegraph

First Nat'l Bank of Miami, "Robber" (Humor), Mike Sloan/Tulchin

Hush Puppies, "Hush Puppies are Dumb" (Music with lyrics), Wells, Rich, Greene/Steve Karmen

Benihana of Tokyo, "Rookie" (Performance—Male), Kracauer & Marvin/Rick Levine

Alka Seltzer, "Wrestling Match" (Performance—female), Wells, Rich, Greene/Gomes-Loew

Activ Panty Hose, "Activ City" (Set design), Young & Rubicam/Horn-Griner

INTERNATIONAL WINNERS

7 Up, "Hippies" (Holland) (Animation), Prad/Anglo-Dutch Group

Ford F-100 Pickup, "You Don't Run Out of Pickup" (Argentina) (Demonstration), J. Walter Thompson/Casares

Pepsi Cola, "Stadium" (Brazil) (Music), Mauro Salles/Filmcenter

Toyota Corona, "Developing the New Corona" (Japan) (Auto), Dentsu/Nippon Recruit Center

Jun-Rope, "Jean" (Japan) (Apparel), Directors Circle

Rambo Hole Sealer, (Holland) (Home maintenance), KVH/Forum

Rank Xerox, "Underground to Moscow" (England) (Office equipment), Young & Rubicam

Nippon Voluntary Insurance, "The Egg" (Japan) (Services) Dentsu/Tokyo Publicity Center

Toronto Energy Conservation (Canada) (Public service), Vickers & Benson/Projections

Coca-Cola, "Surfing" (Australia) (Soft drinks), Hansen Rubensohn-McCann-Erickson/Telemark

Hypermarche Stores, "The Higher We Pile 'Em" (Canada) (Retail), W.B. Doner/Mayday

Cadbury Whole Nut Candy, "Director" (Ireland) (Confections), Peter Owens/GPA Films

Uncle Sam Deodorant, "Uncle Sam" (Australia) (Bath products), Hansen Rubensohn-McCann-Erickson/Eric Porter

Benson & Hedges Special Panatellas, "Hat" (England) (Tobacco), Collett, Dickenson, Pearce/Alan Parker

Ize Electricity, "Helps to Live" (Germany) (Corporate), Die Werbe Euro/Franck Film

Hovis Bread, "Bike Ride" (England) (Foods/photography/direction), Collett, Dickenson, Pearce/RSA

Walls Ice Cream, "Walls Follies" (England) (Production design), Lintas/Illustra

Cockburns Special Reserve, "Shipwrecked" (England) (Beers and wines), Collett, Dickenson, Pearce/AlanPorter

Barclays Bank, "Hands" (England) (Editing), Charles Barker/Michael Warhurst/Studio Lambert

Ricore Cafe, "The Hunt" (France) (Coffee/tea), Publicis Conseil/Hamster

Vicks Vaporub, "Breathing Jar" (England) (Pharmaceuticals), Benton & Bowles/Gillie Potter

Sunday Times, "Wine" (England) (Media promotion), HSL

Gillette Foamy, "Split Screen" (England) (Men's toiletries), J. Walter Thompson/Streich Perkins

La Bonne Vie Cheese, "Monk's Lunch" (England) (Dairy products), Leo Burnett/HSL

Kodak Pocket Instamatic, "Handplay" (England) (Personal/gift items) J. Walter Thompson/Streich Perkins

Cie Railways, "The Super Train" (Ireland) (Travel), Arks/Scope

Swish Curtain Rack, "Bathroom", "Honey-mooners", "Speech" (England) (Home furnishings/overall campaign) Cogent Elliott/Alan Parker

1975 U.S. PRODUCT WINNERS

Southern Airways, "Orgy", "Party", "Bum" (Campaign, Humor, Travel), McDonald Little/Sedelmaier

American Motors Pacer, "Shell" (Automotive), Cunningham & Walsh/Stone

No More Tangles, "Damaged" (Bath products), Compton/Gottlieb

Schaefer Beer, "Kites" (Beers/wines), BBDO/Garrett

Tic Tac Mints, "Bang Out of Life" (Confection/-snacks), Chalek & Dreyer/Wylde, Sunlight

General Electric, "Bull in the Lexan Shop" (Corporate), BBDO/May Day

Pure Magic Lipstick, "Lips" (Cosmetics/toiletries-women), Rosenfeld, Sirowitz, Lawson/Lacy

Ultra-Bright, "Laura Baugh-Love Life" (Dentifrice), William Esty/Filmco

Kodak Film, "First Time Ever I Saw Your Face" (Gift items), J. Walter Thompson/MPO

Duracell Batteries, "Rabbits" (Home maintenance), Dancer Fitzgerald Sample/Lobell
M.O.N.Y., "Cabins" (Insurance), Marschalk/Horn
Mobil Oil, "Masterpiece Theatre" (Media promotion/entertainment), Varied Directions
Delmonte Catsup, "Catsup Moon" (Packaged foods), McCann-Erickson/Harris
Nat'l Alliance of Businessmen, "Toy Soldiers" (Public service), Grey/Ampersand
Kawasaki Motorcycles, "Garage" (Recreation equipment), Cunningham & Walsh/Pytka, Sandler
Big Ten Ford Dealers, "Hubcaps" (Retail auto), Mike Sloan/A&R
Barney's, "You're Big Enough" (Retail department stores), Scali, McCabe, Sloves/Horn
Pepsi Cola, "Pied Piper" (Soft Drinks), BBDO/Garrett
Diet Pepsi Cola, "Zipper" (Soft Drinks), BBDO/Michlin & Hill
Tonka Toys, "Elephant" (Demonstration toys/games) Carl Ally/Horn-Griner
Illinois Bell, "Teenager" (Utilities), N.W. Ayer ABH/Hil Covington

TECHNIQUE WINNERS

Eastern Airlines, "Winter Wonderland" (Animation), Young & Rubicam/Ovation
AT&T, "Maine" (Cinematography), N.W. Ayer ABH/Lear Levin
Burlington, "The Burlington Look" (Costuming), Doyle Dane Bernbach/Garrett
AAA of Michigan, "Travels of Charlie" (Direction), Stockwell-Marcuse/May Day
Gimbels, "Image" (Editing), Wyse/Editors Gas
Seven-Up, "Bubbles" (Film effects), J. Walter Thompson/EUE, Abel
Dr. Pepper, "Board Room" (Male performance) and set Design, Young & Rubicam/Rick Levine
Colt 45 Malt Liquor, "Hotel" (Set design), W.B. Doner/Movie House

INTERNATIONAL WINNERS

Ford F-100, "Air Drop" (Argentina) (Automotive, demonstration), J. Walter Thompson/Casares
Cadbury, "Mona Lisa" (Canada) (Confection/snacks), Doyle Dane Bernbach/Rabko
Crespi, "Pollution" (Argentina) (Corporate), Portillo Olson
Fuji Waste Disposer, "Recycling" (Japan) (Corporate), Hakuhodo/Tohoku Shin Sha
Walls Ice Cream, "Fizz Bang" (United Kingdom) (Dairy products), Lintas/Ridley Scott
Listerine, "Lifeboat Deck" (United Kingdom) (Dentifrice/pharmaceuticals), J. Walter Thompson/GPA
Moulinex, "Electric Knife" (Switzerland) (Home furnishings/appliances), Walther & Leuenberger/Condor
Desk Top Lamps, "Dancing Lamps" (Japan) (Home furnishings/appliances), Hakunodo/O.T.V. Film
Decora, "Stains" (Brazil) (Home maintenance), Casabranca/Robert Bakker
Panasonic Batteries, "Robot" (Japan) (Home maintenance), Dentsu/Dentsu Motion Picture
Marlboro, "Wild Horses" (Australia) (Tobacco), USP Needham/Film House

KLM, "Surprising Amsterdam" (Holland) (Travel/transportation), Vaz/Dies/Producers
Coca-Cola, "Waves" (Australia) (Cinematography), Hansen Rubenson/Telemark
Count Pushkin Vodka, "Transiberian Express" (South Africa) (Animation/graphics), ARL Services/Richard Williams
Country Pale, "Aqua Ballet" (France) (Production design), Dupuy/Compton/ID
Speedy Muffler, "Golfer" (Canada) (Humor), Goodis, Goldberg, Soren/Rabko

1976 U.S. WINNERS

Exxon, "Mark Twain", "Anne Sullivan" (Introduction Campaign)
Chevrolet, "Baseball, Hotdogs '76" (Automotive)
BF Goodrich, "Joan Rivers" (Auto Accessories)
Texaco, "Tortoise & Hare" (Gasolines/lubricants)
Diet Rite, "Hava" (Soft drinks)
Schmidts, "Tell a Coors" (Beers/wines)
Salada, "Saleman" (Coffee/tea)
Nair, "Sport Shorts" (Bath products)
Colgate, "Braces" (Dentifrice)
Pampers, "It's a Girl" (Household items)
Tic Tac, "Ballerina Bang" (Confections/snacks)
Old Home Bread, "Bread Bash" (Foods)
Straw Hat Pizza, "Time Lapse" (Retail food)
Sony Cassette, "Restaurant" (Gifts/personal items)
Celotex, "I'm a Roof" (Home maintenance)
Elmers Glue-All, "Bulldozer" (Product demo)
Tonka, "Factory" (Toys/games)
National Geographic, "Incredible Machine" (Media promotion)
Barney's, "English Room" (Retail specialty)
British Airways, "Horseman" (Travel transportation)
Xerox 9200, "Monks" (Office equipment)
Anti Defamation League, "The Prejudice Test" (Copywriting)
Kodak Trimline, "Scrooge" (Costuming/set design)
Exxon, "Dizzy Dean" (Cinematography)
Pepsi Cola, "Samantha" (Direction)
Boston Red Sox, "Keep Your Sox On" (Editing)
Levis, "Threads" (Animation)
East LA Health Task Force, "Drunk Driving" (Local low budget)
Peugeot, "Test Track" (Musical scoring)
Kodak Film, "In Session" (Music/lyrics)

INTERNATIONAL WINNERS

Eaton's, "Number One," "Timothy E", Canada (Campaign)
Levis, "The First Jean", Argentina (Apparel)
Wool Superwash, "Label", Holland (Apparel)
Tropical Tires, "Highways", Brazil (Auto Accessories)
Master Charge, "Dominoes", Canada (Services)
Lion Lager, "Barbeque", South Africa (Cinematography)
Coca Cola, "Real You", Australia (Soft drinks)
Tetley Tea Bags, "Folk Dance", United Kingdom (Coffee/tea)
Ontario Milk Marketing Board, "Hats/Moustache", Canada (Dairy products)
Mazola Oil, "Growing Seed", Germany (Foods)
National Lamp, "Mosquito", Japan (Home furnishings)

Corco Plasticine, "Plasticine", Puerto Rico (Corporate)

Rapid Cement, "Balloon", Japan (Household items)

Optrex Eye Dew, "Mirror Mirror", United Kingdom (Animation)

Uncle Sam Tooth Paste, "Need All", Australia (Dentifrice)

Chipmonks Potato Chips, "Chipmonks", Canada (Confections/snacks)

Solo, "More Real Than Brown", Norway (Humor)

1977 U.S. WINNERS

Kodak Film, "This Old House", "Time to Sow", (Introduction Campaign)

Fiat, "Over the Years", (Automotive)

Life Savers, "Karen", (Confections/snacks)

Breakstone Cottage Cheese, "Store", (Dairy products/Fruit drinks)

Mueller's Egg Noodles, "Dr. Joyce Brothers' Mother", (Packaged foods)

Sure Anti-Perspirant, "Take Off Your Coat America", (Bath products)

Faberge Babe, "Restaurant", (Women's products)

Downy Fabric Softener, "The Feeling's Fine", (Household items)

Purina Meow Mix, "Letters", (Pet products)

Pace CB Radios, "Girl", (Recreation equipment)

Hallmark Cards, "Moving Day", (Corporate)

Paine Webber Brokerage, "Antique Cars", (Banks/financial)

Illinois Bell Telephone/Disabled, "Alexander Graham Bell", (Utilities)

American Cancer Society, "Money Talks", (Public service)

Dayton's Warehouse Sale, "Mr. Shirley", (Retail specialty/department store)

Pan Am, "Millions of Americans", (Travel/transportation)

N.Y. Shakespeare Festival, "3 Penny Opera", (Media promotion)

General Electric, "Steinmetz", (Copy and male performance)

Farmland Industries, "History", (Cinematography)

National Beer, "Softball", (Editing)

Dean Witter Stocks/Bonds, "Omnibus", (Animation)

ITT, "Fiber Optics", (Film effects)

Wamsutta Sheets, "Designer Sheets", (Musical scoring)

Sugar Free Dr. Pepper, "Pinball", (Set design)

St. Regis, "Bridge", (Product demonstration)

Yamaha Motorcycles, "Police Chief", (Humor)

INTERNATIONAL WINNERS

Overseas Telecommunications, "Greece", "Italy", Australia (Campaign)

Peugeot 104, "Slalom", France (Automotive)

Gilbey's Gin, "Phrase Book-Small", "Talk" World Wide (Beers/wines)

Evergood Coffee, "Evergood", Norway (Coffee/tea)

Johnson's Cotonetes, "Bored Baby", Brazil (Dentifrice/pharmaceuticals)

H.J. Heinz Canned Salad, "Ingredients", England (Packaged foods)

Taubmans Gaylon Paint, "Army", New Zealand (Household items)

The London Sunday Times, "Ageing", England (Media promotion)

Xerox 3103 Copier, "Great Performance", Japan (Office equipment)

Samsonite, "The Elephants", France/Germany/Holland (Gifts/personal items)

Sugar Free 7-Up, "Evolution", Canada (Soft drinks)

Singha Beer, "Monsoon", Thailand (Cinematography)

Martini Bianco, "Because You Know It's Right", England (Editing)

Aron-Alpha Instant Adhesive, "Sticking Power", Japan (Product demonstration)

4711 Eau de Cologne, "Young Generation", Germany (Music/lyrics)

Chrysler Avenger, "Avenger File '77", Ireland (Musical scoring)

Cadbury's Crunchie Bar, "Gold Rush", New Zealand (Confections/snacks and set design)

Advertising Hall of Fame
AMERICAN ADVERTISING FEDERATION
1225 Connecticut Ave. NW, Washington, D.C. 20036
(202/659-1800)

Election to the Advertising Hall of Fame recognizes individuals who have contributed to American advertising by the advancement of social and economic values of advertising and who have applied their expertise to some form of public service. A council of judges reviews nominations and selects new members of the Hall of Fame each year.

1949

Rollin C. Ayres	Cyrus H. K. Curtis
Alfred W. Erickson	William H. Johns
Lewis B. Jones	Theodore F. MacManus
Edwin T. Meredith	John Irving Romer
Walter A. Strong	John Wanamaker

1950

F. Wayland Ayer	Stanley Clague
Benjamin Franklin	James H. McGraw
Merle Sidener	

1951

William Cheever D'Arcy	E. St. Elmo Lewis

1952

Erma Perham Proetz	J. Earle Pearson

1953

Samuel C. Dobbs	Charles Coolidge Parlin
James O'Shaughnessy	

1954

Frank Presbrey	John E. Powers

1955

Henry T. Ewald	George Burton Hotchkiss

1956

No inductees

1957

Herbert S. Houston	Claude Clarence Hopkins

1958

Orlando Clinton Harn	Albert D. Lasker

1959
Merlin Hall Aylesworth   Kerwin Holmes Fulton

1960
Allen Loren Billingsly   James Randolph Adams

1961
Barney Link   Harley Procter

1962
Mac Martin   Donald W. Davis

1963
Gilbert T. Hodges   Paul B. West

1964
Homer J. Buckley   Edgar Kobak
Jesse H. Neal

1965
Robert M. Feemster   Samuel C. Gale
Harrison King McCann

1966
Lee Hastings Bristol   Walter Dill Scott

1967
Ernest Elmo Calkins   Stanley B. Resor
Mrs. Stanley B. Resor   George P. Rowell

1968
Russell T. Gray   Charles W. Mears
Alex F. Osborn

1969
Bruce Barton   Thomas D'Arcy Brophy

1970
Don Belding   Laurence W. Lane
Graham C. Patterson

1971
No inductees

1972
Leo Burnett   Ralph Starr Butler
Philip Livingston Thomson

1973
John P. Cunningham   Bernard C. Duffy

1974
James Webb Young   Raymond Rubicam

1975
Fairfax M. Cone   G. D. Crain, Jr.
Artemas Ward

1976
William Bernbach   David Ogilvy
Victor Elting, Jr.

1977
George Gallup   John Capels

Gold Medal

CIOS—WORLD COUNCIL OF MANAGEMENT
1, rue de Varembe, Case postale 20, CH-1211 Geneva 20,
Switzerland (Tel: 34-14-30)

The CIOS Gold Medal is awarded every three years at
the CIOS World Congress for literary or practical
achievements in scientific management. CIOS members nominate and a medal selection committee
chooses the recipient from six final nominees.

1929 Henri Le Chatelier, France
1932 Charles Adamiecki, Poland
1934 Masaryk Academy of Labor, Czechoslovakia
1935 Edmond Landauer, Great Britain
1938 Harry Arthur Hopf, U.S.A.
1947 Harlow S. Person, U.S.A.
1951 Lyndall F. Urwick, United Kingdom
1954 Lillian M. Gilbreth, U.S.A.
1960 John Ryan, United Kingdom
1963 Erwin H. Schell, U.S.A.
1966 Sir Walter Scott, Australia
1969 No award
1972 Peter F. Drucker, U.S.A.
1975 Not available

Stark Award

COLLECTIVE BARGAINING INSTITUTE
49 E. 68th St., New York, N.Y. 10021 (212/628-1010)

The $1,000 Stark Award is given periodically for excel-
lence in reporting on collective bargaining and labor
relations. The board of directors selects the winner. A
complete list of recipients is not available.

1977 A.H. Raskin, *New York Times*

DPMA Computer Sciences Man-of-the-Year Award

DATA PROCESSING MANAGEMENT ASSOCIATION
505 Busse Hwy., Park Ridge, Ill. 60068 (312/825-8124)

The DPMA Computer Sciences Man-of-the-Year
Award is based on nominations from individual chapters and from the executive council, with the selection
based on an executive council vote, for outstanding contributions and distinguished service in computer
sciences and information processing.

1969 Commander Grace Murray Hopper, U.S. Navy
1970 Frederick Phillips Brooks, Jr., University of North Carolina
1971 No award
1972 Robert C. Cheek, Westinghouse Tele-Computer Systems Corp.
1973 Carl Hammer, UNIVAC Div., Sperry Rand Corp.
1974 Edward L. Glaser, Case Western Reserve University
1975 Willis H. Ware, The Rand Corp.
Donald L. Bitzer, University of Illionois
1976 Gene M. Amdahl, Amdahl Corp.
1977 J. Daniel Cougar, Professor, University of Colorado

Distinguished Service Award
Grace Murray Hooper Award
A.M. Turing Award

ASSOCIATION FOR COMPUTING MACHINERY
1133 Ave. of the Americas, New York, N.Y. 10036
(212/265-6300)

The Distinguished Service Award, which consists of a gift and a certificate, is given on the basis of the value and degree of an individual's services to the computer community, as judged by the awards committee.

1970 Franz L. Alt
1971 Don Madden
1972 George Forsythe
1973 William Atchison
1974 Saul Gorn
1975 John W. Carr III
1976 Richard G. Canning
1977 Thomas B. Steel, Jr.

The $1,000 Grace Murray Hopper Award is given to an outstanding computer professional 30 years of age or under to honor a single recent technical or service contribution. An awards committee selects the winner.

1971 Donald E. Knuth
1972 Paul H. Dirkson
     Paul H. Cress
1973 Lawrence Breed
     Richard Lathwell
     Roger Moore
1974 George N. Baird
1975 Allen L. Scherr
1976 Edward A. Shortliffe
1977 No award

The A.M. Turing Award, which carries a $1,000 honorarium, is a technical award given annually to an individual for lasting and major contributions to the computer field. An awards committee selects the winner.

1966 A.J. Perlis
1967 Maurice Wilkes
1968 Richard W. Hamming
1969 Marvin Minsky
1970 J.H. Wilkinson
1971 John McCarthy
1972 E.W. Dijkstra
1973 Charles Bachman
1974 Donald Knuth
1975 Allen Newell
     Herbert A. Simon
1976 Michael O. Rabin
     Dana S. Scott
1977 John Backus

Best Managed Companies List

DUN'S REVIEW
666 Fifth Ave., New York, N.Y. 10019 (212/489-2200)

In each year's December issue, the editors of *Dun's Review* cite the five companies they view as the best-managed, based on their observations of the American business scene. Corporations honored with designation also receive a silver plaque.

1972 Mobil Oil

Du Pont
Pfizer
Eastman Kodak
Xerox
1973 Citibank
Monsanto
J.C. Penney
Exxon
Weyerhaueser
1974 Southern Railway
American Telephone and Telegraph
R.J. Reynolds
Keer-McGee
Merck
1975 Dow Chemical
Hewlitt-Packard
S.S. Kresge
Merrill Lynch
Procter & Gamble
1976 Haliburton
Ralston-Purina
Bendix
Bank of America
Philip Morris
1977 Beatrice Foods
Delta Air Lines
Emerson Electric
McDonald's
General Motors

Eaton Award

INTERNATIONAL PLATFORM ASSOCIATION
2564 Berkshire Rd., Cleveland Heights, Ohio 44106
(216/932-0505)

The Eaton Award, which consists of an engraved bowl, is given annually to the individual judged by a committee of the International Platform Assn. and the Eaton Corp. to be the best business speaker of the year.

1976 Charles E. Spahr
1977 Fletcher Byrom

Executive of the Year Award

NATIONAL MANAGEMENT ASSOCIATION
2210 Arbor Blvd., Dayton, Ohio 45439 (513/294-0421)

The Executive of the Year Award, which consists of a plaque, honors "outstanding contribution towards the preservation and advancement of the Free Enterprise System." Companies sponsoring membership in the association may make nominations for consideration by the Public Relations Committee and the executive board for ranking. A panel of judges selects the winner from the three finalists.

1915 R.W. Litchfield
1916 C.M. White
1917 A.A. Nicholson
1918 W.J. Cameron
1919 H.D. Bennett
1920 J.S. Thomas
1921 T.G. Graham
1922 B.D. Kunkle
1923 Louis Ruthenburg
1924 J.A. Voss
1925 W.C. Wright

1926	J.S. Strobel
1927	J.G. Jones
1928	A.A. Stockdale
1929	W.H. Hisey
1930	W.D. Henderson
1931	G.C.A. Hantleman
1932	C.C. Smith
1933	H.W. Barclay
1934	F.D. Slutz
1935	C.L. Proctor
1936	Frank H. Adams
1937	A.M. Degner
1938	C.C. Kendrick
1939	H.H. Woodhead
1940	George Spatta
1941	No award
1942	C.E. Wilson
1943	J.A. Robertshaw
1944	S.C. Allyn
1946	C.R. Hook
1947	J.H. Kindelberger and Robert E. Gross
1948	Fred Maytag II
1949	W.D. Robinson and George R. Fink
1950	Frank H. Irelan
1951	Robert F. Loetscher
1952	Mason M. Roberts
1953	Ralph S. Damon
1954	John T. Beatty
1955	Alva W. Phelps
1956	Gen. J.T. McNarney
1957	Gen. H.F. Safford
1958	Thomas E. Millsop
1959	George Romney
1960	Thomas W. Martin
1962	Frank J. Schaeffer
1961	John Mihalic
1963	Albrecht M. Lederer
1964	Floyd Dewey Gottwald
1965	Charles C. Gates, Jr.
1966	Daniel J. Haughton
1967	Russell DeYoung
1968	Lynn A. Townsend
1969	Donald C. Burnham
1970	Robert G. Dunlop
1971	George H. Weyerhaeuser
1972	Frederick G. Jaicks
1973	Melvin C. Holm
1974	W. Michael Blumenthal
1976	Willard F. Rockwell, Jr.
1976	William Plummer Drake
1977	Ray W. Macdonald

1942	Sumner Welles
1943	Juan T. Trippe
1944	Eric A. Johnston
1945	Fred I. Kent
1946	William L. Clayton
1947	John Abbink
1948	Robert F. Loree
1949	Christian A. Herter
1950	Paul G. Hoffman
1951	James A. Farley
1952	Edward Riley
1953	Eugene Holman
1954	Clarence B. Randall
1955	George W. Wolf
1956	William S. Swingle
1957	Howard C. Sheperd
1958	W. Rogers Herod
1959	Samuel C. Waugh
1960	Henry W. Balgooyen
1961	J. Peter Grace
1962	William E. Knox
1963	James A. Farrell, Jr.
1964	David Rockefeller
1965	Thomas J. Watson, Jr.
1966	George S. Moore
1967	William Blackie
1968	Harold F. Linder
1969	Elis S. Hoglund
1970	Rudolph A. Peterson
1971	Henry Kearns
1972	Robert J. Dixson
1973	Walter B. Wriston
1974	George P. Shultz
1975	Stephen D. Bechtel
1976	Reginald H. Jones
1977	Irving S. Shapiro

Captain Robert Dollar Memorial Award

NATIONAL FOREIGN TRADE COUNCIL
10 Rockefeller Plaza, New York, N.Y. 10020 (212/581-6420)

The Captain Robert Dollar Memorial Award is given annually for distinguished contribution to the advancement of American foreign trade and investments. An Annual Award Committee makes the nominations for approval by the board of directors. The recipient is honored with a plaque.

1938	Cordell Hull
1939	James A. Farrell
1940	Thomas J. Watson
1941	Eugene P. Thomas

Fragrance Foundation Award

THE FRAGRANCE FOUNDATION
116 E. 19th St., New York, N.Y. 10003 (212/673-5580)

An abstract column in crystal is annually awarded for various outstanding contributions in the fragrance industry, as voted by industry members.

MOST SUCCESSFUL INTRODUCTION OF A NEW FRAGRANCE

1973 **Chanel #19,** Chanel
1974 **Charlie,** Revlon (women)
       YSL for Men, Yves St. Laurent (men)
1975 **Farouche,** Nina Ricci (women)
       Paco Pour Homme, Paco Rabanne (men)
1976 **Halston,** Halston Fragrances (women, limited distribution)
       Aviance, Prince Matchabelli (women, popular distribution)
       Grey Flannel, Geoffrey Beene (men, limited distribution)
       Chaz, Revlon (men, popular distribution)
1977 **Not available at press time**

HALL OF FAME

1974 **Estee Lauder,** Estee Lauder
1975 **Charles Revson,** Revlon
1976 **H. Gregory Thomas,** Chanel
1977 **Not available at press time**

John Robert Gregg Award

MCGRAW-HILL BOOK COMPANY
1221 Ave. of the Americas, New York, N.Y. 10020
(212/997-1221)

The $500 John Robert Gregg Award annually honors outstanding achievements in business education made during the two previous calendar years or for a series of achievements culminating in one evidenced during the two previous years.

1953 Frederick G. Nichols
1954 Paul S. Lomax
1955 David D. Lessenberry
1956 Elvin S. Eyster
1957 Hamden L. Forkner
1958 Jessie Graham
1959 Ann Brewington
1960 Lloyd V. Douglas
1961 Paul A. Carlson
1962 Herbert A. Tonne
1963 Paul F. Muse
1964 Gladys Bahr
1965 Ray G. Price
1966 Russell J. Hosler
1967 Samuel J. Wanous
1968 McKee Fisk
1969 Bernard A. Shilt
1970 Alton B. Parker Liles
1971 Ruth I. Anderson
1972 J. Marshall Hanna
1973 Warren G. Meyer
1974 Lawrence W. Erickson
1975 Estell L. Popham
1976 John L. Rowe
1977 F. Kendrick Bangs

James A. Hamilton Hospital Administrators' Book Award

AMERICAN COLLEGE OF HOSPITAL
ADMINISTRATORS
810 N. Lake Shore Dr., Chicago, Ill. 60611 (312/943-0544)

The James A. Hamilton Hospital Administrators' Book Award is given in cooperation with the Alumni Assn. of the Graduate Program in Hospital and Health Care Administration of the University of Minnesota for a management book judged outstanding by a special committee. The award, which consists of $500, a bronze medallion and a certificate, honors a work published in the preceding two years.

1958 Herbert A. Simon, *Administrative Behavior*
1959 Chris Argyris, *Personality and Organization*
1960 Harold Leavitt, *Managerial Psychology*
1961 Melville Dalton, *Men Who Manage*
1962 Douglas McGregor, *The Human Side of Enterprise*
1963 Rensis Likert, *New Patterns of Management*
1964 Basil S. Georgopoulos and Floyd C. Mann, *The Community General Hospital*
1965 Richard A. Johnson, Fremont E. Kast and James E. Rosenzweig, *The Theory and Management of Systems*
1966 Alfred P. Sloan, Jr., *My Years With General Motors*
1967 Robert Golembiewski, *Men, Management and Morality: Toward a New Organizational Ethic*

1968 Daniel Katz and Robert Kahn, *The Social Psychology of Organizations*
1969 Paul R. Lawrence and Jay W. Lorsch, *Organization and Environment*
1970 Harry Levinson, *The Exceptional Executive*
1971 Clarence C. Walton, *Ethos and the Executive Values in Managerial Decision Making*
1972 John P. Campbell, Marvin D. Dunnette, Edward E. Lawler and Karl E. Weick, *Managerial Behavior, Performance and Effectiveness*
1973 Anne Ramsay Somers, *Health Care in Transition: Directions for the Future*
1974 Basil S. Georgopoulos, *Organization Research on Health Institutions*
1975 Peter F. Drucker, *Management: Tasks, Responsibilities, Practices*
1976 William Christopher, *The Achieving Enterprise*
1977 Robert N. Anthony and Regina E. Herzlinger, *Management Control and Nonprofit Organizations*

Marketer of the Year Award

AMERICAN MARKETING ASSOCIATION/
CHICAGO CHAPTER
222 S. Riverside Pl., Chicago, Ill. 60606 (312/648-9536)

The Association's Chicago Chapter, the nation's second largest, annually gives the Marketer of the Year Award to an outstanding professional in the Chicago area. Business, civic and academic leaders are asked for nominees, and the winner is selected by the board of directors on the basis of the company's innovative and successful marketing efforts as well as for the individual's social, civic and philanthropic involvement.

1958 Floyd K. Thayer, Abbott Latoratories
1959 Leonard C. Truesdell, Zenith Sales Corp.
1960 Judson B. Branch, Allstate Insurance Co.
1961 B. Edward Bensinger, Brunswick Corp.
1962 Franklin J. Lunding, Jewel Tea Co.
1963 No award
1964 William Wood-Prince, Armour & Co.
1965 David M. Kennedy, Continental Illinois National Bank
1966 Leo Burnett, Leo Burnett, Inc.
1967 George E. Keck, United Air Lines
1968 Harold F. Werhane, Culligan, Inc
1969 Robert D. Stuart, Jr., Quaker Oats Co.
1970 Arthur C. Neilsen, A.C. Neilsen Co.
1971 James W. Button, Sears, Roebuck & Co.
1972 Ray A. Kroc, McDonald's Corp.
1973 Donald S. Perkins, Jewel Co.
1974 William O. Beers, Kraftco Corp.
1975 Edward E. Carlson, United Air Lines and UAL, Inc.
1976 William G. Karnes, Beatrice Foods, Inc.
1977 William B. Graham, Baxter Travenol Laboratories

Marketer of the Year

AMERICAN MARKETING ASSOCIATION/NEW
YORK CHAPTER
420 Lexington Ave., New York, N.Y. 10017 (212/687-3280)

The Marketer of the Year is named annually for marketing excellence and community service. The winner, who receives a trophy, is selected by nominations from the New York Chapter's membership, recommendation by a committee and a final vote by the board of directors. The award had been given previously, was stopped for a number of years and was reinstituted in 1976.

1976 Frank Braynar, Operation Sail
1977 John H. Iselin, WNET Channel 13

McKinsey Award

HARVARD BUSINESS REVIEW
Soldiers Field, Boston, Mass. 02163 (617/495-6175)

The McKinsey Foundation annually sponsors the $1,000 McKinsey Award,which is announced in the January-February issue of the *Harvard Business Review,* for the best article of the preceding year. Every year the editors choose a board of judges who make the selection based on the following criteria: helpfulness to executives in solving major internal management problems and/or in making strategic adjustments of the business to the environment and to competition; contribution to knowledge—innovation or originality of approach; depth of analysis and soundness of reasoning; provocativeness in challenging existing notions and present practices; readability—clarity and simplicity of style and interest of wording. A $500 second-place award is also given annually.

1970 George Cabot Lodge, "Top Priority: Renovating Our Ideology," September-October
1971 J. Sterling Livingston, "Myth of the Well-Educated Manager," January-February
1972 Theodore Levitt, "Production-Line Approach to Service," September-October
1973 C. Jackson Grayson, Jr., "Let's Get Back to the Competitive Market System," November-December
1974 George Cabot Lodge, "Business and the Changing Society," March-April
1975 Henry Mintzberg, "The Manager's Job: Folklore and Fact," July-August
1976 David C. McClelland and David H. Burnham, "Power is the Great Motivator," March-April
1977 Abraham Zaleznik, "Managers and Leaders: Are They Different?", May-June

Domestic Car of the Year

MOTOR TREND
8490 Sunset Blvd., Los Angeles, Calif. 90069 (213/657-5100)

Motor Trend magazine annually selects vehicles of the year in various categories. The list below reflects the choices for the annual Domestic Car of the Year honors.

1949 Cadillac
1950 No award
1951 Chrysler
1952 Cadillac
1953 No award
1954 No award
1955 No award
1956 Ford Motor Co.
1957 Chrysler Corp.
1958 Ford Thunderbird
1959 Pontiac Division
1960 Chevrolet Corvair
1961 Pontiac Tempest
1962 Buick Special

1963 AMC Rambler
1964 Ford Division
1965 Pontiac Division
1966 Oldsmobile Toronado
1967 Mercury Cougar
1968 Pontiac GTO
1969 Plymouth Road Runner
1970 Ford Torino
1971 Chevrolet Vega
1972 Citroen SM
1973 Chevrolet Monte Carlo
1974 Ford Mustang II
1975 Chevrolet Monza 2+2 V8
1976 Chrysler Corp.: Dodge Aspen and Plymouth Volare
1977 Chevrolet Caprice

Thomas Newcomen Award

NEWCOMEN SOCIETY IN NORTH AMERICA
Downington, Pa. 19335 (215/363-6600)

The $1,000 Thomas Newcomen Award, which is given every three years in conjunction with the Harvard Graduate School of Business, honors the author of an outstanding work on business history in the United States and Canada. The book may be about an individual firm, interactions between businesses, analysis of business philosophy or behavior or studies of business adjustments to changes in society. A committee representing the two organizations selects the winner.

1964 Alfred D. Chandler, Jr., *Strategy and Structure: Chapters in the History of the Industrial Enterprise*
1967 Sidney Pollard, *The Genesis of Modern Management: A Study of the Industrial Revolution in Great Britain*
1970 Robert W. Ozanne, *A Century of Labor-Management Relations at McCormick and International Harvester and Wages in Practice and Theory: McCormick and International Harvester, 1860-1960*
1973 Thomas C. Cochran, *Business in American Life: A History*
1976 Irvine H. Anderson, Jr., *The Standard Vacuum-Oil Company and United States East Asian Policy, 1933-1941*

Louis Brownlow Book Award

NATIONAL ACADEMY OF PUBLIC ADMINISTRATION
1225 Connecticut Ave. NW, Washington, D.C. 20036 (202/659-9165)

The Louis Brownlow Book Award, consisting of a plaque and special recognition at the annual meeting, is given for new insights, fresh analysis and original ideas in public administration as expressed in a work published during the specified time period. A selection committee reviews works submitted by publishers.

1969 Frederick C. Mosher, *Democracy and the Public Service*
1970 Emmette S. Redford, *Democracy in the Administrative State*
   James L. Sundquist, *Making Federalism Work*
1975 Harlan Cleveland, *The Future Executive*
   Rufus E. Miles, Jr., *The Department of H.E.W.*
1976 Louis Fisher, *Presidential Spending Power*

Railroad Man of the Year
Golden Freight Car Award

MODERN RAILROADS MAGAZINE
5 S. Wabash Av., Chicago, Ill. 60603 (312/372-6880)

The Railroad Man of the Year is honored by the editors of *Modern Railroads* with a bronze bust of himself to reocognize outstanding contributions to railroading. The award was originally based on a readers' poll.

1964 **D. W. Brosnan,** Southern Railway System
1965 **Stuart T. Saunders,** Pennsylvania Railroad Co.
1966 **Stuart T. Saunders,** Pennsylvania Railroad Co.
1967 **Louis W. Menk,** Northern Pacific Railway
1968 **William B. Johnson,** Illinois Central Railroad
1969 **John W. Barriger,** Missouri-Kansas-Texas Railroad
1970 **John S. Reed,** Atchison, Topeka & Santa Fe Railway Co.
1971 **Jervis Langdon, Jr.,** Penn Central Transportation Co.
1972 **Charles Luna,** United Transportation Union
1973 **James W. Germany,** Southern Pacific Transportation Co.
1974 **L. Stanley Crane,** Southern Railway System
1975 **Frank E. Barnett,** Union Pacific Railroad
1976 **William J. Harris, Jr.,** Assn. of American Railroads
1977 **Edward G. Jordan,** Conrail

The Golden Freight Car Award, which consists of a replica of a railroad freight car, is given annually to the railroad which, in the judgment of the magazine's editors, has made strides in the rail transport of freight.

1973 **Penn Central Transportation Co.**
1974 **Western Pacific**
1975 **Illinois Central Gulf**
1976 No award
1977 **Family Lines System**

Robert E. Slaughter Research Award

MCGRAW-HILL BOOK COMPANY
1221 Ave. of the Americas, New York, N.Y. 10020
(212/997-1221)

The $1,000 Robert E. Slaughter Research Award recognizes outstanding contributions to business and office education by up to three individuals in any given year, at least one of which must be for research in the teaching of Gregg shorthand. Studies may be scholarly, institutional or independent but must have been completed during the preceding 12 months,

1975 **Gary McLean,** University of Minnesota
L. Eugene Jones, Northeastern Louisiana University
1976 **Christine Gilmore,** Bishop College
Thomas O. Stanley, Missouri Southern College
Boyd G. Worthington, Brigham Young University
1977 **Thomas Duff,** University of Minnesota
Rita C. Kutie, Lakeland Community College

Elmer A. Sperry Award

AMERICAN INSTITUTE OF AERONAUTICS AND ASTRONAUTICS
1290 Ave. of the Americas, New York, N.Y. 10019
(212/581-4300)

The Elmer A. Sperry Award, which consists of a bronze

medal and certificate, is given jointly be the AIEE, the Institute of Electrical and Electronic Engineers, the Society of Automotive Engineers, the American Society of Mechnical Engineers and the SNAME in recognition of contributions to transportation engineering.

1965 **William H. Cook**
Richard L. Loesch, Jr.
Commercial Airplane Div., Boeing Co. (citation)
1966 **Hideo Shima**
Matsuataro Fujii
Shigenari Oishi
Japanese National Railways (citation)
1967 **Edward R. Dye**
Hugh DeHaven
Robert A. Wolf
Research Engineers, Cornell Aero. Lab., Cornell University Medical College (citation)
1968 **Christopher S. Cockerell**
Richard Stanton-Jones
British Hovercraft Corp. (citation)
1969 **Douglas C. MacMillan**
M. Nielsen
Edward L. Teale, Jr.
Wilbert C. Gumprich (citation)
George G. Sharp (citation)
Babock and Wilcox Co. (citation)
New York Shipbuilding Corp. (citation)
1970 **Charles Stark Draper**
1971 **Sedwig N. Wight**
George W. Baughman
William D. Hailes (citation)
Lloyd V. Lewis (citation)
Clarence S. Snavely (citation)
Herbert A. Wallace (citation)
Employees of General Railways Signal Co. (Signal and Communications Div.), Westinghouse Air Brake Co.
1972 **Perry W. Pratt**
Leonard S. Hobb
Pratt & Whitney (citation)
1973 No award
1974 No award
1975 **Jerome L. Goldman**
Frank A. Nemec
James J. Henry
Naval Architects & Marine Engineers of Friede & Goldman Inc. (citation)
Alfred H. Schwendtner (citation)
1976 No award
1977 No award

Salute to Women in Business

YWCA OF GREATER NEW YORK
610 Lexington Ave., New York, N.Y. 10022 (212/755-2700)

The initial Salute to Women in Business honored business achievements and public service by women selected by a committee of prominent individuals. The award consisted of a commemorative cube from Tiffany & Co.

1976 **Marion, S. Adams,** Blythe Eastman Dillon & Co., Inc.
Rena R. Bartos, J. Walter Thompson Co.
Caroline Beebe, Bloomingdale's
Meg Bianco, Xerox Corp.
Barbara C. Blake, Chase Manhattan Bank N.A.
Mari Ann Blatch, Reader's Digest Assn., Inc.
Roberta Paula Books, Morgan Stanley & Co.

Joan-Ann Bostic, Pfizer, Inc.
Frankie Cadwell, Compton Advertising
Eleanor E. Campbell, Johnson & Higgins
Emilie Caravasios, American Stock Exchange
Frimet Celnik, New York Telephone
Paula Cholomondeley, International Paper Co.
Jeanne R. Corbett, Metropolitan Life Insurance Co.
Zoe Coulson, Good Housekeeping Institute
Gloria B. Deragon, Lever Brothers
Margaret B. Devlin, General Motors Corp.
Edith Drucker, B. Altman & Co.
Virginia A. Dwyer, American Telephone and Telegraph Co.
Rhoda Erickson, Sullivan & Cromwell
Sophie A. Fiattarone, First Boston Corp.
Josephine Foxworth, Jo Foxworth, Inc.
Dorothy L. Furness, J.C. Penney Co., Inc.
Elaine Garzarelli, Becker Securities Corp.
Dorothy Gregg, Celanese Corp.
Ruth Haase, Blue Cross & Blue Shield of Greater New York
Marjorie L. Hart, Exxon Corp.
Louise S. Hazeltine, Cornell University-New York Hospital School of Nursing
Peggy Healy, Young & Rubicam International, Inc.
Eleanor G. Hirsch, Holt Rinehart & Winston, CBS Educational Publishing
Charlotte Schiff Jones, Manhattan Cable Television, Inc.
Johanna Kaiser, YWCA of Greater New York
Jean D. Keaveny, International Telephone and Telegraph Corp.
Maryann N. Keller, Kidder, Peabody & Co., Inc.
Marion S. Kellogg, General Electric Co.
Moira Kelly, W.R. Grace & Co.
Dagnija D. Lacis, Burroughs Corp.
Natalie S. Lang, Booz, Allen & Hamilton, Inc.
Joy Levien, Singer Co.
Anna Maria Malachi, Port Authority of New York and New Jersey
Theresa A. Marmo, Bulova Watch Co., Inc.
Kay B. Maunsbach, Manhattan Life Insurance Co.
M. Jacqueline McCurdy, Joseph E. Seagram & Sons, Inc.

Sallie C. Melvin, Chemical Bank
Heidi Merrill, *Working Woman* magazine
Anne M. Meschino, Citibank N.A.
Birgit E. Morris, RCA Corp.
Dolores J. Morrissey, Bowery Savings Bank
Patricia Neighbors, Avon Products Inc.
Catherine A. Rein, Continental Group, Inc.
Ann Robb, Sperry and Hutchinson Co.
Marlene Sanders, American Broadcasting Co., Inc.
Eleanor J. Shehane, AT&T Long Lines Dept.
Judith G. Shepard, Goldman, Sachs & Co.
Doris H. Skutch, Burlington Industries, Inc.
Gail A. Wallace, Kennecott Copper Corp.
Dorothy Wayner, Byrde, Richard & Pound
Corrine Williams, Tiffany & Co.
Marjorie Worme, Parkchester Management Corp.
Kristina Wrba, Helena Rubinstein, Inc.
Mary Anne Wrenn, Merrill Lynch Pierce Fenner & Smith, Inc.
Ruth Ziff, Doyle Dane Bernbach, Inc.

Subsequently, Anne Morrow Lindbergh endowed the award, which was renamed in honor of her mother, Elizabeth Cutter Morrow. The award was redesigned in the form of an apple and was limited to 14 women a year, selected by a panel of judges.

1977   Ruth S. Block, Equitable Life Assurance Society of the U.S.
Elizabeth R. Clark, Bowery Savings Bank
Gail Erickson, W.R. Grace & Co.
Marilyn E. LaMarche, Citibank N.A.
Beverly C. Lannquist, Morgan Stanley & Co., Inc.
Helen Meyer, Dell Publishing Co., Inc.
Geraldine E. Rhoads, *Woman's Day* magazine
Mala Rubinstein, Helena Rubinstein
Sheila M. Smythe, Blue Cross & Blue Shield of Greater New York
Patricia Carry Stewart, Edna McConnell Clark Foundation
Carol C. Tatkon, Exxon Corp.
Carol C. Tucker, Avon Products, Inc.
Marilyn S. Watts, RCA Corp.
Shirley Wilkins, Roper Organization, Inc.

International Relations &

Understanding

Contents

Related Awards

Charlemagne Prize (International Prize of the City of Aachen)

THE CITY OF AACHEN
c/o Kur- und Verkehrsamt der Stadt Aachen, Postfach 1210, 51 Aachen, Federal Republic of Germany (Tel: 0241/33491 and 472301)

The International Prize of the City of Aachen, known as the Charlemagne Prize, is awarded annually to people of merit for the promotion of Western unity by political, literary or economic endeavors. The prize consists of 5,000 German marks and a medallion. A jury selects the winner.

1950 Graf Richard Coudenhove-Kalergi, Creator of the Pan-European Movement
1951 Hendrik Brugmans, Rector of the European College, Bruges
1952 Alcide de Gasperi, Italian Prime Minister
1953 Jean Monnet, President of the European Coal and Steel Community, Luxembourg
1954 Konrad Adenauer, Chancellor of the Federal Republic of Germany
1955 Sir Winston S. Churchill, Former Prime Minister of Great Britain
1957 Paul Henri Spaak, Secretary General of North Atlantic Treaty Organization
1958 Robert Schuman, President of European Parliament
1959 George C. Marshall, former U.S. Secretary of State
1960 Joseph Bech, Honorary Minister of State — President of the Chamber of Deputies, Luxembourg
1961 Walter Hallstein, President of the Commission of the European Economic Community
1963 Edward Heath, Lord Privy Seal of Britain
1964 Antonio Segni, President of the Italian Republic
1966 Jens Otto Krag, Prime Minister of Denmark
1967 Joseph Luns, Minister of Foreign Affairs of the Royal Netherlands Government
1969 The Commission of the European Communities
1970 Francois Seydoux de Clausonne, Former French Ambassador to the Federal Republic of Germany
1972 Roy Jenkins, M.P.
1973 Don Salvador de Madariaga
1976 Leo Tindemans, Belgian Prime Minister
1977 Walter Scheel, President of the Federal Republic of Germany

Eisenhower Medallion

PEOPLE-TO-PEOPLE INTERNATIONAL
3 Crown Center, 2440 Pershing Rd., Suite G-30, Kansas City, Mo. 64108 (816/421-6343)

The Eisenhower Medallion is awarded to one or two individuals for exceptional contributions to world peace and understanding over a period of at least five years. Nominees must receive a unanimous vote of the executive committee of the board of trustees to be honored.

1968 Mrs. Carter Collins
Mrs. Renzo Sawada
Mrs. Guido Panteleoni
Louise Kim
Arnold Palmer
James A. McCain

1969 Neil Armstrong, Edwin Aldrin, Jr. and Michael Collins
George Venable Allen
Frank H. Krusen
1970 Melville Bell Grosvenor
1971 Joyce C. Hall
1972 Albert Pick, Jr.
1973 Donald J. Hall
1974 No award
1975 No award
1976 Magnus von Braun
1977 No award

International Lenin Prize for the Promotion of Peace Among the Nations

INTERNATIONAL LENIN PRIZE COMMITTEE
The Kremlin, Moscow, U.S.S.R. (Tel: 224-75-35)

The International Lenin Prize, often called the Lenin Peace Prize, is awarded annually to about five individuals of any nationality for outstanding activities in the promotion of peace, or for scientific achievements, works of literature or art or achievements in any area that contributes to the cause of peace among nations. The recipients are presented with a gold medal bearing a likeness of I.V. Lenin, a certificate and 25,000 rubles. The winners are selected by a committee which considers documentation of candidates' suitability for the honor from nominees suggested to the committee's Secretariat by organizations of all types. These awards, which parallel the Lenin Prizes given to Soviet citizens, were begun in 1950, but the names of early winners are not available

1968-69 Ludvic Svoboda (Czechoslovakia), Statesman and public figure
Linus Pauling (U.S.A.), Scientist and public figure
Shafi Ahmed al Cheih (Sudan), Public figure
Jaroslav Ivaschkevitch (Poland), Writer and public figure
Akira Ivai (Japan), Public figure
Bertil Svanstrem (Sweden), Journalist and public figure
Haled Mohi ad Deem (Egypt), Journalist and public figure
1970-71 A.H.S. Burop (United Kingdom), Scientist and President of the World Scientist Foundation
Renato Guttozo (Italy), Artist and public figure
Tsola Dragoicheva (Bulgaria), Political and public figure
Camal Djumblat (Lebanon), Political and public figure
Ernst Bush (German Democratic Republic), Artist
Alfredo Varela (Argentina), Writer and public figure
1972 L.I. Brezhnev (U.S.S.R.), General Secretary of the Central Committee of the Communist Part of the Soviet Union
James Aldridge (United Kingdom), Writer
Louis Carvalan (Chile), Senator and Secretary General of the Communist Party of Chile
Janne Marten Sisse (Guinea), Political and public figure
Raimon Goor (Belgium), Canon and public figure
1975-76 Janosh Kadar (Hungary), First Secretary of the Central Committee of the Hungarian Socialist Workers Party

Agostinho Neto (Angola), President of Angola

Samora M. Machel (Mozambique), President of Mozambique

Hortenzia Bussi de Allende (Chile), Public figure and honorable vice president of the International Democratic Women's Federation

Sean McBride (Ireland), Political and public figure

Pierre Poyade (France), Public figure

Yannis Ritsos (Greece), Poet and public figure

1977 Gus Hall (U.S.A.), Leader of the Communist Party in the United States

Other winners not available at press time

Ramon Magsaysay Award in International Understanding

RAMON MAGSAYSAY AWARD FOUNDATION
1680 Roxas Blvd., Manila, Philippines (Tel: 59-19-58 and 59-17-20)

The Ramon Magsaysay Award is given annually in each of five areas of achievement to individuals who exemplify the ideals of Ramon Magsaysay. Accomplishments of the previous five years in government service; public service; community leadership; journalism, literature and communication arts; and international understanding are honored. On August 31, the birthday of Ramon Magsaysay, the five awards are made in Manila to Asians regardless of race, creed, sex or nationality. The award consists of $10,000, a gold medal and a certificate.

1958 Operation Brotherhood, For advancement of friendship between the peoples of different countries

1959 No award

1960 Y.C. James Yen (China), For sharing wealth of experience of rural reconstruction in Asia

1961 Genevieve Caulfield, (U.S.A.), International citizenship and help to the blind

1962 Mother Teresa (Yugoslavia/India), Merciful cognizance of the abject poor of a foreign land

1963 U.S. Peace Corps Volunteers (Asia), For voluntary service in the cause of peace and humanity in a direct and personal way

1964 Welthy Honsinger Fisher (U.S.A.), For commitment to the cause of literacy

1965 Bayanihan Folk Arts Center (Philippines), For warm and artistic portrayal of Philippine people to five continents

1966 Committee for Coordination of Investigations of the Lower Mekong Basin and Cooperating Entities (Vietnam), For progress toward harnessing one of the world's great river systems

1967 Shiroshi Nasu (Japan), Humanitarianism enhancing world-wide cooperation in agriculture

1968 Cooperative for American Relief Everywhere (CARE), For constructive humanitarianism

1969 International Rice Research Institute, Innovative interdisciplinary teamwork by Asian and Western scientists

1970 No award

1971 Saburo Okita (Japan), Advocacy of genuine Japanese partnership in the economic progress of her Asian neighbors

1972 No award

1973 Summer Institute of Linguistics, For outreach to non-literate people, recording and teaching them to read their own languages

1974 Father William F. Masterson (U.S.A.), Multinational education and inspiration of rural leaders

1975 Father Patrick J. McGlinchey (Ireland), For mobilizing foreign support and volunteers to modernize livestock farming

1976 Henning Holck-Larsen (Danish/India), Chemist cited for contributions to technical and industrial modernization

1977 Not available at press time

Jawaharlal Nehru Award for International Understanding

INDIAN COUNCIL FOR CULTURAL RELATIONS
Azad Bhavan, I.P. Estate, New Delhi, India (Tel: 272114)

The Jawaharlal Nehru Award for International Understanding, which carries an honorarium of 100,000 rupees and a citation, is given annually for contributions to the promotion of international understanding, goodwill and friendship among the world's people. Nominations in writing may be made by former members of the selection jury, past recipients of the award, members of the Parliament of India, Nobel laureates, the secretary general of the United Nations and leaders of other international organizations whose objectives are the promotion of world peace, presidents or vice chancellors of universities, academicians, professors of social or natural sciences, heads of Indian missions abroad, heads of learned societies or research institutions or anyone else invited by the jury to submit a nomination. A seven-member jury appointed by the government of India selects the recipient.

1965 U Thant, Former secretary general of the United Nations

1966 Martin Luther King, Fighter against racial discrimination

1967 Abdul Ghaffar Khan, Freedom fighter

1968 Yehudi Menuhin, Violinist

1969 Mother Teresa, Missionary

1970 Kenneth D. Kaunda, President of Zambia

1971 Josip Broz Tito, President of Yugoslavia

1972 Andre Malraux, Writer and former French minister of Culture

1973 Julius K. Nyerere, President of Tanzania

1974 Raul Prebisch, Economist

1975 Jonas Salk, Biochemist

1976 Giuseppe Tucci, Indologist

1977 Not available at press time

Nobel Peace Prize

NOBEL FOUNDATION
Nobel House, Sturegatan 14, 11436 Stockholm, Sweden

Of the six Nobel Prizes given annually, the Nobel Peace Prize is generally recognized as the highest honor which can be bestowed upon an individual or organization for furthering fraternity among nations and all humanity, reduction of standing armies and promotion of peace conferences. Although the other Nobel Prizes are awarded on the decision of Swedish juries at ceremonies in Sweden, the Nobel Peace Prize is administered and presented by the Nobel Peace Prize Selection Committee comprised of the Norwegian Parliament and the Norwegian Nobel Institute (address: 19 Dramensveien, Oslo, Norway). The award is presented concurrently with ceremonies in Stockholm on December 10; they take place in the presence of His Majesty, the King of Norway, in the Great Hall of Oslo University. The amount of the honorarium fluctuates. In 1977, it was approximately $145,000.

1901 **Jean H. Dunant,** Switzerland
      Frederick Passy, France
1902 **Elie Ducommun,** Switzerland
      Charles A. Gobat, Switzerland
1903 **Sir William R. Cremer,** Great Britain
1904 **Institute of International Law**
1905 **Baroness Bertha von Shuttner,** Austria
1906 **Theodore Roosevelt,** U.S.A.
1907 **Ernesto T. Moneta,** Italy
      Louis Renault, France
1908 **Klas P. Arnoldson,** Sweden
      Fredik Bajer, Denmark
1909 **Auguste M.F. Beernaert,** Belgium
      Paul H.B.B. d'Estournelles de Constant, France
1910 **Permanent International Peace Bureau**
1911 **Tobias M.C. Asser,** Netherlands
      Alfred H. Fried, Austria
1912 **Elihu Root,** U.S.A.
1913 **Henri La Fontaine,** Belgium
1914 No award
1915 No award
1916 No award
1917 **International Committee of the Red Cross**
1918 No award
1919 **Woodrow Wilson,** U.S.A.
1920 **Loen V. A. Bourgeois,** France
1921 **Karl H. Branting,** Sweden
      Christian L. Lange, Norway
1922 **Fridtjof Nansen,** Norway
1923 No award
1925 No award
1925 **Sir J. Austen Chamberlain,** Great Britain
      Charles G. Dawes, U.S.A.
1926 **Aristide Briand,** France
      Gustav Stresemann, Germany
1927 **Ferdinand E. Buisson,** France
      Ludwig Quidde, Germany
1928 No award
1929 **Frank B. Kellogg,** U.S.A.
1930 **Lars O.N. Soderblom,** Sweden
1931 **Jane Addams,** U.S.A.
      Nicholas Murray Butler, U.S.A.
1932 No award
1933 **Sir Norman Angell,** Great Britain
1934 **Arthur Henderson,** Great Britain
1935 **Carl von Ossietzky,** Germany
1936 **Carlos de Saavedra Lambs,** Argentina
1937 **Viscount Cecil of Chelwood,** Great Britain
1938 **International Office for Refugees**
1939 No award
1940 No award
1941 No award
1942 No award
1943 No award
1944 **International Committee of the Red Cross**
1945 **Cordell Hull,** U.S.A.
1946 **Emily G. Balch,** U.S.A.
      John R. Mott, U.S.A.
1947 **Friends Service Council,** Great Britain
      American Friends Service Committee

1948 No award
1949 **Lord John Boyd Orr of Brechin,** Great Britain
1950 **Ralph J. Bunche,** U.S.A.
1951 **Leon Jouhaux,** France
1952 **Albert Schweitzer,** France (German-born)
1953 **George C. Marshall,** U.S.A.
1954 **Office of U.N. High Commissioner for Refugees**
1955 No award
1956 No award
1957 **Lester B. Pearson,** Canada
1958 **Georges Pire,** Belgium
1959 **Philip J. Noel-Baker,** Great Britain
1960 **Albert J. Luthuli,** South Africa
1961 **Dag Hammarskjold,** Sweden (posthumous)
1962 **Linus C. Pauling,** U.S.A.
1963 **International Committee of the Red Cross**
      Red Cross Societies League
1964 **Martin Luther King, Jr.,** U.S.A.
1965 **United Nations Children's Fund (UNICEF)**
1966 No award
1967 No award
1968 **Rene Cassin,** France
1969 **International Labor Organization (ILO)**
1970 **Norman E. Borlaug,** U.S.A.
1971 **Willy Brandt,** Germany
1972 No award
1973 **Henry A. Kissinger,** U.S.A. (German-born)
      Le Duc Tho, North Vietnam
1974 **Eisaku Sato,** Japan
      Sean MacBride, Ireland
1975 **Andrei D. Sakharov,** U.S.S.R.
1976 **Betty Williams and Mairead Corrigan,** United Kingdom (Northern Ireland)
1977 **Amnesty International**

Robert Schuman Prize
Robert Schuman Medal

STIFTUNG F.V.S.
Georgsplatz 10, 2 Hamburg 1, Federal Republic of Germany
(Tel: 33 04 00 and 33 06 00)

The Robert Schuman Prize, which carries a cash award of 30,000 marks, is given annually in recognition of the furtherance of European unity. The University of Bonn administers the award.

1966 **Jean Monnet,** France
1967 **Joseph Bech** Luxemburg
1968 **Sicco L. Mansholt,** Belgium
1969 **Walter Hallstein,** Federal Republic of Germany
1970 **Denis de Rougemont,** Switzerland
1971 **Alain Poher,** France
      Silvius Magnago, Italy
1972 **Roy Jenkins,** Great Britain
1973 **Jens Otto Krag,** Denmark
1974 **Altiero Spinelli,** Belgium
1975 **Pierre Pflimlin,** France
1976 **Sir Christopher Soames,** Great Britain
1977 **Gaston Thorn,** Luxembourg

The Robert Schuman Medal, which is of gold, is given annually for contributions to Franco-German understanding or European unity. The award is administered by the Society of the the Friends of Robert Schuman in Montigny-les-Metz.

    1966 **Konrad Adenauer**
    1967 **Rene Mayer**
           Walter Hallstein

1968 Emilio Colombo
1969 Paul-Henri Spaak
1970 Louis Armand
1971 Pierre Werner
1972 Hendrik Brugmans
1973 John Lynch
1974 Olivier Reverdin
1975 Francois-Xavier Ortoli
1976 No award
1977 Otto von Habsburg

James Brown Scott Prizes

INSTITUT DE DROIT INTERNATIONAL
82, Ave. du Castel, B-1200, Brussels, Belgium

The James Brown Scott Prizes are 13 honors which go according to pre-set criteria to authors of the best memoirs on the question of international public law. The awards are made every two years for works at least 150 but not more than 500 pages, submitted by anyone but members and former members of the Institute. A jury selects the winner of the James Brown Scott Prize, which carries a cash honorarium, which since 1964 has been 2,000 Swiss francs.

1933 John Westlake Prize: Anton Roth (Germany)
1935 Andres Bello Prize: No award
1937 Carlos Calvo Prize: A. Balasko (France)
1950 Grotius Prize: Martinus Willem Mouton (Netherlands)
1952 Francis Lieber Prize: Hedwig Maier (Germany)
1954 Frederic de Martins Prize: Theodor Schneid (Germany)
1956 Mancini Prize: No award
1958 Pufendorf Prize: Chava Schachor-Landau (Israel)
1960 Louis Renault Prize: No award
1962 G. Rolin-Jaequemyns Prize: No award
1964 Emer de Vattel Prize: No award
1966 Vitoria Prize: No award
1968 JohnWestlake Prize: Hugh W.A. Thirlway (Great Britain
1970 Henri Wheaton Prize: No award
1972 Andres Bellow Prize: No award

1974 Carlos Calvo Prize: No award
1976 Grotius Prize: Will be given on Dec. 31, 1978

United Nations Prizes

UNITED NATIONS
G.C. Box 20, New York, N.Y. 10017 (Tel. Geneva, Switzerland 34-60-11, Ext. 2723)

The United Nations Prizes are given every five years for outstanding contributions to the promotion and protection of human rights and fundamental freedoms embodied in the Universal Declaration of Human Rights. The establishment of this plaque honoring notable individuals was made under General Assembly Resolution 2217 (XXI).

1968 Manuel Bianchi
     Rene Cassia
     Albert Luthuli
     Mehranguiz Manoutchehrian
     P.E. Nedbaila
     Eleanor Roosevelt
1973 Taha Hussein
     Wildred Jenks
     Maria Lavalle-Urbina
     Bishop Abel Muzorewa
     Sir Seewoosagur Ramjodam
     U Thant

U.N. Children's Fund Award

UNITED NATIONS
First Ave. and 42nd St., New York, N.Y. 10017
(212/754-8029)

The United Nations Children's Fund Award for Distinguished Service at the international level is presented annually for efforts on behalf of and for contributions to the United Nations International Children's Emergency Fund.

1976 Danny Kaye
     Robert Debre, France, Founder of UNICEF
1977 Peter Ustinov

Public Service, Humanitarianism

Contents

Related Awards

& Heroism

Advertising Council Award for Public Service

THE ADVERTISING COUNCIL
825 Third Ave., New York, N.Y. 10022 (212/758-0400)

The Advertising Council Award for Public Service is a Sterling silver Paul Revere bowl given annually to an American business leader for notable contributions in public service to the welfare of the country and its citizens. The Council's board of directors selects the winner.

1954	Charles E. Wilson
1955	Clarence Francis
1956	Paul G. Hoffman
1957	Sidney J. Weinberg
1958	George M. Humphrey
1959	Roy E. Larsen
1960	Neil McElroy
1961	Henry Ford II
1962	Lucius D. Clay
1963	John J. McCloy
1964	Charles G. Mortimer
1965	David Sarnoff
1966	John A. McCone
1967	John T. Connor
1968	Robert S. McNamara
1969	Frank Stanton
1970	James M. Roche
1971	David Rockefeller
1972	Thomas J. Watson, Jr.
1973	Howard J. Morgens
1974	Katharine Graham
1975	J. Paul Austin
1976	Arthur M. Wood
1977	William F. May

Murray-Green Award

AFL-CIO
815 16th St. NW, Washington, D.C. 20006 (202/637-5000, Ext. 5189)

The Murray-Green Award, which carries a $5,000 grant and a medallion, is given annually to recognize outstanding contributions to the health, welfare and recreation of people everywhere, to stimulate leadership in the field of social welfare and to honor the memory of two American labor leaders, Philip Murray and William Green, whose lives exemplified the tradition of service. Any AFL-CIO affiliate or member may submit nominations for selection by the organization's Community Services Committee. Until 1956, the honor was known as the Philip Murray Award.

1947	Gen. Omar N. Bradley
1948	Sen. Robert F. Wagner
1949	No award
1950	No award
1951	Sen. James E. Murray
1952	No award
1953	Oscar R. Ewing
	Robert H. MacRae
	Wilbur F. Maxwell
	United Nations Children's Emergency Fund
1954	Menninger Foundation
1955	Eleanor Roosevelt
1956	Herbert H. Lehman

1957	Jonas E. Salk
1958	Bob Hope
1959	President Harry S. Truman
1960	Agnes E. Meyer
1961	No award
1962	Gov. Louis Munoz Marin
1963	Gen. Alfred M. Gruenther
1964	Sen. Estes Kefauver
1965	Henry J. Kaiser
1966	Mr. and Mrs. Sargent Shriver
1967	Albert B. Sabin
1968	Wilbur J. Cohen
1969	Sen. Paul A. Douglas
1970	John W. Gardner
1971	Jerry Lewis
1972	A. Philip Randolph
1973	President Lyndon B. Johnson
1974	Sen. Hubert H. Humphrey
1975	Joseph Beirne
1976	Golda Meir
1977	Walter Mondale

National Law and Social Justice Award

AFRO-AMERICAN PATROLMEN'S LEAGUE
7126 S. Jeffrey Blvd., Chicago, Ill. 60649 (312/667-7384)

The National Law and Social Justice Award, which consists of a plaque, is given each year on decision by the board of directors, for outstanding work in the field of law or social justice.

1971	Ramsey Clark, U.S. Attorney General
1972	Father Theodore Hesburgh, President, Notre Dame University
1973	Robert B. Blackwell, Mayor, Highland Park, Mich.
	Theodore M. Berry, Mayor, Cincinnati, Ohio
	Thomas Bradley, Mayor, Los Angeles, Calif.
	A.J. Cooper, Mayor, Prichard, Ala.
	Doris Davis, Mayor, Compton, Calif.
	Lelia Foley, Mayor, Taft, Okla.
	Kenneth Gibson, Mayor, Newark, N.J.
	William S. Hart, Mayor, East Orange, N.J.
	Richard G. Hatcher, Mayor, Gary, Ind.
	Charles F. Joseph, Mayor, Benton Harbor, Mich.
	James H. McGee, Mayor, Dayton, Ohio
	James Williams, Mayor, East St. Louis, Mo.
	Maynard Jackson, Mayoral candidate, Atlanta, Ga.
1974	No award
1975	Kirkland, Ellis & Rowe, Law firm, Washington, D.C.
	James Johnstone, Kirkland Ellis & Rowe
	Douglas Serdehely, Kirkland, Ellis & Rowe
	Ilana Rovner, Deputy Director of Public Protection, U.S. Attorney's Office
	Donald Pailen, Justice Department, Washington, D.C.
	Francis Cronin, Justice Department, Washington, D.C.
	Arthur Jefferson, Center of National Policy Review, Washington, D.C.
	Judith S. Bernstein, Lawyers' Committee for Civil Rights Under Law, Washington, D.C.
	Harold Himmelman, Lawyers' Committee for Civil Rights Under Law, Washington, D.C.
	Kermit B. Coleman, General Counsel, Afro-American Patrolmen's League
	Eric Graham, General Counsel, Afro-American Patrolmen's League

William H. Brown, Chairman, Equal Opportunity Employment Commission

Leon M. Depres, Alderman, Fifth Ward, Chicago

1976 No award
1977 No award

Agronomic Service Award

AMERICAN SOCIETY OF AGRONOMY
677 S. Segoe Rd., Madison, Wisc. 53711 (608/274-1212)

The $200 Agronomic Service Award annually recognizes development of service programs, practices and products and their acceptance by the public. This includes effective public relations programs designed to promote the understanding and use of agronomic science and technology by the public, government and others.

1961 M.H. McVickar
1962 J. Fieldings Reed
1963 D.E. Western
1964 W.L. Nelson
1965 W.H. Garman
1966 R.M. Love
1967 J.W. Neely
1968 H.H. Tucker
1969 H.D. Loden
1970 I.J. Johnson
1971 L.C. Meade
1972 S.L. Tisdale
1973 W.H. Daniel
1974 W.K. Griffith
1975 T.F. Pratt
1976 R.D. Munson
1977 J.R. Watson, Jr.

American Bar Association Medal

AMERICAN BAR ASSOCIATION
1155 E. 60th St., Chicago, Ill. 60637 (312/947-4000)

The American Bar Association Medal honors "conspicuous service" to American jurisprudence by a lawyer, judge or law professor. While the award is not thus limited, it has frequently honored past presidents of the ABA. The board of governors makes recommendations for the recipient of the annual honor.

1929 Samuel Williston
1930 Elihu Root
1931 Oliver Wendell Holmes
1932 John Henry Wigmore
1933 No award
1934 George Woodward Wickersham
1935 No award
1936 No award
1937 No award
1938 Herbert Harley
1939 Edgar Bronson Tolman
1940 Roscoe Pound
1941 George Wharton Pepper
1942 Charles Evans Hughes
1943 John J. Parker
1944 Hatton W. Sumners
1945 No award
1946 Carl McFarland
1947 William L. Ransom
1948 Arthur T. Vanderbilt

1949 No award
1950 Orie L. Phillips
1951 Reginald Heber Smith
1952 Harrison Tweed
1953 Frank E. Holman
1954 George M. Morris
1955 No award
1956 Robert G. Storey
1957 William Clarke Mason
1958 E. Smythe Gambrell
1959 Greenville Clark
1960 William A. Schnader
1961 Jacob Mark Lashly
1962 Tom C. Clark
1963 Felix Frankfurter
1964 Henry S. Drinker
1965 Edmund M. Morgan
1966 Charles S. Rhyne
1967 Roger J. Traynor
1968 J. Edward Lumbard
1969 Walter V. Schaefer
1970 Frank C. Haymond
1971 Whitney North Seymour
1972 Harold J. Gallagher
1973 William J. Jameson
1974 Ross L. Malone
1975 Leon Jaworski
1976 Bernard D. Segal
1977 Edward L. Wright

Gold Distinguished Service Medal
International Amity Award
Canadian Friendship Award

AMERICAN LEGION
700 N. Pennsylvania, Inidanapolis, Ind. 46204 (317/635-8411)

The Gold Distinguished Service Medal is awarded annually on a vote by the national executive committee for outstanding service to the nation and to the program of the Legion.

1921 Marshall Foch, France
Adm. Beatty, Great Britain
Gen. Baron Jacques, Belgium
Gen. Diaz, Italy
Charles Bertrand, France
1922 Gen. John J. Pershing, U.S.A.
1923 Adm. R. E. Coontz, U.S.A.
Gen. Josef Haller, Poland
1924 No award
1925 No award
1926 Ignace Jan Paderewski, Poland
1927 Comte Francois Marie Robert DeJean, France
1928 Lord Allenby, Great Britain
1929 Judge Kenesaw M. Landis, U.S.A.
1930 Adm. William S. Sims, U.S.A.
1931-41 No awards
1942 Gen. Douglas MacArthur, U.S.A.
1943 Adm. Ernest J. King, U.S.A.
Gen. George C. Marshall, U.S.A.
1944 Gen. H. H. Arnold, U.S.A.
Henry Ford, U.S.A.
Frank Knox, U.S.A.
1945 Franklin D. Roosevelt, U.S.A.
Henry L. Stimson, U.S.A.
Ernest Taylor "Ernie" Pyle, U.S.A.
Adm. Chester Nimitz, U.S.A.

Brig. Gen. Theodore Roosevelt, U.S.A.
Gen. Dwight D. Eisenhower, U.S.A.
1946 William Randolph Hearst, U.S.A.
Bob Hope, U.S.A.
Maj. Gen. Lewis B. Hershey, U.S.A.
J. Edgar Hoover, U.S.A.
Cordell Hull, U.S.A.
1947 Fred M. Vinson, U.S.A.
Edward Martin, U.S.A.
William S. Knudsen, U.S.A.
1948 No award
1949 President Harry S. Truman, U.S.A.
George Herman "Babe" Ruth, U.S.A.
Gen. Frank Parker, U.S.A.
1950 Congresswoman Edith Nourse Rogers, U.S.A.
Maj. Gen. Milton A. Reckord, U.S.A.
Charles F. Johnson, Jr., U.S.A.
1951 Maj. Gen. Charles P. Summerall, U.S.A.
1952 No award
1953 Royal C. Johnson, U.S.A.
1954 Maj. Gen. George A. White, U.S.A.
1955 Jonas E. Salk, U.S.A.
Maj. Gen. Ellard A. Walsh, U.S.A.
1956 V. Adm. Joel T. Boone, U.S.A.
Charles Stewart Mott, U.S.A.
1957 Bishop Fulton J. Sheen, U.S.A.
Gen. Mark. W. Clark, U.S.A.
1958 Bernard M. Baruch, U.S.A.
1959 Sen. Robert S. Kerr, U.S.A.
1961 John F. Kennedy, U.S.A.
1962 Gen. Lucius D. Clay, U.S.A.
Thomas A. Dooley, U.S.A.
1963 Francis Cardinal Spellman, Archbishop of New York, U.S.A.
1964 Charles W. Mayo, U.S.A.
1965 James F. Byrnes, U.S.A.
Herbert Clark Hoover, U.S.A.
1966 Capt. Roger H.D. Donlon, U.S.A.
1967 Tom C. Clark, U.S.A.
1968 Lyndon B. Johnson, U.S.A.
Gen. William C. Westmoreland, U.S.A.
1969 Richard M. Nixon, U.S.A.
1970 Congressman Olin E. Teague, U.S.A.
1971 Hon. Richard Brevard Russell, U.S.A.
Hon. L. Mendel Rivers, U.S.A.
1972 DeWitt Wallace, U.S.A.
Sen. John C. Stennis, U.S.A.
1973 No award
1974 Henry F. Kissinger, U.S.A.
Congressman F. Edward Hebert, U.S.A.
1975 Harry Colmery, U.S.A.
1976 Pat O'Brien, U.S.A.
1977 Howard A. Rusk, U.S.A.

The International Amity Award is a citation given annually to war veterans of any war-time ally of the United States from nominations by any American Legion member and selection by the National Trophies, Awards and Ceremonials Committee for contributions to international good will and service in veterans' affairs.

1962 Raymond Triboulet, France
Jean Louis Bonet-Maury, France
Robert A. Vivien, France
Major-General Sir Richard Howard-Vyse, Great Britain
General Sir Roy Bucher, Great Britain
P. N. Ferstenberg, Belgium
S. L. Woodcock, Canada

Donald Johnston, Canada
Jack Pothecary, Canada
Hugh J. McGivern, Canada
J. P. Nevins, Canada
A. J. Wickens, Canada
L. G. Howard, Canada
James Dickson, Canada
Don H. Thompson, Canada
I. C. Lundberg, Canada
G. R. Lang, Canada
J. D. Baxter, Canada
W. J. Maddison, Canada
C. A. Young, Canada
1963 Antoine Ginee, Belgium
Gen. Wladyslaw Anders, Poland
Jean Sainteny, France
Donald S. McTavish, Canada
Maj. Gen. Lucien Truyers, Belgium
1964 Gen. Rueben Peralta y Alarcon, Mexico
Gen. Roberto Fierro, Mexico
A. J. Carfrae, Canada
Gordon Thomson, Canada
Alex Shirra, Canada
Brigadier James L. Melville, Canada
F. F. Bailey, Canada
John Ewasew, Canada
Lt. Gen. Augustin Olachea Avilez, Secretary of Defense, Mexico
1965 Maj. Gen. Julien Bouhon, Belgium
General of the Armies Martial Valin, France
Gen. Jacques P. L. DeGrancey, France
Henry J. Harvey, Canada
Fred T. O'Brecht, Canada
Ian Beresford, Canada
1966 Byron Wilson, Canada
W. Lorne Manchester, Canada
E. K. Carter, Canada
Gen. Piere Koenig, France
Meir Bar-Rav-Hay, Israel (United Kingdom)
A. J. Lee, Australia
Rev. H. Berry, Canada
Harold Berry, Canada
John Hall, Canada
George Waters, Canada
T. L. Fraser, Canada
1967 Hamilton Mitchell, New Zealand
The Right Honorable Lord Carew, Ireland (United Kingdom)
Thomas D. Bailey, Canada
Leonard Hall Turner, Canada
Montague Herbert Hurst, Canada
1968 General Henri Zeller, France
Pierre Weber, France
Simeon C. Medalla, Philippines
Pham Xuan Chieu, Republic of Vietnam
R. N. Johnson, Canada
J. Albert Walker, Canada
Frank H. Farley, Canada
Albert Bianchini, Canada
Michael Popowich, Canada
L. J. Murphy, Canada
George Smith, Canada
1969 Arthur Wallace, Canada
James Hall, Canada
Edouard Emond Leon Dejean, Belgium
1970 No award
1971 Jae Sung Kim, Republic of South Korea
Stanislas Szewalski, Poland (France)
1972 Jacques Medecin, France
1973 Leon DeCleyre, Belgium

Tsu-Yu Chao, Republic of China (Taiwan)
Victor C.J. Chai, Republic of China (Taiwan)
1974 No award
1975 Adelina Geurin-Beau, France
William Craydon, United Kingdom
1976 Alfonzo Cuellar, Ponce de Leon, Mexico
Claude-Lucien Ferrer, France
1977 Yen Hsaio-Chang, Republic of China (Taiwan)
Alejo S. Santos, Philippines
Andre Rigoine de Fougerolles, France
Glenn Grose, Canada

The Canadian Friendship Award, consisting of a citation and medal, is given annually to a Canadian veteran for outstanding service in the field of veterans' affairs and the perpetuation of good will and friendship between the United States and Canada and the veterans' organizations of the two countries. Any Legion member may make a nomination for selection by the National Trophies, Awards and Ceremonials Committee.

1970

Frank Washbrook	S. Slater
W. B. Morden	Mel Rogers
E. J. Potter	Hugh Gillis
Russell Ward	

1971

Alexander Donald Grant	Robert Kohaly
Mary C. Driscoll	William Albert Johns
Berrien Eaton	

1972

Andrew Hutton Black	John Redmond Roche
J. C. McArthur	George Campbell
J. Hamilton	Richard Rigby
T. Holland	George Kemp
Jessie Iron	J. Stewart
W. J. Ford	R. Dunne
P. Fedosen	W. Talbot
Stan Stiwell	A. G. Winnmill

1973

Rev. E. G. B. Foote	Francis W. Chaplin
F. Gordon Wright	Harry Paul

1974

Joseph J. Savage	Jean E. A. J. Lamy
Robert Murray Whipple	Keith Corrigan
Fred Hake	J. M. Stewart
Ben Miller	Charles M. Thompson
Irwin McNeeley	A. J. Hoyes
K. "Chuck" Karasin	W. J. "Bill" Dobson
R. G. Burns	C. Cunningham
W. G. Smith	Gordon Westman
J. J. Maurice Theoret	W. Pike

1975

Robert McChessney	Sgt. William A. Lorette
Edward Doyle Dimsdale	Oliver Hrynchuk
Howard Goldrup	Alex Cairns

1976

Allan S. Morrison	Lionel Gagne
Walter Homes	Ralph L. Smith

Thomas Goddard	Brian Patrick O'Callaghan
Reginald Swindlehurst	Alfred G. Bull
Renie Crawford	Murray Edmunds
Sam C. Isaacs	Joseph William Johnson
Ronald D. Jones	William E. Lamb
George Mabbe	Harold Z. McKenzie
Stewart Robinson	George Rountree
Wilmont G. Wallace	William S. White
William Whitehouse	

1977

Nelson Leonard Wrommel	Gerard Kit Bellanger
Armand Daigle	George Wakeford
Donald Lester Hansen	Archibald McKenzie
Douglas McDonald	

John Phillip Immroth Award for Intellectual Freedom

AMERICAN LIBRARY ASSOCIATION
50 E. Huron St., Chicago, Ill. 60611 (312/944-6780)

The John Phillip Immroth Award for Intellectual Freedom is given annually by the Association's Intellectual Freedom Roundtable for outstanding contributions to the cause. The Immroth Award Committee selects the winner, who receives a plaque and a $500 cash honorarium.

1976 **I.F. Stone,** Lifelong contributions
1977 **Irene Turin,** Librarian at Island Trees (N.Y.) High School

America's Democratic Legacy Award

ANTI-DEFAMATION LEAGUE OF B'NAI B'RITH
315 Lexington Ave., New York, N.Y. 10016 (212/689-7400)

The Democratic Legacy Award, which consists of a silver medallion, annually honors individuals or organizations for contributions to the enrichment of America's democratic traditions.

1948 **Eleanor Roosevelt**
Darryl Zanuck, Producer
Dore Schary, Writer-producer
Barney Balaban, President, Paramount Pictures
Charles E. Wilson, Chairman, President's Committee on Civil Rights
1949 **President Harry S. Truman**
1950 **J. Howard McGrath,** U.S. Attorney General
1951 **Henry Ford II,** Industrialist
1952 **Herbert H. Lehman,** U.S. Senator
1953 **President Dwight D. Eisenhower**
1954-55 **Carnegie Corporation**
Ford Foundation
Rockefeller Foundation
1956 **Herbert H. Lehman,** U. S. Senator
James P. Mitchell, U. S. Secretary of Labor
Charles P. Taft, Mayor of Cincinnati
1957 **85th Congress of the United States**
1958 **Columbia Broadcasting System**
Look magazine
The *New York Times*
1959 **Actors' Equity Association**
Dramatists Guild
League of New York Theatres
Society of Stage Directors and Choreographers

1960 Harvard University
      University of Notre Dame
      Brandeis University
1961 Adlai E. Stevenson, U.S. Ambassador to the United Nations
1962 President John F. Kennedy
1963 Eugene Carson Blake, United Presbyterian Church
      A. Philip Randolph, Brotherhood of Sleeping Car Porters
      Walter Reuther, United Auto Workers
      Roy Wilkins, NAACP
1964 President Lyndon B. Johnson
1965 Arthur J. Goldberg, U.S. Ambassador to the United Nations
1966 Nicholas deB. Katzenbach, Under Secretary of State
1967 John W. Gardner, National Urban Coalition
1968 No award
1969 Earl Warren, Former Chief Justice, U.S. Supreme Court
1970 No award
1971 Abraham Joshua Heschel, Jewish Theological Seminary of America
1972 No award
1973 Jacob K. Javits, U. S. Senator
      Abraham A. Ribicoff, U. S. Senator
1974 No award
1975 No award
1976 Saul Bellow, Author
1977 Arthur F. Burns, Chairman, Federal Reserve Board

AVCA/AWA Helicopter Heroism Award

AVIATION/SPACE WRITERS ASSOCIATION
Cliffwood Rd., Chester, N.J. 07930

The AVCA/AWA Helicopter Heroism Award recognizes outstanding heroism of a pilot, crew member or other individual involving the use of a helicopter. There is a $500 honorarium with this award, which is sponsored jointly with AVCO Corp.

1967 Maj. Bruce P. Crandall
1968 Maj. Steven Pless
1969 Sgt. Steve Northern, Para-rescueman
1970 Capt. Daniel A. Nicholson
1971 Warrant Officer I Mark M. Feinburg, USA, and Lt. Cdr. James E. Rylee, USN
1972 Maj. Kenneth E. Ernest, USAF, Combat area
      Charles Allred, Non-combat area
1973 Capt. Billy H. Causey, USA, Combat area
      Albert Carriger and John Lockwood, Non-combat area
1974 Flight Lieutenant Bernard Braithwaite and Master Air Electronics Operator Alister More, both Royal Air Force, Great Britain
1975 Lt. Patrick W. Gregory and Crewman Terry E. Richardson, both of the U.S. Coast Guard
1976 N.A.
1977 Cameron Bangs

Bellarmine Medal

BELLARMINE COLLEGE
2000 Norris Place, Louisville, Ky. 40205 (502/452-8011)

The silver Bellarmine Medal is awarded annually to an individual, group or organization exemplifying the characterisitics of St. Robert Bellarmine and exhibiting justice, charity or temperateness when dealing with difficult or controversial subjects. A selection committee chooses the recipient.

1955 Jefferson Caffrey
1956 Gen. Carlos Romulo
1957 John W. McCormack, U.S. Representative
1958 Frank M. Folsom
1959 Robert D. Murphy
1960 James P. Mitchell
1961 Frederick H. Boland
1962 Gen. Alfred M. Gruenther
1963 Henry Cabot Lodge
1964 R. Sargent Shriver
1965 Irene Dunne
1966 Everett M. Dirksen, U.S. Senator
1967 Nicholas Katzenbach
1968 Danny Thomas
1969 J. Irwin Miller
1970 Theodore M. Hesburgh, C.S.C.
1971 John Sherman Cooper, U.S. Senator
1972 No award
1973 William B. Walsh
1974 No award
1975 Rev. Fulton J. Sheen, D.D.
1976 No award
1977 William F. Buckley, Jr.

Silver Buffalo
Distinguished Eagle Scout Award

BOY SCOUTS OF AMERICA
North Brunswick, N.J. 08902 (201/249-6000)

The Silver Buffalo is the highest of the Boy Scouts of America's four service awards, the others being either of a more localized nature or dependent on a direct, long-term association with scouting. The Silver Buffalo is bestowed by the National Court of Honor upon the recommendation of the National Executive Board for distinguished service to youth. It is the only award made by the Boy Scouts of America that has no specific course of action, tests to be met or training as a requirement; rather, it honors committed service to young people.

1926 Sir Robert S. S. Baden-Powell, Gilwell Park, Great Britain, Chief Scout of the World
      The Unknown Scout, Boy Scout
      William D. Boyce, Chicago, Ill., Publisher; incorporator of Boy Scouts of America
      Colin H. Livingstone, Washington, D.C., Financier
      James J. Storrow, Boston, Mass., Banker; President, Boy Scouts of America
      Daniel Carter Beard, Suffern, N.Y., National Scout Commissioner
      Ernest Thompson Seton, New York, N.Y., Chief Scout
      Edgar M. Robinson, Washington, D.C., Coorganizer of the Boy Scouts of America
      Lee F. Hanmer, New York, N.Y., Coorganizer of the Boy Scouts of America
      George W. Wingate, New York, N.Y., Advocate of organized outdoor recreation
      Joseph Lee, Boston, Mass., Advocate of playground and outdoor recreation
      Howard S. Braucher, New York, N.Y., Chairman, Committee on Organization, Boy Scouts of America

Mortimer L. Schiff, New York, N.Y., Philanthropist; President, Boy Scouts of America

Milton A. McRae, Detroit, Mich., Publisher; President, Boy Scouts of America

Frank Presbrey, New York, N.Y., Advertising Man; developer of *Boys' Life*

George D. Pratt, New York, N.Y., Treasurer, Boy Scouts of America

John Sherman Hoyt, Darien, Conn., Manufacturer; Chairman, Finance Committee Boy Scouts of America

Jeremiah W. Jenks, New York, N.Y., Educator; Formulator of Scout Oath and Law

William D. Murray, Plainfield, N.J., Lawyer; Chairman, Editorial Board, Boy Scouts of America

G. Barrett Rich, New York, N.Y., Chairman, National Committee of Badges, Awards, and Scout Requirements

James E. West, New York, N.Y., Lawyer; Chief Scout Executive

George J. Fisher, New York, N.Y., Physician, Deputy Chief Scout Executive

1927 **William Howard Taft,** Washington, D.C., Chief Justice of the United States; First Honorary President, Boy Scouts of America

Hubert S. Martin, C.B.E., London, Great Britain, Director, Boy Scouts International Bureau

William Adams Welch, Washington, D.C., National and State Parks Commissioner

Stuart W. French, Pasadena, Calif., Business executive; Organizer of Region 12

Bolton Smith, Memphis, Tenn., Banker; promoter of interracial understanding

Walter B. Head, Omaha, Neb., Banker; President, Boy Scouts of America

Brother Barnabas, F.S.C., New York, N.Y., Educator; Director, Catholic Bureau, Boy Scouts of America

1928 **The Unknown Soldier,** Patriot

Charles A. Lindbergh, Hopewell, N.J., Aviator; transatlantic pioneer

W. de Bonstetten, Kandersteg, Switzerland, President, Swiss Federation of Boy Scouts

Arthur N. Cotton, Buffalo, N.Y., Promoter of High-Y Clubs

Clarence H. Howard, St. Louis, Mo., Philanthropist; founder of Junior Chamber of Commerce

Charles D. Velie, Minneapolis, Minn., Philanthropist; promoter of scouting for rural boys

William H. Cowles, Spokane, Wash., Publisher, first Chairman, Region 11 Committee

1929 **Calvin Coolidge,** Plymouth, Vt., President, United States of America

Richard E. Byrd, Winchester, Va., Commander, U.S. Navy, Antarctic explorer

Wilbert E. Longfellow, Washington, D.C., Water safety promoter, American Red Cross

John H. Finley, New York, N.Y., Educator; founder of Junior American Red Cross

Howard F. Gillette, Chicago, Ill., Banker; promoter of sea scouting

Charles D. Hart, Philadelphia, Pa., Physician; promoter of troop camping

H.R.H. The Prince of Wales, Scouting enthusiast

1930 **Herbert Clark Hoover,** West Branch, Iowa, President, United States of America

James Earl Russell, New York, N.Y., Educator, scouter

Franklin D. Roosevelt, Hyde Park, N.Y., Governor, State of New York; advocate of scouting

James Austin Wilder, New York, N.Y., Developed and organized the Sea Scouts program

Charles L. Sommers, Minneapolis, Minn., Business executive; Chairman, Region 10

Charles C. Moore, San Francisco, Calif., Engineer, scouter

Lewis Warrington Baldwin, St. Louis, Mo., Railroad president; regional chairman

1931 **Lord Hampton, D.S.O.,** London, Great Britain, Distinguished British scouter

Griffith Ogden Ellis, Detroit, Mich., Editor and publisher, *American Boy* Magazine

Lewis Gawtry, New York, N.Y., Banker; philanthropist

George Welch Olmsted, Warren, Pa., Utilities executive; world scouter

Victor F. Ridder, New York, N.Y., Newspaper publisher; Catholic scouter

Robert P. Sniffen, Yonkers, N.Y., Merchandising consultant; Chairman, Committee on Supply Service

Mell R. Wilkinson, Atlanta, Ga., Manufacturer; National Executive Board Member

1932 **Dwight Filley Davis,** St. Louis, Mo., Public servant; advocate of athletics

William Edwin Hall, Greenwich, Conn., Lawyer; President, Boys' Clubs of America

Alfred W. Dater, Stamford, Conn., Utilities executive; first Chairman, Sea Scout Committee

Barron Collier, New York, N.Y., Philanthropist; promoter of scouting

Frank A. Bean, Minneapolis, Minn., Business executive, advocate of rural scouting

Hermann W. Merkel, New York, N.Y., Creative administrator of parks and camps

1933 **Vincent Massey,** Toronto, Canada, Canadian diplomat; philanthropist

Martin H. Carmody, New York, N.Y., Supreme Knight, Knights of Columbus

John P. Wallace, Des Moines, Iowa, Publisher; advocate of rural scouting

Cyrus Adler, Philadelphia, Pa., Educator; Chairman, Jewish Committee on Scouting

Reginald H. Parsons, Seattle, Wash., Developer of scouting in Pacific Northwest

John A. McGregor, San Francisco, Calif., Region 12 scouter; friend to youth

1934 **Newton D. Baker,** Cleveland, Ohio, Statesman; humanitarian

Paul Percy Harris, Chicago, Ill., Lawyer; founder of Rotary Club Movement

John M. Phillips, Pittsburgh, Pa., Conservationist; recipient of Silver Wolf award

Theodore Roosevelt, Jr., Oyster Bay, N.Y., Public servant; explorer

Charles E. Cotting, Boston, Mass., Philanthropist, promoter of New England scouting

Frederic Kernochan, New York, N.Y., Jurist; pioneer scouter; Urban League Executive

George Albert Smith, Salt Lake City, Utah, Business executive; religious leader; scouter

1935 **Booth Tarkington,** Indianapolis, Ind., Author; immortalizer of youth

Amos Alonzo Stagg, Stockton, Calif., Educator; dean of American coaches

Daniel A. Tobin, New York, N.Y., Banker; scouter; cofounder, Columbian Squires

Fielding Harris Yost, Ann Arbor, Mich., Scout Commissioner; exponent of clean sports

Calvin Derrick, Jamesburg, N.J., Educator; penologist; innovator

R. Tait McKenzie, Philadelphia, Pa., Educator; sculptor of Boy Scout statue

1936 **Frederick Russell Burnham,** Three Rivers, Calif., American-British adventurer

Hugh S. Cumming, Washington, D.C., United States Surgeon General

Lawrence Locke Doggett, Springfield, Mass., Educator; Pioneer for training for boys' work

Charles Horace Mayo, Rochester, Minn., Surgeon; health authority; pioneer scouter

George Edgar Vincent, Greenwich, Conn., Educator; adviser to scouting for health and safety

John Skinner Wilson, Gilwell Park, Great Britain, Gilwell Camp Chief; world scouter

1937 No award

1938 **Thomas E. Wilson,** Chicago, Ill., Promoter for rural youth and 4-H Clubs

William T. Hornaday, Stamford, Conn., Zoologist and conservationist; pioneer, scouter

George A. Allen, Washington, D.C., Presidential Representative to first National Jamboree

Frank Cody, Detroit, Mich., Educator; innovator with schools and scouting

Frank G. Hoover, Canton, Ohio, Longtime scouter; friend to youth

Cornelius "Connie Mack" McGillicuddy, Philadelphia, Pa., Advocate of good sportsmanship

C. B. Smith, Washington, D.C., Public servant; physician; worker for rural scouting

John A. Stiles, Ottawa, Canada, Canadian scouting official; recipient of Silver Wolf award

1939 **William Chalmers Covert,** Pittsburgh, Pa., Clergyman; scouter

Marshall Field, New York, N.Y., Business Executive; philanthropist; scouter

Elbert K. Fretwell, New York, N.Y., Educator; scouter; training innovator

Heber J. Grant, Salt Lake City, Utah, Industrialist; Mormon church official

Francis C. Kelley, Tulsa, Okla., Bishop of Oklahoma City and Tulsa; scouter

John R. Mott, New York, N.Y., Missionary; statesman, world youth leader

Norman Rockwell, Arlington, Vt., Artist; prime creator of scouting's image

1940 **Edward Roberts Moore,** New York, N.Y., Catholic clergyman; youth worker; scouter

George W. Truett, Dallas, Tex., Clergyman; world youth leader; scouter

Eugene D. Nims, St. Louis, Mo., Philanthropist; longtime scouter

1941 **C. Ward Crampton,** New York, N.Y., Scientist; author; physical fitness advocate

Homer Folks, New York, N.Y., Social welfare statesman

Edgar Rickard, Darien, Conn., Mining engineer; humanitarian; friend to scouting

J. E. H. Stevenot, Manila, Philippines, Creator of modern Philippine Scout Organization

Daniel A. Poling, Philadelphia, Pa., Clergyman; editor; scouter

1942 **Frank O. Lowden,** Oregon, Ill., Farmer; lawyer; statesman; philanthropist; scouter

Ragnvald Anderson Nestos, Minot, N.D., Lawyer; statesman; churchman; pioneer in rural scouting

Frank Phillips, Bartlesville, Okla., Banker; philanthropist; enthusiast for scouting

Bernard J. Sheil, Chicago, Il., Auxiliary Bishop of Chicago; founder of CYO; scouter

William Clay Smoot, Bartlesville, Okla., Banker; outdoorsman; worker for rural youth

1943 **J. Edgar Hoover,** Washington, D.C., Lawyer; criminologist; director of the FBI

Harry C. Knight, New Haven, Conn., Business executive; philanthropist; scouter

John Mortimer Schiff, New York, N.Y., Banker; philanthropist; president, Boy Scouts of America

William L. Smith, Louisville, Ky., Surgeon; public servant; author; scouter

Frank W. Wozencraft, Dallas, Tex., Businessman; lawyer; statesman; scouter

1944 **Oscar H. Benson,** Seven Stars, Pa., Educator; founder of the 4-H Clubs

Charles Evans Hughes, Glens Falls, N.Y., Jurist; statesman; diplomat; champion of youth

Elbridge W. Palmer, Kingsport, Tenn., Publisher; worker for crippled youth, racial harmony, and scouting

William C. Menninger, Topeka, Kans., Neuropsychiatrist; enthusiastic scouter

Philip L. Reed, Chicago, Ill., Business executive; scouter; member, advisory council

Edward Vernon Rickenbacker, New York, N.Y., Aviation pioneer; executive; wartime ace of aces; scouter

Arthur Herbert Tennyson Somers-Cocks, 6th Baron Somers, London, Great Britain, Chief Scout of the British Empire

Thomas J. Watson, New York, N.Y., Business executive; philanthropist; educator; scouter

1945 **Francis W. Hatch,** Boston, Mass., Publicist; scouter; chairman, *Boys' Life* committee

Amory Houghton, Corning, N.Y., Manufacturer; philanthropist; vice-president, Boy Scouts of America

Paul W. Litchfield, Akron, Ohio, Industrialist; developed First Air Scout Squadron

Earl C. Sams, New York, N.Y., Merchant; philanthropist; chairman, business division committee

1946 **John M. Bierer,** Wellesley Hills, Mass., Business executive; longtime scouter

William J. Campbell, Chicago, Ill., Jurist; promoter of scouting for Catholic boys

Walter E. Disney, Beverly Hills, Calif., Cinema executive; creator of Mickey Mouse

Dwight D. Eisenhower, Denison, Tex., General of the Army, Supreme Commander of Allied Expeditionary Forces in Europe

Raymond F. Low, Omaha, Neb., Business executive; scouter; Sea Scouting enthusiast

Wheeler McMillen, Trenton, N.J., Journalist; editor; advocate for rural scouting

Chester William Nimitz, Fredericksburg, Tex., Chief of Naval Operations; U.S. signator to Japanese surrender treaty

Vilhjalmur Stefansson, New York, N.Y., Arctic explorer; author; scouter

Frank L. Weil, New York, N.Y., Lawyer; scouter; co-founder, United Service Organizations

1947 **Bernard M. Baruch,** Camden, S.C., Economist; philanthropist; patriot

Manuel Camus, Manila, Philippines, Statesman; jurist; president, Boy Scouts of the Philippines

Cleveland E. Dodge, New York, N.Y., Financier; philanthropist; chairman, International Board of the Y.M.C.A.

Perrin C. Galpin, New York, N.Y., Educator; Scouter; child-health advocate

William H. Pouch, New York, N.Y., Industrialist; longtime scouter; civic leader

Paul A. Siple, Arlington, Pa., Geographer; explorer; author; member, first Byrd Antarctic expedition

Francis Cardinal Spellman, New York, N.Y., Archbishop of New York; author; patriot

R. Douglas Stuart, Chicago, Ill., Manufacturer; pioneer scouter; friend to youth

1948 **Irving Berlin,** New York, N.Y., Composer of "God Bless America"

Belmore Browne, Ross, Calif., Artist; explorer; cold-weather camping expert

Cherry Logan Emerson, Atlanta, Ga., Engineer; educator; servant of youth

Reuben Brooks Hale, San Francisco, Calif., Merchant; civic leader; advocate of Senior Scouting

Robert F. Payne, New York, N.Y., Educator; author; longtime scouter

Lord Rowallan, Ayrshire, Scotland, Chief Scout of British Commonwealth and Empire

Wade Warren Thayer, Honolulu, Hawaii, Attorney; author; exponent of Hawaiian scouting

1949 **David W. Armstrong,** New York, N.Y., Executive director, Boys' Clubs of America

Sheldon Clark, Chicago, Ill., Business executive; national Sea Scout commodore

Richard J. Cushing, Boston, Mass., Archbishop of Boston; lecturer; author; civic leader; head of all youth work of Catholic Chruch in U.S.A.

W. V. M. Fawcett, Boston, Mass., Business executive; civic leader; scouter

Charles R. Hook, Middletown, Ohio, Industrialist; advocate of Junior Achievement; scouter

Luther A. Weigle, New Haven, Conn., Educator; dean; Bible scholar; pioneer scouter

1950 **Harry Messiter Addinsell,** New York, N.Y., Financier; churchman; treasurer, Boy Scouts of America

Kenneth K. Bechtel, San Francisco, Calif., Business executive; vice-president, Boy Scouts of America

Charles Franklin Kettering, Dayton, Ohio, Engineer; manufacturer; philanthropist; innovator

Irving Langmuir, Schenectady, N.Y., Nobel Prize scientist; pioneer scouter

Byrnes MacDonald, New York, N.Y., Business executive; worker ofr underprivileged youth

Owen J. Roberts, Philadelphia, Pa., Jurist; public servant; longtime scouter

Arthur A. Schuck, New Brunswick, N.J., Chief Scout Executive, Boy Scouts of America

Lowell Thomas, Pawling, N.Y., Explorer; author; news commentator; scouter

Harry S. Truman, Independence, Mo., President, United States of America

Milburn Lincoln Wilson, Washington, D.C., National director, 4-H Clubs; scouter

1951 **Ralph J. Bunche,** Jamaica, N.Y., Educator; Nobel Peace Prize winner; scouter

James Lippitt Clark, New York, N.Y., Explorer; author; sculptor; conservationist; scouter

Edgar Albert Guest, Detroit, Mich., Writer; poet; Boys' Club official; friend of youth

Raymond W. Miller, Washington, D.C., Publicist; scouter; advocate of rural scouting

D. C. Spry, Ottawa, Canada, Chief Executive Commissioner, Canadian General Council of the Boy Scouts Association

James H. Douglas, Jr., Chicago, Ill., Attorney; public servant; longtime scouter

Henry Smith Richardson, Greensboro, N.C., Manufacturing chemist; longtime scouter

Jack P. Whitaker, Kansas City, Mo., Manufacturer; scouter; president, American Humanics Foundation

1952 **Julius Ochs Adler,** New York, N.Y., Journalist; patriot; veteran scouter

Roy Chapman Andrews, New York, N.Y., Explorer; zoologist; museum director; author

Frank Learoyd Boyden, Deerfield, Mass., Teacher; headmaster; friend to youth

Harmar D. Denny, Pittsburgh, Pa., Attorney; congressman; longtime scouter

Gale F. Johnston, St. Louis, Mo., Banker; civic leader; philanthropist; scouter

Carlos P. Romulo, Washington, D.C., Author; soldier; diplomat; cofounder, Boy Scouts of the Philippines

Louis John Taber, Columbus, Ohio, Farmer; granger; exponent of rural scouting; scouter

1953 **Alton Fletcher Baker,** Eugene, Ore., Journalist; publisher; civic leader; scouter

Henry B. Grandin, San Marino, Calif., Business executive; scouter; host to 3d National Jamboree

Ross L. Leffler, Pittsburgh, Pa., Business executive; civic leader; veteran scouter

Charles Francis McCahill, Cleveland, Ohio, Newspaper executive; philanthropist; scouter

David O. McKay, Salt Lake City, Utah, President, Church of Jesus Christ of Latter-day Saints

1954 **William H. Albers,** Cincinnati, Ohio, Business executive; philanthropist; scouter

Ellsworth Hunt Augustus, Cleveland, Ohio, Banker; civic leader; scouter

Ezra Taft Benson, Salt Lake City, Utah, Secretary of agriculture; church leader; scouter

Philip David Bookstaber, Harrisburg, Pa., Rabbi; scholar; exponent of scouting for Jewish boys

Norton Clapp, Seattle, Wash., Business executive; civic leader; veteran scouter

J. M. T. Finney, Jr., Baltimore, Md., Surgeon; churchman; civic leader; veteran scouter

Richard Oliver Gerow, Natchez, Miss., Bishop of Natchez, Miss.; longtime scouter

Edward Urner Goodman, Bondville, Vt., Church executive; pioneer scouter; founder, Order of the Arrow

George Lloyd Murphy, Beverly Hills, Calif., Producer; actor; publicist; scouter

Nathan Marvin Ohrbach, New York, N.Y., Business executive; philanthropist; scouter

Dewitt Wallace, Pleasantville, N.Y., Magazine founder; editor; publisher; philanthropist

1955 **Charles Dana Bennett,** Addison, Vt., Author; rural consultant; publicist; scouter

Rex Ivan Brown, Jackson, Miss., Utility executive; civic leader; veteran scouter

William Durant Campbell, New York, N.Y., Naturalist; world traveler; Eagle Scout; scouter

Francis John Chesterman, Philadelphia, Pa., Utilities executive; civic leader; scouter

Leonard Kimball Firestone, Los Angeles, Calif., Industrialist; churchman; civic leader; scouter

Charles William Froessel, Jamaica, N.Y., Jurist; churchman; civic leader; scouter

Robert Tyre Jones, Jr., Atlanta, Ga., Attorney; business executive; sportsman; champion athlete

Lewis Edward Phillips, Eau Claire, Wisc., Manufacturer; philanthropist; scouter

Frank Chambless Rand, Jr., Sante Fe, N.M., Business executive; publisher; civic leader; scouter

Thomas John Watson, Jr., New York, N.Y., Business executive; civic leader, philanthropist; scouter

1956 **Ivan Allen, Jr.,** Atlanta, Ga., Executive; banker; engineer; civic leader; scouter

Gerald F. Beal, New York, N.Y., Banker; financier; cultural and civic leader; scouter

Daniel W. Bell, Washington, D.C., Banker; public servant; community leader; scouter

Hugh Moss Comer, Sylacauga, Ala., Textile manufacturer; philanthropist; scouter

Walter Francis Dillingham, Honolulu, Hawaii, Executive; builder; philanthropist; statesman; scouter

Whitney Haskins Eastman, Minneapolis, Minn., Business executive; engineer; scientist; scouter

William Harrison Fetridge, Chicago, Ill. Editor; publisher; executive; community leader; scouter

William Jansen, New York, N.Y., Educator; author; churchman; administrator; scouter

Guy Lee Noble, Chicago, Ill., National 4-H Club executive; humanitarian

Harry Lloyd Schaeffer, St. Louis, Mo., Railroad executive; scouter

Henry Frederick Schricker, Knox, Ind., Statesman; banker; editor; pioneer scouter

Harold Edward Stassen, St. Paul, Minn., Educator; humanitarian; statesman; author; scouter

Edwin Joel Thomas, Akron, Ohio, Industrialist; civic leader; humanitarian; scouter

1957 **Harold Roe Bartle,** Kansas City, Mo., Attorney; civic leader; humanitarian; scouter

Brooks Hays, Washington D.C., Congressman; lawyer; humanitarian; scouter

Walter David Heller, San Francisco, Calif., Business executive; civic leader; philanthropist; scouter

Henry Cabot Lodge, Beverly, Mass., Journalist; national and international statesman

Abram Leon Sachar, Waltham, Mass., Educator; author; historian; university president

Herman Lee Turner, Atlanta, Ga., Clergyman; humanitarian; civic leader; scouter

Kenneth Dale Wells, Valley Forge, Pa., Economist; educator; president, Freedoms Foundation at Valley Forge

1958 **Robert Bernerd Anderson,** Washington, D.C., Secretary of the Treasury; lawyer; educator; scouter

John Hopkinson Baker, New York, N.Y., Conservation executive; governmental adviser

Hubert Hardison Coffield, Rockdale, Tex., Industrialist; rancher; churchman; humanitarian; scouter

Nathan Dauby, Cleveland, Ohio, Business Executive; civic leader; philanthropist; scouter

Jackson Dodds, Montreal, Canada, Banker; scouter; recipient of Silver Wolf and Bronze Wolf

John Randolph Donnell, Findlay, Ohio, Business executive; civic leader; scouter

Robert Newcomb Gibson, East Lansing, Mich., Business executive; lumberman; scouter

Frank Brittain Kennedy, Cohasset, Mass., Investment dealer; churchman; executive; scouter

Edward Leroy Kohnle, Dayton, Ohio, Business executive; churchman; cultural leader; scouter

Sol George Levy, Seattle, Wash., Import-export business executive; community leader; scouter

John Norton Lord, Detroit, Mich., Business executive; community leader; scouter

James Maitland Stewart, Beverly Hills, Calif., Actor; combat aviator; scouter

1959 **Milo William Bekins,** Los Angeles, Calif., Business executive; community leader; scouter

George Michael Dowd, Franklin, Mass., Clergyman; domestic prelate; youth leader; scout chaplain

Irving Jonas Feist, Newark, N.J., Business executive; community leader; scouter

Roger Stanley Firestone, Bryn Mawr, Pa., Manufacturing executive; humanitarian; scouter

Bob Hope, Beverly Hills, Calif., Cinema, radio, and television comedian; humanitarian

Jeffrey Louis Lazarus, Cincinnati, Ohio, Business executive; community leader; scouter

Walter Lee Lingle, Jr., Cincinnati, Ohio, Business executive; community leader; scouter

George Magar Mardikian, San Francisco, Calif., Restaurateur; author; philanthropist; scouter

Pliny Hunnicut Powers, New Brunswick, N.J., Educator; deputy chief scout executive, Boy Scouts of America

Charles Dudley Pratt, Honolulu, Hawaii, Attorney; civic leader; pioneer scouter

Joseph Frederic Wiese, Coatesville, Pa., Industrial executive; community leader; veteran scouter

1960 **Joe C. Carrington,** Austin, Tex., Insurance executive; rancher; churchman; youth worker; scouter

Thomas Campbell Clark, Washington, D.C., Associate Justice of the United States Supreme Court; humanitarian; veteran scouter

James Thomas Griffin, Cleveland, Ohio, Business executive; humanitarian; churchman; scouter

Alfred M. Gruenther, Washington, D.C., President, American National Red Cross; Supreme Allied Commander in Europe 1953-56; scouter

Roy Edward Larson, New York, N.Y., Publishing executive; civic leader; humanitarian

Robert John Lloyd, Tacoma, Wash., Business executive; community leader; scouter

Alexander White Moffat, Beverly Farms, Mass., Business executive; yachtsman; author; scouter

Clifford A. Randall, Milwaukee, Wisc., Lawyer; executive; humanitarian; Past President, Rotary International

Norman Salit, Lawrence, N.Y., Rabbi; attorney; humanitarian; veteran scouter

1961 **Wyeth Allen,** Ann Arbor, Mich., Educator; community leader; longtime scouter

Carl Otto Janus, Indianapolis, Ind., Business executive; civic leader; veteran scouter

Richard E. McArdle, Washington, D.C., Educator; public servant; conservationist; scouter

Charles B. McCabe, Jr., New York, N.Y., Publisher; broadcasting executive; veteran scouter

Lauris Norstad, Minneapolis, Minn., Supreme Allied Commander, Europe (SHAPE); promulgator of scouting

William T. Spanton, Washington, D.C., Cofounder, Future Farmers of America; scouter

Delbert Leon Stapley, Phoenix, Ariz., Business executive; church leader; veteran scouter

Charles M. White, Cleveland, Ohio, Industrialist; civic leader; youth worker; scouter

Robert E. Wood, Chicago, Ill., Retired army general; business executive; philanthropist; veteran scouter

1962 **Bruce Cooper Clarke,** Adams, N.Y., Commander in Chief, United States Army, Europe; veteran scouter

Zenon Clayton Raymond Hansen, Lansing, Mich., Business executive; civic leader Eagle Scout; scouter

Carl Hayden, Phoenix, Arix., Member, United States Senate; veteran scouter

Wayne Andrew Johnston, Chicago, Ill., Railroad executive; humanitarian; longtime scouter

Thomas J. Keane, Forest Hills, N.Y., Naval officer in two World Wars; veteran scouter

John Cook Parish, St. Paul, Minn., Business executive; civic leader; scouter

John Thurman, Gilwell Park, Great Britain, Camp chief of Gilwell Park; recipient of Silver Wolf and Bronze Wolf

Carl Vinson, Milledgeville, Ga., Member, House of Representatives; friend of scouting

Clarence E. Williams, Woodward, Okla., Physician; surgeon; Jamboree medical officer; scouter

1963 **Erwin Dain Canham,** Boston, Mass., Editor; author; broadcasting commentator; humanitarian

L. Osmond Crosby, Picayune, Miss., Industrialist; community leader; scouter

Herold C. Hunt, Cambridge, Mass., Educator; author; consultant; scouter

Walter H. Judd, Washington, D.C., Statesman; missionary; civic leader; veteran scouter

John T. Kimball, New York, N.Y., Utilities executive; civic leader; scouter

Harold B. Lee, Salt Lake City, Utah, Business executive; educator; church official; scouter

Douglas MacArthur, New York, N.Y., Corporation Chairman; General of the Army; recipient of Congressional Medal of Honor

Jack C. Vowell. El Paso, Tex., Business executive; engineer; civic leader; veteran scouter

Frederick M. Warburg, New York, N.Y., Banker; philanthropist; worker for youth; scouter

1964 **A. Frank Bray,** Martinez, Calif., Jurist; civic leader; friend to youth; scouter

Albert L. Cole, Greenwich, Conn., Publisher; president, Boys' Clubs of America; philanthropist

Lyndon B. Johnson, Johnson City, Tex., President, United States of America

Ralph W. McCreary, Indiana, Pa., Industrialist; civic leader; veteran scouter

Robert Moses, New York, N.Y., Public servant; builder; friend to youth; scouter

Ephraim Laurence Palmer, Ithaca, N.Y., Educator; author; conservationist; veteran scouter

Thomas F. Patton, Cleveland, Ohio, International industrialist; civic leader; scouter

Gilbert R. Pirrung, Bainbridge, Ga., Agriculturist; churchman; world scouter

Howard Tellepsen, Houston, Tex., Business leader; churchman; scouter

1965 **Irving Ben Cooper,** New York, N.Y., Jurist; humanitarian; friend to youth

Austin T. Cushman, Chicago, Ill, Merchandising executive; community leader; scouter

Harry J. Delaney, New York, N.Y., Business leader; churchman; scouter

Royal Firman, Jr., Cleveland, Ohio, Business, cultural, community and church leader; scouter

John H. Glenn, Jr., Houston, Tex., Colonel, Marine Corps (ret.); astronaut; scouter

Harry J. Johnson, New York, N.Y., Physician; educator; administrator; scouter

Harry G. McGavran, Quincy, Ill., Surgeon; community leader; humanitarian; scouter

David Sarnoff, New York, N.Y., Industrialist; communications expert; veteran scouter

Jo. S. Stong, Keosauqua, Iowa, Community leader; scouting enthusiast

Gustavo J. Vollmer, Caracas, Venezuela, Engineer; Venezuelan and world scouter

1966 **Richard W. Darrow,** Scarsdale, N.Y., Publicist; civic leader; Eagle Scout; scouter

John Henry Fischer, New York, N.Y., Educator; civic leader; Eagle Scout; scouter

Charles Zachary Hardwick, Findlay, Ohio, Business executive; humanitarian; scouter

Lewis Blaine Hershey, Washington, D.C., Lieutenant general, United States Army; director, Selective Service; scouter

Basil O'Connor, New York, N.Y., Lawyer; public servant; humanitarian; friend to youth

Philip Henry Powers, Greensburg, Pa., Engineer; educator; pioneer scouter

1967 **Paul G. Benedum,** Pittsburgh, Pa., Business executive; community leader; scouter

Sterling B. Doughty, Sacramento, Calif., Financial and management consultant; world scouter

Harold Keith Johnson, Washington, D.C., Chief of staff, United States Army; educator; scouter

Otto Kerner, Springfield, Ill., Governor of Illinois; scouter

Clarence "Biggie" Munn Lansing, Minn., Athletic director; coach; friend of youth; scouter

Crawford Rainwater, Pensacola, Fla., Business executive; community leader; scouter

Vittz-James Ramsdell, Portland, Ore., Business executive; community leader; scouter

Howard A. Rusk, New York, N.Y., Physician; educator; innovator; humanitarian

Dwight J. Thomson, Cincinnati, Ohio, Business leader; veteran scouter; world scouter

William C. Westmoreland, Washington, D.C., Commander, U.S. Military Assistance Command, Vietnam; CG, U.S. Army, Vietman; Eagle Scout; scouter

1968 **John Cardinal Cody,** Chicago, Ill., Archbiship of Chicago; recipient of the Silver Beaver; energetic scouter

John G. Detwiler, Williamsport, Pa., Industrialist; churchman; recipient of the Silver Beaver and Silver Antelope; National Executive Board Member

Robert T. Gray, Prospect, Ohio, Physician; Eagle Scout; medical officer at many national and world jamborees

Arthur Z. Hirsch, Santa Barbara, Calif., Veteran scouter; recipient of the Silver Beaver and Silver Antelope

John F. Lott, Lubbock, Tex., Rancher; world scouter; recipient of the Silver Beaver and Silver Antelope

William L. Schloss, Indianapolis, Ind., Banker; community leader; recipient of the Silver Beaver

James E. Webb, New York, N.Y., Lawyer; businessman; diplomat; educator; administrator, National Aeronautics and Space Administration

1969 **John M. Budd,** St. Paul, Minn., Executive . . . , champion of youth, dedicated scouter

Arleigh Burke, Washington D.C., Military leader, patriot, distinguished scouter

James F. Burshears, La Junta, Col., Imaginative scouter

M. Scott Carpenter, Houston, Tex., Aquanaut, astronaut, friend of scouting

Vincent T. Lombardi, Washington, D.C., Professional football general manager, friend of youth

John W. H. Miner, Quebec, Canada, Manufacturer, community leader, world scouter

James E. Patrick, Phoenix, Ariz., Banker, community leader, devoted scouter

Robert W. Reneker, Chicago, Ill., Executive, humanitarian, devoted scouter

John W. Starr, Kansas City, Mo., Executive, faithful scouter

N. Eldon Tanner, Salt Lake City, Utah, Churchman, executive, veteran scouter

1970 **Neil A. Armstrong,** El Lago, Tex., Astronaut, first man to walk on the Moon

Francisco Bueso, San Juan, P.R., Chamber of Commerce director, champion of scouting

Antonio C. Delgado, Manila, Philippines, Business executive, world scouter

Laurence C. Jones, Piney Woods, Miss., Educator, author, servant of youth

Aryeh Lev, New York, N.Y., Rabbi, chaplain, dedicated scouter

Leo Perlis, Washington, D.C., Organized labor official, humanitarian, friend of scouting

Bryan S. Reid, Jr., Chicago, Ill., Investment banker, community leader, devoted scouter

William H. Spurgeon III, Santa Ana, Calif., Children's hospital executive, "father" of special-interest exploring

1971 **William G. Connare,** Greensburg, Pa., Bishop, scouter, and champion of scouting

Elbert R. Curtis, Salt Lake City, Utah, Executive, community and church leader, veteran scouter

Thomas Stephens Haggai, High Point, N.C., Gifted public speaker, ordained minister, patriot, scouter

August F. Hook, Indianapolis, Ind., Business executive, community leader, dedicated scouter

William R. Jackson, Sewickley, Pa., Executive, devoted scouter, friend of youth

Fred C. Mills, Aptos, Calif., Outstanding scouter; retired director, Health and Safety Service, Boy Scouts of America

Arch Monson, Jr., San Francisco, Calif., Patron of the arts, humanitarian, executive

Richard Milhous Nixon, Washington, D.C., President, United States of America

Leon Howard Sullivan, Philadelphia, Pa., Humanitarian, peoples' champion

1972 **Louis R. Bruce, Jr.,** Washington, D.C., U.S. commissioner of Indian Affairs, champion of scouting

Harvey C. Christen, Burbank, Calif., Aircraft company executive, civic leader, devoted scouter

Louis G. Feil, Chipita Park, Colo., Consulting engineer, promoter of camping and Order of the Arrow

Edwin H. Gott, Pittsburgh, Pa., Corporate executive, community leader, vigorous promoter of Exploring

Donald P. Hammond, Monticello, N.Y., Business executive, civic leader, scouting enthusiast

Albert M. Jongeneel, Rio Vista, Calif., Retired rancher, dedicated scouter

Arthur L. Jung, Jr., New Orleans, La., Business executive, servant of youth, international scouter

Prime F. Osborn III, Jacksonville, Fla., Company president, friend of youth, advocate of scouting

George W. Pirtle, Tyler, Tex., Consulting geologist and independent oil producer, philanthropist, benefactor of scouting

Penn W. Zeigler, Cincinnati, Ohio, Business executive, humanitarian, veteran scouter

1973 **Ernest Banks,** Chicago, Ill., Baseball great, inspiration for boys, faithful scouter

Joseph A. Brunton, Jr., Matawan, N.J., Servant of youth, former chief scout executive

Victor T. Ehre, Utica, N.Y., Company president, community leader, dedicated scouter

Donald H. Flanders, Fort Smith, Ariz., Company founder and president, distinguished scouter

E. K. Jamison, Atlanta, Ga., Company president, devoted scouter

Max I. Silber, Nashua, N.H., Company president, loyal scouter, benefactor of students

Osborne K. Taylor, Montclair, N.J., Retired corporate executive, veteran scoutmaster, champion of scouting

J. Kimball Whitney, Wayzata, Minn., Company president, friend of youth, veteran scouter

1974 **Stephen A. Derby,** Honolulu, Hawaii, Retired banker, civic leader, faithful scouter

James E. Johnson, Los Angeles, Calif., Corporate board chairman, former assistant secretary of the Navy, distinguished scouter

Allen W. Mathis, Jr., Montgomery, Ala., Company Board Chairman, civic leader, dedicated scouter

James R. Neidhoefer, Menomonee Falls, Wisc., Company president, distinguished scouter, veteran scoutmaster

Melvin B. Neisner, Rochester, N.Y., Company president, community leader, devoted scouter

William H. Quasha, Manila, Philippines, Attorney, international scouter and scoutmaster

John K. Sloan, Los Angeles, Calif., Attorney, advocate of youth loyal scouter

Herman Stern, Valley City, N.D., Merchant, humanitarian, veteran scouter

Leif J. Sverdrup, St. Louis, Mo., Industrialist and engineer, zealous scouter

Wallace E. Wilson, Detroit, Mich., Corporate vice-president, friend of youth, dedicated scouter

1975 **Gerald R. Ford,** Washington, D.C., President, United States of America; symbol of integrity, example for youth

1976 **John T. Acree, Jr.,** Louisville, Ky., Company board chairman, civic leader, dedicated scouter

Perry R. Bass, Fort Worth, Tex., Corporate chairman and president, community benefactor, distinguished scouter

Milton Caniff, Palm Springs, Calif., Cartoonist, humanitarian, friend of scouting

Arthur H. Cromb, Mission Hills, Kans., Company president, inspirational scouter, university alumni leader

Thomas F. Hawkins, River Forest, Ill., University vice-president, scouter extraordinary

Elizabeth G. Knight, Waite Hill, Ohio, Philanthropist, benefactor of scouting

Joseph W. Marshall, Twin Falls, Ida., Retired physician and surgeon, churchman, faithful scouter

Louis W. Menk, South St. Paul, Minn., Company board chairman, transportation industry leader, loyal scouter

Max S. Norris, Indianapolis, Ind., Physician, businessman, devoted scouter

LaVern Watts Parmley, Salt Lake City, Ut., Churchwoman, benefactor of children, Cub Scouting advocate

Simon Rositzky, St. Joseph, Mo., Company president, conservationist, American Humanics chairman

Lester R. Steig, San Francisco, Calif., Educator, author, proponent of scouting

The Distinguished Eagle Scout Award was established in 1969 to honor men who were Eagle Scouts at least 25 years before and who subsequently distinguished themselves in business, one of the professions or in service to their country. The National Court of Honor selects the recipients of this award from nominees made by the Committee of Distinguished Eagle Scouts. The following is an alphabetical listing of the recipients of this honor and the years in which they originally earned their Eagles; the years in which they were made Distinguished Eagle Scouts are not available.

Paul Haynes Abel, 1929
Frederick W. Ackroyd, 1944
Clyde Spears Alexander, 1933
E. Ross Allen, 1927
Thomas L. Allen, 1940
Paul Richard Allyn, Jr., 1928
Maj. Gen. E.H. Almquist, USA, 1933

Bryon Lesley Anderson, 1942
George W. Anderson, 1938
Carlos D. Arguelles, 1932
Neil Alden Armstrong, 1947
Louis C. Bailey, 1937
Alden G. Barber, 1933
Walter Carlyle Barnes, Jr., 1939
J.V. Bauknight, 1930
Louis H. Beechnau, 1942
John M. Belk, 1947
William H. Bell, 1926
Charles E. Bennett, 1925
Maj. Gen. John Charles Bennett, USA, 1938
Lloyd M. Bentsen, Jr., 1938
Louis P. Bergna, 1938
Maj. Gen. Sidney B. Berry, 1940
Morris R. Beschloss, 1948
Frank Blair, 1930
John A. Blatnik, 1926
Gen. Charles H. Bonesteel III, USA, 1925
Marvin Borman, 1937
Max Leo Bramer, 1927
Jack H. Braucht, 1936
James H. Brian, Sr., 1932
John C. Brizendine, 1940
Howell Harris Brooks, 1922
Newton Duncan Brookshire, Jr., 1937
Clarence J. Brown, 1943
Gen. George Scratchley Brown, USAF 1935
J. Royston Brown, 1942
Allen E. Brubaker, 1928
William K. Brumbach, 1929
Joseph A. Brunton, Jr., 1918
Rear Adm. Ross P. Bullard, 1930
M. Caldwell Butler, 1941
John Tyler Caldwell, 1926
William D. Campbell, 1922
Lester F. Canham, Jr., 1946
Milton Caniff, 1923
George Howard Capps, 1930
Gerald P. Carr, 1947
Jack Caskey, 1945
Henry Carroll Chambers, 1943
Hugh McMaster Chapman, 1946
Laurence Dreher Chapman, 1942
Walter E. Chapman, 1943
Paul R. Christen, 1943
Donald N. Clark, 1923
Harold R. Clark, 1939
Thomas Campbell Clark, 1914
Charles T. Clayton, 1924
Hugh C. Clayton, 1937
William P. Clements, Jr., 1930
Conrad P. Cleveland, Jr., 1937
Stephen H. Clink, 1928
Murray L. Cole, 1937
James D. Collins, Jr., 1933
Ralph J. Comstock, Jr., 1933
Lyman C. Conger, 1930
Lt. Gen. Albert O. Connor, 1928
David C. Cook III, 1928
William B. Crawford, 1940
Lon Worth Crow, Jr., 1926
William R. Cumerford, 1933
William J. Cure, 1935
Chester H. Curtis, 1926
Thomas B. Curtis, 1925
Loren S. Dahl, 1937
Richard W. Darrow, 1933
Joseph W. Davis, 1938

Philip Sheridan Davy, 1932
Antonio C. Delgado, 1933
Russell DeYoung, 1927
John E. Dolibois, 1934
Rulon W. Doman, 1923
Maj. Gen. Edwin I. Donley, 1932
Hedley Donovan, 1929
John D. Driggs, 1941
William T. Duboc, 1940
Everett H. Dudley, 1920
Gov. Michael S. Dukakis, 1949
Charles M. Duke, 1946
William W. Duke, 1949
William E. Dukes, Jr., 1946
Oscar Carroll Dunn, 1937
Grover B. Eaker, 1947
Ernest C. Ebrite, 1944
Lt. Gen. James V. Edmundson, 1929
Wallace W. Edwards, 1937
James Erwin Egger, 1937
Victor T. Ehre, 1927
Charles R. Ehrhardt, 1938
Arthur R. Eldred, 1912
Eugene E. Ellis, Jr., 1930
Charles Emmett Engel, 1922
Jacob R. Esser, 1935
Col. Bernhard Ettenson, USA, 1931
Daniel J. Evans, 1941
Bernhard I. Everson, 1929
William Harrison Fetridge, 1924
John L. Feudner, Jr., 1932
Edward Ridley Finch, Jr., 1936
Robert H. Finch, 1940
John H. Fischer, 1931
Donald H. Flanders, 1941
Jerome F. Foley, Jr., 1933
Gerald R. Ford, Jr., 1927
C. Richard Ford, Jr., 1938
Neal Randolph Fosseen, Sr., 1923
Dulany Foster, 1931
Edward M. Friend, 1925
Thomas Teasley Galt, 1942
Theodore R. Gamble, 1940
James F. Gary, 1937
Thomas F. Gilbane, 1928
William J. Gilbane, 1928
Hyde Gillette, 1921
Norman B. Gillis, Jr., 1940
Stanley J. Glaser, 1921
M. Thomas Goedeke, 1935
Robert H. Goldman, 1931
W. Richard Goodwin, 1940
Lawrence W. Gougler, 1936
John Underwood Graham, 1933
Milton H. Gray, 1926
Anthony S. Greene, 1941
Richard Putnam Gripe, 1935
Robert Charles Gunness, 1928
Gen. Ralph E. Haines, Jr., USA, 1928
Ezra A. Hale, 1924
Durward Gorham Hall, 1923
Brig. Gen. Ralph J. Hallenbeck, 1934
Robert D. Hammer, 1928
Gaines Wardlaw Hammond, Sr., 1929
Richardson Miles Hanckel, 1942
Raymond T. Hander, 1929
Zenon C.R. Hansen, 1926
Bernold M. Hanson, 1943
John K. Hanson, 1929
Samuel Elvis Hanvey, 1940

John M. Harbert III, 1937
John P. Harbin, 1931
Jack D. Harby, 1930
William Benjamin Harrell, Jr., 1925
Benjamin L. Harris, 1938
George A. Harris, 1924
James T. Harrison, 1929
Walter Kenneth Hartford, 1935
Robert T. Hartmann, 1933
Allan E. Hassinger, 1936
Thomas F. Hawkins, 1932
Jack A. Hayes, 1938
David Warrington Hedrick, 1932
Paul M. Herring, 1934
Robert R. Herring, 1941
Paul B. Heuston, 1936
Robert G. Hibbard, 1926
Lynn P. Himmelman, 1928
Lawrence L. Hirsch, 1941
Philip Bernhard Hofmann, 1925
Alex A. Hogan, 1930
Billie Holder, 1932
Gen. Joseph R. Holzapple, USAF, 1929
August F. Hook, 1922
Harold Swanson Hook, 1945
Ernest B. Hueter, 1936
James R. Hughes, Jr., 1921
A.D. Hulings, 1929
Robert N. Hunter, 1936
Don Hutson, 1927
Harry T. Ice, 1921
William L. Jeffords, 1944
Reuben R. Jenson, 1936
Bryan Johnson, 1929
George Dean Johnson, 1924
Ted Lincoln Johnson, 1941
William Kenneth Johnson, 1941
Edward Carey Joullian III, 1944
John J. Kamerick, 1935
O. Frank Kattwinkel, 1940
Ewing M. Kauffman, 1931
Brig. Gen. Paul A. Kauttu, USAF, 1947
Lewis Kayton, 1917
William P. Kemp, Jr., 1937
Ernest C. Keppler, 1935
Richard W. Kiefer, 1930
Norman Victor Kinsey, 1934
Robert E. Kirby, 1933
Rufus W. Kiser, 1928
Philip Monroe Klauber, 1930
Louis A. Klewer, 1917
John A. Kley, 1936
Joseph William Koch, 1924
Edward J. Kuntz, 1936
Louis Charles LaCour, Sr., 1943
John W. Lander, Jr., 1943
Carl T. Langford, 1934
John S. Langford, Jr., 1947
Louis A. Langie, Jr., 1945
Walter Philip Leber, 1932
Stanley Levingston, 1940
Lee M. Liberman, 1938
Walter Rearick Lohman, 1931
Thomas D. Long, 1941
Cook O.P. Lougheed, 1938
James A. Lovell, 1943
Richard G. Lugar, 1946
Paul H. Lyle, 1926
William C. MacDonald, Jr., 1921
Bruce G. MacMillan, 1936

Leander A. Malone, 1932
Robert A. Manchester II, 1920
Darrell F. Manley, 1940
William Donald Manly, 1939
H. Edward Manville, Jr., 1919
Robert S. Mars, Jr., 1940
John Otho Marsh, Jr., 1941
Allen W. Mathis, Jr., 1939
Joseph L. Matthews, 1931
Russell G. Mawby, 1944
William J. Maxion, 1934
C. Robert McBrier, 1931
Joseph J. McClelland, 1931
James A. McClure, 1933
James J. McClure, Jr., 1934
William Frazer McColl, Jr., 1944
James R. McConnell, 1934
Harold James McCurry, Jr., 1935
Robert Owen McCurry, 1935
Gen. John A. McDavid, USA, 1930
James Henry McGregor, 1939
Rear Adm. Robert W. McNitt, USN, 1931
Ferdinand Mendenhall, 1924
Ronald Clifford Metevier, 1941
Martin Michael, 1943
Donald P. Miller, 1922
George Fuller Miller, 1921
Morris F. Miller, 1934
Wallace T. Miller, 1937
James Selden Miner, 1928
Frank Warren Mogensen, 1940
O. William Moody, 1931
Lt. Gen. Joseph H. Moore, USAF, 1929
James A. Moreau, 1929
Graham J. Morgan, 1933
Howard J. Morgens, 1924
Charles Shoemaker Morris, Jr., 1933
Josh R. Morriss, Jr., 1939
Jerome Moskow, 1938
Franklin David Murphy, 1931
William Paul Murray, Jr., 1934
James R. Neidhoefer, 1941
Oswald George Nelson, 1920
Maj. Gen. Franklin A. Nichols, USAF, 1933
Max S. Norris, 1941
Edgar A. Oglesby, 1936
H. Ted Olson, 1949
John Roberts Opel, 1940
Jack W. Osborn, 1931
Nathaniel A. Owings, 1922
George M. Pardee, Jr., 1932
John C. Parish, 1926
James E. Patrick, 1923
Robert W. Paul, 1934
William G. Payne, 1931
H. Ross Perot, 1943
Edward Patterson Perrin, 1942
G. Freeland Phillips, 1950
John Temple Phillips, Jr., 1932
Samuel R. Pierce, Jr., 1936
Lt. Gen. Bryce Poe II, USAF, 1940
William Poole, 1923
Boone Powell, 1928
C. Dudley Pratt, 1942
G. Merritt Preston, 1931
Kenneth G. Pringle, 1930
William Howard Quasha, 1931
Paul W. Radichel, 1935
Vittz-James Ramsdell, 1936
Julian R. Rashkind, 1935

L. Edmund Rast, 1931
Fred A. Ratcliffe, 1921
Rulon W. Rawson, 1923
R.P. Reinemer, Jr., 1934
Paul Hansen Reistrup, 1948
Robert Field Ritchie, 1931
C.M.A. Rogers III, 1947
Philip S. Rogers, 1923
Gen. William Rosson, USA, 1933
Gabriel Rouquie, 1930
Herbert J. Rowe, 1944
Donald H. Rumsfeld, 1949
Ray L. Russell, 1946
Paul Salerno, 1930
Harrison Salisbury, 1924
James Terry Sanford, 1932
Thomas D. Sayles, Jr., 1948
Philip H. Schaff, Jr., 1934
John D. Schapiro, 1931
Ralph G. Schimmele, 1940
David G. Schmidt, 1924
Ernest F. Schmidt, 1926
Don B. Scott, 1942
Donald R. Seawell, 1929
Raymond P. Shafer, 1931
Robert H. Shaffer, 1930
Edgar Finley Shannon, Jr., 1932
Louis W. Shelburne, 1928
James Gilbert Shirley, 1932
Thomas M. Shive, 1938
Edward H. Sibley, 1928
Max I. Silber, 1936
Fred W. Sington, 1924
John K. Sloan, 1938
J. Harold Smith, 1927
Lloyd E. Smith, 1925
Marvin Hugh Smith, 1934
Robert L. Smith, 1931
Maj. Gen. Lawrence W. Snowden, 1937
William Layton Spruell, 1943
Frank Stanton, 1926
Jack J. Stark, 1929
Tom Steed, 1921
Richard C. Steele, 1930
Lester R. Steig, 1930
Lloyd M. Steward, 1924
Richard Stoner, 1935
Walter Franklin Story, Jr., 1935
Edmund D. Strang, 1932
Percy E. Sutton, 1936
Maj. Gen. Orwin Clark Talbott, USA, 1936
Thomas L. Tatham, 1927
George Brown Taylor, 1941
Harry D. Thorsen, Jr., 1929
Maj. Gen. William Gay Thrash, USMC, 1931
Bertram William Tremayne, Jr., 1934
Frederick C. Tucker, Jr., 1935
James McClure Turner, 1927
William Keener Ulerich, 1924
Victor Vincent Veysey, 1929
Rev. Frans A. Victorson, 1935
Benjamin Stuart Vincent, 1945
Jack C. Vowell, Jr., 1942
Laurence C. Walker 1938
W.E. Walker, Jr., 1943
J. Richard Walton, 1945
Carl Erwin Wasmuth, 1938
Elmer H. Wavering, 1922
Grady Webb, Jr., 1930
Adm. Maurice Franklin Weisner, USN, 1933

Louie Welch, 1933
Harold L. Wenaas, 1946
Fred W. Wenzel, 1930
Gen. William Childs Westmoreland, USA, 1930
Walter R. Whidden, 1922
Stephen White, 1925
Harold E. Wibberley, Jr., 1936
Harry G. Wiles, 1932
Joseph W. Wilkus, 1940
Charles S. Williams, Jr., 1937
Joseph W. Williams, Jr., 1930
Lyman Perry Williams, 1924
James McCrorry Willson, Jr., 1938
Delmer H. Wilson, 1927
Douglas E. Wilson, 1932
James Robert Gavin Wilson, 1930
R. Baxter Wilson, 1920
Richard Samuel Wilson, 1934
Wallace E. Wilson, 1925
John William Witt, 1949
Halbert O. Woodward, 1932
Earle W. Wright, 1915
Lt. Gen. John M. Wright, Jr., USA, 1929
Walter B. Wriston, 1934
Robert H. Young, Jr., 1937
Adm. Elmo Russell Zumwalt, Jr., USN, 1937

James J. and Jane Hoey Award for Interracial Justice
John Lafarge Memorial Award for Interracial Justice

CATHOLIC INTERRACIAL COUNCIL OF NEW YORK
55 Liberty St., New York, N.Y. 10004 (Last known address)

The James J. and Jane Hoey Award for Interracial Justice, which consists of a silver medal, is given annually to honor a black and a white Catholic for the promotion of interracial justice

1942 Frank A. Hall
     Edward La Salle
1943 Philip Murray
     Ralph H. Metcalfe
1944 Mrs. Edward V. Morrell
     John L. Yancey
1945 Paul D. Williams
     Richard Barthe
1946 Richard Reid
     Charles L. Rawlings
1947 Julian J. Reiss
     Clarence T. Hunter
1948 Anna McGarry
     Ferdinand L. Rousseve
1949 John O'Connor
     M.C. Clarke
1950 J. Howard McGrath
     Lou Montgomery
1951 Mrs. Roger L. Putnam
     Francis M. Hammond
1952 Charles F. Vatterot, Jr.
     Joseph H. Yancey
1953 Joseph J. Morrow
     John B. King
1954 Gladys D. Woods
     Collins J. Seitz
1955 Millard F. Everett

James W. Hose
1956 Frank M. Folsom
Paul G. King
1957 George Meany
James W. Dorsey
1958 James T. Harris
Robert Sargent Shriver, Jr.
1959 Percy H. Steele, Jr.
John P. Nelson
1960 William Duffy, Jr.
George A. Moore
1961 Ralph Fenton
Osma Spurlock
1962 Benjamin Muse
Eugene T. Reed
1963 James T. Carey
Percy H. Williams
1964 Arthur J. Holland
Frederick O'Neal
1965 Gerard E. Sherry
James R. Dumpson
1966 Jane M. Hoey
Mrs. Roy Wilkins
1967 Frank Horne
Lt. Gov. Malcolm Wilson
1968 E.H. Molisani
John Strachan
1969 Harold E. McGannon
Hulan E. Jack
1970 George P. McManus
Alfred Del Bello
Maceo A. Thomas
Cleo Joseph L. Froix
1971 Rev. Francis J. Mugavero
Rev. Harold R. Perry
1972 Joseph F. Crangle
Alen E. Pinado
1973 Meade H. Esposito
Robert B. Boyd
1974 Harold A. Stevens
Thomas Van Arsdale
1975 N.A.
1976 N.A.
1977 N.A.

The John LaFarge Memorial Award for Interracial Justice, which consists of a scroll, annually honors outstanding contributions to justice for all races.

1965 Francis Cardinal Spellman
1966 Sen. Jacob K. Javits
1967 Gov. Nelson A. Rockefeller
1968 George F. Meany
1969 Whitney M. Young, Jr.
1970 Harry Van Arsdale, Jr.
1971 John V. Lindsay
1972 Earl W. Brydges
1973 Louis K. Lefkowitz
1974 Arthur Levitt
1975 Robert J. Wagner
1976 N.A.
1977 N.A.

Humanitarian Awards

UNITED CEREBRAL PALSY OF NEW YORK, INC.
122 E. 23rd St., New York, N.Y. 10010 (212/677-7400)

The United Cerebral Palsy Humanitarian Awards are now given annually for service to victims of the disease. An awards committee selects the winner, who receives a Tiffany crystal and silver obelisk. The award has been annual since 1971. Prior to that, it had been given irregularly and exact dates of the honors ceremony are not available.

EARLIER RECIPIENTS:

Thomas E. Dewey
Peter Grimm
Stanley C. Hope
Joseph A. Martino
Roger S. Firestone
Jinx Falkenberg McCrary
William Clay Ford
Jane Pickens Langley
Gen. Dwight D. Eisenhower
1971 Gov. and Mrs. Nelson A. Rockefeller, New York
1972 William S. Renchard, Chairman of the Board, Chemical Bank
Richard E. Berlin, President, Hearst Corp.
1973 T. Vincent Learson, Chairman of the Board, IBM Corp.
John F. McGillicuddy, President, Manufacturers Hanover Trust Co.
1974 Donald C. Platten, Chairman of the Board, Chemical Bank
Edward R. Rowley, Chairman of the Board, NL Industries, Inc.
1975 Bob Hope, Honorary National UCP Chairman
Emil J. Pattberg, Jr., Chairman of the Board, First Boston Corp.
1976 Mrs. Albert D. Lasker, President, UCP Research & Educational Foundation
Willard C. Butcher, President, Chase Manhattan Bank N. A.
1977 Gov. Hugh L. Carey, New York

CBC Medal

CITIZENS BUDGET COMMISSION
110 E. 42nd St, New York, N.Y. 10017 (212/687-0711)

The CBC Medal, which is of bronze, annually honors distinguished civic service to New York City. An awards committee selects the recipient.

1953 Joseph M. Proskauer
1954 Devereux C. Josephs
1955 Stanley M. Isaacs
1956 David Rockefeller
Bernard F. Gimbel
1957 Herbert H. Lehman
1958 Harrison Tweed
1959 James Felt
1960 Samuel D. Leidesdorf
1961 John D. Rockefeller, 3rd
James Felt
1962 David M. Heyman
Emma Alden Rothblatt
1963 Austin J. Tobin
Mrs. Charles S. Payson
1964 Percy Uris
1965 Othmar Hermann Ammann
1966 Earl B. Schwulst
1967 Thomas P. F. Hoving
1968 McGeorge Bundy
1969 Robert W. Dowling
1970 Walter Cronkite

1971 Jacob K. Javits
1972 Arthur Levitt
1973 William J. Ronan
      George Champion
1974 Abraham Beame
1975 J. Peter Grace
1976 Richard R. Shinn
1977 Gov. Hugh Carey

Secretary of Defense Award for Outstanding Public Service

DEPARTMENT OF DEFENSE
Washington, D.C. 20301 (202/697-3305)

The Secretary of Defense Award for Outstanding Public Service is given for civilian contributions to the nation's defense. Traditionally, the honor is presented most frequently by an outgoing Secretary of Defense to his people. While the award has been in existence for a number of years, only the 1977 winners are listed here.

1977

Ann P. Ulrey	J. Kevin Murphy
Rodney C. Loehr	Henry E. Glass
Robert C. Lewis	John Dunworth
Thurston Hassell	Richard C. Steadman
Lotte Duker	Robert N. Smith
John P. Stenbit	William W. Wisman
Solomon J. Buchsbaum	David O. Cooke
J. Robinson West	James S. Brady
Kenneth L. Adelman	Tod R. Hullin
Maynard W. Glitman	John T. Hughes
Morton S. Abramowitz	Ferderick P. Hitz
Harry E. Bergold, Jr.	Laurence J. Legere
Will Hill Tankersley	Harold Meyer
Julian R. Levine	James A. Messer
Daniel L. Mausser	James E. Frank (USAR-Ret.)
R. W. Henderson	James B. Foley
Edward B. Hudson	
Fount L. Robison	

Distinguished New Yorker Award

CITY CLUB OF NEW YORK
44 E. 43rd St., New York, N.Y. 10017 (212/687-3116)

The Distinguished New Yorker Award, which consists of a bronze medallion and a certificate, is given annually to individuals deemed to "act positively for New York and to have devoted energy, skill and talent to the improvement of the quality of New York life." The club's board of trustees makes the selection.

1967 **George Baehr,** President, Academy of Medicine
      Roger Baldwin, Founder, American Civil Liberties Union
      Detlev W. Bronk, Chairman, National Research Council; President, Johns Hopkins University; President, The Rockefeller University
      Gordon Bunshaft, Partner, Skidmore, Owings & Merrill
      Cass Canfield, Senior Editor, Harper and Brothers; leader, Planned Parenthood
      Richard S. Childs, Past President, City Club; former Chairman, Citizens Union; Chairman, Municipal League; member, New York State Board of Regents

      Kenneth B. Clark, President, Marc Corp.; Distinguished Professor of Psychology, City University of New York; member, New York State Board of Regents
      Lou Crandall, Chairman of the Board, George A. Fuller Co.
      Duke Ellington, Musician, whose 1927 Cotton Club orchestra gained acceptance for jazz as a musical form
      Martha Graham, Creator of new dance form
      Alvin Johnson, Founder, New School, University in Exile
      Robert Moses, "Prime achiever among a forest of non-achievers"
      David Sarnoff, For a career spanning the entire history of electronics and electronic communication
      Earl B. Schwulst, Chairman, Bowery Savings Bank; Temporary Commission on City Finances
      Whitney North Seymour, Partner, Simpson, Thacher & Bartlett; U.S. Attorney, Southern District, New York State
      Arthur Hays Sulzberger, Publisher, *New York Times*
      Austin J. Tobin, Former Chairman, Port Authority

1968 No award
1969 **Jacob S. Potofsky,** President, Amalgamated Clothing Workers of America
1970 **Mary Lasker,** Contributor to health and medicine fields; the Lasker Awards; beautification of New York City
1971 No award
1972 **Andrew Heiskell,** Former Chairman of the Board, Time Inc.
1973 **George Champion,** Former Chairman of the Board, Chase Manhattan Bank; Chairman and President, Economic Development Council of New York
      John Chancellor, Former Director, Voice of America; anchorman and principal reporter, NBC nightly news
      Walter Cronkite, Veteran journalist; space expert; anchorman and principal reporter, CBS Evening News
      George T. Delacorte, Jr., Founder, Make New York Beautiful; publisher
      Paul Foley, President, Inter-Public Group of Companies
      Lloyd Goodrich, Author of distinguished works on American Art; former Director, Whitney Museum
      Ada Louise Huxtable, Architecture critic, *New York Times*
      Winfield H. James, President, publisher, *New York News*
      Whitman Knapp, U.S. Judge, Southern District, New York State; Chairman Knapp Commission
      Willie E. Mays, Baseball star
      John P. McGrath, Chairman of the Board, East New York Savings Bank; lawyer; former Corporation Counsel of the City of New York
      Arthur Mitchell, Former premier danseur, New York City Ballet; Director, Dance Theatre of Harlem
      Bess Myerson, Former Commissioner, Department of Consumer Affairs; distinguished reporter, commentator
      John B. Oakes, Editor of Editorial Page, *New York Times*; supervisor, "Op-Ed"; author, numerous articles on public affairs and conservation
      Joseph Papp, Founder and producer, New York Shakespeare Festival; Public Theatre
      Basil A. Paterson, Lawyer; member, board of editors, *New York Law Journal*; President, Institute for Mediation and Conflict Resolution
      I.M. Pei, Architect, academician
      Lewis Rudin, Executive Vice President, Rudin Management Co.; Chairman, Assn. for a Better New York

Dorothy Schiff, Editor-in-Chief, publisher, *New York Post,* oldest daily newspaper in continuous publication in the U.S.

Neil Simon, Playwright

Franklin A. Thomas, President, Bedford-Stuyvesant Restoration Corp.; former Deputy Police Commissioner

Preston R. Tisch, President, New York City Convention and Visitors Bureau; Chairman of the Board, Convention-Exhibition Center Corp.; builder

Lila Acheson Wallace, Co-chairman, *Reader's Digest*

1974 **George Agrell,** President, Addo Machine Co.; Trustee, Scandinavian-American Foundation

Cecelia Benattar, President, British Commercial Group; originator of financial arrangements for and supervision of construction of General Motors complex

Giovanni Buitoni, Founder, Buitoni Foods Corp.

Antonio Carillo-Flores, Director General, Committee on Population of the United Nations

Ramon Castroviejo, Innovator and leader, corneal surgery

Maurice Galy, President, Lycee Francais de New York

Rod Gilbert, New York Rangers

Soichi Kawazoe, Executive Vice President, Nissan Motor Corp. U.S.A., sponsor of "Plant a Tree" and "Send a Kid to Camp" test drives

Oivind Lorentzen, Jr., President, Flagship Cruises

Raymond J. Picard, Chairman, Rhodia, Inc.

Erwin A. Single, Publisher, *New York Staats-Zeitung und Herold*

Yoshio Teresawa, President, Nomura Securities International, Inc.

Leo Van Munching, President, Van Munching & Co.

1975 **Charles G. Bluhdorn,** Chairman of the Board, Gulf & Western Industries, Inc.

1976 No award

1977 **Donald T. Regan,** Chairman of the Board, Merrill, Lynch & Co.

Hall of Honor
Silver Medal of Valor
Distinguished Service Award

CIVIL AIR PATROL
Maxwell Air Froce Base, Ala. 36112 (205/293-1190)

Of the many honors conferred by the Civil Air Patrol, an auxiliary of the U.S. Air Force, induction into the Hall of Honor is the highest overall honor.

1972 Gill Robb Wilson
 Gen. Carl A. Spaatz, USAF (Ret)
 Brig. Gen. D. Harold Byrd, CAP
 Brig. Gen. William C. Whelen, CAP
 Brig. Gen. Paul W. Turner, CAP
 Brig. Gen. Lyle W. Castle, CAP
 Brig. Gen. F. Ward Reilly, CAP
 Col. Clara E. Livingston, CAP
 Col. Joseph S. Bergin, CAP
 Col. Allan C. Perkinson, CAP
1973 Maj. Gen. Lucas V. Beau, USAF (Ret)
 Col. Edwin Lyons, CAP
1974 Col. James E. Carter, CAP
 Brig. Gen. S. H. duPont, Jr., CAP
 Brig. Gen. Earl L. Johnson
1975 No inductees
1976 Col. Zack T. Mosley, CAP
 Brig. Gen. William M. Patterson, CAP

1977 No inductees

The Silver Medal of Valor is the highest award for bravery. It is given as merited.

1962 Cdt. Ronald Baecher
1965 Lt. Leonard A. Gilliland
1968 Capt. Paul B. Crawford
 Cdt. David R. Jaffe
 Lt. Col. Robert C. Owen
1969 Lt. Eugene E. Dombrowski
 Maj. John L. Elliott
 Cdt. Scott Lyons
 Capt. Herbert F. Santos
1970 Maj. Adelbert C. Cross
 Cdt. David L. White
1971 No award
1972 Lt. Harold P. Parsons
1973 Lt. Raymond E. Bruen
1974 Capt. Bernard Berger
1975 Cdt. Charles T. Hughes
 Cdt. Thomas R. Peoples
1976 Maj. Charles M. Brown
 Capt. James V. Hotsinger
 Lt. Michael J. Martin
 Cdt. Robert J. Scott
1977 Lt. Col. Frank L. Hendrix
 Lt. Col. James T. Higgins
 Sm. Dorothy A. Kelly
 Lt. James R. Pallariot
 Maj. Paul E. Routhier

The Distinguished Service Award is the Civil Air Patrol's highest award for service.

1960

Lt. Col. Virginia C. Capps	Col. James E. Carter
Capt. C.M. Kelley, Jr.	Lt. Col. Leon N. Leboire
Lt. Col. Benjamin F. Miller	Maj. William C. Ooley
Col. Vee L. Phillips	

1961

Col. Marcus R. Barnes	Col. James L. Camp
Col. J Reed Capps	Col. Charles R. Chick
Col. Charles F. Howard	Maj. Margaret L. Howard
Col. James H. Laidlaw	Lt. Col. Edwin T. Lovelace
Col. James J. Mitchell	Lt. Col. Alfred C. Nowitsky
Col. James J. O'Connor	Lt. Col. Richard L. Oliver
Maj. Agnes M. Richards	Col. Raymond A. Smith
Sm. Thomas M. Smith	Col. Herbert H. Stahnke
Lt. Col. Louise M. Thaden	

1962

Lt. Col. Sarah E. Adams	Maj. Elwood R. Angstadt
Col. Marcus R. Barnes	Col. Joseph S. Bergin
Lt. Col. Luther C. Bogard	Col. Paul E. Burbank
Lt. Col. Vir N. James	Col. James H. Laidlaw
Col. James J. O'Connor	Lt. Col. Joseph M. O'Malley
Col. George J. Race	Lt. Col. Lawrence Reibscheid
Col. Herbert H. Stahnke	Col. John D. Swarts

1963

Maj. Ted Bagan	Col. Harlon W. Bement
Col. Homer L. Bigelow, Jr.	Col. Paul E. Burbank
Col. James E. Carter	Col. Robert H. Herweh
Capt. Donald T. Mageen	Col. Maurice A. Marrs

Lt. Col. Charles W. Matthis, Jr.
Col. Malcolm McDermid
Lt. Col. Doris M. Olson
Col. Richard W. Reynard
Col. James A. Wellons

Col. Murray C. McComas
Col. Joseph F. Moody
Col. Joseph J. Princen
Col. Paul W. Turner

1964

Col. Paul C. Ashworth
Col. Lyle W. Castle
Col. John E. Page
Col. Ward F. Reilly
Col. John R. Taylor

Col. Francis A. Blevins
Col. James E. O'Connell
Col. William M. Patterson
Col. Ralph M. Shangraw
Lt. Col. John N. Weaver

1965

Lt. Col. Sarah E. Adams
Capt. Robert L. Camina
Col. S.H. duPont, Jr.
Lt. Col. Vir N. James
Col. Stanhope Lineberry
Lt. Col. Joseph M. O'Malley
Lt. Col. Lawrence Reibscheid
Col. Herbert H. Stahnke
Maj. Theodore H. Walter

Col. Joseph S. Bergin
Lt. Col. James E. Carlton
Lt. Col. Francis G. Gomes
Lt. Col. Kenneth E. Jones
Capt. Andrew E. Mild
Lt. Col. Frank S. Patterson
Lt. Col. Amel Shultz
Lt. Col. Kenna T. Trout

1966

Col. Charles R. Chick

Lt. Col. Sarah E. Duke
Col. Daniel E. Evans
Lt. Col. Robert W. Hemphill
Col. Frank D. Landes
Col. Edwin Lyons
Capt. John L. O'Connor
Lt. Col. Albert Plotkin

Col. Robert M. Shaw
Maj. Theodore W. Walter
Maj. Louis D. Wolff

Lt. Col. Louis Dellamonica
Col. S.H. duPont, Jr.
Col. George S. Hastings
Lt. Col. Gilbert O. Keeton
Col. Clara E. Livingston
Col. Louisa S. Morse
Col. Neil Pansey
Col. Ward F. Reilly (two DSAs in one year)
Col. John R. Taylor
Maj. James R. Williams

1967

Lt. Col. Warren D. Anderson

Col. Donald H. Denton
Col. Roger A. Guilmett
Lt. Col. Reuben M. Katz

Lt. Col. Rupert M. Much

Lt. Col. Howard N. Pratt
Sm. Carl E. Sanders
Col. Wayne E. Smith
Col. Peter J. Stavneak

Lt. Col. Edward C. Beauvais
Lt. Col. Robert L. Forche
Maj. J. David Jones
Capt. Maurice G. Lambert
Lt. Col. Joseph M. O'Malley
Cdt. Alex H. Rocha
Lt. Col. A.H. Saunders
Lt. Col. John P. St. Clair
Col. Jess Strauss

1968

Col. J.F.H. Bottom

Col. Julius Goldman
Lt. Col. Mildred C. Hicks
Lt. Col. Ira L. Kessler

Maj. D. Jean Maire
Col. Richard T. Murphy
Col. James E. O'Connell
Col. Walter M. Sanford

Lt. Col. Lewis H. Freeman
Lt. Col. Douglas E. Hicks
Lt. Col. Jonathan H. Hill
Lt. Col. William D. Madsen
Col. Ben S. McGlashan
Lt. Col. Gerard K. Nash
Lt. Col. Milton N. Popp
Col. Herbert H. Stahnke

1969

Col. Joseph S. Bergin

Lt. Col. William R. Brady

Lt. Col. James H. Cheek, Jr.

Col. Houston H. Doyle
Col. Raymond H. Gaver

Lt. Col. William E.B. Hall

Col. Stanhope Lineberry

Maj. George Loertscher
Lt. Col. Lester G. Maddox
Lt. Col. John J. McNabb

Maj. Robert P. Miller
1st. Lt. Lawrence F. Parker
Col. Arthur F. Putz
Maj. Herbert W. Urry

S/Sgt. Lemmie F. Young

Capt. Bernard P. Dickerson
Lt. Col. Kenneth Dunlap
Lt. Col. George W. Gentner
Lt. Col. Raymond L. Kraemer
Lt. Col. Harland B. Little, Jr.
Col. Edwin Lyons
Capt. O.J. Marlborough
Lt. Col. Benjamin F. Miller
1st Lt. Maurita Nail
Col. William M. Patterson
C.W.O. James D. Rogers
Lt. Col. Ephraim W. Walton

1970

Col. William R. Bass
Col. Howard L. Brookfield
Brig. Gen. Lyle W. Castle
Col. Obed A. Donaldson
1st Lt. James A. Flynt

Col. Donald E. Hale
Lt. Col. Raymond J. Johnson
Col. Edwin Lyons
Col. Richard T. Murphy
Col. F. Ward Reilly
Lt. Col. Wilson W. Ronda
1st. Lt. Walter L. Tribble

Col. Luther C. Bogard
Col. Thomas C. Casaday
Col. Claude L. Chambers
Lt. Col. Sarah E. Duke
Lt. Col. Willard E. Geiger, Jr.
Col. Robert H. Herweh
Col. Kenneth Lebo
Cdt. Julius A. Mink
Col. William M. Patterson
Capt. E.M. Rea
Col. Wayne E. Smith
Brig. Gen. Paul W. Turner

1971

Col. Arlie G. Andrews
Col. Marvin S. Donnaud
Col. David R. Ellsworth
Col. Charles W. Klann
Col. Theodore H. Limmer, Jr.
Col. Walter M. Markey
Lt. Col. Harold M. Mitchell
Col. Alvin S. Rousse
Col. Peter J. Stavneak
Lt. Col. Charles R. Thulin

Col. P.W. Burgmeestre
Col. Richard R. Dooley
Col. Ernest M. Green
Col. Frank D. Landes

Col. Clinton G. Litchfield
Col. Stephen E. Mills
Col. William H. Ramsey
Col. Arthur P. Schneider
Col. John R. Taylor

1972

Col. Luther C. Bogard
Col. James E. Carter
Col. Clarence M. Fountain
Col. Jonathan H. Hill
Col. Richard D. Law
Col. Edwin Lyons
Col. Gerald M. Quilling
Col. Roderick V. Riek
Col. Richard A. Salsman (two DSAs in one year)
Lt. Col. Norman Strauss

Maj. Robert S. Vankeuren

Lt. Col. Noel E. Bullock
Col. Donald D. Dixon
Col. Julius Goldman
Col. Thomas C. Jackson
Col. Clara E. Livingston
Col. William M. Patterson
Col. William H. Ramsey
Maj. Frank H. Rockwell

Col. Jess Strauss
Col. Frank L. Swaim (two DSAs in one year)

1973

Col. Leonard A. Brodsky

Col. Raymond A. Gaver
Capt. James L. Hile

Brig. Gen S.H. duPont, Jr.
Col. Willard D. Gilbert
Lt. Col. Bernice R. Hill

Col. Eugene A. Kerwin
Col. Raymond S. Mabrey
Col. Barry N. Thompson
Lt. Col. Charles L. Wood

Col. Palmer S. Kickland
Col. John M. Piane, Jr.
Col. Earl T. Van Stavern

1974

Maj. Harold W. Bowden
Col. Richard R. Dooley

Col. Jack Ferman
Col. Stanley F. Moyer, Jr.
Col. Edward L. Palka

Col. Carl J. Platter
Maj. John C. Samuel
Maj. Alvin J. Stewart

Col. John A. Vozzo

Col. Thomas C. Casaday
Lt. Col. Edward C.
Feilinger
Col. Zenon C.R. Hansen
Col. Robert C. Owen
Brig. Gen. William M.
Patterson
Col. Joseph F. Roemisch
Col. Lee F. Smith
Brig. Gen. Paul W.
Turner

1975

Lt. Col. Robert E. Benoit
Col. Howard L. Brookfield
Col. William B. Cass
Col. Ivey M. Cook, Jr.
Col. Richard Damerow

Col. Julius Goldman
Col. Jonathan H. Hill
Col. Clark Johnston
Col. David P. Mohr
Col. William H. Ramsey
(two DSAs in one year)
Col. John R. Taylor

Col. Luther C. Bogard
Col. James V. Brown, Jr.
Brig. Gen. Lyle W. Castle
Col. James E. Connor, Jr.
Brig. Gen. S.H. duPont,
Jr.
Maj. Albert E. Henfy
Col. Bob E. James
Col. Roy G. Loughary
Col. E. Lee Morgan

Col. Frank L. Swaim

1976

Col. Marcus R. Barnes
Lt. Col. Robert C. Bess
Col. Johnnie Boyd
Col. Richard T. Davis
Col. Obed A. Donaldson
Lt. Col. Lucille V. Evans
Lt. Col. David Floyd

Dr. James P. Gilligan
Col. Mary C. Harris
Col. Jonathan H. Hill
Col. Eugene G. Isaak
Col. Oscar J. Jolley
Col. Albert D. Lamb
Col. Larry D. Miller
Maj. Barbara Morris
Col. Thomas G. Patton
Col. Lindsey V. Rice
Col. Kermit K. Schaver
Col. Charles X. Suraci

Col. Gordon T. Weir
Col. William T. Winkert

Col. Frederick S. Bell
Maj. Joan C. Birns
Col. Thomas C. Casaday
Lt. Col. Iris T. Donaldson
Col. A. Sidney Evans
Col. Thomas S. Evans
Col. Clarence M. Fountain
Col. Robert E. Gobel
Col. Robert H. Herweh
Col. Harry J. Howes
Col. John T. Johnson
Col. Kenneth Kershner
Gen. Carl S. Miller
Col. Louisa S. Morse
Col. Ceclia A. Patterson
Col. John F. Price
Col. Randolph C. Ritter
Maj. Mark Shirk
Col. John A. Vozzo (two
DSAs in one year)
Col. Robert H. Wilson

1977

Col. Edgar M. Bailey

Col. William H. Cahill
Brig. Gen. S.H. duPont, Jr.
Col. Julius Goldman
Lt. Col. Betty W. McNabb
Col. Rolf H. Mitchel
Col. Leroy S. Riley
Col. Joseph B. Witkin

Lt. Col. Lucille E.
Branscomb
Col. Henri P. Casenov
Col. William H. Everett
Col. Oscar K. Jolley
Col. Angelo A. Milano
Col. William H. Ramsey
Col. Lester W. Snyder

President's Award for Distinguished Federal Civilian Service

U.S. CIVIL SERVICE COMMISSION
1900 E St. NW, Washington, D.C. 20415 (202/632-5563)

The President's Award for Distinguished Federal Civilian Service is presented annually for outstanding performance of duties and execution of office by federal career employees. The award is made in White House ceremonies by the President or Vice President, to individuals selected now by the chairman of the Civil Service Commission. Previously, a special board chose the recipients.

1958 **Loy W. Henderson,** Deputy Under Secretary of State for Administration

Sterling B. Hendricks, Chief Chemist, Department of Agriculture Pioneering Research Laboratory for Mineral Nutrition of Plants

John Edgar Hoover, Director, Federal Bureau of Investigation

Roger W. Jones, Assistant Director for Legislative Reference, Bureau of the Budget

William B. McLean, Technical Director, U.S. Naval Ordnance Test Station (China Lake, Calif.)

1959 **James Bennett,** Director, Bureau of Prisons, Department of Justice

Doyle L. Northrup, Technical Director, Special Weapons Squadron, Department of the Air Force

Hazel K. Stiebeling, Director, Institute of Home Economics, Department of Agriculture

Wernher Von Braun, Director, Development Operations Division, Army Ballistic Missile Agency

1960 **Andrew Barr,** Chief Accountant, Securities and Exchange Commission

Hugh L. Dryden, Deputy Administrator, National Aeronautics and Space Administration

William J. Hopkins, Executive Clerk, White House Office

Winfred Overholser, Superintendent, Saint Elizabeth's Hospital

Robert M. Page, Director of Research, Naval Research Laboratory

1961 **Bert B. Barnes,** Assistant Postmaster General, Bureau of Operations, Post Office Department

Wilbur S. Hinman, Jr., Technical Director, Diamond Ordnance Fuze Laboratories, Department of the Army

Frederick J. Lawton, Commissioner, U.S. Civil Service Commission

Richard E. McArdle, Chief, Forest Service, Department of Agriculture

William McCauley, Director, Bureau of Employee's Compensation, Department of Labor

1962 **J. Stanley Baughman,** President, Federal National Mortgage Association, Housing and Home Finance Agency

Robert R. Gilruth, Director, Manned Spacecraft Center, National Aeronautics and Space Administration (Houston, Tex.)

Donald E. Gregg, Chief, Department of Cardiorespiratory Diseases, Walter Reed Army Institute of Research

Waldo K. Lyon, head, Submarine and Arctic Research Branch, U.S. Navy Electronics Laboratory (San Diego, Calif.)

Llewellyn E. Thompson, Jr., Ambassador to the Union of Soviet Socialist Republics, Department of State

1963 Winthrop G. Brown, career minister, Department of State

Alain C. Enthoven, Deputy Comptroller for Systems Analysis, Office of the Secretary of Defense

Sherman E. Johnson, Deputy Administrator, Foreign Economics, Economic Research Service Department of Agriculture

David D. Thomas, Director, Air Traffic Service, Federal Aviation Agency

Fred L. Whipple, director, Smithsonian Institution Astrophysical Observatory

1964 John Doar, First Assistant to the Assistant Attorney General, Civil Rights Division, Department of Justice

Herbert Friedman, Superintendent, Atmosphere and Astrophysics Division, U.S. Naval Research Laboratory, Department of the Navy

Lyman B. Kirkpatrick, Jr., Executive Director-Comptroller, Central Intelligence Agency

Bromley K. Smith, Executive Secretary, National Security Council

1965 Howard C. Grieves, Assistant Director of the Bureau of the Census, Department of Commerce

Homer E. Newell, Associate Administrator for Space Science and Applications, National Aeronautics and Space Administration

Frank B. Rowlett, Special Assistant to the Director, National Security Agency, Department of Defense

Clyde A. Tolson, Associate Director of Federal Bureau of Investigation, Department of Justice

Philip H. Trezise, Deputy Assistant Secretary for Economic Affairs, Department of State

1966 Elson B. Helwig, Pathologist, Armed Forces Institute of Pathology

Robert E. Hollingsworth

H. Rex Lee, Administrator, American Samoa

Thomas C. Mann

James A. Shannon, scientific administrator

1967 Myrl E. Alexander, director, Federal Bureau of Prisons, Department of Justice

Arthur E. Hess, Deputy Commissioner, Social Security Administration, Department of Health, Education, and Welfare

Sherman Kent, Director, National Estimates and Chairman of the Board, National Estimates, Central Intelligence Agency

C. Payne Lucas, Deputy Director, Africa Region, Peace Corps

William J. Porter, Ambassador to the Republic of South Korea, Department of State

Carl F. Romney, Seismologist, Department of the Air Force

1968 James J. Rowley

1969 No award

1970 No award

1971 Samuel M. Cohn, Assistant Director for Budget Review, Office of Management and Budget

U. Alexis Johnson, career ambassador, Under Secretary for Political Affairs, Department of State

Edward F. Knipling, Director, Entomology Research Division, Agricultural Research Service, Department of Agriculture

Fred Leonard, Scientific Director, Army Medical Biomechanical Research Laboratory, Walter Reed Army Medical Center, Department of the Army

George H. Willis, Deputy to the Assistant Secretary for International affairs, Department of the Treasury

1972-75 No awards

1976 Ernest Ambler, Acting Director, National Bureau of Standards, Department of Commerce

Lawrence S. Eagleburger, Deputy Under Secretary of State for Management and Executive Assistant to the Secretary, Department of State

Alfred J. Eggers, Jr., Assistant Director for Research Applications, National Science Foundation

E. Henry Knoche, Deputy Director of Central Intelligence, Central Intelligence Agency

Dale R. McOmber, Assistant Director for Budget Review, Office of Management and Budget

Barbara Ringer, Register of Copyrights, Library of Congress

1977 Not available at Press Time

Grenville Clark Prize

THE GRENVILLE CLARK FUND AT
DARTMOUTH COLLEGE
2501 Holmes St., Kansas City, Mo. 64108 (816/421-5058)

The Grenville Clark Prize, which carries an honorarium of $15,000, will be given every three years until the end of the 20th Century for a scholarly work or activity which, in the opinion of the Board of Directors of the Fund, exemplifies Grenville Clark's objectives in civil liberties, academic freedom, civic rights, world peace and good government.

1975 Jean Monnet, France

Eugene V. Debs Award

EUGENE V. DEBS FOUNDATION
Box 843, Terre Haute, Ind. 47808 (812/232-2163)

The Eugene V. Debs Award annually honors an individual for contributions in public service, labor or education. The plaque is given to an individual nominated by foundation members and selected by the executive board.

1965 John L. Lewis
1966 Norman Thomas
1967 A. Philip Randolph
1968 Walter Reuther
1969 H.E. Gilbert
1970 Patrick E. Gorman
1971 No award
1972 Dorothy Day
1973 Michael Harrington
1974 Arthur Schlesinger, Jr.
1975 Ruben Levin
1976 Martin Miller
1977 Not available at press time

Splendid American Award

THOMAS A. DOOLEY FOUNDATION
442 Post. St., San Francisco, Calif. 94102 (415/397-0244)

The Splendid American Award, which consists of an engraved Steuben glass dish, is given annually to honor personal accomplishments that have reflected well "the meaning and purpose of the United States to the world community." The board of directors of the foundation selects the American citizen(s) to receive the award.

1964 Henry Cabot Lodge
1965 Bob Hope

Dean Rusk
1966 Danny Kaye
Edwin O. Reischauer
1967 Kirk Douglas
Daniel K. Inouye
1968 Eugene R. Black
John H. Glenn, Jr.
1969 Duke Ellington
Samuel F. Pryor
1970 No award
1971 Perle Mesta
Lowell Thomas
1972 Spiro T. Agnew
Frank Sinatra
1973 No award
1974 No award
1975 No award
1976 No award
1977 No award

Erasmus Prize

ERASMUS PRIZE FOUNDATION (Stichting Praemium Erasmianum)
5, Jan van Goyenkade, Amsterdam, the Netherlands (Tel. 760222)

The Erasmus Prize is given annually to honor individuals or institutions whose work is considered of outstanding merit for the spiritual and cultural values of Europe. The amount of the prize is 10,000 guilders, which is spent partially for cultural, social or socioscientific projects. The winner is selected by the foundation's board of governors in consultation with Dutch and international experts and an international committee.

1958 **People of Austria,** Determination to preserve their European culture and character "under difficult circumstances"
1959 **Karl Jaspers (Germany) and Robert Schuman (France),** Living symbols of the unity of Europe on philosophical and political planes
1960 **Marc Chagall and Oskar Kokoschka,** Contributions to European painting
1961 **No award**
1962 **Romano Guardini,** "For his many-sided contribution to cultivation and intensification of European spiri - tual life"
1963 **Martin Buber,** For serving "the cause of European culture for more than 50 years in many domains"
1964 **Union Academique Internationale,** For initiating and encouraging "many ventures of learning which maintained and enhanced the high standing of the humanities in Europe"
1965 **Charles S. Chaplin and Ingmar Bergman,** Outstanding merits in cinematographic art
1966 **Sir Hubert Read and Rene Huyghe,** For deepening the receptivity of their contemporaries to the artist's message through their writings
1967 **Jan Tinbergen,** For pioneering work in the new science of econometrics and important contributions to economic planning policies of developing countries
1968 **Henry Moore,** For vital contributions to the rebirth of European sculpture
1969 **Gabriel Marcel and Carl Friedrich von Weizsae - cker,** Philosophical contributions to European intel - lectual life

1970 **Hans Scharoun,** For the expression his work has given to spatial architecture
1971 **Olivier Messiaen,** For enriching European music
1972 **Jean Piaget,** Discoveries in the theory of knowledge and the thinking of children
1973 **Claude Levi-Strauss,** Original research into the constants of human nature in primitive and developed societies
1974 **Dame Ninette de Valois and Maurice Bejart,** Development of the art of ballet
1975 **Sir Ernst Gombrich and Willem Sandberg,** For contributions to art
1976 **Rene David,** For work in comparative law
Amnesty International, Activities in human rights.
1977 **Werner Keagi,** Swiss historian
Jean Monnet, French statesman

Ethical Humanist Award

NEW YORK SOCIETY FOR ETHICAL CULTURE
2 W. 64th St., New York, N.Y. 10023 (212/874-5200)

The Ethical Humanist Award, which consists of a $500 donation in the name of the recipient to the cause of his or her choice and a plaque, is given annually by committee selection to "an individual who has performed an extraordinary act of moral courage, fully aware of the potential cost to his own or her life, career or reputation, and without the general sanction of his or her peers or of society, but with broad humanizing implications."

1970 **Michael A. Bernhardt,** Refusal to participate in My Lai Massacre
1971 **George M. Michaels,** Cast the deciding vote for passage of New York State's Abortion Law
1972 **Howard Levy,** Refusal to train Green Berets for ultimately brutal missions
1973 **Joseph A. Yablonski,** (Posthumously) Fight against corruption in United Mine Workers
1974 **No award**
1975 **Judge Bruce McM. Wright,** For moral courage in the vigorous application of Constitutional principles in pursuit of equal justice under law
1976 **No award**
1977 **Orlando Letelier,** (Posthumously) For undaunted pursuit of fundamental, personal and democratic freedoms for all people, which cost him his life.

Henry N. Wilwers Fire Buff of the Year Award

INTERNATIONAL FIRE BUFF ASSOCIATES
2125 Eastern Ave., Baltimore, Md. 21231 (301/327-8323)

The Henry N. Wilwers Fire Buff of the Year Award, which consists of a plaque, is given for contributions to fire service. Nominees are submitted by members to a committee which selects the recipient.

1967 **Henry N. Wilwers,** Chicago, Ill.
1968 **William H. Perkins,** Boston, Mass.
1969 **Edward R. Damaschke,** Ferndale, Mich.
1970 **William A. Brennan,** Trenton, N.J.
1971 **Albert J. Burch,** Detroit, Mich.
1972 **Charles C. Price,** Baltimore, Md.
1973 **Keith F. Franz,** Milwaukee, Wisc.
1974 **John I. Hruska,** Linthicum, Md.
1975 **Arthur D. Devlin,** Newark, N.J.

1976   James H. Blomley, Boston, Mass.
1977   Henry G. Nathan, Baltimore, Md.

Gold Medal
Distinguished American Award

NATIONAL FOOTBALL FOUNDATION
201 E. 42nd St., Suite 1506, New York, N.Y. 10017
(212/682-0255)

The foundation's Gold Medal, its highest honor, is awarded for significant contributions by an individual in a career that "embodies the highest ideals for which the game of football stands." The recipient must have been associated with college football as a player, manager, coach or be a business, political or educational leader who played college football. The recipient must be an American citizen, most of whose business life has been spent in the U.S., and who has a reputation for notable and dedicated public service carrying out the basic values of amateur sport.

1958	Dwight D. Eisenhower
1959	Douglas A. MacArthur
1960	Herbert C. Hoover
	Amos Alonzo Stagg
1961	John F. Kennedy
1962	Byron R. White
1963	Roger M. Blough
1964	Donald B. Lourie
1965	Juan T. Trippe
1966	Earl H. Blaik
1967	Frederick L. Hovde
1968	Chester J. LaRoche
1969	Richard M. Nixon
1970	Thomas J. Hamilton
1971	Ronald W. Reagan
1972	Gerald R. Ford
1973	John Wayne
1974	Gerald B. Zornow
1975	David Packard
1976	Edgar B. Speer
1977	Gen. Louis H. Wilson

The Distinguished American Award, which is a gold medal, is given as merited to men of national or international stature who, through an involvement with college football, have demonstrated that the best qualities of the game can be applied to society.

1966	Capt. William Carpenter
1967	No award
1968	No award
1969	Archibald MacLeish
1970	Vincent Lombardi
1971	Frank Boyden
1972	Jerome H. Holland
1973	No award
1974	Bob Hope
1975	Rev. Theodore Hesburgh
1976	Gen. James A. Van Fleet
1977	Rev. Edmund P. Joyce

George Washington Award
American Statesman Medal
National Service Medal
American Friendship Medal
American Patriots Medal
American Exemplar Medal
Private Enterprise Exemplar Medal
Freedom Leadership Foreign Award
National Recognition Award
Freedom Leadership Medal
Special Awards

FREEDOMS FOUNDATION
Valley Forge, Pa. 19481 (215/933-8825)

The Freedoms Foundation at Valley Forge annually honors hundreds of Americans in public and private life for "significant contributions toward making this nation a better country for all of us." The recipients are selected by a jury, which includes Supreme Court justices, officers of major national veterans' organizations, service organizations and patriotic groups. Each award consists of a medal, plaque or other memento. The following are the major honors given to recipients in public life. The dates in parentheses indicate the inception of the award; a complete list of winners is not available.

GEORGE WASHINGTON AWARD (1949)

1956	J. Edgar Hoover
1957	Herbert Hoover
1958	Arthur A. Schuck
1959	John L. McClellan
1960	No award
1961	J. Edgar Hoover
1962	Walt Disney
1963	Lt. Col. John Herschel Glenn, Jr., USMC
1964	DeWitt and Lila Wallace
1965	Civic Action Program
1966	PFC Hiram D. Strickland, USA (Posthumous)
1967	Frank J. Mrkva
1968	Gen. Harold K. Johnson, USA (Ret.)
1969	Michael Levesque
1970	Bill Pierson
1971	Gen. of the Army Omar N. Bradley
1972	Donald W. Hurrelbrink
1973	John Wayne
1974	No award
1975	No award
1976	No award
1977	Lowell Thomas

AMERICAN STATESMAN MEDAL (1949)

1959	John Foster Dulles
1968	James F. Byrnes
1969	Ellsworth Bunker
1969	Henry Cabot Lodge
1971	Clare Boothe Luce

NATIONAL SERVICE MEDAL (1949)

1966	Bob Hope
1967	Martha Raye
1968	Lawrence Welk
1969	Red Skelton
1970	John Wayne

500 Public Service, Humanitarianism & Heroism

AMERICAN FRIENDSHIP MEDAL (1949)

1965 Fritz Hans Harnisch
1973 Gordon Sinclair, Canada
1975 Alexander Solzhenitsyn, Switzerland
1976 Axel Springer, Federal Republic of Germany

AMERICAN PATRIOTS MEDAL (1949)

1961 Gen. of the Army Dwight D. Eisenhower
1965 Joseph A. Brunton, Jr.
1969 Maj. James N. Rowe, USA
1970 John W. McCormack
     Victor Riesel
1971 No award
1972 Sol Freinstone
1973 William A. Smith
1975 Sr. M. Virgina Geiger
1976 Gene Autry
1977 Clay Smothers

AMERICAN EXEMPLAR MEDAL (1960)

1968 Leon H. Sullivan
1969 Rev. Ralph W. Beiting
1970 Maj. Wesley V. Geary, USA
1971 Henry Viscardi, Jr.
1972 Rev. Melvin Floyd
1973 Earl Hamner, Jr.
1974 Frank E. Harris
1975 Randy Steffen
1976 Arthur Fiedler
1977 Helen Hayes
     Dixy Lee Ray

PRIVATE ENTERPRISE EXEMPLAR MEDAL (1965)

1965 Alfred P. Sloan, Jr.
1968 J. Howard Wood
1969 Zenon C. R. Hansen
1970 Asa T. Spaulding
1971 W. Clement Slone
1972 James W. Walter
1974 Kenneth McFarland
1976 Phillips Petroleum Co.
1977 Milton Friedman

FREEDOM LEADERSHIP FOREIGN AWARD

1955 Carlos Castillo Armas (Supreme Achievement
     Medal)
     Ramon Magsaysay
     Ernst Reuter
1957 Carlos P. Romulo
     Konrad Adenauer
     Ngo Dinh Diem
     Syngman Rhee
     Winston Churchill
1958 Chiang Kai-Shek

NATIONAL RECOGNITION AWARD

1963 Margaret Long Arnold
     Virgil Miller Newton, Jr.
     Russell Potter Reeder, Jr.
     Sharon Sue Rountree
     Elfrieda Freeman Tice
1964 Gen. Thomas S. Power, USAF (Ret)
     Rev. James H. Smythe
     Tournament of Roses Association
1965 Mattie Coney
     Marie Davis Hunt
     Mail Call—Vietnam
     Maj. Gen. H. Nickerson, Jr., USMC
1966 Raymond Burr

Harold C. "Chad" McClellan
Joseph O'Malley
1967 Ernest Crain
     Sheriff Donald S. Genung
     Lt. Col. Samuel R. Loboda, USA
     Ken and Jeanadele Magner
1968 George E. Foreman
     Luke Greene
     Mrs. Chester H. Lehman
     Margaret Moore
     George Putnam
     Alice Widener
1969 Charles L. Gould
     Art Linkletter
     Eugene Ormandy
     Kate Smith
     Wernher von Braun
     DeWitt Wallace
1970 Frank L. Rizzo
     Sgt. Joseph J. Pfister, ANGUS
     James E. Self
1971 Denise Evers
     Walter Trohan
1972 George Mardikian
1973 Joy Eilers
     Thomas Lakan
     Mark Bute
1974 George S. Benson
     Martin DeVries
1975 Vickie L. Jones
     LeRoy Foster, Jr.
     Mary Mullen
     Caroline C. Myers
1977 Robert Moses

FREEDOM LEADERSHIP MEDAL (1949)

1954 William Robertson Coe
     Charles Edward Merrill
     Columbia University
1955 David Lawrence
1957 Gen. Curtis LeMay
     Charles S. Mott
     Gen. Lewis B. Hershey
1959 Wilber M. Brucker
     Cdr. William R. Anderson
     Ward Bond
     Lt. Cdr. Donald M. Hanson
     Armand Penha
     Bob Hope
     Ann Hawkes Hutton
     Hon. Elwood Fouts
     Ian Stuart
1960 Frank M. Tait
     Dave Garroway
     David Taylor
     James McC. Willson
     Cdr. Paul A. Terry
     Arthur Godfrey
1962 Arch N. Booth
     Perry E. Gresham
     Walter Kerr
     Christian Sanderson
     George Todt
1963 Gen. Lauris Norstad, USAF (Ret.)
1964 Gene E. Bradley
     Irving R. Melbo
     Eric Sloane
1965 Capt. Roger H. C. Donlon, USA
     James W. Turpin
1966 Milton Caniff

William H. Spurgeon III
1967 Walter and Cordelia Knott
Kenneth McFarland
William B. Walsh
1968 Stan Musial
1969 Anita Bryant
Eric Hoffer
Paul Harvey
Jenkin Lloyd Jones
1970 H. Ross Perot
1971 George C. Roche III
Alfred J. Barran
Albert M. Ettinger
1972 Armistead Maupin, Jr.
1973 George Foreman
1974 Hugh O'Brian
1975 Rev. Donald E. Mowery
1976 American Freedom Train Foundation, Inc.
1977 Douglas L. Brandow

SPECIAL AWARDS

1952 American Broadcasting Co.
American Legion
Columbia Broadcasting System
National Broadcasting Co.
National Committee for a Free Europe
U.S. Military Academy
Armed Forces I & E
1953 Boy Scouts of America
News Magazine of the Screen
Reader's Digest
1954 Billy Graham
St. John's University
1955 E. I. duPont
Kiwanis International
Daughters of the American Revolution
Armed Forces I & E
1956 Disneyland
Gen. Federation of Women's Clubs
Lawrence C. Lockley
Col. John H. Shenkel
Helen Lynch
Warner Bros. Pictures, Inc.
1957 John Coleman
S/Sgt Herbert P. Weet
1969 National Aeronautics and Space Administration

Henrietta Szold Award

HADASSAH, THE WOMEN'S ZIONIST
ORGANIZATION OF AMERICA
50 W. 58th St., New York, N.Y. 10019 (212/355-7900)

The Henrietta Szold Award and Citation, which carries a cash prize of $1,000, is given annually based on an awards committee recommendation to an individual of any age or nationality, organization, committee or nation to perpetuate the name of Henrietta Szold, the founder of Hadassah.

1949 Eleanor Roosevelt
1950 Selman A. Waksman
1951 President Harry S. Truman
1952 Herbert H. Lehman
1953 William O. Douglas, U.S. Supreme Court Justice
1954 Monnett B. Davis
1955 Mordecai M. Kaplan
1956 Isadore I. Rabi
1957 Louis Lipsky
1958 David Ben Gurion

1959 Rahel Yanait Ben Zvi
1960 Golda Meir, Public Service Centennial Award
Leonard W. Mayo, Youth Welfare Centennial Award
Mary Woodward Lasker, Medicine Centennial Award
Nahum Goldmann, Zionism Centennial Award
Martin Buber, Education Centennial Award
1961 No award
1962 No award
1963 Albert B. Sabin
1964 Moshe Sharett
Queen Mother Elizabeth of Belgium
1965 Hubert H. Humphrey
1966 No award
1967 Michael E. DeBakey
1968 Arthur Goldbert
Mrs. Heinie Heiman-Elkind for Hadassah Nurses
Mrs. James de Rothschild for Rothschild Family
1969 Christiaan Barnaard
Youth Aliyah
1970 Marvin Feldman
1971 Zalman Shazar
1972 Soviet Jewry
1973 The People of the Netherlands
1974 Teddy Kolleck
1975 No award
1976 Sir Harold Wilson
1977 No award

Distinguished Public Service Award

U.S. DEPARTMENT OF HEALTH, EDUCATION
AND WELFARE
330 Independence Ave. SW, Washington, D.C. 20201
(202/245-7456)

The Distinguished Public Service Award, which consists of a plaque, is given as merited for contributions by an individual, or institution, outside of the department to its growth and development. Beginning in 1978, the criteria will change to include recipients from inside the department as well.

1968 Lister Hill
Carl Elliott
1969 No award
1970 No award
1971 Alfred Gilman
William Middleton
Maurice Warsaw
1972 WRC-TV, Washington, D.C.
1973 No award
1974 Elizabeth M. Boggs
1975 No award
1976 No award
1977 No award

Stillman Award

AMERICAN HUMANE ASSOCIATION
4351 S. Roslyn, Englewood, Col. 80110 (303/779-1400)

The Stillman Award, named for Dr. William O. Stillman by a bequest of Mrs. Morris H. Vandegrift, is presented annually to humans showing courage in the face of personal danger to rescue animals or animals who have saved human life. Gold, silver and bronze medals or certificates are awarded to people and animals for such heroism. The award has been given since 1928, but only the most recent recipients are listed here.

1965 Fuzzy, Dayton, Ohio
Comet, collie, Vineland, N.J.
Rocket Bruno, collie, Vineland, N.J.
King, border sheepdog, Austin, Tex.
Laddie, labrador, Helena, Mont.
Randy, poodle, Phoenix, Ariz.
King, German shepherd, Colorado Springs, Colo.
Fox Glen Zipper, terrier, Sharon, Pa.
Duke, German shepherd, Fillmore, Calif.
Pooch, mutt, Pittsburg, Kans.
Randy Simons, Tucson, Ariz
Tiger, terrier, Albany, N.Y.
Prince, chihuahua, Palm Beach, Fla.
Pamela and Jackie Carrico, Elkhart, Ind.
Scott Ray and Gilbert Larochelle, Auburn, Me.
Jerome Renhack, Oconomowoc, Wisc.
James L. Adams, Oregon City, Ore
Donald Serres, Oregon City, Ore.
Dave Stewart, Crescent City, Calif.
Gene Remington, John McDonald and Laurence Seckley, Tacoma, Wash.
Libby (posthumous), great dane, Kent, Wash.
Casey, mutt, Brookline, Mass.
Laddie, collie, Akron, Ohio
Jackie, german shepherd, Myrtle Beach, S.C.
Lady, dalmatian, Inkster, Miss.
Sultan, german shepherd, Hillsboro, Ore.
Midge, mutt, Greenville, Ohio
Spookie, cocker spaniel, Pompano, Fla.
Lassie, collie, Canajoharie, N.Y.
Fox Glen Bustling Buckaroo, terrier, Sharon, Pa.
Shep, collie, Freeport, N.Y.
James "Bucky" Welch, Louisville, Ky.
Rev. Russell Raker, Russell Raker III and Wendy, dog, Allentown, Pa.
1966 Nancee Bickelhaupt, Birmingham, Ala.
Mickey Mouse, Pittsburg, Kans.
Lassie, collie, Osceola, Fla.
Sir Scott and Donar, German shepherds, St. Louis, Mo.
Patrick Delp Colorado Springs, Colo.
Edward Lansberry, Cleveland, Ohio
Earl Boatman and Brownie, Knoxville, Tenn.
Elmer Zellner, Delafield City, Wisc.
Scooter, german shepherd, Waukesha, Wisc.
Misty and Catt Avery, cats, Augusta, Ga.
J.W. Doane and Charlie F. Weaver, Knoxville, Tenn.
Jake Orishan, Troy, N.Y.
James O'Beirne, Jr., Rochester, N.Y.
Charlie, Long Island, N.Y.
Gyp, Labrador, Princeton, Minn.
Bill Radix, Oconomowoc, Wisc.
Mrs. Ernest LeClair, Nassau, N.Y.
Stephen Rasputni and Stanley Odziemiec, Niagara Falls, N.Y.
Timmy Danley, James and Scott Decker and Stephen and Mark Littlewood, Alexandria, Va.
June Kickleiter, St. Petersburg, Fla.
Steris Sturquell, Amarillo, Tex.
David Lee Hess, Lancaster, Pa.
Willie Smith and Greg Williams, Easton, Md.
George Rebar and Charles Opitz, Sarasota, Fla.
April, Gallup, N.M.
Foxy, Kingsport, Tenn.
1967 Sheriff Jorgen and Dwight Booth, Pewaukee, Wisc.

Bodidly, Cleveland, Ohio
Tashka, Afghan hound, Vacaville, Calif.
Duchess, mutt, DeLand, Fla.
Jasper County Emergency Rescue Unit, Webb City, Mo.
Chester O. Young, Ronald Sauls, Russell Logan, Jr. and Tony Logan, Tuscumbia, Ala.
Volunteer Rescue Squad and Nosey, chihuahua, Knoxville, Tenn.
Ken Johnson, Menominee Falls, Wisc.
Donald Moore, Jackson Summit, N.Y.
Bounce, mutt, Florence, Ala.
Douglas Censiba, Palm Beach, Fla.
Mike Hall, Ironton, Ohio
Runt (posthumous), dog, Chesterton, Ind.
Richard Nicholson, Lansing, Mich.
Precious, cat, Wilmington, Del.
Roy J. Hamman, New Orleans, La.
Carbon and Shambie, Malibu, Calif.
Benjamin J. Parker and Randall E. Dotto, Springfield, Ohio
Stripey, cat, St. Paul, Minn.
Wallie, collie, Albuquerque, N.M.
Chuck Parsons, Greg Ballard, Ronnie Kayrouz, Scott Ballard and Marie C. Wiegand, Louisville, Ky.
Cindy, cocker spaniel, **and Bill Morgan,** Stockton, Calif.
Cliff McAdams and Teddy (posthumous), dog, Covina, Calif.
Lee N. Centell, Porterville, Calif,
Thomas J. Cervini, Vineland, N.J.
Roger Burggraf, Anchorage, Alas.
1968 Butchie, mutt, Terre Haute, Ind.
Kenneth Wright, Frankfort, Ind.
Rudolph (posthumous), Norwegian elkhound, Tacoma, Wash.
Thunder, collie, Asheville, N.C.
Sam, boxer, Utica, Mich.
Squeakie, mutt, Montgomery, Ala.
Tuffy, poodle, Medford, Ore.
Leigh Larson, Menominee Falls, Wisc.
Crew of the Rio Grande California Zephyr, Denver, Colo.
Soho Solange, cocker spaniel, Phoenix, Ariz.
Tinker, Australian terrier, Littleton, Colo.
Pepe, mutt, Cleveland, Ohio
Ernest T. Toth and Rodney Miller, Allentown, Pa.
Lassie, collie, **and Our Pup,** collie, Hamilton, Ala.
Taffy, poodle, Fresno, Calif.
Gretchen Rattweiler, Robert Rambo, George Fowler and Robert, Stockton, Calif.
Tweed, scottie, Detroit, Mich.
Big Boy, dog, Wilmington, N.C.
Gary J. Kunz (posthumous), St. Paul, Minn.
Edward Blotzner, Forest Hills, Pa.
Monroe Lerman, Hollywood, Fla.
Pierre, poodle, Cedarburg, Wisc.
1969 Woodrow W. Smith, Joseph H. Armstrong, C. Warren Newbill, William B. Schultz and John Lockwood, Portsmouth, Va.
Little Bit and Kansas, terriers, Spokane, Wash.
Scottie, mutt, Hagerstown, Md.
Elry Tice and Michael W. Becker, Saginaw, Mich.
Frisky Dan, Dalmatian, Richland, Wash.
Ruth, Sharon and Diana Haynes, Claremont, N.H.
Dick Yates, Springfield, Ore.
Harry Peterson, R. A. Linsley and Albert O'Neil, Barstow, Calif.
Don R. Griffin, Montgomery, Ala.

Bernie Ross, John Gustofson and Bill Richardson, Wheat Ridge, Colo.
Ladybird, Australian terrier, Oak Run, Calif.
Ricky, dog, Sacramento, Calif.
Rusty, Doberman pinscher, Salem, Mass.
Pokey (posthumous), terrier, Jacksonville, Fla.
1970 **Allen Bobb, Jr.,** Port Jervis, N.Y.
Tinkerbelle, Pekingese, Alexandria, Va.
Natalie Korniloff, Woodridge, N.Y.
Gene Fehlman and Jay Crockett, Logan, Utah
Christopher Hewells, Manakin, Va.
Raymond Pertinaci and John Hardy, W. Mifflin, Ohio
Amos, Persian cat, Centralia, Ill.
Suzanne Marie Smith, Minneapolis, Minn.
King E. Jordan, Savannah, Ga.
Ginger (posthumous), dog, Kenosha, Wisc.
Don Smetana, N.A.
Richard "Buster" Campbell, Missouri
Maybelle Neuguth (posthumous), Pennsylvania
Boris (posthumous), Michigan
John E. Ward, Georgia
Thomas Thelan, Wisconsin
Nallannna Chetty Venugopal, Madras, India
Samuel Lopez, California
Curly (posthumous), Pennsylvania
Heidi, boxer, Ohio
1971 **Ruby Katheryn,** mutt, Herrin, Ill.
Norman Blake, Denver, Colo.
James Turner, New Berlin, Wisc.
Gerald Slemmer, Philadelphia, Pa.
John J. Mahoney, Beverly, Mass.
Sheila, German shepherd, Braddock, Pa.
Jim Hawes, Boston, Mass.
Duchess and Polly, mutts, Tacoma, Wash.
Hooligan, St. Bernard, Clinton, Ill.
Cheryl Haugen, Aurora, Colo.
Shadow, German shepherd, Westfall, N.Y.
Boy Scout Troop # 413, Richmond, Va.
Anthony Zito and Alfred Mueller, Melrose Park, Ill.
Tim, Labrador, Marsh Hill, N.H.
Gigi, poodle, Ford City, Pa.
R.D. Hayes and L.I. Slife, Dayton, Ohio
Brandy, Chesapeake Bay retriever, Pelican, Minn
John D. MacArthur, Palm Beach Gardens, Fla.
Fraulein, German shepherd, Oak Brook, Ill
Tony Kelley, Kingston N.C.
Linda and Roger, collies, Vienna, Mich.
1972 **Tony,** mutt, Greenville, S.C.
Thomas Gonia, Point Place, Ohio
Brownie (posthumous), German shorthair, Milwaukee, Wisc.
Misty, collie, Minneapolis, Minn.
Hercules (posthumous), Maine coon cat, Arvada, Colo.
William Whelan, Peoria, Ill.
Lynn Parker (posthumous), Missoula, Mont.
Leon Norris, Robert Defresne and Louis Pennetti, Auburn, Me.
Tink, Labrador, Lafayette, La.
Thumper, German shepherd, Rapid City, S.D.
Lester Beard and Wayne Jet, Birmingham, Ala.
Fred, mutt, S. Williamsport, Pa.
Budweiser, St. Bernard, John's Island, S.C.
1973 **Cinders,** spaniel mixed, Minneapolis, Minn.
Homer Ellett, Castro Valley, Calif.
Baylor Horvath, Portsmouth, N.H.
King, Boston, Mass.
Patrick, German shepherd, Portland, Me.
Huntington Fire Companies 4 and 8, Huntington, W. Va.

Tony Rodriguez and Steve Chayka, Michigan
Dingaling, German shepherd, Indiana
Joe Matty, New Hampshire
Maurice, Florida
Frostie, terrier mixed, Missouri
Tom Anderson and John Grishaber, Wisconsin
Gary Hamilton (posthumous), Oregon
Fraulein, German shepherd, Oak Brook, Ill.
Ed Bottorff, Indiana
Fawnee, chihuahua, Pennsylvania
J. Marshall Hughes, Kentucky
Steve Epps, California
Ace of Spades, great Dane, Alabama
Queenie, Doberman pinscher, N.A.
Peanuts, poodle, South Carolina
Mort, cat, Indiana
William Wakeland, Illinois
1974 **Teddy,** German shepherd, Pennsylvania
Ladybug, mutt, North Carolina
Glen, Craig, Bobbi and Terry Wood, Washington
James H. Dula, North Carolina
Romie Bryant, Delaware
Tippy (posthumous), chihuahua, Wyoming
Kurt Gorbutt, Michigan
Tinny (posthumous), beagle, California
Duke, Labrador, Oregon
Gidget, Michigan
James Stremeckus (posthumous), Massachusetts
Taiwan, Siamese cat, Colorado
Smokey, Hawaii
Heidi, dachshund, Booth Bay Harbor, Maine
Martin Senna, Roland O'Neil and Clarence O'Neil, Barstow, California
Charlie, Mutt, South Carolina
Thomas Gherardi, Mt. Vernon, N.Y.
David Douglas Johnson (posthumous), Oregon
1975 **Barbara Sandblom, Ruth Colby, Fritz Haubner and Douglas Cole,** North Eastham, Mass.
Muffin, peekapoo, Birmingham, Ala.
Baron, dachshund, Rock Island Ill
Creek, Labrador, Charlottesville, Va.
Skipper (posthumous), pomeranian, Billings, Mont.
Buster, mutt, Salem, Oregon
Laddie, cocker/poodle, Lahaska, Pa.
Michael Walsh, Clear Lake, Ida.
Heidi, mutt, Medford, Ore.
Whitey, dog, Kingsport, Tenn.
Citizens of Ranier, Ranier, Minn.
Arnold Rose, Milwaukee, Wisc.
Chang Lo, s'hih-tzu, Dallas, Tex.
Jenny, cat, Peabody, Mass
Poochie, mutt, Westfield, N.J.
Moon, Afghan hound, Birmingham, Ala.
Barbetta Sherrer, Montgomery, Ala.
Bill Tabor and John Strodi, Terre Haute, Ind.
Roy Harvey, Toledo, Ohio
John Szczepanick (posthumous) **and Dennis J. Scheffer,** Newark, N.J.
Charles Southworth, Jackson, Mid.
Baron, golden retriever, St. Paul, Minn.
Bootsie, schnauzer, Rock Island, Ill.
Warren Sims, Milwaukee, Wisc.
1976 **Thomas V. Di Puma** (posthumous), Bronx, N.Y.
Sampson, German shepherd, Hartwell, Ohio
James Blake, Marine City, Mich.
Zorro, German shepherd, Oakland, Calif.
Snap, mutt, Natchez, Miss.
Kenneth Encarnacao, Dartmouth, Mass
St. Paul Fire Department Ladder Company #7 and Rescue Squad #1, St. Paul, Minn.

Red, Irish setter, St. Louis, Mo.
Samantha, Burmese cat, Vallejo, Calif.
Misty, poodle, Benton, Ark.
Sissy (posthumous), poodle, Brainard, Mass.
Tina, Shiloh and Midnight (posthumous), chihuahuas, N.A.

1977 Jerry Morland and Dennis Jacobs, Columbus, Ind.
Toby Krominga, St. Paul, Minn.
Snowball, Cocoa, Fla.
Bridgette, Clark Lake, Mich.
Mr. and Mrs. Donald White, Douglas and Brian Pardee, and Ernest Labidueur, Niagara Falls, N.Y.
Mark Bairel (posthumous), Wisconsin Rapids, Wisc.
Corky, Detroit, Mich.
Duke Sudell and Bruce Roed, Grand Forks, N.D.
Chipper, El Dorado, Ark.
George Hesse, Newark, N.J.
John Elmer Smith, Columbia, Pa.
Javier Garcia Chavez, Mexico
Ebony, Ohio
Soul, Ohio
Zachary, Michigan
Clyde Haggerty, Michigan
Meatball, New Jersey
William Dana Fish, California
Meatball, Alabama
Candy, South Carolina
Charles Ross (posthumous), Michigan

Man of the Year

SOCIETY OF PROFESSIONAL INVESTIGATORS
Box 1197, Church Street Station, New York, N.Y. 10008

The plaque given annually to the Man of the Year commemorates outstanding service in law enforcement and the combat against crime, rackets and corruption.

1957 Robert F. Kennedy, Chief Counsel, U.S. Senate Select Committee on Improper Activities in the Labor or Management Field

1958 Edgar D. Croswell, State Police sergeant who uncovered the organized crime meeting at Apalachin, N.Y.

1959 Detective Division, New York City Police Department

1960 Arthur H. Christy, Chief of the Criminal Division, U.S. Attorney's Office, Southern District, New York

1961 Urbanus Edmund Baughman, Chief, U.S. Secret Service

1962 Charles "Pat" Ward, Agent-in-Charge, New York office, Federal Bureau of Narcotics

1963 Joseph Kaitz, New York Commissioner, Waterfront Commission of New York Harbor

1964 Michael J. Murphy, Police Commissioner, New York

1965 William A. O'Connor, Superintendent, Port of New York Authority Police Department

1966 Alfred J. Scotti, Chief Assistant, District Attorney's Office, New York County

1967 Sanford D. Garelik, Chief Inspector, New York City Police Department

1968 John F. Malone, Assistant Director, Federal Bureau of Investigation

1969 Albert E. Whitaker, Agent-in-Charge, U.S. Secret Service, New York

1970 John L. Barry, Police Commissioner, Suffolk County (N.Y.) Police Department

1971 Louis J. Lefkowitz, Attorney General, State of New York

1972 Myles J. Ambrose, Special Assistant Attorney General for Drug Abuse Law Enforcement

1973 Clarence M. Kelley, Director, Federal Bureau of Investigation

1974 Michael J. Codd, Police Commissioner, New York

1975 William C. Connelie, Superintendent, New York State Police

1976 Mario Merola, District Attorney of Bronx County, New York

1977 Not available at press time

Jefferson Award

AMERICAN INSTITUTE FOR PUBLIC SERVICE
1028 Connecticut Ave., Washington, D.C. 20036
(202/293-1050)

The Jefferson Award, which consists of $5,000 and a gold-on-silver medallion, is given each year for distinguished public service in five categories. Anyone may submit nominations, which are voted on by a large and distinguished board of selectors.

THE AWARD FOR THE GREATEST PUBLIC SERVICE PERFORMED BY AN ELECTED OR APPOINTED OFFICIAL:

1973 Henry A. Kissinger, Assistant to the President for National Security Affairs, "for his efforts to strengthen world peace by opening doors to China and by initiating closer economic and social ties with Russia."

1974 Elliot L. Richardson, Attorney General, "for upholding the principle that no man can stand above the law and for sacrificing private position for the good of the country."

1975 Peter W. Rodino, U.S. House of Representatives, "for his fair and bipartisan leadership as Chairman of the House Judiciary Committee."

1976 Arthur F. Burns, Chairman, Federal Reserve Board and Alan Greenspan, Chairman, President's Council of Economic Advisers and William E. Simon Secretary of the Treasury, "for their joint efforts as chief architects of our national economic policy, and for their combined courage and conviction in cutting government spending to stop inflation and to stimulate economic recovery."

1977 Michael J. Mansfied, U.S. Ambassador to Japan

THE AWARD FOR THE GREATEST PUBLIC SERVICE PERFORMED BY A PRIVATE CITIZEN:

1973 John W. Gardner, Chairman, Common Cause, "for the zeal and imagination which he has brought to the creation of an effective national citizens' lobby."

1974 Ralph Nader, consumer advocate, "for being champion and protector of the rights of the American consumer."

1975 Katharine Graham, Chairman of the Board, The Washington Post Co., "for her relentless pursuit of the truth, and for her courage in using the media to uphold the principle of the people's right to know."

1976 John D. Rockefeller III, Honorary Chairman, The Rockefeller Foundation, "for a lifetime of dedication to public service and for his effective dramatization of the need to control national and world population growth."

1977 Art Buchwald, essayist

THE AWARD FOR THE GREATEST PUBLIC SERVICE BENEFITING THE DISADVANTAGED:

1973 **Cesar Chavez, President, United Farm Workers,** "for his efforts in protecting the rights of migrant workers."

1974 **Thomas Szasz, Professor of Psychiatry, State University of New York,** "for his campaign to defend the civil rights of the mentally retarded."

1975 **Rev. Leon Sullivan, Founder, Opportunities Industrialization Centers,** "for his special leadership in founding the IOCs across the country to offer job training to unskilled, low-income people."

1976 **Rev. Theodore M. Hesburgh, President, Notre Dame University,** "for his unwavering, long-term commitment to protect and expand the civil rights of the nation's minorities."

1977 **Howard Rusk, director,** New York University Rehabilitation center

THE AWARD FOR THE GREATEST PUBLIC SERVICE PERFORMED BY AN INDIVIDUAL THIRTY-FIVE YEARS OR UNDER:

1973 **Joseph A. Yablonski, General Counsel, United Mine Workers,** "for his courageous campaign to restore integrity to unionism."

1974 **Maynard Jackson, Mayor, Atlanta, Ga.,** "as the first black mayor of a major Southern city since Reconstruction."

1975 **R. Emmett Tyrrell, Jr., Editor,** *The Alternative,* "for his work as founder and editor of *The Alternative* magazine for offering an alternative and conservative viewpoint to college students in America."

1976 **Vilma S. Martinez, President, Mexican-American Legal Defense and Educational Fund,** "for her substantial accomplishments in expanded bilingual education and voting rights for Mexican-Americans and women through legal processes."

1977 **Max Cleland,** administrator, U.S. Veterans' Administration

THE AWARD FOR THE GREATEST PUBLIC SERVICE BENEFITING LOCAL COMMUITIES:

1974 **Robert T. Bates, interior designer,** "for his efforts to save a small Midwestern town, Albia, Iowa, by building industry and job opportunities."
James Ellis, lawyer, "for his leadership in the battle against the pollution of Lake Washington."
James Masten, former sociology instructor, California State University, "for his varied contributions to improving the lives of retired people in Fresno, Calif."
Ellen S. Straus, founder, Call for Action, "for origination the program that now functions as an ombudsman in 50 cities."
Peter Wilson, Mayor, San Diego, Calif., "for his attack on the problems of urban growth."

1975 **No award**

1976 **Felix G. Rohatyn, Chairman, Municipal Assistance Corp.,** "for utilizing his special skills and toughness to restore fiscal integrity to New York City, averting default and a potential national economic crisis."

1977 **Rev. Alfred Boddeker, founder,** St. Anthony's Dining Room, San Francisco
Jean Chaudhuri, founder, Traditional Indian Alliance, Tucson, Ariz.
Leonard Cobb, director of cardiology, Harborview Medical Center, Seattle, Wash.
Olga Mele, family counselor, Community Renewal Team, Hartford, Conn.

Marjory Taylor, founder, First Marlboro-Westboro Mental Health Association, Southboro, Mass.

Freedom Award

INTERNATIONAL RESCUE COMMITTEE
486 Park Ave. S., New York, N.Y. 10016 (212/OR 9-0010)

The Freedom Award is given as merited for contributions to the cause of refugees and human freedom. The board of directors chooses the winner, who is given a plaque. The Committee maintains no records as to the year in which the following individuals were given the Freedom Award.

Winston Churchill
Adm. Richard E. Byrd
David Dubinsky
Gen. W.J. "Wild Bill" Donovan
Willy Brandt
Geaorge Meany
David Sarnoff
Gen. Lucius D. Clay
Jacob K. Javits
Leo Cherne
Bruno Kreisky

Lyndon Baines Johnson Foundation Award

LYNDON BAINES JOHNSON FOUNDATION
2313 Red River, Austin, Tex. 78705 (512/478-7829)

The Lyndon Baines Johnson Foundation Award, which carries a $25,000 honorarium, is given annually to an American citizen for outstanding contributions to the national well-being in fields such as civil rights, urban affairs and solar energy. An award committee of prominent Americans selects the recipient.

1973 **Roy Wilkins,** Civil rights
1974 **Ivan Allen and Franklin Thomas,** Urban affairs
1975 **No award**
1976 **George O.G. Lof,** Solar energy.
1977 **Sidney R. Garfield,** Medical care

Helen Keller International Award

HELEN KELLER INTERNATIONAL
22 W. 17th St., New York, N.Y. 10011 (212/924-0420)

The Helen Keller International Award is presented to recognize outstanding contributions in the field of blindness. The award, which consists of a trophy, is given as merited. The recipient is selected from nominees from various sources by the executive director with the approval of the board of directors.

1960 **Col. Edwin A. Baker,** founder and managing director, Canadian National Institute for the Blind
1968 **Georges L. Raverat,** (France), European office director, American Foundation for the Overseas Blind
1970 **Sir John F. Wilson,** (United Kingdom), director and chief executive officer, Royal Commonwealth Society for the Blind
1971 **Lord Fraser of Lonsdale,** (United Kingdom), chairman, St. Dunstan's, London
1973 **James S. Adams,** (U.S.A.), industrialist, investment banker and president, Research to Prevent Blindness

1976 **John Feree,** (U.S.A.), director, National Society for the Prevention of Blindness, and member, American Foundation for Overseas Blind Advisory Committee on Blindness Prevention

1977 **Henry Labouisse,** director, United Nations Children's Emergency Fund (UNICEF)

Philip Arnow Award
Service Awards
U.S. DEPARTMENT OF LABOR
200 Constitution Ave. NW, NDOL Bldg., Room N5458, Washington, D.C. 20210 (202/523-6557)

The $1,000 Philip Arnow Award is given annually in recognition of consistently outstanding performance and service to the department over a 15-year period. The Secretary's Honors Awards Committee selects the winners.

1973 Alfred G. Albert
1974 William B. Hewitt
1975 Beatrice J. Dvorak
1976 No award
1977 Al Zuck

The Secretary of Labor's Service Awards recognize outstanding career employees by underwriting a year's training in an academic institution or government agency other than the Labor group. It is given annually to employees who have demonstrated ability, achievement and growth potential on the recommendation of the Secretary's Honors awards committee.

1966 Robert M. Guttman
       Denis Foster Johnston
1967 No award
1968 No award
1969 No award
1970 No award
1971 Paul A. Heise
       Henry Rose
1972 Irving I. Kramer
       Lauriston Hardin Long
1973 Donald J. McNulty
       Gresham C. Smith
1974 No award
1975 Alfred G. Albert
       Elaine Louise Sealock
1976 No award
1977 Paul M. Ryscavage

Fiorello LaGuardia Award
NEW SCHOOL FOR SOCIAL RESEARCH
66 W. 12th St., New York, N.Y. 10011 (212/741-5667)

The Fiorello LaGuardia Award, which consists of a bronze statue of New York City's former mayor, is given annually for outstanding public service.

1973

Amyas Ames   Kenneth B. Clark
Gustave L. Levy   Ellen Stewart

1974

WNET, Channel 13   Mrs. John L. Loeb
David Rose   Francisco Trilla
Roy Wilkins

1975

James Reed Ellis   Kenneth A. Gibson
Ada Louise Huxtable   Richard Green Lugar
Patrick Vincent Murphy   Pete Seeger
Leon Howard Sullivan

1976

William M. Ellinghaus   Richard Ravitch
Felix G. Rohatyn

1977

J. Richardson Dilworth   Emil Mosbacher, Jr.
Preston Robert Tisch

Ramon Magsaysay Awards
RAMON MAGSAYSAY AWARD FOUNDATION
1680 Roxas Blvd., Manila, Philippines (Tel: 59-19-59 and 59-17-20)

The Ramon Magsaysay Award is given annually in each of five areas of achievement to individuals who exemplify the ideals of Ramon Magsaysay. Accomplishments of the previous five years in government service, public service and community leadership are honored. On August 31, the birthday of Ramon Magsaysay, the awards are made in Manila to Asians regardless of race, creed, sex or nationality. The award consists of $10,000, a gold medal and a certificate.

GOVERNMENT SERVICE

1958 **Chiang Mon-Ling** (China), Rural reconstruction
1959 **Chintaman Dwarkanath Deshmukh** (India) **and Jose Vasquez Aquilar** (Philippines), Exemplary service
1960 No award
1961 **Raden Kodijat** (Indonesia), Directed yaws campaign
1962 **Francisca Reyes Aquino** (Philippines), Research to preserve national folk heritage
1963 **Akhter Hameed Khan** (Pakistan), Rural reform in East Pakistan
1964 **Yukiharu Miki** (Japan), Community-wide modernization
1965 **Puey Ungphakorn** (Thailand), Management of public finance
1966 **Phon Sangsingkeo** (Thailand), Mental Health services
1967 **Keo Viphakone** (Laos), Public services for villagers
1968 **K.T. Li** (China), Economics
1969 **Hsu Shih-Chu** (China), Rural health, sanitation and family planning
1970 No award
1971 **Ali Sadikin** (Indonesia), Modern administration
1972 **Goh Keng Swee** (Singapore), Industrialization of Singapore
1973 **Balachandra Chakkingal Sekhar** (Malaysia), Scientific and technical developments in rubber
1974 **Hiroshi Kuroki** (Japan), Administrative modernization of a Prefecture
1975 **Tun Mohamed Suffian bin Hashim** (Malaysia), Adaptation of Western legal forms to own Asian society
1976 **Elsie Elliot** (Hong Kong), leader of crusade to make government more responsive to the poor
1977 Not available at press time

PUBLIC SERVICE

1958 Mary Rutnam (Ceylon), Dedicated service as private citizen

1959 Father Joaquin Vilallonga (Spaniard) **and Daw Tee Tee Luce** (Burma),For compassionate service to others

1960 Sir Henry Holland (Pakistan) **and Ronald Holland** (British), For selfless dedication of surgical skills

1961 Nilawan Pintong (Thailand), Leadership of effective civil action

1962 Lawrence and Horace Kadoorie (British), Practical philanthropy to promote rural welfare

1963 Helen Kim (Korea), Leadership in emancipation of Korean women

1964 Father Nguyen Lac Hoa (Vietnam), Extraordinary valor in defence of freedom

1965 Jayaprakash Narayan (India), Constructive articulation of public conscience

1966 Kim Yong-Ki (Korea), Improvement of rural life through application of Christian principles

1967 M.C. Sithiporn Kridakara (Thailand), Pioneering experiments and education in agriculture

1968 Seiichi Tobata (Japan), Modernization of agriculture

1969 Kim Hyung Seo (Korea), Leadership of refugees in reclaiming new agricultural lands

1970 No award

1971 Pedro T. Orata (Philippines), Creative work in education, especially of rural youth

1972 Cecile R. Guidote and Gilopez Kabayao (Philippines), Leadership in the performing arts

1973 Msgr. Antonia Y. Fortich and Benjamin C. Gaston (Philippines), Rural development

1974 M.S. Subbulakshmi (India), For devotional song and support of numerous public causes

1975 Phra Charoon Parnchandara (Thailand), Curing drug addicts with herbal and spiritual treatments

1976 Hermenegild Joseph (Sri Lanka), missionary schoolteacher devoted to helping youth

1977 Not available at press time

COMMUNITY LEADERSHIP

1958 Acharya Vinoba Bhave (India), Inspiration and help to "the man on the land"

1959 His Holiness, the Dalai Lama of Tibet (Tibet), For defense of his people's right to live and worship in their own way

1960 Tunku Abdul Rahman Putra Al-Haj (Malaysia), For guiding a multi-racial socity toward communal alliance and national solidarity

1961 Gus Borgeest (British/Hong Kong), For human concern and courage on "Sunshine Island"

1962 H. Koesna Poeradiredja (Indonesia) **and P.P. Narayanan** (Malayasia), For their championship of the workers' cause through responsible unionism

1963 Dara N. Khorody, Tribhuvandas K. Patel and Verghese Kurien (India), For coordination of government and private efforts in improving the supply of essential food and sanitation in a major city, and living standards in villages

1964 Pablo Torres Tapia (Philippines), For mobilizing the savings of a community for its productive needs

1965 Lim Kim San (Singapore), Decent, moderately priced housing

1966 Kamaladevi Chattopadhyay (India), Creativity in handicrafts, cooperatives, politics, art and theatre

1967 Tun Abdul Razak bin Hussein (Malaysia), Administration

1968 Silvino and Rosario Encarnacion (Philippines), Management of a credit cooperative

1969 Ahangamage T. Ariyaratne (Ceylon), Services to villages

1970 No award

1971 Moncompu Sambasiva Swaminathan (India), Scientist, educator and administrator

1972 Hans Westenberg (Indonesia), Practical propagation of new crops and better methods among small farmers

1973 Krasae Chanawongse (Thailand), Establishment of medical services

1974 Fusaye Ichikawa (Japan), Advancement of her countrywomen's public and personal freedom

1975 Lee Tai-Young (Korea), For the cause of equal juridical rights for the liberation of Korean women

1976 Toshikazu Wakatsuki (Japan), For medical service to less privileged countrymen

1977 Not available at press time

Distinguished Service Award
MILITARY ORDER OF THE WORLD WARS
1100 17th St. NW, Suite 1000, Washington, D.C. 20036
(202/296-3923)

The Distinguished Service Award annually honors an American citizen for notable contributions to national defense and the preservation of American constitutional liberties. A selection committee studies the records of accomplishment and selects the winner of the gold medallion and scroll.

1963 Sen. Barry Goldwater
1964 Sen. J. Strom Thurmond
1965 Commander Copley, Copley Press
1966 Gen. Lewis B. Hershey
1967 Francis Cardinal Spellman
1968 Sen. John Stennis
1969 Gen. William C. Westmoreland
1970 Gen. Lyman L. Lemnitzer
1971 Adm. Thomas H. Moorer
1972 F. Edward Hebert, Member of Congress
1973 Richard M. Nixon
1974 Gen. Harold K. Johnson
1975 Gen. George S. Brown
1976 James R. Schlesinger (Dept. of Energy)
1977 Willard F. Rockwell, Jr., Chairman, Rockwell International

All-America City Awards
NATIONAL MUNICIPAL LEAGUE
47 E. 68th., New York, N.Y. 10021 (212/535-5700)

The All-America City Awards are given annually to cities for community improvement through citizen action. Cities submit entry forms describing community projects, which are reviewed by staff and by two impartial panels of experts in citizen organization and community development. The winners are awarded citations plus special recognition in the media.

1949

Bayonne, N.J.	Boston, Mass.
Cincinnati, Ohio	Cleveland, Ohio
Des Moines, Iowa	Grand Rapids, Mich.
Philadelphia, Pa.	Pittsburgh, Pa.
Poughkeepsie, N.Y.	San Antonio, Tex.
Worcester, Mass.	

1950

Cincinnati, Ohio
Kansas City, Mo.
Montgomery County, Md.
Phoenix, Ariz.
Richmond, Va.
Youngstown, Ohio

Hartford, Conn.
Montclair, N.J.
New Orleans, La.
Portland, Me.
Toledo, Ohio

1951

Atlanta, Ga.

Boston, Mass.
Dayton, Ohio
Kansas City, Mo.
Pawtucket, R.I.
San Antonio, Tex.

Asheville-Buncombe Co., N.C.
Columbia, S.C.
Kalamazoo, Mich.
Mount Vernon, Ill.
Philadelphia, Pa.

1952

Torrance, Calif.
Worcester, Mass.
Setauket, N.Y.
Pawtucket, R.I.
Houston, Tex.
Richmond, Va.

Daytona Beach, Fla.
Kansas City, Mo.
Wilkes-Barre, Pa.
Columbia, S.C.
San Antonio, Tex.

1953

Richmond, Calif.
Park Forest, Ill.
Shreveport, La.
De Soto, Mo.
Scranton, Pa.
Port Angeles, Wash.

Daytona Beach, Fla.
Peoria, Ill.
Flint, Mich.
Canton, Ohio
Petersburg, Va.

1954

Maricopa County, Ariz.
Modesto, Calif.
Chicago, Ill.
Rockville, Md.
Mexico, Mo.
Warren, Ohio

Decatur, Ark.
Pueblo, Colo.
Rock Island, Ill.
Richfield, Minn.
Newark, N.J.

1955

Phenix City, Ala.
Savannah, Ga.
Joliet, Ill.
Port Huron, Mich.
Cambridge, Ohio
Bellevue, Wash.

Riverside, Calif.
Bloomington, Ill.
St. Paul, Minn.
Grand Island, Neb.
Reading, Pa.

1956

Anchorage, Alas.
Torrance, Calif.
St. Louis, Mo.
Laurinburg, N.C.
Altus, Okla.
Tacoma, Wash.

Oakland, Calif.
Elgin, Ill.
Springfield, Mo.
Zanesville, Ohio
Brattleboro, Vt.

1957

Albuquerque, N.M.
Galesburg, Ill.
Miami-Dade County, Fla.
Neosho, Mo.
Philadelphia, Pa.
Yankton, S.D.

Clarksburg, W.Va.
Ketchikan, Alas.
Middletown, Ohio
Omaha, Neb.
Vancouver, Wash.

1958

Bloomington, Ind.
Granite City, Ill.

Columbus, Ohio
Hayden, Ariz.

Highland Park, Ill.
Leadville, Colo.
Phoenix, Ariz.
Westport, Conn.

Huntington, W.Va.
New Haven, Conn.
Sheridan, Wyo.

1959

Alton, Ill.
East St. Louis, Ill.
Lamar, Colo.
San Juan, P.R.
Seattle, Wash.
Winston-Salem, N.C.

De Soto, Mo.
Fargo, N.D.
Norfolk, Va.
Santa Fe Springs, Calif.
Vallejo, Calif.

1960

Bloomington, Minn.
East Providence, R.I.
Town of Las Vegas, N.M.
Radford, Va.
Salem, Ore.
Worcester, Mass.

Decatur, Ill.
Grand Rapids, Mich.
Marin County, Calif.
Richland, Wash.
San Jose, Calif.

1961

Anacortes, Wash.
Galveston, Tex.
Independence, Mo.
Milton-Freewater, Ore.
Salisbury, N.C.
Wichita, Kans.

Falls Church, Va.
Hartford, Conn.
Lynwood, Calif.
Rockville, Md.
Sioux City, Iowa

1962

Allentown, Pa.
Boston, Mass.
Dade County, Fla.
Grand Junction, Colo.
Knoxville, Tenn.
San Diego, Calif.

Bartlesville, Okla.
Chattanooga, Tenn.
Grafton, W.Va.
High Point, N.C.
Quincy, Ill.

1963

Alexandria, Va.
Gastonia, N.C.
Minneapolis, Minn.
Roseville, Calif.
Sidney, Ohio
Woodstock, Ill.

Aztec, N.M.
Louisville, Ky.
Oil City, Pa.
Seward, Alas.
Woodbridge, N.J.

1964

Bluefield, W.Va.
Fort Worth, Tex.
Hazleton, Pa.
Keene, N.H.
South Portland, Me.
Winston-Salem, N.C.

Columbia, S.C.
Green Bay, Wisc.
Hopkinsville, Ky.
Niles, Ill.
White Bear Lake, Minn.

1965

Anchorage, Alas.
Florence, S.C.
Michigan City, Ind.
Ogallala, Neb.
Seward, Alaska
Valdez, Alaska
Worcester, Mass.

Flat River, Mo.
La Crosse, Wisc.
Mount Vernon, Ohio
Pikeville, Ky.
Trenton, N.J.
Wilmington, N.C.

1966

Ann Arbor, Mich.
Cohoes, N.Y.
Greensboro, N.C.
Peoria, Ill.
Presque Isle, Me.
Seattle, Wash.

Clearfield, Pa.
Detroit, Mich.
Malden, Mass.
Pinellas Co., Fla.
Richmond, Va.

1967

Auburn, Me.
Fresno, Calif.
Hickory, N.C.
Leavenworth, Wash.
South Bend, Ind.
Wheaton, Ill.

Cape Girardeau, Mo.
Grand Island, Neb.
Laurinburg, N.C.
Royal Oak, Mich.
Tupelo, Miss.

1968

Charlotte, N.C.
Danville, Ky.
Fairbanks, Alas.
New Albany, Ind.
San Diego, Calif.
Snyder, Tex.

Cottage Grove, Ore.
Edinburg, Tex.
Jacksonville, Fla.
Saginaw, Mich.
Savannah, Ga.

1969

Asheville, N.C.
Cuero, Tex.
Eugene, Ore.
Martinsville, Va.
Rock Hill, S.C.
Springfield, Ill.

Borger, Tex.
El Paso, Tex.
Kalamazoo, Mich.
Maryville, Mo.
Rocky Mount, N.C.

1970

Ardmore, Okla.
Bloomfield, Conn.
Enfield, Conn.
Gainesville, Fla.
Lakeland, Fla.
Shelby, N.C.

Birmingham, Ala.
Dallas, Tex.
Fitchburg, Mass.
Indianapolis, Ind.
Lumberton, N.C.

1971

Beloit, Wisc.
Chickasha, Okla.
Lowell, Mass.
Placentia, Calif.
Twin Cities, Minn.

Carbondale, Ill.
Jamaica, N.Y.
North Branford, Conn.
Santa Fe Springs, Calif.

1972

Chewelah, Wash.
Hampton, Va.
Modesto, Calif.
St. Petersburg, Fla.
Verdigre, Neb.
Wilson, N.C.

Erie, Pa.
Johnstown, Pa.
Poplar Bluff, Mo.
Somerville, Mass.
Wilmington, Del.

1973

Albion, Mich.
LaHabra, Calif.
Lexington, Neb.
North Adams, Mass.
St. Cloud, Minn.

Jameston, N.Y.
Lewistown, Pa.
Macon, Mo.
Port Arthur, Tex.
Tulsa, Okla.

1974

Allentown, Pa.
Fall River, Mass.
Grand Prairie, Tex.
Pontiac, Mich.
South El Monte, Calif.
Spokane, Wash.

Excelsior Springs, Mo.
Gardner, Mass.
Norfolk, Neb.
Raleigh, N.C.
Spencer, W.Va.
Wooster, Ohio

1975

Cleveland Heights, Ohio
Harbor Springs, Mich.
Montebello, Calif.
Plainfield, N.J.
San Pablo, Calif.

Frederick, Md.
Marshall, Tex.
Oak Park, Ill.
Portsmouth, Va.
Toccoa, Ga.

1976

Anderson, Ind.
Danville, Va.
Newton, Mass.
Rockville, Md.
Tarboro, N.C.

Baltimore, Md.
Des Moines, Iowa
Park Forest, Ill.
San Bernardino, Calif.
Union, N.J.

1977

Anniston, Ala.
Cleveland Heights, Ohio
Dennis, Mass.
Lincoln, Neb.
Mankato, Minn.
Ottumwa, Iowa

Charleston, S.C.
Dayton, Ohio
Duluth, Minn.
Madison, Wisc.
Oklahoma City, Okla.
Ravenna, Neb.

Award of Valor

NATIONAL COLLEGIATE ATHLETIC ASSOCIATION
Box 1906, Shawnee Mission, Kans. 66222 (913/384-3220)

The Award of Valor, which consists of a medal, is awarded as merited to any current or former intercollegiate varsity letterman from an NCAA school who has averted or minimized potential disaster by courageous action in a non-military situation.

1973 Ursinus College Basketball Team—Robert E. Cattell, William J. Downy, Warren Fry, (head coach), Robert Handwerk, (assistant coach), George P. Kinek, Jack S. Messenger, Norman Reichenback, (trainer), Randy D. Stubits, Thomas E. Sturgeon, and Michael C. Weston
Charles C. Driesell, University of Maryland
William Jeffrey Miller, University of Texas, Arlington
1974-76 No awards
1977 Dwayne A. Wright, St. Mary's of California

Charles Evans Hughes Medallion

NATIONAL CONFERENCE OF CHRISTIANS AND JEWS
43 W. 57th St., New York, N.Y. 10019 (212/688-7530)

The Charles Evans Hughes Medallion, accompanied by a hand-lettered scroll, is presented annually for "courageous leadership in governmental, civic and humanitarian affairs." The conference executive board selects the recipient.

1965 Gov. Edmund (Pat) G. Brown, California
Gov. Leroy Collins, Florida
Gov. Nelson A. Rockefeller, New York
Gov. George Romney, Michigan
1966 General of the Army Dwight D. Eisenhower
1967 Harry S. Truman
Sen. Edward W. Brooke
Paul H. Douglas
1968 Adm. Lewis L. Strauss, (Ret.)
John W. Gardner
Mayor Ivan Allen, Jr.
1969 Chief Justice Earl Warren, (Ret.)
1970 Constance Baker Motley
Rev. Theodore M. Hesburgh
1971 Gen. Lucius D. Clay, (Ret.)
Associate Justice Tom C. Clark, (Ret.)
Walter E. Washington

1972 Ambassador Jerome H. Holland
1973 Secretary of State Henry A. Kissinger
1974 David Rockefeller
1975 Brooks Hays
      Linwood Holton
      Ambassador Robert D. Murphy
1976 John D. deButts
1977 Betty Ford
      Gerald R. Ford

James Forrestal Memorial Award

NATIONAL SECURITY INDUSTRIAL
ASSOCIATION
740 Fifteenth St. NW, Washington, D.C. 20005
(202/393-3620)

The James Forrestal Memorial Award, consisting of a
gold medal and citation, is "given annually to the individual who most effectively applied the concept of a
continuing close-working partnership between industry and government in the interest of national
security." The Forrestal Award Selection Committee
chooses the winner for nominations by member companies of the organization.

1954 Dwight David Eisenhower, President of the United
      States
1955 Gen. David Sarnoff, Chairman of the Board, Radio
      Corp. of America
1956 Gen. Alfred M. Gruenther, Supreme Allied Com-
      mander, Europe
1957 Arthur W. Radford, Chairman, Joint Chiefs of Staff
1958 Mervin J. Kelley, President, Bell Telephone
      Laboratories
1959 Wilfred J. McNeil, Assistant Secretary of Defense
      Donald A. Quarles, Deputy Secretary of Defense
1960 Gen. N.F. Twining, Chairman Joint Chiefs of Staff
1961 Adm. Arleigh A. Burke, Chief of Naval Operations
1962 Gen. Lauris Norstad, Supreme Allied Commander,
      Europe
1963 Robert S. McNamara, Secretary of Defense
1964 Gen. Curtis E. LeMay, Chief of Staff, U.S. Air Force
1965 Vice Adm. William F. Raborn, Jr., Director, Polaris
      Project
1966 H. Mansfield Horner, Chairman of the Board, United
      Aircraft Corp.
1967 William M. Allen, Chairman of the Board, The Boeing
      Co.
1968 Richard B. Russell, U.S. Senator from Georgia
1969 John S. Foster, Jr., Director, Defense Research and
      Engineering
1970 L. Mendel Rivers, Chairman, Committee on Armed
      Services, U.S. House of Representatives
1971 David Packard, Deputy Secretary of Defense
1972 James S. McDonnell, Chairman of the Board,
      McDonnell Douglas Corp.
1973 Adm. Thomas H. Moorer, Chairman, Joint Chiefs of
      Staff
1974 John C. Stennis, Chairman, Armed Services Commit-
      tee, U.S. Senate
1975 T.A. Wilson, Chairman and Chief Executive Officer,
      The Boeing Co.
1976 George A. Mahon, Chairman, Appropriations Com-
      mittee, U.S. House of Representatives

1977 Vice Adm. Levering Smith, Office, U.S. Navy Direc-
      tor, Strategic Systems Project

Museum Medal

NETHERLANDS GOVERNMENT
The Hague, The Netherlands

The Museum Medal (Museummedaille) is given as merited to those who have benefited art and scientific col-
lections open to the public. Gold, silver and bronze
medals are awarded as tokens of recognition upon
recommendation and consultation with the State Committee for Museums. All awards are not given every
year.

GOLD MEDAL
1891 W.G.A.C. Christan
1900 F. Uldall
1901 Sir Henry Howard
1908 Mohamed Siranoedin
1911 Ch. L.J. Palmer v.d. Broek
1913 A. Mauritz
1916 The London family
1920 A.J. Gooszen
      C.P.D. Pape
1922 J.P. van der Schilden
1923 M.L. Drucker-Fraser
      F.G. Waller
1925 de Wed. de Basel-Oorschot
1926 Ir. C. Hofstede de Groot
      J.H. Holwerda
      A.J.E.A. Bik
      J.Th. de Visser
1930 Eduina van Heek-Erving
1931 Princess de Croy, nee Countess de l'Espine
1932 D.G. van Beuningen
      W.J.M. d'Ablaing
1933 E. Heldring
1934 J.G. de Bruyn-Van der Leeuw
1935 Edwin van Rath
      H.E.L.J. Kroller-Muller
      H.E. van Gelder
1937 P. Boendermaker
1938 W. van de Verm
      Kaichiro Netsu
1939 H.E. ten Cate
1940 E.A. van Beresteyn
      H.K. Westendorp
1946 J.K. van der Haagen
      P.A. Regnault
1947 J.C. Bierens de Haan
      W. Martin
      I.S. Scholton
1953 J.H. van Heek
      Henry v.d. Velde
1954 Fritz Lugt
      N. Ottema
1957 J. Lugt-Klever
1960 P. Sybrandy
1964 R.M.A. Willemsen-Widdershoven
1966 Joh. G. Wertheim
1970 Ir. V.W. van Gogh
1972 C.H. van der Leeuw
      L.R.J. Ridder van Rappard

1974   Frank D. Robson
       F.J.E. van Lennep
1975   J.G. van Gelder
       D.W.F. Langelaan
1976   Netherlands Museum Society

SILVER MEDAL

1906   J.N.A. Panken
1914   P. van Hulstijn
1915   W. Zweerts de Jongh
1919   J.A. Saurel
       J.L. Cadet-Kempers
       P.F.T. Van Veen
1920   C.W. Bruinvis
       N.J.A.P.H. van Es
       F.J.G. ten Raa
       H.A. le Bron de Vexela
       A.E. Brinckmann
       P. Muller Heymer
1921   H.M. Werner
       J.S. Goekoop de Jongh
1922   J. Hoynck van Papendrecht
1923   G.M. Kam
       T.A. Boeree
1924   W. Spijer
       A. Baron van Aerssen Beyeren van Voshol
1925   R. Magnee de Horn
       J.J.H. Sieben
1926   H.J. Voskuil
       H.J.S. Terstappen
1927   Pangeran Hario Hadiwidjojo
1928   J. Valckenier Suringar
       J.G. Kist
1929   D.S. van Zuiden
1931   J.A.H. Alexander
       H. van Oort van Lauwenrecht
1933   W. van Rijn
       A. Averkamp
1935   P.G. van Tienhoven
1936   L.A. Springer
       Eugene Stiels
       Pangeran Ario Poerbonagoro
1937   Kaspar   Freiherr   von   Furstenberg-Kortling-
       hausen
       L.C.F. Engelen
1938   J.M. Somer
       D.L. Warsinck
1947   M.P.T. van Mastenbroek-Wellsted
       C.A. van Woelderen
1948   E.L.L. Colin
       C.A. Crommelin
       C.J. van der Klaauw
1949   A. Preston Pearce
1950   J.J. Vost tot Nederveen Cappel
1952   J.B. Bernik
       K. Tinholt
1953   H. Muller
       J.R. Schuiling
       C.F. Venema
1954   J.J.H.H. Asselberghs
       W.F. Bax
       M.J. van Sambeek
1955   C. Eisneo
1956   D.H. Huygen
1957   H.K. Remmers
1958   H.A. Fonteyn-Kuypers
       H. van Hoogdalen
       H.M.A.F. Six

1959   C. Franssen
       D.J. Kamminga
1960   R. Wartena
       P.J. Yperlaan
1961   C.B. Nicolas
       H.S. Christoffelsz
1962   J.M. de Nooyer
       B.W. Schot
1963   J.W.G.H.M. Huysmans
       Ir. J. Struik Dalm
       A.M. Sustring
1965   D. Barneveld
1968   D. Fledderus
1969   E.D. van Wijngaarden
       F. G. de Wilde
1970   General Hoefer Military Museum, Leyden
       H.J. Feyfer
       F.E. Feyfer-Teutelink
1971   C.E. Smit-Dyserinck
       Pater J.B. van Croonenburg
1972   J.J.A. Jongenelen
       H. Offerhaus
       A. Komter
       E.J. Nieuwenhuijs
1975   J. Zibrandtsen
1976   W. Stroman
       P.C. van den Berg

BRONZE MEDAL

1930   H. de Jongh
1931   F. Bloemen
       C.J. Kortenbach
1953   A. Hollander
1955   S.B. Slipjer
1960   H. Boon
       J.G.C.C. Hendriks
       O. Koster

ASPO Medal
Planner of the Year Award

AMERICAN SOCIETY OF PLANNING OFFICIALS
1313 E. 60th St., Chicago, Ill. 60637 (312/947-2560)

The ASPO Medal is awarded annually for continual leadership and outstanding contribution in the field, with special consideration for non-professionals and professionals in other fields. The silver medal was designed by sculptor John Amore. A three-member committee nominates the winner for approval by the board of directors.

1949   **Harold Buttenheim,** In tribute of 40th anniversary as
       editor of *The American City*
1950   **No award**
1951   **No award**
1952   **Lawson Purdy,** Lawyer, for developing zoning princi-
       ples and techniques
       Frank B. Williams, Lawyer, for major contributions
       in drafting New York Zoning Resolution of 1916, the
       nation's first comprehensive zoning ordinance
1953   **Edward H. Bennett,** Architect and city planner, pion-
       eer planner (e.g., 1905 San Francisco plan and 1906
       Chicago plan)
       Louis Brownlow, Public administrator on various na-
       tional committees and contributor to planning and
       zoning literature

1954 Elizabeth Herlihy, Planner, for 40-year career in Massachusetts
Harlean James, Executive Secretary of American Planning and Civic Assn.
Katherine McNamara, Librarian, for 40 years' service to planning and landscape architecture library at Harvard University and lecturer in city planning department
1955 Clarence Stein, Architect, author and civic designer
1956 No award
1957 Benjamin Kizer, Lawyer, influential citizen, for service to planning boards in the Northwest
1958 John Ihlder, Planner, especially in the field of good housing
1959 Walter H. Blucher, Planner, ASPO Executive Director and consultant for 25 years
1960 Sir Frederic Osborn, Planner, for advocacy of greenbelts and new towns
1961 Francis A. Pitkin, Planner, for outstanding role in state planning
1962 Harold Osborne, Engineer and municipal official, for pioneering contributions in telephone communications and second career in municipal and regional planning
1963 L. Perry Cookingham, City planner, for imaginative planning and leadership
Hugh R. Pomeroy, Planner, for 37-year career in planning, zoning, housing and government
1964 Harland Bartholomew, Planner, in tribute of his unparalleled career as head of a planning agency, consulting firm, chairman of the National Capitol Planning Commission and professor
1965 Lewis Mumford, Author and critic, for illuminations of potentials and problems of cities
Catherine Bauer Wurster, Planner, for contributions to national policy for housing and planning
1966 Ernest J. Bohn, Legislator, administrator, planning commissioner and presidential advisor, for pioneering policy in law of housing and slum clearance
Sears-Roebuck Foundation, In tribute to leadership in initiating a large-scale program of financial assistance for education of planners and other projects
1967 Tracy Augur, Planner, for urban, regional, national and international planning as public official, private consultant and author
Rexford Guy Tugwell, Planner, public official, educator and author
1968 Dennis O'Harrow, "The Conscience of the Profession" for contributions to literature and techniques of planning
1969 Fairfield Osborn and The Conservation Foundation, For pioneering and continued influence to expand the concept of conservation
1970 Charles Abrams, Planner, author, lawyer and public servant
1971 Charles McKim Norton, For major influence on New York region and on the concepts and laws of regional planning during 31 years as leader in the Regional Plan Assn. of New York
1972 Rene Dubos, Scientist and humanist, in tribute to his writings on effects of environment on human life
Charles W. Eliot II, Planner, for bridging gap between early landscape architecture and later city and regional planning
Ladislas Segoe, Planner, for rare quality of his products during 50 years of practice, including directing the National Resources Committee landmark report on American cities

1973 No award
1974 Robert E. Simon, For value and objectives embodied in plan of Reston, Va., a symbol of aspiration for the contemporary new town
William L.C. Wheaton, Planner and teacher
1975 Hans Blumenfeld, Planner, for contributions to planning analysis
T.J. Kent, Jr., Planner, for work on the general urban plan, political and planning practice, and planning education
John T. Howard, Planner, for work on the general urban plan, political and planning practice, and planning education
John R. Parker, For leadership in planning education and teaching
1976 No award
1977 No award

The Planner of the Year Award is given annually to honor specific achievements in advancing the field of planning, as recognized and evaluated by the groups affected. A three- to five-member committee of professionals and citizen representatives selects the recipient of the certificate from nominations made by ASPO members. Winners may be ASPO members or nonmembers, individuals or groups.

1974 Frank G. Colley, Citizen-planner of Meeker, Colo., for vision and leadership in public awareness in region threatened by oil-shale development
Ralph D. Smith, Citizen-planner of Boston for leading and validating a neighborhood voice, initiating plans and implementing techniques to upgrade inner-city development
1975 Anthony H. Mason, Planning commissioner of Phoenix for inspiring the confidence upon which an independent planning commission depends
1976 No award
1977 No award

Daniel Webster Award
INTERNATIONAL PLATFORM ASSOCIATION
2564 Berkshire Rd., Cleveland Heights, Ohio 44106
(216/932-0505)

The Daniel Webster Award, which consists of an engraved bowl, is given annually for the speech judged to deal with the most important problem facing the United States and its citizens.

1976 Glenn Seaborg
1977 Kenneth H. Cooper

Margaret Sanger Award
PLANNED PARENTHOOD FEDERATION OF AMERICA
810 Seventh Ave., New York, N.Y. 10019 (212/541-7800)

The $1,000 Margaret Sanger Award is presented annually for service to the cause of family planning and population control. The award includes a statue and a citation. The Margaret Sanger Awards Committee selects the winner.

1966 Gen. William H. Draper
Carl G. Hartman
Lyndon B. Johnson
Rev. Martin Luther King, Jr.
1967 John D. Rockefeller III
1968 Ernest Gruening
1969 Lord Caradon
1970 Joseph D. Tydings
1971 Louis M. Hellman
1972 Alan F. Guttmacher
1973 Sarah Lewit
Christopher Tietze
1974 Harriet F. Pilpel
1975 Cass Canfield
1976 John Rock
1977 Bernard Berelson

Henry Medal

SMITHSONIAN INSTITUTION
1000 Jefferson Dr. SW, Washington, D.C. 20560
(202/628-4422)

The Henry Medal, which is of gold, is given as merited with an honorarium for distinguished service, achievement or contributions to the prestige and growth of the Smithsonian Institution. The board of regents bestows this honor.

1967 David E. Finley, First director, National Gallery of Art
1968 Frank A. Taylor, Smithsonian's Director General of Museums and Director, United States National Museum
1970 Charles G. Abbot, For 16 years, Secretary of the Smithsonian, and prior to that, Director of the Smithsonian Astrophysical Observatory and founder and Director of the Radiation Biology Laboratory
1973 Fred L. Whipple, Director, Smithsonian Astrophysical Observatory
Edward K. Thompson, Editor, *Smithsonian* magazine
1975 John Nicholas Brown, Citizen regent of the Smithsonian for 18 years
1976 T. Dale Stewart, Smithsonian Anthropologist Emeritus
Martin H. Moynihan, Founder and former director, Smithsonian Tropical Research Institute
1977 Hubert H. Humphrey, U.S. Senator, and former Vice President and Smithsonian regent

Gold Medal

NATIONAL INSTITUTE OF SOCIAL SCIENCES
150 Amsterdam Ave., New York, N.Y. 10023 (212/787-1000)

The Institute's Gold Medal is given annually to distinguished individuals—usually Americans—who have served their country and humanity in an outstanding capacity. The medals committee selects and the president and board of trustees approve the winners.

1913

Archer M. Huntington	Samuel L. Parrish
William H. Taft	

1914

Charles W. Eliot	Gen. George W. Goethals
Abraham Jacobi	Henry Fairfield Osborn

1915

Luther Burbank	Andrew Carnegie

1916

Robert Bacon	Mrs. H. Hartley Jenkins
Adolph Lewisohn	

1917

George W. Crile	Surgeon-Gen. William Gorgas
John Purroy Mitchell	Michael Idvorsky Pupin

1918

Henry P. Davison	Herbert C. Hoover
William J. Mayo	

1919

Samuel Gompers	William Henry Welch

1920

Alexis Carrel	H. Holbrook Curtis
Sir Wilfred T. Grenfell	Harry Pratt Judson

1921

Charles Frederick Chandler	Calvin Coolidge
Marie Curie	Cleveland H. Dodge

1923

Charles B. Davenport	Sir Auckland Geddes
Emory R. Johnson	Jules J. Jusserand
John D. Rockefeller, Sr.	

1924

Walter Hampden	Charles E. Hughes
Mrs. C. Lorillard Spencer	

1925

Mrs. E.H. Harriman	William H. Park
Elihu Root	

1926

S. Parkes Cadman	Clarence Hungerford Mackay
Stephen Tying Mather	Mary Schenck Woolman

1927

George Pierce Baker	Walter Damrosch
Harry Emerson Fosdick	Adolph S. Ochs

1928

Liberty Hyde Bailey	Robert W. deForest
Willis R. Whitney	

1929

Valeria Langeloth	Rose Livingston
John D. Rockefeller, Jr.	James T. Shotwell
Daniel Willard	

1930

Anna Billings Gallup	George R. Minot

William Lyon Phelps

1931
Grace Abbott
Mrs. Grace Goodhue
Coolidge

1932
Edward E. Allen
William C. Redfield

1933
Newton D. Baker
Evangeline Booth

1934
Eleanor Robson Belmont
Samuel Seabury

1935
Cornelius N. Bliss
Carter Glass

1936
Nicholas Murray Butler
William Edwin Hall

1937
James Rowland Angell
J. Edgar Hoover

1938
John W. Davis
Dorothy Thompson

1939
Martha Berry
George Wharton Pepper

1940
Carrie Chapman Catt
Wendell L. Willkie

1941
Norman H. Davis
Alfred E. Smith

1942
Rufus B. von KleinSmid
Donald M. Nelson

1943
Madame Chiang Kai-shek
Cdr. Mildred H. McAffee,
USNR

1944
Bernard M. Baruch
James G.K. McClure

1945
Vannevar Bush
William Mather Lewis

Nathan Straus

Richard Clarke Cabot
Frank B. Kellogg

James Howell Post
Gerard Swope

Clifford W. Beers

Walter B. Cannon

Harvey Cushing
George E. Vincent

Mrs. Harrison Eustis
J. Pierpont Morgan

Mrs. Edward W. Bok
Wesley Clair Mitchell

Walter S. Gifford

William Church Osborn

James E. West

Mrs. J. Borden Harriman

Anne O'Hare McCormick

Edwin Grant Conklin
Juan Terry Trippe

Mrs. Henry Pomeroy
Davison

Mrs. John Henry
Hammond

1946
Virginia C. Gildersleeve
Edwin R. Stettinius. Jr.

Robert Moses

1947
Katharine F. Lenroot
Thomas J. Watson, Sr.

Edward Johnson

1948
Georgiana Farr Sibley
Warren R. Austin

Basil O'Connor

1949
Lillian M. Gilbreth
General of the Army
George Catlett Marshall

Alfred P. Sloan. Jr.

1950
Henry Bruere
Gen. Carlos P. Romulo

Sarah Gibson Blanding

1951
Bayard Foster Pope
John Foster Dulles
General of the Army
Douglas MacArthur

Paul G. Hoffman
Lewis W. Douglas

1952
Harold Raymond Medina
John Jay McCloy

Helen Adams Keller
Robert Abercrombie
Lovett

1953
E. Roland Harriman
Charles F. Kettering

Oveta Culp Hobby

1954
Howard A. Rusk
Gen. Walter Bedell Smith

Mrs. Lytle Hull

1955
Samuel D. Leidesdorf
Henry Cabot Lodge, Jr.

Elizabeth Luce Moore

1956
Clarence G. Michalis
Henry T. Heald

Mary Pillsbury Lord

1957
William F. Graham, Jr.
Gen. Alfred M. Gruenther

Clare Boothe Luce

1958
Marian Anderson
Robert Bernerd Anderson

James R. Killian, Jr.
Herbert Hoover

1959
Helen Hayes
Jonas E. Salk

Laurance S. Rockefeller

1960
Sir Rudolf Bing
Millicent C. McIntosh

Gilbert Darlington
Grayson L. Kirk

1961
Marie L. Bullock
William C. Menninger

Karl Menninger
Edward Durell Stone

1962

Mary I. Bunting	Ralph J. Bunche
John W. Gardner	Gen. Lucius D. Clay

1963

Arthur H. Dean	Katharine E. McBride
Nathan M. Pusey	Frank Stanton

1964

Margaret Chase Smith	Dean Rusk
Frederick R. Kappel	Bob Hope

1965

Dorothy Buffam Chandler	Gen. Maxwell D. Taylor
James A. Perkins	

1966

Lady Bird Johnson	Francis Cardinal Spellman
David Sarnoff	Keith Funston
Danny Kaye	

1967

John D. Rockefeller, 3rd	Nelson A. Rockefeller
Laurance S. Rockefeller	Winthrop Rockefeller
David Rockefeller	The Rockefeller Family

1968

Anne Morrow Lindbergh	Ralph W. Sockman
Eugene R. Black	Charles A. Lindbergh

1969

Lady Jackson	Col. Frank Borman
Rev. Theodore M. Hesburgh	Lester B. Pearson

1970

Katharine Graham	Gen. Lauris Norstad
Eric Sevareid	William P. Rogers. Jr.

1971

Joan Ganz Cooney	Charles H. Malik
Arthur K. Watson	Thomas J. Watson, Jr.

1972

George Bush	Henry A. Kissinger
Mrs. Laurance Rockefeller	Rev. Fulton J. Sheen

1973

Brig. Gen. John T. Flynn	Jean Kerr
Rev. Paul Moore, Jr.	Elliott L. Richardson

1974

Col. Peter M. Dawkins	Golda Meir
George P. Schultz	Roy Wilkins

1975

Nancy Hanks	William E. Simon
Donald K. Slayton	Lowell Thomas
Lowell Thomas, Jr.	

1976

Barry M. Goldwater	Norman Vincent Peale
John J. McCloy	Barbara Walters
Peter J. Peterson	

1977

Anne Armstrong	Sir Edwin Leather, Bermuda
Mr. and Mrs. Clifford Robertson	William Rockefeller
	William B. Walsh

Secretary's Award
Award for Heroism
Award for Valor

U.S. DEPARTMENT OF STATE
Awards Office, Washington, D.C. 20520 (202/655-4000)

The Secretary's Award, which consists of a plaque, is given annually to individuals in government service abroad who have performed official duties at the sacrifice of personal health or life. The Department Awards Committee selects the recipients. (* Posthumous)

1968-70 Robert D. Handy*, Vietnam
    Don Mitrione*, Vietnam
    Donald M. Sladkin, Vietnam
1970-72 Joseph A. Smith*, Vietnam
1972-73 Thomas M. Gompertz*, Vietnam
    Robert R. Little*, Vietnam
    Jeffrey S. Lundstedt*, Vietnam
    George Curtis Moore*, Khartoum, Sudan
    Cleo A. Noel, Jr.*, Khartoum, Sudan
    Thomas W. Ragsdale*, Vietnam
1973-74 Steven A. Haukness, Vietnam
    Roger P. Davies*, Nicosia, Cyprus
    John P. Egan*, Cordoba, Spain
    Alfred A. Laun III, Cordoba, Spain
    Antoinette M. Varnava*, Nicosia, Cyprus
1974-75 Francis E. Meloy, Jr.*, Beirut, Lebanon
    Robert O. Waring*, Beirut, Lebanon
    Zohair Moghrabi*, Beirut, Lebanon
1976 No award
1977 No award

The Award for Heroism, which consists of a plaque, is given annually to individuals in government service abroad for performance of an act of heroism without regard for personal safety, related to his or her official duties or not. The Department Awards Committee selects the recipients. (* Posthumous)

1968-70 Hugh G. Appling, Vietnam
    Paul E. Barbian, Vietnam
    David L. Buckles, Vietnam
    Francis B. Corry, Vietnam
    Thomas W. Culbertson, Vietnam
    Curtis C. Cutter, Porto Alegre, Brazil
    Frederick D. Elfers, Vietnam
    Peter F. Hurst, Vietnam
    Terry L. Lambacher, Vietnam
    Thomas D. Maher, Vietnam
    Kenneth R. Mahony, Vietnam
    Edward L. Merseth, Vietnam
    Hawthorne Q. Mills, Vietnam
    John S. Powley, Vietnam
    Thomas J. Rice, Frankfurt, Federal Republic of Germany
    Stephen H. Rimmer, Vietnam
    Robert E. Runyon, Vietnam
    William H. Saunders, Vietnam
    Edward W. Schaefer, Mogadishu, Somalia
    Samuel L. Turner, Vietnam
    Loring A. Waggoner, Vietnam
    John C. Ziegler, Vietnam

1970-72 Eugenia Antonescu, Bucharest, Rumania
  William A. Levis, Vientiane, Laos
  Sanda Pansitescu, Bucharest, Rumania
  Charles E. Sothan, Vietnam
  Angela Voicu, Bucharest, Rumania
1972-73 No award
1973-74 No award
1974-75 Barbara A. Hutchinson, Santo Domingo, Dominican Republic
  Ronald A. Webb*, Cambridge, England
1975-76 No award
1976-77 Bernard A. Johnson, New York
  George R. Mitchell, New York

The Award for Valor, which consists of a plaque, is given annually to individuals in government service abroad for performance under dangerous circumstances that required personal bravery and perseverance to complete an assignment. The Department Awards Committee selects the recipients. (* Posthumous)

1968-70 Group Award to the staff of 43 of the American Embassy in Amman, Jordan
1970-72 Thomas O. Brennan, Vietnam
  Martin S. Christie, Vietnam
  John Hollingsworth, Jordan
  William P. Hovis, La Paz, Bolivia
  Desaix B. Myers, Dacca, Bangladesh
  Richard B. Peterson, Vietnam
  Thomas Polgar, Buenos Aires, Argentina
  David A. Reinhardt, Vietnam
  Herbert W. Timrud, Vietnam
1972-73 Susan A. Beauvais, Vietnam
  Michael D. Benge, Vietnam
  Norman J. Brookens, Vietnam
  William A. Cole, Addis Ababa, Ethiopia
  Philip W. Manhard, Vietnam
  Douglas K. Ramsay, Vietnam
  Edward W. Sprague, Vietnam
  Richard W. Utrecht, Vietnam
  Charles E. Willis, Vietnam
1973-74 Thomas J. Barnes, Vietnam
  Henry B. Cushing, Vietnam
1974-75 Mark E. Mulvey, Nicosia, Cyprus
  Frixos Yerolemou, Nicosia Cyprus
  Group Award to American Embassy Staff, Nicosia, Cyprus
1975-76 Rached Mohamed Bahi, Tunis, Tunisia
  Ted D. Morse, Addis Ababa, Ethiopia
  Paul A. Struharik, Vietnam
  Reinaldo Vieira-Ribeiro, Hong Kong
  Group Award to Political Section (Consulate General), Asmara, Saudi Arabia
1976-77 Philip R. Cook, Jr., Nha Trang, Vietnam
  Julio Correia, Luanda, Angola
  William Dykes*, Beirut, Lebanon
  Charles Gallagher, Beirut, Lebanon
  Nicholas MacNeil, Beirut, Lebanon
  Brunson McKinley, Da Nang, Vietnam
  Horace H. Mitchell, Philadelphia
  Dough Van Nghia, Danang, Vietnam
  Kenneth N. Rogers, Angola
  Sidney T. Telford, Beirut, Lebanon

Distinguished Service Award

U.S. DEPARTMENT OF THE TREASURY
15th St. and Pennsylvania Ave., Washington, D.C. 20220
(202/376-0282)

The Distinguished Service Award is given annually for outstanding service to the Department of the Treasury by an individual or individuals not employed by the Department. The Secretary of the Treasury approves of the winners from nominees submitted. A gold medal and a certificate are presented to the recipient of the award.

1964
J. Vaughan Gary
Robert G. Rouse

1965
Frank R. Milliken

1966
William C. Decker

1967
No award

1968

Francis M. Bator	Eugene N. Beesley
Edward M. Bernstein	Roger M. Blough
Harold Boeschenstein	Charles A. Coombs
Bert S. Cross	Paul L. Davies
Frederic G. Donner	Edward R. Fried
G. Keith Funston	Thomas S. Gates, Jr.
Kermit Gordon	Walter W. Heller
Robert M. McKinney	William McChesney Martin, Jr.
Andre Mayer	Frank R. Milliken
Albert L. Nickerson	Reno Odlin
David Packard	David Rockefeller
Robert V. Roosa	Sidney J. Weinberg
Frazer B. Wilde	Henry S. Wingate

1969
Alfred Hayes
J. L. Robertson

1970
No award

1971
James M. Roche

1972-75
No awards

1976
James S. Fish

1977
Arthur M. Burns

Woman of the Year

UNITED SERVICE ORGANIZATIONS
110 E. 42nd St., New York, N.Y. 10017 (212/697-3840)

The United Service Organization annually honors a Woman of the Year at a luncheon designed as a fundraising activity for USO projects. The recipient of the award, who is presented with jewelry, is a woman who has benefited the military, either by entertaining service personnel or in another capacity. A committee, consisting of representatives of the board of directors and the USO's Women's Division, selects the Woman of the Year.

1961	Mary Martin
1962-64	No award
1965	Joan Crawford
1966	No award
1967	Martha Raye
1968	Pearl Bailey
1969	Gypsy Rose Lee
1970	No award
1971	No award
1972	Mrs. Dwight D. Eisenhower
1973	Mrs. Douglas MacArthur
1974	Helen Hayes
1975	Kitty Carlisle
1976	Mrs. Bob Hope
1977	Mrs. Gerald R. Ford

Freiherr von Stein Prize

STIFTUNG F.V.S.
Georgplatz 10, 2 Hamburg 1, Federal Republic of Germany
(Tel: 33 04 00 and 33 06 00)

The Freiherr von Stein Prize, which carries a cash award of 25,000 German marks, is now given every two years to honor public service in the Federal Republic of Germany. A jury selects the winner.

1954	Klaus von Bismarck
1955	Alfred Flender
1956	Otto A. Friedrich
1957	August Schmidt
1958	Fritz Freiherr von Babo
	Heinrich Blum
	Friedrich Greiff
1960	Alexander Rustow
1962	Kurt Hahn
1964	Gen. Johann Adolf Graf von Kielmannsegg
	Lt. Gen. Wolf Graf Baudissin
	Lt. Gen. Ulrich de Maiziere
1966	Wilhelm Kaisen
1968	President Kurt Baurichter
1970	Franz Bohm
1972	Etta Grafin Waldersee
1973	Herbert Weichmann
1974	Ludwig Erhard
	Alfred Muller-Armack
1976	Ludwig Raiser

Federal Woman's Award

FEDERAL WOMAN'S AWARD BOARD OF TRUSTEES
c/o V. Oldham, Veterans Administration, 810 Vermont Ave. NW, Washington, D.C. 20420 (202/389-2530)

The Federal Woman's Award, which consists of a medallion, a pendant and a certificate, is given annually to a female employee of the federal government for outstanding contributions to the efficiency and quality of government career service. Federal agencies, including the District of Columbia government, make nominations to the Board of Trustees of the Federal Woman's Award, the independent organization which selects six recipients for the honor. The Federal Woman's Award has been suspended.

1961 Beatrice Aitchison, Director, Transportation Research, Post Office Dept.
Ruth Elizabeth Bacon, Charge D'Affairs, American Embassy, New Zealand
Nina Kinsella, Warden, Federal Reformatory for Women
Charlotte Moore Sitterly, Physicist, Department of Commerce
Aryness Joy Wickens, Economic Adviser, Department of Labor
Rosalyn S. Yalow, Physicist and Principal Scientist, Veterans Administration Hospital, Bronx, N.Y.
1962 Katherine W. Bracken, Director, Office of Central American and Panamanian Affairs, Department of State
Margaret H. Brass, Chief, General Litigation Section, Department of Justice
Thelma B. Dunn, Head, Cancer Induction and Pathogenesis Section, Department of Health, Education and Welfare
Evelyn Harrison, Deputy Director, Bureau of Programs and Standards, U.S. Civil Service Commission
Allene R. Jeanes, Research Chemist, Department of Agriculture
Nancy Grace Roman, Chief of Astronomy and Solar Physics, National Aeronautics and Space Administration
1963 Eleanor L. Makel, Supervisory Medical Officer, Department of Health, Education and Welfare
Bessie Margolin, Associate Solicitor, Department of Labor
Katherine Mather, Chief, Petrography Section, Department of the Army
Verna C. Mohagen, Director of Personnel, Soil Conservation Service, Department of Agriculture
Blanche W. Hoyes, Air Marketing Specialist, Federal Aviation Agency
Eleanor C. Pressly, Head, Vehicles Section, National Aeronautics and Space Administration
1964 Evelyn Anderson, Research Scientist, Ames Research Center, National Aeronautics and Space Administration
Gertrude Blanch, Air Force Scientist, Wright-Patterson Air Force Base
Selene Gifford, Assistant Commissioner, Bureau of Indian Affairs
Elizabeth F. Messer, Assistant to the Deputy Director, Bureau of Retirement and Insurance, U.S. Civil Service Commission
Margaret Wolman Schwartz, Director, Office of Foreign Assets Control, Department of the Treasury
Patricia G. van Delden, Deputy Public Affairs Officer, Attache, American Embassy, U.S. Information Agency, Germany
1965 Ann Z. Caracristi, Senior Intelligence Research Analyst, National Security Agency
Elizabeth B. Drewry, Director, Franklin D. Roosevelt Library
Dorothy Morrow Gilford, Director, Mathematical Sciences Division, Department of the Navy
Carol C. Laise, Deputy Director, Office of South Asian Affairs, Department of State
Sarah E. Stewart, Head, Human Virus Studies Section, Department of Health, Education and Welfare

Penelope Hartland Thunberg, Deputy Chief, International Division, Central Intelligence Agency

1966 Fannie M. Boyls, Hearing Examiner, National Labor Relations Board

Stella E. Davis, Desk Officer for East and South Africa, U.S. Information Agency

Jocelyn R. Gill, Program Chief, National Aeronautics and Space Administration

Ida Craven Merriam, Assistant Commissioner for Research and Statistics, Department of Health, Education and Welfare

Irene Parsons, Assistant Administrator and Director of Personnel, Veterans Administration

Ruth G. Van Cleve, Director, Office of Territories, Department of the Interior

1967 Elizabeth Ann Brown, Director of the Office of the United Nations, Department of State

Barbara Moulton, Medical Officer, Federal Trade Commission

Anne Mason Roberts, Deputy Regional Administrator, New York Region, Department of Housing and Urban Development

Kathryn Grove Shipp, Research Chemist, Department of the Navy

Wilma Louise Victor, Superintendent, Intermountain Indian School, Department of the Interior

Marjorie J. Williams, Director, Pathology and Allied Sciences Service, Veterans Administration

1968 Ruth Rogan Benerito, Research Chemist and Investigations Leader, Department of Agriculture

Mabel Kunce Gibby, Clinical Psychologist and Coordinator of Counseling Psychology, Veterans Administration Hospital, Coral Gables, Fla.

Frances M. James, Chief Statistician, Council of Economic Advisors, Executive Office of the President

Ruby Grant Martin, Director, Operations Division, Office for Civil Rights, Department of Health, Education and Welfare

Lucille Farrier Stickel, Wildlife Research Biologist, Department of the Interior

Rogene L. Thompson, Supervisory Air Traffic Control Specialist and Crew Leader, Department of Transportation

Nina Bencich Woodside, Chief, Bureau of Chronic Disease Control, District of Columbia Department of Public Health

1969 Mary Hughes Budenbach, Senior Cryptologist and Deputy Group Chief, National Security Agency

Edith N. Cook, Associate Solicitor, Department of Labor

Eileen R. Donovan, Assistant Director, Office of Caribbean Affairs, Department of State

Jo Ann Smith Kinney, Supervisory Psychologist, Vision Branch, Submarine Medical Research Laboratory, Department of the Navy

Esther Christian Lawton, Assistant Director of Personnel, Department of the Treasury

Dorothy L. Starbuck, Area Field Director, Veterans Administration

1970 Jean Apgar, Research Chemist, Department of Agriculture

Sarah B. Glindmeyer, Chief, Bureau of Nursing, District of Columbia Department of Public Health

Margaret Pittman, Chief, Laboratory of Bacterial Products, Department of Health, Education and Welfare

Valerija B. Raulinaitis, Chief of Staff, Veterans Administration Hospital, Downey, Ill.

Naomi R. Sweeney, Assistant Director, Office of Legislative Reference, Bureau of the Budget

Margaret Joy Tibbetts, Deputy Assistant Secretary for European Affairs, Department of State

1971 Jeanne Wilson Davis, Staff Secretary, National Security Council

Florence Johnson Hicks, Special Assistant to the Director of Public Health, District of Columbia Dept. of Human Resources

Juanita Morris Moody, Chief, Information and Reporting Element, National Security Agency

Essie Davis Morgan, Chief, Socio-economic Rehabilitation and Staff Development, Veterans Administration

Rita M. Rapp, Subsystems Manager for Apollo Food and Personal Hygiene Items, National Aeronautics and Space Administration

Joan Raup Rosenblatt, Chief, Statistical Engineering Laboratory, Department of Commerce

1972 Lois Albro Chatham, Chief, Narcotics Addict Rehabilitation Branch, Department of Health, Education and Welfare

Phyllis Dixon Clemmons, Director, Suicide Prevention and Emergency Mental Health Consultation Service, District of Columbia Department of Human Resources

Ruth M. Davis, Director, Center for Computer Sciences and Technology, Department of Commerce

Mary Harrover Ferguson, Comptroller, Office of Naval Research and Special Assistant to the Assistant Secretary for Research and Development, Department of the Navy

Ruth Mandeville Leverton, Science Advisor, Department of Agriculture

Patricia Ann McCreedy, Public Health Physician, Vientiane, Laos (Agency for International Development)

1973 Bernice L. Bernstein, Director, Region II, Department of Health, Education and Welfare

Marguerite S. Chang, Research Chemist, Naval Ordnance Systems Command, Department of the Navy

Janet Hart, Assistant Director, Division of Supervision and Regulations, Board of Governors of the Federal Reserve System

Marilyn E. Jacox, Research Chemist, National Bureau of Standards

Isabella L. Karle, Research Physicist, Office of Naval Research, Department of the Navy

Marjorie R. Townsend, Project Manager, Small Astronomy Satellite, Goddard Space Flight Center, National Aeronautics and Space Administration

1974 Henriette D. Avram, Library of Congress

Edna A. Boorady, Agency for International Development

Roselyn Payne Epps, Physician, District of Columbia Government

Brigid Gray Leventhal, Physician, National Cancer Institute

Gladys P. Rogers, Department of State

Madge Skelly, Veterans Administration

1975 Anita F. Alpern, Assistant Commissioner, Internal Revenue Service

Beatrice J. Dvorak, Supervisory Personel Research Psychologist, Employment and Training Administration, Department of Labor

Evans Hayward, Nuclear Physicist, National Bureau of Standards, Department of Commerce

Wilda H. Martinez, Research Chemist, Department of Agriculture

Marie U. Nylen, Chief, Laboratory of Biological Structure, National Institutes of Health

Marguerite M. Rogers, Assistant Technical Director for Systems and Head, Systems Development Department, Naval Weapons Center, China Lake, Calif.

1976 **I. Blanche Bourne,** Deputy Director of Public Health, District of Columbia Department of Human Resources

Carin Ann Clauss, Associate Solicitor for Fair Labor Standards, Department of Labor

Dorothy I. Fennell, Microbiologist, Dept. of Agriculture, North Regional Research Center, Peoria, Ill.

Marion J. Finkel, Associate Director for New Drug Evaluation, Food and Drug Administration

M. Patricia Murray, Chief, Kinesiology Research Laboratory, Veterans Administration Center, Wood, Wisc.

Joyce J. Walker, Deputy Associate Director for Economics and Government, Office of Management and Budget

1977 **No award**

Contents

Sports

Related Awards

Association Progress Award
Public Recreation Award
Public Relations Award
Henry Stone Award
James E. Sullivan Memorial Award
Arthur Callins Toner, Jr. Memorial Award
Veterans Awards

AMATEUR ATHLETIC UNION OF THE UNITED STATES

3400 W. 86th St., Indianapolis, Ind. 46268 (317/297-2900)

The Association Progress Award is awarded annually to the district association showing the greatest increase in activities over the previous years.

1934 Missouri Valley Association
1935 Ozark Association
1936 Adirondack Association
1937 Oklahoma Association
1938 Southwestern Association
1939 Iowa Association
1940 Hawaiian Association
1941 Niagara Association
1942 Niagara Association
1943 Rocky Mountain Association
1944 Southeastern Association
1945 Pacific Association
1946 South Texas Association
1947 Michigan Association
1948 Central Association
1949 Central Association
1950 District of Columbia Association
1951 Georgia Association
1952 Southern Pacific Association
1953 Oklahoma Association
1954 Southern Pacific Association
1955 Florida Association
1956 Lake Erie Association
1957 Lake Erie Association
1958 Southern Pacific Association
1959 South Texas Association
1960 Montana Association
1961 Carolinas Association
1962 Southern Pacific Association
1963 Pacific Association
1964 District of Columbia Association
1965 Pacific Association
1966 Pacific Association
1967 Missouri Valley Association
1968 Pacific Association
1969 Southern Pacific Association
1970 Pacific Association
1971 Missouri Valley Association
1972 Pacific Association
1973 Lake Erie Association
1974 Indiana Association
1975 Lake Erie Association
1976 Pacific Association
1977 Pacific Association

The Public Recreation Award was established to honor the outstanding leaders, generally one man and one woman, in the field of public recreation during the year.

1963 Eugene Fuller, Florida Association

Beryl Kelly, Central Association
1964 Ben York, Florida Gold Coast Association
Dorothy Boyce, Central Association
1965 Nathan Mallison, Florida Association
Elizabeth Falbisaner, Central Association
Hertha Goedde, New Jersey Association
1966 Eugene Fuller, South Carolina Association
Dorothy Boyce, Central Association
1967 Ray Kisiah, North Carolina Association
Lucille Wilson, Central Association
1968 George Cron, New Jersey Association
Arlene Illsman, Central Association
1969 Herman Riese, Central California Association
Ethel Stevens, Central Association
1970 Ralph Hileman, Missouri Valley Association
John A. Bauer, Central Association
1971 David Scheuermann, Southern Association
Erna Wachtel, Central Association
1972 John Lawson, Missouri Valley Association
1973 George R. Hoagland, New Jersey Association
Jane Dickens, Central Association
1974 Dalby Shirley, Southern Nevada Association
Betty Baldwin, Lake Erie Association
1975 Bret McGinnis, Ohio Association
Betty Baldwin, Lake Erie Association
1976 Joseph B. Sharpless, Potomac Valley Association
1977 Morris Weissbrot, Queens, N.Y.

The Public Relations Award is awarded annually by the Public Relations Committee for outstanding public relations contribution on behalf of amateur athletes.

1966 June Fergusson
1967 George Thornber
1968 George Thornber
1969 No award
1970 No award
1971 Denny Hawkins
1972 John B. Kelly, Jr.
1973 Jane Dickens
1974 No award
1975 No award
1976 Marvin Thomas
1977 "Buck" Johnson

The AAU Media Man of the Year honors journalistic achivement.

1977 Don Hurlburt, *Arizona Republic* (Phoenix)

The Henry Stone Award is a plaque given annually to an individual for sustained contributions to the development of sport.

1968 E. K. Koiwai
1969 Joseph Fitzsimmons
1970 Yosh Uchido
1971 Thomas Dalton
1972 Tom Nagamatsu
1973 Shag Okada
1974 Frank Fullerton
1975 Wey Seng Kim
     James Takemori
1976 James Colgan
1977 No award

The James E. Sullivan Memorial Award, which consists of a trophy, is given annually to the outstanding amateur athlete in the United States, based on a ballot of the media and the AAU's board of governors from nominees selected at the organization's annual convention.

1930 Bobby Jones, Golf

1931 **Bernard Berlinger,** Track and field
1932 **James Bausch,** Track and field
1933 **Glenn Cunningham,** Track and field
1934 **Bill Bonthron,** Track and field
1935 **Lawson Little,** Golf
1936 **Glenn Morris,** Track and field
1937 **Don Budge,** Tennis
1938 **Don Lash,** Track and field
1939 **Joseph Burk,** Crew
1940 **Greg Rice,** Track and field
1941 **Leslie McMitchell,** Track and field
1942 **Cornelius Warmerdam,** Track and field
1943 **Gil Dodds,** Track and field
1944 **Ann Curtis,** Swimming
1945 **Felix Blanchard,** Football
1946 **Arnold Tucker,** Football
1947 **Jack Kelly,** Crew
1948 **Bob Mathias,** Track and field
1949 **Dick Button,** Figure skating
1950 **Fred Wilt,** Track and field
1951 **Bob Richards,** Track and field
1952 **Horace Ashenfelter,** Track and field
1953 **Sammy Lee,** Diving
1954 **Mal Whitfield,** Track and field
1955 **Harrison Dillard,** Track and field
1956 **Patricia McCormick,** Diving
1957 **Bobby Morrow,** Track and field
1958 **Glenn Davis,** Track and field
1959 **Parry O'Brien,** Track and field
1960 **Rafer Johnson,** Track and field
1961 **Wilma Rudolph,** Track and field
1962 **James Beatty,** Track and field
1963 **John Pennel,** Track and field
1964 **Don Schollander,** Swimming
1965 **Bill Bradley,** Basketball
1966 **Jim Ryun,** Track and field
1967 **Randy Matson,** Track and field
1968 **Debbie Meyer,** Swimming
1969 **Bill Toomey,** Track and field
1970 **John Kinsella,** Swimming
1971 **Mark Spitz,** Swimming
1972 **Frank Shorter,** Track and field
1973 **Bill Walton,** Basketball
1974 **Rich Wohlhuter,** Track and field
1975 **Tim Shaw,** Swimming
1976 **Bruce Jenner,** Track and field
1977 **John Naber,** Swimming

The Arthur Carling Toner, Jr. Memorial Award annually honors distinguished registration service to the Amateur Athletic Union of the United States.

1974   **Warren Emery**
1975   **Harold W. Heller**
1976   **Charles O. Roeser**
1977   **Pincus Sober**

The Veterans Award is annually presented to any individual who has served the Amateur Athletic Union at the national level for 50 years and has attained the age of 80.

1970   **Daniel J. Ferris**
       Avery Brundage
       Emil Breitkreutz
1971   **Fred Schmertz**
       Al Sandell
1972   **Mrs. E. Fullard-Leo**
1973   **Edward Rosenblum**
1974   No award
1975   **Paul Staff**
1976   **Beth Kaufman**

1977 **Harry Hainsworth**
      Ray Moore
      Mrs. Charles Ornstein

Masters Athlete of the Year (for active competitors in Masters Class)

1977 **Herb Anderson**

Athlete of the Year
ASSOCIATED PRESS
50 Rockefeller Plaza, New York, N.Y. 10020 (212/262-4000)

Sports editors of Associated Press member newspapers annually select the male and female Athlete of the Year from both professional and amateur ranks.

MEN
1931 **Pepper Martin,** Baseball
1932 **Gene Sarazen,** Golf
1933 **Carl Hubbell,** Baseball
1934 **Dizzy Dean,** Baseball
1935 **Joe Louis,** Boxing
1936 **Jesse Owens,** Track and field
1937 **Don Budge,** Tennis
1938 **Don Budge,** Tennis
1939 **Nile Kinnick,** Football
1940 **Tommy Harmon,** Football
1941 **Joe DiMaggio,** Baseball
1942 **Frank Sinkwich,** Football
1943 **Gunder Haegg,** Track and field
1944 **Byron Nelson,** Golf
1945 **Byron Nelson,** Golf
1946 **Glenn Davis,** Football
1947 **Johnny Lujack,** Football
1948 **Lou Boudreau,** Baseball
1949 **Leon Hart,** Football
1950 **Jim Konstanty,** Baseball
1951 **Dick Kazmaier,** Football
1952 **Bob Mathias,** Track and field, Football
1953 **Ben Hogan,** Golf
1954 **Willie Mays,** Baseball
1955 **"Hopalong" Cassady,** Football
1956 **Mickey Mantle,** Baseball
1957 **Ted Williams,** Baseball
1958 **Herb Elliott,** Track and field
1959 **Ingemar Johansson,** Boxing
1960 **Rafer Johnson,** Track and field
1961 **Roger Maris,** Baseball
1962 **Maury Wills,** Baseball
1963 **Sandy Koufax,** Baseball
1964 **Don Schollander,** Swimming
1965 **Sandy Koufax,** Baseball
1966 **Frank Robinson,** Baseball
1967 **Carl Yastrzemski,** Baseball
1968 **Denny McLain,** Baseball
1969 **Tom Seaver,** Baseball
1970 **George Blanda,** Football
1971 **Lee Trevino,** Golf
1972 **Mark Spitz,** Swimming
1973 **O.J. Simpson,** Football
1974 **Muhammad Ali,** Boxing
1975 **Fred Lynn,** Baseball
1976 **Bruce Jenner,** Track and field
1977 **Steve Cauthen,** Horse Racing

WOMEN
1931 **Helene Madison,** Swimming
1932 **Babe Didrikson,** Track and field

1933 **Helen Jacobs,** Tennis
1934 **Virginia Van Wie,** Golf
1935 **Helen Wills Moody,** Tennis
1936 **Helen Stephens,** Track and field
1937 **Katherine Rawls,** Swimming
1938 **Patty Berg,** Golf
1939 **Alice Marble,** Tennis
1940 **Alice Marble,** Tennis
1941 **Betty Hicks Newell,** Golf
1942 **Gloria Callen,** Swimming
1943 **Patty Berg,** Golf
1944 **Ann Curtis,** Swimming
1945 **Babe Didrikson Zaharias,** Golf
1946 **Babe Didrikson Zaharias,** Golf
1947 **Babe Didrikson Zaharias,** Golf
1948 **Fanny Blankers-Koen,** Track and field
1949 **Marlene Bauer,** Golf
1950 **Babe Didrikson Zaharias,** Golf
1951 **Maureen Connolly,** Tennis
1952 **Maureen Connolly,** Tennis
1953 **Maureen Connolly,** Tennis
1954 **Babe Didrikson Zaharias,** Golf
1955 **Patty Berg,** Golf
1956 **Pat McCormick,** Diving
1957 **Althea Gibson,** Tennis
1958 **Althea Gibson,** Tennis
1959 **Maria Bueno,** Tennis
1960 **Wilma Rudolph,** Track and field
1961 **Wilma Rudolph,** Track and field
1962 **Dawn Fraser,** Swimming
1963 **Mickey Wright,** Golf
1964 **Mickey Wright,** Golf
1965 **Kathy Whitworth,** Golf
1966 **Kathy Whitworth,** Golf
1967 **Billie Jean King,** Tennis
1968 **Peggy Fleming,** Figure skating
1969 **Debbie Meyer,** Swimming
1970 **Chi Cheng,** Track and field
1971 **Evonne Goolagong,** Tennis
1972 **Olga Korbut,** Gymnastics
1973 **Billie Jean King,** Tennis
1974 **Chris Evert,** Tennis
1975 **Chris Evert,** Tennis
1976 **Nadia Comaneci,** Gymnastics
1977 **Chris Evert,** Tennis

Honorary Membership

THE ATHLETIC INSTITUTE
200 Castlewood Dr., N. Palm Beach, Fla. 33408
(305/842-3600)

Honorary membership in the Athletic Institute and a bowl are awarded annually to those who distinguish themselves in service to athletics, physical education and recreation in the opinion of the Institute's executive committee.

1974 **G. Marvin Shutt,** Executive Director, National Sporting Goods Assn.
1975 **Carl Benkert,** President, Athletic Institute
1976 **C.C. Johnson Spink,** Editor, *The Sporting Goods Dealer*
1977 **H.W. Colburn,** President, Athletic Institute

Induction

CANADA'S SPORTS HALL OF FAME
Exhibition Place, Toronto, Ont. M6K 3C3, Canada
(416/366-7551)

Athletes selected annually are awarded a Lucite mounted crest and a permanent citation displayed in Canada's Sports Hall of Fame for excellence nationally and internationally in sport or for significant contributions to the development of sports.

1955 **Frank Amyot,** Paddling
      Norman Baker, Basketball
      Norris Bowden, Figure skating
      Lou Brouillard, Boxing
      Tommy (Noah Brusso) Burns, Boxing
      The Bluenose, Schooner
      Ethel Catherwood, High jumping
      Lionel Conacher, All-round athlete
      Johnny Coulon, Boxing
      Louis Cyr, Weightlifting
      Francis Dafoe, Figure skating
      Jack Delaney, Boxing
      Etienne Desmarteau, Hammer throwing
      George Dixon, Boxing
      Jack Guest, Sr., Sculling
      George Genereux, Trap shooting
      George Goulding, Walking
      Charles Gorman, Speed skating
      Horace ("Lefty") Gwynne, Boxing
      Ned Hanlan, Sculling
      Doug Hepburn, Weightlifting
1956 **Albert ("Frenchy") Belanger,** Boxing
      Cal Bricker, Broad jumping
      Eugene Brosseau, Boxing
      George Brown, Sculling
      Cyril Coafee, Sprints
      Gerard Cote, Marathon running
      Jake Gaudaur, Sculling
      The Paris Crew (Robert Fulton, Samuel Hutton, George Price, Elija Ross), Rowing
      Emile St. Godard, Dogsled racing
      George Woolf, Jockey
1957 **Gerry Ouellette,** Rifle shooting
      Robert Paul, Figure skating
      Barbara Wagner, Figure skating
      University of British Columbia Crew (Donald Arnold, Walter d'Hondt, Lorne Loomer, Archie McKinnon), Rowing
1958 **Marilyn Bell,** Marathon swimming
      Gilmour S. Boa, Rifle shooting
      Walter Ewing, Trap shooting
      George ("Mooney") Gibson, Baseball
      Johnny Longden, Jockey
      Lucille Wheeler, Skiing
1959 **James A. Ball,** Running
      Frank S McGill, Swimming/Football
      Edward ("Ted") Reeve, Lacrosse/Football
      George Hodgson, Swimming
      Sam Langford, Boxing
      Edouard ("Newsy") Lalonde, Lacrosse
      Tom Longboat, Marathon running
      George S. Lyon, Golf
      Ada Mackenzie, Golf
      Howie Morenz, Hockey
      Jimmy McLarnin, Boxing
      Duncan McNaughton, High jumping
      James Naismith, Basketball
      J. Percy Page, Basketball
      William ("Torchy") Peden, Cycling
      Relay Team (Bobbie Rosenfeld, Myrtle Cook, Florence Bell, Ethel Smith), Sprint relay team
      Bobbie Rosenfeld, All-round athlete

William J. Roue, *Bluenose* designer
Louis Rubenstein, Marathon running
Bert Schneider, Boxing
Lou F. Scholes, Sculling
Barbara Ann Scott, Figure skating
Bill Sherring, Marathon running
Sandy Somerville, Golf
David Turner, Soccer
Captain Angus Walters, *Bluenose* Skipper
Jean Wilson, Speed skating
Jack Wright, Tennis
Joe Wright, Sr., Rowing
Joe Wright, Jr., Sculling
Percy Williams, Sprints
George Young, Swimming
Bobby Kerr, Sprints
Walter Knox, All-round athlete
Jack Purcell, Badminton
Earl Thompson, Hurdles
1960 Robert Hayward, Speedboat racing
Anne Heggtveit, Skiing
Jack Laviolette, Lacrosse
Jack McCulloch, Speed skating
Miss Supertest III, Speedboat
James Thompson, Speedboat designing
James Trifunov, Wrestling
1961 William Fitzgerald, Lacrosse
Daniel A. MacKinnon, Harness racing
Dorothy Walton, Badminton/Tennis
1962 George Herrick Duggan, Yachting
Donald Jackson, Figure skating
Maria Jelinek, Figure skating
Otto Jelinek, Figure skating
Wilbert Martel, Candlepin bowling
Marlene Stewart Streit, Golf
1963 Norval Baptie, Speed skating
R.S. McLaughlin, Horse racing
Donald McPherson, Figure skating
Gus Ryder, Swimming
1964 Douglas Anakin, Bobsledding
John Emery, Bobsledding
Victor Emery, Bobsledding
Edouard Fabre, Marathon running
George Hungerford, Rowing
Roger Jackson, Rowing
Peter Kirby, Bobsledding
Stanley Leonard, Golf
Alvin Ritchie, Hockey/Football
1965 Petra Burka, Figure skating
Patrick Joseph Lally, Lacrosse
Northern Dancer, Horse racing
Joseph Cyril O'Brien, Harness racing
Gerald Presley, Bobsledding
Michael Young, Bobsledding
1966 John O'Neil, Rowing
Peggy Seller, Synchronized swimming
R. James Speers, Horse racing
1967 Gary Cowan, Golf
Nancy Greene, Skiing
Earl McCready, Wrestling
Johnny Miles, Marathon running
1968 James Day, Equestrian team
James Elder, Equestrian team
Elmer Ferguson, Sports writing
Tom Gayford, Equestrian team
Bruce Kidd, Marathon running
Richardson Rink (Arnold Richardson, Ernie Richardson, Garnet Richardson, Wes Richardson), Curling
1969 Al Balding, Golf

Jackie Callura, Boxing
George Duthie, Administration
Herve Filion, Harness racing
George Knudson, Golf
R. A. ("Bob") Porter, All round athlete
Ken Watson, Curling
1970 Betsy Clifford, Skiing
Ron Northcott, Curling
Harry L. Price, Administration
Marjory Shedd, Badminton
1971 Donald H. ("Dan") Bain, All round athlete
George Chenier, Snooker pool
Eric Coy, Track and field
William Crothers, Track and field
Phyllis Dewar, Swimming
Harry Jerome, Sprints
Charles Mayer, Administration
Noel MacDonald, Basketball
Graydon ("Blondie") Robinson, Bowling
Fred J. Robson, Speed skating
Thomas F. Ryan, Bowling
William Simpson, Soccer
Elaine Tanner, Swimming
Nick Weslock, Golf
1972 Lela Brooks, Speed skating
Desmond Burke, Marksmanship
J.W. ("Jack") Hamilton, Builder
Richard ("Kid") Howard, Boxing
Msgr. Athol Murray, Builder
Hilda Strike, Sprints
Walter Windeyer, Sailing
1973 George Anderson, Soccer builder
Matt Baldwin, Curling
David Bauer, Hockey builder
Victor Delamarre, Weightlifting
George Gray, Shotput
Karen Magnussen, Figure skating
Ray Mitchell, Bowling
Levi ("Shorty") Rodgers, Rowing
Keith Waples, Harness racing
1974 George Athans, Jr., Waterskiing
Conrad S. Riley, Builder
Frank Stack, Speed skating
Edward P. Taylor, Builder
Frank J. Shaughnessy, Jr., Builder
1975 Yvon Durelle, Boxing
Pat Fletcher, Golf
H.R. ("Bobby") Pearce, Sculls
Jack Dennett, Builder
H.A. Wilson, Speedboat racing

The following hockey players were admitted in 1975:

Jack Adams
Jean Beliveau
Hector ("Toe") Blake
Frank Boucher
C.S. Campbell
Francis Clancy
Charlie Conacher
Bill Cook
Syl Apps, Sr.
Aubrey ("Dit") Clapper
Charlie Gardiner
Eddie Gerard
Doug Harvey
Foster Hewitt
Gordon Howe
Dick Irvin
Leonard ("Red") Kelly
Aurel Joliat

Edouard ("Newsy") Lalonde
Joe Malone
Frank Nighbor
Lester Patrick
Maurice Richard
Frank Patrick
Joe Primeau
Art Ross
Terry Sawchuk
Milt Schmidt
Frank J. Selke
Eddie Shore
Joe Simpson
Conn Smythe
Nels Stewart
Fred ("Cyclone") Taylor
Harvey Jackson

The following football players were admitted in 1975:

Harry Batstone
Ab Box
Joseph M. Breen
Wes Cutler
Ernest Cox
Ross Brown Craig
John DeGruchy
Eddie Emerson
A.H. ("Cap") Fear
Hugh Gall
Tony Golab
Harry Griffith
G. Sydney Halter
Robert Isbister, Sr.
Russ Jackson
Eddie ("Dynamite") James
Joe Krol
Normie Kwong
Smirle Lawson
Frank R. ("Pep") Leadley
Percy Molson
Ted Morris
Gordon Perry
Norman Perry
S.P. ("Silver") Quilty
Jeff Russel
Paul Rowe
Joseph B. Ryan
David Sprague
Hugh Stirling
Brian Timmis
Joe Tubman
Benjamin L. Simpson
Hawley ("Huck") Welch
1976 Bob Abate, Builder
Kathy Kreiner, Skiing
Cliff Lumsdon, Swimming
Hartland MacDougall, All-round athlete
Phil Marchildon, Baseball
Lloyd Percival, Builder
W. Harold Rea, Builder
Andy Tommy, Football
1977 Arnie Boldt, High jump
Sylvia Burka, Speed skating
Toller Cranston, Figure skating
Sylvie Fortier, Synchronized swimming
Ralph Hutton, Swimming
Lucille Lessard, Archery
Dorothy Lidstone, Archery
Susan Nattrass, Shooting
George Orton, Track and field

The Outer Cove Crew, Rowing
John Primrose, Trapshooting
Bruce Robertson, Swimming
Doug Rogers, Judo
Cathy Townnsend, Bowling
Howard Wood, Curling

World Trophy
Athletes of the Year
College Basketball National Championship Team
College Basketball Player of the Year
College Football Championship Team of the Year
College Football Player of the Year

CITIZENS SAVINGS ATHLETIC FOUNDATION
9800 S. Sepulveda Blvd., Los Angeles, Calif. 90045
(213/670-7550)

The World Trophy is presented each year to the foremost amateur athlete from each of the six continents, as selected by the Citizens Savings Hall board. Although the awards were not instituted until 1948, selections were dated back to 1896 for Australasia, Europe and North America and to 1920 for Africa, Asia and South-America/Caribbean, following several years of research and contacts with amateur sports authorities throughout the world.

AFRICA
1920 Bevil Rudd (South Africa), Track and field
1921 B. I. C. Norton (South Africa), Tennis
1922 Herbert Taylor (South Africa), Cricket
1923 Louis Raymomd (South Africa), Tennis
1924 William Smith (South Africa), Boxing
1925 Arthur Newton (South Africa), Distance running
1926 Pierre Albertjin (South Africa), Rugby
1927 Sydney Atkinson (South Africa), Track and field
1928 Mohamed El Ouafi (Algeria), Marathon
1929 E. L. Heine (South Africa), Tennis
1930 Benjamin Osler (South Africa), Rugby
1931 Daniel J. Joubert (South Africa), Track and field
1932 David E. Carstens (South Africa), Boxing
1933 William Zeller (South Africa), Rugby
1934 Harry B. Hart (South Africa), Track and field
1935 Arthur B. Locke (South Africa), Golf
1936 Khadr El Touni (Egypt), Weightlifting
1937 Hardy R. Ballington (South Africa), Distance running
1938 Thomas P. Lavery (South Africa), Track and field
1939 Ibrahim Shams (Egypt), Weightlifting
1940 No selections
1941 No selections
1942 No selections
1943 No selections
1944 No selections
1945 Denis Shore (South Africa), Track and field
1946 Aaron Geffin (South Africa), Rugby
1947 Bruce Mitchell (South Africa), Cricket
1948 George Hunter (South Africa), Boxing
1949 Eric Sturgess (South Africa), Tennis

1950 Thiam Papa Gallo (French W. Africa), Track and field
1951 Wally Hayward (South Africa), Distance running
1952 Joan Harrison (South Africa), Swimming
1953 John Cheetham (South Africa), Cricket
1954 Emmanuel Ifeajuna (Nigeria), Track and field
1955 Jan Barnard (South Africa), Distance running
1956 Julius Chigbolu (Nigeria), Track and field
1957 Gerhardus Potgieter (South Africa), Track and field
1958 Grant Webster (South Africa), Boxing
1959 Sandra Reynolds (South Africa), Tennis
1960 Abebe Bikila (Ethiopia), Marathon
1961 Abdul Amu (Nigeria), Track and field
1962 Seraphino Antao (Kenya), Track and field
1963 George Hazle (South Africa), Track and field
1964 Mohamed Gammoudi (Tunisia), Track and field
1965 Kipchoge Keino (Kenya), Track and field
1966 Karen Muir (South Africa), Swimming
1967 Naftali Temu (Kenya), Track and field
1968 Mamo Wolde (Ethiopia), Marathon
1969 Charles Asati (Kenya), Track and field
1970 Philip Waruinge (Kenya), Boxing
1971 Eric Broberg (South Africa), Track and field
1972 John Akii-Bua (Uganda), Track and field
1973 Benjamin Jipcho (Kenya), Track and field
1974 Filbert Bayi (Tanzania), Track and field
1975 Mike Boit (Kenya), Track and field
1976 Jonty Skinner (South Africa), Track and field
1977 Miruts Yifter (Ethiopia), Track and field

ASIA

1920 Ichiya Kumagae (Japan), Tennis
1921 J.K. Taduran (Philippines), Decathlon
1922 Zenzo Shimizu (Japan), Tennis
1923 Masonosuke Fukuda (Japan), Tennis
1924 Katsuo Takaishi (Japan), Swimming
1925 Takeichi Harada (Japan), Tennis
1926 Sekio Tawara (Japan), Tennis
1927 Mikio Oda (Japan), Track and field
1928 Yoshiyuki Tsuruta (Japan), Swimming
1929 Kinuye Hitomi (Japan), Track and field
1930 Simeon Toribio (Philippines), Track and field
1931 Chuhei Nambu (Japan), Track and field
1932 Kusuo Kitamura (Japan), Swimming
1933 Jiro Satoh (Japan), Tennis
1934 Masao Harada (Japan), Track and field
1935 Shozo Makino (Japan), Swimming
1936 Kee Chung Sohn (Japan), Marathon
1937 Sueo Oe (Japan), Track and field
1938 Tomikatsu Amano (Japan), Swimming
1939 Hiroshi Tanaka (Japan), Track and field
1940 Chengkong Kin (Japan), Track and field
1941 No selections
1942 No selections
1943 No selections
1944 No selections
1945 No selections
1946 No selections
1947 Yun Bok Suh (Korea), Distance running
1948 Duncan White (Ceylon), Track and field
1949 Hironoshin Furuhashi (Japan), Swimming
1950 Kee Yong Ham (South Korea), Distance running
1951 Shigeki Tanaka (Japan), Distance running
1952 K. D. "Babu" Singh (India), Field hockey
1953 Keizo Yamada (Japan), Marathon
1954 Shazo Sasahara (Japan), Wrestling
1955 Hideo Hamamura (Japan), Marathon
1956 Masura Furukawa (Japan), Swimming
1957 Takashi Ishimoto (Japan), Swimming
1958 Chuan-Kwang Yang (Formosa), Track and field

1959 Milkha Singh (India), Track and field
1960 Naseer Ahmad (Pakistan), Field hockey
1961 Tsuyoshi Yamanaka (Japan), Swimming
1962 Satoko Tanaka (Japan), Swimming
1963 Takeo Sugahara (Japan), Track and field
1964 Yukio Endo (Japan), Gymnastics
1965 Morio Shigematsu (Japan), Marathon
1966 Ramanathan Krishnan (India), Tennis
1967 Kenji Kimihara (Japan), Marathon
1968 Sawao Katoh (Japan), Gymnastics
1969 Chi Cheng (Formosa), Track and field
1970 Ni Chih-Chin (China), Track and field
1971 Shigenobu Murofushi (Japan), Track and field
1972 Yukio Kasaya (Japan), Skiing
1973 Mohammed Nassiri (Iran), Weightlifting
1974 Shigeru Kasamatsu (Japan), Gymnastics
1975 Shozo Fujii (Japan), Judo
1976 Mitsuo Tsukahara (Japan), Gymnastics
1977 Yuji Takada (Japan), Wrestling

AUSTRALASIA

1896 Edwin H. Flack (Australia), Track and field
1897 A. B. Sloan (Australia), Rowing
1898 Victor Trumper (Australia), Cricket
1899 Stanley R. Rowley (Australia), Track and field
1900 Frederick C. V. Lane (Australia), Swimming
1901 G. A. Moir (Australia), Track and field
1902 James Donald (Australia), Rowing
1903 Richmond Cavill (Australia), Swimming
1904 H. H. Hunter (Australia), Track and field
1905 Barney B. Kieran (Australia), Swimming
1906 Nigel C. Barker (Australia), Track and field
1907 Norman E. Brookes (Australia), Tennis
1908 Reginald L. Baker (Australia), All-around
1909 Anthony Wilding (New Zealand), Tennis
1910 Frank E. Beaurepaire (Australia), Swimming
1911 Harold Hardwick (Australia), Swimming
1912 Cecil Healy (Australia), Swimming
1913 Cecil McVilly (Australia), Rowing
1914 William Longworth (Australia), Swimming
1915 Fanny Durack (Australia), Swimming
1916 No selections
1917 No selections
1918 No selections
1919 H. C. Disher (Australia), Rowing
1920 Ivo H. Whitton (Australia), Golf
1921 Edward W. Carr (Australia), Track and field
1922 Gerald L. Patterson (Australia), Tennis
1923 Anthony Winter (Australia), Track and field
1924 Andrew M. Charlton (Australia), Swimming
1925 Victor S. Richardson (Australia), All-around
1926 R. Rose (New Zealand), Track and field
1927 Stanley Lay (New Zealand), Track and field
1928 H. Robert Pearce (Australia), Rowing
1929 James A. Carlton (Australia), Track and field
1930 Donald G. Bradman (Australia), Cricket
1931 Noel P. Ryan (Australia), Swimming
1932 Edgar L. Gray (Australia), Cycling
1933 John B. Crawford (Australia), Tennis
1934 John P. Metcalfe (Australia), Track and field
1935 Cecil H. Matthews (New Zealand), Distance running
1936 John E. Lovelock (New Zealand), Track and field
1937 Robin Biddulph (Australia), Swimming
1938 James B. Ferrier (Australia), Golf
1939 D. Brian Dunn (Australia), Track and field
1940 No selections
1941 No selections
1942 No selections
1943 No selections
1944 No selections

1945 No selections
1946 John Treloar (Australia), Track and field
1947 John A. Winter (Australia), Track and field
1948 Mervyn T. Wood (Australia), Rowing
1949 Syd Patterson (Australia), Cycling
1950 John B. Marshall (Australia), Swimming
1951 Frank A. Sedgman (Australia), Tennis
1952 Marjorie Jackson (Australia), Track and field
1953 John Landy (Australia), Track and field
1954 Jon Henricks (Australia), Swimming
1955 Shirley S. de la Hunty (Australia), Track and field
1956 Lorraine Crapp (Australia), Swimming
1957 Stuart MacKenzie (Australia), Rowing
1958 Herbert Elliott (Australia), Track and field
1959 Jon Konrads (Australia), Swimming
1960 Peter Snell (New Zealand), Track and field
1961 Dawn Fraser (Australia), Swimming
1962 Murray Rose (Australia), Swimming
1963 Tony Sneazwell (Australia), Track and field
1964 Betty Cuthbert (Australia), Track and field
1965 Ron Clarke (Australia), Track and field
1966 Fred Stolle (Australia), Tennis
1967 Judy Pollock (Australia), Track and field
1968 Michael Wenden (Australia), Swimming
1969 Pamela Kilborn (Australia), Track and field
1970 Kerry O'Brien (Australia), Track and field
1971 Shane Gould (Australia), Swimming
1972 Gail Neall (Australia), Swimming
1973 Stephan Holland (Australia), Swimming
1974 Jenny Turrall (Australia), Swimming
1975 John Walker (New Zealand), Track and field
1976 Dick Quax (New Zealand), Track and field
1977 Edward Palubinskas (Australia), Basketball

EUROPE

1896 Spiridon Luis (Greece), Marathon
1897 William G. Grace (England), Cricket
1898 Reginald F. Doherty (England), Tennis
1899 John Ball (England), Golf
1900 Michel Theato (France), Marathon
1901 Peter J. O'Connor (Ireland), Track and field
1902 Joseph Binks (England), Track and field
1903 Hugh L. Doherty (England), Tennis
1904 Alfred Shrubb (England), Track and field
1905 Frederick S. Kelly (England), Rowing
1906 H. Jalmar Mellander (Sweden), Pentat.lon
1907 Con Leahy (Ireland), Track and field
1908 Henry Taylor (England), Swimming
1909 A. W. Gore (England), Tennis
1910 Hannes Kolehmainen (Finland), Distance running
1911 Harold H. Hilton (England), Golf
1912 Erik V. Lemning (Sweden), Track and field
1913 Jean Bouin (France), Distance running
1914 Mrs. Lambert Chambers (England), Golf
1915 No selections
1916 No selections
1917 No selections
1918 No selections
1919 Jean Vermeulen (France), Distance running
1920 Helge Lovland (Norway), Decathlon
1921 Cecil Leitch (England), Golf
1922 Paavo Nurmi (Finland), Distance running
1923 Suzanne Lenglen (France), Tennis
1924 Willie Ritola (Finland), Distance running
1925 Joyce Wethered (England), Golf
1926 Jack Beresford, Jr. (England), Rowing
1927 Rene Lacoste (France), Tennis
1928 Paavo Yrjola (Finland), Decathlon
1929 Henri Cochet (France), Tennis
1930 Jules Ladoumegue (France), Track and field

1931 Klas Thunberg (Finland), Speed skating
1932 Jean Borotra (France), Tennis
1933 Matti Jarvinen (Finland), Track and field
1934 Hans H. Sievert (Germany), Decathlon
1935 Frederick J. Perry (England), Tennis
1936 Sonja Henie (Norway), Figure skating
1937 Sidney C. Wooderson (England), Distance running
1938 Ragnhild Hveger (Denmark), Swimming
1939 Taisto Maki (Finland), Distance running
1940 Rudolf Harbig (Germany), Track and field
1941 Mario Lanzi (Italy), Track and field
1942 Gunder Haegg (Sweden), Distance running
1943 Arne Andersson (Sweden), Distance running
1944 Verner Hardmo (Sweden), Walking
1945 Viljo Heino (Finland), Distance running
1946 Rune Gustafson (Sweden), Distance running
1947 Lennart Strand (Sweden), Distance running
1948 Fanny Blankers-Koen (Netherlands), Track and field
1949 Emil Zatopek (Czechoslovakia), Distance running
1950 Ignace Heinrich (France), Decathlon
1951 Adolfo Consolini (Italy), Track and field
1952 Joseph Barthel (Luxemburg), Track and field
1953 Gordon Pirie (England), Track and field
1954 Roger Bannister (England), Track and field
1955 Sandor Iharos (Hungary), Track and field
1956 Vladimir Kuts (USSR), Track and field
1957 Ron Delany (Ireland), Track and field
1958 Vasiliy Kuznyetsov (USSR), Track and field
1959 Karl Martin Lauer (Germany), Track and field
1960 Livio Berruti (Italy), Track and field
1961 Valeriy Brumel (USSR), Track and field
1962 Vyacheslav Ivanov (USSR), Rowing
1963 Tamara Press (USSR), Track and field
1964 Gaston Roelants (Belgium), Track and field
1965 Michel Jazy (France), Track and field
1966 Manolo Santana (Spain), Tennis
1967 Liesel Westermann (W. Germany), Track and field
1968 Jean-Claude Killy (France), Skiing
1969 Liese Prokop (Austria), Track and field
1970 Chris Papanicolaou (Greece), Track and field
1971 Walter Schmidt (W. Germany), Track and field
1972 Lasse Viren (Finland), Track and field
1973 Klaus Wolfermann (W. Germany), Track and field
1974 Irena Szewinska (Poland), Track and field
1975 Ludmila Turischeva (USSR), Gymnastics
1976 Nadia Comaneci (Rumania), Gymnastics
    Kornelia Ender (E. Germany), Swimming
1977 Ulrike Tauber (E. Germany), Swimming

NORTH AMERICA (All U.S.A. except 1928 - Percy Williams, Canada)

1896 Robert Garrett, Track and field
1897 Robert D. Wrenn, Tennis
1898 Juliette P. Atkinson, Tennis
1899 T. Truxton Hare, Football
1900 Alvin C. Kraenzlein, Track and field
1901 Charles Daly, Football
1902 William A. Larned, Tennis
1903 Walter J. Travis, Golf
1904 James Lightbody, Track and field
1905 May Sutton, Tennis
1906 Walter Eckersall, Football
1907 Martin J. Sheridan, Track and field
1908 Melvin Sheppard, Track and field
1909 Charles M. Daniels, Swimming
1910 Fred C. Thomson, Track and field
1911 Hazel Hotchkiss, Tennis
1912 James Thorpe, Football, track and field
1913 Maurice McLoughlin, Tennis

1914 Francis Ouimet, Golf
1915 Jerome D. Travers, Golf
1916 J. E. "Ted" Meredith, Track and field
1917 Molla Bjurstedt, Tennis
1918 Avery Brundage, Track and field
1919 William Johnston, Tennis
1920 Charles W. Paddock, Track and field
1921 William T. Tilden II, Tennis
1922 Thomas Hitchcock, Jr., Polo
1923 John Weissmuller, Swimming
1924 Harold "Red" Grange, Football
1925 Ernest Nevers, Football
1926 Robert T. Jones, Golf
1927 Benjamin Oosterbaan, Football, basketball
1928 Percy Williams, Track and field
1929 Helen Wills, Tennis
1930 Glenna Collett, Golf
1931 Helene Madison, Swimming
1932 H. Ellsworth Vines, Tennis
1933 Glenn Cunningham, Track and field
1934 W. Lawson Little, Golf
1935 Jesse Owens, Track and field
1936 Glenn Morris, Track and field
1937 J. Donald Budge, Tennis
1938 Angelo Luisetti, Basketball
1939 Alice Marble, Tennis
1940 J. Gregory Rice, Track and field
1941 Robert L. Riggs, Tennis
1942 Cornelius Warmerdam, Track and field
1943 Gilbert Dodds, Track and field
1944 Ann Curtis, Swimming
1945 Glenn Davis, Football
1946 Pauline Betz, Tennis
1947 John A. Kramer, Tennis
1948 Robert Mathias, Track and field
1949 Melvin Patton, Track and field
1950 Richard Attlesey, Track and field
1951 Robert Richards, Track and field
1952 Horace Ashenfelter, Track and field
1953 Malvin Whitfield, Track and field
1954 Wes Santee, Track and field
1955 Patricia McCormick, Diving
1956 Parry O'Brien, Track and field
1957 Robert Gutowski, Track and field
1958 Rafer Johnson, Track and field
1959 Ray Norton, Track and field
1960 Wilma Rudolph, Track and field
1961 Ralph Boston, Track and field
1962 Terry Baker, Football
1963 Brian Sternberg, Track and field
1964 Alfred Oerter, Track and field
1965 Michael Garrett, Football
1966 James Ryun, Track and field
1967 J. Randel Matson, Track and field
1968 Robert Beamon, Track and field
1969 William Toomey, Track and field
1970 Gary Hall, Swimming
1971 Pat Matzdorf, Track and field
1972 Mark Spitz, Swimming
1973 Keena Rothhammer, Swimming
1974 Tim Shaw, Swimming
1975 Shirley Babashoff, Swimming
1976 John Naber, Swimming
1977 Edwin Moses, Track and field

SOUTH AMERICA/CARIBBEAN

1920 Juan Jorquera (Chile), Distance running
1921 Lewis L. Lacey (Argentina), Polo
1922 John B. Miles (Argentina), Polo
1923 J. A. E. Traill (Argentina), Polo

1924 Luis Brunetto (Argentina), Track and field
1925 Jack D. Nelson (Argentina), Polo
1926 Miguel Plaza (Chile), Distance running
1927 Erwin Gevert (Chile), Decathlon
1928 Alberto Zorilla (Argentina), Swimming
1929 Pedro J. C. Velarde (Peru), Track and field
1930 Arturo Kenny (Argentina), Polo
1931 Juan C. Zabala (Argentina), Marathon
1932 Santiago Lovell (Argentina), Boxing
1933 Lucio A. P. Castro (Brazil), Track and field
1934 Manuel Andrada (Argentina), Polo
1935 Jose Ribas (Argentina), Distance running
1936 Oscar Cassanovas (Argentina), Boxing
1937 Anita Lizana (Chile), Tennis
1938 Oscar Bringas (Peru), Track and field
1939 S. de M. Padilha (Brazil), Track and field
1940 Jose B. de Assis (Brazil), Track and field
1941 Raul Ibarra (Argentina), Distance running
1942 Maria Lenk (Brazil), Swimming
1943 Francisco Segura (Ecuador), Tennis
1944 Mario Gonzales (Argentina), Golf
1945 Elisabeth Muller (Brazil), Track and field
1946 Mario Recordion (Chile), Track and field
1947 Unrique Kistenmacher (Argentina), Track and field
1948 Delfo Cabrera (Argentina), Marathon
1949 Roberto Cavanaugh (Argentina), Polo
1950 Oscar Furlong (Argentina), Basketball
1951 Adhemar Da Silva (Brazil), Track and field
1952 Reinaldo Gorno (Argentina), Distance running
1953 Pedro Galvao (Argentina), Swimming
1954 Jose I. de Conceicao (Brazil), Track and field
1955 Oswaldo Suarez (Argentina), Track and field
1956 Miguel Agostini (Trinidad), Track and field
1957 Luis Ayala (Chile), Tennis
1958 Alejandro Olmedo (Peru), Tennis
1959 Maria Bueno (Brazil), Tennis
1960 Manoel Dos Santos (Brazil), Swimming
1961 Wlamir Marques (Brazil), Basketball
1962 Luis Nicolao (Argentina), Swimming
1963 Juan C. Dyrzka (Argentina), Track and field
1964 Wendell Mottley (Trinidad), Track and field
1965 Edwin Roberts (Trinidad), Track and field
1966 Alvaro Mejia (Colombia), Track and field
1967 Jose Fiolo (Brazil), Swimming
1968 Nelson Prudencio (Brazil), Track and field
1969 Juan Bello (Peru), Swimming
1970 F. A. Brito-Rodriguez (Venezuela), Boxing
      Olga de Angulo (Colombia), Swimming
1971 Alberto Dimiddi (Argentina), Rowing
1972 Teofilo Stevenson (Cuba), Boxing
1973 Donald Quarrie (Jamaica), Track and field
1974 Silvio Leonard (Cuba), Track and field
1975 Joao Carlos de Oliveira (Brazil), Track and field
1976 Alberto Juantorena (Cuba), Track and field
1977 Alejandro Cadanas (Cuba), Track and field

In addition to an Athlete of the Month honor (not listed here), which involves display in the Circle of Champions in the Hall of the Athletic Foundation, Athletes of the Year are chosen for Northern and Southern California, resulting in permanent enshrinement in the Hall. The Southern California Awards were instituted in 1939 and dated back to 1900, while the Northern California awards were established in 1973 and dated back to 1890. The individuals honored receive medals.

SOUTHERN CALIFORNIA

1900 James J. Jeffries, Boxing

1901 **Dean Cromwell,** Football, basketball, track and field
1902 **Ralph Noble,** Football and other sports
1903 **Charles Bazata,** Football, basketball and other sports
1904 **Eustace Newton,** Baseball
         John Hagerman, Track and field and other sports
1905 **May Sutton,** Tennis
1906 **Charles Parsons,** Track and field
1907 **Stanislaus Burek,** Football, baseball
1908 **Frank "Cap" Dillon,** Baseball
1909 **William Tozer,** Baseball
1910 **Fred Thompson,** Track and field, football
1911 **Walter Carlisle,** Baseball
1912 **Fred Kelly,** Track and field
1913 **Harry Kirkpatrick,** Football and other sports
1914 **Mary K. Browne,** Tennis
         Sidney Foster, Football and other sports
1915 **Sam McClung,** Football and other sports
1916 **Olen Finch,** Football and other sports
1917 **Earl Cooper,** Auto racing
1918 **Bruce Kirkpatrick,** Football and other sports
1919 **Charles Paddock,** Track and field
1920 **Roy Evans,** Football and other sports
1921 **Samuel Thomson,** Track and field
1922 **Jakie May,** Baseball
1923 **Jack Dempsey,** Boxing
1924 **Clarence "Bud" Houser,** Track and field,
1925 **Morton Kaer,** Football and other sports
1926 **Arnold Statz,** Baseball
         George Von Elm, Golf
1927 **Morley Drury,** Football and other sports
1928 **Jesse Mortensen,** Football, track and field, basketball
1929 **Harlow Rothert,** Football, track and field, basketball
1930 **Eric Pedley,** Polo
1931 **Frank Wykoff,** Track and field
1932 **H. Ellsworth Vines,** Tennis
1933 **Harry Hinkel,** Walking
1934 **Olin Dutra,** Golf
1935 **Floyd Vaughn,** Baseball
1936 **Louis Meyer,** Auto racing
1937 **Earle Meadows,** Track and field
         William Sefton, Track and field
1938 **Henry Armstrong,** Boxing
1939 **Kenneth Washington,** Football, baseball
1940 **Alice Marble,** Tennis
1941 **Frank Albert,** Football
1942 **Frederick Schroeder,** Tennis
1943 **Manuel Ortiz,** Boxing
1944 **James Hardy,** Football, baseball
1945 **Glenn Davis,** Football and other sports
1946 **Jack Kramer,** Tennis
1947 **Ralph Kiner,** Baseball
1948 **Victoria Draves,** Diving
1949 **Melvin Patton,** Track and field
1950 **Richard Attlesey,** Track and field
1951 **Florence Chadwick,** Swimming
1952 **Malvin Whitfield,** Track and field
         Cy Young, Track and field
1953 **Maureen Connolly,** Tennis
1954 **Parry O'Brien,** Track and field
1955 **Edwin "Duke" Snider,** Baseball
1956 **Patricia McCormick,** Diving
1957 **Sam Hanks,** Auto racing
1958 **Greta Andersen,** Swimming
1959 **Wally Moon,** Baseball
         Larry Sherry, Baseball
1960 **Rafer Johnson,** Track and field, basketball
1961 **Jerry Barber,** Golf
1962 **Jim Beatty,** Track and field
1963 **Sandy Koufax,** Baseball
1964 **Michael Larrabee,** Track and field

1965 **Michael Garrett,** football
1966 **John Longden,** Horse racing
1967 **Gary Beban,** Football
         O.J. Simpson, Football
1968 **David Jones,** Football
1969 **William Toomey,** Track and field
1970 **William Shoemaker,** Horse racing
1971 **Frank Heckl,** Swimming
1972 **Sandra Nielson,** Swimming
         Merlin Olsen, Football
1973 **Nolan Ryan,** Baseball
1974 **Steve Garvey,** Baseball
1975 **Randy Jones,** Baseball
1976 **John Naber,** Swimming
1977 **Carlos Palomino,** Boxing

NORTHERN CALIFORNIA

1890 **Joe Choynski,** Boxing
1891 **Young Mitchell,** Boxing
1892 **James Corbett,** Boxing
1893 **Harry Walton,** Football, baseball
1894 **Guy Cochran,** Football
1895 **William Lange,** Baseball
1896 **Charles Fickert,** Football, track and field
1897 **Solly Smith,** Boxing
1898 **Lawrence Kaarsberg,** Football, baseball
1899 **James Hughes,** Baseball
1900 **Alfred Plaw,** Track and field
1901 **Orval Overall,** Football, baseball
1902 **James Britt,** Boxing
1903 **Francis Neil,** Boxing
1904 **Sam Berger,** Boxing
1905 **Michael Donlin,** Baseball
1906 **Harold Chase,** Baseball
1907 **Theodore Vandervoort,** Rugby, track and field
1908 **Ralph Rose,** Track and field
1909 **Harry Krause,** Baseball
1910 **Frank Bodie,** Baseball
1911 **Hazel Hotchkiss,** Tennis
1912 **Willie Ritchie,** Boxing
1913 **Maurice McLoughlin,** Tennis
1914 **William James,** Baseball
1915 **William Johnston,** Tennis
1916 **Fred Murray,** Track and field
1917 **Norman Ross,** Swimming
1918 **R. Lindley Murray,** Track and field
1919 **Harry Liversedge,** Track and field
         Robert Templeton, Football, track and field
1920 **Walter Mails,** Baseball
1921 **Harold Muller,** Football, track and field
1922 **William Kamm,** Baseball
1923 **Harry Heilmann,** Baseball
1924 **Helen Wills,** Tennis
1925 **Ernest Nevers,** Football, baseball
1926 **Albert White,** Diving
1927 **Lawrence Bettencourt,** Football, baseball
1928 **Robert King,** Track and field
1929 **Frank O'Doul,** Baseball
         Lewis Fonseca, Baseball
1930 **Joe Cronin,** Baseball
1931 **Alfred Banuet,** Handball
         Charles Hafey, Baseball
1932 **Benjamin Eastman,** Track and field
1933 **Helen Jacobs,** Tennis
         Max Baer, Boxing
1934 **W. Lawson Little,** Golf
         Vernon Gomez, Baseball
1935 **Robert Clark,** Track and field
         Oscar Eckhardt, Baseball
1936 **Archie Williams,** Track and field

1937	**J. Donald Budge,** Tennis
1938	**Angelo Luisetti,** Basketball
	Ernest Lombardi, Baseball
1939	**Joe DiMaggio,** Baseball
1940	**Alice Marble,** Tennis
1941	**Grover Klemmer,** Track and field
1942	**Cornelius Warmerdam,** Track and field
1943	**Harold Davis,** Track and field
1944	**Ann Curtis,** Swimming
1945	**Helen Crlenkovitch,** Diving
1946	**Zoe Ann Olsen,** Diving
1947	**Margaret Osborne,** Tennis
1948	**Jack Jensen,** Football, baseball
1949	**Joe Perry,** Football
1950	**Arthur Larsen,** Tennis
1951	**William McColl,** Football
1952	**Robert Mathias,** Football, track and field
1953	**Carl Olson,** Boxing
1954	**Billy Vukovitch,** Auto racing
1955	**Harvie Ward,** Golf
1956	**Bill Russell,** Basketball
1957	**Don Bowden,** Track and field
1958	**Willie Mays,** Baseball
1959	**Ray Norton,** Track and field
1960	**Darrall Imhoff,** Basketball
1961	**Orlando Cepeda,** Baseball
1962	**Jack Sanford,** Baseball
1963	**Juan Marichal,** Baseball
1964	**Don Schollander,** Swimming
1965	**John Brodie,** Football
	Tony Lema, Golf
1966	**Rick Barry,** Basketball
	Gaylord Perry, Baseball
1967	**Claudia Kolb,** Swimming
	Daryle Lamonica, Football
1968	**Deborah Meyer,** Swimming
1969	**Willie McCovey,** Baseball
1970	**George Blanda,** Football
	Jim Plunkett, Football
1971	**Vida Blue,** Baseball
1972	**Mark Spitz,** Swimming
1973	**Johnny Miller,** Golf
1974	**Joe Rudi,** Baseball
1975	**Chuck Muncie,** Football
1976	**Bruce Jenner,** Track and field
1977	**John Lofton,** Track and field

The Citizens Savings Athletic Foundation names the College Basketball National Championship Team by compiling the records to determine which team scored to the greatest degree for an over-all season, with consideration also given for postseason play in the selection. The coach's name appears with the team.

1901	**Yale,** No coach
1902	**Minnesota,** Louis Cooke
1903	**Yale,** No coach
1904	**Columbia,** No coach
1905	**Columbia,** No coach
1906	**Dartmouth,** No coach
1907	**Chicago,** Joseph Raycroft
1908	**Chicago,** Joseph Raycroft
1909	**Chicago,** Joseph Raycroft
1910	**Columbia,** Harry A. Fisher
1911	**St. John's (Brooklyn),** Claude B. Allen
1912	**Wisconsin,** Walter Meanwell
1913	**U.S. Naval Academy,** Louis P. Wenzell
1914	**Wisconsin,** Walter Meanwell
1915	**Illinois,** Ralph R. Jones
1916	**Wisconsin,** Walter Meanwell

1917	**Washington State,** J. Fred Bohler
1918	**Syracuse,** Edmund A. Dollard
1919	**Minnesota,** Louis Cooke
1920	**Pennsylvania,** Lon W. Jourdet
1921	**Pennsylvania,** Edward McNichol
1922	**Kansas,** Forrest C. Allen
1923	**Kansas,** Forrest C. Allen
1924	**North Carolina,** Norman Shepard
1925	**Princeton,** Albert Wittmer
1926	**Syracuse,** Lewis P. Andreas
1927	**Notre Dame,** George E. Keogan
1928	**Pittsburgh,** Clifford Carlson
1929	**Montana State,** Schubert Dyche
1930	**Pittsburgh,** Clifford Carlson
1931	**Northwestern,** Arthur Lonborg
1932	**Purdue,** Ward Lambert
1933	**Kentucky,** Adolph Rupp
1934	**Wyoming,** Willard Witte
1935	**New York University,** Howard Cann
1936	**Notre Dame,** George Keogan
1937	**Stanford,** John W. Bunn
1938	**Temple,** James Usilton
1939	**Long Island,** Clair F. Bee
1940	**Southern California,** Justin M. Barry
1941	**Wisconsin,** Harold E. Foster
1942	**Stanford,** Everett S. Dean
1943	**Wyoming,** Everett Shelton
1944	**U.S. Military Academy,** Edward Kelleher
1945	**Oklahoma State,** Henry P. Iba
1946	**Oklahoma State,** Henry P. Iba
1947	**Holy Cross,** Alvin F. Julian
1948	**Kentucky,** Adolph Rupp
1949	**Kentucky,** Adolph Rupp
1950	**City College of New York,** Nat Holman
1951	**Kentucky,** Adolph Rupp
1952	**Kansas,** Forrest C. Allen
1953	**Indiana,** Branch McCracken
1954	**Kentucky,** Adolph Rupp
1955	**San Francisco,** Phil Woolpert
1956	**San Francisco,** Phil Woolpert
1957	**North Carolina,** Frank McGuire
1958	**Kentucky,** Adolph Rupp
1959	**California,** Pete Newell
1960	**Ohio State,** Fred Taylor
1961	**Cincinnati,** Ed Jucker
1962	**Cincinnati,** Ed Jucker
1963	**Loyola (Chicago),** George Ireland
1964	**UCLA,** John Wooden
1965	**UCLA,** John Wooden
1966	**Texas Western,** Don Haskins
1967	**UCLA,** John Wooden
1968	**UCLA,** John Wooden
1969	**UCLA,** John Wooden
1970	**UCLA,** John Wooden
1971	**UCLA,** John Wooden
1972	**UCLA,** John Wooden
1973	**UCLA,** John Wooden
1974	**North Carolina State,** Norman Sloan
1975	**UCLA,** John Wooden
1976	**Indiana,** Bob Knight
1977	**Marquette,** Al McGuire

COLLEGE BASKETBALL PLAYER OF THE YEAR

1905	**Chris Steinmetz,** Wisconsin
1906	**George Grebenstein,** Dartmouth
1907	**Gilmore Kinney,** Yale
1908	**Charles Keinath,** Pennsylvania
1909	**John Schommer,** Chicago
1910	**Harlan "Pat" Page,** Chicago
1911	**Theodore Kiendl,** Columbia

1912 **Otto Stangel,** Wisconsin
1913 **Eddie Calder,** St. Lawrence
1914 **Gil Halstead,** Cornell
1915 **Ernest Houghton,** Union
1916 **George Levis,** Wisconsin
1917 **Ray Woods,** Illinois
1918 **William Chandler,** Wisconsin
1919 **Erling Platou,** Minnesota
1920 **Howard Cann,** New York
1921 **George Williams,** Missouri
1922 **Charles Carney,** Illinois
1923 **Paul Endacott,** Kansas
1924 **Charles Black,** Kansas
1925 **Earl Mueller,** Colorado College
1926 **John Cobb,** North Carolina
1927 **Victor Hanson,** Syracuse
1928 **Victor Holt,** Oklahoma
1929 **John A. Thompson,** Montana State
1930 **Charles Hyatt,** Pittsburgh
1931 **Bart Carlton,** East Central Oklahoma
1932 **John Wooden,** Purdue
1933 **Forest Sale,** Kentucky
1934 **Wesley Bennett,** Westminster (Pa.)
1935 **Leroy Edwards,** Kentucky
1936 **John Moir,** Notre Dame
1937 **Angelo Luisetti,** Stanford
1938 **Angelo Luisetti,** Stanford
1939 **Chester Jaworski,** Rhode Island
1940 **George Glamack,** North Carolina
1941 **George Glamack,** North Carolina
1942 **Stan Modzelewski,** Rhode Island
1943 **George Senesky,** St. Joseph's
1944 **George Mikan,** De Paul
1945 **George Mikan,** De Paul
1946 **Robert Kurland,** Oklahoma State
1947 **Gerald Tucker,** Oklahoma
1948 **Ed Macauley,** St. Louis
1949 **Anthony Lavelli,** Yale
1950 **Paul Arizin,** Villanova
1951 **Richard Groat,** Duke
1952 **Clyde Lovellette,** Kansas
1953 **Robert Houbregs,** Washington
1954 **Tom Gola,** La Salle
1955 **Bill Russell,** San Francisco
1956 **Bill Russell,** San Francisco
1957 **Leonard Rosenbluth,** North Carolina
1958 **Elgin Baylor,** Seattle
1959 **Oscar Robertson,** Cincinnati
1960 **Oscar Robertson,** Cincinnati
1961 **Jerry Lucas,** Ohio State
1962 **Paul Hogue,** Cincinnati
1963 **Arthur Heyman,** Duke
1964 **Walter Hazzard,** U.C.L.A.
1965 **Bill Bradley,** Princeton
     Gail Goodrich, U.C.L.A.
1966 **Cazzie Russell,** Michigan
1967 **Lew Alcindor,** U.C.L.A.
1968 **Lew Alcindor,** U.C.L.A.
1969 **Lew Alcindor,** U.C.L.A.
1970 **Pete Maravich,** Louisiana State
     Sidney Wicks, U.C.L.A.
1971 **Sidney Wicks,** U.C.L.A.
     Austin Carr, Notre Dame
1972 **Bill Walton,** U.C.L.A.
1973 **Bill Walton,** U.C.L.A.
1974 **David Thompson,** N.Caro. St.
     Bill Walton, U.C.L.A.
1975 **Kevin Grevey,** Kentucky
     David Meyers, U.C.L.A.
1976 **Kent Benson,** Indiana

     Scott May, Indiana
1977 **Marques Johnson,** U.C.L.A.

The Citizens Savings Athletic Foundation names the College Football Championship Team of the Year, based primarily on season-long play but also considering postseason play and other honors accorded to players on the team. The coach's name appears with the team, unless otherwise designated.

1883 **Yale,** Ray Tompkins, captain
1884 **Yale,** Eugene Richards, captain
1885 **Princeton,** C.M. DeCamp, captain
1886 **Yale,** Robert Corwin, captain
1887 **Yale,** Harry Beecher, captain
1888 **Yale,** Walter Camp
1889 **Princeton,** Edgar A. Poe, captain
1890 **Harvard,** George A. Stewart
     George C. Adams
1891 **Yale,** Walter Camp
1892 **Yale,** Walter Camp
1893 **Princeton,** Alex Moffatt
1894 **Yale,** William C. Rhodes
1895 **Pennsylvania,** George W. Woodruff
1896 **Princeton,** Langdon Lea
1897 **Pennsylvania,** George W. Woodruff
1898 **Harvard,** W. Cameron Forbes
1899 **Harvard,** Benjamin H. Dibblee
1900 **Yale,** Malcolm L. McBride
1901 **Michigan,** Fielding H. Yost
1902 **Michigan,** Fielding H. Yost
1903 **Princeton,** A.R.T. Hillebrand
1904 **Pennsylvania,** Carl S. Williams
1905 **Chicago,** Amos Alonzo Stagg
1906 **Princeton,** William W. Roper
1907 **Yale,** William Knox
1908 **Pennsylvania,** Sol Metzger
1909 **Yale,** Howard H. Jones
1910 **Harvard,** Percy D. Haughton
1911 **Princeton,** William W. Roper
1912 **Harvard,** Percy D. Haughton
1913 **Harvard,** Percy D. Haughton
1914 **U.S. Military Academy,** Charles Daly
1915 **Cornell,** Albert H. Sharpe
1916 **Pittsburgh,** Glenn S. Warner
1917 **Georgia Tech,** John W. Heisman
1918 **Pittsburgh,** Glenn S. Warner
1919 **Harvard,** Robert Fisher
1920 **California,** Andrew L. Smith
1921 **Cornell,** Gilmour Dobie
1922 **Cornell,** Gilmour Dobie
1923 **Illinois,** Robert Zuppke
1924 **Notre Dame,** Knute K. Rockne
1925 **Alabama,** W. Wallace Wade
1926 **Alabama,** W. Wallace Wade
     Stanford, Glenn S. Warner
1927 **Illinois,** Robert Zuppke
1928 **Georgia Tech,** William A. Alexander
1929 **Notre Dame,** Knute K. Rockne
1930 **Notre Dame,** Knute K. Rockne
1931 **Southern California,** Howard H. Jones
1932 **Southern California,** Howard H. Jones
1933 **Michigan,** Harry Kipke
1934 **Minnesota,** Bernard W. Bierman
1935 **Minnesota,** Bernard W. Bierman
1936 **Minnesota,** Bernard W. Bierman
1937 **California,** Leonard B. Allison
1938 **Texas Christian,** Leo R. Meyer
1939 **Texas A & M,** Homer H. Norton
1940 **Stanford,** Clark Shaughnessy

1941	Minnesota, Bernard W. Bierman
1942	Wisconsin, Harry Stuhldreher
1943	Notre Dame, Frank W. Leahy
1944	U.S. Military Academy, Earl H. Blaik
1945	U.S. Military Academy, Earl H. Blaik
1946	U.S. Military Academy, Earl H. Blaik
	Notre Dame, Frank W. Leahy
1947	Notre Dame, Frank W. Leahy
	Michigan, Herbert O. Crisler
1948	Michigan, Benjamin G. Oosterbaan
1949	Notre Dame, Frank W. Leahy
1950	Oklahoma, Charles Wilkinson
1951	Michigan State, Clarence Munn
1952	Michigan State, Clarence Munn
1953	Notre Dame, Frank W. Leahy
1954	U.C.L.A., Henry R. Sanders
	Ohio State, W. Woodrow Hayes
1955	Oklahoma, Charles Wilkinson
1956	Oklahoma, Charles Wilkinson
1957	Auburn, Ralph Jordan
1958	Louisiana State, Paul F. Dietzel
1959	Syracuse, Floyd Schwartzwalder
1960	Washington, James Owens
1961	Alabama, Paul W. Bryant
1962	Southern California, John McKay
1963	Texas, Darrell Royal
1964	Arkansas, Frank Broyles
1965	Michigan State, Hugh Daugherty
1966	Notre Dame, Ara Parseghian
	Michigan State, Hugh Daugherty
1967	Southern California, John McKay
1968	Ohio State, W. Woodrow Hayes
1969	Texas, Darrell Royal
1970	Nebraska, Robert S. Davaney
1971	Nebraska, Robert S. Devaney
1972	Southern California, John McKay
1973	Notre Dame, Ara Parseghian
1974	Oklahoma, Barry Switzer
	Southern California, John McKay
1975	Ohio State, W. Woodrow Hayes
	Oklahoma, Barry Switzer
1976	Pittsburgh, John Majors
1977	Pittsburgh, John Majors

COLLEGE FOOTBALL PLAYER OF THE YEAR (B-Back, C-Center, E-End, G-Guard, T-Tackle)

1900	Truxton Hare, University of Pennsylvania (G)
1901	Charles Daly, U.S. Military Academy (B)
1902	James Hogan, Yale (T)
1903	John DeWitt, Princeton (G)
1904	William Heston, University of Michigan (B)
1905	Thomas Shevlin, Yale (E)
1906	Walter Eckersall, Chicago (B)
1907	Adolph Schulz, Michigan (C)
1908	Walter Steffen, Chicago (B)
1909	Edward Coy, Yale (B)
1910	John Kilpatrick, Yale (E)
1911	Sanford White, Princeton (E)
1912	James Thorpe, Carlisle (B)
1913	Charles Brickley, Harvard (B)
1914	H. Hardwick, Harvard (E)
1915	Edward Mahan, Harvard (B)
1916	Elmer Oliphant, U.S. Military Academy (B)
1917	Wilbur Henry, Washington-Jefferson (T)
1918	Paul Robeson, Rutgers (E)
1919	Alvin McMillin, Centre (B)
1920	George Gipp, Notre Dame (B)
1921	Harold Muller, California (E)
1922	Harry Kipke, Michigan (B)
1923	George Pfann, Cornell (B)

1924	Harold "Red" Grange, Illinois (B)
1925	Ernest Nevers, Stanford (B)
1926	Ben Oosterbaan, Michigan (E)
1927	Morley Drury, So. Calif. (B)
1928	Christian Cagle, U.S. Military Academy (B)
1929	Jack Cannon, Notre Dame (G)
1930	Frank Carideo, Notre Dame (B)
1931	John Baker, Southern California (G)
1932	Harry Newman, Michigan (B)
1933	Beattie Feathers, Tennessee (B)
1934	Millard Howell, Alabama (B)
1935	Jay Berwanger, Chicago (B)
1936	Sammy Baugh, Texas Christian (B)
1937	Byron White, Colorado (B)
1938	Davey O'Brien, Texas Christian (B)
1939	Tom Harmon, Michigan (B)
1940	Frank Albert, Stanford (B)
1941	Bruce Smith, Minnesota (B)
1942	Frank Sinkwich, Georgia (B)
1943	Angelo Bertelli, Notre Dame (B)
1944	Glenn Davis, U.S. Military Academy (B)
1945	Felix Blanchard, U.S. Military Academy (B)
1946	Glenn Davis, U.S. Military Academy (B)
1947	Charles Conerly, Mississippi (B)
1948	Charles Bednarik, Pennsylvania University (C)
1949	Leon Hart, Notre Dame (E)
1950	Francis Bagnell, Pennsylvania University (B)
1951	William McColl, Stanford (E)
1952	Steve Meilinger, Kentucky (E)
1953	John Lattner, Notre Dame (B)
1954	Kurt Burris, Oklahoma (C)
1955	Howard Cassady, Ohio St. (B)
1956	Paul Hornung, Notre Dame (B)
1957	John Crow, Texas A & M (B)
1958	Randy Duncan, Iowa (B)
1959	Billy Cannon, Louisiana State (B)
1960	Joseph Bellino, U.S. Naval Academy (B)
1961	Bobby Bell, Minnesota (T)
1962	Terry Baker, Oregon State (B)
1963	Roger Staubach, U.S. Naval Academy (B)
1964	John Huarte, Notre Dame (B)
1965	Michael Garrett, University of Southern California (B)
1966	Steve Spurrier, Florida (B)
1967	Gary Beban, U.C.L.A. (B)
1968	O.J. Simpson, University of Southern California (B)
1969	Steve Owens, Oklahoma (B)
1970	Jim Plunkett, Stanford (B)
1971	Jerry Tagge, Nebraska (B)
1972	Johnny Rodgers, Nebraska (B)
1973	John Cappelletti, Penn State (B)
1974	Archie Griffin, Ohio State (B)
1975	Archie Griffin, Ohio State (B)
1976	Tony Dorsett, Pittsburgh (B)
1977	Earl Campbell, Texas (B)

Theodore Roosevelt Award Silver Anniversary Top Five Today's Top Five

NATIONAL COLLEGIATE ATHLETIC ASSOCIATION
Box 1906, Shawnee Mission, Kans. 66222 (913/384-3220)

The Theodore Roosevelt Award, the NCAA's highest honor, recognizes an individual whose distinguished career has been influenced by competitive collegiate athletics. A trophy and medal are presented to the winner.

1967 Dwight D. Eisenhower, General of the Army and former President of the United States
1968 Leverett Saltonstall, former Unites States Senator and Governor of Massachusetts
1969 Byron R. White, United States Supreme Court Justice
1970 Frederick L. Hovde, president, Purdue University
1971 Christopher C. Kraft, Jr., National Aeronautics and Space Administration
1972 Jerome H. Holland, U.S. Ambassador to Sweden
1973 Omar N. Bradley, General of the Army
1974 Jesse Owens, Jesse Owens, Inc.
1975 Gerald R. Ford, President of the United States and former House Minority Leader
1976 Thomas J. Hamilton, Rear Admiral, U.S. Navy
1977 Tom Bradley, Mayor of Los Angeles

The Silver Anniversary Top Five Awards honor five former collegiate athletes 25 years after their graduation from college, based both on their collegiate years and career achievement since graduation. A medal is presented to the winners.

1973 Ray R. Evans, (University of Kansas), bank president
John Feraro, (University of Southern California), city councilman
John D. Hopper, (Dickinson College), insurance consultant
Donald G. Mulder, (Hope College), surgeon
Stewart L. Udall, (University of Arizona), lawyer and former Cabinet Secretary
1974 Howard H. Callaway, (United States Military Academy), Secretary of the Army
Robert S. Dorsey, (Ohio State University), jet engine expert
Robert B. McCurry, Jr., (Michigan State University), vice-president Chrysler Corp.
Robert J. Robinson, (Baylor University), minister
Eugene T. Rossides, (Columbia University), lawyer
1975 Robert S. Folsom, (Southern Methodist University), investor
Billy M. Jones, (Vanderbilt University), president, Memphis State University
William J. Keating, (University of Cincinnati), president, *Cincinnati Enquirer*
Ralph E. O'Brien, (Butler University), insurance
Philip J. Ryan, (U.S. Naval Academy), commander, U.S. Navy
1976 Napolean A. Bell, (Mount Union College), attorney
Ernest Jackson Curtis, (Vanderbilt University), corporate marketing
H. Samuel Greenawalt, (University of Pennsylvania), banking
Ross J. Pritchard, (University of Arkansas), president, Arkansas State University
Wade Roger Stinson, (University of Kansas), banking
1977 Donald E. Coleman, (Michigan State University), minority programs director, College of Osteopathic Medicine, Michigan State University
Richard W. Kazmaier, (Princeton University), president, L & R Industries, Inc., and Eastern Sports Sales, Inc.
Vincent George Rhoden, (Morgan State University), podiatrist and surgeon
William J. Wade, (Vanderbilt University), assistant vice-president, Third National Bank
Frederick A. Yonkman, (Hope College), executive vice president and general counsel, American Express Company

The Today's Top Five Awards are presented annually to the five seniors judged to be the most outstanding, based on academic achievement and character as well as on sports accomplishments. Medals are presented to the winners.

1973 Robert Wesley Ash, (Cornell College), football
Bruce Patrick Bannon, (Pennsylvania State University), football
Blake Lynn Ferguson, (Drexel University), lacrosse
Jerry Alan Heidenreich, (Southern Methodist University), swimming
Sidney Allen Sink, (Bowling Green State University), track and field
1974 David A. Bladino, (University of Pittsburgh), football
Paul Douglas Collins, (Illinois State), basketball
David D. Gallagher, (University of Michigan), football
Gary W. Hall, (Indiana University), swimming
David J. Wottle, (Bowling Green State University), track and field
1975 John R. Baiorunos, (Pennsylvania State University), football
Patrick C. Haden, (University of Southern California), football
Randy L. Hall, (University of Alabama), football
Jarrett T. Hubbard, (University of Michigan), wrestling
Tony G. Waldrop, (University of North Carolina), track and field
1976 Marvin Lawrence Cobb, (University of Southern California), baseball and football
Archie Griffin, (Ohio State University), football
Bruce Alan Hamming, (Augustana College), basketball
Patrick Timothy Moore, (Ohio State University), diving
John Michael Sciarra, (UCLA), football
1977 Jeffrey Dankworth, (UCLA), football
Randolph Dean, (Northwestern University), football
Steven Furniss, (University of Southern California), swimming
John Hencken, (Stanford University), swimming
Gerald Huesken, (Susquehanna University), football

Hickok Belt

HICKOK MANUFACTURING COMPANY
845 Ave. G East, Arlington, Tex. 76011 (817/640-1800)

The Hickok Belt is a trophy of gold, diamonds and other jewels currently worth about $35,000, which is awarded annually to the leading professional athlete of the year. A poll of 270 leading newspaper sports editors in the U.S. determines the recipient.

1950 Phil Rizzuto, Baseball
1951 Allie Reynolds, Baseball
1952 Rocky Marciano, Boxing
1953 Ben Hogan, Golf
1954 Willie Mays, Baseball
1955 Otto Graham, Football
1956 Mickey Mantle, Baseball
1957 Carmen Basilio, Boxing
1958 Bob Turley, Baseball
1959 Ingemar Johansson, Boxing
1960 Arnold Palmer, Golf
1961 Roger Maris, Baseball
1962 Maury Wills, Baseball
1963 Sandy Koufax, Baseball

1964 Jim Brown, Football
1965 Sandy Koufax, Baseball
1966 Frank Robinson, Baseball
1967 Carl Yastrzemski, Baseball
1968 Joe Namath, Football
1969 Tom Seaver, Baseball
1970 Brooks Robinson, Baseball
1971 Lee Trevino, Golf
1972 Steve Carlton, Baseball
1973 O.J. Simpson, Football
1974 Muhammad Ali, Boxing
1975 Pete Rose, Baseball
1976 Kenny Stabler, Football
1977 No award

National Sports Award

UNITED STATES OF MEXICO, UNDER-
SECRETARIAT OF YOUTH RECREATION AND
SPORTS
Argentina #28, Mexico, D.F., Mexico (Tel: 512.55.93)

The Mexican National Sports Award is given annually for distinguished performance in or contributions to sports by individuals or teams. Individuals must be under 25 years of age. The winner is nominated by Mexican sports federations, organizations and similar institutions and selected by a panel of judges. The award is a gold medal and a diploma signed by the president of the Republic.

1975 Carlos Giron, Diving
1976 Daniel Bautista, 20,000-meter walk
1977 Not available at press time

Seven Crowns of Sports Awards

JOSEPH E. SEAGRAM & SONS, INC.
375 Park Ave., New York, N.Y. 10022 (212/572-7000)

The $10,000 Seagram's Seven Crowns of Sports Award honors excellence in a season's competition in each of seven major professional spectator sports. A complex mathematical formula has been established to determine the top performers in both team and individual sports. In team sports, the individual player's performance is evaluated in light of to what degree it contributes to the team's accomplishment, while in individual sports, the evaluation is made on the basis of head-to-head competition with other athletes.

FOOTBALL
1975 Otis Armstrong
1976 O.J. Simpson
1977 Walter Payton

BASEBALL
1975 Joe Morgan
1976 Joe Morgan
1977 Rod Carew

TENNIS—MEN
1975 Manuel Orantes
1976 Jimmy Connors
1977 Bjorn Borg

TENNIS—WOMEN
1975 Chris Evert
1976 Chris Evert
1977 Chris Evert

GOLF—MEN
1975 Jack Nicklaus
1976 Jack Nicklaus
1977 Jack Nicklaus

GOLF—WOMEN
1975 Sandra Palmer
1976 JoAnne Carner
1977 Judy Rankin

BASKETBALL
1975 Bob McAdoo
1976 Kareem Abdul-Jabbar
1977 Bobby Jones

HOCKEY
1975 Bernie Parent
1976 Guy Lafleur
1977 Marcel Dionne

HORSERACING
1975 Bill Shoemaker
1976 Jorge Tejeira
1977 Steve Cauthen

Most Valuable Player

SPORT MAGAZINE
641 Lexington Ave., New York, N.Y. 10022 (212/935-4100)

The editors of Sport magazine annually select the Most Valuable Player in the championship tournaments of various professional (and one college) sports.

BASEBALL (World Series)
1955 Johnny Podres, Brooklyn Dodgers
1956 Don Larsen, New York Yankees
1957 Lew Burdette, Milwaukee Braves
1958 Bob Turley, New York Yankees
1959 Larry Sherry, Los Angeles Dodgers
1960 Bobby Richardson, New York Yankees
1961 Whitey Ford, New York Yankees
1962 Ralph Terry, New York Yankees
1963 Sandy Koufax, Los Angeles Dodgers
1964 Bob Gibson, St. Louis Cardinals
1965 Sandy Koufax, Los Angeles Dodgers
1966 Frank Robinson, Baltimore Orioles
1967 Bob Gibson, St. Louis Cardinals
1968 Mickey Lolich, Detroit Tigers
1969 Donn Clendenon, New York Mets
1970 Brooks Robinson, Baltimore Orioles
1971 Roberto Clemente, Pittsburgh Pirates
1972 Gene Tenace, Oakland A's
1973 Reggie Jackson, Oakland A's
1974 Rollie Fingers, Oakland A's
1975 Pete Rose, Cincinnati Reds
1976 Johnny Bench, Cincinnati Reds
1977 Reggie Jackson, New York Yankees

BASKETBALL (National Basketball Association Playoffs)
1969 Jerry West, Los Angeles Lakers
1970 Willis Reed, New York Knicks
1971 Kareem Abdul-Jabbar, Milwaukee Bucks
1972 Wilt Chamberlain, Los Angeles Lakers

1973 **Willis Reed,** New York Knicks
1974 **John Havlicek,** Boston Celtics
1975 **Rick Barry,** Golden State Warriors
1976 **Jojo White,** Boston Celtics
1977 **Bill Walton,** Portland Trailblazers

BASKETBALL (American Basketball Association Playoffs)
1973 **George McGinnis,** Indiana Pacers
1974 **Julius Erving,** New York Nets
1975 **Artis Gilmore,** Kentucky Colonels
1976 **Julius Erving,** New York Nets

BASKETBALL (College Basketball Player of the Year)
1977 **Marques Johnson,** UCLA

FOOTBALL (National Football Association Championship Games)
1958 **Johnny Unitas,** Baltimore Colts
1959 **Johnny Unitas,** Baltimore Colts
1960 **Norm Van Brocklin,** Philadelphia Eagles
1961 **Paul Hornung,** Green Bay Packers
1962 **Ray Nitschke,** Green Bay Packers
1963 **Larry Morris,** Chicago Bears
1964 **Gary Collins,** Cleveland Browns
1965 **Jim Taylor,** Green Bay Packers

FOOTBALL (Super Bowl)
1967 **Bart Starr,** Green Bay Packers
1968 **Bart Starr,** Green Bay Packers
1969 **Joe Namath,** New York Jets
1970 **Len Dawson,** Kansas City Chiefs
1971 **Chuck Howley,** Dallas Cowboys
1972 **Roger Staubach,** Dallas Cowboys
1973 **Jake Scott,** Miami Dolphins
1974 **Larry Csonka,** Miami Dolphins
1975 **Franco Harris,** Pittsburgh Steelers
1976 **Lynn Swann,** Pittsburgh Steelers
1977 **Fred Biletnikoff,** Oakland Raiders

HOCKEY (Stanley Cup)
1971 **Ken Dryden,** Montreal Canadiens
1972 **Bobby Orr,** Boston Bruins
1973 **Yvan Cournoyer,** Montreal Canadiens
1974 **Bernie Parent,** Philadelphia Flyers
1975 **Bernie Parent,** Philadelphia Flyers
1976 **Larry Robinson,** Montreal Canadiens
1977 **Guy Lafleur,** Montreal Canadiens

Man of the Year
SPORTING NEWS
1212 N. Lindbergh Blvd., St. Louis, Mo. 63132
(314/997-7111)

The editors of *The Sporting News* annually select outstanding athletes and teams in various sports as well as the Man of the Year. That latter honor, whose recipients are listed here, is given for the greatest sports accomplishment during the calendar year. A trophy is presented to the athlete selected.

1968 **Denny McLain,** Baseball
1969 **Tom Seaver,** Baseball
1970 **John Wooden,** College basketball
1971 **Lee Trevino,** Golf
1972 **Charles O. Finley,** Baseball
1973 **O.J. Simpson,** Professional football
1974 **Lou Brock,** Baseball

1975 **Archie Griffith,** College football
1976 **Lawrence O'Brien,** National Basketball Association
1977 **Steve Cauthen,** Horseracing

Sportsman of the Year
SPORTS ILLUSTRATED
Time & Life Bldg., 1271 Ave. of the Americas, New York, N.Y. 10020 (212/586-1212)

The editors of *Sports Illustrated* annually select a male or female amateur or professional athlete as Sportsman of the Year, based on excellence in sport, either over an extended period or for a single, outstanding victory. The honor, therefore, is for *arete*—pure excellence. The trophy is a reproduction of a Greek amphora, or vase, with a sport motif dated at least 510 B.C.

1954 **Roger Bannister,** Track and field
1955 **Johnny Podres,** Baseball
1956 **Bobby Morrow,** Football
1957 **Stan Musial,** Baseball
1958 **Rafer Johnson,** Track and field
1959 **Ingemar Johansson,** Boxing
1960 **Arnold Palmer,** Golf
1961 **Jerry Lucas,** Basketball
1962 **Terry Baker,** Football
1963 **Pete Rozelle,** Football
1964 **Ken Venturi,** Golf
1965 **Sandy Koufax,** Baseball
1966 **Jim Ryun,** Track and field
1967 **Carl Yastrzemski,** Baseball
1968 **Bill Russell,** Basketball
1969 **Tom Seaver,** Baseball
1970 **Bobby Orr,** Hockey
1971 **Lee Trevino,** Golf
1972 **John Wooden,** Basketball coach
     Billie Jean King, Tennis
1973 **Jackie Stewart,** Auto racing
1974 **Muhammad Ali,** Boxing
1975 **Pete Rose,** Baseball
1976 **Chris Evert,** Tennis
1977 **Steve Cauthen,** Horse racing

Fair Play Trophy
UNITED NATIONS EDUCATIONAL, SCIENTIFIC AND CULTURAL ORGANIZATION
7 Place de Fontenoy, 75007 Paris, France (Tel: 976 22 54)

The Fair Play Trophy, given by the International Committee for Fair Play (Comite International pour le Fair-Play, 16 Rue Peron, Croixxy-sur-Seine, France), annually recognizes the highest standards of sport spirit. The committee selects the winner, who receives a medallion and a certificate, on the recommendation of national Olympic committees.

1964 **Eugenio Monti,** (Italy), Bobsled
1965 **Willye White,** (U.S.A.), Long Jump
     West Ham United, (England), Soccer
     Munich 60, (Federal Republic of Germany), Soccer
     Isztvan Zsolt, (Hungary), Soccer
1966 **Stevan Horvat,** (Yugoslavia), Wrestling
1967 **Istvan Gulyas,** (Hungary), Tennis
1968 **Japanese National Team,** (Japan), Soccer
1969 **Pedro Zaballa,** (Spain), Soccer
     Francisco Buscato, (Spain), Basketball
1970 **Ryszard Szurkowski,** (Poland), Cycling

1971 **Meta Antenen,** (Switzerland), Long Jump
1972 **Stan Smith,** (U.S.A.), Tennis
     Emiliano Rodriguez, (Spain), Basketball
1973 **Yan Hallam, Will Moore, Mick Bennettand, Rick Evans,** (England), Cycling
     Bobby Charlton, (England), Soccer
1974 **Claude Rovonel,** (Switzerland), Karate
     Lia Manoliu, (Rumania), Discus
1975 **Victor Niederhoffer,** (U.S.A.), Squash racquets
     Bob Mathias, (U.S.A.), Decathlon
     Emil Zatopek, (Czechoslovakia), Marathon
1976 **No award**
1977 **No award**

Most Valuable Player Award
Joe Cronin Award
AMERICAN LEAGUE OF PROFESSIONAL BASEBALL CLUBS
280 Park Ave., New York, N.Y. 10017 (212/682-7000)

The American League Most Valuable Player Award is an honor based on season-long performance

1931 **Lefty Grove,** Philadelphia
1932 **Jimmie Foxx,** Philadelphia
1933 **Jimmie Foxx,** Philadelphia
1934 **Mickey Cochrane,** Detroit
1935 **Hank Greenberg,** Detroit
1936 **Lou Gehrig,** New York
1937 **Charlie Gehringer,** Detroit
1938 **Jimmie Foxx,** Boston
1939 **Joe DiMaggio,** New York
1940 **Hank Greenberg,** Detroit
1941 **Joe DiMaggio,** New York
1942 **Joe Gordon,** New York
1943 **Spud Chandler,** New York
1944 **Hal Newhouser,** Detroit
1945 **Hal Newhouser,** Detroit
1946 **Ted Williams,** Boston
1947 **Joe DiMaggio,** New York
1948 **Lou Boudreau,** Cleveland
1949 **Ted Williams,** Bostons
1950 **Phil Rizzuto,** New York
1951 **Yogi Berra,** New York
1952 **Bobby Schantz,** Philadelphia
1953 **Al Rosen,** Cleveland
1954 **Yogi Berra,** New York
1955 **Yogi Berra,** New York
1956 **Mickey Mantle,** New York
1957 **Mickey Mantle,** New York
1958 **Jackie Jensen,** Boston
1959 **Nellie Fox,** Chicago
1960 **Roger Maris,** New York
1961 **Roger Maris,** New York
1962 **Mickey Mantle,** New York
1963 **Elston Howard,** New York
1964 **Brooks Robinson,** Baltimore
1965 **Zoilo Versalles,** Minnesota
1966 **Frank Robinson,** Baltimore
1967 **Carl Yastrzemski,** Boston
1968 **Denny McLain,** Detroit
1969 **Harmon Killebrew,** Minnesota
1970 **Boog Powell,** Baltimore
1971 **Vida Blue,** Oakland
1972 **Dick Allen,** Chicago
1973 **Reggie Jackson,** Oakland
1974 **Jeff Burroughs,** Texas
1975 **Fred Lynn,** Boston

1976 **Thurman Munson,** New York
1977 **Rod Carew,** Minnesota

The Joe Cronin Award, which consists of a trophy and two special watches, is given annually for significant achievement in baseball during the season or through a career. Member clubs nominate players for a vote by League executives.

1973 **Nolan Ryan,** (California Angels), Record 383 strikeouts in season
1974 **Al Kaline,** (Detroit Tigers), 3,000 hits in 22-year career
1975 **Rod Carew,** (Minnesota Twins), Fourth consecutive batting championship
1976 **Jim Palmer,** (Baltimore Orioles), Winner of 20 or more games in six of previous seven years; three-time Cy Young Award winner
1977 **Brooks Robinson,** (Baltimore Orioles), 23-year career in which he recorded the highest field average of all third basemen (.971), played on 18 consecutive American League All-Star Teams and won 16 consecutive Golden Glove Awards for the best fielding in the League, among other honors

Induction
NATIONAL BASEBALL HALL OF FAME
Cooperstown, N.Y. 13326 (607/547-9988)

The Baseball Writers' Association of America annually elects new members of the National Baseball Hall of Fame from the ranks of retired players who were active in the Major Leagues during a period beginning 20 years before and ending five years prior to the election. Playing ability, integrity, sportsmanship, character and contributions to their teams and to the sport are considered, first by a screening committee and then by active members of the BWAA. The Committee on Veterans selects inductees active more than 25 years before. Baseball managers and executives are eligible for election, but no member of the Baseball Hall of Fame Committee may be considered while he is serving on the committee.

1936

Tyrus R. Cobb	Walter P. Johnson
Christopher Mathewson	George H. "Babe" Ruth
John P. "Honus" Wagner	

1937

Morgan G. Bulkeley	Byron B. "Ban" Johnson
Napoleon "Larry" Lajoie	John J. McGraw
Connie Mack	Tristram E. Speaker
George Wright	Denton T. "Cy" Young

1938

Grover C. Alexander	Alexander J. Cartwright, Jr.
Henry Chadwick	

1939

Adrian C. "Cap" Anson	Edward T. Collins
Charles A. Comiskey	William A. "Candy" Cummings
William B. "Buck" Ewing	H. Louis Gehrig
William H. "Willie" Keeler	Charles G. Radbourne
George H. Sisler	Albert G. Spalding

1942
Rogers Hornsby

1944
Kenesaw M. Landis

1945
Roger P. Bresnahan
Frederick C. Clarke
Edward J. Delahanty
Hugh A. Jennings
James H. O'Rourke

Dennis "Dan" Brouthers
James J. Collins
Hugh Duffy
Michael J. "King" Kelly
Wilbert Robinson

1946
Jesse C. Burkett
John D. Chesbro
Clark C. Griffith
Joseph J. McGinnity
Joseph B. Tinker

Frank L. Chance
John J. Evers
Thomas F. McCarthy
Edward S. Plank
George E. "Rube"
Waddell

Edward A. Walsh

1947
Gordon S. "Mickey"
Cochrane
Robert M. "Lefty" Grove

Frank F. Frisch

Carl O. Hubbell

1948
Herbert J. Pennock

Harold J. "Pie" Traynor

1949
Mordecai P. Brown
Charles A. "Kid" Nichols

Charles L. Gehringer

1951
James E. Foxx

Melvin T. Ott

1952
Harry E. Heilmann

Paul G. Waner

1953
Edward G. Barrow

Thomas H. Connolly
William J. Klem
Roderick J. "Bobby"
Wallace

Charles A. "Chief"
Bender
Jay H. "Dizzy" Dean
Aloysius H. Simmons
William H. "Harry"
Wright

1954
William M. Dickey

William H. Terry

Walter J. "Rabbit"
Maranville

1955
J. Franklin Baker
Charles L. "Gabby" Hartnett
Raymond W. Schalk

Joseph P. DiMaggio
Theodore A. Lyons
Arthur C. "Dazzy" Vance

1956
Joseph E. Cronin

Henry B. Greenberg

1957
Samuel E. Crawford

Joseph V. McCarthy

1959
Zachariah D. Wheat

1960
No inductees

1961
Max G. Carey

William R. Hamilton

1962
Robert W.A. Feller
Jack R. Robinson

William B. McKechnie
Edd J. Roush

1963
John G. Clarkson
Edgar C. "Sam" Rice

Elmer H. Flick
Eppa Rixey

1964
Lucius B. "Luke" Appling
Burleigh A. Grimes
Timothy J. Keefe

John M. Ward

Urban C. "Red" Faber
Miller J. Huggins
Henry E. "Heinie"
Manush

1965
James F. "Pud" Galvin

1966
Charles D. "Casey" Stengel Theodore S. Williams

1967
W. Branch Rickey
Lloyd J. Waner

Charles H. "Red" Ruffing

1968
Hazen S. "Kiki" Cuyler
Joseph M. Medwick

Leon A. "Goose" Goslin

1969
Roy Campanella
Waite C. Hoyt

Stanley A. Coveleski
Stanley F. Musial

1970
Louis Boudreau
Ford C. Frick

Earle B. Combs
Jesse J. "Pop" Haines

1971
David J. Bancroft
Charles J. "Chick" Hafey
Joseph J. Kelley

Leroy R. "Satchel" Paige

Jacob P. Beckley
Harry B. Hooper
Richard W. "Rube"
Marquard
George M. Weiss

1972
Lawrence P. "Yogi" Berra
Vernon L. "Lefty" Gomez
Sanford Koufax

Early Wynn

Joshua Gibson
William Harridge
Walter F. "Buck"
Leonard
Ross M. Youngs

1973
Roberto W. Clemente
Monford "Monte" Irvin
Warren E. Spahn

William G. Evans
George L. Kelly
Michael F. Welch

1974
James T. "Cool Papa" Bell
John B. "Jocko" Conlan
Mickey C. Mantle

James L. Bottomley
Edward C. "Whitey" Ford
Samuel L. Thompson

1975

H. Earl Averill	Stanley R. "Bucky" Harris
William J. Herman	William J. "Judy" Johnson
Ralph M. Kiner	

1976

Oscar M. Charleston	Roger Connor
R. Cal Hubbard	Robert G. Lemon
Frederick C. Lindstrom	Robin E. Roberts

1977

Ernest Banks	Martin Dihigo
John H. Lloyd	Alfonso R. Lopez
Amos W. Rusie	Joseph W. Sewell

Most Valuable Player

NATIONAL LEAGUE OF BASEBALL CLUBS
One Rockefeller Plaza, Suite 1602, New York, N.Y. 10020
(212/582-4213)

The Most Valuable Player is selected by a vote of the Baseball Writers Association of America members for season-long performance. A trophy is presented to the winner.

1931 Frank Frisch, Cardinals
1932 Chuck Klein, Phillies
1933 Carl Hubbell, Giants
1934 Dizzy Dean, Cardinals
1935 Gabby Hartnett, Cubs
1936 Carl Hubbell, Giants
1937 Joe Medwick, Cardinals
1938 Ernie Lombardi, Reds
1939 Bucky Walters, Reds
1940 Frank McCormick, Reds
1941 Dolph Camilli, Dodgers
1942 Mort Cooper, Cardinals
1943 Stan Musial, Cardinals
1944 Marty Marion, Cardinals
1945 Phil Cavarretta, Cubs
1946 Stan Musial, Cardinals
1947 Bob Elliott, Braves
1948 Stan Musial, Cardinals
1949 Jackie Robinson, Dodgers
1950 Jim Konstanty, Phillies
1951 Roy Campanella, Dodgers
1952 Hank Sauer, Cubs
1953 Roy Campanella, Dodgers
1954 Willie Mays, Giants
1955 Roy Campanella, Dodgers
1956 Don Newcombe, Dodgers
1957 Hank Aaron, Braves
1958 Ernie Banks, Cubs
1959 Ernie Banks, Cubs
1960 Dick Groat, Pirates
1961 Frank Robinson, Reds
1962 Maury Wills, Dodgers
1963 Sandy Koufax, Dodgers
1964 Ken Boyer, Cardinals
1965 Willie Mays, Giants
1966 Roberto Clemente, Pirates
1967 Orlando Cepeda, Cardinals
1968 Bob Gibson, Cardinals
1969 Willie McCovey, Giants
1970 Johnny Bench, Reds
1971 Joe Torre, Cardinals

1972 Johnny Bench, Reds
1973 Pete Rose, Reds
1974 Steve Garvey, Dodgers
1975 Joe Morgan, Reds
1976 Joe Morgan, Reds
1977 George Foster, Reds

Major League Player of the Year

THE SPORTING NEWS
1212 N. Lindbergh, St. Louis, Mo. 63132 (314/997-7171)

The editors of *The Sporting News* annually select the outstanding baseball player of the season as the Major League Player of the Year. An engraved watch is presented to the winner.

1936 Carl Hubbell, New York (National League)
1937 Johnny Allen, Cleveland (American League)
1938 Johnny Vander Meer, Cincinnati (National League)
1939 Joe DiMaggio, New York (American League)
1940 Bob Feller, Cleveland (American League)
1941 Ted Williams, Boston (American League)
1942 Ted Williams, Boston (American League)
1943 Spud Chandler, New York (American League)
1944 Marty Marion, St. Louis (National League)
1945 Hal Newhouser, Detroit (American League)
1946 Stan Musial, St. Louis (National League)
1947 Ted Williams, Boston (American League)
1948 Lou Boudreau, Cleveland (American League)
1949 Ted Williams, Boston (American League)
1950 Phil Rizzuto, New York (American League)
1951 Stan Musial, St. Louis (National League)
1952 Robin Roberts, Philadelphia (National League)
1953 Al Rosen, Cleveland (American League)
1954 Willie Mays, New York (National League)
1955 Duke Snider, Brooklyn (National League)
1956 Mickey Mantle, New York (American League)
1957 Ted Williams, Boston (American League)
1958 Bob Turley, New York (American League)
1959 Early Wynn, Chicago (American League)
1960 Bill Mazeroski, Pittsburgh (National League)
1961 Roger Maris, New York (American League)
1962 Maury Wills, Los Angeles (National League)
       Don Drysdale, Los Angeles (National League)
1963 Sandy Koufax, Los Angeles (National League)
1964 Ken Boyer, St. Louis (National League)
1965 Sandy Koufax, Los Angeles (National League)
1966 Frank Robinson, Baltimore (American League)
1967 Carl Yastrzemski, Boston (American League)
1968 Denny McLain, Detroit (American League)
1969 Willie McCovey, San Francisco (National League)
1970 Johnny Bench, Cincinnati (National League)
1971 Joe Torre, St. Louis (National League)
1972 Billy Williams, Chicago (National League)
1973 Reggie Jackson, Oakland (American League)
1974 Lou Brock, St. Louis (National League)
1975 Joe Morgan, Cincinnati (National League)
1976 Joe Morgan, Cincinnati (National League)
1977 Rod Carew, Minnesota (American League)

Relief Man Award

WARNER-LAMBERT COMPANY
201 Tabor Rd., Morris Plains, N.J. 07950 (201/540-2000)

Recognizing the growing importance of the relief pitcher (or "fireman") in major league baseball, Rolaids present the Relief Man Award to the most outstanding relief pitchers in the American and National Leagues each season, based on wins and saves versus losses. The winners receive trophies.

AMERICAN LEAGUE
1976 Bill Campbell, Minnesota Twins
1977 Bill Campbell, Minnesota Twins

NATIONAL LEAGUE
1976 Rawly Eastwick, Cincinnati Reds
1977 Rollie Fingers, San Diego Padres

Player of the Year
Rookie of the Year
Cy Young Award
BASEBALL WRITERS ASSOCIATION OF AMERICA
7 Oregon Dr., Huntington Station, N.Y. 11746

The Association votes for the American League and National Player of the Year for the baseball season. This is officially—though infrequently—called the Kenesaw M. Landis Award.

AMERICAN LEAGUE
1931 Robert M. Grove (Philadelphia), Pitcher
1932 James E. Foxx (Philadelphia), First baseman
1933 James E. Foxx (Philadelphia), First baseman
1934 Gordon Cochrane (Detroit), Catcher
1935 Henry B. Greenberg (Detroit), First baseman
1936 Henry L. Gehrig (New York), First baseman
1937 Charles L. Gehringer (Detroit), Second baseman
1938 James E. Foxx (Boston), First baseman
1939 Joseph P. DiMaggio (New York), Outfielder
1940 Henry B. Greenberg (Detroit), Outfielder
1941 Joseph P. DiMaggio (New York), Outfielder
1942 Joseph L. Gordon (New York), Second baseman
1943 Spurgeon F. Chandler (New York), Pitcher
1944 Harold Newhouser (Detroit), Pitcher
1945 Harold Newhouser (Detroit), Pitcher
1946 Theodore S. Williams (Boston), Outfielder
1947 Joseph P. DiMaggio (New York), Outfielder
1948 Louis Boudreau (Cleveland), Shortstop
1949 Theodore S. Williams (Boston), Outfielder
1950 Philip F. Rizzuto (New York), Shortstop
1951 Lawrence P. "Yogi" Berra (New York), Catcher
1952 Robert C. Schantz (Philadelphia), Pitcher
1953 Albert C. Rosen (Cleveland), Third baseman
1954 Lawrence P. "Yogi" Berra (New York), Catcher
1955 Lawrence P. "Yogi" Berra (New York), Catcher
1956 Mickey C. Mantle (New York), Outfielder
1957 Mickey C. Mantle (New York), Outfielder
1958 Jack E. Jensen (Boston), Outfielder
1959 J. Nelson Fox (Chicago), Second baseman
1960 Roger E. Maris (New York), Outfielder
1961 Roger E. Maris (New York), Outfielder
1962 Mickey C. Mantle (New York), Outfielder
1963 Elston G. Howard (New York), Catcher
1964 Brooks C. Robinson (Baltimore), Third baseman
1965 Zoilo C. Versalles (Minnesota), Shortstop
1966 Frank Robinson (Baltimore), Outfielder
1967 Carl M. Yastrzemski (Boston), Outfielder
1968 Dennis D. McLain (Detroit), Pitcher
1969 Harmon C. Killebrew (Minnesota), Third baseman
1970 John W. Powell (Baltimore), First baseman
1971 Vida Blue (Oakland), Pitcher

1972 Richard A. Allen (Chicago), Third baseman
1973 Reggie Jackson (Oakland), Outfielder
1974 Jeff Burroughs (Texas), Outfielder
1975 Fred Lynn (Boston), Outfielder
1976 Thurman Munson (New York), Catcher
1977 Rod Carew (Minnesota), Second baseman

NATIONAL LEAGUE
1931 Frank Frisch (St. Louis), Second baseman
1932 Charles H. Klein (Philadelphia) Outfielder
1933 Carl O. Hubbell (New York), Pitcher
1934 Jerome H. Dean (St. Louis), Pitcher
1935 Charles L. Hartnett (Chicago), Catcher
1936 Carl O. Hubbell (New York), Pitcher
1937 Joseph M. Medwick (St. Louis), Outfielder
1938 Ernest N. Lombardi (Cincinnati), Catcher
1939 William H. Walters (Cincinnati), Pitcher
1940 Frank A. McCormick (Cincinnati), First baseman
1941 Adolph L. Camilli (Brooklyn), First baseman
1942 Morton C. Cooper (St. Louis), Pitcher
1943 Stanley F. Musial (St. Louis), Outfielder
1944 Martin W. Marion (St. Louis), Shortstop
1945 Philip J. Cavarretta (Chicago), First baseman
1946 Stanley F. Musial (St. Louis), First baseman
1947 Robert I. Elliott (Boston), Third baseman
1948 Stanley F. Musial (St. Louis), Outfielder
1949 Jack R. Robinson (Brooklyn), Second baseman
1950 C. James Konstanty (Philadelphia), Pitcher
1951 Roy Campanella (Brooklyn) Catcher
1952 Henry J. Sauer (Chicago), Outfield
1953 Roy Campanella (Brooklyn), Catcher
1954 Willie H. Mays (New York), Outfielder
1955 Roy Campanella (Brooklyn), Catcher
1956 Donald Newcombe (Brooklyn), Pitcher
1957 Henry L. Aaron (Milwaukee), Outfielder
1958 Ernest Banks (Chicago), Shortstop
1959 Ernest Banks (Chicago), Shortstop
1960 Richard M. Groat (Pittsburgh), Shortstop
1961 Frank Robinson (Cincinnati), Outfielder
1962 Maurice M. Wills (Los Angeles), Shortstop
1963 Sanford Koufax (Los Angeles), Pitcher
1964 Kenton L. Boyer (St. Louis), Third baseman
1965 Willie H. Mays (San Francisco), Outfielder
1966 Roberto W. Clemente (Pittsburgh), Outfielder
1967 Orlando M. Cepeda (St. Louis), First baseman
1968 Robert Gibson (St. Louis), Pitcher
1969 Willie L. McCovey (San Francisco), First baseman
1970 Johnny L. Bench (Cincinnati), Catcher
1971 Joseph P. Torre (St. Louis), Third baseman
1972 Johnny L. Bench (Cincinnati), Catcher
1973 Pete Rose (Cincinnati), Outfielder
1974 Steve Garvey (Los Angeles), First baseman
1975 Joe Morgan (Cincinnati), Second baseman
1976 Joe Morgan (Cincinnati), Second baseman
1977 George Foster (Cincinnati), Outfielder

The Rookie of the Year selection honors one American League and one National League player as the best during the first year of major league play.

AMERICAN LEAGUE
1947 Only one selection; see National League listing
1948 Only one selection; see National League listing
1949 Roy E. Sievers (St. Louis), Outfielder
1950 Walter O. Dropo (Boston), First baseman
1951 Gilbert J. McDougald (New York), Third baseman
1952 Harry G. Byrd (Philadelphia), Pitcher
1953 Harvey E. Kuenn (Detroit), Shortstop
1954 Robert A. Grim (New York), Pitcher
1955 Herbert J. Score (Cleveland), Pitcher

1956 Luis E. Aparicio (Chicago), Shortstop
1957 Anthony Kubek (New York), Outfielder
1958 Albert Pearson (Washington), Outfielder
1959 W. Robert Allison (Washington), Outfielder
1960 Ronald L. Hansen (Baltimore), Shortstop
1961 Donald B. Schwall (Boston), Pitcher
1962 Thomas M. Tresh (New York), Shortstop
1963 Gary C. Peters (Chicago), Pitcher
1964 A. Pedro Oliva (Minnesota), Outfielder
1965 Curtis L. Blefary (Baltimore), Outfielder
1966 Tommie L. Agee (Chicago), Outfielder
1967 Rodney C. Carew (Minnesota), Second baseman
1968 Stanley R. Bahnsen (New York), Pitcher
1969 Louis V. Piniella (Kansas City), Outfielder
1970 Thurman L. Munson (New York), Catcher
1971 C. Christopher Chambliss (Cleveland), First baseman
1972 Carlton E. Fisk (Boston), Catcher
1973 Al Bumbry (Baltimore), Outfielder
1974 Mike Hargrove (Texas), First baseman
1975 Fred Lynn (Boston), Outfielder
1976 Mark Fidrych (Detroit), Pitcher
1977 Eddie Murray (Baltimore), Designated hitter

NATIONAL LEAGUE

1947 Jack R. Robinson (Brooklyn), First baseman
1948 Alvin R. Dark (Boston), Shortstop
1949 Donald Newcombe (Brooklyn), Pitcher
1950 Samuel Jethroe (Boston), Outfielder
1951 Willie H. Mays (New York), Outfielder
1952 Joseph Black (Brooklyn), Pitcher
1953 James W. Gilliam (Brooklyn), Second baseman
1954 Wallace W. Moon (St. Louis), Outfielder
1955 William C. Virdon (St. Louis), Outfielder
1956 Frank Robinson (Cincinnati), Outfielder
1957 John S. Sanford (Philadelphia), Pitcher
1958 Orlando M. Cepeda (San Francisco), First baseman
1959 Willie L. McCovey (SanFrancisco), First baseman
1960 Frank O. Howard (Los Angeles), Outfielder
1961 Billy L. Williams (Chicago), Outfielder
1962 Kenneth D. Hubbs (Chicago), Second baseman
1963 Peter E. Rose (Cincinnati), Second baseman
1964 Richard A. Allen (Philadelphia), Third baseman
1965 James K. Lefebvre (Los Angeles), Second baseman
1966 Tommy V. Helms (Cincinnati), Third baseman
1967 G. Thomas Seaver (New York), Pitcher
1968 Johnny L. Bench (Cincinnati), Catcher
1969 Ted C. Sizemore (Los Angeles), Second baseman
1970 Carl W. Morton (Montreal), Pitcher
1971 Earl C. Williams (Atlanta), Catcher
1972 Jonathan T. Matlack (New York), Pitcher
1973 Gary Matthews (San Francisco), Outfielder
1974 Bake McBride (St. Louis), Outfielder
1975 John Montefusco (San Francisco), Pitcher
1976 Pat Zachry (Cincinnati), Pitcher
       Butch Metzger (San Diego), Pitcher
1977 Andre Dawson (Montreal), Outfielder

The Cy Young Award is awarded annually to the best pitcher in each league. Through 1966, only one award was made for both leagues.

1956 Donald Newcomb (National League), Brooklyn
1957 Warren E. Spahn (National League), Milwaukee
1958 Robert Turley (American League), New York
1959 Early Wynn (American League), Chicago
1960 Vernon Law (National League), Pittsburgh
1961 Edward C. Ford (American League), New York
1962 Donald S. Drysdale (National League), Los Angeles
1963 Sanford Koufax (National League), Los Angeles
1964 W. Dean Chance (American League), Los Angeles

1965 Sanford Koufax (National League), Los Angeles
1966 Sanford Koufax (National League), Los Angeles

AMERICAN LEAGUE

1967 James R. Lonborg, Boston
1968 Dennis D. McLain, Detroit
1969 Miguel A. Cuellar, Baltimore
       Dennis D. McLain, Detroit
1970 James E. Perry, Minnesota
1971 Vida Blue, Oakland
1972 Gaylord J. Perry, Cleveland
1973 James Palmer, Baltimore
1974 James Hunter, Oakland
1975 James Palmer, Baltimore
1976 James Palmer, Baltimore
1977 Sparky Lyle, New York

NATIONAL LEAGUE

1967 Michael F. McCormick, San Francisco
1968 Robert Gibson, St. Louis
1969 G. Thomas Seaver, New York
1970 Robert Gibson, St. Louis
1971 Ferguson A. Jenkins, Chicago
1972 Steven N. Carlton, Philadelphia
1973 G. Thomas Seaver, New York
1974 Michael Marshall, Los Angeles
1975 G. Thomas Seaver, New York
1976 Randy Jones, San Diego
1977 Steven N. Carlton, Philadelphia

Colonel Harry D. Henshel Award
Louis G. Wilke Memorial Award

AMATEUR ATHLETIC UNION OF THE UNITED STATES
3400 W. 86th St., Indianapolis, Ind. 46268 (317/297-2900)

The Colonel Harry D. Henshel Award is a trophy presented annually to the winning team in the Men's AAU National Basketball Championship.

1963 Phillips 66
1964 Goodyear Wingfoots
1965 Armed Forces All-Stars
1966 Ford Mustangs
1967 Akron Goodyear
1968 Armed Forces All-Stars
1969 Armed Forces All-Stars
1970 Armed Forces All-Stars
1971 Armed Forces All-Stars
1972 Armed Forces All-Stars
1973 Marathon Oil
1974 Jacksonville, Fla., AAU
1975 Capitol Insulation, Los Angeles, Calif.
1976 Athletes in Action, Tustin, Calif.
1977 Armed Forces All-Stars

In 1962, the Louis G. Wilke Memorial Award, was set up as the official trophy for the Most Valuable Player of the National AAU Basketball Tournament.

1954 George Macuga, U.S. Army
1955 George Bales, U.S. Marine Corps
1956 Jim Bond, Pasadena Mirror Glaze
1957 Tom Meschery, San Francisco Olympic Club
1958 Harvey Schmidt, D-C Truckers
1959 Dick Boushka, Wichita Vickers
1960 Bob Boozer, Peoria Cats
1961 Horace Walker, D-C Truckers
1962 Gary Thompson, Phillips "66"

1963 Don Kojis, Phillips "66"
1964 Larry Brown, Goodyear Wingfoots
1965 Verne Benson, Armed Forces All-Stars
1966 Cazzie Russell, Ford Mustangs
1967 Harold Sergent, Phillips "66"
1968 Mike Barrett, Armed Forces All-Stars
1969 Garfield Smith, Armed Forces All-Stars
1970 Michael Silliman, Armed Forces All-Stars
1971 Darnell Hillman, Armed Forces All-Stars
1972 Richard Harris, Marion-Kay
1973 George Bryant, Marathon Oil
1974 Rick Coleman, Jacksonville, Fla. AAU
1975 Larry Hollifield, Capitol Insulation
1976 Irvin Kiffin, Athletes in Action
1977 Jyrona Ralston, Armed Forces All-Stars

John W. Bunn Award
Frances P. Naismith Hall of Fame Award

NAISMITH MEMORIAL BASKETBALL HALL OF FAME
Springfield, Mass. 01109 (413/781-6500)

The John W. Bunn Award is given annually for outstanding contributions to basketball in particular and sports in general. The Hall of Fame board of trustees select the recipient of the silver bowl.

1973 John W. Bunn, Coach, author, prime mover in founding the Hall of Fame
1974 John Wooden, "The most successful coach ever in the history of collegiate basketball"; first at Indiana State and then at UCLA
1975 J. Walter Kennedy, National Basketball Assn. Commissioner
1976 Henry P. Iba, Collegiate coach at University of Colorado State and Oklahoma State Universities; three-time U.S. Olympic basketball coach
1977 Clifford B. Fagan, President of the Basketball Hall of Fame, Secretary of the National Basketball Committee of the United States and Canada, Board of Directors of the U.S. Olympic Committee, President of the Basketball Federation of the U.S.A., President of the Amateur Basketball Assn. of the U.S.A. and official of other basketball and sports organizations

The Frances P. Naismith Hall of Fame Award honors exceptional all-round basketball ability and special qualities of character, leadership and loyalty as demonstrated by a national college senior player under six feet tall. Collegiate coaches nominate players, and the recipient is selected by a committee of basketball writers and members of the Hall of Fame board of trustees.

1969 William C. Keller, Purdue University
1970 John Rinka, Kenyon College
1971 Charlie Johnson, University of California at Berkeley
1972 Scott Martin, University of Oklahoma
1973 Cadet Robert Sherwin, U.S. Military Academy
1974 Mike Robinson, Michigan State University
1975 Monte Towe, North Carolina State University
1976 Frank Alagia, Jr., St. John's University (Queens, N.Y.)
1977 Jeff Jonas, University of Utah

Most Valuable Player
Rookie of the Year
Coach of the Year

NATIONAL BASKETBALL ASSOCIATION
645 Fifth Ave., New York, N.Y. 10022 (212/826-7000)

The Podoloff Cup, named after former league Commissioner Maurice Podoloff, is given annually to the Most Valuable Player of the season, based on a vote of players on National Basketball Association teams.

1956 Bob Pettit, St. Louis
1957 Bob Cousy, Boston
1958 Bill Russell, Boston
1959 Bob Pettit, St. Louis
1960 Wilt Chamberlain, Philadelphia
1961 Bill Russell, Boston
1962 Bill Russell, Boston
1963 Bill Russell, Boston
1964 Oscar Robertson, Cincinnati
1965 Bill Russell, Boston
1966 Wilt Chamberlain, Philadelphia
1967 Wilt Chamberlain, Philadelphia
1968 Wilt Chamberlain, Philadelphia
1969 Wes Unseld, Baltimore
1970 Willis Reed, New York
1971 Lew Alcindor, Milwaukee
1972 Kareem Abdul-Jabbar, Milwaukee
1973 Dave Cowens, Boston
1974 Kareem Abdul-Jabbar, Milwaukee
1975 Bob McAdoo, Buffalo
1976 Kareem Abdul-Jabbar, Los Angeles
1977 Kareem Abdul-Jabbar, Los Angeles

The writers and broadcasters who cover basketball annually vote for the Rookie of the Year for outstanding performance in the first season of NBA play. The winner receives a trophy.

1953 Don Meineke, Ft. Wayne
1954 Ray Felix, Baltimore
1955 Bob Pettit, Milwaukee
1956 Maurice Stokes, Rochester
1957 Tom Heinsohn, Boston
1958 Woody Sauldsberry, Philadelphia
1959 Elgin Baylor, Minneapolis
1960 Wilt Chamberlain, Philadelphia
1961 Oscar Robertson, Cincinnati
1962 Walt Bellamy, Chicago
1963 Terry Dischinger, Chicago
1964 Jerry Lucas, Cincinnati
1965 Willis Reed, New York
1966 Rick Barry, San Francisco
1967 Dave Bing, Detroit
1968 Earl Monroe, Baltimore
1969 Wes Unseld, Baltimore
1970 Lew Alcindor, Milwaukee
1971 Dave Cowens, Boston
     Geoff Petrie, Portland
1972 Sidney Wicks, Portland
1973 Bob McAdoo, Buffalo
1974 Ernie DiGregorio, Buffalo
1975 Keith Wilkes, Golden State
1976 Alvan Adams, Phoenix
1977 Adrian Dantley, Buffalo

The writers and broadcasters who cover basketball annually select the Coach of the Year. The winner receives a clock.

1963 Harry Gallatin, St. Louis

1964 Alex Hannum, San Francisco
1965 Red Auerbach, Boston
1966 Dolph Schayes, Philadelphia
1967 Johnny Kerr, Chicago
1968 Richie Guerin, St. Louis
1969 Gene Shue, Baltimore
1970 Red Holzman, New York
1971 Dick Motta, Chicago
1972 Bill Sharman, Los Angeles
1973 Tom Heinsohn, Boston
1974 Ray Scott, Detroit
1975 Phil Johnson, K.C.-Omaha
1976 Bill Fitch, Cleveland
1977 Tom Nissalke, Houston

Until the merger of the American Basketball Association into the National Basketball Association, comparable awards were made in that league as well.

MOST VALUABLE PLAYER

1968 Connie Hawkins, Pittsburgh
1969 Mel Daniels, Indiana
1970 Spencer Haywood, Denver
1971 Mel Daniels, Indiana
1972 Artis Gilmore, Kentucky
1973 Billy Cunningham, Carolina
1974 Julius Erving, New York
1975 George McGinnis, Indiana
     Julius Erving, New York
1976 Julius Erving, New York

ROOKIE OF THE YEAR

1968 Mel Daniels, Minnesota
1969 Warren Armstrong, Oakland
1970 Spencer Haywood, Denver
1971 Charlie Scott, Virginia
     Dan Issel, Kentucky
1972 Artis Gilmore, Kentucky
1973 Brian Taylor, New York
1974 Swen Nater, San Antonio
1975 Marvin Barnes, St. Louis
1976 David Thompson, Denver

COACH OF THE YEAR

1968 Vince Cazetta, Pittsburgh
1969 Alex Hannum, Oakland
1970 Bill Sharman, Los Angeles
     Joe Belmont, Denver
1971 Al Bianchi, Virginia
1972 Tom Nissalke, Dallas
1973 Larry Brown, Carolina
1974 Babe McCarthy, Kentucky
     Joe Mullaney, Utah
1975 Larry Brown, Denver
1976 Larry Brown, Denver

Baton Twirling Achievement Award
AMATEUR ATHLETIC UNION OF THE UNITED STATES
3400 W. 86th St., Indianapolis, Ind. 46268 (317/297-2900)

No additional information is available on this award or the method of selecting the winners.

BATON TWIRLING ACHIEVEMENT AWARD

1973 Edith Pratt
     Kathy Stewart

1974 No award
1975 Peter Villerea
1976 Ernestine Mignone
     Niagara Association AAU
1977 Vikki Vallone
     Chuck Medre

Bowler of the Year
BOWLING WRITERS ASSOCIATION OF AMERICA
c/o Jim Fitzgerald, Chicago Tribune, 435 N. Michigan Ave., Chicago, Ill. 60611 (312/222-3232)

The Bowler of the Year, named by the bowling writers, receives a large trophy to recognize year-long excellence in professional bowling competition.

MEN

1942 Johnny Crimmins, Detroit, Mich.
1943 Ned Day, Milwaukee, Wisc.
1944 Ned Day, Milwaukee, Wisc.
1945 Buddy Bomar, Chicago, Ill.
1946 Joe Wilman, Chicago, Ill.
1947 Buddy Bomar, Chicago, Ill.
1948 Andy Varipapa, Brooklyn, N.Y.
1949 Connie Schwoegler, Madison, Wisc.
1950 Junie McMahon, Fairlawn, N.J.
1951 Lee Jouglard, Detroit, Mich.
1952 Steve Nagy, Cleveland, Ohio
1953 Don Carter, St. Louis, Mo.
1954 Don Carter, St. Louis, Mo
1955 Steve Nagy, Cleveland, Ohio
1956 Bill Lilliard, Chicago, Ill
1957 Don Carter, St. Louis, Mo
1958 Don Carter, St. Louis, Mo.
1959 Ed Lubanski, Detroit, Mich.
1960 Don Carter, St. Louis, Mo.
1961 Dick Weber, St. Louis, Mo.
1962 Don Carter, St. Louis, Mo.
1963 Dick Weber, St. Louis, Mo.
1964 Billy Hardwick, Louisville, Ky.
1965 Dick Weber, St. Louis, Mo
1966 Wayne Zahn, Atlanta, Ga.
1967 Dave Davis, Phoenix, Ariz.
1968 Jim Stefanich, Joiet, Ill.
1969 Billy Hardwick, Louisville, Ky.
1970 Nelson Burton Jr., St. Louis, Mo.
1971 Don Johnson, Akron, Ohio
1972 Don Johnson, Akron, Ohio
1973 Don McCune, Munster, Ind.
1974 Earl Anthony, Tacoma, Wash.
1975 Earl Anthony, Tacoma, Wash.
1976 Earl Anthony, Tacoma, Wash.
1977 Mark Roth, Staten Island, N.Y.

WOMEN

1948 Val Mikiel, Detroit, Mich.
1949 Val Mikiel, Detroit, Mich.
1950 Marion Ladewig, Grand Rapids, Mich.
1951 Marion Ladewig, Grand Rapids, Mich.
1952 Marion Ladewig, Grand Rapids, Mich.
1953 Marion Ladewig, Grand Rapids, Mich.
1954 Marion Ladewig, Grand Rapids, Mich.
1955 Sylvia Martin, Philadelphia, Pa.
1956 Anita Cantaline, Detroit, Mich.
1957 Marion Ladewig, Grand Rapids, Mich.
1958 Marion Ladewig, Grand Rapids, Mich.

1959 **Marion Ladewig,** Grand Rapids, Mich.
1960 **Sylvia Martin,** Philadelphia, Pa.
1961 **Shirley Garms,** Chicago, Ill.
1962 **Shirley Garms,** Chicago, Ill.
1963 **Marion Ladewig,** Grand Rapids, Mich.
1964 **LaVerne Carter,** St. Louis, Mo.
1965 **Betty Kuczynski,** Chicago, Ill.
1966 **Joy Able,** Chicato, Ill.
1967 **Millie Martorella,** Rochester, N.Y.
1968 **Dotty Fothergill,** North Attleboro, Mass.
1969 **Dotty Fothergill,** North Attleboro, Mass.
1970 **Mary Baker,** Central Islip, N.Y.
1971 **Paula Sperber,** Miami, Fla.
1972 **Patty Costello,** New Carollton, Md.
1973 **Judy Cook,** Grandview, Mo.
1974 **Betty Morris,** Stockton, Calif.
1975 **Judy Soutar,** Kansas City, Mo.
1976 **Patty Costello,** Scranton, Pa.
1977 **Berry Morris,** Stockton, Calif.

Boxer of the Year Award
Boxing Hall of Fame Award
Boxing Sportsman of the Year Award
Arthur Morse Boxing Coach of the Year

AMATEUR ATHLETIC UNION OF THE UNITED STATES
3400 W. 86th St., Indianapolis, Ind. 46268 (317/297-2900)

BOXER OF THE YEAR

1973 **Mike Hess**
1974 **No award**
1975 **No award**
1976 **No award**
1977 **No award**

The Boxing Hall of Fame Award is a plaque presented annually to an individual for outstanding services to amateur boxing. It is donated by the *San Francisco Examiner.*

1967 **John J. "Tam" Sheehan**
     Al Sandell
1968 **F. X. "Pat" Duffy**
1969 **Paul Staff**
1970 **Ben Becker**
1971 **Leo Salakin**
1972 **Roland Schwartz**
1973 **Bill Downey**
1974 **No award**
1975 **Robert J. Surkein**
     Clyde Quisenberry
1976 **Vern Woodward**
1977 **Matthew Cusak**

SPORTSMAN OF THE YEAR (BOXING)

1976 **Marvin Sugarman**
1977 **No award**

The Arthur Morse Boxing Coach of the Year Award is a plaque presented by the *New York Daily News,* to an outstanding boxing coach.

1969 **Pat Nappi**
1970 **Arrington B. Klice**
1971 **Tom Johnson**
1972 **Joe Clough**
1973 **William Cummings, Jr.**
1974 **No award**
1975 **William Cummings, Jr.**
1976 **Joe Clough**
1977 **Joe Clough**

Cat of the Year

CATS MAGAZINES
Box 4106, Pittsburgh, Pa. 15202 (412/225-3753)

Cats Magazine Cat of the Year selections are based on point evaluations of various breeds of cats accumulated through the cat show season. The winning cat receives a ribbon and a certificate. In addition to the Cat of the Year honors listed here, the Best Longhair and Shorthair are also cited.

1947 **Wimauma Masterpiece of Chalsu,** Blue Persian male
1948 **Dixi-Land's Pearl Harbor Yank,** Blue Persian male
1949 **Dixi-Land's Felice of Nor-Mont,** Blue Persian male
1950 **Lavender Liberty Beau,** Blue Persian male
1951 **Pied Piper of Barbe Bleue,** Black Persian male
1952 **Great Lakes Timothy of Rosemont,** Blue Persian male
1953 **Arlington's Sensation II,** Chinchilla Persian female
1954 **Kerry Lu Ramon of Casa Contenta,** Chinchilla Persian male
1955 **Kerry Lu Ramon of Casa Contenta**
1956 **Tempura Yours Truly,** Bluepoint Siamese male
1957 **Dixi-Land's Sir Gai of Nor-Mont,** Blue Persian male
1958 **Rosemont Golden Boy,** Cream Persian male
1959 **Vel-Vene's Voodoo,** Black Persian male
1960 **Shawnee Moonflight,** Copper-Eyed White Persian male
1961 **Shawnee Moonflight**
1962 **Chez Moumette Cal of Nor-Mont,** Cream Persian male
1963 **Azulita Paleface of Casa Cielo,** Copper-Eyed White Persian male
1964 **Shawnee Moonflight**
1965 **Shawnee Trademark,** Silver Tabby American male
1966 **Pharoh Ramses II,** Ruddy Abyssinian male
1967 **Mizpah's Ferdnand of Brierwood,** Sable Burmese male
1968 **Burm-Si's Sir Henry,** Sable Burmese male
1969 **Conalan's Miss Prettee of Walhall,** Black Persian female
1970 **Walhall's Isolde,** Black Persian female
1971 **Lowland's Zeus of Lin-Lea,** Cream Persian male
1972 **Joelwyn Columbyan,** Silver Tabby American male
1973 **Joelwyn The Wild One III of Nile,** Ruddy Abyssinian male
1974 **Kalico's Mary Poppins of Marvonack,** Blue British Shorthair female
1975 **Hawthorne Nite Liter of Lee,** Black Persian male
1976 **Thaibok Tyrone,** Sealpoint Siamese male
1977 **Kalico's Lolly of Welcome,** British Blue shorthair male

Best in Show

WESTMINSTER KENNEL CLUB
14 E. 60th St., New York, N.Y. 10022 (212/755-2275)

The annual Westminster Kennel Club Show is generally regarded as the most prestigious dog show in the United States. One hundred twenty-two breeds are recognized by the American Kennel Club. Champions of record and dogs credited with championship points from among these breeds may be entered in the Westminster show, which takes place in New York. Judges select the winners in various categories, the most significant of which is the Best in Show citation. The list below includes the name of the dog, the breed and the owner's name.

1907 **Ch. Warren Remedy,** Fox terrier (smooth), Winthrop Rutherfurd
1908 **Ch. Warren Remedy,** Fox terrier (smooth), Winthrop Rutherfurd
1909 **Ch. Warren Remedy,** Fox terrier (smooth), Winthrop Rutherfurd
1910 **Ch. Sabine Rarebit,** Fox terrier (smooth), Sabine Kennels
1911 **Ch. Tickle Em Jock,** Scottish terrier, A. Albright, Jr.
1912 **Ch. Kenmare Sorceress,** Airedale terrier, William P. Wolcott
1913 **Ch. Strathtay Prince Albert,** Bulldog, Alex H. Stewart
1914 **Ch. Slumber,** Old English sheepdog, Mrs. Tylor Morse
1915 **Ch. Matford Vic,** Fox terrier (wire), George W. Quintard
1916 **Ch. Matford Vic,** Fox terrier (wire), George W. Quintard
1917 **Ch. Conejo Wycollar Boy,** Fox terrier (wire), Mrs. Roy A. Rainey
1918 **Ch. Haymarket Fruitless,** Bull terrier, R. H. Elliott
1919 **Ch. Briergate Bright Beauty,** Airedale terrier, G. L. L. Davis
1920 **Ch. Conejo Wycollar Boy,** Fox terrier (wire), Mrs. Roy A. Rainey
1921 **Ch. Midkiff Seductive,** Cocker spaniel, William T. Payne
1922 **Ch. Boxwood Barkentine,** Airedale terrier, Frederic C. Hood
1923 **No Best in Show award.**
1924 **Ch. Barberyhill Bootlegger,** Sealyham terrier, Bayard Warren
1925 **Ch. Governor Moscow,** Pointer, Robert F. Maloney
1926 **Ch. Signal Circuit of Halleston,** Fox Terrier (wire), Halleston Kennels
1927 **Ch. Pinegrade Perfection,** Sealyham terrier, Frederic C. Brown
1928 **Ch. Talavera Margaret,** Fox terrier (wire), R. M. Lewis
1929 **Laund Loyalty of Bellhaven,** Collie, Florence B. Ilch
1930 **Ch. Pendley Calling of Blarney,** Fox terrier (wire) John G. Bates
1931 **Ch. Pendley Calling of Blarney,** Fox terrier (wire) John G. Bates
1932 **Ch. Nancolleth Markable,** Pointer, Giralda Farms
1933 **Ch. Warland Protector of Shelterock,** Airedale terrier, S. M. Stewart
1934 **Ch. Flornell Spicy Bit of Halleston,** Fox terrier (wire), Halleston Kennels
1935 **Ch. Nunsoe Duc de la Terrace of Blackeen,** Standard poodle, Blakeen Kennels
1936 **Ch. St. Margaret Magnificent of Clairedale,** Sealyham terrier, Clairedale Kennels

1937 **Ch. Flornell Spicy Piece of Halleston,** Fox terrier (wire), Halleston Kennels
1938 **Ch. Daro of Maridor,** English setter, Maridor Kennels
1939 **Ch. Ferry v. Rauhfelsen of Giralda,** Doberman pinscher, Giralda Farms
1940 **Ch. My Own Brucie,** Cocker spaniel, H. E. Mellenthin
1941 **Ch. My Own Brucie,** Cocker spaniel, H. E. Mellenthin
1942 **Ch. Wolvey Pattern of Edgerstoune,** West Highland white terrier, Mrs. J. G. Winant
1943 **Ch. Pitter Patter of Piperscroft,** Miniature poodle, Mrs. P. H. B. Frelinghuysen
1944 **Ch. Flornell Rare-Bit of Twin Ponds,** Welsh terrier, Mrs. Edward P. Alker
1945 **Ch. Shieling's Signature,** Scottish terrier, Mr. and Mrs. T. H. Snethen
1946 **Ch. Hetherington Model Rhythm,** Fox terrier (wire), Mr. and Mrs. T. H. Carruthers, III
1947 **Ch. Warlord of Mezelaine,** Boxer, Mr. and Mrs. Richard C. Kettles, Jr.
1948 **Ch. Rock Ridge Night Rocket,** Bedlington terrier, Mr. and Mrs. William A. Rockefeller
1949 **Ch. Mezelaine Zazarac Brandy,** Boxer, Mr. and Mrs. John Phelps Wagner
1950 **Ch. Walsing Winning Trick of Edgerstoune,** Scottish terrier, Mrs. J. G. Winant
1951 **Ch. Bang Away of Sirrah Crest,** Boxer, Dr. and Mrs. R. C. Harris
1952 **Ch. Rancho Dobe's Storm,** Doberman pinscher, Mr. and Mrs. Len Carey
1953 **Ch. Rancho Dobe's Storm,** Doberman pinscher, Mr. and Mrs. Len Carey
1954 **Ch. Carmor's Rise and Shine,** Cocker spaniel, Mrs. Carl E. Morgan
1955 **Ch. Kippax Fearnought,** Bulldog, John A. Saylor
1956 **Ch. Wilber White Swan,** Toy poodle, Bertha Smith
1957 **Ch. Shirkhan of Grandeur,** Afghan hound, Sunny Shay and Dorothy Chenade
1958 **Ch. Puttencove Promise,** Standard poodle, Puttencove Kennels
1959 **Ch. Fontclair Festoon,** Miniature poodle, Dunwalke Kennels
1960 **Ch. Chik T'Sun of Caversham,** Pekingese, Mr. and Mrs. C. C. Venable
1961 **Ch. Cappoquin Little Sister,** Toy poodle, Florence Michelson
1962 **Ch. Elfinbrook Simon,** West Highland white terrier, Wishing Well Kennels
1963 **Ch. Wakefield's Black Knight,** English springer spaniel, Mrs. W. J. S. Borie
1964 **Ch. Courtenay Fleetfoot of Pennyworth,** Whippet Pennyworth Kennels
1965 **Ch. Carmichael's Fanfare,** Scottish terrier, Mr. and Mrs. Charles C. Stalter
1966 **Ch. Zeloy Moormaide's Magic,** Fox terrier (wire), Marion G. Bunker
1967 **Ch. Bardene Bingo,** Scottish terrier, E. H. Stuart
1968 **Ch. Stingray of Derryabah,** Lakeland terrier, Mr. and Mrs. James A. Farrell, Jr.
1969 **Ch. Glamoor Good News,** Skye terrier, Walter F. and Adele F. Goodman
1970 **Ch. Arriba's Prima Donna,** Boxer, Dr. and Mrs. P. J. Pagano and Dr. Theodore S. Fickes
1971 **Ch. Chinoe's Adamant James,** English springer spaniel, Milton E. Prickett
1972 **Ch. Chinoe's Adamant James,** English springer spaniel, Milton E. Prickett
1973 **Ch. Acadia Command Performance,** Standard poodle, E. B. Jenner and J. Sering

1974   Ch. Gretchenhof Columbia River, German shor-
thaired pointer, Richard P. Smith
1975   Ch. Sir Lancelot of Barvan, Old English sheepdog,
Mr. and Mrs. R. Vanword
1976   Ch. Jo Ni's Red Baron of Crofton, Lakeland terrier,
Virginia K. Dickson
1977   Ch. Dersade Bobby's Girl, Sealyham terrier, Pool
Forge Kennels

Coach of the Year
Tuss McLaughery Award
Amos Alonzo Stagg Award
AMERICAN FOOTBALL COACHES
ASSOCIATION
Box 8705, Durham, N.C. 27707

The Coach of the Year is elected by a vote of active
members of the association and is honored at a presentation dinner. Beginning in 1960, two awards have
been given annually—one to a major school and one to
a minor school.

1935   Lynn Waldorf, Northwestern
1936   Dick Harlow, Harvard
1937   Hooks Mylin, Lafayette
1938   Bill Kern, Carnegie Tech
1939   Eddie Anderson, Iowa
1940   Clark Shaughnessy, Stanford
1941   Frank Leahy, Notre Dame
1942   Bill Alexander, Georgia Tech
1943   Amos Alonzo Stagg, College of Pacific
1944   Carroll Widdoes, Ohio State
1945   Bo McMillin, Indiana
1946   Red Blaik, Army
1947   Fritz Crisler, Michigan
1948   Benny Oosterbaan, Michigan
1949   Bud Wilkinson, Oklahoma
1950   Charley Caldwell, Princeton
1951   Chuck Taylor, Stanford
1952   Biggie Munn, Michigan State
1953   Jim Tatum, Maryland
1954   Red Sanders, U.C.L.A.
1955   Duffy Daugherty, Michigan State
1956   Bowden Wyatt, Tennessee
1957   Woody Hayes, Ohio State
1958   Paul Dietzel, Louisiana State
1959   Floyd Schwartzwalder, Syracuse
1960   Murray Warmath, Minnesota
Warren Woodson, New Mexico State
1961   Paul W. Bryant, Alabama
Alonzo S. Gaither, Florida A&M
1962   John McKay, Southern California
William M. Edwards, Wittenberg
1963   Darrell Royal, Texas
William M. Edwards, Wittenberg
1964   Frank Broyles, Arkansas
Ara Parseghian, Notre Dame
Clarence Stasavich, East Carolina College
1965   Tommy Prothro, U.C.L.A.
Jack Curtice, Univ. of Cal. at Santa Barbara
1966   Tom Cahill, U.S. Military Academy
Dan Jessee, Trinity College
1967   John Pont, Indiana
A. C. (Scrappy) Moore, Chattanooga
1968   Joe Paterno, Penn State
Jim Root, New Hampshire
1969   Bo Schembechler, Michigan

Larry Naviaux, Boston University
1970   Darrell Royal, Texas
Charles McClendon, L.S.U.
Bennie Ellender, Arkansas State
1971   Paul Bryant, Alabama
Harold Raymond, Delaware
1972   John McKay, Southern California
Harold Raymond, Delaware
1973   Paul Bryant, Alabama
Dave Maurer, Wittenberg
1974   Grant Teaff, Baylor
Roy Kramer, Central Michigan
1975   Frank Kush, Arizona State
Dave Maurer, Wittenberg
1976   N.A.
N.A.
1977   Don James, University of Washington
Bill Manlove, Widener College

The Tuss McLaughery Award is given annually to a
distinguished American to honor service to others.

1964   Gen. Douglas MacArthur
1965   Bob Hope
1966   Lyndon B. Johnson
1967   Dwight D. Eisenhower
1968   J. Edgar Hoover
1969   Rev. Billy Graham
1970   Richard M. Nixon
1971   Neil Armstrong, Michael Collins and Edwin
Aldrin
1972   No award
1973   John Wayne
1974   Gerald R. Ford
1975   No award
1976   Gen. James A. Van Fleet
1977   N.A.

The Amos Alonzo Stagg Award is given annually to the
individual, group or institution whose services have
advanced the best interests of football.

1940   Donald G. Herring, Jr., and family
1941   William H. Crowell
1946   Grantland Rice
1947   William Alexander
1948   Gilmour Dobie, Glenn S. Warner and Robert
C. Zuppke
1949   Richard C. Harlow
1950   No award
1951   DeOrmond McLaughrey
1952   A.N. (Bo) McMillin
1953   Lou Little
1954   Dana X. Bible
1955   Joseph J. Tomlin
1956   No award
1957   Robert R. Neyland
1958   Bernard Bierman
1959   John W. Wilce
1960   Harvey J. Harman
1961   Ray Elior
1962   E.E. (Tad) Wieman
1963   Andrew Kerr
1964   Don Faurot
1965   Harry Stuhldreher
1966   Bernie Moore
1967   Jess Neeley
1968   Abe Martin

1969 Rip Engle
1970 Lynn Waldorf
1971 Bill Murray
1972 Jack Curtice
1973 Lloyd Jordan
1974 A.S. (Jake) Gaither
1975 Gerald B. Zornow
1976 N.A.
1977 N.A.

Heisman Trophy

DOWNTOWN ATHLETIC CLUB
19 West St., New York, N.Y. 10004 (212/425-7000)

The Heisman Trophy is awarded annually to the individual voted by the members as the best college football player of the year. The trophy is a bronze statue of a running back. (RB=running back; HB=halfback; QB =quarter back; FB=Fullback; E=end; TB=tailback)

1935 Jay Berwanger, Chicago, HB
1936 Larry Kelley, Yale, E
1937 Clint Frank, Yale, HB
1938 Davey O'Brien, T.C.U., QB
1939 Nile Kinnick, Iowa, HB
1940 Tom Harmon, Michigan, HB
1941 Bruce Smith, Minnesota, HB
1942 Frank Sinkwich, Georgia, HB
1943 Angelo Bertelli, Notre Dame, QB
1944 Les Horvath, Ohio State, QB
1945 Doc Blanchard, U.S. Military Academy, FB
1946 Glenn Davis, U.S. Military Academy, HB
1947 John Lujack, Notre Dame, QB
1948 Doak Walker, S.M.U., HB
1949 Leon Hart, Notre Dame, E
1950 Vic Janowicz, Ohio State, HB
1951 Dick Kazmaier, Princeton, HB
1952 Billy Vessels, Oklahoma, HB
1953 John Lattner, Notre Dame, HB
1954 Alan Ameche, Wisconsin, FB
1955 Howard Cassady, Ohio State, HB
1956 Paul Hornung, Notre Dame, QB
1957 John Crow, Texas A & M, HB
1958 Pete Dawkins, U.S. Military Academy, HB
1959 Billy Cannon, L.S.U., HB
1960 Joe Bellino, U.S. Naval Academy, HB
1961 Ernie Davis, Syracuse, HB
1962 Terry Baker, Oregon State, QB
1963 Roger Staubach, U.S. Naval Academy, QB
1964 John Huarte, Notre Dame, QB
1965 Mike Garrett, Southern California, HB
1966 Steve Spurrier, Florida, QB
1967 Gary Beban, U.C.L.A., QB
1968 O. J. Simpson, Southern California, TB
1969 Steve Owens, Oklahoma, HB
1970 Jim Plunkett, Stanford, QB
1971 Pat Sullivan, Auburn, QB
1972 Johnny Rodgers, Nebraska, RB
1973 John Cappelletti, Penn State, TB
1974 Archie Griffin, Ohio State, TB
1975 Archie Griffin, Ohio State, TB
1976 Tony Dorsett, Pittsburgh, TB
1977 Earl Campbell, Texas, RB

Grantland Rice Trophy
Outland Trophy
Coach of the Year
Bert McGrane Award

FOOTBALL WRITERS ASSOCIATION OF AMERICA
Box 1022, Edmond, Okla. 73034 (405/341-4731)

A five-man committee of football writers annually votes for the best collegiate football team of the season to receive the Grantland Rice Trophy, which is a bronze football mounted on a base.

1954 U.C.L.A.
1955 Oklahoma
1956 Oklahoma
1957 Ohio State
1958 Iowa
1959 Syracuse
1960 Mississippi
1961 Ohio State
1962 Southern California
1963 Texas
1964 Arkansas
1965 Michigan State
     Alabama
1966 Notre Dame
1967 Southern California
1968 Ohio State
1969 Texas
1970 Nebraska
1971 Nebraska
1972 Southern California
1973 Notre Dame
1974 Southern California
1975 Oklahoma
1976 Pittsburgh
1977 Notre Dame

The Outland Trophy, which consists of a plaque, is given for the outstanding interior lineman of the year on a vote by the membership of the assocation, subject to confirmation by the FWAA All-America Committee.

1946 George Connor, Notre Dame
1947 Joe Steffy, U.S. Military Academy
1948 Bill Fischer, Notre Dame
1949 Ed Bagdon, Michigan State
1950 Bob Gain, Kentucky
1951 Jim Weatherall, Oklahoma
1952 Dick Modzelewski, Maryland
1953 J.D. Roberts, Oklahoma
1954 William (Bud) Brooks, Arkansas
1955 Calvin Jones, Iowa
1956 Jim Parker, Ohio State
1957 Alex Karras, Iowa
1958 Zeke Smith, Auburn
1959 Mike McGee, Duke
1960 Tom Brown, Minnesota
1961 Merlin Olson, Utah State
1962 Bobby Bell, Minnesota
1963 Gordon Scott, Appleton, Texas
1964 Steve DeLong, Tennessee
1965 Tommy Nobis, Texas
1966 Lloyd Phillips, Arkansas
1967 Ron Yary, Southern California
1968 Bill Stanfill, Georgia
1969 Mike Reid, Penn State
1970 Jim Stillwagon, Ohio State

1971 Larry Jacobson, Nebraska
1972 Rich Glover, Nebraska
1973 John Hicks, Ohio State
1974 Randy White, Maryland
1975 Leroy Selmon, Oklahoma
1976 Ross Browner, Notre Dame
1977 Brad Shearer, University of Texas

The full membership of the FWAA votes on the Coach of the Year for the individual doing the most outstanding coaching job in college football. A plaque is given to the winner.

1957 Woody Hayes, Ohio State
1958 Paul Dietzel, Louisiana State
1959 Ben Schwartzwalder, Syracuse
1960 Murray Warmath, Minnesota
1961 Darrell Royal, Texas
1962 John McKay, Southern California
1963 Darrell Royal, Texas
1964 Ara Parseghian, Notre Dame
1965 Duffy Daugherty, Michigan State
1966 Tom Cahill, U.S. Military Academy
1967 John Pont, Indiana
1968 Woody Hayes, Ohio State
1969 Bo Schembechler, Michigan
1970 Alex Agase, Northwestern
1971 Bob Devaney, Nebraska
1972 John McKay, Southern California
1973 Johnny Majors, Pittsburgh
1974 Grant Teaff, Baylor
1975 Woody Hayes, Ohio State
1976 Johnny Majors, Pittsburgh
1977 Lou Holtz, Arkansas

The Bert McGrane Award, which consists of a plaque, is given annually on committee decision to a member of FWAA for meritorious service to the association.

1974 Charley Johnson, *Minneapolis Star*
1975 Wilfrid Smith, *Chicago Tribune*
1976 Paul Zimmerman, *Los Angeles Times*
1977 Dick Cullum, *Minneapolis Tribune*

Scholar Athlete Award
MacArthur Bowl

NATIONAL FOOTBALL FOUNDATION
201 E. 42nd St., Suite 1506, New York, N.Y. 10017
(212/682-0255)

The Scholar Athlete Award, which consists of a silver bowl and $1,000, is given annually to college seniors who have demonstrated academic application and performance as well as outstanding football ability and performance and school leadership. College athletic directors nominate candidates who are voted on by the foundation's award committee and approved by the executive committee.

1959 Paul Choquette, Brown
Gerhard Schwedes, Syracuse
Neyle Solle, Univ. of Tennessee
Philip Ross, Ohio Wesleyan
Harry Tolly, Univ. of Nebraska
Maurice Doke, Univ. of Texas
Pat Smyth, Univ. of Wyoming
Donald Patrick Newell, Univ. of California
1960 Alan Rozycki, Dartmouth
Paul Benke, Rutgers
Edmund Dyas, Auburn

John Easterbrook, Illinois
Frederick Brossart, Missouri
Jerry Mays, Southern Methodist
Bruce Henry, Colorado School of Mines
Barry Bullard, Washington
1961 Davey Thompson, Tufts
Alex Kroll, Rutgers
Wade Butcher, Vanderbilt
Albert Iosue, Western Reserve
Joseph Romig, Colorado
Bob E. Johnson, Rice
Merlin Olsen, Utah State
Mike Kline, Oregon State
1962 Al Snyder, Holy Cross
Tim Callard, Princeton
Gary Cuozzo, Virginia
Robert Heckman, Dayton
Rex Russell, Oklahoma State
John Pat Culpepper, Texas
Ron Joseph Manno, Utah
Terry Wayne Baker, Oregon State
1963 Kenneth Ancell, Colorado School of Mines
Mike Briggs, Washington
Richard Deller, Illinois
Frank Drigotas, Bowdoin
David Gill, Missouri
Algis Grigaliunas, Pittsburgh
Joe Ince, U.S. Naval Academy
Don Trull, Baylor
Russell Walls, Davidson
1964 Cosmo Iacavazzi, Princeton
Arnold Chonko, Ohio State
Bill Zadel, U.S. Military Academy
Bob Timberlake, Michigan
Archie Roberts, Columbia
Ron Oelshlager, Kansas
Jimmy Bell, Clemson
Kenneth Gousens, Amherst
Mel Carpenter, Utah
Horst Paul, Houston
Bill Douglas, Washington
1965 Charles Arrobio, Southern California
Sam Champi, U.S. Military Academy
John Cochran, Auburn
David Fronek, Wisconsin
Stephen Juday, Michigan State
Dan Jones, Texas Christian
Allen Roodhouse, U.S. Naval Academy
Williard Sander, Ohio State
1966 Thomas Allen, Bowdoin
Robert Etter, Georgia
Stanley Juk, South Carolina
James R. Lynch, Notre Dame
Charles Peters, Princeton
William Powell, Missouri
John Richards, Texas Christian
Michael Ryan, Washington
1967 Gary Beban, UCLA
Alan Douglas Bersin, Harvard
William P. Eastman, Georgia Tech
Barry Furst, Ohio Wesleyan
Robert Johnson, Tennessee
Thomas W. Lawhorne, Georgia
John R. McCarthy, Yale
Keith Miles, Trinity
Bohdan Neswiacheny, U.S. Military Academy
John Pierson Root, Stanford
John Scovell, Texas Tech
Steve F. Warren, North Carolina State
Robert Weber, Princeton

1968 Allen Brenner, Michigan State
David Foley, Ohio State
John Hendricks, Iowa
Stephen Hindman, Mississippi
George Kunz, Notre Dame
William Moody, Arizona
William Payne, Georgia
Michael Perrin, Texas
David Rea, Amherst
Richard Sandler, Princeton
Robert Stein, Minnesota
1969 Tim Callaway, Georgia
John Cramer, Harvard
Harry Gonso, Indiana
George Joseph, Penn
Harry Khasigian, Southern California
Charles Longenecker, U.S. Air Force Academy
Mike Oriard, Notre Dame
Daniel Pike, U.S. Naval Academy
Theodore Shahid, U.S. Military Academy
Terry Stewart, Arkansas
1970 William Bogan, Dartmouth
James Cooch, Colorado
Don Denbo, Tennessee
Leo Dillon, Dayton
Larry DiNardo, Notre Dame
Dennis Dummit, U.C.L.A.
David Elmendorf, Texas A&M
Rex Kern, Ohio State
Thomas Lyons, Georgia
Thomas Neville, Yale
Robert Parker, U.S. Air Force Academy
John Sande III, Stanford
Willie Frank Zapalac, Texas
1971 William Brafford, North Carolina
Dennis Ferguson, Utah State
Thomas Gatewood, Jr., Notre Dame
Darryl Owen Hass, U.S. Air Force Academy
David M. Joyner, Penn State
John Sefcik, Columbia
William Thomson, Indiana
Michael McCoy, Kansas
Larry Mildren, Jr., Oklahoma
John Musso, Alabama
Thomas Nach, Jr., Georgia
1972 Bruce Bannon, Penn State
William Cahill, Washington
Frank Dowsing, Mississippi State
Floyd Harvey, Grambling
Richard Homburg, U.S. Air Force Academy
Richard Jauron, Yale
Greg Marx, Notre Dame
Timothy Quinn, Dayton
Fred Radke, Dartmouth
Charles Whitener, Southern Methodist
Joe Wylie, Oklahoma
1973 Forrest Anderson, Nebraska
Richard Len Bland, Colorado
David Arthur Blandino, Pittsburgh
David John Casper, Notre Dame
David Dillon Gallagher, Michigan
Randolph C. Gradishar, Ohio State
Thomas Mark Harmon, U.C.L.A.
James H. Jennings, Rutgers
Patrick Michael Kelly, Texas
Mark Markovich, Penn State
Norris Lee Weese, Mississippi
1974 John R. Baiorunos, Penn State
David Lynn Chambers, Colorado
William R. Cregar, South Carolina

Peter K. Demmerle, Notre Dame
Patrick C. Haden, Southern California
Randall L. Hall, Alabama
Timothy S. Harden, U.S. Naval Academy
J. Randy Hughes, Oklahoma
Douglas H. Martin, Vanderbilt
Patrick J. McInally, Harvard
Todd W. Toerper, Pittsburgh
1975 Brian Dale Baschnagel, Ohio State
Robert Joseph Elliott, Univ. of Iowa
Scott Dale Gillogly, U.S. Military Academy
Thomas Heiser, Univ. of Nebraska
Darryl W. Jackson, North Carolina State
Ralph Abraham Jackson, New Mexico State
Richard T. Lawrence, U.C.L.A.
Kirk John Lewis, Michigan
John M. Sciarra, Univ. of California
LeRoy Selmon, Univ. of Oklahoma
Randall J. Stockham, Utah State
1976 John R. Bushy, Univ. of Arkansas
Jeffrey A. Dankworth, U.C.L.A.
Randolph H. Dean, Northwestern
Vince A. Ferragamo, Univ. of Nebraska
Kevin R. Fox, Princeton
Gerry Huesken, Susquehanna
Michael G. Mauck, Univ. of Tennessee
Duncan McColl, Stanford
Stephen D. Miller, Brigham Young
Stone S. Phillips, Yale
Patrick M. Sullivan, Dartmouth
1977 Gary Wayne Bethel, U.C.L.A.
Jonathan E. Claiborne, Univ. of Maryland
Morgan Lee Copeland, Jr., Univ. of Texas
Curtis J. Downs, U.S. Military Academy
Tom Robert Fitch, Univ. of Kansas
Joseph E. Holland, Cornell
Jeffrey Young Lewis, Univ. of Georgia
Kevin Monk, Texas A&M
Richard Scudellari, Boston College
David Williams Vinson, Notre Dame
Mark Wichman, Bowling Green State Univ.

The MacArthur Bowl, named after Gen. Douglas MacArthur, is awarded annually to the season's outstanding college football team. It is made of silver, fashioned in the form of a football stadium, and was created by Tiffany.

1959 Syracuse University
1960 Univ. of Minnesota
1961 Univ. of Alabama
1962 Univ. of Southern California
1963 Univ. of Texas
1964 Univ. of Notre Dame
1965 Michigan State
1966 Michigan State
Univ. of Notre Dame
1967 Ohio State Univ.
1968 Ohio State Univ.
1969 Univ. of Texas
1970 Ohio State Univ.
Univ. of Texas
1971 Univ. of Nebraska
1972 Univ. of Southern California
1973 Univ. of Notre Dame
1974 Univ. of Southern California
1975 Univ. of Oklahoma
1976 Univ. of Pittsburgh
1977 Univ. of Notre Dame

Jim Thorpe Trophy
Joe F. Carr Trophy
George Halas Trophy
Player of the Year
National Football Conference Player of the Year Award
Rookie of the Year

NEWSPAPER ENTERPRISE ASSOCIATION
200 Park Ave., New York, N.Y. 10017 (212/557-5870)

The Jim Thorpe Trophy is awarded annually to the most valuable National Football League player as determined by a poll conducted by the Newspaper Enterprise Association of the players on the 26 league teams.

1955 Narlon Hill, N.A.
1956 Frank Gifford, New York Giants
1957 John Unitas, Baltimore Colts
1958 Jim Brown, Cleveland Browns
1959 Charley Conerly, New York Giants
1960 Norm Van Brocklin, Philadelphia Eagles
1961 Y.A. Tittle, New York Giants
1962 Jim Taylor, Green Bay Packers
1963 Jim Brown, Cleveland Browns
      Y.A. Tittle, New York Giants
1964 Lenny Moore, Baltimore Colts
1965 Jim Brown, Cleveland Browns
1966 Bart Starr, Green Bay Packers
1967 John Unitas, Baltimore Colts
1968 Earl Morrall, Baltimore Colts
1969 Roman Gabriel, Los Angeles Rams
1970 John Brodie, San Francisco 49ers
1971 Bob Griese, Miami Dolphins
1972 Larry Brown, Washington Redskins
1973 O.J. Simpson, Buffalo Bills
1974 Ken Stabler, Oakland Raiders
1975 Fran Tarkenton, Minnesota Vikings
1976 Bert Jones, Baltimore Colts
1977 Walter Payton, Chicago Bears

The Joe F. Carr Trophy was an award given until 1946 to the league's Most Valuable Player.

1938 Mel Hein, New York Giants
1939 Parker Hall, Cleveland Rams
1940 Ace Parker, Brooklyn Dodgers
1941 Don Hutson, Green Bay Packers
1942 Don Hutson, Green Bay Packers
1943 Sid Luckman, Chicago Bears
1944 Frank Sinkwich, Detroit Lions
1945 Bob Waterfield, Los Angeles Rams
1946 Bill Dudley, Pittsburgh Steelers

The George Halas Trophy is given annually to the year's outstanding defensive player, based on a vote by news service sports editors.

1966 Larry Wilson, St. Louis Cardinals
1967 Deacon Jones, Los Angeles Rams
1968 Deacon Jones, Los Angeles Rams
1969 Dick Butkus, Chicago Bears
1970 Dick Butkus, Chicago Bears
1971 Alan Page, Minnesota Vikings
      Carl Eller, Minnesota Vikings
1972 Joe Greene, Pittsburgh Steelers
1973 Dick Anderson, Miami Dolphins
      Alan Page, Minnesota Vikings
1974 Joe Greene, Pittsburgh Steelers
1975 Mel Blount, Dallas Cowboys

      Curley Culp, Kansas City Chiefs
      Jack Youngblood, Los Angeles Rams
1976 Wally Chambers, Chicago Bears
      Jack Lambert, Pittsburgh Steelers
      Jerry Sherk, Cleveland Browns
1977 Harvey Martin, Dallas Cowboys

The American Football League was merged with the National Football League in 1969, becoming the American Football Conference. News service sports editors annually select a Player of the Year from the teams in this group.

1960 Abner Haynes, Dallas Texans
1961 George Blanda, Houston Oilers
1962 Len Dawson, Kansas City Chiefs
1963 Clem Daniels, Oakland Raiders
1964 Gino Cappelletti, Boston Patriots
1965 Paul Lowe, San Diego Chargers
1966 Jim Nance, Boston Patriots
1967 Daryle Lamonica, Oakland Raiders
1968 George Blanda, Oakland Raiders
1971 Bob Griese, Miami Dolphins
      Otis Taylor, Kansas City Chiefs
1972 Earl Morrall, Miami Dolphins
      O.J. Simpson, Buffalo Bills
1973 O.J. Simpson, Buffalo Bills
1974 Ken Stabler, Oakland Raiders
1975 O.J. Simpson, Buffalo Bills
1976 Bert Jones, Baltimore Colts
1977 No award

The National Football League's own Player of the Year Award became the National Football Conference Player of the Year Award after the merger of the two leagues in 1969. News service sports editors select the winner.

1953 Otto Graham, Cleveland Browns
1954 Joe Perry, San Francisco 49ers
1955 Otto Graham, Cleveland Browns
1956 Frank Gifford, New York Giants
1957 Y.A. Tittle, San Francisco 49ers
1958 Jim Brown, Cleveland Browns
1959 John Unitas, Baltimore Colts
1960 Norm Van Brocklin, Philadelphia Eagles
1961 Paul Hornung, Green Bay Packers
1962 Y.A. Tittle, New York Giants
1963 Jim Brown, Celeveland Browns
1964 John Unitas, Baltimore Colts
1965 Jim Brown, Cleveland Browns
1966 Bart Starr, Green Bay Packers
1967 John Unitas, Baltimore Colts
1968 Earl Morrall, Baltimore Colts
1969 Roman Gabriel, Los Angeles Rams
1970 John Brodie, San Francisco 49ers
1971 Alan Page, Minnesota Vikings
1972 Larry Brown, Washington Redskins
1973 John Hadl, Los Angeles Rams
1974 Jim Hart, St. Louis Cardinals
1975 Fran Tarkenton, Minnesota Vikings
1976 Chuck Foreman, Minnesota Vikings
1977 No award

The Rookie of the Year selection, made by news service sports editors, honors the player deemed to be the most outstanding from the group playing their first year of professional football. One American Football Conference and one National Football Conference player are now chosen annually.

1958 Bobby Mitchell, Cleveland Browns

1959	Nick Pietrosante, Detroit Lions	
1960	Gail Cogdill, Detroit Lions (NFL)	
	Abner Haynes, Dallas Texans (AFL)	
1961	Mike Ditka, Chicago Bears (NFL)	
	Earl Faison, San Diego Chargers (AFL)	
1962	Ronnie Bull, Chicago Bears (NFL)	
	Curtis McClinton, Kansas City Chiefs (AFL)	
1963	Paul Flatley, Minnesota Vikings (NFL)	
	Billy Joe, Denver Broncos (AFL)	
1964	Charlie Taylor, Washington Redskins (NFL)	
	Matt Snell, New York Jets (AFL)	
1965	Gale Sayers, Chicago Bears (NFL)	
	Joe Namath, New York Jets (AFL)	
1966	John Roland, St. Louis Cardinals (NFL)	
	Bobby Burnett, Buffalo Bills (AFL)	
1967	Mel Farr, Detroit Lions (NFL)	
	George Webster, Houston Oilers (AFL)	
1968	Earl McCullouch, Detroit Lions (NFL)	
	Paul Robinson, Cincinnati Bengals (AFL)	
1969	Calvin Hill, Dallas Cowboys (NFL)	
	Carl Garrett, Boston Patriots (AFL)	
1970	Dennis Shaw, Buffalo Bills (AFC)	
	Bruce Taylor, San Francisco 49ers (NFC)	
	Ray Chester, Oakland Raiders (AFC)	
1971	John Brockington, Green Bay Packers (NFC)	
	Jim Plunkett, New England Patriots (AFC)	
	Isaiah Robertson, Los Angeles Rams (NFC)	
1972	Franco Harris, Pittsburgh Steelers (AFC)	
	Willie Buchanan, Green Bay Packers (NFC)	
	Chester Marcol, Green Bay Packers (NFC)	
1973	Chuck Foreman, Minnesota Vikings (NFC)	
	Bobby Clark, Cincinnati Bengals (AFC)	
	Wally Chambers, Chicago Bears (NFC)	
	Charles Young, Philadelphia Eagles (NFC)	
1974	Don Woods, San Diego Chargers (AFC)	
	Jack Lambert, Pittsburgh Steelers (AFC)	
1975	Mike Thomas, Washington Redskins (NFC)	
	Robert Brazile, Houston Oilers (AFC)	
1976	Mike Haynes, New England Patriots (AFC)	
	Sammy White, Minnesota Vikings (NFC)	
1977	Tony Dorsett, Dallas Cowboys (NFL)	
	No AFC award	

Induction

PRO FOOTBALL HALL OF FAME

2121 Harrison Ave, NW, Canton, Ohio 44708 (216/456-8207)

Induction in the Pro Football Hall of Fame honors any professional football player, owner or coach who has been retired for at least five years for an outstanding career. Anyone may nominate candidates for consideration by a board of selection, which consists of a football writer or broadcaster from each city with a professional football team and one officer from the Pro Football Writers Association. At least 80 per cent of the the selectors must be in favor of the candidate for permanent enshrinement in the Hall of Fame. The years below are the years of induction into the Hall of Fame.

1963

Sammy Baugh	Bert Bell
Joe Carr	Dutch Clark
"Red" Grange	George Halas
Mel Hein	Pete Henry
Cal Hubbard	Don Hutson
Curly Lambeau	Tim Mara
George Marshall	Johnny Blood McNally

Bronko Nagurski	Ernie Nevers
Jim Thorpe	

1964

Jimmy Conzelman	Ed Healey
Clarke Hinkle	Link Lyman
Mike Michalske	Art Rooney
George Trafton	

1965

Guy Chamberlin	Paddy Driscoll
Dan Fortmann	Otto Graham
Sid Luckman	Steve Van Buren
Bob Waterfield	

1966

Bill Dudley	Joe Guyon
Arnie Herber	Walt Kiesling
George McAfee	Steve Owen
"Shorty" Ray	"Bulldog" Turner

1967

Chuck Bednarik	Charles Bidwill, Sr.
Paul Brown	Bobby Layne
Dan Reeves	Ken Strong
Joe Stydahar	Emlen Tunnell

1968

Cliff Battles	Art Donovan
Elroy Hirsch	Wayne Millner
Marion Motley	Charley Trippi
Alex Wojciechowicz	

1969

Turk Edwards	"Greasy" Neale
Leo Nomellini	Joe Perry
Ernie Stautner	

1970

Jack Christiansen	Tom Fears
Hugh McElhenny	Pete Pihos

1971

Jim Brown	Bill Hewitt
"Bruiser" Kinard	Vince Lombardi
Andy Robustelli	Y. A. Tittle
Norm Van Brocklin	

1972

Lamar Hunt	Gino Marchetti
Ollie Matson	Ace Parker

1973

Raymond Berry	Jim Parker
Joe Schmidt	

1974

Tony Canadeo	Bill George
Lou Groza	"Night Train" Lane

1975

Roosevelt Brown	George Connor
Dante Lavelli	Lenny Moore

1976

Ray Flaherty	Len Ford
Jim Taylor	

1977

Frank Gifford	Forrest Gregg
Gale Sayers	Bart Starr
Bill Willis	

Lombardi Award
ROTARY CLUB OF HOUSTON FOUNDATION
911 Walker, Suite 1145, Houston, Tex. 77002
(713/228-1327)

The Lombardi Award, which consists of a trophy, is presented annually to the nation's best lineman in college football during the previous season.

1971 Jim Stillwagon, Ohio State
1972 Walt Patulski, Notre Dame
1973 Rich Glover, Nebraska
1974 John Hicks, Ohio State
1975 Randy White, Maryland
1976 LeRoy Selmon, Oklahoma
1977 Wilson Whitley, Houston

Most Improved (Men) Golfer
Most Improved (Women) Golfer
Rookie of the Year (Men)
Rookie of the Year (Women)
Mickey Wright Award for Tournament Victories
Byron Nelson Award for Tournament Victories
GOLF DIGEST
495 Westport Ave., Norwalk, Conn. 06856 (203/847-5811)

Golf Digest magazine keeps tabs on performances of top golfers and cites a number of outstanding accomplishments in the sport. The editors select the winners on the basis of performance during the previous year.

MOST IMPROVED (men)
1953 Doug Ford
1954 Bob Toski
1955 Mike Souchak
1956 Dow Finsterwald
1957 Paul Harney
1958 Ernie Vossler
1959 Don Whitt
1960 Don January
1961 Gary Player
1962 Bobby Nichols
1963 Tony Lema
1964 Ken Venturi
1965 Randy Glover
1966 Gay Brewer
1967 Dave Stockton
1968 Bob Lunn
1969 Dave Hill
1970 Dick Lotz
1971 Jerry Heard
1972 Jim Jamieson
1973 Tom Weiskopf
1974 Tom Watson
1975 Pat Fitzsimons
1976 Ben Crenshaw

1977 Bruce Litzke

MOST IMPROVED (women)
1954 Beverly Hanson
1955 Fay Crocker
1956 Marlene Hagge
1957 Mickey Wright
1958 Bonnie Randolph
1959 Murle MacKenzie
1960 Kathy Whitworth
1961 Mary Lena Faulk
1962 Kathy Whitworth
1963 Marilynn Smith
1964 Judy Torluemke
1965 Carol Mann
1966 Gloria Ehret
1967 Susie Maxwell
1968 Gerda Whalen
1969 Donna Caponi
1970 Jane Blalock
1971 Jane Blalock
1972 Betty Burfeindt
1973 Mary Mills
1974 JoAnne Carner
1975 JoAnn Washam
1976 Pat Bradley
1977 Debbie Austin

ROOKIE OF THE YEAR (men)
1957 Ken Venturi
1958 Bob Goalby
1959 Joe Campbell
1960 Mason Rudolph
1961 Jacky Cupit
1962 Jack Nicklaus
1963 Raymond Floyd
1964 R. H. Sikes
1965 Homero Blancas
1966 John Schlee
1967 Lee Trevino
1968 Bob Murphy
1969 Grier Jones
1970 Ted Hayes, Jr.
1971 Hubert Green
1972 Lanny Wadkins
1973 Tom Kite
1974 Ben Crenshaw
1975 Roger Maltbie
1976 Jerry Pate
1977 Graham Marsh

ROOKIE OF THE YEAR (women)
1962 Mary Mills
1963 Clifford Ann Creed
1964 Susie Maxwell
1965 Margie Masters
1966 Jan Ferraris
1967 Sharron Moran
1968 Sandra Post
1969 Jane Blalock
1970 JoAnne Carner
1971 Sally Little
1972 Jocelyne Bourassa
1973 Laura Baugh
1974 Jan Stephenson
1975 Amy Alcott
1976 Tu Ai-Yu
1977 Nancy Lopez

MICKEY WRIGHT AWARD FOR TOURNAMENT VICTORIES (wins in parentheses)

1955 Patty Berg, (6)
1956 Marlene Hagge, (8)
1957 Patty Berg, (5)
1958 Mickey Wright, (5)
1959 Betsy Rawls, (10)
1960 Mickey Wright, (6)
1961 Mickey Wright, (10)
1962 Mickey Wright, (10)
1963 Mickey Wright, (13)
1964 Mickey Wright, (11)
1965 Kathy Whitworth, (8)
1966 Kathy Whitworth, (9)
1967 Kathy Whitworth, (8)
1968 Kathy Whitworth, (10)
1969 Carol Mann, (8)
1970 Shirley Englehorn, (4)
1971 Kathy Whitworth, (4)
1972 Kathy Whitworth, (5)
1973 Kathy Whitworth, (7)
1974 JoAnne Carner, (6)
1975 Sandra Haynie, (4)
1976 Judy Rankin, (6)
1977 Judy Rankin, (N.A.)

BYRON NELSON AWARD FOR TOURNAMENT VICTORIES (wins in parentheses)

1955 Cary Middlecoff, (5)
1956 Ted Kroll, (3)
1957 Arnold Palmer, (4)
1958 Ken Venturi, (4)
1959 Gene Littler, (5)
1960 Arnold Palmer, (8)
1961 Arnold Palmer, (5)
1962 Arnold Palmer, (7)
1963 Arnold Palmer, (7)
1964 Jack Nicklaus, (4)
1965 Jack Nicklaus, (5)
1966 Billy Casper, (4)
1967 Jack Nicklaus, (5)
1968 Billy Casper, (6)
1969 Dave Hill, (3)
1970 Billy Casper, (4)
1971 Lee Trevino, (5)
1972 Jack Nicklaus, (7)
1973 Jack Nicklaus, (7)
1974 Johnny Miller, (8)
1975 Jack Nicklaus, (5)
1976 Ben Crenshaw, (3)
1977 Tom Watson, (N.A.)

Charlie Bartlett Award
Ben Hogan Award
Richardson Award
Player of the Year

GOLF WRITERS ASSOCIATION OF AMERICA
1720 Section Rd., Suite 210, Cincinnati, Ohio 45237
(513/631-4400)

The Charlie Bartlett Award annually honors a playing professional for unselfish contributions to the betterment of society.

1971 Billy Casper
1972 Lee Trevino
1973 Gary Player
1974 Chi Chi Rodriguez
1975 Gene Littler
1976 Arnold Palmer
1977 Lee Elder

The Ben Hogan Award, which consists of a trophy, recognizes the achievements of an individual who has continued to be active in golf in spite of a physical handicap.

1954 Babe Didrikson Zaharias
1955 Ed Furgol
1956 President Dwight D. Eisenhower
1957 Clint Russell
1958 Dale Bourisseau
1959 Charlie Boswell
1960 Skip Alexander
1961 Horton Smith
1962 Jimmy Nichols
1963 Bobby Nichols
1964 Bob Morgan
1965 Ernest Jones
1966 Ken Venturi
1967 Warren Pease
1968 Shirley Englehorn
1969 Curtis Person
1970 Joe Lazaro
1971 Larry Hinson
1972 Ruth Jessen
1973 Gene Littler
1974 Gay Brewer
1975 Patty Berg
1976 Paul Hahn
1977 Des Sullivan

The Richardson Award, which consists of a plaque, is presented annually to the individual who has consistently made outstanding contributions to golf.

1948 Robert A. Hudson
1949 Scotty Fessenden
1950 Bing Crosby
1951 Richard Tufts
1952 Chick Evans
1953 Bob Hope
1954 Babe Didrikson Zaharias
1955 President Dwight D. Eisenhower
1956 George S. May
1957 Francis Ouimet
1958 Bob Jones
1959 Patty Berg
1960 Fred Corcoran
1961 Joseph C. Dey
1962 Walter Hagen
1963 Joe and Herb Graffis
1964 Cliff Roberts
1965 Gene Sarazen
1966 Robert E. Harlow
1967 Max Elbin
1968 Charles Bartlett
1969 Arnold Palmer
1970 Roberto de Vicenzo
1971 Lincoln Werden
1972 Leo Fraser
1973 Ben Hogan
1974 Byron Nelson
1975 Gary Player
1976 Herbert W. Wind
1977 Mark Cox

The Golf Writers Association of America annually selects a man and a woman active in golf competition as Player of the Year.

1968	Billy Casper
1969	Orville Moody
1970	Billy Casper
1971	Lee Trevino
1972	Jack Nicklaus
	Kathy Whitworth
1973	Tom Weiskopf
	Kathy Whitworth
1974	Johnny Miller
	JoAnne Carner
1975	Jack Nicklaus
	Sandra Palmer
1976	Jack Nicklaus, Jerry Pate (co-winners)
	Judy Rankin
1977	Tom Watson
	Judy Rankin

Player of the Year
Rookie of the Year
Vare Trophy
Teacher of the Year
Hall of Fame

LADIES' PROFESSIONAL GOLF ASSOCIATION
919 Third Ave., New York, N.Y. 10022 (212/751-8181)

The Player of Year selection is based on the most consistent and outstanding record in LPGA-sponsored events during the tournament year.

1966	Kathy Whitworth
1967	Kathy Whitworth
1968	Kathy Whitworth
1969	Kathy Whitworth
1970	Sandra Haynie
1971	Kathy Whitworth
1972	Kathy Whitworth
1973	Kathy Whitworth
1974	JoAnne Carner
1975	Sandra Palmer
1976	Judy T. Rankin
1977	Judy T. Rankin

The Rookie of the Year title honors the most outstanding tournament performance during the first year of professional play.

1962	Mary Mills
1963	Clifford Ann Creed
1964	Susie Maxwell Berning
1965	Margie Masters
1966	Jan Ferraris
1967	Sharron Moran
1968	Sandra Post
1969	Jane Blalock
1970	JoAnne Gunderson Carner
1971	Sally Little
1972	Jocelyne Bourassa
1973	Laura Baugh
1974	Jan Stephenson
1975	Amy Alcott
1976	Bonnie Lauer
1977	Debbie Massey

The Vare Trophy honors the LPGA player for consistency in professional competition as shown in low strokes-per-round during tournament play.

1953	Patty Berg
1954	Babe Didrikson Zaharias
1955	Patty Berg
1956	Patty Berg
1957	Louise Suggs
1958	Beverly Hanson
1959	Betsy Rawls
1960	Mickey Wright
1961	Mickey Wright
1962	Mickey Wright
1963	Mickey Wright
1964	Mickey Wright
1965	Kathy Whitworth
1966	Kathy Whitworth
1967	Kathy Whitworth
1968	Carol Mann
1969	Kathy Whitworth
1970	Kathy Whitworth
1971	Kathy Whitworth
1972	Kathy Whitworth
1973	Judy Rankin
1974	JoAnne Carner
1975	JoAnne Carner
1976	Judy T. Rankin
1977	Judy T. Rankin

The Teacher of the Year Award recognizes an LPGA Teaching Division Class A member for dedication, leadership and promotion of the sport of golf. Teaching Division members nominate candidates for selection by a vote of the membership.

1958	Helen Dettweiler
1959	Shirley Spork
1960	Barbara Rotvig
1961	Peggy Kirk Bell
1962	Ellen Griffin
1963	Vonnie Colby
1964	Sally Doyle
1965	Goldie Bateson
1966	Ann Casey Johnstone
1967	Jackie Pung
1968	Gloria Fecht
1969	JoAnne Winter
1970	Gloria Armstrong
1971	Jeannette Rector
1972	Lee Spencer
1973	Penny Zavichas
1974	Mary Dagraedt
1975	Carol Johnson
1976	Marge Burns
1977	DeDe Owens

Induction into the LPGA Hall of Fame honors a woman's professional golf career. She must be an association member for at least 10 consecutive years and the winner of at least 30 tour events with two championships, 40 events with one championship or 40 events. The Hall of Fame is a wing of the World Golf Hall of Fame in Pinehurst, Ga. Induction is as merited.

1951	Patty Berg
	Betty Jameson
	Louise Suggs
	Babe Didrikson Zaharias
1960	Betsy Rawls
1964	Mickey Wright
1975	Kathy Whitworth
1977	Sandra Haynie
	Carol Mann

Player of the Year
Professional of the Year
Vardon Trophy
Ed Dudley Award
Horton Smith Award

PROFESSIONAL GOLFERS' ASSOCIATION OF
AMERICA
Box 12458, Lake Park, Fla. 33403 (305/848-3481)

The Player of the Year is selected by a poll of the PGA
Executive Committee as the most outstanding competitor in professional golf. The winner receives a plaque.

1948 Ben Hogan
1949 Sam Snead
1950 Ben Hogan
1951 Ben Hogan
1952 Julius Boros
1953 Ben Hogan
1954 Ed Furgol
1955 Doug Ford
1956 Jack Burke, Jr.
1957 Dick Mayer
1958 Dow Finsterwald
1959 Art Wall
1960 Arnold Palmer
1961 Jerry Barber
1962 Arnold Palmer
1963 Julius Boros
1964 Ken Venturi
1965 Dave Marr
1966 Billy Casper
1967 Jack Nicklaus
1968 No award
1969 Orville Moody
1970 Billy Casper
1971 Lee Trevino
1972 Jack Nicklaus
1973 Jack Nicklaus
1974 Johnny Miller
1975 Jack Nicklaus
1976 Jack Nicklaus
1977 Tom Watson

A plaque is presented to the working club professional
chosen as Professional of the Year based on service to
golf in general and the association, to the club and to
promotion of the sport of golf. The winner must be a
PGA member for a minimum of 10 years.

1955 Bill Gordon, Tam O'Shanter C.C., Chicago, Ill.
1956 Harry Shepard, Mark Twain Community G.C., Elmira, N.Y.
1957 Dugan Aycock, Lexington C.C., Lexington, N.C.
1958 Harry Pezzullo, Mission Hills G.C., Northbrook, Ill.
1959 Eddie Duino, San Jose C.C., San Jose, Calif.
1960 Warren Orlick, Tam O'Shanter C.C., Orchard Lake,
Mich.
1961 Don Padgett, Green Hills C.C., Selma, Ind.
1962 Tom Lo Presti, Haggin Oaks G.C., Sacramento, Calif.
1963 Bruce Herd, Flossmoor C.C., Flossmoor, Ill.
1964 Lyle Wehrman, Merced G.&C.C., Merced, Calif.
1965 Hubby Habjan, Onwentsia Club, Lake Forest, Ill.
1966 Bill Strausbaugh Jr., Turf Valley C.C., Ellicott City,
Md.
1967 Ernie Vossler, Quail Creek C.C., Oklahoma City,
Okla.

1968 Hardy Loudermilk, Oak Hills, C.C., San Antonio,
Tex.
1969 A. Hubert Smith, Arnold Center C.C., Tullahoma,
Tenn.
1969 Wally Mund, Midland Hills C.C., St. Paul, Minn.
1970 Grady Shumate, Tanglewood G.C., Clemmons, N.C.
1971 Ross Collins, Dallas A. C. C. C., Dallas, Tex.
1972 Howard Morrette, Twin Lakes C.C., Kent, Ohio
1973 Warren Smith, Cherry-Hills C.C., Englewood, Colo.
1974 Paul Harney, Paul Harney's G.C., Hatchville, Mass.
1975 Walker Inman, Jr., Scioto C.C., Columbus, Ohio
1976 Ron Letellier, Cold Spring Harbor C.C., N.Y.
1977 Don Soper, Royal Oak, Mich.

The Vardon Trophy honors consistency in professional
competition as shown in low strokes-per-round during
tournament play.

1937 Harry Cooper
1938 Sam Snead
1939 Byron Nelson
1940 Ben Hogan
1941 Ben Hogan
1942-46 No awards
1947 Jimmy Demaret
1948 Ben Hogan
1949 Sam Snead
1950 Sam Snead
1951 Lloyd Mangrum
1952 Jackie Burke
1953 Lloyd Mangrum
1954 Dutch Harrison
1955 Sam Snead
1956 Cary Middlecoff
1957 Dow Finsterwald
1958 Bob Rosburg
1959 Art Wall
1960 Billy Casper
1961 Arnold Palmer
1962 Arnold Palmer
1963 Billy Casper
1964 Arnold Palmer
1965 Billy Casper
1966 Billy Casper
1967 Arnold Palmer
1968 Billy Casper
1969 Dave Hill
1970 Lee Trevino
1971 Lee Trevino
1972 Lee Trevino
1973 Bruce Crampton
1974 Lee Trevino
1975 Bruce Crampton
1976 Don January
1977 Tom Watson

The Ed Dudley Award is now given twice annually to
the low-qualifying player in the PGA Players' Division
qualification tournament.

1965 John Schlee, (144 holes)
1966 Harry Toscano, (144 holes)
1967 Bobby Cole, (144 holes)
1968 (Spring) Bob Dickson, (144 holes)
(Fall) Grier Jones, (144 holes)
Martin Roesink, (144 holes)
1969 (Spring) Bobby Eastwood, (72 holes)
(Fall) Doug Olson, (72 holes)
1970 Bob Barbarossa, (72 holes)
1971 Bob Zender, (108 holes)
1972 Larry Stubblefield, (108 holes)
1973 Ben Crenshaw, (144 holes)

1974 **Fuzzy Zoeller,** (144 holes)
1975 (Spring) **Joey Dills,** (108 holes)
(Fall) **Jerry Pate,** (108 holes)
1976 (Spring) **Woody Blackburn,** (108 holes)
(Fall) **Keith Fergus,** (108 holes)
1977 (Spring) **Phil Hancock,** (108 holes)
(Fall) **Ed Fiori**

The Horton Smith Award honors the professional who is judged to have made the greatest contributions to professional education.

1965 **Emil Beck,** Black River C.C., Port Huron, Mich.
1966 **Gene C. Mason,** Columbia-Edgewater C.C., Portland, Ore.
1967 **Donald E. Fischesser,** Evansville C.C., Evansville, Ind.
1968 **R. William Clarke,** Hillendale C.C., Phoenix, Md.
1969 **Paul Hahn,** Miami, Fla.
1970 **Joe Walser,** Oklahoma City C.C., Oklahoma City, Okla.
1971 **Irving Schloss,** Dunedin, Fla.
1972 **John Budd,** New Port Richey, Fla.
1973 **George Aulbach,** Pecan Valley C.C., San Antonio, Tex.
1974 **Bill Hardy,** Chevy Chase Club, Chevy Chase, Md.
1975 **John P. Henrich,** Elma Meadows G.C., Elma, N.Y.
1976 **Jim Bailey,** Adams Park Golf Course, Brighton, Colo.
1977 **Paul Runyan,** Green Gables C.C., Denver, Colo.

Bob Jones Award
Green Section Award

U.S. GOLF ASSOCIATION
Golf House, Far Hills, N.J. 07931 (201/234-2300)

The Bob Jones Award is given annually to honor individuals whose personal qualities exemplify those which are esteemed in sports, such as generosity of spirit, manner of playing or behaving so as to show respect for the game and the people in it, unselfishness, self-control and fair play.

1955 Michael Bonallack
1956 Francis D. Ouimet
1957 William C. Campbell
1958 Mildred "Babe" Didrikson Zaharias
1959 Margaret Curtis
1960 Findlay S. Douglas
1961 Charles Evans, Jr.
1962 Joseph B. Carr
1963 Horton Smith
1964 Patty Berg
1965 Charles R. Coe
1966 Mrs. Edwin H. Vare, Jr.
1967 Gary Player
1968 Richard S. Tufts
1969 Robert B. Dickson
1970 Gerald H. Micklem
1971 Roberto DeVicenzo
1972 Arnold Palmer
1973 Gene Littler
1974 Byron Nelson
1975 Jack Nicklaus
1976 Ben Hogan
1977 Joseph C. Dey, Jr.

The Green Section Award recognizes service to golf through work with turfgrass. Nominees may be involved with research, extension, superintendence, maintenance or any other direct work.

1961 John Monteith
1962 Lawrence S. Dickinson
1963 O.J. Noer
1964 Joseph Valentine
1965 Glenn W. Burton
1966 H. Burton Musser
1967 Elmer J. Michael
1968 James L. Haines
1969 Fred V. Grau
1970 Eberhardt R. Steiniger
1971 Thomas Mascaro
1972 Herb and Joe Graffis
1973 Marvin Ferguson
1974 Howard B. Sprague
1975 Fannie Fern Davis
1976 James R. Watson
1977 Edward J. Casey

Milton B. Davis Trampoline Coach of the Year Rotating Trophy Award
Roy E. Moore Award
James A. Rozanas Memorial Tumbling Coach of the Year

AMATEUR ATHLETIC UNION OF THE UNITED STATES
3400 W. 86th St., Indianapolis, Ind. 46268 (317/297-2900)

The Milton B. Davis Trampoline Coach of the Year Rotating Trophy Award is given to the coach for outstanding dedication to faith and morals, athletics, the betterment of the sport and the principles of competition and sportsmanship.

1976 David Coons
1977 Donald Waters

SERVICE AWARD
1977 Robert Thurston

The Roy E. Moore Award is awarded annually to the team winning the Men's Senior National Gymnastic Championship.

1957 Los Angeles Turners
1958 Los Angeles Turners
1959 Los Angeles Turners
1960 Pennsylvania State University
1961 Southern Illinois University
1962 Los Angeles Turners
1963 Los Angeles Turners
1964 Los Angeles Turners
1965 Southern Connecticut Gymnastics Club
1966 Southern Connecticut Gymnastics Club
1967 Northwestern Louisiana State College
1968 Husky Gymnastics Club (Seattle, Wash.)
1969 Husky Gymnastics Club (Seattle, Wash.)
1970 New York Athletic Club
1971 New York Athletic Club
1972 New York Athletic Club
1973 New York Athletic Club
1974 New York Athletic Club
1975 New York Athletic Club
1976 National Gymnastics Center, (Woodward, Pa.)
1977 New York Athletic Club

The James A. Ronzanas Memorial Tumbling Coach of the Year award is given for outstanding dedication, commitment, enthusiasm and tireless efforts in teaching not only the skills but also the morals and discipline of good sportsmanship in furthering the sport of tumbling.

    1976 Dave Green
          Roger Brown
    1977 Pat Henderson

Prince of Wales Trophy
Clarence S. Campbell Bowl
Hart Memorial Trophy
Calder Memorial Trophy
James Norris Memorial Trophy
Art Ross Trophy
Vezina Trophy
Lady Byng Memorial Trophy
Lester Patrick Trophy
Conn Smythe Memorial Trophy
Bill Masterton Memorial Trophy

NATIONAL HOCKEY LEAGUE
920 Sun Life Bldg., Montreal H3B 2W2, Canada
(514/871-9220)

The Prince of Wales Trophy, originally donated by His Royal Highness and given until 1974 for team excellence in league division performance in regular-season play, is now awarded to the winner of the Prince of Wales Conference at the end of the regular championship season.

    1925 Montreal Canadiens
    1926 Montreal Maroons
    1927 Ottawa Senators
    1928 Boston Bruins
    1929 Boston Bruins
    1930 Boston Bruins
    1931 Boston Bruins
    1932 New York Rangers
    1933 Boston Bruins
    1934 Detroit Red Wings
    1935 Boston Bruins
    1936 Detroit Red Wings
    1937 Detroit Red Wings
    1938 Boston Bruins
    1939 Boston Bruins
    1940 Boston Bruins
    1941 Boston Bruins
    1942 New York Rangers
    1943 Detroit Red Wings
    1944 Montreal Canadiens
    1945 Montreal Canadiens
    1946 Montreal Canadiens
    1947 Montreal Canadiens
    1948 Toronto Maple Leafs
    1949 Detroit Red Wings
    1950 Detroit Red Wings
    1951 Detroit Red Wings
    1952 Detroit Red Wings
    1953 Detroit Red Wings

    1954 Detroit Red Wings
    1955 Detroit Red Wings
    1956 Montreal Canadiens
    1957 Detroit Red Wings
    1958 Montreal Canadiens
    1959 Montreal Canadiens
    1960 Montreal Canadiens
    1961 Montreal Canadiens
    1962 Montreal Canadiens
    1963 Toronto Maple Leafs
    1964 Montreal Canadiens
    1965 Detroit Red Wings
    1966 Montreal Canadiens
    1967 Chicago Black Hawks
    1968 Montreal Canadiens
    1969 Montreal Canadiens
    1970 Chicago Black Hawks
    1971 Boston Bruins
    1972 Boston Bruins
    1973 Montreal Canadiens
    1974 Boston Bruins
    1975 Buffalo Sabres
    1976 Montreal Canadiens
    1977 Montreal Canadiens

The Clarence S. Campbell Bowl is presented annually to the team finishing with the most points in the Clarence S. Campbell Conference.

    1968 Philadelphia Flyers
    1969 St. Louis Blues
    1970 St. Louis Blues
    1971 Chicago Black Hawks
    1972 Chicago Black Hawks
    1973 Chicago Black Hawks
    1974 Philadelphia Flyers
    1975 Philadelphia Flyers
    1976 Philadelphia Flyers
    1977 Philadelphia Flyers

The Hart Memorial Trophy, which carries a cash award of $1,500, is awarded annually to the player judged to be the most valuable to his team by a poll of the Professional Hockey Writers' Association.

    1924 Frank Nighbor, Ottawa Senators
    1925 Billy Burch, Hamilton
    1926 Nels Stewart, Montreal Maroons
    1927 Herb Gardiner, Montreal Canadiens
    1928 Howie Morenz, Montreal Canadiens
    1929 Ray Worters, New York Americans
    1930 Nels Stewart, Montreal Maroons
    1931 Howie Morenz, Montreal Canadiens
    1932 Howie Morenz, Montreal Canadiens
    1933 Eddie Shore, Boston Bruins
    1934 Aurel Joliat, Montreal Canadiens
    1935 Eddie Shore, Boston Bruins
    1936 Eddie Shore, Boston Bruins
    1937 "Babe" Siebert, Montreal Canadiens
    1938 Eddie Shore, Boston Bruins
    1939 Toe Blake, Montreal Canadiens
    1940 Ebbie Goodfellow, Detroit Redwings
    1941 Bill Cowley, Boston Bruins
    1942 Tommy Anderson, New York Americans
    1943 Bill Cowley, Boston Bruins
    1944 "Babe" Pratt, Toronto Maple Leafs
    1945 Elmer Lach, Montreal Canadiens
    1946 Max Bentley, Chicago Black Hawks
    1947 Maurice Richard, Montreal Canadiens
    1948 Buddy O'Connor, New York Rangers
    1949 Sid Abel, Detroit Red Wings
    1950 Chuck Rayner, New York Rangers

1951 Milt Schmidt, Boston Bruins
1952 Gordie Howe, Detroit Red Wings
1953 Gordie Howe, Detroit Red Wings
1954 Al Rollins, Chicago Black Hawks
1955 Ted Kennedy, Toronto Maple Leafs
1956 Jean Beliveau, Montreal Canadiens
1957 Gordie Howe, Detroit Red Wings
1958 Gordie Howe, Detroit Red Wings
1959 Andy Bathgate, New York Rangers
1960 Gordie Howe, Detroit Red Wings
1961 Bernie Geoffrion, Montreal Canadiens
1962 Jacques Plante, Montreal Canadiens
1963 Gordie Howe, Detroit Red Wings
1964 Jean Beliveau, Montreal Canadiens
1965 Bobby Hull, Chicago Black Hawks
1966 Bobby Hull, Chicago Black Hawks
1967 Stan Mikita, Chicago Black Hawks
1968 Stan Mikita, Chicago Black Hawks
1969 Phil Esposito, Boston Bruins
1970 Bobby Orr, Boston Bruins
1971 Bobby Orr, Boston Bruins
1972 Bobby Orr, Boston Bruins
1973 Bobby Clarke, Philadelphia Flyers
1974 Phil Esposito, Boston Bruins
1975 Bobby Clarke, Philadelphia Flyers
1976 Bobby Clarke, Philadelphia Flyers
1977 Guy Lafleur, Montreal Canadiens

The Calder Memorial Trophy, which carries a cash award of $1,500, is awarded annually to the player selected as the most proficient in his first year of competition in the National Hockey League in a poll by the Professional Hockey Writers' Association.

1952 Bernie Geoffrion, Montreal Canadiens
1953 Gump Worsley, New York Rangers
1954 Camille Henry, New York Rangers
1955 Ed Litzenberger, Chicago Black Hawks
1956 Glenn Hall, Detroit Red Wings
1957 Larry Regan, Boston Bruins
1958 Frank Mahovlich, Toronto Maple Leafs
1959 Ralph Backstrom, Montreal Canadiens
1960 Bill Hay, Chicago Black Hawks
1961 Dave Keon, Toronto Maple Leafs
1962 Bobby Rousseau, Montreal Canadiens
1963 Kent Douglas, Toronto Maple Leafs
1964 Jacques Laperriere, Montreal Canadiens
1965 Roger Crozier, Detroit Reg Wings
1966 Brit Selby, Toronto Maple Leafs
1967 Bobby Orr, Boston Bruins
1968 Derek Sanderson, Boston Bruins
1969 Danny Grant, Minnesota North Stars
1970 Tony Esposito, Chicago Black Hawks
1971 Gilbert Perreault, Buffalo Sabres
1972 Ken Dryden, Montreal Canadiens
1973 Steve Vickers, New York Rangers
1974 Denis Potvin, New York Islanders
1975 Eric Vail, Atlanta Flames
1976 Bryan Trottier, New York Islanders
1977 Willi Plett, Atlanta Flames

The James Norris Memorial Trophy, which carries a cash award of $1,500, is awarded annually to the defensive player in the National Hockey League who demonstrates the greatest season-long ability, as selected in a poll of the Professional Hockey Writers' Association.

1954 Red Kelly, Detroit Red Wings
1955 Doug Harvey, Montreal Canadiens
1956 Doug Harvey, Montreal Canadiens
1957 Doug Harvey, Montreal Canadiens

1958 Doug Harvey, Montreal Canadiens
1959 Tom Johnson, Montreal Canadiens
1960 Doug Harvey, Montreal Canadiens
1961 Doug Harvey, Montreal Canadiens
1962 Doug Harvey, New York Rangers
1963 Pierre Pilote, Chicago Black Hawks
1964 Pierre Pilote, Chicago Black Hawks
1965 Pierre Pilote, Chicago Black Hawks
1966 Jacques Laperriere, Montreal Canadiens
1967 Harry Howell, New York Rangers
1968 Bobby Orr, Boston Bruins
1969 Bobby Orr, Boston Bruins
1970 Bobby Orr, Boston Bruins
1971 Bobby Orr, Boston Bruins
1972 Bobby Orr, Boston Bruins
1973 Bobby Orr, Boston Bruins
1974 Bobby Orr, Boston Bruins
1975 Bobby Orr, Boston Bruins
1976 Denis Potvin, New York Islanders
1977 Larry Robinson, Montreal Canadiens

The Art Ross Trophy, which carries a cash award of $1,000, is given annually to the league player who leads in scoring during the regular season.

1952 Gordie Howe, Detroit Red Wings
1953 Gordie Howe, Detroit Red Wings
1954 Gordie Howe, Detroit Red Wings
1955 Bernie Geoffrion, Montreal Canadien
1956 Jean Beliveau, Montreal Canadiens
1957 Gordie Howe, Detroit Red Wings
1958 Dickie Moore, Montreal Canadiens
1959 Dickie Moore, Montreal Canadiens
1960 Bobby Hull, Chicago Black Hawks
1961 Bernie Geoffrion, Montreal Canadiens
1962 Bobby Hull, Chicago Black Hawks
1963 Gordie Howe, Detroit Red Wings
1964 Stan Mikita, Chicago Black Hawks
1965 Stan Mikita, Chicago Black Hawks
1966 Bobby Hull, Chicago Black Hawks
1967 Stan Mikita, Chicago Black Hawks
1968 Stan Mikita, Chicago Black Hawks
1969 Phil Esposito, Boston Bruins
1970 Bobby Orr, Boston Bruins
1971 Phil Esposito, Boston Bruins
1972 Phil Esposito, Boston Bruins
1973 Phil Esposito, Boston Bruins
1974 Phil Esposito, Boston Bruins
1975 Bobby Orr, Boston Bruins
1976 Guy Lafleur, Montreal Canadiens
1977 Guy Lafleur, Montreal Canadiens

The Vezina Trophy, which carries a cash award of $1,500, is given annually to the goalkeeper(s) playing at least 25 games for the team with the fewest goals scored against it.

1952 Terry Sawchuk, Detroit Red Wings
1953 Terry Sawchuk, Detroit Red Wings
1954 Harry Lumley, Toronto Maple Leafs
1955 Terry Sawchuk, Detroit Red Wings
1956 Jacques Plante, Montreal Canadiens
1957 Jacques Plante, Montreal Canadiens
1958 Jacques Plante, Montreal Canadiens
1959 Jacques Plante, Montreal Canadiens
1960 Jacques Plante, Montreal Canadiens
1961 Johnny Bower, Toronto Maple Leafs
1962 Jacques Plante, Montreal Canadiens
1963 Glenn Hall, Chicago Black Hawks
1964 Charlie Hodge, Montreal Canadiens
1965 Terry Sawchuk, Toronto Maple Leafs
     Johnny Bower, Toronto Maple Leafs

1966	**Gump Worsley,** Montreal Canadiens
	Charlie Hodge, Montreal Canadiens
1967	**Glenn Hall,** Chicago Black Hawks
	Denis DeJordy, Chicago Black Hawks
1968	**Gump Worsley,** Montreal Canadiens
	Rogatien Vachon, Montreal Canadiens
1969	**Jacques Plante,** St. Louis Blues
	Glenn Hall, St. Louis Blues
1970	**Tony Esposito,** Chicago Black Hawks
1971	**Ed Giacomin,** New York Rangers
	Gilles Villemure, New York Rangers
1972	**Tony Esposito,** Chicago Black Hawks
	Gary Smith, Chicago Black Hawks
1973	**Ken Dryden,** Montreal Canadiens
1974	**Bernie Parent,** Philadelphia Flyers
	Tony Esposito, Chicago Black Hawks
1975	**Bernie Parent,** Philadelphia Flyers
1976	**Ken Dryden,** Montreal Canadiens
1977	**Ken Dryden,** Montreal Canadiens
	Michel Larocque, Montreal Canadiens

The Lady Byng Memorial Trophy, which carries a cash award of $1,500, is given annually to the player judged to have "exhibited the best type of sportsmanship and gentlemanly conduct combined with a high standard of playing ability" during the previous playing season, as selected by a poll of the Professional Hockey Writers' Association.

1925	**Frank Nighbor,** Ottawa Senators
1926	**Frank Nighbor,** Ottawa Senators
1927	**Billy Burch,** New York Americans
1928	**Frank Boucher,** New York Rangers
1929	**Frank Boucher,** New York Rangers
1930	**Frank Boucher,** New York Rangers
1931	**Frank Boucher,** New York Rangers
1932	**Joe Primeau,** Toronto Maple Leafs
1933	**Frank Boucher,** New York Rangers
1934	**Frank Boucher,** New York Rangers
1935	**Frank Boucher,** New York Rangers
1936	**Doc Romney,** Chicago Black Hawks
1937	**Marty Barry,** Detroit Red Wings
1938	**Gordie Drillon,** Toronto Maple Leafs
1939	**Clint Smith,** New York Rangers
1940	**Bobby Baver,** Boston Bruins
1941	**Bobby Baver,** Boston Bruins
1942	**Phil Apps,** Toronto Maple Leafs
1943	**Max Bentley,** Chicago Black Hawks
1944	**Clint Smith,** Chicago Black Hawks
1945	**Bill Mosienko,**Chicago Black Hawks
1946	**"Toe" Black,** Montreal Canadiens
1947	**Bobby Baver,** Boston Bruins
1948	**Buddy O'Connor,** New York Rangers
1949	**Bill Quackenbush,** Detroit Red Wings
1950	**Edgar Laprade,** New York Rangers
1951	**Red Kelly,** Detroit Red Wings
1952	**Sid Smith,** Toronto Maple Leafs
1953	**Red Kelly,** Detroit Red Wings
1954	**Red Kelly,** Detroit Red Wings
1955	**Sid Smith,** Toronto Maple Leafs
1956	**Earl Reibel,** Detroit Red Wings
1957	**Andy Hebenton,** New York Rangers
1958	**Camille Henry,** New York Rangers
1959	**Alex Delvecchio,** Detroit Red Wings
1960	**Don McKenney,** Boston Bruins
1961	**Red Kelly,** Toronto Maple Leafs
1962	**Dave Keon,** Toronto Maple Leafs
1963	**Dave Keon,** Toronto Maple Leafs
1964	**Ken Wharram,** Chicago Black Hawks
1965	**Bobby Hull,** Chicago Black Hawks

1966	**Alex Delvecchio,** Detroit Red Wings
1967	**Stan Mikita,** Chicago Black Hawks
1968	**Stan Mikita,** Chicago Black Hawks
1969	**Alex Delvecchio,** Detroit Red Wings
1970	**Phil Goyette,** St. Louis Blues
1971	**Johnny Bucyk,** Boston Bruins
1972	**Jean Ratelle,** New York Rangers
1973	**Gilbert Perreault,** Buffalo Sabres
1974	**Johnny Bucyk,** Boston Bruins
1975	**Marcel Dionne,** Detroit Red Wings
1976	**Jean Ratelle,** New York Rangers and Boston Bruins
1977	**Marcel Dionne,** Los Angeles Kings

The Lester Patrick Trophy is awarded annually to the players, officials, coaches and referees judged to have given the most outstanding service to hockey in the United States. The winner is selected by an award committee consisting of the NHL president, NHL governor, a hockey writer for a U.S. national news service, a nationally syndicated sports columnist, an ex-player in the Hockey Hall of Fame and a sports director of a national broadcast network.

1966	**Jack Adams**
1967	**Gordie Howe**
	Charles F. Adams
	James Norris, Sr.
1968	**Thomas F. Lockhart**
	Walter Brown
	Gen. John R. Kilpatrick
1969	**Bobby Hull**
	Edward Jeremiah
1970	**Eddie Shore**
	James Hendy
1971	**William M. Jennings**
	John B. Sollenberger
	Terry Sawchuk
1972	**Clarence S. Campbell**
	John Kelley
	Cooney Weiland
1973	**Walter L. Bush, Jr.**
1974	**Alex Delvecchio**
	Murray Murdoch
	Weston W. Adams, Sr.
	Charles L. Crovat
1975	**Donald M. Clark**
	William L. Chadwick
	Thomas N. Ivan
1976	**Stan Mikita**
	George A. Leader
	Bruce A. Norris
1977	**John Bucyk**
	Murray Armstrong
	John Mariucci

The Conn Smythe Memorial Trophy is given to the individual deemed the most valuable player in the league play-offs.

1965	**Jean Beliveau,** Montreal Canadiens
1966	**Roger Crozier,** Detroit Red Wings
1967	**Dave Keon,** Toronto Maple Leafs
1968	**Glenn Hall,** St. Louis Blues
1969	**Serge Savard,** Montreal Canadiens
1970	**Bobby Orr,** Boston Bruins
1971	**Ken Dryden,** Montreal Canadiens
1972	**Bobby Orr,** Boston Bruins
1973	**Yvan Cournoyer,** Montreal Canadiens
1974	**Bernie Parent,** Philadelphia Flyers
1975	**Bernie Parent,** Philadelphia Flyers

1976 **Reggie Leach,** Philadelphia Flyers
1977 **Guy Lafleur,** Montreal Canadiens

The Bill Masterton Memorial Trophy honors perseverence, sportsmanship and dedication to professional hockey.

1968 **Claude Provost,** Montreal Canadiens
1969 **Ted Hampson,** Oakland
1970 **Pit Martin,** Chicago Black Hawks
1971 **Jean Ratelle,** New York Rangers
1972 **Bobby Clarke,** Philadelphia Flyers
1973 **Lowell MacDonald,** Pittsburgh Penguins
1974 **Henri Richard,** Montreal Canadiens
1975 **Don Luce,** Buffalo Sabres
1976 **Rod Gilbert,** New York Rangers
1977 **Ed Westfall,** New York Islanders

Avco World Trophy
Gordie Howe Trophy
W.D. "Bill" Hunter Trophy
WORLD HOCKEY ASSOCIATION
Suite 1700, 1 Financial Plaza, Hartford Conn. 06103
(203/278-4240)

The Avco World Trophy is award to the WHA championship team.

1973 **New England Whalers**
1974 **Houston Aeros**
1975 **Houston Aeros**
1976 **Winnipeg Jets**
1977 **Quebec Nordiques**

The Gordie Howe Trophy honors the Most Valuable Player in the league, selected by a vote of the media people covering WHA teams.

1973 **Bobby Hull,** Winnipeg Jets
1974 **Gordie Howe,** Houston Aeros
1975 **Bobby Hull,** Winnipeg Jets
1976 **Marc Tardif,** Quebec Nordiques
1977 **Robbie Ftorek,** Phoenix Roadrunners

The W.D. "Bill" Hunter Trophy is given to the league scoring leader.

1973 **Andre Lacroix,** Philadelphia Blazers
1974 **Mike Walton,** Minnesota Fighting Saints
1975 **Andre Lacroix,** San Diego Mariners
1976 **Marc Tardif,** Quebec Nordiques
1977 **Real Cloutier,** Quebec Nordiques

Horseman of the Year
HORSEMAN AND FAIR WORLD PUBLISHING CO.
Box 11688, Lexington, Ky. 40511 (606/254-4026)

The subscribers to *Horseman and Fair World* annually vote on the individual to be honored as the Horseman of the Year on the basis of contributions to harness racing. The winner receives a set of silver mint julep cups on a silver tray and is the subject of a feature in the magazine.

1956 **Delvin Miller**
1957 **John Simpson, Sr.**
1958 **William Haughton**
1959 **Joe O'Brien**
1960 **Clint Hodgins**

1961 **Frank Ervin**
1962 **Stanley Dancer**
1963 **Ralph Baldwin**
1964 **Frank Ervin**
1965 **Frank Ervin**
1966 **Robert Farrington**
1967 **William Haughton**
1968 **Stanley Dancer**
1969 **Mr. and Mrs. Frederick Van Lennep**
1970 **Stanley F. Bergstein**
1971 **William R. Hayes II**
1972 **Mr. and Mrs. H. Willis Nichols**
1973 **E. Roland Harriman**
1974 **Elgin Armstrong**
1975 **Henry C. Thomson**
1976 **Norman Woolworth and David Johnston**
1977 **Lloyd Arnold**

Eclipse Awards
THOROUGHBRED RACING ASSOCIATION
3000 Marcus Ave., Suite 2W4, Lake Success, N.Y. 11040
(516/328-2660)

The Eclipse Awards, which are statuettes, are given annually to various individuals and horses for contributions to and achievements in thoroughbred horseracing.

HORSE OF THE YEAR

1971 **Ack Ack**
1972 **Secretariat**
1973 **Secretariat**
1974 **Forego**
1975 **Forego**
1976 **Forego**
1977 **Seattle Slew**

OLDER COLT, HORSE OR GELDING

1971 **Ack Ack**
1972 **Autobiography**
1973 **Riva Ridge**
1974 **Forego**
1975 **Forego**
1976 **Forego**
1977 **Forego**

OLDER FILLY OR MARE

1971 **Shuvee**
1972 **Typecast**
1973 **Susan's Girl**
1974 **Desert Vixen**
1975 **Susan's Girl**
1976 **Proud Delta**
1977 **Cascapedia**

THREE-YEAR-OLD COLT

1971 **Canonero II**
1972 **Key to the Mint**
1973 **Secretariat**
1974 **Little Current**
1975 **Wajima**
1976 **Bold Forbes**
1977 **Seattle Slew**

THREE-YEAR-OLD FILLY

1971 **Turkish Trousers**
1972 **Susan's Girl**

1973 Desert Vixen
1974 Chris Evert
1975 Ruffian
1976 Revidere
1977 Our Mims

TWO-YEAR-OLD COLT

1971 Riva Ridge
1972 Secretariat
1973 Protagonist
1974 Foolish Pleasure
1975 Honest Pleasure
1976 Seattle Slew
1977 Affirmed

TWO-YEAR-OLD FILLY

1971 Numbered Account
1972 La Prevolante
1973 Talking Picture
1974 Ruffian
1975 Dearly Precious
1976 Sensational
1977 Lakeville Miss

TURF HORSE

1971 Run the Gantlet
1972 Cougar II
1973 Secretariat
1974 Dahlia
1975 Snow Knight
1976 Youth
1977 Johnny D.

SPRINTER

1971 Ack Ack
1972 Chou Croute
1973 Shecky Greene
1974 Forego
1975 Gallant Bob
1976 My Juliet
1977 What a Summer

STEEPLECHASE OR HURDLE HORSE

1971 Shadowbrook
1972 Soothsayer
1973 Athenian Idol
1974 Gran Kan
1975 Life's Illusion
1976 Straight and True
1977 Cafe Prince

MAN OF THE YEAR

1972 John W. Galbreath
1973 Edward Plunket Taylor
1974 William L. McKnight
1975 John A. Morris

ECLIPSE AWARD OF MERIT

1976 Jack J. Dreyfus
1977 Steve Cauthen

OUTSTANDING OWNER

1971 Mr. and Mrs. E. E. Fogelson
1974 Dan Lasater
1975 Dan Lasater
1976 Dan Lasater
1977 Maxwell Gluck

OUTSTANDING BREEDER

1974 John W. Galbreath
1975 Fred W. Hooper
1976 Nelson Bunker Hunt
1977 Edward Plunket Taylor

OUTSTANDING OWNER-BREEDER

1971 Paul Mellon
1972 Meadow Stable/Meadow Stud (C. T. Chenery)
1973 Meadow Stable/Meadow Stud (C. T. Chenery)

OUTSTANDING TRAINER

1971 Charles Whittingham
1972 Lucien Laurin
1973 H. Allen Jerkens
1974 Sherrill Ward
1975 Steve DiMauro
1976 Lazaro Barrera
1977 Lazaro Barrera

OUTSTANDING JOCKEY

1971 Laffit Pincay, Jr.
1972 Braulio Baeza
1973 Laffit Pincay, Jr.
1974 Laffit Pincay, Jr.
1975 Braulio Baeza
1976 Sandford D. Hawley
1977 Steve Cauthen

OUTSTANDING APPRENTICE JOCKEY

1971 Gene St. Leon
1972 Thomas Wallis
1973 Steve Valdez
1974 Chris McCarron
1975 Jimmy Edwards
1976 George Martens
1977 Steve Cauthen

SPECIAL AWARD

1971 Robert J. Klebert
1974 Charles Hatton
1976 Bill Shoemaker

OUTSTANDING ACHIEVEMENT AWARD

1971 Charles Engelhard
1972 Arthur B. Hancock, Jr.

Meritorious Service Award

HORSEMEN'S BENEVOLENT & PROTECTIVE ASSOCIATION
6000 Executive Blvd., Suite 317, Rockville, Md. 20852
(301/881-7191)

The Association annually honors an individual for meritorious service to racing. A selection committee chooses the person to be honored. Unofficially, the recipient of this award is usually referred to as the Man of the Year. A trophy is presented to the winner.

1953 George Widener
1954 Marshall Cassidy
1955 Lou Smith
1956 Charles H. Strub
1957 Benjamin Lindheimer
1958 Leo O'Donnell

1959 J. Samuel Perlman
1960 J. J. "Jake" Isaacson
1961 James D. Stewart
1962 Irving Gushen
1963 Wathen Knebelkamp
1964 Neil J. Curry
1965 Edward P. Taylor
1966 Raymond R. Guest
1967 William H. May
1968 Thomas J. Brogan
1969 No award
1970 Harry Farnham
1971 Herve Racivitch
1972 Eugene Bierhaus
1973 Burt Bacharach
       Bill Shoemaker
1974 William McKnight
1975 Ray H. Freeark
1976 American Horse Council
1977 David A. "Sonny" Werblin

Racehorse of the Year Award
National Hunt Champion Award

RACECOURSE ASSOCIATION
42 Portman Sq., London W1H 0JE, U.K. (Tel: 01-486 4571)

The Racehorse of the Year Award, a bronze statuette of a horse and jockey, is given annually for outstanding achievements by a horse racing on the flat. A committee of racing writers votes on the winner, which must have raced on a British course during the season for which the award is made.

1965 Sea Bird II
1966 Charlottown
1967 Busted
1968 Sir Ivor
1969 Park Top
1970 Nijinsky
1971 Mill Reef
1972 Brigadier Gerard
1973 Dahlia
1974 Dahlia
1975 Grundy
1976 Pawneese
1977 The Minstrel

The National Hunt Champion Award, a bronze statuette of a horse and jockey, is given annually to the outstanding horse that has competed in a British steeplechase or hurdle course during the previous season. A committee of racing writers selects the winner.

1966 Arkle, Steeplechaser
1967 Mill House, Steeplechaser
1968 Persian War, Hurdler
1969 Persian War, Hurdler
1970 Persian War, Hurdler
1971 Bula, Hurdler
1972 Bula, Hurdler
1973 Pendil, Steeplechaser
1974 Red Rum, Steeplechaser
1975 Comedy of Errors, Hurdler
1976 Night Nurse, Hurdler
1977 Midnight Court

Induction

RACING HALL OF FAME
Union Ave., Saratoga Springs, N.Y. 12866 (518/584-0400)

The Hall of Fame honors trainers, jockeys and horses (thoroughbred male and female horses, flat runners and steeplechasers). A nominating committee of three or more members appointed by the executive committee of the National Museum of Racing proposes candidates in all three categories for selection by a 100-member voting committee comprised of sportswriters and radio and television racing announcers. To be eligible, a horse must have been retired from racing , and a person must have retired or served as a jockey or trainer for more than 20 years in the United States.

TRAINERS

1955 William P. Burch
       Thomas J. Healey
       Sam Hildreth
       Andrew J. Joyner
       John W. Rogers
       James Rowe, Sr.
1956 William Duke
       John J. Hyland
       Henry McDaniel
1957 No new inductees
1958 Sunny Jim Fitzsimmons
       Hirsch Jacobs
       Ben Jones
1959 Max Hirsch
       H.A. "Jimmy" Jones
1960 William Molter, Jr.
1961 No new inductees
1962 No new inductees
1963 Preston M. Burch
1964 Louis Feustel
1965 No new inductees
1966 John M. Gaver
1967 J. Dallett "Dolly" Byers
       Burt Mulholland
1968 Frank Childs
1969 J. Howard Lewis
       Herbert J. Thompson
1970 Marion H. Van Berg
       R.W. Walden
1971 Harvey Guy Bedwell
       William C. Winfrey
1972 John Nerud
1973 Fred Burlew
       Thomas Hitchcock, Sr.
       Hollie Hughes
1974 Alfred P. Smithwick
       Charlie Whittingham
1975 D. Michael Smithwick
1976 Robert A. "Whistling Bob" Smith
       W.C. "Woody" Stephens
1977 Lucien Lauren
       Sylvester Veitch

JOCKEYS

1955 Laverne Fator
       Edward R. Garrison
       Daniel Mahrer
       James McLaughlin
       Walter Miller
       Isaac Murphy
       George M. Odom

Earl Sande
Tod Sloan
Fred Taral
Nash Turner
George Woolf
1956 Henry Griffin
Linus McAtee
Winnie O'Connor
Frank O'Neill
John Reiff
1957 Ted Atkinson
1958 Eddie Arcaro
John Longden
William Lee "Willie" Shoemaker
1959 William John Hartack
John Loftus
1960 Ralph Reeves
1961 No new inductees
1962 Lavelle "Buddy" Ensor
1963 Steve Brooks
Joseph A. "Joe" Notter
1964 No new inductees
1965 John Adams
1966 No new inductees
1967 Charles F. Kurtsinger
1968 Rigan McKinney
Jimmy Stout
1969 George H. Bostwick
Mack Garner
Willie Knapp
1970 Frank David Adams
Frank Coltiletti
Gilbert Patrick
Samuel Purdy
Carroll Shilling
1971 Albert Johnson
1972 Carroll K. Bassett
Eric Guerin
Clarence Kummer
1973 Sam Boulmetis
Robert H. Crawford
Bayard Tuckermen, Jr.
Raymond Workman
1974 Conn McCreary
1975 Laffit Pincay, Jr.
1976 Braulio Baeza
1977 Willie Simms
Manuel Ycaza

HORSES

1955 Ben Brush
Boston
Domino
Hanover
Hindoo
Kingston
Lexington
Luke Blackburn
Salvator
Sir Archy
1956 Artful
Beldame
Broomstick
Colin
Commando
Fair Play
Good and Plenty
Peter Pan
Roseben
Sysonby

1957 Blue Larkspur
Equipoise
Exterminator
Gallant Fox
Grey Lag
Man O'War
Regret
Sarazen
Sir Barton
Twenty Grand
1958 Seabiscuit
War Admiral
1959 Citation
Whirlaway
1960 Tom Fool
1961 No election
1962 Count Fleet
1963 Armed
Gallorette
Native Dancer
Twilight Tear
1964 Assault
Busher
1965 Imp
Jolly Roger
Nashua
Omaha
1966 Elkridge
Neji
Swaps
Top Flight
1967 Bushranger
Cicada
Kelso
Miss Woodford
1968 Old Rosebud
1969 Battleship
Discovery
1970 American Eclipse
Buckpasser
1971 Dr. Fager
Jay Trump
Longfellow
1972 Pan Zareta
Round Table
1973 Bold Ruler
1974 Damascus
Dark Mirage
Secretariat
1975 Carry Back
Ruthless
Shuvee
Stymie
1976 Alsab
Bed O'Roses
L'Escargot

Joe Palmer Award

NATIONAL TURF WRITERS ASSOCIATION
6000 Executive Blvd., Suite 317, Rockville, Md. 20852
(301/881-2266)

The Joe Palmer Award is given annually for meritorious service to racing. A plaque is presented to the winner of a balloting of the association membership.

1964 Wathen Knebelkamp
1965 John D. Schapiro

1966 Marshall Cassidy
1967 John Longden
1968 Marion Van Berg
1969 Raymond Guest
1970 Warner L. Jones
1971 Bill Shoemaker
1972 Paul Mellon
1973 John Galbreath
1974 Secretariat
1975 I. J. Collins
1976 Fred W. Hooper
1977 Nelson Bunker Hunt

Karate Award

AMATEUR ATHLETIC UNION OF THE UNITED
STATES
3400 W. 86th St., Indianapolis, Ind. 46268 (317/297-2900)

1976 Jerry Thomson
1977 Jon Evans

Governor's Trophy

UNITED STATES OF AMERICA RUGBY
FOOTBALL UNION
27 E. State St., Sherburne, N.Y. 13460 (607/674-5381 and
334-9332 [summer])

The Governor's Trophy is awarded annually for excellence in the Round Robin Tournament among
USARFU Territorial Union Members.

1977 Pacific Coast Rugby Union

Competitor of the Year
World Cup Competitor of the Year - Male
World Cup Competitor of the Year - Female
Pro Racer of the Year
U.S. Alpine Racer of the Year - Male
U.S. Alpine Racer of the Year - Female
International Nordic Competitor of the Year - Male
International Nordic Competitor of the Year - Female
U.S. Nordic Competitor of the Year - Male
U.S. Nordic Competitor of the Year - Female

Freestyle Competitor of the Year - Male
Freestyle Competitor of the Year - Female

SKI RACING
75 Main St., Fair Haven, Vt. 05743 (802/265-3434)

Ski Racing's editors annually select the top skiers —
amateur and professional, Alpine and Nordic — as the
most outstanding performers in their specialties during the previous year.

COMPETITOR OF THE YEAR

1975 Gustavo Thoeni, Italy
1976 Rosi Mittermaier, Federal Republic of Germany
1977 Ingemar Stenmark, Sweden

WORLD CUP COMPETITOR OF THE YEAR - MALE

1975 Gustavo Thoeni, Italy
1976 Ingemar Stenmark, Sweden
1977 Ingemar Stenmark, Sweden

WORLD CUP COMPETITOR OF THE YEAR - FEMALE

1975 Annemarie Moser-Proell, Austria
1976 Rosi Mittermaier, Federal Republic of Germany
1977 Lise-Marie Morerod, Switzerland

PRO RACER OF THE YEAR

1975 Hank Kashiwa
1976 Henri Duvillard
1977 Henri Duvillard

U.S. ALPINE RACER OF THE YEAR - MALE

1975 Greg Jones, Tahoe City, Calif.
1976 Phil Mahre, White Pass, Wash.
1977 Phil Mahre, White Pass, Wash.

U.S. ALPINE RACER OF THE YEAR - FEMALE

1975 Cindy Nelson, Lutsen, Ninn.
1976 Cindy Nelson, Lutsen, Minn.
1977 Abbi Fisher, South Conway, N.H.

**INTERNATIONAL NORDIC COMPETITOR OF THE YEAR -
MALE**

1975 Oddvar Braa, Norway
1976 Anton Innauer, Austria
1977 Walter Steiner, Switzerland

**INTERNATIONAL NORDIC COMPETITOR OF THE YEAR -
FEMALE**

1975 Galina Kulakova, USSR
1976 Raisa Smetanina, USSR
1977 Galina Kulakova, USSR

U.S. NORDIC COMPETITOR OF THE YEAR - MALE

1975 Bill Koch, Putney, Vt.
1976 Bill Koch, Putney, Vt.
1977 Jim Denney, Duluth, Minn.

U.S. NORDIC COMPETITOR OF THE YEAR - FEMALE

1975 Martha Rockwell, West Lebanon, N.H.
1976 Martha Rockwell, West Lebanon, N.H.
1977 Alison Owen Spencer, Anchorage, Alas.

FREESTYLE COMPETITOR OF THE YEAR - MALE
1975 Mark Stiegemeier, Boise, Idaho
1976 Scott Brooksbank, Stillwater, Minn.
1977 John Eaves, Montreal, Que., Canada

FREESTYLE COMPETITOR OF THE YEAR - FEMALE
1975 Genia Fuller, Framingham, Mass.
1976 Marion Post, Averill Park, N.Y.
1977 Marion Post, Averill Park, N.Y.

Golden Quill
Outstanding Competitor Award
U.S. SKI WRITERS ASSOCIATION
7 Kensington Rd., Glens Falls, N.Y. 12801 (518/793-1201)

The Golden Quill, which is depicted as a sculpture, is awarded annually upon nomination by the Golden Quill Committee and ratification by the board of directors for outstanding contributions to skiing.

1968 Merritt H. Stiles, U.S. Ski Association
1969 Ralph "Doc" Des Roches, Ski Industries America
1970 Robert P. Beattie, International Ski Racers Association
1971 Harold S. Hirsch, White Stag, Inc.
1972 Dorice Taylor, Sun Valley resort, Idaho
1973 Willy Schaeffler, U.S. Ski Association
1974 Fred Pabst, Jr., Bromley Mt., Vt.
1975 Robert Parker, Vail Associates, Colo.
1976 Rudi Mattesich, Ski Touring Council
1977 Lowell Thomas, Skier, broadcaster, author

The Outstanding Competitor Award is given annually to the ski racer, Alpine or Nordic, amateur or professional, who has contributed most to American skiing.

1967 Jimmy Heuga
1968 John Bower
1969 No award
1970 Billy Kidd
1971 Cochran family
1972 Barbara Ann Cochran
1973 Jean-Claude Killy
1974 Martha Rockwell
1975 Hank Kashiwa
1976 Bill Koch
1977 Phil Mahre

College Soccer Award
INTERCOLLEGIATE SOCCER ASSOCIATION OF AMERICA
University of Wisconsin, Parkside, Kenosha, Wisc. 53140 (414/553-2245)

A plaque is awarded annually for an outstanding contribution to college soccer in the previous year to a recipient nominated by the membership and selected by a committee.

1972 Wayne Sunderland, National rating system
1973 Dettmar Cramer, National Coaching School
1974 John McKeon, National Soccer Bowl
1975 No award
1976 Don Yonker, Editor, *National Soccer Coaches' Association Journal*
1977 Frank Longo, Quincy (Ill.) College

Most Valuable Player
Rookie of the Year
Lead Goalkeeper
Coach of the Year
Hermann Trophy
NORTH AMERICAN SOCCER LEAGUE
1133 Ave. of the Americas, New York, N.Y. 10036 (212/575-0066)

The Most Valuable Player is selected annually by a poll of players on North American Soccer League teams conducted by *The Sporting News*. The winner currently receives a Toyota automobile.

1967 Ruben Navarro (Philadelphia Spartans)
1968 John Kowalik (Chicago Mustangs)
1969 Cirilio Fernandez (Kansas City Spurs)
1970 Carlos Metidieri (Rochester Lancers)
1971 Carlos Metidieri (Rochester Lancers)
1972 Randy Horton (New York Cosmos)
1973 Warren Archibald (Miami Toros)
1974 Peter Silvester (Baltimore Comets)
1975 Steven David (Miami Toros)
1976 Pele (New York Cosmos)
1977 Franz Beckenbauer (New York Cosmos)

The Rookie of the Year is selected annually by a poll of players on North American Soccer League teams conducted by *The Sporting News*.

1967 Willie Roy (Chicago Spurs)
1968 Kaizer Motaung (Atlanta Chiefs)
1969 Siegfried Stritzi (Baltimore Bays)
1970 Jim Leeker (St. Louis Stars)
1971 Randy Horton (New York Cosmos)
1972 Mike Winter (St. Louis Stars)
1973 Kyle Rote, Jr. (Dallas Tornado)
1974 Douglas McMillan (Los Angeles Aztecs)
1975 Chris Bahr (Philadelphia Atoms)
1976 Steve Pecher (Dallas Tornado)
1977 Jim McAlister (Seattle Sounders)

Lead Goalkeeper honors go annually to the athlete with the most saves in the season's North American Soccer League play.

1967 Mirko Stojanovic (Oakland Clippers)
1968 Ataulfo Sanchez (San Diego Toros)
1969 Manfred Kammerer (Atlanta Chiefs)
1970 Lincoln Phillips (Washington Darts)
1971 Mirko Stojanovic (Dallas Tornado)
1972 Ken Cooper (Dallas Tornado)
1973 Bob Rigby (Philadelphia Atoms)
1974 Barry Watling (Seattle Sounders)
1975 Shep Messing (Boston Minutemen)
1976 Tony Chursky (Seattle Sounders)
1977 Ken Cooper (Dallas Tornado)

Coaches and general managers of North American Soccer League teams annually select an individual as Coach of the Year.

1968 Phil Woosnam (Atlanta Chiefs)
1969 No information available
1970 No information available
1971 No information available
1972 Casey Frankiewicz (St. Louis Stars)
1973 Al Miller (Philadelphia Atoms)
1974 John Young (Miami Toros)
1975 John Sewell (St. Louis Stars)

1976 Eddie Firmani (Tampa Bay Rowdies)
1977 Ron Newman (Fort Lauderdale Strikers)

The Hermann Trophy is given annually to the individual chosen as the leading college soccer player of the year, based on a poll conducted by *The Sporting News* of college soccer coaches.

1967 Dov Markus (Long Island University, N.Y.)
1968 Mani Hernandez (San Jose State, Calif.)
1969 Al Trost (St. Louis University, Mo.)
1970 Al Trost (St. Louis University, Mo.)
1971 Mike Seerey (St. Louis University, Mo.)
1972 Mike Seerey (St. Louis University, Mo.)
1973 Dan Counce (St. Louis University, Mo.)
1974 Farrukh Quraishi (Oneonta State, N.Y.)
1975 Steve Ralbovsky (Brown University, R.I.)
1976 Glenn Myernick (Hartwick College, N.Y.)
1977 Bill Gazonas (Hartwick College, N.Y.)

Duke Kahanamoku Trophy
AMERICAN SURFING ASSOCIATION
2131 Kalakaua Avenue, Honolulu, Hawaii 96815

A bronze bust of the late Duke Kahanamoku is awarded as the Duke Kahanamoku Trophy for the highest individual contribution to the sport.

1977 James Nystrom, coach, Marina High School, Huntington Beach, Calif.

AAU Swimming and Diving Awards
AMATEUR ATHLETIC UNION OF THE UNITED STATES
3400 W. 86th St., Indianapolis, Ind. 46268 (317/297-2900)

The Lawrence J. Johnson Award is an aquatics award, presented annually in rotation to an outstanding male swimmer, female swimmer, male diver, female diver, synchronized swimmer and water polo player.

1964 Don Schollander
1965 Cathy Ferguson
1966 Bernie Wrightson
1967 Leslie Bush
1968 Margo McGrath
1969 Gary P. Sheerer
1970 Michael J. Burton
1971 Susie Atwood
1972 Dick Rydze
1973 Cynthia Potter
1974 Gail Johnson
1975 Bruce Bradley
1976 John Naber
1977 Wendy Boglioli

The AAU Swimming Award is a bronze replica of a life-size statue located in the Payne Whitney Gymnasium at Yale University that is awarded annually to an individual or organization for outstanding contributions to the advancement of swimming.

1954 Federation Internationale De Natation Amateur
1955 Amateur Swimming Federation of Japan
1956 Beth Kaufman, Chairman, National AAU Age Group Committee

1957 Amateur Swimming Union of Australia
1958 Lawrence J. Johnson, ASUA
Robert J.H. Kiphuth, Yale University
R. Max Ritter, FINA
1959 Carl O. Bauer, Missouri Athletic Club
1960 F. Jeffery Farrell, New Haven Swim Club
1961 Mary Freeman Kelly, Vesper Boat Club
1962 I. Murray Rose, Los Angeles Athletic Club ASU of Australia
1963 James Counsilman, Indiana University
1964 Harold W. Henning, Chairman, National AAU Men's Swimming Committee
1965 George F. Haines, Santa Clara Swim Club
1966 College Swimming Coaches Association of America
Harry Hainsworth, AAU Aquatics Administrator
1967 Albert Schoenfield, Swimming World
1968 Deborah Meyer, Arden Hills Swim Club
1969 Federacion Mexicana de Natacion
1970 Michael J. Burton
Charles McCaffree, Jr.
1971 A. R. "Red" Barr
1972 Mark Spitz
Kenneth Treadway
1973 Edwin Olson
1974 John Bogert
1975 Peter Daland
1976 John Naber
1977 Phillips Petroleum Co., Bartlesville, Okla.

The Robert J. H. Kiphuth Award is awarded to the male and female high point scorers in the Short Course and Long Course Swimming Championships.

1968 Charles Hickcox, Short Course
Deborah Meyer, Short Course
Mark Spitz, Long Course
Sue Pedersen, Long Course
1969 Mike Burton, Short Course
Susie Atwood, Short Course
Gary Hall, Long Course
Sue Pedersen, Long Course
1970 Gary Hall, Short Course
Susie Atwood, Short Course
Gary Hall, Long Course
Susie Atwood, Long Course
1971 Frank Heckl, Short Course
Susie Atwood, Short Course
Mark Spitz, Long Course
Susie Atwood, Long Course
1972 Mark Spitz, Short Course
Susie Atwood, Short Course
No championship held, Long Course
1973 Shane Gould, Short Course
Rick Colella, Short Course
Lynn Colella, Long Course
Keena Rothhammer, Long Course
Rick Colella, Long Course
1974 Shirley Babashoff, Short Course
Rick Colella, Short Course
Shirley Babashoff, Long Course
Bruce Furniss, Long Course
1975 Shirley Babashoff, Short Course
John Naber, Short Course
Shirley Babashoff, Long Course
Bruce Furniss, Long Course
1976 John Naber, Indoor Long Course
Shirley Babashoff, Indoor Long Course
John Naber, Long Course
Donnalee Wennerstrom, Long Course
1977 Scott Spann, Short Course

Tracy Caulkins, Short Course
Brian Goodell, Long Course
Tracy Caulkins, Long Course

AMERICAN SWIMMING COACHES ASSOCIATION APPRECIATION AWARD

1972 John B. Kelly, Jr.
1973 Bob Miller
1974 George Breen
1975 Mark Schubert
1976 Mark Schubert
1977 Paul Bergen

MAX RITTER AWARD FOR ADVANCEMENT OF INTERNATIONAL AQUATICS

1977 Yugoslavian Swim Federation

SWIM COACH OF THE YEAR

1977 Paul Bergen

SPECIAL AWARD

1977 Ken Pettigrew, for outstanding service as a swimming official

The Lillan MacKeller Award goes to an individual who has given unselfishly of herself for synchronized swimming without thought of personal gain, and with a particular emphasis on working for the benefit of the athlete.

1971 Lillian MacKellar
1972 Joy Cushman
1973 Dawn Ben
1974 No award
1975 Kay Vilen
1976 No award
1977 Theresa Anderson

SPECIAL AWARD

1977 Harold Henning, for the advancement of synchronized swimming

DIVING COACH OF THE YEAR

1977 Ron O'Brien, Ohio State University

AGE GROUP DIVING COACH OF THE YEAR

1972 Paul Flack
1973 Don Gartiez
1974 Charles Casuto
1975 Richard Kimball
1976 Glen McCormick
1977 Dave Glander

MIKE MALONE MEMORIAL DIVING AWARD

1969 Al White
1970 R. Jackson Smith
1971 Stan Kistler
1972 Richard Kimball
1973 Hobie Billingsley
1974 Ron O'Brien
1975 Mike Peppe
1976 Robert A. Rydze
1977 Betty Perkins

Induction

INTERNATIONAL SWIMMING HALL OF FAME

1 Hall of Fame Dr., Ft. Lauderdale, Fla. 33316
(305/462-6536)

Induction in the Hall of Fame honors an outstanding swimmer, diver, coach or contributor. Any aquatic personality in the world is eligible for nomination and a vote by 1,700 aquatic coaches and other swimming authorities. Those honored are permanently recognized with an alcove displaying his or her achievements in the sport.

1965 Buster Crabbe
C. M. "Charlie" Daniels
Gertrude Ederle
Dawn Fraser
Beulah Gundling
Jamison Handy
Duke Kahanamoku
Adolph Kiefer
Robert J. H. Kiphuth
Kusuo Kitamura
Commodore Longfellow
Pat McCormick
Matt Mann II
Pam Morris
R. Max Ritter
Murray Rose
Don Schollander
Matthew Webb
Johnny Weissmuller
Al White
Katherine Rawls
1966 Dave Armbruster
Bill Bachrach
Arne Borg
Ernst Brandsten
Steve Clark
Georgia Coleman
Ann Curtis
Pete Desjardins
Alan Ford
Alfred Hajos
Eleanor Holm
Ragnhild Hveger
Edward T. Kennedy
Helene Madison
Shelly Mann
Jack Medica
Wally O'Connor
Mike Peppe
Clarence Pinkston
Wally Ris
Soichi Sakamoto
Bill Smith
Joe Verdeur
Chris Von Saltza
Esther Williams
1967 Miller Anderson
Carl Bauer
Sybil Bauer
Sir Frank Beaurepaire
Ethelda Bleibtrey
"Ma" Braun
Teddy Cann
Jacques Yves Cousteau
Fanny Durack
Hironoshin Furuhashi
L. deB. Handley
Beth Kaufman
Al Neuschaefer
Martha Norelius
Betty Becker Pinkston
Paul Radmilovic

Aileen Riggin
Norman Ross
The Spence Brothers
1968 Jeff Farrell
Benjamin Franklin
Zolten de Halmay
Harry Hebner
George Hodgson
John Jarvis
Warren Kealoha
George Kojac
Sammy Lee
Hendrika Mastenbroek
Emil Rausch
E. Carroll Schaeffer
Dorothy Poynton
David Theile
Yoshiyuki Tsuruta
1969 Greta Andersen
Fred Cady
Donna deVarona
Vickie Draves
Stephen Hunyadfi
Barney Kieran
Ethel Lackie
Freddie Lane
Michael McDermott
James Nemeth
Al Patnik
Henry Taylor
1970 Walter Bathe
Cavill Family
Florence Chadwick
Jack Cody
Willy den Ouden
Olga Dorfner
Claire Galligan
Richard R. Hough
Jimmy McLane
Henri Padou
Charlie Sava
Robert Webster
1971 George Corsan, Sr.
Ray Daughters
Dick Degener
Jennie Fletcher
Budd Goodwin
John Higgins
Martin Homonnay
Cor Kint
Konrads Kids
Helen Meany
Mike Troy
Bill Yorzyk
1972 Stan Brauninger
Andrew M. "Boy" Charlton
Earl Clark
Lorraine Crapp
Ford Konno
Mario Majoni
Erich Rademacher
Sharon Stouder
Helen Wainwright
1973 Greta Brandsten
Bruce Harlan
John Henricks
Walter Laufer
John Marshall
Eva and Ilona Novak
Yoshi Oyakawa

Jan Stender
Nell Van Vliet
1974 Capt. Bert Cummins
Charlotte Epstein
Harold Fern
Ellen Fullard-Leo
William Henry
Annette Kellerman
Fred Luehring
John Trudgeon
Alick Wickham
1975 George Breen
David "Skippy" Browning
Karen Harup
Claudia Kolb
Ingrid Kramer
Frank McKinney
Keo Nakama
Tom Robinson
Mina Wylie
1976 Catie Ball
Joaquin Capilla
Forbes Carlile
James Counsilman
Marjorie Gestring
Dezso Gyarmati
Charles Hickcox
Ada Kok
Charles McCaffree
Carl Robie
Sylvia Ruuska
Roy Saari
Charles Silvia
Eva Szekely
Alberto Zorrilla
1977 Mike Burton
Sherm Chavoor
Peter Daland
Shane Gould
George Haines
Alex Jany
Chet Jastremski
Debbie Meyer
Galina Prozumenshikova
Mickey and Johnny Riley
Mark Spitz

Rookie of the Year (Male)
Rookie of the Year (Female)
Most Improved Player (Male)
Most Improved Player (Female)

TENNIS MAGAZINE
495 Westport Ave., Norwalk, Conn. 06856 (203/847-5811)

The editors of this publication spotlight noteworthy achievements among professional tennis players.

ROOKIE OF THE YEAR (male)

1972 Jimmy Connors
1973 Brian Gottfried
1974 Paul Ramirez
1975 Sandy Mayer
1976 Billy Martin
1977 John McEnroe

ROOKIE OF THE YEAR (female)

1974 Martina Navratilova
1975 Greer Stevens
1976 Natasha Chmyreva
1977 Tracy Austin

MOST IMPROVED PLAYER (male)

1976 Wojtek Fibak
1977 Brian Gottfried

MOST IMPROVED PLAYER (female)

1976 Sue Barker
1977 Wendy Turnbull

DiBenedetto Award
Colonel Charles J. Dieges Award
Scott Hamilton Award for
Leadership in Road Running
J.B. "Cap" Haralson Award
Long Distance Running Merit Award
Reddock Award
Joseph Robichaux Award
Seattel Award
WomenSports Team Championship
Award
WomenSports Foundation Female
Long Distance Runner of the Year

AMATEUR ATHLETIC UNION OF THE UNITED
STATES
3400 W. 86th St., Indianapolis, Ind. 46268 (317/297-2900)

The Lawrence DiBeneditto Award is a trophy awarded
annually for the outstanding individual track and field
performance of the year.

1959 Parry O'Brien
1960 Ralph Boston
1961 Ralph Boston
1962 James Beatty
1963 John Pennel
1964 Lt. Billy Mills
1965 Randy Matson
1966 James Ryun
1967 James Ryun
1968 Bob Beamon
1969 George Young
1970 Ralph Mann
1971 Patrick Matzdorf
1972 Rodney Milburn, Jr.
1973 Rodney Milburn, Jr.
1974 Rick Wohlhuter
1975 William Rodgers
1976 Edwin Moses
1977 Edwin Moses

The Colonel Charles J. Dieges Award is presented to
the outstanding performer at the National Men's Indoor and Outdoor AAU Track and Field Championships. For a time, women were also honored.

INDOOR

1954 Parry O'Brien
1955 Arnie Sowell
1956 Parry O'Brien
1957 Phil Reavis
1958 Ron Delaney
1959 John Thomas
1960 Allan Lawrence
1961 Ralph Boston
1962 Jim Beatty
1963 Jim Beatty
1964 Ron Clarke
1965 Billy Mills
1966 Bob Seagren
      Edith McGuire
1967 Tracy Smith
      Madeline Manning
1968 Eleanor Montgomery
      Pat Van Wolvelaere
1969 George Young
1970 Martin McGrady
1971 Frank Shorter
1972 Kjell Isaksson
1973 Tracy Smith
1974 Richard Wohlhuter
1975 Miruts Yifter
1976 Filbert Bayi
1977 No award

OUTDOOR

1954 Arthur Bragg
1955 Arnie Sowell
1956 No award
1957 Reggie Pearman
1958 No award
1959 Ray Norton
1960 No award
1961 No award
1962 No award
1963 Bob Hayes
1964 No award
1965 No award
1966 Jim Ryun
1967 No award
1968 No award
1969 No award
1970 Frank Shorter
1971 Rod Milburn
1972 No award
1973 No award
1974 Richard Wohlhuter
1975 Donald Quarrie
1976 Mac Wilkins
1977 No award

SCOTT HAMILTON AWARD FOR LEADERSHIP IN ROAD RUNNING

1976 Harold DeMoss
      Fred Brown
1977 Vincent Fandetti

The J. B. "Cap" Haralson Award is a plaque awarded
annually for outstanding service as an AAU Track and
Field official.

1967 Robert Giegengack
1968 S. B. "Si" Tyler
1969 Albert Post
1970 Daniel J. Ferris
1971 Lawrence E. Houston

1972 Pincus Sober
1973 George Wilson
1974 Hilmer Lodge
1975 John Oelkers
1977 Ted Haydon
1977 Ralph Colson

LONG DISTANCE RUNNING MERIT AWARD

1969 H. Browning Ross
1970 Robert S. Campbell
1971 Ted Corbitt
1972 Frank Shorter
1973 Robert E. DeCelle
1974 Aldo M. Scandurra
1975 Harold Canfield
1976 John Brennand
1977 Joseph Kleinman

The *Redbook* Award is presented to the outstanding female athlete at both the National Women's Indoor and Outdoor Track and Field Championships.

1973 Mable Fergerson
1974 No award
1975 Madeline Manning Jackson
1976 Jan Merrill
1977 Francie Larrieu
      Evelyn Ashford

The Joseph Robichaux Award is given annually to one who has made an outstanding contribution to the women's track and field program in the United States.

1972 Edward Temple
1973 C. C. Jackson
1974 Juner Bellew
1975 Conrad Ford
1976 Roxanne Andersen
1977 Harmon Brown

The Seattel Award, awarded annually by the Women's Track and Field Committee to the female track and field competitor who exhibits the most outstanding performance for the year, has been replaced by the Female Track and Field Star of the Year Award.

SEATTEL AWARD

1965 Wyomia Tyus
1966 Charlotte Cook
1967 Doris Brown
1968 Madeline Manning
1969 Elinor Montgomery
1970 Willye White
1971 Iris Davis
1972 Kathy Hammond
1973 Martha Watson
1974 Francie Larrieu
1975 No award
1976 Joni Huntley
      Jane Frederick

FEMALE TRACK AND FIELD STAR OF THE YEAR

1977 Kathy McMillan

Originated by *WomenSports* magazine, the Female Long Distance Runner of the Year and Team Championship Awards are now continued by the publication's successor, the WomenSports Foundation, and honor excellence in women's athletics

WOMENSPORTS TEAM CHAMPIONSHIP AWARD

1974 Atoms Track Club
1975 Sports International Track Club
1976 Atoms Track Club
1977 Los Angeles Mercurettes Track Club

WOMENSPORT FOUNDATION FEMALE LONG DISTANCE RUNNER OF THE YEAR

1977 Miki Gorman

Induction

NATIONAL TRACK AND FIELD HALL OF FAME
1524 Kanawha Blvd. E., Charleston, W.Va. 25311
(304/345-0087)

Induction in the National Track and Field Hall of Fame honors American athletes whose accomplishments, in the judgment of the board of governors, has been exemplary.

1974

Ralph H. Boston	Avery Brundage
Lee Q. Calhoun	Dean B. Cromwell
Glenn Cunningham	Glenn Davis
Harold Davis	Mildred "Babe" Didrikson Zaharias
Harrison Dillard	
Daniel J. Ferris	Ray Ewry
Rafer Johnson	Brutus Hamilton
Robert B. Mathias	Alvin Kraenzlein
Lawrence Myers	Michael C. Murphy
Al Oerter	Parry O'Brien
Jesse Owens	Harold M. Osborn
Robert I. Simpson	Wilma Rudolph
Cornelius "Dutch" Warmerdam	Lester Steers
	Malvin G. Whitfield

1975

Horace Ashenfelter III	Alice Coachman Davis
M.E. "Bill" Easton	John J. Flanagan
Edward M. "Ted" Haydon	Edward P. Hurt
Ralph Metcalfe	Bobby Joe Morrow
Rob Richards	Helen Stephens
James Francis Thrope	William A. Toomey
Stella Walsh	

1976

Dee Boeckmann	J. Kenneth Doherty
Robert L. Hayes	Hayes Wendell Jones
Billy Mills	Charles Paddock
Steve Prefontaine	Joie Ray
Mae Faggs Star	Forrest Towns

1977

Bob Beamon	Wilbur Hutsell
Thomas Jones	Greg Rice
Jackson V. Scholz	Elizabeth Robinson Schwartz
Andy Stanfield	James E. Sullivan
Earl Thompson	Frank Wykoff

Emil Breitkreutz Leadership Award

AMATEUR ATHLETIC UNION OF THE UNITED STATES
3400 W. 86th St., Indianapolis, Ind. 46268 (317/297-2900)

Established by the National A.A.U. Volleyball Committee, the Emil Breitkreutz Leadership Award honors contributions to volleyball.

1970   Emil Breitkreutz
1971   Dorothy Boyce
1972   Joe Sharpless
1973   No award
1974   Ethel Stevens
1975   Dorothy Boyce
1976   James J. Fox
1977   No award

AAU Racewalking Awards
AMATEUR ATHLETIC UNION
3400 W. 86th St., Indianapolis, Ind. 46268 (317/297-2900)

Achievements in and contributions to racewalking are recognized by the AAU.

RON ZINN MEMORIAL AWARD (TO THE OUTSTANDING U.S. RACEWALKER)

1977   Neal Pike

ACHIEVEMENT AWARD

1977   Wisconsin Association AAU

OUTSTANDING CONTRIBUTIONS AWARD

1977   Charles Silcock

SPECIAL AWARD

1977   Joseph Tigerman, for meritorious service

John J. Curren Award
James W. Lee Award
AMATEUR ATHLETIC UNION OF THE UNITED STATES
3400 W. 86th St., Indianapolis, Ind. 46268 (317/297-2900)

The John J. Curren Award is given annually by the New York Athletic Club to the outstanding player in the National AAU Men's Indoor Water Polo Championships.

1962   William Kooistra
1963   Charles Bittick
1964   Edward Jaworski
1965   Charles Harris
1966   Dean Willeford
1967   Sam Kooistra
1968   Irwin Okumura
1969   Patrick McClellan
1970   Jerry Christy
1971   Gary Sheerer
1972   No award
1973   William Harris

1974   No award
1975   Charles Harris
1976   No award
1977   William Harris

The James W. Lee Award is given annually to the outstanding player in the National AAU Men's Outdoor Water Polo Championship.

1963   Stan Sprague
1964   George Stransky
        Chuck Bittick
1965   Dave Ashleigh
1966   Gary Sheerer
1967   Dean Willeford
1968   Tony Van Dorp
1969   Steve Barnett
1970   Gary Sheerer
1971   Thomas Walsh
1972   Doug Arth
1973   Eric Ferguson
1974   Eric Lindroth
1975   Peter Asch
1956   Steve Hamann
1977   Gary Figueroa

AAU Exemplary Wrestling Award
Sustained Superior Performance Award
AMATEUR ATHLETIC UNION OF THE UNITED STATES
3400 W. 86th St., Indianapolis, Ind. 46268 (317/297-2900)

AAU EXEMPLARY WRESTLING AWARD

1972   Fendley Collins
1973   Ivan Olsen
1974   No award
1975   No award
1976   Newt Copple
1977   No award

The Sustained Superior Performance Award is a plaque given annually to an individual who "at the grass roots level" has made an outstanding contribution to wrestling for a number of years. The award is sponsored by the U.S. Wrestling Foundation.

1967   Bill Schriver
1968   Maurice E. "Pat" McGill
1969   John K. Eareckson
1970   Steere Noda
1971   George Myerson
1972   Fendley Collins
1973   Ivan Olsen
1974   Billy Martin
1975   Cy Mitchell
1976   Roy Moore
1977   Andrew Kovacz

Beauty & Fashion

Contents

Related Awards

Miss America

MISS AMERICA PAGEANT
1325 Boardwalk, Boardwalk and Tennessee Ave., Atlantic City, N.J. 08401 (609/345-7571)

Miss America is chosen annually from contestants from the 50 states, the District of Columbia and U.S. territories by a panel of celebrity judges on the basis of beauty, talent, poise and charm. The winner, who is crowned on a national telecast, receives a year's appearance contract and various prizes, including a $20,000 scholarship. In addition to the scholarship awarded to Miss America, 10 runnersup and several non-finalists are given scholarships as well. The winner for any given year is selected at the Atlantic City pageant the previous September.

1921 **Margaret Gorman,** Washington, D.C.
1922 **Mary Campbell,** Columbus, Ohio
1923 **No pageant**
1924 **Ruth Malcolmson,** Philadelphia, Pa.
1925 **Fay Lanphier,** Oakland, Calif.
1926 **Norma Smallwood,** Tulsa, Okla.
1927 **Lois Delaner,** Joliet, Ill.
1928-32 **No pageants**
1933 **Marion Bergeron,** West Haven, Conn.
1934 **No pageant**
1935 **Henrietta Leaver,** Pittsburgh, Pa.
1936 **Rose Coyle,** Philadelphia, Pa.
1937 **Bette Cooper,** Bertrand Island, N.J.
1938 **Marilyn Meseke,** Marion, Ohio
1939 **Patricia Donnelly,** Detroit, Mich.
1940 **Frances Marie Burke,** Philadelphia, Pa.
1941 **Rosemary LaPlanche,** Los Angeles, Calif.
1942 **Jo-Carroll Dennison,** Tyler, Tex.
1943 **Jean Bartel,** Los Angeles, Calif.
1944 **Venus Ramey,** Washington D.C.
1945 **Bess Myerson,** New York, N.Y.
1946 **Marilyn Buferd,** Los Angeles, Calif.
1947 **Barbara Walker,** Memphis, Tenn.
1948 **BeBe Shopp,** Hopkins, Minn.
1939 **Jacque Mercer,** Litchfield, Ariz.
1950 **No pageant**
1951 **Yolande Betbeze,** Mobile, Ala.
1952 **Coreen Kay Hutchins,** Salt Lake City, Utah
1953 **Neva Jane Langley,** Macon, Ga.
1954 **Evelyn Margaret Ay,** Ephrata, Pa.
1955 **Lee Meriwether,** San Francisco, Calif.
1956 **Sharon Ritchie,** Denver, Colo.
1957 **Marian McKnight,** Manning, S.C.
1958 **Marilyn Van Derbur,** Denver, Colo.
1959 **Mary Ann Mobley,** Brandon, Miss.
1960 **Lynda Lee Mead,** Natchez, Miss.
1961 **Nancy Fleming,** Montague, Mich.
1962 **Maria Fletcher,** Asheville, N.C.
1963 **Jacquelyn Mayer,** Sandusky, Ohio
1964 **Donna Axum,** El Dorado, Ark.
1965 **Vonda Kay Van Dyke,** Phoenix, Ariz.
1966 **Deborah Irene Bryant,** Overland Park, Kans.
1967 **Jane Anne Jayroe,** Laverne, Okla.
1968 **Debra Dene Barnes,** Moran, Kans.
1969 **Judith Anne Ford,** Belvidere, Ill.
1970 **Pamela Anne Eldred,** Birmingham, Mich.
1971 **Phyllis Ann George,** Denton, Tex.
1972 **Laurie Lea Schaefer,** Columbus, Ohio
1973 **Terre Anne Meeuwsen,** DePere, Wisc.
1974 **Rebecca Ann King,** Denver Colo.
1975 **Shirley Cothran,** Fort Worth, Tex.
1976 **Tawny Elaine Godin,** Yonkers, N.Y.
1977 **Dorothy Kathleen Benham,** Edina, Minn.

Miss Black America

J. MORRIS ANDERSON PRODUCTIONS, INC.
24 W. Chilton Ave., Philadelphia, Pa. 19144 (215/VI 4-8872)

Miss Black America is selected on a national telecast pageant by a panel of judges based on beauty, talent and personality criteria after competitions on local and state levels. The winner receives cash, merchandise and trips, currently including $10,000, screen tests and performance contracts and a variety of other prizes.

1968 **Sandy Williams,** Pennsylvania
1969 **"G.O." Smith,** New York
1970 **Stephanie Clark,** Washington, D.C.
1971 **Joyce Warner,** Florida
1972 **Linda Barney,** New Jersey
1973 **Arnice Russell,** New York
1974 **VonGretchen Sheppard,** California
1975 **Helen Ford,** Mississippi
1976 **Twanna Kilgore,** Washington, D.C.
1977 **Claire Ford,** Tennessee

Playmate of the Year

PLAYBOY MAGAZINE
919 N. Michigan Ave., Chicago, Ill. 60611 (312/PL 1-8000)

The editors of *Playboy* annually vote for the Playmate of the Year from among the previous year's Playmates of the Month. In addition to the original modeling fee, the Playmate of the Year receives $10,000 and a variety of merchandise prizes.

1960 **Ellen Stratton**
1961 **Linda Gamble**
1962 **Christa Speck**
1963 **June Cochran**
1964 **Donna Michelle**
1965 **Jo Collins**
1966 **Allison Parks**
1967 **Lisa Baker**
1968 **Angela Dorian**
1969 **Connie Kreski**
1970 **Claudia Jennings**
1971 **Sharon Clark**
1972 **Liv Lindeland**
1973 **Marilyn Cole**
1974 **Cyndi Wood**
1975 **Marilyn Lange**
1976 **Lillian Muller**
1977 **Patti McGuire**

Miss U.S.A.
Miss Universe

MISS UNIVERSE, INC.
666 Fifth Ave., New York, N.Y. 10019 (212/757-9396)

In nationally televised pageants each year, a panel of celebrity judges selects the winner of the annual Miss U.S.A. and Miss Universe titles. Miss U.S.A. is chosen from among contestants in franchised pageants in the various states and the District of Columbia, while Miss Universe is selected from international contestants. The winner of the Miss U.S.A. contest receives an

$11,000 cash award, a cash scholarship, a year-long $10,000 personal appearance contract and various prizes, principally clothing, a fur coat and a car. Miss Universe receives a $10,000 cash award, a $3,500 scholarship, a one-year contract with Paramount Pictures with a guarantee of at least $15,000, a $10,000 year-long personal-appearance contract and various prizes, principally clothing, a fur coat and a car.

MISS U.S.A.

1952 Jackie Loughery, New York
1953 Myrna Hansen, Illinois
1954 Miriam Stevenson, South Carolina
1955 Carlene King Johnson, Vermont
1956 Carol Morris, Iowa
1957 Charlotte Sheffield, Utah
1958 Arlene Howell, Louisiana
1959 Terry Lynn Huntington, California
1960 Linda Bement, Utah
1961 Sharon Brown, Louisiana
1962 Macel Wilson, Hawaii
1963 Marite Ozers, Illinois
1964 Bobbie Johnson, District of Columbia
1965 Sue Downey, Ohio
1966 Maria Remenyi, California
1967 Cheryl-Ann Patton, Florida
1968 Didi Anstett, Washington
1969 Wendy Dascomb, Virginia
1970 Debbie Shelton, Virginia
1971 Michele McDonald, Pennsylvania
1972 Tanya Wilson, Hawaii
1973 Amanda Jones, Illinois
1974 Karen Morrison, Illinois
1975 Summer Bartholomew, California
1976 Barbara Peterson, Minnesota
1977 Kimberly Louise Tomes, Texas

MISS UNIVERSE

1952 Armi Kuusela, Finland
1953 Christiane Martel, France
1954 Miriam Stevenson, U.S.A.
1955 Hellevi Rombin, Sweden
1956 Carol Morris, U.S.A.
1957 Gladys Zender, Peru
1958 Luz Marina Zuluaga, Colombia
1959 Akiko Kojima, Japan
1960 Linda Bement, U.S.A.
1961 Marlene Schmidt, Federal Republic of Germany
1962 Norma Nolan, Argentina
1963 Ieda Maria Vargas, Brazil
1964 Corinna Tsopei, Greece
1965 Apasra Hongsakula, Thailand
1966 Margareta Arvidsson, Sweden
1967 Sylvia Hitchcock, U.S.A.
1968 Martha Vasconellos, Brazil
1969 Gloria Diaz, Philippines
1970 Marisol Malaret, Puerto Rico
1971 Georgina Risk, Lebanon
1972 Kerry Anne Wells, Australia
1973 Margarita Moran, Philippines
1974 Amparo Munoz, Spain
1975 Anne Marie Pohtamo, Finland
1976 Rina Messinger, Israel
1977 Janelle Commissiong, Trinidad & Tobago

Best Dressed Women
Best Dressed Men
Hall of Fame Entrants
NEW YORK COUTURE GROUP
32 E. 57th St., New York, N.Y. 10022 (212/MU 8-2130)

Qualified experts and observers in the fields of women's and men's fashions vote by ballot for the Best Dressed Women and Men and Hall of Fame entrants each year. The ballots are tabulated by a committee of fashion editors. The criteria for these honors are "distinguished application of fashion to contemporary living, without extravagance or ostentation." Individuals named to the Best Dressed List do not receive anything but publicity. The Best Dressed List has at times been compiled according to relative voting strength of the individuals named to the list; at other times, it has appeared alphabetically. The lists have refered to married women in different ways in different years, using their own first names or their husband's. In each case, we have reproduced each year's list as we received it from the coordinator.

BEST-DRESSED WOMEN
1940 Mrs. Harrison Williams
Mrs. Ronald Balcom (Millicent Rogers)
Mrs. Thomas Shevlin
Mrs. Byron Foy
Countess Haugwitz Reventlow, (Barbara Hutton)
Mrs. William Paley
Mrs. Howard Linn
Gladys Swarthout
Ina Claire
Mrs. Gilbert Miller
Mrs. Lawrence Tibbett
Lynn Fontanne
Mrs. S. Kent Legare
Mrs. Harold Talbott
Mrs. William Rhinelander Stewart
1941 The Duchess of Windsor
Mrs. Stanley Mortimer
Mrs. Byron Foy
Mrs. Harrison Williams
Mrs. Rodman Arturo de Heeren
Mrs. Thomas Shevlin
Mme. Felipe A. Espil
Mrs. Robert W. Miller
Mrs. Robert Sherwood
Rosalind Russell
1942 No list
1943 Clare Boothe Luce
The Duchess of Windsor
Mrs. Byron Foy
Mrs. Walter Hoving
Mrs. Harrison Williams
Mrs. Andre Embiricos
Mme. Chiang Kai-Shek
Lily Pons
Mrs. Harold Talbott
Mrs. Lawrence Tibbett
Rosalind Russell
1944 Mrs. Stanley Mortimer
Mrs. Byron Foy
Mrs. William Rhinelander Stewart
Mrs. S. Kent Legare
The Hon. Clare Boothe Luce

Mrs. William Paley
Mrs. Andre Embiricos
Mrs. Michael Phipps
Mrs. Howard Hawks
The Duchess of Windsor
1945 Mrs. Stanley Mortimer
Mrs. Byron Foy
Mrs. Millicent Rogers
Mrs. Lawrence Tibbett
The Duchess of Windsor
Mrs. George Schlee (Valentina)
Mrs. Harry Hopkins
Rosalind Russell
Mrs. Robert Sarnoff
The Hon. Clare Boothe Luce
1946 Mrs. Howard Hawks
The Duchess of Windsor
Mrs. Cushing Mortimer
Mrs. Byron Foy
Mrs. Thomas Shevlin
Mrs. Millicent Rogers
Mrs. Harrison Williams
Mrs. William Rhinelander Stewart
Mrs. William Paley
The Hon. Clare Boothe Luce
1947 The Duchess of Windsor
Mrs. William Paley
Mrs. Harrison Williams
Mrs. William Rhinelander Stewart
Mrs. Byron Foy
Mrs. John C. Wilson
Mrs. Millicent Rogers
Mrs. Howard Hawks
Mrs. Geoffrey Gates
Mrs. William Wallace (Ina Claire)
1948 Mrs. William Paley
Mrs. Millicent Rogers
The Duchess of Windsor
Mrs. Andre Embiricos
Mrs. Alfred Gwynne Vanderbilt
Mrs. William Randolph Hearst, Jr.
Mrs. Harrison Williams
The Duchess of Kent
Mme. Louis Arpels
Mrs. Howard Hawks
1949 Mrs. William Paley
The Duchess of Windsor
Mrs. Harrison Williams
The Duchess of Kent
Mrs. Leland Hayward
Mrs. William Randolph Hearst, Jr.
Mary Martin
Mrs. Byron Foy
Mme. Louis Arpels
Mrs. Kingman Douglass (Adele Astaire)
1950 The Duchess of Windsor
Mrs. William Paley
Mrs. Byron Foy
Mrs. William O'Dwyer (Sloane Simpson)
Mrs. William Randolph Hearst, Jr.
Faye Emerson
Gloria Swanson
Mme. Louis Arpels
Mrs. Andre Embiricos
Mrs. Leland Hayward
1951 The Duchess of Windsor
Mrs. William Paley
Mme. Louis Arpels
Mrs. Byron Foy
Irene Dunne

Mrs. William Randolph Hearst, Jr.
Marlene Dietrich
The Duchess of Kent
Mrs. Alfred Gwynne Vanderbilt
Mrs. Douglas MacArthur
Mrs. George McGhee
Mrs. Henry Ford II
Princess Margaret Rose
Countess Uberto Corti
1952 The Duchess of Windsor
Mrs. William Paley
The Duchess of Kent
Mrs. Byron Foy
Mme. Louis Arpels
Marlene Dietrich
Mrs. William Randolph Hearst, Jr.
Mrs. Winston Guest
Countess Rodolfo Crespi
Mme. Henri Bonnet
Mrs. Dwight D. Eisenhower
Mrs. Oveta Culp Hobby
1953 Mrs. William Paley
Mrs. Winston Guest
Mrs. Byron Foy
Mme. Henri Bonnet
Mrs. William Randolph Hearst, Jr.
Oveta Culp Hobby
Mme. Louis Arpels
Princess Margaret Rose
Mrs. Henry Ford II
Mrs. Alfred G. Vanderbilt
The Duchess of Windsor
Mary Martin
1954 Mrs. William Paley
The Duchess of Windsor
Mrs. Byron Foy
Princess Margaret Rose
Mme. Henri Bonnet
Mme. Louis Arpels
Mrs. Alfred Gwynne Vanderbilt
Ambassador Clare Boothe Luce
Mme. Arturo Lopez-Willshaw
Mrs. William Randolph Hearst, Jr.
Mrs. Harold E. Talbott
Queen Frederica
1955 Mrs. William Paley
Grace Kelly
The Duchess of Windsor
Princess Margaret Rose
Mrs. Byron Foy
Countess Rodolfo Crespi
Mrs. Winston Guest
Mrs. William Randolph Hearst, Jr.
Mme. Jacques Balsan
Mrs. Alfred Gwynne Vanderbilt
Mrs. Henry Ford II
Mme. Arturo Lopez-Willshaw
The Countess of Quintanilla
Mrs. Oveta Culp Hobby
1956 Mrs. William Paley
The Duchess of Windsor
Princess Grace of Monaco
Mrs. Winston Guest
Audrey Hepburn
Marlene Dietrich
Mrs. William Randolph Hearst, Jr.
Countess Consuelo Crespi
Rosalind Russell
The Duchess of Kent
Princess Margaret Rose

Countess of Quintanilla
Mrs. Henry Ford II
Countess Mona von Bismarck
1957 Mrs. William Paley
The Duchess of Windsor
Mrs. Winston Guest
Countess Consuelo Crespi
Queen Elizabeth II
Audrey Hepburn
Mrs. Henry Ford II
Vicomtesse Jacqueline de Ribes
Claudette Colbert
Mrs. William R. Hearst, Jr.
The Countess of Quintanilla
Countess Mona Von Bismarck
Mrs. Norman K. Winston
Mrs. Thomas Bancroft, Jr.
1958 Mrs. Winston Guest
Countess Rodolfo Crespi
Mrs. Henry Ford II
Princess Margaret Rose
Countess of Quintanilla
Mme. Arturo Lopez-Willshaw
Mrs. William Randolph Hearst, Jr.
Kay Kendall
Mrs. Thomas Bancroft
Mrs. Norman K. Winston
Audrey Hepburn
Dina Merrill
Mrs. David K. Bruce
Merle Oberon
1959 Donna Marella Agnelli
HRH Princess Alexandra of Kent
Mme. Herve Alphand
Mrs. Thomas Bancroft, Jr.
Mrs. Walther de Moreira Salles
Vicomtesse Jacqueline de Ribes
Princess Grace of Monaco
Mrs. Loel Guinness
Audrey Hepburn
Mrs. Bruno Pagliai
Mrs. John Barry Ryan III
Mrs. Norman K. Winston
1960 Mrs. John F. Kennedy
Vicomtesse Jacqueline de Ribes
Audrey Hepburn
Mrs. Norman K. Winston
Donna Marella Agnelli
Mrs. Loel Guinness
Mrs. Patrick Guinness
Princess Alexandra of Kent
Mrs. John Barry Ryan III
Mrs. David K. Bruce
Mrs. Stavros Niarchos
Queen Sirikit of Thailand
1961 Mrs. John F. Kennedy
Mrs. Loel Guinness
Princess Stanislas Radziwill
Queen Sirikit of Thailand
Signora Gianni Agnelli
Vicomtesse Jacqueline de Ribes
Mrs. David Bruce
Mme. Herve Alphand
Princess Alexandra of Kent
Mrs. Charles Wrightsman
Mrs. John Barry Ryan III
Signora Uberto Agnelli
1962 Mrs. John F. Kennedy
Mrs. Loel Guinness
Princess Lee Radziwill

Mrs. Gianni Agnelli
Mme. Herve Alphand
Mrs. David Bruce
Mrs. Gloria Vanderbilt Lumet
Mrs. Walther Moreire-Salles
Mrs. John Barry Ryan III
Mrs. Charles Wrightsman
Mrs. Frederick Eberstadt
Baroness Henry Thyssen-Bornemisza
1963 Mrs. Loel Guinness
Princess Lee Radziwill
Dina Merrill
Gloria Vanderbilt (Mrs. Wyatt Cooper)
Baroness Henry Thyssen-Bornemisza
Mrs. Walther Moreira-Salles
Mrs. David Bruce
Queen Farah Pahlavi
Mrs. Charles Wrightsman
Princess Alexandra of Kent
Mrs. T. Charlton Henry
Mrs. Alfred G. Vanderbilt
1964 Queen Sirikit of Thailand
Mrs. John F. Kennedy
Mrs. Joseph P. Kennedy
Mrs. Charles Wrightsman
Princess Lee Radziwill
Dina Merrill (Mrs. Stanley Rumbough, Jr.)
Mrs. Wyatt Cooper
Mrs. Alfred Gwynne Vanderbilt
Mrs. William McCormick Blair, Jr.
Mrs. Paul Mellon
Mrs. Alfred Bloomingdale
The Misses Anne and Charlotte Ford
1965 Mrs. Carter Burden
Mrs. Alfred Gwynne Vanderbilt
Mrs. Wyatt Cooper (Gloria Vanderbilt)
Anne and Charlotte Ford (Mrs. Giancarlo Uzielli
and Mme. Stavros Niarchos)
Mrs. Joseph P. Kennedy
Mrs. Kirk Douglas
Mrs. Angus Ogilvy (Princess Alexandra of Kent)
Barbra Streisand
Mrs. Charles Engelhard
Mrs. William McCormick Blair
Princess Luciana Pignatelli
Princess Paola of Belgium
1966 Princess Lee Radziwill
Mrs. S. Carter Burden
Lauren Bacall
Mrs. Wyatt Cooper (Gloria Vanderbilt)
Mrs. Lyndon B. Johnson
Mrs. Alfred Gwynne Vanderbilt
Mrs. Patrick Guinness
Mrs. Charlotte Niarchos
Sophia Loren
Mrs. Angier Biddle Duke
Mrs. Henry Ford II
Mrs. Harilaos Theodoracopulos
1967 Mrs. Wyatt Emory Cooper (Gloria Vanderbilt)
Mrs. Carter A. Burden,
Mrs. Charlotte Ford Niarchos
Mrs. Harilaos Theodoracopulos
Mrs. Angier Biddle Duke
Princess Lee Radziwill
Lauren Bacall
Mrs. Henry Ford II
Mrs. Charles Spittal Robb (Lynda Bird Johnson)
Mrs. Ronald Reagan
Princess Alexandra of Kent (Mrs. Angus Ogilvy)
Faye Dunaway

1968   Mrs. Alfred Bloomingdale
Mrs. Chalres Revson
Mrs. Graham Mattison
Mrs. Charles Engelhard, Jr.
Princess Ira Furstenberg
Mrs. Gianni Uzielli (Anne Ford)
Mrs. Harilos Theodoracopulos
Marquesa Carol de Portago
Mrs. Liberman Savitt
Mrs. Vincente Minnelli
The Duchess de Cadaval
Mme. Ahmed Benhima

MOST IMAGINATIVE DRESSERS

Barbra Streisand (Mrs. Elliott Gould)
Baroness Philippe de Rothschild
Miss Marisa Berenson
Mrs. Thomas Kempner
Mrs. Wyatt Cooper (Gloria Vanderbilt)
Mrs. Renny Saltzman
Mrs. Ahmet Ertegun
Mrs. William Rayner
Diahann Carroll
Mrs. Robin Butler
Mme. Maya Plisetskaya
Marisol (Escobar)

1969   Mrs. William McCormick Blair, Jr.
Mrs. Wyatt Cooper (Gloria Vanderbilt)
Mrs. Kirk Douglas
Mrs. Ahmet Ertegun
Mrs. Robert Evans (Ali McGraw)
Mrs. Patrick Guinness
Her Highness Princess Salima wife of the Aga Khan
(Lady Sarah Chrichton-Stuart)
Mrs. Graham Mattison
Mrs. Charlotte Niarchos (Charlotte Ford)
Mrs. Robert Sakowitz
Mrs. Harilaos Theodoracopulos

1970   H.R.H. The Begum Aga Khan (Lady Sarah Crichton-Stuart)
Mme. Ahmed Benhima
Diahann Carroll
Catherine Deneuve
Sophia Loren
Mrs. Denise Minnelli
Mme. Georges Pompidou
Mrs. Richard Pistell (Marquesa Carol de Portago)
Mrs. Ronald Reagan
Mrs. Samuel P. Reed
Mrs. Charles Revson
Mrs. Harilaos Theodoracopulos

1971   H.R.H. The Begum Aga Khan (Lady Sarah Crichton-Stuart)
Mrs. Ronald Reagan
Mrs. Richard Pistell
Mme Francios Catroux (Betsy Saint)
Mrs. Frederick Melhado (Louise Savitt)
Mrs. Sidney Brody
Miss Liza Minnelli
Mme. Pierre Schlumberger
Mrs. Reinaldo Herrera, Jr.
Cher Bono
Twiggy (Leslie Hornby)
Kitty Hawks
Jan Weymouth

1972   Marisa Berenson
Baroness Thierry van Zuylen
H.R.H. Princess Salima Khan (Lady Sarah Crichton-Stuart)
Mrs. Henry Ford II

Mrs. Reinaldo Herrera
Mrs. Ronald Reagan
Mrs. Frederick Melhado
Signora Gianluigi Gabetti
Mrs. Mick Jagger
Mrs. William Buckley, Jr.
Mrs. William Clay Ford

1973   Marisa Berenson
Countess Brando Brandolini
Mrs. Sidney Brody
Mme. Bernard Camu
Duchess de Cadaval
Duchess de Cadiz Carmencita Martinez-Bordiu y Franco
Mme. Francois Catroux
Baroness Arnaud de Rosnay (Isabelle Goldsmith)
Senora Reinaldo Herrera, Jr.
Mrs. Harding Lawrence (Mary Wells)
Baroness Thierry van Zuylen
Mrs. Oscar Wyatt, Jr.

1974   Mrs. William F. Buckley, Jr.
Mme. Bernard Camu
Princess Caroline of Monaco
Mme Francois Catroux
Baroness Arnaud de Rosnay (Isabelle Goldsmith)
Senora Gabriel Echevarria (Pilar Crespi)
Mrs. Gerald Ford
Mrs. Kay Graham
Mrs. Henry Kissinger
Mrs. Harding Lawrence (Mary Wells)
Mrs. Frederick Melhado
Mrs. Jan (Lally) Weymouth

1975   Marisa Berenson
Mme. Francois Catroux
Miss Kitty Hawks
Mrs. Reinaldo Herrera, Jr.
Mrs. Irving Lazar
H.R.H. Princess Edouard de Lobkowicz
Silvana Mangano (Sra. Dino de Laurentiis)
Mme. Manuel Machado-Macedo
Mrs. Frederick Melhado
Mrs. Paul Peralta-Ramos
Mrs. Charles Percy
Mrs. Oscar Wyatt, Jr.

1976   Louise Nevelson
Baronne David (Olympia) de Rothschild
H.H. Farah Diba Empress of Iran
Mary Tyler Moore
Sra. Reinaldo (Carolina) Herrera, Jr.
Sra. Manuel (Jacqueline) Machado-Macedo
Mrs. Oscar (Lynn) Wyatt, Jr.
Mrs. Irving (Mary) Lazar
H.R.H. Princesse Francoise de Bourbon-Parme
Mrs. William Averill Harriman
Mrs. Thomas (Olive) Watson, Jr.
Lady Antonia Fraser

1977   Diane Keaton
Mrs. Smith Begley
Olive Behrendt
Sra. Manuela Macado de Macedo
Countess Hubert d'Orano
Mrs. Gordon Getty
Sra. Reinaldo Herrera, Jr.
Mrs. Irving Lazar
Sra. Antonio A. Mayrank Veiga
Lacey Newhouse
Mrs. T. Suffern Tailer
Baronne Thierry van Zuylen

BEST DRESSED MEN

1968 Prince Philip Duke of Edinburgh
Wyatt Cooper
Bill Blass
Patrick Earl of Litchfield
George Hamilton
Baron Alexis de Rede
George W. Widener
Cecil Beaton
Jean-Claude Killy
Bernard Lanvin
Count Rudolfo Crespi
Hubert de Givenchy
1969 Gianni Agnelli
Adolphus Andrews
Harry Belafonte
Gianni Bulgari
Michael Butler
James Coburn
Wyatt Cooper
Frank Gifford
George Hamilton
Jean-Claude Killy
Baron Eric de Rothschild
David Susskind
1970 Frederic Byers III
Yul Brynner
Hernando Courtwright
John Galliher
Hon. Angus Ogilvy
Armando Orsini
Giorgio Pavone
Baron Alexis de Rede
Thomas Shevlin
Bobby Short
Lord Snowdon (Antony Armstrong-Jones)
Hon. Sargent Shriver
1971 Baron Alexis de Rede
Gianni Bulgari
Hon. John V. Lindsay
Billy (William) Baldwin
Sidney Poitier
Mick Jagger
Harry Belafonte
Lord Snowdon (Antony Armstrong-Jones)
Robert Redford
Marques de Villaverde
Thomas Schippers
Frank Gifford
1972 Gianni Bulgari
Mayor John V. Lindsay
Billy Baldwin
David Mahoney
Robert Evans
Mick Jagger
John Galliher
Fred Hughes
Armando Orsini
Richard Roundtree
1973 Count Brando Brandolini
Reinaldo Herrera, Jr.
Hon. David Bruce
Luiz Gastal
Senator Barry Goldwater
Horace Kelland
Peter Revson
David Rothschild
Valerian Stux-Rybar
Yves Vidal
Billy Dee Williams

Michael York
1974 President Valery Giscard d'Estaing
Charles Prince of Wales
Guy Burgos
Angelo Donghia
Frank Gifford
J.J. Hooker
Johnny Miller
Thomas Schippers
Telly Savalas
Senator John Tunney
Yves Vidal
Fred Williamson
1975 Marquis of Bath
Alistair Cooke
Ahmet Ertegun
President Valery Giscard d'Estaing
George Hamilton
H.I.M. Mohammed Reza Pahlavi Shah of Iran
Hon. John V. Lindsay
Marcello Mastroianni
Joel Schumacher
O.J. Simpson
Dick van Dyke
Michael York
1976 Count Brando Brandolini
Jeffrey Butler
Angelo Donghia
Walt Frazier
Fred Hughes
Governor John Love
Marcello Mastroianni
Marques Anthony de Portago
Roberto Rosellini, Jr.
Joel Schumacher
Valerian Stux-Rybar
Marquis of Tavistock
1977 Mikhail Baryshnikov
Earl Blackwell
Jeffrey Burlet
Kim d'Estainville
Arthur Levitt, Jr.
Gov. John Love Colorado
David Mahoney
Gerry Mulligan
President Anwar Sadat, Egypt
O.J. Simpson
Thomas Tryon
Ambassador Andrew Young

SUPPLEMENTAL LIST—WOMEN INVOLVED IN THE FASHION INDUSTRY

This category was initially called the "Professional" category, honoring actresses and professional women. Over the years, the category was modified and changed to recognize professionals in the fashion industry (designers, models, retail executives and editors) and women married to men in the fashion industry.

1947 Mrs. Adam Gimbel
Mrs. George Schlee (Valentina)
Mrs. Orson D. Munn
Mrs. Gilbert Adrian
1948 Mrs. Adam Gimbel
Mrs. George Schlee (Valentina)
Gene Tierney
Janet Gaynor Adrian
Mrs. John C. Wilson
1949 Valentina (Mrs. George Schlee)
Mrs. Adam Gimbel

Mrs. John C. Wilson
Janet Gaynor (Mrs. Gilbert Adrian)
Countess Alain de la Falaise
1950 Janet Gaynor (Mrs. Gilbert Adrian)
Valentina (Mrs. George Schlee)
Mrs. Adam Gimbel
Mrs. John C. Wilson
1951 Janet Gaynor (Mrs. Gilbert Adrian)
Gene Tierney
Gloria Swanson
Valentina (Mrs. George Schlee)
Mrs. Adam Gimbel
Mme. Jacques Fath
Mrs. John C. Wilson
Mrs. Orson D. Munn
Margaret Case
Mrs. Leon Mandel
1952 Valentina (Mrs. George Schlee)
Janet Gaynor (Mrs. Gilbert Adrian)
Mrs. Adam Gimbel
Mme. Jacques Fath
Mrs. Orson D. Munn
Mrs. Leon Mandel
Bettina Ballard
Mrs. Andrew Goodman
Gene Tierney
1953 Sophie Gimbel
Mrs. Leon Mandel
Mrs. T. Reed Vreeland
Mrs. Walter Hoving
Simonetta Fabiani
Mme. Jacques Fath
Mrs. John C. Wilson
Mrs. Ira Haupt
Valentina (Mrs. George Schlee)
1954 Margaret Case
Mrs. Adam Gimbel
Janet Gaynor
Valentina (Mrs. George Schlee)
Mme. Jacques Fath
Mrs. John C. Wilson
Mrs. Orson Munn
Mrs. Andrew Goodman
Margaret Case
Mrs. Leon Mandel
1955 Mrs. Adam Gimbel
Simonetta Fabiani
Genevieve Fath
Mrs. Stanley Marcus
Mrs. George Schlee (Valentina)
Mrs. T. Reed Vreeland
Mrs. Carmel Snow
Anne Fogarty
Mrs. Digby Morton
Mrs. Andrew Goodman
1956 Mme. Henri Bonnet
Vicomtesse de Ribes
Mrs. Carmel Snow
Katherine McManus
Mrs. Leon Mandel
Mrs. Hector Escoboza
Phyllis Digby-Morton
Valentina Schlee
Signora Simonetta Fabiani
Mrs. Stanley Marcus
1957 Gabrielle Chanel
Signora Simonetta Fabiani
Mrs. Carmel Snow
Helene Arpels
Mrs. Earl E. T. Smith

Mrs. T. Reed Vreeland
Mrs. Stanley Marcus
Mrs. Ira Haupt
Sybil Connolly
Pauline Trigere
Margaret Case
1958 Sophie Gimbel
Simonetta Fabiani
Gabrielle Chanel
Pauline Trigere
Carmel Snow
Enid Haupt
Sybil Connolly
Janet Gaynor (Mrs. Gilbert Adrian)
Mrs. Stanley Marcus
Mrs. Leon Mandel
Mrs. Tom May
Helene Arpels
1959 Gabrielle Chanel
Simonetta Fabiani
Princess Irene Galitzine
Sophie Gimbel
Mrs. Leon Mandel
Mrs. Lawrence Marcus
Mrs. Tom May
Geraldine Stutz
Mrs. Carmel Snow
Pauline Trigere
1960 Pauline Trigere
Simonetta Fabiani
Gabrielle Chanel
Sophie Gimbel
Mrs. Stanley Marcus
Mrs. T. Reed Vreeland
Enid Haupt
Mrs. Carmel Snow
Sybil Connolly
Helene Rochas
1961 Pauline Trigere
Simonetta Fabiani
Gabrielle Chanel
Mrs. T. Reed Vreeland
Mrs. Adam Gimbel
Sybil Connolly
Helene Rochas
Helene Arpels
Mrs. Tom May
Mrs. Lawrence Marcus
1962 Mrs. T. Reed Vreeland
Gabrielle Chanel
Simonetta Fabiani
Pauline Trigere
Anita Colby
Helene Rochas
Enid Haupt
Mrs. Samuel I. Newhouse
Mrs. Stanley Marcus
Mrs. Adam Gimbel
Sybil Connolly
Mrs. Tom May
1963 Gabrielle Chanel
Diana Vreeland
Pauline Trigere
Donna Simonetta Fabiani
Mrs. Adam Gimbel
Mrs. Stanley Marcus
Mrs. S. I. Newhouse
Geraldine Stutz
Princess Irene Galitzine
Margaret Case

Mrs. David Evins
Mrs. Milton Greene
1964   Mrs. Richard Rodgers
Mrs. S. I. Newhouse
Mrs. Frederick Eberstadt
Helena Rubinstein
Geraldine Stutz
Mrs. William Rose
Mrs. Milton Greene
Mollie Parnis
Mary Quant
Mrs. David Evins
Mrs. Robin Butler
Gloria Schiff
1965   Marisa Berenson
Mrs. Richard Rodgers
Mrs. Frederick Eberstadt
Mrs. Robin Butler
Mrs. David Evins
Mary Quant
Amy Greene
Mollie Parnis
Emanuelle Khanh
Mrs. William Rose
Caterine Milinaire
Mrs. Mark Miller
1966   Mrs. Robin Butler
Princess Luciana Pignatelli
Mrs. David Evins
Mollie Parnis Livingston
Mrs. Frank Schiff
Mrs. Frederick Eberstadt
Baroness Fiona Thyssen-Bornemisza
Mrs. Montague Hackett
Francoise de Langlade
Mrs. Thomas (Nan) Kempner
Caterine Milinaire
Marisa Berenson
1967   Mrs. David Evins
Mrs. Oscar de la Renta
Princess Luciana Pignatelli
Mrs. Thomas (Nan) Kempner
Marisa Berenson
Mrs. Frank (Gloria) Schiff
Countess Vera Lehndorff (Verouschka)
Mrs. Montagne Hackett
Elieth Roux
Mary Quant
Mme. Bernard Lanvin
Mrs. Renny (Ellen) Saltzman
1968   No list
1969   Marisa Berenson
Berry Berenson
Mrs. Robin Butler
Mrs. Oscar de la Renta (Francoise de Langlade)
Mrs. David Evins
Pamela, Lady Harlech
Mrs. Thomas (Nan) Kempner
Mme. Minouche Le Blan
Miss Eve Orton
Mrs. Renny Saltzman
Mrs. Frank Schiff
Countess Vera von Lehndorff (Verouschka)
1970   Marisa Berenson
Pilar Crespi
Mrs. David Evins
Pamela, Lady Harlech
Mrs. Thomas (Nan) Kempner
Anne Klein (Mrs. Matthew Rubenstein)
Eve Orton

Sonia Rykiel
Mrs. Robert Sackowitz
Mrs. Renny Saltzman
Naomi Sims
1971   Mrs. Bruce Addison
Marisa Berenson
Francoise (Mrs. Oscar) la Renta
Diane (Princess Egon) von Furstenberg
Mary McFadden
Mrs. Even Orton
Elsa Peretti
Mrs. Robert Sackowitz
Mrs. Renny Saltzman
Mrs. Frank (Gloria) Schiff
Naomi Sims
1972   Naomi Sims
Princess Diane von Furstenberg
Mary McFadden
Elsa Peretti
Jean Muir
Contessa Lulu de la Falaise
Maxime de la Falaise McKendry
Mrs. Bruce Addison
Francoise de la Renta
Mrs. Renny Saltzman
Grace Mirabella
Eve Orton
1973   Contessa Lulu de la Falaise
Countess Alessandro di Montezemolo (Catherine Murray)
Carrie Donovan
Princess Diane von Furstenberg
Angelica Huston
Grace Mirabella
Jean Muir
Audrey Smaltz
Mrs. Robert Sackowitz
1974   Carrie Donovan
Princess Diane von Furstenberg
Mary McFadden
Marchesa Catherine de Montezemolo
Grace Mirabella (Mrs. William Cahan)
Mrs. David Neusteter
Mme. Jacques Rouet
Mary Russell
Mrs. Robert Sackowitz
Marina Schiano
Audrey Smaltz
Baroness Hubert (Lorna) de Wangen
1975   Mrs. Bernard Camu
Contessa Lulu de la Falaise
Carrie Donovan
Sra. Gabriel Echaverria (Pilar Crespi)
Donna Karan
Mary McFadden
Mme. Jacques Rouet
Naomi Sims
1976   Mary McFadden
Mrs. Herbert (Minnie) Marcus
Ellen Saltzman
Naomi Sims
Marina Schiano
Contessa Donina Cicogna
1977   Grace Cuddington
Countess Donina Cicogna
Contessa Lulu de Falaise
Carrie Donovan
Pilar Crespi Echevarria
Muriel Grateau
Norma Kalami

Donna Karan
Elsa Klensch
Mme. Jacques Rouet
Mme. Elie Thoux
Diane von Furstenburg

MEN INVOLVED IN THE FASHION INDUSTRY

1966   Pierre Cardin
Norman Parkinson
Bill Blass
John Weitz
I.S.V. Patcevitch
Patrick O'Higgins
1967   No list
1968   No separate category; several men in the fashion field were included in the year's Best-Dressed List.
1969   Bill Blass
Hubert de Givenchy
Luis Estevez
Robert L. Green
Baron Nicolas de Gunzberg
Walter Halle
Sixten Herrgard
Bernard Lanvin
Patrick, Earl of Litchfield
Robert Sakowitz
Philippe Venet
John Weitz
1970   Hardy Amies
Antonia Cerutti
Baron Nicolaus de Gunzburg
Kenneth Jay Lane
Oscar de la Renta
Thomas Nutter
Andre Oliver
Robert Sakowitz
Alexander Shields
Chip Tolbert
Philippe Venet
Daniel Zaren
1971   Oscar de la Renta
Philippe Venet
Hardy Amies
Robert Sakowitz
Andre Oliver
Robert L. Green
Chip Tolbert
Daniel Zaren
Thomas Nutter
Kenneth Jay Lane
1972   Oscar de la Renta
Hardy Amies
Thomas Nutter
Andre Olivier
Philippe Venet
Kenneth Jay Lane
Halston Frowick
James Galanos
Yves Saint-Laurent
Joel Schumacher
Max Evans
Henry Sell
1973   Max Evans
James Galanos
Giancarlo Giametti
Kenneth Jay Lane
Ralph Lauren
Piero Nuti
Carlo Palazzi
Anthony Nutter

Jose Mildano
Yves Saint-Laurent
Chip Tolbert
Daniel Zarem
1974   Giorgio Armani
Robert Bryan
Aldo Cipullo
James Galanos
Uva Harden
Jose Maldonado
Nando Miglio
Ottavio Missoni
Anthony Thomas Nutter
Yves Saint-Laurent
Robert Sakowitz
Joel Schumacher
1975   Giorgio Armani
James Galanos
Calvin Klein
Ralph Lauren
Jerry Magnin
Ottavio Missoni
Anthony Nutter
Carlo Palazzi
Daniel Zarem
1976   Giorgio Armonai
James Galanos
Calvin Klein
Ralph Lauren
Jerry Magnin
Ottavio Missoni
1977   Giorgio Armani
Ted Dawson
Tom Fallon
James Galanos
Alexander Julian
Calvin Klein
Robert Lycett-Green
Jerry Magnin
Ottavio Missoni
Daniel Zarem

To honor individuals who have consistently been voted to the Best Dressed List—and to make room for new names on the List—the Hall of Fame was instituted as a permanent honor. The Hall of Fame designation is sometimes also given to individuals whose affect on fashion has been great, even though they have not been voted Best Dressed.

SUPER DRESSER OF OUR TIME
1974   Mrs. William Paley

WOMEN
1958   Duchess of Windsor
Mrs. William Paley
Countess Edward Von Bismarck
Queen Elizabeth II
Mme. Jacques Balsan
Mary Martin
Irene Dunne
Claudette Colbert
1959   Countess Consuelo Crespi
Mrs. Henry Ford II
Mrs. Winston Guest
Mrs. William Randolph Hearst, Jr.
1960   The Duchess of Kent
Mrs. Bruno Pagliai
Princess Grace of Monaco

Mme. Arturo Lopez-Willshaw
1961 Audrey Hepburn
Mrs. Norman K. Winston
1962 Vicomtesse Jacqueline de Ribes
Countess Aline Quintanilla
1963 Signora Gianni Agnelli
Mme. Herve Alphand
Mrs. John Barry Ryan III
1964 Mrs. Loel Guinness
Mrs. David Bruce
Mrs. Walther Moreira Salles
Mrs. T. Charlton Henry
Rosalind Russell
1965 Mrs. John F. Kennedy
Mrs. Charles Wrightsman
Queen Sirikit of Thailand
Dame Margot Fonteyn
Dina Merrill
Mrs. Gilbert Miller
1966 Mrs. Joseph P. Kennedy
1967 No award
1968 No award
1969 Baronesse Philippe Rothschild
1970 Mrs. William McCormick Blair, Jr.
Mrs. Alfred Bloomingdale
Mrs. Wyatt Cooper (Gloria Vanderbilt)
Mrs. Kirk Douglas
Mrs. Patrick Guinness
1971 Mrs. Charles Revson
Betsy Pickering Theodoracopulos
Mrs. Thomas (Nan) Kempner
Mrs. Ahmet (Mica) Ertegun
Mrs. William (Chessie) Rayner
1972 Mrs. Charles Engelhard, Jr.
Mrs. Graham Mattison
Mrs. David Evins
Mme. Gres
Mrs. Richard Pistell
1973 Mrs. Oscar (Francoise) de la Renta
Mrs. Henry Ford II
Princess Salima Aga Khan
Elsa Peretti
Mrs. Ronald Reagan
Mrs. Samuel P. Reed
1974 Mrs. Paley voted "Super Dresser of Our Time"
1975 Mme. Ahmed Benhima
Mrs. William F. Buckley, Jr.
Countess Brando Brandolini
Mrs. Kingman Douglas (Adele Astaire)
Mrs. Prestis Cobb Hale
Mrs. Paul Mellon
Grace Mirabella (Mrs. William Cahan)
Mrs. Pierre Schlumberger
1976 Mrs. Frederick (Louise) Melhado
Mrs. Mick (Bianca) Jagger
Mrs. Robin Hambro
1977 Empress Farah Diba, Iran
Mary Wells Lawrence
Mary McFadden
Princess Edouard de Lobkowicz
Mrs. Oscar Wyatt, Jr.

PROFESSIONALS
1964 Gabrielle Chanel
Diana Vreeland
Pauline Trigere
Mrs. Sophie Gimbel
Mrs. Tom May
Mme. Helene Rochas
Donna Simonetta Fabiani

Miss Margaret Case
Mrs. Stanley Marcus
1965 Sybil Connolly
Enid Haupt
Mrs. S. I. Newhouse
Geraldine Stutz Gibbs
Anita Colby
Princess Irene Galitzine
1967 Mollie Parnis Livingston
Mrs. Robin Butler
Mrs. Frederick Eberstadt

MEN
1968 Duke of Windsor
1969 Prince Philip, Duke of Edinburgh
Angier Biddle Duke
Douglas Fairbanks
Cary Grant
Dean Acheson
1970 No award
1971 No award
1972 Patrick, Earl of Lichthfield
Baron Nicolas Gunzburg
1973 Earl of Airlie
Hon. Angus Ogilvy
Harry Belafonte
Sidney Poitier
Baron Alexis de Rede
Robert L. Green
1974 Oscar de La Renta
Nino Cerutti
Hernando Courtwright
John Galliher
Andre Oliver
Philippe Venet
1975 Hardy Amies
Billy Baldwin
Max Evans
Kenneth Jay Lane
Chip Tolbert
Van Day Truex
1976 Gianni Bulgari
Robert Evans
Frank Gifford
Prince Philip, Duke of Edinburgh
Horace Kelland
Yves Saint-Laurent
Robert Sakowitz
1977 Angelo Donghia
Yves Vidal
Joel Schumacher
Michael York

Coty American Fashion Critics Awards

COTY INC.
c/o Eleanor Lambert, 32 E. 57th, New York, N.Y. 10022
(212/MU 8-2130)

The Coty American Fashion Critics Awards are presented annually to American designers whose work during the previous year has had a significant effect on American dress. A nominating committee composed of fashion editors of national magazines, newspaper syndicates and newspapers makes recommendations which are submitted to a 400-judge panel, which makes the final selections

The Winnie Award, which is a sculpture by Malvina Hoffman, is given annually to the individual selected as the leading designer of American women's fashion. In addition, a Winnie is presented to the winner of the Return Award, given to a designer whose work merits a top award for a second time.

WINNIE

1943 Norman Norell
1944 Claire MacCardell
1945 Gilbert Adrian
      Tina Leser
      Emily Wilkens
1946 Clare Potter
      Omar Kiam of Ben Reig
      Vincent Monte-Sano
1947 Nettie Rosenstein
      Mark Morring
      Jack Horwitz
      Adele Simpson
1948 Hattie Carnegie
1949 Pauline Trigere
1950 Bonnie Cashin
      Charles James
1951 Jane Derby
1952 Ben Zuckerman
      Ben Sommers
1953 Thomas F. Brigance
1954 James Galanos
1955 Jeanne Campbell
      Anne Klein
      Herbert Kasper
1956 Luis Estevez
      Sally Victor
1957 Leslie Morris
      Sydney Wragge
1958 Arnold Scaasi
1959 No award
1960 Ferdinando Sarmi
      Jacques Tiffeau
1961 Bill Blass
      Gustave Tassell
1962 Donald Brooks
1963 Rudi Gernreich
1964 Geoffrey Beene
1965 No award
1966 Dominic
1967 Oscar de la Renta
1968 George Halley
      Luba
1969 Stan Herman
      Victor Joris
1970 Giorgio Di Sant'Angelo
      Chester Weinberg
1971 Halston
      Betsey Johnson
1972 John Anthony
1973 Stephen Burrows
      Calvin Klein
1974 Ralph Lauren
1975 Carol Horn
1976 Mary McFadden
1977 Donna Karan and Louis Dell'Olio
      Stephen Burrows

RETURN AWARD

1951 Norman Norell
1952 No award
1953 No award

1954 No award
1955 No award
1956 James Galanos
1957 No award
1958 Ben Zuckerman
1959 No award
1960 No award
1961 No award
1962 No award
1963 Bill Blass
1964 Jacques Tiffeau
      Sylvia Pedlar
1965 No award
1966 Rudi Gernreich
      Geoffrey Beene
1967 Donald Brooks
1968 Oscar de la Renta
1969 Anne Klein
1970 Herbert Kasper
1971 No award
1972 Halston
1973 No award
1974 Calvin Klein
1975 No award
1976 Ralph Lauren
1977 No award

Special Awards are given as merited to honor noteworthy contributions to fashion ideas. The award consists of a bronze plaque decorated with a bas-relief Malvina Hoffman figurine.

1943 Lilly Dache
      John Frederics
1944 Sally Victor
      Phelps Associates
1945 No award
1946 No award
1947 No award
1948 Ester Dorothy
      Joseph De Leo
      Maximilian
1949 Toni Owen
      David Evins
1950 Mabel and Charles Julianelli
      Nancy Melcher
1951 Vera Maxwell
      Anne Fogarty
      Sylvia Pedlar
1952 Harvey Berin and Karen Stark
      Sydney Wragge
1953 Helen Lee
      Mattie Talmack and John Moore
1954 Charles James
1955 Adolfo
1956 Gertrude and Robert Goldworm
1957 Emeric Partos
1958 Donald Brooks
      Jean Schlumberger
1959 No award
1960 Rudi Gernreich
      Sol Klein
      Roxane
1961 Bonnie Cashin
      Mr. Kenneth
1962 Halston
1963 Arthur and Theodora Edelman
      Betty Yokova
1964 David Webb
1965 Anna Potok
      Tzaims Luksus

Gertrude Seperack
Pablo
Joint Special Award: Sylvia de Gay, Bill Smith, Victor Joris, Leo Narducci, Don Simonelli, Gayle Kirkpatrick, Stanley Herman, Edie Gladstone and Deanna Littell
1966 Kenneth Jay Lane
1967 Beth and Herbert Levine
1968 Count Giorgio di Sant'Angelo
1969 Adolfo
Halston
Julian Tomchin
1970 Will and Eileen Richardson
Joint Special Awards for Costume Jewelry: Alexis Kirk, Cliff Nicholson, Marty Ruza, Bill Smith, and Daniel Stoenescu and Eileen Richardson
1971 John Kloss of Cira
Nancy Knox of Renegades
Elsa Peretti
Levi Strauss
1972 Dorothy Weatherford
Special Men's Fashion Awards: Alexander Sheilds,
Pinky Wolman and Dianne Beaudry, Alan Rosanes and Robert Margolis
1973 Clovis Ruffin
Special Accessory Awards: Michael Moraux, Joe Famolare, Don Kline, Herbert and Beth Levine, Judith Leiber and Celia Sebiri
1974 Special Menswear Award for Jewelry: Bill Kaiserman for Rafael
Special Lingerie Awards: Fernando Sanchez, Stan Herman, John Kloss, Bill Tice and Stephen Burrows
Special Menswear Awards: Sal Cesarani and John Weitz
1975 Special Award for Swimsuits: Monika Tilley
Special Menswear Award for Leather Design: Nancy Knox
Special Awards for Fur Design: Bill Blass, Fernando Sanchez, Calvin Klein and Viola Sylbert
1976 Special Menswear Award for Neckwear: Vicky Davis
Special Menswear Award for Loungewear: Robert Schafer, Lowell Judson and Ronald Kolodzie
Barbara Dulien
Special Citations: Abercrombie & Fitch, Miller's Riding Clothes, L.L. Bean, Eddie Bauer and Gokey's
1977 Special Award for Jewelry Design: Ted Muehling
Special Award for Lingerie Design: Fernando Sanchez
Special Menswear Award for Hats: Marsha Akens
Special Menswear Award for Furs: Jeffrey Banks

The Coty Menswear Fashion Award carries a trophy, designed by Forrest Myers, which is a free-form aluminum sculpture.

1968 Bill Blass
1969 No award
1970 Ralph Lauren
1971 Larry Kane
1972 No award
1973 Piero Dimitri
1974 Bill Kaiserman
1975 Chuck Howard and Peter Wrigley
1976 Sal Ceserani
1977 Alexander Julian

MENSWEAR RETURN AWARD
1973 Ralph Lauren

1974 No award
1975 Bill Kaiserman
1976 No award
1977 No award

The Hall of Fame Award, which consists of a gold medallion, was established as a higher accolade for the Winnie designer chosen three times as the best of the year.

1956 Norman Norell
1957 No award
1958 Claire McCardell
1959 Pauline Trigere
James Galanos
1960 No award
1961 Ben Zuckerman
1962 No award
1963 No award
1964 No award
1965 No award
1966 No award
1967 Rudi Gernreich
1968 No award
1969 No award
1970 Bill Blass
1971 Bill Blass
Anne Klein
1972 Bonnie Cashin
1973 Oscar de la Renta
1974 Geoffrey Beene
Halston
1975 Geoffrey Beene (Hall of Fame Citation)
Calvin Klein
Hall of Fame for Menswear: Bill Kaiserman
1976 Kasper
Hall of Fame for Menswear: Bill Kaiserman
Hall of Fame for Menswear: Ralph Lauren
1977 No award

Lulu Award

MEN'S FASHION ASSOCIATION OF AMERICA
1290 Ave. of the Americas, New York, N.Y. 10019
(212/581-8210)

The Lulu Awards are given annually to journalists for covering men's fashions in an outstanding way. Print and broadcast reporters and commentators are considered in up to about 10 categories, the exact criteria for which are not available. The awards have been given since 1959, but only the last few years are available. In addition to the winners listed here, first and second runner-up honors are also made.

1972 Hope Strong, *Lima* (Ohio) *News*
Mildred Whiteaker, *San Antonio* (Tex.) *Express and News*
Esther Walker, *San Jose* (Calif.) *Mercury-News*
Robert Heilman, *Seattle Times*
Marji Kunz, *Detroit Free Press*
Yvonne Petrie, *Detroit News*
Berta Mohr, Berta Mohr Fashion Syndicate, New York
John Camposa, *New York Times Magazine* (two awards)
Nancy Welch, *Nancy Welch Show,* WSPA-TV (Spartanburg, S. Ca.)
Bob Carr, *Midday,* WDSU-TV (New Orleans, La.)

1973 Elviretta Walker, *Oklahoma Journal* (Oklahoma City)
Mildred Whiteaker, *San Antonio* (Tex.) *Express-News*
Esther Walker, *San Jose* (Calif.) *Mercury-News*
Jason Thomas, *Cleveland Plain Dealer*
Genevieve Buck, *Chicago Tribune*
Walter Logan, United Press International (New York)
John Camposa, *New York Times Magazine* (two awards)
Rita Davenport, *Phoenix at Midday/Open House*, KPHO-TV (Phoenix, Ariz.)
Barbara Walters, *Not for Women Only*, NBC-TV (New York)
Mike Douglas, *The Mike Douglas Show*, syndicated (Philadelphia)
1974 Elviretta Walker, *Oklahoma Journal* (Oklahoma City)
Charles F. Hoch, *Corpus Christi* (Tex.) *Caller-Times*
Esther Walker, *San Jose* (Calif.) *Mercury-News*
Jason Thomas, *Cleveland Plain Dealer*
Genevieve Buck, *Chicago Tribune* (two awards)
Walter Logan, United Press International (New York)
John Camposa, *New York Times Magazine*
Kity Broman, *Kitty Today*, WWLP-TV (Springfield, Mass.)
Pia Lindstrom, "Newscenter 4 Lifestyles," WNBC-TV (New York)
Hazel Stebbins, *Hazel Stebbins Show*, KFOR-Radio (Lincoln, Neb.)
Arlene Sachs, WINS Radio (New York)
1975 Barbara Schuler, *Arizona Daily Star* -Tucson, Ariz.)
Sarah C. Teague, *Birmingham* (Ala.) *Post Herald*
Mary C. Jackson, *Sacramento* (Calif.) *Bee*
Genevieve Buck, *Chicago Tribune* (two awards)
Jason Thomas, *Chicago Sun-Times*
Addis Durning, *New York News*
Audrey West, *Ask Audrey/Montage*, WKNO-TV (Memphis, Tenn.)
Larry Angelo, *Larry Angelo Show*, WJZO-TV (Baltimore)
Barbara Walters, *Not For Women Only*, NBC-TV (New York)
Pat DiSalvo, *Feminine Angle*, WIOU-Radio (Kokomo, Ind.)
Richard Pyatt, *Fashions for Males*, WNYC-Radio (New York)
1976 Sarah Teague, *Birmingham* (Ala.) *Post-Herald*
Dois Hjorth, *Oakland* (Calif.) *Tribune*
Esther Walker, *San Jose* (Calif.) *Mercury-News*
Addis Durning, *New York News* (two awards)
Charles Hix, Newspaper Enterprise Association (New York)
MaeBelle Pendergast, *Sacramento* (Calif.) *Union*
Leta Powell Drake, *The Morning Show*, KOLN-TV (Lincoln, Neb.)
Eyewitness News, WABC-TV (New York)
Pat DiSalvo, *Feminine Angle*, WIOU-Radio (Kokomo, Ind.)
Paige Palmer, *Paige Palmer Show*, WELW-Radio (Bath, Ohio)
1977 Doris Dale Paysour, *Greensboro* (N. C.) *Record*
Elviretta Walker, *Oklahoma Journal* (Oklahoma City)
Judy Jeannin, *The Record* (Hackensack, N.J.)
Janice Munson, *Cleveland Plain Dealer*
Marji Kinz, *Detroit News*
Charles Hix, Newspaper Enterprise Association (New York)

MaeBelle Pendergast, *Sacramento* (Calif.) *Union*
Becky Livas, *People, Places and Things*, WTAR-TV (Norfolk, Va.)
Anna Bond, *Eyewitness News*, WABC-TV (New York)
Pat DiSalvo, *Feminine Angle, WIOU-Radio (Kokomo, Ind.)*
Sally Jessy Raphael, *The Sally Jessy Raphael Show*, WMCA-Radio, New York

Worst Dressed List
MR. BLACKWELL
719 S. Los Angeles St., Los Angeles, Calif. 90014
(213/627-5202)

Richard Blackwell, known professionally as Mr. Blackwell, annually issues a Worst Dressed List, to cite women who he feels have violated "fashion's prime purpose, to glorify womanhood." While the list has been issued each year since 1959, only the most recent are available, and of these just the last three years are complete. We are including Mr. Blackwell's occassionally acerbic reasons for his selections.

1970 Sophia Loren
Angie Dickinson
Gloria Vanderbilt
1971 Ali MacGraw
Jacqueline Onassis
Princess Anne
1972 Raquel Welch
Julie Andrews
Mia Farrow
1973 Bette Midler
Princess Anne
Raquel Welch
1974 Helen Reddy
Princess Elizabeth of Yugoslavia
Fanne Fox
1975 Caroline Kennedy, "A shaggy dog in pants"
Helen Reddy, "She spent the year proving I was right . . . she should have saved her costumes for the Bicentennial explosion!"
Nancy Kissinger, "A traveling fashion stew!"
Bette Midler, "Betsy Bloomer . . . didn't pantaloons go out with the hoopskirt?"
Sally Struthers, "Certainly not in the 'fashion family'"
Princess Anne, "A royal auto mechanic"
Tammy Wynette and Donna Fargo, Both for "country music dressed in a circus tent"
Tatum O'Neal, "Twelve going on forty"
Sonia Rykiel, "She put the 'Fanny Wrap' back in and out of fashion"
Elton John, "Would be the campiest spectacle in the Rose Parade"
1976 Louise Lasser, "Mary Hartman, Mary Hartman . . . last summer's Tumble Weed, Tumble Weed!"
Maralin Niska, "Carmen dressed like Sadie Thompson!"
Angie Dickinson, "The policewoman that has caught everything but fashion!"
Charo, "A rumble seat with a pushed-up front!"
Ann Miller, "A 1937 screen test!"
Queen Juliana, "All the Queen's horses and all of the Queen's men couldn't make Julie look good again!"
Lee Radziwill, "Did Lee's designer go down with the *Titanic?*"

Loretta Lynn, "The right dress in the wrong century!"

Nancy Walker, "Vacuum cleaners have better covers!"

Dinah Shore, "Wild again, beguiled again and constantly contrived again!"

1977 Farrah Fawcett-Majors, "Enough splits in her dress for an earthquake!"

Linda Ronstadt, "Bought her entire wardrobe during a five minute bus stop!"

Charo, "Cuchi, Cuchi . . . is that a dress or a bug killer?"

Anita Bryant, "She should go to the 'Queen's' dressmaker!"

Diane Keaton, "Ash Can fashions from her local alley!"

Dolly Parton, "Scarlet O'Hara dressed like Mae West in *My Little Chickadee!*"

Marie Osmond, "Over-done and over-dressed. *The Good Ship Lollipop* in dry dock!"

Dyan Cannon, "Looks like she was blown out of one in a circus!"

Chris Evert, "If tailored is in . . . so is boring!"

Margaret Trudeau, "Canada's loss is New York's loss!"

MR. BLACKWELL'S LIST OF FABULOUS FASHION INDEPENDENTS

1975 Marisa Berenson
Nancy Reagan
Mary Tyler Moore
Rose Kennedy
Princess Caroline of Monaco
Diana Ross

1976 Judy Collins
Farrah Fawcett-Majors
Vivian Reed
Jacqueline Bissett
Princess Caroline of Monaco
Mary Tyler Moore
Marthe Keller

1977 Princess Grace of Monaco
Meg Newhouse
Suzanne Somers
Lady Lichfield
Natalie Wood
Contessa Chon
Princess Yasmin Kahn
Gena Rowlands

HALL OF FAME

Elizabeth Taylor
Zsa Zsa Gabor
Barbra Streisand
Raquel Welch

Lord & Taylor Creative Design Award

LORD & TAYLOR, INC.
424 Fifth Ave., New York, N.Y. 10018 (212/381-3344)

The Lord & Taylor Creative Design Award, a Tiffany crystal trophy, has been established to honor excellence and creativity in the field. A panel of the department store's creative executives selects the winner.

1977 Harriet Selwyn

Culinary Arts &

Homemaking

Contents

Related Awards

National Mother of the Year
AMERICAN MOTHERS COMMITTEE
The Waldorf-Astoria, 301 Park Ave., New York, N.Y. 10022
(212/755-2755)

The American Mothers Committee, which seeks to "strengthen the moral and spiritual foundations of the home," annually selects a woman who sets a high standard for family life as the National Mother of the Year.

1935 Lucy Keen Johnson, Georgia
1936 Frances Eleanor Smith, California
1937 Henriette Flora Gray, Nebraska
1938 Grace Noll Crowell, Texas
1939 Otelia K. Compton, Ohio
1940 Edith Graham Mayo, Minnesota
1941 Dena Shelby Diehl, Kentucky
1942 Elizabeth Vize Berry, North Carolina
1943 Mary Dabney Thompson, Ohio
1944 Harriet Duff Phillips, Pennsylvania
1945 Georgiana Farr Sibley, New York
1946 Emma Clarissa Clement, Kentucky
1947 Janette Stevenson Murray, Iowa
1948 Helen Gartside Hines, Illinois
1949 Pearl Owens Gillis, Texas
1950 Elizabeth Roe Cloud, Oregon
1951 Mary Martin Sloop, North Carolina
1952 Toy Lin Goon, Maine
1953 Ethlyn Wisengarver Bott, Illinois
1954 Love McDuffie Tolbert, Georgia
1955 Lavina Christensen Fugal, Utah
1956 Jane Maxwell Pritchard, Michigan
1957 Hazel Hempel Abel, Nebraska
1958 May Roper Coker, South Carolina
1959 Jennie Loitman Barron, Massachusetts
1960 Emerald Barman Arbogast, California
1961 Louis Giddings Currey, Tennessee
1962 Mary Celesta Weatherly, Alabama
1963 Olga Pearson Engdahl, Nebraska
1964 Cora Hjertaas Stavig, South Dakota
1965 Lorena Chipman Fletcher, Utah
1966 Bertha Holt, Oregon
1967 Minnie Knoop Guenther, Arizona
1968 E. Grossman Bodine, North Dakota
1969 E. Peterson Le Tourneau, Texas
1970 Dorothy Lee Wilson, Tennessee
1971 Betty Anthony Zahn, Oklahoma
1972 Esther Hunt Moore, North Carolina
1973 Ruth Youngdahl Nelson, Minnesota
1974 Phyllis Brown Marriott, District of Columbia
1975 Josephine Wainman Burson, Tennessee
1976 M. Garnett Grindstaff, New Mexico
1977 Gloria Berry Landon, Oklahoma

WORLD MOTHER
1962 Clara Sproat Glenn, Ohio

Pillsbury Bake-Off Grand Prize
THE PILLSBURY CO.
608 Second Ave. S., Minneapolis, Minn. 55402
(612/330-4719)

The Pillsbury Bake-Off is an annual contest currently offering two $25,000 Grand Prizes and 10 other cash prizes. Any resident of the United States 10 years of age or older may enter the contest. Initial participation is by mail. A professional judging agency, home econo-mists and a consumer panel narrow the field to 100 finalists, who are invited to the Bake-Off site to prepare their entries for evaluation by another panel of judges. Each recipe entered requires the use of at least one Pillsbury brand product.

1949 Mrs. Ralph E. Smafield, Rockford, Ill., Water-Rising Twists
1950 Mrs. Peter Wuebel, Menlo Park, Calif., Orange Kiss Me Cake
1951 Mrs. Samuel P. Weston, La Jolla, Calif., Starlight Double Delight Cake
1952 Mrs. Peter Harlib, Chicago, Ill., Snappy Turtle Cook-ies
1953 Mrs. Bernard Kanago, Denver, Colo., My Inspiration Cake
1954 Mrs. Bernard A. Koteen, Washington, D.C., Open Sesame Pie
1955 Mrs. Henry Jorgenson, Portland, Ore., Ring-A-Lings
1956 Mrs. Hildreth H. Hatheway, Santa Barbara, Calif., California Casserole
1957 Gerda Roderer, Hayward, Calif., Accordian Treats
1958 Mrs. Donald DeVault, Delaware, Ohio, Spicy Apple Twists
1959 Eunice Surles, Lake Charles, La., Mardi Gras Party Cake
1960 Leona P. Schnuelle, Beatrice, Neb., Dilly Casserole Bread
1961 Mrs. Vernon Resse, Minneapolis, Minn., Candy Bar Cookies
1962 Mrs. Erwin J. Smogor, South Bend, Ind., Apple Pie '63
1963 Mrs. Roman Walilko, Detroit, Mich, Hungry Boys' Casserole
1964 Janis Boykin Risley, Sarasota, Fla., Peacheesy Pie
1965 No award
1966 Mrs. John Petrelli, Ely, Nev., Golden Gate Snack Bread
1967 Mrs. Carol Bullock, Spring City, Tenn., Muffin Mix Buffet Bread
1968 Phillis Lidert, Fort Lauderdale, Fla., Buttercream Pound Cake
1969 Edna Holmgren, Hopkins, Minn., Magic Marshmal-low Crescent Puffs
1970 Nan Robb, Huachuca City, Ariz., Onion Lover's Twist
1971 Pearl Hall, Snohomish, Wash., Pecan Surprise Bars

REFRIGERATED
1972 Mrs. Gerald Collins, Elk River, Minn., Quick 'n Chewy Crescent Bars
1973 Mrs. Jerome Flieller, Jr., Floresville, Tex., Quick Crescent Pecan Pie Bars
1974 Mrs. James S. Castle, River Forest, Ill., Savory Cres-cent Chicken Squares
1975 Barbara Gibson, Ft. Wayne, Ind., Easy Crescent Dan-ish Rolls
1976 Mrs. Bert Groves, San Antonio, Tex., Crescent Caramel Swirl
1977 No award

GROCERY
1972 Mrs. Carl DeDominicis, Verona, Pa., Streusel Spice Cake
1973 Mrs. Ronald L. Brooks, Salisbury, Md., Banana Crunch Cake
1974 Mrs. Emil Jerzak, Porter, Minn., Chocolate Cherry Bars
1975 Luella Maki, Ely, Minn., Sour Cream Apple Squares
1976 Mrs. Edward F. Smith, Harahan, La., Whole Wheat Raisin Loaf
1977 No award

Tableau D'Honneur des Concours Culinaires

SOCIÉTE CULINAIRE PHILANTHROPIQUE
250 W. 57th St., New York, N.Y. 10019 (212/246-6754)

The winner of the annual Tableau d'Honneur des Concours Culinaires is awarded a medal by the Government of France for outstanding achievement in the culinary arts. The 1977 competition was part of the 109th annual Salon of Culinary Art in New York. In addition to the Grand Prize winners listed here, individual honors are given in 27 other fields, including cooking, artistic preparation of food, pastry, management and service. These are too numerous to mention here.

1912　O. Gentsch
1913　L. Canal
1914　A. Foussat
1915-20　No awards
1921　E. Miserez
1922　L. Paquet
1923　Ed. Maitre
1924　Ch. Scotto
1925　P. Bedard
1926　A. Gamard
1927　A. Paschetto
1928　G. Brusati
1929　Ch. Champion
1930　G. K. Waldner
1931　J. Chiarle
1932　E. Griesshaber
1933　V. Fattori
1934　G. Banino
1935　J. Dincauze
1936　J. Gruny
1937　G. Hertrich
1938　E. Banino
1939　Waldorf Astoria Hotel
1940-46　No awards
1947　Paul Jourcin
1948　Plaza Hotel
1949　Aime Patran
　　　Hermann G. Rusch
1950　Paul Laesecke
1951　Robert Audelan
1952　Arthur Irminger
1953　Traugott Schneider
1954　Humbert Gatti
1955　Manuel Orta
1956　Clement Grangier
1957　Georges Blanc
1958　Henri P. Sidoli
1959　Joseph Castaybert
1960　Henry Haller
1961　Greenbrier Hotel
1962　Marcel Haentzler
1963　Andre Rene
1964　Andre Pujol
1965　Herbert Barath
1966　Andre Soltner
1967　Ferdinand Metz
1968　Willy Ritz
1969　Claude Swartvagher
　　　Joseph Tarantino
1970　Culinary Institute of America
1971　William Spry
1972　New York City Community College

1973　Jean-Jacques Rachou
1974　Matthew Ryan
1975　Joseph Trombetti
1976　Gerold Berger
1977　Jean Jacques Dietrich

Tastemaker Awards

R.T. FRENCH CO.
1 Mustard Pl., Rochester, N.Y. 14609 (716/482-8000)

The $500 Tastemaker Awards are given annually for the best American cookbooks of the previous year, as selected by a panel of magazine, newspaper and cookbook writers, editors and publishers.

1967　Gloria Bley Miller, *The Thousand Recipe Chinese Cookbook*
1968　Anne Seranne, *America Cooks* ("best of show")
　　　Jose Wilson, *House and Garden's New Cook Book* (basic)
　　　Elizabeth Lambert Ortiz, *The Complete Book of Mexican Cooking* (foreign or regional)
　　　Helen McCully, *Nobody Ever Tells You These Things About Food and Drink* (specialty)
　　　Clementine Paddleford, *Clementine Paddleford's Cook Young* (soft cover)
1969　Jean Hewitt, *New York Times Large Type Cookbook* ("best of show" and basic)
　　　Dale Brown, *American Cooking* (foreign or American regional)
　　　Annemarie Huste, *Annemarie's Personal Cookbook* (specialty)
　　　Better Homes and Gardens Cooking for Two (specialty)
　　　Sunset Cook Book of Desserts (soft cover)
1970　Craig Claiborne, *Kitchen Primer* (basic)
　　　Adi Boni, *Italian Regional Cooking* (foreign or American regional)
　　　Better Homes and Gardens Ground Meat Cook Book (specialty)
　　　Jean Hewitt, *The New York Times Main Dish Cookbook* (soft cover)
1971　Albert Stockli, *Splendid Fare* ("best of show" and basic)
　　　Jeanne Voltz, *California Cookbook* (foreign or American regional)
　　　Michael Field, *All Manner of Food* (specialty)
　　　Sunset Magazine Editors, *Sunset Oriental Cook Book* (soft cover)
1972　Craig Claiborne, *The New York Times International Cookbook* ("best of show" and foreign or American regional)
　　　Charlotte Adams, *The Four Seasons Cookbook* (basic)
　　　Jean Hewitt, *The New York Times Natural Foods Cookbook* (specialty)
　　　Helen Worth, *Hostess Without Help* (entertaining)
　　　Alan Hooker, *Herb Cookery* (soft cover)
1973　James Beard, *American Cookery* ("best of show" and basic)
　　　Craig Claiborne and Virginia Lee, *The Chinese Cookbook* (foreign or American regional)
　　　Dorothy Ivens, *Pates and Other Marvelous Meat Loves* (specialty)
　　　Marian Burros and Lois Levine, *Summertime Cookbook* (entertaining)
　　　Beatrice Trum Hunter, *The Natural Foods Primer* (organic)

Nancy Bryal, *Better Homes and Gardens Low-Calorie Desserts* (specialty diet)
Sunset Magazine Editors, *Cooking With Wine* (soft cover)

1974 Perla Myers, *The Seasonal Kitchen* ("best of show," basic and best first cookbook)
Marcella Hazan, *The Classic Italian Cookbook* (foreign or American regional)
Madeleine Kamman, *Dinner Against the Clock* (specialty)
Diana Collier and Joan Weiner, *Bread: Making It the Natural Way* (organic)
Paul Rubinstein, *Feasts for Two* (entertaining)
Anne Seranne, *Anne Seranne's Good Food Without Meat* (specialty diet)
Sunset Magazine Editors, *Sunset Ideas for Cooking Vegetables* (soft cover)

1975 Nika Hazelton, *I Cook as I Please* (basic)
Richard Olney, *Simple French Food* ("best of show" and foreign or American regional)
Bernard Clayton, Jr., *The Complete Book of Breads* (specialty and best first cookbook)
Helen Corbitt, *Helen Corbitt Cooks for Company* (entertaining)
Beryl M. Marton, *Dinner for One and All* (health and diet)
Daphne Metaxas, *Classic Greek Cooking* (soft cover)

1976 Jean Anderson and Elaine Hanna, *The Doubleday Cookbook* ("best of show" and basic)
Nancy Morton, *Better Homes and Gardens Heritage Cook Book* (foreign or American regional)
Craig Claiborne, *Craig Claiborne's Favorites from the New York Times* (specialty)
Jean Hewitt, *The New York Times Weekend Cookbook* (entertaining)
June Roth, *Salt Free Cooking with Herbs and Spices* (natural and specialty diet)

Mable Hoffman, *Crockery Cookery* (soft cover)
Evan Jones, *American Food, The Gastronomic Story* (best first cookbook)

1977 Michel Guerard, *Michel Guerard's Cuisine Minceur* ("best of show," best first cookbook and foreign or American regional)
Carol Cutler, *The Six-Minute Souffle and Other Culinary Delights* (basic)
Nika Hazelton, *The Unabridged Vegetable Cookbook* (specialty)
Diana and Paul von Welanetz, *The Pleasure of Your Company* (entertaining)
Barbara Gibbons, *The Slim Gourmet* (health)
Mable Hoffman, *Crepe Cookery* (soft cover)

Award of Merit

AMERICAN WINE SOCIETY
4218 Rosewold, Royal Oak, Mich. 48073 (313/549-2303)

The Award of Merit is given annually for significant contribution to the advancement of knowledge of American wine.

1971 Konstantin Frank, Growing vinifera
1972 Charles Fournier, Contributions to vinifera
1973 Leon D. Adams, Author and founder of the Wine Institute
1974 Willard Robinson, Chairman, Department of Enology, State University of New York at Geneva
1975 Philip and Jocelyn Wagner, Authors and French hybrid researchers
1976 Maynard Amerine, Professor, University of California at Davis, for 20 point scale research
1977 G.H. Mowbray, Montbray Winery, for pioneering research with vinifera and hybrids

Humorous &

Satirical Awards

Contents

Related Awards

Preceptorial Accolade
Sweet Fanny Award
ARCANE ORDER
c/o Studio of Contemplation, 5340 Weller Ave., Jacksonville, Fla. 32211 (904/724-4185)

The Preceptorial Accolade is given semiannually ("unless no one is deemed worthy") to the individual who has "done the most for the order and to prominent speakers, artists, etc., who conduct programs for the order."

1970 **Lorraine Albert,** Oil on canvas
     Peggy Mohrer, Service
1971 **Steve Lotz,** Pen and ink drawing
1972 **Leonard Mather,** Collage
1973 **Elihu Edelson,** Lecture
1974 **Carl Begley,** Lecture
     Sandy Merriman, Serigraph
1975 **Virginia Cathey,** Poem
1976 **Faith Britton,** Produced ceremony
     John Darling, Lecture
1977 **Fielding West,** Lecture
     Jean Marie Cornwell, Lecture

The Sweet Fanny Award is given "as specified in 'Academic Research Centograph,' Vol. XXIII, No. 3 (1973), including a callipygian classification chart." The name of the winner is inscribed on a "sublime pot" and a certificate is awarded by judges' decision to male and female members of the order.

    1975 **Barbara Nagle**
    1976 **Nancy Redfern**
    1977 **Harriet Smith**

Dame Maria Van Slyke Medal
INTERNATIONAL CONFEDERATION OF BOOK ACTORS
1364 Rockrimmon Rd., Stamford, Conn. 06903
(203/322-6186)

A Dame Maria Van Slyke Medal, which is actually a scroll, awarded quadriennially, for "exceptional achievement in protean portrayals in works of fiction where characters are assigned names of living persons. The living person must be represented in works of living authors. . . . Membership in ICOBA gives preferred status in consideration." Winners are selected "by a select committee of members selected by the president." (ICOBA also indicates that it offers the Fiona Wergel Citation for Canine Achievement, which has never been awarded.)

1959 **Dame Maria Van Slyke,** *The Manchurian Candidate,* by Richard Condon
1966 **Bennett Reyes,** *Any God Will Do,* by Richard Condon
1970 **Abraham Weiler,** *The Ecstasy Business,* by Richard Condon
1974 **Norman Keifetz,** *Winter Kills,* by Richard Condon
     Franklin Heller, *The Star Spangled Crunch,* by Richard Condon

Bore of the Year
SHOW MAGAZINE
708 Third Ave., New York, N.Y. 10017 (212/687-2545)

The readers of *Show* are invited to fill out a ballot to select the Bore of the Year in six categories. The editors select nominees from whom the readers choose. Space is allowed for write-in votes as well.

1977 Television: **Lee Majors,** "For the best imitation of a robot on-screen and off"
     Movies: **Elizabeth Taylor,** "For John Warner"
     Sports: **Muhammad Ali,** "For not being more retiring"
     Music: **Anita Bryant,** "For obvious reasons"
     Publishing: **Larry Flynt,** "For being the biggest hustler of them all"
     Broadcast: **Barbara Walters,** "For proving that a million dollars doesn't buy what it used to"

Doublespeak Award

NATIONAL COUNCIL OF TEACHERS OF ENGLISH
1111 Kenyon Rd., Urbana, Ill. 61820 (217/328-3870)

The Doublespeak Award is made annually to cite "outstanding examples of misuse of public language" by government, media, advertising or other organizations. Examples of obscure language and euphemistic downplaying in communications to the public are sought as nominees for the Doublespeak Award. The Committee on Public Doublespeak selects the winners, who now must be Americans.

1974 **Col. Opfer,** U.S. Air Force Press Officer in Cambodia, after a U.S. bombing raid for telling reporters, "You always write it's bombing, bombing, bombing. It's *not* bombing! It's air support." (Award in Misuse of Euphemisms category)
     Ron Ziegler, Press Secretary to President Richard M. Nixon, for replying to a question on whether a batch of Watergate tapes were all intact, which required a "yes" or "no" answer, by saying the following:
     "I would feel that most of the conversations that took place in those areas of the White House that did have the recording system would in almost their entirety be in existence but the special prosecutor, the court, and, I think, the American people are sufficiently familiar with the recording system to know where the recording devices existed and to know the situation in terms of the recording process but I feel, although the process has not been undertaken yet in preparation of the material to abide by the court decision, really, what the answer to that question is." (Award in Gobbledygook category)

Don J. Willower of Pennsylvania State University for the following remarks in the presidential address to the University Council for Education Administration: 1. "The point in all this is not that frameworks that stress the individual and commonly exhibit a psychological orientation are full of error. They are not. To the contrary, they often furnish important insights. But such modes have dominated the thinking of many educators; a state of affairs reinforced by the tangibility of the person as an object of analysis as contrasted with the misty, obstruse quality of system concepts." 2. "Yet, the most basic problems that arise in connection with knowledge utilization may be those that stem from the social and organizational character of educational institutions. A few university adaptations already have been highlighted. Public schools display a myriad of normative and other regulatory structures that promote internal predictability, as well as a host of adaptive mechanisms that reduce external uncertainties." (Award in Educationeze category)

M&M/Mars Candy Co., for a commercial aimed at children which it claimed in a press release was reviewed by the American Dental Association. The company failed to say that the ADA refused M&M/Mars permission to use the ADA's "statement of scientific accuracy," because the commercial claimed that the "bad guy" in tooth decay is plaque rather than the interaction between plaque and sugar. (Award in Language of Silence category)

1975 Yasir Arafat, leader of the Palestinian Liberation Organization for replying to an interviewer's comment that "the Israelis say this means you want to destroy their state over the long term instead of the short term," by saying, "They are wrong. We do not want to destroy any people. It is precisely because we have been advocating coexistence that we have already shed so much blood."

1976 Government employee who drew up a job description for the position of Consumer Affairs Coordinator for the State Department. One portion reads, "The purpose of the Department's plan is two-fold, to confirm and reinforce the Department's sensitivity to consumer rights and interests as they impact upon the Department and to take those steps necessary to promote and channel these rights and interests with respect to the maintenance and expansion of an international dialogue and awareness." A second passage states that the job would be "to review existing mechanisms of consumer input, thruput and output, and seek ways of improving these linkages via the consumer communication channel."

1977 Pentagon and Energy Research and Development Agency for attempting to slip through the appropriations for the neutron bomb by means of euphemistic jargon and by hiding the item in an obscure section of ERDA's budget request. In Pentagon slang, the weapon which kills people but leaves buildings intact is called the "cookie cutter."

Flat Earth Scientist Certificate of Award
Seeker of Truth Award

INTERNATIONAL FLAT EARTH RESEARCH SOCIETY
Box 2533, Lancaster, Calif. 93534

The Flat Earth Scientist Certificate of Award is given to the individual who "has proved himself to be a diligent Seeker of Truth; has shown in the face of opposition; has sought out the Truth; completed Study conducted by the Flat Earth Society; knows the Earth is flat." Society President Charles K. Johnson refuses to release the names of Award winners. As he says, "through fear of retaliation, holders of this award prefer not to have their names made public."

The Seeker of Truth Award, which was established in 1972, goes to "any citizen or official of either sex or any age who, in the face of ridicule or persecution or opposition, has acted or spoken on what he believed to be the Truth." Sadly, no one has yet deserved this award in the eyes of the President and Officers, and it therefore has not yet been given.

Fleece of the Month
Fleece of the Year

SENATOR WILLIAM PROXMIRE
5241 Senate Office Building, Washington, D.C.
(202/224-5653)

The Fleece of the Month is given "for the biggest, most ridiculous or ironic example of waste of the taxpayers' money or government activity which fleeces the taxpayer for the month." It culminates in a Fleece of the Year designation each December. While we have not generally reported monthly honors — or dishonors — in this volume, the amount of money involved in activities which make the monthly list are frequently great enough to warrant their inclusion. Furthermore, the activity is frequently national in scope, or at least, according to the Senator, affects all American taxpayers. Occasionally, Awards of Merit are made to honor praiseworthy actions. The selections are named from activities by the federal government, or a federal government-sponsored program, that come to the attention of the Senator's staff, which selects the winner and makes a public statement concerning its selection.

GOLDEN FLEECE AWARD

March 1975 National Science Foundation, "For squandering $84,000 to try to find out why people fall in love." Other citations to the NSF go for a $15,000 study on hitchhiking, an $81,000 study on the social behavior of the Alaskan brown bear, $25,000 to study primate teeth and $112,000 to study the African climate during the last Ice Age.

April 1975 National Science Foundation, National Aeronautics and Space Administration and Office of Naval Research, "For spending over $500,000 in the last seven years to determine under what conditions rats, monkeys and humans bite and clench their jaws, of which more than $100,000 were federal funds."

May 1975 Selective Service System, "For a $98,029 contract it awarded Mr. Kenneth Coffey to study the all-volunteer army concept in a number of foreign countries two years after the all-volunteer army had been put into effect in the U.S."

Army Corps of Engineers, "For their back-door attempt to commit $6- to $10- billion to build a series of new locks and dams on the Mississippi River under a little-known law designed merely for the maintenance, repair or replacement of existing structures . . . If [they] get by with this action, they can replace any of the other 27 locks and dams on the Mississippi and the seven locks and dams on the Illinois River without specific approval."

June 1975 U.S. Congress, "For living high off the hog while much of the rest of the country is suffering economic disaster." Cited were approval of up to three new committee staffers per senator at a $33,975 each salary, increase of House travel allowances by $23,000 per member, the construction of a new $85-million office building and the installation of 19 automatic elevators at $1.3 million in the House Office Building, while retaining operators to run them.

July 1975 Bureau of Land Management, "For requiring useless paperwork on a contract that resulted in a $4,-000 piece of equipment costing over $15,000." The equipment: fire equipment to be placed on two pick-up trucks.

August 1975 Federal Aviation Administration, "For a $57,800, 103-page study of body measurements of airline stewardess trainees."

September 1975 Department of the Navy, "For using 64 aircraft to fly 1,334 officers to the Hilton Hotel in Las Vegas for a reunion of a private organization during the height of the energy crisis."

October 1975 National Institute on Alcohol Abuse and Alcoholism, "For spending millions of dollars to find out if drunk fish are more aggressive than sober fish, if young rats are more likely than adult rats to drink booze in order to reduce anxiety and if rats can be systematically turned into alcoholics."

November 1975 Frank Zarb, Administrator of the Federal Energy Administration, "For spending $25,000 and using almost 19,000 gallons of fuel in 10 months since January 1, 1975, jetting about the country in chartered aircraft urging businessmen and civic groups to economize on energy resources."

December 1975 The White House, "For its efforts to add to its empire through increased funds for consultants, contingencies, travel and high-level personnel while calling for austerity from the rest of the government." Specifically cited were an increase of $1.6 million in consultants fees in the Ford Administration, a 100 per cent increase to $1 million of the discretionary contingency fund, an increase of $60,000 in White House staff travel funds without legislative authorization and for having on staff 54 White House aides earning between $37,800 and $44,600 a year.

January 1976 National Endowment for the Humanities, "For grants to well-heeled doctors, lawyers and school administrators to attend tuition-free, vacation-like, month-long humanistic bull sessions at some of the choicest watering holes in the country next summer. This boon-doggle will cost the hard-pressed taxpayer at least $750,000 this year."

February 1976 Department of the Navy, "For exploding an expected $15,000 in repair and maintenance of Vice President Rockefeller's temporary home to a $537,000 expenditure."

March 1976 National Science Foundation, "For a study supported by an NSF grant on 'Environmental Determinants of Human Aggression.' The method of operation: the researcher's assistant would pull his car to a stop at a red light. . . . When the light turned green, the assistant would refuse to move the car for about 15 seconds . . . to determine when and and how often the driver immediately behind would become impatient and aggressive enough to honk his horn."

April 1976 National Aeronautics and Space Administration, "For requesting $2.8 million to construct an addition to the existing Lunar Receiving Laboratory at the Johnson Space Center to house 100 pounds of moon rocks."

May 1976 Federal Aviation Administration, "The FAA, according to its own Public Affairs Office newsletter, spent over $417,000 for 95 new meteorological instruments so that its employees can make rain predictions while remaining indoors despite the fact that existing instruments perform the same function but must be read outdoors."

June 1976 National Center for Health Services, "An examination of over $20 million of their grants and demonstration contracts indicates that routinely they were not completed on time, cost up to five times the original contract and contained low quality and highly questionable results."

July 1976 National Science Foundation's Research Applied to National Needs program, "RANN awarded a $397,000 contract allegedly to perform an unbiased and scientific study of consumer legislation and services to a principal investigator and research center having an overwhelming bias in favor of the credit industry."

August 1976 General Services Adminstration, "For spending $1,015,000 for 15 statues, murals or works of art at federal buildings under the Art in Architecture program." Works included: a $100,000 80- to 100-foot red-painted steel baseball bat.

September 1976 National Aeronautics and Space Administration, "For a sole source contract award of $140,000 for a 6,000-word article and a follow-up book-length history of the Viking Mars Landing project."

October 1976 Housing and Urban Development Department, "For a $245,000 study of New Towns. Over the last decade New Towns and New Communities have been studied to death while most New Towns are dead or dying."

November 1976 Treasury Department, "For its failure to collect as much as $4.8 million in taxes owed by government big shots who are chauffered to and from home in government cars. As much as $17-$18 million in costs to the taxpayer and taxes not collected have been lost because of the Treasury's inaction."

December 1976 Army Corps of Engineers, "For the worst record of cost overruns in the entire federal government . . . [which] cannot be explained away by inflation."

January 1977 Agriculture Department, "For spending nearly $46,000 to find out how long it takes to cook breakfast."

February 1977 Law Enforcement Assistance Administration, "For spending nearly $27,000 to determine why inmates want to escape from prison."

March 1977 In lieu of a Fleece of the Month Award, a Special Merit Award to Max Cleland, Veterans Administration Director, "Notwithstanding the fact that he is a triple amputee, he is driving himself to and from work in his own car, thereby saving taxpayers at least $16,000 a year."

April 1977 Smithsonian Institute, "For spending $89,000 of public funds in producing a dictionary of Tzotzil, an obscure and unwritten Mayan language spoken by 120,000 corn-farming peasants in southern Mexico."

May 1977 National Endowment for the Humanities, "For making a $2,500 grant through the state to Arlington

County, Va., to study why people are rude, cheat and lie on local tennis courts" and "for $132 million of taxpayers' money this year to determine why tennis players hog the courts, become frustrated when they have to wait to play for hours or go from court to court to find one with which to play."

June 1977 In lieu of a Fleece of the Month Award, Merit Awards were made to the following:
Smithsonian Institution, "For building its Air and Space Museum on time, for less money than originally requested and for an improvement rather than a reduction of its quality."
Farmers Home Administration, "For the 1972-76 period the FHA had a 32 per cent increase in the weighted total of the loans and grants it made and serviced with a 3 per cent reduction in the number of persons doing the job."
National Science Foundation, "For funding work to build a man-made working gene . . . which may pave the way for supplies of infection-fighting chemicals, insulin or other medically important substances, . . . to find methods to improve on nature's own way of replenishing nitrogen in the soil . . . and pioneering research on how the brain recovers after being damaged."

July 1977 U. S. Postal Service, "For spending over $3.4 million on a Madison Avenue ad campaign to write more letters . . . [and] almost $775,000 more in a seemingly futile effort to test whether the campaign works."

August 1977 Transportation Department, "For spending $225,000 on a report which forecasts transportation needs in the year 2025 under four separate science fiction 'scenarios'—where the United States undergoes an Ice Age, becomes a dictatorship, is transformed into a hippie culture or blossoms into a society the authors term 'the American Dream.' "

September 1977 National Endowment for the Arts, "For making a $6,025 grant to an artist to film the throwing of crepe paper and burning gases out of high-flying airplanes . . . 'to document on film an event designed to alter an audiences immediate environment for a short period of time.' "

October 1977 Labor Department, "For granting a $384,-948 contract to hire 101 persons under the Comprehensive Employment and Training Act to do a door-to-door survey to count the dogs, cats and horses at the 160,000 houses and apartments in Ventura County, Calif."

November 1977 Pentagon civilian and military brass, "For misusing military aircraft on a massive scale at a cost of at least $52.3 million, including support and personal flights instead of combat training and for flights where commercial transportation was many times cheaper."

December 1977 Federal Deposit Insurance Corp., "For a series of outrageous expenditure's for its former Chairman's personal use as revealed in a General Accounting Office report," including travel expenses of Robert E. Barnett's wife who accompanied him on seven trips to such exotic places as Puerto Rico, Manila and Mexico, billing the FDIC over $6,000; using agency vehicles to transport Mrs. Barnett to her doctor and Mrs. Barnett and her children to visit the Hirschhorn Museum. In one case the Barnett children were chauffeured to Rehobeth Beach by two FDIC employees using an agency car. The FDIC also paid Mr. Barnett's membership fees in a private tennis club in Virginia.

FLEECE OF THE YEAR

1975 U.S. Air Force, "For operating a $66 million fleet of 23 plush jets used solely to transport top government

officials at a cost to the taxpayers of over $6 million a year. This little-known airline is called the 89th Military Aircraft Wing and is based at Andrews Air Force Base near Washington, D.C."
1976 No award
1977 Treasury Department, "For its zealous support of an end-of-the-year, end-run attempt to amend the tax laws at a cost to the taxpayers of over $400 million this year," by continuing to exempt U.S. residents abroad $20,000 of earned-income on their federal income tax base.

Lefthander of the Year
All-Lefty Pro Baseball Team
LEFTHANDERS INTERNATIONAL
3601 SW 29th St., Topeka, Kans. 66614 (913/273-0680)

The Lefthander of the Year is a new award that will be given annually for outstanding achievement by left-handed public personalities, entertainers and athletes. A plaque is presented to the winner, who is selected by membership vote.

1977 Gerald R. Ford

All-Lefty Pro Baseball Team selections receive a plaque for members of the team, who are chosen by a vote of the membership of Lefthanders International.

1976 Ted Simmons, (St. Louis Cardinals), catcher
Vida Blue, (Oakland As), Pitcher
Randy Jones, (San Diego Padres), Pitcher
Al Hrabosky, (St. Louis Cardinals), Pitcher
John Mayberry, (Kansas City Royals), First Base
Rod Carew, (Minnesota Twins), Second Base
George Brett, (Kansas City Royals), Third Base
Joe Morgan, (Cincinnati Reds), Shortstop
Lou Brock, (St. Louis Cardinals), Left Fielder
Fred Lynn, (Boston Red Sox), Center Fielder
Dave Parker, (Pittsburgh Pirates), Right Fielder
1977 No awards

Procrastinator of the Year Award
PROCRASTINATORS CLUB OF AMERICA
111 Broad-Locust Bldg., Philadelphia, Pa. 19102 (215/KI 6-3861)

The Procrastinator of the Year Award, which consists of a "plaque to be inscribed later," is given annually, more or less, to honor recognizable fulfillment in the art of procrastination—not too recently. An awards committee selects the recipient.

1969 Unnamed topless dancer, For putting things off
1970 Jack Benny, For never getting around to turning 40
1971 Dean Martin and Jerry Lewis, "Comedy Team of the Year"
1972 Methodist Hospital, Philadelphia, "For placing their cornerstone, dated 1968, in 1972
1973 Murray Rappaport, Breaking the world record for an overdue library book
1974 Illinois Central Railroad, Latest train: departed 1903, still not arrived
1975 Postmaster General Elmer T. Klassen, Late delivery of mail
1976 No award, Committee didn't select in time
1977 Committee hasn't responded to questionnaire yet

Sour Apple Award

HOLLYWOOD WOMEN'S PRESS CLUB
4446 Ledge Ave., Hollywood, Calif. 91602 (213/769-2506)

The Sour Apple Award was established originally to "chastise" the "least cooperative" stars at the time when the Hollywood Women's Press Club had a membership largely of correspondents and reporters. By 1970, when more press agents had joined the association and might be reluctant to have their own clients so cited, the criteria changed to rap the individual or group who had presented an unfavorable image of Hollywood. At the same time, the name of the award officially became the Sour Apple, to balance the Golden Apple given to the Star of the Year. A committee nominates and the membership votes on the recipient.

LEAST COOPERATIVE MALE

1941	Fred Astaire
1942	George Sanders
1943	Errol Flynn
1944	Walter Pidgeon
1945	Fred MacMurray
1946	Frank Sinatra
1947	Gary Cooper
1948	Errol Flynn
1949	Humphrey Bogart
1950	Robert Mitchum
1951	Frank Sinatra
1952	Mario Lanza
1953	Dale Robertson
1954	Edmund Purdom
1955	No awards
1960	Elvis Presley
1961	Marlon Brando
1962	Warren Beatty

1963	James Franciscus
1964	Tony Curtis
1965	Vince Edwards
1966	Elvis Presley

LEAST COOPERATIVE FEMALE

1941	Ginger Rogers
1942	Jean Arthur
1943	Joan Fontaine
1944	Sonja Henie
1945	Greer Garson
1946	Ingrid Bergman
1947	Jennifer Jones
1948	Rita Hayworth
1949	Hedy Lamarr
1950	Olivia de Havilland
1951	Esther Williams
1952	Rita Hayworth
1953	Esther Williams
1954	Doris Day
1955	No awards
1960	Debbie Reynolds
1961	Debbie Reynolds
1962	Doris Day
1963	Ann-Margret
1964	Doris Day
1965	Ann-Margret
1966	Natalie Wood

SOUR APPLE

1970	Jane Fonda
1971	No award
1972	No award
1973	Norman Mailer
1974	Frank Sinatra
1975	No award
1976	Porno film producers
1977	Truman Capote

Miscellaneous

Awards

Contents

Johnny Appleseed Award
Silver Medal
Gold Medal
Woodson K. Jones Memorial Plaque

MEN'S GARDEN CLUBS OF AMERICA
5560 Merle Hay Rd., Des Moines, Iowa 50323
(515/278-0295)

The Johnny Appleseed Award, which consists of a medal, is given annually to a man who in a local, regional or national sense has pioneered in some branch of horticulture in a spirit of service, as exemplified by John Chapman, known as Johnny Appleseed. Any member of MGCA may nominate candidates for consideration by the Awards Committee.

1939	Carleton Morse
	John Marvin Yoste
1940	John McLaren
	August Kock
1941	Adolph Mueller
1942	Henry Hicks
	Jens Jenson
1943	No award
1944	No award
1945	John Bacher
	Adolph Jaenicke
1946	Fred Edmunds
	Lester Morris
1947	No award
1948	Liberty Hyde Bailey
1949	David Fairchild
1950	E. J. Kraus
1951	Arie den Boer
1952	No award
1953	George Terziev
1954	George W. Kelly
1955	James Henry, Jr.
1956	Henry J. Benninger
1957	A. H. Hermann
1958	No award
1959	Herbert Ferris Crisler
1960	Arthur W. Solomon, Sr.
1961	Harvey Foster Stoke
1962	Wister Henry
1963	No award
1964	George Redlow
1965	David Cowan
1966	Clarence E. Godshalk
1967	Rupert Streets
1968	Perry Davis
1969	Frank Curto
1970	Leo F. Simon
1971	Barnie Kennedy
1972	George E. Allen
1973	Edgar Friedrich
1974	Robert Vines
1975	No award
1976	No award
1977	George E. Hughes

The Silver Medal is awarded annually to a member of the Men's Garden Clubs of America who has rendered outstanding service to the organization. Any member may nominate candidates for consideration by the awards committee.

1953	Charles Hudson, Jr.
1954	Milton Carleton
	W. H. Thorne
1955	Clair Johnson
1956	No award
1957	A. Ray Tillman
1958	Herbert E. Kahlert
1959	Harold Laing
1960	Larry Hubbard
1961	Raymond C. Allen
1962	Leo C. Nack
1963	Edgar Weikhorst
1964	J. Bryant Horne
1965	Robert L. Waln
1966	William L. Hull
1967	Frank Leech
1968	C. Hal Nelson
1969	Edwin Engelbrecht
1970	Harold J. Parnham
1971	W. O. Ezell
1972	Carroll Greenman
1973	Larry Grove
1974	George Spader
1975	Leland Fetzer
1976	Sam Fairchild
1977	Ray Cheetham

The Gold Medal is awarded annually to a man who has made outstanding achievements in the field of horticulture. Any MGCA member may nominate candidates for consideration by the awards committee.

1949	C. Eugene Pfister
1950	No award
1951	William Lathrop
1952	No award
1953	No award
1954	No award
1955	Fred Rockwell
1956	Arno Nehrling
1957	Jan De Graff
1958	Edgar Anderson
1959	George Lewis Slate
1960	Clement Bowers
1961	George Pring
1962	Eugene S. Boerner
1963	Leon C. Snyder
1964	Grant Mitsch
1965	Glen W. Burton
1966	Connie, Robert
	Barnard Schreiner
1967	Max Watson
1968	No award
1969	John Nash Ott
1970	No award
1971	Arvil L. Stark
1972	Albert Wilson
1973	No award
1974	Clarence Barbre
1975	Wheelock Wilson
1976	Paul Mangelsdorf
1977	No award

The Woodson K. Jones Memorial Plaque is awarded to an affiliated club for outstanding projects and service to the community, region and MGCA. Clubs may submit records of their accomplisments for consideration.

1959	Jackson, Miss.
1960	Findlay, Ohio
1961	North Shore, Highland Park, Ill.
1962	Beaumont, Tex.
1963	Spartanburg, S.C.
1964	Reidsville, N.C.

1965 Reidsville, N.C.
1966 East Jefferson, Colo.
1967 Spartanburg, S.C.
1968 East Jefferson, Colo.
1969 Spartanburg, S.C.
1970 Marietta, Ga.
1971 Marietta, Ga.
1972 Grosse Pointe, Mich.
1973 Austin, Tex.
1974 Austin, Tex.
1975 Fort Worth, Tex.
1976 Libertvville-Mundelein, Ill.
1977 San Antonio, Tex.

All-America Rose Selection Award
ALL-AMERICA ROSE SELECTIONS, INC.
Box 218, 513 W. Sheridan Ave., Shenandoah, Iowa 51601
(712/246-2884)

The All-America Rose Selection Award, which consists of a plaque and assistance in distributing the winning rose, honors the variety of the flower which shows outstanding performance in official gardens through the U.S. during a two-year period. Official judges check entries during the two-year trial and score them on a point basis to determine the winner(s). The list below includes the name of the winning rose, its color and type and its originator.

1940 Dickson's Red (Scarlet hybrid tea), A. Dickson
Flash (Oriental red climbing bybrid tea), Hatton
The Chief (Salmon red hybrid tea), Lammerts
World's Fair (Deep red floribunda), Minna Kordes
1941 Apricot Queen (Apricot hybrid tea), F.H. Howard
California (Golden yellow hybrid tea), F.H. Howard
Charlotte Armstrong (Cerise red hybrid tea), Lammerts
1942 Heart's Desire (Deep rose pink hybrid tea), F.H. Howard
1943 Grand Duchess Charlotte (Wine red hybrid tea), Ketten Brothers
Mary Margaret McBride (Rose pink hybrid tea), Nicolas
1944 Fred Edmunds (Apricot hybrid tea), F. Meilland
Katherine T. Marshall (Deep pink hybrid tea), Boerner
Lowell Thomas (Butter yellow hybrid tea), Mallerin
Mme. Chiang Kai-Shek (Light yellow hybrid tea), Duehrsen
Mme. Marie Curie (Golden yellow hybrid tea), Gaujard
1945 Floradora (Salmon rose floribunda), Tantau
Horace McFarland (Buff pink hybrid tea), Mallerin
Mirandy (Crimson hybrid tea), Lammerts
1946 Peace (Pale gold hybrid tea), Mme. A. Meilland
1947 Rubaiyat (Cerise red hybrid tea), McGredy
1948 Diamond Jubilee (Buff hybrid tea), Boerner
High Noon (Yellow climbing hybrid tea), Lammerts
Nocturne (Dark red hybrid tea), Swim
Pinkie (Light rose pink floribunda), H.C. Swim
San Fernando (Currant red hybrid tea), Morris
Taffeta (Carmine hybrid tea), Lammerts
1949 Forty-Niner (Red and yellow hybrid tea), H.C. Swim
Tallyho (Two-tone pink hybrid tea), H.C. Swim
1950 Capistrano (Pink hybrid tea), Morris
Fashion (Coral pink floribunda), Boerner
Mission Bells (Salmon hybrid tea), Morris
Sutters Gold (Golden yellow hybrid tea), H.C. Swim

1951 No awards
1952 Fred Howard (Yellow, pencilled-pink hybrid tea), F.H. Howard
Helen Traubel (Apricot pink hybrid tea), H.C. Swim
Vogue (Cherry coral floribunda), Boerner
1953 Chrysler Imperial (Crimson red hybrid tea), Lammerts
Ma Perkins (Coral-shell pink floribunda), Boerner
1954 Lilibet (Dawn pink floribunda), Lindquist
Mojave (Apricot orange hybrid tea), H.C. Swim
1955 Jiminy Cricket (Coral orange floribunda), Boerner
Queen Elizabeth (Clear pink grandiflora), Lammerts
Tiffany (Orchid Pink hybrid tea), Lindquist
1956 Circus (Multicolored floribunda), H.C. Swim
1957 Golden Showers (Daffodil yellow climber), Lammerts
White Bouquet (White floribunda), Boerner
1958 Fusilier (Orange-red Floribunda), Morey
Gold Cup (Golden yellow floribunda), Boerner
White Knight (White hybrid tea), F. Meilland
1959 Ivory Fashion (Ivory floribunda), Boerner
Starfire (Cherry red grandiflora), Lammerts
1960 Fire King (Vermillion floribunda), F. Meilland
Garden Party (White hybrid tea), H.C. Swim
Sarabande (Scarlet orange floribunda), F. Meilland
1961 Duet (Salmon pink and orange-red hybrid tea), H.C. Swim
Pink Parfait (Dawn pink grandiflora), H.C. Swim
1962 Christian Dior (Crimson-scarlet hybrid tea), F. Meilland
Golden Slippers (Orange gold floribunda), Von Abrams
John S. Armstrong (Deep red grandiflora), H.C. Swim
King's Ransom (Chrome yellow hybrid tea), Morey
1963 Royal Highness (Clear pink hybrid tea), H.C. Swim and O.L. Weeks
Tropicana (Orange-red hybrid tea), Matthias Tantau
1964 Granada (Scarlet, nasturtium and yellow hybrid tea), Lindquist
Saratoga (White floribunda), Boerner
1965 Camelot (Shrimp pink grandiflora), H.C. Swim and O.L. Weeks
Mister Lincoln (Deep red hybrid tea), H.C. Swim and O.L. Weeks
1966 American Heritage (Ivory-tinged carmine hybrid tea), Lammerts
Apricot Nectar (Apricot floribunda), Boerner
Matterhorn (White hybrid tea), D.L. Armstrong and H.C. Swim
1967 Bewitched (Clear, phlox-pink hybrid tea), Lammerts
Gay Princess (Sheel pink floribunda), Boerner
Lucky Lady (Creamy shrimp-pink grandiflora), D.L. Armstrong and H.C. Swim
Roman Holiday (Orange-red floribunda), Lindquist
1968 Europeana (Red floribunda), G. deRuiter
Miss All-American Beauty (Pink hybrid tea), Meilland
Scarlet Knight (Scarlet red grandiflora), Meilland
1969 Angel Face (Lavender floribunda), H.C. Swim and O.L. Weeks
Comanche (Scarlet-orange grandiflora), H.C. Swim and O.L. Weeks
Gene Boerner (Pink floribunda), Boerner
Pascali (White hybrid tea), Louis Lens
1970 First Prize (Rose-red hybrid tea), Boerner
1971 Aquarius (Pink blend grandiflora), D.L. Armstrong
Command Performance (Orange-red hybrid tea), Lindquist
Redgold (Red edge on yellow floribunda), Dickson
1972 Apollo (Sunrise yellow hybrid tea), D.L. Armstrong
Portrait (Pink hybrid tea), Carl Meyer

1973 **Electron** (Rose-pink hybrid tea), Sam McGredy IV
Gypsy (Orange-red hybrid tea), O.L. Weeks
Medallion (Apricot pink hybrid tea), William Warriner
1974 **Bahia** (Orange-pink floribunda), Lammerts
Bon Bon (Pink and white bi-color floribunda), William Warriner
Perfume Delight (Clear pink hybrid tea), O.L. Weeks
1975 **Arizona** (Bronze-copper grandiflora), O.L. Weeks
Oregold (Pure yellow hybrid tea), Matthias Tantau
Rose Parade (Pink floribunda), J. Benjamin Williams
1976 **America** (Salmon climber), William Warriner
Cathedral (Golden apricot floribunda), Sam McGredy IV
Seashell (Peach and salmon hybrid tea), Reimer Kordes
Yankee Doodle (Sherbet-orange hybrid rea), Reimer Kordes
1977 **Double Delight** (Red and white bi-color hybrid tea), H.C. Swim
First Edition (Coral floribunda), Georges Delbard
Prominent (Hot organe grandiflora), Reimer Kordes

Honorary Globetrotter

HARLEM GLOBETROTTERS
5746 Sunset Blvd., Los Angeles, Calif., 90028
(213/464-3111)

The comedy-oriented basketball team known as the Harlem Globetrotters annually honors a well-traveled public figure with a lifetime honorary membership in the Globetrotter organization. The recipient is presented with a personalized uniform.

   1976 Henry Kissinger
   1977 Bob Hope

Harry S. Truman Good Neighbor Award

HARRY S. TRUMAN GOOD NEIGHBOR AWARD FOUNDATION
Box 6566, Leawood, Kans. 66206 (913/782-7500)

The Harry S. Truman Good Neighbor Award is annually presented on May 8, the late President's birthday, to an individual for meritorious public service. A committee selects the recipient, who is honored at a luncheon.

   1973 Earl Warren
   1974 Thomas F. Eagleton
   1975 Lt. Gen. Louis W. Truman, USA (Ret.)
   1976 Clarence M. Kelley
   1977 Gerald R. Ford

Western Heritage Awards

NATIONAL COWBOY HALL OF FAME
1700 NE 63, Oklahoma City, Okla. 73111 (405/478-2252)

After several years of annual presentation, the Western Heritage Awards are now given biennially to recognize the drama and heritage of the Old West in art, literature, music, film and theater which depict the history and legends of America's West. Winners, who are selected by the board of trustees which reviews entries, receive the Wrangler Trophy, a replica of Charles Russell's painting *Night Herder*. The next awards will be in 1978.

THEATRICAL MOTION PICTURES
1961 *The Alamo*
1962 *The Comancheros*
1963 *The Man Who Shot Liberty Valance*
1964 *How The West Was Won*
1965 *Cheyenne Autumn*
1966 *Sons of Katie Elder*
1967 *Appaloosa*
1968 *The War Wagon*
1969 *Will Penny*
1970 *True Grit*
1971 *A Man Called Horse*
1972 *The Cowboys*
1973 *Jeremiah Johnson*
1974 *The New Land*
1975 No award
1976 *Bite the Bullet*

FACTUAL TELEVISION PROGRAMS
1961 "The Greatest Lounsberry Scoop," *Death Valley Days*
1962 "The Real West," *Project Twenty*
1963 "The Hat That Wore The West," *Death Valley Days*
1964 "The American Cowboy," *Discovery '63*
1965 "The Hanging Judge"
      "They Went That-a-Way"
1966 "Custer to the Little Big Horn"
      "The Journals of Lewis and Clark"
1967 "An Iron Horse In Silver Pastures," *Discovery*
1968 "The End of the Trail," *Project Twenty*
1969 "The Bonanza Years"
1970 "The West of Charles Russell," *Project Twenty*
1971 "The Last of the Westerners," ABC News
1972 No award
1973 "Gone West," *The America Series*
1974 "Conrad Schwiering—Mountain Painter"
1975 "The American Parade: The 34th Star"
1976 "I Will Fight No More Forever"

NON-FICTION BOOKS
1961 No award
1962 *The American Heritage Book Of Indians,* Alvin M. Josephy, Jr. (Ed.)
1963 *Where The West Stayed Young,* John Rolph Burroughs
1964 *Furs By Astor,* John Upton Terrell
1965 *Standing Up Country,* C. Gregory Crampton
1966 *The American Heritage History Of The Great West,* Alvin M. Josephy, Jr. (Ed.)
1967 *Gold Fever,* George W. Groh
1968 *America's Western Frontiers,* John A. Hawgood
1969 *The Cattle Towns,* Robert Dykstra
      The Enduring Navajo, Laura Gilpin
1970 *The Great Platte River Road,* Merrill J. Mattes
1971 *The Great Range Wars,* Harry Siclair Drago
1972 *North America Divided: The Mexican War,* Odie B. Faulk and Seymour V. Connor
1973 *The Time of the Buffalo,* Tom McHugh
      Carson Valley, Grace Dangberg
      Crimsoned Prairie, S.L.A. Marshall
1974 *Bell Ranch As I Knew It,* George Ellis
      Will Rogers: The Man and His Times, Richard Ketchum
      Owyhee Trails, Mike Hanley and Ellis Lucia

Colorado Summer/Fall/Winter/Spring, David Muench, photographs and N. Scott Momaday, text
- **1975** *The Warren Wagontrain Raid,* Benjamin Capps
  Idaho—Pictorial Overview, Robert O. Beatty
  Born Grown, Roy P. Stewart
  Colonel Green and the Copper Skyrocket, C.S. Sonnichsen
  American, Margaret Sanborn
- **1976** *Fifty Great Western Illustrators,* Jeff C. Dykes
  Butte's Memory Book, Don James
  Charles F. Lummis: The Man and His West, Turbese Lummis Fisk and Keith Lummis

FICTION TELEVISION PROGRAMS

- **1961** "Incident At Dragoon Crossing," *"Rawhide*
- **1962** "The Sendoff," *Rawhide*
- **1963** "The Contender," *Stoney Burke*
- **1964** "Incident of Iron Bull" *Rawhide*
- **1965** "Corporal Dasovik," *Rawhide*
- **1966** "The Horse Fighter," *The Virginian*
- **1967** "The Intruders," *The Monroes*
  "Deathwatch," *Gunsmoke*
- **1968** "Bitter Autumn," *The Virginian*
- **1969** "The Buffalo Soldiers," *The High Chaparral*
- **1970** "The Wish," *Bonanza*
- **1971** "Run, Simon, Run," *Movie of the Week*
- **1972** "Pike," *Gunsmoke*
- **1973** "Hec," *Hec Ramsey*
- **1974** "Pioneer Woman," *Movie of the Week*
- **1975** *The Little House on the Prairie*
- **1976** "The Macahans"

WESTERN DOCUMENTARY FILMS

- **1961** *Four Seasons West*
- **1962** *101*
- **1963** *Appaloosa*
- **1964** *Pioneer Painter*
- **1965** *Age of the Buffalo*
- **1966** *The Beautiful Tree, Chishkale*
- **1967** *The Five Civilized Tribes*
- **1968** *Colorado: Prehistoric Man*
  Time Of The West
- **1969** *Born To Buck*
- **1970** *The Golden Spike*
- **1971** *Rodeo*
- **1972** *The Last of the Wild Mustang*
- **1973** *Bighorn*
- **1974** *The Great American Cowboy*
- **1975** *Going Down The Road*
- **1976** *Red Sunday: The Battle of the Little Bighorn*

NOVELS

- **1961** No award
- **1962** *The Shadow Catcher,* James D. Horan
- **1963** *Fire On The Mountain,* Edward Abbey
- **1964** *Honor Thy Father,* Robert Roripaugh
- **1965** *Little Big Man,* Thomas Berger
- **1966** *Mountain Man,* Vardis Fisher
- **1967** *They Came To A Valley, Bill Gulick*
- **1968** *North To Yesterday,* Robert Flynn
- **1969** *The Buffalo Runners,* Fred Grove
- **1970** *The White Man's Road,* Benjamin Capps
- **1971** *Arfive,* A. B. Guthrie
- **1972** *Pike's Peak: A Family Saga,* Frank Waters
- **1973** *Chiricahua,* Will Henry
- **1974** *The Time It Never Rained,* Elmer Kelton
- **1975** *Centennial,* James Michener
- **1976** No award

JUVENILE BOOKS

- **1961** No award
- **1962** *King Of The Mountain,* Gene Caesar
- **1963** *The Book Of The West,* Charles Clifton
- **1964** *Killer-of-Death,* Betty Baker
- **1965** *The Greatest Cattle Drive,* Paul Wellman
- **1966** *Land Rush,* Carl G. Hodges
- **1967** *Mustang: Wild Spirit Of The West,* Marguerite Henry
- **1968** *Down The Rivers, Westward Ho!,* Eric Scott
- **1969** *Edge Of Two Worlds,* Weyman Jones
- **1970** *An Awful Name To Live Up To,* Jessie Hosford
- **1971** *And One Was A Wooden Indian,* Betty Baker
- **1972** *The Black Mustanger,* Richard Wormser
- **1973** *Famous American Explorers,* Bern Keating
- **1974** No award
- **1975** *Susy's Scoundrel,* Harold Keith
- **1976** *Owl in the Cedar Trees,* Natachee Scott Momaday

ART BOOKS

- **1961-67** No awards
- **1968** *George Caleb Bingham: The Evolution Of An Artist,* E. Maurice Bloch
- **1969** *The Cowboy In Art,* Ed Ainsworth
- **1970** *Olaf Wieghorst,* William Reed
- **1971** *The Story of Harvey Dunn, Artist: Where Your Heart Is,* Robert F. Karolevitz
- **1972** *The Art of the Old West,* Paul E. Rossi and David Hunt
- **1973** *Harold Von Schmidt Draws and Paints the Old West,* Walt Reed
- **1974** *The Lure of the Great West,* Frank Getlein
- **1975** *Edward Borein Cowboy Artist,* Harold Davidson
- **1976** *Hans Kleiber: Artist of the Bighorn Mountains,* Emmie D. Myghet and Roberta Cheney

MAGAZINE ARTICLES, SHORT STORIES OR POETRY

- **1961** "The Old Chisholm Trail," W. Bruce Bell, Article in *Kiwanis Magazine*
  "All Legal And Proper," Steve Frazee, Short Story in *Ellery Queen Magazine*
- **1962** "Comanche Son," Fred Grove, Short Story in *Boys' Life*
  "The Look Of The Last Frontier," Mari Sandoz, Article in *American Heritage*
- **1963** "The Prairie Schooner Got Them There," George Stewart, Article in *American Heritage*
- **1964** "Nine Years Among The Indians," Herman Lehmann, Article in *Frontier Times*
- **1965** "Titans Of Western Art," J. Frank Dobie, Article in *American Heritage*
- **1966** "How Lost Was Zebulon Pike," Donald Jackson, Article in *American Heritage*
- **1967** "The Red Man's Last Struggle," Jack Guinn, Article in *Empire Magazine*
- **1968** "The Snows Of Rimrock Ridge," Carolyn Woirhaye, Article in *The Farm Quarterly*
- **1969** "W. R. Leigh: The Artist's Studio Collection," Donnie D. Good, Article in *The American Scene*
- **1970** "Bennett Howell's Cow Country," May Howell Dodson, Article in *Frontier Times*
- **1971** "Cattle, Guns, and Cowboys," James E. Serven, Article in *Arizona Highways Magazine*
- **1972** "Echoes of the Little Bighorn," David Humphreys Miller, Article in *American Heritage*
- **1973** "Horses of the West," James E. Serven, Article in *Arizona Highways Magazine*
  "The Donner Party," George Keithley, George Braziller, Inc.

1974 "40 Years Gatherins'," Spike Van Cleve, Article in *The Dude Rancher Magazine*

1975 "George Humphreys, Half Century With 6666," Jim Jennings, Article in *Quarter Horse Journal*

1976 "The Pioneer Woman: Image of Bronze," Patricia J. Broder, *American Art Review*

MUSIC

1961 *The Alamo,* Dmitri Tiomkin, Motion picture score

1962 *Charles Russell Contata, William J. May for Historical Society of Montana*

1963 No award

1964 *How the West Was Won,* Alfred Newman and Ken Darby, Motion picture score

1965 *Damon's Road,* Herschel Burke Gilbert, From "Corporal Dasovik" (*Rawhide*), television program

1966 *Hallelujah Trail,* Elmer Bernstein, Motion picture score

1967 No award

1968 *The End Of The Trail,* Robert Russell Bennett, *Project Twenty* television score

1969 No award

1970 *True Grit,* Elmer Bernstein and Don Black, Motion picture score

1971 *Snow Train,* John Parker, From *Gunsmoke* "Snow Train" television program

1972 *The Cowboys,* John Williams, Motion picture score.

1973 *The Train Robbers,* Dominic Frontiere, Motion picture score

1974 *Cahill U.S. Marshall,* Elmer Bernstein, Motion picture score

1975 *Little House on the Prairie,* David Rose, NBC television program

1976 "Bite the Bullet," Alex North, motion picture score

SPECIAL AWARDS

1970 *Arizona Highways* Magazine; *Death Valley Days;* Swiss National Television Network's documentary, *Far West: The Indians*

1971 *The Autobiography Of Charles Francis Colcord, 1859-1934*
Yakima Canutt
The Marlboro Man
The Sons Of The Pioneers
Survival On The Prairie NBC News Documentary

1972 John Ford
Dorthy Harmsen, *Harmsen's Western Americana*
Wyoming Stock Growers Association
Winchester-Western

1973 William H. Clother
Ben K. Green, *Some More Horse Tradin"*
Agnes Wright Spring
Dale Robertson

1974 Alfred Y. Allee
Howard Hawks
Luke Short
Dmitri Tiomkin
Korczak Ziolkowski
National Park Service documentary, *The Excavation of Mound Seven*

1975 Bob Wills and His Texas Playboys: For The Last Time (record album)
Delmer Daves
James Whitmore; Watt R. Matthews
Robert Adams, author of *The Architecture and Art of Early Hispanic Colorado*
Oklahoma Today Magazine

1976 *Mustang Country,* TV short starring Joel McCrea
W. C. Lawrence, historian of the fur trade
George O'Brien, Western film actor
Spike Van Cleeve: An American Portrait, TV short
Margaret Harper, founder, Texas Pageant
George Shirk, leader in historical preservation

Index

PAGANINI International Violin
Competition Prize, N.—283
PAGE, Alan—550
PAGE, Chester H.—379
PAGE, Geraldine—8, 122, 125, 228,
239
PAGE, Harlan (Pat)—531
PAGE, Irvine E.—405
PAGE, Irvine H.—404, 410, 413, 417
PAGE, J. Percy—524
PAGE, Col. John E.—495
PAGE, P. K.—28, 60
PAGE, R. M.—379
PAGE, Robert—271
PAGE, Robert M.—496
PAGE, Tony—68, 70
PAGEL, Al—83
PAGER, Antal—220
PAGLIA, Anthony—210
PAGLIAI, Mrs. Bruno—577, 582
PAGNIEZ, Yvonne—18
PAHL, Ellen—256
PAHLAVI, Empress Farah (Iran)—
577, 578, 583
PAHLAVI, Princess Achraf (Iran)—
420
PAHLAVI Prize, Mohammed Reza
—342
PAHLAVI, Shah Mohammed Reza
(Iran)—579
PAICH, David—134, 267
PAICH, Marty—134
PAIGE, Jeffrey—336
PAIGE, Leroy R. (Satchel)—538
PAIK, K. Kenneth—84, 87
PAIK Kun-Woo—279
PAILEN, Donald—478
PAILLERETS, Yoland Bonnet de—
422
PAINE, John Knowles—278
PAINE Prize, Robert Troup—34, 35
PAINE, Thomas—7
PAINE Webber Jackson & Curtis
Co.—462
PAINTER, Emlen—424
PAINTER, Theophilus Shickel—350
PAINTING—See ART; ART History
PAINTINGS, Annual Exhibition of
Contemporary American—298
PAISAN (movie)—234, 242
PAJAMA Game, The (musical)—
187
PAKENHAM, Michael—100
PAKISTAN—25, 342
PAKULA, Alan J.—242
PAL, George—202, 212
PAL Joey (musical)—179
PALADE, George E.—406, 412, 413,
414
PALANCE, Jack—116
PALAY, Sanford L.—405
PALAZZESCHI, Aldo—6, 45
PALAZZI, Carlo—582
PALEONTOLOGY—5, 6, 350, 351,
352, 385, 387, 389
PALESTINE—See MIDDLE East
PALEY, Grace—20
PALEY Park (NYC)—169
PALEY, Mrs. William—575, 576,
582, 583
PALKA, Col. Edward L.—496
PALLADINO, Nunzio J.—376
PALLARIOT, Lt. James R.—494
PALLE, Albert—53
PALLE Seul au Monde (movie)—
216
PALM, Sister Martha—421
PALMA, Sandro de—250
PALMEN, Erik—392, 395
PALMER, Alice—7
PALMER, Allison Ralph—351
PALMER, Arnold—472, 534, 536,
553, 555, 556
PALMER Award, Joe—563
PALMER, B.—358

PALMER, Elbridge W.—484
PALMER, Ephraim Laurence—487
PALMER, Ernest—197
PALMER, Gene—224
PALMER, James—537, 541
PALMER, John—87
PALMER, Paige—586
PALMER, R.R.—23
PALMER, Robert—276
PALMER, Sandra—535, 554
PALMER, William—293
PALMIERI, Eddie—265
PALMQUIST, Philip V.—211
PALMSTIERNA-WEISS, Gunilla—
189
PALOMA Blanca (recording)—281
PALOMINO, Carlos—530
PALUBINSKAS, Edward—528
PAMPERS (diapers)—461
PAN American World Airways, Inc.
—394, 440, 441, 462
PAN, Hermes—118, 201
PAN (movie)—219
PAN Zareta (race horse)—563
PAN-AFRICAN Congress—12
PANAMA City News-Herald—98
PANAS, Marie Balil—418
PANASONIC Co.—461
PANAVISION, Inc.—206, 207, 210,
211
PANDA, Edie—138
PANETTA, George—179
PANETTI, Joan—253
PANGBORN, Franklin—238
PANIC in Needle Park (movie)—
221
PANIC in the Streets (movie)—234
PANIS, Janine—274
PANITZ, Sol—159
PANKEN, J.N.A.—511
PANOFSKY, Hans A.—392, 393
PANOFSKY, W.K.H.—353
PANORAMA (program)—150
PANORAMEN, Die (book)—45
PANSCHAR, William—340
PANSCHAR, William G.—340
PANSEY, Col. Nell—495
PANSHIN, Alexei—37, 43
PANSITESCU, Sanda—516
PANTELEONI, Mrs. Guido—472
PANTHEON Books—23
PANTOMIME Quiz Time (program)
—114
PAOLA Princess (Belgium)—577
PAOLELLA, Domenico—216
PAPA Gallo, Thiam—527
PAPADATOU, Aristea—423
PAPAILIOLULOS, Sister Stefania—
419
PAPAIOANNOU, Yannis A.—164
PAPAKYRIAKOPOULOS, C.D.—391
PAPANICOLAOU, Chris—528
PAPANICOLAOU, George Nicholas
—413, 428
PAPE, C.P.D.—510
PAPENDRECHT, J. Hoynck van—
511
PAPENEK, Jan—15
PAPENFUSS, George F.—359
PAPER Bag Players, The—170, 183
PAPERNY, Myra—29
PAPERS of Thomas Jefferson, The
(book)—29
PAPINCOLAOU, George—408
PAPP, Joseph—110, 166, 170, 175,
176, 493, 493
PAPPAS, Charles—166
PAPPAS, Georges—274
PAPPAS, Ike—85, 86
PAPPAS, Irene—239
PAQUET, L.—591
PARADE (publication)—68, 77, 79
PARAMOUNT Studios—201, 202,
205, 206, 208, 209, 210, 405, 481
PARAPLUIES de Cherbourg, Les
(movie)—220

PARASKEVOPOULA, Helene—419
Parbaj (movie)—219
PARCHMAN, William—190
PARDE, Jean—448
PARDEE, Arthur B.—414
PARDEE, Brian—87
PARDEE Jr., George M.—490
PARDI, Leo—5
PARDUE, Leonard G.—359
PARE, George—335
PARENT, Bernie—535, 536, 559
PARENT, Gail—132, 157
PARENT, Lise—32
PARIS International Voice
Competition—283
PARIS, Jerry—121
PARIS La Belle (movie)—219
PARIS La Nuit (movie)—214
PARIS National Opera—268, 271
PARIS Review (publication—92
PARIS 1900 (movie)—236
PARISH, John C.—486, 490
PARK, Andy—286
PARK Central (Dallas, Tex.)—448
PARK, Charlotte—294
PARK, Edwards A.—404
PARK Forest, Ill.—508, 509
PARK High School (Ill.)—318
PARK, Robert H.—378
PARK, Thomas—447
PARK Top (race horse)—562
PARK, William C.—433
PARK, William H.—350, 428, 513
PARKER, Ace—550, 551
PARKER, Annette—258
PARKER, Benjamin J.—502
PARKER, Bruce C.—359
PARKER, Charles E. Robert—404
PARKER, Charlie—265, 278
PARKER, Dan—93
PARKER, Dave—599
PARKER, Dorothy—168
PARKER, E. N.—358
PARKER, Eugene N.—349, 390, 436
PARKER, Everett—113
PARKER, Gen. Frank—480
PARKER, George B.—96
PARKER, George Howard—350
PARKER, Gordon Rod—157
PARKER, Horatio—278
PARKER, Jim—547, 551
PARKER, John—108
PARKER, John J.—479
PARKER, John R.—512
PARKER, Lynn—503
PARKER Prize, William Riley—46
PARKER, Robert Andrew—49, 294
PARKER, Robert (football)—549
PARKER, Robert L.—390
PARKER, Robert (skiing)—565
PARKER, William—274, 283
PARKER, William Stanley—308
PARKER, 1st. Lt. Lawrence F.—495
PARKINS, Barbara—170
PARKINSON, Norman—582
PARKMAN Award, Francis—333,
334
PARKMAN, Francis—7
PARKS, Allison—574
PARKS, Charles—296
PARKS, Christopher—296, 297
PARKS, Eric—296, 297
PARKS, Gordon—13, 103, 292
PARKS, James—90
PARKS, Lloyd M.—425, 426, 427
PARKS, Robert J.—433
PARKS, W. George—368
PARLIN, Charles Coolidge—462
PARLO, Dita—238
PARMEE, Douglas—55
PARMENTIER, Juliette—418
PARMLEY, LaVern Watts—488
PARNCHANDARA, Phra Charoon—
507
PARNELL, Jack—134, 135
PARNHAM, Harold J.—604
PARNIS, Mollie—581, 583

PARRAN, Thomas—409, 428
PARRES, Maurice—24
PARRINGTON, Vernon Louis—50
PARRIS, Bill—108
PARRISH Kenneth—459
PARRISH, Robert—203
PARRISH, Samuel L.—513
PARRISH, Wayne—70, 439
PARRONDO, Gil—197
PARRY, Gordon—272
PARRY, Leslie—134, 224
PARRY, Robert W.—363
PARSEGHIAN, Ara—533, 546, 548
PARSONS Award, Charles Lathrop
—367
PARSONS Award, Louella O.—225,
226
PARSONS, Charles—530
PARSONS, Charles L.—367
PARSONS, Chuck—502
PARSONS Co., Ralph M.—305
PARSONS, Elizabeth—19
PARSONS, Estelle—165, 181, 196
PARSONS, Geoffrey—96
PARSONS, Irene—518
PARSONS, John H—397
PARSONS, Louella H.—232
PARSONS, Lt. Harold P.—494
PARSONS, Reginald H.—483
PARTCH, Harry—168
PARTON, Dolly—163, 259, 587
PARTON, Margaret—81
PARTOS, Emeric—584
PARTOS, Frank—245, 246
PARTRIDGE, Everett P.—376
PARTRIDGE Family, The (program)
—153
PARTY With Betty Comden and
Adolph Green, A (musical)—179
PAS de Deux (movie)—224
PASADENA Public Library (Calif.)
—320
PASCAGOULA Chronicle—100
PASCAL Duarte (movie)—222
PASCAL, Jean Louis—307
PASCAL, Roy—164
PASCHETTO, A.—591
PASCKE, Olive—420
PASCUAL, Psyche Anne—62
PASHALINSKI, Lola—181
PASINETTI, P. M.—20
PASOLINI, Pier Paulo—218, 222
PASQUIN, John—182
PASQUINI, Pasquale—5
PASS, Joe—265, 283
PASSAGERE, La (movie)—220
PASSANO Foundation Award—413
PASSION of Anna, The (movie)—
237
PASSWORD (program)—135
PASSY, Frederick—474
PASTAN, Linda—62
PASTENAK, Boris L.—46
PASTERNAK, Jr.—190
PASTEUR, Louis—347
PASTREICH, Peter—449
PATAI, Raphael—21, 41
PATCEVITCH, I.S.V.—582
PATCH, Maj. Gen. Alexander M.—
386
PATCHETT, Tom—132
PATCH of Blue, A (movie)—240
PATE, Jerry—552, 554, 556
PATE, Maurice—409
PATEL, C. Kumar N.—379
PATEL, Tribhuvandas K.—507
PATERNO, Joe—546
PATERSON, Basil A.—493
PATERSON, Clifford C.—398
PATERSON, Neil—198
PATHER Panchali (movie)—217,
237
PATHOLOGY—See Medicine
PATNIK, Al—568
PATON, Alan—21

WIENER, Norbert—40, 352
WIENER Prize in Applied
  Mathematics, Norbert—390, 391
WIEPKING, Heinrich—314
WIERZBICKA, Alice—420
WIESE, Joseph Frederic—486
WIESEL, Elie—38, 41, 42, 52
WIESEL, Torstein N.—413
WIESEL, Uzi—255
WIESENBERGER, Arthur—456
WIESENSOMMER (movie)—218
WIESENTHAL, Simon—4
WIESNER, Jerome B.—378
WIETING, David W.—375
WIGGERS, Carl J.—410
WIGGINS, Ira—359
WIGGINS, James R.—104
WIGGLESWORTH, Frank—276
WIGHT, G. Earle—414
WIGHT, Sedwig N.—468
WIGMORE, John Henry—479
WIGNER, Eugene P.—352, 396
WIHURI FOUNDATION, JENNY
  AND ANTTI—14, 287
WIHURI-SIBELIUS Prize—287
WIJNGAARDEN, E.D. van—511
WIK, Reynold M.—332
WIKANDER, Oscar R.—373
WIKINSON, Stephan—439
WIKLICKY, Leopold—358
WIL-KIN, Inc.—211
WILARDEBO, Carlos—221
WILBUR, Capt. Carl E.—415
WILBUR, Curtis D.—386
WILBUR, Richard—34, 49, 59, 60,
  63
WILCE, John W.—546
WILCOCK, Donald F.—372
WILCOX, Carolyn—140
WILCOX, Colin—174
WILCOX, Dan—127
WILCOX, Max—269
WILD Cherry (group)—281
WILD Child, The (movie)—237, 240
WILD, Frank—383
WILD Kingdom (program)—122,
  123, 125, 127
WILD Wings (movie)—204
WILD, Paul J.—349
WILD River (movie)—235
WILD Strawberries (movie)—214,
  227, 237
WILDE, F. G. de—511
WILDE, Frazer B.—516
WILDER, Alec—153, 251
WILDER, Amos—31
WILDER, Billy—190, 198, 215, 229,
  230, 242, 245, 246
WILDER, Carol—256
WILDER, Clinton—186
WILDER, Gene—174
WILDER, James Austin—483
WILDER, Laura Ingalls—57
WILDER Medal, Laura Ingalls—57
WILDER, Russell M.—404
WILDER, Thornton—11, 40, 47, 50,
  110, 167, 169
WILDER, William—253
WILDERMUTH, Ora L.—323
WILDERNESS Kingdom: The
  Journals and Paintings of Father
  Nicolas Point (book)—29
WILDFIRE (dog)—243
WILDHABER, Ernest—372
WILDING, Anthony—527
WILDLIFE FEDERATION,
  NATIONAL—451
WILDLIFE Management Institute—
  451
WILENSKY, Otis—255
WILES, Gordon—196
WILES, Harry G.—491
WILES, John—53
WILEY, Frank H.—425
WILFORD, John Noble—69
WILHELM, Kate—36, 43

WILHELM, Paulina Perelman de—
  421
WILHELM, Richard H.—367
WILHOUSKY, Peter—166
WILK, Max—156, 251
WILKE Memorial Award, Louis G.—
  541
WILKENS, Emily—584
WILKES & Braun, Inc.—272
WILKES, Keith—542
WILKES, Maurice Vincent—369, 464
WILKES, Paul—73
WILKES, Ray—313
WILKES-BARRE, Pa.—508
WILKINS, Sir George Hubert—384
WILKINS, H. Percy—359
WILKINS, Lawson—428
WILKINS, Leslie—329
WILKINS, M.H.F.—408
WILKINS, Mac—569
WILKINS, Maurice H. F.—412
WILKINS, Robert W.—408
WILKINS, Roy—11, 13, 482, 492,
  505, 506, 515
WILKINS, Shirley—469
WILKINS, Sophie—55
WILKINSON, Bud—546
WILKINSON, Charles—533
WILKINSON, Denys Haigh—397,
  398
WILKINSON, Eleanore—439
WILKINSON, Ernest L.—459
WILKINSON, Geoffrey—364
WILKINSON Jr., George D.—375
WILKINSON, J.H.—464
WILKINSON, John A.—207
WILKINSON, Kenneth—272
WILKINSON, Meil R.—483
WILKINSON, Paul H.—439
WILKINSON, Ray—208
WILKINSON, Stephan—69, 70
WILKONSKA, Marie—420
WILKUS, Joseph W.—491
WILL, Frederick—64
WILL, George F.—97
WILL Penny (movie)—606
WILL, Robert—314
WILL Rogers: The Man and His
  Times (book)—606
WILLARD, Daniel—513
WILLARD, Emma—6
WILLARD, Frances Elizabeth—7
WILLARD, John E.—364
WILLARD, M. H.—364
WILLARD, William R.—404
WILLCOX, William B.—23
WILLEFORD, Dean—571
WILLEMSEN-WIDDERSHOVEN,
  R.M.A.—510
WILLESTON, Kim—87
WILLETT, H.G.—436
WILLETT, Hurd Curtis—392
WILLEY, Gordon Randolph—329
WILLIAMS Jr., Albert J.—373, 379
WILLIAMS, Andy—244
WILLIAMS, Archie—544
WILLIAMS, Betty—474
WILLIAMS, Billy—539
WILLIAMS, Billy Dee—579
WILLIAMS, Billy L.—541
WILLIAMS, Camelia—285
WILLIAMS, Carl S.—532
WILLIAMS, Carlos—60
WILLIAMS Jr., Charles S.—491
WILLIAMS, Cicely D.—404
WILLIAMS, Clarence E.—487
WILLIAMS, Corrine—469
WILLIAMS, Dave—127, 140
WILLIAMS, Judge David W.—14
WILLIAMS, Donald D.—433
WILLIAMS, Douglas—202
WILLIAMS, E. Virginia—177, 260
WILLIAMS, Earl C.—541
WILLIAMS, Edward—116
WILLIAMS, Elmo—203
WILLIAMS, Emlyn—178

WILLIAMS, Esther—293, 321, 567,
  600
WILLIAMS, F. Carter—308
WILLIAMS, Frank B.—511
WILLIAMS, Frank S.G.—373
WILLIAMS, Frederick Calland—399
WILLIAMS, G. Lowell—375
WILLIAMS, George—54, 532
WILLIAMS, Gordon L.—72, 87
WILLIAMS, Gordon S.—440
WILLIAMS, Grant—256
WILLIAMS, Greg—502
WILLIAMS, Guy Neal—81
WILLIAMS, Hank—278
WILLIAMS, Harold M.—14
WILLIAMS, Mrs. Harrison—575,
  576
WILLIAMS, Heathcote—180
WILLIAMS, Jackie—458
WILLIAMS, James—478
WILLIAMS, Maj. James R.—495
WILLIAMS, Joan—19
WILLIAMS, John—40, 54, 184, 200,
  230, 239, 263, 264, 268, 270
WILLIAMS, John A.—19
WILLIAMS, John F.—433
WILLIAMS, John T.—125, 130
WILLIAMS, John W.—363
WILLIAMS, Joseph—159
WILLIAMS Jr., Joseph W.—491
WILLIAMS, L. Pearce—353
WILLIAMS, La Verne—274
WILLIAMS, Lyman Perry—491
WILLIAMS, Marjorie J.—518
WILLIAMS, Martin—251
WILLIAMS, Mason—263
WILLIAMS, Maynard Owen—386
WILLIAMS, Pat—263
WILLIAMS, Paul—201, 230, 262
WILLIAMS, Paul D.—491
WILLIAMS, Paul R.—13
WILLIAMS, Percy—525, 529
WILLIAMS, Percy H.—492
WILLIAMS, Capt. Randolph P.—
  386, 387
WILLIAMS, Roger—7, 297, 298
WILLIAMS, Sammy—181, 185
WILLIAMS, Sandy—574
WILLIAMS, T. Harry—29, 40, 52
WILLIAMS, Ted—523, 537, 539
WILLIAMS, Tennessee—19, 110,
  168, 178, 186
WILLIAMS, Theodore S.—538, 540
WILLIAMS, Thomas—40
WILLIAMS, W. Ewart—399
WILLIAMS, Walter—293
WILLIAMS, Walter C.—435, 436
WILLIAMS, Wheeler—295
WILLIAMS, William Carlos—49, 57,
  58, 59, 61, 64, 168
WILLIAMS, William Taylor Burwell
  —12
WILLIAMS-ASHMAN, Howard Guy
  —428
WILLIAMSBURG Restoration (Va.)
  —304
WILLIAMSON, Fred—579
WILLIAMSON, Frederick C.—449
WILLIAMSON, Gerald V.—372
WILLIAMSON, Jack—43, 47
WILLIAMSON Jr., Samuel R.—331
WILLINGHAM, Calder—245
WILLIS, Bailey—388
WILLIS, Bill—552
WILLIS, Charles E.—516
WILLIS, Edwin B.—201
WILLIS, George H.—497
WILLIS, Walter A.—38
WILLISTON Medal, Arthur L.—370,
  374
WILLISTON, Samuel—479
WILLKIE, Wendell L.—4, 514
WILLMAN, Noel—186
WILLMS, James A.—375
WILLOWBROOK Case, The
  (program)—138

WILLOWBROOK, The Last Great
  Disgrace (program)—152
WILLOWER, Don J.—596
WILLS, Bob—278, 608
WILLS, Hasel M.—323
WILLS, Helen—529, 530
WILLS, Mary—199
WILLS, Maury—523, 534, 539, 540
WILLSON, David Harris—333
WILLSON Jr., James McCrory—
  491, 500
WILLSON, Meredith—179, 187, 188,
  267
WILLSTATTER, Richard M.—361
WILMAN, Joe—543
WILMINGTON, Del.—509
WILMINGTON, N.C.—508
WILSON, Albert—604
WILSON, Angus—24, 30, 45
WILSON, Arthur M.—40, 331
WILSON, Bill—100
WILSON, Byron—480
WILSON, Charles—294
WILSON, Charles E.—456, 465, 478,
  481
WILSON, Charles Thomson Rees—
  399
WILSON Co., H.W.—318
WILSON Co. Library Periodical
  Award, H.W.—323
WILSON, Connie—321
WILSON, Dave—139
WILSON, David E.—81
WILSON, David R.—308
WILSON, Delmer H.—491
WILSON, Dorothy Lee—590
WILSON, Doug—125
WILSON, Douglas E.—491
WILSON, E. Bright—353, 355
WILSON Jr., Edgar Bright—6, 365
WILSON, Edmund—11, 31, 167
WILSON, Edmund Beecher—349,
  350
WILSON, Edward O.—353
WILSON, Elizabeth—181, 185
WILSON, Erica—295
WILSON, Flip—146, 162, 225, 265
WILSON, Forrest—51
WILSON, Fred R.—209, 210
WILSON, George—276, 570
WILSON, George W.—100
WILSON, Gill Robb—494
WILSON, Grace Margaret—418
WILSON, H.A.—525
WILSON, Halsey W.—321
WILSON, Sir Harold—501
WILSON, J. J.—9
WILSON, J. Tuzo—388, 389, 390
WILSON, James—124
WILSON, James Robert Gavin—
  491
WILSON, Jane B.—320
WILSON, Jean—525
WILSON, Jean D.—428
WILSON, Joan Hoff—334
WILSON, John—56
WILSON, Mrs. John C.—576, 579,
  580
WILSON, Sir John F.—505
WILSON, John Skinner—484
WILSON, Jose—591
WILSON, Kemmons—458
WILSON, Lanford—20, 178, 179
WILSON, Larry—550
WILSON, Gen. Louis H.—499
WILSON, Louis Round—320, 322
WILSON, Lucille—522
WILSON, Macel—575
WILSON, Malcolm—492
WILSON, Margaret—50
WILSON, Mark E.—254
WILSON, Michael—230, 246
WILSON, Milburn Lincoln—485
WILSON, Mona Gordon—422
WILSON, Morley Evans—388
WILSON, N.C.—509
WILSON, Nancy—266

Z